**RANDOM HOUSE
WEBSTER'S**

STUDENT notebook SPANISH DICTIONARY

2nd Ed.

English Abbreviations/Abreviaturas inglesas

a.	adjective		*interrog.*	interrogative
abbr.	abbreviation		*Leg.*	legal
adv.	adverb		*m.*	masculine
Aero.	aeronautics		*Mech.*	mechanics
Agr.	agriculture		*Mex.*	Mexico
Anat.	anatomy		*Mil.*	military
art.	article		*Mus.*	music
Auto.	automotive		*n.*	noun
Biol.	biology		*Naut.*	nautical
Bot.	botany		*Phot.*	photography
Carib.	Caribbean		*pl.*	plural
Chem.	chemistry		*Pol.*	politics
Colloq.	colloquial		*prep.*	preposition
Com.	commerce		*pron.*	pronoun
conj.	conjunction		*Punct.*	punctuation
dem.	demonstrative		*rel.*	relative
Econ.	economics		*Relig.*	religion
Elec.	electrical		*S.A.*	Spanish America
esp.	especially		*Theat.*	theater
f.	feminine		*v.*	verb
Fig.	figurative			
Fin.	finance			
Geog.	geography			
Govt.	government			
Gram.	grammar			
interj.	interjection			

Note: If a main entry term is repeated in a boldface subentry in exactly the same form, it is abbreviated. Example: **comedor** *n.m.* dining room. **coche c.,** dining car.

Spanish Stress

In a number of words, spoken stress is marked by an accent (´): *nación, país, médico, día.*

Words which are not so marked are, generally speaking, stressed on the next-to-the-last syllable if they end in a vowel, *n,* or *s;* and on the last syllable if they end in a consonant other than *n* or *s.*

Note: An accent is placed over some words to distinguish them from others having the same spelling and pronunciation but differing in meaning.

Spanish Alphabetization

In Spanish, *ch* and *ll* are no longer considered to be separate letters of the alphabet. They are now alphabetized as they would be in English. However, words with *ñ* are alphabetized after *n.*

PRONUNCIATION KEY FOR SPANISH

IPA Symbols	Key Words	Approximate Equivalents
a	alba, banco, cera	father, depart
e	esto, del, parte, mesa	bet; like rain when e ends syllable and is not followed by r, rr, or t
i	ir, fino, adiós, muy	like beet, but shorter
o	oler, flor, grano	like vote, but shorter
u	un, luna, cuento, vergüenza, guarda	fool, group
b	bajo, ambiguo, vaca	by, abet
β	hablar, escribir, lavar	like vehicle, but with lips almost touching
d	dar, desde, andamio, dueña	deal, adept
ð	pedir, edredón, verdad	that, gather
f	fecha, afectar, golf	fan, after
g	gato, grave, gusto, largo, guerra	garden, ugly
h	gemelo, giro, junta, bajo	horse
k	cacao, claro, cura, cuenta, que, quinto	kind, actor
l	lado, lente, habla, papel	lot, altar
ʎ	(in Spain) llama, calle, olla	like million, but with tongue behind teeth
m	mal, amor	more, commit
n	nada, nuevo, mano, bien	not, enter
ɲ	ñapa, año	canyon, companion
ŋ	angosto, aunque	ring, anchor
p	peso, guapo	pill, applaud
r	real, faro, deber	like rice, but with single flap of tongue on roof of mouth
rr	perro, sierra	like rice, but with trill, or vibration of tongue, against upper teeth
s	sala, espejo, mas;	say, clasp
	(in Latin America) cena, hacer, vez	
θ	(in Spain) cena, hacer, cierto, cine, zarzuela, lazo, vez	thin, myth
t	tocar, estado, cenit	table, attract
y	ya, ayer; (in Latin America) llama, calle	you, voyage
tʃ	chica, mucho	chill, batch

Diphthongs

ai, ay	baile, hay	high, rye
au	audacia, laudable	out, round
ei, ey	veinte, seis, rey	ray
ie	miel, también	fiesta
oi, oy	estoico, hoy	coin, loyal
ua	cuanto	quantity
ue	buena, suerte	sway, quaint

Guía de Pronunciación del Inglés

Símbolos del AFI	Ejemplos
/æ/	*ingl.* h**a**t; como la **a** de *esp.* p**a**ro, pero más cerrada
/ei/	*ingl.* st**ay**; *esp.* r**ei**na
/ɛə/ [followed by /r/]	*ingl.* h**air**; *esp.* v**er**
/ɑ/	*ingl.* f**a**ther; similar a las **a**s de *esp.* c**a**s**a**, pero más larga
/ɛ/	*ingl.* b**e**t; *esp.* **e**ntre
/i/	*ingl.* b**ee**; como la **i** de *esp.* v**i**da, pero más larga
/ɪə/ [followed by /r/]	*ingl.* h**ear**; como la **i** de *esp.* ven**i**r, pero menos cerrada
/ɪ/	*ingl.* s**i**t; como la **i** de *esp.* Ch**i**le, pero menos cerrada
/ai/	*ingl.* tr**y**; *esp.* h**ay**
/ɒ/	*ingl.* h**o**t; *esp.* p**o**ner
/o/	*ingl.* b**oa**t; similar a la **o** de *esp.* sac**o**, pero más cerrada
/ɔ/	*ingl.* s**aw**; similar a la **o** de *esp.* c**o**rte, pero más cerrada
/ɔi/	*ingl.* t**oy**; *esp.* h**oy**
/ʊ/	*ingl.* b**oo**k; como la **u** de *esp.* ins**u**lto, pero menos cerrada
/u/	*ingl.* t**oo**; como la **u** de *esp.* l**u**na, pero más larga
/au/	*ingl.* c**ow**; *esp.* p**au**sa
/ʌ/	*ingl.* **u**p; entre la **o** de *esp.* b**o**rde y la **a** de *esp.* b**a**rro
/ɜ/ [followed by /r/]	*ingl.* b**ur**n; *fr.* fl**eur**
/ə/	*ingl.* **a**lone; *fr.* d**e**main
/ₒ/	*ingl.* f**i**re (fiᵣr); *fr.* bastill**e**
/b/	*ingl.* **b**oy; como la **b** de *esp.* **b**oca, pero más aspirada
/tʃ/	*ingl.* **ch**ild; *esp.* mu**ch**o
/d/	*ingl.* **d**ad; *esp.* **d**ar
/f/	*ingl.* **f**or; *esp.* **f**echa
/g/	*ingl.* **g**ive; *esp.* **g**ato
/h/	*ingl.* **h**appy; como la **j** de *esp.* **j**abón, pero más aspirada y menos aspera
/dʒ/	*ingl.* **j**ust; *it.* **gi**orno
/k/	*ingl.* **k**ick; similar a la **k** de *esp.* **k**ilogramo, pero más aspirada
/l/	*ingl.* **l**ove; *esp.* **l**ibro
/m/	*ingl.* **m**other; *esp.* li**mb**o
/n/	*ingl.* **n**ow; *esp.* **n**oche
/ŋ/	*ingl.* si**ng**; *esp.* bla**n**co
/p/	*ingl.* **p**ot; como las **p**s de *esp.* **p**a**p**a, pero más aspirada
/r/	*ingl.* **r**ead; como la **r** de *esp.* pa**r**a, pero con la lengua elevada hacia el paladar, sin tocarlo
/s/	*ingl.* **s**ee; *esp.* ha**s**ta
/ʃ/	*ingl.* **sh**op; *fr.* **ch**er**ch**er
/t/	*ingl.* **t**en; similar a la **t** de *esp.* **t**omar, pero más aspirada
/θ/	*ingl.* **th**ing; *esp.* (en España) **c**erdo, **z**apato
/ð/	*ingl.* fa**th**er; *esp.* co**d**o
/v/	*ingl.* **v**ictory; como la **b** de *esp.* ha**b**a, pero es labiodental en vez de bilabial
/w/	*ingl.* **w**itch; como la **u** de *esp.* p**u**esto, pero con labios más cerrados
/y/	*ingl.* **y**es; *esp.* **y**acer
/z/	*ingl.* **z**ipper; *fr.* **z**éro
/ʒ/	*ingl.* plea**s**ure; *fr.* **j**eune

Las consonantes /l̩/, /m̩/, y /n̩/ son similares a las **l**, **m**, y **n** del español, pero alargadas y resonantes

Spanish–English

español–inglés

A

a /a/ *prep.* to; at.

abacería /aβaθe'ria; aβase'ria/ *n. f.* grocery store.

abacero /aβa'θero; aβa'sero/ *n. m.* grocer.

ábaco /'aβako/ *n. m.* abacus.

abad /a'βað/ *n. m.* abbot.

abadía /aβa'ðia/ *n. f.* abbey.

abajar /aβa'har/ *v.* lower; go down.

abajo /a'βaho/ *adv.* down; downstairs.

abandonar /aβando'nar/ *v.* abandon.

abandono /aβan'dono/ *n. m.* abandonment.

abanico /aβa'niko/ *n. m.* fan. **—abanicar,** *v.*

abaratar /aβara'tar/ *v.* cheapen.

abarcar /aβar'kar/ *v.* comprise; clasp.

abastecer /aβaste'θer; aβaste'ser/ *v.* supply, provide.

abatido /aβa'tiðo/ *a.* dejected, despondent.

abatir /aβa'tir/ *v.* knock down; dismantle; depress, dishearten.

abdicación /aβðika'θion; aβðika'sion/ *n. f.* abdication.

abdicar /aβði'kar/ *v.* abdicate.

abdomen /aβ'ðomen/ *n. m.* abdomen.

abdominal /aβðomi'nal/ *a.* **1.** abdominal. **—n. 2.** *m.* sit-up.

abecé /aβe'θe; aβe'se/ *n. m.* ABCs, rudiments.

abecedario /aβeθe'ðario; aβese'ðario/ *n. m.* alphabet; reading book.

abeja /a'βeha/ *n. f.* bee.

abejarrón /aβeha'rron/ *n. m.* bumblebee.

aberración /aβerra'θion; aβerra'sion/ *n. f.* aberration.

abertura /aβer'tura/ *n. f.* opening, aperture, slit.

abeto /a'βeto/ *n. m.* fir.

abierto /a'βierto/ *a.* open; overt.

abismal /aβis'mal/ *a.* abysmal.

abismo /a'βismo/ *n. m.* abyss, chasm.

ablandar /aβlan'dar/ *v.* soften.

abnegación /aβnega'θion; aβnega'sion/ *n. f.* abnegation.

abochornar /aβot ʃor'nar/ *v.* overheat; embarrass.

abogado /aβo'gaðo/ **-da** *n.* lawyer, attorney.

abolengo /aβo'lengo/ *n. m.* ancestry.

abolición /aβoli'θion; aβoli'sion/ *n. f.* abolition.

abolladura /aβoʎa'ðura; aβoya'ðura/ *n. f.* dent. **—abollar,** *v.*

abominable /aβomi'naβle/ *a.* abominable.

abominar /aβomi'nar/ *v.* abhor.

abonado /aβo'naðo/ **-da** *n. m. & f.* subscriber.

abonar /aβo'nar/ *v.* pay; fertilize.

abonarse /aβo'narse/ *v.* subscribe.

abono /a'βono/ *n. m.* fertilizer; subscription; season ticket.

aborigen /aβo'rihen/ *a. & n.* aboriginal.

aborrecer /aβorre'θer; aβorre'ser/ *v.* hate, loathe, abhor.

abortar /aβor'tar/ *v.* abort, miscarry.

aborto /a'βorto/ *n. m.* abortion.

abovedar /aβoβe'ðar/ *v.* vault.

abrasar /aβra'sar/ *v.* burn.

abrazar /aβra'θar; aβra'sar/ *v.* embrace; clasp.

abrazo /a'βraθo; a'βraso/ *n. m.* embrace.

abrelatas /aβre'latas/ *n. m.* can opener.

abreviar /aβre'βiar/ *v.* abbreviate, abridge, shorten.

abreviatura /aβreβia'tura/ *n. f.* abbreviation.

abrigar /aβri'gar/ *v.* harbor, shelter.

abrigarse /aβri'garse/ *v.* bundle up.

abrigo /a'βrigo/ *n. m.* overcoat; shelter; (*pl.*) wraps.

abril /a'βril/ *n. m.* April.

abrir /a'βrir/ *v.* open; *Med.* lance.

abrochar /aβro'tʃar/ *v.* clasp.

abrogación /aβroga'θion; aβroga'sion/ *n. f.* abrogation, repeal.

abrogar /aβro'gar/ *v.* abrogate.

abrojo /a'βroho/ *n. m.* thorn.

abrumar /aβru'mar/ *v.* overwhelm, crush, swamp.

absceso /aβs'θeso; aβ'sseso/ *n. m.* abscess.

absolución /aβsolu'θion; aβsolu'sion/ *n. f.* absolution; acquittal.

absoluto /aβso'luto/ *a.* absolute; downright.

absolver /aβsol'βer/ *v.* absolve, pardon.

absorbente /aβsor'βente/ *a.* absorbent.

absorber /aβsor'βer/ *v.* absorb.

absorción /aβsor'θion; aβsor'sion/ *n. f.* absorption.

abstemio /aβs'temio/ *a.* abstemious.

abstenerse /aβste'nerse/ *v.* abstain; refrain.

abstinencia /aβsti'nenθia; aβsti'nensia/ *n. f.* abstinence.

abstracción /aβstrak'θion; aβstrak'sion/ *n. f.* abstraction.

abstracto /aβs'trakto/ *a.* abstract.

abstraer /aβstra'er/ *v.* abstract.

absurdo /aβ'surðo/ *a.* **1.** absurd. **—n. 2.** *m.* absurdity.

abuchear /aβutʃe'ar/ *v.* boo.

abuela /a'βuela/ *n. f.* grandmother.

abuelo /a'βuelo/ *n. m.* grandfather; (*pl.*) grandparents.

abultado /aβul'taðo/ *a.* bulky.

abultamiento /aβulta'miento/ *n. m.* bulge. **—abultar,** *v.*

abundancia /aβun'danθia; aβun'dansia/ *n. f.* abundance, plenty.

abundante /aβun'dante/ *a.* abundant, plentiful.

abundar /aβun'dar/ *v.* abound.

aburrido /aβu'rriðo/ *a.* boring, tedious.

aburrimiento /aβurri'miento/ *n. m.* boredom.

aburrir /aβu'rrir/ *v.* bore.

abusar /aβu'sar/ *v.* abuse, misuse.

abusivo /aβu'siβo/ *a.* abusive.

abuso /a'βuso/ *n. m.* abuse.

abyecto /aβ'yekto/ *a.* abject, low.

a.C., *abbr.* (**antes de Cristo**) BC.

acá /a'ka/ *adv.* here.

acabar /aka'βar/ *v.* finish. **a. de...,** to have just....

acacia /a'kaθia; a'kasia/ *n. f.* acacia.

academia /aka'ðemia/ *n. f.* academy.

académico /aka'ðemiko/ *a.* academic.

acaecer /akae'θer; akae'ser/ *v.* happen.

acanalar /akana'lar/ *v.* groove.

acaparar /akapa'rar/ *v.* hoard; monopolize.

acariciar /akari'θiar; akari'siar/ *v.* caress, stroke.

acarrear /akarre'ar/ *v.* cart, transport; occasion, entail.

acaso /a'kaso/ *n. m.* chance. **por si a.,** just in case.

acceder /akθe'ðer; akse'ðer/ *v.* accede.

accesible /akθe'siβle; akse'siβle/ *a.* accessible.

acceso /ak'θeso; ak'seso/ *n. m.* access, approach.

accesorio /akθe'sorio; akse'sorio/ *a.* accessory.

accidentado /akθiðen'taðo; aksiðen'taðo/ *a.* hilly.

accidental /akθiðen'tal; aksiðen'tal/ *a.* accidental.

accidente /akθi'ðente; aksi'ðente/ *m.* accident, wreck.

acción /ak'θion; ak'sion/ *n. f.* action, act; *Com.* share of stock.

accionista /akθio'nista; aksio'nista/ *n. m. & f.* shareholder.

acechar /aθe'tʃar; ase'tʃar/ *v.* ambush, spy on.

acedía /aθe'ðia; ase'ðia/ *n. f.* heartburn.

aceite /a'θeite; a'seite/ *n. m.* oil.

aceite de hígado de bacalao /a'θeite de i'gaðo de baka'lao; a'seite/ cod-liver oil.

aceitoso /aθei'toso; asei'toso/ *a.* oily.

aceituna /aθei'tuna; asei'tuna/ *n. f.* olive.

aceleración /aθelera'θion; aselera'sion/ *n. f.* acceleration.

acelerar /aθele'rar; asele'rar/ *v.* accelerate, speed up.

acento /a'θento; a'sento/ *n. m.* accent.

acentuar /aθen'tuar; asen'tuar/ *v.* accent, accentuate, stress.

acepillar /aθepi'ʎar; asepi'yar/ *v.* brush; plane (wood).

aceptable /aθep'taβle; asep'taβle/ *a.* acceptable.

aceptación /aθepta'θion; asepta'sion/ *n. f.* acceptance.

aceptar /aθep'tar; asep'tar/ *v.* accept.

acequía /a'θekia; a'sekia/ *n. f.* ditch.

acera /a'θera; a'sera/ *n. f.* sidewalk.

acerca de /a'θerka de; a'serka de/ *prep.* about, concerning.

acercar /aθer'kar; aser'kar/ *v.* bring near.

acercarse /aθer'karse; aser'karse/ *v.* approach, come near, go near.

acero /a'θero; a'sero/ *n. m.* steel.

acero inoxidable /a'θero inoksi'ðaβle; a'sero inoksi'ðaβle/ stainless steel.

acertar /aθer'tar; aser'tar/ *v.* guess right. **a. en,** hit (a mark).

acertijo /aθer'tiho; aser'tiho/ *n. m.* puzzle, riddle.

achicar /atʃi'kar/ *v.* diminish, dwarf; humble.

acidez /aθi'ðeθ; asi'ðes/ *n. f.* acidity.

ácido /'aθiðo; 'asiðo/ *a.* **1.** sour. **—n. 2.** *m.* acid.

aclamación /aklama'θion; aklama'sion/ *n. f.* acclamation.

aclamar /akla'mar/ *v.* acclaim.

aclarar /akla'rar/ *v.* brighten; clarify, clear up.

acoger /ako'her/ *v.* welcome, receive.

acogida /ako'hiða/ *n. f.* welcome, reception.

acometer /akome'ter/ *v.* attack.

acomodador /akomoða'ðor/ *n. m.* usher.

acomodar /akomo'ðar/ *v.* accommodate, fix up.

acompañamiento /akompaɲa'miento/ *n. m.* accompaniment; following.

acompañar /akompa'ɲar/ *v.* accompany.

acondicionar /akondiθio'nar; akondisio'nar/ *v.* condition.

aconsejable /akonse'haβle/ *a.* advisable.

aconsejar /akonse'har/ *v.* advise.

acontecer /akonte'θer; akonte'ser/ *v.* happen.

acontecimiento /akonteθi'miento; akontesi'miento/ *n. m.* event, happening.

acorazado /akora'θaðo; akora'saðo/ *n.* **1.** *m.* battleship. **—a. 2.** armor-plated, ironclad.

acordarse /akor'ðarse/ *v.* remember, recollect.

acordeón /akorðe'on/ *n. m.* accordion.

acordonar /akorðo'nar/ *v.* cordon off.

acortar /akor'tar/ *v.* shorten.

acosar /ako'sar/ *v.* beset, harry.

acostar /ako'star/ *v.* lay down; put to bed.

acostarse /akos'tarse/ *v.* lie down; go to bed.

acostumbrado /akostum'braðo/ *a.* accustomed; customary.

acostumbrar /akostum'brar/ *v.* accustom.

acrecentar /akreθen'tar; akresen'tar/ *v.* increase.

acreditar /akreði'tar/ *v.* accredit.

acreedor /akree'ðor/ **-ra** *n.* creditor.

acróbata /a'kroβata/ *n. m. & f.* acrobat.

acrobático /akro'βatiko/ *a.* acrobatic.

actitud /akti'tuð/ *n. f.* attitude.

actividad /aktiβi'ðað/ *n. f.* activity.

activista /akti'βista/ *a. & n.* activist.

activo /ak'tiβo/ *a.* active.

acto /'akto/ *n. m.* act.

actor /ak'tor/ *n. m.* actor.

actriz /ak'triθ; ak'tris/ *n. f.* actress.

actual /ak'tual/ *a.* present; present day.

actualidades /aktuali'ðaðes/ *n. f.pl.* current events.

actualmente /aktual'mente/ *adv.* at present; nowadays.

actuar /ak'tuar/ *v.* act.

acuarela /akua'rela/ *n. f.* watercolor.

acuario /a'kuario/ *n. m.* aquarium.

acuático /a'kuatiko/ *a.* aquatic.

acuchillar /akutʃi'ʎar; akutʃi'yar/ *v.* slash, knife.

acudir /aku'ðir/ *v.* rally; hasten; be present.

acuerdo /a'kuerðo/ *n. m.* accord, agreement; settlement. **de a.,** in agreement, agreed.

acumulación /akumula'θion; akumula'sion/ *n. f.* accumulation.

acumular /akumu'lar/ *v.* accumulate.

acuñar /aku'ɲar/ *v.* coin, mint.

acupuntura /akupun'tura/ *n. f.* acupuncture.

acusación /akusa'θion; akusa'sion/ *n. f.* accusation, charge.

acusado /aku'saðo/ **-da** *a. & n.* accused; defendant.

acusador /akusa'ðor/ **-ra** *n.* accuser.

acusar /aku'sar/ *v.* accuse; acknowledge.

acústica /a'kustika/ *n. f.* acoustics.

adaptación /aðapta'θion; aðapta'sion/ *n. f.* adaptation.

adaptador /aðapta'ðor/ *n. m.* adapter.

adaptar /aðap'tar/ *v.* adapt.

adecuado /aðe'kuaðo/ *a.* adequate.

adelantado /aðelan'taðo/ *a.* advanced; fast (clock).

adelantamiento /aðelanta'miento/ *n. m.* advancement, promotion.

adelantar /aðelan'tar/ *v.* advance.

adelante /aðe'lante/ *adv.* ahead, forward, onward, on.

adelanto /aðe'lanto/ *n. m.* advancement, progress, improvement.

adelgazar /aðelga'θar; aðelga'sar/ *v.* make thin.

ademán /aðe'man/ *n. m.* attitude; gesture.

además /aðe'mas/ *adv.* in addition, besides, also.

adentro /a'ðentro/ *adv.* in, inside.

adepto /a'ðepto/ *a.* adept.

aderezar /aðere'θar; aðere'sar/ *v.* prepare; trim.

adherirse /aðe'rirse/ *v.* adhere, stick.

adhesivo /aðe'siβo/ *a.* adhesive.

adicción /aðik'θion; aðik'sion/ *n. f.* adiction.

adición /aði'θion; aði'sion/ *n. f.* addition.

adicional /aðiθio'nal; aðisio'nal/ *a.* additional, extra.

adicto /a'ðikto/ **-ta** *a. & n.* addicted; addict.

adinerado /aðine'raðo/ **-a** *a.* wealthy.

adiós /a'ðios/ *n. m. & interj.* good-bye, farewell.

adivinar /aðiβi'nar/ *v.* guess.

adjetivo /aðhe'tiβo/ *n. m.* adjective.

adjunto /að'hunto/ *a.* enclosed.

administración /aðministra'θion; aðministra'sion/ *n. f.* administration.

administrador /aðministra'ðor/ **-ra** *n.* administrator.

administrar /aðminis'trar/ *v.* administer; manage.

administrativo /aðministra'tiβo/ *a.* administrative.

admirable /aðmi'raβle/ *a.* admirable.

admiración. /aðmira'θion; aðmira'o-prim;sion/ *n. f.* admiration; wonder.

admirar /aðmiˈrar/ v. admire.

admisión /aðmiˈsion/ n. f. admission.

admitir /aðmiˈtir/ v. admit, acknowledge.

ADN, abbr. **(ácido desoxirribonucleico)** DNA (deoxyribonucleic acid).

adobar /adoˈβar/ v. marinate.

adolescencia /aðolesˈθenθia; aðolesˈsensia/ n. f. adolescence, youth.

adolescente /aðolesˈθente; aðolesˈsente/ a. & n. adolescent.

adónde /aˈðonde/ adv. where.

adondequiera /a͵ðondeˈkiera/ conj. wherever.

adopción /aðopˈθion; aðopˈsion/ n. f. adoption.

adoptar /aðopˈtar/ v. adopt.

adoración /aðoraˈθion; aðoraˈsion/ n. f. worship, love, adoration. **—adorar,** v.

adormecer /aðormeˈθer; aðormeˈser/ v. drowse.

adornar /aðorˈnar/ v. adorn; decorate.

adorno /aˈðorno/ n. m. adornment, trimming.

adquirir /aðkiˈrir/ v. acquire, obtain.

adquisición /aðkisiˈθion; aðkisiˈsion/ n. f. acquisition, attainment.

aduana /aˈðuana/ n. f. custom house, customs.

adujada /aðuˈhaða/ n. f. Naut. coil of rope.

adulación /aðulaˈθion; aðulaˈsion/ n. f. flattery.

adular /aðuˈlar/ v. flatter.

adulterar /aðulteˈrar/ v. adulterate.

adulterio /aðulˈterio/ n. m. adultery.

adulto /aˈðulto/ **-ta** a. & n. adult.

adusto /aˈðusto/ a. gloomy; austere.

adverbio /aðˈβerβio/ n. m. adverb.

adversario /aðβerˈsario/ n. m. adversary.

adversidad /aðβersiˈðað/ n. f. adversity.

adverso /aðˈβerso/ a. adverse.

advertencia /aðβerˈtenθia; aðβerˈtensia/ n. f. warning.

advertir /aðβerˈtir/ v. warn; notice.

adyacente /aðyaˈθente; aðyaˈsente/ a. adjacent.

aéreo /ˈaereo/ a. aerial; air.

aerodeslizador /aeroðesliθaˈðor; aeroðeslisaˈðor/ n. m. hovercraft.

aeromoza /aeroˈmoθa; aeroˈmosa/ n. f. stewardess, flight attendant.

aeroplano /aeroˈplano/ n. m. light plane.

aeropuerto /aeroˈpuerto/ n. m. airport.

aerosol /aeroˈsol/ n. m. aerosol, spray.

afable /aˈfaβle/ a. affable, pleasant.

afanarse /afaˈnarse/ v. toil.

afear /afeˈar/ v. deface, mar, deform.

afectación /afektaˈθion; afektaˈsion/ n. f. affectation.

afectar /afekˈtar/ v. affect.

afecto /aˈfekto/ n. m. affection, attachment.

afeitada /afeiˈtaða/ n. f. shave. **—afeitarse,** v.

afeminado /afemiˈnaðo/ a. effeminate.

afición /afiˈθion; afiˈsion/ n. f. fondness, liking; hobby.

aficionado /afiθioˈnaðo; afisioˈnaðo/ a. fond.

aficionado -da n. fan, devotee; amateur.

aficionarse a /afiθioˈnarse a; afisioˈnarse a/ v. become fond of.

afilado /afiˈlaðo/ a. sharp.

afilar /afiˈlar/ v. sharpen.

afiliación /afiliaˈθion; afiliaˈsion/ n. f. affiliation.

afiliado /afiˈliaðo/ **-da** n. affiliate. **—afiliar,** v.

afinar /afiˈnar/ v. polish; tune up.

afinidad /afiniˈðað/ n. f. relationship, affinity.

afirmación /afirmaˈθion; afirmaˈsion/ n. f. affirmation, statement.

afirmar /afirˈmar/ v. affirm, assert.

afirmativa /afirmaˈtiβa/ n. f. affirmative. **—afirmativo,** a.

aflicción /aflikˈθion; aflikˈsion/ n. f. affliction; sorrow, grief.

afligido /afliˈhiðo/ a. sorrowful, grieved.

afligir /afliˈhir/ v. grieve, distress.

aflojar /afloˈhar/ v. loosen.

afluencia /aˈfluenθia; aˈfluensia/ n. f. influx.

afortunado /afortuˈnaðo/ a. fortunate, successful, lucky.

afrenta /aˈfrenta/ n. f. insult, outrage, affront. **—afrentar,** v.

afrentoso /afrenˈtoso/ a. shameful.

africano /afriˈkano/ **-na** a. & n. African.

afuera /aˈfuera/ adv. out, outside.

afueras /aˈfueras/ n. f.pl. suburbs.

agacharse /agaˈtʃarse/ v. squat, crouch; cower.

agarrar /agaˈrrar/ v. seize, grasp, clutch.

agarro /aˈgarro/ n. m. clutch, grasp.

agencia /aˈhenθia; aˈhensia/ n. f. agency.

agencia de colocaciones /aˈhenθia de kolokaˈθiones; aˈhensia de kolokaˈsiones/ employment agency.

agencia de viajes /aˈhenθia de ˈbiahes; aˈhensia de ˈbiahes/ travel agency.

agente /aˈhente/ n. m. & f. agent, representative.

agente de aduana /aˈhente de aˈðuana/ mf. customs officer.

agente inmobiliario /aˈhente imoβiˈliario/ **-ria** n. real-estate agent.

ágil /ˈahil/ a. agile, spry.

agitación /ahitaˈθion; ahitaˈsion/ n. f. agitation, ferment.

agitado /ahiˈtaðo/ a. agitated; excited.

agitador /ahitaˈðor/ n. m. agitator.

agitar /ahiˈtar/ v. shake, agitate, excite.

agobiar /agoˈβiar/ v. oppress, burden.

agosto /aˈgosto/ n. m. August.

agotamiento /a͵gotaˈmiento/ n. m. exhaustion.

agotar /agoˈtar/ v. exhaust, use up, sap.

agradable /agraˈðaβle/ a. agreeable, pleasant.

agradar /agraˈðar/ v. please.

agradecer /agraðeˈθer; agraðeˈser/ v. thank; appreciate, be grateful for.

agradecido /agraðeˈθiðo; agraðeˈsiðo/ a. grateful, thankful.

agradecimiento /agraðeθiˈmiento; agraðesiˈmiento/ n. m. gratitude, thanks.

agravar /agraˈβar/ v. aggravate, make worse.

agravio /aˈgraβio/ n. m. wrong. **—agraviar,** v.

agregado /agreˈgaðo/ a. & n. aggregate; Pol. attaché.

agregar /agreˈgar/ v. add; gather.

agresión /agreˈsion/ n. f. aggression; Leg. battery.

agresivo /agreˈsiβo/ a. aggressive.

agresor /agreˈsor/ **-ra** n. aggressor.

agrícola /aˈgrikola/ a. agricultural.

agricultor /agrikulˈtor/ n. m. farmer.

agricultura /agrikulˈtura/ n. f. agriculture, farming.

agrio /ˈagrio/ a. sour.

agrupar /agruˈpar/ v. group.

agua /ˈagua/ n. f. water. **—aguar,** v.

aguacate /aguaˈkate/ n. m. avocado, alligator pear.

aguafuerte /͵aguaˈfuerte/ n. f. etching.

agua mineral /ˈagua mineˈral/ mineral water.

aguantar /aguanˈtar/ v. endure, stand, put up with.

aguardar /aguarˈðar/ v. await; expect.

aguardiente /aguarˈðiente/ n. m. brandy.

aguas abajo /ˈaguas aˈβaho/ adv. downriver, downstream.

aguas arriba /ˈaguas aˈrriβa/ adv. upriver, upstream.

agudo /aˈguðo/ a. sharp, keen, shrill, acute.

agüero /aˈguero/ n. m. omen.

águila /ˈagila/ n. f. eagle.

aguja /aˈguha/ n. f. needle.

agujero /aguˈhero/ n. m. hole.

aguzar /aguˈθar; aguˈsar/ v. sharpen.

ahí /aˈi/ adv. there.

ahogar /aoˈgar/ v. drown; choke; suffocate.

ahondar /aonˈdar/ v. deepen.

ahora /aˈora/ adv. now.

ahorcar /aorˈkar/ v. hang (execute).

ahorrar /aoˈrrar/ v. save, save up; spare.

ahorros /aˈorros/ n. m.pl. savings.

ahumar /auˈmar/ v. smoke.

airado /aiˈraðo/ a. angry, indignant.

aire /ˈaire/ n. m. air. **—airear,** v.

aire acondicionado /ˈaire akondiθioˈnaðo; ˈaire akondisioˈnaðo/ air conditioning.

aislamiento /aislaˈmiento/ n. m. isolation.

aislar /aisˈlar/ v. isolate.

ajedrez /aheˈðreθ; aheˈðres/ n. m. chess.

ajeno /aˈheno/ a. alien; someone else's.

ajetreo /aheˈtreo/ n. m. hustle and bustle.

ají /aˈhi/ n. m. chili.

ajo /ˈaho/ n. m. garlic.

ajustado /ahusˈtaðo/ a. adjusted; trim; exact.

ajustar /ahusˈtar/ v. adjust.

ajuste /aˈhuste/ n. m. adjustment, settlement.

al /al/ contr. of **a** + **el.**

ala /ˈala/ n. f. wing; brim (of hat).

alabanza /alaˈβanθa; alaˈβansa/ n. f. praise. **—alabar,** v.

alabear /alaβeˈar/ v. warp.

ala delta /ˈala ˈdelta/ hang glider.

alambique /alamˈbike/ n. m. still.

alambre /aˈlambre/ n. m. wire. **a. de púas,** barbed wire.

alarde /aˈlarðe/ n. m. boasting, ostentation.

alargar /alarˈgar/ v. lengthen; stretch out.

alarma /aˈlarma/ n. f. alarm. **—alarmar,** v.

alba /ˈalβa/ n. f. daybreak, dawn.

albanega /alβaˈnega/ n. f. hair net.

albañil /alβaˈɲil/ n. m. bricklayer; mason.

albaricoque /alβariˈkoke/ n. m. apricot.

alberca /alˈβerka/ n. f. swimming pool.

albergue /alˈβerge/ n. m. shelter. **—albergar,** v.

alborotar /alβoroˈtar/ v. disturb, make noise, brawl, riot.

alboroto /alβoˈroto/ n. m. brawl, disturbance, din, tumult.

álbum /ˈalβum/ n. m. album.

álbum de recortes /ˈalβum de reˈkortes/ scrapbook.

alcachofa /alkaˈtʃofa/ n. f. artichoke.

alcalde /alˈkalde/ n. m. mayor.

alcance /alˈkanθe; alˈkanse/ n. m. reach; range, scope.

alcanfor /alkanˈfor/ n. m. camphor.

alcanzar /alkanˈθar; alkanˈsar/ v. reach, overtake, catch.

alcayata /alkaˈyata/ n. f. spike.

alce /ˈalθe; ˈalse/ n. m. elk.

alcoba /alˈkoβa/ n. f. bedroom; alcove.

alcoba de huéspedes /alˈkoβa de ˈuespeðes/ guest room.

alcoba de respeto /alˈkoβa de rresˈpeto/ guest room.

alcohol /alˈkool/ n. m. alcohol.

alcohólico /alkoˈoliko/ **-ca** a. & n. alcoholic.

aldaba /alˈdaβa/ n. f. latch.

aldea /alˈdea/ n. f. village.

alegación /alegaˈθion; alegaˈsion/ n. f. allegation.

alegar /aleˈgar/ v. allege.

alegrar /aleˈgrar/ v. make happy, brighten.

alegrarse /aleˈgrarse/ v. be glad.

alegre /aˈlegre/ a. glad, cheerful, merry.

alegría /aleˈgria/ n. f. gaiety, cheer.

alejarse /aleˈharse/ v. move away, off.

alemán /aleˈman/ **-ana** a. & n. German.

Alemania /aleˈmania/ n. f. Germany.

alentar /alenˈtar/ v. cheer up, encourage.

alergia /alerˈhia/ n. f. allergy.

alerta /aˈlerta/ adv. on the alert.

aleve /aˈleβe/ **alevoso** a. treacherous.

alfabeto /alfaˈβeto/ n. m. alphabet.

alfalfa /alˈfalfa/ n. f. alfalfa.

alfarería /alfareˈria/ n. f. pottery.

alférez /alˈfereθ; alˈferes/ n. m. (naval) ensign.

alfil /alˈfil/ n. m. (chess) bishop.

alfiler /alfiˈler/ n. m. pin.

alfombra /alˈfombra/ n. f. carpet, rug.

alforja /alˈforha/ n. f. knapsack; saddlebag.

alga /ˈalga/ n. f. seaweed.

alga marina /ˈalga maˈrina/ seaweed.

algarabía /algaraˈβia/ n. f. jargon; din.

álgebra /ˈalheβra/ n. f. algebra.

algo /ˈalgo/ pron. & adv. something, somewhat; anything.

algodón /algoˈðon/ n. m. cotton.

algodón hidrófilo /algoˈðon iˈðrofilo/ absorbent cotton.

alguien /ˈalgien/ pron. somebody, someone; anybody, anyone.

algún /alˈgun/ **-no -na** a. & pron. some; any.

alhaja /aˈlaha/ n. f. jewel.

aliado /aˈliaðo/ **-da** a. & n. allied; ally. **—aliar,** v.

alianza /aˈlianθa; aˈliansa/ n. f. alliance.

alicates /aliˈkates/ n. m.pl. pliers.

aliento /aˈliento/ n. m. breath. **dar a.,** encourage.

aligerar /aliheˈrar/ v. lighten.

alimentar /alimenˈtar/ v. feed, nourish.

alimento /aliˈmento/ n. m. nourishment, food.

alinear /alineˈar/ v. line up; Pol. align.

aliñar /aliˈɲar/ v. dress (a salad).

aliño /aˈliɲo/ n. m. salad dressing.

alisar /aliˈsar/ v. smooth.

alistamiento /alistaˈmiento/ n. m. enlistment.

alistar /alisˈtar/ v. make ready, prime.

alistarse /alisˈtarse/ v. get ready; Mil. enlist.

aliviar /aliˈβiar/ v. alleviate, relieve, ease.

alivio /aˈliβio/ n. m. relief.

allá /aˈʎa; aˈya/ adv. there. **más a.,** beyond, farther on.

allanar /aʎaˈnar; ayaˈnar/ v. flatten, smooth, plane.

allí /aˈʎi; aˈyi/ adv. there. **por a.,** that way.

alma /ˈalma/ n. f. soul.

almacén /almaˈθen; almaˈsen/ n. m. department store; storehouse, warehouse.

almacenaje /almaθeˈnahe; almaseˈnahe/ n. m. storage.

almacenar /almaθeˈnar; almaseˈnar/ v. store.

almanaque /almaˈnake/ n. m. almanac.

almeja /alˈmeha/ n. f. clam.

almendra /alˈmendra/ n. f. almond.

almíbar /alˈmiβar/ n. m. syrup.

almidón /almiˈðon/ n. m. starch. **—almidonar,** v.

almirante /almiˈrante/ n. m. admiral.

almohada /almoˈaða/ n. f. pillow.

almuerzo /al'muerθo; al'muerso/ *n. m.* lunch. —**almorzar**, *v.*

alojamiento /aloha'miento/ *n. m.* lodging, accommodations.

alojar /alo'har/ *v.* lodge, house.

alojarse /alo'harse/ *v.* stay, room.

alquiler /alki'ler/ *n. m.* rent. —**alquilar**, *v.*

alrededor /alreðe'ðor/ *adv.* around.

alrededores /alreðe'ðores/ *n. m.pl.* environs.

altanero /alta'nero/ *a.* haughty.

altar /al'tar/ *n. m.* altar.

altavoz /ˌalta'βoθ; ˌalta'βos/ *n. m.* loudspeaker.

alteración /altera'θion; altera'sion/ *n. f.* alteration.

alterar /alte'rar/ *v.* alter.

alternativa /alterna'tiβa/ *n. f.* alternative. —**alternativo**, *a.*

alterno /al'terno/ *a.* alternate. —**alternar**, *v.*

alteza /al'teθa; al'tesa/ *n. f.* highness.

altivo /al'tiβo/ *a.* proud, haughty; lofty.

alto /'alto/ *a.* **1.** high, tall; loud. —*n.* **2.** *m.* height, story (house).

altura /al'tura/ *n. f.* height, altitude.

alud /a'luð/ *n. m.* avalanche.

aludir /alu'ðir/ *v.* allude.

alumbrado /alum'braðo/ *n. m.* lighting.

alumbrar /alum'brar/ *v.* light.

aluminio /alu'minio/ *n. m.* aluminum.

alumno /a'lumno/ **-na** *n.* student, pupil.

alusión /alu'sion/ *n. f.* allusion.

alza /'alθa; 'alsa/ *n. f.* rise; boost.

alzar /al'θar; al'sar/ *v.* raise, lift.

ama /'ama/ *n. f.* housewife, mistress (of house). **a. de llaves,** housekeeper.

amable /a'maβle/ *a.* kind; pleasant, sweet.

amalgamar /amalga'mar/ *v.* amalgamate.

amamantar /amaman'tar/ *v.* suckle, nurse.

amanecer /amane'θer; amane'ser/ *n.* **1.** *m.* dawn, daybreak. —*v.* **2.** dawn; awaken.

amante /a'mante/ *n. m. & f.* lover.

amapola /ama'pola/ *n. f.* poppy.

amar /a'mar/ *v.* love.

amargo /a'margo/ *a.* bitter.

amargón /amar'gon/ *n. m.* dandelion.

amargura /amar'gura/ *n. f.* bitterness.

amarillo /ama'riʎo; ama'riyo/ *a.* yellow.

amarradero /amarra'ðero/ *n. m.* mooring.

amarrar /ama'rrar/ *v.* hitch, moor, tie up.

amartillar /amarti'ʎar; amarti'yar/ *v.* hammer; cock (a gun).

amasar /ama'sar/ *v.* knead, mold.

ámbar /'ambar/ *n. m.* amber.

ambarino /amba'rino/ *a.* amber.

ambición /ambi'θion; ambi'sion/ *n. f.* ambition.

ambicionar /ambiθio'nar; ambisio'nar/ *v.* aspire to.

ambicioso /ambi'θioso; ambi'sioso/ *a.* ambitious.

ambientalista /ambienta'lista/ *n. m. & f.* environmentalist.

ambiente /am'biente/ *n. m.* environment, atmosphere.

ambigüedad /ambigue'ðað/ *n. f.* ambiguity.

ambiguo /am'biguo/ *a.* ambiguous.

ambos /'ambos/ *a. & pron.* both.

ambulancia /ambu'lanθia; ambu'lansia/ *n. f.* ambulance.

amenaza /ame'naθa; ame'nasa/ *n. f.* threat, menace.

amenazar /amena'θar; amena'sar/ *v.* threaten, menace.

ameno /a'meno/ *a.* pleasant.

americana /ameri'kana/ *n. f.* suit coat.

americano /ameri'kano/ **-na** *a. & n.* American.

ametralladora /ametraʎa'ðora; ametraya'ðora/ *n. f.* machine gun.

amigable /ami'gaβle/ *a.* amicable, friendly.

amígdala /a'migdala/ *n. f.* tonsil.

amigo /a'migo/ **-ga** *n.* friend.

aminorar /amino'rar/ *v.* lessen, reduce.

amistad /amis'tað/ *n. f.* friendship.

amistoso /amis'toso/ *a.* friendly.

amniocéntesis /amnioθen'tesis; amniosen'tesis/ *n. m.* amniocentesis.

amonestaciones /amonesta'θiones; amonesta'siones/ *n. f.pl.* banns.

amonestar /amones'tar/ *v.* admonish.

amoníaco /amo'niako/ *n. m.* ammonia.

amontonar /amonto'nar/ *v.* amass, pile up.

amor /a'mor/ *n. m.* love. **a. propio,** self-esteem.

amorío /amo'rio/ *n. m.* romance, love affair.

amoroso /amo'roso/ *a.* amorous; loving.

amortecer /amorte'θer; amorte'ser/ *v.* deaden.

amparar /ampa'rar/ *v.* aid, befriend; protect, shield.

amparo /am'paro/ *n. m.* protection.

ampliar /amp'liar/ *v.* enlarge; elaborate.

amplificar /amplifi'kar/ *v.* amplify.

amplio /'amplio/ *a.* ample, roomy.

ampolla /am'poʎa; am'poya/ *n. f.* bubble; bulb; blister.

amputar /ampu'tar/ *v.* amputate.

amueblar /amue'βlar/ *v.* furnish.

analfabeto /analfa'βeto/ **-ta** *a. & n.* illiterate.

analgésico /anal'hesiko/ *n. m.* pain killer.

análisis /a'nalisis/ *n. m.* analysis.

analizar /anali'θar; anali'sar/ *v.* analyze.

analogía /analo'hia/ *n. f.* analogy.

análogo /a'nalogo/ *a.* similar, analogous.

anarquía /anar'kia/ *n. f.* anarchy.

anatomía /anato'mia/ *n. f.* anatomy.

ancho /'antʃo/ *a.* wide, broad.

anchoa /an'tʃoa/ *n. f.* anchovy.

anchura /an'tʃura/ *n. f.* width, breadth.

anciano /an'θiano; an'siano/ **-na** *a. & n.* old, aged (person).

ancla /'ankla/ *n. f.* anchor. —**anclar,** *v.*

anclaje /an'klahe/ *n. m.* anchorage.

andamio /an'damio/ *n. m.* scaffold.

andar /an'dar/ *v.* walk; move, go.

andén /an'den/ *n. m.* (railroad) platform.

andrajoso /andra'hoso/ *a.* ragged, uneven.

anécdota /a'nekðota/ *n. f.* anecdote.

anegar /ane'gar/ *v.* flood, drown.

anestesia /anes'tesia/ *n. f.* anesthetic.

anexar /anek'sar/ *v.* annex.

anexión /anek'sion/ *n. f.* annexation.

anfitrión /anfitri'on/ **-na** *n.* host.

ángel /'anhel/ *n. m.* angel.

angosto /aŋ'gosto/ *a.* narrow.

anguila /aŋ'gila/ *n. f.* eel.

angular /aŋgu'lar/ *a.* angular.

ángulo /'aŋgulo/ *n. m.* angle.

angustia /aŋ'gustia/ *n. f.* anguish, agony.

angustiar /aŋgus'tiar/ *v.* distress.

anhelar /ane'lar/ *v.* long for.

anidar /ani'ðar/ *v.* nest, nestle.

anillo /a'niʎo; a'niyo/ *n. m.* ring; circle.

animación /anima'θion; anima'sion/ *n. f.* animation; bustle.

animado /ani'maðo/ *a.* animated, lively; animate.

animal /ani'mal/ *a. & n.* animal.

ánimo /'animo/ *n. m.* state of mind, spirits; courage.

aniquilar /aniki'lar/ *v.* annihilate, destroy.

aniversario /aniβer'sario/ *n. m.* anniversary.

anoche /a'notʃe/ *adv.* last night.

anochecer /anotʃe'θer; anotʃe'ser/ *n.* **1.** *m.* twilight, nightfall. —*v.* **2.** get dark.

anónimo /a'nonimo/ *a.* anonymous.

anorexia /ano'reksia/ *n. f.* anorexia.

anormal /anor'mal/ *a.* abnormal.

anotación /anota'θion; anota'sion/ *n. f.* annotation.

anotar /ano'tar/ *v.* annotate.

ansia /'ansia/ **ansiedad** *n. f.* anxiety.

ansioso /an'sioso/ *a.* anxious.

antagonismo /antago'nismo/ *n. m.* antagonism.

antagonista /antago'nista/ *n. m. & f.* antagonist, opponent.

anteayer /antea'yer/ *adv.* day before yesterday.

antebrazo /ante'βraθo; ante'βraso/ *n. m.* forearm.

antecedente /anteθe'ðente; antese'ðente/ *a. & m.* antecedent.

anteceder /anteθe'ðer; antese'ðer/ *v.* precede.

antecesor /anteθe'sor; antese'sor/ *n. m.* ancestor.

antemano /ante'mano/ *de a.,* in advance.

antena /an'tena/ *n. f.* antenna.

antena parabólica /an'tena para'βolika/ satellite dish.

anteojos /ante'ohos/ *n. m.pl.* eyeglasses.

antepasado /antepa'saðo/ *n. m.* ancestor.

antepenúltimo /antepe'nultimo/ *a.* antepenultimate.

anterior /ante'rior/ *a.* previous, former.

antes /'antes/ *adv.* before; formerly.

antibala /anti'bala/ *a.* bulletproof.

anticipación /antiθipa'θion; antisipa'sion/ *n. f.* anticipation.

anticipar /antiθi'par; antisi'par/ *v.* anticipate; advance.

anticonceptivo /antikonθep'tiβo; antikonsep'tiβo/ *a. & n.* contraceptive.

anticongelante /antikoŋge'lante/ *n. m.* antifreeze.

anticuado /anti'kuaðo/ *a.* antiquated, obsolete.

antídoto /an'tiðoto/ *n. m.* antidote.

antigüedad /antigue'ðað/ *n. f.* antiquity; antique.

antiguo /an'tiguo/ *a.* former; old; antique.

antihistamínico /antiista'miniko/ *n. m.* antihistamine.

antílope /an'tilope/ *n. m.* antelope.

antinuclear /antinukle'ar/ *a.* antinuclear.

antipatía /antipa'tia/ *n. f.* antipathy.

antipático /anti'patiko/ *a.* disagreeable, nasty.

antiséptico /anti'septiko/ *a. & m.* antiseptic.

antojarse /anto'harse/ *v.* **se me antoja...** etc., I desire..., take a fancy to..., etc.

antojo /an'toho/ *n. m.* whim, fancy.

antorcha /an'tortʃa/ *n. f.* torch.

antracita /antra'θita; antra'sita/ *n. f.* anthracite.

anual /a'nual/ *a.* annual, yearly.

anudar /anu'ðar/ *v.* knot; tie.

anular /anu'lar/ *v.* annul, void.

anunciar /anun'θiar; anun'siar/ *v.* announce; proclaim, advertise.

anuncio /a'nunθio; a'nunsio/ *n. m.* announcement; advertisement.

añadir /aɲa'ðir/ *v.* add.

añil /a'ɲil/ *n. m.* bluing; indigo.

año /'aɲo/ *n. m.* year.

apacible /apa'θiβle; apa'siβle/ *a.* peaceful, peaceable.

apaciguamiento /aˌpaθigua'miento;

apaciguar /apaθi'guar; apasi'guar/ *v.* appease; placate.

apagado /apa'gaðo/ *a.* dull.

apagar /apa'gar/ *v.* extinguish, quench, put out.

apagón /apa'gn/ *n. m.* blackout.

aparador /apara'ðor/ *n. m.* buffet, cupboard.

aparato /apa'rato/ *n. m.* apparatus; machine; appliance, set.

aparcamiento /aparka'miento/ *n. m.* parking lot; parking space.

aparecer /apare'θer; apare'ser/ *v.* appear, show up.

aparejo /apa'reho/ *n. m.* rig. —**aparejar,** *v.*

aparentar /aparen'tar/ *v.* pretend; profess.

aparente /apa'rente/ *a.* apparent.

apariencia /apa'rienθia; apa'riensia/ **aparición** *n. f.* appearance.

apartado /apar'taðo/ *a.* **1.** aloof; separate. —*n.* **2.** *m.* post-office box.

apartamento /aparta'mento/ *n. m.* apartment. **a. en propiedad,** condominium.

apartar /apar'tar/ *v.* separate; remove.

aparte /a'parte/ *adv.* apart; aside.

apartheid /apar'teið/ *n. m.* apartheid.

apasionado /apasio'naðo/ *a.* passionate.

apatía /apa'tia/ *n. f.* apathy.

apearse /ape'arse/ *v.* get off, alight.

apedrear /apeðre'ar/ *v.* stone.

apelación /apela'θion; apela'sion/ *n. f.* appeal. —**apelar,** *v.*

apellido /ape'ʎiðo; ape'yiðo/ *n. m.* family name.

apellido materno /ape'ʎiðo ma'terno; ape'yiðo ma'terno/ mother's family name.

apellido paterno /ape'ʎiðo pa'terno; ape'yiðo pa'terno/ father's family name.

apenas /a'penas/ *adv.* scarcely, hardly.

apéndice /a'pendiθe; a'pendise/ *n. m.* appendix.

apercibir /aperθi'βir; apersi'βir/ *v.* prepare, warn.

aperitivo /aperi'tiβo/ *n. m.* appetizer.

aperos /a'peros/ *n. m.pl.* implements.

apestar /apes'tar/ *v.* infect; stink.

apetecer /apete'θer; apete'ser/ *v.* desire, have appetite for.

apetito /ape'tito/ *n. m.* appetite.

ápice /'apiθe; 'apise/ *n. m.* apex.

apilar /api'lar/ *v.* stack.

apio /'apio/ *n. m.* celery.

aplacar /apla'kar/ *v.* appease; placate.

aplastar /aplas'tar/ *v.* crush, flatten.

aplaudir /aplau'ðir/ *v.* applaud, cheer.

aplauso /a'plauso/ *n. m.* applause.

aplazar /apla'θar; apla'sar/ *v.* postpone, put off.

aplicable /apli'kaβle/ *a.* applicable.

aplicado /apli'kaðo/ *a.* industrious, diligent.

aplicar /apli'kar/ *v.* apply.

aplomo /a'plomo/ *n. m.* aplomb, poise.

apoderado /apoðe'raðo/ **-da** *n.* attorney.

apoderarse de /apoðe'rarse de/ *v.* get hold of, seize.

apodo /a'poðo/ *n. m.* nickname. —**apodar,** *v.*

apologético /apolo'hetiko/ *a.* apologetic.

apoplejía /apople'hia/ *n. f.* apoplexy.

aposento /apo'sento/ *n. m.* room, flat.

apostar /apos'tar/ *v.* bet, wager.

apóstol /a'postol/ *n. m.* apostle.

apoyar /apo'yar/ *v.* support, prop; lean.

apoyo /a'poyo/ *n. m.* support; prop; aid; approval.

apreciable /apreθia'βle; apresia'βle/ *a.* appreciable.

apreciar /apre'θiar; apre'siar/ v. appreciate, prize.

aprecio /a'preθio; a'presio/ n. m. appreciation, regard.

apremio /a'premio/ n. m. pressure, compulsion.

aprender /apren'der/ v. learn.

aprendiz /apren'diθ; apren'dis/ n. m. apprentice.

aprendizaje /aprendi'θahe; aprendi'sahe/ n. m. apprenticeship.

aprensión /apren'sion/ n. f. apprehension.

aprensivo /apren'siβo/ a. apprehensive.

apresurado /apresu'raðo/ a. hasty, fast.

apresurar /apresu'rar/ v. hurry, speed up.

apretado /apre'taðo/ a. tight.

apretar /apre'tar/ v. squeeze, press; tighten.

apretón /apre'ton/ n. m. squeeze.

aprieto /a'prieto/ n. m. plight, predicament.

aprobación /aproβa'θion; aproβa'sion/ n. f. approbation, approval.

aprobar /apro'βar/ v. approve.

apropiación /apropia'θion; apropia'sion/ n. f. appropriation.

apropiado /apro'piaðo/ a. appropriate. —**apropiar,** v.

aprovechar /aproβe't ʃar/ v. profit by.

aprovecharse /aproβe't ʃarse/ v. take advantage.

aproximado /aproksi'maðo/ a. approximate.

aproximarse a /aproksi'marse a/ v. approach.

aptitud /apti'tuð/ n. f. aptitude.

apto /'apto/ a. apt.

apuesta /a'puesta/ n. f. bet, wager, stake.

apuntar /apun'tar/ v. point, aim; prompt; write down.

apunte /a'punte/ n. m. annotation, note; promptings, cue.

apuñalar /apuɲa'lar/ v. stab.

apurar /apu'rar/ v. hurry; worry.

apuro /a'puro/ n. m. predicament, scrape, trouble.

aquel /a'kel/ **aquella** dem. a. that.

aquél /a'kel/ **aquélla** dem. pron. that (one); the former.

aquello /a'keʎo; a'keyo/ dem. pron. that.

aquí /a'ki/ adv. here. **por a.,** this way.

aquietar /akie'tar/ v. allay; lull, pacify.

ara /'ara/ n. f. altar.

árabe /'araβe/ a. & n. Arab, Arabic.

arado /a'raðo/ n. m. plow. —**arar,** v.

arándano /a'randano/ n. m. cranberry.

araña /a'raɲa/ n. f. spider. **a. de luces,** chandelier.

arbitración /arβitra'θion; arβitra'sion/ n. f. arbitration.

arbitrador /arβitra'ðor/ -ra n. arbitrator.

arbitraje /arβi'trahe/ n. m. arbitration.

arbitrar /arβi'trar/ v. arbitrate.

arbitrario /arβi'trario/ a. arbitrary.

árbitro /'arβitro/ n. m. arbiter, umpire, referee.

árbol /'arβol/ n. m. tree; mast.

árbol genealógico /'arβol henea'lohiko/ family tree.

arbusto /ar'βusto/ n. m. bush, shrub.

arca /'arka/ n. f. chest; ark.

arcada /ar'kaða/ n. f. arcade.

arcaico /ar'kaiko/ a. archaic.

arce /'arθe; 'arse/ n. m. maple.

archipiélago /art ʃi'pielago/ n. m. archipelago.

archivador /art ʃiβa'ðor/ n. m. file cabinet.

archivo /ar't ʃiβo/ n. m. archive; file. —**archivar,** v.

arcilla /ar'θiʎa; ar'siya/ n. f. clay.

arco /'arko/ n. m. arc; arch; (archer's) bow. **a. iris,** rainbow.

arder /ar'ðer/ v. burn.

ardid /ar'ðið/ n. m. stratagem, cunning.

ardiente /ar'ðiente/ a. ardent, burning, fiery.

ardilla /ar'ðiʎa; ar'ðiya/ n. f. squirrel.

ardor /ar'ðor/ n. m. ardor, fervor.

ardor de estómago /ar'ðor de es'tomago/ heartburn.

arduo /'arðuo/ a. arduous.

área /'area/ n. f. area.

arena /a'rena/ n. f. sand; arena.

arenoso /are'noso/ a. sandy.

arenque /a'renke/ n. m. herring.

arete /a'rete/ n. earring.

argentino /arhen'tino/ -na a. & n. Argentine.

argüir /ar'guir/ v. dispute, argue.

árido /'ariðo/ a. arid.

aristocracia /aristo'kraθia; aristo'krasia/ n. f. aristocracy.

aristócrata /aris'tokrata/ n. f. aristocrat.

aristocrático /aristo'kratiko/ a. aristocratic.

aritmética /arit'metika/ n. f. arithmetic.

arma /'arma/ n. f. weapon, arm.

armadura /arma'ðura/ n. f. armor; reinforcement; framework.

armamento /arma'mento/ n. m. armament.

armar /ar'mar/ v. arm.

armario /ar'mario/ n. m. cabinet, bureau, wardrobe.

armazón /arma'θon; arma'son/ n. f. framework, frame.

armería /arme'ria/ n. f. armory.

armisticio /armis'tiθio; armis'tisio/ n. m. armistice.

armonía /armo'nia/ n. f. harmony.

armonioso /armo'nioso/ a. harmonious.

armonizar /armoni'θar; armoni'sar/ v. harmonize.

arnés /ar'nes/ n. m. harness.

aroma /a'roma/ n. f. aroma, fragrance.

aromático /aro'matiko/ a. aromatic.

arpa /'arpa/ n. f. harp.

arquear /arke'ar/ v. arch.

arquitecto /arki'tekto/ n. m. architect.

arquitectura /arkitek'tura/ n. f. architecture.

arquitectural /arkitektu'ral/ a. architectural.

arrabal /arra'βal/ n. m. suburb.

arraigar /arrai'gar/ v. take root, settle.

arrancar /arran'kar/ v. pull out, tear out; start up.

arranque /a'rranke/ n. m. dash, sudden start; fit of anger.

arrastrar /arras'trar/ v. drag.

arrebatar /arreβa'tar/ v. snatch, grab.

arrebato /arre'βato/ n. m. sudden attack, fit of anger.

arrecife /arre'θife; arre'sife/ n. m. reef.

arreglar /arre'glar/ v. arrange; repair, fix; adjust, settle.

arreglárselas /arre'glarselas/ v. manage, shift for oneself.

arreglo /a'rreglo/ n. m. arrangement, settlement.

arremangarse /arremaŋ'garse/ v. roll up one's sleeves; roll up one's pants.

arremeter /arreme'ter/ v. attack.

arrendar /arren'dar/ v. rent.

arrepentimiento /arrepenti'miento/ n. m. repentance.

arrepentirse /arrepen'tirse/ v. repent.

arrestar /arres'tar/ v. arrest.

arriba /a'rriβa/ adv. up; upstairs.

arriendo /a'rriendo/ n. m. lease.

arriero /a'rriero/ n. m. muleteer.

arriesgar /arries'gar/ v. risk.

arrimarse /arri'marse/ v. lean.

arrodillarse /arroði'ʎarse; arroði'yarse/ v. kneel.

arrogancia /arro'ganθia; arro'gansia/ n. f. arrogance.

arrogante /arro'gante/ a. arrogant.

arrojar /arro'har/ v. throw, hurl; shed.

arrollar /arro'ʎar; arro'yar/ v. roll, coil.

arroyo /a'rroyo/ n. m. brook; gully; gutter.

arroz /a'rroθ; a'rros/ n. m. rice.

arruga /a'rruga/ n. f. ridge; wrinkle.

arrugar /arru'gar/ v. wrinkle, crumple.

arruinar /arrui'nar/ v. ruin, destroy, wreck.

arsenal /arse'nal/ n. m. arsenal; armory.

arsénico /ar'seniko/ n. m. arsenic.

arte /'arte/ n. m. (f. in pl.) art, craft; wiliness.

arteria /ar'teria/ n. f. artery.

artesa /ar'tesa/ n. f. trough.

artesano /arte'sano/ -na n. artisan, craftsman.

ártico /'artiko/ a. arctic.

articulación /artikula'θion; artikula'sion/ n. f. articulation; joint.

articular /artiku'lar/ v. articulate.

artículo /ar'tikulo/ n. m. article.

artífice /ar'tifiθe; ar'tifise/ n. m. & f. artisan.

artificial /artifi'θial; artifi'sial/ a. artificial.

artificio /arti'fiθio; arti'fisio/ n. m. artifice, device.

artificioso /artifi'θioso; artifi'sioso/ a. affected.

artillería /artiʎe'ria; artiye'ria/ n. f. artillery.

artista /ar'tista/ n. m. & f. artist.

artístico /ar'tistiko/ a. artistic.

artritis /ar'tritis/ n. f. arthritis.

arzobispo /arθo'βispo; arso'βispo/ n. m. archbishop.

as /as/ n. m. ace.

asado /a'saðo/ a. & n. roast.

asaltador /asalta'ðor/ -ra n. assailant.

asaltante /asal'tante/ n. m. & f. mugger.

asaltar /asal'tar/ v. assail, attack.

asalto /a'salto/ n. m. assault. —**asaltar,** v.

asamblea /asam'βlea/ n. f. assembly.

asar /a'sar/ v. roast; broil, cook (meat).

asaz /a'saθ; a'sas/ adv. enough; quite.

ascender /asθen'der; assen'der/ v. ascend, go up; amount.

ascenso /as'θenso; as'senso/ n. m. ascent.

ascensor /asθen'sor; assen'sor/ n. m. elevator.

ascensorista /asθenso'rista; assenso'rista/ n. m. & f. (elevator) operator.

asco /'asko/ n. m. nausea; disgusting thing. **qué a.,** how disgusting.

aseado /ase'aðo/ a. tidy. —**asear,** v.

asediar /ase'ðiar/ v. besiege.

asedio /a'seðio/ n. m. siege.

asegurar /asegu'rar/ v. assure; secure.

asegurarse /asegu'rarse/ v. make sure.

asemejarse a /aseme'harse a/ v. resemble.

asentar /asen'tar/ v. settle; seat.

asentimiento /asenti'miento/ n. m. assent. —**asentir,** v.

aseo /a'seo/ n. m. neatness, tidiness.

aseos /a'seos/ n. m.pl. restroom.

asequible /ase'kiβle/ a. attainable; affordable.

aserción /aser'θion; aser'sion/ n. f. assertion.

aserrar /ase'rrar/ v. saw.

asesinar /asesi'nar/ v. assassinate; murder, slay.

asesinato /asesi'nato/ n. m. assassination, murder.

asesino /ase'sino/ -na n. murderer, assassin.

aseveración /aseβera'θion; aseβera'sion/ n. f. assertion.

aseverar /aseβe'rar/ v. assert.

asfalto /as'falto/ n. m. asphalt.

así /a'si/ adv. so, thus, this way, that way. **a. como,** as well as. **a. que,** as soon as.

asiático /a'siatiko/ -ca a. & n. Asiatic.

asiduo /a'siðuo/ a. assiduous.

asiento /a'siento/ n. m. seat; chair; site.

asiento delantero /a'siento delan'tero/ front seat.

asiento trasero /a'siento tra'sero/ back seat.

asignar /asig'nar/ v. assign; allot.

asilo /a'silo/ n. m. asylum, sanctuary.

asimilar /asimi'lar/ v. assimilate.

asir /a'sir/ v. grasp.

asistencia /asis'tenθia; asistensia/ n. f. attendance, presence.

asistir /asis'tir/ v. be present, attend.

asno /'asno/ n. m. donkey.

asociación /asoθia'θion; asosia'sion/ n. f. association.

asociado /aso'θiaðo; aso'siaðo/ n. m. associate, partner.

asociar /aso'θiar; aso'siar/ v. associate.

asolar /aso'lar/ v. desolate; burn, parch.

asoleado /asole'aðo/ a. sunny.

asomar /aso'mar/ v. appear, loom up, show up.

asombrar /asom'βrar/ v. astonish, amaze.

asombro /a'sombro/ n. m. amazement, astonishment.

aspa /'aspa/ n. f. reel. —**aspar,** v.

aspecto /as'pekto/ n. m. aspect.

aspereza /aspe'reθa; aspe'resa/ n. f. harshness.

áspero /'aspero/ a. rough, harsh.

aspiración /aspira'θion; aspira'sion/ n. f. aspiration.

aspirador /aspira'ðor/ n. m. vacuum cleaner.

aspirar /aspi'rar/ v. aspire.

aspirina /aspi'rina/ n. f. aspirin.

asqueroso /aske'roso/ a. dirty, nasty, filthy.

asta /'asta/ n. f. shaft.

asterisco /aste'risko/ n. m. asterisk.

astilla /as'tiʎa; as'tiya/ n. f. splinter, chip. —**astillar,** v.

astillero /asti'ʎero; asti'yero/ n. m. dry dock.

astro /'astro/ n. m. star.

astronauta /astro'nauta/ n. m. & f. astronaut.

astronave /astro'naβe/ n. f. spaceship.

astronomía /astrono'mia/ n. f. astronomy.

astucia /as'tuθia; as'tusia/ n. f. cunning.

astuto /as'tuto/ a. astute, sly, shrewd.

asumir /asu'mir/ v. assume.

asunto /a'sunto/ n. m. matter, affair, business; subject.

asustar /asus'tar/ v. frighten, scare, startle.

atacar /ata'kar/ v. attack, charge.

atajo /a'taho/ n. m. shortcut.

ataque /a'take/ n. m. attack, charge; spell, stroke.

ataque cardíaco /a'take kar'ðiako/ heart attack.

atar /a'tar/ v. tie, bind, fasten.

atareado /atare'aðo/ a. busy.

atascar /atas'kar/ v. stall, stop, obstruct.

atasco /a'tasko/ n. m. traffic jam.

ataúd /ata'uð/ n. m. casket, coffin.

atavío /ata'βio/ n. m. dress; gear, equipment.

atemorizar /atemori'θar; atemori'sar/ v. frighten.

atención /aten'θion; aten'sion/ n. f. attention.

atender /aten'der/ v. heed; attend to, wait on.

atenerse a /ate'nerse a/ v. count on, depend on.

atentado /aten'taðo/ n. m. crime, offense.

atento /a'tento/ *a.* attentive, courteous.

ateo /a'teo/ *n. m.* atheist.

aterrizaje /aterri'θahe; aterri'sahe/ *n. m.* landing (of aircraft).

aterrizaje forzoso /aterri'θahe for-'θoso; aterri'sahe for'soso/ emergency landing, forced landing.

aterrizar /aterri'θar; aterri'sar/ *v.* land.

atesorar /ateso'rar/ *v.* hoard.

atestar /ates'tar/ *v.* witness.

atestiguar /atesti'guar/ *v.* attest, testify.

atinar /ati'nar/ *v.* hit upon.

atisbar /atis'βar/ *v.* scrutinize, pry.

Atlántico /at'lantiko/ *n. m.* Atlantic.

atlántico *a.* Atlantic.

atlas /'atlas/ *n. m.* atlas.

atleta /at'leta/ *n. m. & f.* athlete.

atlético /at'letiko/ *a.* athletic.

atletismo /atle'tismo/ *n. m.* athletics.

atmósfera /at'mosfera/ *n. f.* atmosphere.

atmosférico /atmos'feriko/ *a.* atmospheric.

atolladero /atoʎa'ðero; atoya'ðero/ *n. m.* dead end, impasse.

atómico /a'tomiko/ *a.* atomic.

átomo /'atomo/ *n. m.* atom.

atormentar /atormen'tar/ *v.* torment, plague.

atornillar /atorni'ʎar; atorni'yar/ *v.* screw.

atracción /atrak'θion; atrak'sion/ *n. f.* attraction.

atractivo /atrak'tiβo/ *a.* **1.** attractive. —*n.* **2.** *m.* attraction.

atraer /atra'er/ *v.* attract; lure.

atrapar /atra'par/ *v.* trap, catch.

atrás /a'tras/ *adv.* back; behind.

atrasado /atra'saðo/ *a.* belated; backward; slow (clock).

atrasar /atra'sar/ *v.* delay, retard; be slow.

atraso /a'traso/ *n. m.* delay; backwardness; (*pl.*) arrears.

atravesar /atraβe'sar/ *v.* cross.

atreverse /atre'βerse/ *v.* dare.

atrevido /atre'βiðo/ *a.* daring, bold.

atrevimiento /atreβi'miento/ *n. m.* boldness.

atribuir /atri'βuir/ *v.* attribute, ascribe.

atributo /atri'βuto/ *n. m.* attribute.

atrincherar /atrintʃe'rar/ *v.* entrench.

atrocidad /atroθi'ðað; atrosi'ðað/ *n. f.* atrocity, outrage.

atronar /atro'nar/ *v.* deafen.

atropellar /atrope'ʎar; atrope'yar/ *v.* trample; fell.

atroz /a'troθ; a'ntros/ *a.* atrocious.

atún /a'tun/ *n. m.* tuna.

aturdir /atur'ðir/ *v.* daze, stun, bewilder.

audacia /au'ðaθia; au'ðasia/ *n. f.* audacity.

audaz /au'ðaθ; au'ðas/ *a.* audacious, bold.

audible /au'ðiβle/ *a.* audible.

audífono /au'ðifono/ *n. m.* hearing aid.

audiovisual /auðioβi'sual/ *a.* audiovisual.

auditorio /auði'torio/ *n. m.* audience.

aula /'aula/ *n. f.* classroom, hall.

aullar /au'ʎar; au'yar/ *v.* howl, bay.

aullido /au'ʎiðo; au'yiðo/ *n. m.* howl.

aumentar /aumen'tar/ *v.* augment; increase, swell.

aun /a'un/ *adv.* still; even. **a. cuando,** even though, even if.

aunque /'aunke/ *conj.* although, though.

áureo /'aureo/ *a.* golden.

aureola /aure'ola/ *n. f.* halo.

auriculares /auriku'lares/ *n. m.pl.* headphones.

aurora /au'rora/ *n. f.* dawn.

ausencia /au'senθia; au'sensia/ *n. f.* absence.

ausentarse /ausen'tarse/ *v.* stay away.

ausente /au'sente/ *a.* absent.

auspicio /aus'piθio; aus'pisio/ *n. m.* auspice.

austeridad /austeri'ðað/ *n. f.* austerity.

austero /aus'tero/ *a.* austere.

austriaco /aus'triako/ **-ca** *a. & n.* Austrian.

auténtico /au'tentiko/ *a.* authentic.

auto /'auto/ **automóvil** *n. m.* auto, automobile.

autobús /auto'βus/ *n. m.* bus.

autocine /auto'θine; auto'sine/ **autocinema** *n. m.* drive-in (movie theater).

automático /auto'matiko/ *a.* automatic.

autonomía /autono'mia/ *n. f.* autonomy.

autopista /auto'pista/ *n. f.* expressway.

autor /au'tor/ *n. m.* author.

autoridad /autori'ðað/ *n. f.* authority.

autoritario /autori'tario/ *a.* authoritarian; authoritative.

autorizar /autori'θar; autori'sar/ *v.* authorize.

autostop /auto'stop/ *n. m.* hitchhiking. **hacer a.,** to hitchhike.

auxiliar /auksi'liar/ *a.* **1.** auxiliary. —*v.* **2.** assist, aid.

auxilio /auk'silio/ *n. m.* aid, assistance.

avaluar /aβa'luar/ *v.* evaluate, appraise.

avance /a'βanθe; a'βanse/ *n. m.* advance. —**avanzar,** *v.*

avaricia /aβa'riθia; aβa'risia/ *n. f.* avarice.

avariento /aβa'riento/ *a.* miserly, greedy.

avaro /a'βaro/ **-ra** *a. & n.* miser; miserly.

ave /'aβe/ *n. f.* bird.

avellana /aβe'ʎana; aβe'yana/ *n. f.* hazelnut.

Ave María /aβema'ria/ *n. m.* Hail Mary.

avena /a'βena/ *n. f.* oat.

avenida /aβe'niða/ *n. f.* avenue; flood.

avenirse /aβe'nirse/ *v.* compromise; agree.

aventajar /aβenta'har/ *v.* surpass, get ahead of.

aventar /aβen'tar/ *v.* fan; scatter.

aventura /aβen'tura/ *n. f.* adventure.

aventurar /aβentu'rar/ *v.* venture, risk, gamble.

aventurero /aβentu'rero/ **-ra** *a. & n.* adventurous; adventurer.

avergonzado /aβergon'θaðo; aβergon'saðo/ *a.* ashamed, abashed.

avergonzar /aβergon'θar; aβergon'sar/ *v.* shame, abash.

avería /aβe'ria/ *n. f.* damage. —**averiar,** *v.*

averiguar /aβeri'guar/ *v.* ascertain, find out.

aversión /aβer'sion/ *n. f.* aversion.

avestruz /aβes'truθ; aβes'trus/ *n. m.* ostrich.

aviación /aβia'θion; aβia'sion/ *n. f.* aviation.

aviador /aβia'ðor/ **-ra** *n.* aviator.

ávido /'aβiðo/ *a.* avid; eager.

avión /a'βion/ *n. m.* airplane.

avisar /aβi'sar/ *v.* notify, let know; warn, advise.

aviso /a'βiso/ *n. m.* notice, announcement; advertisement; warning.

avispa /a'βispa/ *n. f.* wasp.

avivar /aβi'βar/ *v.* enliven, revive.

axila /ak'sila/ *n. f.* armpit.

aya /'aya/ *n. f.* governess.

ayatolá /aya'tola/ *n. m.* ayatollah.

ayer /a'yer/ *adv.* yesterday.

ayuda /a'yuða/ *n. f.* help, aid. —**ayudar,** *v.*

ayudante /ayu'ðante/ *a.* assistant, helper; adjutant.

ayuno /a'yuno/ *n. m.* fast. —**ayunar,** *v.*

ayuntamiento /ayunta'miento/ *n. m.* city hall.

azada /a'θaða; a'saða/ *n. f.*, **azadón,** *m.* hoe.

azafata /aθa'fata; asa'fata/ *n. f.* stewardess, flight attendant.

azar /a'θar; a'sar/ *n. m.* hazard, chance. **al a.,** at random.

azotar /aθo'tar; aso'tar/ *v.* whip, flog; belabor.

azote /a'θote; a'sote/ *n. m.* scourge, lash.

azúcar /a'θukar; a'sukar/ *n. m.* sugar.

azucarero /aθuka'rero; asuka'rero/ *n. m.* sugar bowl.

azúcar moreno /a'θukar mo'reno; a'sukar mo'reno/ brown sugar.

azul /a'θul; a'sul/ *a.* blue.

azulado /aθu'laðo; asu'laðo/ *a.* blue, bluish.

azulejo /aθu'leho; asu'leho/ *n. m.* tile; bluebird.

azul marino /a'θul ma'rino; a'sul ma'rino/ navy blue.

B

baba /'baβa/ *n. f.* drivel. —**babear,** *v.*

babador /baβa'ðor, ba'βero/ *n. m.* bib.

babucha /ba'βutʃa/ *n. f.* slipper.

bacalao /baka'lao/ *n. m.* codfish.

bachiller /batʃi'ʎer; batʃi'yer/ **-ra** *n.* bachelor (degree).

bacía /ba'θia; ba'sia/ *n. f.* washbasin.

bacterias /bak'terias/ *n. f.pl.* bacteria.

bacteriología /bakteriolo'hia/ *n. f.* bacteriology.

bahía /ba'ia/ *n. f.* bay.

bailador /baila'ðor/ **-ra** *n.* dancer.

bailar /bai'lar/ *v.* dance.

bailarín /baila'rin/ **-ina** *n.* dancer.

baile /'baile/ *n. m.* dance.

baja /'baha/ *n. f.* fall (in price); *Mil.* casualty.

bajar /ba'har/ *v.* lower; descend.

bajeza /ba'heθa; ba'hesa/ *n. f.* baseness.

bajo /'baho/ *prep.* **1.** under, below. —*a.* **2.** low; short; base.

bala /'bala/ *n. f.* bullet; ball; bale.

balada /ba'laða/ *n. f.* ballad.

balancear /balanθe'ar; balanse'ar/ *v.* balance; roll, swing, sway.

balanza /ba'lanθa; ba'lansa/ *n. f.* balance; scales.

balbuceo /balβu'θeo; balβu'seo/ *n. m.* stammer; babble. —**balbucear,** *v.*

Balcanes /bal'kanes/ *n. m.pl.* Balkans.

balcón /bal'kon/ *n. m.* balcony.

balde /'balde/ *n. m.* bucket, pail. **de b.,** gratis. **en b.,** in vain.

balística /ba'listika/ *n. f.* ballistics.

ballena /ba'ʎena; ba'yena/ *n. f.* whale.

balneario /balne'ario/ *n. m.* bathing resort; spa.

balompié /balom'pie/ *n. m.* football.

balón /ba'lon/ *n. m.* football; *Auto.* balloon tire.

baloncesto /balon'θesto; balon'sesto/ *n. m.* basketball.

balota /ba'lota/ *n. f.* ballot, vote. —**balotar,** *v.*

balsa /'balsa/ *n. f.* raft.

bálsamo /'balsamo/ *n. m.* balm.

baluarte /ba'luarte/ *n. m.* bulwark.

bambolearse /bambole'arse/ *v.* sway.

bambú /bam'βu/ *n. m.* bamboo.

banal /ba'nal/ *a.* banal, trite.

banana /ba'nana/ *n. f.* banana.

banano /ba'nano/ *n. m.* banana tree.

bancarrota /banka'rrota/ *n. f.* bankruptcy.

banco /'banko/ *n. m.* bank; bench; school of fish.

banco cooperativo /'banko koopera'tiβo/ credit union.

banda /'banda/ *n. f.* band.

bandada /ban'daða/ *n. f.* covey; flock.

banda sonora /'banda so'nora/ *n. f.* soundtrack.

bandeja /ban'deha/ *n. f.* tray.

bandera /ban'dera/ *n. f.* flag; banner; ensign.

bandido /ban'diðo/ **-da** *n.* bandit.

bando /'bando/ *n. m.* faction.

bandolero /bando'lero/ **-ra** *n.* bandit, robber.

banquero /ban'kero/ **-ra** *n.* banker.

banqueta /ban'keta/ *n. f.* stool; (Mex.) sidewalk.

banquete /ban'kete/ *n. m.* feast, banquet.

banquillo /ban'kiʎo; ban'kiyo/ *n. m.* stool.

bañar /ba'ɲar/ *v.* bathe.

bañera /ba'ɲera/ *n. f.* bathtub.

baño /'baɲo/ *n. m.* bath; bathroom.

bar /bar/ *n. m.* bar, pub.

baraja /ba'raha/ *n. f.* pack of cards; game of cards.

baranda /ba'randa/ *n. f.* railing, banister.

barato /ba'rato/ *a.* cheap.

barba /'barβa/ *n. f.* beard; chin.

barbacoa /barβa'koa/ *n. f.* barbecue; stretcher.

barbaridad /barβari'ðað/ *n. f.* barbarity; *Colloq.* excess (in anything).

bárbaro /'barβaro/ *a.* barbarous; crude.

barbería /barβe'ria/ *n. f.* barbershop.

barbero /bar'βero/ *n. m.* barber.

barca /'barka/ *n. f.* (small) boat.

barcaza /bar'kaθa; bar'kasa/ *n. f.* barge.

barco /'barko/ *n. m.* ship, boat.

barniz /bar'niθ; bar'nis/ *n. m.* varnish. —**barnizar,** *v.*

barómetro /ba'rometro/ *n. m.* barometer.

barón /ba'ron/ *n. m.* baron.

barquilla /bar'kiʎa; bar'kiya/ *n. f.* *Naut.* log.

barra /'barra/ *n. f.* bar.

barraca /ba'rraka/ *n. f.* hut, shed.

barrear /barre'ar/ *v.* bar, barricade.

barreno /ba'rreno/ *n. m.* blast, blasting. —**barrenar,** *v.*

barrer /ba'rrer/ *v.* sweep.

barrera /ba'rrera/ *n. f.* barrier.

barricada /barri'kaða/ *n. f.* barricade.

barriga /ba'rriga/ *n. f.* belly.

barril /ba'rril/ *n. m.* barrel; cask.

barrio /'barrio/ *n. m.* district, ward, quarter.

barro /'barro/ *n. m.* clay, mud.

base /'base/ *n. f.* base; basis. —**basar,** *v.*

base de datos /'base de 'datos/ database.

bastante /bas'tante/ *a.* **1.** enough, plenty of. —*adv.* **2.** enough; rather, quite.

bastar /bas'tar/ *v.* suffice, be enough.

bastardo /bas'tarðo/ **-a** *a. & n.* bastard.

bastear /baste'ar/ *v.* baste.

bastidor /basti'ðor/ *n. m.* wing (in theater).

bastón /bas'ton/ *n. m.* (walking) cane.

bastos /'bastos/ *n. m.pl.* clubs (cards).

basura /ba'sura/ *n. f.* refuse, dirt; garbage; junk.

basurero /basu'rero/ **-ra** *n.* scavenger.

batalla /ba'taʎa; ba'taya/ *n. f.* battle. —**batallar,** *v.*

batallón /bata'ʎon; bata'yon/ *n. m.* batallion.

batata /ba'tata/ *n. f.* sweet potato.

bate /'bate/ *n. m.* bat. —**batear,** *v.*

batería /bate'ria/ *n. f.* battery.

batido /ba'tiðo/ *n. m.* (cooking) batter; milkshake.

batidora /bati'ðora/ *n. f.* mixer (for food).

batir /ba'tir/ v. beat; demolish; conquer.

baúl /ba'ul/ n. m. trunk.

bautismo /bau'tismo/ n. m. baptism.

bautista /bau'tista/ n. m. & f. Baptist.

bautizar /bauti'θar; bauti'sar/ v. christen, baptize.

bautizo /bau'tiðo; bau'tiso/ n. m. baptism.

baya /'baia/ n. f. berry.

bayoneta /bayo'neta/ n. f. bayonet.

beato /be'ato/ a. blessed.

bebé /be'βe/ n. m. baby.

beber /be'βer/ v. drink.

bebible /be'βiβle/ a. drinkable.

bebida /be'βiða/ n. f. drink, beverage.

beca /'beka/ n. f. grant, scholarship.

becado /be'kaðo/ **-da** n. scholar.

becerro /be'θerro; be'serro/ n. m. calf; calfskin.

beldad /bel'dað/ n. f. beauty.

belga /'belɣa/ a. & n. Belgian.

Bélgica /'belhika/ n. f. Belgium.

belicoso /beli'koso/ a. warlike.

beligerante /belihe'rante/ a. & n. belligerent.

bellaco /be'ʎako; be'yako/ a. **1.** sly, roguish. —n. **2.** m. rogue.

bellas artes /'beʎas 'artes; 'beyas 'artes/ n. f.pl. fine arts.

belleza /be'ʎeθa; be'yesa/ n. f. beauty.

bello /'beʎo; 'beyo/ a. beautiful.

bellota /be'ʎota; be'yota/ n. f. acorn.

bendecir /bende'θir; bende'sir/ v. bless.

bendición /bendi'θion; bendi'sion/ n. f. blessing, benediction.

bendito /ben'dito/ a. blessed.

beneficio /bene'fiθio; bene'fisio/ n. m. benefit. —**beneficiar**, v.

beneficioso /benefi'θioso; benefi'sioso/ a. beneficial.

benevolencia /beneβo'lenθia; beneβo'lensia/ n. f. benevolence.

benévolo /be'neβolo/ a. benevolent.

benigno /be'niɣno/ a. benign.

beodo /be'oðo/ **-da** a. & n. drunk.

berenjena /beren'hena/ n. f. eggplant.

beso /'beso/ n. m. kiss. —**besar**, v.

bestia /'bestia/ n. f. beast, brute.

betabel /beta'βel/ n. m. beet.

Biblia /'biβlia/ n. f. Bible.

bíblico /'biβliko/ a. Biblical.

biblioteca /biβlio'teka/ n. f. library.

bicarbonato /bikarβo'nato/ n. m. bicarbonate.

bicicleta /biθi'kleta; bisi'kleta/ n. f. bicycle.

bien /bien/ adv. **1.** well. —n. **2.** good; (pl.) possessions.

bienes inmuebles /'bienes i'mueβles/ n. m.pl. real estate.

bienestar /bienes'tar/ n. m. well-being, welfare.

bienhechor /biene'tʃor/ **-ra** n. benefactor.

bienvenida /biembe'niða/ n. f. welcome.

bienvenido /biembe'niðo/ a. welcome.

biftec /bif'tek/ n. m. steak.

bifurcación /bifurka'θion; bifurka'sion/ n. f. fork. —**bifurcar**, v.

bigamia /bi'gamia/ n. f. bigamy.

bígamo /'bigamo/ **-a** n. bigamist.

bigotes /bi'gotes/ n. m.pl. mustache.

bikini /bi'kini/ n. m. bikini.

bilingüe /bi'lingue/ a. bilingual.

bilingüismo /bilin'guismo/ n. m. bilingualism.

bilis /'bilis/ n. f. bile.

billar /bi'ʎar; bi'yar/ n. m. billiards.

billete /bi'ʎete; bi'yete/ n. m. ticket; bank note, bill.

billete de banco /bi'ʎete de 'banko; bi'yete de 'banko/ bank note.

billón /bi'ʎon; bi'yon/ n. m. billion.

bingo /'bingo/ n. m. bingo.

biodegradable /bioðeɣra'ðaβle/ a. biodegradable.

biografía /biogra'fia/ n. f. biography.

biología /biolo'hia/ n. f. biology.

biombo /'biombo/ n. m. folding screen.

bisabuela /bisa'βuela/ n. f. great-grandmother.

bisabuelo /bisa'βuelo/ n. m. great-grandfather.

bisel /bi'sel/ n. m. bevel. —**biselar**, v.

bisonte /bi'sonte/ n. m. bison.

bisté /bis'te/ **bistec** n. m. steak.

bisutería /bisute'ria/ n. f. costume jewelry.

bizarro /bi'θarro; bi'sarro/ a. brave; generous; smart.

bizco /'biθko/ **-ca** n. **1.** cross-eyed person. —a. **2.** cross-eyed, squinting.

bizcocho /biθ'kotʃo; bis'kotʃo/ n. m. biscuit, cake.

blanco /'blanko/ a. **1.** white; blank. —n. **2.** m. white; target.

blandir /blan'dir/ v. brandish, flourish.

blando /'blando/ a. soft.

blanquear /blanke'ar/ v. whiten; bleach.

blasfemar /blasfe'mar/ v. blaspheme, curse.

blasfemia /blas'femia/ n. f. blasphemy.

blindado /blin'daðo/ a. armored.

blindaje /blin'dahe/ n. m. armor.

bloque /'bloke/ n. m. block. —**bloquear**, v.

bloqueo /blo'keo/ n. m. blockade. —**bloquear**, v.

blusa /'blusa/ n. f. blouse.

bobada /bo'βaða/ n. f. stupid, silly thing.

bobo /'boβo/ **-ba** a. & n. fool; foolish.

boca /'boka/ n. f. mouth.

bocado /bo'kaðo/ n. m. bit; bite, mouthful.

bocanada /boka'naða/ n. f. puff (of smoke); mouthful (of liquor).

bocazas /bo'kaθas/ n. m. & f. Colloq. bigmouth.

bochorno /bo'tʃorno/ n. m. sultry weather; embarrassment.

bocina /bo'θina; bo'sina/ n. f. horn.

boda /'boða/ n. f. wedding.

bodega /bo'ðeɣa/ n. f. wine cellar; Naut. hold; (Carib.) grocery store.

bofetada /bofe'taða/ n. f. **bofetón**, m. slap.

boga /'boɣa/ n. f. vogue; fad.

bogar /bo'gar/ v. row (a boat).

bohemio /bo'emio/ **-a** a. & n. Bohemian.

boicoteo /boiko'teo/ n. m. boycott. —**boicotear**, v.

boina /'boina/ n. f. beret.

bola /'bola/ n. f. ball.

bola de nieve /'bola de 'nieβe/ snowball.

bolas de billar /bolas de bi'ʎar; 'bolas de bi'yar/ billiard balls.

bolera /bo'lera/ n. f. bowling alley.

boletín /bole'tin/ n. m. bulletin.

boletín informativo /bole'tin informa'tiβo/ news bulletin.

boleto /bo'leto/ n. m. ticket. **b. de embarque**, boarding pass.

boliche /bo'litʃe/ n. m. bowling alley.

bolígrafo /bo'liɣrafo/ n. m. ballpoint pen.

boliviano /boli'βiano/ **-a** a. & n. Bolivian.

bollo /'boʎo; 'boyo/ n. m. bun, loaf.

bolos /'bolos/ n. m.pl. bowling.

bolsa /'bolsa/ n. f. purse; stock exchange.

bolsa de agua caliente /'bolsa de 'agua ka'liente/ hot-water bottle.

bolsillo /bol'siʎo; bol'siyo/ n. m. pocket.

bomba /'bomba/ n. f. pump; bomb; gas station.

bombardear /bombarðe'ar/ v. bomb; bombard, shell.

bombear /bombe'ar/ v. pump.

bombero /bom'βero/ n. m. fireman.

bombilla /bom'βiʎa; bom'βiya/ n. f. (light) bulb.

bonanza /bo'nanθa; bo'nansa/ n. f. prosperity; fair weather.

bondad /bon'dað/ n. f. kindness; goodness.

bondadoso /bonda'ðoso/ a. kind, kindly.

bongó /boŋ'go/ n. m. bongo drum.

bonito /bo'nito/ a. pretty.

bono /'bono/ n. m. bonus; Fin. bond.

boqueada /boke'aða/ n. f. gasp; gape. —**boquear**, v.

boquilla /bo'kiʎa; bo'kiya/ n. f. cigarette holder.

bordado /bor'ðaðo/ n. m., **bordadura**, f. embroidery.

bordar /bor'ðar/ v. embroider.

borde /'borðe/ n. m. border, rim, edge, brink, ledge.

borde de la carretera /'borðe de la karre'tera/ roadside.

borla /'borla/ n. f. tassel.

borracho /bo'rratʃo/ **-a** a. & n. drunk.

borrachón /borra'tʃon/ **-na** n. drunkard.

borrador /borra'ðor/ n. m. eraser.

borradura /borra'ðura/ n. f. erasure.

borrar /bo'rrar/ v. erase, rub out.

borrasca /bo'rraska/ n. f. squall, storm.

borrico /bo'rriko/ n. m. donkey.

bosque /'boske/ n. m. forest, wood.

bosquejo /bos'keho/ n. m. sketch, draft. —**bosquejar**, v.

bostezo /bos'teθo; bos'teso/ n. m. yawn. —**bostezar**, v.

bota /'bota/ n. f. boot.

botalón /bota'lon/ n. m. Naut. boom.

botánica /bo'tanika/ n. f. botany.

botar /bo'tar/ v. throw out, throw away.

bote /'bote/ n. m. boat; can, box.

bote salvavidas /'bote salβa'βiðas/ lifeboat.

botica /bo'tika/ n. f. pharmacy, drugstore.

boticario /boti'kario/ n. m. pharmacist, druggist.

botín /bo'tin/ n. m. booty, plunder, spoils.

botiquín /boti'kin/ n. m. medicine chest.

boto /'boto/ a. dull, stupid.

botón /bo'ton/ n. m. button.

botones /bo'tones/ n. m. bellboy (in a hotel).

bóveda /b'oβeða/ n. f. vault.

boxeador /boksea'ðor/ n. m. boxer.

boxeo /bok'seo/ n. m. boxing. —**boxear**, v.

boya /'boya/ n. f. buoy.

boyante /bo'yante/ a. buoyant.

bozal /bo'θal; bo'sal/ n. m. muzzle.

bragas /'bragas/ n. f.pl. panties.

bramido /bra'miðo/ n. m. roar, bellow. —**bramar**, v.

brasa /'brasa/ n. f. embers, grill. —**brasear**, v.

brasileño /brasi'leɲo/ **-ña** a. & n. Brazilian.

bravata /bra'βata/ n. f. bravado.

bravear /braβe'ar/ v. bully.

braza /'braθa; 'brasa/ n. f. fathom.

brazada /bra'θaða; bra'saða/ n. f. (swimming) stroke.

brazalete /braθa'lete; brasa'lete/ n. m. bracelet.

brazo /'braθo; 'braso/ n. m. arm.

brea /'brea/ n. f. tar, pitch.

brecha /'bretʃa/ n. f. gap, breach.

brécol /'brekol/ n. m. broccoli.

bregar /bre'ɣar/ v. scramble.

breña /'breɲa/ n. f. rough country with brambly shrubs.

Bretaña /bre'taɲa/ n. f. Britain.

breve /'breβe/ a. brief, short. **en b.**, shortly, soon.

brevedad /breβe'ðað/ n. f. brevity.

bribón /bri'βon/ **-na** n. rogue, rascal.

brida /'briða/ n. f. bridle.

brigada /bri'gaða/ n. f. brigade.

brillante /bri'ʎante; bri'yante/ a. **1.** brilliant, shiny. —n. **2.** m. diamond.

brillo /'briʎo; 'briyo/ n. m. shine, glitter. —**brillar**, v.

brinco /'brinko/ n. m. jump; bounce, skip. —**brincar**, v.

brindis /'brindis/ n. m. toast. —**brindar**, v.

brío /'brio/ n. m. vigor.

brioso /'brioso/ a. vigorous, spirited.

brisa /'brisa/ n. f. breeze.

brisa marina /'brisa ma'rina/ sea breeze.

británico /bri'taniko/ a. British.

brocado /bro'kaðo/ **-da** a. & n. brocade.

brocha /'brotʃa/ n. f. brush.

broche /'brotʃe/ n. m. brooch, clasp, pin.

broma /'broma/ n. f. joke. —**bromear**, v.

bronca /'bronka/ n. f. Colloq. quarrel, row, fight.

bronce /'bronθe; 'bronse/ n. m. bronze; brass.

bronceador /bronθea'ðor; bronsea'ðor/ n. m. suntan lotion, suntan oil.

bronquitis /bron'kitis/ n. f. bronchitis.

brotar /bro'tar/ v. gush; sprout; bud.

brote /'brote/ n. m. bud, shoot.

bruja /'bruha/ n. f. witch.

brújula /'bruhula/ n. f. compass.

bruma /'bruma/ n. f. mist.

brumoso /bru'moso/ a. misty.

brusco /'brusko/ a. brusque; abrupt, curt.

brutal /bru'tal/ a. savage, brutal.

brutalidad /brutali'ðað/ n. f. brutality.

bruto /'bruto/ **-ta** a. **1.** brutish; ignorant. —n. **2.** blockhead.

bucear /buθe'ar; buse'ar/ v. dive.

bueno /'bueno/ a. good, fair; well (in health).

buey /buei/ n. m. ox, steer.

búfalo /'bufalo/ n. m. buffalo.

bufanda /bu'fanda/ n. f. scarf.

bufón /bu'fon/ **-ona** a. & n. fool, buffoon, clown.

búho /'buo/ n. m. owl.

buhonero /buo'nero/ n. m. peddler, vendor.

bujía /bu'hia/ n. f. spark plug.

bulevar /bule'βar/ n. m. boulevard.

bulimia /bu'limia/ n. f. bulimia.

bullicio /bu'ʎiθio; bu'yisio/ n. m. bustle, noise.

bullicioso /buʎi'θioso; buyi'sioso/ a. boisterous, noisy.

bulto /'bulto/ n. m. bundle; lump.

buñuelo /bu'ɲuelo/ n. m. bun.

buque /'buke/ n. m. ship.

buque de guerra /'buke de 'gerra/ warship.

buque de pasajeros /'buke de pasa'heros/ passenger ship.

burdo /'burðo/ a. coarse.

burgués /bur'ges/ **-esa** a. & n. bourgeois.

burla /'burla/ n. f. mockery; fun.

burlador /burla'ðor/ **-ra** n. trickster, jokester.

burlar /bur'lar/ v. mock, deride.

burlarse de /bur'larse de/ v. scoff at; make fun of.

burro /'burro/ n. m. donkey.

busca /'buska/ n. f. search, pursuit, quest.

buscar /bus'kar/ v. seek, look for; look up.

busto /'busto/ n. m. bust.

butaca /bu'taka/ n. f. armchair; Theat. orchestra seat.

buzo /'buθo; 'buso/ n. m. diver.

buzón /bu'θon; bu'son/ n. m. mailbox.

C

cabal /ka'βal/ a. exact; thorough.

cabalgar /kaβal'gar/ v. ride horseback.

caballeresco /kaβaʎe'resko; kaβaye-'resko/ *a.* gentlemanly, chivalrous.

caballería /kaβaʎe'ria; kaβaye'ria/ *n. f.* cavalry; chivalry.

caballeriza /kaβaʎe'riθa; kaβaye'risa/ *n. f.* stable.

caballero /kaβa'ʎero; kaβa'yero/ *n. m.* gentleman; knight.

caballete /kaβa'ʎete; kaβa'yete/ *n. m.* sawhorse; easel; ridge (of roof).

caballo /ka'βaʎo; ka'βayo/ *n. m.* horse.

cabaña /ka'βaɲa/ *n. f.* cabin; booth.

cabaré /kaβa're/ *n. m.* nightclub.

cabaretero /kaβare'tero/ **-a** *n. m. & f.* nightclub owner.

cabecear /kaβeθe'ar; kaβese'ar/ *v.* pitch (as a ship).

cabecera /kaβe'θera; kaβe'sera/ *n. f.* head (of bed, table).

cabello /ka'βeʎo; ka'βeyo/ *n. m.* hair.

caber /ka'βer/ *v.* fit into, be contained in. **no cabe duda,** there is no doubt.

cabeza /ka'βeθa; ka'βesa/ *n. f.* head; warhead.

cabildo /ka'βildo/ *n. m.* city hall.

cabildo abierto /ka'βildo a'βierto/ town meeting.

cabizbajo /kaβiθ'βaho; kaβis'βaho/ *a.* downcast.

cablegrama /kaβle'grama/ *n. m.* cablegram.

cabo /'kaβo/ *n. m.* end; *Geog.* cape; *Mil.* corporal. **llevar a c.,** carry out, accomplish.

cabra /'kaβra/ *n. f.* goat.

cacahuete /kaka'uete/ *n. m.* peanut.

cacao /ka'kao/ *n. m.* cocoa; chocolate.

cacerola /kaθe'rola; kase'rola/ *n. f.* pan, casserole.

cachondeo /katʃon'deo/ *n. m.* fun, hilarity.

cachondo /ka'tʃondo/ *a.* funny; *Colloq.* horny.

cachorro /ka'tʃorro/ *n. m.* cub; puppy.

cada /'kaða/ *a.* each, every.

cadáver /ka'ðaβer/ *n. m.* corpse.

cadena /ka'ðena/ *n. f.* chain.

cadera /ka'ðera/ *n. f.* hip.

cadete /ka'ðete/ *n. m.* cadet.

caer /ka'er/ *v.* fall.

café /ka'fe/ *n. m.* coffee; café.

café exprés /ka'fe eks'pres/ espresso.

café soluble /ka'fe so'luβle/ instant coffee.

cafetal /kafe'tal/ *n. m.* coffee plantation.

cafetera /kafe'tera/ *n. f.* coffee pot.

caída /ka'iða/ *n. f.* fall, drop; collapse.

caimán /kai'man/ *n. m.* alligator.

caja /'kaha/ *n. f.* box, case; checkout counter.

caja de ahorros /'kaha de a'orros/ savings bank.

caja de cerillos /'kaha de θe'riʎos; 'kaha de se'riyos/ matchbox.

caja de fósforos /'kaha de 'fosforos/ matchbox.

caja torácica /'kaha to'raθika; 'kaha to'rasika/ rib cage.

cajero /ka'hero/ **-ra** *n.* cashier.

cajón /ka'hon/ *n. m.* drawer.

cal /kal/ *n. f.* lime.

calabaza /kala'βaθa; kala'βasa/ *n. f.* calabash, pumpkin.

calabozo /kala'βoθo; kala'βoso/ *n. m.* jail, cell.

calambre /ka'lambre/ *n. m.* cramp.

calamidad /kalami'ðað/ *n. f.* calamity, disaster.

calcetín /kalθe'tin; kalse'tin/ *n. m.* sock.

calcio /'kalθio; 'kalsio/ *n. m.* calcium.

calcular /kalku'lar/ *v.* calculate, figure.

cálculo /'kalkulo/ *n. m.* calculation, estimate.

caldera /kal'dera/ *n. f.* kettle, caldron; boiler.

caldo /'kaldo/ *n. m.* broth.

calefacción /kalefak'θion; kalefak-'sion/ *n. f.* heat, heating.

calendario /kalen'dario/ *n. m.* calendar.

calentar /kalen'tar/ *v.* heat, warm.

calidad /kali'ðað/ *n. f.* quality, grade.

caliente /ka'liente/ *a.* hot, warm.

calificar /kalifi'kar/ *v.* qualify.

callado /ka'ʎaðo; ka'yaðo/ *a.* silent, quiet.

callarse /ka'ʎarse; ka'yarse/ *v.* quiet down; keep still; stop talking.

calle /'kaʎe; 'kaye/ *n. f.* street.

callejón /kaʎe'hon; kaye'hon/ *n. m.* alley.

calle sin salida /'kaʎe sin sa'liða; 'kaye sin sa'liða/ dead end.

callo /'kaʎo; 'kayo/ *n. m.* callus, corn.

calma /'kalma/ *n. f.* calm, quiet.

calmado /kal'maðo/ *a.* calm.

calmante /kal'mante/ *a.* soothing, calming.

calmar /kal'mar/ *v.* calm, quiet, lull, soothe.

calor /ka'lor/ *n.* heat, warmth. **tener c.,** to be hot, warm; feel hot, warm. **hacer c.,** to be hot, warm (weather).

calorífero /kalo'rifero/ *a.* **1.** heat-producing. —*n.* **2.** *m.* radiator.

calumnia /ka'lumnia/ *n. f.* slander. —**calumniar,** *v.*

caluroso /kalu'roso/ *a.* warm, hot.

calvario /kal'βario/ *n. m.* Calvary.

calvo /'kalβo/ *a.* bald.

calzado /kal'θaðo; kal'saðo/ *n. m.* footwear.

calzar /kal'θar; kal'sar/ *v.* wear (as shoes).

calzoncillos /kalθon'θiʎos; kalson'si-yos/ *n. m.pl.* shorts.

calzones /kal'θones; kal'sones/ *n. m.pl.* trousers.

cama /'kama/ *n. f.* bed.

cámara /'kamara/ *n. f.* chamber; camera.

camarada /kama'raða/ *n. m. & f.* comrade.

camarera /kama'rera/ *n. f.* chambermaid; waitress.

camarero /kama'rero/ *n. m.* steward; waiter.

camarón /kama'ron/ *n. m.* shrimp.

camarote /kama'rote/ *n. m.* stateroom, berth.

cambiar /kam'βiar/ *v.* exchange, change, trade; cash.

cambio /'kambio/ *n. m.* change, exchange. **en c.,** on the other hand.

cambista /kam'βista/ *n. m. & f.* money changer; banker, broker.

cambur /kam'βur/ *n. m.* banana.

camello /ka'meʎo; ka'meyo/ *n. m.* camel.

camilla /ka'miʎa; ka'miya/ *n. f.* stretcher.

caminar /kami'nar/ *v.* walk.

caminata /kami'nata/ *n. f.* tramp, hike.

camino /ka'mino/ *n. m.* road; way.

camión /ka'mion/ *n. m.* truck.

camisa /ka'misa/ *n. f.* shirt.

camisería /kamise'ria/ *n. f.* haberdashery.

camiseta /kami'seta/ *n. f.* undershirt; T-shirt.

campamento /kampa'mento/ *n. m.* camp.

campana /kam'pana/ *n. f.* bell.

campanario /kampa'nario/ *n. m.* bell tower, steeple.

campaneo /kampa'neo/ *n. m.* chime.

campaña /kam'paɲa/ *n. f.* campaign.

campeón /kampe'on/ **-na** *n.* champion.

campeonato /kampeo'nato/ *n. m.* championship.

campesino /kampe'sino/ **-na** *n.* peasant.

campestre /kam'pestre/ *a.* country, rural.

campo /'kampo/ *n. m.* field; (the) country.

campo de concentración /'kampo de konθentra'θion; 'kampo de konsentra'sion/ concentration camp.

campo de golf /'kampo de 'golf/ golf course.

Canadá /kana'ða/ *n. m.* Canada.

canadiense /kana'ðiense/ *a. & n.* Canadian.

canal /ka'nal/ *n. m.* canal; channel.

Canal de la Mancha /ka'nal de la 'mantʃa/ *n. m.* English Channel.

canalla /ka'naʎa; ka'naya/ *n. f.* rabble.

canario /ka'nario/ *n. m.* canary.

canasta /ka'nasta/ *n. f.* basket.

cáncer /'kanθer; 'kanser/ *n. m.* cancer.

cancha de tenis /'kantʃa de 'tenis/ *n. f.* tennis court.

canciller /kanθi'ʎer; kansi'yer/ *n. m.* chancellor.

canción /kan'θion; kan'sion/ *n. f.* song.

candado /kan'daðo/ *n. m.* padlock.

candela /kan'dela/ *n. f.* fire; light; candle.

candelero /kande'lero/ *n. m.* candlestick.

candidato /kandi'ðato/ **-ta** *n.* candidate; applicant.

candidatura /kandiða'tura/ *n. f.* candidacy.

canela /ka'nela/ *n. f.* cinnamon.

cangrejo /kaŋ'greho/ *n. m.* crab.

caníbal /ka'niβal/ *n. m.* cannibal.

caniche /ka'nitʃe/ *n. m.* poodle.

canje /'kanhe/ *n. m.* exchange, trade. —**canjear,** *v.*

cano /'kano/ *a.* gray.

canoa /ka'noa/ *n. f.* canoe.

cansado /kan'saðo/ *a.* tired, weary.

cansancio /kan'sanθio; kan'sansio/ *n. m.* fatigue.

cansar /kan'sar/ *v.* tire, fatigue, wear out.

cantante /kan'tante/ *n. m. & f.* singer.

cantar /kan'tar/ *n.* **1.** *m.* song. —*v.* **2.** sing.

cántaro /'kantaro/ *n. m.* pitcher.

cantera /kan'tera/ *n. f.* (stone) quarry.

cantidad /kanti'ðað/ *n. f.* quantity, amount.

cantina /kan'tina/ *n. f.* bar, tavern; restaurant.

canto /'kanto/ *n. m.* chant, song, singing; edge.

caña /'kaɲa/ *n. f.* cane, reed; sugar cane; small glass of beer.

cañón /ka'ɲon/ *n. m.* canyon; cannon; gun barrel.

caoba /ka'oβa/ *n. f.* mahogany.

caos /'kaos/ *n. m.* chaos.

caótico /ka'otiko/ *a.* chaotic.

capa /'kapa/ *n. f.* cape, cloak; coat (of paint).

capacidad /kapaθi'ðað; kapasi'ðað/ *n. f.* capacity; capability.

capacitar /kapaθi'tar; kapasi'tar/ *v.* enable.

capataz /kapa'taθ; kapa'tas/ *n. m.* foreman.

capaz /ka'paθ; ka'pas/ *a.* capable, able.

capellán /kape'ʎan; kape'yan/ *n. m.* chaplain.

caperuza /kape'ruθa; kape'rusa/ *n. f.* hood.

capilla /ka'piʎa; ka'piya/ *n. f.* chapel.

capital /kapi'tal/ *n.* **1.** *m.* capital. **2.** *f.* capital (city).

capitalista /kapita'lista/ *a. & n.* capitalist.

capitán /kapi'tan/ *n. m.* captain.

capitular /kapitu'lar/ *v.* yield.

capítulo /ka'pitulo/ *n. m.* chapter.

capota /ka'pota/ *n. f.* hood.

capricho /ka'pritʃo/ *n. m.* caprice; fancy, whim.

caprichoso /kapri'tʃoso/ *a.* capricious.

cápsula /'kapsula/ *n. f.* capsule.

capturar /kaptu'rar/ *v.* capture.

capucha /ka'putʃa/ *n. f.* hood.

capullo /ka'puʎo; ka'puyo/ *n. m.* cocoon.

cara /'kara/ *n. f.* face.

caracol /kara'kol/ *n. m.* snail.

carácter /ka'rakter/ *n. m.* character.

característica /karakte'ristika/ *n. f.* characteristic.

característico /karakte'ristiko/ *a.* characteristic.

caramba /ka'ramba/ mild exclamation.

caramelo /kara'melo/ *n. m.* caramel; candy.

carátula /ka'ratula/ *n. f.* dial.

caravana /kara'βana/ *n. f.* caravan.

carbón /kar'βon/ *n. m.* carbon; coal.

carbonizar /karβoni'θar; karβoni'sar/ *v.* char.

carburador /karβura'ðor/ *n. m.* carburetor.

carcajada /karka'haða/ *n. f.* burst of laughter.

cárcel /'karθel; 'karsel/ *n. f.* prison, jail.

carcelero /karθe'lero; karse'lero/ *n. m.* jailer.

carcinogénico /karθino'heniko; karsino'heniko/ *a.* carcinogenic.

cardenal /karðe'nal/ *n. m.* cardinal.

cardiólogo /kar'ðiologo/ **-a** *m & f.* cardiologist.

carecer /kare'θer; kare'ser/ *v.* lack.

carestía /kares'tia/ *n. f.* scarcity; famine.

carga /'karga/ *n. f.* cargo; load, burden; freight.

cargar /kar'gar/ *v.* carry; load; charge.

cargo /'kargo/ *n. m.* load; charge, office.

caricatura /karika'tura/ *n. f.* caricature; cartoon.

caricaturista /karikatu'rista/ *n. m. & f.* caricaturist; cartoonist.

caricia /ka'riθia; ka'risia/ *n. f.* caress.

caridad /kari'ðað/ *n. f.* charity.

cariño /ka'riɲo/ *n. m.* affection, fondness.

cariñoso /kari'ɲoso/ *a.* affectionate, fond.

carisma /ka'risma/ *n. m.* charisma.

caritativo /karita'tiβo/ *a.* charitable.

carmesí /karme'si/ *a. & m.* crimson.

carnaval /karna'βal/ *n. m.* carnival.

carne /'karne/ *n. f.* meat, flesh; pulp.

carne acecinada /'karne aθeθi'naða; 'karne asesi'naða/ *n. f.* corned beef.

carnero /kar'nero/ *n. m.* ram; mutton.

carnicería /karniθe'ria; karnise'ria/ *n. f.* meat market; massacre.

carnicero /karni'θero; karni'sero/ **-ra** *n.* butcher.

carnívoro /kar'niβoro/ *a.* carnivorous.

caro /'karo/ *a.* dear, costly, expensive.

carpa /'karpa/ *n. f.* tent.

carpeta /kar'peta/ *n. f.* folder; briefcase.

carpintero /karpin'tero/ *n. m.* carpenter.

carrera /ka'rrera/ *n. f.* race; career.

carrera de caballos /ka'rrera de ka'βaʎos; ka'rrera de ka'βayos/ horse race.

carreta /ka'rreta/ *n. f.* wagon, cart.

carrete /ka'rrete/ *n. m.* reel, spool.

carretera /karre'tera/ *n. f.* road, highway.

carril /ka'rril/ *n. m.* rail.

carrillo /ka'rriʎo; ka'rriyo/ *n. m.* cart (for baggage or shopping).

carro /'karro/ *n. m.* car, automobile; cart.

carroza /ka'rroθa; ka'rrosa/ *n. f.* chariot.

carruaje /ka'rruahe/ *n. m.* carriage.

carta /'karta/ *n. f.* letter; (*pl.*) cards.

cartel /kar'tel/ *n. m.* placard, poster; cartel.

cartelera /karte'lera/ *n. f.* billboard.

cartera /kar'tera/ *n. f.* pocketbook, handbag, wallet; portfolio.

cartero /kar'tero/ **(-ra)** *n.* mail carrier.

cartón /kar'ton/ *n. m.* cardboard.

cartón piedra /kar'ton 'pieðra/ *n. m.* papier-mâché.

cartucho /kar'tutʃo/ *n. m.* cartridge; cassette.

casa /'kasa/ *n. f.* house, dwelling; home.

casaca /ka'saka/ *n. f.* dress coat.

casa de pisos /'kasa de 'pisos/ apartment house.

casado /ka'saðo/ *a.* married.

casamiento /kasa'miento/ *n. m.* marriage.

casar /ka'sar/ *v.* marry, marry off.

casarse /ka'sarse/ *v.* get married. **c. con,** marry.

cascabel /kaska'βel/ *n. m.* jingle bell.

cascada /kas'kaða/ *n. f.* waterfall, cascade.

cascajo /kas'kaho/ *n. m.* gravel.

cascanueces /kaska'nueθes; kaska'nueses/ *n. m.* nutcracker.

cascar /kas'kar/ *v.* crack, break, burst.

cáscara /'kaskara/ *n. f.* shell, rind, husk.

casco /'kasko/ *n. m.* helmet; hull.

casera /ka'sera/ *n. f.* landlady; housekeeper.

caserío /kase'rio/ *n. m.* settlement.

casero /ka'sero/ *a.* **1.** homemade. —*n.* **2.** *m.* landlord, superintendent.

caseta /ka'seta/ *n. f.* cottage, hut.

casi /'kasi/ *adv.* almost, nearly.

casilla /ka'siʎa; ka'siya/ *n. f.* booth; ticket office; pigeonhole.

casimir /kasi'mir/ *n. m.* cashmere.

casino /ka'sino/ *n. m.* club; clubhouse.

caso /'kaso/ *n. m.* case. **hacer c. a,** pay attention to.

casorio /ka'sorio/ *n. m.* informal wedding.

caspa /'kaspa/ *n. f.* dandruff.

casta /'kasta/ *n. f.* caste.

castaña /kas'taɲa/ *n. f.* chestnut.

castaño /kas'taɲo/ *a.* **1.** brown. —*n.* **2.** *m.* chestnut tree.

castañuela /kasta'ɲuela/ *n. f.* castanet.

castellano /kaste'ʎano; kaste'yano/ **-na** *a. & n.* Castilian.

castidad /kasti'ðað/ *n. f.* chastity.

castigar /kasti'gar/ *v.* punish, castigate.

castigo /kas'tigo/ *n. m.* punishment.

castillo /kas'tiʎo; kas'tiyo/ *n. m.* castle.

castizo /kas'tiθo; kas'tiso/ *a.* pure, genuine; noble.

casto /'kasto/ *a.* chaste.

castor /kas'tor/ *n. m.* beaver.

casual /ka'sual/ *adj.* accidental, coincidental.

casualidad /kasuali'ðað/ *n. f.* coincidence. **por c.,** by chance.

casuca /ka'suka/ *n. f.* hut, shanty, hovel.

cataclismo /kata'klismo/ *n. m.* cataclysm.

catacumba /kata'kumba/ *n. f.* catacomb.

catadura /kata'ðura/ *n. f.* act of tasting; appearance.

catalán /kata'lan/ **-na** *a. & n.* Catalonian.

catálogo /ka'talogo/ *n. m.* catalogue. —**catalogar,** *v.*

cataputta /kata'putta/ *n. f.* catapult.

catar /ka'tar/ *v.* taste; examine, try; bear in mind.

catarata /kata'rata/ *n. f.* cataract, waterfall.

catarro /ka'tarro/ *n. m.* head cold, catarrh.

catástrofe /ka'tastrofe/ *n. f.* catastrophe.

catecismo /kate'θismo; kate'sismo/ *n. m.* catechism.

cátedra /'kateðra/ *n. f.* professorship.

catedral /kate'ðral/ *n. f.* cathedral.

catedrático /kate'ðratiko/ **-ca** *n.* professor.

categoría /katego'ria/ *n. f.* category.

categórico /kate'goriko/ *a.* categorical.

catequismo /kate'kismo/ *n. m.* catechism.

catequizar /kateki'θar; kateki'sar/ *v.* catechize.

cátodo /'katoðo/ *n. m.* cathode.

catolicismo /katoli'θismo; katoli'sismo/ *n. m.* Catholicism.

católico /ka'toliko/ **-ca** *a. & n.* Catholic.

catorce /ka'torθe; ka'torse/ *a. & pron.* fourteen.

catre /'katre/ *n. m.* cot.

cauce /'kauθe; 'kause/ *n. m.* riverbed; ditch.

cauchal /kau'tʃal/ *n. m.* rubber plantation.

caucho /'kautʃo/ *n. m.* rubber.

caución /kau'θion; kau'sion/ *n. f.* precaution; security, guarantee.

caudal /kau'ðal/ *n. m.* means, fortune; (*pl.*) holdings.

caudaloso /kauða'loso/ *a.* prosperous, rich.

caudillaje /kauði'ʎahe; kauði'yahe/ *n. m.* leadership; tyranny.

caudillo /kau'ðiʎo; kau'ðiyo/ *n. m.* leader, chief.

causa /'kausa/ *n. f.* cause. —**causar,** *v.*

cautela /kau'tela/ *n. f.* caution.

cauteloso /kaute'loso/ *a.* cautious.

cautivar /kauti'βar/ *v.* captivate.

cautiverio /kauti'βerio/ *n. m.* captivity.

cautividad /kautiβi'ðað/ *n. f.* captivity.

cautivo /kau'tiβo/ **-va** *a. & n.* captive.

cauto /'kauto/ *a.* cautious.

cavar /ka'βar/ *v.* dig.

caverna /ka'βerna/ *n. f.* cavern, cave.

cavernoso /kaβer'noso/ *a.* cavernous.

cavidad /kaβi'ðað/ *n. f.* cavity, hollow.

cavilar /kaβi'lar/ *v.* criticize, cavil.

cayado /ka'yaðo/ *n. m.* shepherd's staff.

cayo /'kayo/ *n. m.* small rocky islet, key.

caza /'kaθa; 'kasa/ *n. f.* hunting, pursuit, game.

cazador /kaθa'ðor; kasa'ðor/ *n. m.* hunter.

cazar /ka'θar; ka'sar/ *v.* hunt.

cazatorpedero /kaθatorpe'ðero; kasatorpe'ðero/ *n. m.* torpedo-boat, destroyer.

cazo /'kaθo; 'kaso/ *n. m.* ladle, dipper; pot.

cazuela /ka'θuela; ka'suela/ *n. f.* crock.

cebada /θe'βaða; se'βaða/ *n. f.* barley.

cebiche /θe'bitʃe/ *n. m.* dish of marinated raw fish.

cebo /'θeβo; 'seβo/ *n. m.* bait. —**cebar,** *v.*

cebolla /θe'βoʎa; se'βoya/ *n. f.* onion.

cebolleta /θeβo'ʎeta; seβo'yeta/ *n. f.* spring onion.

ceceo /θe'θeo; se'seo/ *n. m.* lisp. —**cecear,** *v.*

cecina /θe'θina; se'sina/ *n. f.* dried beef.

cedazo /θe'ðaθo; se'ðaso/ *n. m.* sieve, sifter.

ceder /θe'ðer; se'ðer/ *v.* cede; transfer; yield.

cedro /'θeðro; 'seðro/ *n. m.* cedar.

cédula /'θeðula; 'seðula/ *n. f.* decree. **c. personal,** identification card.

céfiro /'θefiro; 'sefiro/ *n. m.* zephyr.

cegar /θe'gar; se'gar/ *v.* blind.

ceguedad /θege'ðað, θe'gera; sege'ðað, se'gera/ **ceguera** /θe'gera; se'gera/ *n. f.* blindness.

ceja /'θeha; 'seha/ *n. f.* eyebrow.

cejar /θe'har; se'har/ *v.* go backwards; yield, retreat.

celada /θe'laða; se'laða/ *n. f.* trap; ambush.

celaje /θe'lahe; se'lahe/ *n. m.* appearance of the sky.

celar /θe'lar; se'lar/ *v.* watch carefully, guard.

celda /'θelda; 'selda/ *n. f.* cell.

celebración /θeleβra'θion; seleβra'sion/ *n. f.* celebration.

celebrante /θele'βrante; sele'βrante/ *n. m.* officiating priest.

celebrar /θele'βrar; sele'βrar/ *v.* celebrate, observe.

célebre /'θeleβre; 'seleβre/ *a.* celebrated, noted, famous.

celebridad /θeleβri'ðað; seleβri'ðað/ *n. f.* fame; celebrity; pageant.

celeridad /θeleri'ðað; seleri'ðað/ *n. f.* speed, rapidity.

celeste /θe'leste; se'leste/ *a.* celestial.

celestial /θeles'tial; seles'tial/ *a.* heavenly.

celibato /θeli'βato; seli'βato/ *n. m.* celibacy.

célibe /'θeliβe; 'seliβe/ *a.* **1.** unmarried. —*n.* **2.** *m. & f.* unmarried person.

celista /θe'lista; se'lista/ *n. m. & f.* cellist.

cellisca /θe'ʎiska; se'yiska/ *n. f.* sleet. —**cellisquear,** *v.*

celo /'θelo; 'selo/ *n. m.* zeal; (*pl.*) jealousy.

celofán /θelo'fan; selo'fan/ *n. m.* cellophane.

celosía /θelo'sia; selo'sia/ *n. f.* Venetian blind.

celoso /θe'loso; se'loso/ *a.* jealous; zealous.

céltico /'θeltiko; 'seltiko/ *a.* Celtic.

célula /'θelula; 'selula/ *n. f. Biol.* cell.

celuloide /θelu'loiðe; selu'loiðe/ *n. m.* celluloid.

cementar /θemen'tar; semen'tar/ *v.* cement.

cementerio /θemen'terio; semen'terio/ *n. m.* cemetery.

cemento /θe'mento; se'mento/ *n. m.* cement.

cena /'θena; 'sena/ *n. f.* supper.

cenagal /θena'gal; sena'gal/ *n. m.* swamp, marsh.

cenagoso /θena'goso; sena'goso/ *a.* swampy, marshy, muddy.

cenar /θe'nar; se'nar/ *v.* dine, eat.

cencerro /θen'θerro; sen'serro/ *n. m.* cowbell.

cendal /θen'dal; sen'dal/ *n. m.* thin, light cloth; gauze.

cenicero /θeni'θero; seni'sero/ *n. m.* ashtray.

ceniciento /θeni'θiento; seni'siento/ *a.* ashen.

cenit /'θenit; 'senit/ *n. m.* zenith.

ceniza /θe'niθa; se'nisa/ *n. f.* ash, ashes.

censo /'θenso; 'senso/ *n. m.* census.

censor /θen'sor; sen'sor/ *n. m.* censor.

censura /θen'sura; sen'sura/ *n. f.* reproof, censure; censorship.

censurable /θensu'raβle; sensu'raβle/ *a.* objectionable.

censurar /θensu'rar; sensu'rar/ *v.* censure, criticize.

centavo /θen'taβo; sen'taβo/ *n. m.* cent.

centella /θen'teʎa; sen'teya/ *n. f.* thunderbolt, lightning.

centellear /θenteʎe'ar; senteye'ar/ *v.* twinkle, sparkle.

centelleo /θente'ʎeo; sente'yeo/ *n. m.* sparkle.

centenar /θente'nar; sente'nar/ *n. m.* (a) hundred.

centenario /θente'nario; sente'nario/ *n. m.* centennial, centenary.

centeno /θen'teno; sen'teno/ *n. m.* rye.

centígrado /θen'tigraðo; sen'tigraðo/ *a.* centigrade.

centímetro /θenti'metro; senti'metro/ *n. m.* centimeter.

céntimo /'θentimo; 'sentimo/ *n. m.* cent.

centinela /θenti'nela; senti'nela/ *n. m.* sentry, guard.

central /θen'tral; sen'tral/ *a.* central.

centralita /θentra'lita; sentra'lita/ *n. f.* switchboard.

centralizar /θentrali'θar; sentrali'sar/ *v.* centralize.

centrar /θen'trar; sen'trar/ *v.* center.

céntrico /'θentriko; 'sentriko/ *a.* central.

centro /'θentro; 'sentro/ *n. m.* center.

centroamericano /θentroameri'kano; sentroameri'kano/ **-na** *a. & n.* Central American.

centro de mesa /'θentro de 'mesa; 'sentro de 'mesa/ centerpiece.

ceñidor /θeɲi'ðor; seɲi'ðor/ *n. m.* belt, sash; girdle.

ceñir /θe'ɲir; se'ɲir/ *v.* gird.

ceño /'θeɲo; 'seɲo/ *n. m.* frown.

ceñudo /θe'ɲuðo; se'ɲuðo/ *a.* frowning, grim.

cepa /'θepa; 'sepa/ *n. f.* stump.

cepillo /θe'piʎo; se'piyo/ *n. m.* brush; plane. —**cepillar,** *v.*

cera /'θera; 'sera/ *n. f.* wax.

cerámica /θe'ramika; se'ramika/ *n. m.* ceramics.

cerámico /θe'ramiko; se'ramiko/ *a.* ceramic.

cerca /'θerka; 'serka/ *adv.* **1.** near. —*n.* **2.** *f.* fence, hedge.

cercado /θer'kaðo; ser'kaðo/ *n. m.* enclosure; garden.

cercamiento /θerka'miento; serka'miento/ *n. m.* enclosure.

cercanía /θerka'nia; serka'nia/ *n. f.* proximity.

cercano /θer'kano; ser'kano/ *a.* near, nearby.

cercar /θer'kar; ser'kar/ *v.* surround.

cercenar /θerθe'nar; serse'nar/ *v.* clip; lessen, reduce.

cerciorar /θerθio'rar; sersio'rar/ *v.* make sure; affirm.

cerco /'θerko; 'serko/ *n. m.* hoop; siege.

cerda /'θerða; 'serða/ *n. f.* bristle.

cerdo /'θerðo; 'serðo/ **-da** *n.* hog.

cerdoso /θer'ðoso; ser'ðoso/ *a.* bristly.

cereal /θere'al; sere'al/ *a. & m.* cereal.

cerebro /θe'reβro; se'reβro/ *n. m.* brain.

ceremonia /θere'monia; sere'monia/ *n. f.* ceremony.

ceremonial /θeremo'nial; seremo'nial/ *a. & m.* ceremonial, ritual.

ceremonioso /θeremo'nioso; seremo'nioso/ *a.* ceremonious.

cereza /θe'reθa; se'resa/ *n. f.* cherry.

cerilla /θe'riʎa; se'riya/ *n. f.,* **cerillo,** *m.* match.

cerner /θer'ner; ser'ner/ *v.* sift.

cero /'θero; 'sero/ *n. m.* zero.

cerrado /θe'rraðo; se'rraðo/ *a.* closed; cloudy; obscure; taciturn.

cerradura /θerra'ðura; serra'ðura/ *n. f.* lock.

cerrajero /θerra'hero; serra'hero/ *n. m.* locksmith.

cerrar /θe'rrar; se'rrar/ *v.* close, shut.

cerro /'θerro; 'serro/ *n. m.* hill.

cerrojo /θe'rroho; se'rroho/ *n. m.* latch, bolt.

certamen /θer'tamen; ser'tamen/ *n. m.* contest; competition.

certero /θer'tero; ser'tero/ *a.* accurate, exact; certain, sure.

certeza /θer'teθa; ser'tesa/ *n. f.* certainty.

certidumbre /θerti'ðumbre; serti'ðumbre/ *n. f.* certainty.

certificado /θertifi'kaðo; sertifi'kaðo/ *n. m.* certificate.

certificado de compra /θertifi'kaðo de 'kompra; sertifi'kaðo de 'kompra/ proof of purchase.

certificar /θertifi'kar; sertifi'kar/ *v.* certify; register (a letter).

cerúleo /θe'ruleo; se'ruleo/ *a.* cerulean, sky-blue.

cervecería /θerβeθe'ria; serβese'ria/ *n. f.* brewery; beer saloon.

cervecero /θerβe'θero; serβe'sero/ *n. m.* brewer.

cerveza /θer'βeθa; ser'βesa/ *n. f.* beer.

cesante /θe'sante; se'sante/ *a.* unemployed.

cesar /θe'sar; se'sar/ *v.* cease.

césped /'θespeð; 'sespeð/ *n. m.* sod, lawn.

cesta /'θesta; 'sesta/ *n. f.,* **cesto,** *m.* basket.

cetrino /θe'trino; se'trino/ *a.* yellow, lemon-colored.

cetro /'θetro; 'setro/ *n. m.* scepter.

chabacano /tʃaβa'kano/ *a.* vulgar.

chacal /tʃa'kal/ *n. m.* jackal.

chacó /'tʃako/ *n. m.* shako.

chacona /tʃa'kona/ *n. f.* chaconne.

chacota /tʃa'kota/ *n. f.* fun, mirth.

chacotear /tʃakote'ar/ *v.* joke.

chacra /'tʃakra/ *n. f.* small farm.

chafallar /tʃafa'ʎar; tʃafa'yar/ *v.* mend badly.

chagra /'tʃagra/ *n. m.* rustic; rural person.

chal /tʃal/ *n. m.* shawl.

chalán /tʃa'lan/ *n. m.* horse trader.

chaleco /tʃa'leko/ *n. m.* vest.

chaleco salvavidas /tʃa'leko salβa'βiðas/ life jacket.

chalet /tʃa'le; tʃa'let/ *n. m.* chalet.

challí /tʃa'ʎi; tʃa'yi/ *n. m.* challis.

chamada /tʃa'maða/ *n. f.* brushwood.

chamarillero /tʃamari'ʎero; tʃamari'yero/ *n. m.* gambler.

chamarra /tʃa'marra/ *n. f.* coarse linen jacket.

chambelán /tʃambe'lan/ *n. m.* chamberlain.

champaña /tʃam'paɲa/ *n. m.* champagne.

champú /tʃam'pu/ *n. m.* shampoo.

chamuscar /tʃamus'kar/ *v.* scorch.

chancaco /tʃan'kako/ *a.* brown.

chance /'tʃanθe/ *n. m. & f.* opportunity, break.

chancear /tʃanθe'ar; tʃanse'ar/ *v.* jest, joke.

chanciller /tʃanθi'ʎer; tʃansi'yer/ *n. m.* chancellor.

chancillería /tʃanθiʎe'ria; tʃansiye'ria/ *n. f.* chancery.

chancla /'tʃankla/ *n. f.* old shoe.

chancleta /tʃan'kleta/ *n. f.* slipper.

chanclos /'tʃanklos/ *n. m.pl.* galoshes.

chancro /'tʃankro/ *n. m.* chancre.

changador /tʃaŋga'ðor/ *n. m.* porter; handyman.

chantaje /tʃan'tahe/ *n. m.* blackmail.

chantajista /tʃanta'hista/ *n. m. & f.* blackmailer.

chantejear /tʃantehe'ar/ *v.* blackmail.

chanto /'tʃanto/ *n. m.* flagstone.

chantre /'tʃantre/ *n. m.* precentor.

chanza /'tʃanθa; 'tʃansa/ *n. f.* joke, jest. **—chancear,** *v.*

chanzoneta /tʃanθo'neta; tʃanso'neta/ *n. f.* chansonette.

chapa /'tʃapa/ *n. f.* (metal) sheet, plate; lock.

chapado en oro /tʃa'paðo en 'oro/ *a.* gold-plated.

chapado en plata /tʃa'paðo en 'plata/ *a.* silver-plated.

chaparrada /tʃapa'rraða/ *n. f.* downpour.

chaparral /tʃapa'rral/ *n. m.* chaparral.

chaparreras /tʃapa'rreras/ *n. f.pl.* chaps.

chaparrón /tʃapa'rron/ *n. m.* downpour.

chapear /tʃape'ar/ *v.* veneer.

chapeo /tʃa'peo/ *n. m.* hat.

chapero /tʃa'pero/ *n. m. Colloq.* male homosexual prostitute.

chapitel /tʃapi'tel/ *n. m.* spire, steeple; (architecture) capital.

chapodar /tʃapo'ðar/ *v.* lop.

chapón /tʃa'pon/ *n. m.* inkblot.

chapotear /tʃapote'ar/ *v.* paddle or splash in the water.

chapoteo /tʃapo'teo/ *n. m.* splash.

chapucear /tʃapuθe'ar; tʃapuse'ar/ *v.* fumble, bungle.

chapucero /tʃapu'θero; tʃapu'sero/ *a.* sloppy, bungling.

chapurrear /tʃapurre'ar/ *v.* speak (a language) brokenly.

chapuz /tʃa'puθ; tʃa'pus/ *n. m.* dive; ducking.

chapuzar /tʃapu'θar; tʃapu'sar/ *v.* dive; duck.

chaqueta /tʃa'keta/ *n. f.* jacket, coat.

chaqueta deportiva /tʃa'keta depor'tiβa/ sport jacket.

charada /tʃa'raða/ *n. f.* charade.

charamusca /tʃara'muska/ *n. f.* twisted candy stick.

charanga /tʃa'raŋga/ *n. f.* military band.

charanguero /tʃaraŋ'guero/ *n. m.* peddler.

charca /'tʃarka/ *n. f.* pool, pond.

charco /'tʃarko/ *n. m.* pool, puddle.

charla /'tʃarla/ *n. f.* chat; chatter, prattle. **—charlar,** *v.*

charladuría /tʃarlaðu'ria/ *n. f.* chatter.

charlatán /tʃarla'tan/ **-ana** *n.* charlatan.

charlatanismo /tʃarlata'nismo/ *n. m.* charlatanism.

charol /tʃa'rol/ *n. m.* varnish.

charolar /tʃaro'lar/ *v.* varnish; polish.

charquear /tʃarke'ar/ *v.* jerk (beef).

charquí /tʃar'ki/ *n. m.* jerked beef.

charrán /tʃa'rran/ *a.* roguish.

chascarillo /tʃaska'riʎo; tʃaska'riyo/ *n. m.* risqué story.

chasco /'tʃasko/ *n. m.* disappointment, blow; practical joke.

chasis /'tʃasis/ *n. m.* chassis.

chasquear /tʃaske'ar/ *v.* fool, trick; disappoint; crack (a whip).

chasquido /tʃas'kiðo/ *n. m.* crack (sound).

chata /'tʃata/ *n. f.* bedpan.

chatear /tʃate'ar/ *v.* chat (on the Internet).

chato /'tʃato/ *a.* flat-nosed, pug-nosed.

chauvinismo /tʃauβi'nismo/ *n. m.* chauvinism.

chauvinista /tʃauβi'nista/ *n. & a.* chauvinist.

chelín /tʃe'lin/ *n. m.* shilling.

cheque /'tʃeke/ *n. m.* (bank) check.

chica /'tʃika/ *n. f.* girl.

chicana /tʃi'kana/ *n. f.* chicanery.

chicha /'tʃitʃa/ *n. f.* an alcoholic drink.

chícharo /'tʃitʃaro/ *n. f.* pea.

chicharra /tʃi'tʃarra/ *n. f.* cicada; talkative person.

chicharrón /tʃitʃa'rron/ *n. m.* crisp fried scrap of meat.

chichear /tʃitʃe'ar/ *v.* hiss in disapproval.

chichón /tʃi'tʃon/ *n. m.* bump, bruise, lump.

chicle /'tʃikle/ *n. m.* chewing gum.

chico /'tʃiko/ *a.* **1.** little. **—***n.* **2.** *m.* boy.

chicote /tʃi'kote/ *n. m.* cigar; cigar butt.

chicotear /tʃikote'ar/ *v.* whip, flog.

chifladura /tʃifla'ðura/ *n. f.* mania; whim; jest.

chiflar /tʃi'flar/ *v.* whistle; become insane.

chiflido /tʃi'fliðo/ *n. m.* shrill whistle.

chile /'tʃile/ *n. m.* chili.

chileno /tʃi'leno/ **-na** *a. & n.* Chilean.

chillido /tʃi'ʎiðo; tʃi'yiðo/ *n. m.* shriek, scream, screech. **—chillar,** *v.*

chillón /tʃi'ʎon; tʃi'yon/ *a.* shrill.

chimenea /tʃime'nea/ *n. f.* chimney, smokestack; fireplace.

china /'tʃina/ *n. f.* pebble; maid; Chinese woman.

chinarro /tʃi'narro/ *n. m.* large pebble, stone.

chinche /'tʃintʃe/ *n. f.* bedbug; thumbtack.

chincheta /tʃin'tʃeta/ *n. f.* thumbtack.

chinchilla /tʃin'tʃiʎa; tʃin'tʃiya/ *n. f.* chinchilla.

chinchorro /tʃin'tʃorro/ *n. m.* fishing net.

chinela /tʃi'nela/ *n. f.* slipper.

chinero /tʃi'nero/ *n. m.* china closet.

chino /'tʃino/ **-na** *a. & n.* Chinese.

chipirón /tʃipi'ron/ *n. m.* baby squid.

chiquero /tʃi'kero/ *n. m.* pen for pigs, goats, etc.

chiquito /tʃi'kito/ **-ta** *a.* **1.** small, tiny. **—***n.* **2.** *m. & f.* small child.

chiribitil /tʃiriβi'til/ *n. m.* small room, den.

chirimía /tʃiri'mia/ *n. f.* flageolet.

chiripa /tʃi'ripa/ *n. f.* stroke of good luck.

chirla /'tʃirla/ *n. f.* mussel.

chirle /'tʃirle/ *a.* insipid.

chirona /tʃi'rona/ *n. f.* prison, jail.

chirrido /tʃi'rriðo/ *n. m.* squeak, chirp. **—chirriar,** *v.*

chis /tʃis/ *interj.* hush!

chisgarabís /tʃisgara'βis/ *n.* meddler; unimportant person.

chisguete /tʃis'gete/ *n. m.* squirt, splash.

chisme /'tʃisme/ *n. m.* gossip. **—chismear,** *v.*

chismero /tʃis'mero/ **-ra** *n.* gossiper.

chismoso /tʃis'moso/ *adj.* gossiping.

chispa /'tʃispa/ *n. f.* spark.

chispeante /tʃispe'ante/ *a.* sparkling.

chispear /tʃispe'ar/ *v.* sparkle.

chisporrotear /tʃisporrote'ar/ *v.* emit sparks.

chistar /tʃis'tar/ *v.* speak.

chiste /'tʃiste/ *n. m.* joke, gag; witty saying.

chistera /tʃis'tera/ *n. f.* fish basket; top hat.

chistoso /tʃis'toso/ *a.* funny, comic, amusing.

chito /'tʃito/ *interj.* hush!

chiva /'tʃiβa/ *n. f.* female goat.

chivato /tʃi'βato/ *n. m.* kid, young goat.

chivo /'tʃiβo/ *n. m.* male goat.

chocante /tʃo'kante/ *a.* striking; shocking; unpleasant.

chocar /tʃo'kar/ *v.* collide, clash, crash; shock.

chocarrear /tʃokarre'ar/ *v.* joke, jest.

chochear /tʃotʃe'ar/ *v.* be in one's dotage.

chochera /tʃo'tʃera/ *n. f.* dotage, senility.

choclo /'tʃoklo/ *n. m.* clog; overshoe; ear of corn.

chocolate /tʃoko'late/ *n. m.* chocolate.

chocolate con leche /tʃoko'late kon 'letʃe/ milk chocolate.

chocolatería /tʃokolate'ria/ *n. f.* chocolate shop.

chofer /'tʃofer/ **chófer** *n. m.* chauffeur, driver.

chofeta /tʃo'feta/ *n. f.* chafing dish.

cholo /'tʃolo/ *n. m.* half-breed.

chopo /'tʃopo/ *n. m.* black poplar.

choque /'tʃoke/ *n. m.* collision, clash, crash; shock.

chorizo /tʃo'riθo; tʃo'riso/ *n. m.* sausage.

chorrear /tʃorre'ar/ *v.* spout; drip.

chorro /'tʃorro/ *n. m.* spout; spurt, jet. **llover a chorros,** to pour (rain).

choto /'tʃoto/ *n. m.* calf, kid.

choza /'tʃoθa; 'tʃosa/ *n. f.* hut, cabin.

chozno /'tʃoθno; 'tʃosno/ **-na** *n.* great-great-great-grandchild.

chubasco /tʃu'βasko/ *n. m.* shower, squall.

chubascoso /tʃuβas'koso/ *a.* squally.

chuchería /tʃutʃe'ria/ *n. f.* trinket, knickknack.

chucho /'tʃutʃo/ *n. m. Colloq.* mutt.

chulería /tʃule'ria/ *n. f.* pleasant manner.

chuleta /tʃu'leta/ *n. f.* chop, cutlet.

chulo /'tʃulo/ *n. m.* rascal, rogue; joker.

chupa /'tʃupa/ *n. f.* jacket.

chupada /tʃu'paða/ *n. f.* suck, sip.

chupado /tʃu'paðo/ *a.* very thin.

chupaflor /tʃupa'flor/ *n. m.* hummingbird.

chupar /tʃu'par/ *v.* suck.

churrasco /tʃu'rrasko/ *n. m.* roasted meat.

churros /'tʃuros/ *n. m.pl.* long, slender fritters.

chuscada /tʃus'kaða/ *n. f.* joke, jest.

chusco /'tʃusko/ *a.* funny, humorous.

chusma /'tʃusma/ *n. f.* mob, rabble.

chuzo /'tʃuθo; 'tʃuso/ *n. m.* pike.

CI, *abbr.* **(coeficiente intelectual)** IQ (intelligence quotient).

ciberespacio /θiβeres'paθio/ *n. m.* cyberspace.

cibernauta /θiβer'nauta/ *n. m. & f.* cybernaut.

cicatero /θika'tero; sika'tero/ *a.* stingy.

cicatriz /θika'triθ; sika'tris/ *n. f.* scar.

cicatrizar /θikatri'θar; sikatri'sar/ *v.* heal.

ciclamato /θi'klamato; si'klamato/ *n. m.* cyclamate.

ciclista /θi'klista; si'klista/ *m & f.* cyclist.

ciclo /'θiklo; 'siklo/ *n. m.* cycle.

ciclón /θi'klon; si'klon/ *n. m.* cyclone.

ciego /'θiego; 'siego/ **-ga** *a.* **1.** blind. **—***n.* **2.** blind person.

cielo /'θielo; 'sielo/ *n. m.* heaven; sky, heavens; ceiling.

ciempiés /θiem'pies; siem'pies/ *n. m.* centipede.

cien /θien; sien/ **ciento** *a. & pron.* hundred. **por c.,** per cent.

ciénaga /'θienaga; 'sienaga/ *n. f.* swamp, marsh.

ciencia /'θienθia; 'siensia/ *n. f.* science.

cieno /'θieno; 'sieno/ *n. m.* mud.

científico /θien'tifiko; sien'tifiko/ **-ca** *a.* **1.** scientific. **—***n.* **2.** scientist.

cierre /'θierre; 'sierre/ *n. m.* fastener, snap, clasp.

cierto /'θierto; 'sierto/ *a.* certain, sure, true.

ciervo /'θierβo; 'sierβo/ *n. m.* deer.

cierzo /'θierθo; 'sierso/ *n. m.* northerly wind.

cifra /'θifra; 'sifra/ *n. f.* cipher, number. **—cifrar,** *v.*

cigarra /θi'garra; si'garra/ *n. f.* locust.

cigarrera /θiga'rrera; siga'rrera/ **cigarrillera** *f.* cigarette case.

cigarrillo /θiga'rriʎo; siga'rriyo/ *n. m.* cigarette.

cigarro /θi'garro; si'garro/ *n. m.* cigar; cigarette.

cigüeña /θi'gueɲa; si'gueɲa/ *n. f.* stork.

cilíndrico /θi'lindriko; si'lindriko/ *a.* cylindrical.

cilindro /θi'lindro; si'lindro/ *n. m.* cylinder.

cima /'θima; 'sima/ *n. f.* summit, peak.

cimarrón /θima'rron; sima'rron/ *a.* **1.** wild, untamed. **—***n.* **2.** *m.* runaway slave.

címbalo /'θimbalo; 'simbalo/ *n. m.* cymbal.

cimbrar /θim'βrar, θimbre'ar; sim'βrar, simbre'ar/ *v.* shake, brandish.

cimientos /θi'mientos; si'mientos/ *n. m.pl.* foundation.

cinc /θink; sink/ *n. m.* zinc.

cincel /θin'θel; sin'sel/ *n. m.* chisel. **—cincelar,** *v.*

cincha /'θintʃa; 'sintʃa/ *n. f.* (harness) cinch. **—cinchar,** *v.*

cinco /'θinko; 'sinko/ *a. & pron.* five.

cincuenta /θin'kuenta; sin'kuenta/ *a. & pron.* fifty.

cine /'θine; 'sine/ n. m. movies; movie theater.

cíngulo /'θiŋgulo; 'siŋgulo/ n. m. cingulum.

cínico /'θiniko; 'siniko/ -ca a. & n. cynical; cynic.

cinismo /θi'nismo; si'nismo/ n. m. cynicism.

cinta /'θinta; 'sinta/ n. f. ribbon, tape; (movie) film.

cintilar /θinti'lar; sinti'lar/ v. glitter, sparkle.

cinto /'θinto; 'sinto/ n. m. belt; girdle.

cintura /θin'tura; sin'tura/ n. f. waist.

cinturón /θintu'ron; sintu'ron/ n. m. belt.

cinturón de seguridad /θintu'ron de seguri'ðað; sintu'ron de seguri'ðað/ safety belt.

ciprés /θi'pres; si'pres/ n. m. cypress.

circo /'θirko; 'sirko/ n. m. circus.

circuito /θir'kuito; sir'kuito/ n. m. circuit.

circulación /θirkula'θion; sirkula'sion/ n. f. circulation.

circular /θirku'lar; sirku'lar/ a. & m. 1. circular. —v. 2. circulate.

círculo /'θirkulo; 'sirkulo/ n. m. circle, club.

circundante /θirkun'dante; sirkun'dante/ a. surrounding.

circundar /θirkun'dar; sirkun'dar/ v. encircle, surround.

circunferencia /θirkunfe'renθia; sirkunfe'rensia/ n. f. circumference.

circunlocución /θirkunloku'θion; sirkunloku'sion/ n. circumlocution.

circunscribir /θirkunskri'βir; sirkunskri'βir/ v. circumscribe.

circunspección /θirkunspek'θion; sirkunspek'sion/ n. decorum, propriety.

circunspecto /θirkuns'pekto; sirkuns'pekto/ a. circumspect.

circunstancia /θirkuns'tanθia; sirkuns'tansia/ n. f. circumstance.

circunstante /θirkuns'tante; sirkuns'tante/ n. m. bystander.

circunvecino /θirkunbe'θino; sirkumbe'sino/ a. neighboring, adjacent.

cirio /'θirio; 'sirio/ n. m. candle.

cirrosis /θi'rrosis; si'rrosis/ n. f. cirrhosis.

ciruela /θi'ruela; si'ruela/ n. f. plum; prune.

cirugía /θiru'hia; siru'hia/ n. f. surgery.

cirujano /θiru'hano; siru'hano/ n. m. surgeon.

cisne /'θisne; 'sisne/ n. m. swan.

cisterna /θis'terna; sis'terna/ n. f. cistern.

cita /'θita; 'sita/ n. f. citation; appointment, date.

citación /θita'θion; sita'sion/ n. f. citation; (legal) summons.

citar /θi'tar; si'tar/ v. cite, quote; summon; make an appointment with.

cítrico /'θitriko; 'sitriko/ a. citric.

ciudad /θiu'ðað; siu'ðað/ n. f. city.

ciudadanía /θiuða'ðania; siuða'ða'nia/ n. f. citizenship.

ciudadano /θiuða'ðano; siuða'ðano/ -na n. citizen.

ciudadela /θiuða'ðela; siuða'ðela/ n. f. fortress, citadel.

cívico /'θiβiko; 'siβiko/ a. civic.

civil /θi'βil; si'βil/ a. & n. civil; civilian.

civilidad /θiβili'ðað; siβili'ðað/ n. f. politeness, civility.

civilización /θiβiliθa'θion; siβilisa'sion/ n. f. civilization.

civilizador /θiβiliθa'ðor; siβilisa'ðor/ a. civilizing.

civilizar /θiβili'θar; siβili'sar/ v. civilize.

cizallas /θi'θaʎas; si'sayas/ n. f.pl. shears. —cizallar, v.

cizaña /θi'θaɲa; si'saɲa/ n. f. weed; vice.

clamar /kla'mar/ v. clamor.

clamor /kla'mor/ n. m. clamor.

clamoreo /klamo'reo/ n. m. persistent clamor.

clamoroso /klamo'roso/ a. clamorous.

clandestino /klandes'tino/ a. secret, clandestine.

clara /'klara/ n. f. white (of egg).

claraboya /klara'βoya/ n. m. skylight; bull's-eye.

clara de huevo /'klara de 'ueβo/ egg white.

clarear /klare'ar/ v. clarify; become light, dawn.

clarete /kla'rete/ n. m. claret.

claridad /klari'ðað/ n. f. clarity.

clarificar /klarifi'kar/ v. clarify.

clarín /kla'rin/ n. m. bugle, trumpet.

clarinete /klari'nete/ n. m. clarinet.

clarividencia /klariβi'ðenθia; klariβi'ðensia/ n. f. clairvoyance.

clarividente /klariβi'ðente/ a. clairvoyant.

claro /'klaro/ a. clear; bright; light (in color); of course.

clase /'klase/ n. f. class; classroom; kind, sort.

clase nocturna /'klase nok'turna/ evening class.

clásico /'klasiko/ a. classic, classical.

clasificar /klasifi'kar/ v. classify, rank.

claustro /'klaustro/ n. m. cloister.

claustrofobia /klaustro'foβia/ n. f. claustrophobia.

cláusula /'klausula/ n. f. clause.

clausura /klau'sura/ n. f. cloister; inner sanctum; closing.

clavado /kla'βaðo/ a. 1. nailed. —n. 2. m. & f. dive.

clavar /kla'βar/ v. nail, peg, pin.

clave /'klaβe/ n. f. code; Mus. key.

clavel /kla'βel/ n. m. carnation.

clavetear /klaβete'ar/ v. nail.

clavícula /kla'βikula/ n. f. collarbone.

clavija /kla'βiha/ n. f. pin, peg.

clavo /'klaβo/ n. m. nail, spike; clove.

clemencia /kle'menθia; kle'mensia/ n. f. clemency.

clemente /kle'mente/ a. merciful.

clementina /klemen'tina/ n. f. tangerine.

clerecía /klere'θia; klere'sia/ n. f. clergy.

clerical /kleri'kal/ a. clerical.

clérigo /'klerigo/ n. m. clergyman.

clero /'klero/ n. m. clergy.

cliente /'kliente/ n. m. & f. customer, client.

clientela /klien'tela/ n. f. clientele, practice.

clima /'klima/ n. m. climate.

clímax /'klimaks/ n. m. climax.

clínca de reposo /'klinka de rre'poso/ convalescent home.

clínica /'klinika/ n. f. clinic.

clínico /'kliniko/ a. clinical.

clíper /'kliper/ n. m. clipper ship.

cloaca /klo'aka/ n. f. sewer.

cloquear /kloke'ar/ v. cluck, cackle.

cloqueo /klo'keo/ n. m. cluck.

cloro /'kloro/ n. m. chlorine.

cloroformo /kloro'formo/ n. m. chloroform.

club /kluβ/ n. m. club, association.

club juvenil /kluβ huβe'nil/ youth club.

clueca /'klueka/ n. f. brooding hen.

coacción /koak'θion; koak'sion/ n. compulsion.

coagular /koagu'lar/ v. coagulate, clot.

coágulo /ko'agulo/ n. m. clot.

coalición /koali'θion; koali'sion/ n. coalition.

coartada /koar'taða/ n. f. alibi.

coartar /koar'tar/ v. limit.

cobarde /ko'βarðe/ a. & n. cowardly; coward.

cobardía /koβar'ðia/ n. f. cowardice.

cobayo /ko'βayo/ n. m. guinea pig.

cobertizo /koβer'tiθo; koβer'tiso/ n. m. shed.

cobertor /koβer'tor/ n. m., cobija, f. blanket.

cobertura /koβer'tura/ n. f. cover, wrapping.

cobijar /koβi'har/ v. cover; protect.

cobrador /koβra'ðor/ n. m. collector.

cobranza /ko'βranθa; ko'βransa/ n. f. collection or recovery of money.

cobrar /ko'βrar/ v. collect; charge; cash.

cobre /'koβre/ n. m. copper.

cobrizo /ko'βriθo; ko'βriso/ a. coppery.

cobro /'koβro/ n. m. collection or recovery of money.

coca /'koka/ n. f. coca leaves.

cocaína /koka'ina/ n. f. cocaine.

cocal /ko'kal/ n. m. coconut plantation.

cocear /koθe'ar; kose'ar/ v. kick; resist.

cocer /ko'θer; ko'ser/ v. cook, boil, bake.

coche /'kotʃe/ n. m. coach; car, automobile.

cochecito de niño /kotʃe'θito de 'niɲo; kotʃe'sito de 'niɲo/ baby carriage.

coche de choque /'kotʃe de 'tʃoke/ dodgem.

cochera /ko'tʃera/ n. f. garage.

cochero /ko'tʃero/ n. m. coachman; cab driver.

cochinada /kotʃi'naða/ n. f. filth; herd of swine.

cochino /ko'tʃino/ n. m. pig, swine.

cocido /ko'θiðo; ko'siðo/ n. m. stew.

cociente /ko'θiente; ko'siente/ n. m. quotient.

cocimiento /koθi'miento; kosi'miento/ n. m. cooking.

cocina /ko'θina; ko'sina/ n. f. kitchen.

cocinar /koθi'nar; kosi'nar/ v. cook.

cocinero /koθi'nero; kosi'nero/ -ra n. cook.

coco /'koko/ n. m. coconut; coconut tree.

cocodrilo /koko'ðrilo/ n. m. crocodile.

cóctel /kok'tel/ n. m. cocktail.

codazo /ko'ðaθo; ko'ðaso/ n. m. nudge with the elbow.

codicia /ko'ðiθia; ko'ðisia/ n. f. avarice, greed; lust.

codiciar /koðiθi'ar; koðisi'ar/ v. covet.

codicioso /koðiθi'oso; koðisi'oso/ a. covetous; greedy.

código /'koðigo/ n. m. (law) code.

codo /'koðo/ n. m. elbow.

codorniz /koðor'niθ; koðor'nis/ n. f. quail.

coeficiente /koefi'θiente; koefi'siente/ n. m. quotient.

coeficiente intelectual /koefi'θiente intelek'tual; koefi'siente intelek'tual/ intelligence quotient.

coetáneo /koe'taneo/ a. contemporary.

coexistir /koeksis'tir/ v. coexist.

cofrade /ko'fraðe/ n. m. fellow member of a club, etc.

cofre /'kofre/ n. m. coffer; chest; trunk.

coger /ko'her/ v. catch; pick; take.

cogote /ko'gote/ n. m. nape.

cohecho /ko'etʃo/ n. m. bribe. —cohechar, v.

coheredero /koere'ðero/ -ra n. coheir.

coherente /koe'rente/ a. coherent.

cohesión /koe'sion/ n. f. cohesion.

cohete /ko'ete/ n. m. firecracker; rocket.

cohibición /koiβi'θion; koiβi'sion/ n. restraint; repression.

cohibir /koi'βir/ v. restrain; repress.

coincidencia /koinθi'ðenθia; koinsi'ðensia/ n. f. coincidence.

coincidir /koinθi'ðir; koinsi'ðir/ v. coincide.

cojear /kohe'ar/ v. limp.

cojera /ko'hera/ n. m. limp.

cojín /ko'hin/ n. m. cushion.

cojinete /kohi'nete/ n. m. small cushion, pad.

cojo /'koho/ -a a. 1. lame. —n. 2. lame person.

col /kol/ n. f. cabbage.

cola /'kola/ n. f. tail; glue; line, queue. hacer c., stand in line.

colaboración /kolaβora'θion; kolaβora'sion/ n. f. collaboration.

colaborar /kolaβo'rar/ v. collaborate.

cola de caballo /'kola de ka'βaʎo; 'kola de ka'βayo/ ponytail.

coladera /kola'ðera/ n. f. strainer.

colador /kola'ðor/ n. m. colander, strainer.

colapso /ko'lapso/ n. m. collapse, prostration.

colar /ko'lar/ v. strain; drain.

colateral /kolate'ral/ a. collateral.

colcha /'koltʃa/ n. f. bedspread, quilt.

colchón /kol'tʃon/ n. m. mattress.

colear /kole'ar/ v. wag the tail.

colección /kolek'θion; kolek'sion/ n. f. collection, set.

coleccionar /kolekθio'nar; koleksio'nar/ v. collect.

colecta /ko'lekta/ n. f. collection; collect (a prayer).

colectivo /kolek'tiβo/ a. collective.

colector /kolek'tor/ n. m. collector.

colega /ko'lega/ n. m. & f. colleague.

colegial /kole'hial/ n. m. college student.

colegiatura /kolehia'tura/ n. f. scholarship; tuition.

colegio /ko'lehio/ n. m. (private) school, college.

colegir /kole'hir/ v. infer, deduce.

cólera /'kolera/ n. 1. f. rage, wrath. 2. m. cholera.

colérico /ko'leriko/ adj. angry, irritated.

colesterol /koleste'rol/ n. m. cholesterol.

coleta /ko'leta/ n. f. pigtail; postscript.

coleto /ko'leto/ n. m. leather jacket.

colgado /kol'gaðo/ -da n. 1. crazy person. —a. 2. hanging, pending.

colgador /kolga'ðor/ n. m. rack, hanger.

colgaduras /kolga'ðuras/ n. f.pl. drapery.

colgante /kol'gante/ a. hanging.

colgar /kol'gar/ v. hang up, suspend.

colibrí /koli'βri/ n. m. hummingbird.

coliflor /koli'flor/ n. f. cauliflower.

coligarse /koli'garse/ v. band together, unite.

colilla /ko'liʎa; ko'liya/ n. f. butt of a cigar or cigarette.

colina /ko'lina/ n. f. hill, hillock.

colinabo /koli'naβo/ n. m. turnip.

colindante /kolin'dante/ a. neighboring, adjacent.

colindar /kolin'dar/ v. neighbor, abut.

coliseo /koli'seo/ n. m. theater; coliseum.

colisión /koli'sion/ n. f. collision.

collado /ko'ʎaðo; ko'yaðo/ n. m. hillock.

collar /ko'ʎar; ko'yar/ n. m. necklace; collar.

colmar /kol'mar/ v. heap up, fill liberally.

colmena /kol'mena/ n. f. hive.

colmillo /kol'miʎo; kol'miyo/ n. m. eyetooth; tusk; fang.

colmo /'kolmo/ n. m. height, peak, extreme.

colocación /koloka'θion; koloka'sion/ n. f. place, position; employment, job; arrangement.

colocar /kolo'kar/ v. place, locate, put, set.

colombiano /kolom'biano/ -na a. & n. Colombian.

colon /'kolon/ n. m. colon (of intestines).

colonia /ko'lonia/ n. 1. f. colony; eau de Cologne.

Colonia n. 2. f. Cologne.

colonial /kolo'nial/ a. colonial.

colonización /koloniθa'θion; kolonisa'sion/ n. f. colonization.

colonizador /koloniθa'ðor; kolonisa'ðor/ **-ra** n. colonizer.

colonizar /koloni'θar; koloni'sar/ v. colonize.

colono /ko'lono/ n. m. colonist; tenant farmer.

coloquio /ko'lokio/ n. m. conversation, talk.

color /ko'lor/ n. m. color. —**colorar,** v.

coloración /kolora'θion; kolora'sion/ n. f. coloring.

colorado /kolo'raðo/ a. red, ruddy.

colorar /kolo'rar/ v. color, paint; dye.

colorete /kolo'rete/ n. m. rouge.

colorido /kolo'riðo/ n. m. color, coloring. —**colorir,** v.

colosal /kolo'sal/ a. colossal.

columbrar /kolum'brar/ v. discern.

columna /ko'lumna/ n. f. column, pillar, shaft.

columpiar /kolum'piar/ v. swing.

columpio /ko'lumpio/ n. m. swing.

coma /'koma/ n. f. coma; comma.

comadre /ko'maðre/ n. f. midwife; gossip; close friend.

comadreja /koma'ðreha/ n. f. weasel.

comadrona /koma'ðrona/ n. f. midwife.

comandancia /koman'danθia; koman'dansia/ n. m. command; command post.

comandante /koman'dante/ n. m. commandant; commander; major.

comandar /koman'dar/ v. command.

comandita /koman'dita/ n. f. silent partnership.

comanditario /komandi'tario/ **-ra** n. silent partner.

comando /ko'mando/ n. m. command.

comarca /ko'marka/ n. f. region; border, boundary.

comba /'komba/ n. f. bulge.

combar /kom'bar/ v. bend; bulge.

combate /kom'bate/ n. m. combat. —**combatir,** v.

combatiente /komba'tiente/ a. & m. combatant.

combinación /kombina'θion; kombina'sion/ n. f. combination; slip (garment).

combinar /kombi'nar/ v. combine.

combustible /kombus'tiβle/ a. **1.** combustible. —n. **2.** m. fuel.

combustión /kombus'tion/ n. f. combustion.

comedero /kome'ðero/ n. m. trough.

comedia /ko'meðia/ n. f. comedy; play.

comediante /kome'ðiante/ n. m. actor; comedian.

comedido /kome'ðiðo/ a. polite, courteous; obliging.

comedirse /kome'ðirse/ v. to be polite or obliging.

comedor /kome'ðor/ n. m. dining room. **coche c.,** dining car.

comendador /komenda'ðor/ n. m. commander.

comensal /komen'sal/ n. m. table companion.

comentador /komenta'ðor/ **-ra** n. commentator.

comentario /komen'tario/ n. m. commentary.

comento /ko'mento/ n. m. comment. —**comentar,** v.

comenzar /komen'θar; komen'sar/ v. begin, start, commence.

comer /ko'mer/ v. eat, dine.

comercial /komer'θial; komer'sial/ a. commercial.

comercializar /komerθiali'θar; komersiali'sar/ v. market.

comerciante /komer'θiante; komer'siante/ **-ta** n. merchant, trader, businessperson.

comerciar /komer'θiar; komer'siar/ v. trade, deal, do business.

comercio /ko'merθio; ko'mersio/ n. m. commerce, trade, business; store.

comestible /komes'tiβle/ a. **1.** edible. —n. **2.** m. (pl.) groceries, provisions.

---

cometa /ko'meta/ n. **1.** m. comet. **2.** f. kite.

cometer /kome'ter/ v. commit.

cometido /kome'tiðo/ n. m. commission; duty; task.

comezón /kome'θon; kome'son/ n. f. itch.

comicios /ko'miθios; ko'misios/ n. m.pl. primary elections.

cómico /'komiko/ **-ca** a. & m. comic, comical; comedian.

comida /ko'miða/ n. f. food; dinner; meal.

comidilla /komi'ðiʎa; komi'ðiya/ n. f. light meal; gossip.

comienzo /ko'mienθo; ko'mienso/ n. m. beginning.

comilitona /komili'tona/ n. f. spread, feast.

comillas /ko'miʎas; ko'miyas/ n. f.pl. quotation marks.

comilón /komi'lon/ **-na** n. glutton; heavy eater.

comisario /komi'sario/ n. m. commissary.

comisión /komi'sion/ n. f. commission. —**comisionar,** v.

comisionado /komisio'naðo/ **-da** n. agent, commissioner.

comisionar /komisio'nar/ v. commission.

comiso /ko'miso/ n. m. (law) confiscation of illegal goods.

comistrajo /komis'traho/ n. m. mess, hodgepodge.

comité /komi'te/ n. m. committee.

comitiva /komi'tiβa/ n. f. retinue.

como /'komo/ conj. & adv. like, as.

cómo adv. how.

cómoda /'komoða/ n. f. bureau, chest (of drawers).

cómodamente /komoða'mente/ adv. conveniently.

comodidad /komoði'ðað/ n. f. convenience, comfort; commodity.

comodín /komo'ðin/ n. m. joker (playing card).

cómodo /'komoðo/ a. comfortable; convenient.

comodoro /komo'ðoro/ n. m. commodore.

compacto /kom'pakto/ a. compact.

compadecer /kompaðe'θer; kompaðe'ser/ v. be sorry for, pity.

compadraje /kompa'ðrahe/ n. m. clique.

compadre /kom'paðre/ n. m. close friend.

compaginar /kompahi'nar/ v. put in order; arrange.

compañerismo /kompaɲe'rismo/ n. m. companionship.

compañero /kompa'ɲero/ **-ra** n. companion, partner.

compañía /kompa'ɲia/ n. f. company.

comparable /kompa'raβle/ a. comparable.

comparación /kompara'θion; kompara'sion/ n. f. comparison.

comparar /kompa'rar/ v. compare.

comparativamente /komparatiβa'mente/ adv. comparatively.

comparativo /kompara'tiβo/ a. comparative.

comparecer /kompare'θer; kompare'ser/ v. appear.

comparendo /kompa'rendo/ n. m. summons.

comparsa /kom'parsa/ n. f. carnival masquerade; retinue.

compartimiento /komparti'miento/ n. m. compartment.

compartir /kompar'tir/ v. share.

compás /kom'pas/ n. m. compass; beat, rhythm.

compasar /kompa'sar/ v. measure exactly.

compasión /kompa'sion/ n. f. compassion.

compasivo /kompa'siβo/ a. compassionate.

compatibilidad /kompatiβili'ðað/ n. f. compatibility.

---

compatible /kompa'tiβle/ a. compatible.

compatriota /kompa'triota/ n. m. & f. compatriot.

compeler /kompe'ler/ v. compel.

compendiar /kompen'diar/ v. summarize; abridge.

compendiariamente /kompendiaria'mente/ adv. briefly.

compendio /kom'pendio/ n. m. summary; abridgment.

compendiosamente /kompendiosa'mente/ adv. briefly.

compensación /kompensa'θion; kompensa'sion/ n. f. compensation.

compensar /kompen'sar/ v. compensate.

competencia /kompe'tenθia; kompe'tensia/ n. f. competence; competition.

competente /kompe'tente/ a. competent.

competentemente /kompetente'mente/ adv. competently.

competición /kompeti'θion; kompeti'sion/ n. f. competition.

competidor /kompeti'ðor/ **-ra** a. & n. competitive; competitor.

competir /kompe'tir/ v. compete.

compilación /kompila'θion; kompila'sion/ n. f. compilation.

compilar /kompi'lar/ v. compile.

compinche /kom'pintʃe/ n. m. pal.

complacencia /kompla'θenθia; kompla'sensia/ n. f. complacency.

complacer /kompla'θer; kompla'ser/ v. please, oblige, humor.

complaciente /kompla'θiente; kompla'siente/ a. pleasing, obliging.

complejidad /komplehi'ðað/ n. f. complexity.

complejo /kom'pleho/ **-ja** a. & n. complex.

complemento /komple'mento/ n. m. complement; Gram. object.

completamente /kompleta'mente/ adv. completely.

completamiento /kompleta'miento/ n. m. completion, finish.

completar /komple'tar/ v. complete.

completo /kom'pleto/ a. complete, full, perfect.

complexión /komplek'sion/ n. f. nature, temperament.

complicación /komplika'θion; komplika'sion/ n. f. complication.

complicado /kompli'kaðo/ a. complicated.

complicar /kompli'kar/ v. complicate.

cómplice /'kompliθe; 'komplise/ n. m. & f. accomplice, accessory.

complicidad /kompliθi'ðað; komplisi'ðað/ n. f. complicity.

complot /kom'plot/ n. m. conspiracy.

componedor /kompone'ðor/ **-ra** n. typesetter.

componenda /kompo'nenda/ n. f. compromise; settlement.

componente /kompo'nente/ a. & m. component.

componer /kompo'ner/ v. compose; fix, repair.

componible /kompo'niβle/ a. reparable.

comportable /kompor'taβle/ a. endurable.

comportamiento /komportamiento/ n. m. behavior.

comportarse /kompor'tarse/ v. behave.

comporte /kom'porte/ n. m. behavior.

composición /komposi'θion; komposi'sion/ n. f. composition.

compositivo /komposi'tiβo/ a. synthetic; composite.

compositor /komposi'tor/ **-ra** n. composer.

compost /kom'post/ n. m. compost.

compostura /kompos'tura/ n. f. composure; repair; neatness.

compota /kom'pota/ n. f. (fruit) sauce.

compra /'kompra/ n. f. purchase. **ir de compras,** to go shopping.

---

comprador /kompra'ðor/ **-ra** n. buyer, purchaser.

comprar /kom'prar/ v. buy, purchase.

comprender /kompren'der/ v. comprehend, understand; include, comprise.

comprensibilidad /komprensiβili'ðað/ n. f. comprehensibility.

comprensible /kompren'siβle/ a. understandable.

comprensión /kompren'sion/ n. f. comprehension, understanding.

comprensivo /kompren'siβo/ a. m. comprehensive.

compresa /kom'presa/ n. f. medical compress.

compresión /kompre'sion/ n. f. compression.

comprimir /kompri'mir/ v. compress; restrain, control.

comprobación /komproβa'θion; komproβa'sion/ n. f. proof.

comprobante /kompro'βante/ a. **1.** proving. —n. **2.** m. proof.

comprobar /kompro'βar/ v. prove; verify, check.

comprometer /komprome'ter/ v. compromise.

comprometerse /komprome'terse/ v. become engaged.

compromiso /kompro'miso/ n. m. compromise; engagement.

compuerta /kom'puerta/ n. f. floodgate.

compuesto /kom'puesto/ n. m. composition; compound.

compulsión /kompul'sion/ n. f. compulsion.

compulsivo /kompul'siβo/ a. compulsive.

compunción /kompun'θion; kompun'sion/ n. f. compunction.

compungirse /kompuɲ'girse/ v. regret, feel remorse.

computación /komputa'θion; komputa'sion/ n. f. computation.

computador /komputa'ðor/ n. m. computer.

computadora de sobremesa /komputa'ðora de soβre'mesa/ n. f. desktop computer.

computadora doméstica /komputa'ðora do'mestika/ n. f. home computer.

computar /kompu'tar/ v. compute.

cómputo /'komputo/ n. m. computation.

comulgar /komul'gar/ v. take communion.

comulgatorio /komulga'torio/ n. m. communion altar.

común /ko'mun/ a. common, usual.

comunal /komu'nal/ a. communal.

comunero /komu'nero/ n. m. commoner.

comunicable /komuni'kaβle/ a. communicable.

comunicación /komunika'θion; komunika'sion/ n. f. communication.

comunicante /komuni'kante/ n. m. & f. communicant.

comunicar /komuni'kar/ v. communicate; convey.

comunicativo /komunika'tiβo/ a. communicative.

comunidad /komuni'ðað/ n. f. community.

comunión /komu'nion/ n. f. communion.

comunismo /komu'nismo/ n. m. communism.

comunista /komu'nista/ a. & n. communistic; communist.

comúnmente /komu'mente/ adv. commonly; usually; often.

con /kon/ prep. with.

concavidad /konkaβi'ðað/ n. f. concavity.

cóncavo /'konkaβo/ a. **1.** concave. —n. **2.** m. concavity.

concebible /konθe'βiβle; konse'βiβle/ *a.* conceivable.

concebir /konθe'βir; konse'βir/ *v.* conceive.

conceder /konθe'ðer; konse'ðer/ *v.* concede.

concejal /konθe'hal; konse'hal/ *n. m.* councilman.

concejo /kon'θeho; kon'seho/ *n. m.* city council.

concento /kon'θento; kon'sento/ *n. m.* harmony (of singing voices).

concentración /konθentra'θion; konsentra'sion/ *n. f.* concentration.

concentrar /konθen'trar; konsen'trar/ *v.* concentrate.

concepción /konθep'θion; konsep'sion/ *n. f.* conception.

conceptible /konθep'tiβle; konsep'tiβle/ *a.* conceivable.

concepto /kon'θepto; kon'septo/ *n. m.* concept; opinion.

concerniente /konθer'niente; konser'niente/ *a.* concerning.

concernir /konθer'nir; konser'nir/ *v.* concern.

concertar /konθer'tar; konser'tar/ *v.* arrange.

concertina /konθer'tina; konser'tina/ *n. f.* concertina.

concesión /konθe'sion; konse'sion/ *f.* concession.

concha /'kontʃa/ *n. f.* S.A. shell.

conciencia /kon'θienθia; kon'siensia/ *n. f.* conscience; consciousness; conscientiousness.

concienzudo /konθien'θuðo; konsien'suðo/ *a.* conscientious.

concierto /kon'θierto; kon'sierto/ *n. m.* concert.

conciliación /konθilia'θion; konsilia'sion/ *n. f.* conciliation.

conciliador /konθilia'ðor; konsilia'ðor/ **-ra** *n.* conciliator.

conciliar /konθi'liar; konsi'liar/ *v.* conciliate.

concilio /kon'θilio; kon'silio/ *n. m.* council.

concisión /konθi'sion; konsi'sion/ *n. f.* conciseness.

conciso /kon'θiso; kon'siso/ *a.* concise.

concitar /konθi'tar; konsi'tar/ *v.* instigate, stir up.

conciudadano /konθiuða'ðano; konsiuða'ðano/ **-na** *n.* fellow citizen.

concluir /kon'kluir/ *v.* conclude.

conclusión /konklu'sion/ *n. f.* conclusion.

conclusivo /konklu'siβo/ *a.* conclusive.

concluso /kon'kluso/ *a.* concluded; closed.

concluyentemente /konkluyente'mente/ *adv.* conclusively.

concomitante /konkomi'tante/ *a.* concomitant, attendant.

concordador /konkorða'ðor/ **-ra** *n.* moderator; conciliator.

concordancia /konkor'ðanθia; konkor'ðansia/ *n. f.* agreement, concord.

concordar /konkor'ðar/ *v.* agree; put or be in accord.

concordia /kon'korðia/ *n. f.* concord, agreement.

concretamente /konkreta'mente/ *adv.* concretely.

concretar /konkre'tar/ *v.* summarize; make concrete.

concretarse /konkre'tarse/ *v.* limit oneself to.

concreto /kon'kreto/ *a. & m.* concrete.

concubina /konku'βina/ *n. f.* concubine, mistress.

concupiscente /konkupis'θente; konkupis'sente/ *a.* lustful.

concurrencia /konku'rrenθia; konku'rrensia/ *n. f.* assembly; attendance; competition.

concurrente /konku'rrente/ *a.* concurrent.

concurrido /konku'rriðo/ *a.* heavily attended or patronized.

concurrir /konku'rrir/ *v.* concur; attend.

concurso /kon'kurso/ *n. m.* contest, competition; meeting.

conde /'konde/ *n. m.* (title) count.

condecente /konde'θente; konde'sente/ *a.* appropriate, proper.

condecoración /kondekora'θion; kondekora'sion/ *n. f.* decoration; medal; badge.

condecorar /kondeko'rar/ *v.* decorate with a medal.

condena /kon'dena/ *n. f.* prison sentence.

condenación /kondena'θion; kondena'sion/ *n. f.* condemnation.

condenar /konde'nar/ *v.* condemn; damn; sentence.

condensación /kondensa'θion; kondensa'sion/ *n. f.* condensation.

condensar /konden'sar/ *v.* condense.

condesa /kon'desa/ *n. f.* countess.

condescendencia /kondesθen'denθia; kondessen'densia/ *n. f.* condescension.

condescender /kondesθen'der; kondessen'der/ *v.* condescend, deign.

condescendiente /kondesθen'diente; kondessen'diente/ *a.* condescending.

condición /kondi'θion; kondi'sion/ *n. f.* condition.

condicional /kondiθio'nal; kondisio'nal/ *a.* conditional.

condicionalmente /kondiθional'mente; kondisional'mente/ *adv.* conditionally.

condimentar /kondimen'tar/ *v.* season, flavor.

condimento /kondi'mento/ *n. m.* condiment, seasoning, dressing.

condiscípulo /kondis'θipulo; kondis'sipulo/ **-la** *n.* schoolmate.

condolencia /kondo'lenθia; kondo'lensia/ *n. f.* condolence, sympathy.

condolerse de /kondo'lerse de/ *v.* sympathize with.

condominio /kondo'minio/ *n. m.* condominium.

condómino /kon'domino/ *n. m.* co-owner.

condonar /kondo'nar/ *v.* condone.

cóndor /'kondor/ *n. m.* condor (bird).

conducción /konduk'θion; konduk'sion/ *n. f.* conveyance.

conducente /kondu'θente; kondu'sente/ *a.* conducive.

conducir /kondu'θir; kondu'sir/ *v.* conduct, escort, lead; drive.

conducta /kon'dukta/ *n. f.* conduct, behavior.

conducto /kon'dukto/ *n. m.* pipe, conduit; sewer.

conductor /konduk'tor/ **-ra** *n.* driver; conductor.

conectar /konek'tar/ *v.* connect.

conejera /kone'hera/ *n. f.* rabbit warren; place of ill repute.

conejillo de Indias /kone'hiʎo de 'indias; kone'hiyo de 'indias/ guinea pig.

conejo /ko'neho/ **-ja** *n.* rabbit.

conexión /konek'sion/ *n. f.* connection; coupling.

conexivo /konek'siβo/ *a.* connective.

conexo /ko'nekso/ *a.* connected, united.

confalón /konfa'lon/ *n. m.* ensign, standard.

confección /konfek'θion; konfek'sion/ *n. f.* workmanship; ready-made article; concoction.

confeccionar /konfekθio'nar; konfeksio'nar/ *v.* concoct.

confederación /konfeðera'θion; konfeðera'sion/ *n. f.* confederation.

confederado /konfeðe'raðo/ **-da** *a. & n.* confederate.

confederar /konfeðe'rar/ *v.* confederate, unite, ally.

conferencia /konfe'renθia; konfe'rensia/ *n. f.* lecture; conference. **c. interurbana**, long-distance call.

conferenciante /konferen'θiante;

konferen'siante/ *n. m. & f.* lecturer, speaker.

conferenciar /konferen'θiar; konferen'siar/ *v.* confer.

conferencista /konferen'θista; konferen'sista/ *n. m. & f.* lecturer, speaker.

conferir /konfe'rir/ *v.* confer.

confesar /konfe'sar/ *v.* confess.

confesión /konfe'sion/ *n. f.* confession.

confesionario /konfesio'nario, konfeso'nario/ *n. m.* confessional.

confesor /konfe'sor/ **-ra** *n.* confessor.

confeti /kon'feti/ *n. m.pl.* confetti.

confiable /kon'fiaβle/ *a.* dependable.

confiado /kon'fiaðo/ *a.* confident; trusting.

confianza /kon'fianθa; kon'fiansa/ *n. f.* confidence, trust, faith.

confiar /kon'fiar/ *v.* entrust; trust, rely.

confidencia /konfi'ðenθia; konfi'ðensia/ *n. f.* confidence, secret.

confidencial /konfiðen'θial; konfiðen'sial/ *a.* confidential.

confidente /konfi'ðente/ *n. m. & f.* confidant.

confidentemente /konfiðente'mente/ *adv.* confidently.

confín /kon'fin/ *n. m.* confine.

confinamiento /konfina'miento/ *n. m.* confinement.

confinar /konfi'nar/ *v.* confine, imprison; border on.

confirmación /konfirma'θion; konfirma'sion/ *n. f.* confirmation.

confirmar /konfir'mar/ *v.* confirm.

confiscación /konfiska'θion; konfiska'sion/ *n. f.* confiscation.

confiscar /konfis'kar/ *v.* confiscate.

confitar /konfi'tar/ *v.* sweeten; make into candy or jam.

confite /kon'fite/ *n. m.* candy.

confitería /konfite'ria/ *n. f.* confectionery; candy store.

confitura /konfi'tura/ *n. f.* confection.

conflagración /konflagra'θion; konflagra'sion/ *n. f.* conflagration.

conflicto /kon'flikto/ *n. m.* conflict.

confluencia /kon'fluenθia; kon'fluensia/ *n. f.* confluence, junction.

confluir /kon'fluir/ *v.* flow into each other.

conformación /konforma'θion; konforma'sion/ *n. f.* conformation.

conformar /konfor'mar/ *v.* conform.

conforme /kon'forme/ *a.* **1.** acceptable, right, as agreed; in accordance, in agreement. —*conj.* **2.** according, as.

conformidad /konformi'ðað/ *n. f.* conformity; agreement.

conformismo /konfor'mismo/ *n. m.* conformism.

conformista /konfor'mista/ *n. m. & f.* conformist.

confortar /konfor'tar/ *v.* comfort.

confraternidad /konfraterni'ðað/ *n. f.* brotherhood, fraternity.

confricar /konfri'kar/ *v.* rub vigorously.

confrontación /konfronta'θion; konfronta'sion/ *n. f.* confrontation.

confrontar /konfron'tar/ *v.* confront.

confucianismo /konfuθia'nismo; konfusia'nismo/ *n. m.* Confucianism.

confundir /konfun'dir/ *v.* confuse; puzzle, mix up.

confusamente /konfusa'mente/ *adv.* confusedly.

confusión /konfu'sion/ *n. f.* confusion, mix-up; clutter.

confuso /kon'fuso/ *a.* confused; confusing.

confutación /konfuta'θion; konfuta'sion/ *n. f.* disproof.

confutar /konfu'tar/ *v.* refute, disprove.

congelable /koŋge'laβle/ *a.* congealable.

congelación /koŋhela'θion; kon-

hela'sion/ *n. f.* congealment; deep freeze.

congelado /koŋge'laðo/ *a.* frozen, congealed.

congelar /koŋhe'lar/ *v.* congeal, freeze.

congenial /koŋge'nial/ *a.* congenial; analogous.

congeniar /koŋhe'niar/ *v.* be congenial.

congestión /koŋhes'tion/ *n. f.* congestion.

conglomeración /koŋglomera'θion; koŋglomera'sion/ *n. f.* conglomeration.

congoja /koŋ'goha/ *n. f.* grief, anguish.

congraciamiento /koŋgraθia'miento; koŋgrasia'miento/ *n. m.* flattery; ingratiation.

congraciar /koŋgra'θiar; koŋgra'siar/ *v.* flatter; ingratiate oneself.

congratulación /koŋgratula'θion; koŋgratula'sion/ *n. f.* congratulation.

congratular /koŋgratu'lar/ *v.* congratulate.

congregación /koŋgrega'θion; koŋgrega'sion/ *n. f.* congregation.

congregar /koŋgre'gar/ *v.* congregate.

congresista /koŋgre'sista/ *n. m. & f.* congressional representative.

congreso /koŋ'greso/ *n. m.* congress; conference.

conjetura /konhe'tura/ *n. f.* conjecture. —**conjeturar,** *v.*

conjetural /konhetu'ral/ *a.* conjectural.

conjugación /konhuga'θion; konhuga'sion/ *n. f.* conjugation.

conjugar /konhu'gar/ *v.* conjugate.

conjunción /konhun'θion; konhun'sion/ *n. f.* union; conjunction.

conjuntamente /konhunta'mente/ *adv.* together, jointly.

conjunto. /kon'hunto/ *a.* **1.** joint, unified. —*n.* **2.** *m.* whole.

conjuración /konhura'θion; konhura'sion/ *n. f.* conspiracy, plot.

conjurado /konhu'raðo/ **-da** *n.* conspirator, plotter.

conjurar /konhu'rar/ *v.* conjure.

conjuro /kon'huro/ *n. m.* exorcism; spell; plea.

conllevador /konʎeβa'ðor; konyeβa'ðor/ *n. m.* helper, aide.

conmemoración /komemora'θion; komemora'sion/ *n. f.* commemoration; remembrance.

conmemorar /komemo'rar/ *v.* commemorate.

conmemorativo /komemora'tiβo/ *a.* commemorative, memorial.

conmensal /komen'sal/ *n. m.* messmate.

conmigo /ko'migo/ *adv.* with me.

conmilitón /komili'ton/ *n. m.* fellow soldier.

conminación /komina'θion; komina'sion/ *n. f.* threat, warning.

conminar /komi'nar/ *v.* threaten.

conminatorio /komina'torio/ *a.* threatening, warning.

conmiseración /komisera'θion; komisera'sion/ *n. f.* sympathy.

conmoción /komo'θion; komo'sion/ *n. f.* commotion, stir.

conmovedor /komoβe'ðor/ *a.* moving, touching.

conmover /komo'βer/ *v.* move, affect, touch.

conmutación /komuta'θion; komuta'sion/ *n. f.* commutation.

conmutador /komuta'ðor/ *n. m.* electric switch.

conmutar /komu'tar/ *v.* exchange.

connatural /konnatu'ral/ *a.* innate, inherent.

connotación /konnota'θion; konnota'sion/ *n. f.* connotation.

connotar /konno'tar/ *v.* connote.

connubial /konnu'βial/ *a.* connubial.

connubio /ko'nnuβio/ *n. m.* matrimony.

cono /'kono/ *n. m.* cone.

conocedor /konoθe'ðor; konose'ðor/ **-ra** *n.* expert, connoisseur.

conocer /kono'θer; kono'ser/ *v.* know, be acquainted with; meet, make the acquaintance of.

conocible /kono'θiβle; kono'siβle/ *a.* knowable.

conocido /kono'θiðo; kono'siðo/ **-da** *a.* **1.** familiar, well-known. —*n.* **2.** acquaintance, person known.

conocimiento /konoθi'miento; konosi'miento/ *n. m.* knowledge, acquaintance; consciousness.

conque /'konke/ *conj.* so then; and so.

conquista /kon'kista/ *n. f.* conquest.

conquistador /konkista'ðor/ **-ra** *n.* conqueror.

conquistar /konkis'tar/ *v.* conquer.

consabido /konsa'βiðo/ *a.* aforesaid.

consagración /konsagra'θion; konsagra'sion/ *n. f.* consecration.

consagrado /konsa'graðo/ *a.* consecrated.

consagrar /konsa'grar/ *v.* consecrate, dedicate, devote.

consanguinidad /konsaŋguini'ðað/ *n. f.* consanguinity.

consciente /kons'θiente; kons'siente/ *a.* conscious, aware.

conscientemente /konsθiente'mente; konssiente'mente/ *adv.* consciously.

conscripción /konskrip'θion; konskrip'sion/ *n. f.* conscription for military service.

consecución /konseku'θion; konseku'sion/ *n. f.* attainment.

consecuencia /konse'kuenθia; konse'kuensia/ *n. f.* consequence.

consecuente /konse'kuente/ *a.* consequent; consistent.

consecuentemente /konsekuente'mente/ *adv.* consequently.

consecutivamente /konsekutiβa'mente/ *adv.* consecutively.

consecutivo /konseku'tiβo/ *a.* consecutive.

conseguir /konse'gir/ *v.* obtain, get, secure; succeed in, manage to.

conseja /kon'seha/ *n. f.* fable.

consejero /konse'hero/ **-ra** *n.* adviser, counselor.

consejo /kon'seho/ *n. m.* council; counsel; (piece of) advice. **c. de redacción**, editorial board.

consenso /kon'senso/ *n. m.* consensus.

consentido /konsen'tiðo/ *a.* spoiled, bratty.

consentimiento /konsenti'miento/ *n. m.* consent.

consentir /konsen'tir/ *v.* allow, permit.

conserje /kon'serhe/ *n. m.* superintendent, keeper.

conserva /kon'serβa/ *n. f.* conserve, preserve.

conservación /konserβa'θion; konserβa'sion/ *n. f.* conservation.

conservador /konserβa'ðor/ **-ra** *a. & n.* conservative.

conservar /konser'βar/ *v.* conserve.

conservativo /konserβa'tiβo/ *a.* conservative, preservative.

conservatorio /konserβa'torio/ *n. m.* conservatory.

considerable /konsiðe'raβle/ *a.* considerable, substantial.

considerablemente /konsiðeraβle'mente/ *adv.* considerably.

consideración /konsiðera'θion; konsiðera'sion/ *n. f.* consideration.

consideradamente /konsiðeraða'mente/ *adv.* considerably.

considerado /konsiðe'raðo/ *a.* considerate; considered.

considerando /konsiðe'rando/ *conj.* whereas.

considerar /konsiðe'rar/ *v.* consider.

consigna /kon'signa/ *n. f.* watchword.

consignación /konsigna'θion; konsigna'sion/ *n. f.* consignment.

consignar /konsig'nar/ *v.* consign.

consignatorio /konsigna'torio/ **-ria** *n.* consignee; trustee.

consigo /kon'sigo/ *adv.* with herself, with himself, with oneself, with themselves, with yourself, with yourselves.

consiguiente /konsi'giente/ *a.* **1.** consequent. —*n.* **2.** *m.* consequence.

consiguientemente /konsigiente'mente/ *adv.* consequently.

consistencia /konsis'tenθia; konsis'tensia/ *n. f.* consistency.

consistente /konsis'tente/ *a.* consistent.

consistir /konsis'tir/ *v.* consist.

consistorio /konsis'torio/ *n. m.* consistory.

consocio /kon'soθio; kon'sosio/ *n. m.* associate; partner; comrade.

consola /kon'sola/ *n. f.* console.

consolación /konsola'θion; konsola'sion/ *n. f.* consolation.

consolar /konso'lar/ *v.* console.

consolativo /konsola'tiβo/ *a.* consolatory.

consolidación /konsoliða'θion; konsoliða'sion/ *n.* consolidation.

consolidado /konsoli'ðaðo/ *a.* consolidated.

consolidar /konsoli'ðar/ *v.* consolidate.

consonancia /konso'nanθianb; konso'nansia/ *n. f.* agreement, accord, harmony.

consonante /konso'nante/ *a. & f.* consonant.

consonar /konso'nar/ *v.* rhyme.

consorte /kon'sorte/ *n. m. & f.* consort, mate.

conspicuo /kons'pikuo/ *a.* conspicuous.

conspiración /konspira'θion; konspira'sion/ *n. f.* conspiracy, plot.

conspirador /konspira'ðor/ **-ra** *n.* conspirator.

conspirar /konspi'rar/ *v.* conspire, plot.

constancia /kons'tanθia; kons'tansia/ *n. f.* perseverance; record.

constante /kons'tante/ *a.* constant.

constantemente /konstante'mente/ *adv.* constantly.

constar /kons'tar/ *v.* consist; be clear, be on record.

constelación /konstela'θion; konstela'sion/ *n. f.* constellation.

consternación /konsterna'θion; konsterna'sion/ *n. f.* consternation.

consternar /konster'nar/ *v.* dismay.

constipación /konstipa'θion; konstipa'sion/ *n. f.* head cold.

constipado /konsti'paðo/ *a.* **1.** having a head cold. —*n.* **2.** *m.* head cold.

constitución /konstitu'θion; konstitu'sion/ *n. f.* constitution.

constitucional /konstituθio'nal; konstitusio'nal/ *a.* constitutional.

constitucionalidad /konstituθionali'ðað; konstitusionali'ðað/ *n. f.* constitutionality.

constituir /konsti'tuir/ *v.* constitute.

constitutivo /konstitu'tiβo/ *n. m.* constituent.

constituyente /konstitu'yente, konstitu'tiβo/ *a.* constituent.

constreñidamente /konstreɲiða'mente/ *adv.* compulsively; with constraint.

constreñimiento /konstreɲi'miento/ *n. m.* compulsion; constraint.

constreñir /konstre'ɲir/ *v.* constrain.

constricción /konstrik'θion; konstrik'sion/ *n. f.* constriction.

construcción /konstruk'θion; konstruk'sion/ *n. f.* construction.

constructivo /konstruk'tiβo/ *a.* constructive.

constructor /konstruk'tor/ **-ra** *n.* builder.

construir /kons'truir/ *v.* construct, build.

consuelo /kon'suelo/ *n. m.* consolation.

cónsul /'konsul/ *n. m.* consul.

consulado /konsu'laðo/ *n. m.* consulate.

consular /konsu'lar/ *a.* consular.

consulta /kon'sulta/ *n. f.* consultation.

consultación /konsulta'θion; konsulta'sion/ *n. f.* consultation.

consultante /konsul'tante/ *n. m. & f.* consultant.

consultar /konsul'tar/ *v.* consult.

consultivo /konsul'tiβo/ *a.* consultative.

consultor /konsul'tor/ **-ra** *n.* adviser.

consumación /konsuma'θion; konsuma'sion/ *n. f.* consummation; end.

consumado /konsu'maðo/ *a.* consummate, downright.

consumar /konsu'mar/ *v.* consummate.

consumidor /konsumi'ðor/ **-ra** *n.* consumer.

consumir /konsu'mir/ *v.* consume.

consumo /kon'sumo/ *n. m.* consumption.

consunción /konsun'θion; konsun'sion/ *n. m.* consumption, tuberculosis.

contabilidad /kontaβili'ðað/ *n. f.* accounting, bookkeeping.

contabilista /kontaβi'lista/ **contable** *n. m. & f.* accountant.

contacto /kon'takto/ *n. m.* contact.

contado /kon'taðo/ *n. m.* **al c.**, (for) cash.

contador /konta'ðor/ **-ra** *n.* accountant, bookkeeper; meter.

contagiar /konta'hiar/ *v.* infect.

contagio /kon'tahio/ *n. m.* contagion.

contagioso /konta'hioso/ *a.* contagious.

contaminación /kontamina'θion; kontamina'sion/ *n. f.* contamination, pollution. **c. del aire, c. atmosférica,** air pollution.

contaminar /kontami'nar/ *v.* contaminate, pollute.

contar /kon'tar/ *v.* count; relate, recount, tell. **c. con,** count on.

contemperar /kontempe'rar/ *v.* moderate.

contemplación /kontempla'θion; kontempla'sion/ *n. f.* contemplation.

contemplador /kontempla'ðor/ **-ra** *n.* thinker.

contemplar /kontem'plar/ *v.* contemplate.

contemplativamente /kontemplatiβa'mente/ *adv.* thoughtfully.

contemplativo /kontempla'tiβo/ *a.* contemplative.

contemporáneo /kontempo'raneo/ **-nea** *a. & n.* contemporary.

contención /konten'θion; konten'sion/ *n. f.* contention.

contencioso /konten'θioso; konten'sioso/ *a.* quarrelsome; argumentative.

contender /konten'der/ *v.* cope, contend; conflict.

contendiente /konten'diente/ *n. m. & f.* contender.

contenedor /kontene'ðor/ *n. m.* container.

contener /konte'ner/ *v.* contain; curb, control.

contenido /konte'niðo/ *n. m.* contents.

contenta /kon'tenta/ *n. f.* endorsement.

contentamiento /kontenta'miento/ *n. m.* contentment.

contentar /konten'tar/ *v.* content, satisfy.

contentible /konten'tiβle/ *a.* contemptible.

contento /kon'tento/ *a.* **1.** contented, happy. —*n.* **2.** *m.* contentment, satisfaction, pleasure.

contérmino /kon'termino/ *a.* adjacent, abutting.

contestable /kontes'taβle/ *a.* disputable.

contestación /kontesta'θion; kontesta'sion/ *n. f.* answer. —**contestar,** *v.*

contestador automático /kontesta'ðor automatiko/ *n. m.* answering machine.

contextura /konteks'tura/ *n. f.* texture.

contienda /kon'tienda/ *n. f.* combat; match; strife.

contigo /kon'tigo/ *adv.* with you.

contiguamente /kontigua'mente/ *adv.* contiguously.

contiguo /kon'tiguo/ *a.* adjoining, next.

continencia /konti'nenθia; konti'nensia/ *n. f.* continence, moderation.

continental /konti'nental/ *a.* continental.

continente /konti'nente/ *n. m.* continent; mainland.

continentemente /kontinente'mente/ *adv.* in moderation.

contingencia /kontin'henθia; kontin'hensia/ *n. f.* contingency.

contingente /kontin'hente/ *a.* contingent; incidental.

continuación /kontinua'θion; kontinua'sion/ *n. f.* continuation. **a c.,** thereupon, hereupon.

continuamente /kontinua'mente/ *adv.* continuously.

continuar /konti'nuar/ *v.* continue, keep on.

continuidad /kontinui'ðað/ *n. f.* continuity.

continuo /kon'tinuo/ *a.* continual; continuous.

contorcerse /kontor'θerse; kontor'serse/ *v.* writhe, twist.

contorción /kontor'θion; kontor'sion/ *n. f.* contortion.

contorno /kon'torno/ *n. m.* contour; profile, outline; neighborhood.

contra /'kontra/ *prep.* against.

contraalmirante /kontraalmi'rante/ *n. m.* rear admiral.

contraataque /kontraa'take/ *n. m.* counterattack.

contrabajo /kontra'βaho/ *n. m.* double bass.

contrabalancear /kontraβalanθe'ar; kontraβalanse'ar/ *v.* counterbalance.

contrabandear /kontraβande'ar/ *v.* smuggle.

contrabandista /kontraβan'dista/ *n. m. & f.* smuggler.

contrabando /kontra'βando/ *n. m.* contraband, smuggling.

contracción /kontrak'θion; kontrak'sion/ *n. f.* contraction.

contracepción /kontraθep'θion; kontrasep'sion/ *n. f.* contraception, birth control.

contractual /kontrak'tual/ *a.* contractual.

contradecir /kontraðe'θir; kontraðe'sir/ *v.* contradict.

contradicción /kontraðik'θion; kontraðik'sion/ *n. f.* contradiction.

contradictorio /kontraðik'torio/ *adj.* contradictory.

contraer /kontra'er/ *v.* contract; shrink.

contrahacedor /kontraaθe'ðor; kontraase'ðor/ **-ra** *n.* imitator.

contrahacer /kontraa'θer; kontraa'ser/ *v.* forge.

contralor /kontra'lor/ *n. m.* comptroller.

contramandar /kontraman'dar/ *v.* countermand.

contraorden /kontra'orðen/ *n. f.* countermand.

contraparte /kontra'parte/ *n. f.* counterpart.

contrapesar /kontrape'sar/ *v.* counterbalance; offset.

contrapeso /kontra'peso/ *n. m.* counterweight.

contraproducente /kontrap-

contraproductivo /kontraproδu'sente/ *a.* counterproductive.

contrapunto /kontra'punto/ *n. m.* counterpoint.

contrariamente /kontraria'mente/ *adv.* contrarily.

contrariar /kontra'riar/ *v.* contradict; vex; antagonize; counteract.

contrariedad /kontrarie'δaδ/ *n. f.* contrariness; opposition; contradiction; disappointment; trouble.

contrario /kon'trario/ *a. & m.* contrary, opposite.

contrarrestar /kontrarres'tar/ *v.* resist; counteract.

contrasol /kontra'sol/ *n. m.* sunshade.

contraste /kon'traste/ *n. m.* contrast. —**contrastar,** *v.*

contratar /kontra'tar/ *v.* engage, contract.

contratiempo /kontra'tiempo/ *n. m.* accident; misfortune.

contratista /kontra'tista/ *n. m. & f.* contractor.

contrato /kon'trato/ *n. m.* contract.

contribución /kontriβu'θion; kontriβu'sion/ *n. f.* contribution; tax.

contribuir /kontri'βuir/ *v.* contribute.

contribuyente /kontriβu'yente/ *n. m. & f.* contributor; taxpayer.

contrición /kontri'θion; kontri'sion/ *n. f.* contrition.

contristar /kontris'tar/ *v.* afflict.

contrito /kon'trito/ *a.* contrite, remorseful.

control /kon'trol/ *n. m.* control. —**controlar,** *v.*

controlador aéreo /kontrola'δor a'ereo/ *n. m.* air traffic controller.

controversia /kontro'βersia/ *n. f.* controversy.

controversista /kontroβer'sista/ *n. m. & f.* controversialist.

controvertir /kontroβer'tir/ *v.* dispute.

contumacia /kontu'maθia; kontu'masia/ *n. f.* stubbornness.

contumaz /kontu'maθ; kontu'mas/ *adj.* stubborn.

contumelia /kontu'melia/ *n. f.* contumely; abuse.

conturbar /kontur'βar/ *v.* trouble, disturb.

contusión /kontu'sion/ *n. f.* contusion; bruise.

convalecencia /kombale'θenθia; kombale'sensia/ *n. f.* convalescence.

convalecer /kombale'θer; kombale'ser/ *v.* convalesce.

convaleciente /kombale'θiente; kombale'siente/ *a.* convalescent.

convecino /kombe'θino; kombe'sino/ -na *a.* 1. near, close. —*n.* 2. neighbor.

convencedor /kombenθe'δor; kombense'δor/ *adj.* convincing.

convencer /komben'θer; komben'ser/ *v.* convince.

convencimiento /kombenθi'miento; kombensi'miento/ *n. m.* conviction, firm belief.

convención /komben'θion; komben'sion/ *n. f.* convention.

convencional /kombenθio'nal; kombensio'nal/ *a.* conventional.

conveniencia /kombe'nienθia; kombe'niensia/ *n. f.* suitability; advantage, interest.

conveniente /kombe'niente/ *a.* suitable; advantageous, opportune.

convenio /kom'benio/ *n. m.* pact, treaty; agreement.

convenir /kombe'nir/ *v.* assent, agree, concur; be suitable, fitting, convenient.

convento /kom'bento/ *n. m.* convent.

convergencia /komber'henθia; komber'hensia/ *n. f.* convergence.

convergir /komber'hir/ *v.* converge.

conversación /kombersa'θion; kombersa'sion/ *n. f.* conversation.

conversar /komber'sar/ *v.* converse.

conversión /komber'sion/ *n. f.* conversion.

convertible /komber'tiβle/ *a.* convertible.

convertir /komber'tir/ *v.* convert.

convexidad /kombeksi'δaδ/ *n. f.* convexity.

convexo /kom'bekso/ *a.* convex.

convicción /kombik'θion; kombik'sion/ *n. f.* conviction.

convicto /kom'bikto/ *a.* found guilty.

convidado /kombi'δaδo/ -da *n.* guest.

convidar /kombi'δar/ *v.* invite.

convincente /kombin'θente; kombin'sente/ *a.* convincing.

convite /kom'bite/ *n. m.* invitation, treat.

convocación /komboka'θion; komboka'sion/ *n. f.* convocation.

convocar /kombo'kar/ *v.* convoke, assemble.

convoy /kom'boi/ *n. m.* convoy, escort.

convoyar /kombo'yar/ *v.* convey; escort.

convulsión /kombul'sion/ *n. f.* convulsion.

convulsivo /kombul'siβo/ *a.* convulsive.

conyugal /konyu'gal/ *a.* conjugal.

cónyuge /'konyuhe/ *n. m. & f.* spouse, mate.

coñac /ko'ɲak/ *n. m.* cognac, brandy.

cooperación /koopera'θion; koopera'sion/ *n. f.* cooperation.

cooperador /koopera'δor/ *a.* cooperative.

cooperar /koope'rar/ *v.* cooperate.

cooperativa /koopera'tiβa/ *n. f.* (food, etc.) cooperative, co-op.

cooperativo /koopera'tiβo/ *a.* cooperative.

coordinación /koorδina'θion; koorδina'sion/ *n. f.* coordination.

coordinar /koorδi'nar/ *v.* coordinate.

copa /'kopa/ *n. f.* goblet.

copartícipe /kopar'tiθipe; kopar'tisipe/ *m & f.* partner.

copete /ko'pete/ *n. m.* tuft; toupee.

copia /'kopia/ *n. f.* copy. —**copiar,** *v.*

copiadora /kopia'δora/ *n. f.* copier.

copioso /ko'pioso/ *a.* copious.

copista /ko'pista/ *n. m. & f.* copyist.

copla /'kopla/ *n. f.* popular song.

coplero /kop'lero/ *n. m.* poetaster.

cópula /'kopula/ *n. f.* connection.

coqueta /ko'keta/ *n. f.* flirt. —**coquetear,** *v.*

coraje /ko'rahe/ *n. m.* courage, bravery; anger.

coral /ko'ral/ *a.* 1. choral. —*n.* 2. *m.* coral.

coralino /kora'lino/ *a.* coral.

Corán /ko'ran/ *n. m.* Koran.

corazón /kora'θon; kora'son/ *n. m.* heart.

corazonada /koraθo'naδa; koraso'naδa/ *n. f.* foreboding.

corbata /kor'βata/ *n. f.* necktie.

corbeta /kor'βeta/ *n. f.* corvette.

corcho /'kortʃo/ *n. m.* cork.

corcova /kor'koβa/ *n. f.* hump, hunchback.

corcovado /korko'βaδo/ -da *a. & n.* hunchback.

cordaje /kor'δahe/ *n. m.* rigging.

cordel /kor'δel/ *n. m.* string, cord.

cordero /kor'δero/ *n. m.* lamb.

cordial /kor'δial/ *a.* cordial; hearty.

cordialidad /korδiali'δaδ/ *n. f.* cordiality.

cordillera /korδi'ʎera; korδi'yera/ *n. f.* mountain range.

cordón /kor'δon/ *n. m.* cord; (shoe) lace.

cordura /kor'δura/ *n. f.* sanity.

Corea /ko'rea/ *n. f.* Korea.

coreano /kore'ano/ -a *a. & n.* Korean.

coreografía /koreogra'fia/ *n. f.* choreography.

corista /ko'rista/ *n. f.* chorus girl.

corneja /kor'neha/ *n. f.* crow.

córneo /'korneo/ *a.* horny.

corneta /kor'neta/ *n. f.* bugle, horn, cornet.

corniforme /korni'forme/ *a.* horn-shaped.

cornisa /kor'nisa/ *n. f.* cornice.

cornucopia /kornu'kopia/ *n. f.* cornucopia.

coro /'koro/ *n. m.* chorus; choir.

corola /ko'rola/ *n. f.* corolla.

corolario /koro'lario/ *n. m.* corollary.

corona /ko'rona/ *n. f.* crown; halo; wreath.

coronación /korona'θion; korona'sion/ *n. f.* coronation.

coronamiento /korona'miento/ *n. m.* completion of a task.

coronar /koro'nar/ *v.* crown.

coronel /koro'nel/ *n. m.* colonel.

coronilla /koro'niʎa; koro'niya/ *n. f.* crown, top of the head.

corporación /korpora'θion; korpora'sion/ *n. f.* corporation.

corporal /korpo'ral/ *adj.* corporeal, bodily.

corpóreo /kor'poreo/ *a.* corporeal.

corpulencia /korpu'lenθia; korpu'lensia/ *n. f.* corpulence.

corpulento /korpu'lento/ *a.* corpulent, stout.

corpuscular /korpusku'lar/ *a.* corpuscular.

corpúsculo /kor'puskulo/ *n. m.* corpuscle.

corral /ko'rral/ *n. m.* corral, pen, yard.

correa /ko'rrea/ *n. f.* belt, strap.

correa transportadora /korrea transporta'δora/ conveyor belt.

corrección /korrek'θion; korrek'sion/ *n. f.* correction.

correcto /ko'rrekto/ *a.* correct, proper, right.

corrector /korrek'tor/ -ra *n.* corrector, proofreader.

corredera /korre'δera/ *n. f.* race course.

corredizo /korre'δiθo; korre'δiso/ *a.* easily untied.

corredor /korre'δor/ *n. m.* corridor; runner.

corregible /korre'hiβle/ *a.* corrigible.

corregidor /korrehi'δor/ *n. m.* corrector; magistrate, mayor.

corregir /korre'hir/ *v.* correct.

correlación /korrela'θion; korrela'sion/ *n. f.* correlation.

correlacionar /korrelaθio'nar; korrelasio'nar/ *v.* correlate.

correlativo /korrela'tiβo/ *a.* correlative.

correo /ko'rreo/ *n. m.* mail.

correoso /korre'oso/ *a.* leathery.

correr /ko'rrer/ *v.* run.

correría /korre'ria/ *n. f.* raid; escapade.

correspondencia /korrespon'denθia; korrespon'densia/ *n. f.* correspondence.

corresponder /korrespon'der/ *v.* correspond.

correspondiente /korrespon'diente/ *a. & m.* corresponding; correspondent.

corresponsal /korrespon'sal/ *n. m.* correspondent.

corretaje /korre'tahe/ *n. m.* brokerage.

correvedile /korreβe'δile/ *n. m.* tale bearer; gossip.

corrida /ko'rriδa/ *n. f.* race. **c. (de toros),** bullfight.

corrido /ko'rriδo/ *a.* abashed; expert.

corriente /ko'rriente/ *a.* 1. current, standard. —*n.* 2. *f.* current, stream. 3. *m.* **al c.,** informed, up to date. **contra la c.,** against the current; upriver, upstream.

corroboración /korroβora'θion; korroβora'sion/ *n. f.* corroboration.

corroborar /korroβo'rar/ *v.* corroborate.

corroer /korro'er/ *v.* corrode.

corromper /korrom'per/ *v.* corrupt.

corrompido /korrom'piδo/ *a.* corrupt.

corrupción /korrup'θion; korrup'sion/ *n. f.* corruption.

corruptela /korrup'tela/ *n. f.* corruption; vice.

corruptibilidad /korruptiβili'δaδ/ *n. f.* corruptibility.

corruptor /korrup'tor/ -ra *n.* corrupter.

corsario /kor'sario/ *n. m.* corsair.

corsé /kor'se/ *n. m.* corset.

corso /'korso/ *n. m.* piracy.

cortacésped /korta'θespeδ; korta'sespeδ/ *n. m.* lawnmower.

cortadillo /korta'δiʎo; korta'δiyo/ *n. m.* small glass.

cortado /kor'taδo/ *a.* cut.

cortadura /korta'δura/ *n. f.* cut.

cortante /kor'tante/ *a.* cutting, sharp, keen.

cortapisa /korta'pisa/ *n. f.* obstacle.

cortaplumas /korta'plumas/ *n. m.* penknife.

cortar /kor'tar/ *v.* cut, cut off, cut out.

corte /'korte/ *n. f.* court, *m.* cut.

cortedad /korte'δaδ/ *n. f.* smallness; shyness.

cortejar /korte'har/ *v.* pay court to, woo.

cortejo /kor'teho/ *n. m.* court; courtship; sweetheart.

cortés /kor'tes/ *a.* civil, courteous, polite.

cortesana /korte'sana/ *n. f.* courtesan.

cortesano. 1. /korte'sano/ *a.* 1. courtly, courteous. —*n.* 2. *m.* courtier.

cortesía /korte'sia/ *n. f.* courtesy.

corteza /kor'teθa; kor'tesa/ *n. f.* bark; rind; crust.

cortijo /kor'tiho/ *n. m.* farmhouse.

cortina /kor'tina/ *n. f.* curtain.

corto /'korto/ *a.* short.

corva /'korβa/ *n. f.* back of the knee.

cosa /'kosa/ *n. f.* thing. **c. de,** a matter of, roughly.

cosecha /ko'setʃa/ *n. f.* crop, harvest. —**cosechar,** *v.*

coser /ko'ser/ *v.* sew, stitch.

cosmético /kos'metiko/ *a. & m.* cosmetic.

cósmico /'kosmiko/ *a.* cosmic.

cosmonauta /kosmo'nauta/ *n. m. & f.* cosmonaut.

cosmopolita /kosmopo'lita/ *a. & n.* cosmopolitan.

cosmos /'kosmos/ *n. m.* cosmos.

coso /'koso/ *n. m.* arena for bull fights.

cosquilla /kos'kiʎa; kos'kiya/ *n. f.* tickle. —**cosquillar,** *v.*

cosquilloso /koski'ʎoso; koski'yoso/ *a.* ticklish.

costa /'kosta/ *n. f.* coast; cost, expense.

costado /kos'taδo/ *n. m.* side.

costal /kos'tal/ *n. m.* sack, bag.

costanero /kosta'nero/ *a.* coastal.

costar /kos'tar/ *v.* cost.

costarricense /kostarri'θense; kostarri'sense/ *a. & n.* Costa Rican.

coste /'koste/ *n. m.* cost, price.

costear /koste'ar/ *v.* defray, sponsor; sail along the coast of.

costilla /kos'tiʎa; kos'tiya/ *n. f.* rib; chop.

costo /'kosto/ *n. m.* cost, price.

costoso /kos'toso/ *a.* costly.

costra /'kostra/ *n. f.* crust.

costumbre /kos'tumbre/ *n. f.* custom, practice, habit.

costura /kos'tura/ *n. f.* sewing; seam.

costurera /kostu'rera/ *n. f.* seamstress, dressmaker.

costurero /kostu'rero/ *n. m.* sewing basket.

cota de malla /'kota de 'maʎa; 'kota de 'maya/ coat of mail.

cotejar /kote'har/ *v.* compare.

cotidiano /koti'ðiano/ *a.* daily; everyday.

cotillón /koti'ʎon; koti'yon/ *n. m.* cotillion.

cotización /kotiθa'θion; kotisa'sion/ *n. f.* quotation.

cotizar /koti'θar; koti'sar/ *v.* quote (a price).

coto /'koto/ *n. m.* enclosure; boundary.

cotón /ko'ton/ *n. m.* printed cotton cloth.

cotufa /ko'tufa/ *n. f.* Jerusalem artichoke.

coturno /ko'turno/ *n. m.* buskin.

covacha /ko'βatʃa/ *n. f.* small cave.

coxal /kok'sal/ *a.* of the hip.

coy /koi/ *n. m.* hammock.

coyote /ko'yote/ *n. m.* coyote.

coyuntura /koyun'tura/ *n. f.* joint; juncture.

coz /koθ; kos/ *n. f.* kick.

crac /krak/ *n. m.* failure.

cráneo /'kraneo/ *n. m.* skull.

craniano /kra'niano/ *a.* cranial.

crapuloso /krapu'loso/ *a.* drunken.

crasiento /kra'siento/ *a.* greasy, oily.

craso /'kraso/ *a.* fat; gross.

cráter /'krater/ *n. m.* crater.

craza /'kraθa; 'krasa/ *n. f.* crucible.

creación /krea'θion; krea'sion/ *n. f.* creation.

creador /krea'ðor/ **-ra** *a. & n.* creative; creator.

crear /kre'ar/ *v.* create.

creativo /krea'tiβo/ *a.* creative.

crébol /'kreβol/ *n. m.* holly tree.

crecer /kre'θer; kre'ser/ *v.* grow, grow up; increase.

creces /'kreθes; 'kreses/ *n. f.pl.* increase, addition.

crecidamente /kreθiða'mente; kresiða'mente/ *adv.* abundantly.

crecido /kre'θiðo; kre'siðo/ *a.* increased, enlarged; swollen.

creciente /kre'θiente; kre'siente/ *a.* **1.** growing. —*n.* **2.** *m.* crescent.

crecimiento /kreθi'miento; kresi'miento/ *n. m.* growth.

credenciales /kreðen'θiales; kreðen'siales/ *f.pl.* credentials.

credibilidad /kreðiβili'ðað/ *n. f.* credibility.

crédito /'kreðito/ *n. m.* credit.

credo /'kreðo/ *n. m.* creed, belief.

crédulamente /kreðula'mente/ *adv.* credulously, gullibly.

credulidad /kreðuli'ðað/ *n. f.* credulity.

crédulo /'kreðulo/ *a.* credulous.

creedero /kree'ðero/ *a.* credible.

creedor /kree'ðor/ *a.* credulous, believing.

creencia /kre'enθia; kre'ensia/ *n. f.* belief.

creer /kre'er/ *v.* believe; think.

creíble /kre'iβle/ *a.* credible, believable.

crema /'krema/ *n. f.* cream.

cremación /krema'θion; krema'sion/ *n. f.* cremation.

crema dentífrica /'krema den'tifrika/ toothpaste.

cremallera /krema'ʎera; krema'yera/ *n. f.* zipper.

crémor tártaro /'kremor 'tartaro/ *n. m.* cream of tartar.

cremoso /kre'moso/ *a.* creamy.

creosota /kreo'sota/ *n. f.* creosote.

crepitar /krepi'tar/ *v.* crackle.

crepuscular /krepusku'lar/ *a.* of or like the dawn or dusk; crepuscular.

crépusculo /kre'puskulo/ *n. m.* dusk, twilight.

crescendo /kres'θendo; kres'sendo/ *n. m.* crescendo.

crespo /'krespo/ *a.* curly.

crespón /kres'pon/ *n. m.* crepe.

cresta /'kresta/ *n. f.* crest; heraldic crest.

crestado /kres'taðo/ *a.* crested.

creta /'kreta/ *n. f.* chalk.

cretáceo /kre'taθeo; kre'taseo/ *a.* chalky.

cretinismo /kreti'nismo/ *n. m.* cretinism.

cretino /kre'tino/ **-na** *n. & a.* cretin.

cretona /kre'tona/ *n. f.* cretonne.

creyente /kre'yente/ *a.* **1.** believing. —*n.* **2.** believer.

creyón /kre'yon/ *n. m.* crayon.

cría /'kria/ *n. f.* (stock) breeding; young (of an animal), litter.

criada /kri'aða/ *n. f.* maid.

criadero /kria'ðero/ *n. m. Agr.* nursery.

criado /kri'aðo/ **-da** *n.* servant.

criador /kria'ðor/ *a.* fruitful, prolific.

crianza /kri'anθa; kri'ansa/ *n. f.* breeding; upbringing.

criar /kri'ar/ *v.* raise, rear; breed.

criatura /kria'tura/ *n. f.* creature; infant.

criba /'kriβa/ *n. f.* sieve.

cribado /kri'βaðo/ *a.* sifted.

cribar /kri'βar/ *v.* sift.

crimen /'krimen/ *n. m.* crime.

criminal /krimi'nal/ *a. & n.* criminal.

criminalidad /kriminali'ðað/ *n. f.* criminality.

criminalmente /kriminal'mente/ *adv.* criminally.

criminología /kriminolo'hia/ *n. f.* criminology.

criminoso /krimi'noso/ *a.* criminal.

crines /'krines/ *n. f.pl.* mane of a horse.

crinolina /krino'lina/ *n. f.* crinoline.

criocirugía /krioθiru'hia; kriosiru'hia/ *n. f.* cryosurgery.

criollo /'krioʎo; 'krioyo/ **-lla** *a. & n.* native; Creole.

cripta /'kripta/ *n. f.* crypt.

criptografía /kriptogra'fia/ *n. f.* cryptography.

crisantemo /krisan'temo/ *n. m.* chrysanthemum.

crisis /'krisis/ *n. f.* crisis.

crisis nerviosa /'krisis ner'βiosa/ nervous breakdown.

crisma /'krisma/ *n. m.* chrism.

crisol /kri'sol/ *n. m.* crucible.

crispamiento /krispa'miento/ *n. m.* twitch, contraction.

crispar /kris'par/ *v.* contract (the muscles); twitch.

cristal /kri'stal/ *n. m.* glass; crystal; lens.

cristalería /kristale'ria/ *n. f.* glassware.

cristalino /krista'lino/ *a.* crystalline.

cristalización /kristaliθa'θion; kristalisa'sion/ *n. f.* crystallization.

cristalizar /kristali'θar; kristali'sar/ *v.* crystallize.

cristianar /kristia'nar/ *v.* baptize.

cristiandad /kristian'dað/ *n. f.* Christendom.

cristianismo /kristia'nismo/ *n. m.* Christianity.

cristiano /kris'tiano/ **-na** *a. & n.* Christian.

Cristo /'kristo/ *n. m.* Christ.

criterio /kri'terio/ *n. m.* criterion; judgment.

crítica /'kritika/ *n. f.* criticism; critique.

criticable /kriti'kaβle/ *a.* blameworthy.

criticador /kritika'ðor/ *a.* critical.

criticar /kriti'kar/ *v.* criticize.

crítico /'kritiko/ **-ca** *a. & n.* critical; critic.

croar /kro'ar/ *v.* croak.

crocante /kro'kante/ *n. m.* almond brittle.

crocitar /kroθi'tar; krosi'tar/ *v.* crow.

cromático /kro'matiko/ *a.* chromatic.

cromo /'kromo/ *n. m.* chromium.

cromosoma /kromo'soma/ *n. m.* chromosome.

cromotipia /kromo'tipia/ *n. f.* color printing.

crónica /'kronika/ *n. f.* chronicle.

crónico /'kroniko/ *a.* chronic.

cronicón /kroni'kon/ *n. m.* concise chronicle.

cronista /kro'nista/ *n. m. & f.* chronicler.

cronología /kronolo'hia/ *n. f.* chronology.

cronológicamente /kronolohika'mente/ *adv.* chronologically.

cronológico /krono'lohiko/ *a.* chronologic.

cronometrar /kronome'trar/ *v.* time.

cronómetro /kro'nometro/ *n. m.* stopwatch; chronometer.

croqueta /kro'keta/ *n. f.* croquette.

croquis /'krokis/ *n. m.* sketch; rough outline.

crótalo /'krotalo/ *n. m.* rattlesnake; castanet.

cruce /'kruθe; 'kruse/ *n. m.* crossing, crossroads, junction.

crucero /kru'θero; kru'sero/ *n. m.* cruiser.

crucífero /kru'θifero; kru'sifero/ *a.* cross-shaped.

crucificado /kruθifi'kaðo; krusifi'kaðo/ *a.* crucified.

crucificar /kruθifi'kar; krusifi'kar/ *v.* crucify.

crucifijo /kruθi'fiho; krusi'fiho/ *n. m.* crucifix.

crucifixión /kruθifik'sion; krusifik'sion/ *n. f.* crucifixion.

crucigrama /kruθi'grama; krusi'grama/ *n. m.* crossword puzzle.

crudamente /kruða'mente/ *adv.* crudely.

crudeza /kru'ðeθa; kru'ðesa/ *n. f.* crudeness.

crudo /'kruðo/ *a.* crude, raw.

cruel /kruel/ *a.* cruel.

crueldad /kruel'dað/ *n. f.* cruelty.

cruelmente /kruel'mente/ *adv.* cruelly.

cruentamente /kruenta'mente/ *adv.* bloodily.

cruento /'kruento/ *a.* bloody.

crujía /kru'hia/ *n. f.* corridor.

crujido /kru'hiðo/ *n. m.* creak.

crujir /kru'hir/ *v.* crackle; creak; rustle.

cruórico /'kruoriko/ *a.* bloody.

crup /krup/ *n. m.* croup.

crupié /kru'pie/ *n. m. & f.* croupier.

crustáceo /krus'taθeo; krus'taseo/ *n. & a.* crustacean.

cruz /kruθ; krus/ *n. f.* cross.

cruzada /kru'θaða; kru'saða/ *n. f.* crusade.

cruzado /kru'θaðo; kru'saðo/ **-da** *n.* crusader.

cruzamiento /kruθa'miento; krusa'miento/ *n. m.* crossing.

cruzar /kru'θar; kru'sar/ *v.* cross.

cruzarse con /kru'θarse kon; kru'sarse kon/ *v.* to (meet and) pass.

cuaderno /kua'ðerno/ *n. m.* notebook.

cuadra /'kuaðra/ *n. f.* block; (hospital) ward.

cuadradamente /kuaðraða'mente/ *adv.* exactly, precisely; completely, in full.

cuadradillo /kuaðra'ðiʎo; kuaðra'ðiyo/ *n. m.* lump of sugar.

cuadrado /kua'ðraðo/ **-da** *a. & n.* square.

cuadrafónico /kuaðra'foniko/ *a.* quadraphonic.

Cuadragésima /kuaðra'hesima/ *n. f.* Lent.

cuadragesimal /kuaðrahesi'mal/ *a.* Lenten.

cuadrángulo /kua'ðraŋgulo/ *n. m.* quadrangle.

cuadrante /kua'ðrante/ *n. m.* quadrant; dial.

cuadrar /kua'ðrar/ *v.* square; suit.

cuadricular /kuaðriku'lar/ *a.* in squares.

cuadrilátero /kuaðri'latero/ *a.* quadrilateral.

cuadrilla /kua'ðriʎa; kua'ðriya/ *n. f.* band, troop, gang.

cuadro /'kuaðro/ *n. m.* picture; painting; frame. **a cuadros,** checked, plaid.

cuadro de servicio /'kuaðro de ser'βiθio; 'kuaðro de ser'βisio/ timetable.

cuadrupedal /kuaðrupe'ðal/ *a.* quadruped.

cuádruplo /'kuaðruplo/ *a.* fourfold.

cuajada /kua'haða/ *n. f.* curd.

cuajamiento /kuaha'miento/ *n. m.* coagulation.

cuajar /kua'har/ *v.* coagulate; overdecorate.

cuajo /'kuaho/ *n. m.* rennet; coagulation.

cual /kual/ *rel. pron.* which.

cuál *a. & pron.* what, which.

cualidad /kuali'ðað/ *n. f.* quality.

cualitativo /kualita'tiβo/ *a.* qualitative.

cualquiera /kual'kiera/ *a. & pron.* whatever, any; anyone.

cuando /'kuando/ *conj.* when.

cuando *adv.* when. **de cuando en cuando,** from time to time.

cuantía /kuan'tia/ *n. f.* quantity; amount.

cuantiar /kuan'tiar/ *v.* estimate.

cuantiosamente /kuantiosa'mente/ *adv.* abundantly.

cuantioso /kuan'tioso/ *a.* abundant.

cuantitativo /kuantita'tiβo/ *a.* quantitative.

cuanto /'kuanto/ *a., adv. & pron.* as much as, as many as; all that which. **en c.,** as soon as. **en c. a,** as for. **c. antes,** as soon as possible. **c. más... tanto más,** the more... the more. **unos cuantos,** a few.

cuánto *a. & adv.* how much, how many.

cuaquerismo /kuake'rismo/ *n. m.* Quakerism.

cuáquero /'kuakero/ **-ra** *n. & a.* Quaker.

cuarenta /kua'renta/ *a. & pron.* forty.

cuarentena /kuaren'tena/ *n. f.* quarantine.

cuaresma /kua'resma/ *n. f.* Lent.

cuaresmal /kuares'mal/ *a.* Lenten.

cuarta /'kuarta/ *n. f.* quarter; quadrant; quart.

cuartear /kuarte'ar/ *v.* divide into quarters.

cuartel /kuar'tel/ *n. m. Mil.* quarters; barracks; *Naut.* hatch. **c. general,** headquarters. **sin c.,** giving no quarter.

cuartelada /kuarte'laða/ *n. f.* military uprising.

cuarterón /kuarte'ron/ *n. & a.* quadroon.

cuarteto /kuar'teto/ *n. m.* quartet.

cuartillo /kuar'tiʎo; kuar'tiyo/ *n. m.* pint.

cuarto /'kuarto/ *a.* **1.** fourth. —*n.* **2.** *m.* quarter; room.

cuarto de baño /'kuarto de 'baɲo/ bathroom.

cuarto de dormir /'kuarto de dor'mir/ bedroom.

cuarto para invitados /'kuarto para imbi'taðos/ guest room.

cuarzo /'kuarθo; 'kuarso/ *n. m.* quartz.

cuasi /'kuasi/ *adv.* almost, nearly.

cuate /'kuate/ *n. & a.* twin.

cuatrero /kua'trero/ *n. m.* cattle rustler.

cuatrillón /kuatri'ʎon; kuatri'yon/ *n. m.* quadrillion.

cuatro /'kuatro/ *a. & pron.* four.

cuatrocientos /kuatro'θientos; kuatro'sientos/ *a. & pron.* four hundred.

cuba /'kuβa/ *n. f.* cask, tub, vat.

cubano /ku'βano/ **-na** *a. & n.* Cuban.

cubero /ku'βero/ *n. m.* cooper.

cubeta /ku'βeta/ *n. f.* small barrel, keg.

cúbico /'kuβiko/ *a.* cubic.

cubículo /ku'βikulo/ *n. m.* cubicle.

cubierta /ku'βierta/ *n. f.* cover; envelope; wrapping; tread (of a tire); deck.

cubiertamente /kuβierta'mente/ *adv.* secretly, stealthily.

cubierto /ku'βierto/ *n. m.* place (at table).

cubil /ku'βil/ *n. m.* lair.

cubismo /ku'βismo/ *n. m.* cubism.

cubito de hielo /ku'βito de 'ielo/ *n. m.* ice cube.

cubo /'kuβo/ *n. m.* cube; bucket.

cubo de la basura /'kuβo de la ba'sura/ trash can.

cubrecama /kuβre'kama/ *n. f.* bedspread.

cubrir /ku'βrir/ *v.* cover.

cubrirse /ku'βrirse/ *v.* put on one's hat.

cucaracha /kuka'ratʃa/ *n. f.* cockroach.

cuchara /ku'tʃara/ *n. f.* spoon, tablespoon.

cucharada /kutʃa'raða/ *n. f.* spoonful.

cucharita /kutʃa'rita/ **cucharilla** *n. f.* teaspoon.

cucharón /kutʃa'ron/ *n. m.* dipper, ladle.

cuchicheo /kutʃi'tʃeo/ *n. m.* whisper. —**cuchichear,** *v.*

cuchilla /ku'tʃiʎa; ku'tʃiya/ *n. f.* cleaver.

cuchillada /kutʃi'ʎaða; kutʃi'yaða/ *n. f.* slash.

cuchillería /kutʃiʎe'ria; kutʃiye'ria/ *n. f.* cutlery.

cuchillo /ku'tʃiʎo; ku'tʃiyo/ *n. m.* knife.

cucho /'kutʃo/ *n. m.* fertilizer.

cuchufleta /kutʃu'fleta/ *n. f.* jest.

cuclillo /ku'kliʎo; ku'kliyo/ *n. m.* cuckoo.

cuco /'kuko/ *a.* sly.

cuculla /ku'kuʎa; ku'kuya/ *n. f.* hood, cowl.

cuelga /'kuelga/ *n. f.* cluster, bunch.

cuelgacapas /kuelga'kapas/ *n. m.* coat rack.

cuello /'kueʎo; 'kueyo/ *n. m.* neck; collar.

cuenca /'kuenka/ *n. f.* socket; (river) basin; wooden bowl.

cuenco /'kuenko/ *n. m.* earthen bowl.

cuenta /'kuenta/ *n. f.* account; bill. **darse c.,** to realize. **tener en c.,** to keep in mind.

cuenta bancaria /'kuenta baŋ'karia/ bank account.

cuenta de ahorros /'kuenta de a'orros/ savings account.

cuentagotas /kuenta'gotas/ *n. m.* dropper (for medicine).

cuentista /kuen'tista/ *n. m. & f.* storyteller; informer.

cuento /'kuento/ *n. m.* story, tale.

cuerda /'kuerða/ *n. f.* cord; chord; rope; string; spring (of clock). **dar c. a,** to wind (clock).

cuerdamente /kuerða'mente/ *adv.* sanely; prudently.

cuerdo /'kuerðo/ *a.* sane; prudent.

cuerno /'kuerno/ *n. m.* horn.

cuero /'kuero/ *n. m.* leather; hide.

cuerpo /'kuerpo/ *n. m.* body; corps.

cuervo /'kuerβo/ *n. m.* crow, raven.

cuesco /'kuesko/ *n. m.* pit, stone (of fruit).

cuesta /'kuesta/ *n. f.* hill, slope. **llevar a cuestas,** to carry on one's back.

cuestación /kuesta'θion; kuesta'sion/ *n. f.* solicitation for charity.

cuestión /kues'tion/ *n. f.* question; affair; argument.

cuestionable /kuestio'naβle/ *a.* questionable.

cuestionar /kuestio'nar/ *v.* question; discuss; argue.

cuestionario /kuestio'nario/ *n. m.* questionnaire.

cuete /'kuete/ *n. m.* firecracker.

cueva /'kueβa/ *n. f.* cave; cellar.

cuguar /ku'guar/ *n. m.* cougar.

cugujada /kugu'haða/ *n. f.* lark.

cuidado /kui'ðaðo/ *n. m.* care, caution, worry. **tener c.,** to be careful.

cuidadosamente /kuiðaðosa'mente/ *adv.* carefully.

cuidadoso /kuiða'ðoso/ *a.* careful, painstaking.

cuidante /kui'ðante/ *n.* caretaker, custodian.

cuidar /kui'ðar/ *v.* take care of.

cuita /'kuita/ *n. f.* trouble, care; grief.

cuitado /kui'taðo/ *a.* unfortunate; shy, timid.

cuitamiento /kuita'miento/ *n. m.* timidity.

culata /ku'lata/ *n. f.* haunch, buttock; butt of a gun.

culatada /kula'taða/ *n. f.* recoil.

culatazo /kula'taθo; kula'taso/ *n. m.* blow with the butt of a gun; recoil.

culebra /ku'leβra/ *n. f.* snake.

culero /ku'lero/ *a.* lazy, indolent.

culinario /kuli'nario/ *a.* culinary.

culminación /kulmina'θion; kulmina'sion/ *n. f.* culmination.

culminar /kulmi'nar/ *v.* culminate.

culpa /'kulpa/ *n. f.* fault, guilt, blame. **tener la c.,** to be at fault. **echar la culpa a,** to blame.

culpabilidad /kulpaβili'ðað/ *n. f.* guilt, fault, blame.

culpable /kul'paβle/ *a.* at fault, guilty, to blame, culpable.

culpar /kul'par/ *v.* blame, accuse.

cultamente /kulta'mente/ *adv.* politely, elegantly.

cultivable /kulti'βaβle/ *a.* arable.

cultivación /kultiβa'θion; kultiβa'sion/ *n. f.* cultivation.

cultivador /kultiβa'ðor/ **-ra** *n.* cultivator.

cultivar /kulti'βar/ *v.* cultivate.

cultivo /kul'tiβo/ *n. m.* cultivation; (growing) crop.

culto /'kulto/ *a.* 1. cultured, cultivated. —*n.* 2. *m.* cult; worship.

cultura /kul'tura/ *n. f.* culture; refinement.

cultural /kultu'ral/ *a.* cultural.

culturar /kultu'rar/ *v.* cultivate.

culturismo /kultu'rismo/ *n. m.* body building.

culturista /kultu'rista/ *n. m. & f.* body builder.

cumbre /'kumbre/ *n. m.* summit, peak.

cumpleaños /kumple'aɲos/ *n. m.pl.* birthday.

cumplidamente /kumpliða'mente/ *adv.* courteously, correctly.

cumplido /kum'pliðo/ *a.* polite, polished.

cumplimentar /kumplimen'tar/ *v.* compliment.

cumplimiento /kumpli'miento/ *n. m.* fulfillment; compliment.

cumplir /kum'plir/ *v.* comply; carry out, fulfill; reach (years of age).

cumulativo /kumula'tiβo/ *a.* cumulative.

cúmulo /'kumulo/ *n. m.* heap, pile.

cuna /'kuna/ *n. f.* cradle.

cundir /kun'dir/ *v.* spread; expand; propagate.

cuneiforme /kunei'forme/ *a.* cuneiform, wedge-shaped.

cuneo /ku'neo/ *n. m.* rocking.

cuña /'kuɲa/ *n. f.* wedge.

cuñada /ku'ɲaða/ *n. f.* sister-in-law.

cuñado /ku'ɲaðo/ *n. m.* brother-in-law.

cuñete /ku'ɲete/ *n. m.* keg.

cuota /'kuota/ *n. f.* quota; dues.

cuotidiano /kuoti'ðiano/ *a.* daily.

cupé /ku'pe/ *n. m.* coupé.

Cupido /ku'piðo/ *n. m.* Cupid.

cupo /'kupo/ *n. m.* share; assigned quota.

cupón /ku'pon/ *n. m.* coupon.

cúpula /'kupula/ *n. f.* dome.

cura /'kura/ *n. m.* priest; *f.* treatment, (medical) care. **c. de urgencia,** first aid.

curable /ku'raβle/ *a.* curable.

curación /kura'θion; kura'sion/ *n. f.* healing; cure; (surgical) dressing.

curado /ku'raðo/ *a.* cured, healed.

curador /kura'ðor/ **-ra** *n.* healer.

curandero /kuran'dero/ **-ra** *n.* healer, medicine man.

curar /ku'rar/ *v.* cure, heal, treat.

curativo /kura'tiβo/ *a.* curative, healing.

curia /'kuria/ *n. f.* ecclesiastical court.

curiosear /kuriose'ar/ *v.* snoop, pry, meddle.

curiosidad /kuriosi'ðað/ *n. f.* curiosity.

curioso /ku'rioso/ *a.* curious.

curro /'kurro/ *a.* showy, loud, flashy.

cursante /kur'sante/ *n.* student.

cursar /kur'sar/ *v.* frequent; attend.

cursi /'kursi/ *a.* vulgar, shoddy, in bad taste.

curso /'kurso/ *n. m.* course.

curso por correspondencia /'kurso por korrespon'denθia; 'kurso por korrespon'densia/ *n. m.* correspondence course.

cursor /kur'sor/ *n. m.* cursor.

curtidor /kurti'ðor/ *n. m.* tanner.

curtir /kur'tir/ *v.* tan.

curva /'kurβa/ *n. f.* curve; bend.

curvatura /kurβa'tura, kurβi'ðað/ *n. f.* curvature.

cúspide /'kuspiðe/ *n. f.* top, peak.

custodia /kus'toðia/ *n. f.* custody.

custodiar /kusto'ðiar/ *v.* guard, watch.

custodio /kus'toðio/ *n. m.* custodian.

cutáneo /ku'taneo/ *a.* cutaneous.

cutícula /ku'tikula/ *n. f.* cuticle.

cutis /'kutis/ *n. m. or f.* skin, complexion.

cutre /'kutre/ *a.* shoddy.

cuyo /'kuyo/ *a.* whose.

D

dable /'daβle/ *a.* possible.

dactilógrafo /dakti'lografo/ **-fa** *n.* typist.

dádiva /'daðiβa/ *n. f.* gift.

dadivosamente /daðiβosa'mente/ *adv.* generously.

dadivoso /daði'βoso/ *a.* generous, bountiful.

dado /'daðo/ *n. m.* die.

dador /da'ðor/ **-ra** *n.* giver.

dados /'daðos/ *n. m.pl.* dice.

daga /'daga/ *n. f.* dagger.

dalia /'dalia/ *n. f.* dahlia.

dallador /daʎa'ðor; daya'ðor/ *n. m.* lawn mower.

dallar /da'ʎar; da'yar/ *v.* mow.

daltonismo /dalto'nismo/ *n. m.* color blindness.

dama /'dama/ *n. f.* lady.

damasco /da'masko/ *n. m.* apricot; damask.

damisela /dami'sela/ *n. f.* young lady, girl.

danés /da'nes/ **-esa** *a. & n.* Danish, Dane.

danza /'danθa; 'dansa/ *n. f.* (the) dance. —**danzar,** *v.*

danzante /dan'θante; dan'sante/ **-ta** *n.* dancer.

dañable /da'ɲaβle/ *a.* condemnable.

dañar /da'ɲar/ *v.* hurt, harm; damage.

dañino /da'ɲino/ *a.* harmful.

daño /'daɲo/ *n. m.* damage; harm.

dañoso /da'ɲoso/ *a.* harmful.

dar /dar/ *v.* give; strike (clock). **d. a,** face, open on. **d. con,** find, locate. **¡Dalo por hecho!** Consider it done!

dardo /'darðo/ *n. m.* dart.

dársena /'darsena/ *n. f.* dock.

datar /'datar/ *v.* date.

dátil /'datil/ *n. m.* date (fruit).

dativo /da'tiβo/ *n. m. & a.* dative.

datos /'datos/ *n. m.pl.* data.

de /de/ *prep.* of; from; than.

debajo /de'βaho/ *adv.* underneath. **d. de,** under.

debate /de'βate/ *n. m.* debate.

debatir /deβa'tir/ *v.* debate, argue.

debe /'deβe/ *n. m.* debit.

debelación /deβela'θion; deβela'sion/ *n. f.* conquest.

debelar /deβe'lar/ *v.* conquer.

deber /de'βer/ *v.* **1.** owe; must; be to, be supposed to. —*n.* **2.** *m.* obligation.

deberes /de'βeres/ *n. m.pl.* homework.

debido /de'βiðo/ *a.* due.

débil /'deβil/ *a.* weak, faint.

debilidad /deβili'ðað/ *n. f.* weakness.

debilitación /deβilita'θion; deβilita'sion/ *n. f.* weakness.

debilitar /deβili'tar/ *v.* weaken.

débito /'deβito/ *n. m.* debit.

debutar /deβu'tar/ *v.* make a debut.

década /'dekaða/ *n. f.* decade.

decadencia /deka'ðenθia; dekaðen'sia/ *n. f.* decadence, decline, decay.

decadente /deka'ðente/ *a.* decadent, declining, decaying.

decaer /deka'er/ *v.* decay, decline.

decalitro /deka'litro/ *n. m.* decaliter.

decálogo /de'kalogo/ *n. m. m.* decalogue.

decámetro /de'kametro/ *n. m.* decameter.

decano /de'kano/ *n. m.* dean.

decantado /dekan'taðo/ *a.* much discussed; overexalted.

decapitación /dekapita'θion; dekapitasion/ *n. f.* beheading.

decapitar /dekapi'tar/ *v.* behead.

decencia /de'θenθia; de'sensia/ *n. f.* decency.

decenio /de'θenio; de'senio/ *n. m.* decade.

decente /de'θente; de'sente/ *a.* decent.

decentemente /deθente'mente; desente'mente/ *adv.* decently.

decepción /deθep'θion; desep'sion/ *n. f.* disappointment, letdown; delusion.

decepcionar /deθepθio'nar; desepsio'nar/ *v.* disappoint, disillusion.

dechado /de'tʃaðo/ *n. m.* model; sample; pattern; example.

decibelio /deθi'βelio; desi'βelio/ *n. m.* decibel.

decididamente /deθiðiða'mente; desiðiða'mente/ *adv.* decidedly.

decidir /deθi'ðir; desi'ðir/ *v.* decide.

decigramo /deθi'gramo; desi'gramo/ *n. m.* decigram.

decilitro /deθi'litro; desi'litro/ *n. m.* deciliter.

décima /'deθima; 'desima/ *n. f.* tenline stanza.

decimal /deθi'mal; desi'mal/ *a.* decimal.

décimo /'deθimo; 'desimo/ *a.* tenth.

decir /de'θir; de'sir/ *v.* tell, say. **es d.,** that is (to say).

decisión /deθi'sion; desi'sion/ *n. f.* decision.

decisivamente /deθisiβa'mente; desisiβa'mente/ *adv.* decisively.

decisivo /deθi'siβo; desi'siβo/ *a.* decisive.

declamación /deklama'θion; deklama'sion/ *n. f.* declamation, speech.

declamar /dekla'mar/ *v.* declaim.

declaración /deklara'θion; deklara'sion/ *n. f.* declaration; statement; plea.

declaración de la renta /deklara'θion de la 'rrenta; deklara'sion de la 'rrenta/ tax return.

declarar /dekla'rar/ *v.* declare, state.

declarativo /deklara'tiβo, dekla'torio/ *a.* declarative.

declinación /deklina'θion; deklina'sion/ *n. f.* descent; decay; decline; declension.

declinar /dekli'nar/ *v.* decline.

declive /de'kliβe,/ *n. m.* declivity, slope.

decocción /dekok'θion; dekok'sion/ *n. f.* decoction.

decomiso /deko'miso/ *n. m.* seizure, confiscation.

decoración /dekora'θion; dekora'sion/ *n. f.* decoration, trimming.

decorado /deko'raðo/ *n. m. Theat.* scenery, set.

decorar /deko'rar/ *v.* decorate, trim.

decorativo /dekora'tiβo/ *a.* decorative, ornamental.

decoro /de'koro/ *n. m.* decorum; decency.

decoroso /deko'roso/ *a.* decorous.

decrecer /dekre'θer; dekre'ser/ *v.* decrease.

decrépito /de'krepito/ *a.* decrepit.

decreto /de'kreto/ *n. m.* decree. —**decretar,** *v.*

dedal /de'ðal/ *n. m.* thimble.

dédalo /'deðalo/ *n. m.* labyrinth.

dedicación /deðika'θion; deðika'sion/ *n. f.* dedication.

dedicar /deði'kar/ *v.* devote; dedicate.

dedicatoria /deðika'toria/ *n. f.* dedication, inscription.

dedo /'deðo/ *n. m.* finger, toe.

dedo anular /'deðo anu'lar/ ring finger.

dedo corazón /'deðo kora'θon; 'deðo kora'son/ middle finger.

dedo índice /'deðo 'indiθe; 'deðo 'indise/ index finger.

dedo meñique /'deðo me'ɲike/ little finger, pinky.

dedo pulgar /'deðo pul'gar/ thumb.

deducción /deðuk'θion; deðuk'sion/ *n. f.* deduction.

deducir /deðu'θir; deðu'sir/ *v.* deduce; subtract.

defectivo /defek'tiβo/ *a.* defective.

defecto /de'fekto/ *n. m.* defect, flaw.

defectuoso /defek'tuoso/ *a.* defective, faulty.

defender /defen'der/ *v.* defend.

defensa /de'fensa/ *n. f.* defense.

defensivo /defen'siβo/ *a.* defensive.

defensor /defen'sor/ -**ra** *n.* defender.

deferencia /defe'renθia; defe'rensia/ *n. f.* deference.

deferir /defe'rir/ *v.* defer.

deficiente /defi'θiente; defi'siente/ *a.* deficient.

déficit /'defiθit; 'defisit/ *n. m.* deficit.

definición /defini'θion; defini'sion/ *n. f.* definition.

definido /defi'niðo/ *a.* definite.

definir /defi'nir/ *v.* define; establish.

definitivamente /definitiβa'mente/ *adv.* definitely.

definitivo /defini'tiβo/ *a.* definitive.

deformación /deforma'θion; deforma'sion/ *n. f.* deformation.

deformar /defor'mar/ *v.* deform.

deforme /de'forme/ *a.* deformed; ugly.

deformidad /deformi'ðað/ *n. f.* deformity.

defraudar /defrau'ðar/ *v.* defraud.

defunción /defun'θion; defun'sion/ *n. f.* death.

degeneración /dehenera'θion; dehenera'sion/ *n. f.* degeneration.

degenerado /dehene'raðo/ *a.* degenerate. —**degenerar,** *v.*

deglutir /deglu'tir/ *v.* swallow.

degollar /dego'ʎar; dego'yar/ *v.* behead.

degradación /degraða'θion; degraða'sion/ *n. f.* degradation.

degradar /degra'ðar/ *v.* degrade, debase.

deidad /dei'ðað/ *n. f.* deity.

deificación /deifika'θion; deifika'sion/ *n. f.* deification.

deificar /deifi'kar/ *v.* deify.

deífico /de'ifiko/ *a.* divine, deific.

deísmo /de'ismo/ *n. m.* deism.

dejadez /deha'ðeθ; deha'ðes/ *n. f.* neglect, untidiness; laziness.

dejado /de'haðo/ *a.* untidy; lazy.

dejar /de'har/ *v.* let, allow; leave. **d. de,** stop, leave off. **no d. de,** not fail to.

dejo /'deho/ *n. m.* abandonment; negligence; aftertaste; accent.

del /del/ *contr. of* de + el.

delantal /delan'tal/ *n. m.* apron; pinafore. **delantal de niña,** pinafore.

delante /de'lante/ *adv.* ahead, forward; in front.

delantero /delan'tero/ *a.* forward, front, first.

delator /dela'tor/ *n. m.* informer; accuser.

delegación /delega'θion; delega'sion/ *n. f.* delegation.

delegado /dele'gaðo/ -**da** *n.* delegate. —**delegar,** *v.*

deleite /de'leite/ *n. m.* delight. —**deleitar,** *v.*

deleitoso /delei'toso/ *a.* delightful.

deletrear /deletre'ar/ *v.* spell; decipher.

delfín /del'fin/ *n. m.* dolphin; dauphin.

delgadez /delga'ðeθ; delga'ðes/ *n. f.* thinness, slenderness.

delgado /del'gaðo/ *a.* thin, slender, slim, slight.

deliberación /deliβera'θion; deliβera'sion/ *n. f.* deliberation.

deliberadamente /deliβeraða'mente/ *adv.* deliberately.

deliberar /deliβe'rar/ *v.* deliberate.

deliberativo /deliβera'tiβo/ *a.* deliberative.

delicadamente /delikaða'mente/ *adv.* delicately.

delicadeza /delika'ðeθa; delika'ðesa/ *n. f.* delicacy.

delicado /deli'kaðo/ *a.* delicate, dainty.

delicia /deli'θia; deli'sia/ *n. f.* delight; deliciousness.

delicioso /deli'θioso; deli'sioso/ *a.* delicious.

delincuencia /delin'kuenθia; delin'kuensia/ *n. f.* delinquency.

delincuencia de menores /delin'kuenθia de me'nores; delin'kuensia de me'nores/ **delincuencia juvenil** juvenile delinquency.

delincuente /delin'kuente/ *a. & n.* delinquent; culprit, offender.

delineación /delinea'θion; delinea'sion/ *n. f.* delineation, sketch.

delinear /deline'ar/ *v.* delineate, sketch.

delirante /deli'rante/ *a.* delirious.

delirar /deli'rar/ *v.* rave, be delirious.

delirio /de'lirio/ *n. m.* delirium; rapture, bliss.

delito /de'lito/ *n. m.* crime, offense.

delta /'delta/ *n. m.* delta (of river); hang glider.

demacrado /dema'kraðo/ *a.* emaciated.

demagogia /dema'gohia/ *n. f.* demagogy.

demagogo /dema'gogo/ *n. m.* demagogue.

demanda /de'manda/ *n. f.* demand, claim.

demandador /demanda'ðor/ -**ra** *n.* plaintiff.

demandar /deman'dar/ *v.* sue; demand.

demarcación /demarka'θion; demarka'sion/ *n. f.* demarcation.

demarcar /demar'kar/ *v.* demarcate, limit.

demás /de'mas/ *a. & n.* other; (the) rest (of). **por d.,** too much.

demasía /dema'sia/ *n. f.* excess; audacity; iniquity.

demasiado /dema'siaðo/ *a. & adv.* too; too much; too many.

demencia /de'menθia; de'mensia/ *n. f.* dementia; insanity.

demente /de'mente/ *a.* demented.

democracia /demo'kraθia; demo'krasia/ *n. f.* democracy.

demócrata /de'mokrata/ *n. m. & f.* democrat.

democrático /demo'kratiko/ *a.* democratic.

demoler /demo'ler/ *v.* demolish, tear down.

demolición /demoli'θion; demoli'sion/ *n. f.* demolition.

demonio /de'monio/ *n. m.* demon, devil.

demontre /de'montre/ *n. m.* devil.

demora /de'mora/ *n. f.* delay. —**demorar,** *v.*

demostración /demostra'θion; demostra'sion/ *n. f.* demonstration.

demostrador /demostra'ðor/ -**ra** *n.* demonstrator.

demostrar /demos'trar/ *v.* demonstrate, show.

demostrativo /demostra'tiβo/ *a.* demonstrative.

demudar /demu'ðar/ *v.* change; disguise, conceal.

denegación /denega'θion; denega'sion/ *n. f.* denial; refusal.

denegar /dene'gar/ *v.* deny; refuse.

dengue /'dengue/ *n. f.* prudishness; dengue.

denigración /denigra'θion; denigra'sion/ *n. f.* defamation, disgrace.

denigrar /deni'grar/ *v.* defame, disgrace.

denodado /deno'ðaðo/ *a.* brave, dauntless.

denominación /denomina'θion; denomina'sion/ *n. f.* denomination.

denominar /denomi'nar/ *v.* name, call.

denotación /denota'θion; denota'sion/ *n. f.* denotation.

denotar /deno'tar/ *v.* denote, betoken, express.

densidad /densi'ðað/ *n. f.* density.

denso /'denso/ *a.* dense.

dentado /den'taðo/ *a.* toothed; serrated; cogged.

dentadura /denta'ðura/ *n. f.* set of teeth.

dentadura postiza /denta'ðura pos'tiθa; denta'ðura pos'tisa/ false teeth, dentures.

dental /den'tal/ *a.* dental.

dentífrico /den'tifriko/ *n. m.* dentifrice, toothpaste.

dentista /den'tista/ *n. m. & f.* dentist.

dentistería /dentiste'ria/ *n. f.* dentistry.

dentro /'dentro/ *adv.* within, inside. **d. de poco,** in a short while.

dentudo /den'tuðo/ *a.* toothy (person).

denuedo /de'nueðo/ *n. m.* bravery, courage.

denuesto /de'nuesto/ *n. m.* insult, offense.

denuncia /de'nunθia; de'nunsia/ *n. f.* denunciation; declaration; complaint.

denunciación /denunθia'θion; denunsia'sion/ *n. f.* denunciation.

denunciar /denun'θiar; denun'siar/ *v.* denounce.

deparar /depa'rar/ *v.* offer; grant.

departamento /departa'mento/ *n. m.* department, section.

departir /depar'tir/ *v.* talk, chat.

dependencia /depen'denθia; depen'densia/ *n. f.* dependence; branch office.

depender /depen'der/ *v.* depend.

dependiente /depen'diente/ *a. & m.* dependent; clerk.

depilar /depi'lar/ *v.* depilate, pluck.

depilatorio /depila'torio/ *a. & n.* depilatory.

depistar *v.* mislead, put off the track.

deplorable /deplo'raβle/ *a.* deplorable, wretched.

deplorablemente /deploraβle'mente/ *adv.* deplorably.

deplorar /deplo'rar/ *v.* deplore.

deponer /depo'ner/ *v.* depose.

deportación /deporta'θion; deporta'sion/ *n. f.* deportation; exile.

deportar /depor'tar/ *v.* deport.

deporte /de'porte/ *n. m.* sport. —**deportivo,** *a.*

deposición /deposi'θion; deposi'sion/ *n. f.* assertion, deposition; removal; movement.

depositante /deposi'tante/ *n. m. & f.* depositor.

depósito /de'posito/ *n. m.* deposit. —**depositar,** *v.*

depravación /depraβa'θion; depraβa'sion/ *n. f.* depravation; depravity.

depravado /depra'βaðo/ *a.* depraved, wicked.

depravar /depra'βar/ *v.* deprave, corrupt, pervert.

depreciación /depreθia'θion; depresia'sion/ *n. f.* depreciation.

depreciar /depre'θiar; depre'siar/ *v.* depreciate.

depredación /depreða'θion; depreða'sion/ *n. f.* depredation.

depredar /depre'ðar/ *v.* pillage, depredate.

depresión /depre'sion/ *n. f.* depression.

depresivo /depre'siβo/ *a.* depressive.

deprimir /depri'mir/ *v.* depress.

depurar /depu'rar/ *v.* purify.

derecha /de'retʃa/ *n. f.* right (hand, side).

derechera /dere'tʃera/ *n. f.* shortcut.

derecho /de'retʃo/ *a.* **1.** right; straight. —*n.* **2.** *m.* right; (the) law. **derechos,** *Com.* duty.

derechos civiles /de'retʃos θi'βiles; de'retʃos si'βiles/ *n. m.pl.* civil rights.

derechos de aduana /de'retʃos de a'ðuana/ *n. m.pl.* customs duty.

derechura /dere'tʃura/ *n. f.* straightness.

derelicto /dere'likto/ *a.* abandoned, derelict.

deriva /de'riβa/ *n. f. Naut.* drift.

derivación /deriβa'θion; deriβa'sion/ *n. f.* derivation.

derivar /deri'βar/ *v.* derive.

dermatólogo /derma'tologo/ -**a** *n.* dermatologist, skin doctor.

derogar /dero'gar/ *v.* derogate; repeal, abrogate.

derramamiento /derrama'miento/ *n. m.* overflow.

derramar /derra'mar/ *v.* spill, pour, scatter.

derrame /de'rrame/ *n. m.* overflow; discharge.

derretir /derre'tir/ *v.* melt, dissolve.

derribar /derri'βar/ *v.* demolish, knock down; bowl over, floor, fell.

derrocamiento /derroka'miento/ *n. m.* overthrow.

derrocar /derro'kar/ *v.* overthrow; oust; demolish.

derrochar /derro'tʃar/ *v.* waste.

derroche /de'rrotʃe/ *n. m.* waste.

derrota /de'rrota/ *n. f.* rout, defeat. —**derrotar,** *v.*

derrotismo /derro'tismo/ *n. m.* defeatism.

derruir /de'rruir/ *v.* destroy, devastate.

derrumbamiento /derrumba'miento/ **derrumbe** *m.* collapse; landslide.

derrumbarse /derrum'βarse/ *v.* collapse, tumble.

derviche /der'βitʃe/ *n. m.* dervish.

desabotonar /desaβoto'nar/ *v.* unbutton.

desabrido /desa'βriðo/ *a.* insipid, tasteless.

desabrigar /desaβri'gar/ *v.* uncover.

desabrochar /desaβro'tʃar/ *v.* unbutton, unclasp.

desacato /desa'kato/ *n. m.* disrespect, lack of respect.

desacierto /desa'θierto; desa'sierto/ *n. m.* error.

desacobardar /desakoβar'ðar/ *v.* remove fear; embolden.

desacomodadamente /desakomo-ðaða'mente/ *adv.* inconveniently.

desacomodado /desakomo'ðaðo/ *a.* unemployed.

desacomodar /desakomo'ðar/ *v.* molest; inconvenience; dismiss.

desacomodo /desako'moðo/ *n. m.* loss of employment.

desaconsejar /desakonse'har/ v. dissuade (someone); advise against (something).

desacordadamente /desakorða-ða'mente/ adv. unadvisedly.

desacordar /desakor'ðar/ v. differ, disagree; be forgetful.

desacorde /desa'korðe/ a. discordant.

desacostumbradamente /desakostumbraða'mente/ adv. unusually.

desacostumbrado /desakostum-'braðo/ a. unusual, unaccustomed.

desacostumbrar /desakostum'brar/ v. give up a habit or custom.

desacreditar /desakreði'tar/ v. discredit.

desacuerdo /desa'kuerðo/ n. m. disagreement.

desadeudar /desaðeu'ðar/ v. pay one's debts.

desadormecer /desaðorme'θer; desaðorme'ser/ v. waken, rouse.

desadornar /desaðor'nar/ v. divest of ornament.

desadvertidamente /desaðβertiða'mente/ adv. inadvertently.

desadvertido /desaðβer'tiðo/ a. imprudent.

desadvertimiento /desaðβerti-'miento/ n. m. imprudence, rashness.

desadvertir /desaðβer'tir/ v. act imprudently.

desafección /desafek'θion; desafek-'sion/ n. f. disaffection.

desafecto /desa'fekto/ a. disaffected.

desafiar /desa'fiar/ v. defy; challenge.

desafinar /desafi'nar/ v. be out of tune.

desafío /desa'fio/ n. m. defiance; challenge.

desaforar /desafo'rar/ v. infringe one's rights; be outrageous.

desafortunado /desafortu'naðo/ a. unfortunate.

desafuero /desa'fuero/ n. m. violation of the law; outrage.

desagraciado /desagra'θiaðo; desagra'siaðo/ a. graceless.

desagradable /desagra'ðaβle/ a. disagreeable, unpleasant.

desagradablemente /desagra-ðaβle'mente/ adv. disagreeably.

desagradecido /desagraðe'θiðo; desagraðe'siðo/ a. ungrateful.

desagradecimiento /desagraðe-θi'miento; desagraðesimiento/ n. m. ingratitude.

desagrado /desa'graðo/ n. m. displeasure.

desagraviar /desagra'βiar/ v. make amends.

desagregar /desagre'gar/ v. separate, disintegrate.

desagriar /desa'griar/ v. mollify, appease.

desaguadero /desagua'ðero/ n. m. drain, outlet; cesspool; sink.

desaguador /desagua'ðor/ n. m. water pipe.

desaguar /desa'guar/ v. drain.

desaguisado /desagi'saðo/ n. m. offense; injury.

desahogadamente /desaogaða-'mente/ adv. impudently; brazenly.

desahogado /desao'gaðo/ a. impudent, brazen; cheeky.

desahogar /desao'gar/ v. relieve.

desahogo /desa'ogo/ n. m. relief; nerve, cheek.

desahuciar /desau'θiar; desau'siar/ v. give up hope for; despair of.

desairado /desai'raðo/ a. graceless.

desaire /des'aire/ n. m. slight; scorn. —desairar, v.

desajustar /desahus'tar/ v. mismatch, misfit; make unfit.

desalar /desa'lar/ v. hurry, hasten.

desalentar /desalen'tar/ v. make out of breath; discourage.

desaliento /desa'liento/ n. m. discouragement.

desaliñar /desali'nar/ v. disarrange; make untidy.

desaliño /desa'lino/ n. m. slovenliness, untidiness.

desalivar /desali'βar/ v. remove saliva from.

desalmadamente /desalmaða-'mente/ adv. mercilessly.

desalmado /desal'maðo/ a. merciless.

desalojamiento /desaloha'miento/ n. m. displacement; dislodging.

desalojar /desalo'har/ v. dislodge.

desalquilado /desalki'laðo/ a. vacant, unrented.

desamar /desa'mar/ v. cease loving.

desamasado /desama'saðo/ a. dissolved, disunited, undone.

desamistarse /desamis'tarse/ v. quarrel, disagree.

desamor /desa'mor/ n. m. disaffection, dislike; hatred.

desamorado /desamo'raðo/ a. cruel; harsh; rude.

desamparador /desampara'ðor/ n. m. deserter.

desamparar /desampa'rar/ v. desert, abandon.

desamparo /desam'paro/ n. m. desertion, abandonment.

desamueblado /desamue'βlaðo/ a. unfurnished.

desamueblar /desamue'βlar/ v. remove furniture from.

desandrajado /desandra'haðo/ a. shabby, ragged.

desanimadamente /desanimaða-'mente/ adv. in a discouraged manner; spiritlessly.

desanimar /desani'mar/ v. dishearten, discourage.

desánimo /des'animo/ n. m. discouragement.

desanudar /desanu'ðar/ v. untie; loosen; disentangle.

desapacible /desapa'θiβle; desapa'siβle/ a. rough, harsh; unpleasant.

desaparecer /desapare'θer; desapare'ser/ v. disappear.

desaparición /desapari'θion; desapari'sion/ n. f. disappearance.

desapasionadamente /desapasionaða'mente/ adv. dispassionately.

desapasionado /desapasio'naðo/ a. dispassionate.

desapego /desa'pego/ n. m. impartiality.

desapercibido /desaperθi'βiðo; desapersi'βiðo/ a. unnoticed; unprepared.

desapiadado /desapia'ðaðo/ a. merciless, cruel.

desaplicación /desaplika'θion; desaplika'sion/ n. f. indolence, laziness; negligence.

desaplicado /desapli'kaðo/ a. indolent, lazy; negligent.

desaposesionar /desaposesio'nar/ v. dispossess.

desapreciar /desapre'θiar; desapre'siar/ v. depreciate.

desapretador /desapreta'ðor/ n. m. screwdriver.

desapretar /desapre'tar/ v. loosen; relieve, ease.

desaprisionar /desaprisio'nar/ v. set free, release.

desaprobación /desaproβa'θion; desaproβa'sion/ n. f. disapproval.

desaprobar /desapro'βar/ v. disapprove.

desaprovechado /desaproβe't ʃaðo/ a. useless, profitless; backward.

desaprovechar /desaproβe't ʃar/ v. waste; be backward.

desarbolar /desarβo'lar/ v. unmast.

desarmado /desar'maðo/ a. disarmed, defenseless.

desarmar /desar'mar/ v. disarm.

desarme /de'sarme/ n. m. disarmament.

desarraigado /desarrai'gaðo/ a. rootless.

desarraigar /desarrai'gar/ v. uproot; eradicate; expel.

desarreglar /desarre'glar/ v. disarrange, mess up.

desarrollar /desarro'ʎar; desarro'yar/ v. develop.

desarrollo /desa'rroʎo; des'arroyo/ n. m. development.

desarropar /desarro'par/ v. undress; uncover.

desarrugar /desarru'gar/ v. remove wrinkles from.

desaseado /desase'aðo/ a. dirty; disorderly.

desasear /desase'ar/ v. make dirty or disorderly.

desaseo /desa'seo/ n. m. dirtiness; disorder.

desasir /desa'sir/ v. loosen; disengage.

desasociable /desaso'θiaβle; desaso'siaβle/ a. unsociable.

desasosegar /desasose'gar/ v. disturb.

desasosiego /desaso'siego/ n. m. uneasiness.

desastrado /desas'traðo/ a. ragged, wretched.

desastre /de'sastre/ n. m. disaster.

desastroso /desas'troso/ a. disastrous.

desatar /desa'tar/ v. untie, undo.

desatención /desaten'θion; desaten'sion/ n. f. inattention; disrespect; rudeness.

desatender /desaten'der/ v. ignore; disregard.

desatentado /desaten'taðo/ a. inconsiderate; imprudent.

desatinado /desati'naðo/ a. foolish; insane, wild.

desatino /desa'tino/ n. m. blunder. —desatinar, v.

desatornillar /desatorni'ʎar; desatorni'yar/ v. unscrew.

desautorizado /desautori'θaðo; desautori'saðo/ a. unauthorized.

desautorizar /desautori'θar; desautori'sar/ v. deprive of authority.

desavenencia /desaβe'nenθia; desaβe'nensia/ n. f. disagreement, discord.

desaventajado /desaβenta'haðo/ a. disadvantageous.

desayuno /desa'yuno/ n. m. breakfast. —desayunar, v.

desazón /desa'θon; desa'son/ n. f. insipidity; uneasiness.

desazonado /desaθo'naðo; desaso'naðo/ a. insipid; uneasy.

desbandada /desβan'daða/ n. f. disbanding.

desbandarse /desβan'darse/ v. disband.

desbarajuste /desβara'huste/ n. m. disorder, confusion.

desbaratar /desβara'tar/ v. destroy.

desbastar /desβas'tar/ v. plane, smoothen.

desbocado /desβo'kaðo/ a. foulspoken, indecent.

desbocarse /desβo'karse/ v. use obscene language.

desbordamiento /desβorða'miento/ n. m. overflow; flood.

desbordar /desβor'ðar/ v. overflow.

desbrozar /desβro'θar; desβro'sar/ v. clear away rubbish.

descabal /deska'βal/ a. incomplete.

descabalar /deskaβa'lar/ v. render incomplete; impair.

descabellado /deskaβe'ʎaðo; deskaβe'yaðo/ a. absurd; preposterous.

descabezar /deskaβe'θar; deskaβe'sar/ v. behead.

descaecimiento /deskaeθi'miento; deskaesi'miento/ n. m. weakness; dejection.

descafeinado /deskafei'naðo/ a. decaffeinated.

descalabrar /deskala'βrar/ v. injure, wound (esp. the head).

descalabro /deska'laβro/ n. m. accident, misfortune.

descalzarse /deskal'θarse; deskal'sarse/ v. take off one's shoes.

descalzo /des'kalθo; des'kalso/ a. shoeless; barefoot.

descaminado /deskami'naðo/ a. wrong, misguided.

descaminar /deskami'nar/ v. mislead; lead into error.

descamisado /deskami'saðo/ a. shirtless; shabby.

descansillo /deskan'siʎo; deskan'siyo/ n. m. landing (of stairs).

descanso /des'kanso/ n. m. rest. —descansar, v.

descarado /deska'raðo/ a. saucy, fresh.

descarga /des'karga/ n. f. discharge.

descargar /deskar'gar/ v. discharge, unload, dump.

descargo /des'kargo/ n. m. unloading; acquittal.

descarnar /deskar'nar/ v. skin.

descaro /des'karo/ n. m. gall, effrontery.

descarriar /deska'rriar/ v. lead or go astray.

descarrilamiento /deskarrila-'miento/ n. m. derailment.

descarrilar /deskarri'lar/ v. derail.

descartar /deskar'tar/ v. discard.

descascarar /deskaska'rar/ v. peel; boast, brag.

descendencia /desθen'denθia; des-ssen'densia/ n. f. descent, origin; progeny.

descender /desθen'der; dessen'der/ v. descend.

descendiente /desθen'diente; ds-ssen'diente/ n. m. & f. descendant.

descendimiento /desθendi'miento; dessendi'miento/ n. m. descent.

descenso /des'θenso; des'senso/ n. m. descent.

descentralización /desθentrali-liθa'θion; dessentralisa'sion/ n. f. decentralization.

descifrar /desθi'frar; dessi'frar/ v. decipher, puzzle out.

descoco /des'koko/ n. m. boldness, brazenness.

descolgar /deskol'gar/ v. take down.

descollar /desko'ʎar; desko'yar/ v. stand out; excel.

descolorar /deskolo'rar/ v. discolor.

descolorido /deskolo'riðo/ a. pale, faded.

descomedido /deskome'ðiðo/ a. disproportionate; rude.

descomedirse /deskome'ðirse/ v. be rude.

descomponer /deskompo'ner/ v. decompose; break down, get out of order.

descomposición /deskomposi'θion; deskomposi'sion/ n. f. discomposure; disorder, confusion.

descompuesto /deskom'puesto/ a. impudent, rude.

descomulgar /deskomul'gar/ v. excommunicate.

descomunal /deskomu'nal/ a. extraordinary, huge.

desconcertar /deskonθer'tar; deskonser'tar/ v. disconcert, baffle.

desconcierto /deskon'θierto; deskon'sierto/ n. m. confusion, disarray.

desconectar /deskonek'tar/ v. disconnect.

desconfiado /deskon'fiaðo/ a. distrustful.

desconfianza /deskon'fianθa; deskon'fiansa/ n. f. distrust.

desconfiar /deskon'fiar/ v. distrust, mistrust; suspect.

descongelar /deskonge'lar/ v. defrost.

descongestionante /deskongestio-'nante/ n. m. decongestant.

desconocer /deskono'θer; deskono-'ser/ v. ignore, fail to recognize.

desconocido /deskono'θiðo; deskono'siðo/ a. stranger.

desconocimiento /deskonoθi'miento; deskonosi'miento/ n. m. ingratitude; ignorance.

desconsejado /deskonse'haðo/ a. imprudent, ill advised, rash.

desconsolado /deskonso'laðo/ *a.* disconsolate, wretched.

desconsuelo /deskon'suelo/ *n. m.* grief.

descontar /deskon'tar/ *v.* discount, subtract.

descontentar /deskonten'tar/ *v.* dissatisfy.

descontento /deskon'tento/ *n. m.* discontent.

descontinuar /deskonti'nuar/ *v.* discontinue.

desconvenir /deskombe'nir/ *v.* disagree.

descorazonar /deskoraθo'nar; deskoraso'nar/ *v.* dishearten.

descorchar /deskor't∫ar/ *v.* uncork.

descortés /deskor'tes/ *a.* discourteous, impolite, rude.

descortesía /deskorte'sia/ *n. f.* discourtesy, rudeness.

descortezar /deskorte'θar; deskor;te'sar/ *v.* peel.

descoyuntar /deskoyun'tar/ *v.* dislocate.

descrédito /des'kreðito/ *n. m.* discredit.

describir /deskri'βir/ *v.* describe.

descripción /deskrip'θion; deskrip'sion/ *n. f.* description.

descriptivo /deskrip'tiβo/ *a.* descriptive.

descuartizar /deskuarti'θar; deskuarti'sar/ *v.* dismember, disjoint.

descubridor /deskuβri'ðor/ -ra *n.* discoverer.

descubrimiento /deskuβri'miento/ *n. m.* discovery.

descubrir /desku'βrir/ *v.* discover; uncover; disclose.

descubrirse /desku'βrirse/ *v.* take off one's hat.

descuento /des'kuento/ *n. m.* discount.

descuidado /deskui'ðaðo/ *a.* reckless, careless; slack.

descuido /des'kuiðo/ *n. m.* neglect. —descuidar, *v.*

desde /'desðe/ *prep.* since; from. **d. luego**, of course.

desdén /des'ðen/ *n. m.* disdain. —desdeñar, *v.*

desdeñoso /desðe'noso/ *a.* contemptuous, disdainful, scornful.

desdicha /des'ðit∫a/ *n. f.* misfortune.

deseable /dese'aβle/ *a.* desirable.

desear /dese'ar/ *v.* desire, wish.

desecar /dese'kar/ *v.* dry, desiccate.

desechable /dese't∫aβle/ *a.* disposable.

desechar /dese't∫ar/ *v.* scrap, reject.

desecho /de'set∫o/ *n. m.* remainder, residue; (*pl.*) waste.

desembalar /desemba'lar/ *v.* unpack.

desembarazado /desembara'θaðo; desembara'saðo/ *a.* free; unrestrained.

desembarazar /desembara'θar; desembara'sar/ *v.* free; extricate; unburden.

desembarcar /desembar'kar/ *v.* disembark, go ashore.

desembocar /desembo'kar/ *v.* flow into.

desembolsar /desembol'sar/ *v.* disburse; expend.

desembolso /desem'bolso/ *n. m.* disbursement.

desemejante /deseme'hante/ *a.* unlike, dissimilar.

desempacar /desempa'kar/ *v.* unpack.

desempeñar /desempe'nar/ *v.* carry out; redeem.

desempeño /desem'peno/ *n. m.* fulfillment.

desencajar /desenka'har/ *v.* disjoint; disturb.

desencantar /desenkan'tar/ *v.* disillusion.

desencanto /desen'kanto/ *n. m.* disillusion.

desencarcelar /desenkarθe'lar; desenkarse'lar/ *v.* set free; release.

desenchufar /desent∫u'far/ *v.* unplug.

desenfadado /desenfa'ðaðo/ *a.* free; unembarrassed; spacious.

desenfado /desen'faðo/ *n. m.* freedom; ease; calmness.

desenfocado /desenfo'kaðo/ *a.* out of focus.

desengaño /deseŋ'gano/ *m.* disillusion. —desengañar *v.*

desenlace /desen'laθe; desen'lase/ *n. m.* outcome, conclusion.

desenredar /desenre'ðar/ *v.* disentangle.

desensartar /desensar'tar/ *v.* unthread (pearls).

desentenderse /desenten'derse/ *v.* overlook; avoid noticing.

desenterrar /desente'rrar/ *v.* disinter, exhume.

desenvainar /desembai'nar/ *v.* unsheath.

desenvoltura /desembol'tura/ *n. f.* confidence; impudence, boldness.

desenvolver /desembol'βer/ *v.* evolve, unfold.

deseo /de'seo/ *n. m.* wish, desire, urge.

deseoso /dese'oso/ *a.* desirous.

deserción /deser'θion; deser'sion/ *n. f.* desertion.

desertar /deser'tar/ *v.* desert.

desertor /deser'tor/ -ra *n.* deserter.

desesperación /desespera'θion; desespera'sion/ *n. f.* despair, desperation.

desesperado /desespe'raðo/ *a.* desperate; hopeless.

desesperar /desespe'rar/ *v.* despair.

desfachatez /desfat∫a'teθ; desfat∫a'tes/ *n. f.* cheek (gall).

desfalcar /desfal'kar/ *v.* embezzle.

desfase horario /des'fase o'rario/ *n. m.* jet lag.

desfavorable /desfaβo'raβle/ *a.* unfavorable.

desfigurar /desfigu'rar/ *v.* disfigure, mar.

desfiladero /desfila'ðero/ *n. m.* defile.

desfile /des'file/ *n. m.* parade. —desfilar, *v.*

desfile de modas /des'file de 'moðas/ fashion show.

desgaire /des'gaire/ *n. m.* slovenliness.

desgana /des'gana/ *n. f.* lack of appetite; unwillingness; repugnance.

desgarrar /desga'rrar/ *v.* tear, lacerate.

desgastar /desgas'tar/ *v.* wear away; waste; erode.

desgaste /des'gaste/ *n. m.* wear; erosion.

desgracia /des'graθia; des'grasia/ *n. f.* misfortune.

desgraciado /desgra'θiaðo; desgra'siaðo/ *a.* unfortunate.

desgranar /desgra'nar/ *v.* shell.

desgreñar /desgre'nar/ *v.* dishevel.

deshacer /desa'θer; desa'ser/ *v.* undo, take apart, destroy.

deshacerse de /desa'θerse de; desa'serse de/ *v.* get rid of, dispose of.

deshecho /des'et∫o/ *a.* undone; wasted.

deshelar /dese'lar/ *v.* thaw; melt.

desheredamiento /desereða'miento/ *n. m.* disinheriting.

desheredar /desere'ðar/ *v.* disinherit.

deshielo /des'ielo/ *n. m.* thaw, melting.

deshinchar /desin't∫ar/ *v.* reduce a swelling.

deshojarse /deso'harse/ *v.* shed (leaves).

deshonestidad /desonesti'ðað/ *n. f.* dishonesty.

deshonesto /deso'nesto/ *a.* dishonest.

deshonra /de'sonra/ *n. f.* dishonor.

deshonrar /deson'rar/ *v.* disgrace; dishonor.

deshonroso /deson'roso/ *a.* dishonorable.

desierto /de'sierto/ *n. m.* desert, wilderness.

designar /desig'nar/ *v.* appoint, name.

designio /de'signio/ *n. m.* purpose, intent.

desigual /desi'gual/ *a.* uneven, unequal.

desigualdad /desigual'dað/ *n. f.* inequality.

desilusión /desilu'sion/ *n. f.* disappointment.

desinfección /desinfek'θion; desinfek'sion/ *n. f.* disinfection.

desinfectar /desinfek'tar/ *v.* disinfect.

desintegrar /desinte'grar/ *v.* disintegrate, zap.

desinterés /desinte'res/ *n. m.* indifference.

desinteresado /desintere'saðo/ *a.* disinterested, unselfish.

desistir /desis'tir/ *v.* desist, stop.

desleal /desle'al/ *a.* disloyal.

deslealtad /desleal'tað/ *n. f.* disloyalty.

desleir /desle'ir/ *v.* dilute, dissolve.

desligar /desli'gar/ *v.* untie, loosen; free, release.

deslindar /deslin'dar/ *v.* make the boundaries of.

deslinde /des'linde/ *n. m.* demarcation.

desliz /des'liθ; des'lis/ *n. m.* slip; false step; weakness.

deslizarse /desli'θarse; desli'sarse/ *v.* slide; slip; glide; coast.

deslumbramiento /deslumbra'miento/ *n. m.* dazzling glare; confusion.

deslumbrar /deslumb'rar/ *v.* dazzle; glare.

deslustre /des'lustre/ *n. m.* tarnish. —deslustrar, *v.*

desmán /des'man/ *n. m.* mishap; misbehavior; excess.

desmantelar /desmante'lar/ *v.* dismantle.

desmañado /desma'naðo/ *a.* awkward, clumsy.

desmaquillarse /desmaki'∫arse; desmaki'yarse/ *v.* remove one's makeup.

desmayar /desma'yar/ *v.* depress, dishearten.

desmayo /des'mayo/ *n. m.* faint. —desmayarse, *v.*

desmejorar /desmeho'rar/ *v.* make worse; decline.

desmembrar /desmem'brar/ *v.* dismember.

desmemoria /desme'moria/ *n. f.* forgetfulness.

desmemoriado /desmemo'riaðo/ *a.* forgetful.

desmentir /desmen'tir/ *v.* contradict, disprove.

desmenuzable /desmenu'θaβle; desmenu'saβle/ *a.* crisp, crumbly.

desmenuzar /desmenu'θar; desmenu'sar/ *v.* crumble, break into bits.

desmesurado /desmesu'raðo/ *a.* excessive.

desmobilizar /desmoβili'θar; desmoβili'sar/ *v.* demobilize.

desmonetización /desmoneti'θa'θion; desmonetisa'sion/ *n. f.* demonetization.

desmonetizar /desmoneti'θar; desmoneti'sar/ *v.* demonetize.

desmontado /desmon'taðo/ *a.* dismounted.

desmontar /desmon'tar/ *v.* dismantle.

desmontarse /desmon'tarse/ *v.* dismount.

desmoralización /desmorali'θa'θion; desmoralisa'sion/ *n. f.* demoralization.

desmoralizar /desmorali'θar; desmorali'sar/ *v.* demoralize.

desmoronar /desmoro'nar/ *v.* crumble, decay.

desmovilizar /desmoβili'θar; desmoβili'sar/ *v.* demobilize.

desnatar /desna'tar/ *v.* skim.

desnaturalización /desnaturaliθa'θion; desnaturalisa'sion/ *n. f.* denaturalization.

desnaturalizar /desnaturali'θar; desnaturali'sar/ *v.* denaturalize.

desnegamiento /desnega'miento/ *n. m.* denial, contradiction.

desnervar /desner'βar/ *v.* enervate.

desnivel /desni'βel/ *n. m.* unevenness or difference in elevation.

desnudamente /desnuða'mente/ *adv.* nakedly.

desnudar /desnu'ðar/ *v.* undress.

desnudez /desnu'ðeθ; desnu'ðes/ *n. f.* bareness, nudity.

desnudo /des'nuðo/ *a.* bare, naked.

desnutrición /desnutri'θion; desnutri'sion/ *n. f.* malnutrition.

desobedecer /desoβeðe'θer; desoβeðe'ser/ *v.* disobey.

desobediencia /desoβeðien'θia; desoβeðien'sia/ *n. f.* disobedience.

desobediente /desoβe'ðiente/ *a.* disobedient.

desobedientemente /desoβeðiente'mente/ *adv.* disobediently.

desobligar /desoβli'gar/ *v.* release from obligation; offend.

desocupado /desoku'paðo/ *a.* idle, not busy; vacant.

desocupar /desoku'par/ *v.* vacate.

desolación /desola'θion; desola'sion/ *n. f.* desolation; ruin.

desolado /deso'laðo/ *a.* desolate. —desolar, *v.*

desollar /deso'∫ar; deso'yar/ *v.* skin.

desorden /de'sorðen/ *n. m.* disorder.

desordenar /desorðe'nar/ *v.* disarrange.

desorganización /desorganiθa'θion; desorganisa'sion/ *n. f.* disorganization.

desorganizar /desorgani'θar; desorgani'sar/ *v.* disorganize.

despabilado /despaβi'laðo/ *a.* vigilant, watchful; lively.

despachar /despa't∫ar/ *v.* dispatch, ship, send.

despacho /despa't∫o/ *n. m.* shipment; dispatch, promptness; office.

despacio /des'paθio; des'pasio/ *adv.* slowly.

desparpajo /despar'paho/ *n. m.* glibness; fluency of speech.

desparramar /desparra'mar/ *v.* scatter.

despavorido /despaβo'riðo/ *a.* terrified.

despecho /des'pet∫o/ *n. m.* spite.

despedazar /despeða'θar; despeða'sar/ *v.* tear up.

despedida /despe'ðiða/ *n. f.* farewell; leave-taking; discharge.

despedir /despe'ðir/ *v.* dismiss, discharge; see off.

despedirse de /despe'ðirse de/ *v.* say good-bye to, take leave of.

despegar /despe'gar/ *v.* unglue; separate; *Aero.* take off.

despego /des'pego/ *n. m.* indifference; disinterest.

despejar /despe'har/ *v.* clear, clear up.

despejo /des'peho/ *n. m.* sprightliness; clarity; without obstruction.

despensa /des'pensa/ *n. f.* pantry.

despensero /despen'sero/ *n. m.* butler.

despeñar /despe'nar/ *v.* throw down.

desperdicio /desper'ðiθio; desper'sio/ *n. m.* waste. —desperdiciar, *v.*

despertador /desperta'ðor/ *n. m.* alarm clock.

despertar /desper'tar/ *v.* wake, wake up.

despesar /despe'sar/ *n. m.* dislike.

despicar /despi'kar/ *v.* satisfy.

despidida /despi'ðiða/ *n. f.* gutter.

despierto /des'pierto/ *a.* awake; alert, wide-awake.

despilfarrado /despilfa'rraðo/ *a.* wasteful, extravagant.

despilfarrar /despilfa'rrar/ *v.* waste, squander.

despilfarro /despil'farro/ *n. m.* waste, extravagance.

despique /des'pike/ *n. m.* revenge.

despistar /despis'tar/ *v.* mislead, put off the track.

desplazamiento /desplaθa'miento; desplasa'miento/ *n. m.* displacement.

desplegar /desple'gar/ *v.* display; unfold.

desplome /des'plome/ *n. m.* collapse. **—desplomarse,** *v.*

desplumar /desplu'mar/ *v.* defeather, pluck.

despoblar /despo'βlar/ *v.* depopulate.

despojar /despo'har/ *v.* strip; despoil, plunder.

despojo /des'poho/ *n. m.* plunder, spoils; (*pl.*) remains, debris.

desposado /despo'saðo/ *a.* newly married.

desposar /despo'sar/ *v.* marry.

desposeer /despose'er/ *v.* dispossess.

déspota /'despota/ *n. m.* & *f.* despot.

despótico /des'potiko/ *a.* despotic.

despotismo /despo'tismo/ *n. m.* despotism, tyranny.

despreciable /despre'θiaβle; despre'siaβle/ *a.* contemptible.

despreciar /despre'θiar; despre'siar/ *v.* spurn, despise, scorn.

desprecio /des'preθio; des'presio/ *n. m.* scorn, contempt.

desprender /despren'der/ *v.* detach, unfasten.

desprenderse /despren'derse/ *v.* loosen, come apart. **d. de,** part with.

desprendido /despren'diðo/ *a.* disinterested.

despreocupado /despreoku'paðo/ *a.* unconcerned; unprejudiced.

desprevenido /despreβe'niðo/ *a.* unprepared, unready.

desproporción /despropor'θion; despropor'sion/ *n. f.* disproportion.

despropósito /despro'posito/ *n. m.* nonsense.

desprovisto /despro'βisto/ *a.* devoid.

después /des'pues/ *adv.* afterwards, later; then, next. **d. de, d. que,** after.

despuntar /despun'tar/ *v.* blunt; remove the point of.

desquiciar /deski'θiar; deski'siar/ *v.* unhinge; disturb, unsettle.

desquitar /deski'tar/ *v.* get revenge, retaliate.

desquite /des'kite/ *n. m.* revenge, retaliation.

desrazonable /desraθo'naβle; desraso'naβle/ *a.* unreasonable.

destacamento /destaka'mento/ *n. m. Mil.* detachment.

destacarse /desta'karse/ *v.* stand out, be prominent.

destajero /desta'hero/ **-a** *n.* **destajista,** *m.* & *f.* pieceworker.

destapar /desta'par/ *v.* uncover.

destello /des'teʎo; deste'yo/ *n. m.* sparkle, gleam.

destemplar /destem'plar/ *v. Mus.* untune; disturb, upset.

desteñir /deste'ɲir/ *v.* fade, discolor.

desterrado /deste'rraðo/ **-da** *n.* exile.

desterrar /deste'rrar/ *v.* banish, exile.

destetar /deste'tar/ *v.* wean.

destierro /des'tierro/ *n. m.* banishment, exile.

destilación /destila'θion; destila'sion/ *n. f.* distillation.

destilar /desti'lar/ *v.* distill.

destilería /destile'ria/ *n. f.* distillery.

destilería de petróleo /destile'ria de pe'troleo/ oil refinery.

destinación /destina'θion; destina'sion/ *n. f.* destination.

destinar /desti'nar/ *v.* destine, intend.

destinatario /destina'tario/ **-ria** *n.* addressee (mail); payee (money).

destino /des'tino/ *n. m.* destiny, fate; destination.

destitución /destitu'θion; destitu'sion/ *n. f.* dismissal; abandonment.

destituido /desti'tuiðo/ *a.* destitute.

destorcer /destor'θer; destor'ser/ *v.* undo, straighten out.

destornillado /destorni'ʎaðo; destorni'yaðo/ *a.* reckless, careless.

destornillador /destorni'ʎaðor; destorni'yaðor/ *n. m.* screwdriver.

destraillar /destrai'ʎar; destrai'yar/ *v.* unleash; set loose.

destral /des'tral/ *n. m.* hatchet.

destreza /des'treθa; des'tresa/ *n. f.* cleverness; dexterity, skill.

destripar /destri'par/ *v.* eviscerate, disembowel.

destrísimo /des'trisimo/ *a.* extremely dexterous.

destronamiento /destrona'miento/ *n. m.* dethronement.

destronar /destro'nar/ *v.* dethrone.

destrozador /destroθa'ðor; destrosa'ðor/ *n. m.* destroyer, wrecker.

destrozar /destro'θar; destro'sar/ *v.* destroy, wreck.

destrozo /des'troθo; des'troso/ *n. m.* destruction, ruin.

destrucción /destruk'θion; destruk'sion/ *n. f.* destruction.

destructibilidad /destruktiβili'ðað/ *n. f.* destructibility.

destructible /destruk'tiβle/ *a.* destructible.

destructivamente /destruktiβa'mente/ *adv.* destructively.

destructivo /destruk'tiβo/ *a.* destructive.

destruir /destruir/ *v.* destroy; wipe out.

desuello /desue'ʎo; desue'yo/ *n. m.* impudence.

desunión /desu'nion/ *n. f.* disunion; discord; separation.

desunir /desu'nir/ *v.* disconnect, sever.

desusadamente /desusaða'mente/ *adv.* unusually.

desusado /desu'saðo/ *a.* archaic; obsolete.

desuso /de'suso/ *n. m.* disuse.

desvalido /des'βaliðo/ *a.* helpless; destitute.

desvalijador /desβaliha'ðor/ *n. m.* highwayman.

desván /des'βan/ *n. m.* attic.

desvanecerse /desβane'θerse; desβane'serse/ *v.* vanish; faint.

desvariado /desβa'riaðo/ *a.* delirious; disorderly.

desvarío /desβa'rio/ *n. m.* raving. **—desvariar,** *v.*

desvedado /desβe'ðaðo/ *a.* free; unrestrained.

desveladamente /desβelaða'mente/ *adv.* watchfully, alertly.

desvelado /desβe'laðo/ *a.* watchful; alert.

desvelar /desβe'lar/ *v.* be watchful; keep awake.

desvelo /des'βelo/ *n. m.* vigilance; uneasiness; insomnia.

desventaja /desβen'taha/ *n. f.* disadvantage.

desventar /desβen'tar/ *v.* let air out of.

desventura /desβen'tura/ *n. f.* misfortune.

desventurado /desβentu'raðo/ *a.* unhappy; unlucky.

desvergonzado /desβergon'θaðo; desβergonsaðo/ *a.* shameless, brazen.

desvergüenza /desβer'guenθa; desβer'guensa/ *n. f.* shamelessness.

desvestir /desβes'tir/ *v.* undress.

desviación /desβia'θion; desβia'sion/ *n. f.* deviation.

desviado /des'βiaðo/ *a.* deviant; remote.

desviar /des'βiar/ *v.* divert; deviate, detour.

desvío /des'βio/ *n. m.* detour; side track; indifference.

desvirtuar /desβir'tuar/ *v.* decrease the value of.

deszumar /desθu'mar; dessu'mar/ *v.* remove the juice from.

detalle /de'taʎe; de'taye/ *n. m.* detail. **—detallar,** *v.*

detective /de'tektiβe/ *n. m.* & *f.* detective.

detención /deten'θion; deten'sion/ *n. f.* detention, arrest.

detenedor /detene'ðor/ **-ra** *n.* stopper; catch.

detener /dete'ner/ *v.* detain, stop; arrest.

detenidamente /deteniða'mente/ *adv.* carefully, slowly.

detenido /dete'niðo/ *adv.* stingy; thorough.

detergente /deter'hente/ *a.* detergent.

deterioración /deteriora'θion; deteriora'sion/ *n. f.* deterioration.

deteriorar /deterio'rar/ *v.* deteriorate.

determinable /determi'naβle/ *a.* determinable.

determinación /determina'θion; determina'sion/ *n. f.* determination.

determinar /determi'nar/ *v.* determine, settle, decide.

determinismo /determi'nismo/ *n. m.* determinism.

determinista /determi'nista/ *n.* & *a.* determinist.

detestable /detes'taβle/ *a.* detestable, hateful.

detestablemente /detestaβle'mente/ *adv.* detestably, hatefully, abhorrently.

detestación /detesta'θion; detesta'sion/ *n. f.* detestation, hatefulness.

detestar /detes'tar/ *v.* detest.

detonación /detona'θion; detona'sion/ *n. f.* detonation.

detonar /deto'nar/ *v.* detonate, explode.

detracción /detrak'θion; detrak'sion/ *n. f.* detraction, defamation.

detractar /detrak'tar/ *v.* detract, defame, vilify.

detraer /detra'er/ *v.* detract.

detrás /de'tras/ *adv.* behind; in back.

detrimento /detri'mento/ *n. m.* detriment, damage.

deuda /'deuða/ *n. f.* debt.

deudo /'deuðo/ **-da** *n.* relative, kin.

deudor /deu'ðor/ **-ra** *n.* debtor.

Deuteronomio /deutero'nomio/ *n. m.* Deuteronomy.

devalar /deβa'lar/ *v.* drift off course.

devanar /deβa'nar/ *v.* to wind, as on a spool.

devanear /deβane'ar/ *v.* talk deliriously, rave.

devaneo /deβa'neo/ *n. m.* frivolity; idle pursuit; delirium.

devastación /deβasta'θion; deβasta'sion/ *n. f.* devastation, ruin, havoc.

devastador /deβasta'ðor/ *a.* devastating.

devastar /deβas'tar/ *v.* devastate.

devenir /deβe'nir/ *v.* happen, occur; become.

devoción /deβo'θion; deβo'sion/ *n. f.* devotion.

devocionario /deβoθio'nario; deβosio'nario/ *n. m.* prayer book.

devocionero /deβoθio'nero; deβosio'nero/ *a.* devotional.

devolver /deβol'βer/ *v.* return, give back.

devorar /deβo'rar/ *v.* devour.

devotamente /deβota'mente/ *adv.* devotedly, devoutly, piously.

devoto /de'βoto/ *a.* devout; devoted.

deyección /deiek'θion; deiek'sion/ *n. f.* depression, dejection.

día /dia/ *n. m.* day. **buenos días,** good morning.

diabetes /dia'βetes/ *n. f.* diabetes.

diabético /dia'βetiko/ *a.* diabetic.

diablear /diaβle'ar/ *v.* play pranks.

diablo /'diaβlo/ *n. m.* devil.

diablura /dia'βlura/ *n. f.* mischief.

diabólicamente /diaβolika'mente/ *adv.* diabolically.

diabólico /dia'βoliko/ *a.* diabolic, devilish.

diaconato /diako'nato/ *n. m.* deaconship.

diaconía /diako'nia/ *n. f.* deaconry.

diácono /'diakono/ *n. m.* deacon.

diacrítico /dia'kritiko/ *a.* diacritic.

diadema /dia'ðema/ *n. f.* diadem; crown.

diáfano /'diafano/ *a.* transparent.

diafragma /dia'fragma/ *n. m.* diaphragm.

diagnosticar /diagnosti'kar/ *v.* diagnose.

diagonal /diago'nal/ *n. f.* diagonal.

diagonalmente /diagonal'mente/ *adv.* diagonally.

diagrama /dia'grama/ *n. m.* diagram.

dialectal /dialek'tal/ *a.* dialectal.

dialéctico /dia'lektiko/ *a.* dialectic.

dialecto /dia'lekto/ *n. m.* dialect.

diálogo /'dialogo/ *n. m.* dialogue.

diamante /dia'mante/ *n. m.* diamond.

diamantista /diaman'tista/ *n. m.* & *f.* diamond cutter; jeweler.

diametral /diame'tral/ *a.* diametric.

diametralmente /diametral'mente/ *adv.* diametrically.

diámetro /'diametro/ *n. m.* diameter.

diana /'diana/ *n. f.* reveille; dartboard.

diapasón /diapa'son/ *n. m.* standard pitch; tuning fork.

diaplejía /diaple'hia/ *n. f.* paralysis.

diariamente /diaria'mente/ *adv.* daily.

diario /'diario/ *a.* & *m.* daily; daily paper; diary; journal.

diarrea /dia'rrea/ *n. f.* diarrhea.

diatriba /dia'triβa/ *n. f.* diatribe, harangue.

dibujo /di'βuho/ *n. m.* drawing, sketch. **—dibujar,** *v.*

dicción /dik'θion; dik'sion/ *n. f.* diction.

diccionario /dikθio'nario; diksio'nario/ *n. m.* dictionary.

diccionarista /dikθiona'rista; diksiona'rista/ *n. m.* & *f.* lexicographer.

dicha /'ditʃa/ *n. f.* happiness.

dicho /'ditʃo/ *n. m.* saying.

dichoso /di'tʃoso/ *a.* happy; fortunate.

diciembre /di'θiembre; di'siembre/ *n. m.* December.

dicotomía /dikoto'mia/ *n. f.* dichotomy.

dictado /dik'taðo/ *n. m.* dictation.

dictador /dikta'ðor/ **-ra** *n.* dictator.

dictadura /dikta'ðura/ *n. f.* dictatorship.

dictamen /dik'tamen/ *n. m.* dictate.

dictar /dik'tar/ *v.* dictate; direct.

dictatorial /diktato'rial/ **dictatorio** *a.* dictatorial.

didáctico /di'ðaktiko/ *a.* didactic.

diecinueve /dieθi'nueβe; diesi'nueβe/ *a.* & *pron.* nineteen.

dieciocho /die'θiotʃo; die'siotʃo/ *a.* & *pron.* eighteen.

dieciseis /dieθi'seis; diesi'seis/ *a.* & *pron.* sixteen.

diecisiete /dieθi'siete; diesi'siete/ *a.* & *pron.* seventeen.

diente /diente/ *n. m.* tooth.

diestramente /diestra'mente/ *adv.* skillfully, ably; ingeniously.

diestro /'diestro/ *a.* dexterous, skillful; clever.

dieta /'dieta/ *n. f.* diet; allowance.

dietética /die'tetika/ *n. f.* dietetics.

dietético /die'tetiko/ *a.* **1.** dietetic; dietary. **—*n.* 2. -ca.** dietician.

diez /dieθ; dies/ *a.* & *pron.* ten.

diezmal /dieθ'mal; dies'mal/ *a.* decimal.

diezmar /dieθ'mar; dies'mar/ *v.* decimate.

difamación /difama'θion; difama'sion/ *n. f.* defamation, smear.

difamar /difa'mar/ *v.* defame, smear, libel.

difamatorio /difama'torio/ *a.* defamatory.

diferencia /dife'renθia; dife'rensia/ *n. f.* difference.

diferencial /diferen'θial; diferen'sial/ *a. & f.* differential.

diferenciar /diferen'θiar; diferen'siar/ *v.* differentiate, distinguish.

diferente /dife'rente/ *a.* different.

diferentemente /diferente'mente/ *adv.* differently.

diferir /dife'rir/ *v.* differ; defer; put off.

difícil /di'fiθil; di'fisil/ *a.* difficult, hard.

difícilmente /difiθil'mente; difisil'mente/ *adv.* with difficulty or hardship.

dificultad /difikul'taθ/ *n. f.* difficulty.

dificultar /difikul'tar/ *v.* make difficult.

dificultoso /difikul'toso/ *a.* difficult, hard.

difidencia /difi'ðenθia; difi'ðensia/ *n. f.* diffidence.

difidente /difi'ðente/ *a.* diffident.

difteria /dif'teria/ *n. f.* diphtheria.

difundir /difun'dir/ *v.* diffuse, spread.

difunto /di'funto/ *a.* **1.** deceased, dead, late. —*n.* **2. -ta,** deceased person.

difusamente /difusa'mente/ *adv.* diffusely.

difusión /difu'sion/ *n. f.* diffusion, spread.

digerible /dihe'riβle/ *a.* digestible.

digerir /dihe'rir/ *v.* digest.

digestible /dihes'tiβle/ *a.* digestible.

digestión /dihes'tion/ *n. f.* digestion.

digestivo /dihes'tiβo/ *a.* digestive.

digesto /di'hesto/ *n. m.* digest or code of laws.

digitado /dihi'taðo/ *a.* digitate.

digital /dihi'tal/ *a.* **1.** digital. —*n.* **2.** *f.* foxglove, digitalis.

dignación /digna'θion; digna'sion/ *f.* condescension; deigning.

dignamente /digna'mente/ *adv.* with dignity.

dignarse /dig'narse/ *v.* condescend, deign.

dignatario /digna'tario/ **-ra** *n.* dignitary.

dignidad /digni'ðaθ/ *n. f.* dignity.

dignificar /dignifi'kar/ *v.* dignify.

digno /'digno/ *a.* worthy; dignified.

digresión /digre'sion/ *n. f.* digression.

digresivo /digre'siβo/ *a.* digressive.

dij, dije /dih; 'dihe/ *n. m.* trinket, piece of jewelry.

dilación /dila'θion; dila'sion/ *n. f.* delay.

dilapidación /dilapiða'θion; dilapi'ðasion/ *n. f.* dilapidation.

dilapidado /dilapi'ðaðo/ *a.* dilapidated.

dilatación /dilata'θion; dilata'sion/ *n. f.* dilatation, enlargement.

dilatar /dila'tar/ *v.* dilate; delay; expand.

dilatoria /dila'toria/ *n. f.* delay.

dilatorio /dila'torio/ *a.* dilatory.

dilecto /di'lekto/ *a.* loved.

dilema /di'lema/ *n. m.* dilemma.

diligencia /dili'henθia; dili'hensia/ *n. f.* diligence, industriousness.

diligente /dili'hente/ *a.* diligent, industrious.

diligentemente /dilihente'mente/ *adv.* diligently.

dilogía /dilo'hia/ *n. f.* ambiguous meaning.

dilución /dilu'θion; dilu'sion/ *n. f.* dilution.

diluir /di'luir/ *v.* dilute.

diluvial /dilu'βial/ *a.* diluvial.

diluvio /di'luβio/ *n. m.* flood, deluge.

dimensión /dimen'sion/ *n. f.* dimension; measurement.

diminución /diminu'θion; diminu'sion/ *n. f.* diminution.

diminuto /dimi'nuto/ **diminutivo** *a.* diminutive, little.

dimisión /dimi'sion/ *n. f.* resignation.

dimitir /dimi'tir/ *v.* resign.

Dinamarca /dina'marka/ *n. f.* Denmark.

dinamarqués /dinamar'kes/ **-esa** *a. & n.* Danish, Dane.

dinámico /di'namiko/ *a.* dynamic.

dinamita /dina'mita/ *n. f.* dynamite.

dinamitero /dinami'tero/ **-ra** *n.* dynamiter.

dínamo /'dinamo/ *n. m.* dynamo.

dinasta /di'nasta/ *n. m.* dynast, king, monarch.

dinastía /dinas'tia/ *n. f.* dynasty.

dinástico /di'nastiko/ *a.* dynastic.

dinero /di'nero/ *n. m.* money, currency.

dinosauro /dino'sauro/ *n. m.* dinosaur.

diócesis /'dioθesis; 'diosesis/ *n. f.* diocese.

Dios /dios/ *n.* **1.** *m.* God.

dios -sa *n.* **2.** god, goddess.

diploma /di'ploma/ *n. m.* diploma.

diplomacia /diplo'maθia; diplo'masia/ *n. f.* diplomacy.

diplomado /diplo'maðo/ **-da** *n.* graduate.

diplomarse /diplo'marse/ *v.* graduate (from a school).

diplomática /diplo'matika/ *n. f.* diplomacy.

diplomático /diplo'matiko/ **-ca** *a. & n.* diplomat; diplomatic.

dipsomanía /dipsoma'nia/ *n. f.* dipsomania.

diptongo /dip'toŋgo/ *n. m.* diphthong.

diputación /diputa'θion; diputa'sion/ *n. f.* deputation, delegation.

diputado /dipu'taðo/ **-da** *n.* deputy; delegate.

diputar /dipu'tar/ *v.* depute, delegate; empower.

dique /'dike/ *n. m.* dike; dam.

dirección /direk'θion; direk'sion/ *n. f.* direction; address; guidance; *Com.* management.

directamente /direkta'mente/ *adv.* directly.

directo /di'rekto/ *a.* direct.

director /direk'tor/ **-ra** *n.* director; manager.

directorio /direk'torio/ *n. m.* directory.

dirigente /diri'hente/ *a.* directing, controlling, managing.

dirigible /diri'hiβle/ *n. m.* dirigible.

dirigir /diri'hir/ *v.* direct; lead; manage.

dirigirse a /diri'hirse a/ *v.* address; approach, turn to; head for.

disanto /di'santo/ *n. m.* holy day.

discantar /diskan'tar/ *v.* sing (esp. in counterpoint); discuss.

disceptación /disθepta'θion; dissepta'sion/ *n. f.* argument, quarrel.

disceptar /disθep'tar; dissep'tar/ *v.* argue, quarrel.

discernimiento /disθerni'miento; disserni'miento/ *n. m.* discernment.

discernir /disθer'nir; disser'nir/ *v.* discern.

disciplina /disθi'plina; dissi'plina/ *n. f.* discipline.

disciplinable /disθipli'naβle; dissipli'naβle/ *a.* disciplinable.

disciplinar /disθipli'nar; dissipli'nar/ *v.* discipline, train, teach.

discípulo /dis'θipulo; dis'sipulo/ **-la** *n.* disciple, follower; pupil.

disco /'disko/ *n. m.* disk; (phonograph) record.

disco compacto /'disko kom'pakto/ compact disk.

disco duro /'disko 'duro/ hard disk.

disco flexible /'disko flek'siβle/ floppy disk.

discontinuación /diskontinua'θion;

diskontinua'sion/ *n. f.* discontinuation.

discontinuar /diskonti'nuar/ *v.* discontinue, break off, cease.

discordancia /diskor'ðanθia; diskor'ðansia/ *n. f.* discordance.

discordar /diskor'ðar/ *v.* disagree, conflict.

discordia /dis'korðia/ *n. f.* discord.

discoteca /disko'teka/ *n. f.* disco, discotheque.

discreción /diskre'θion; diskre'sion/ *n. f.* discretion.

discrecional /diskreθio'nal; diskresio'nal/ *a.* optional.

discrecionalmente /diskreθional'mente; diskresional'mente/ *adv.* optionally.

discrepancia /diskre'panθia; diskre'pansia/ *n. f.* discrepancy.

discretamente /diskreta'mente/ *adv.* discreetly.

discreto /dis'kreto/ *a.* discreet.

discrimen /dis'krimen/ *n. m.* risk, hazard.

discriminación /diskrimina'θion; diskrimina'sion/ *n. f.* discrimination.

discriminar /diskrimi'nar/ *v.* discriminate.

disculpa /dis'kulpa/ *n. f.* excuse; apology.

disculpar /diskul'par/ *v.* excuse; exonerate.

disculparse /diskul'parse/ *v.* apologize.

discurrir /disku'rrir/ *v.* roam; flow; think; plan.

discursante /diskur'sante/ *n.* lecturer, speaker.

discursivo /diskur'siβo/ *a.* discursive.

discurso /dis'kurso/ *n. m.* speech, talk.

discusión /disku'sion/ *n. f.* discussion.

discutible /disku'tiβle/ *a.* debatable.

discutir /disku'tir/ *v.* discuss; debate; contest.

disecación /diseka'θion; diseka'sion/ *n. f.* dissection.

disecar /dise'kar/ *v.* dissect.

disección /disek'θion; disek'sion/ *n. f.* dissection.

diseminación /disemina'θion; disemina'sion/ *n. f.* dissemination.

diseminar /disemi'nar/ *v.* disseminate, spread.

disensión /disen'sion/ *n. f.* dissension; dissent.

disenso /di'senso/ *n. m.* dissent.

disentería /disente'ria/ *n. f.* dysentery.

disentir /disen'tir/ *v.* disagree, dissent.

diseñador /diseɲa'ðor/ **-ra** *n.* designer.

diseño /di'seɲo/ *n. m.* design. **—diseñar,** *v.*

disertación /diserta'θion; diserta'sion/ *n. f.* dissertation.

disforme /dis'forme/ *a.* deformed, monstrous, ugly.

disformidad /disformi'ðaθ/ *n. f.* deformity.

disfraz /dis'fraθ; dis'fras/ *n. m.* disguise. **—disfrazar,** *v.*

disfrutar /disfru'tar/ *v.* enjoy.

disfrute /dis'frute/ *n. m.* enjoyment.

disgustar /disgus'tar/ *v.* displease; disappoint.

disgusto /dis'gusto/ *n. m.* displeasure; disappointment.

disidencia /disi'ðenθia; disi'ðensia/ *n. f.* dissidence.

disidente /disi'ðente/ *a. & n.* dissident.

disímil /di'simil/ *a.* unlike.

disimilitud /disimili'tuθ/ *n. f.* dissimilarity.

disimulación /disimula'θion; disimula'sion/ *n. f.* dissimulation.

disimulado /disimu'laðo/ *a.* dissembling, feigning; sly.

disimular /disimu'lar/ *v.* hide; dissemble.

disimulo /di'simulo/ *n. m.* pretense.

disipación /disipa'θion; disipa'sion/ *n. f.* dissipation.

disipado /disi'paðo/ *a.* dissipated; wasted; scattered.

disipar /disi'par/ *v.* waste; scatter.

dislexia /dis'leksia/ *n. f.* dyslexia.

disléxico /dis'leksiko/ *a.* dyslexic.

dislocación /disloka'θion; disloka'sion/ *n. f.* dislocation.

dislocar /dislo'kar/ *v.* dislocate; displace.

disminuir /dismi'nuir/ *v.* diminish, lessen, reduce.

disociación /disoθia'θion; disosia'sion/ *n. f.* dissociation.

disociar /diso'θiar; diso'siar/ *v.* dissociate.

disolubilidad /disoluβili'ðaθ/ *n. f.* dissolubility.

disoluble /diso'luβle/ *a.* dissoluble.

disolución /disolu'θion; disolu'sion/ *n. f.* dissolution.

disolutamente /disoluta'mente/ *adv.* dissolutely.

disoluto /diso'luto/ *a.* dissolute.

disolver /disol'βer/ *v.* dissolve.

disonancia /diso'nanθia; diso'nansia/ *n. f.* dissonance; discord.

disonante /diso'nante/ *a.* dissonant; discordant.

disonar /diso'nar/ *v.* be discordant; clash in sound.

dísono /di'sono/ *a.* dissonant.

dispar /dis'par/ *a.* unlike.

disparadamente /disparaða'mente/ *adv.* hastily, hurriedly.

disparar /dispa'rar/ *v.* shoot, fire (a weapon).

disparatado /dispara'taðo/ *a.* nonsensical.

disparatar /dispara'tar/ *v.* talk nonsense.

disparate /dispa'rate/ *n. m.* nonsense, tall tale.

disparejo /dispa'reho/ *a.* uneven, unequal.

disparidad /dispari'ðaθ/ *n. f.* disparity.

disparo /dis'paro/ *n. m.* shot.

dispendio /dis'pendio/ *n. m.* extravagance.

dispendioso /dispen'dioso/ *a.* expensive; extravagant.

dispensa /dis'pensa/ **dispensación** *n. f.* dispensation.

dispensable /dispen'saβle/ *a.* dispensable; excusable.

dispensar /dispen'sar/ *v.* dispense, excuse; grant.

dispensario /dispen'sario/ *n. m.* dispensary.

dispepsia /dis'pepsia/ *n. f.* dyspepsia.

dispéptico /dis'peptiko/ *a.* dyspeptic.

dispersar /disper'sar/ *v.* scatter; dispel; disband.

dispersión /disper'sion/ *n. f.* dispersion, dispersal.

disperso /dis'perso/ *a.* dispersed.

displicente /displi'θente; displi'sente/ *a.* unpleasant.

disponer /dispo'ner/ *v.* dispose. **d. de,** have at one's disposal.

disponible /dispo'niβle/ *a.* available.

disposición /disposi'θion; disposi'sion/ *n. f.* disposition; disposal.

dispuesto /dis'puesto/ *a.* disposed, inclined; attractive.

disputa /dis'puta/ *n. f.* dispute, argument.

disputable /dispu'taβle/ *a.* disputable.

disputador /disputa'ðor/ **-ra** *n.* disputant.

disputar /dispu'tar/ *v.* argue; dispute.

disquete /dis'kete/ *n. m.* diskette.

disquetera /diske'tera/ *n. f.* disk drive.

disquisición /diskisi'θion; diskisi'sion/ *n. f.* disquisition.

distancia /dis'tanθia; dis'tansia/ *n. f.* distance.

distante /dis'tante/ *a.* distant.

distantemente /distante'mente/ *adv.* distantly.

distar /dis'tar/ *v.* be distant, be far.

distender /disten'der/ *v.* distend, swell, enlarge.

distensión /disten'sion/ *n. f.* distension, swelling.

dístico /'distiko/ *n. m.* couplet.

distinción /distin'θion; distin'sion/ *n. f.* distinction, difference.

distingo /dis'tiŋgo/ *n. m.* restriction.

distinguible /distiŋ'guiβle/ *a.* distinguishable.

distinguido /distiŋ'guiðo/ *a.* distinguished, prominent.

distinguir /distiŋ'guir/ *v.* distinguish; make out, spot.

distintamente /distinta'mente/ *adv.* distinctly, clearly; differently.

distintivo /distin'tiβo/ *a.* distinctive.

distintivo del país /distin'tiβo del pa'is/ country code.

distinto /dis'tinto/ *a.* distinct; different.

distracción /distrak'θion; distrak'sion/ *n. f.* distraction, pastime; absent-mindedness.

distraer /distra'er/ *v.* distract.

distraídamente /distraiða'mente/ *adv.* absent-mindedly, distractedly.

distraído /distra'iðo/ *a.* absent-minded; distracted.

distribución /distriβu'θion; distriβu'sion/ *n. f.* distribution.

distribuidor /distriβui'ðor/ **-ra** *n.* distributor.

distribuir /distri'βuir/ *v.* distribute.

distributivo /distriβu'tiβo/ *a.* distributive.

distributor /distriβu'tor/ *n. m.* distributor.

distrito /dis'trito/ *n. m.* district.

disturbar /distur'βar/ *v.* disturb, trouble.

disturbio /dis'turβio/ *n. m.* disturbance, outbreak; turmoil.

disuadir /disua'ðir/ *v.* dissuade.

disuasión /disua'sion/ *n. f.* dissuasion; deterrence.

disuasivo /disua'siβo/ *a.* dissuasive.

disyunción /disyun'θion; disyun'sion/ *n. f.* disjunction.

ditirambo /diti'rambo/ *n. m.* dithyramb.

diurno /'diurno/ *a.* diurnal.

diva /'diβa/ *n. f.* diva, prima donna.

divagación /diβaga'θion; diβaga'sion/ *n. f.* digression.

divagar /diβa'gar/ *v.* digress, ramble.

diván /di'βan/ *n. m.* couch.

divergencia /diβer'henθia; diβer'hensia/ *n. f.* divergence.

divergente /diβer'hente/ *a.* divergent, differing.

divergir /diβer'hir/ *v.* diverge.

diversamente /diβersa'mente/ *adv.* diversely.

diversidad /diβersi'ðað/ *n. f.* diversity.

diversificar /diβersifi'kar/ *v.* diversify, vary.

diversión /diβer'sion/ *n. f.* diversion, pastime.

diverso /di'βerso/ *a.* diverse, different; (*pl.*) various, several.

divertido /diβer'tiðo/ *a.* humorous, amusing.

divertimiento /diβerti'miento/ *n. m.* diversion; amusement.

divertir /diβer'tir/ *v.* entertain, amuse.

divertirse /diβer'tirse/ *v.* enjoy oneself, have a good time.

dividendo /diβi'ðendo/ *n. m.* dividend.

divididero /diβiði'ðero/ *a.* to be divided.

dividido /diβi'ðiðo/ *a.* divided.

dividir /diβi'ðir/ *v.* divide; separate.

divieso /di'βieso/ *n. m. Med.* boil.

divinamente /diβina'mente/ *adv.* divinely.

divinidad /diβini'ðað/ *n. f.* divinity.

divinizar /diβini'θar; diβini'sar/ *v.* deify.

divino /di'βino/ *a.* divine; heavenly.

divisa /di'βisa/ *n. f.* badge, emblem.

divisar /diβi'sar/ *v.* sight, make out.

divisibilidad /diβisiβili'ðað/ *n. f.* divisibility.

divisible /diβi'siβle/ *a.* divisible.

división /diβi'sion/ *n. f.* division.

divisivo /diβi'siβo/ *a.* divisive.

divo /'diβo/ *n. m.* movie star.

divorcio /di'βorθio; di'βorsio/ *n. m.* divorce. —**divorciar,** *v.*

divulgable /diβul'gaβle/ *a.* divulgable.

divulgación /diβulga'θion; diβulga'sion/ *n. f.* divulgation.

divulgar /diβul'gar/ *v.* divulge, reveal.

dobladamente /doβlaða'mente/ *adv.* doubly.

dobladillo /doβla'ðiʎo; doβla'ðiyo/ *n. m.* hem of a skirt or dress.

dobladura /doβla'ðura/ *n. f.* fold; bend.

doblar /do'βlar/ *v.* fold; bend.

doble /'doβle/ *a.* double.

doblegable /doβle'gaβle/ *a.* flexible, foldable.

doblegar /doβle'gar/ *v.* fold, bend; yield.

doblez /do'βleθ; doβles/ *n. m.* fold; duplicity.

doblón /do'βlon/ *n. m.* doubloon.

doce /'doθe; 'dose/ *a. & pron.* twelve.

docena /do'θena; do'sena/ *n. f.* dozen.

docente /do'θente; do'sente/ *a.* educational.

dócil /'doθil; 'dosil/ *a.* docile.

docilidad /doθili'ðað; dosili'ðað/ *n. f.* docility, tractableness.

dócilmente /doθil'mente; dosil'mente/ *adv.* docilely, meekly.

doctamente /dokta'mente/ *adv.* learnedly, profoundly.

docto /'dokto/ *a.* learned, expert.

doctor /dok'tor/ **-ra** *n.* doctor.

doctorado /dokto'raðo/ *n. m.* doctorate.

doctoral /dokto'ral/ *a.* doctoral.

doctrina /dok'trina/ *n. f.* doctrine.

doctrinador /doktrina'ðor/ **-ra** *n.* teacher.

doctrinal /doktri'nal/ *n. m.* doctrinal.

doctrinar /doktri'nar/ *v.* teach.

documentación /dokumenta'θion; dokumenta'sion/ *n. f.* documentation.

documental /dokumen'tal/ *a.* documentary.

documento /doku'mento/ *n. m.* document.

dogal /do'gal/ *n. m.* noose.

dogma /'dogma/ *n. m.* dogma.

dogmáticamente /dog'matikamente/ *adv.* dogmatically.

dogmático /dog'matiko/ *n. m.* dogmatic.

dogmatismo /dogma'tismo/ *n. m.* dogmatism.

dogmatista /dogma'tista/ *n. m. & f.* dogmatist.

dogo /'dogo/ *n. m.* bulldog.

dolar /'dolar/ *v.* cut, chop, hew.

dólar /'dolar/ *n. m.* dollar.

dolencia /do'lenθia; do'lensia/ *n. f.* pain; disease.

doler /do'ler/ *v.* ache, hurt, be sore.

doliente /do'liente/ *a.* ill; aching.

dolor /do'lor/ *n. m.* pain; grief, sorrow, woe.

dolor de cabeza /do'lor de ka'βeθa; do'lor de ka'βesa/ headache.

dolor de espalda /do'lor de es'palda/ backache.

dolor de estómago /do'lor de es'tomago/ stomachache.

dolorido /dolo'riðo/ *a.* painful, sorrowful.

dolorosamente /dolorosa'mente/ *adv.* painfully, sorrowfully.

doloroso /dolo'roso/ *a.* painful, sorrowful.

dolosamente /dolosa'mente/ *adv.* deceitfully.

doloso /do'loso/ *a.* deceitful.

domable /do'maβle/ *a.* that can be tamed or managed.

domar /do'mar/ *v.* tame; subdue.

dombo /'dombo/ *n. m.* dome.

domesticable /domesti'kaβle/ *a.* that can be domesticated.

domesticación /domestika'θion; domestika'sion/ *n. f.* domestication.

domésticamente /domestika'mente/ *adv.* domestically.

domesticar /domesti'kar/ *v.* tame, domesticate.

domesticidad /domestiθi'ðað; domestisi'ðað/ *n. f.* domesticity.

doméstico /do'mestiko/ *a.* domestic.

domicilio /domi'θilio; domi'silio/ *n. m.* dwelling, home, residence, domicile.

dominación /domina'θion; domina'sion/ *n. f.* domination.

dominador /domina'ðor/ *a.* dominating.

dominante /domi'nante/ *a.* dominant.

dominar /domi'nar/ *v.* rule, dominate; master.

dómine /'domine/ *n. m.* teacher.

domingo /do'miŋgo/ *n. m.* Sunday.

dominio /do'minio/ *n. m.* domain; rule; power.

dominó /domi'no/ *n. m.* domino.

domo /'domo/ *n. m.* dome.

don /don/ *title used before a man's first name.*

don *n. m.* gift.

donación /dona'θion; dona'sion/ *n. f.* donation.

donador /dona'ðor/ **-ra** *n.* giver, donor.

donaire /do'naire/ *n. m.* grace.

donairosamente /donairosa'mente/ *adv.* gracefully.

donairoso /donai'roso/ *a.* graceful.

donante /do'nante/ *n.* giver, donor.

donar /do'nar/ *v.* donate.

donativo /dona'tiβo/ *n. m.* donation, contribution; gift.

doncella /don'θeʎa; don'seya/ *n. f.* lass; maid.

donde /'donde/ **dónde** *conj. & adv.* where.

dondequiera /donde'kiera/ *adv.* wherever, anywhere.

donosamente /donosa'mente/ *adv.* gracefully; wittily.

donoso /do'noso/ *a.* graceful; witty.

donosura /dono'sura/ *n. f.* gracefulness; wittiness.

doña /'doɲa/ *title used before a lady's first name.*

dopar /do'par/ *v.* drug, dope.

dorado /do'raðo/ *a.* gilded.

dorador /dora'ðor/ **-ra** *n.* gilder.

dorar /do'rar/ *v.* gild.

dórico /'doriko/ *a.* Doric.

dormidero /dormi'ðero/ *a.* sleep-inducing; soporific.

dormido /dor'miðo/ *a.* asleep.

dormir /dor'mir/ *v.* sleep.

dormirse /dor'mirse/ *v.* fall asleep, go to sleep.

dormitar /dormi'tar/ *v.* doze.

dormitorio /dormi'torio/ *n. m.* dormitory; bedroom.

dorsal /dor'sal/ *a.* dorsal.

dorso /'dorso/ *n. m.* spine.

dos /dos/ *a. & pron.* two. **los d.,** both.

dosañal /dosa'ɲal/ *a.* biennial.

doscientos /dos'θientos; dos'sientos/ *a. & pron.* two hundred.

dosel /do'sel/ *n. m.* canopy; platform, dais.

dosificación /dosifika'θion; dosifika'sion/ *n. f.* dosage.

dosis /'dosis/ *n. f.* dose.

dotación /dota'θion; dota'sion/ *n. f.* endowment; *Naut.* crew.

dotador /dota'ðor/ **-ra** *n.* donor.

dotar /do'tar/ *v.* endow; give a dowry to.

dote /'dote/ *n. f.* dowry; (*pl.*) talents.

dragaminas /draga'minas/ *n. m.* mine sweeper.

dragar /dra'gar/ *v.* dredge; sweep.

dragón /dra'gon/ *n. m.* dragon; dragoon.

dragonear /dragone'ar/ *v.* pretend to be.

drama /'drama/ *n. m.* drama; play.

dramática /dra'matika/ *n. f.* drama, dramatic art.

dramáticamente /dramatika'mente/ *adv.* dramatically.

dramático /dra'matiko/ *a.* dramatic.

dramatizar /dramati'θar; dramati'sar/ *v.* dramatize.

dramaturgo /drama'turgo/ **-ga** *n.* playwright, dramatist.

drástico /'drastiko/ *a.* drastic.

drenaje /dre'nahe/ *n. m.* drainage.

dríade /'driaðe/ *n. f.* dryad.

dril /dril/ *n. m.* denim.

driza /'driθa; 'drisa/ *n. f.* halyard.

droga /'droga/ *n. f.* drug.

drogadicto /droga'ðikto/ **-ta** *n.* drug addict.

droguería /droge'ria/ *n. f.* drugstore.

droguero /dro'gero/ *n. m.* druggist.

dromedario /drome'ðario/ *n. m.* dromedary.

druida /'druiða/ *n. m. & f.* Druid.

dualidad /duali'ðað/ *n. f.* duality.

dubitable /duβi'taβle/ *a.* doubtful.

dubitación /duβita'θion; duβita'sion/ *n. f.* doubt.

ducado /du'kaðo/ *n. m.* duchy.

ducal /du'kal/ *a.* ducal.

ducha /'dutʃa/ *n. f.* shower (bath).

ducharse /du'tʃarse/ *v.* take a shower.

dúctil /'duktil/ *a.* ductile.

ductilidad /duktili'ðað/ *n. f.* ductility.

duda /'duða/ *n. f.* doubt.

dudable /du'ðaβle/ *a.* doubtful.

dudar /du'ðar/ *v.* doubt; hesitate; question.

dudosamente /duðosa'mente/ *adv.* doubtfully.

dudoso /du'ðoso/ *a.* dubious; doubtful.

duela /'duela/ *n. f.* stave.

duelista /due'lista/ *n. m. & f.* duelist.

duelo /'duelo/ *n. m.* duel; grief; mourning.

duende /'duende/ *n. m.* elf, hobgoblin.

dueño /'dueɲo/ **-ña** *n.* owner; landlord -lady; master, mistress.

dulce /'dulθe; dulse/ *a.* **1.** sweet. **agua d.,** fresh water. —*n.* **2.** *m.* piece of candy; (*pl.*) candy.

dulcedumbre /dulθe'ðumbre; dulse'ðumbre/ *n. f.* sweetness.

dulcemente /dulθe'mente; dulse'mente/ *adv.* sweetly.

dulcería /dulθe'ria; dulse'ria/ *n. f.* confectionery; candy shop.

dulcificar /dulθifi'kar; dulsifi'kar/ *v.* sweeten.

dulzura /dul'θura; dul'sura/ *n. f.* sweetness; mildness.

duna /'duna/ *n. f.* dune.

dúo /'duo/ *n. m.* duo, duet.

duodenal /duoðe'nal/ *a.* duodenal.

duplicación /duplika'θion; duplika'sion/ *n. f.* duplication; doubling.

duplicadamente /duplikaða'mente/ *adv.* doubly.

duplicado /dupli'kaðo/ *a. & m.* duplicate.

duplicar /dupli'kar/ *v.* double, duplicate, repeat.

duplicidad /dupliθi'ðað; duplisi'ðað/ *n. f.* duplicity.

duplo /'duplo/ *a.* double.

duque /'duke/ *n. m.* duke.

duquesa /du'kesa/ *n. f.* duchess.

durabilidad /duraβili'ðað/ *n. f.* durability.

durable /du'raβle/ *a.* durable.

duración /dura'θion; dura'sion/ *n. f.* duration.

duradero /duraˈðero/ *a.* lasting, durable.

duramente /duraˈmente/ *adv.* harshly, roughly.

durante /duˈrante/ *prep.* during.

durar /duˈrar/ *v.* last.

durazno /duˈraθno; duˈrasno/ *n. m.* peach; peach tree.

dureza /duˈreθa; duˈresa/ *n. f.* hardness.

durmiente /durˈmiente/ *a.* sleeping.

duro /ˈduro/ *a.* hard; stiff; stern; stale.

dux /duks/ *n. m.* doge.

E

e /e/ *conj.* and.

ebanista /eβaˈnista/ *n. m. & f.* cabinetmaker.

ebanizar /eβaniˈθar; eβaniˈsar/ *v.* give an ebony finish to.

ébano /ˈeβano/ *n. m.* ebony.

ebonita /eβoˈnita/ *n. f.* ebonite.

ebrio /ˈeβrio/ *a.* drunken, inebriated.

ebullición /eβuʎiˈθion; eβuyiˈsion/ *n. f.* boiling.

echada /eˈtʃaða/ *n. f.* throw.

echadillo /etʃaˈðiʎo; etʃaˈðiyo/ *n. m.* foundling; orphan.

echar /eˈtʃar/ *v.* throw, toss; pour. **e. a,** start to. **e. a perder,** spoil, ruin. **e. de menos,** miss.

echarse /eˈtʃarse/ *v.* lie down.

eclecticismo /eklektiˈθismo; eklektiˈsismo/ *n. m.* eclecticism.

ecléctico /eˈklektiko/ *n. & a.* eclectic.

eclesiástico /ekleˈsiastiko/ *a. & m.* ecclesiastic.

eclipse /eˈklipse/ *n. m.* eclipse. **—eclipsar,** *v.*

écloga /ˈekloga/ *n. f.* eclogue.

eco /ˈeko/ *n. m.* echo.

ecología /ekoloˈhia/ *n. f.* ecology.

ecológico /ekoˈlohiko/ *n. f.* ecological.

ecologista /ekoloˈhista/ *n. m. & f.* ecologist.

economía /ekonoˈmia/ *n. f.* economy; thrift; economics. **e. política,** political economy.

económicamente /ekonomikaˈmente/ *adv.* economically.

económico /ekoˈnomiko/ *a.* economic; economical, thrifty; inexpensive.

economista /ekonoˈmista/ *n. m. & f.* economist.

economizar /ekonomiˈθar; ekonomiˈsar/ *v.* save, economize.

ecuación /ekuaˈθion; ekuaˈsion/ *n. f.* equation.

ecuador /ekuaˈðor/ *n. m.* equator.

ecuanimidad /ekuanimiˈðað/ *n. f.* equanimity.

ecuatorial /ekuatoˈrial/ *a.* equatorial.

ecuatoriano /ekuatoˈriano/ **-na** *a. & n.* Ecuadorian.

ecuestre /eˈkuestre/ *a.* equestrian.

ecuménico. /ekuˈmeniko/ *a.* ecumenical.

edad /eˈðað/ *n. f.* age.

edecán /eðeˈkan/ *n. m.* aide-de-camp.

Edén /eˈðen/ *n. m.* Eden.

edición /eðiˈθion; eðiˈsion/ *n. f.* edition; issue.

edicto /eˈðikto/ *n. m.* edict, decree.

edificación /eðifikaˈθion; eðifikaˈsion/ *n. f.* construction; edification.

edificador /eðifikaˈðor/ *n.* constructor; builder.

edificar /eðifiˈkar/ *v.* build.

edificio /eðiˈfiθio; eðiˈfisio/ *n. m.* edifice, building.

editar /eðiˈtar/ *v.* publish, issue; edit.

editor /eðiˈtor/ *n. m.* publisher; editor.

editorial /eðitoˈrial/ *n. m.* editorial; publishing house.

edredón /eðreˈðon/ *n. m.* quilt.

educación /eðukaˈθion; eðukaˈsion/ *n. f.* upbringing; breeding; education.

educado /eðuˈkaðo/ *a.* well-mannered; educated.

educador /eðukaˈðor/ **-ra** *n.* educator.

educar /eðuˈkar/ *v.* educate; bring up; train.

educativo /eðukaˈtiβo/ *a.* educational.

educción /eðukˈθion; eðukˈsion/ *n. f.* deduction.

educir /eðuˈθir; eðuˈsir/ *v.* educe.

efectivamente /efektiβaˈmente/ *adv.* actually, really.

efectivo /efekˈtiβo/ *a.* effective; actual, real. **en e.,** *Com.* in cash.

efecto /eˈfekto/ *n. m.* effect.

efecto invernáculo /eˈfekto imberˈnakulo/ greenhouse effect.

efectuar /efekˈtuar/ *v.* effect; cash.

eferente /efeˈrente/ *a.* efferent.

efervescencia /eferβesˈθenθia; eferβesˈsensia/ *n. f.* effervescence; zeal.

eficacia /efiˈkaθia; efiˈkasia/ *n. f.* efficacy.

eficaz /efiˈkaθ; efiˈkas/ *a.* efficient, effective.

eficazmente /efikaθˈmente; efikasˈmente/ *adv.* efficaciously.

eficiencia /efiˈθienθia; efiˈsiensia/ *n. f.* efficiency.

eficiente /efiˈθiente; efiˈsiente/ *a.* efficient.

efigie /eˈfihie/ *n. f.* effigy.

efímera /efiˈmera/ *n. f.* mayfly.

efímero /eˈfimero/ *a.* ephemeral, passing.

efluvio /eˈfluβio/ *n. m.* effluvium.

efundir /efunˈdir/ *v.* effuse; pour out.

efusión /efuˈsion/ *n. f.* effusion.

egipcio /eˈhipθio; eˈhipsio/ **-cia** *a. & n.* Egyptian.

Egipto /eˈhipto/ *n. m.* Egypt.

egoísmo /egoˈismo/ *n. m.* egoism, egotism, selfishness.

egoísta /egoˈista/ *a. & n.* selfish, egoistic; egoist.

egotismo /egoˈtismo/ *n. m.* egotism.

egotista /egoˈtista/ *n. m. & f.* egotist.

egreso /eˈgreso/ *n. m.* expense, outlay.

eje /ˈehe/ *n. m.* axis; axle.

ejecución /ehekuˈθion; ehekuˈsion/ *n. f.* execution; performance; enforcement.

ejecutar /ehekuˈtar/ *v.* execute; enforce; carry out.

ejecutivo /ehekuˈtiβo/ **-va** *a. & n.* executive.

ejecutor /ehekuˈtor/ **-ra** *n.* executor.

ejemplar /ehemˈplar/ *a.* **1.** exemplary. —*n.* **2.** *m.* copy.

ejemplificación /ehemplifikaˈθion; ehemplifikaˈsion/ *n. f.* exemplification.

ejemplificar /ehemplifiˈkar/ *v.* illustrate.

ejemplo /eˈhemplo/ *n. m.* example.

ejercer /eherˈθer; eherˈser/ *v.* exert; practice.

ejercicio /eherˈθiθio; eherˈsisio/ *n. m.* exercise, drill. —**ejercitar,** *v.*

ejercitación /eherθitaˈθion; ehersitaˈsion/ *n. f.* exercise, training, drill.

ejercitar /eherθiˈtar; ehersiˈtar/ *v.* exercise, train, drill.

ejército /eˈherθito; eˈhersito/ *n. m.* army.

ejotes /eˈhotes/ *n. m.pl.* string beans.

el /el/ *art. & pron.* the; the one.

él *pron.* he, him; it.

elaboración /elaβoraˈθion; elaβoraˈsion/ *n. f.* elaboration; working up.

elaborado /elaβoˈraðo/ *a.* elaborate.

elaborador /elaβoraˈðor/ *n.* manufacturer, maker.

elaborar /elaβoˈrar/ *v.* elaborate; manufacture; brew.

elación /elaˈθion; elaˈsion/ *n. f.* elation; magnanimity; turgid style.

elasticidad /elastiθiˈðað; elastisiˈðað/ *n. f.* elasticity.

elástico /eˈlastiko/ *a.* elastic.

elección /elekˈθion; elekˈsion/ *n. f.* election; option, choice.

electivo /elekˈtiβo/ *a.* elective.

electo /eˈlekto/ *a.* elected, chosen, appointed.

electorado /elektoˈraðo/ *n. m.* electorate.

electoral /elektoˈral/ *a.* electoral.

electricidad /elektriθiˈðað; elektrisiˈðað/ *n. f.* electricity.

electricista /elektriˈθista; elektriˈsista/ *n. m. & f.* electrician.

eléctrico /eˈlektriko/ *a.* electric.

electrización /elektriθaˈθion; elektrisaˈsion/ *n. f.* electrification.

electrocardiograma /e,lektrokarˈðioˈgrama/ *n. m.* electrocardiogram.

electrocución /elektrokuˈθion; elektrokuˈsion/ *n. f.* electrocution.

electrocutar /elektrokuˈtar/ *v.* electrocute.

electrodo /elekˈtroðo/ *n. m.* electrode.

electrodoméstico /e,lektroðoˈmestiko/ *n. m.* electrical appliance, home appliance.

electroimán /elektroiˈman/ *n. m.* electromagnet.

electrólisis /elekˈtrolisis/ *n. f.* electrolysis.

electrólito /elekˈtrolito/ *n. m.* electrolyte.

electrón /elekˈtron/ *n. m.* electron.

electrónico /elekˈtroniko/ *a.* electronic.

elefante /eleˈfante/ *n. m.* elephant.

elegancia /eleˈganθia; eleˈgansia/ *n. f.* elegance.

elegante /eleˈgante/ *a.* elegant, smart, stylish, fine.

elegantemente /eleganteˈmente/ *adv.* elegantly.

elegía /eleˈhia/ *n. f.* elegy.

elegibilidad /elehiβiliˈðað/ *n. f.* eligibility.

elegible /eleˈhiβle/ *a.* eligible.

elegir /eleˈhir/ *v.* select, choose; elect.

elemental /elemenˈtal/ *a.* elementary.

elementalmente /elementalˈmente/ *adv.* elementally; fundamentally.

elemento /eleˈmento/ *n. m.* element.

elepé /eleˈpe/ *n. m.* long-playing (record), LP.

elevación /eleβaˈθion; eleβaˈsion/ *n. f.* elevation; height.

elevador /eleβaˈðor/ *n. m.* elevator.

elevamiento /eleβaˈmiento/ *n. m.* elevation.

elevar /eleˈβar/ *v.* elevate; erect, raise.

elidir /eliˈðir/ *v.* elide.

eliminación /eliminaˈθion; eliminaˈsion/ *n. f.* elimination.

eliminar /elimiˈnar/ *v.* eliminate.

elipse /eˈlipse/ *n. f.* ellipse.

elipsis /eˈlipsis/ *n. f.* ellipsis.

elíptico /eˈliptiko/ *a.* elliptic.

ella /ˈeʎa; ˈeya/ *pron.* she, her; it.

ello /ˈeʎo; ˈeyo/ *pron.* it.

ellos /ˈeʎos; ˈeyos/ **-as** *pron. pl.* they, them.

elocuencia /eloˈkuenθia; eloˈkuensia/ *n. f.* eloquence.

elocuente /eloˈkuente/ *a.* eloquent.

elocuentemente /elokuenteˈmente/ *adv.* eloquently.

elogio /eˈlohio/ *n. m.* praise, compliment. —**elogiar,** *v.*

elucidación /eluθiðaˈθion; elusiðaˈsion/ *n. f.* elucidation.

elucidar /eluθiˈðar; elusiˈðar/ *v.* elucidate.

eludir /eluˈðir/ *v.* elude.

emanar /emaˈnar/ *v.* emanate, stem.

emancipación /emanθipaˈθion; emansipaˈsion/ *n. f.* emancipation; freeing.

emancipador /emanθipaˈðor; emansipaˈðor/ **-ra** *n.* emancipator.

emancipar /emanθiˈpar; emansiˈpar/ *v.* emancipate; free.

embajada /embaˈhaða/ *n. f.* embassy; legation; *Colloq.* errand.

embajador /embahaˈðor/ **-ra** *n.* ambassador.

embalar /embaˈlar/ *v.* pack, bale.

embaldosado /embaldoˈsaðo/ *n. m.* tile floor.

embalsamador /embalsamaˈðor/ *n. m.* embalmer.

embalsamar /embalsaˈmar/ *v.* embalm.

embarazada /embaraˈθaða; embaraˈsaða/ *a.* pregnant.

embarazadamente /embaraθaðaˈmente; embarasaðaˈmente/ *adv.* embarrassedly.

embarazar /embaraˈθar; embaraˈsar/ *v.* make pregnant; embarrass.

embarazo /embaˈraθo; embaˈraso/ *n. m.* embarrassment; pregnancy.

embarbascado /embarβasˈkaðo/ *a.* difficult; complicated.

embarcación /embarkaˈθion; embarkaˈsion/ *n. f.* boat, ship; embarkation.

embarcadero /embarkaˈðero/ *n. m.* wharf, pier, dock.

embarcador /embarkaˈðor/ *n. m.* shipper, loader, stevedore.

embarcar /embarˈkar/ *v.* embark, board ship.

embarcarse /embarˈkarse/ *v.* embark; sail.

embargador /embargaˈðor/ *n. m.* one who impedes; one who orders an embargo.

embargante /embarˈgante/ *a.* impeding, hindering.

embargar /embarˈgar/ *v.* impede, restrain; *Leg.* seize, embargo.

embargo /emˈbargo/ *n. m.* seizure, embargo. **sin e.,** however, nevertheless.

embarnizar /embarniˈθar; embarniˈsar/ *v.* varnish.

embarque /emˈbarke/ *n. m.* shipment.

embarrador /embarraˈðor/ **-ra** *n.* plasterer.

embarrancar /embarranˈkar/ *v.* get stuck in mud; *Naut.* run aground.

embarrar /embaˈrrar/ *v.* plaster; besmear with mud.

embasamiento /embasaˈmiento/ *n. m.* foundation of a building.

embastecer /embasteˈθer; embasteˈser/ *v.* get fat.

embaucador /embaukaˈðor/ **-ra** *n.* impostor.

embaucar /embauˈkar/ *v.* deceive, trick, hoax.

embaular /embauˈlar/ *v.* pack in a trunk.

embausamiento /embausaˈmiento/ *n. m.* amazement.

embebecer /embeβeˈθer; embeβeˈser/ *v.* amaze, astonish; entertain.

embeber /embeˈβer/ *v.* absorb; incorporate; saturate.

embelecador /embelekaˈðor/ **-ra** *n.* impostor.

embeleco /embeˈleko/ *n. m.* fraud, perpetration.

embeleñar /embeleˈɲar/ *v.* fascinate, charm.

embelesamiento /embelesaˈmiento/ *n. m.* rapture.

embelesar /embeleˈsar/ *v.* fascinate, charm.

embeleso /embeˈleso/ *n. m.* rapture, bliss.

embellecer /embeʎeˈθer; embeyeˈser/ *v.* beautify, embellish.

embestida /embesˈtiða/ *n. f.* violent assault; attack.

emblandecer /emblandeˈθer; emblandeˈser/ *v.* soften; moisten; move to pity.

emblema /emˈblema/ *n. m.* emblem.

emblemático /embleˈmatiko/ *a.* emblematic.

embocadura /embokaˈðura/ *n. f.* narrow entrance; mouth of a river.

embocar /emboˈkar/ *v.* eat hastily; gorge.

embolia /emˈbolia/ *n. f.* embolism.

émbolo /ˈembolo/ *n. m.* piston.

embolsar /embolˈsar/ *v.* pocket.

embonar /emboˈnar/ *v.* improve, fix, repair.

emborrachador /emborratʃa'ðor/ a. intoxicating.

emborrachar /emborra'tʃar/ v. get drunk.

emboscada /embos'kaða/ n. f. ambush.

emboscar /embos'kar/ v. put or lie in ambush.

embotado /embo'taðo/ a. blunt, dull (edged). —**embotar**, v.

embotadura /embota'ðura/ n. f. bluntness; dullness.

embotellamiento /emboteʎa'miento; emboteya'miento/ n. m. bottling (liquids); traffic jam.

embotellar /embote'ʎar; embote'yar/ v. put in bottles.

embozado /embo'θaðo; embo'saðo/ v. muzzled; muffled.

embozar /embo'θar; embo'sar/ v. muzzle; muffle.

embozo /em'boθo; em'boso/ n. m. muffler.

embrague /em'brage/ n. m. Auto. clutch.

embravecer /embraβe'θer; embraβe'ser/ v. be or make angry.

embriagado /embria'gaðo/ a. drunken, intoxicated.

embriagar /embria'gar/ v. intoxicate.

embriaguez /embria'geθ; embria'ges/ n. f. drunkenness.

embrión /em'brion/ n. m. embryo.

embrionario /embrio'nario/ a. embryonic.

embrochado /embro'tʃaðo/ a. embroidered.

embrollo /em'broʎo; em'broyo/ n. m. muddle. —**embrollar**, v.

embromar /embro'mar/ v. tease; joke.

embuchado /embu'tʃaðo/ n. m. pork sausage.

embudo /em'buðo/ n. m. funnel.

embuste /em'buste/ n. m. lie, fib.

embustear /embuste'ar/ v. lie, fib.

embustero /embus'tero/ **-ra** n. liar.

embutir /embu'tir/ v. stuff, cram.

emergencia /emer'henθia; emer'hensia/ n. f. emergency.

emérito /e'merito/ a. emeritus.

emético /e'metiko/ n. m. & a. emetic.

emigración /emigra'θion; emigra'sion/ n. f. emigration.

emigrante /emi'grante/ a. & n. emigrant.

emigrar /emi'grar/ v. emigrate.

eminencia /emi'nenθia; emi'nensia/ n. f. eminence, height.

eminente /emi'nente/ a. eminent.

emisario /emi'sario/ **-ria** n. emissary, spy; outlet.

emisión /emi'sion/ n. f. issue; emission.

emisor /emi'sor/ n. m. radio transmitter.

emitir /emi'tir/ v. emit.

emoción /emo'θion; emo'sion/ n. f. feeling, emotion, thrill.

emocional /emo'θional; emo'sional/ a. emotional.

emocionante /emoθio'nante; emosio'nante/ a. exciting.

emocionar /emoθio'nar; emosio'nar/ v. touch, move, excite.

emolumento /emolu'mento/ n. m. emolument; perquisite.

empacar /empa'kar/ v. pack.

empacho /em'patʃo/ n. m. shyness, timidity; embarrassment.

empadronamiento /empaðrona'miento/ n. m. census; list of taxpayers.

empalizada /empali'θaða; empali'saða/ n. f. palisade, stockade.

empanada /empa'naða/ n. f. meat pie.

empañar /empa'ɲar/ v. blur; soil, sully.

empapar /empa'par/ v. soak.

empapelado /empape'laðo/ n. m. wallpaper.

empapelar /empape'lar/ v. wallpaper.

empaque /em'pake/ n. m. packing; appearance, mien.

empaquetar /empake'tar/ v. pack, package.

emparedado /empare'ðaðo/ n. m. sandwich.

emparejarse /empare'harse/ v. match, pair off; level, even off.

emparentado /emparen'taðo/ a. related by marriage.

emparrado /empa'rraðo/ n. m. arbor.

empastadura /empasta'ðura/ n. f. (dental) filling.

empastar /empas'tar/ v. fill (a tooth); paste.

empate /em'pate/ n. m. tie, draw. —**empatarse**, v.

empecer /empe'θer; empe'ser/ v. hurt, harm, injure; prevent.

empedernir /empeðer'nir/ v. harden.

empeine /em'peine/ n. m. groin; instep; hoof.

empellar /empe'ʎar; empe'yar/ v. shove, jostle.

empellón /empe'ʎon; empe'yon/ n. m. hard push, shove.

empeñar /empe'ɲar/ v. pledge; pawn.

empeñarse en /empe'ɲarse en/ v. persist in, be bent on.

empeño /em'peɲo/ n. m. persistence; pledge; pawning.

empeoramiento /empeora'miento/ n. m. deterioration.

empeorar /empeo'rar/ v. get worse.

emperador /empera'ðor/ n. m. emperor.

emperatriz /empera'triθ; empera'tris/ n. f. empress.

empernar /emper'nar/ v. bolt.

empero /em'pero/ conj. however; but.

emperramiento /emperra'miento/ n. m. stubbornness.

empezar /empe'θar; empe'sar/ v. begin, start.

empinado /empi'naðo/ a. steep.

empinar /empi'nar/ v. raise; exalt.

empíreo /em'pireo/ a. celestial, heavenly; divine.

empíricamente /empirika'mente/ adv. empirically.

empírico /em'piriko/ a. empirical.

empirismo /empi'rismo/ n. m. empiricism.

emplastarse /emplas'tarse/ v. get smeared.

emplasto /em'plasto/ n. m. salve.

emplazamiento /emplaθa'miento; emplasa'miento/ n. m. court summons.

emplazar /empla'θar; empla'sar/ v. summon to court.

empleado /emple'aðo/ **-da** n. employee.

emplear /emple'ar/ v. employ; use.

empleo /em'pleo/ n. m. employment, job; use.

empobrecer /empoβre'θer; empoβre'ser/ v. impoverish.

empobrecimiento /empoβreθi'miento; empoβresi'miento/ n. m. impoverishment.

empollador /empoʎa'ðor; empoya'ðor/ n. m. incubator.

empollar /empo'ʎar; empo'yar/ v. hatch.

empolvado /empol'βaðo/ a. dusty.

empolvar /empol'βar/ v. powder.

emporcar /empor'kar/ v. soil, make dirty.

emporio /em'porio/ n. m. emporium.

emprendedor /emprende'ðor/ a. enterprising.

emprender /empren'der/ v. undertake.

empreñar /empre'ɲar/ v. make pregnant; beget.

empresa /em'presa/ n. f. enterprise, undertaking; company.

empresario /empre'sario/ **-ria** n. businessperson; impresario.

empréstito /em'prestito/ n. m. loan.

empujón /empu'hon/ n. m. push; shove. —**empujar**, v.

empuñar /empu'ɲar/ v. grasp, seize; wield.

emulación /emula'θion; emula'sion/ n. f. emulation; envy; rivalry.

emulador /emula'ðor/ n. m. emulator; rival.

émulo /'emulo/ a. rival. —**emular**, v.

emulsión /emul'sion/ n. f. emulsion.

emulsionar /emulsio'nar/ v. emulsify.

en /en/ prep. in, on, at.

enaguas /e'naguas/ n. f.pl. petticoat; skirt.

enajenable /enahe'naβle/ a. alienable.

enajenación /enahena'θion; enahena'sion/ n. f. alienation; derangement, insanity.

enajenar /enahe'nar/ v. alienate.

enamoradamente /enamoraða'mente/ adv. lovingly.

enamorado /enamo'raðo/ a. in love.

enamorador /enamora'ðor/ n. m. wooer; suitor; lover.

enamorarse /enamo'rarse/ v. fall in love.

enano /e'nano/ **-na** n. midget; dwarf.

enardecer /enarðe'θer; enarðe'ser/ v. inflame.

enastado /enas'taðo/ a. horned.

encabestrar /enkaβe'strar/ v. halter.

encabezado /enkaβe'θaðo; enkaβe'saðo/ n. m. headline.

encabezamiento /enkaβeθa'miento; enkaβesa'miento/ n. m. title; census; tax roll.

encabezar /enkaβe'θar; enkaβe'sar/ v. head.

encachar /enka'tʃar/ v. hide.

encadenamiento /enkaðena'miento/ n. m. connection, linkage.

encadenar /enkaðe'nar/ v. chain; link, connect.

encajar /enka'har/ v. fit in, insert.

encaje /en'kahe/ n. m. lace.

encalar /enka'lar/ v. whitewash.

encallarse /enka'ʎarse; enka'yarse/ v. be stranded.

encallecido /enkaʎe'θiðo; enkaye'siðo/ a. hardened; calloused.

encalvecer /enkalβe'θer; enkalβe'ser/ v. lose one's hair.

encaminar /enkami'nar/ v. guide; direct; be on the way to.

encandilar /enkandi'lar/ v. dazzle; daze.

encantación /enkanta'θion; enkanta'sion/ n. f. incantation.

encantado /enkan'taðo/ a. charmed, fascinated, enchanted.

encantador /enkanta'ðor/ a. charming, delightful.

encante /en'kante/ n. m. public auction.

encanto /en'kanto/ n. m. charm, delight. —**encantar**, v.

encapillado /enkapi'ʎaðo; enkapi'yaðo/ n. m. clothes one is wearing.

encapotar /enkapo'tar/ v. cover, cloak; muffle.

encaprichamiento /enkapritʃa'miento/ n. m. infatuation.

encaramarse /enkara'marse/ v. perch; climb.

encararse con /enka'rarse kon/ v. face.

encarcelación /enkarθela'θion; enkarsela'sion/ n. f. imprisonment.

encarcelar /enkarθe'lar; enkarse'lar/ v. jail, imprison.

encarecer /enkare'θer; enkare'ser/ v. recommend; extol.

encarecidamente /enkareθiða'mente; enkaresiða'mente/ adv. extremely; ardently.

encargado /enkar'gaðo/ **-da** n. agent; attorney; representative.

encargar /enkar'gar/ v. entrust; order.

encargarse /enkar'garse/ v. take charge, be in charge.

encargo /en'kargo/ n. m. errand; assignment; Com. order.

encarnación /enkarna'θion; enkarna'sion/ n. f. incarnation.

encarnado /enkar'naðo/ a. red.

encarnar /enkar'nar/ v. embody.

encarnecer /enkarne'θer; enkarne'ser/ v. grow fat or heavy.

encarnizado /enkarni'θaðo; enkarni'saðo/ a. bloody, fierce.

encarrilar /enkarri'lar/ v. set right; put on the track.

encartar /enkar'tar/ v. ban, outlaw; summon.

encastar /enkas'tar/ v. improve by crossbreeding.

encastillar /enkasti'ʎar; enkasti'yar/ v. be obstinate or unyielding.

encatarrado /enkata'rraðo/ a. suffering from a cold.

encausar /enkau'sar/ v. prosecute; take legal action against.

encauzar /enkau'θar; enkau'sar/ v. channel; direct.

encefalitis /enθefa'litis; ensefa'litis/ n. f. encephalitis.

encelamiento /enθela'miento; ensela'miento/ n. m. envy, jealousy.

encelar /enθe'lar; ense'lar/ v. make jealous.

encenagar /enθena'gar; ensena'gar/ v. wallow in mud.

encendedor /enθende'ðor; ensende'ðor/ n. m. lighter.

encender /enθen'der; ensen'der/ v. light; set fire to, kindle; turn on.

encendido /enθen'diðo; ensen'diðo/ n. m. ignition.

encerado /enθe'raðo; ense'raðo/ n. m. oilcloth; tarpaulin.

encerar /enθe'rar; ense'rar/ v. wax.

encerrar /enθe'rrar; ense'rrar/ v. enclose; confine, shut in.

enchapado /entʃa'paðo/ n. m. veneer.

enchufe /en'tʃufe/ n. m. Elec. plug, socket.

encía /en'θia; en'sia/ n. f. gum.

encíclico /en'θikliko; en'sikliko/ a. **1.** encyclic. —n. **2.** f. encyclical.

enciclopedia /enθiklo'peðia; ensiklo'peðia/ n. f. encyclopedia.

enciclopédico /enθiklo'peðiko; ensiklo'peðiko/ a. encyclopedic.

encierro /en'θierro; en'sierro/ n. m. confinement; enclosure.

encima /en'θima; en'sima/ adv. on top. **e. de**, on. **por e. de**, above.

encina /en'θina; en'sina/ n. f. oak.

encinta /en'θinta; en'sinta/ a. pregnant.

enclavar /enkla'βar/ v. nail.

enclenque /en'klenke/ a. frail, weak, sickly.

encogerse /enko'herse/ v. shrink. **e. de hombros**, shrug the shoulders.

encogido /enko'hiðo/ a. shy, bashful, timid.

encojar /enko'har/ v. make or become lame; cripple.

encolar /enko'lar/ v. glue, paste, stick.

encolerizar /enkoleri'θar; enkoleri'sar/ v. make or become angry.

encomendar /enkomen'dar/ v. commend; recommend.

encomiar /enko'miar/ v. praise, laud, extol.

encomienda /enko'mienda/ n. f. commission, charge; (postal) package.

encomio /en'komio/ n. m. encomium, eulogy.

enconar /enko'nar/ v. irritate, annoy, anger.

encono /en'kono/ n. m. rancor, resentment.

enconoso /enko'noso/ a. rancorous, resentful.

encontrado /enkon'traðo/ a. opposite.

encontrar /enkon'trar/ v. find; meet.

encorajar /enkora'har/ v. encourage; incite.

encornar /enkor'nar/ v. gore.

encorralar /enkorra'lar/ v. corral.

encorvadura /enkorβa'ðura/ n. f. bend, curvature.

encorvar /enkorˈβar/ v. arch, bend.

encorvarse /enkorˈβarse/ v. stoop.

encrucijada /enkruθiˈhaða; enkrusiˈhaða/ n. f. crossroads.

encuadrar /enkuaðˈrar/ v. frame.

encubierta /enkuˈβierta/ a. **1.** secret, fraudulent. —n. **2.** f. fraud.

encubrir /enkuβˈrir/ v. hide, conceal.

encuentro /enˈkuentro/ n. m. encounter; match, bout.

encurtido /enkurˈtiðo/ n. m. pickle.

endeble /enˈdeβle/ a. rail, weak, sickly.

enderezar /endereˈθar; endereˈsar/ v. straighten; redress.

endeudarse /endeuˈðarse/ v. get into debt.

endiablado /endiaˈβlaðo/ a. devilish.

endibia /enˈdiβia/ n. f. endive.

endiosar /endioˈsar/ v. deify.

endorso /enˈdorso/ **endoso** n. m. endorsement.

endosador /endosaˈðor/ **-ra** n. endorser.

endosar /endoˈsar/ v. endorse.

endosatario /endosaˈtario/ **-ria** n. endorsee.

endulzar /endulˈθar; endulˈsar/ v. sweeten; soothe.

endurar /enduˈrar/ v. harden.

endurecer /endureˈθer; endureˈser/ v. harden.

enemigo /eneˈmigo/ **-ga** n. foe, enemy.

enemistad /enemisˈtað/ n. f. enmity.

éneo /ˈeneo/ a. brass.

energía /enerˈhia/ n. f. energy.

energía nuclear /enerˈhia nukleˈar/ atomic energy, nuclear energy.

energía vital /enerˈhia biˈtal/ élan vital, vitality.

enérgicamente /eˈnerhikamente/ adv. energetically.

enérgico /eˈnerhiko/ a. forceful; energetic.

enero /eˈnero/ n. m. January.

enervación /enerβaˈθion; enerβaˈsion/ n. f. enervation.

enfadado /enfaˈðaðo/ a. angry.

enfadar /enfaˈðar/ v. anger, vex.

enfado /enˈfaðo/ n. m. anger, vexation.

énfasis /ˈenfasis/ n. m. or f. emphasis, stress.

enfáticamente /enˈfatikamente/ adv. emphatically.

enfático /enˈfatiko/ a. emphatic.

enfermar /enferˈmar/ v. make ill; fall ill.

enfermedad /enfermeˈðað/ n. f. illness, sickness, disease.

enfermera /enferˈmera/ n. f. nurse.

enfermería /enfermeˈria/ n. f. sanatorium.

enfermo /enˈfermo/ **-ma** a. & n. ill, sick; sickly; patient.

enfilar /enfiˈlar/ v. line up; put in a row.

enflaquecer /enflakeˈθer; enflakeˈser/ v. make thin; grow thin.

enfoque /enˈfoke/ n. m. focus. —enfocar, v.

enfrascamiento /enfraskaˈmiento/ n. m. entanglement.

enfrascar /enfrasˈkar/ v. bottle; entangle oneself.

enfrenar /enfreˈnar/ v. bridle, curb; restrain.

enfrentamiento /enfrentaˈmiento/ n. m. clash, confrontation.

enfrente /enˈfrente/ adv. across, opposite; in front.

enfriadera /enfriaˈðera/ n. f. icebox; cooler.

enfriar /enfˈriar/ v. chill, cool.

enfurecer /enfureˈθer; enfureˈser/ v. infuriate, enrage.

engalanar /eŋgalaˈnar/ v. adorn, trim.

enganchar /eŋganˈtʃar/ v. hook, hitch, attach.

engañar /eŋgaˈɲar/ v. deceive, cheat.

engaño /eŋˈgaɲo/ n. m. deceit; delusion.

engañoso /eŋgaˈɲoso/ a. deceitful.

engarce /eŋˈgarθe; eŋgarˈse/ n. m. connection, link.

engastar /eŋgasˈtar/ v. to put (gems) in a setting.

engaste /eŋˈgaste/ n. m. setting.

engatusar /eŋgatuˈsar/ v. deceive, trick.

engendrar /enhenˈdrar/ v. engender, beget, produce.

engendro /enˈhendro/ n. m. fetus, embryo.

englobar /eŋgloˈβar/ v. include.

engolfar /eŋgolˈfar/ v. be deeply absorbed.

engolosinar /eŋgolosiˈnar/ v. allure, charm, entice.

engomar /eŋgoˈmar/ v. gum.

engordador /eŋgorðaˈðor/ a. fattening.

engordar /eŋgorˈðar/ v. fatten; grow fat.

engranaje /eŋgraˈnahe/ n. m. Mech. gear.

engranar /eŋgraˈnar/ v. gear; mesh together.

engrandecer /eŋgrandeˈθer; eŋgrandeˈser/ v. increase, enlarge; exalt; exaggerate.

engrasación /eŋgrasaˈθion; eŋgrasaˈsion/ n. f. lubrication.

engrasar /eŋgraˈsar/ v. grease, lubricate.

engreído /eŋgreˈiðo/ a. conceited.

engreimiento /eŋgreiˈmiento/ n. m. conceit.

engullidor /eŋguʎiˈðor; eŋguyiˈðor/ **-ra** n. devourer.

engullir /eŋguˈʎir; eŋguˈyir/ v. devour.

enhebrar /eneˈβrar/ v. thread.

enhestadura /enestaˈðura/ n. f. raising.

enhestar /enesˈtar/ v. raise, erect, set up.

enhiesto /enˈiesto/ a. erect, upright.

enhorabuena /enoraˈβuena/ n. f. congratulations.

enigma /eˈnigma/ n. m. enigma, puzzle.

enigmáticamente /enigmatikaˈmente/ adv. enigmatically.

enigmático /enigˈmatiko/ a. enigmatic.

enjabonar /enhaβoˈnar/ v. soap, lather.

enjalbegar /enhalβeˈgar/ v. whitewash.

enjambradera /enhambraˈðera/ n. f. queen bee.

enjambre /enˈhambre/ n. m. swarm. —enjambrar, v.

enjaular /enhauˈlar/ v. cage, coop up.

enjebe /enˈheβe/ n. m. lye.

enjuagar /enhuaˈgar/ v. rinse.

enjuague bucal /enˈhuage buˈkal/ n. m. mouthwash.

enjugar /enhuˈgar/ v. wipe, dry off.

enjutez /enhuˈteθ; enhuˈtes/ n. f. dryness.

enjuto /enˈhuto/ a. dried; lean, thin.

enlace /enˈlaθe; enˈlase/ n. m. attachment; involvement; connection.

enladrillador /enlaðriʎaˈðor; enlaðriyaˈðor/ **-ra** n. bricklayer.

enlardar /enlarˈðar/ v. baste.

enlatado /enlaˈtaðo/ **-da** a. canned (food).

enlatar /enlaˈtar/ v. can (food).

enlazar /enlaˈθar; enlaˈsar/ v. lace; join, connect; wed.

enlodar /enloˈðar/ v. cover with mud.

enloquecer /enlokeˈθer; enlokeˈser/ v. go insane; drive crazy.

enloquecimiento /enlokeθiˈmiento; enlokesiˈmiento/ n. m. insanity.

enlustrecer /enlustreˈθer; enlustreˈser/ v. polish, brighten.

enmarañar /emaraˈɲar/ v. entangle.

enmendación /emendaˈθion; emendaˈsion/ n. f. emendation.

enmendador /emendaˈðor/ **-ra** n. emender, reviser.

enmendar /emenˈdar/ v. amend, correct.

enmienda /eˈmienda/ n. f. amendment; correction.

enmohecer /emoeˈθer; emoeˈser/ v. rust; mold.

enmohecido /emoeˈθiðo; emoeˈsiðo/ a. rusty; moldy.

enmudecer /emuðeˈθer; emuðeˈser/ v. silence; become silent.

ennegrecer /ennegreˈθer; ennegreˈser/ v. blacken.

ennoblecer /ennoβleˈθer; ennoβleˈser/ v. ennoble.

enodio /eˈnoðio/ n. m. young deer.

enojado /enoˈhaðo/ a. angry, cross.

enojarse /enoˈharse/ v. get angry.

enojo /eˈnoho/ n. m. anger. —enojar, v.

enojosamente /enohosaˈmente/ adv. angrily.

enorme /eˈnorme/ a. enormous, huge.

enormemente /enormeˈmente/ adv. enormously; hugely.

enormidad /enormiˈðað/ n. f. enormity; hugeness.

enraizar /enraiˈθar; enraiˈsar/ v. take root, sprout.

enramada /enraˈmaða/ n. f. bower.

enredadera /enreðaˈðera/ n. f. climbing plant.

enredado /enreˈðaðo/ a. entangled, snarled.

enredar /enreˈðar/ v. entangle, snarl; mess up.

enredo /enˈreðo/ n. m. tangle, entanglement.

enriquecer /enrikeˈθer; enrikeˈser/ v. enrich.

enrojecerse /enroheˈθerse; enroheˈserse/ v. color; blush.

enrollar /enroˈʎar; enroˈyar/ v. wind, coil, roll up.

enromar /enroˈmar/ v. make dull, blunt.

enronquecimiento /enronkeθiˈmiento; enronkesiˈmiento/ n. m. hoarseness.

enroscar /enrosˈkar/ v. twist, curl, wind.

ensacar /ensaˈkar/ v. put in a bag.

ensalada /ensaˈlaða/ n. f. salad.

ensaladera /ensalaˈðera/ n. f. salad bowl.

ensalmo /enˈsalmo/ n. m. charm, enchantment.

ensalzamiento /ensalθaˈmiento; ensalsaˈmiento/ n. m. praise.

ensalzar /ensalˈθar; ensalˈsar/ v. praise, laud, extol.

ensamblar /ensamˈblar/ v. join; unite; connect.

ensanchamiento /ensantʃaˈmiento/ n. m. widening, expansion, extension.

ensanchar /ensanˈtʃar/ v. widen, expand, extend.

ensangrentado /ensaŋgrenˈtaðo/ a. bloody; bloodshot.

ensañar /ensaˈɲar/ v. enrage, infuriate; rage.

ensayar /ensaˈyar/ v. try out; rehearse.

ensayista /ensaˈyista/ n. m. & f. essayist.

ensayo /enˈsayo/ n. m. attempt; trial; rehearsal.

ensenada /enseˈnaða/ n. f. cove.

enseña /enˈseɲa/ n. f. ensign, standard.

enseñador /enseɲaˈðor/ **-ra** n. teacher.

enseñanza /enseˈɲanθa; enseˈɲansa/ n. f. education; teaching.

enseñar /enseˈɲar/ v. teach, train; show.

enseres /enˈseres/ n. m.pl. household goods.

ensilaje /ensiˈlahe/ n. m. ensilage.

ensillar /ensiˈʎar; ensiˈyar/ v. saddle.

ensordecedor /ensorðeθeˈðor; ensorðeseˈðor/ a. deafening.

ensordecer /ensorðeˈθer; ensorðeˈser/ v. deafen.

ensordecimiento /ensorðeθiˈmiento; ensorðesiˈmiento/ n. m. deafness.

ensuciar /ensuˈθiar; ensuˈsiar/ v. dirty, muddy, soil.

ensueño /enˈsueɲo/ n. m. illusion, dream.

entablar /entaˈβlar/ v. board up; initiate, begin.

entallador /entaʎaˈðor; entayaˈðor/ n. m. sculptor, carver.

entapizar /entapiˈθar; entapiˈsar/ v. upholster.

ente /ˈente/ n. m. being.

entenada /enteˈnaða/ n. f. stepdaughter.

entenado /enteˈnaðo/ n. m. stepson.

entender /entenˈder/ v. understand.

entendimiento /entendiˈmiento/ n. m. understanding.

entenebrecer /enteneβreˈθer; enteneβreˈser/ v. darken.

enterado /enteˈraðo/ a. aware, informed.

enteramente /enteraˈmente/ adv. entirely, completely.

enterar /enteˈrar/ v. inform.

enterarse /enteˈrarse/ v. find out.

entereza /enteˈreθa; enteˈresa/ n. f. entirety; integrity; firmness.

entero /enˈtero/ a. entire, whole, total.

enterramiento /enterraˈmiento/ n. m. burial, interment.

enterrar /enteˈrrar/ v. bury.

entestado /entesˈtaðo/ a. stubborn, willful.

entibiar /entiˈβiar/ v. to cool; moderate.

entidad /entiˈðað/ n. f. entity.

entierro /enˈtierro/ n. m. interment, burial.

entonación /entonaˈθion; entonaˈsion/ n. f. intonation.

entonamiento /entonaˈmiento/ n. m. intonation.

entonar /entoˈnar/ v. chant; harmonize.

entonces /enˈtonθes; entonses/ adv. then.

entono /enˈtono/ n. m. intonation; arrogance; affectation.

entortadura /entortaˈðura/ n. f. crookedness.

entortar /entorˈtar/ v. make crooked; bend.

entrada /enˈtraða/ n. f. entrance; admission, admittance.

entrambos /enˈtrambos/ a. & pron. both.

entrante /enˈtrante/ a. coming, next.

entrañable /entraˈɲaβle/ a. affectionate.

entrañas /enˈtraɲas/ n. f.pl. entrails, bowels; womb.

entrar /enˈtrar/ v. enter, go in, come in.

entre /ˈentre/ prep. among; between.

entreabierto /entreaˈβierto/ a. ajar, half-open.

entreabrir /entreaˈβrir/ v. set ajar.

entreacto /entreˈakto/ n. m. intermission.

entrecejo /entreˈθeho; entreˈseho/ n. m. frown; space between the eyebrows.

entrecuesto /entreˈkuesto/ n. m. spine, backbone.

entredicho /entreˈðitʃo/ n. m. prohibition.

entrega /enˈtrega/ n. f. delivery.

entregar /entreˈgar/ v. deliver, hand; hand over.

entrelazar /entrelaˈθar; entrelaˈsar/ v. intertwine, entwine.

entremedias /entreˈmedias/ adv. meanwhile; halfway.

entremés /entreˈmes/ n. m. side dish.

entremeterse /entremeˈterse/ v. meddle, intrude.

entremetido /entremeˈtiðo/ **-da** n. meddler.

entrenador /entrena'ðor/ **-ra** n. coach. —**entrenar,** v.

entrenarse /entre'narse/ v. train.

entrepalado /entrepa'laðo/ a. variegated; spotted.

entrerenglonar /entrereŋglo'nar/ v. interline.

entresacar /entresa'kar/ v. select, choose; sift.

entresuelo /entre'suelo/ n. m. mezzanine.

entretanto /entre'tanto/ adv. meanwhile.

entretenedor /entretene'ðor/ **-ra** n. entertainer.

entretener /entrete'ner/ v. entertain, amuse; delay.

entretenimiento /entreteni'miento/ n. m. entertainment, amusement.

entrevista /entre'βista/ n. f. interview. —**entrevistar,** v.

entrevistador /entreβista'ðor/ **-ra** n. interviewer.

entristecedor /entristeθe'ðor/ entristese'ðor/ a. sad.

entristecer /entriste'θer; entriste'ser/ v. sadden.

entronar /entro'nar/ v. enthrone.

entroncar /entron'kar/ v. be related or connected.

entronización /entroniθa'θion; entronisa'sion/ n. f. enthronement.

entronque /entron'ke/ n. m. relationship; connection.

entumecer /entume'θer; entume'ser/ v. become or be numb; swell.

entusiasmado /entusias'maðo/ a. enthusiastic.

entusiasmo /entu'siasmo/ n. m. enthusiasm.

entusiasta /entu'siasta/ n. m. & f. enthusiast.

entusiástico /entu'siastiko/ a. enthusiastic.

enumeración /enumera'θion; enumera'sion/ n. f. enumeration.

enumerar /enume'rar/ v. enumerate.

enunciación /enunθia'θion; enunsia'sion/ n. f. enunciation; statement.

enunciar /enun'θiar; enun'siar/ v. enunciate.

envainar /embai'nar/ v. sheathe.

envalentonar /embalento'nar/ v. encourage, embolden.

envanecimiento /embaneθimiento; embanesi'miento/ n. m. conceit, vanity.

envasar /emba'sar/ v. put in a container; bottle.

envase /em'base/ n. m. container.

envejecer /embehe'θer; embehe'ser/ v. age, grow old.

envejecimiento /embeheθi'miento; embehesi'miento/ n. m. oldness, aging.

envenenar /embene'nar/ v. poison.

envés /em'bes/ n. m. wrong side; back.

envestir /embes'tir/ v. put in office; invest.

enviada /em'biaða/ n. f. shipment.

enviado /em'biaðo/ **-da** n. envoy.

enviar /em'biar/ v. send; ship.

envidia /em'biðia/ n. f. envy. —**envidiar,** v.

envidiable /embi'ðiaβle/ a. enviable.

envidioso /embi'ðioso/ a. envious.

envilecer /embile'θer; embile'ser/ v. vilify, debase, disgrace.

envío /em'bio/ n. m. shipment.

envión /em'bion/ n. m. shove.

envoltura /embol'tura/ n. f. wrapping.

envolver /embol'βer/ v. wrap, wrap up.

enyesar /enye'sar/ v. plaster.

enyugar /enyu'gar/ v. yoke.

eperlano /eper'lano/ n. m. smelt (fish).

épica /'epika/ n. f. epic.

épico /'epiko/ a. epic.

epicureísmo /epikure'ismo/ n. m. epicureanism.

epicúreo /epi'kureo/ n. & a. epicurean.

epidemia /epi'ðemia/ n. f. epidemic.

epidémico /epi'ðemiko/ a. epidemic.

epidermis /epi'ðermis/ n. f. epidermis.

epigrama /epi'grama/ n. m. epigram.

epigramático /epigra'matiko/ **-ca** a. epigrammatic.

epilepsia /epi'lepsia/ n. f. epilepsy.

epiléptico /epi'leptiko/ **-ca** n. & a. epileptic.

epílogo /e'pilogo/ n. m. epilogue.

episcopado /episko'paðo/ n. m. bishopric; episcopate.

episcopal /episko'pal/ a. episcopal.

episódico /epi'soðiko/ a. episodic.

episodio /epi'soðio/ n. m. episode.

epístola /e'pistola/ n. f. epistle, letter.

epitafio /epi'tafio/ n. m. epitaph.

epitomadamente /epitomaða'mente/ adv. concisely.

epitomar /epito'mar/ v. epitomize, summarize.

época /'epoka/ n. f. epoch, age.

epopeya /epo'peya/ n. f. epic.

epsomita /epso'mita/ n. f. Epsom salts.

equidad /eki'ðað/ n. f. equity.

equilibrado /ekili'βraðo/ a. stable.

equilibrio /eki'liβrio/ n. m. equilibrium, balance.

equinoccio /eki'nokθio; ekinoksio/ n. m. equinox.

equipaje /eki'pahe/ n. m. luggage, baggage. **e. de mano,** luggage.

equipar /eki'par/ v. equip.

equiparar /ekipa'rar/ v. compare.

equipo /e'kipo/ n. m. equipment; team.

equitación /ekita'θion; ekita'sion/ f. horsemanship; horseback riding, riding.

equitativo /ekita'tiβo/ a. fair, equitable.

equivalencia /ekiβa'lenθia; ekiβa'lensia/ n. f. equivalence.

equivalente /ekiβa'lente/ a. equivalent.

equivaler /ekiβa'ler/ v. equal, be equivalent.

equivocación /ekiβoka'θion; ekiβoka'sion/ n. f. mistake.

equivocado /ekiβo'kaðo/ a. wrong, mistaken.

equivocarse /ekiβo'karse/ v. make a mistake, be wrong.

equívoco /e'kiβoko/ a. equivocal, ambiguous.

era /'era/ n. f. era, age.

erario /e'rario/ n. m. exchequer.

erección /erek'θion; erek'sion/ n. f. erection; elevation.

eremita /ere'mita/ n. m. hermit.

erguir /er'gir/ v. erect; straighten up.

erigir /eri'hir/ v. erect, build.

erisipela /erisi'pela/ n. f. erysipelas.

erizado /eri'θaðo; eri'saðo/ a. bristly.

erizarse /eri'θarse; eri'sarse/ v. bristle.

erizo /e'riθo; e'riso/ n. m. hedgehog; sea urchin.

ermita /er'mita/ n. f. hermitage.

ermitaño /ermi'taɲo/ n. m. hermit.

erogación /eroga'θion; eroga'sion/ n. f. expenditure. —**erogar,** v.

erosión /ero'sion/ n. f. erosion.

erótico /e'rotiko/ a. erotic.

erradicación /erraðika'θion; erraðika'sion/ n. f. eradication.

erradicar /erraði'kar/ v. eradicate.

errado /e'rraðo/ a. mistaken, erroneous.

errante /e'rrante/ a. wandering, roving.

errar /e'rrar/ v. be mistaken.

errata /e'rrata/ n. f. erratum.

errático /e'rratiko/ a. erratic.

erróneamente /erronea'mente/ adv. erroneously.

erróneo /e'rroneo/ a. erroneous.

error /e'rror/ n. m. error, mistake.

eructo /e'rukto/ n. m. belch. —**eructar,** v.

erudición /eruði'θion; eruði'sion/ n. f. scholarship, learning.

eruditamente /eruðita'mente/ adv. learnedly.

erudito /eru'ðito/ **-ta** n. **1.** scholar. —a. **2.** scholarly.

erupción /erup'θion; erup'sion/ n. f. eruption; rash.

eruptivo /erup'tiβo/ a. eruptive.

esbozo /es'βoθo; es'βoso/ n. m. outline, sketch. —**esbozar,** v.

escabechar /eskaβe't∫ar/ v. pickle; preserve.

escabeche /eska'βet∫e/ n. m. brine.

escabel /eska'βel/ n. m. small stool or bench.

escabroso /eska'βroso/ a. rough, irregular; craggy; rude.

escabullirse /eskaβu'ʎirse; eskaβu'yirse/ v. steal away, sneak away.

escala /es'kala/ n. f. scale; ladder. **hacer e.,** to make a stop.

escalada /eska'laða/ n. f. escalation.

escalador /eskala'ðor/ **-ra** n. climber.

escalar /eska'lar/ v. climb; scale.

escaldar /eskal'dar/ v. scald.

escalera /eska'lera/ n. f. stairs, staircase; ladder.

escalfado /eskal'faðo/ a. poached.

escalofriado /eskalo'friaðo/ a. chilled.

escalofrío /eskalo'frio/ n. m. chill.

escalón /eska'lon/ n. m. step.

escalonar /eskalo'nar/ v. space out, stagger.

escaloña /eska'loɲa/ n. f. scallion.

escalpar /eskal'par/ v. scalp.

escalpelo /eskal'pelo/ n. m. scalpel.

escama /es'kama/ n. f. (fish) scale. —**escamar,** v.

escamondar /eskamon'dar/ v. trim, cut; prune.

escampada /eskam'paða/ n. f. break in the rain, clear spell.

escandalizar /eskandali'θar; eskandali'sar/ v. shock, scandalize.

escandalizativo /eskandaliθa'tiβo; eskandalisa'tiβo/ a. scandalous.

escándalo /es'kandalo/ n. m. scandal.

escandaloso /eskanda'loso/ a. scandalous; disgraceful.

escandinavo /eskandi'naβo/ **-va** n. & a. Scandinavian.

escandir /eskan'dir/ v. scan.

escanear /eskane'ar/ v. scan (on a computer).

escáner /es'kaner/ v. scanner (of a computer).

escanilla /eska'niʎa; eska'niya/ n. f. cradle.

escañuelo /eska'ɲuelo/ n. m. small footstool.

escapada /eska'paða/ n. f. escapade.

escapar /eska'par/ v. escape.

escaparate /eskapa'rate/ n. m. shop window, store window.

escape /es'kape/ n. m. escape; Auto. exhaust.

escápula /es'kapula/ n. f. scapula.

escarabajo /eskara'βaho/ n. m. black beetle; scarab.

escaramucear /eskaramuθe'ar; eskaramuse'ar/ v. skirmish; dispute.

escarbadientes /eskarβa'ðientes/ n. m. toothpick.

escarbar /eskar'βar/ v. scratch; poke.

escarcha /es'kart∫a/ n. f. frost.

escardar /eskar'ðar/ v. weed.

escarlata /eskar'lata/ n. f. scarlet.

escarlatina /eskarla'tina/ n. f. scarlet fever.

escarmentar /eskarmen'tar/ v. correct severely.

escarnecedor /eskarneθe'ðor; eskarneseðor/ **-ra** n. scoffer; mocker.

escarnecer /eskarne'θer; eskarne'ser/ v. mock, make fun of.

escarola /eska'rola/ n. f. endive.

escarpa /es'karpa/ n. m. escarpment.

escarpado /eskar'paðo/ a. **1.** steep. —n. **2.** m. bluff.

escasamente /eskasa'mente/ adv. scarcely; sparingly; barely.

escasear /eskase'ar/ v. be scarce.

escasez /eska'seθ; eska'ses/ n. f. shortage, scarcity.

escaso /es'kaso/ a. scant; scarce.

escatimar /eskati'mar/ v. be stingy, skimp; save.

escatimoso /eskati'moso/ a. malicious; sly, cunning.

escena /es'θena; es'sena/ n. f. scene; stage.

escenario /esθe'nario; esse'nario/ n. m. stage (of theater); scenario.

escénico /es'θeniko; es'seniko/ a. scenic.

escépticamente /esθeptika'mente; esseptika'mente/ adv. skeptically.

escepticismo /esθepti'θismo; essepti'sismo/ n. m. skepticism.

escéptico /es'θeptiko; es'septiko/ **-ca** a. & n. skeptic; skeptical.

esclarecer /esklare'θer; esklare'ser/ v. clear up.

esclavitud /esklaβi'tuð/ n. f. slavery; bondage.

esclavizar /esklaβi'θar; esklaβi'sar/ v. enslave.

esclavo /es'klaβo/ **-va** n. slave.

escoba /es'koβa/ n. f. broom.

escocés /esko'θes; esko'ses/ **-esa** a. & n. Scotch, Scottish; Scot.

Escocia /es'koθia; eskosia/ n. f. Scotland.

escofinar /eskofi'nar/ v. rasp.

escoger /esko'her/ v. choose, select.

escogido /esko'hiðo/ a. chosen, selected.

escogimiento /eskohi'miento/ n. m. choice.

escolar /esko'lar/ a. **1.** scholastic, (of) school. —n. **2.** m.& f. student.

escolasticismo /eskolasti'θismo; eskolasti'sismo/ n. m. scholasticism.

escollo /es'koʎo; es'koyo/ n. m. reef.

escolta /es'kolta/ n. f. escort. —**escoltar,** v.

escombro /es'kombro/ n. m. mackerel.

escombros /es'kombros/ n. m.pl. debris, rubbish.

esconce /es'konθe; es'konse/ n. m. corner.

escondedero /eskonde'ðero/ n. m. hiding place.

esconder /eskon'der/ v. hide, conceal.

escondidamente /eskondiða'mente/ adv. secretly.

escondimiento /eskondi'miento/ n. m. concealment.

escondrijo /eskon'driho/ n. m. hiding place.

escopeta /esko'peta/ n. f. shotgun.

escopetazo /eskope'taθo; eskope'taso/ n. m. gunshot.

escoplo /es'koplo/ n. m. chisel.

escorbuto /eskor'βuto/ n. m. scurvy.

escorpena /eskor'pena/ n. f. grouper.

escorpión /eskor'pion/ n. m. scorpion.

escorzón /eskor'θon; eskor'son/ n. m. toad.

escotado /esko'taðo/ a. low-cut, with a low neckline.

escote /es'kote/ n. m. low neckline.

escribiente /eskri'βiente/ n. m. & f. clerk.

escribir /eskri'βir/ v. write.

escritor /eskri'tor/ **-ra** n. writer, author.

escritorio /eskri'torio/ n. m. desk.

escritura /eskri'tura/ n. f. writing, handwriting.

escrófula /es'krofula/ n. f. scrofula.

escroto /es'kroto/ n. m. scrotum.

escrúpulo /es'krupulo/ n. m. scruple.

escrupuloso /eskrupu'loso/ a. scrupulous.

escrutinio /eskru'tinio/ n. m. scrutiny; examination.

escuadra /es'kuaðra/ *n. f.* squad; fleet.

escuadrón /eskuaðˈron/ *n. m.* squadron.

escualidez /eskualiˈðeθ; eskualiˈðes/ *n. f.* squalor; poverty; emaciation.

escuálido /es'kualiðo/ *a.* squalid.

escualo /es'kualo/ *n. m.* shark.

escuchar /esku'tʃar/ *v.* listen; listen to.

escudero /esku'ðero/ *n. m.* squire.

escudo /es'kuðo/ *n. m.* shield; protection; coin of certain countries.

escuela /es'kuela/ *n. f.* school.

escuela nocturna /es'kuela nokˈturna/ night school.

escuela por correspondencia /es'kuela por korresponˈdenθia; es'kuela por korresponˈdensia/ correspondence school.

escuerzo /es'kuerθo; es'kuerso/ *n. m.* toad.

esculpir /eskul'pir/ *v.* carve, sculpture.

escultor /eskul'tor/ **-ra** *n.* sculptor.

escultura /eskul'tura/ *n. f.* sculpture.

escupidera /eskupi'ðera/ *n. f.* cuspidor.

escupir /esku'pir/ *v.* spit.

escurridero /eskurri'ðero/ *n. m.* drain board.

escurridor /eskurri'ðor/ *n. m.* colander, strainer.

escurrir /esku'rrir/ *v.* drain off; wring out.

escurrirse /esku'rrirse/ *v.* slip; sneak away.

ese /'ese/ **esa** *dem. a.* that.

ése, ésa *dem. pron.* that (one).

esencia /e'senθia; e'sensia/ *n. f.* essence; perfume.

esencial /esen'θial; esen'sial/ *a.* essential.

esencialmente /esenθial'mente; esensial'mente/ *adv.* essentially.

esfera /es'fera/ *n. f.* sphere.

esfinge /es'finhe/ *n. f.* sphinx.

esforzar /esfor'θar; esfor'sar/ *v.* strengthen.

esforzarse /esfor'θarse; esfor'sarse/ *v.* strive, exert oneself.

esfuerzo /es'fuerθo; es'fuerso/ *n. m.* effort, attempt; vigor.

esgrima /es'grima/ *n. f.* fencing.

esguince /es'ginθe; es'ginse/ *n. m.* sprain.

eslabón /esla'ßon/ *n. m.* link (of a chain).

eslabonar /eslaßo'nar/ *v.* link, join, connect.

eslavo /es'laßo/ **-va** *a. & n.* Slavic; Slav.

esmalte /es'malte/ *n. m.* enamel, polish. —**esmaltar,** *v.*

esmerado /esme'raðo/ *a.* careful, thorough.

esmeralda /esme'ralda/ *n. f.* emerald.

esmerarse /esme'rarse/ *v.* take pains, do one's best.

esmeril /es'meril/ *n. m.* emery.

eso /'eso/ *dem. pron.* that.

esófago /e'sofago/ *n. m.* esophagus.

esotérico /eso'teriko/ *a.* esoteric.

espacial /espa'θial; espa'sial/ *a.* spatial.

espacio /es'paθio; es'pasio/ *n. m.* space. —**espaciar,** *v.*

espaciosidad /espaθiosi'ðað; espasiosi'ðað/ *n. f.* spaciousness.

espacioso /espa'θioso; espa'sioso/ *a.* spacious.

espada /es'paða/ *n. f.* sword; spade (in cards).

espadarte /espa'ðarte/ *n. m.* swordfish.

espaguetis /espa'getis/ *n. m.pl.* spaghetti.

espalda /es'palda/ *n. f.* back.

espaldera /espal'dera/ *n. f.* espalier.

espantar /espan'tar/ *v.* frighten, scare; scare away.

espanto /es'panto/ *n. m.* fright.

espantoso /espan'toso/ *a.* frightening, frightful.

España /es'paɲa/ *n. f.* Spain.

español /espa'ɲol/ **-ola** *a. & n.* Spanish; Spaniard.

esparcir /espar'θir; espar'sir/ *v.* scatter, disperse.

espárrago /es'parrago/ *n. m.* asparagus.

espartano /espar'tano/ **-na** *n. & a.* Spartan.

espasmo /es'pasmo/ *n. m.* spasm.

espasmódico /espas'moðiko/ *a.* spasmodic.

espata /es'pata/ *n. f.* spathe.

espato /es'pato/ *n. m.* spar (mineral).

espátula /es'patula/ *n. f.* spatula.

especia /es'peθia; es'pesia/ *n. f.* spice. —**especiar,** *v.*

especial /espe'θial; espe'sial/ *a.* special, especial.

especialidad /espeθiali'ðað; espesiali'ðað/ *n. f.* specialty.

especialista /espeθia'lista; espesia'lista/ *n. m. & f.* specialist.

especialización /espeθialiθa'θion; espesialisa'sion/ *n. f.* specialization.

especialmente /espeθial'mente; espesial'mente/ *adv.* especially.

especie /es'peθie; es'pesie/ *n. f.* species; sort.

especiería /espeθie'ria; espesie'ria/ *n. f.* grocery store; spice store.

especiero /espe'θiero; espe'siero/ **-ra** *n.* spice dealer; spice box.

especificar /espeθifi'kar; espesifi'kar/ *v.* specify.

específico /espe'θifiko; espe'sifiko/ *a.* specific.

espécimen /es'peθimen; es'pesimen/ *n. m.* specimen.

especioso /espe'θioso; espe'sioso/ *a.* neat; polished; specious.

espectacular /espektaku'lar/ *a.* spectacular.

espectáculo /espek'takulo/ *n. m.* spectacle, show.

espectador /espekta'ðor/ **-ra** *n.* spectator.

espectro /es'pektro/ *n. m.* specter, ghost.

especulación /espekula'θion; espekula'sion/ *n. f.* speculation.

especulador /espekula'ðor/ **-ra** *n.* speculator.

especular /espeku'lar/ *v.* speculate.

especulativo /espekula'tißo/ *a.* speculative.

espejo /es'peho/ *n. m.* mirror.

espelunca /espe'lunka/ *n. f.* dark cave, cavern.

espera /es'pera/ *n. f.* wait.

esperanza /espe'ranθa; espe'ransa/ *n. f.* hope, expectation.

esperar /espe'rar/ *v.* hope; expect; wait, wait for, watch for.

espesar /espe'sar/ *v.* thicken.

espeso /es'peso/ *a.* thick, dense, bushy.

espesor /espe'sor/ *n. m.* thickness, density.

espía /es'pia/ *n. m. & f.* spy. —**espiar,** *v.*

espigón /espi'gon/ *n. m.* bee sting.

espina /es'pina/ *n. f.* thorn.

espinaca /espi'naka/ *n. f.* spinach.

espina dorsal /es'pina dor'sal/ spine.

espinal /espi'nal/ *a.* spinal.

espinazo /espi'naθo; espi'naso/ *n. m.* backbone.

espineta /espi'neta/ *n. f.* spinet.

espino /es'pino/ *n. m.* briar.

espinoso /espi'noso/ *a.* spiny, thorny.

espión /es'pion/ *n. m.* spy.

espionaje /espio'nahe/ *n. m.* espionage.

espiral /espi'ral/ *a. & m.* spiral.

espirar /espi'rar/ *v.* expire; breathe, exhale.

espíritu /es'piritu/ *n. m.* spirit.

espiritual /espiri'tual/ *a.* spiritual.

espiritualidad /espirituali'ðað/ *n. f.* spirituality.

espiritualmente /espiritual'mente/ *adv.* spiritually.

espita /es'pita/ *n. f.* faucet, spigot.

espléndido /es'plendiðo/ *a.* splendid.

esplendor /esplen'dor/ *n. m.* splendor.

espolear /espole'ar/ *v.* incite, urge on.

espoleta /espo'leta/ *n. f.* wishbone.

esponja /es'ponha/ *n. f.* sponge.

esponjoso /espon'hoso/ *a.* spongy.

esponsales /espon'sales/ *n. m.pl.* engagement, betrothal.

esponsalicio /esponsa'liθio; esponsa'lisio/ *a.* nuptial.

espontáneamente /espontanea'mente/ *adv.* spontaneously.

espontaneidad /espontanei'ðað/ *n. f.* spontaneity.

espontáneo /espon'taneo/ *a.* spontaneous.

espora /es'pora/ *n. f.* spore.

esporádico /espo'raðiko/ *a.* sporadic.

esposa /es'posa/ *n. f.* wife.

esposar /espo'sar/ *v.* shackle; handcuff.

esposo /es'poso/ *n. m.* husband.

espuela /es'puela/ *n. f.* spur. —**espolear,** *v.*

espuma /es'puma/ *n. f.* foam. —**espumar,** *v.*

espumadera /espuma'ðera/ *n. f.* whisk; skimmer.

espumajear /espumahe'ar/ *v.* foam at the mouth.

espumajo /espu'maho/ *n. m.* foam.

espumar /espu'mar/ *v.* foam, froth; skim.

espumoso /espu'moso/ *a.* foamy; sparkling (wine).

espurio /es'purio/ *a.* spurious.

esputar /espu'tar/ *v.* spit, expectorate.

esputo /es'puto/ *n. m.* spit, saliva.

esquela /es'kela/ *n. f.* note.

esqueleto /eske'leto/ *n. m.* skeleton.

esquema /es'kema/ *n. f.* scheme; diagram.

esquero /es'kero/ *n. m.* leather sack, leather pouch.

esquiar /es'kiar/ *v.* ski.

esquiciar /eski'θiar; eski'siar/ *v.* outline, sketch.

esquicio /es'kiθio; es'kisio/ *n. m.* rough sketch, rough outline.

esquife /es'kife/ *n. m.* skiff.

esquilar /eski'lar/ *v.* fleece, shear.

esquilmo /es'kilmo/ *v.* harvest.

esquimal /eski'mal/ *n. & a.* Eskimo.

esquina /es'kina/ *n. f.* corner.

esquivar /eski'ßar/ *v.* evade, shun.

estabilidad /estaßili'ðað/ *n. f.* stability.

estable /es'taßle/ *a.* stable.

establecedor /estaßleθe'ðor; estaßlese'ðor/ *n. m.* founder, originator.

establecer /estaßle'θer; estaßle'ser/ *v.* establish, set up.

establecimiento /estaßleθi'miento; estaßlesi'miento/ *n. m.* establishment.

establero /estaß'lero/ *n. m.* groom.

establo /es'taßlo/ *n. m.* stable.

estaca /es'taka/ *n. f.* stake.

estación /esta'θion; esta'sion/ *n. f.* station; season.

estacionamiento /estaθiona'miento; estasiona'miento/ *n. m.* parking; parking lot; parking space.

estacionar /estaθio'nar; estasio'nar/ *v.* station; park (a vehicle).

estacionario /estaθio'nario; estasio'nario/ *a.* stationary.

estación de servicio /esta'θion de ser'ßiθio; esta'sion de ser'ßisio/ service station.

estación de trabajo /esta'θion de tra'ßaho; esta'sion de tra'ßaho/ work station.

estadista /esta'ðista/ *n. m. & f.* statesman.

estadística /esta'ðistika/ *n. f.* statistics.

estadístico /esta'ðistiko/ *a.* statistical.

estado /es'taðo/ *n. m.* state; condition; status.

Estados Unidos /es'taðos u'niðos/ *n. m.pl.* United States.

estafa /es'tafa/ *n. f.* swindle, fake. —**estafar,** *v.*

estafeta /esta'feta/ *n. f.* post office.

estagnación /estagna'θion; estagna'sion/ *n. f.* stagnation.

estallar /esta'ʎar; esta'yar/ *v.* explode; burst; break out.

estallido /esta'ʎiðo; esta'yiðo/ *n. m.* crash; crack; explosion.

estampa /es'tampa/ *n. f.* stamp. —**estampar,** *v.*

estampado /estam'paðo/ *n. m.* printed cotton cloth.

estampida /estam'piða/ *n. f.* stampede.

estampilla /estam'piʎa; estam'piya/ *n. f.* (postage) stamp.

estancado /estan'kaðo/ *a.* stagnant.

estancar /estan'kar/ *v.* stanch, stop, check.

estancia /es'tanθia; es'tansia/ *n. f.* stay; (S.A.) small farm.

estanciero /estan'θiero; estan'siero/ **-ra** *n.* small farmer.

estandarte /estan'darte/ *n. m.* banner.

estanque /es'tanke/ *n. m.* pool; pond.

estante /es'tante/ *n. m.* shelf.

estaño /es'taɲo/ *n. m.* tin. —**estañar,** *v.*

estar /es'tar/ *v.* be; stand; look.

estática /es'tatika/ *n. f.* static.

estático /es'tatiko/ *a.* static.

estatua /es'tatua/ *n. f.* statue.

estatura /esta'tura/ *n. f.* stature.

estatuto /esta'tuto/ *n. m.* statute, law.

este /'este/ *n. m.* east.

este, esta *dem. a.* this.

éste, ésta *dem. pron.* this (one); the latter.

estelar /este'lar/ *a.* stellar.

estenografía /estenogra'fia/ *n. f.* stenography.

estenógrafo /este'nografo/ **-fa** *n.* stenographer.

estera /es'tera/ *n. f.* mat, matting.

estereofónico /estereo'foniko/ *a.* stereophonic.

estéril /es'teril/ *a.* barren; sterile.

esterilidad /esterili'ðað/ *n. f.* sterility, fruitlessness.

esterilizar /esterili'θar; esterili'sar/ *v.* sterilize.

esternón /ester'non/ *n. m.* breastbone.

estética /es'tetika/ *n. f.* esthetics.

estético /es'tetiko/ *a.* esthetic.

estetoscopio /esteto'skopio/ *n. m.* stethoscope.

estibador /estißa'ðor/ *n. m.* stevedore.

estiércol /es'tierkol/ *n. m.* dung, manure.

estigma /es'tigma/ *n. m.* stigma; disgrace.

estilarse /esti'larse/ *v.* be in fashion, be in vogue.

estilo /es'tilo/ *n. m.* style; sort.

estilográfica /estilo'grafika/ *n. f.* (fountain) pen.

estima /es'tima/ *n. f.* esteem.

estimable /esti'maßle/ *a.* estimable, worthy.

estimación /estima'θion; estima'sion/ *n. f.* estimation.

estimar /esti'mar/ *v.* esteem; value; estimate; gauge.

estimular /estimu'lar/ *v.* stimulate.

estímulo /es'timulo/ *n. m.* stimulus.

estío /es'tio/ *n. m.* summer.

estipulación /estipula'θion; estipula'sion/ *n. f.* stipulation.

estipular /estipu'lar/ *v.* stipulate.

estirar /esti'rar/ *v.* stretch.

estirpe /es'tirpe/ *n. m.* stock, lineage.

esto /'esto/ *dem. pron.* this.

estocada /esto'kaða/ *n. f.* stab, thrust.

estofado /esto'faðo/ *n. m.* stew. —**estofar,** *v.*

estoicismo /estoi'θismo; estoi'sismo/ *n. m.* stoicism.

estoico /es'toiko/ *n.* & *a.* stoic.

estómago /es'tomago/ *n. m.* stomach.

estorbar /estor'βar/ *v.* bother, hinder, interfere with.

estorbo /es'torβo/ *n. m.* hindrance.

estornudo /estor'nuðo/ *n. m.* sneeze. —**estornudar,** *v.*

estrabismo /estra'βismo/ *n. m.* strabismus.

estrago /es'trago/ *n. m.* devastation, havoc.

estrangulación /estraŋgula'θion; estraŋgula'sion/ *n. f.* strangulation.

estrangular /estraŋgu'lar/ *v.* strangle.

estraperlista /estraper'lista/ *n. m.* & *f.* black marketeer.

estraperlo /estra'perlo/ *n. m.* black market.

estratagema /estrata'hema/ *n. f.* stratagem.

estrategia /estra'tehia/ *n. f.* strategy.

estratégico /estra'tehiko/ *a.* strategic.

estrato /es'trato/ *n. m.* stratum.

estrechar /estre't∫ar/ *v.* tighten; narrow.

estrechez /estre't∫eθ; estre't∫es/ *n. f.* narrowness; tightness.

estrecho /es'tret∫o/ *a.* **1.** narrow, tight. —*n.* **2.** *m.* strait.

estregar /estre'gar/ *v.* scour, scrub.

estrella /es'treʎa; es'treya/ *n. f.* star.

estrellamar /estreʎa'mar; estreya'mar/ *n. f.* starfish.

estrellar /estre'ʎar; estre'yar/ *v.* shatter, smash.

estremecimiento /estremeθi'miento; estremesi'miento/ *n. m.* shudder. —**estremecerse,** *v.*

estrenar /estre'nar/ *v.* wear for the first time; open (a play).

estreno /es'treno/ *n. m.* debut, first performance.

estrenuo /es'trenuo/ *a.* strenuous.

estreñido /estre'ɲiðo/ **-da** *a.* constipated.

estreñimiento /estreɲi'miento/ *n. m.* constipation.

estreñir /estre'ɲir/ *v.* constipate.

estrépito /es'trepito/ *n. m.* din.

estreptococo /estrepto'koko/ *n. m.* streptococcus.

estría /es'tria/ *n. f.* groove.

estribillo /estri'βiʎo; estri'βiyo/ *n. m.* refrain.

estribo /es'triβo/ *n. m.* stirrup.

estribor /estri'βor/ *n. m.* starboard.

estrictamente /estrikta'mente/ *adv.* strictly.

estrictez /estrik'teθ; estrik'tes/ *n. f.* strictness.

estricto /es'trikto/ *a.* strict.

estrofa /es'trofa/ *n. f.* stanza.

estropajo /estro'paho/ *n. m.* mop.

estropear /estrope'ar/ *v.* cripple, damage, spoil.

estructura /estruk'tura/ *n. f.* structure.

estructural /estruktu'ral/ *a.* structural.

estruendo /es'truendo/ *n. m.* din, clatter.

estuario /es'tuario/ *n. m.* estuary.

estuco /es'tuko/ *n. m.* stucco.

estudiante /estu'ðiante/ **-ta** *n.* student.

estudiar /estu'ðiar/ *v.* study.

estudio /es'tuðio/ *n. m.* study; studio.

estudioso /estu'ðioso/ *a.* studious.

estufa /es'tufa/ *n. f.* stove.

estufa de aire /es'tufa de 'aire/ fan heater.

estulto /es'tulto/ *a.* foolish.

estupendo /estu'pendo/ *a.* wonderful, grand, fine.

estupidez /estupi'ðeθ; estupi'ðes/ *n. f.* stupidity.

estúpido /es'tupiðo/ *a.* stupid.

estupor /estu'por/ *n. m.* stupor.

estuque /es'tuke/ *n. m.* stucco.

esturión /estu'rion/ *n. m.* sturgeon.

etapa /e'tapa/ *n. f.* stage.

éter /'eter/ *n. m.* ether.

etéreo /e'tereo/ *a.* ethereal.

eternal /eter'nal/ *a.* eternal.

eternidad /eterni'ðað/ *n. f.* eternity.

eterno /e'terno/ *a.* eternal.

ética /'etika/ *n. f.* ethics.

ético /'etiko/ *a.* ethical.

etimología /etimolo'hia/ *n. f.* etymology.

etiqueta /eti'keta/ *n. f.* etiquette; tag, label.

étnico /'etniko/ *a.* ethnic.

etrusco /e'trusko/ **-ca** *n.* & *a.* Etruscan.

eucaristía /eukaris'tia/ *n. f.* Eucharist.

eufemismo /eufe'mismo/ *n. m.* euphemism.

eufonía /eufo'nia/ *n. f.* euphony.

Europa /eu'ropa/ *n. f.* Europe.

europeo /euro'peo/ **-pea** *a.* & *n.* European.

eutanasia /euta'nasia/ *n. f.* euthanasia.

evacuación /eβakua'θion; eβakua'sion/ *n. f.* evacuation.

evacuar /eβa'kuar/ *v.* evacuate.

evadir /eβa'ðir/ *v.* evade.

evangélico /eβan'heliko/ *a.* evangelical.

evangelio /eβan'helio/ *n. m.* gospel.

evangelista /eβanhe'lista/ *n. m.* evangelist.

evaporación /eβapora'θion; eβapora'sion/ *n. f.* evaporation.

evaporarse /eβapo'rarse/ *v.* evaporate.

evasión /eβa'sion; eβa'siβa/ *n. f.* evasion.

evasivamente /eβasiβa'mente/ *adv.* evasively.

evasivo /eβa'siβo/ *a.* evasive.

evento /e'βento/ *n. m.* event, occurrence.

eventual /eβen'tual/ *a.* eventual.

eventualidad /eβentuali'ðað/ *n. f.* eventuality.

evicción /eβik'θion; eβik'sion/ *n. f.* eviction.

evidencia /eβi'ðenθia; eβiðensia/ *n. f.* evidence.

evidenciar /eβiðen'θiar; eβiðen'siar/ *v.* prove, show.

evidente /eβi'ðente/ *a.* evident.

evitación /eβita'θion; eβita'sion/ *n. f.* avoidance.

evitar /eβi'tar/ *v.* avoid, shun.

evocación /eβoka'θion; eβoka'sion/ *n. f.* evocation.

evocar /eβo'kar/ *v.* evoke.

evolución /eβolu'θion; eβolu'sion/ *n. f.* evolution.

exacerbar /eksaθer'βar; eksaser'βar/ *v.* irritate deeply; exacerbate.

exactamente /eksakta'mente/ *adv.* exactly.

exactitud /eksakti'tuð/ *n. f.* precision, accuracy.

exacto /ek'sakto/ *a.* exact, accurate.

exageración /eksahera'θion; eksahera'sion/ *n. f.* exaggeration.

exagerar /eksahe'rar/ *v.* exaggerate.

exaltación /eksalta'θion; eksalta'sion/ *n. f.* exaltation.

exaltamiento /eksalta'miento/ *n. m.* exaltation.

exaltar /eksal'tar/ *v.* exalt.

examen /ek'samen/ *n. m.* test, examination.

examen de ingreso /ek'samen de iŋ'greso/ entrance examination.

examinar /eksami'nar/ *v.* test, examine.

exánime /eksa'nime/ *a.* spiritless, weak.

exasperación /eksaspera'θion; eksaspera'sion/ *n. f.* exasperation.

exasperar /eksaspe'rar/ *v.* exasperate.

excavación /ekskaβa'θion; ekskaβa'sion/ *n. f.* excavation.

excavar /ekska'βar/ *v.* excavate.

exceder /ekse'ðer; eksse'ðer/ *v.* exceed, surpass; outrun.

excelencia /ekse'lenθia; eksse'lensia/ *n. f.* excellence.

excelente /ekse'lente; eksse'lente/ *a.* excellent.

excéntrico /ek'θentriko; eks'sentriko/ *a.* eccentric.

excepción /eksθep'θion; ekssep'sion/ *n. f.* exception.

excepcional /eksθepθio'nal; ekssepsio'nal/ *a.* exceptional.

excepto /eks'θepto; eks'septo/ *prep.* except, except for.

exceptuar /eksθep'tuar; ekssep'tuar/ *v.* except.

excesivamente /eksθesiβa'mente; ekssesiβa'mente/ *adv.* excessively.

excesivo /eksθe'siβo; eksse'siβo/ *a.* excessive.

exceso /eks'θeso; eks'seso/ *n. m.* excess.

excitabilidad /eksθitaβili'ðað; ekssitaβili'ðað/ *n. f.* excitability.

excitación /eksθita'θion; eksssita'sion/ *n. f.* excitement.

excitar /eksθi'tar; ekssi'tar/ *v.* excite.

exclamación /eksklama'θion; ekssklama'sion/ *n. f.* exclamation.

exclamar /ekskla'mar/ *v.* exclaim.

excluir /eksk'luir/ *v.* exclude, bar, shut out.

exclusión /eksklu'sion/ *n. f.* exclusion.

exclusivamente /eksklusiβa'mente/ *adv.* exclusively.

exclusivo /eksklu'siβo/ *a.* exclusive.

excomulgar /ekskomul'gar/ *v.* excommunicate.

excomunión /ekskomu'nion/ *n. f.* excommunication.

excreción /ekskre'θion; ekskre'sion/ *n. f.* excretion.

excremento /ekskre'mento/ *n. m.* excrement.

excretar /ekskre'tar/ *v.* excrete.

exculpar /ekskul'par/ *v.* exonerate.

excursión /ekskur'sion/ *n. f.* excursion.

excursionista /ekskursio'nista/ *n. m.* & *f.* excursionist; tourist.

excusa /eks'kusa/ *n. f.* excuse. —**excusar,** *v.*

excusado /eksku'saðo/ *n. m.* toilet.

excusarse /eksku'sarse/ *v.* apologize.

exención /eksen'θion; eksen'sion/ *n. f.* exemption.

exento /ek'sento/ *a.* exempt. —**exentar,** *v.*

exhalación /eksala'θion; eksala'sion/ *n. f.* exhalation.

exhalar /eksa'lar/ *v.* exhale, breathe out.

exhausto /ek'sausto/ *a.* exhausted.

exhibición /eksiβi'θion; eksiβi'sion/ *n. f.* exhibit, exhibition.

exhibir /eksi'βir/ *v.* exhibit, display.

exhortación /eksorta'θion; eksorta'sion/ *n. f.* exhortation.

exhortar /eksor'tar/ *v.* exhort, admonish.

exhumación /eksuma'θion; eksuma'sion/ *n. f.* exhumation.

exhumar /eksu'mar/ *v.* exhume.

exigencia /eksi'henθia; eksi'hensia/ *n. f.* requirement, demand.

exigente /eksi'hente/ *a.* exacting, demanding.

exigir /eksi'hir/ *v.* require, exact, demand.

eximir /eksi'mir/ *v.* exempt.

existencia /eksis'tenθia; eksis'tensia/ *n. f.* existence; *Econ.* supply.

existente /eksis'tente/ *a.* existent.

existir /eksis'tir/ *v.* exist.

éxito /'eksito/ *n. m.* success.

éxodo /'eksoðo/ *n. m.* exodus.

exoneración /eksonera'θion; eksonera'sion/ *n. f.* exoneration.

exonerar /eksone'rar/ *v.* exonerate, acquit.

exorar /ekso'rar/ *v.* beg, implore.

exorbitancia /eksorβi'tanθia; eksorβi'tansia/ *n. f.* exorbitance.

exorbitante /eksorβi'tante/ *a.* exorbitant.

exorcismo /eksor'θismo; eksor'sismo/ *n. m.* exorcism.

exornar /eksor'nar/ *v.* adorn, decorate.

exótico /ek'sotiko/ *a.* exotic.

expansibilidad /ekspansiβili'ðað/ *n. f.* expansibility.

expansión /ekspan'sion/ *n. f.* expansion.

expansivo /ekspan'siβo/ *a.* expansive; effusive.

expatriación /ekspatria'θion; ekspatria'sion/ *n. f.* expatriation.

expatriar /ekspa'triar/ *v.* expatriate.

expectación /ekspekta'θion; ekspekta'sion/ *n. f.* expectation.

expectorar /ekspekto'rar/ *v.* expectorate.

expedición /ekspeði'θion; ekspeði'sion/ *n. f.* expedition.

expediente /ekspe'ðiente/ *n. m.* expedient; means.

expedir /ekspe'ðir/ *v.* send off, ship; expedite.

expeditivo /ekspeði'tiβo/ *a.* speedy, prompt.

expedito /ekspe'ðito/ *a.* speedy, prompt.

expeler /ekspe'ler/ *v.* expel, eject.

expendedor /ekspende'ðor/ **-ra** *n.* dealer.

expender /ekspen'der/ *v.* expend.

expensas /ek'spensas/ *n. f.pl.* expenses, costs.

experiencia /ekspe'rienθia; ekspe'riensia/ *n. f.* experience.

experimentado /eksperimen'taðo/ *a.* experienced.

experimental /eksperimen'tal/ *a.* experimental.

experimentar /eksperimen'tar/ *v.* experience.

experimento /eksperi'mento/ *n. m.* experiment.

expertamente /eksperta'mente/ *adv.* expertly.

experto /ek'sperto/ **-ta** *a.* & *n.* expert.

expiación /ekspia'θion; ekspia'sion/ *n. f.* atonement.

expiar /eks'piar/ *v.* atone for.

expiración /ekspira'θion; ekspira'sion/ *n. f.* expiration.

expirar /ekspi'rar/ *v.* expire.

explanación /eksplana'θion; eksplana'sion/ *n. f.* explanation.

explanar /ekspla'nar/ *v.* make level.

expletivo /eksple'tiβo/ *n.* & *a.* expletive.

explicable /ekspli'kaβle/ *a.* explicable.

explicación /eksplika'θion; eksplika'sion/ *n. f.* explanation.

explicar /ekspli'kar/ *v.* explain.

explicativo /eksplika'tiβo/ *a.* explanatory.

explícitamente /ekspliθita'mente; eksplisita'mente/ *adv.* explicitly.

explícito /eks'pliθito; eksplisito/ *adj.* explicit.

exploración /eksplora'θion; eksplora'sion/ *n. f.* exploration.

explorador /eksplora'ðor/ **-ra** *n.* explorer; scout.

explorar /eksplo'rar/ *v.* explore; scout.

exploratorio /eksplora'torio/ *a.* exploratory.

explosión /eksplo'sion/ *n. f.* explosion; outburst.

explosivo /eksplo'siβo/ *a. & m.* explosive.

explotación /eksplota'θion; eksplota'sion/ *n. f.* exploitation.

explotar /eksplo'tar/ *v.* exploit.

exponer /ekspo'ner/ *v.* expose; set forth.

exportación /eksporta'θion; eksporta'sion/ *n. f.* exportation; export.

exportador /eksporta'ðor/ **-ra** *n.* exporter.

exportar /ekspor'tar/ *v.* export.

exposición /eksposi'θion; eksposi'sion/ *n. f.* exhibit; exposition; exposure.

expósito /eks'posito/ **-ta** *n.* foundling; orphan.

expresado /ekspre'saðo/ *a.* aforesaid.

expresamente /ekspresa'mente/ *adv.* clearly, explicitly.

expresar /ekspre'sar/ *v.* express.

expresión /ekspre'sion/ *n. f.* expression.

expresivo /ekspre'siβo/ *a.* expressive; affectionate.

expreso /eks'preso/ *a. & m.* express.

exprimidera de naranjas /eksprimi'ðera de na'ranhas/ *n. f.* orange squeezer.

exprimir /ekspri'mir/ *v.* squeeze.

expropiación /ekspropia'θion; ekspropia'sion/ *n. f.* expropriation.

expropiar /ekspro'piar/ *v.* expropriate.

expulsar /ekspul'sar/ *v.* expel, eject; evict.

expulsión /ekspul'sion/ *n. f.* expulsion.

expurgación /ekspurga'θion; ekspurga'sion/ *n. f.* expurgation.

expurgar /ekspur'gar/ *v.* expurgate.

exquisitamente /ekskisita'mente/ *adv.* exquisitely.

exquisito /eks'kisito/ *a.* exquisite.

éxtasis /'ekstasis/ *n. m.* ecstasy.

extemporáneo /ekstempo'raneo/ *a.* extemporaneous, impromptu.

extender /eksten'der/ *v.* extend; spread; widen; stretch.

extensamente /ekstensa'mente/ *adv.* extensively.

extensión /eksten'sion/ *n. f.* extension, spread, expanse.

extenso /eks'tenso/ *a.* extensive, widespread.

extenuación /ekstenua'θion; ekstenua'sion/ *n. f.* weakening; emaciation.

extenuar /ekste'nuar/ *v.* extenuate.

exterior /ekste'rior/ *a. & m.* exterior; foreign.

exterminar /ekstermi'nar/ *v.* exterminate.

exterminio /ekster'minio/ *n. m.* extermination, ruin.

extinción /ekstin'θion; ekstin'sion/ *n. f.* extinction.

extinguir /ekstiŋ'guir/ *v.* extinguish.

extinto /eks'tinto/ *a.* extinct.

extintor /ekstin'tor/ *n. m.* fire extinguisher.

extirpar /ekstir'par/ *v.* eradicate.

extorsión /ekstor'sion/ *n. f.* extortion.

extra /'ekstra/ *n.* extra.

extracción /ekstrak'θion; ekstrak'sion/ *n. f.* extraction.

extractar /ekstrak'tar/ *v.* summarize.

extracto /eks'trakto/ *n. m.* extract; summary.

extradición /ekstraði'θion; ekstraði'sion/ *n. f.* extradition.

extraer /ekstra'er/ *v.* extract.

extranjero /ekstran'hero/ **-ra** *a.* **1.** foreign. —*n.* **2.** foreigner; stranger.

extrañar /ekstra'ɲar/ *v.* surprise; miss.

extraño /eks'traɲo/ *a.* strange, queer.

extraordinariamente /ˌekstraorðinaria'mente/ *adv.* extraordinarily.

extraordinario /ekstraorði'nario/ *a.* extraordinary.

extravagancia /ekstraβa'ganθia; ekstraβa'gansia/ *n. f.* extravagance.

extravagante /ekstraβa'gante/ *a.* extravagant.

extraviado /ekstra'βiaðo/ *a.* lost, misplaced.

extraviarse /ekstra'βiarse/ *v.* stray, get lost.

extravío /ekstra'βio/ *n. m.* misplacement; aberration, deviation.

extremadamente /ekstremaða'mente/ *adv.* extremely.

extremado /ekstre'maðo/ *a.* extreme.

extremaunción /ekstremaun'θion; ekstremaun'sion/ *n. f.* extreme unction.

extremidad /ekstremi'ðað/ *n. f.* extremity.

extremista /ekstre'mista/ *n. & a.* extremist.

extremo /eks'tremo/ *a. & m.* extreme, end.

extrínseco /ekstrin'seko/ *a.* extrinsic.

exuberancia /eksuβe'ranθia; eksuβeransia/ *n. f.* exuberance.

exuberante /eksuβe'rante/ *a.* exuberant.

exudación /eksuða'θion; eksuða'sion/ *n. f.* exudation.

exudar /eksu'ðar/ *v.* exude, ooze.

exultación /eksulta'θion; eksulta'sion/ *n. f.* exultation.

eyaculación /eyakula'θion; eyakula'sion/ *n. f.* ejaculation.

eyacular /eyaku'lar/ *v.* ejaculate.

eyección /eyek'θion; eyek'sion/ *n. f.* ejection.

eyectar /eyek'tar/ *v.* eject.

F

fábrica /'faβrika/ *n. f.* factory.

fabricación /faβrika'θion; faβrika'sion/ *n. f.* manufacture, manufacturing.

fabricante /faβri'kante/ *n. m. & f.* manufacturer, maker.

fabricar /faβri'kar/ *v.* manufacture, make.

fabril /fa'βril/ *a.* manufacturing, industrial.

fábula /'faβula/ *n. f.* fable, myth.

fabuloso /faβu'loso/ *a.* fabulous.

facción /fak'θion; fak'sion/ *n. f.* faction, party; (*pl.*) features.

faccioso /fak'θioso; fak'sioso/ *a.* factious.

fachada /fa'tʃaða/ *n. f.* façade, front.

fácil /'faθil; 'fasil/ *a.* easy.

facilidad /faθili'ðað; fasili'ðað/ *n. f.* facility, ease.

facilitar /faθili'tar; fasili'tar/ *v.* facilitate, make easy.

fácilmente /ˌfaθil'mente; ˌfasil'mente/ *adv.* easily.

facsímile /fak'simile/ *n. m.* facsimile.

factible /fak'tiβle/ *a.* feasible.

factor /fak'tor/ *n. m.* factor.

factótum /fak'totum/ *n. m.* factotum; jack of all trades.

factura /fak'tura/ *n. f.* invoice, bill.

facturar /faktu'rar/ *v.* bill; check (baggage).

facultad /fakulta'ð/ *n. f.* faculty; ability.

facultativo /fakulta'tiβo/ *a.* optional.

faena /fa'ena/ *n. f.* task; work.

faisán /fai'san/ *n. m.* pheasant.

faja /'faha/ *n. f.* band; sash; zone.

falacia /fa'laθia; fa'lasia/ *n. f.* fallacy; deceitfulness.

falda /'falda/ *n. f.* skirt; lap.

falibilidad /faliβili'ðað/ *n. f.* fallibility.

falla /'faʎa; faya/ *n. f.* failure; fault.

fallar /fa'ʎar; fa'yar/ *v.* fail.

fallecer /faʎe'θer; faye'ser/ *v.* pass away, die.

fallo /'faʎo; 'fayo/ *n. m.* verdict; shortcoming.

falsear /false'ar/ *v.* falsify, counterfeit, forge.

falsedad /false'ðað/ *n. f.* falsehood; lie; falseness.

falsificación /falsifika'θion; falsifika'sion/ *n. f.* falsification; forgery.

falsificar /falsifi'kar/ *v.* falsify, counterfeit, forge.

falso /'falso/ *a.* false; wrong.

falta /'falta/ *n. f.* error, mistake; fault; lack. **hacer f.,** to be lacking, to be necessary. **sin f.,** without fail.

faltar /fal'tar/ *v.* be lacking, be missing; be absent.

faltriquera /faltri'kera/ *n. f.* pocket.

fama /'fama/ *n. f.* fame; reputation; glory.

familia /fa'milia/ *n. f.* family; household.

familiar /fami'liar/ *a.* familiar; domestic; (of) family.

familiaridad /familiari'ðað/ *n. f.* familiarity, intimacy.

familiarizar /familiari'θar; familiari'sar/ *v.* familiarize, acquaint.

famoso /fa'moso/ *a.* famous.

fanal /fa'nal/ *n. m.* lighthouse; lantern, lamp.

fanático /fa'natiko/ **-ca** *a. & n.* fanatic.

fanatismo /fana'tismo/ *n. m.* fanaticism.

fanfarria /fan'farria/ *n. f.* bluster. —**fanfarrear,** *v.*

fango /'faŋgo/ *n. m.* mud.

fantasía /fanta'sia/ *n. f.* fantasy; fancy, whim.

fantasma /fan'tasma/ *n. m.* phantom; ghost.

fantástico /fan'tastiko/ *a.* fantastic.

faquín /fa'kin/ *n. m.* porter.

faquir /fa'kir/ *n. m.* fakir.

farallón /fara'ʎon; fara'yon/ *n. m.* cliff.

Faraón /fara'on/ *n. m.* Pharaoh.

fardel /far'ðel/ *n. m.* bag; package.

fardo /far'ðo/ *n. m.* bundle.

farináceo /fari'naθeo; fari'naseo/ *a.* farinaceous.

faringe /fa'rinhe/ *n. f.* pharynx.

fariseo /fari'seo/ *n. m.* pharisee, hypocrite.

farmacéutico /farma'θeutiko; farma'seutiko/ **-ca** **1.** pharmaceutical. —*n.* **2.** pharmacist.

farmacia /far'maθia; far'masia/ *n. f.* pharmacy.

faro /'faro/ *n. m.* beacon; lighthouse; headlight.

farol /fa'rol/ *n. m.* lantern; (street) light, street lamp.

farra /'farra/ *n. f.* spree.

fárrago /'farrago/ *n. m.* medley; hodgepodge.

farsa /'farsa/ *n. f.* farce.

fascinación /fasθina'θion; fassina'sion/ *n. f.* fascination.

fascinar /fasθi'nar; fassi'nar/ *v.* fascinate, bewitch.

fase /'fase/ *n. f.* phase.

fastidiar /fasti'ðiar/ *v.* disgust; irk, annoy.

fastidio /fasti'ðio/ *n. m.* disgust; annoyance.

fastidioso /fasti'ðioso/ *a.* annoying; tedious.

fasto /'fasto/ *a.* happy, fortunate.

fatal /fa'tal/ *a.* fatal.

fatalidad /fatali'ðað/ *n. f.* fate; calamity, bad luck.

fatalismo /fata'lismo/ *n. m.* fatalism.

fatalista /fata'lista/ *n. & a.* fatalist.

fatiga /fa'tiga/ *n. f.* fatigue. —**fatigar,** *v.*

fauna /'fauna/ *n. f.* fauna.

fauno /'fauno/ *n. m.* faun.

favor /fa'βor/ *n. m.* favor; behalf. **por f.,** please.

¡Favor! Puh-lease!

favorable /faβo'raβle/ *a.* favorable.

favorablemente /faβoraβle'mente/ *adv.* favorably.

favorecer /faβore'θer; faβore'ser/ *v.* favor; flatter.

favoritismo /faβori'tismo/ *n. m.* favoritism.

favorito /faβo'rito/ **-ta** *a. & n.* favorite.

fax /faks/ *n. m.* fax.

faz /faθ; fas/ *n. f.* face.

fe /fe/ *n. f.* faith.

fealdad /feal'dað/ *n. f.* ugliness, homeliness.

febrero /fe'βrero/ *n. m.* February.

febril /fe'βril/ *a.* feverish.

fecha /'fetʃa/ *n. f.* date. —**fechar,** *v.*

fecha de caducidad /'fetʃa de kaðuθi'ðað; 'fetʃa de kaðusi'ðað/ expiration date.

fécula /'fekula/ *n. f.* starch.

fecundar /fekun'dar/ *v.* fertilize.

fecundidad /fekundi'ðað/ *n. f.* fecundity, fertility.

fecundo /fe'kundo/ *a.* fecund, fertile.

federación /feðera'θion; feðera'sion/ *n. f.* federation.

federal /feðe'ral/ *a.* federal.

felicidad /feliθi'ðað; felisi'ðað/ *n. f.* happiness; bliss.

felicitación /feliθita'θion; felisita'sion/ *n. f.* congratulation.

felicitar /feliθi'tar; felisi'tar/ *v.* congratulate.

feligrés /feli'gres/ **-esa** *n.* parishioner.

feliz /fe'liθ; fe'lis/ *a.* happy; fortunate.

felón /fe'lon/ *n. m.* felon.

felonía /felo'nia/ *n. f.* felony.

felpa /'felpa/ *n. f.* plush.

felpudo /fel'puðo/ *n. m.* doormat.

femenino /feme'nino/ *a.* feminine.

feminismo /femi'nismo/ *n. m.* feminism.

feminista /femi'nista/ *n. m. & f.* feminist.

fenecer /fene'θer; fene'ser/ *v.* conclude; die.

fénix /'feniks/ *n. m.* phoenix; model.

fenomenal /fenome'nal/ *a.* phenomenal.

fenómeno /fe'nomeno/ *n. m.* phenomenon.

feo /'feo/ *a.* ugly, homely.

feracidad /feraθi'ðað; ferasi'ðað/ *n. f.* feracity, fertility.

feraz /'feraθ; 'feras/ *a.* fertile, fruitful; copious.

feria /'feria/ *n. f.* fair; market.

feriado /fe'riaðo/ *a.* **día f.,** holiday.

fermentación /fermenta'θion; fermenta'sion/ *n. f.* fermentation.

fermento /fer'mento/ *n. m.* ferment. —**fermentar,** *v.*

ferocidad /feroθi'ðað; ferosi'ðað/ *n. f.* ferocity, fierceness.

feroz /fe'roθ; fe'ros/ *a.* ferocious, fierce.

férreo /'ferreo/ *a.* of iron.

ferrería /ferre'ria/ *n. f.* ironworks.

ferretería /ferrete'ria/ *n. f.* hardware; hardware store.

ferrocarril /ferroka'rril/ *n. m.* railroad.

fértil /'fertil/ *a.* fertile.

fertilidad /fertili'ðað/ *n. f.* fertility.

fertilizar /fertili'θar; fertili'sar/ *v.* fertilize.

férvido /'ferβiðo/ *a.* fervid, ardent.

ferviente /fer'βiente/ *a.* fervent.

fervor /fer'βor/ *n. m.* fervor, zeal.

fervoroso /ferβo'roso/ *a.* zealous, eager.

festejar /feste'har/ *v.* entertain, fete.

festejo /fes'teho/ *n. m.* feast.

festín /fes'tin/ *n. m.* feast.

festividad /festiβi'ðað/ *n. f.* festivity.

festivo /fes'tiβo/ *a.* festive.

fétido /'fetiðo/ *adj.* fetid.

feudal /feu'ðal/ *a.* feudal.

feudo /'feuðo/ *n. m.* fief; manor.

fiado /'fiaðo, al/ *adj.* on trust, on credit.

fiambrera /fiam'brera/ *n. f.* lunch box.

fianza /'fianθa; 'fiansa/ *n. f.* bail.

fiar /fi'ar/ *v.* trust, sell on credit; give credit.

fiarse de /'fiarse de/ *v.* trust (in), rely on.

fiasco /'fiasko/ *n. m.* fiasco.
fibra /'fiβra/ *n. f.* fiber; vigor.
fibroso /fi'βroso/ *a.* fibrous.
ficción /fik'θion; fik'sion/ *n. f.* fiction.
ficha /'fitʃa/ *n. f.* slip, index card; chip.
fichero /fi'tʃero/ *n. m.* computer file, filing cabinet, card catalog.
ficticio /fik'tiθio; fik'tisio/ *a.* fictitious.
fidedigno /fiðe'ðigno/ *a.* trustworthy.
fideicomisario /fiðeikomi'sario/ **-ria** *n.* trustee.
fideicomiso /fiðeiko'miso/ *n. m.* trust.
fidelidad /fiðeli'ðað/ *n. f.* fidelity.
fideo /fi'ðeo/ *n. m.* noodle.
fiebre /'fieβre/ *n. f.* fever.
fiebre del heno /'fieβre del 'eno/ hayfever.
fiel /fiel/ *a.* faithful.
fieltro /'fieltro/ *n. m.* felt.
fiera /'fiera/ *n. f.* wild animal.
fiereza /fie'reθa; fie'resa/ *n. f.* fierceness, wildness.
fiero /'fiero/ *a.* fierce; wild.
fiesta /'fiesta/ *n. f.* festival, feast; party.
figura /fi'gura/ *n. f.* figure. **—figurar,** *v.*
figurarse /figu'rarse/ *v.* imagine.
figurón /figu'ron/ *n. m.* dummy.
fijar /fi'har/ *v.* fix; set, establish; post.
fijarse en /fi'harse en/ *v.* notice.
fijeza /fi'heθa; fi'hesa/ *n. f.* firmness.
fijo /'fiho/ *a.* fixed, stationary, permanent, set.
fila /'fila/ *n. f.* row, rank, file, line.
filantropía /filantro'pia/ *n. f.* philanthropy.
filatelia /fila'telia/ *n. f.* philately, stamp collecting.
filete /fi'lete/ *n. m.* fillet; steak.
film /film/ *n. m.* film. **—filmar,** *v.*
filo /'filo/ *n. m.* (cutting) edge.
filón /fi'lon/ *n. m.* vein (of ore).
filosofía /filoso'fia/ *n. f.* philosophy.
filosófico /filo'sofiko/ *a.* philosophical.
filósofo /fi'losofo/ **-fa** *n.* philosopher.
filtro /'filtro/ *n. m.* filter. **—filtrar,** *v.*
fin /fin/ *n. m.* end, purpose, goal. **a f. de que,** in order that. **en f.,** in short. **por f.,** finally, at last.
final /fi'nal/ *a.* **1.** final. **—***n.* **2.** *m.* end.
finalidad /finali'ðað/ *n. f.* finality.
finalmente /final'mente/ *adv.* at last.
financiero /finan'θiero; finan'siero/ **-ra** *a.* **1.** financial. **—***n.* **2.** financier.
finca /'finka/ *n. f.* real estate; estate; farm.
finés /fi'nes/ **-esa** *a.* & *n.* Finnish; Finn.
fineza /fi'neθa; fi'nesa/ *n. f.* courtesy, politeness; fineness.
fingimiento /finhi'miento/ *n. m.* pretense.
fingir /fin'hir/ *v.* feign, pretend.
fino /'fino/ *a.* fine; polite, courteous.
firma /'firma/ *n. f.* signature; *Com.* firm.
firmamento /firma'mento/ *n. m.* firmament, heavens.
firmar /fir'mar/ *v.* sign.
firme /'firme/ *a.* firm, fast, steady, sound.
firmemente /firme'mente/ *adv.* firmly.
firmeza /fir'meθa; fir'mesa/ *n. f.* firmness.
fisco /'fisko/ *n. m.* exchequer, treasury.
física /'fisika/ *n. f.* physics.
físico /'fisiko/ **-ca** *a.* & *n.* physical; physicist.
fisiología /fisiolo'hia/ *n. f.* physiology.
fláccido /'flakθiðo; 'flaksiðo/ *a.* flaccid, soft.
flaco /'flako/ *a.* thin, gaunt.
flagelación /flahela'θion; flahela'sion/ *n. f.* flagellation.
flagelar /flahe'lar/ *v.* flagellate, whip.
flagrancia /fla'granθia; fla'gransia/ *n. f.* flagrancy.
flagrante /fla'grante/ *a.* flagrant.
flama /'flama/ *n. f.* flame; ardor, zeal.
flamante /fla'mante/ *a.* flaming.
flamenco /fla'menko/ *n. m.* flamingo.
flan /flan/ *n. m.* custard.
flanco /'flanko/ *n. m.* side; *Mil.* flank.
flanquear /flanke'ar/ *v.* flank.
flaqueza /fla'keθa; fla'kesa/ *n. f.* thinness; weakness.
flauta /'flauta/ *n. f.* flute.
flautín /flau'tin/ *n. m.* piccolo.
flautista /flau'tista/ *n. m.* & *f.* flutist, piper.
flecha /'fletʃa/ *n. f.* arrow.
flechazo /fle'tʃaθo; fle'tʃaso/ *n. m.* love at first sight.
flechero /fle'tʃero/ **-ra** *n.* archer.
fleco /'fleko/ *n. m.* fringe; flounce.
flema /'flema/ *n. f.* phlegm.
flemático /fle'matiko/ *a.* phlegmatic.
flequillo /fle'kiʎo; fle'kiyo/ *n. m.* fringe; bangs (of hair).
flete /'flete/ *n. m.* freight. **—fletar,** *v.*
flexibilidad /fleksiβili'ðað/ *n. f.* flexibility.
flexible /fle'ksiβle/ *a.* flexible, pliable.
flirtear /flirte'ar/ *v.* flirt.
flojo /'floho/ *a.* limp; loose, flabby, slack.
flor /flor/ *n. f.* flower; compliment.
flora /'flora/ *n. f.* flora.
floral /flo'ral/ *a.* floral.
florecer /flore'θer; flore'ser/ *v.* flower, bloom; flourish.
floreo /flo'reo/ *n. m.* flourish.
florero /flo'rero/ *n. m.* flower pot; vase.
floresta /flo'resta/ *n. f.* forest.
florido /flo'riðo/ *a.* flowery; flowering.
florista /flo'rista/ *n. m.* & *f.* florist.
flota /'flota/ *n. f.* fleet.
flotante /flo'tante/ *a.* floating.
flotar /flo'tar/ *v.* float.
flotilla /flo'tiʎa; flo'tiya/ *n. f.* flotilla, fleet.
fluctuación /fluktua'θion; fluktua'sion/ *n. f.* fluctuation.
fluctuar /fluktu'ar/ *v.* fluctuate.
fluente /'fluente/ *a.* fluent; flowing.
fluidez /flui'ðeθ; flui'ðes/ *n. f.* fluency.
fluido /'fluiðo/ *a.* & *m.* fluid, liquid.
fluir /flu'ir/ *v.* flow.
flujo /'fluho/ *n. m.* flow, flux.
fluor /fluor/ *n. m.* fluorine.
fluorescencia /fluores'θenθia; fluores'sensia/ *n. f.* fluorescence.
fluorescente /fluores'θente; fluores'sente/ *a.* fluorescent.
fobia /'foβia/ *n. f.* phobia.
foca /'foka/ *n. f.* seal.
foco /'foko/ *n. m.* focus, center; floodlight.
fogata /fo'gata/ *n. f.* bonfire.
fogón /fo'gon/ *n. m.* hearth, fireplace.
fogosidad /fogosi'ðað/ *n. f.* vehemence, ardor.
fogoso /fo'goso/ *a.* vehement, ardent.
folclore /fol'klore/ *n. m.* folklore.
follaje /fo'ʎahe; fo'yahe/ *n. m.* foliage.
folleto /fo'ʎeto; fo'yeto/ *n. m.* pamphlet, booklet.
follón /fo'ʎon; fo'yon/ *n. m.*mess, chaos.
fomentar /fomen'tar/ *v.* develop, promote, further, foster.
fomento /fo'mento/ *n. m.* fomentation.
fonda /'fonda/ *n. f.* eating house, inn.
fondo /'fondo/ *n. m.* bottom; back (part); background; (*pl.*) funds; finances. **a f.,** thoroughly.
fonética /fo'netika/ *n. f.* phonetics.
fonético /fo'netiko/ *a.* phonetic.
fonógrafo /fo'nografo/ *n. m.* phonograph.
fontanero /fonta'nero/ **-era** *n.* plumber.
forastero /foras'tero/ **-ra** *a.* **1.** foreign, exotic. **—***n.* **2.** stranger.
forjar /for'har/ *v.* forge.
forma /'forma/ *n. f.* form, shape. **—formar,** *v.*
formación /forma'θion; forma'sion/ *n. f.* formation.
formal /for'mal/ *a.* formal.
formaldehido /formalde'iðo/ *n. m.* formaldehyde.
formalidad /formali'ðað/ *n. f.* formality.
formalizar /formali'θar; formali'sar/ *v.* finalize; formulate.
formidable /formi'ðaβle/ *a.* formidable.
formidablemente /formiðaβle'mente/ *adv.* formidably.
formón /for'mon/ *n. m.* chisel.
fórmula /'formula/ *n. f.* formula.
formular /formu'lar/ *v.* formulate, draw up.
formulario /formu'lario/ *n. m.* form.
foro /'foro/ *n. m.* forum.
forrado /fo'rraðo/ *a.* stuffed; *Colloq.* filthy rich.
forraje /fo'rrahe/ *n. m.* forage, fodder.
forrar /fo'rrar/ *v.* line.
forro /'forro/ *n. m.* lining; condom.
fortalecer /fortale'θer; fortale'ser/ *v.* fortify.
fortaleza /forta'leθa; forta'lesa/ *n. f.* fort, fortress; fortitude.
fortificación /fortifika'θion; fortifika'sion/ *n. f.* fortification.
fortitud /forti'tuð/ *n. f.* fortitude.
fortuitamente /fortuita'mente/ *adv.* fortuitously.
fortuito /for'tuito/ *a.* fortuitous.
fortuna /for'tuna/ *n. f.* fortune; luck.
forúnculo /fo'runkulo/ *n. m.* boil.
forzar /for'θar; for'sar/ *v.* force, compel, coerce.
forzosamente /forθosa'mente; forsosa'mente/ *adv.* compulsorily; forcibly.
forzoso /for'θoso; for'soso/ *a.* compulsory; necessary. **paro f.,** unemployment.
forzudo /for'θuðo; for'suðo/ *a.* powerful, vigorous.
fosa /'fosa/ *n. f.* grave; pit.
fósforo /'fosforo/ *n. m.* match; phosphorus.
fósil /'fosil/ *n. m.* fossil.
foso /'foso/ *n. m.* ditch, trench; moat.
fotocopia /foto'kopia/ *n. f.* photocopy.
fotocopiadora /fotokopia'ðora/ *n. f.* photocopier.
fotografía /fotogra'fia/ *n. f.* photograph; photography. **—fotografiar,** *v.*
frac /frak/ *n. m.* dress coat.
fracasar /fraka'sar/ *v.* fail.
fracaso /fra'kaso/ *n. m.* failure.
fracción /frak'θion; frak'sion/ *n. f.* fraction.
fractura /frak'tura/ *n. f.* fracture, break.
fragancia /fra'ganθia; fra'gansia/ *n. f.* fragrance; perfume; aroma.
fragante /fra'gante/ *a.* fragrant.
frágil /'frahil/ *a.* fragile, breakable.
fragilidad /frahili'ðað/ *n. f.* fragility.
fragmentario /fragmen'tario/ *a.* fragmentary.
fragmento /frag'mento/ *n. m.* fragment, bit.
fragor /fra'gor/ *n. m.* noise, clamor.
fragoso /fra'goso/ *a.* noisy.
fragua /'fragua/ *n. f.* forge. **—fraguar,** *v.*
fraile /'fraile/ *n. m.* monk.
frambuesa /fram'buesa/ *n. f.* raspberry.
francamente /franka'mente/ *adv.* frankly, candidly.
francés /fran'θes; fran'ses/ **-esa** *a.* & *n.* French; Frenchman, Frenchwoman.
Francia /'franθia; 'fransia/ *n. f.* France.
franco /'franko/ *a.* frank.
franela /fra'nela/ *n. f.* flannel.
frangible /fraŋ'giβle/ *a.* breakable.
franqueo /fran'keo/ *n. m.* postage.
franqueza /fran'keθa; fran'kesa/ *n. f.* frankness.
franquicia /fran'kiθia; fran'kisia/ *n. f.* franchise.
frasco /'frasko/ *n. m.* flask, bottle.
frase /'frase/ *n. f.* phrase; sentence.
fraseología /fraseolo'hia/ *n. f.* phraseology; style.
fraternal /frater'nal/ *a.* fraternal, brotherly.
fraternidad /fraterni'ðað/ *n. f.* fraternity, brotherhood.
fraude /'frauðe/ *n. m.* fraud.
fraudulento /frauðu'lento/ *a.* fraudulent.
frazada /fra'θaða; fra'saða/ *n. f.* blanket.
frecuencia /fre'kuenθia; fre'kuensia/ *n. f.* frequency.
frecuente /fre'kuente/ *a.* frequent.
frecuentemente /frekuente'mente/ *adv.* frequently, often.
fregadero /frega'ðero/ *n. m.* sink.
fregadura /frega'ðura/ *n. f.* scouring, scrubbing.
fregar /fre'gar/ *v.* scour, scrub, mop.
fregona /fre'gona/ *n. f.* mop.
freír /fre'ir/ *v.* fry.
fréjol /'frehol/ *n. m.* kidney bean.
frenazo /fre'naθo; fre'naso/ *n. m.* sudden braking, slamming on the brakes.
frenesí /frene'si/ *n. m.* frenzy.
frenéticamente /fre'netikamente/ *adv.* frantically.
frenético /fre'netiko/ *a.* frantic, frenzied.
freno /'freno/ *n. m.* brake. **—frenar,** *v.*
freno de auxilio /'freno de auk'silio/ emergency brake.
freno de mano /'freno de 'mano/ hand brake.
frente /'frente/ *n.* **1.** *f.* forehead. **2.** *m.* front. **en f., al f.,** opposite, across. **f. a,** in front of.
fresa /'fresa/ *n. f.* strawberry.
fresca /'freska/ *n. f.* fresh, cool air.
fresco /'fresko/ *a.* fresh; cool; crisp.
frescura /fres'kura/ *n. f.* coolness, freshness.
fresno /'fresno/ *n. m.* ash tree.
fresquería /freske'ria/ *n. f.* soda fountain.
friabilidad /friaβili'ðað/ *n. f.* brittleness.
friable /'friaβle/ *a.* brittle.
frialdad /frial'dað/ *n. f.* coldness.
fríamente /fria'mente/ *adv.* coldly; coolly.
fricandó /'frikando/ *n. m.* fricandeau.
fricar /fri'kar/ *v.* rub together.
fricción /frik'θion; frik'sion/ *n. f.* friction.
friccionar /frikθio'nar; friksio'nar/ *v.* rub.
friega /'friega/ *n. f.* friction; massage.
frigidez /frihi'ðeθ; frihi'ðes/ *n. f.* frigidity.
frígido /'frihiðo/ *a.* frigid.
frijol /fri'hol/ *n. m.* bean.
frío /'frio/ *a.* & *n. m.* cold. **tener f.,** to be cold, feel cold. **hacer f.,** to be cold (weather).
friolento /frio'lento/ **friolero** *a.* chilly; sensitive to cold.
friolera /frio'lera/ *n. f.* trifle, trinket.
friso /'friso/ *n. m.* frieze.
fritillas /fri'tiʎas; fri'tiyas/ *n. f.pl.* fritters.
frito /'frito/ *a.* fried.
fritura /fri'tura/ *n. f.* fritter.
frívolamente /'friβolamente/ *adv.* frivolously.
frivolidad /friβoli'ðað/ *n. f.* frivolity.
frívolo /'friβolo/ *a.* frivolous.
frondoso /fron'doso/ *a.* leafy.
frontera /fron'tera/ *n. f.* frontier; border.
frotar /fro'tar/ *v.* rub.

fructífero /fruk'tifero/ *a.* fruitful.
fructificar /fruktifi'kar/ *v.* bear fruit.
fructuosamente /fruktuosa'mente/ *adv.* fruitfully.
fructuoso /fruk'tuoso/ *a.* fruitful.
frugal /fru'gal/ *a.* frugal; thrifty.
frugalidad /frugali'ðað/ *n. f.* frugality; thrift.
frugalmente /frugal'mente/ *adv.* frugally, thriftily.
fruncir /frun'θir; frun'sir/ *v.* gather, contract. **f. el entrecejo,** frown.
fruslería /frusle'ria/ *n. f.* trinket.
frustrar /frus'trar/ *v.* frustrate, thwart.
fruta /'fruta/ *n. f.* fruit.
frutería /frute'ria/ *n. f.* fruit store.
fruto /'fruto/ *n. m.* fruit; product; profit.
fucsia /'fuksia/ *n. f.* fuchsia.
fuego /'fuego/ *n. m.* fire.
fuelle /'fueʎe; 'fueye/ *n. m.* bellows.
fuente /'fuente/ *n. f.* fountain; source; platter.
fuera /'fuera/ *adv.* without, outside.
fuero /'fuero/ *n. m.* statute.
fuerte /'fuerte/ *a.* **1.** strong; loud. —*n.* **2.** *m.* fort.
fuertemente /fuerte'mente/ *adv.* strongly; loudly.
fuerza /'fuerθa; 'fuersa/ *n. f.* force, strength.
fuga /'fuga/ *n. f.* flight, escape.
fugarse /fu'garse/ *v.* flee, escape.
fugaz /fu'gaθ; fu'gas/ *a.* fugitive, passing.
fugitivo /fuhi'tiβo/ **-va** *a. & n.* fugitive.
fulano /fu'lano/ **-na** *n.* Mr., Mrs. so-and-so.
fulcro /'fulkro/ *n. m.* fulcrum.
fulgor /ful'gor/ *n. m.* gleam, glow. —**fulgurar,** *v.*
fulminante /fulmi'nante/ *a.* explosive.
fumador /fuma'ðor/ **-ra** *n.* smoker.
fumar /fu'mar/ *v.* smoke.
fumigación /fumiga'θion; fumiga'sion/ *n. f.* fumigation.
fumigador /fumiga'ðor/ **-ra** *n.* fumigator.
fumigar /fumi'gar/ *v.* fumigate.
fumoso /fu'moso/ *a.* smoky.
función /fun'θion; fun'sion/ *n. f.* function; performance, show.
funcionar /funθio'nar; funsio'nar/ *v.* function; work, run.
funcionario /funθio'nario; funsio'nario/ **-ria** *n.* official, functionary.
funda /'funda/ *n. f.* case, sheath, slipcover.
fundación /funda'θion; funda'sion/ *n. f.* foundation.
fundador /funda'ðor/ **-ra** *n.* founder.
fundamental /funda'mental/ *a.* fundamental, basic.
fundamentalmente /fundamental'mente/ *adv.* fundamentally.
fundamento /funda'mento/ *n. m.* base, basis, foundation.
fundar /fun'dar/ *v.* found, establish.
fundición /fundi'θion; fundi'sion/ *n. f.* foundry; melting; meltdown.
fundir /fun'dir/ *v.* fuse; smelt.
fúnebre /'funeβre/ *a.* dismal.
funeral /fune'ral/ *n. m.* funeral.
funeraria /fune'raria/ *n. f.* funeral home, funeral parlor.
funestamente /funesta'mente/ *adv.* sadly.
fungo /'fuŋgo/ *n. m.* fungus.
furente /fu'rente/ *a.* furious, enraged.
furgoneta /furgo'neta/ *n. f.* van.
furia /'furia/ *n. f.* fury.
furiosamente /furiosa'mente/ *adv.* furiously.
furioso /fu'rioso/ *a.* furious.
furor /fu'ror/ *n. m.* furor; fury.
furtivamente /furtiβa'mente/ *adv.* furtively.
furtivo /fur'tiβo/ *a.* furtive, sly.
furúnculo /fu'runkulo/ *n. m.* boil.
fusibilidad /fusiβili'ðað/ *n. f.* fusibility.
fusible /fu'siβle/ *n. m.* fuse.
fusil /fu'sil/ *n. m.* rifle, gun.
fusilar /fusi'lar/ *v.* shoot, execute.
fusión /fu'sion/ *n. f.* fusion; merger.
fusionar /fusio'nar/ *v.* unite, fuse, merge.
fútbol /'futβol/ *n. m.* football, soccer.
fútil /'futil/ *a.* trivial.
futilidad /futili'ðað/ *n. f.* triviality.
futuro /fu'turo/ *a. & m.* future.
futurología /futurolo'hia/ *n. f.* futurology.

G

gabán /ga'βan/ *n. m.* overcoat.
gabardina /gaβar'ðina/ *n. f.* raincoat.
gabinete /gaβi'nete/ *n. m.* closet; cabinet; study.
gacela /ga'θela; ga'sela/ *n. f.* gazelle.
gaceta /ga'θeta; ga'seta/ *n. f.* gazette, newspaper.
gacetilla /gaθe'tiʎa; gase'tiya/ *n. f.* personal news section of a newspaper.
gaélico /ga'eliko/ *a.* Gaelic.
gafas /'gafas/ *n. f.pl.* eyeglasses.
gaguear /gage'ar/ *v.* stutter, stammer.
gaita /'gaita/ *n. f.* bagpipes.
gaje /'gahe/ *n. m.* salary; fee.
gala /'gala/ *n. f.* gala, ceremony; (*pl.*) regalia. **tener a g.,** be proud of.
galán /ga'lan/ *n. m.* gallant.
galano /ga'lano/ *a.* stylishly dressed; elegant.
galante /ga'lante/ *a.* gallant.
galantería /galante'ria/ *n. f.* gallantry, compliment.
galápago /ga'lapago/ *n. m.* freshwater turtle.
galardón /galar'ðon/ *n. m.* prize; reward.
gáleo /'galeo/ *n. m.* swordfish.
galera /ga'lera/ *n. f.* wagon; shed; galley.
galería /gale'ria/ *n. f.* gallery, *Theat.* balcony.
galés /'gales/ **-esa** *a. & n.* Welsh; Welshman, Welshwoman.
galgo /'galgo/ *n. m.* greyhound.
galillo /ga'liʎo; ga'liyo/ *n. m.* uvula.
galimatías /galima'tias/ *n. m.* gibberish.
gallardete /gaʎar'ðete; gayar'ðete/ *n. m.* pennant.
galleta /ga'ʎeta; ga'yeta/ *n. f.* cracker.
gallina /ga'ʎina; ga'yina/ *n. f.* hen.
gallinero /gaʎi'nero; gayi'nero/ *n. m.* chicken coop.
gallo /ga'ʎo; ga'yo/ *n. m.* rooster.
galocha /ga'lotʃa/ *n. f.* galosh.
galón /ga'lon/ *n. m.* gallon; *Mil.* stripe.
galope /ga'lope/ *n. m.* gallop. —**galopar,** *v.*
galopín /galo'pin/ *n. m.* ragamuffin, urchin (child).
gamba /'gamba/ *n. f.* prawn.
gamberro /gam'βerro/ **-ra** *n.* hooligan.
gambito /gam'bito/ *n. m.* gambit.
gamuza /ga'muθa; ga'musa/ *n. f.* chamois.
gana /'gana/ *n. f.* desire, wish, mind (to). **de buena g.,** willingly. **tener ganas de,** to feel like.
ganado /ga'naðo/ *n. m.* cattle.
ganador /gana'ðor/ **-ra** *n.* winner.
ganancia /ga'nanθia; ga'nansia/ *n. f.* gain, profit; (*pl.*) earnings.
ganapán /gana'pan/ *n. m.* drudge.
ganar /ga'nar/ *v.* earn; win; beat.
ganchillo /gan'tʃiʎo; gan'tʃiyo/ *n. m.* crochet work.
gancho /'gantʃo/ *n. m.* hook, hanger, clip, hairpin.
gandul /gan'dul/ **-la** *n.* idler, tramp, hobo.
ganga /'gaŋga/ *n. f.* bargain.
gangrena /gaŋ'grena/ *n. f.* gangrene.
gansarón /gansa'ron/ *n. m.* gosling.
ganso /'ganso/ *n. m.* goose.
garabato /gara'βato/ *n. m.* hook; scrawl, scribble.
garaje /ga'rahe/ *n. m.* garage.
garantía /garan'tia/ *n. f.* guarantee; collateral, security.
garantizar /garanti'θar; garanti'sar/ *v.* guarantee, secure, pledge.
garbanzo /gar'βanθo; gar'βanso/ *n. m.* chickpea.
garbo /'garβo/ *n. m.* grace.
garboso /gar'βoso/ *a.* graceful, sprightly.
gardenia /gar'ðenia/ *n. f.* gardenia.
garfa /'garfa/ *n. f.* claw, talon.
garganta /gar'ganta/ *n. f.* throat.
gárgara /'gargara/ *n. f.* gargle. —**gargarizar,** *v.*
garita /ga'rita/ *n. f.* sentry box.
garito /ga'rito/ *n. m.* gambling house.
garlopa /gar'lopa/ *n. f.* carpenter's plane.
garra /'garra/ *n. f.* claw.
garrafa /ga'rrafa/ *n. f.* decanter, carafe.
garrideza /garri'ðeθa; garri'ðesa/ *n. f.* elegance, handsomeness.
garrido /ga'rriðo/ *a.* elegant, handsome.
garrote /ga'rrote/ *n. m.* club, cudgel.
garrotillo /garro'tiʎo; garro'tiyo/ *n. m.* croup.
garrudo /ga'rruðo/ *a.* powerful, brawny.
garza /'garθa; 'garsa/ *n. f.* heron.
gas /gas/ *n. m.* gas.
gasa /'gasa/ *n. f.* gauze.
gaseosa /gase'osa/ *n. f.* carbonated water.
gaseoso /gase'oso/ *a.* gaseous.
gasolina /gaso'lina/ *n. f.* gasoline.
gasolinera /gasoli'nera/ *n. f.* gas station.
gastar /gas'tar/ *v.* spend; use up, wear out; waste.
gastritis /gas'tritis/ *n. f.* gastritis.
gastrómano /gas'tromano/ *n. m.* glutton.
gastrónomo /gas'tronomo/ **-ma** *n.* gourmet, epicure, gastronome.
gatear /gate'ar/ *v.* creep.
gatillo /ga'tiʎo; ga'tiyo/ *n. m.* trigger.
gato /'gato/ **-ta** *n.* cat.
gaucho /'gautʃo/ *n. m.* Argentine cowboy.
gaveta /ga'βeta/ *n. f.* drawer.
gavilla /ga'βiʎa; ga'βiya/ *n. f.* sheaf.
gaviota /ga'βiota/ *n. f.* seagull.
gayo /ga'yo/ *a.* merry, gay.
gayola /ga'yola/ *n. m.* cage; *Colloq.* prison.
gazapera /gaθa'pera; gasa'pera/ *n. f.* rabbit warren.
gazapo /ga'θapo; ga'sapo/ *n. m.* rabbit.
gazmoñada /gaθmo'ɲaða; gasmo'ɲaða/ *n. f.* prudishness.
gazmoño /gaθ'moɲo; gas'moɲo/ *n. m.* prude.
gaznate /gaθ'nate; gas'nate/ *n. m.* windpipe.
gazpacho /gaθ'patʃo; gas'patʃo/ *n. m.* cold tomato soup; gazpacho.
gelatina /hela'tina/ *n. f.* gelatine.
gemelo /he'melo/ **-la** *n.* twin.
gemelos /he'melos/ *n. m.pl.* cuff links; opera glasses; **-as,** twins.
gemido /he'miðo/ *n. m.* moan, groan, wail. —**gemir,** *v.*
genciana /hen'θiana; hen'siana/ *n. f.* gentian.
genealogía /henealo'hia/ *n. f.* genealogy, pedigree.
generación /henera'θion; henera'sion/ *n. f.* generation.
generador /henera'ðor/ *n. m.* generator.
general /hene'ral/ *a. & m.* general.
generalidad /henerali'ðað/ *n. f.* generality.
generalización /heneraliθa'θion; heneralisa'sion/ *n. f.* generalization.
generalizar /henerali'θar; henerali'sar/ *v.* generalize.
generalmente /heneral'mente/ *adv.* generally.
género /'henero/ *n.* **1.** *m.* gender; kind. **2.** (*pl.*) goods, material.
generosidad /henerosi'ðað/ *n. f.* generosity.
generoso /hene'roso/ *a.* generous.
génesis /'henesis/ *n. m.* genesis.
genético /he'netiko/ *a.* genetic.
genial /he'nial/ *a.* genial; brilliant.
genio /'henio/ *n. m.* genius; temper; disposition.
genitivo /heni'tiβo/ *n. m.* genitive.
genocidio /heno'θiðio; heno'siðio/ *n. m.* genocide.
gente /'hente/ *n. f.* people, folk.
gentil /hen'til/ *a.* gracious; graceful.
gentileza /henti'leθa; henti'lesa/ *n. f.* grace, graciousness.
gentío /hen'tio/ *n. m.* mob, crowd.
genuino /he'nuino/ *a.* genuine.
geografía /heogra'fia/ *n. f.* geography.
geográfico /heo'grafiko/ *a.* geographical.
geométrico /heo'metriko/ *a.* geometric.
geranio /he'ranio/ *n. m.* geranium.
gerencia /he'renθia; he'rensia/ *n. f.* management.
gerente /he'rente/ *n. m. & f.* manager, director.
germen /'hermen/ *n. m.* germ.
germinar /hermi'nar/ *v.* germinate.
gerundio /he'rundio/ *n. m.* gerund.
gesticulación /hestikula'θion; hestikula'sion/ *n. f.* gesticulation.
gesticular /hestiku'lar/ *v.* gesticulate, gesture.
gestión /hes'tion/ *n. f.* conduct; effort; action.
gesto /'hesto/ *n. m.* gesture, facial expression.
gigante /hi'gante/ *a. & n.* gigantic, giant.
gigantesco /higan'tesko/ *a.* gigantic, huge.
gilipollas /gili'poʎas; gili'poyas/ *n. m. & f. Colloq.* fool, idiot.
gimnasio /him'nasio/ *n. m.* gymnasium.
gimnástica /him'nastika/ *n. f.* gymnastics.
gimotear /himote'ar/ *v.* whine.
ginebra /hi'neβra/ *n. f.* gin.
ginecólogo /hine'kologo/ **-ga** *n.* gynecologist.
gira /'hira/ *n. f.* tour, trip.
girado /hi'raðo/ **-da** *n. Com.* drawee.
girador /hira'ðor/ **-ra** *n. Com.* drawer.
girar /hi'rar/ *v.* revolve, turn, spin, whirl.
giratorio /hira'torio/ *a.* rotary, revolving.
giro /'hiro/ *n. m.* whirl, turn, spin; *Com.* draft. **g. postal,** money order.
gitano /hi'tano/ **-na** *a. & n.* Gypsy.
glacial /gla'θial; gla'sial/ *a.* glacial, icy.
glaciar /gla'θiar; gla'siar/ *n. m.* glacier.
gladiador /glaðia'ðor/ *n. m.* gladiator.
glándula /'glandula/ *n. f.* gland.
glándula endocrina /'glandula endo'krina/ endocrine gland.
glándula pituitaria /'glandula pitui'taria/ pituitary gland.
glándula prostática /'glandula pros'tatika/ prostate gland.
glasé /gla'se/ *n. m.* glacé.
glicerina /gliθe'rina; glise'rina/ *n. f.* glycerine.
globo /'gloβo/ *n. m.* globe; balloon.
gloria /'gloria/ *n. f.* glory.
glorieta /glo'rieta/ *n. f.* bower.
glorificación /glorifika'θion; glorifika'sion/ *n. f.* glorification.
glorificar /glorifi'kar/ *v.* glorify.
glorioso /glo'rioso/ *a.* glorious.

glosa /'glosa/ n. f. gloss. —**glosar,** v.

glosario /glo'sario/ n. m. glossary.

glotón /glo'ton/ **-ona** a. & n. gluttonous; glutton.

glucosa /glu'kosa/ n. f. glucose.

gluten /'gluten/ n. m. gluten; glue.

gobernación /goβerna'θion; goβerna'sion/ n. f. government.

gobernador /goβerna'ðor/ **-ra** n. governor.

gobernalle /goβer'naʎe; goβer'naye/ n. m. rudder, tiller, helm.

gobernante /goβer'nante/ n. m. & f. ruler.

gobernar /goβer'nar/ v. govern.

gobierno /go'βierno/ n. m. government.

goce /'goθe; 'gose/ n. m. enjoyment.

gola /'gola/ n. f. throat.

golf /golf/ n. m. golf.

golfista /gol'fista/ n. m. & f. golfer.

golfo /'golfo/ n. m. gulf.

gollete /go'ʎete; go'yete/ n. m. upper portion of one's throat.

golondrina /golon'drina/ n. f. swallow.

golosina /golo'sina/ n. f. delicacy.

goloso /go'loso/ a. sweet-toothed.

golpe /'golpe/ n. m. blow, stroke. **de g.,** suddenly.

golpear /golpe'ar/ v. strike, beat, pound.

goma /'goma/ n. f. rubber; gum; glue; eraser.

góndola /'gondola/ n. f. gondola.

gordo /'gorðo/ a. fat.

gordura /gor'ðura/ n. f. fatness.

gorila /go'rila/ n. m. gorilla.

gorja /'gorha/ n. f. gorge.

gorjeo /gor'heo/ n. m. warble, chirp. —**gorjear,** v.

gorrión /go'rrion/ n. m. sparrow.

gorro /'gorro/ n. m. cap.

gota /'gota/ n. f. drop (of liquid).

gotear /gote'ar/ v. drip, leak.

goteo /go'teo/ n. m. leak.

gotera /go'tera/ n. f. leak; gutter.

gótico /'gotiko/ a. Gothic.

gozar /go'θar; go'sar/ v. enjoy.

gozne /'goθne; 'gosne/ n. m. hinge.

gozo /'goθo; 'goso/ n. m. enjoyment, delight, joy.

gozoso /go'θoso; go'soso/ a. joyful, joyous.

grabado /gra'βaðo/ n. **1.** m. engraving, cut, print. —a. **2.** recorded.

grabador /graβa'ðor/ n. m. engraver.

grabadora /graβa'ðora/ n. f. tape recorder.

grabar /gra'βar/ v. engrave; record.

gracia /'graθia; 'grasia/ n. f. grace; wit, charm. **hacer g.,** to amuse, strike as funny. **tener g.,** to be funny, to be witty.

gracias /'graθias; 'grasias/ n. f.pl. thanks, thank you.

gracioso /gra'θioso; gra'sioso/ a. witty, funny.

grada /'graða/ n. f. step.

gradación /graða'θion; graða'sion/ n. f. gradation.

grado /'graðo/ n. m. grade; rank; degree.

graduado /gra'ðuaðo/ **-da** n. graduate.

gradual /gra'ðual/ a. gradual.

graduar /gra'ðuar/ v. grade; graduate.

gráfico /'grafiko/ a. graphic, vivid.

grafito /gra'fito/ n. m. graphite.

grajo /'graho/ n. m. jackdaw.

gramática /gra'matika/ n. f. grammar.

gramo /'gramo/ n. m. gram.

gran /gran/ **grande** a. big, large; great.

granada /gra'naða/ n. f. grenade; pomegranate.

granar /gra'nar/ v. seed.

grandes almacenes /'grandes alma'θenes; 'grandes alma'senes/ n. m.pl. department store.

grandeza /gran'deθa; gran'desa/ n. f. greatness.

grandiosidad /grandiosi'ðað/ n. f. grandeur.

grandioso /gran'dioso/ a. grand, magnificent.

grandor /gran'dor/ n. m. size.

granero /gra'nero/ n. m. barn; granary.

granito /gra'nito/ n. m. granite.

granizada /grani'θaða; grani'saða/ n. f. hailstorm.

granizo /gra'niθo; gra'niso/ n. m. hail. —**granizar,** v.

granja /'granha/ n. f. grange; farm; farmhouse.

granjear /granhe'ar/ v. earn, gain; get.

granjero /gran'hero/ **-era** n. farmer.

grano /'grano/ n. m. grain; kernel.

granuja /gra'nuha/ n. m. waif, urchin.

grapa /'grapa/ n. f. clamp, clip.

grapadora /grapa'ðora/ n. f. stapler.

grasa /'grasa/ n. f. grease, fat.

grasiento /gra'siento/ a. greasy.

gratificación /gratifika'θion; gratifika'sion/ n. f. gratification; reward; tip.

gratificar /gratifi'kar/ v. gratify; reward; tip.

gratis /'gratis/ adv. gratis, free.

gratitud /grati'tuð/ n. f. gratitude.

grato /'grato/ a. grateful; pleasant.

gratuito /gra'tuito/ a. gratuitous; free.

gravamen /gra'βamen/ n. m. tax; burden; obligation.

grave /'graβe/ a. grave, serious, severe.

gravedad /graβe'ðað/ n. f. gravity, seriousness.

gravitación /graβita'θion; graβita'sion/ n. f. gravitation.

gravitar /graβi'tar/ v. gravitate.

gravoso /gra'βoso/ a. burdensome.

graznido /graθ'niðo; gras'niðo/ n. m. croak. —**graznar,** v.

Grecia /'greθia; 'gresia/ n. f. Greece.

greco /'greko/ **-ca** a. & n. Greek.

greda /'greða/ n. f. clay.

gresca /'greska/ n. f. revelry; quarrel.

griego /'griego/ **-ga** a. & n. Greek.

grieta /'grieta/ n. f. opening; crevice, crack.

grifo /'grifo/ n. m. faucet.

grillo /'griʎo; 'griyo/ n. m. cricket.

grima /'grima/ n. f. fright.

gringo /'gringo/ **-ga** n. foreigner (usually North American).

gripa /'gripa/ **gripe** n. f. grippe.

gris /gris/ a. gray.

grito /'grito/ n. m. shout, scream, cry. —**gritar,** v.

grosella /gro'seʎa; gro'seya/ n. f. currant.

grosería /grose'ria/ n. f. grossness; coarseness.

grosero /gro'sero/ a. coarse, vulgar, discourteous.

grotesco /gro'tesko/ a. grotesque.

grúa /'grua/ n. f. crane; tow truck.

gruesa /'gruesa/ n. f. gross.

grueso /'grueso/ a. **1.** bulky; stout; coarse, thick. —n. **2.** m. bulk.

grulla /'gruʎa; 'gruya/ n. f. crane.

gruñido /gru'niðo/ n. m. growl, snarl, mutter. —**gruñir,** v.

grupo /'grupo/ n. m. group, party.

gruta /'gruta/ n. f. cavern.

guacamol /guaka'mol/ **guacamole** n. m. avocado sauce; guacamole.

guadaña /gua'ðaɲa/ n. f. scythe. —**guadañar,** v.

guagua /'guagua/ n. f. (S.A.) baby; (Carib.) bus.

gualdo /'gualdo/ n. m. yellow, golden.

guano /'guano/ n. m. guano (fertilizer).

guante /'guante/ n. m. glove.

guantera /guan'tera/ n. f. glove compartment.

guapo /'guapo/ a. handsome.

guarda /'guarða/ n. m. or f. guard.

guardabarros /guarða'βarros/ n. m. fender.

guardacostas /guarða'kostas/ n. m. revenue ship.

guardaespaldas /,guarðaes'paldas/ n. m. & f. bodyguard.

guardameta /guarða'meta/ n. m. & f. goalkeeper.

guardar /guar'ðar/ v. keep, store, put away; guard.

guardarropa /guarða'rropa/ n. f. coat room.

guardarse de /guar'ðarse de/ v. beware of, avoid.

guardia /'guarðia/ n. **1.** f. guard; watch. —n. **2.** m. policeman.

guardián /guar'ðian/ **-na** n. guardian, keeper, watchman.

guardilla /guar'ðiʎa; guar'ðiya/ n. f. attic.

guarida /gua'riða/ n. f. den.

guarismo /gua'rismo/ n. m. number, figure.

guarnecer /guarne'θer; guarne'ser/ v. adorn.

guarnición /guarni'θion; guarni'sion/ n. f. garrison; trimming.

guasa /'guasa/ n. f. joke, jest.

guayaba /gua'yaβa/ n. f. guava.

gubernativo /guβerna'tiβo/ a. governmental.

guerra /'gerra/ n. f. war.

guerrero /ge'rrero/ **-ra** n. warrior.

guía /'gia/ n. **1.** m. & f. guide. **2.** f. guidebook, directory.

guiar /giar/ v. guide; steer, drive.

guija /'giha/ n. f. pebble.

guillotina /giʎo'tina; giyo'tina/ n. f. guillotine.

guindar /gin'dar/ v. hang.

guinga /'ginga/ n. f. gingham.

guiñada /gi'naða/ n. f., **guiño,** m. wink. —**guiñar,** v.

guión /gi'on/ n. m. dash, hyphen; script.

guirnalda /gir'nalda/ n. f. garland, wreath.

guisa /'gisa/ n. f. guise, manner.

guisado /gi'saðo/ n. m. stew.

guisante /gi'sante/ n. m. pea.

guisar /gi'sar/ v. cook.

guiso /'giso/ n. m. stew.

guita /'gita/ n. f. twine.

guitarra /gi'tarra/ n. f. guitar.

guitarrista /gita'rrista/ n. m. & f. guitarist.

gula /'gula/ n. f. gluttony.

gurú /gu'ru/ n. m. guru.

gusano /gu'sano/ n. m. worm, caterpillar.

gustar /gus'tar/ v. please; taste.

gustillo /gus'tiʎo; gus'tiyo/ n. m. aftertaste, slight pleasure.

gusto /'gusto/ n. m. pleasure; taste; liking.

gustoso /gus'toso/ a. pleasant; tasteful.

gutural /gutu'ral/ a. guttural.

H

haba /'aβa/ n. f. bean.

habanera /aβa'nera/ n. f. Cuban dance melody.

haber /a'βer/ v. have. **h. de,** be to, be supposed to.

haberes /a'βeres/ n. m.pl. property; worldly goods.

habichuela /aβi't ʃuela/ n. f. bean.

hábil /'aβil/ a. skillful; capable; clever.

habilidad /aβili'ðað/ n. f. ability; skill; talent.

habilidoso /aβili'ðoso/ a. able, skillful, talented.

habilitado /aβili'taðo/ **-da** n. paymaster.

habilitar /aβili'tar/ v. qualify; supply, equip.

hábilmente /'aβilmente/ adv. ably.

habitación /aβita'θion; aβita'sion/ n. f. dwelling; room. **h. individual,** single room.

habitante /aβi'tante/ n. m. & f. inhabitant.

habitar /aβi'tar/ v. inhabit; dwell.

hábito /'aβito/ n. m. habit; custom.

habitual /aβi'tual/ a. habitual.

habituar /aβi'tuar/ v. accustom, habituate.

habla /'aβla/ n. f. speech.

hablador /aβla'ðor/ a. talkative.

hablar /a'βlar/ v. talk, speak.

haca /'aka/ n. f. pony.

hacedor /aθe'ðor; ase'ðor/ n. m. maker.

hacendado /aθen'daðo; asen'daðo/ **-da** n. hacienda owner; farmer.

hacendoso /aθen'doso; asen'doso/ a. industrious.

hacer /a'θer; a'ser/ v. do; make. **hace dos años,** etc., two years ago, etc.

hacerse /a'θerse; a'serse/ v. become, get to be.

hacha /'atʃa/ n. f. ax, hatchet.

hacia /'aθia; 'asia/ prep. toward.

hacienda /a'θienda; a'sienda/ n. f. property; estate; ranch; farm; Govt. treasury.

hada /'aða/ n. f. fairy.

hado /'aðo/ n. m. fate.

halagar /ala'gar/ v. flatter.

halar /a'lar/ v. haul, pull.

halcón /al'kon/ n. m. hawk, falcon.

haleche /a'letʃe/ n. m. anchovy.

hallado /a'ʎaðo; a'yaðo/ a. found. **bien h.,** welcome. **mal h.,** uneasy.

hallar /a'ʎar; a'yar/ v. find, locate.

hallarse /a'ʎarse; a'yarse/ v. be located; happen to be.

hallazgo /a'ʎaθgo; a'yasgo/ n. m. find, thing found.

hamaca /a'maka/ n. f. hammock.

hambre /'ambre/ n. f. hunger. **tener h., estar con h.,** to be hungry.

hambrear /ambre'ar/ v. hunger; starve.

hambriento /am'briento/ a. starving, hungry.

hamburguesa /ambur'gesa/ n. f. beefburger, hamburger.

haragán /ara'gan/ **-na** n. idler, lazy person.

haraganear /aragane'ar/ v. loiter.

harapo /a'rapo/ n. m. rag, tatter.

haraposo /ara'poso/ a. ragged, shabby.

harén /a'ren/ n. m. harem.

harina /a'rina/ n. f. flour, meal.

harnero /ar'nero/ n. m. sieve.

hartar /ar'tar/ v. satiate.

harto /'arto/ a. stuffed; fed up.

hartura /ar'tura/ n. f. superabundance, glut.

hasta /'asta/ prep. **1.** until, till; as far as, up to. **h. luego,** good-bye, so long. —adv. **2.** even.

hastío /as'tio/ n. m. distaste, loathing.

hato /'ato/ n. m. herd.

hay /ai/ v. there is, there are. **h. que,** it is necessary to. **no h. de qué,** you're welcome, don't mention it.

haya /'aya/ n. f. beech tree.

haz /aθ; as/ n. f. bundle, sheaf; face.

hazaña /a'θaɲa; a'saɲa/ n. f. deed; exploit, feat.

hebdomadario /eβðoma'ðario/ a. weekly.

hebilla /e'βiʎa; e'βiya/ n. f. buckle.

hebra /'eβra/ n. f. thread, string.

hebreo /e'βreo/ **-rea** a. & n. Hebrew.

hechicero /etʃi'θero; etʃi'sero/ **-ra** n. wizard, witch.

hechizar /etʃi'θar; etʃi'sar/ v. bewitch.

hechizo /e'tʃiθo; e'tʃiso/ n. m. spell.

hecho /'etʃo/ n. m. fact; act; deed.

hechura /e'tʃura/ n. f. workmanship, make.

hediondez /eðion'deθ; eðion'des/ n. f. stench.

hégira /'ehira/ n. f. hegira.

helada /e'laða/ n. f. frost.

heladería /elaðe'ria/ n. f. ice-cream parlor.

helado /e'laðo/ n. m. ice cream.

helar /e'lar/ *v.* freeze.

helecho /e'letʃo/ *n. m.* fern.

hélice /'eliθe; 'elise/ *n. f.* propeller; helix.

helicóptero /eli'koptero/ *n. m.* helicopter.

helio /'elio/ *n. m.* helium.

hembra /'embra/ *n. f.* female.

hemisferio /emis'ferio/ *n. m.* hemisphere.

hemoglobina /emoglo'βina/ *n. f.* hemoglobin.

hemorragia /emo'rrahia/ *n. f.* hemorrhage.

hemorragia nasal /emo'rrahia na'sal/ nosebleed.

henchir /en'tʃir/ *v.* stuff.

hendedura /ende'ðura/ *n. f.* crevice, crack.

hendido /en'diðo/ *a.* cloven, cleft (lip).

heno /'eno/ *n. m.* hay.

hepática /e'patika/ *n. f.* liverwort.

hepatitis /epa'titis/ *n. f.* hepatitis.

heraldo /e'raldo/ *n. m.* herald.

herbáceo /er'βaθeo; er'βaseo/ *a.* herbaceous.

herbívoro /er'βiβoro/ *a.* herbivorous.

heredar /ere'ðar/ *v.* inherit.

heredero /ere'ðero/ **-ra** *n.* heir; successor.

hereditario /ereði'tario/ *a.* hereditary.

hereje /e'rehe/ *n. m. & f.* heretic.

herejía /ere'hia/ *n. f.* heresy.

herencia /e'renθia; e'rensia/ *n. f.* inheritance; heritage.

herético /e'retiko/ *a.* heretical.

herida /e'riða/ *n. f.* wound, injury.

herir /e'rir/ *v.* wound, injure.

hermafrodita /ermafro'ðita/ *a. & n.* hermaphrodite.

hermana /er'mana/ *n. f.* sister.

hermano /er'mano/ *n. m.* brother.

hermético /er'metiko/ *a.* airtight.

hermoso /er'moso/ *a.* beautiful, handsome.

hermosura /ermo'sura/ *n. f.* beauty.

hernia /'ernia/ *n. f.* hernia, rupture.

héroe /'eroe/ *n. m.* hero.

heroico /e'roiko/ *a.* heroic.

heroína /ero'ina/ *n. f.* heroine.

heroísmo /ero'ismo/ *n. m.* heroism.

herradura /erra'ðura/ *n. f.* horseshoe.

herramienta /erra'mienta/ *n. f.* tool; implement.

herrería /erre'ria/ *n. f.* blacksmith's shop.

herrero /e'rrero/ *n. m.* blacksmith.

herrumbre /e'rrumbre/ *n. f.* rust.

hertzio /'ertθio; 'ertsio/ *n. m.* hertz.

hervir /er'βir/ *v.* boil.

hesitación /esita'θion; esita'sion/ *n. f.* hesitation.

heterogéneo /etero'heneo/ *a.* heterogeneous.

heterosexual /eterosek'sual/ *a.* heterosexual.

hexagonal /eksago'nal/ *a.* hexagonal.

hexágono /e'ksagono/ *n. m.* hexagon.

hez /eθ; es/ *n. f.* dregs, sediment.

híbrido /'iβriðo/ **-da** *n. & a.* hybrid.

hidalgo /i'ðalgo/ **-ga** *a. & n.* noble.

hidalguía /iðal'gia/ *n. f.* nobility; generosity.

hidráulico /i'ðrauliko/ *a.* hydraulic.

hidroavión /iðroa'βion/ *n. m.* seaplane, hydroplane.

hidrofobia /iðro'foβia/ *n. f.* rabies.

hidrógeno /i'ðroheno/ *n. m.* hydrogen.

hidropesía /iðrope'sia/ *n. f.* dropsy.

hiedra /'ieðra/ *n. f.* ivy.

hiel /iel/ *n. f.* gall.

hielo /'ielo/ *n. m.* ice.

hiena /'iena/ *n. f.* hyena.

hierba /'ierβa/ *n. f.* grass; herb; marijuana.

hierbabuena /ierβa'βuena/ *n. f.* mint.

hierro /'ierro/ *n. m.* iron.

hígado /'igaðo/ *n. m.* liver.

higiene /i'hiene/ *n. f.* hygiene.

higiénico /i'hieniko/ *a.* sanitary, hygienic.

higo /'igo/ *n. m.* fig.

higuera /i'gera/ *n. f.* fig tree.

hija /'iha/ *n. f.* daughter.

hija adoptiva /'iha aðop'tiβa/ adopted daughter.

hijastro /i'hastro/ **-tra** *n.* stepchild.

hijo /'iho/ *n. m.* son.

hijo adoptivo /'iho aðop'tiβo/ *n. m.* adopted child, adopted son.

hila /'ila/ *n. f.* line.

hilandero /ilan'dero/ **-ra** *n.* spinner.

hilar /i'lar/ *v.* spin.

hilera /i'lera/ *n. f.* row, line, tier.

hilo /'ilo/ *n. m.* thread; string; wire; linen.

himno /'imno/ *n. m.* hymn.

hincar /in'kar/ *v.* drive, thrust; sink into.

hincarse /in'karse/ *v.* kneel.

hinchar /in'tʃar/ *v.* swell.

hindú /in'du/ *n. & a.* Hindu.

hinojo /i'noho/ *n. m.* knee.

hiperenlace /iperen'laθe, iperen'lase/ *n. m.* hyperlink.

hipermercado /ipermer'kaðo/ *n. m.* hypermarket.

hipertexto /iper'teksto/ *n. m.* hypertext.

hipnótico /ip'notiko/ *a.* hypnotic.

hipnotismo /ipno'tismo/ *n. m.* hypnotism.

hipnotista /ipno'tista/ *n. m. & f.* hypnotist.

hipnotizar /ipnoti'θar; ipnoti'sar/ *v.* hypnotize.

hipo /'ipo/ *n. m.* hiccough.

hipocresía /ipokre'sia/ *n. f.* hypocrisy.

hipócrita /i'pokrita/ *a. & n.* hypocritical; hypocrite.

hipódromo /i'poðromo/ *n. m.* race track.

hipoteca /ipo'teka/ *n. f.* mortgage. —**hipotecar,** *v.*

hipótesis /i'potesis/ *n. f.* hypothesis.

hirsuto /ir'suto/ *a.* hairy, hirsute.

hispano /is'pano/ *a.* Hispanic, Spanish American.

Hispanoamérica /ispanoa'merika/ *f.* Spanish America.

hispanoamericano /ispanoameri'kano/ **-na** *a. & n.* Spanish American.

histerectomía /isterekto'mia/ *n. f.* hysterectomy.

histeria /is'teria/ *n. f.* hysteria.

histérico /is'teriko/ *a.* hysterical.

historia /is'toria/ *n. f.* history; story.

historiador /istoria'ðor/ **-ra** *n.* historian.

histórico /is'toriko/ *a.* historic, historical.

histrión /is'trion/ *n. m.* actor.

hocico /o'θiko; o'siko/ *n. m.* snout, muzzle.

hogar /o'gar/ *n. m.* hearth; home.

hoguera /o'gera/ *n. f.* bonfire, blaze.

hoja /'oha/ *n. f.* leaf; sheet (of paper); pane; blade.

hoja de cálculo /'oha de 'kalkulo/ spreadsheet.

hoja de inscripción /'oha de inskrip'θion; 'oha de inskrip'sion/ entry blank.

hoja de pedidos /'oha de pe'ðiðos/ order blank.

hoja informativa /'oha informa'tiβa/ newsletter.

hojalata /oha'lata/ *n. f.* tin.

hojalatero /ohala'tero/ **-ra** *n.* tinsmith.

hojear /ohe'ar/ *v.* scan, skim through.

hola /'ola/ *interj.* hello.

Holanda /o'landa/ *n. f.* Holland, Netherlands.

holandés /olan'des/ **-esa** *a. & n.* Dutch; Hollander.

holganza /ol'ganθa; ol'gansa/ *n. f.* leisure; diversion.

holgazán /olga'θan; olga'san/ **-ana** *a.*

1. idle, lazy. —*n.* 2. *m.* idler, loiterer, tramp.

holgazanear /olgaθane'ar; olgasane'ar/ *v.* idle, loiter.

hollín /o'ʎin; o'yin/ *n. m.* soot.

holografía /ologra'fia/ *n. f.* holography.

holograma /olo'grama/ *n. m.* hologram.

hombre /'ombre/ *n. m.* man.

hombría /om'βria/ *n. f.* manliness.

hombro /'ombro/ *n. m.* shoulder.

hombruno /om'bruno/ *a.* mannish, masculine (woman).

homenaje /ome'nahe/ *n. m.* homage.

homeópata /ome'opata/ *n. m.* homeopath.

homicidio /omi'θiðio; omi'siðio/ *n. m.* homicide.

homilía /omi'lia/ *n. f.* homily.

homosexual /omose'ksual/ *a.* homosexual, gay.

honda /'onda/ *n. f.* sling.

hondo /'ondo/ *a.* deep.

hondonada /ondo'naða/ *n. f.* ravine.

hondura /on'dura/ *n. f.* depth.

honestidad /onesti'ðað/ *n. f.* modesty, unpretentiousness.

honesto /o'nesto/ *a.* honest; pure; just.

hongo /'oŋgo/ *n. m.* fungus; mushroom.

honor /o'nor/ *n. m.* honor.

honorable /ono'raβle/ *a.* honorable.

honorario /ono'rario/ *a.* 1. honorary. —*n.* 2. *m.* honorarium, fee.

honorífico /ono'rifiko/ *a.* honorary.

honra /'onra/ *n. f.* honor. —**honrar,** *v.*

honradez /onra'ðeθ; onra'ðes/ *n. f.* honesty.

honrado /on'raðo/ *a.* honest, honorable.

hora /'ora/ *n. f.* hour; time (of day).

horadar /ora'ðar/ *v.* perforate.

hora punta /'ora 'punta/ rush hour.

horario /o'rario/ *n. m.* timetable, schedule.

horca /'orka/ *n. f.* gallows; pitchfork.

horda /'orða/ *n. f.* horde.

horizontal /oriθon'tal; orison'tal/ *a.* horizontal.

horizonte /ori'θonte; ori'sonte/ *n. m.* horizon.

hormiga /or'miga/ *n. f.* ant.

hormiguear /ormige'ar/ *v.* itch.

hormiguero /ormi'gero/ *n. m.* ant hill.

hornero /or'nero/ **-ra** *n.* baker.

hornillo /or'niʎo; or'nijo/ *n. m.* stove.

horno /'orno/ *n. m.* oven; kiln.

horóscopo /o'roskopo/ *n. m.* horoscope.

horrendo /o'rrendo/ *a.* dreadful, horrendous.

horrible /o'rriβle/ *a.* horrible, hideous, awful.

hórrido /'orriðo/ *a.* horrid.

horror /o'rror/ *n. m.* horror.

horrorizar /orrori'θar; orrori'sar/ *v.* horrify.

horroroso /orro'roso/ *a.* horrible, frightful.

hortelano /orte'lano/ *n. m.* horticulturist.

hospedaje /ospe'ðahe/ *n. m.* lodging.

hospedar /ospe'ðar/ *v.* give or take lodgings.

hospital /ospi'tal/ *n. m.* hospital.

hospitalario /ospita'lario/ *a.* hospitable.

hospitalidad /ospitali'ðað/ *n. f.* hospitality.

hospitalmente /ospital'mente/ *adv.* hospitably.

hostia /'ostia/ *n. f.* host; *Colloq.* hit, blow.

hostil /'ostil/ *a.* hostile.

hostilidad /ostili'ðað/ *n. f.* hostility.

hotel /'otel/ *n. m.* hotel.

hoy /oi/ *adv.* today. **h. día, h. en día,** nowadays.

hoya /'oya/ *n. f.* dale, valley.

hoyo /'oyo/ *n. m.* pit, hole.

hoyuelo /o'yuelo/ *n. m.* dimple.

hoz /oθ; os/ *n. f.* sickle.

hucha /'utʃa/ *n. f.* chest, money box; savings.

hueco /'ueko/ *a.* 1. hollow, empty. —*n.* 2. *m.* hole, hollow.

huelga /'uelga/ *n. f.* strike.

huelgista /uel'hista/ *n. m. & f.* striker.

huella /'ueʎa; 'ueya/ *n. f.* track, trace; footprint.

huérfano /'uerfano/ **-na** *a. & n.* orphan.

huero /'uero/ *a.* empty.

huerta /'uerta/ *n. f.* (vegetable) garden.

huerto /'uerto/ *n. m.* orchard.

hueso /'ueso/ *n. m.* bone; fruit pit.

huésped /'uespeð/ *n. m. & f.* guest.

huesudo /ue'suðo/ *a.* bony.

huevo /'ueβo/ *n. m.* egg.

huída /'uiða/ *n. f.* flight, escape.

huir /uir/ *v.* flee.

hule /'ule/ *n. m.* oilcloth.

humanidad /umani'ðað/ *n. f.* humanity, mankind; humaneness.

humanista /uma'nista/ *n. m. & f.* humanist.

humanitario /umani'tario/ *a.* humane.

humano /u'mano/ *a.* human; humane.

humareda /uma'reða/ *n. f.* dense cloud of smoke.

humear /ume'ar/ *v.* emit smoke or steam.

humedad /ume'ðað/ *n. f.* humidity, moisture, dampness.

humedecer /umeðe'θer; umeðe'ser/ *v.* moisten, dampen.

húmedo /'umeðo/ *a.* humid, moist, damp.

humildad /umil'dað/ *n. f.* humility, meekness.

humilde /u'milde/ *a.* humble, meek.

humillación /umiʎa'θion; umiya'sion/ *n. f.* humiliation.

humillar /umi'ʎar; umi'yar/ *v.* humiliate.

humo /'umo/ *n. m.* smoke; (*pl.*) airs, affectation.

humor /u'mor/ *n. m.* humor, mood.

humorista /umo'rista/ *n. m. & f.* humorist.

hundimiento /undi'miento/ *n. m.* collapse.

hundir /un'dir/ *v.* sink; collapse.

húngaro /'uŋgaro/ **-ra** *a. & n.* Hungarian.

Hungría /uŋ'gria/ *n. f.* Hungary.

huracán /ura'kan/ *n. m.* hurricane.

huraño /u'raɲo/ *a.* shy, bashful.

hurgar /ur'gar/ *v.* stir.

hurón /u'ron/ *n. m.* ferret.

hurtadillas /urta'ðiʎas; urta'ðiyas/ *n. f.pl.* **a h.,** on the sly.

hurtador /urta'ðor/ **-ra** *n.* thief.

hurtar /ur'tar/ *v.* steal, rob of; hide.

hurtarse /ur'tarse/ *v.* hide; withdraw.

husmear /usme'ar/ *v.* scent, smell.

huso /'uso/ *n. m.* spindle; bobbin.

huso horario /'uso o'rario/ time zone.

I

ibérico /i'βeriko/ *a.* Iberian.

iberoamericano /iβeroameri'kano/ **-na** *a. & n.* Latin American.

ida /'iða/ *n. f.* departure; trip out. **i. y vuelta,** round trip.

idea /i'ðea/ *n. f.* idea.

ideal /i'ðeal/ *a. & m.* ideal.

idealismo /iðea'lismo/ *n. m.* idealism.

idealista /iðea'lista/ *n. m. & f.* idealist.

idear /iðe'ar/ *v.* plan, conceive.

idéntico /i'ðentiko/ *a.* identical.

identidad /iðenti'ðað/ *n. f.* identity; identification.

identificar /iðentifi'kar/ *v.* identify.

idilio /i'ðilio/ *n. m.* idyll.

idioma /i'ðioma/ *n. m.* language.

idiota /i'ðiota/ *a. & n.* idiotic; idiot.

idiotismo /iðio'tismo/ *n. m.* idiom; idiocy.

idolatrar /iðola'trar/ *v.* idolize, adore.

ídolo /'iðolo/ *n. m.* idol.

idóneo /i'ðoneo/ *a.* suitable, fit, apt.

iglesia /i'glesia/ *n. f.* church.

ignición /igni'θion; igni'sion/ *n. f.* ignition.

ignominia /igno'minia/ *n. f.* ignominy, shame.

ignominioso /ignomi'nioso/ *a.* ignominious, shameful.

ignorancia /igno'ranθia; igno'ransia/ *n. f.* ignorance.

ignorante /igno'rante/ *a.* ignorant.

ignorar /igno'rar/ *v.* be ignorant of, not know.

ignoto /ig'noto/ *a.* unknown.

igual /i'gual/ *a.* equal; the same; (*pl.*) alike. *m.* equal.

igualar /igua'lar/ *v.* equal; equalize; match.

igualdad /igual'daθ/ *n. f.* equality; sameness.

ijada /i'haða/ *n. f.* flank (of an animal).

ilegal /ile'gal/ *a.* illegal.

ilegítimo /ile'hitimo/ *a.* illegitimate.

ileso /i'leso/ *a.* unharmed.

ilícito /i'liθito; i'lisito/ *a.* illicit, unlawful.

iluminación /ilumina'θion; ilumina'sion/ *n. f.* illumination.

iluminar /ilumi'nar/ *v.* illuminate.

ilusión /ilu'sion/ *n. f.* illusion.

ilusión de óptica /ilu'sion de 'optika/ optical illusion.

ilusorio /ilu'sorio/ *a.* illusive.

ilustración /ilustra'θion; ilustra'sion/ *n. f.* illustration; learning.

ilustrador /ilustra'ðor/ **-ra** *n.* illustrator.

ilustrar /ilus'trar/ *v.* illustrate.

ilustre /i'lustre/ *a.* illustrious, honorable, distinguished.

imagen /i'mahen/ *n. f.* image.

imaginación /imahina'θion; imahina'sion/ *n. f.* imagination.

imaginar /imahi'nar/ *v.* imagine.

imaginario /imahi'nario/ *a.* imaginary.

imaginativo /imahina'tiβo/ *a.* imaginative.

imán /i'man/ *n. m.* magnet; imam.

imbécil /im'beθil; im'besil/ *a. & n.* imbecile; stupid, foolish; fool.

imbuir /im'buir/ *v.* imbue, instil.

imitación /imita'θion; imita'sion/ *n. f.* imitation.

imitador /imita'ðor/ **-ra** *n.* imitator.

imitar /imi'tar/ *v.* imitate.

impaciencia /impa'θienθia; impa'siensia/ *n. f.* impatience.

impaciente /impa'θiente; impa'siente/ *a.* impatient.

impar /im'par/ *a.* unequal, uneven, odd.

imparcial /impar'θial; impar'sial/ *a.* impartial.

impasible /impa'siβle/ *a.* impassive, unmoved.

impávido /im'paβiðo/ *adj.* fearless, intrepid.

impedimento /impeði'mento/ *n. m.* impediment, obstacle.

impedir /impe'ðir/ *v.* impede, hinder, stop, obstruct.

impeler /impe'ler/ *v.* impel; incite.

impensado /impen'saðo/ *a.* unexpected.

imperar /impe'rar/ *v.* reign; prevail.

imperativo /impera'tiβo/ *a.* imperative.

imperceptible /imperθep'tiβle; impersep'tiβle/ *a.* imperceptible.

imperdible /imper'ðiβle/ *n. m.* safety pin.

imperecedero /impereθe'ðero; imperese'ðero/ *a.* imperishable.

imperfecto /imper'fekto/ *a.* imperfect, faulty.

imperial /impe'rial/ *a.* imperial.

imperialismo /imperia'lismo/ *n. m.* imperialism.

impericia /impe'riθia; impe'risia/ *n. f.* inexperience.

imperio /im'perio/ *n. m.* empire.

imperioso /impe'rioso/ *a.* imperious, domineering.

impermeable /imperme'aβle/ *a.* waterproof. *m.* raincoat.

impersonal /imperso'nal/ *a.* impersonal.

impertinencia /impertinen'θia; impertinen'sia/ *n. f.* impertinence.

ímpetu /'impetu/ *n. m.* impulse; impetus.

impetuoso /impe'tuoso/ *a.* impetuous.

impiedad /impie'ðaθ/ *n. f.* impiety.

impío /im'pio/ *a.* impious.

implacable /impla'kaβle/ *a.* implacable, unrelenting.

implicar /impli'kar/ *v.* implicate, involve.

implorar /implo'rar/ *v.* implore.

imponente /impo'nente/ *a.* impressive.

imponer /impo'ner/ *v.* impose.

impopular /impopu'lar/ *a.* unpopular.

importación /importa'θion; importa'sion/ *n. f.* importation, importing.

importador /importa'ðor/ **-ra** *n.* importer.

importancia /impor'tanθia; impor'tansia/ *n. f.* importance.

importante /impor'tante/ *a.* important.

importar /impor'tar/ *v.* be important, matter; import.

importe /im'porte/ *n. m.* value; amount.

importunar /importu'nar/ *v.* beg, importune.

imposibilidad /imposiβili'ðaθ/ *n. f.* impossibility.

imposibilitado /imposiβili'taðo/ *a.* helpless.

imposible /impo'siβle/ *a.* impossible.

imposición /imposi'θion; imposi'sion/ *n. f.* imposition.

impostor /impos'tor/ **-ra** *n.* imposter, faker.

impotencia /impo'tenθia; impo'tensia/ *n. f.* impotence.

impotente /impo'tente/ *a.* impotent.

imprecar /impre'kar/ *v.* curse.

impreciso /impre'θiso; impre'siso/ *adj.* inexact.

impregnar /impreg'nar/ *v.* impregnate.

imprenta /im'prenta/ *n. f.* press; printing house.

imprescindible /impresθin'diβle; impressin'diβle/ *a.* essential.

impresión /impre'sion/ *n. f.* impression.

impresionable /impresio'naβle/ *a.* impressionable.

impresionar /impresio'nar/ *v.* impress.

impresor /impre'sor/ *n. m.* printer.

imprevisión /impreβi'sion/ *n. f.* oversight; thoughtlessness.

imprevisto /impre'βisto/ *a.* unexpected, unforeseen.

imprimir /impri'mir/ *v.* print; imprint.

improbable /impro'βaβle/ *a.* improbable.

improbo /im'proβo/ *a.* dishonest.

improductivo /improðuk'tiβo/ *a.* unproductive.

improperio /impro'perio/ *n. m.* insult.

impropio /im'propio/ *a.* improper.

improvisación /improβisa'θion; improβisa'sion/ *n. f.* improvisation.

improvisar /improβi'sar/ *v.* improvise.

improviso /impro'βiso; impro'βisto/ *a.* unforeseen.

imprudencia /impru'ðenθia; impru'ðensia/ *n. f.* imprudence.

imprudente /impru'ðente/ *a.* imprudent, reckless.

impuesto /im'puesto/ *n. m.* tax.

impuesto sobre la renta /im'puesto soβre la 'rrenta/ income tax.

impulsar /impul'sar/ *v.* prompt, impel.

impulsivo /impul'siβo/ *a.* impulsive.

impulso /im'pulso/ *n. m.* impulse.

impureza /impu'reθa; impu'resa/ *n. f.* impurity.

impuro /im'puro/ *a.* impure.

imputación /imputa'θion; imputa'sion/ *n. f.* imputation.

imputar /impu'tar/ *v.* impute, attribute.

inaccesible /inakθe'siβle; inakse'siβle/ *a.* inaccessible.

inacción /inak'θion; inak'sion/ *n. f.* inaction; inactivity.

inaceptable /inaθep'taβle; inasep'taβle/ *a.* unacceptable.

inactivo /inak'tiβo/ *a.* inactive; sluggish.

inadecuado /inaðe'kuaðo/ *a.* inadequate.

inadvertencia /inaðβer'tenθia; inaðβer'tensia/ *n. f.* oversight.

inadvertido /inaðβer'tiðo/ *a.* inadvertent, careless; unnoticed.

inagotable /inago'taβle/ *a.* inexhaustible.

inalterado /inalte'raðo/ *a.* unchanged.

inanición /inani'θion; inani'sion/ *n. f.* starvation.

inanimado /inani'maðo/ *adj.* inanimate.

inapetencia /inape'tenθia; inape'tensia/ *n. f.* lack of appetite.

inaplicable /inapli'kaβle/ *a.* inapplicable; unfit.

inaudito /inau'ðito/ *a.* unheard of.

inauguración /inaugura'θion; inaugura'sion/ *n. f.* inauguration.

inaugurar /inaugu'rar/ *v.* inaugurate, open.

incandescente /inkandes'θente; inkandes'sente/ *a.* incandescent.

incansable /inkan'saβle/ *a.* tireless.

incapacidad /inkapaθi'ðaθ; inkapasi'ðaθ/ *n. f.* incapacity.

incapacitar /inkapaθi'tar; inkapasi'tar/ *v.* incapacitate.

incapaz /inka'paθ; inka'pas/ *a.* incapable.

incauto /in'kauto/ *a.* unwary.

incendiar /inθen'diar; insen'diar/ *v.* set on fire.

incendio /in'θendio; in'sendio/ *n. m.* fire; conflagration.

incertidumbre /inθerti'ðumbre; inserti'ðumbre/ *n. f.* uncertainty, suspense.

incesante /inθe'sante; inse'sante/ *a.* continual, incessant.

incidente /inθi'ðente; insi'ðente/ *m.* incident, event.

incienso /in'θienso; in'sienso/ *n. m.* incense.

incierto /in'θierto; in'sierto/ *a.* uncertain, doubtful.

incinerar /inθine'rar; insine'rar/ *v.* incinerate; cremate.

incisión /inθi'sion; insi'sion/ *n. f.* incision, cut.

incitamiento /inθita'miento; insita'miento/ *n. m.* incitement, motivation.

incitar /inθi'tar; insi'tar/ *v.* incite, instigate.

incivil /inθi'βil; insi'βil/ *a.* impolite, rude.

inclemencia /inkle'menθia; inkle'mensia/ *n. f.* inclemency.

inclemente /inkle'mente/ *a.* inclement, merciless.

inclinación /inklina'θion; inklina'sion/ *n. f.* inclination, bent; slope.

inclinar /inkli'nar/ *v.* incline; influence.

inclinarse /inkli'narse/ *v.* slope; lean, bend over; bow.

incluir /in'kluir/ *v.* include; enclose.

inclusivo /inklu'siβo/ *a.* inclusive.

incluso /in'kluso/ *prep.* including.

incógnito /in'kognito/ *a.* unknown.

incoherente /inkoe'rente/ *a.* incoherent.

incombustible /inkombus'tiβle/ *a.* fireproof.

incomible /inko'miβle/ *a.* inedible.

incomodar /inkomo'ðar/ *v.* disturb, bother, inconvenience.

incomodidad /inkomoði'ðaθ/ *n. f.* inconvenience.

incómodo /in'komoðo/ *n. m.* uncomfortable; cumbersome; inconvenient.

incomparable /inkompa'raβle/ *a.* incomparable.

incompatible /inkompa'tiβle/ *a.* incompatible.

incompetencia /inkompe'tenθia; inkompe'tensia/ *n. f.* incompetence.

incompetente /inkompe'tente/ *a.* incompetent.

incompleto /inkom'pleto/ *a.* incomplete.

incondicional /inkondiθio'nal; inkondisio'nal/ *a.* unconditional.

inconexo /inkone'kso/ *a.* incoherent; unconnected.

incongruente /inkoŋgru'ente/ *a.* incongruous.

inconsciencia /inkon'sθienθia; inkon'ssiensia/ *n. f.* unconsciousness.

inconsciente /inkon'sθiente; inkons'siente/ *a.* unconscious.

inconsecuencia /inkonse'kuenθia; inkonse'kuensia/ *n. f.* inconsistency.

inconsecuente /inkonse'kuente/ *a.* inconsistent.

inconsiderado /inkonsiðe'raðo/ *a.* inconsiderate.

inconstancia /inkons'tanθia; inkons'tansia/ *n. f.* changeableness.

inconstante /inkons'tante/ *a.* changeable.

inconveniencia /inkombe'nienθia; inkombe'niensia/ *n. f.* inconvenience; unsuitability.

inconveniente /inkombe'niente/ *a.* unsuitable. *m.* disadvantage; objection.

incorporar /inkorpo'rar/ *v.* incorporate, embody.

incorporarse /inkorpo'rarse/ *v.* sit up.

incorrecto /inko'rrekto/ *a.* incorrect, wrong.

incredulidad /inkreðuli'ðaθ/ *n. f.* incredulity.

incrédulo /in'kreðulo/ *a.* incredulous.

increíble /inkre'iβle/ *a.* incredible.

incremento /inkre'mento/ *n. m.* increase.

incubadora /inkuβa'ðora/ *n. f.* incubator.

incubar /inku'βar/ *v.* hatch.

inculto /in'kulto/ *a.* uncultivated.

incumplimento de contrato /inkumpli'mento de kon'trato/ *n. m.* breach of contract.

incurable /inku'raβle/ *a.* incurable.

incurrir /inku'rrir/ *v.* incur.

indagación /indaga'θion; indaga'sion/ *n. f.* investigation, inquiry.

indagador /indaga'ðor/ **-ra** *n.* investigator.

indagar /inda'gar/ *v.* investigate, inquire into.

indebido /inde'βiðo/ *a.* undue.

indecencia /inde'θenθia; inde'sensia/ *n. f.* indecency.

indecente /inde'θente; inde'sente/ *a.* indecent.

indeciso /inde'θiso; inde'siso/ *a.* undecided.

indefenso /inde'fenso/ *a.* defenseless.

indefinido /indefi'niðo/ *a.* indefinite; undefined.

indeleble /inde'leβle/ *a.* indelible.

indemnización de despido /indemniθaˈθion de desˈpiðo; indemnisaˈsion de desˈpiðo/ n. f. severance pay.

indemnizar /indemniˈθar; indemniˈsar/ v. indemnify.

independencia /indepenˈdenθia; indepenˈdensia/ n. f. independence.

independiente /indepenˈdiente/ a. independent.

indesmallable /indesmaˈʎaβle; indesmaˈyaβle/ a. runproof.

India /ˈindia/ n. f. India.

indicación /indikaˈθion; indikaˈsion/ n. f. indication.

indicar /indiˈkar/ v. indicate, point out.

indicativo /indikaˈtiβo/ a. & m. indicative.

índice /ˈindiθe; ˈindise/ n. m. index; forefinger.

índice de materias /ˈindiθe de maˈterias; ˈindise de maˈterias/ table of contents.

indicio /inˈdiθio; inˈdisio/ n. m. hint, clue.

indiferencia /indifeˈrenθia; indifeˈrensia/ n. f. indifference.

indiferente /indifeˈrente/ a. indifferent.

indígena /inˈdihena/ a. & n. native.

indigente /indiˈhente/ a. indigent, poor.

indignación /indignaˈθion; indignaˈsion/ n. f. indignation.

indignado /indigˈnaðo/ a. indignant, incensed.

indignar /indigˈnar/ v. incense.

indigno /inˈdigno/ a. unworthy.

indio /ˈindio/ **-dia** a. & n. Indian.

indirecto /indiˈrekto/ a. indirect.

indiscreción /indiskreˈθion; indiskreˈsion/ n. f. indiscretion.

indiscreto /indisˈkreto/ a. indiscreet.

indiscutible /indiskuˈtiβle/ a. unquestionable.

indispensable /indispenˈsaβle/ a. indispensable.

indisposición /indisposiˈθion; indisposiˈsion/ n. f. indisposition, ailment; reluctance.

indistinto /indisˈtinto/ a. indistinct, unclear.

individual /indiβiˈðual/ a. individual.

individualidad /indiβiðualiˈðað/ n. f. individuality.

individuo /indiˈβiðuo/ a. & m. individual.

indócil /inˈdoθil; inˈdosil/ a. headstrong, unruly.

índole /ˈindole/ n. f. nature, character, disposition.

indolencia /indoˈlenθia; indoˈlensia/ n. f. indolence.

indolente /indoˈlente/ a. indolent.

indómito /inˈdomito/ a. untamed, wild; unruly.

inducir /induˈθir; induˈsir/ v. induce, persuade.

indudable /induˈðaβle/ a. certain, indubitable.

indulgencia /indulˈhenθia; indulˈhensia/ n. f. indulgence.

indulgente /indulˈhente/ a. indulgent.

indultar /indulˈtar/ v. free; pardon.

industria /inˈdustria/ n. f. industry.

industrial /indusˈtrial/ a. industrial.

industrioso /indusˈtrioso/ a. industrious.

inédito /iˈneðito/ a. unpublished.

ineficaz /inefiˈkaθ; inefiˈkas/ a. inefficient.

inepto /iˈnepto/ a. incompetent.

inequívoco /ineˈkiβoko/ a. unmistakable.

inercia /iˈnerθia; iˈnersia/ n. f. inertia.

inerte /iˈnerte/ a. inert.

inesperado /inespeˈraðo/ a. unexpected.

inestable /inesˈtaβle/ a. unstable.

inevitable /ineβiˈtaβle/ a. inevitable.

inexacto /ineˈksakto/ a. inexact.

inexperto /ineksˈperto/ a. unskilled.

inexplicable /inekspliˈkaβle/ a. inexplicable, unexplainable.

infalible /infaˈliβle/ a. infallible.

infame /inˈfame/ a. infamous, bad.

infamia /inˈfamia/ n. f. infamy.

infancia /inˈfanθia; inˈfansia/ n. f. infancy; childhood.

infante /inˈfante/ **-ta** n. infant.

infantería /infanteˈria/ n. f. infantry.

infantil /infanˈtil/ a. infantile, childish.

infarto (de miocardio) /inˈfarto de mioˈkarðio/ n. m. heart attack.

infatigable /infatiˈgaβle/ a. untiring.

infausto /inˈfausto/ a. unlucky.

infección /infekˈθion; infekˈsion/ n. f. infection.

infeccioso /infekˈθioso; infekˈsioso/ a. infectious.

infectar /infekˈtar/ v. infect.

infeliz /infeˈliθ; infeˈlis/ a. unhappy, miserable.

inferior /infeˈrior/ a. inferior; lower.

inferir /infeˈrir/ v. infer; inflict.

infernal /inferˈnal/ a. infernal.

infestar /infesˈtar/ v. infest.

infiel /inˈfiel/ a. unfaithful.

infierno /inˈfierno/ n. m. hell.

infiltrar /infilˈtrar/ v. infiltrate.

infinidad /infiniˈðað/ n. f. infinity.

infinito /infiˈnito/ a. infinite.

inflación /inflaˈθion; inflaˈsion/ n. f. inflation.

inflamable /inflaˈmaβle/ a. flammable.

inflamación /inflamaˈθion; inflamaˈsion/ n. f. inflammation.

inflamar /inflaˈmar/ v. inflame, set on fire.

inflar /inˈflar/ v. inflate, pump up, puff up.

inflexible /infleˈksiβle/ a. inflexible, rigid.

inflexión /infleˈksion/ n. f. inflection.

infligir /infliˈhir/ v. inflict.

influencia /influˈenθia; influˈensia/ n. f. influence.

influenza /inˈfluenθa; inˈfluensa/ n. f. influenza, flu.

influir /inˈfluir/ v. influence, sway.

influyente /influˈyente/ a. influential.

información /informaˈθion; informaˈsion/ n. f. information.

informal /inforˈmal/ a. informal.

informar /inforˈmar/ v. inform; report.

informática /inforˈmatika/ n. f. computer science; information technology.

informe /inˈforme/ n. m. report; (pl.) information, data.

infortunio /inforˈtunio/ n. m. misfortune.

infracción /infrakˈθion; infrakˈsion/ n. f. violation.

infraestructura /infraeˈstrukˈtura; infraestrukˈtura/ n. f. infrastructure.

infrascrito /infrasˈkrito/ **-ta** n. signer, undersigned.

infringir /infrinˈhir/ v. infringe, violate.

infructuoso /infrukˈtuoso/ a. fruitless.

infundir /infunˈdir/ v. instil, inspire with.

ingeniería /inhenieˈria/ n. f. engineering.

ingeniero /inheˈniero/ **-ra** n. engineer.

ingenio /inˈhenio/ n. m. wit; talent.

ingeniosidad /inheniosiˈðað/ n. f. ingenuity.

ingenioso /inheˈnioso/ a. witty; ingenious.

ingenuidad /inhenuiˈðað/ n. f. candor; naïveté.

ingenuo /inˈhenuo/ a. ingenuous, naïve, candid.

Inglaterra /inglaˈterra/ n. f. England.

ingle /ˈingle/ n. f. groin.

inglés /inˈgles/ **-esa** a. & n. English; Englishman; Englishwoman.

ingratitud /ingratiˈtuð/ n. f. ingratitude.

ingrato /inˈgrato/ a. ungrateful.

ingravidez /ingraβiˈðeθ; ingraβiˈðes/ n. f. weightlessness.

ingrávido /inˈgraβiðo/ a. weightless.

ingrediente /ingreˈðiente/ n. m. ingredient.

ingresar en /ingreˈsar en/ v. enter; join.

ingreso /inˈgreso/ n. m. entrance; (pl.) earnings, income.

inhábil /inˈaβil/ a. unskilled; incapable.

inhabilitar /inaβiliˈtar/ v. disqualify.

inherente /ineˈrente/ a. inherent.

inhibir /iniˈβir/ v. inhibit.

inhumano /inuˈmano/ a. cruel, inhuman.

iniciador /iniθiaˈðor; inisiaˈðor/ **-ra** n. initiator.

inicial /iniˈθial; iniˈsial/ a. initial.

iniciar /iniˈθiar; iniˈsiar/ v. initiate, begin.

iniciativa /iniθiaˈtiβa; inisiaˈtiβa/ n. f. initiative.

inicuo /iniˈkuo/ a. wicked.

iniquidad /inikiˈðað/ n. f. iniquity; sin.

injuria /inˈhuria/ n. f. insult. —**injuriar**, v.

injusticia /inhusˈtiθia; inhusˈtisia/ n. f. injustice.

injusto /inˈhusto/ a. unjust, unfair.

inmaculado /imakuˈlaðo/ a. immaculate; pure.

inmediato /imeˈðiato/ a. immediate.

inmensidad /imensiˈðað/ n. f. immensity.

inmenso /iˈmenso/ a. immense.

inmersión /imerˈsion/ n. f. immersion.

inmigración /imigraˈθion; imigraˈsion/ n. f. immigration.

inmigrante /imiˈgrante/ a. & n. immigrant.

inmigrar /imiˈgrar/ v. immigrate.

inminente /imiˈnente/ a. imminent.

inmoderado /imoðeˈraðo/ a. immoderate.

inmodesto /imoˈðesto/ a. immodest.

inmoral /imoˈral/ a. immoral.

inmoralidad /imoraliˈðað/ n. f. immorality.

inmortal /imorˈtal/ a. immortal.

inmortalidad /imortaliˈðað/ n. f. immortality.

inmóvil /iˈmoβil/ a. immobile, motionless.

inmundicia /imunˈdiθia; imunˈdisia/ n. f. dirt, filth.

inmune /iˈmune/ a. immune; exempt.

inmunidad /imuniˈðað/ n. f. immunity.

innato /inˈnato/ a. innate, inborn.

innecesario /inneθeˈsario; inneseˈsario/ a. unnecessary, needless.

innegable /inneˈgaβle/ a. undeniable.

innoble /inˈnoβle/ a. ignoble.

innocuo /innoˈkuo/ a. innocuous.

innovación /innoβaˈθion; innoβaˈsion/ n. f. innovation.

innumerable /innumeˈraβle/ a. innumerable, countless.

inocencia /inoˈθenθia; inoˈsensia/ n. f. innocence.

inocentada /inoθenˈtaða; inosenˈtaða/ n. f. practical joke.

inocente /inoˈθente; inoˈsente/ a. innocent.

inocular /inokuˈlar/ v. inoculate.

inodoro /inoˈðoro/ n. m. toilet.

inofensivo /inofenˈsiβo/ a. inoffensive, harmless.

inolvidable /inolβiˈðaβle/ a. unforgettable.

inoportuno /inoporˈtuno/ a. inopportune.

inoxidable /inoksiˈðaβle/ a. stainless.

inquietante /inkieˈtante/ a. disturbing, worrisome, worrying, upsetting.

inquietar /inkieˈtar/ v. disturb, worry, trouble.

inquieto /inˈkieto/ a. anxious, uneasy, worried; restless.

inquietud /inkieˈtuð/ n. f. concern, anxiety, worry; restlessness.

inquilino /inkiˈlino/ **-na** n. occupant, tenant.

ingrávido /inˈgraβiðo/ a. weightless.

inquirir /inkiˈrir/ v. inquire into, investigate.

inquisición /inkisiˈθion; inkisiˈsion/ n. f. inquisition, investigation.

insaciable /insaˈθiaβle; insaˈsiaβle/ a. insatiable.

insalubre /insaˈluβre/ a. unhealthy.

insano /inˈsano/ a. insane.

inscribir /inskriˈβir/ v. inscribe; record.

inscribirse /inskriˈβirse/ v. register, enroll.

inscripción /inskripˈθion; inskripˈsion/ n. f. inscription; registration.

insecticida /insektiˈθiða; insektiˈsiða/ n. m. insecticide.

insecto /inˈsekto/ n. m. insect.

inseguro /inseˈguro/ a. unsure, uncertain; insecure, unsafe.

insensato /insenˈsato/ a. stupid, senseless.

insensible /insenˈsiβle/ a. unfeeling, heartless.

inseparable /insepaˈraβle/ a. inseparable.

inserción /inserˈθion; inserˈsion/ n. f. insertion.

insertar /inserˈtar/ v. insert.

inservible /inserˈβiβle/ a. useless.

insidioso /insiˈðioso/ a. insidious, crafty.

insigne /inˈsigne/ a. famous, noted.

insignia /inˈsignia/ n. f. insignia, badge.

insignificante /insignifiˈkante/ a. insignificant, negligible.

insincero /insinˈθero; insinˈsero/ a. insincere.

insinuación /insinuaˈθion; insinuaˈsion/ n. f. insinuation; hint.

insinuar /insiˈnuar/ v. insinuate, suggest, hint.

insipidez /insipiˈðeθ; insipiˈðes/ n. f. insipidity.

insípido /inˈsipiðo/ a. insipid.

insistencia /insisˈtenθia; insisˈtensia/ n. f. insistence.

insistente /insisˈtente/ a. insistent.

insistir /insisˈtir/ v. insist.

insolación /insolaˈθion; insolaˈsion/ n. f. sunstroke.

insolencia /insoˈlenθia; insoˈlensia/ n. f. insolence.

insolente /insoˈlente/ a. insolent.

insólito /inˈsolito/ a. unusual.

insolvente /insolˈβente/ a. insolvent.

insomnio /inˈsomnio/ n. m. insomnia.

insonorizado /insonoriˈθaðo; insonoriˈsaðo/ a. soundproof.

insonorizar /insonoriˈθar; insonoriˈsar/ v. soundproof.

insoportable /insoporˈtaβle/ a. unbearable.

inspección /inspekˈθion; inspekˈsion/ n. f. inspection.

inspeccionar /inspekθioˈnar; inspeksioˈnar/ v. inspect, examine.

inspector /inspekˈtor/ **-ra** n. inspector.

inspiración /inspiraˈθion; inspiraˈsion/ n. f. inspiration.

inspirar /inspiˈrar/ v. inspire.

instalación /instalaˈθion; instalaˈsion/ n. f. installation, fixture.

instalar /instaˈlar/ v. install, set up.

instantánea /instanˈtanea/ n. f. snapshot.

instantáneo /instanˈtaneo/ a. instantaneous.

instante /insˈtante/ a. & m. instant. **al i.,** at once.

instar /insˈtar/ v. coax, urge.

instigar /instiˈgar/ v. instigate, urge.

instintivo /instinˈtiβo/ a. instinctive.

instinto /insˈtinto/ n. m. instinct. **por i.,** by instinct, instinctively.

institución /instituˈθion; instituˈsion/ n. f. institution.

instituto /insti'tuto/ *n. m.* institute. **—instituir,** *v.*
institutriz /institu'triθ; institu'tris/ *n. f.* governess.
instrucción /instruk'θion; instruk'sion/ *n. f.* instruction; education.
instructivo /instruk'tiβo/ *a.* instructive.
instructor /instruk'tor/ **-ra** *n.* instructor.
instruir /ins'truir/ *v.* instruct, teach.
instrumento /instru'mento/ *n. m.* instrument.
insuficiente /insufi'θiente; insufi'siente/ *a.* insufficient.
insufrible /insu'friβle/ *a.* intolerable.
insular /insu'lar/ *a.* island, insular.
insulto /in'sulto/ *n. m.* insult. **—insultar,** *v.*
insuperable /insupe'raβle/ *a.* insuperable.
insurgente /insur'hente/ *n. & a.* insurgent, rebel.
insurrección /insurrek'θion; insurrek'sion/ *n. f.* insurrection, revolt.
insurrecto /insu'rrekto/ **-ta** *a. & n.* insurgent.
intacto /in'takto/ *a.* intact.
integral /inte'gral/ *a.* integral.
integridad /integri'ðað/ *n. f.* integrity; entirety.
íntegro /'integro/ *a.* entire; upright.
intelecto /inte'lekto/ *n. m.* intellect.
intelectual /intelek'tual/ *a. & n.* intellectual.
inteligencia /inteli'henθia; inteli'hensia/ *n. f.* intelligence.
inteligente /inteli'hente/ *a.* intelligent.
inteligible /inteli'hiβle/ *a.* intelligible.
intemperie /intem'perie/ *n. f.* bad weather.
intención /inten'θion; inten'sion/ *n. f.* intention.
intendente /inten'dente/ *n. m.* manager.
intensidad /intensi'ðað/ *n. f.* intensity.
intensificar /intensifi'kar/ *v.* intensify.
intensivo /inten'siβo/ *a.* intensive.
intenso /in'tenso/ *a.* intense.
intentar /inten'tar/ *v.* attempt, try.
intento /in'tento/ *n. m.* intent; attempt.
intercambiable /interkam'biaβle/ *a.* interchangeable.
intercambiar /interkam'βiar/ *v.* exchange, interchange.
interceptar /interθep'tar; intersep'tar/ *v.* intercept.
intercesión /interθe'sion; interse'sion/ *n. f.* intercession.
interés /inte'res/ *n. m.* interest; concern; appeal.
interesante /intere'sante/ *a.* interesting.
interesar /intere'sar/ *v.* interest, appeal to.
interfaz /inter'faθ; inter'fas/ *n. f.* interface.
interferencia /interfe'renθia; interfe'rensia/ *n. f.* interference.
interino /inte'rino/ *a.* temporary.
interior /inte'rior/ *a.* **1.** interior, inner. **—***n.* **2.** *m.* interior.
interjección /interhek'θion; interhek'sion/ *n. f.* interjection.
intermedio /inter'meðio/ *a.* **1.** intermediate. **—***n.* **2.** *m.* intermediary; intermission.
interminable /intermi'naβle/ *a.* interminable, endless.
intermisión /intermi'sion/ *n. f.* intermission.
intermitente /intermi'tente/ *a.* intermittent.
internacional /internaθio'nal; internasio'nal/ *a.* international.
internarse en /inter'narse en/ *v.* enter into, go into.
Internet, el /inter'net/ *n. m.* the Internet.
interno /in'terno/ *a.* internal.
interpelar /interpe'lar/ *v.* ask questions; implore.
interponer /interpo'ner/ *v.* interpose.
interpretación /interpreta'θion; interpreta'sion/ *n. f.* interpretation.
interpretar /interpre'tar/ *v.* interpret; construe.
intérprete /in'terprete/ *n. m. & f.* interpreter; performer.
interrogación /interroga'θion; interroga'sion/ *n. f.* interrogation.
interrogar /interro'gar/ *v.* question, interrogate.
interrogativo /interroga'tiβo/ *a.* interrogative.
interrumpir /interrum'pir/ *v.* interrupt.
interrupción /interrup'θion; interrup'sion/ *n. f.* interruption.
intersección /intersek'θion; intersek'sion/ *n. f.* intersection.
intervalo /inter'βalo/ *n. m.* interval.
intervención /interβen'θion; interβen'sion/ *n. f.* intervention.
intervenir /interβe'nir/ *v.* intervene, interfere.
intestino /intes'tino/ *n. m.* intestine.
intimación /intima'θion; intima'sion/ *n. f.* intimation, hint.
intimar /inti'mar/ *v.* suggest, hint.
intimidad /intimi'ðað/ *n. f.* intimacy.
intimidar /intimi'ðar/ *v.* intimidate.
íntimo /'intimo/ **-ma** *a. & n.* intimate.
intolerable /intole'raβle/ *a.* intolerable.
intolerancia /intole'ranθia; intole'ransia/ *n. f.* intolerance, bigotry.
intolerante /intole'rante/ *a.* intolerant.
intoxicación alimenticia /intoksika'θion alimen'tiθia; intoksika'sion alimen'tisia/ *n. f.* food poisoning.
intranquilo /intran'kilo/ *a.* uneasy.
intravenoso /intraβe'noso/ *a.* intravenous.
intrepidez /intrepi'ðeθ; intrepi'ðes/ *n. f.* daring.
intrépido /in'trepiðo/ *a.* intrepid.
intriga /in'triga/ *n. f.* intrigue, plot, scheme. **—intrigar,** *v.*
intrincado /intrin'kaðo/ *a.* intricate, involved; impenetrable.
introducción /introðuk'θion; introðuk'sion/ *n. f.* introduction.
introducir /introðu'θir; introðu'sir/ *v.* introduce.
intruso /in'truso/ **-sa** *n.* intruder.
intuición /intui'θion; intui'sion/ *n. f.* intuition.
inundación /inunda'θion; inunda'sion/ *n. f.* flood. **—inundar,** *v.*
inútil /i'nutil/ *a.* useless.
invadir /imba'ðir/ *v.* invade.
inválido /im'baliðo/ **-da** *a. & n.* invalid.
invariable /imba'riaβle/ *a.* constant.
invasión /imba'sion/ *n. f.* invasion.
invasor /imba'sor/ **-ra** *n.* invader.
invencible /imben'θiβle; imben'siβle/ *a.* invincible.
invención /imben'θion; imben'sion/ *n. f.* invention.
inventar /imben'tar/ *v.* invent; devise.
inventario /imben'tario/ *n. m.* inventory.
inventivo /imben'tiβo/ *a.* inventive.
invento /im'bento/ *n. m.* invention.
inventor /imben'tor/ **-ra** *n.* inventor.
invernáculo /imber'nakulo/ *n. m.* greenhouse.
invernal /imber'nal/ *a.* wintry.
inverosímil /imbero'simil/ *a.* improbable, unlikely.
inversión /imber'sion/ *n. f.* inversion; *Com.* investment.
inverso /im'berso/ *a.* inverse, reverse.
inversor /imber'sor/ **-ra** *n.* investor.
invertir /imber'tir/ *v.* invert; reverse; *Com.* invest.
investigación /imbestiga'θion; imbestiga'sion/ *n. f.* investigation.
investigador /imbestiga'ðor/ **-ra** *n.* investigator; researcher.
investigar /imbesti'gar/ *v.* investigate.
invierno /im'bierno/ *n. m.* winter.
invisible /imbi'siβle/ *a.* invisible.
invitación /imbita'θion; imbita'sion/ *n. f.* invitation.
invitar /imbi'tar/ *v.* invite.
invocar /imbo'kar/ *v.* invoke.
involuntario /imbolun'tario/ *a.* involuntary.
inyección /inyek'θion; inyek'sion/ *n. f.* injection.
inyectar /inyek'tar/ *v.* inject.
ir /ir/ *v.* go. **irse,** go away, leave.
ira /'ira/ *n. f.* anger, ire.
iracundo /ira'kundo/ *a.* wrathful, irate.
iris /'iris/ *n. m.* iris. **arco i.,** rainbow.
Irlanda /ir'landa/ *n. f.* Ireland.
irlandés /irlan'des/ **-esa** *a. & n.* Irish; Irishman, Irishwoman.
ironía /iro'nia/ *n. f.* irony.
irónico /i'roniko/ *a.* ironical.
irracional /irraθio'nal; irrasio'nal/ *a.* irrational; insane.
irradiación /irraðia'θion; irraðia'sion/ *n. f.* irradiation.
irradiar /irra'ðiar/ *v.* radiate.
irrazonable /irraθo'naβle; irraso'naβle/ *a.* unreasonable.
irregular /irregu'lar/ *a.* irregular.
irreligioso /irreli'hioso/ *a.* irreligious.
irremediable /irreme'ðiaβle/ *a.* irremediable, hopeless.
irresistible /irresis'tiβle/ *a.* irresistible.
irresoluto /irreso'luto/ *a.* irresolute, wavering.
irrespetuoso /irrespe'tuoso/ *a.* disrespectful.
irreverencia /irreβe'renθia; irreβe'rensia/ *n. f.* irreverence.
irreverente /irreβe'rente/ *adj.* irreverent.
irrigación /irriga'θion; irriga'sion/ *n. f.* irrigation.
irrigar /irri'gar/ *v.* irrigate.
irritación /irrita'θion; irrita'sion/ *n. f.* irritation.
irritar /irri'tar/ *v.* irritate.
irrupción /irrup'θion; irrup'sion/ *n. f.* raid, attack.
isla /'isla/ *n. f.* island.
isleño /is'leɲo/ **-ña** *n.* islander.
israelita /israe'lita/ *n. & a.* Israelite.
Italia /i'talia/ *n. f.* Italy.
italiano /ita'liano/ **-na** *a. & n.* Italian.
itinerario /itine'rario/ *n. m.* itinerary; timetable.
IVA, *abbrev.* **(impuesto sobre el valor añadido)** VAT (value-added tax).
izar /i'θar; i'sar/ *v.* hoist.
izquierda /iθ'kierða; is'kierða/ *n. f.* left (hand, side).
izquierdista /iθ'kierðista; is'kierðista/ *n. & a.* leftist.
izquierdo /iθ'kierðo; is'kierðo/ *a.* left.

J

jabalí /haβa'li/ *n. m.* wild boar.
jabón /ha'βon/ *n. m.* soap. **j. en polvo,** soap powder.
jabonar /haβo'nar/ *v.* soap.
jaca /'haka/ *n. f.* nag.
jacinto /ha'θinto; ha'sinto/ *n. m.* hyacinth.
jactancia /hak'tanθia; hak'tansia/ *n. f.* boast. **—jactarse,** *v.*
jactancioso /haktan'θioso; haktan'sioso/ *a.* boastful.
jadear /haðe'ar/ *v.* pant, puff.
jaez /ha'eθ; ha'es/ *n. m.* harness; kind.
jalar /ha'lar/ *v.* haul, pull.
jalea /ha'lea/ *n. f.* jelly.
jaleo /ha'leo/ *n. m.* row, uproar; hassle.
jamás /ha'mas/ *adv.* never, ever.
jamón /ha'mon/ *n. m.* ham.
Japón /ha'pon/ *n. m.* Japan.
japonés /hapo'nes/ **-esa** *a. & n.* Japanese.
jaqueca /ha'keka/ *n. f.* headache.
jarabe /ha'raβe/ *n. m.* syrup.
jaranear /harane'ar/ *v.* jest; carouse.
jardín /har'ðin/ *n. m.* garden.
jardín de infancia /har'ðin de in'fanθia; har'ðin de in'fansia/ nursery school.
jardinero /harði'nero/ **-ra** *n.* gardener.
jarra /'harra/ *n. f.* jar; pitcher.
jarro /'harro/ *n. m.* jug, pitcher.
jaspe /'haspe/ *n. m.* jasper.
jaula /'haula/ *n. f.* cage; coop.
jauría /hau'ria/ *n. f.* pack of hounds.
jazmín /haθ'min; has'min/ *n. m.* jasmine.
jefatura /hefa'tura/ *n. f.* headquarters.
jefe /'hefe/ **-fa** *n.* chief, boss.
jefe de comedor /'hefe de kome'ðor/ headwaiter.
jefe de sala /'hefe de 'sala/ maître d'.
jefe de taller /'hefe de ta'ʎer; 'hefe de ta'yer/ foreman.
Jehová /heo'βa/ *n. m.* Jehovah.
jengibre /hen'hiβre/ *n. m.* ginger.
jerez /he'reθ; he'res/ *n. m.* sherry.
jerga /'herga/ *n. f.* slang.
jergón /her'gon/ *n. m.* straw mattress.
jerigonza /heri'gonθa; heri'gonsa/ *n. f.* jargon.
jeringa /he'riŋga/ *n. f.* syringe.
jeringar /heriŋ'gar/ *v.* inject; annoy.
jeroglífico /hero'glifiko/ *n. m.* hieroglyph.
jersey /her'sei/ *n. m.* pullover; **j. de cuello alto,** turtleneck sweater.
Jerusalén /herusa'len/ *n. m.* Jerusalem.
jesuita /he'suita/ *n. m.* Jesuit.
Jesús /he'sus/ *n. m.* Jesus.
jeta /'heta/ *n. f.* snout.
jícara /'hikara/ *n. f.* cup.
jinete /hi'nete/ **-ta** *n.* horseman.
jingoísmo /hiŋgo'ismo/ *n. m.* jingoism.
jingoísta /hiŋgo'ista/ *n. & a.* jingoist.
jira /'hira/ *n. f.* picnic; outing.
jirafa /hi'rafa/ *n. f.* giraffe.
jiu-jitsu /hiu'hitsu/ *n. m.* jujitsu.
jocundo /ho'kundo/ *a.* jovial.
jornada /hor'naða/ *n. f.* journey; day's work.
jornal /hor'nal/ *n. m.* day's wage.
jornalero /horna'lero/ *n. m.* day laborer, workman.
joroba /ho'roβa/ *n. f.* hump.
jorobado /horo'βaðo/ *a.* humpbacked.
joven /'hoβen/ *a.* **1.** young. **—***n.* **2.** *m. & f.* young person.
jovial /ho'βial/ *a.* jovial, jolly.
jovialidad /hoβiali'ðað/ *n. f.* joviality.
joya /'hoia/ *n. f.* jewel, gem.
joyas de fantasía /'hoias de fanta'sia/ *n. f.pl.* costume jewelry.
joyelero /hoie'lero/ *n. m.* jewel box.
joyería /hoie'ria/ *n. f.* jewelry; jewelry store.
joyero /ho'iero/ *n. m.* jeweler; jewel case.
juanete /hua'nete/ *n. m.* bunion.
jubilación /huβila'θion; huβila'sion/ *n. f.* retirement; pension.
jubilar /huβi'lar/ *v.* retire, pension.
jubileo /huβi'leo/ *n. m.* jubilee, public festivity.
júbilo /'huβilo/ *n. m.* glee, rejoicing.
jubiloso /huβi'loso/ *a.* joyful, gay.
judaico /hu'ðaiko/ *a.* Jewish.
judaísmo /huða'ismo/ *n. m.* Judaism.
judía /hu'ðia/ *n. f.* bean, string bean.
judicial /huði'θial; huði'sial/ *a.* judicial.
judío /hu'ðio/ **-día** *a. & n.* Jewish; Jew.
juego /'huego/ *n. m.* game; play;

gambling; set. **j. de damas,** checkers. **j. limpio,** fair play.

Juegos Olímpicos /huegos o'limpi-kos/ *n. m.pl.* Olympic Games.

juerga /'huerga/ *n. f.* spree.

jueves /'hueβes/ *n. m.* Thursday.

juez /hueθ; hues/ *n. m.* judge.

jugador /huga'ðor/ **-ra** *n.* player.

jugar /hu'gar/ *v.* play; gamble.

juglar /hug'lar/ *n. m.* minstrel.

jugo /'hugo/ *n. m.* juice. **j. de naranja,** orange juice.

jugoso /hu'goso/ *a.* juicy.

juguete /hu'gete/ *n. m.* toy, plaything.

juguetear /hugete'ar/ *v.* trifle.

juguetón /huge'ton/ *a.* playful.

juicio /'huiθio; 'huisio/ *n. m.* sense, wisdom, judgment; sanity; trial.

juicioso /hui'θioso; hui'sioso/ *a.* wise, judicious.

julio /'hulio/ *n. m.* July.

jumento /hu'mento/ *n. m.* donkey.

junco /'hunko/ *n. m.* reed, rush.

jungla /'huŋgla/ *n. f.* jungle.

junio /'hunio/ *n. m.* June.

junípero /hu'nipero/ *n. m.* juniper.

junquillo /hun'kiʎo; hun'kiyo/ *n. m.* jonquil.

junta /'hunta/ *n. f.* board, council; joint, coupling.

juntamente /hunta'mente/ *adv.* jointly.

juntar /hun'tar/ *v.* join; connect; assemble.

junto /'hunto/ *a.* together. **j. a,** next to.

juntura /hun'tura/ *n. f.* joint, juncture.

jurado /hu'raðo/ *n. m.* jury.

juramento /hura'mento/ *n. m.* oath.

jurar /hu'rar/ *v.* swear.

jurisconsulto /huriskon'sulto/ *n. m.* jurist.

jurisdicción /hurisðik'θion; hurisðik-'sion/ *n. f.* jurisdiction; territory.

jurisprudencia /hurispru'ðenθia; hu-rispru'ðensia/ *n. f.* jurisprudence.

justa /'husta/ *n. f.* joust. —**justar,** *v.*

justicia /hus'tiθia; hus'tisia/ *n. f.* justice, equity.

justiciero /husti'θiero; husti'siero/ *a.* just.

justificación /hustifika'θion; hustifi-ka'sion/ *n. f.* justification.

justificadamente /hustifikaða'men-te/ *adv.* justifiably.

justificar /hustifi'kar/ *v.* justify, warrant.

justo /'husto/ *a.* right; exact; just; righteous.

juvenil /huβe'nil/ *a.* youthful.

juventud /huβen'tuð/ *n. f.* youth.

juzgado /huθ'gaðo; hus'gaðo/ *n. m.* court.

juzgar /huθ'gar; hus'gar/ *v.* judge, estimate.

K

káiser /'kaiser/ *n. m.* kaiser.

karate /ka'rate/ *n. m.* karate.

kepis /'kepis/ *n. m.* military cap.

kerosena /kero'sena/ *n. f.* kerosene.

kilo /'kilo/ **kilogramo** *n. m.* kilogram.

kilohercio /kilo'erθio; kilo'ersio/ *n. m.* kilohertz.

kilolitro /kilo'litro/ *n. m.* kiloliter.

kilometraje /kilome'trahe/ *n. m.* mileage.

kilómetro /ki'lometro/ *n. m.* kilometer.

kiosco /'kiosko/ *n. m.* newsstand; pavilion.

L

la /la/ *art. & pron.* **1.** the; the one. —*pron.* **2.** her, it, you; (*pl.*) them, you.

laberinto /laβe'rinto/ *n. m.* labyrinth, maze.

labia /'laβia/ *n. f.* eloquence, fluency.

labio /'laβio/ *n. m.* lip.

labor /la'βor/ *n. f.* labor, work.

laborar /laβo'rar/ *v.* work; till.

laboratorio /laβora'torio/ *n. m.* laboratory.

laborioso /laβo'rioso/ *a.* industrious.

labrador /laβra'ðor/ *n. m.* farmer.

labranza /la'βranθa; la'βransa/ *n. f.* farming; farmland.

labrar /la'βrar/ *v.* work, till.

labriego /la'βriego/ **-ga** *n.* peasant.

laca /'laka/ *n. f.* shellac.

lacio /'laθio; 'lasio/ *a.* withered; limp; straight.

lactar /lak'tar/ *v.* nurse, suckle.

lácteo /'lakteo/ *a.* milky.

ladear /laðe'ar/ *v.* tilt, tip; sway.

ladera /la'ðera/ *n. f.* slope.

ladino /la'ðino/ *a.* cunning, crafty.

lado /'laðo/ *n. m.* side. **al l. de,** beside. **de l.,** sideways.

ladra /'laðra/ *n. f.* barking. —**ladrar,** *v.*

ladrillo /la'ðriʎo; la'ðriyo/ *n. m.* brick.

ladrón /la'ðron/ **-ona** *n.* thief, robber.

lagarto /la'garto/ *n. m.* lizard; (Mex.) alligator.

lago /'lago/ *n. m.* lake.

lágrima /'lagrima/ *n. f.* tear.

lagrimear /lagrime'ar/ *v.* weep, cry.

laguna /la'guna/ *n. f.* lagoon; gap.

laico /'laiko/ *a.* lay.

laja /'laha/ *n. f.* stone slab.

lamentable /lamen'taβle/ *a.* lamentable.

lamentación /lamenta'θion; la-menta'sion/ *n. f.* lamentation.

lamentar /lamen'tar/ *v.* lament; wail; regret, be sorry.

lamento /la'mento/ *n. m.* lament, wail.

lamer /la'mer/ *v.* lick; lap.

lámina /'lamina/ *n. f.* print, illustration.

lámpara /'lampara/ *n. f.* lamp.

lampiño /lam'piɲo/ *a.* beardless.

lana /'lana/ *n. f.* wool.

lanar /la'nar/ *a.* woolen.

lance /'lanθe; 'lanse/ *n. m.* throw; episode; quarrel.

lancha /'lantʃa/ *n. f.* launch; small boat.

lanchón /lan'tʃon/ *n. m.* barge.

langosta /laŋ'gosta/ *n. f.* lobster; locust.

langostino /laŋgos'tino/ *n. m.* king prawn.

languidecer /laŋguiðe'θer; laŋguiðe-'ser/ *v.* languish, pine.

languidez /laŋgui'ðeθ; laŋgui'ðes/ *n. f.* languidness.

lánguido /'laŋguiðo/ *a.* languid.

lanza /'lanθa; 'lansa/ *n. f.* lance, spear.

lanzada /lan'θaða; lan'saða/ *n. f.* thrust, throw.

lanzar /lan'θar; lan'sar/ *v.* hurl; launch.

lañar /la'ɲar/ *v.* cramp; clamp.

lapicero /lapi'θero; lapi'sero/ *n. m.* mechanical pencil.

lápida /'lapiða/ *n. f.* stone; tombstone.

lápiz /'lapiθ; 'lapis/ *n. m.* pencil; crayon.

lápiz de ojos /'lapiθ de 'ohos; 'lapis de 'ohos/ *n. m.* eyeliner.

lapso /'lapso/ *n. m.* lapse.

lardo /'larðo/ *n. m.* lard.

largar /lar'gar/ *v.* loosen; free.

largo /'largo/ *a.* **1.** long. **a lo l. de,** along. —*n.* **2.** *m.* length.

largometraje /largome'trahe/ *n. m.* feature film.

largor /lar'gor/ *n. m.* length.

largueza /lar'geθa; lar'gesa/ *n. f.* generosity; length.

largura /lar'gura/ *n. f.* length.

laringe /la'rinhe/ *n. f.* larynx.

larva /'larβa/ *n. f.* larva.

lascivia /las'θiβia; las'siβia/ *n. f.* lasciviousness.

lascivo /las'θiβo; las'siβo/ *a.* lascivious.

láser /'laser/ *n. m.* laser.

laso /'laso/ *a.* weary.

lástima /'lastima/ *n. f.* pity. **ser l.,** to be a pity, to be too bad.

lastimar /lasti'mar/ *v.* hurt, injure.

lastimoso /lasti'moso/ *a.* pitiful.

lastre /'lastre/ *n. m.* ballast. —**lastrar,** *v.*

lata /'lata/ *n. f.* tin can; tin (plate); *Colloq.* annoyance, bore.

latente /la'tente/ *a.* latent.

lateral /late'ral/ *a.* lateral, side.

latigazo /lati'gaθo; lati'gaso/ *n. m.* lash, whipping.

látigo /'latigo/ *n. m.* whip.

latín /la'tin/ *n. m.* Latin (language).

latino /la'tino/ *a.* Latin.

latir /la'tir/ *v.* beat, pulsate.

latitud /lati'tuð/ *n. f.* latitude.

latón /la'ton/ *n. m.* brass.

laúd /la'uð/ *n. m.* lute.

laudable /lau'ðaβle/ *a.* laudable.

láudano /'lauðano/ *n. m.* laudanum.

laurel /lau'rel/ *n. m.* laurel.

lava /'laβa/ *n. f.* lava.

lavabo /la'βaβo/ **lavamanos** *n. m.* washroom, lavatory.

lavadora /laβa'ðora/ *n. f.* washing machine.

lavandera /laβan'dera/ *n. f.* washerwoman, laundress.

lavandería /laβande'ria/ *f.* laundry; laundromat.

lavaplatos /laβa'platos/ *n.* **1.** *m.* dishwasher (machine). —*n.* **2.** *m. & f.* dishwasher (person).

lavar /la'βar/ *v.* wash.

lavatorio /laβa'torio/ *n. m.* lavatory.

laya /'laia/ *n. f.* spade. —**layar,** *v.*

lazar /la'θar; la'sar/ *v.* lasso.

lazareto /laθa'reto; lasa'reto/ *n. m.* isolation hospital; quarantine station.

lazo /'laθo; 'laso/ *n. m.* tie, knot; bow; loop.

le /le/ *pron.* him, her, you; (*pl.*) them, you.

leal /le'al/ *a.* loyal.

lealtad /leal'tað/ *n. f.* loyalty.

lebrel /le'βrel/ *n. m.* greyhound.

lección /lek'θion; lek'sion/ *n. f.* lesson.

leche /'letʃe/ *n. f.* milk.

lechería /letʃe'ria/ *n. f.* dairy.

lechero /le'tʃero/ *n. m.* milkman.

lecho /'letʃo/ *n. m.* bed; couch.

lechón /le'tʃon/ *n. m.* pig.

lechoso /le'tʃoso/ *a.* milky.

lechuga /le'tʃuga/ *n. f.* lettuce.

lechuza /le'tʃuθa; le'tʃusa/ *n. f.* owl.

lecito /le'θito; le'sito/ *n. m.* yolk.

lector /lek'tor/ **-ra** *n.* reader.

lectura /lek'tura/ *n. f.* reading.

leer /le'er/ *v.* read.

legación /lega'θion; lega'sion/ *n. f.* legation.

legado /le'gaðo/ *n. m.* bequest.

legal /le'gal/ *a.* legal, lawful.

legalizar /legali'θar; legali'sar/ *v.* legalize.

legar /le'gar/ *v.* bequeath, leave, will.

legible /le'hiβle/ *a.* legible.

legión /le'hion/ *n. f.* legion.

legislación /lehisla'θion; lehisla'sion/ *n. f.* legislation.

legislador /lehisla'ðor/ **-ra** *n.* legislator.

legislar /lehis'lar/ *v.* legislate.

legislativo /lehisla'tiβo/ *a.* legislative.

legislatura /lehisla'tura/ *n. f.* legislature.

legítimo /le'hitimo/ *a.* legitimate.

lego /'lego/ *n. m.* layman.

legua /'legua/ *n. f.* league (measure).

legumbre /le'gumbre/ *n. f.* vegetable.

lejano /le'hano/ *a.* distant, far-off.

lejía /le'hia/ *n. f.* lye.

lejos /'lehos/ *adv.* far. **a lo l.,** in the distance.

lelo /'lelo/ *a.* stupid, foolish.

lema /'lema/ *n. m.* theme; slogan.

lengua /'leŋgua/ *n. f.* tongue; language.

lenguado /leŋ'guaðo/ *n. m.* sole, flounder.

lenguaje /leŋ'guahe/ *n. m.* speech; language.

lenguaraz /leŋgua'raθ; leŋgua'ras/ *a.* talkative.

lente /'lente/ *n.* **1.** *m. or f.* lens. **2.** *m.pl.* eyeglasses.

lenteja /len'teha/ *n. f.* lentil.

lentilla /len'tiʎa; len'tiya/ *n. f.* contact lens.

lentitud /lenti'tuð/ *n. f.* slowness.

lento /'lento/ *a.* slow.

leña /'leɲa/ *n. f.* wood, firewood.

león /le'on/ *n. m.* lion.

leopardo /leo'parðo/ *n. m.* leopard.

lerdo /'lerðo/ *a.* dull-witted.

lesbiana /les'βiana/ *n. f.* lesbian.

lesión /le'sion/ *n. f.* wound; damage.

letanía /leta'nia/ *n. f.* litany.

letárgico /le'tarhiko/ *a.* lethargic.

letargo /le'targo/ *n. m.* lethargy.

letra /'letra/ *n. f.* letter (of alphabet); print; words (of a song).

letrado /le'traðo/ *a.* **1.** learned. —*n.* **2.** *m.* lawyer.

letrero /le'trero/ *n. m.* sign, poster.

leva /'leβa/ *n. f. Mil.* draft.

levadura /leβa'ðura/ *n. f.* yeast, leavening, baking powder.

levantador /leβanta'ðor/ *n. m.* lifter; rebel, mutineer.

levantar /leβan'tar/ *v.* raise, lift.

levantarse /leβan'tarse/ *v.* rise, get up; stand up.

levar /le'βar/ *v.* weigh (anchor).

leve /'leβe/ *a.* slight, light.

levita /le'βita/ *n. f.* frock coat.

léxico /'leksiko/ *n. m.* lexicon, dictionary.

ley /lei/ *n. f.* law, statute.

leyenda /le'ienda/ *n. f.* legend.

lezna /'leθna; 'lesna/ *n. f.* awl.

libación /liβa'θion; liβa'sion/ *n. f.* libation.

libelo /li'βelo/ *n. m.* libel.

libélula /li'βelula/ *n. f.* dragonfly.

liberación /liβera'θion; liβera'sion/ *n. f.* liberation, release.

liberal /liβe'ral/ *a.* liberal.

libertad /liβer'tað/ *n. f.* freedom.

libertador /liβerta'ðor/ **-ra** *n.* liberator.

libertar /liβer'tar/ *v.* free, liberate.

libertinaje /liβerti'nahe/ *n. m.* licentiousness.

libertino /liβer'tino/ **-na** *n.* libertine.

libídine /li'βiðine/ *n. f.* licentiousness; lust.

libidinoso /liβiði'noso/ *a.* lustful.

libra /'liβra/ *n. f.* pound.

libranza /li'βranθa; li'βransa/ *n. f.* draft, bill of exchange.

librar /li'βrar/ *v.* free, rid.

libre /'liβre/ *a.* free, unoccupied.

librería /liβre'ria/ *n. f.* bookstore.

librero /li'βrero/ **-ra** *n.* bookseller.

libreta /li'βreta/ *n. f.* notebook; booklet.

libreto /li'βreto/ *n. m.* libretto.

libro /'liβro/ *n. m.* book.

libro de texto /'liβro de 'teksto/ textbook.

licencia /li'θenθia; li'sensia/ *n. f.* permission, license, leave; furlough. **l. de armas,** gun permit.

licenciado /liθen'θiaðo; lisen'siaðo/ **-da** *n.* graduate.

licencioso /liθen'θioso; lisen'sioso/ *a.* licentious.

lícito /'liθito; 'lisito/ *a.* lawful.

licor /li'kor/ *n. m.* liquor.

licuadora /likua'ðora/ *n. f.* blender (for food).

lid /lið/ *n. f.* fight. —**lidiar,** *v.*

líder /'liðer/ *n. m. & f.* leader.

liebre /'lieβre/ *n. f.* hare.

lienzo /'lienθo; 'lienso/ *n. m.* linen.

liga /'liga/ n. f. league, confederacy; garter.
ligadura /liga'ðura/ n. f. ligature.
ligar /li'gar/ v. tie, bind, join.
ligero /li'hero/ a. light; fast, nimble.
ligustro /li'gustro/ n. m. privet.
lija /'liha/ n. f. sandpaper.
lijar /li'har/ v. sandpaper.
lima /'lima/ n. f. file; lime.
limbo /'limbo/ n. m. limbo.
limitación /limita'θion; limita'sion/ n. f. limitation.
límite /'limite/ n. m. limit. —**limitar,** v.
limo /'limo/ n. m. slime.
limón /li'mon/ n. m. lemon.
limonada /limo'naða/ n. f. lemonade.
limonero /limo'nero/ n. m. lemon tree.
limosna /li'mosna/ n. f. alms.
limosnero /limos'nero/ -ra n. beggar.
limpiabotas /limpia'βotas/ n. m. bootblack.
limpiadientes /limpia'ðientes/ n. m. toothpick.
limpiar /lim'piar/ v. clean, wash, wipe.
límpido /'limpiðo/ a. limpid, clear.
limpieza /lim'pieθa; lim'piesa/ n. f. cleanliness.
limpio /'limpio/ n. m. clean.
limusina /limu'sina/ n. f. limousine.
linaje /li'nahe/ n. m. lineage, ancestry.
linaza /li'naθa; li'nasa/ n. f. linseed.
lince /'linθe; 'linse/ a. sharp-sighted, observing.
linchamiento /lintʃa'miento/ n. m. lynching.
linchar /lin'tʃar/ v. lynch.
lindar /lin'dar/ v. border, bound.
linde /'linde/ n. m. boundary; landmark.
lindero /lin'dero/ n. m. boundary.
lindo /'lindo/ a. pretty, lovely, nice.
línea /'linea/ n. f. line.
línea de puntos /'linea de 'puntos/ dotted line.
lineal /line'al/ a. lineal.
linfa /'linfa/ n. f. lymph.
lingüista /liŋ'guista/ n. m. & f. linguist.
lingüístico /liŋ'guistiko/ a. linguistic.
linimento /lini'mento/ n. m. liniment.
lino /'lino/ n. m. linen; flax.
linóleo /li'noleo/ n. m. linoleum.
linterna /lin'terna/ n. f. lantern; flashlight.
lío /'lio/ n. m. pack, bundle; mess, scrape; hassle.
liquidación /likiða'θion; likiða'sion/ n. f. liquidation.
liquidar /liki'ðar/ v. liquidate; settle up.
líquido /'likiðo/ a. & m. liquid.
lira /'lira/ n. f. lyre.
lírico /'liriko/ a. lyric.
lirio /'lirio/ n. m. lily.
lirismo /li'rismo/ n. m. lyricism.
lis /lis/ n. f. lily.
lisiar /li'siar/ v. cripple, lame.
liso /'liso/ a. smooth, even.
lisonja /li'sonha/ n. f. flattery.
lisonjear /lisonhe'ar/ v. flatter.
lisonjero /lison'hero/ -ra n. flatterer.
lista /'lista/ n. f. list; stripe; menu.
lista negra /'lista 'negra/ blacklist.
listar /lis'tar/ v. list; put on a list.
listo /'listo/ a. ready; smart, clever.
listón /lis'ton/ n. m. ribbon.
litera /li'tera/ n. f. litter, bunk, berth.
literal /lite'ral/ a. literal.
literario /lite'rario/ a. literary.
literato /lite'rato/ n. m. literary person, writer.
literatura /litera'tura/ n. f. literature.
litigación /litiga'θion; litiga'sion/ n. f. litigation.
litigio /li'tihio/ n. m. litigation; lawsuit.
litoral /lito'ral/ n. m. coast.
litro /'litro/ n. m. liter.
liturgia /li'turhia/ n. f. liturgy.
liviano /li'βiano/ a. light (in weight).

lívido /'liβiðo/ a. livid.
llaga /'ʎaga; 'yaga/ n. f. sore.
llama /'ʎama; 'yama/ n. f. flame; llama.
llamada /ʎa'maða; ya'maða/ n. f. call; knock. —**llamar,** v.
llamarse /ʎa'marse; ya'marse/ v. be called, be named. **se llama...** etc., his name is... etc.
llamativo /ʎama'tiβo; yama'tiβo/ a. gaudy, showy.
llamear /ʎame'ar; yame'ar/ v. blaze.
llaneza /ʎa'neθa; ya'nesa/ n. f. simplicity.
llano /'ʎano; 'yano/ a. 1. flat, level, plain. —n. 2. m. plain.
llanta /'ʎanta; 'yanta/ n. f. tire.
llanto /'ʎanto; 'yanto/ n. m. crying, weeping.
llanura /ʎa'nura; ya'nura/ n. f. prairie, plain.
llave /'ʎaβe; 'yaβe/ n. f. key; wrench; faucet; Elec. switch. **ll. inglesa,** monkey wrench.
llegada /ʎe'gaða; ye'gaða/ n. f. arrival.
llegar /ʎe'gar; ye'gar/ v. arrive; reach. **ll. a ser,** become, come to be.
llenar /ʎe'nar; ye'nar/ v. fill.
lleno /'ʎeno; 'yeno/ a. full.
llenura /ʎe'nura; ye'nura/ n. f. abundance.
llevadero /ʎeβa'ðero; yeβa'ðero/ a. tolerable.
llevar /ʎe'βar; ye'βar/ v. take, carry, bear; wear (clothes). **ll. a cabo,** carry out.
llevarse /ʎe'βarse; ye'βarse/ v. take away, run away with. **ll. bien,** get along well.
llorar /ʎo'rar; yo'rar/ v. cry, weep.
lloroso /ʎo'roso; yo'roso/ a. sorrowful, tearful.
llover /ʎo'βer; yo'βer/ v. rain.
llovido /ʎo'βiðo; yo'βiðo/ n. m. stowaway.
llovizna /ʎo'βiθna; yo'βisna/ n. f. drizzle, sprinkle. —**lloviznar,** v.
lluvia /'ʎuβia; 'yuβia/ n. f. rain.
lluvia ácida /'ʎuβia 'aθiða; 'yuβia 'asiða/ acid rain.
lluvioso /ʎu'βioso; yu'βioso/ a. rainy.
lo /lo/ pron. the; him, it, you; (pl.) them, you.
loar /lo'ar/ v. praise, laud.
lobina /lo'βina/ n. f. striped bass.
lobo /'loβo/ n. m. wolf.
lóbrego /'loβrego/ a. murky; dismal.
local /lo'kal/ a. 1. local. —n. 2. m. site.
localidad /lokali'ðað/ n. f. locality, location; seat (in theater).
localizar /lokali'θar; lokali'sar/ v. localize.
loción /lo'θion; lo'sion/ n. f. lotion.
loco /'loko/ -ca a. 1. crazy, insane, mad. —n. 2. lunatic.
locomotora /lokomo'tora/ n. f. locomotive.
locuaz /lo'kuaθ; lo'kuas/ a. loquacious.
locución /loku'θion; loku'sion/ n. f. locution, expression.
locura /lo'kura/ n. f. folly; madness, insanity.
lodo /'loðo/ n. m. mud.
lodoso /lo'ðoso/ a. muddy.
lógica /'lohika/ n. f. logic.
lógico /'lohiko/ a. logical.
lograr /lo'grar/ v. achieve; succeed in.
logro /'logro/ n. m. accomplishment.
lombriz /lom'βriθ; lom'βris/ n. f. earthworm.
lomo /'lomo/ n. m. loin; back (of an animal).
lona /'lona/ n. f. canvas, tarpaulin.
longevidad /lonheβi'ðað/ n. f. longevity.
longitud /lonhi'tuð/ n. f. longitude; length.
lonja /'lonha/ n. f. shop; market.
lontananza /lonta'nanθa; lonta'nansa/ n. f. distance.

loro /'loro/ n. m. parrot.
losa /'losa/ n. f. slab.
lote /'lote/ n. m. lot, share.
lotería /lote'ria/ n. f. lottery.
loza /'loθa; 'losa/ n. f. china, crockery.
lozanía /loθa'nia; losa'nia/ n. f. freshness, vigor.
lozano /lo'θano; lo'sano/ a. fresh, spirited.
lubricación /luβrika'θion; luβrika-'sion/ n. f. lubrication.
lubricar /luβri'kar/ v. lubricate.
lucero /lu'θero; lu'sero/ n. m. (bright) star.
lucha /'lutʃa/ n. f. fight, struggle; wrestling. —**luchar,** v.
luchador /lutʃa'ðor/ -ra n. fighter, wrestler.
lúcido /lu'θiðo; lu'siðo/ a. lucid, clear.
luciente /lu'θiente; lu'siente/ a. shining, bright.
luciérnaga /lu'θiernaga; lu'siernaga/ n. f. firefly.
lucimiento /luθi'miento; lusi'miento/ n. m. success; splendor.
lucir /lu'θir; lu'sir/ v. shine, sparkle; show off.
lucrativo /lukra'tiβo/ a. lucrative, profitable.
luego /'luego/ adv. right away; afterwards, next. **l. que,** as soon as. **desde l.,** of course. **hasta l.,** goodbye, so long.
lugar /lu'gar/ n. m. place, spot; space, room.
lúgubre /'luguβre/ a. gloomy; dismal.
lujo /'luho/ n. m. luxury. **de l.,** deluxe.
lujoso /lu'hoso/ a. luxurious.
lumbre /'lumbre/ n. f. fire; light.
luminoso /lumi'noso/ a. luminous.
luna /'luna/ n. f. moon.
lunar /lu'nar/ n. m. beauty mark, mole; polka dot.
lunático /lu'natiko/ -ca a. & n. lunatic.
lunes /'lunes/ n. m. Monday.
luneta /lu'neta/ n. f. Theat. orchestra seat.
lupa /'lupa/ n. f. magnifying glass.
lustre /'lustre/ n. m. polish, shine. —**lustrar,** v.
lustroso /lus'troso/ a. shiny.
luto /'luto/ n. m. mourning.
luz /luθ; lus/ n. f. light. **dar a l.,** give birth to.

M

maca /'maka/ n. f. blemish, flaw.
macaco /ma'kako/ a. ugly, horrid.
macareno /maka'reno/ a. boasting.
macarrones /maka'rrones/ n. m.pl. macaroni.
macear /maθe'ar; mase'ar/ v. molest, push around.
macedonia de frutas /maθe'ðonia de 'frutas; mase'ðonia de 'frutas/ n. f. fruit salad.
maceta /ma'θeta; ma'seta/ n. f. vase; mallet.
machacar /matʃa'kar/ v. pound; crush.
machina /ma'tʃina/ n. f. derrick.
machista /ma'tʃista/ a. macho.
macho /'matʃo/ n. m. male.
machucho /ma'tʃutʃo/ a. mature, wise.
macizo /ma'θiθo; ma'siso/ a. 1. solid. —n. 2. m. bulk; flower bed.
macular /maku'lar/ v. stain.
madera /ma'ðera/ n. f. lumber; wood.
madero /ma'ðero/ n. m. beam, timber.
madrastra /ma'ðrastra/ n. f. stepmother.
madre /'maðre/ n. f. mother. **m. política,** mother-in-law.
madreperla /maðre'perla/ n. f. mother-of-pearl.
madriguera /maðri'gera/ n. f. burrow; lair, den.
madrina /ma'ðrina/ n. f. godmother.

madroncillo /maðron'θiʎo; maðron-'siyo/ n. m. strawberry.
madrugada /maðru'gaða/ n. f. daybreak.
madrugar /maðru'gar/ v. get up early.
madurar /maðu'rar/ v. ripen.
madurez /maðu'reθ; maðu'res/ n. f. maturity.
maduro /ma'ðuro/ a. ripe; mature.
maestría /maes'tria/ n. f. mastery; master's degree.
maestro /ma'estro/ n. m. master; teacher.
mafia /'mafia/ n. f. mafia.
maganto /ma'ganto/ a. lethargic, dull.
magia /'mahia/ n. f. magic.
mágico /'mahiko/ a. & m. magic; magician.
magistrado /mahis'traðo/ n. m. magistrate.
magnánimo /mag'nanimo/ a. magnanimous.
magnético /mag'netiko/ a. magnetic.
magnetismo /magne'tismo/ n. m. magnetism.
magnetófono /magne'tofono/ n. m. tape recorder.
magnificar /magnifi'kar/ v. magnify.
magnificencia /magnifi'θenθia; magnifi'sensia/ n. f. magnificence.
magnífico /mag'nifiko/ a. magnificent.
magnitud /magni'tuð/ n. f. magnitude.
magno /'magno/ a. great, grand.
magnolia /mag'nolia/ n. f. magnolia.
mago /'mago/ n. m. magician; wizard.
magosto /ma'gosto/ n. m. chestnut roast; picnic fire for roasting chestnuts.
magro /'magro/ a. meager; thin.
magullar /magu'ʎar; magu'yar/ v. bruise.
mahometano /maome'tano/ n. & a. Mohammedan.
mahometismo /maome'tismo/ n. m. Mohammedanism.
maíz /ma'iθ; ma'is/ n. m. corn.
majadero /maha'ðero/ -ra a. & n. foolish; fool.
majar /ma'har/ v. mash.
majestad /mahes'tað/ n. f. majesty.
majestuoso /mahes'tuoso/ a. majestic.
mal /mal/ adv. 1. badly; wrong. —n. 2. m. evil, ill; illness.
mala /'mala/ n. f. mail.
malacate /mala'kate/ n. m. hoist.
malandanza /malan'danθa; malan'dansa/ n. f. misfortune.
malaventura /malaβen'tura/ n. f. misfortune.
malcomido /malko'miðo/ a. underfed; malnourished.
malcontento /malkon'tento/ a. dissatisfied.
maldad /mal'dað/ n. f. badness; wickedness.
maldecir /malde'θir; malde'sir/ v. curse, damn.
maldición /maldi'θion; maldi'sion/ n. f. curse.
maldito /mal'dito/ a. accursed, damned.
malecón /male'kon/ n. m. embankment.
maledicencia /maleði'θenθia; maleði'sensia/ n. f. slander.
maleficio /male'fiθio; male'fisio/ n. m. spell, charm.
malestar /males'tar/ n. m. indisposition.
maleta /ma'leta/ n. f. suitcase, valise.
malévolo /ma'leβolo/ a. malevolent.
maleza /ma'leθa; ma'lesa/ n. f. weeds; underbrush.
malgastar /malgas'tar/ v. squander.
malhechor /male'tʃor/ -ra n. malefactor, evildoer.
malhumorado /malumo'raðo/ a. morose, ill-humored.

malicia /ma'liθia; ma'lisia/ *n. f.* malice.

maliciar /mali'θiar; mali'siar/ *v.* suspect.

malicioso /mali'θioso; mali'sioso/ *a.* malicious.

maligno /ma'ligno/ *a.* malignant, evil.

malla /'maʎa; 'maya/ *n. f.* mesh, net.

mallas /'maʎas; 'mayas/ *n. f.pl.* leotard.

mallete /ma'ʎete; ma'yete/ *n. m.* mallet.

malo /'malo/ *a.* bad; evil, wicked; naughty; ill.

malograr /malo'grar/ *v.* miss, lose.

malparto /mal'parto/ *n. m.* abortion, miscarriage.

malquerencia /malke'renθia; malke'rensia/ *n. f.* hatred.

malquerer /malke'rer/ *v.* dislike; bear ill will.

malsano /mal'sano/ *a.* unhealthy; unwholesome.

malsín /mal'sin/ *n. m.* malicious gossip.

malta /'malta/ *n. f.* malt.

maltratar /maltra'tar/ *v.* mistreat.

malvado /mal'βaðo/ **-da** *a.* **1.** wicked. —*n.* **2.** villain.

malversar /malβer'sar/ *v.* embezzle.

malvís /mal'βis/ *n. m.* redwing.

mamá /'mama/ *n. f.* mama, mother.

mamar /ma'mar/ *v.* suckle; suck.

mamífero /ma'mifero/ *n. m.* mammal.

mampara /mam'para/ *n. f.* screen.

mampostería /mamposte'ria/ *n. f.* masonry.

mamut /ma'mut/ *n. m.* mammoth.

manada /ma'naða/ *n. f.* flock, herd, drove.

manantial /manan'tial/ *n. m.* spring (of water).

manar /ma'nar/ *v.* gush, flow out.

mancebo /man'θeβo; man'seβo/ *n. m.* young man.

mancha /'mantʃa/ *n. f.* stain, smear, blemish, spot. —**manchar,** *v.*

mancilla /man'θiʎa; man'siya/ *n. f.* stain; blemish.

manco /'manko/ *a.* armless; one-armed.

mandadero /manda'ðero/ *n. m.* messenger.

mandado /man'daðo/ *n. m.* order, command.

mandamiento /manda'miento/ *n. m.* commandment; command.

mandar /man'dar/ *v.* send; order, command.

mandatario /manda'tario/ *n. m.* attorney; representative.

mandato /man'dato/ *n. m.* mandate, command.

mandíbula /man'diβula/ *n. f.* jaw; jawbone.

mando /'mando/ *n. m.* command, order; leadership.

mando a distancia /'mando a dis'tanθia; 'mando a dis'tansia/ remote control.

mandón /man'don/ *a.* domineering.

mandril /man'dril/ *n. m.* baboon.

manejar /mane'har/ *v.* handle, manage; drive (a car).

manejo /ma'neho/ *n. m.* management; horsemanship.

manera /ma'nera/ *n. f.* way, manner, means. **de m. que,** so, as a result.

manga /'manga/ *n. f.* sleeve.

mangana /maŋ'gana/ *n. f.* lariat, lasso.

manganeso /maŋga'neso/ *n. m.* manganese.

mango /'maŋgo/ *n. m.* handle; mango (fruit).

mangosta /maŋ'gosta/ *n. f.* mongoose.

manguera /maŋ'guera/ *n. f.* hose.

manguito /maŋ'guito/ *n. m.* muff.

maní /ma'ni/ *n. m.* peanut.

manía /ma'nia/ *n. f.* mania, madness; hobby.

maníaco /ma'niako/ **-ca, maniático -ca** *a. & n.* maniac.

manicomio /mani'komio/ *n. m.* insane asylum.

manicura /mani'kura/ *n. f.* manicure.

manifactura /manifak'tura/ *n. f.* manufacture.

manifestación /manifesta'θion; manifesta'sion/ *n. f.* manifestation.

manifestar /manifes'tar/ *v.* manifest, show.

manifiesto /mani'fiesto/ *a. & m.* manifest.

manija /ma'niha/ *n. f.* handle; crank.

maniobra /ma'nioβra/ *n. f.* maneuver. —**maniobrar,** *v.*

manipulación /manipula'θion; manipula'sion/ *n. f.* manipulation.

manipular /manipu'lar/ *v.* manipulate.

maniquí /mani'ki/ *n. m.* mannequin.

manivela /mani'βela/ *n. f. Mech.* crank.

manjar /man'har/ *n. m.* food, dish.

manlieve /man'lieβe/ *n. m.* swindle.

mano /'mano/ *n. f.* hand.

manojo /ma'noho/ *n. m.* handful; bunch.

manómetro /ma'nometro/ *n. m.* gauge.

manopla /ma'nopla/ *n. f.* gauntlet.

manosear /manose'ar/ *v.* handle, feel, touch.

manotada /mano'taða/ *n. f.* slap, smack. —**manotear,** *v.*

mansedumbre /manse'ðumbre/ *n. f.* meekness, tameness.

mansión /man'sion/ *n. f.* mansion; abode.

manso /'manso/ *a.* tame, gentle.

manta /'manta/ *n. f.* blanket.

manteca /man'teka/ *n. f.* fat, lard; butter.

mantecado /mante'kaðo/ *n. m.* ice cream.

mantecoso /mante'koso/ *a.* buttery.

mantel /man'tel/ *n. m.* tablecloth.

mantener /mante'ner/ *v.* maintain, keep; sustain; support.

mantenimiento /manteni'miento/ *n. m.* maintenance.

mantequera /mante'kera/ *n. f.* butter dish; churn.

mantequilla /mante'kiʎa; mante'ki-ya/ *n. f.* butter.

mantilla /man'tiʎa; man'tiya/ *n. f.* mantilla; baby clothes.

mantillo /man'tiʎo; man'tiyo/ *n. m.* humus; manure.

manto /'manto/ *n. m.* mantle, cloak.

manual /ma'nual/ *a. & m.* manual.

manubrio /ma'nuβrio/ *n. m.* handle; crank.

manufacturar /manufaktu'rar/ *v.* manufacture; make.

manuscrito /manus'krito/ *n. m.* manuscript.

manzana /man'θana; man'sana/ *n. f.* apple; block (of street).

manzanilla /manθa'niʎa; mansa'niya/ *n. f.* dry sherry.

manzano /man'θano; man'sano/ *n. m.* apple tree.

maña /'maɲa/ *n. f.* skill; cunning; trick.

mañana /ma'ɲana/ *adv.* **1.** tomorrow. —*n.* **2.** *f.* morning.

mañanear /maɲane'ar/ *v.* rise early in the morning.

mañero /ma'ɲero/ *a.* clever; skillful; lazy.

mapa /'mapa/ *n. m.* map, chart.

mapache /ma'patʃe/ *n. m.* raccoon.

mapurito /mapu'rito/ *n. m.* skunk.

máquina /'makina/ *n. f.* machine. **m. de coser,** sewing machine. **m. de lavar,** washing machine.

maquinación /makina'θion; makina-'sion/ *n. f.* machination; plot.

maquinador /makina'ðor/ **-ra** *n.* plotter, schemer.

maquinal /maki'nal/ *a.* mechanical.

maquinar /maki'nar/ *v.* scheme, plot.

maquinaria /maki'naria/ *n. f.* machinery.

maquinista /maki'nista/ *n. m.* machinist; engineer.

mar /mar/ *n. m. or f.* sea.

marabú /mara'βu/ *n. m.* marabou.

maraña /ma'raɲa/ *n. f.* tangle; maze; snarl; plot.

maravilla /mara'βiʎa; mara'βiya/ *n. f.* marvel, wonder. —**maravillarse,** *v.*

maravilloso /maraβi'ʎoso; maraβi-'yoso/ *a.* marvelous, wonderful.

marbete /mar'βete/ *n. m.* tag, label; check.

marca /'marka/ *n. f.* mark, sign; brand, make.

marcador /marka'ðor/ *n. m.* highlighter.

marcapáginas /marka'pahinas/ *n. m.* bookmark.

marcar /mar'kar/ *v.* mark; observe, note.

marcha /'martʃa/ *n. f.* march; progress. —**marchar,** *v.*

marchante /mar'tʃante/ *n. m.* merchant; customer.

marcharse /mar'tʃarse/ *v.* go away, depart.

marchitable /martʃi'taβle/ *a.* perishable.

marchitar /martʃi'tar/ *v.* fade, wilt, wither.

marchito /mar'tʃito/ *a.* faded, withered.

marcial /mar'θial; mar'sial/ *a.* martial.

marco /'marko/ *n. m.* frame.

marea /ma'rea/ *n. f.* tide.

mareado /mare'aðo/ *a.* seasick.

marearse /mare'arse/ *v.* get dizzy; be seasick.

mareo /ma'reo/ *n. m.* dizziness; seasickness.

marfil /mar'fil/ *n. m.* ivory.

margarita /marga'rita/ *n. f.* pearl; daisy.

margen /'marhen/ *n. m. or f.* margin, edge, rim.

marido /ma'riðo/ *n. m.* husband.

marijuana /mari'huana/ *n. f.* marijuana.

marimacha /mari'matʃa/ *n. f.* lesbian.

marimacho /mari'matʃo/ *n. m.* mannish woman.

marimba /ma'rimba/ *n. f.* marimba.

marina /ma'rina/ *n. f.* navy; seascape.

marinero /mari'nero/ *n. m.* sailor, seaman.

marino /ma'rino/ *a. & m.* marine, (of) sea; mariner, seaman.

marión /ma'rion/ *n. m.* sturgeon.

mariposa /mari'posa/ *n. f.* butterfly.

mariquita /mari'kita/ *n. f.* ladybird.

mariscal /maris'kal/ *n. m.* marshal.

marisco /ma'risko/ *n. m.* shellfish; mollusk.

marital /mari'tal/ *a.* marital.

marítimo /ma'ritimo/ *a.* maritime.

marmita /mar'mita/ *n. f.* pot, kettle.

mármol /'marmol/ *n. m.* marble.

marmóreo /mar'moreo/ *a.* marble.

maroma /ma'roma/ *n. f.* rope.

marqués /mar'kes/ *n. m.* marquis.

marquesa /mar'kesa/ *n. f.* marquise.

Marruecos /ma'rruekos/ *n. m.* Morocco.

Marte /'marte/ *n. m.* Mars.

martes /'martes/ *n. m.* Tuesday.

martillo /mar'tiʎo; mar'tiyo/ *n. m.* hammer. —**martillar,** *v.*

mártir /'martir/ *n. m. & f.* martyr.

martirio /mar'tirio/ *n. m.* martyrdom.

martirizar /martiri'θar; martiri'sar/ *v.* martyrize.

marzo /'marθo; 'marso/ *n. m.* March.

mas /mas/ *conj.* but.

más /mas/ *a. & adv.* more, most; plus. **no m.,** only; no more.

masa /'masa/ *n. f.* mass; dough.

masaje /ma'sahe/ *n. m.* massage.

mascar /mas'kar/ *v.* chew.

máscara /'maskara/ *n. f.* mask.

mascarada /maska'raða/ *n. f.* masquerade.

mascota /mas'kota/ *n. f.* mascot; good-luck charm.

masculino /masku'lino/ *a.* masculine.

mascullar /masku'ʎar; masku'yar/ *v.* mumble.

masón /ma'son/ *n. m.* Freemason.

masticar /masti'kar/ *v.* chew.

mástil /'mastil/ *n. m.* mast; post.

mastín /mas'tin/ *n. m.* mastiff.

mastín danés /mas'tin da'nes/ Great Dane.

mastuerzo /mas'tuerθo; mas'tuerso/ *n. m.* fool, ninny.

mata /'mata/ *n. f.* plant; bush.

matadero /mata'ðero/ *n. m.* slaughterhouse.

matador /mata'ðor/ **-ra** *n.* matador.

matafuego /mata'fuego/ *n. m.* fire extinguisher.

matanza /ma'tanθa; ma'tansa/ *n. f.* killing, bloodshed, slaughter.

matar /ma'tar/ *v.* kill, slay; slaughter.

matasanos /mata'sanos/ *n. m.* quack.

mate /'mate/ *n. m.* checkmate; Paraguayan tea.

matemáticas /mate'matikas/ *n. f.pl.* mathematics.

matemático /mate'matiko/ *a.* mathematical.

materia /ma'teria/ *n. f.* material; subject (matter).

material /mate'rial/ *a. & m.* material.

materialismo /materia'lismo/ *n. m.* materialism.

materializar /materiali'θar; materiali'sar/ *v.* materialize.

maternal /mater'nal/ **materno** *a.* maternal.

maternidad /materni'ðað/ *n. f.* maternity; maternity hospital.

matiné /mati'ne/ *n. f.* matinee.

matiz /ma'tiθ; ma'tis/ *n. m.* hue, shade.

matizar /mati'θar; mati'sar/ *v.* blend; tint.

matón /ma'ton/ *n. m.* bully.

matorral /mato'rral/ *n. m.* thicket.

matoso /ma'toso/ *a.* weedy.

matraca /ma'traka/ *n. f.* rattle. —**matraquear,** *v.*

matrícula /ma'trikula/ *n. f.* registration; tuition.

matricularse /matriku'larse/ *v.* enroll, register.

matrimonio /matri'monio/ *n. m.* matrimony, marriage; married couple.

matriz /ma'triθ; ma'tris/ *n. f.* womb; *Mech.* die, mold.

matrona /ma'trona/ *n. f.* matron.

maullar /mau'ʎar; mau'yar/ *v.* mew.

máxima /'maksima/ *n. f.* maxim.

máxime /'maksime/ *a.* principally.

máximo /'maksimo/ *a. & m.* maximum.

maya /'maya/ *n. f.* daisy.

mayo /'mayo/ *n. m.* May.

mayonesa /mayo'nesa/ *n. f.* mayonnaise.

mayor /ma'yor/ *a.* larger, largest; greater, greatest; elder, eldest, senior. **m. de edad,** major, of age. **al por m.,** at wholesale. *m.* major.

mayoral /mayo'ral/ *n. m.* head shepherd; boss; foreman.

mayordomo /mayor'ðomo/ *n. m.* manager; butler, steward.

mayoría /mayo'ria/ *n. f.* majority, bulk.

mayorista /mayo'rista/ *n. m. & f.* wholesaler.

mayúscula /ma'yuskula/ *n. f.* capital letter, upper-case letter.

mazmorra /maθ'morra; mas'morra/ *n. f.* dungeon.

mazorca /ma'θorka; ma'sorka/ *n. f.* ear of corn.

me /me/ *pron.* me; myself.

mecánico /me'kaniko/ **-ca** *a. & n.* mechanical; mechanic.

mecanismo /meka'nismo/ *n. m.* mechanism.

mecanizar /mekani'θar; mekani'sar/ *v.* mechanize.

mecanografía /mekanogra'fia/ *n. f.* typewriting.

mecanógrafo /meka'nografo/ **-fa** *n.* typist.

mecedor /meθe'ðor; mese'ðor/ *n. m.* swing.

mecedora /meθe'ðora; mese'ðora/ *n. f.* rocking chair.

mecer /me'θer; me'ser/ *v.* rock; swing, sway.

mecha /'metʃa/ *n. f.* wick; fuse.

mechón /me'tʃon/ *n. m.* lock (of hair).

medalla /me'ðaʎa; me'ðaya/ *n. f.* medal.

médano /'meðano/ *n. m.* sand dune.

media /'meðia/ *n. f.* stocking.

mediación /meðia'θion; meðia'sion/ *n. f.* mediation.

mediador /meðia'ðor/ **-ra** *n.* mediator.

mediados /me'ðiaðos/ *n. m.pl.* **a m. de,** about the middle of (a period of time).

medianero /meðia'nero/ *n. m.* mediator.

medianía /meðia'nia/ *n. f.* mediocrity.

mediano /me'ðiano/ *a.* medium; moderate; mediocre.

medianoche /meðia'notʃe/ *n. f.* midnight.

mediante /me'ðiante/ *prep.* by means of.

mediar /me'ðiar/ *v.* mediate.

medicamento /meðika'mento/ *n. m.* medicine, drug.

medicastro /meði'kastro/ *n. m.* quack.

medicina /meði'θina; meði'sina/ *n. f.* medicine.

medicinar /meðiθi'nar; meðisi'nar/ *v.* treat (as a doctor).

médico /'meðiko/ *a.* **1.** medical. —*n.* **2.** *m. & f.* doctor, physician.

medida /me'ðiða/ *n. f.* measure, step.

medidor /meði'ðor/ *n. m.* meter.

medieval /meðie'βal/ *a.* medieval.

medio /'meðio/ *a.* **1.** half; mid; middle of. —*n.* **2.** *m.* middle; means.

mediocre /me'ðiokre/ *a.* mediocre.

mediocridad /meðiokri'ðað/ *n. f.* mediocrity.

mediodía /meðio'ðia/ *n. m.* midday, noon.

medir /me'ðir/ *v.* measure, gauge.

meditación /meðita'θion; meðita'sion/ *n. f.* meditation.

meditar /meði'tar/ *v.* meditate.

mediterráneo /meðite'rraneo/ *a.* Mediterranean.

medrar /'meðrar/ *v.* thrive; grow.

medroso /me'ðroso/ *a.* fearful, cowardly.

megáfono /me'gafono/ *n. m.* megaphone.

megahercio /mega'erθio; mega'ersio/ *n. f.* megahertz.

mejicano /mehi'kano/ **-na** *a. & n.* Mexican.

mejilla /me'hiʎa; me'hiya/ *n. f.* cheek.

mejillón /mehi'ʎon; mehi'yon/ *n. m.* mussel.

mejor /me'hor/ *a. & adv.* better; best. **a lo m.,** perhaps.

mejora /me'hora/ *n. f.,* **mejoramiento,** *m.* improvement.

mejorar /meho'rar/ *v.* improve, better.

mejoría /meho'ria/ *n. f.* improvement; superiority.

melancolía /melanko'lia/ *n. f.* melancholy.

melancólico /melan'koliko/ *a.* melancholy.

melaza /me'laθa; me'lasa/ *n. f.* molasses.

melena /me'lena/ *n. f.* mane; long or loose hair.

melenudo /mele'nuðo/ **-da** *a.* longhaired.

melindroso /melin'droso/ *a.* fussy.

mella /'meʎa; 'meya/ *n. f.* notch; dent. —**mellar,** *v.*

mellizo /me'ʎiθo; me'yiso/ **-za** *n. & a.* twin.

melocotón /meloko'ton/ *n. m.* peach.

melodía /melo'ðia/ *n. f.* melody.

melodioso /melo'ðioso/ *a.* melodious.

melón /me'lon/ *n. m.* melon.

meloso /me'loso/ *a.* like honey.

membrana /mem'brana/ *n. f.* membrane.

membrete /mem'brete/ *n. m.* memorandum; letterhead.

membrillo /mem'briʎo; mem'briyo/ *n. m.* quince.

membrudo /mem'bruðo/ *a.* strong, muscular.

memorable /memo'raβle/ *a.* memorable.

memorándum /memo'randum/ *n. m.* memorandum; notebook.

memoria /me'moria/ *n. f.* memory; memoir; memorandum.

mención /men'θion; men'sion/ *n. f.* mention. —**mencionar,** *v.*

mendigar /mendi'gar/ *v.* beg (for alms).

mendigo /men'digo/ **-a** *n.* beggar.

mendrugo /men'drugo/ *n. m.* (hard) crust, chunk.

menear /mene'ar/ *v.* shake, wag; stir.

menester /menes'ter/ *n. m.* need, want; duty, task. **ser m.,** to be necessary.

menesteroso /meneste'roso/ *a.* needy.

mengua /'meŋgua/ *n. f.* decrease; lack; poverty.

menguar /meŋ'guar/ *v.* abate, decrease.

meningitis /meniŋ'gitis/ *n. f.* meningitis.

menopausia /meno'pausia/ *n. f.* menopause.

menor /me'nor/ *a.* smaller, smallest; lesser, least; younger, youngest, junior. **m. de edad,** minor, under age. **al por m.,** at retail.

menos /'menos/ *a. & adv.* less, least; minus. **a m. que,** unless. **echar de m.,** to miss.

menospreciar /menospre'θiar; menospre'siar/ *v.* cheapen; despise; slight.

mensaje /men'sahe/ *n. m.* message.

mensajero /mensa'hero/ **-ra** *n.* messenger.

menstruar /menstru'ar/ *v.* menstruate.

mensual /men'sual/ *a.* monthly.

mensualidad /mensuali'ðað/ *n. f.* monthly income or allowance; monthly payment.

menta /'menta/ *n. f.* mint, peppermint.

mentado /men'taðo/ *a.* famous.

mental /men'tal/ *a.* mental.

mentalidad /mentali'ðað/ *n. f.* mentality.

menta romana /'menta rro'mana/ spearmint.

mente /'mente/ *n. f.* mind.

mentecato /mente'kato/ *a.* foolish, stupid.

mentir /men'tir/ *v.* lie, tell a lie.

mentira /men'tira/ *n. f.* lie, falsehood. **parece m.,** it seems impossible.

mentiroso /menti'roso/ *a.* lying, untruthful.

mentol /men'tol/ *n. m.* menthol.

menú /me'nu/ *n. m.* menu.

menudeo /menu'ðeo/ *n. m.* retail.

menudo /menu'ðo/ *a.* small, minute. **a m.,** often.

meñique /me'ɲike/ *a.* tiny.

meple /'meple/ *n. m.* maple.

merca /'merka/ *n. f.* purchase.

mercader /merka'ðer/ *n. m.* merchant.

mercaderías /merkaðe'rias/ *n. f.pl.* merchandise, commodities.

mercado /mer'kaðo/ *n. m.* market.

Mercado Común /mer'kaðo ko'mun/ Common Market.

mercado negro /mer'kaðo 'negro/ black market.

mercancía /merkan'θia; merkan'sia/ *n. f.* merchandise; (*pl.*) wares.

mercante /mer'kante/ *a.* merchant.

mercantil /merkan'til/ *a.* mercantile.

merced /mer'θeð; mer'seð/ *n. f.* mercy, grace.

mercenario /merθe'nario; merse'nario/ **-ria** *a. & n.* mercenary.

mercurio /mer'kurio/ *n. m.* mercury.

merecedor /mereθe'ðor; merese'ðor/ *a.* worthy.

merecer /mere'θer; mere'ser/ *v.* merit, deserve.

merecimiento /mereθi'miento; meresi'miento/ *n. m.* merit.

merendar /meren'dar/ *v.* eat lunch; snack.

merendero /meren'dero/ *n. m.* lunchroom.

meridional /meriðio'nal/ *a.* southern.

merienda /me'rienda/ *n. f.* midday meal, lunch; afternoon snack.

mérito /'merito/ *n. m.* merit, worth.

meritorio /meri'torio/ *a.* meritorious.

merla /'merla/ *n. f.* blackbird.

merluza /mer'luθa; mer'lusa/ *n. f.* haddock.

mermelada /merme'laða/ *n. f.* marmalade.

mero /'mero/ *a.* mere.

merodeador /meroðea'ðor/ **-ra** *n.* prowler.

mes /'mes/ *n. m.* month.

mesa /'mesa/ *n. f.* table.

meseta /me'seta/ *n. f.* plateau.

mesón /me'son/ *n. m.* inn.

mesonero /meso'nero/ **-ra** *n.* innkeeper.

mestizo /mes'tiθo; mes'tiso/ **-za** *a. & n.* half-caste.

meta /'meta/ *n. f.* goal, objective.

metabolismo /metaβo'lismo/ *n. m.* metabolism.

metafísica /meta'fisika/ *n. f.* metaphysics.

metáfora /me'tafora/ *n. f.* metaphor.

metal /me'tal/ *n. m.* metal.

metálico /me'taliko/ *a.* metallic.

metalurgia /metalur'hia/ *n. f.* metallurgy.

meteoro /mete'oro/ *n. m.* meteor.

meteorología /meteorolo'hia/ *n. f.* meteorology.

meter /me'ter/ *v.* put (in).

meterse /me'terse/ *v.* interfere, meddle; go into.

metódico /me'toðiko/ *a.* methodic.

método /'metoðo/ *n. m.* method, approach.

metralla /me'traʎa; me'traya/ *n. f.* shrapnel.

métrico /'metriko/ *a.* metric.

metro /'metro/ *n. m.* meter (measure); subway.

metrópoli /me'tropoli/ *n. f.* metropolis.

mexicano /meksi'kano/ **-na** *a. & n.* Mexican.

mezcla /'meθkla; 'meskla/ *n. f.* mixture; blend.

mezclar /meθ'klar; mes'klar/ *v.* mix; blend.

mezcolanza /meθko'lanθa; mesko'lansa/ *n. f.* mixture; hodgepodge.

mezquino /meθ'kino; mes'kino/ *a.* stingy; petty.

mezquita /meθ'kita; mes'kita/ *n. f.* mosque.

mi /'mi/ *a.* my.

mí /'mi/ *pron.* me; myself.

microbio /mi'kroβio/ *n. m.* microbe, germ.

microbús /mikro'βus/ *n. m.* minibus.

microchip /mikro'tʃip/ *n. m.* microchip.

microficha /mikro'fitʃa/ *n. f.* microfiche.

micrófono /mi'krofono/ *n. m.* microphone.

microforma /mikro'forma/ *n. f.* microform.

microscópico /mikros'kopiko/ *a.* microscopic.

microscopio /mikros'kopio/ *n. m.* microscope.

microtaxi /mikro'taksi/ *n. m.* minicab.

miedo /'mieðo/ *n. m.* fear. **tener m.,** fear, be afraid.

miedoso /mie'ðoso/ *a.* fearful.

miel /miel/ *n. f.* honey.

miembro /mi'embro/ *n. m. & f.* member; limb.

mientras /'mientras/ *conj.* while. **m. tanto,** meanwhile. **m. más... más,** the more... the more.

miércoles /'mierkoles/ *n. m.* Wednesday.

miércoles de ceniza /'mierkoles de θe'niθa; 'mierkoles de se'nisa/ Ash Wednesday.

miga /'miga/ **migaja** *n. f.* scrap; crumb.

migración /migra'θion; migra'sion/ *n. f.* migration.

migratorio /migra'torio/ *a.* migratory.

mil /mil/ *a. & pron.* thousand.

milagro /mi'lagro/ *n. m.* miracle.

milagroso /mila'groso/ *a.* miraculous.

milicia /mi'liθia; mi'lisia/ *n. f.* militia.

militante /mili'tante/ *a.* militant.

militar /mili'tar/ *a.* **1.** military. —*n.* **2.** *m.* military man.

militarismo /milita'rismo/ *n. m.* militarism.

milla /'miʎa; 'miya/ *n. f.* mile.

millar /mi'ʎar; mi'yar/ *n. m.* (a) thousand.

millón /mi'ʎon; mi'yon/ *n. m.* million.

millonario /miʎo'nario; miyo'nario/ **-ria** *n.* millionaire.

mimar /mi'mar/ *v.* pamper, spoil (a child).

mimbre /'mimbre/ *n. m.* willow; wicker.

mímico /'mimiko/ *a.* mimic.

mimo /'mimo/ *n. m.* mime, mimic.

mina /'mina/ *n. f.* mine. —**minar,** *v.*

mineral /mine'ral/ *a. & m.* mineral.

minero /mi'nero/ **-ra** *n.* miner.

miniatura /minia'tura/ *n. f.* miniature.

miniaturizar /miniaturi'θar; miniaturi'sar/ *v.* miniaturize.

mínimo /'minimo/ *a. & m.* minimum.

ministerio /minis'terio/ *n. m.* ministry; cabinet.

ministro /mi'nistro/ **-a** *n. Govt.* minister, secretary.

minoría /mino'ria/ *n. f.* minority.

minoridad /minori'ðað/ *n. f.* minority (of age).

minucioso /minu'θioso; minu'sioso/ *a.* minute; thorough.

minué /mi'nue/ *n. m.* minuet.

minúscula /mi'nuskula/ *n. f.* lowercase letter, small letter.

minuta /mi'nuta/ *n. f.* draft.

mío /'mio/ *a.* mine.

miopía /mio'pia/ *n. f.* myopia.

mira /'mira/ *n. f.* gunsight.

mirada /mi'raða/ *n. f.* look; gaze, glance.

miramiento /mira'miento/ *n. m.* consideration; respect.

mirar /mi'rar/ *v.* look, look at; watch. **m. a,** face.

miríada /mi'riaða/ *n. f.* myriad.

mirlo /'mirlo/ *n. m.* blackbird.

mirón /mi'ron/ **-ona** *n.* bystander, observer.

mirra /'mirra/ *n. f.* myrrh.

mirto /'mirto/ *n. m.* myrtle.

misa /'misa/ *n. f.* mass, church service.

misceláneo /misθe'laneo; misse'laneo/ *a.* miscellaneous.

miserable /mise'raβle/ *a.* miserable, wretched.

miseria /mi'seria/ *n. f.* misery.

misericordia /miseri'korðia/ *n. f.* mercy.

misericordioso /miserikor'ðioso/ *a.* merciful.

misión /mi'sion/ *n. f.* assignment; mission.

misionario /misio'nario/ **-ria, misionero -ra** *n.* missionary.

mismo /'mismo/ *a. & pron.* **1.** same; -self, -selves. —*adv.* **2.** right, exactly.

misterio /mis'terio/ *n. m.* mystery.

misterioso /miste'rioso/ *a.* mysterious, weird.

místico /'mistiko/ **-ca** *a. & n.* mystical, mystic.

mitad /mi'tað/ *n. f.* half.

mítico /'mitiko/ *a.* mythical.

mitigar /miti'gar/ *v.* mitigate.

mitin /'mitin/ *n. m.* meeting; rally.

mito /'mito/ *n. m.* myth.

mitón /mi'ton/ *n. m.* mitten.

mitra /'mitra/ *n. f.* miter (bishop's).

mixto /'miksto/ *a.* mixed.

mixtura /miks'tura/ *n. f.* mixture.

mobiliario /moβi'liario/ *n. m.* household goods.

mocasín /moka'sin/ *n. m.* moccasin.

mocedad /moθe'ðað; mose'ðað/ *n. f.* youthfulness.

mochila /mo'tʃila/ *n. f.* knapsack, backpack.

mocho /'motʃo/ *a.* cropped, trimmed, shorn.

moción /mo'θion; mo'sion/ *n. f.* motion.

mocoso /mo'koso/ **-sa** *n.* brat.

moda /'moða/ *n. f.* mode, fashion, style.

modales /mo'ðales/ *n. m.pl.* manners.

moďelo /mo'ðelo/ *n. m.* model, pattern.

módem /'moðem/ *n. m.* modem.

moderación /moðera'θion; moðera'sion/ *n. f.* moderation.

moderado /moðe'raðo/ *a.* moderate. —**moderar,** *v.*

modernizar /moðerni'θar; moðerni'sar/ *v.* modernize.

moderno /mo'ðerno/ *a.* modern.

modestia /mo'ðestia/ *n. f.* modesty.

modesto /mo'ðesto/ *a.* modest.

módico /'moðiko/ *a.* reasonable, moderate.

modificación /moðifi'kaθion; moðifika'sion/ *n. f.* modification.

modificar /moðifi'kar/ *v.* modify.

modismo /mo'ðismo/ *n. m. Gram.* idiom.

modista /mo'ðista/ *n. f.* dressmaker; milliner.

modo /'moðo/ *n. m.* way, means.

modular /moðu'lar/ *v.* modulate.

mofarse /mo'farse/ *v.* scoff, sneer.

mofletudo /mofle'tuðo/ *a.* fat-cheeked.

mohín /mo'in/ *n. m.* grimace.

moho /'moo/ *n. m.* mold, mildew.

mohoso /mo'oso/ *a.* moldy.

mojar /mo'har/ *v.* wet.

mojón /mo'hon/ *n. m.* landmark; heap.

molde /'molde/ *n. m.* mold, form.

molécula /mo'lekula/ *n. f.* molecule.

moler /mo'ler/ *v.* grind, mill.

molestar /moles'tar/ *v.* molest, bother, disturb, annoy, trouble.

molestia /mo'lestia/ *n. f.* bother, annoyance, trouble; hassle.

molesto /mo'lesto/ *a.* bothersome; annoyed; uncomfortable.

molicie /mo'liθie; mo'lisie/ *n. f.* softness.

molinero /moli'nero/ *n. m.* miller.

molino /mo'lino/ *n. m.* mill. **m. de viento,** windmill.

mollera /mo'ʎera; mo'yera/ *n. f.* top of the head.

molusco /mo'lusko/ *n. m.* mollusk.

momentáneo /momen'taneo/ *a.* momentary.

momento /mo'mento/ *n. m.* moment.

mona /'mona/ *n. f.* female monkey.

monarca /mo'narka/ *n. m. & f.* monarch.

monarquía /monar'kia/ *n. f.* monarchy.

monarquista /monar'kista/ *n. & a.* monarchist.

monasterio /mona'sterio/ *n. m.* monastery.

mondadientes /monda'ðientes/ *n. m.* toothpick.

moneda /mo'neða/ *n. f.* coin; money.

monetario /mone'tario/ *a.* monetary.

monición /moni'θion; moni'sion/ *n. m.* warning.

monigote /moni'gote/ *n. m.* puppet.

monja /'monha/ *n. f.* nun.

monje /'monhe/ *n. m.* monk.

mono /'mono/ **-na** *a.* **1.** *Colloq.* cute. —*n.* **2.** *m. & f.* monkey.

monólogo /mo'nologo/ *n. m.* monologue.

monopatín /monopa'tin/ *n. m.* skateboard.

monopolio /mono'polio/ *n. m.* monopoly.

monopolizar /monopoli'θar; monopoli'sar/ *v.* monopolize.

monosílabo /mono'silaβo/ *n. m.* monosyllable.

monotonía /monoto'nia/ *n. f.* monotony.

monótono /mo'notono/ *a.* monotonous, dreary.

monstruo /'monstruo/ *n. m.* monster.

monstruosidad /monstruosi'ðað/ *n. f.* monstrosity.

monstruoso /mon'struoso/ *a.* monstrous.

monta /'monta/ *n. f.* amount; price.

montaña /mon'taɲa/ *n. f.* mountain.

montañoso /monta'ɲoso/ *a.* mountainous.

montar /mon'tar/ *v.* mount, climb; amount; *Mech.* assemble. **m. a caballo,** ride horseback.

montaraz /monta'raθ; monta'ras/ *a.* wild, barbaric.

monte /'monte/ *n. m.* mountain; forest.

montón /mon'ton/ *n. m.* heap, pile.

montuoso /mon'tuoso/ *a.* mountainous.

montura /mon'tura/ *n. f.* mount; saddle.

monumental /monumen'tal/ *a.* monumental.

monumento /monu'mento/ *n. m.* monument.

mora /'mora/ *n. f.* blackberry.

morada /mo'raða/ *n. f.* residence, dwelling.

morado /mo'raðo/ *a.* purple.

moral /mo'ral/ *a.* **1.** moral. —*n.* **2.** *f.* morale.

moraleja /mora'leha/ *n. f.* moral.

moralidad /morali'ðað/ *n. f.* morality, morals.

moralista /mora'lista/ *n. m. & f.* moralist.

morar /mo'rar/ *v.* dwell, live, reside.

mórbido /'morβiðo/ *a.* morbid.

mordaz /mor'ðaθ; mor'ðas/ *a.* caustic, sarcastic.

mordedura /morðe'ðura/ *n. f.* bite.

morder /mor'ðer/ *v.* bite.

moreno /mo'reno/ **-na** *a. & n.* brown; dark-skinned; dark-haired, brunette.

morfina /mor'fina/ *n. f.* morphine.

moribundo /mori'βundo/ *a.* dying.

morir /mo'rir/ *v.* die.

morisco /mo'risko/ **-ca, moro -ra** *a. & n.* Moorish; Moor.

morriña /mo'rriɲa/ *n. f.* sadness.

morro /'morro/ *n. m.* bluff; snout.

mortaja /mor'taha/ *n. f.* shroud.

mortal /mor'tal/ *a. & n.* mortal.

mortalidad /mortali'ðað/ *n. f.* mortality.

mortero /mor'tero/ *n. m.* mortar.

mortífero /mor'tifero/ *a.* fatal, deadly.

mortificar /mortifi'kar/ *v.* mortify.

mortuorio /mor'tuorio/ *a.* funereal.

mosaico /mo'saiko/ *a. & m.* mosaic.

mosca /'moska/ *n. f.* fly.

mosquito /mos'kito/ *n. m.* mosquito.

mostacho /mos'tatʃo/ *n. m.* mustache.

mostaza /mos'taθa; mos'tasa/ *n. f.* mustard.

mostrador /mostra'ðor/ *n. m.* counter; showcase.

mostrar /mos'trar/ *v.* show, display.

mote /'mote/ *n. m.* nickname; alias.

motel /mo'tel/ *n. m.* motel.

motín /mo'tin/ *n. m.* mutiny; riot.

motivo /mo'tiβo/ *n. m.* motive, reason.

motocicleta /motoθi'kleta; motosi'kleta/ *n. f.* motorcycle.

motociclista /motoθi'klista; motosi'klista/ *n. m. & f.* motorcyclist.

motor /mo'tor/ *n. m.* motor.

motorista /moto'rista/ *n. m. & f.* motorist.

movedizo /moβe'ðiθo; moβe'ðiso/ *a.* movable; shaky.

mover /mo'βer/ *v.* move; stir.

movible /mo'βiβle/ *a.* movable.

móvil /'moβil/ *a.* mobile.

movilización /moβiliθa'θion; moβilisa'sion/ *n. f.* mobilization.

movilizar /moβili'θar; moβili'sar/ *v.* mobilize.

movimiento /moβi'miento/ *n. m.* movement, motion.

mozo /'moθo; 'moso/ *n. m.* boy; servant, waiter, porter.

muaré /mua're/ *n. m.* moiré.

muchacha /mu'tʃatʃa/ *n. f.* girl, youngster; maid (servant).

muchachez /mutʃa'tʃeθ; mutʃa'tʃes/ *n. m.* boyhood, girlhood.

muchacho /mu'tʃatʃo/ *n. m.* boy; youngster.

muchedumbre /mutʃe'ðumbre/ *n. f.* crowd, mob.

mucho /'mutʃo/ *a.* **1.** much, many. —*adv.* **2.** much.

mucoso /mu'koso/ *a.* mucous.

muda /'muða/ *n. f.* change.

mudanza /mu'ðanθa; muðansa/ *n. f.* change; change of residence.

mudar /mu'ðar/ *v.* change, shift.

mudarse /mu'ðarse/ *v.* change residence, move.

mudo /'muðo/ **-da** *a. & n.* mute.

mueble /'mueβle/ *n. m.* piece of furniture; (*pl.*) furniture.

mueca /'mueka/ *n. f.* grimace.

muela /'muela/ *n. f.* (back) tooth.

muelle /'mueʎe; 'mueye/ *n. m.* pier, wharf; *Mech.* spring.

muerte /'muerte/ *n. f.* death.

muerto /'muerto/ **-ta** *a.* **1.** dead. —*n.* **2.** dead person.

muesca /'mueska/ *n. f.* notch; groove.

muestra /'muestra/ *n. f.* sample, specimen; sign.

mugido /mu'hiðo/ *n. m.* lowing; mooing.

mugir /mu'hir/ *v.* low, moo.

mugre /'mugre/ *n. f.* filth, dirt.

mugriento /mu'griento/ *a.* dirty.

mujer /mu'her/ *f.* woman; wife. **m. de la limpieza,** cleaning lady, charwoman.

mujeril /muhe'ril/ *a.* womanly, feminine.

mula /'mula/ *n. f.* mule.

mulato /mu'lato/ **-ta** *a. & n.* mulatto.

muleta /mu'leta/ *n. f.* crutch; prop.

mulo /'mulo/ **-la** *n. m.* mule.

multa /'multa/ *n. f.* fine, penalty.

multicolor /multiko'lor/ *a.* many-colored.

multinacional /multinaθio'nal; multinasio'nal/ *a.* multinational.

múltiple /'multiple/ *a.* multiple.

multiplicación /multiplika'θion; multiplika'sion/ *n. f.* multiplication.

multiplicar /multipli'kar/ *v.* multiply.

multiplicidad /multipliθi'ðað; multiplisi'ðað/ *n. f.* multiplicity.

multitud /multi'tuð/ *n. f.* multitude, crowd.

mundanal /munda'nal, mun'dano/ *a.* worldly.

mundano /mun'dano/ *a.* worldly, mundane.

mundial /mun'dial/ *a.* worldwide; (of the) world.

mundo /'mundo/ *n. m.* world.

munición /muni'θion; muni'sion/ *n. f.* ammunition.

municipal /muniθi'pal; munisi'pal/ *a.* municipal.

municipio /muni'θipio; muni'sipio/ *n. m.* city hall.

muñeca /mu'ɲeka/ *n. f.* doll; wrist.

muñeco /mu'ɲeko/ *n. m.* doll; puppet.

mural /mu'ral/ *a. & m.* mural.

muralla /mu'raʎa; mu'raya/ *n. f.* wall.

murciélago /mur'θielago; mur'sielago/ *n. m.* bat.

murga /'murga/ *n. f.* musical band.

murmullo /mur'muʎo; mur'muyo/ *n. m.* murmur; rustle.

murmurar /murmu'rar/ *v.* murmur, rustle; grumble.

musa /'musa/ *n. f.* muse.

muscular /musku'lar/ *a.* muscular.

músculo /'muskulo/ *n. m.* muscle.

muselina /muse'lina/ *n. f.* muslin.

museo /mu'seo/ *n. m.* museum.

música /'musika/ *n. f.* music.

musical /musi'kal/ *a.* musical.

músico /'musiko/ **-ca** *a. & n.* musical; musician.

muslo /'muslo/ *n. m.* thigh.

mustio /'mustio/ *a.* sad.

musulmano /musul'mano/ **-na** *a. & n.* Muslim.

muta /'muta/ *n. f.* pack of hounds.

mutabilidad /mutaβili'ðað/ *n. f.* mutability.

mutación /muta'θion; muta'sion/ *n. f.* mutation.

mutilación /mutila'θion; mutila'sion/ *n. f.* mutilation.

mutilar /muti'lar/ *v.* mutilate; mangle.

mutuo /'mutuo/ *a.* mutual.

muy /'mui/ *adv.* very.

N Ñ

nabo /'naβo/ *n. m.* turnip.

nácar /'nakar/ *n. m.* mother-of-pearl.

nacarado /naka'raðo, na'kareo/ *a.* pearly.

nacer /na'θer; na'ser/ *v.* be born.

naciente /na'θiente; na'siente/ *a.* rising; nascent.

nacimiento /naθi'miento; nasi'miento/ *n. m.* birth.

nación /na'θion; na'sion/ *n. f.* nation.

nacional /naθio'nal; nasio'nal/ *a.* national.

nacionalidad /naθionali'ðað; nasionali'ðað/ *n. f.* nationality.

nacionalismo /naθiona'lismo; nasiona'lismo/ *n. m.* nationalism.

nacionalista /naθiona'lista; nasiona'lista/ *n. & a.* nationalist.

nacionalización /naθionaliθa'θion; nasionalisa'sion/ *n. f.* nationalization.

nacionalizar /naθionali'θar; nasionali'sar/ *v.* nationalize.

Naciones Unidas /na'θiones u'niðas; na'siones u'niðas/ *n. f.pl.* United Nations.

nada /'naða/ *pron.* **1.** nothing; anything. **de n.,** you're welcome. —*adv.* **2.** at all.

nadador /naða'ðor/ **-ra** *n.* swimmer.

nadar /na'ðar/ *v.* swim.

nadie /'naðie/ *pron.* no one, nobody; anyone, anybody.

nafta /'nafta/ *n. f.* naphtha.

naipe /'naipe/ *n. m.* (playing) card.
naranja /na'ranha/ *n. f.* orange.
naranjada /naran'haða/ *n. f.* orangeade.
naranjo /na'ranho/ *n. m.* orange tree.
narciso /nar'θiso; nar'siso/ *n. m.* daffodil; narcissus.
narcótico /nar'kotiko/ *a.* & *m.* narcotic.
nardo /'narðo/ *n. m.* spikenard.
nariz /na'riθ; na'ris/ *n. f.* nose; (*pl.*) nostrils.
narración /narra'θion; narra'sion/ *n. f.* account.
narrador /narra'ðor/ **-ra** *n.* narrator.
narrar /na'rrar/ *v.* narrate.
narrativa /narra'tiβa/ *n. f.* narrative.
nata /'nata/ *n. f.* cream.
nata batida /'nata ba'tiða/ whipped cream.
natación /nata'θion; nata'sion/ *n. f.* swimming.
natal /na'tal/ *a.* native; natal.
natalicio /nata'liθio; nata'lisio/ *n. m.* birthday.
natalidad /natali'ðað/ *n. f.* birth rate.
natillas /na'tiʎas; na'tiyas/ *n. f.pl.* custard.
nativo /na'tiβo/ *a.* native; innate.
natural /natu'ral/ *a.* **1.** natural. —*n.* **2.** *m.* & *f.* native. **3.** *m.* nature, disposition.
naturaleza /natura'leθa; natura'lesa/ *n. f.* nature.
naturalidad /naturali'ðað/ *n. f.* naturalness; nationality.
naturalista /natura'lista/ *a.* & *n.* naturalistic; naturalist.
naturalización /naturaliθa'θion; naturalisa'sion/ *n. f.* naturalization.
naturalizar /naturali'θar; naturali'sar/ *v.* naturalize.
naufragar /naufra'gar/ *v.* be shipwrecked; fail.
naufragio /nau'frahio/ *n. m.* shipwreck; disaster.
náufrago /'naufrago/ **-ga** *a.* & *n.* shipwrecked (person).
náusea /'nausea/ *n. f.* nausea.
nausear /nause'ar/ *v.* feel nauseous.
náutico /'nautiko/ *a.* nautical.
navaja /na'βaha/ *n. f.* razor; pen knife.
naval /na'βal/ *a.* naval.
navasca /na'βaska/ *n. f.* blizzard, snowstorm.
nave /'naβe/ *n. f.* ship.
nave espacial /'naβe espa'θial; 'naβe es'pasial/ spaceship.
navegable /naβe'gaβle/ *a.* navigable.
navegación /naβega'θion; naβega'sion/ *n. f.* navigation.
navegador /naβega'ðor/ **-ra** *n.* navigator.
navegante /naβe'gante/ *n. m.* & *f.* navigator.
navegar /naβe'gar/ *v.* sail; navigate.
Navidad /naβi'ðað/ *n. f.* Christmas.
navío /na'βio/ *n. m.* ship.
neblina /ne'βlina/ *n. f.* mist, fog.
nebuloso /neβu'loso/ *a.* misty; nebulous.
necedad /neθe'ðað; nese'ðað/ *n. f.* stupidity; nonsense.
necesario /neθe'sario; nese'sario/ *a.* necessary.
necesidad /neθesi'ðað; nesesi'ðað/ *n. f.* necessity, need, want.
necesitado /neθesi'taðo; nesesi'taðo/ *a.* needy, poor.
necesitar /neθesi'tar; nesesi'tar/ *v.* need.
necio /'neθio; 'nesio/ **-cia** *a.* **1.** stupid, silly. —*n.* **2.** fool.
néctar /'nektar/ *n. m.* nectar.
nectarina /nekta'rina/ *n. f.* nectarine.
nefando /ne'fando/ *a.* nefarious.
nefasto /ne'fasto/ *a.* unlucky, ill-fated.
negable /ne'gaβle/ *a.* deniable.
negación /nega'θion; nega'sion/ *n. f.* denial, negation.
negar /ne'gar/ *v.* deny.
negarse /ne'garse/ *v.* refuse, decline.
negativa /nega'tiβa/ *n. f.* negative, refusal.
negativamente /negatiβa'mente/ *adv.* negatively.
negativo /nega'tiβo/ *a.* negative.
negligencia /negli'henθia; negli'hensia/ *n. f.* negligence, neglect.
negligente /negli'hente/ *a.* negligent.
negociación /negoθia'θion; negosia'sion/ *n. f.* negotiation, deal.
negociador /negoθia'ðor; negosia'ðor/ **-ra** *n.* negotiator.
negociante /nego'θiante; nego'siante/ **-ta** *n.* businessperson.
negociar /nego'θiar; nego'siar/ *v.* negotiate, trade.
negocio /ne'goθio; ne'gosio/ *n. m.* trade; business.
negro /'negro/ **-gra** *a.* **1.** black. —*n.* **2.** *m.* Black.
nene /'nene/ **-na** *n.* baby.
neo /'neo/ **neón** *n. m.* neon.
nervio /'nerβio/ *n. m.* nerve.
nerviosamente /nerβiosa'mente/ *adv.* nervously.
nervioso /ner'βioso/ *a.* nervous.
nesciencia /nesθien'θia; nessien'sia/ *n. f.* ignorance.
nesciente /nes'θiente; nes'siente/ *a.* ignorant.
neto /'neto/ *a.* net.
neumático /neu'matiko/ *a.* **1.** pneumatic. —*n.* **2.** *m.* (pneumatic) tire.
neumático de recambio /neu'matiko de rre'kambio/ spare tire.
neumonía /neumo'nia/ *n. f.* pneumonia.
neurótico /neu'rotiko/ *a.* neurotic.
neutral /neu'tral/ *a.* neutral.
neutralidad /neutrali'ðað/ *n. f.* neutrality.
neutro /'neutro/ *a.* neuter; neutral.
neutrón /neu'tron/ *n. m.* neutron.
nevada /ne'βaða/ *n. f.* snowfall.
nevado /ne'βaðo/ *a.* snow-white; snow-capped.
nevar /ne'βar/ *v.* snow.
nevera /ne'βera/ *n. f.* icebox.
nevoso /ne'βoso/ *a.* snowy.
ni /ni/ *conj.* **1.** nor. **ni... ni,** neither... nor. —*adv.* **2.** not even.
nicho /'nitʃo/ *n. m.* recess; niche.
nido /'niðo/ *n. m.* nest.
niebla /'nieβla/ *n. f.* fog; mist.
nieto /'nieto/ **-ta** *n.* grandchild.
nieve /'nieβe/ *n. f.* snow.
nilón /ni'lon/ *n. m.* nylon.
nimio /'nimio/ *adj.* stingy.
ninfa /'ninfa/ *n. f.* nymph.
ningún /niŋ'gun/ **-no -na** *a.* & *pron.* no, none, neither (one); any, either (one).
niñera /ni'ɲera/ *n. f.* nursemaid, nanny.
niñez /ni'ɲeθ; ni'ɲes/ *n. f.* childhood.
niño /'niɲo/ **-ña 1.** *a.* **1.** young; childish; childlike. —*n.* **2.** child.
níquel /'nikel/ *n. m.* nickel.
niquelado /nike'laðo/ *a.* nickel-plated.
nítido /'nitiðo/ *a.* neat, clean, bright.
nitrato /ni'trato/ *n. m.* nitrate.
nitro /'nitro/ *n. m.* niter.
nitrógeno /ni'troheno/ *n. m.* nitrogen.
nivel /ni'βel/ *n. m.* level; grade. —**nivelar,** *v.*
no /no/ *adv.* **1.** not. **no más,** only. —*interj.* **2.** no.
noble /'noβle/ *a.* & *m.* noble; nobleman.
nobleza /no'βleθa; no'βlesa/ *n. f.* nobility; nobleness.
noche /'notʃe/ *n. f.* night; evening.
Nochebuena /notʃe'βuena/ *n. f.* Christmas Eve.
noción /no'θion; no'sion/ *n. f.* notion, idea.
nocivo /no'θiβo; no'siβo/ *a.* harmful.
noctiluca /nokti'luka/ *n. f.* glowworm.
nocturno /nok'turno/ *a.* nocturnal.
nodriza /no'ðriθa; no'ðrisa/ *n. f.* wet nurse.
no fumador /no fuma'ðor/ **-ra** *n. m.* & *f.* nonsmoker.
nogal /no'gal/ *n. m.* walnut.
nombradía /nom'βraðia/ *n. f.* fame.
nombramiento /nombra'miento/ *n. m.* appointment, nomination.
nombrar /nom'βrar/ *v.* name, appoint, nominate; mention.
nombre /'nombre/ *n. m.* name; noun.
nombre y apellidos /'nombre i ape'ʎiðos; 'nombre i ape'yiðos/ (person's) full name.
nómina /'nomina/ *n. f.* list; payroll.
nominación /nomina'θion; nomina'sion/ *n. f.* nomination.
nominal /nomi'nal/ *a.* nominal.
nominar /nomi'nar/ *v.* nominate.
non /non/ *a.* uneven, odd.
nonada /no'naða/ *n. f.* trifle.
nordeste /nor'ðeste/ *n. m.* northeast.
nórdico /'norðiko/ *a.* Nordic; northerly.
norma /'norma/ *n. f.* norm, standard.
normal /nor'mal/ *a.* normal, standard.
normalidad /normali'ðað/ *n. f.* normality.
normalizar /normali'θar; normali'sar/ *v.* normalize; standardize.
noroeste /noro'este/ *n. m.* northwest.
norte /'norte/ *n. m.* north.
norteamericano /norteameri'kano/ **-na** *a.* & *n.* North American.
Noruega /no'ruega/ *n. f.* Norway.
noruego /no'ruego/ **-ga** *a.* & *n.* Norwegian.
nos /nos/ *pron.* us; ourselves.
nosotros /no'sotros, no'sotras/ **-as** *pron.* we, us; ourselves.
nostalgia /nos'talhia/ *n. f.* nostalgia, homesickness.
nostálgico /nos'talhiko/ *a.* nostalgic.
nota /'nota/ *n. f.* note; grade, mark.
notable /no'taβle/ *a.* notable, remarkable.
notación /nota'θion; nota'sion/ *n. f.* notation; note.
notar /no'tar/ *v.* note, notice.
notario /no'tario/ **-ria** *n.* notary.
noticia /no'tiθia; no'tisia/ *n. f.* notice; piece of news; (*pl.*) news.
noticia de última hora /no'tiθia de 'ultima 'ora; no'tisia de 'ultima 'ora/ news flash.
notificación /notifika'θion; notifika'sion/ *n. f.* notification.
notificación de reclutamiento /notifika'θion de rrekluta'miento; notifika'sion de rrekluta'miento/ draft notice.
notificar /notifi'kar/ *v.* notify.
notorio /no'torio/ *a.* well-known.
novato /no'βato/ **-ta** *n.* novice.
novecientos /noβe'θientos; noβe'sientos/ *a.* & *pron.* nine hundred.
novedad /noβe'ðað/ *n. f.* novelty; piece of news.
novel /no'βel/ *a.* new; inexperienced.
novela /no'βela/ *n. f.* novel.
novelista /noβe'lista/ *n. m.* & *f.* novelist.
novena /no'βena/ *n. f.* novena.
noveno /no'βeno/ *a.* ninth.
noventa /no'βenta/ *a.* & *pron.* ninety.
novia /'noβia/ *n. f.* bride; sweetheart; fiancée.
noviazgo /no'βiaθgo; no'βiasgo/ *n. m.* engagement.
novicio /no'βiθio; no'βisio/ **-cia** *n.* novice, beginner.
noviembre /no'βiembre/ *n. m.* November.
novilla /no'βiʎa; no'βiya/ *n. f.* heifer.
novio /'noβio/ *n. m.* bridegroom; sweetheart; fiancé.
nube /'nuβe/ *n. f.* cloud.
núbil /'nuβil/ *a.* marriageable.
nublado /nu'βlaðo/ *a.* cloudy.
nuclear /nukle'ar/ *a.* nuclear.
núcleo /'nukleo/ *n. m.* nucleus.
nudo /'nuðo/ *n. m.* knot.
nuera /'nuera/ *n. f.* daughter-in-law.
nuestro /'nuestro/ *a.* our, ours.
nueva /'nueβa/ *n. f.* news.
nueve /'nueβe/ *a.* & *pron.* nine.
nuevo /'nueβo/ *a.* new. **de n.,** again, anew.
nuez /nueθ; nues/ *n. f.* nut; walnut.
nulidad /nuli'ðað/ *n. f.* nonentity; nullity.
nulo /'nulo/ *a.* null, void.
numeración /numera'θion; numera'sion/ *n. f.* numeration.
numerar /nume'rar/ *v.* number.
numérico /nu'meriko/ *a.* numerical.
número /'numero/ *n. m.* number; size (of shoe, etc.) **n. impar,** odd number. **n. par,** even number.
numeroso /nume'roso/ *a.* numerous.
numismática /numis'matika/ *n. f.* numismatics.
nunca /'nunka/ *adv.* never; ever.
nupcial /nup'θial; nup'sial/ *a.* nuptial.
nupcias /'nupθias; 'nupsias/ *n. f.pl.* nuptials, wedding.
nutrición /nutri'θion; nutri'sion/ *n. f.* nutrition.
nutrimento /nutri'mento/ *n. m.* nourishment.
nutrir /nu'trir/ *v.* nourish.
nutritivo /nutri'tiβo/ *a.* nutritious.
nylon /'nilon/ *n. m.* nylon.
ñame /'ɲame/ *n. m.* yam.
ñapa /'ɲapa/ *n. f.* something extra.
ñoñeria /ɲoɲe'ria/ *n. f.* dotage.
ñoño /'ɲoɲo/ *a.* feeble-minded, senile.

O

o /o/ *conj.* or. **o... o,** either... or.
oasis /o'asis/ *n. m.* oasis.
obedecer /oβeðe'θer; oβeðe'ser/ *v.* obey, mind.
obediencia /oβe'ðienθia; oβe'ðiensia/ *n. f.* obedience.
obediente /oβe'ðiente/ *a.* obedient.
obelisco /oβe'lisko/ *n. m.* obelisk.
obertura /oβer'tura/ *n. f.* overture.
obeso /o'βeso/ *a.* obese.
obispo /o'βispo/ *n. m.* bishop.
obituario /oβi'tuario/ *n. m.* obituary.
objeción /oβhe'θion; oβhe'sion/ *n. f.* objection.
objetivo /oβhe'tiβo/ *a.* & *m.* objective.
objeto /oβ'heto/ *n. m.* object. —**objetar,** *v.*
objetor de conciencia /oβhe'tor de kon'θienθia; oβhe'tor de kon'siensia/ *n. m.* conscientious objector.
oblicuo /o'βlikuo/ *a.* oblique.
obligación /oβliga'θion; oβliga'sion/ *n. f.* obligation, duty.
obligar /oβli'gar/ *v.* oblige, require, compel; obligate.
obligatorio /oβliga'torio/ *a.* obligatory, compulsory.
oblongo /o'βloŋgo/ *a.* oblong.
oboe /o'βoe/ *n. m.* oboe.
obra /'oβra/ *n. f.* work. —**obrar,** *v.*
obrero /o'βrero/ **-ra** *n.* worker, laborer.
obscenidad /oβsθeni'ðað; oβsseni'ðað/ *n. f.* obscenity.
obsceno /oβs'θeno; oβs'seno/ *a.* obscene.
obscurecer /oβskure'θer; oβskure'ser/ *v.* obscure; darken.
obscuridad /oβskuri'ðað/ *n. f.* obscurity; darkness.
obscuro /oβs'kuro/ *a.* obscure; dark.
obsequiar /oβse'kiar/ *v.* court; make presents to, fete.
obsequio /oβ'sekio/ *n. m.* obsequiousness; gift; attention.
observación /oβserβa'θion; oβserβa'sion/ *n. f.* observation.
observador /oβserβa'ðor/ **-ra** *n.* observer.
observancia /oβser'βanθia; oβser'βansia/ *n. f.* observance.
observar /oβser'βar/ *v.* observe, watch.

observatorio /oβserβa'torio/ n. m. observatory.

obsesión /oβse'sion/ n. f. obsession.

obstáculo /oβs'takulo/ n. m. obstacle.

obstante /oβs'tante/ adv. **no o.**, however, yet, nevertheless.

obstar /oβs'tar/ v. hinder, obstruct.

obstetricia /oβste'triθia; oβste'trisia/ n. f. obstetrics.

obstinación /oβstina'θion; oβstina'sion/ n. f. obstinacy.

obstinado /oβsti'naðo/ a. obstinate, stubborn.

obstinarse /oβsti'narse/ v. persist, insist.

obstrucción /oβstruk'θion; oβstruk'sion/ n. f. obstruction.

obstruir /oβs'truir/ v. obstruct, clog, block.

obtener /oβte'ner/ v. obtain, get, secure.

obtuso /oβ'tuso/ a. obtuse.

obvio /'oββio/ a. obvious.

ocasión /oka'sion/ n. f. occasion; opportunity, chance. **de o.**, secondhand.

ocasional /okasio'nal/ a. occasional.

ocasionalmente /okasional'mente/ adv. occasionally.

ocasionar /okasio'nar/ v. cause, occasion.

occidental /okθiðen'tal; oksiðen'tal/ a. western.

occidente /okθi'ðente; oksi'ðente/ n. m. west.

océano /o'θeano; o'seano/ n. m. ocean.

Océano Atlántico /o'θeano a'tlantiko; o'seano a'tlantiko/ Atlantic Ocean.

Océano Pacífico /o'θeano pa'θifiko; o'seano pa'sifiko/ Pacific Ocean.

ocelote /oθe'lote; ose'lote/ n. m. ocelot.

ochenta /o'tʃenta/ a. & pron. eighty.

ocho /'otʃo/ a. & pron. eight.

ochocientos /otʃo'θientos; otʃo'sientos/ a. & pron. eight hundred.

ocio /'oθio; 'osio/ n. m. idleness, leisure.

ociosidad /oθiosi'ðað; osiosi'ðað/ n. f. idleness, laziness.

ocioso /o'θioso; o'sioso/ a. idle, lazy.

ocre /'okre/ n. m. ochre.

octagonal /oktago'nal/ a. octagonal.

octava /ok'taβa/ n. f. octave.

octavo /ok'taβo/ a. eighth.

octubre /ok'tuβre/ n. m. October.

oculista /oku'lista/ n. m. & f. oculist.

ocultación /okulta'θion; okulta'sion/ n. f. concealment.

ocultar /okul'tar/ v. hide, conceal.

oculto /o'kulto/ a. hidden.

ocupación /okupa'θion; okupa'sion/ n. f. occupation.

ocupado /oku'paðo/ a. occupied; busy.

ocupante /oku'pante/ n. m. & f. occupant.

ocupar /oku'par/ v. occupy.

ocuparse de /oku'parse de/ v. take care of, take charge of.

ocurrencia /oku'rrenθia; oku'rrensia/ n. f. occurrence; witticism.

ocurrente /oku'rrente/ a. witty.

ocurrir /oku'rrir/ v. occur, happen.

oda /'oða/ n. f. ode.

odio /'oðio/ n. m. hate. —**odiar**, v.

odiosidad /oðiosi'ðað/ n. f. odiousness; hatred.

odioso /o'ðioso/ a. obnoxious, odious.

odisea /oði'sea/ n. f. odyssey.

OEA, abbr. (**Organización de los Estados Americanos**). OAS (Organization of American States).

oeste /o'este/ n. m. west.

ofender /ofen'der/ v. offend, wrong.

ofenderse /ofen'derse/ v. be offended, take offense.

ofensa /o'fensa/ n. f. offense.

ofensiva /ofen'siβa/ n. f. offensive.

ofensivo /ofen'siβo/ a. offensive.

ofensor /ofen'sor/ **-ra** n. offender.

oferta /o'ferta/ n. f. offer, proposal.

ofertorio /ofer'torio/ n. m. offertory.

oficial /ofi'θial; ofi'sial/ a. & m. official; officer.

oficialmente /ofiθial'mente; ofisial'mente/ adv. officially.

oficiar /ofi'θiar; ofi'siar/ v. officiate.

oficina /ofi'θina; ofi'sina/ n. f. office.

oficio /o'fiθio; o'fisio/ n. m. office; trade; church service.

oficioso /ofi'θioso; ofi'sioso/ a. officious.

ofrecer /ofre'θer; ofre'ser/ v. offer.

ofrecimiento /ofreθi'miento; ofresi'miento/ n. m. offer, offering. **o. de presentación,** introductory offer.

ofrenda /o'frenda/ n. f. offering.

oftalmía /oftal'mia/ n. f. ophthalmia.

ofuscamiento /ofuska'miento/ n. m. obfuscation; bewilderment.

ofuscar /ofus'kar/ v. obfuscate; bewilder.

ogro /'ogro/ n. m. ogre.

oído /o'iðo/ n. m. ear; hearing.

oír /o'ir/ v. hear; listen.

ojal /o'hal/ n. m. buttonhole.

ojalá /oha'la/ interj. expressing wish or hope. **o. que...** would that...

ojeada /ohe'aða/ n. f. glance; peep; look.

ojear /ohe'ar/ v. eye, look at, glance at, stare at.

ojeriza /ohe'riθa; ohe'risa/ n. f. spite; grudge.

ojiva /o'hiβa/ n. f. pointed arch, ogive.

ojo /'oho/ n. m. eye. **¡Ojo!** Look out!

ola /'ola/ n. f. wave.

olaje /o'lahe/ n. m. surge of waves.

oleada /ole'aða/ n. f. swell.

oleo /o'leo/ n. m. oil; holy oil; extreme unction.

oleoducto /oleo'ðukto/ n. m. pipeline.

oleomargarina /oleomarga'rina/ n. f. oleomargarine.

oleoso /ole'oso/ a. oily.

oler /o'ler/ v. smell.

olfatear /olfate'ar/ v. smell.

olfato /ol'fato/ n. m. scent, smell.

oliva /o'liβa/ n. f. olive.

olivar /oli'βar/ n. m. olive grove.

olivo /o'liβo/ n. m. olive tree.

olla /'oʎa; 'oya/ n. f. pot, kettle. **o. podrida,** stew.

olmo /'olmo/ n. m. elm.

olor /o'lor/ n. m. odor, smell, scent.

oloroso /olo'roso/ a. fragrant, scented.

olvidadizo /olβiða'ðiθo; olβiða'ðiso/ a. forgetful.

olvidar /olβi'ðar/ v. forget.

olvido /ol'βiðo/ n. m. omission; forgetfulness.

ombligo /om'βligo/ n. m. navel.

ominar /omi'nar/ v. foretell.

ominoso /omi'noso/ a. ominous.

omisión /omi'sion/ n. f. omission.

omitir /omi'tir/ v. omit, leave out.

ómnibus /'omniβus/ n. m. bus.

omnipotencia /omnipo'tenθia; omnipo'tensia/ n. f. omnipotence.

omnipotente /omnipo'tente/ a. almighty.

omnipresencia /omnipre'senθia; omnipre'sensia/ n. f. omnipresence.

omnisciencia /omnis'θienθia; omnis'siensia/ n. f. omniscience.

omnívoro /om'niβoro/ a. omnivorous.

omóplato /omo'plato/ n. m. shoulder blade.

once /'onθe; 'onse/ a. & pron. eleven.

onda /'onda/ n. f. wave, ripple.

ondear /onde'ar/ v. ripple.

ondulación /ondula'θion; ondula'sion/ n. f. wave, undulation.

ondular /ondu'lar/ v. undulate, ripple.

onza /'onθa; 'onsa/ n. f. ounce.

opaco /o'pako/ a. opaque.

ópalo /'opalo/ n. m. opal.

opción /op'θion; op'sion/ n. f. option.

ópera /'opera/ n. f. opera.

operación /opera'θion; opera'sion/ n. f. operation.

operar /ope'rar/ v. operate; operate on.

operario /ope'rario/ **-ria** n. operator; (skilled) worker.

operarse /ope'rarse/ v. have an operation.

operativo /opera'tiβo/ a. operative.

opereta /ope'reta/ n. f. operetta.

opiato /o'piato/ n. m. opiate.

opinar /opi'nar/ v. opine.

opinión /opi'nion/ n. f. opinion, view.

opio /'opio/ n. m. opium.

oponer /opo'ner/ v. oppose.

Oporto /o'porto/ n. m. port (wine).

oportunidad /oportuni'ðað/ n. f. opportunity.

oportunismo /oportu'nismo/ n. m. opportunism.

oportunista /oportu'nista/ n. & a. opportunist.

oportuno /opor'tuno/ a. opportune, expedient.

oposición /oposi'θion; oposi'sion/ n. f. opposition.

opresión /opre'sion/ n. f. oppression.

opresivo /opre'siβo/ a. oppressive.

oprimir /opri'mir/ v. oppress.

oprobio /o'proβio/ n. m. infamy.

optar /op'tar/ v. select, choose.

óptica /'optika/ n. f. optics.

óptico /'optiko/ a. optic.

optimismo /opti'mismo/ n. m. optimism.

optimista /opti'mista/ a. & n. optimistic; optimist.

óptimo /'optimo/ a. best.

opuesto /o'puesto/ a. opposite; opposed.

opugnar /opug'nar/ v. attack.

opulencia /opu'lenθia; opu'lensia/ n. f. opulence, wealth.

opulento /opu'lento/ a. opulent, wealthy.

oración /ora'θion; ora'sion/ n. f. sentence; prayer; oration.

oráculo /o'rakulo/ n. m. oracle.

orador /ora'ðor/ **-ra** n. orator, speaker.

oral /o'ral/ a. oral.

orangután /orangu'tan/ n. m. orangutan.

orar /o'rar/ v. pray.

oratoria /ora'toria/ n. f. oratory.

oratorio /ora'torio/ a. oratorical.

orbe /'orβe/ n. m. orb; globe.

órbita /'orβita/ n. f. orbit.

orden /'orðen/ n. m. or f. order.

ordenador /orðena'ðor/ n. m. computer; regulator.

ordenador de sobremesa /orðena'ðor de soβre'mesa/ desktop computer.

ordenador doméstico /orðena'ðor do'mestiko/ home computer.

ordenanza /orðe'nanθa; orðe'nansa/ n. f. ordinance.

ordenar /orðe'nar/ v. order; put in order; ordain.

ordeñar /orðe'ɲar/ v. milk.

ordinal /orði'nal/ a. & m. ordinal.

ordinario /orði'nario/ a. ordinary; common, usual.

oreja /o'reha/ n. f. ear.

orejera /ore'hera/ n. f. earmuff.

orfanato /orfa'nato/ n. m. orphanage.

organdí /organ'di/ n. m. organdy.

orgánico /or'ganiko/ a. organic.

organigrama /organi'grama/ n. m. flow chart.

organismo /orga'nismo/ n. m. organism.

organista /orga'nista/ n. m. & f. organist.

organización /organiθa'θion; organisa'sion/ n. f. organization.

organizar /organi'θar; organi'sar/ v. organize.

órgano /'organo/ n. m. organ.

orgía /or'hia/ n. f. orgy, revel.

orgullo /or'guʎo; or'guyo/ n. m. pride.

orgulloso /orgu'ʎoso; orgu'yoso/ a. proud.

orientación /orienta'θion; orienta'sion/ n. f. orientation.

oriental /orien'tal/ a. Oriental; eastern.

orientar /orien'tar/ v. orient.

oriente /o'riente/ n. m. orient, east.

orificación /orifika'θion; orifika'sion/ n. f. gold filling (for tooth).

origen /o'rihen/ n. m. origin; parentage, descent.

original /orihi'nal/ a. original.

originalidad /orihinali'ðað/ n. f. originality.

originalmente /orihinal'mente/ adv. originally.

originar /orihi'nar/ v. originate.

orilla /o'riʎa; o'riya/ n. f. shore; bank; edge.

orín /o'rin/ n. m. rust.

orina /o'rina/ n. f. urine.

orinar /ori'nar/ v. urinate.

orines /o'rines/ n. m.pl. urine.

oriol /o'riol/ n. m. oriole.

orla /'orla/ n. f. border; edging.

ornado /or'naðo/ a. ornate.

ornamentación /ornamenta'θion; ornamenta'sion/ n. f. ornamentation.

ornamento /orna'mento/ n. m. ornament. —**ornamentar,** v.

ornar /or'nar/ v. ornament, adorn.

oro /'oro/ n. m. gold.

oropel /oro'pel/ n. m. tinsel.

orquesta /or'kesta/ n. f. orchestra.

ortiga /or'tiga/ n. f. nettle.

ortodoxo /orto'ðokso/ a. orthodox.

ortografía /ortogra'fia/ n. f. orthography, spelling.

ortóptero /or'toptero/ a. orthopterous.

oruga /o'ruga/ n. f. caterpillar.

orzuelo /or'θuelo; or'suelo/ n. m. sty.

os /os/ pron. you (pl.); yourselves.

osadía /osa'ðia/ n. f. daring.

osar /o'sar/ v. dare.

oscilación /osθila'θion; ossila'sion/ n. f. oscillation.

oscilar /osθi'lar; ossi'lar/ v. oscillate, rock.

ósculo /'oskulo/ n. m. kiss.

oscurecer /oskure'θer; oskure'ser/ **oscuridad, oscuro** = obscur-.

oso /'oso/ **osa** n. bear.

oso de felpa /'oso de 'felpa/ teddy bear.

ostentación /ostenta'θion; ostenta'sion/ n. f. ostentation, showiness.

ostentar /osten'tar/ v. show off.

ostentoso /osten'toso/ a. ostentatious, flashy.

ostra /'ostra/ n. f. oyster.

ostracismo /ostra'θismo; ostra'sismo/ n. m. ostracism.

otalgia /o'talhia/ n. f. earache.

otero /o'tero/ n. m. hill, knoll.

otoño /o'toɲo/ n. m. autumn, fall.

otorgar /otor'gar/ v. grant, award.

otro /'otro/ a. & pron. other, another. **o. vez,** again. **el uno al o.,** one another, each other.

ovación /oβa'θion; oβa'sion/ n. f. ovation.

oval /o'βal/ **ovalado** a. oval.

óvalo /'oβalo/ n. m. oval.

ovario /o'βario/ n. m. ovary.

oveja /o'βeha/ n. f. sheep.

ovejero /oβe'hero/ n. m. sheep dog.

ovillo /o'βiʎo; o'βiyo/ n. m. ball of yarn.

OVNI /'oβni/ abbr. (objeto volador no identificado) UFO (unidentified flying object).

oxidación /oksiða'θion; oksiða'sion/ n. f. oxidation.

oxidar /oksi'ðar/ v. oxidize; rust.

óxido /'oksiðo/ n. m. oxide.

oxígeno /ok'siheno/ n. m. oxygen.

oyente /o'iente/ n. m. & f. hearer; (pl.) audience.

ozono /o'θono; o'sono/ *n. m.* ozone.

P

pabellón /paβe'ʎon; paβe'yon/ *n. m.* pavilion. **p. de deportes,** sports center.

pabilo /pa'βilo/ *n. m.* wick.

paciencia /pa'θienθia; pa'siensia/ *n. f.* patience.

paciente /pa'θiente; pa'siente/ *a. & n.* patient.

pacificar /paθifi'kar; pasifi'kar/ *v.* pacify.

pacífico /pa'θifiko; pa'sifiko/ *a.* pacific.

pacifismo /paθi'fismo; pasi'fismo/ *n. m.* pacifism.

pacifista /paθi'fista; pasi'fista/ *n. & a.* pacifist.

pacto /'pakto/ *n. m.* pact, treaty.

padecer /paðe'θer; paðe'ser/ *v.* suffer. **p. del corazón,** have heart trouble.

padrastro /pa'ðrastro/ *n. m.* stepfather.

padre /'paðre/ *n. m.* father; priest; (*pl.*) parents.

padrenuestro /paðre'nuestro/ *n. m.* paternoster, Lord's Prayer.

padrino /pa'ðrino/ *n. m.* godfather; sponsor.

paella /pa'eʎa; pa'eya/ *n. f.* dish of rice with meat or chicken.

paga /'paga/ *n. f.* pay, wages. **p. extra bonus.**

pagadero /paga'ðero/ *a.* payable.

pagador /paga'ðor/ **-ra** *n.* payer.

paganismo /paga'nismo/ *n. m.* paganism.

pagano /pa'gano/ **-na** *a. & n.* heathen, pagan.

pagar /pa'gar/ *v.* pay, pay for. **p. en metálico,** pay cash.

página /'pahina/ *n. f.* page.

pago /'pago/ *n. m.* pay, payment.

país /pa'is/ *n. m.* country, nation.

paisaje /pai'sahe/ *n. m.* landscape, scenery, countryside.

paisano /pai'sano/ **-na** *n.* countryman; compatriot; civilian.

paja /'paha/ *n. f.* straw.

pajar /pa'har/ *n. m.* barn.

pajarita /paha'rita/ *n. f.* bow tie.

pájaro /'paharo/ *n. m.* bird.

paje /'pahe/ *n. m.* page (person).

pala /'pala/ *n. f.* shovel, spade.

palabra /pa'laβra/ *n. f.* word.

palabrero /pala'βrero/ *a.* talkative; wordy.

palabrista /pala'βrista/ *n. m. & f.* talkative person.

palacio /pa'laθio; pa'lasio/ *n. m.* palace.

paladar /pala'ðar/ *n. m.* palate.

paladear /palaðe'ar/ *v.* taste; relish.

palanca /pa'lanka/ *n. f.* lever. **p. de cambio,** gearshift.

palangana /palaŋ'gana/ *n. f.* washbasin.

palco /'palko/ *n. m.* theater box.

palenque /pa'lenke/ *n. m.* palisade.

paleta /pa'leta/ *n. f.* mat, pallet.

paletilla /pale'tiʎa; pale'tiya/ *n. f.* shoulder blade.

palidecer /paliðe'θer; paliðe'ser/ *v.* turn pale.

palidez /pali'ðeθ; pali'ðes/ *n. f.* paleness.

pálido /'paliðo/ *a.* pale.

paliza /pa'liθa; pa'lisa/ *n. f.* beating.

palizada /pali'θaða; pali'saða/ *n. m.* palisade.

palma /'palma/ **palmera** *n. f.* palm (tree).

palmada /pal'maða/ *n. f.* slap, clap.

palmear /palme'ar/ *v.* applaud.

palo /'palo/ *n. m.* pole, stick; suit (in cards); *Naut.* mast.

paloma /pa'loma/ *n. f.* dove, pigeon.

palpar /pal'par/ *v.* touch, feel.

palpitación /palpita'θion; palpita'sion/ *n. f.* palpitation.

palpitar /palpi'tar/ *v.* palpitate.

paludismo /palu'ðismo/ *n. m.* malaria.

pampa /'pampa/ *n. f.* (*S.A.*) prairie, plain.

pan /pan/ *n. m.* bread; loaf. **p. de centeno,** rye bread.

pana /'pana/ *n. f.* corduroy.

panacea /pana'θea; pana'sea/ *n. f.* panacea.

panadería /panaðe'ria/ *n. f.* bakery.

panadero /pana'ðero/ **-ra** *n.* baker.

panameño /pana'meɲo/ **-ña** *a. & n.* Panamanian, of Panama.

panamericano /panameri'kano/ *a.* Pan-American.

páncreas /'pankreas/ *n. m.* pancreas.

pandeo /pan'deo/ *n. m.* bulge.

pandilla /pan'diʎa; pan'diya/ *n. f.* band, gang.

panecillo /pane'θiʎo; pane'siyo/ *n. m.* roll, muffin.

panegírico /pane'hiriko/ *n. m.* panegyric.

pánico /'paniko/ *n. m.* panic.

panocha /pa'notʃa/ *n. f.* ear of corn.

panorama /pano'rama/ *n. m.* panorama.

panorámico /pano'ramiko/ *a.* panoramic.

pantalla /pan'taʎa; pan'taya/ *n. f.* (movie) screen; lamp shade.

pantalones /panta'lones/ *n. m.pl.* trousers, pants.

pantano /pan'tano/ *n. m.* bog, marsh, swamp.

pantanoso /panta'noso/ *a.* swampy, marshy.

pantera /pan'tera/ *n. f.* panther.

pantomima /panto'mima/ *n. f.* pantomime.

pantorrilla /panto'rriʎa; panto'rriya/ *n. f.* calf (of body).

panza /'panθa; 'pansa/ *n. f.* belly, paunch.

pañal /pa'ɲal/ *n. m.* diaper.

paño /'paɲo/ *n. m.* piece of cloth.

pañuelo /pa'ɲuelo/ *n. m.* handkerchief.

Papa /'papa/ *n. m.* Pope.

papa *n. f.* potato.

papá /pa'pa/ *n. m.* papa, father.

papado /pa'paðo/ *n. m.* papacy.

papagayo /papa'gaio/ *n. m.* parrot.

papal /pa'pal/ *a.* papal.

Papá Noel /pa'pa no'el/ *n. m.* Santa Claus.

papel /pa'pel/ *n. m.* paper; role, part.

papel crespón /pa'pel kres'pon/ crepe paper.

papel de aluminio /pa'pel de alu'minio/ aluminum foil.

papel de escribir /pa'pel de es-kri'βir/ writing paper.

papel de estaño /pa'pel de es'taɲo/ tin foil.

papel de lija /pa'pel de 'liha/ sandpaper.

papelera /pape'lera/ *n. f.* file cabinet; wastepaper basket.

papelería /papele'ria/ *n. f.* stationery store.

papel moneda /pa'pel mo'neða/ paper money.

paperas /pa'peras/ *n. f.pl.* mumps.

paquete /pa'kete/ *n. m.* package.

par /par/ *a.* **1.** even, equal. —*n.* **2.** *m.* pair; equal, peer. **abierto de p. en p.,** wide open.

para /'para/ *prep.* for; in order to. **p. que,** in order that. **estar p.,** to be about to.

parabién /para'βien/ *n. m.* congratulation.

parabrisa /para'βrisa/ *n. m.* windshield.

paracaídas /paraka'iðas/ *n. m.* parachute.

parachoques /para'tʃokes/ *n. m. Auto.* bumper.

parada /pa'raða/ *n. f.* stop, halt; stopover; parade.

paradero /para'ðero/ *n. m.* whereabouts; stopping place.

paradigma /para'ðigma/ *n. m.* paradigm.

paradoja /para'ðoha/ *n. f.* paradox.

parafina /para'fina/ *n. f.* paraffin.

parafrasear /parafrase'ar/ *v.* paraphrase.

paraguas /pa'raguas/ *n. m.* umbrella.

paraguayao /paragua'yao/ **-a** *n. & a.* Paraguayan.

paraíso /para'iso/ *n. m.* paradise.

paralelo /para'lelo/ *a. & m.* parallel.

parálisis /pa'ralisis/ *n. f.* paralysis.

paralizar /parali'θar; parali'sar/ *v.* paralyze.

paramédico /para'meðiko/ *n. m.* paramedic.

parámetro /pa'rametro/ *n. m.* parameter.

parapeto /para'peto/ *n. m.* parapet.

parar /pa'rar/ *v.* stop, stem, ward off; stay.

pararse /pa'rarse/ *v.* stop; stand up.

parasítico /para'sitiko/ *a.* parasitic.

parásito /pa'rasito/ *n. m.* parasite.

parcela /par'θela; par'sela/ *n. f.* plot of ground.

parcial /par'θial; par'sial/ *a.* partial.

parcialidad /parθiali'ðað; parsiali-'ðað/ *n. f.* partiality; bias.

parcialmente /parθial'mente; parsial-'mente/ *adv.* partially.

pardo /'parðo/ *a.* brown.

parear /pare'ar/ *v.* pair; match; mate.

parecer /pare'θer; pare'ser/ *n.* **1.** *m.* opinion. —*v.* **2.** seem, appear, look.

parecerse /pare'θerse; pare'serse/ *v.* look alike. **p. a,** look like.

parecido /pare'θiðo; pare'siðo/ *a.* similar.

pared /pa'reð/ *n. f.* wall.

pareja /pa'reha/ *n. f.* pair, couple; (dancing) partner.

parentela /paren'tela/ *n. f.* kinfolk.

parentesco /paren'tesko/ *n. m.* parentage, lineage; kin.

paréntesis /pa'rentesis/ *n. m.* parenthesis.

paria /'paria/ *n. f.* outcast, pariah.

paricipante /pariθi'pante; parisi'pan-te/ *n. m. & f.* participant.

paridad /pari'ðað/ *n. f.* parity.

pariente /pa'riente/ *n. m. & f.* relative.

parir /pa'rir/ *v.* give birth.

parisiense /pari'siense/ *n. & a.* Parisian.

parlamentario /parlamen'tario/ *a.* parliamentary.

parlamento /parla'mento/ *n. m.* parliament.

paro /'paro/ *n. m.* stoppage; strike. **p. forzoso,** unemployment.

parodia /pa'roðia/ *n. f.* parody.

parodista /paro'ðista/ *n. m. & f.* parodist.

paroxismo /parok'sismo/ *n. m.* paroxysm.

párpado /'parpaðo/ *n. m.* eyelid.

parque /'parke/ *n. m.* park.

parquímetro /par'kimetro/ *n. m.* parking meter.

parra /'parra/ *n. f.* grapevine.

párrafo /'parrafo/ *n. m.* paragraph.

parranda /pa'rranda/ *n. f.* spree.

parrandear /parrande'ar/ *v.* carouse.

parrilla /pa'rriʎa; pa'rriya/ *n. f.* grill; grillroom.

párroco /'parroko/ *n. m.* parish priest.

parroquia /pa'rrokia/ *n. f.* parish.

parroquial /parro'kial/ *a.* parochial.

parsimonia /parsi'monia/ *n. f.* economy, thrift.

parsimonioso /parsimo'nioso/ *a.* economical, thrifty.

parte /'parte/ *n. f.* part. **de p. de,** on behalf of. **alguna p.,** somewhere. **por otra p.,** on the other hand. **dar p. a,** to notify.

partera /par'tera/ *n. f.* midwife.

partición /parti'θion; parti'sion/ *n. f.* distribution.

participación /partiθipa'θion; partisi-pa'sion/ *n. f.* participation.

participar /partiθi'par; partisi'par/ *v.* participate; announce.

participio /parti'θipio; parti'sipio/ *n. m.* participle.

partícula /par'tikula/ *n. f.* particle.

particular /partiku'lar/ *a.* **1.** particular; private. —*n.* **2.** *m.* particular; detail; individual.

particularmente /partikular'mente/ *adv.* particularly.

partida /par'tiða/ *n. f.* departure; *Mil.* party; (sport) game.

partida de defunción /par'tiða de defun'θion; par'tiða de defun'sion/ death certificate.

partida de matrimonio /par'tiða de matri'monio/ marriage certificate.

partida de nacimiento /par'tiða de naθi'miento; par'tiða de nasi'miento/ birth certificate.

partidario /parti'ðario/ **-ria** *n.* partisan.

partido /par'tiðo/ *n. m.* side, party; faction; game, match.

partir /par'tir/ *v.* leave, depart; part, cleave, split.

parto /'parto/ *n. m.* delivery, childbirth.

pasa /'pasa/ *n. f.* raisin.

pasado /pa'saðo/ *a.* **1.** past; last. —*n.* **2.** *m.* past.

pasaje /pa'sahe/ *n. m.* passage, fare.

pasajero /pasa'hero/ **-ra** *a.* **1.** passing, transient. —*n.* **2.** *m.* passenger.

pasamano /pasa'mano/ *n. m.* banister.

pasaporte /pasa'porte/ *n. m.* passport.

pasar /pa'sar/ *v.* pass; happen; spend (time). **p. por alto,** overlook. **p. lista,** call the roll. **p. sin,** do without.

pasatiempo /pasa'tiempo/ *n. m.* pastime; hobby.

pascua /'paskua/ *n. f.* religious holiday; (*pl.*) Christmas (season). **P. Florida,** Easter.

pase de modelos /'pase de mo'ðelos/ *n. m.* fashion show.

paseo /pa'seo/ *n. m.* walk, stroll; drive. —**pasear,** *v.*

pasillo /pa'siʎo; pa'siyo/ *n. m.* aisle; hallway.

pasión /pa'sion/ *n. f.* passion.

pasivo /pa'siβo/ *a.* passive.

pasmar /pas'mar/ *v.* astonish, astound, stun.

pasmo /'pasmo/ *n. m.* spasm; wonder.

paso /'paso/ *a.* **1.** dried (fruit). —*n.* **2.** *m.* pace, step; (mountain) pass.

paso cebra /'paso 'θeβra; 'paso 'seβra/ crosswalk.

paso de ganso /'paso de 'ganso/ goose step.

paso de peatones /'paso de pea'tones/ pedestrian crossing.

pasta /'pasta/ *n. f.* paste; batter; plastic.

pasta dentífrica /'pasta den'tifrika/ toothpaste.

pastar /pas'tar/ *v.* graze.

pastel /pas'tel/ *n. m.* pastry; pie.

pastelería /pastele'ria/ *n. f.* pastry; pastry shop.

pasteurización /pasteuriθa'θion; pasteurisa'sion/ *n. f.* pasteurization.

pasteurizar /pasteuri'θar; pasteuri-'sar/ *v.* pasteurize.

pastilla /pas'tiʎa; pas'tiya/ *n. f.* tablet, lozenge, coughdrop.

pasto /'pasto/ *n. m.* pasture; grass.

pastor /pas'tor/ *n. m.* pastor; shepherd.

pastorear /pastore'ar/ *v.* pasture, tend (a flock).

pastrón /pas'tron/ *n. m.* pastrami.

pastura /pas'tura/ *n. f.* pasture.

pata /'pata/ *n. f.* foot (of animal).

patada /pa'taða/ *n. f.* kick.

patán /pa'tan/ *n. m.* boor.

patanada /pata'naða/ *n. f.* rudeness.

patata /pa'tata/ *n. f.* potato. **p. asada**, baked potato.

patear /pate'ar/ *v.* stamp, tramp, kick.

patente /pa'tente/ *a. & m.* patent. **—patentar,** *v.*

paternal /pater'nal/ **paterno** *a.* paternal.

paternidad /paterni'ðað/ *n. f.* paternity, fatherhood.

patético /pa'tetiko/ *a.* pathetic.

patíbulo /pa'tiβulo/ *n. m.* scaffold; gallows.

patín /pa'tin/ *n. m.* skate. **—patinar,** *v.*

patín de ruedas /pa'tin de 'rrueðas/ roller skate.

patio /'patio/ *n. m.* yard, court, patio.

pato /'pato/ *n. m.* duck.

patria /'patria/ *n. f.* native land.

patriarca /pa'triarka/ *n. m. & f.* patriarch.

patrimonio /patri'monio/ *n. m.* inheritance.

patriota /pa'triota/ *n. m. & f.* patriot.

patriótico /pa'triotiko/ *a.* patriotic.

patriotismo /patrio'tismo/ *n. m.* patriotism.

patrocinar /patroθi'nar/ patrosi'nar/ *v.* patronize, sponsor.

patrón /pa'tron/ **-ona** *n.* patron; boss; (dress) pattern.

patrulla /pa'truʎa; pa'truya/ *n. f.* patrol. **—patrullar,** *v.*

paulatino /paula'tino/ *a.* gradual.

pausa /'pausa/ *n. f.* pause. **—pausar,** *v.*

pausa para el café /'pausa 'para el ka'fe/ coffee break.

pauta /'pauta/ *n. f.* guideline.

pavesa /pa'βesa/ *n. f.* spark, cinder.

pavimentar /paβimen'tar/ *v.* pave.

pavimento /paβi'mento/ *n. m.* pavement.

pavo /'paβo/ *n. m.* turkey. **p. real,** peacock.

pavor /pa'βor/ *n. m.* terror.

payaso /pa'iaso/ **-sa** *n.* clown.

paz /paθ; pas/ *n. f.* peace.

peatón /pea'ton/ **-na** *n.* pedestrian.

peca /'peka/ *n. f.* freckle.

pecado /pe'kaðo/ *n. m.* sin. **—pecar,** *v.*

pecador /peka'ðor/ **-ra** *a. & n.* sinful; sinner.

pecera /pe'θera; pe'sera/ *n. f.* aquarium, fishbowl.

pechera /pe'tʃera/ *n. f.* shirt front.

pecho /'petʃo/ *n. m.* chest; breast; bosom.

pechuga /pe'tʃuga/ *n. f.* breast (of fowl).

pecoso /pe'koso/ *a.* freckled, freckly.

peculiar /peku'liar/ *a.* peculiar.

peculiaridad /pekuliari'ðað/ *n. f.* peculiarity.

pedagogía /peðago'hia/ *n. f.* pedagogy.

pedagogo /peða'gogo/ **-ga** *n.* pedagogue, teacher.

pedal /pe'ðal/ *n. m.* pedal.

pedantesco /peðan'tesko/ *a.* pedantic.

pedazo /pe'ðaθo; pe'ðaso/ *n. m.* piece.

pedernal /peðer'nal/ *n. m.* flint.

pedestal /peðes'tal/ *n. m.* pedestal.

pediatra /pe'ðiatra/ *n. m. & f.* pediatrician.

pediatría /peðia'tria/ *n. f.* pediatrics.

pedicuro /peði'kuro/ *n. m.* chiropodist.

pedir /pe'ðir/ *v.* ask, ask for, request; apply for; order.

pedo /'peðo/ *n. m.* fart; intoxication.

pedregoso /peðre'goso/ *a.* rocky.

pegajoso /pega'hoso/ *a.* sticky.

pegamento /pega'mento/ *n. m.* glue.

pegar /pe'gar/ *v.* beat, strike; adhere, fasten, stick.

peinado /pei'naðo/ *n. m.* coiffure, hairdo.

peine /'peine/ *n. m.* comb. **—peinar,** *v.*

peineta /pei'neta/ *n. f.* (ornamental) comb.

pelagra /pe'lagra/ *n. f.* pellagra.

pelar /pe'lar/ *v.* skin, pare, peel.

pelea /pe'lea/ *n. f.* fight, row. **—pelearse,** *v.*

pelícano /pe'likano/ *n. m.* pelican.

película /pe'likula/ *n. f.* movie, motion picture, film. **p. de terror** horror film.

peligrar /peli'grar/ *v.* be in danger.

peligro /pe'ligro/ *n. m.* peril, danger.

peligroso /peli'groso/ *a.* perilous, dangerous.

pelirrojo /peli'rroho/ **-ja** *a. & n.* redhead.

pellejo /pe'ʎeho; pe'yeho/ *n. m.* skin; peel (of fruit).

pellizco /pe'ʎiθko; pe'yisko/ *n. m.* pinch. **—pellizcar,** *v.*

pelo /'pelo/ *n. m.* hair.

pelota /pe'lota/ *n. f.* ball.

peltre /'peltre/ *n. m.* pewter.

peluca /pe'luka/ *n. f.* wig.

peludo /pe'luðo/ *a.* hairy.

peluquería /peluke'ria/ *n. f.* hairdresser's shop, beauty parlor.

peluquero /pelu'kero/ **-ra** *n.* hairdresser.

pena /'pena/ *n. f.* pain, grief, trouble, woe; penalty. **valer la p.,** to be worthwhile.

penacho /pe'natʃo/ *n. m.* plume.

penalidad /penali'ðað/ *n. f.* trouble; penalty.

pender /pen'der/ *v.* hang, dangle; be pending.

pendiente /pen'diente/ *a.* **1.** hanging; pending. **—n. 2.** *m.* incline, slope; earring, pendant.

pendón /pen'don/ *n. m.* pennant, flag.

penetración /penetra'θion; penetra'sion/ *n. f.* penetration.

penetrar /pene'trar/ *v.* penetrate, pierce.

penicilina /peniθi'lina; penisi'lina/ *n. f.* penicillin.

península /pe'ninsula/ *n. f.* peninsula.

penitencia /peni'tenθia; peni'tensia/ *n. f.* penitence, penance.

penitenciaría /penitenθia'ria; penitensia'ria/ *n. f.* penitentiary.

penoso /pe'noso/ *a.* painful, troublesome, grievous, distressing.

pensador /pensa'ðor/ **-ra** *n.* thinker.

pensamiento /pensa'miento/ *n. m.* thought.

pensar /pen'sar/ *v.* think; intend, plan.

pensativo /pensa'tiβo/ *a.* pensive, thoughtful.

pensión /pen'sion/ *n. f.* pension; boardinghouse.

pensionista /pensio'nista/ *n. m. & f.* boarder.

pentagonal /pentago'nal/ *a.* pentagonal.

penúltimo /pe'nultimo/ *a.* next-to-the-last, last but one, penultimate.

penuria /pe'nuria/ *n. f.* penury, poverty.

peña /'pena/ *n. f.* rock.

peñascoso /penas'koso/ *a.* rocky.

peñón /pe'non/ *n. m.* rock, crag.

Peñón de Gibraltar /pe'non de hiβral'tar/ Rock of Gibraltar.

peón /pe'on/ *n. m.* unskilled laborer; infantryman.

peonada /peo'naða/ *n. f.* group of laborers.

peonía /peo'nia/ *n. f.* peony.

peor /pe'or/ *a.* worse, worst.

pepino /pe'pino/ *n. m.* cucumber.

pepita /pe'pita/ *n. f.* seed (in fruit).

pequeñez /peke'neθ; peke'nes/ *n. f.* smallness; trifle.

pequeño /pe'keno/ **-ña** *a.* **1.** small, little, short, slight. **—n. 2.** child.

pera /'pera/ *n. f.* pear.

peral /pe'ral/ *n. m.* pear tree.

perca /'perka/ *n. f.* perch (fish).

percal /per'kal/ *n. m.* calico, percale.

percance /per'kanθe; per'kanse/ *n. m.* mishap, snag, hitch.

percepción /perθep'θion; persep'sion/ *n. f.* perception.

perceptivo /perθep'tiβo; persep'tiβo/ *a.* perceptive.

percha /'pertʃa/ *n. f.* perch; clothes hanger, rack.

percibir /perθi'βir; persi'βir/ *v.* perceive, sense; collect.

perder /per'ðer/ *v.* lose; miss; waste. **echar a p.,** spoil. **p. el conocimiento,** lose consciousness.

perdición /perði'θion; perði'sion/ *n. f.* perdition, downfall.

pérdida /'perðiða/ *n. f.* loss.

perdiz /per'ðiθ; per'ðis/ *n. f.* partridge.

perdón /per'ðon/ *n. m.* pardon, forgiveness.

perdonar /perðo'nar/ *v.* forgive, pardon; spare.

perdurable /perðu'raβle/ *a.* enduring, everlasting.

perdurar /perðu'rar/ *v.* endure, last.

perecedero /pereθe'ðero; perese'ðero/ *a.* perishable.

perecer /pere'θer; pere'ser/ *v.* perish.

peregrinación /peregrina'θion; peregrina'sion/ *n. f.* peregrination; pilgrimage.

peregrino /pere'grino/ **-na** *n.* pilgrim.

perejil /pere'hil/ *n. m.* parsley.

perenne /pe'renne/ *a.* perennial.

pereza /pe'reθa; pe'resa/ *n. f.* laziness.

perezoso /pere'θoso; pere'soso/ *a.* lazy, sluggish.

perfección /perfek'θion; perfek'sion/ *n. f.* perfection.

perfeccionar /perfekθio'nar; perfeksio'nar/ *v.* perfect.

perfeccionista /perfekθio'nista; perfeksio'nista/ *a. & n.* perfectionist.

perfectamente /perfekta'mente/ *adv.* perfectly.

perfecto /per'fekto/ *a.* perfect.

perfidia /per'fiðia/ *n. f.* falseness, perfidy.

pérfido /'perfiðo/ *a.* perfidious.

perfil /per'fil/ *n. m.* profile.

perforación /perfora'θion; perfora'sion/ *n. f.* perforation.

perforar /perfo'rar/ *v.* pierce, perforate.

perfume /per'fume/ *n. m.* perfume, scent. **—perfumar,** *v.*

pergamino /perga'mino/ *n. m.* parchment.

pericia /pe'riθia; pe'risia/ *n. f.* skill, expertness.

perico /pe'riko/ *n. m.* parakeet.

perímetro /pe'rimetro/ *n. m.* perimeter.

periódico /pe'rioðiko/ *a.* **1.** periodic. **—n. 2.** *m.* newspaper.

periodista /perio'ðista/ *n. m. & f.* journalist.

período /pe'rioðo/ *n. m.* period.

periscopio /peris'kopio/ *n. m.* periscope.

perito /pe'rito/ **-ta** *a. & n.* experienced; expert, connoisseur.

perjudicar /perhuði'kar/ *v.* damage, hurt; impair.

perjudicial /perhuði'θial; perhuði'sial/ *a.* harmful, injurious.

perjuicio /per'huiθio; per'huisio/ *n. m.* injury, damage.

perjurar /perhu'rar/ *v.* commit perjury.

perjurio /per'hurio/ *n. m.* perjury.

perla /'perla/ *n. f.* pearl.

permanecer /permane'θer; permane'ser/ *v.* remain, stay.

permanencia /perma'nenθia; perma'nensia/ *n. f.* permanence; stay.

permanente /perma'nente/ *a.* permanent.

permiso /per'miso/ *n. m.* permission; permit; furlough.

permitir /permi'tir/ *v.* permit, enable, let, allow.

permuta /per'muta/ *n. f.* exchange, barter.

pernicioso /perni'θioso; perni'sioso/ *a.* pernicious.

perno /'perno/ *n. m.* bolt.

pero /'pero/ *conj.* but.

peróxido /pe'roksiðo/ *n. m.* peroxide.

perpendicular /perpendiku'lar/ *n. m. & a.* perpendicular.

perpetración /perpetra'θion; perpetra'sion/ *n. f.* perpetration.

perpetrar /perpe'trar/ *v.* perpetrate.

perpetuar /perpe'tuar/ *v.* perpetuate.

perpetuidad /perpetui'ðað/ *n. f.* perpetuity.

perpetuo /per'petuo/ *a.* perpetual.

perplejo /per'pleho/ *a.* perplexed, puzzled.

perrito caliente /pe'rrito ka'liente/ *n. m.* hot dog.

perro /'perro/ **-rra** *n.* dog.

persecución /perseku'θion; perseku'sion/ *n. f.* persecution.

perseguir /perse'gir/ *v.* pursue; persecute.

perseverancia /perseβe'ranθia; perseβe'ransia/ *n. f.* perseverance.

perseverar /perseβe'rar/ *v.* persevere.

persiana /per'siana/ *n. f.* shutter, Venetian blind.

persistente /persis'tente/ *a.* persistent.

persistir /persis'tir/ *v.* persist.

persona /per'sona/ *n. f.* person.

personaje /perso'nahe/ *n. m.* personage; *Theat.* character.

personal /perso'nal/ *a.* **1.** personal. **—n. 2.** *m.* personnel, staff.

personalidad /personali'ðað/ *n. f.* personality.

personalmente /personal'mente/ *adv.* personally.

perspectiva /perspek'tiβa/ *n. f.* perspective; prospect.

perspicaz /perspi'kaθ; perspi'kas/ *a.* perspicacious, acute.

persuadir /persua'ðir/ *v.* persuade.

persuasión /persua'sion/ *n. f.* persuasion.

persuasivo /persua'siβo/ *a.* persuasive.

pertenecer /pertene'θer; pertene'ser/ *v.* pertain; belong.

pertinencia /perti'nenθia; perti'nensia/ *n. f.* pertinence.

pertinente /perti'nente/ *a.* pertinent; relevant.

perturbar /pertur'βar/ *v.* perturb, disturb.

peruano /pe'ruano/ **-na** *a. & n.* Peruvian.

perversidad /perβersi'ðað/ *n. f.* perversity.

perverso /per'βerso/ *a.* perverse.

pesadez /pesa'ðeθ; pesa'ðes/ *n. f.* dullness.

pesadilla /pesa'ðiʎa; pesa'ðiya/ *n. f.* nightmare.

pesado /pe'saðo/ *a.* heavy; dull, dreary, boring.

pésame /'pesame/ *n. m.* condolence.

pesar /pe'sar/ *n. m.* sorrow; regret. **a p. de,** in spite of. *v.* weigh.

pesca /'peska/ *n. f.* fishing; catch (of fish).

pescadería /peskaðe'ria/ *n. f.* fish store.

pescado /pes'kaðo/ *n. m.* fish. **—pescar,** *v.*

pescador /peska'ðor/ *n. m.* fisherman.

pesebre /pe'seβre/ *n. m.* stall, manger; crib.

peseta /pe'seta/ *n. f.* peseta (monetary unit).

pesimismo /pesi'mismo/ *n. m.* pessimism.

pesimista /pesi'mista/ *a. & n.* pessimistic; pessimist.

pésimo /'pesimo/ *a.* awful, terrible, very bad.
peso /'peso/ *n. m.* weight; load; peso (monetary unit).
pesquera /pes'kera/ *n. f.* fishery.
pesquisa /pes'kisa/ *n. f.* investigation.
pestaña /pes'taɲa/ *n. f.* eyelash.
pestañeo /pesta'ɲeo/ *n. m.* wink, blink. **—pestañear,** *v.*
peste /'peste/ *n. f.* plague.
pesticida /pesti'θiða; pesti'siða/ *n. m.* pesticide.
pestilencia /pesti'lenθia; pesti'lensia/ *n. f.* pestilence.
pétalo /'petalo/ *n. m.* petal.
petardo /pe'tarðo/ *n. m.* firecracker.
petición /peti'θion; peti'sion/ *n. f.* petition.
petirrojo /peti'rroho/ *n. m.* robin.
petrel /pe'trel/ *n. m.* petrel.
pétreo /'petreo/ *a.* rocky.
petrificar /petrifi'kar/ *v.* petrify.
petróleo /pe'troleo/ *n. m.* petroleum.
petrolero /petro'lero/ *n. m.* oil tanker.
petunia /pe'tunia/ *n. f.* petunia.
pez /peθ; pes/ *n.* **1.** *m.* fish (in the water). **—***n.* **2.** *f.* pitch, tar.
pezuña /pe'θuɲa; pe'suɲa/ *n. f.* hoof.
piadoso /pia'ðoso/ *a.* pious; merciful.
pianista /pia'nista/ *n. m. & f.* pianist.
piano /'piano/ *n. m.* piano.
picadero /pika'ðero/ *n. m.* riding school.
picadura /pika'ðura/ *n. f.* sting, bite, prick.
picamaderos /pikama'ðeros/ *n. m.* woodpecker.
picante /pi'kante/ *a.* hot, spicy.
picaporte /pika'porte/ *n. m.* latch.
picar /pi'kar/ *v.* sting, bite, prick; itch; chop up, grind up.
pícaro /'pikaro/ **-ra** *a.* **1.** knavish, mischievous. **—***n.* **2.** rogue, rascal.
picarse /pi'karse/ *v.* be offended, piqued.
picazón /pika'θon; pika'son/ *n. f.* itch.
pícea /'piθea; 'pisea/ *n. f.* spruce.
pichón /pi'tʃon/ *n. m.* pigeon, squab.
pico /'piko/ *n. m.* peak; pick; beak; spout; small amount.
picotazo /piko'taθo; piko'taso/ *n. m.* peck. **—picotear,** *v.*
pictórico /pik'toriko/ *a.* pictorial.
pie /pie/ *n. m.* foot. **al p. de la letra,** literally; thoroughly.
piedad /pie'ðað/ *n. f.* piety; pity, mercy.
piedra /'pieðra/ *n. f.* stone.
piel /piel/ *n. f.* skin, hide; fur.
pienso /'pienso/ *n. m.* fodder.
pierna /'pierna/ *n. f.* leg.
pieza /'pieθa; 'piesa/ *n. f.* piece; room; *Theat.* play.
pijama /pi'hama/ *n. m. or m.pl.* pajamas.
pila /'pila/ *n. f.* pile, stack; battery; sink.
pilar /pi'lar/ *n. m.* pillar, column.
píldora /'pildora/ *n. f.* pill.
pillo /'piʎo; 'piyo/ **-a** *n.* thief; rascal.
piloto /pi'loto/ *n. m. & f.* pilot.
pimentón /pimen'ton/ *n. m.* paprika.
pimienta /pi'mienta/ *n. f.* pepper (spice).
pimiento /pi'miento/ *n. m.* pepper (vegetable).
pináculo /pi'nakulo/ *n. m.* pinnacle.
pincel /pin'θel; pin'sel/ *n. m.* (artist's) brush.
pinchadiscos /pintʃa'ðiskos/ *m. & f.* disk jockey.
pinchazo /pin'tʃaθo; pin'tʃaso/ *n. m.* puncture; prick. **—pinchar,** *v.*
pingajo /piŋ'gaho/ *n. m.* rag, tatter.
pino /'pino/ *n. m.* pine.
pinta /'pinta/ *n. f.* pint.
pintar /pin'tar/ *v.* paint; portray, depict.
pintor /pin'tor/ **-ra** *n.* painter.
pintoresco /pinto'resko/ *a.* picturesque.
pintura /pin'tura/ *n. f.* paint; painting.
pinzas /'pinθas; 'pinsas/ *n. f.pl.* pincers, tweezers; claws.
piña /'piɲa/ *n. f.* pineapple.
pío /'pio/ *a.* pious; merciful.
piojo /'pioho/ *n. m.* louse.
pionero /pio'nero/ **-ra** *n.* pioneer.
pipa /'pipa/ *n. f.* tobacco pipe.
pique /'pike/ *n. m.* resentment, pique. **echar a p.,** sink (ship).
pira /'pira/ *n. f.* pyre.
piragua /pi'ragua/ *n. f.* canoe.
piragüismo /pira'guismo/ *n. m.* canoeing.
piragüista /pira'guista/ *n. m. & f.* canoeist.
pirámide /pi'ramiðe/ *n. f.* pyramid.
pirata /pi'rata/ *n. m. & f.* pirate. **p. de aviones,** hijacker.
pisada /pi'saða/ *n. f.* tread, step. **—pisar,** *v.*
pisapapeles /pisapa'peles/ *n. m.* paperweight.
piscina /pis'θina; pis'sina/ *n. f.* fishpond; swimming pool.
piso /'piso/ *n. m.* floor.
pista /'pista/ *n. f.* trace, clue, track; racetrack.
pista de tenis /'pista de 'tenis/ tennis court.
pistola /pis'tola/ *n. f.* pistol.
pistón /pis'ton/ *n. m.* piston.
pitillo /pi'tiʎo; pi'tiyo/ *n. m.* cigarette.
pito /'pito/ *n. m.* whistle. **—pitar,** *v.*
pizarra /pi'θarra; pi'sarra/ *n. f.* slate; blackboard.
pizca /'piθka; 'piska/ *n. f.* bit, speck; pinch.
pizza /'piθθa; 'pissa/ *n. f.* pizza.
placentero /plaθen'tero; plasen'tero/ *a.* pleasant.
placer /pla'θer; pla'ser/ *n.* **1.** *m.* pleasure. **—***v.* **2.** please.
plácido /'plaθiðo; 'plasiðo/ *a.* placid.
plaga /'plaga/ *n. f.* plague, scourge.
plagio /'plahio/ *n. m.* plagiarism; (*S.A.*) kidnapping.
plan /plan/ *n. m.* plan. **—planear,** *v.*
plancha /'plantʃa/ *n. f.* plate; slab, flatiron.
planchar /plan'tʃar/ *v.* iron, press.
planeta /pla'neta/ *n. m.* planet.
planificación /planifika'θion; planifika'sion/ *n. f.* planning.
planificar /planifi'kar/ *v.* plan.
plano /'plano/ *a.* **1.** level, flat. **—***n.* **2.** *m.* plan; plane.
planta /'planta/ *n. f.* plant; sole (of foot).
planta baja /'planta 'baha/ *n. f.* ground floor.
plantación /planta'θion; planta'sion/ *n. f.* plantation.
plantar /plan'tar/ *v.* plant.
plantear /plante'ar/ *v.* pose, present.
plantel /plan'tel/ *n. m.* educational institution; *Agr.* nursery.
plasma /'plasma/ *n. m.* plasma.
plástico /'plastiko/ *a. & m.* plastic.
plata /'plata/ *n. f.* silver; *Colloq.* money.
plataforma /plata'forma/ *n. f.* platform.
plátano /'platano/ *n. m.* plantain; banana.
platel /pla'tel/ *n. m.* platter.
plática /'platika/ *n. f.* chat, talk. **—platicar,** *v.*
platillo /pla'tiʎo; pla'tiyo/ *n. m.* saucer.
platillo volante /pla'tiʎo bo'lante; pla'tiyo bo'lante/ flying saucer.
plato /'plato/ *n. m.* plate, dish.
playa /'plaia/ *n. f.* beach, shore.
plaza /'plaθa; 'plasa/ *n. f.* square. **p. de toros,** bullring.
plazo /'plaθo; 'plaso/ *n. m.* term, deadline; installment.
plebe /'pleβe/ *n. f.* common people; masses.
plebiscito /pleβis'θito; pleβis'sito/ *n. m.* plebiscite.
plegable /ple'gaβle/ *a.* foldable, folding.
plegadura /plega'ðura/ *n. f.* fold, pleat. **—plegar,** *v.*
pleito /'pleito/ *n. m.* lawsuit; dispute.
plenitud /pleni'tuð/ *n. f.* fullness; abundance.
pleno /'pleno/ *a.* full. **en pleno...** in the middle of...
pliego /'pliego/ *n. m.* sheet of paper.
pliegue /'pliege/ *n. m.* fold, pleat, crease.
plomería /plome'ria/ *n. f.* plumbing.
plomero /plo'mero/ *n. m.* plumber.
plomizo /plo'miθo; plo'miso/ *a.* leaden.
plomo /'plomo/ *n. m.* lead; fuse.
pluma /'pluma/ *n. f.* feather; (writing) pen.
pluma estiglográfica /'pluma estiglo'grafika/ fountain pen.
plumafuente /pluma'fuente/ *n. f.* fountain pen.
plumaje /plu'mahe/ *n. m.* plumage.
plumero /plu'mero/ *n. m.* feather duster; plume.
plumoso /plu'moso/ *a.* feathery.
plural /plu'ral/ *a. & m.* plural.
pluriempleo /pluriem'pleo/ *n. m.* moonlighting.
PNB, *abbr.* (producto nacional bruto), GNP (gross national product).
población /poβla'θion; poβla'sion/ *n. f.* population; town.
poblador /poβla'ðor/ **-ra** *n.* settler.
poblar /po'βlar/ *v.* populate; settle.
pobre /'poβre/ *a. & n.* poor; poor person.
pobreza /po'βreθa; po'βresa/ *n. f.* poverty, need.
pocilga /po'θilga; po'silga/ *n. f.* pigpen.
poción /po'θion; po'sion/ *n. f.* drink; potion.
poco /'poko/ *a. & adv.* **1.** little, not much, (*pl.*) few. **por p.,** almost, nearly. **—***n.* **2.** *m.* **un p. (de),** a little, a bit (of).
poder /po'ðer/ *n.* **1.** *m.* power. **—***v.* **2.** be able to, can; be possible, may, might. **no p. menos de,** not be able to help.
poder adquisitivo /po'ðer aðkisi'tiβo/ purchasing power.
poderío /poðe'rio/ *n. m.* power, might.
poderoso /poðe'roso/ *a.* powerful, mighty, potent.
podrido /po'ðriðo/ *a.* rotten.
poema /po'ema/ *n. m.* poem.
poesía /poe'sia/ *n. f.* poetry; poem.
poeta /po'eta/ *n. m. & f.* poet.
poético /po'etiko/ *a.* poetic.
polaco /po'lako/ **-ca** *a. & n.* Polish; Pole.
polar /po'lar/ *a.* polar.
polaridad /polari'ðað/ *n. f.* polarity.
polea /po'lea/ *n. f.* pulley.
polen /'polen/ *n. m.* pollen.
policía /poli'θia; poli'sia/ *n.* **1.** *f.* police. **—***n.* **2.** *m.* policeman.
polideportivo /poliðepor'tiβo/ *n. m.* sports center.
poliéster /poli'ester/ *n. m.* polyester.
poligamia /poli'gamia/ *n. f.* polygamy.
poligloto /poli'gloto/ **-ta** *n.* polyglot.
polígono industrial /po'ligono indus'trial/ *n. m.* industrial park.
polilla /po'liʎa; po'liya/ *n. f.* moth.
política /po'litika/ *n. f.* politics; policy.
político /po'litiko/ **-ca** *a. & n.* politic; political; politician.
póliza /'poliθa; 'polisa/ *n. f.* (insurance) policy; permit, ticket.
polizonte /poli'θonte; poli'sonte/ *n. m.* policeman.
pollada /po'ʎaða; po'yaða/ *n. f.* brood.
pollería /poʎe'ria; poye'ria/ *n. f.* poultry shop.
pollino /po'ʎino; po'yino/ *n. m.* donkey.
pollo /'poʎo; 'poyo/ *n. m.* chicken.
polo /'polo/ *n. m.* pole; polo; popsicle.
polonés /polo'nes/ *a.* Polish.
Polonia /po'lonia/ *n. f.* Poland.
polvera /pol'βera/ *n. f.* powder box; powder puff.
polvo /'polβo/ *n. m.* powder; dust.
pólvora /'polβora/ *n. f.* gunpowder.
pompa /'pompa/ *n. f.* pomp.
pomposo /pom'poso/ *a.* pompous.
pómulo /'pomulo/ *n. m.* cheekbone.
ponche /'pontʃe/ *n. m.* punch (beverage).
ponchera /pon'tʃera/ *n. f.* punch bowl.
ponderar /ponde'rar/ *v.* ponder.
ponderoso /ponde'roso/ *a.* ponderous.
poner /po'ner/ *v.* put, set, lay, place.
ponerse /po'nerse/ *v.* put on; become, get; set (sun). **p. a,** start to.
poniente /po'niente/ *n. m.* west.
pontífice /pon'tifiθe; pon'tifise/ *n. m.* pontiff.
popa /'popa/ *n. f.* stern.
popular /popu'lar/ *a.* popular.
popularidad /populari'ðað/ *n. f.* popularity.
populazo /popu'laθo; popu'laso/ *n. m.* populace; masses.
por /por/ *prep.* by, through, because of; via; for. **¿p. qué?,** why?
porcelana /porθe'lana; porse'lana/ *n. f.* porcelain, chinaware.
porcentaje /porθen'tahe; porsen'tahe/ *n. m.* percentage.
porche /'portʃe/ *n. m.* porch; portico.
porción /por'θion; por'sion/ *n. f.* portion, lot.
porfiar /por'fiar/ *v.* persist; argue.
pormenor /porme'nor/ *n. m.* detail.
pornografía /pornogra'fia/ *n. f.* pornography.
poro /'poro/ *n. m.* pore.
poroso /po'roso/ *a.* porous.
porque /'porke/ *conj.* because.
porqué *n. m.* reason, motive.
porra /'porra/ *n. f.* stick, club.
porrazo /po'rraθo; po'rraso/ *n. m.* blow.
porro /'porro/ *n. m. Colloq.* joint (marijuana).
portaaviones /portaa'βiones/ *n. m.* aircraft carrier.
portador /porta'ðor/ **-ra** *n.* bearer.
portal /por'tal/ *n. m.* portal.
portar /por'tar/ *v.* carry.
portarse /por'tarse/ *v.* behave, act.
portátil /por'tatil/ *a.* portable.
portavoz /porta'βoθ; porta'βos/ *n.* **1.** *m.* megaphone. **2.** *m. & f.* spokesperson.
porte /'porte/ *n. m.* bearing; behavior; postage.
portero /por'tero/ *n. m.* porter; janitor.
pórtico /'portiko/ *n. m.* porch.
portorriqueño /portorri'keɲo/ **-ña** *n. & a.* Puerto Rican.
portugués /portu'ges/ **-esa** *a. & n.* Portuguese.
posada /po'saða/ *n. f.* lodge, inn.
posar /po'sar/ *v.* pose.
posdata /pos'ðata/ *n. f.* postscript.
poseer /pose'er/ *v.* possess, own.
posesión /pose'sion/ *n. f.* possession.
posibilidad /posiβili'ðað/ *n. f.* possibility.
posible /po'siβle/ *a.* possible.
posiblemente /posiβle'mente/ *adv.* possibly.
posición /posi'θion; posi'sion/ *n. f.* position, stand.
positivo /posi'tiβo/ *a.* positive.
posponer /pospo'ner/ *v.* postpone.
postal /pos'tal/ *a.* postal; postcard.
poste /'poste/ *n. m.* post, pillar.
posteridad /posteri'ðað/ *n. f.* posterity.

posterior /poste'rior/ *a.* posterior, rear.

postizo /pos'tiθo; pos'tiso/ *a.* false, artificial.

postrado /pos'traðo/ *a.* prostrate. —**postrar,** *v.*

postre /'postre/ *n. m.* dessert.

póstumo /'postumo/ *a.* posthumous.

postura /pos'tura/ *n. f.* posture, pose; bet.

potable /po'taβle/ *a.* drinkable.

potaje /po'tahe/ *n. m.* porridge; pot stew.

potasa /po'tasa/ *n. f.* potash.

potasio /po'tasio/ *n. m.* potassium.

pote /'pote/ *n. m.* pot, jar.

potencia /po'tenθia; po'tensia/ *n. f.* potency, power.

potencial /poten'θial; poten'sial/ *a. & m.* potential.

potentado /poten'taðo/ *n. m.* potentate.

potente /po'tente/ *a.* potent, powerful.

potestad /potes'taθ/ *n. f.* power.

potro /'potro/ *n. m.* colt.

pozo /'poθo; 'poso/ *n. m.* well.

práctica /'praktika/ *n. f.* practice. —**practicar,** *v.*

práctico /'praktiko/ *a.* practical.

pradera /pra'ðera/ *n. f.* prairie, meadow.

prado /'praðo/ *n. m.* meadow; lawn.

pragmatismo /pragma'tismo/ *n. m.* pragmatism.

preámbulo /pre'ambulo/ *n. m.* preamble.

precario /pre'kario/ *a.* precarious.

precaución /prekau'θion; prekau'sion/ *n. f.* precaution.

precaverse /preka'βerse/ *v.* beware.

precavido /preka'βiðo/ *a.* cautious, guarded, wary.

precedencia /preθe'ðenθia; prese'ðensia/ *n. f.* precedence, priority.

precedente /preθe'ðente; prese'ðente/ *a. & m.* preceding; precedent.

preceder /preθe'ðer; prese'ðer/ *v.* precede.

precepto /pre'θepto; pre'septo/ *n. m.* precept.

preciar /pre'θiar; pre'siar/ *v.* value, prize.

preciarse de /pre'θiarse de; pre'siarse de/ *v.* take pride in.

precio /'preθio; 'presio/ *n. m.* price. **p. del billete de avión** air fare. **p. del cubierto** cover charge.

precioso /pre'θioso; pre'sioso/ *a.* precious; beautiful, gorgeous.

precipicio /preθi'piθio; presi'pisio/ *n. m.* precipice, cliff.

precipitación /preθipita'θion; presipita'sion/ *n. f.* precipitation.

precipitar /preθipi'tar; presipi'tar/ *v.* precipitate, rush; throw headlong.

precipitoso /preθipi'toso; presipi'toso/ *a.* precipitous; rash.

precisar /preθi'sar; presi'sar/ *v.* fix, specify; be necessary.

precisión /preθi'sion; presi'sion/ *n. f.* precision; necessity.

preciso /pre'θiso; pre'siso/ *a.* precise; necessary.

precocidad /prekoθi'ðaθ; prekosi'ðaθ/ *n. f.* precocity.

precocinado /prekoθi'naðo; prekosi'naðo/ *a.* precooked, ready-cooked.

precoz /pre'koθ; pre'kos/ *a.* precocious.

precursor /prekur'sor/ **-ra** *a.* **1.** preceding. —*n.* **2.** precursor, forerunner.

predecesor /preðeθe'sor; preðese'sor/ **-ra** *a. & n.* predecessor.

predecir /preðe'θir; preðe'sir/ *v.* predict, foretell.

predicación /preðika'θion; preðika'sion/ *n. f.* sermon.

predicador /preðika'ðor/ **-ra** *n.* preacher.

predicar /preði'kar/ *v.* preach.

predicción /preðik'θion; preðik'sion/ *n. f.* prediction.

predilecto /preði'lekto/ *a.* favorite, preferred.

predisponer /preðispo'ner/ *v.* predispose.

predisposición /preðisposi'θion; preðisposi'sion/ *n. f.* predisposition; bias.

predominante /preðomi'nante/ *a.* prevailing, prevalent, predominant.

predominar /preðomi'nar/ *v.* prevail, predominate.

predominio /preðo'minio/ *n. m.* predominance, sway.

prefacio /pre'faθio; pre'fasio/ *n. m.* preface.

preferencia /prefe'renθia; prefe'rensia/ *n. f.* preference.

preferentemente /preferente'mente/ *adv.* preferably.

preferible /prefe'riβle/ *a.* preferable.

preferir /prefe'rir/ *v.* prefer.

prefijo /pre'fiho/ *n. m.* prefix; area code, dialing code. —**prefijar,** *v.*

pregón /pre'gon/ *n. m.* proclamation; street cry.

pregonar /prego'nar/ *v.* proclaim; cry out.

pregunta /pre'gunta/ *n. f.* question, inquiry. **hacer una p.,** to ask a question.

preguntar /pregun'tar/ *v.* ask, inquire.

preguntarse /pregun'tarse/ *v.* wonder.

prehistórico /preis'toriko/ *a.* prehistoric.

prejuicio /pre'huiθio; pre'huisio/ *n. m.* prejudice.

prelacía /prela'θia; prela'sia/ *n. f.* prelacy.

preliminar /prelimi'nar/ *a. & m.* preliminary.

preludio /pre'luðio/ *n. m.* prelude.

prematuro /prema'turo/ *a.* premature.

premeditación /premeðita'θion; premeðita'sion/ *n. f.* premeditation.

premeditar /premeði'tar/ *v.* premeditate.

premiar /pre'miar/ *v.* reward; award a prize to.

premio /'premio/ *n. m.* prize, award; reward. **p. de consuelo,** consolation prize.

premisa /pre'misa/ *n. f.* premise.

premura /pre'mura/ *n. f.* pressure; urgency.

prenda /'prenda/ *n. f.* jewel; (personal) quality. **p. de vestir,** garment.

prender /pren'der/ *v.* seize, arrest, catch; pin, clip. **p. fuego a,** set fire to.

prensa /'prensa/ *n. f.* printing press; (the) press.

prensar /pren'sar/ *v.* press, compress.

preñado /pre'ɲaðo/ *a.* pregnant.

preocupación /preokupa'θion; preokupa'sion/ *n. f.* worry, preoccupation.

preocupar /preoku'par/ *v.* worry, preoccupy.

preparación /prepara'θion; prepara'sion/ *n. f.* preparation.

preparar /prepa'rar/ *v.* prepare.

preparativo /prepara'tiβo/ *n. m.* preparation.

preparatorio /prepara'torio/ *n. m.* preparatory.

preponderante /preponde'rante/ *a.* preponderant.

preposición /preposi'θion; preposi'sion/ *n. f.* preposition.

prerrogativa /prerroga'tiβa/ *n. f.* prerogative, privilege.

presa /'presa/ *n. f.* capture; (water) dam.

presagiar /presa'hiar/ *v.* presage, forebode.

presbiteriano /presβite'riano/ **-na** *n. & a.* Presbyterian.

presbítero /pres'βitero/ *n. m.* priest.

prescindir de /presθin'dir de; pressin'dir de/ *v.* dispense with; omit.

prescribir /preskri'βir/ *v.* prescribe.

prescripción /preskrip'θion; preskrip'sion/ *n. f.* prescription.

presencia /pre'senθia; pre'sensia/ *n. f.* presence.

presenciar /presen'θiar; presen'siar/ *v.* witness, be present at.

presentable /presen'taβle/ *a.* presentable.

presentación /presenta'θion; presenta'sion/ *n. f.* presentation; introduction.

presentar /presen'tar/ *v.* present; introduce.

presente /pre'sente/ *a. & m.* present.

presentimiento /presenti'miento/ *n. m.* premonition.

preservación /preserβa'θion; preserβa'sion/ *n. f.* preservation.

preservar /preser'βar/ *v.* preserve, keep.

preservativo /preserβa'tiβo/ *a. & m.* preservative; condom.

presidencia /presi'ðenθia; presi'ðensia/ *n. f.* presidency.

presidencial /presiðen'θial; presiðen'sial/ *a.* presidential.

presidente /presi'ðente/ **-ta** *n.* president.

presidiario /presi'ðiario/ **-ria** *n. m. & f.* prisoner.

presidio /pre'siðio/ *n. m.* prison; garrison.

presidir /presi'ðir/ *v.* preside.

presión /pre'sion/ *n. f.* pressure.

presión arterial /pre'sion arte'rial/ blood pressure.

preso /'preso/ **-sa** *n.* prisoner.

presta /'presta/ *n. f.* mint (plant).

prestador /presta'ðor/ **-ra** *n.* lender.

prestamista /presta'mista/ *n. m. & f.* money lender.

préstamo /'prestamo/ *n. m.* loan.

prestar /pres'tar/ *v.* lend.

presteza /pres'teθa; pres'tesa/ *n. f.* haste, promptness.

prestidigitación /prestiðihita'θion; prestiðihita'sion/ *n. f.* sleight of hand.

prestigio /pres'tihio/ *n. m.* prestige.

presto /'presto/ *a.* **1.** quick, prompt; ready. —*adv.* **2.** quickly; at once.

presumido /presu'miðo/ *a.* conceited, presumptuous.

presumir /presu'mir/ *v.* presume; boast; claim; be conceited.

presunción /presun'θion; presun'sion/ *n. f.* presumption; conceit.

presunto /pre'sunto/ *a.* presumed; prospective.

presuntuoso /presun'tuoso/ *a.* presumptuous.

presupuesto /presu'puesto/ *n. m.* premise; budget.

pretender /preten'der/ *v.* pretend; intend; aspire.

pretendiente /preten'diente/ *n. m.* suitor; pretender (to throne).

pretensión /preten'sion/ *n. f.* pretension; claim.

pretérito /pre'terito/ *a. & m.* preterit, past (tense).

pretexto /pre'teksto/ *n. m.* pretext.

prevalecer /preβale'θer; preβale'ser/ *v.* prevail.

prevención /preβen'θion; preβen'sion/ *n. f.* prevention.

prevenir /preβe'nir/ *v.* prevent; forewarn; prearrange.

preventivo /preβen'tiβo/ *a.* preventive.

prever /pre'βer/ *v.* foresee.

previamente /preβia'mente/ *adv.* previously.

previo /'preβio/ *a.* previous.

previsible /preβi'siβle/ *a.* predictable.

previsión /preβi'sion/ *n. f.* foresight. **p. social,** social security.

prieto /'prieto/ *a.* blackish, very dark.

primacía /prima'θia; prima'sia/ *n. f.* primacy.

primario /pri'mario/ *a.* primary.

primavera /prima'βera/ *n. f.* spring (season).

primero /pri'mero/ *a. & adv.* first.

primitivo /primi'tiβo/ *a.* primitive.

primo /'primo/ **-ma** *n.* cousin.

primor /pri'mor/ *n. m.* beauty; excellence; lovely thing.

primoroso /primo'roso/ *a.* exquisite, elegant; graceful.

princesa /prin'θesa; prin'sesa/ *n. f.* princess.

principal /prinθi'pal; prinsi'pal/ *a.* **1.** principal, main. —*n.* **2.** *m.* chief, head, principal.

principalmente /prinθipal'mente; prinsipal'mente/ *adv.* principally.

príncipe /'prinθipe; 'prinsipe/ *n. m.* prince.

príncipe azul /'prinθipe a'θul; 'prinsipe a'sul/ Prince Charming.

principiar /prinθi'piar; prinsi'piar/ *v.* begin, initiate.

principio /prin'θipio; prin'sipio/ *n. m.* beginning, start; principle.

pringado /priŋ'gaðo/ *n. m.* low-life, loser.

prioridad /priori'ðaθ/ *n. f.* priority.

prisa /'prisa/ *n. f.* hurry, haste. **darse p.,** hurry, hasten. **tener p.,** be in a hurry.

prisión /pri'sion/ *n. f.* prison; imprisonment.

prisionero /prisio'nero/ **-ra** *n.* captive, prisoner.

prisma /'prisma/ *n. m.* prism.

prismático /pris'matiko/ *a.* prismatic.

privación /priβa'θion; priβa'sion/ *n. f.* privation, want.

privado /pri'βaðo/ *a.* private, secret; deprived.

privar /pri'βar/ *v.* deprive.

privilegio /priβi'lehio/ *n. m.* privilege.

pro /pro/ *n. m. or f.* benefit, advantage. **en p. de,** in behalf of. **en p. y en contra,** pro and con.

proa /'proa/ *n. f.* prow, bow.

probabilidad /proβaβili'ðaθ/ *n. f.* probability.

probable /pro'βaβle/ *a.* probable, likely.

probablemente /proβaβle'mente/ *adv.* probably.

probador /proβa'ðor/ *n. m.* fitting room.

probar /pro'βar/ *v.* try, sample; taste; test; prove.

probarse /pro'βarse/ *v.* try on.

probidad /proβi'ðaθ/ *n. f.* honesty, integrity.

problema /pro'βlema/ *n. m.* problem.

probo /'proβo/ *a.* honest.

procaz /pro'kaθ; pro'kas/ *a.* impudent, saucy.

proceder /proθe'ðer; prose'ðer/ *v.* proceed.

procedimiento /proθeði'miento; proseði'miento/ *n. m.* procedure.

procesar /proθe'sar; prose'sar/ *v.* prosecute; sue; process.

procesión /proθe'sion; prose'sion/ *n. f.* procession.

proceso /pro'θeso; pro'seso/ *n. m.* process; (court) trial.

proclama /pro'klama/ **proclamación** *n. f.* proclamation.

proclamar /prokla'mar/ *v.* proclaim.

procreación /prokrea'θion; prokrea'sion/ *n. f.* procreation.

procrear /prokre'ar/ *v.* procreate.

procurar /proku'rar/ *v.* try; see to it; get, procure.

prodigalidad /proðigali'ðaθ/ *n. f.* prodigality.

prodigar /proði'gar/ *v.* lavish; squander, waste.

prodigio /pro'ðihio/ *n. m.* prodigy.

pródigo /'proðigo/ *a.* prodigal; profuse; lavish.

producción /proðuk'θion; proðuk'sion/ *n. f.* production.

producir /proðu'θir; proðu'sir/ *v.* produce.

productivo /proðuk'tiβo/ *a.* productive.

producto /pro'ðukto/ *n. m.* product.

producto nacional bruto /pro'ðukto naθio'nal 'bruto; pro'ðukto nasio'nal 'bruto/ gross national product.

proeza /pro'eθa; pro'esa/ *n. f.* prowess.

profanación /profana'θion; profana'sion/ *n. f.* profanation.

profanar /profa'nar/ *v.* defile, desecrate.

profanidad /profani'ðað/ *n. f.* profanity.

profano /pro'fano/ *a.* profane.

profecía /profe'θia; profe'sia/ *n. f.* prophecy.

proferir /profe'rir/ *v.* utter, express.

profesar /profe'sar/ *v.* profess.

profesión /profe'sion/ *n. f.* profession.

profesional /profesio'nal/ *a.* professional.

profesor /profe'sor/ **-ra** *n.* professor, teacher.

profeta /pro'feta/ *n. m.* prophet.

profético /pro'fetiko/ *a.* prophetic.

profetizar /profeti'θar; profeti'sar/ *v.* prophesy.

proficiente /profi'θiente; profi'siente/ *a.* proficient.

profundamente /profunda'mente/ *adv.* profoundly, deeply.

profundidad /profundi'ðað/ *n. f.* profundity, depth.

profundizar /profundi'θar; profundi'sar/ *v.* deepen.

profundo /pro'fundo/ *a.* profound, deep.

profuso /pro'fuso/ *a.* profuse.

progenie /pro'henie/ *n. f.* progeny, offspring.

programa /pro'grama/ *n. m.* program; schedule.

programador /programa'ðor/ **-ra** *n.* (computer) programmer.

progresar /progre'sar/ *v.* progress, advance.

progresión /progre'sion/ *n. f.* progression.

progresista /progre'sista/ **progresivo** *a.* progressive.

progreso /pro'greso/ *n. m.* progress.

prohibición /proiβi'θion; proiβi'sion/ *n. f.* prohibition.

prohibir /proi'βir/ *v.* prohibit, forbid.

prohibitivo /proiβi'tiβo, proiβi'torio/ *a.* prohibitive.

prole /'prole/ *n. f.* progeny.

proletariado /proleta'riaðo/ *n. m.* proletariat.

proliferación /prolifera'θion; prolifera'sion/ *n. f.* proliferation.

prolijo /pro'liho/ *a.* prolix, tedious; long-winded.

prólogo /'prologo/ *n. m.* prologue; preface.

prolongar /prolon'gar/ *v.* prolong.

promedio /pro'meðio/ *n. m.* average.

promesa /pro'mesa/ *n. f.* promise.

prometer /prome'ter/ *v.* promise.

prometido /prome'tiðo/ *a.* promised; engaged (to marry).

prominencia /promi'nenθia; promi'nensia/ *n. f.* prominence.

promiscuamente /promiskua'mente/ *adv.* promiscuously.

promiscuo /pro'miskuo/ *a.* promiscuous.

promisorio /promi'sorio/ *a.* promissory.

promoción /promo'θion; promo'sion/ *n. f.* promotion.

promocionar /promoθio'nar; promosio'nar/ *v.* advertise, promote.

promover /promo'βer/ *v.* promote, further.

promulgación /promulga'θion; promulga'sion/ *n. f.* promulgation.

promulgar /promul'gar/ *v.* promulgate.

pronombre /pro'nombre/ *n. m.* pronoun.

pronosticación /pronostika'θion;

pronosticar /pronosti'kar/ *v.* predict, forecast.

pronóstico /pro'nostiko/ *n. m.* prediction.

prontamente /pronta'mente/ *adv.* promptly.

prontitud /pronti'tuð/ *n. f.* promptness.

pronto /'pronto/ *a.* **1.** prompt; ready. —*adv.* **2.** soon; quickly. **de p.,** abruptly.

pronunciación /pronunθia'θion; pronunsia'sion/ *n. f.* pronunciation.

pronunciar /pronun'θiar; pronun'siar/ *v.* pronounce.

propagación /propaga'θion; propaga'sion/ *n. f.* propagation.

propaganda /propa'ganda/ *n. f.* propaganda.

propagandista /propagan'dista/ *m. & f.* propagandist.

propagar /propa'gar/ *v.* propagate.

propicio /pro'piθio; pro'pisio/ *a.* propitious, auspicious, favorable.

propiedad /propie'ðað/ *n. f.* property.

propietario /propie'tario/ **-ria** *n.* proprietor; owner; landlord, landlady.

propina /pro'pina/ *n. f.* gratuity, tip.

propio /'propio/ *a.* proper, suitable; typical; (one's) own; -self.

proponer /propo'ner/ *v.* propose.

proporción /propor'θion; propor'sion/ *n. f.* proportion.

proporcionado /proporθio'naðo; proporsio'naðo/ *a.* proportionate.

proporcionar /proporθio'nar; proporsio'nar/ *v.* provide with, supply, afford.

proposición /proposi'θion; proposi'sion/ *n. f.* proposition, offer; proposal.

propósito /pro'posito/ *n. m.* purpose; plan; **a p.,** by the way, apropos; on purpose.

propuesta /pro'puesta/ *n. f.* proposal, motion.

prorrata /pro'rrata/ *n. f.* quota.

prórroga /'prorroga/ *n. f.* renewal, extension.

prorrogar /prorro'gar/ *v.* renew, extend.

prosa /'prosa/ *n. f.* prose.

prosaico /pro'saiko/ *a.* prosaic.

proscribir /proskri'βir/ *v.* prohibit, proscribe, ban.

prosecución /proseku'θion; proseku'sion/ *n. f.* prosecution.

proseguir /prose'gir/ *v.* pursue; proceed, go on.

prosélito /pro'selito/ **-ta** *n.* proselyte.

prospecto /pros'pekto/ *n. m.* prospectus.

prosperar /prospe'rar/ *v.* prosper, thrive, flourish.

prosperidad /prosperi'ðað/ *n. f.* prosperity.

próspero /'prospero/ *a.* prosperous, successful.

prosternado /proster'naðo/ *a.* prostrate.

prostitución /prostitu'θion; prostitu'sion/ *n. f.* prostitution.

prostituir /prosti'tuir/ *v.* prostitute; debase.

prostituta /prosti'tuta/ *n. f.* prostitute.

protagonista /protago'nista/ *n. m. & f.* protagonist, hero, heroine.

protección /protek'θion; protek'sion/ *n. f.* protection.

protector /protek'tor/ **-ra** *a. & n.* protective; protector.

proteger /prote'her/ *v.* protect, safeguard. **p. contra escritura,** write-protect (diskette).

protegido /prote'hiðo/ **-da** *n.* **1.** protégé. —*a.* **2.** protected. **p. contra escritura,** write-protected.

proteína /prote'ina/ *n. f.* protein.

protesta /pro'testa/ *n. f.* protest. —**protestar,** *v.*

protestante /protes'tante/ *a. & n.* Protestant.

protocolo /proto'kolo/ *n. m.* protocol.

protuberancia /protuβe'ranθia; protuβe'ransia/ *n. f.* protuberance, lump.

protuberante /protuβe'rante/ *a.* bulging.

provecho /pro'βetʃo/ *n. m.* profit, gain, benefit. **¡Buen provecho!** May you enjoy your meal!

provechoso /proβe'tʃoso/ *a.* beneficial, advantageous, profitable.

proveer /proβe'er/ *v.* provide, furnish.

provenir de /proβe'nir de/ *v.* originate in, be due to, come from.

proverbial /proβer'βial/ *a.* proverbial.

proverbio /pro'βerβio/ *n. m.* proverb.

providencia /proβi'ðenθia; proβi'ðensia/ *n. f.* providence.

providente /proβi'ðente/ *a.* provident.

provincia /pro'βinθia; pro'βinsia/ *n. f.* province.

provincial /proβin'θial; proβin'sial/ *a.* provincial.

provinciano /proβin'θiano; proβin'siano/ **-na** *a. & n.* provincial.

provisión /proβi'sion/ *n. f.* provision, supply, stock.

provisional /proβisio'nal/ *a.* provisional.

provocación /proβoka'θion; proβoka'sion/ *n. f.* provocation.

provocador /proβoka'ðor/ **-ra** *n.* provoker.

provocar /proβo'kar/ *v.* provoke, excite.

provocativo /proβoka'tiβo/ *a.* provocative.

proximidad /proksimi'ðað/ *n. f.* proximity, vicinity.

próximo /'proksimo/ *a.* next; near.

proyección /proiek'θion; proiek'sion/ *n. f.* projection.

proyectar /proiek'tar/ *v.* plan, project.

proyectil /proyek'til/ *n. m.* projectile, missile, shell.

proyecto /pro'iekto/ *n. m.* plan, project, scheme.

proyector /proiek'tor/ *n. m.* projector.

prudencia /pru'ðenθia; pru'ðensia/ *n. f.* prudence.

prudente /pru'ðente/ *a.* prudent.

prueba /'prueβa/ *n. f.* proof; trial; test.

psicoanálisis /psikoa'nalisis/ *n. m.* psychoanalysis.

psicoanalista /psikoana'lista/ *n. m. & f.* psychoanalyst.

psicodélico /psiko'ðeliko/ *a.* psychedelic.

psicología /psikolo'hia/ *n. f.* psychology.

psicológico /psiko'lohiko/ *a.* psychological.

psicólogo /psi'kologo/ **-ga** *n.* psychologist.

psiquiatra /psi'kiatra/ *n. m. & f.* psychiatrist.

psiquiatría /psikia'tria/ *n. f.* psychiatry.

publicación /puβlika'θion; puβlika'sion/ *n. f.* publication.

publicar /puβli'kar/ *v.* publish.

publicidad /puβliθi'ðað; puβlisi'ðað/ *n. f.* publicity.

publicista /puβli'θista; puβli'sista/ *n. m. & f.* publicity agent.

público /'puβliko/ *a. & m.* public.

puchero /pu'tʃero/ *n. m.* pot.

pudiente /pu'ðiente/ *a.* powerful; wealthy.

pudín /pu'ðin/ *n. m.* pudding.

pudor /pu'ðor/ *n. m.* modesty.

pudoroso /puðo'roso/ *a.* modest.

pudrirse /pu'ðrirse/ *v.* rot.

pueblo /'pueβlo/ *n. m.* town, village; (the) people.

puente /'puente/ *n. m.* bridge.

puente para peatones /'puente para pea'tones/ *n. m.* footbridge.

puerco /'puerko/ **-ca** *n.* pig.

puericultura /puerikul'tura/ *n. f.* pediatrics.

pueril /pue'ril/ *a.* childish.

puerilidad /puerili'ðað/ *n. f.* puerility.

puerta /'puerta/ *n. f.* door; gate.

puerta giratoria /'puerta hira'toria/ revolving door.

puerta principal /'puerta prinθi'pal; 'puerta prinsi'pal/ front door.

puerto /'puerto/ *n. m.* port, harbor.

puertorriqueño /puertorri'keno/ **-ña** *a. & n.* Puerto Rican.

pues /pues/ *adv.* **1.** well... —*conj.* **2.** as, since, for.

puesto /'puesto/ *n. m.* appointment, post, job; place; stand. **p. que,** since.

pugilato /puhi'lato/ *n. m.* boxing.

pugna /'pugna/ *n. f.* conflict.

pugnacidad /pugnaθi'ðað; pugnasi'ðað/ *n. f.* pugnacity.

pugnar /pug'nar/ *v.* fight; oppose.

pulcritud /pulkri'tuð/ *n. f.* neatness; exquisiteness.

pulga /'pulga/ *n. f.* flea.

pulgada /pul'gaða/ *n. f.* inch.

pulgar /pul'gar/ *n. m.* thumb.

pulir /pu'lir/ *v.* polish; beautify.

pulmón /pul'mon/ *n. m.* lung.

pulmonía /pulmo'nia/ *n. f.* pneumonia.

pulpa /'pulpa/ *n. f.* pulp.

púlpito /'pulpito/ *n. m.* pulpit.

pulque /'pulke/ *n. m.* pulque (fermented maguey juice).

pulsación /pulsa'θion; pulsa'sion/ *n. f.* pulsation, beat.

pulsar /pul'sar/ *v.* pulsate, beat.

pulsera /pul'sera/ *n. f.* wristband; bracelet.

pulso /'pulso/ *n. m.* pulse.

pulverizar /pulβeri'θar; pulβeri'sar/ *v.* pulverize.

puma /'puma/ *n. m.* puma.

pundonor /pundo'nor/ *n. m.* point of honor.

punta /'punta/ *n. f.* point, tip, end.

puntada /pun'taða/ *n. f.* stitch.

puntapié /punta'pie/ *n. m.* kick.

puntería /punte'ria/ *n. f.* (marksman's) aim.

puntiagudo /puntia'guðo/ *a.* sharp-pointed.

puntillas /pun'tiʎas; pun'tiyas/ *n. f.pl.* **de p., en p.,** on tiptoe.

punto /'punto/ *n. m.* point; period; spot, dot. **dos puntos,** *Punct.* colon. **a p. de,** about to. **al p.,** instantly.

punto de admiración /'punto de aðmira'θion; 'punto de aðmira'sion/ exclamation mark.

punto de congelación /'punto de konɡela'θion; 'punto de konɡela'sion/ freezing point.

punto de ebullición /'punto de eβuʎi'θion; 'punto de eβuyi'sion/ boiling point.

punto de vista /'punto de 'bista/ point of view, viewpoint.

puntuación /puntua'θion; puntua'sion/ *n. f.* punctuation.

puntual /pun'tual/ *a.* punctual, prompt.

puntuar /pun'tuar/ *v.* punctuate.

puñada /pu'naða/ *n. f.* punch.

puñado /pu'naðo/ *n. m.* handful.

puñal /pu'nal/ *n. m.* dagger.

puñalada /puna'laða/ *n. f.* stab.

puñetazo /pune'taθo; pune'taso/ *n. m.* punch, fist blow.

puño /'puno/ *n. m.* fist; cuff; handle.

pupila /pu'pila/ *n. f.* pupil (of eye).

pupitre /pu'pitre/ *n. m.* writing desk, school desk.

pureza /pu'reθa; pu'resa/ *n. f.* purity; chastity.

purgante /pur'gante/ *n. m.* laxative.

purgar /pur'gar/ *v.* purge, cleanse.

purgatorio /purga'torio/ *n. m.* purgatory.

puridad /puri'ðað/ *n. f.* secrecy.

purificación /purifika'θion; purifika-'sion/ *n. f.* purification.
purificar /purifi'kar/ *v.* purify.
purismo /pu'rismo/ *n. m.* purism.
purista /pu'rista/ *n. m. & f.* purist.
puritanismo /purita'nismo/ *n. m.* puritanism.
puro /'puro/ *a.* **1.** pure. —*n.* **2.** *m.* cigar.
púrpura /'purpura/ *n. f.* purple.
purpúreo /pur'pureo/ *a.* purple.
purulencia /puru'lenθia; puru'lensia/ *n. f.* purulence.
purulento /puru'lento/ *a.* purulent.
pus /pus/ *n. m.* pus.
pusilánime /pusi'lanime/ *a.* pusillanimous.
puta /'puta/ **-to** *n.* prostitute.
putrefacción /putrefak'θion; putrefak'sion/ *n. f.* putrefaction, rot.
putrefacto /putre'fakto/ *a.* putrid, rotten.
pútrido /'putriðo/ *a.* putrid.
puya /'puya/ *n. f.* goad.

Q

que /ke/ *rel. pron.* **1.** who, whom; that, which. —*conj.* **2.** than.
qué *a. & pron.* what. **por q., para q.,** why? *adv.* how.
quebrada /ke'βraða/ *n. f.* ravine, gully, gulch; stream.
quebradizo /keβra'ðiθo; keβra'ðiso/ *a.* fragile, brittle.
quebrantaley /keβran'lei/ *n. m. & f.* lawbreaker, outlaw.
quebrar /ke'βrar/ *v.* break.
queda /'keða/ *n. f.* curfew.
quedar /ke'ðar/ *v.* remain, be located; be left. **q. bien a,** be becoming to.
quedarse /ke'ðarse/ *v.* stay, remain. **q. con,** keep, hold on to; remain with.
quedo /'keðo/ *a.* quiet; gentle.
quehacer /kea'θer; kea'ser/ *n. m.* task; chore.
queja /'keha/ *n. f.* complaint.
quejarse /ke'harse/ *v.* complain, grumble.
quejido /ke'hiðo/ *n. m.* moan.
quejoso /ke'hoso/ *a.* complaining.
quema /'kema/ *n. f.* burning.
quemadura /kema'ðura/ *n. f.* burn.
quemar /ke'mar/ *v.* burn.
querella /ke'reʎa; ke'reya/ *n. f.* quarrel; complaint.
querencia /ke'renθia; ke'rensia/ *n. f.* affection, liking.
querer /ke'rer/ *v.* want, wish; will; love (a person). **q. decir,** mean. **sin q.,** without meaning to; unwillingly.
querido /ke'riðo/ *a.* dear, loved, beloved.
quesería /kese'ria/ *n. f.* dairy.
queso /'keso/ *n. m.* cheese.
queso crema /'keso 'krema/ cream cheese.
quetzal /ket'θal; ket'sal/ *n. m.* quetzal.
quiche /'kitʃe/ *n. f.* quiche.
quiebra /'kieβra/ *n. f.* break, fracture; damage; bankruptcy.
quien /kien/ *rel. pron.* who, whom.
quién *interrog. pron.* who, whom.
quienquiera /kien'kiera/ *pron.* whoever, whomever.
quietamente /kieta'mente/ *adv.* quietly.
quieto /'kieto/ *a.* quiet, still.
quietud /kie'tuð/ *n. f.* quiet, quietude.
quijada /ki'haða/ *n. f.* jaw.
quijotesco /kiho'tesko/ *a.* quixotic.
quilate /ki'late/ *n. m.* carat.
quilla /'kiʎa; 'kiya/ *n. f.* keel.
quimera /ki'mera/ *n. f.* chimera; vision; quarrel.
química /'kimika/ *n. f.* chemistry.
químico /'kimiko/ **-ca** *a. & n.* chemical; chemist.

quimoterapia /kimote'rapia/ *n. f.* chemotherapy.
quincalla /kin'kaʎa; kin'kaya/ *n. f.* (computer) hardware.
quincallería /kinkaʎe'ria; kinkaye'ria/ *n. f.* hardware store.
quince /'kinθe; 'kinse/ *a. & pron.* fifteen.
quinientos /ki'nientos/ *a. & pron.* five hundred.
quinina /ki'nina/ *n. f.* quinine.
quintana /kin'tana/ *n. f.* country home.
quinto /'kinto/ *a.* fifth.
quirúrgico /ki'rurhiko/ *a.* surgical.
quiste /'kiste/ *n. m.* cyst.
quitamanchas /kita'mantʃas/ *n. m.* stain remover.
quitanieves /kita'nieβes/ *n. m.* snowplow.
quitar /ki'tar/ *v.* take away, remove.
quitarse /ki'tarse/ *v.* take off; get rid of.
quitasol /kita'sol/ *n. m.* parasol, umbrella.
quitasueño /kita'sueɲo/ *n. m. Colloq.* nightmare; worry.
quizá /ki'θa; ki'sa/ **quizás** *adv.* perhaps, maybe.
quórum /'korum/ *n. m.* quorum.

R

rábano /'rraβano/ *n. m.* radish.
rabí /rra'βi/ **rabino** *n. m.* rabbi.
rabia /'rraβia/ *n. f.* rage; grudge; rabies.
rabiar /rra'βiar/ *v.* rage, be furious.
rabieta /rra'βieta/ *n. f.* tantrum.
rabioso /rra'βioso/ *a.* furious; rabid.
rabo /'rraβo/ *n. m.* tail.
racha /'rratʃa/ *n. f.* streak.
racimo /rra'θimo; rra'simo/ *n. m.* bunch, cluster.
ración /rra'θion; rra'sion/ *n. f.* ration. —**racionar,** *v.*
racionabilidad /rraθionaβili'ðað; rrasionaβili'ðað/ *n. f.* rationality.
racional /rraθio'nal; rrasio'nal/ *a.* rational.
racionalismo /rraθiona'lismo; rrasiona'lismo/ *n. m.* rationalism.
racionalmente /rraθional'mente; rrasional'mente/ *adv.* rationally.
radar /rra'ðar/ *n. m.* radar.
radiación /rraðia'θion; rraðia'sion/ *n. f.* radiation.
radiador /rraðia'ðor/ *n. m.* radiator.
radiante /rra'ðiante/ *a.* radiant.
radical /rraði'kal/ *a. & n.* radical.
radicalismo /rraðika'lismo/ *n. m.* radicalism.
radicoso /rraði'koso/ *a.* radical.
radio /'rraðio/ *n. m. or f.* radio.
radioactividad /rraðioaktiβi'ðað/ *n. f.* radioactivity.
radioactivo /rraðioak'tiβo/ *a.* radioactive.
radiocasete /rraðioka'sete/ *n. m.* radio cassette.
radiodifundir /rraðioðifun'dir/ *v.* broadcast.
radiodifusión /rraðioðifu'sion/ *n. f.* (radio) broadcasting.
radiografía /rraðiogra'fia/ *n. f.* X-ray.
radiografiar /rraðiogra'fiar/ *v.* X-ray.
ráfaga /'rrafaga/ *n. f.* gust (of wind).
raíz /rra'iθ; rra'is/ *n. f.* root.
raja /'rraha/ *n. f.* rip; split, crack. —**rajar,** *v.*
ralea /rra'lea/ *n. f.* stock, breed.
ralo /'rralo/ *a.* thin, scattered.
rama /'rrama/ *n. f.* branch, bough.
ramillete /rrami'ʎete; rrami'yete/ *n. m.* bouquet.
ramo /'rramo/ *n. m.* branch, bough; bouquet.
ramonear /rramone'ar/ *v.* browse.
rampa /'rrampa/ *n. f.* ramp.
rana /'rrana/ *n. f.* frog.

ranchero /rran'tʃero/ **-ra** *n.* small farmer.
rancho /'rrantʃo/ *n. m.* ranch.
rancidez /rranθi'ðeθ; rransi'ðes/ *n. f.* rancidity.
rancio /'rranθio; 'rransio/ *a.* rancid, rank, stale, sour.
rango /'rrango/ *n. m.* rank.
ranúnculo /rra'nunkulo/ *n. m.* ranunculus; buttercup.
ranura /rra'nura/ *n. f.* slot.
ranura de expansión /rra'nura de ekspan'sion/ expansion slot.
rapacidad /rrapaθi'ðað; rrapasi'ðað/ *n. f.* rapacity.
rapaz /rra'paθ; rra'pas/ *a.* **1.** rapacious. —*n.* **2.** *m.* young boy.
rapé /'rrape/ *n. m.* snuff.
rápidamente /rrapiða'mente/ *adv.* rapidly.
rapidez /rrapi'ðeθ; rrapi'ðes/ *n. f.* rapidity, speed.
rápido /'rrapiðo/ *a.* **1.** rapid, fast, speedy. —*n.* **2.** *m.* express (train).
rapiña /rra'piɲa/ *n. f.* robbery, plundering.
rapsodia /rrap'soðia/ *n. f.* rhapsody.
rapto /'rrapto/ *n. m.* kidnapping.
raquero /rra'kero/ **-ra** *n.* beachcomber.
raqueta /rra'keta/ *n. f.* (tennis) racket.
rareza /rra'reθa; rra'resa/ *n. f.* rarity; freak.
raridad /rrari'ðað/ *n. f.* rarity.
raro /'rraro/ *a.* rare, strange, unusual, odd, queer.
rasar /rra'sar/ *v.* skim.
rascacielos /rraska'θielos; rraska'sielos/ *n. m.* skyscraper.
rascar /rras'kar/ *v.* scrape; scratch.
rasgadura /rrasga'ðura/ *n. f.* tear, rip. —**rasgar,** *v.*
rasgo /'rrasgo/ *n. m.* trait.
rasgón /rras'gon/ *n. m.* tear.
rasguño /rras'guɲo/ *n. m.* scratch. —**rasguñar,** *v.*
raso /'rraso/ *a.* **1.** plain. **soldado r.,** *Mil.* private. —*n.* **2.** *m.* satin.
raspar /rras'par/ *v.* scrape; erase.
rastra /'rrastra/ *n. f.* trail, track. —**rastrear,** *v.*
rastrillar /rrastri'ʎar; rrastri'yar/ *v.* rake.
rastro /'rrastro/ *n. m.* track, trail, trace; rake; flea market.
rata /'rrata/ *n. f.* rat.
ratificación /rratifika'θion; rratifika'sion/ *n. f.* ratification.
ratificar /rratifi'kar/ *v.* ratify.
rato /'rrato/ *n. m.* while, spell, short time.
ratón /rra'ton/ *n. m.* mouse.
ratonera /rrato'nera/ *n. f.* mousetrap.
raya /'rraya/ *n. f.* dash, line, streak, stripe.
rayar /rra'yar/ *v.* rule, stripe; scratch; cross out.
rayo /'rrayo/ *n. m.* lightning bolt; ray; flash.
rayón /rra'yon/ *n. m.* rayon.
raza /'rraθa; 'rrasa/ *n. f.* race; breed, stock.
razón /rra'θon; rra'son/ *n. f.* reason; ratio. **a r. de,** at the rate of. **tener r.,** to be right.
razonable /rraθo'naβle; rraso'naβle/ *a.* reasonable, sensible.
razonamiento /rraθona'miento; rrasona'miento/ *n. m.* argument.
razonar /rraθo'nar; rraso'nar/ *v.* reason.
reacción /rreak'θion; rreak'sion/ *n. f.* reaction.
reaccionar /rreakθio'nar; rreaksio'nar/ *v.* react.
reaccionario /rreakθio'nario; rreaksio'nario/ *a. & n.* reactionary.
reacondicionar /rreakondiθio'nar; rreakondisio'nar/ *v.* recondition.
reactivo /rreak'tiβo/ *a. & m.* reactive; *Chem.* reagent.
reactor /rreak'tor/ *n. m.* reactor.

real /rre'al/ *a.* royal, regal; real, actual.
realdad /rreal'dað/ *n. f.* royal authority.
realeza /rrea'leθa; rrea'lesa/ *n. f.* royalty.
realidad /rreali'ðað/ *n. f.* reality.
realidad virtual /rreali'ðað βir'tual/ virtual reality.
realista /rrea'lista/ *a. & n.* realistic; realist.
realización /rrealiθa'θion; rrealisa'sion/ *n. f.* achievement, accomplishment.
realizar /rreali'θar; rreali'sar/ *v.* accomplish; fulfill; effect; *Com.* realize.
realmente /rreal'mente/ *adv.* in reality, really.
realzar /rreal'θar; rreal'sar/ *v.* enhance.
reata /rre'ata/ *n. f.* rope; lasso, lariat.
rebaja /rre'βaha/ *n. f.* reduction.
rebajar /rreβa'har/ *v.* cheapen; reduce (in price); lower.
rebanada /rreβa'naða/ *n. f.* slice. —**rebanar,** *v.*
rebaño /rre'βaɲo/ *n. m.* flock, herd.
rebato /rre'βato/ *n. m.* alarm; sudden attack.
rebelarse /rreβe'larse/ *v.* rebel, revolt.
rebelde /rre'βelde/ *a. & n.* rebellious; rebel.
rebelión /rreβe'lion/ *n. f.* rebellion, revolt.
reborde /rre'βorðe/ *n. m.* border.
rebotar /rreβo'tar/ *v.* rebound.
rebozo /rre'βoθo; rre'βoso/ *n. m.* shawl.
rebuscar /rreβus'kar/ *v.* search thoroughly.
rebuznar /rreβuθ'nar; rreβus'nar/ *v.* bray.
recado /rre'kaðo/ *n. m.* message; errand.
recaída /rreka'iða/ *n. f.* relapse. —**recaer,** *v.*
recalcar /rrekal'kar/ *v.* stress, emphasize.
recalentar /rrekalen'tar/ *v.* reheat.
recámara /rre'kamara/ *n. f.* (Mex.) bedroom.
recapitulación /rrekapitula'θion; rrekapitula'sion/ *n. f.* recapitulation.
recapitular /rrekapitu'lar/ *v.* recapitulate.
recatado /rreka'taðo/ *n. m.* coy; prudent.
recaudador /rrekauða'ðor/ **-ra** *n.* tax collector.
recelar /rreθe'lar; rrese'lar/ *v.* fear, distrust.
receloso /rreθe'loso; rrese'loso/ *a.* distrustful.
recepción /rreθep'θion; rresep'sion/ *n. f.* reception.
recepcionista /rreθepθio'nista; rresepsio'nista/ *n. m. & f.* desk clerk.
receptáculo /rreθep'takulo; rresep'takulo/ *n. m.* receptacle.
receptividad /rreθeptiβi'ðað; rresseptiβi'ðað/ *n. f.* receptivity.
receptivo /rreθep'tiβo; rresep'tiβo/ *a.* receptive.
receptor /rreθep'tor; rresep'tor/ *n. m.* receiver.
receta /rre'θeta; rre'seta/ *n. f.* recipe; prescription.
recetar /rreθe'tar; rrese'tar/ *v.* prescribe.
rechazar /rretʃa'θar; rretʃa'sar/ *v.* reject, spurn, discard.
rechinar /rretʃi'nar/ *v.* chatter.
recibimiento /rreθiβi'miento; rresiβi'miento/ *n. m.* reception; welcome; anteroom.
recibir /rreθi'βir; rresi'βir/ *v.* receive.
recibo /rre'θiβo; rre'siβo/ *n. m.* receipt.
reciclaje /reθi'klahe; resi'klahe/ *n. m.* recycling.
reciclar /rreθi'klar; rresi'klar/ *v.* recycle.

recidiva /rreθi'ðiβa; rresi'ðiβa/ *n. f.* relapse.

recién /rre'θien; rre'sien/ *adv.* recently, newly, just.

reciente /rre'θiente; rre'siente/ *a.* recent.

recinto /rre'θinto; rre'sinto/ *n. m.* enclosure.

recipiente /rreθi'piente; rresi'piente/ *n. m.* recipient.

reciprocación /rreθiproka'θion; rresiproka'sion/ *n. f.* reciprocation.

recíprocamente /rreθiproka'mente; rresiproka'mente/ *adv.* reciprocally.

reciprocar /rreθipro'kar; rresipro'kar/ *v.* reciprocate.

reciprocidad /rreθiproθi'ðað; rresiprosi'ðað/ *n. f.* reciprocity.

recitación /rreθita'θion; rresita'sion/ *n. f.* recitation.

recitar /rreθi'tar; rresi'tar/ *v.* recite.

reclamación /rreklama'θion; rreklama'sion/ *n. f.* claim; complaint.

reclamar /rrekla'mar/ *v.* claim; complain.

reclamo /rre'klamo/ *n. m.* claim; advertisement, advertising; decoy.

reclinar /rrekli'nar/ *v.* recline, repose, lean.

recluta /rre'kluta/ *n. m. & f.* recruit.

reclutar /rreklu'tar/ *v.* recruit, draft.

recobrar /rreko'βrar/ *v.* recover, salvage, regain.

recobro /rre'koβro/ *n. m.* recovery.

recoger /rreko'her/ *v.* gather; collect; pick up. **r. el conocimiento,** regain consciousness.

recogerse /rreko'herse/ *v.* retire (for night).

recolectar /rrekolek'tar/ *v.* gather, assemble; harvest.

recomendación /rrekomenda'θion; rrekomenda'sion/ *n. f.* recommendation; commendation.

recomendar /rrekomen'dar/ *v.* recommend; commend.

recompensa /rrekom'pensa/ *n. f.* recompense; compensation.

recompensar /rrekompen'sar/ *v.* reward; compensate.

reconciliación /rrekonθilia'θion; rrekonsilia'sion/ *n. f.* reconciliation.

reconciliar /rrekonθi'liar; rrekonsi'liar/ *v.* reconcile.

reconocer /rrekono'θer; rrekono'ser/ *v.* recognize; acknowledge; inspect, examine; *Mil.* reconnoiter.

reconocimiento /rrekonoθi'miento; rrekonosi'miento/ *n. m.* recognition; appreciation, gratitude.

reconstituir /rrekonsti'tuir/ *v.* reconstitute.

reconstruir /rrekons'truir/ *v.* reconstruct, rebuild.

record /'rrekorð/ *n. m.* (sports) record.

recordar /rrekor'ðar/ *v.* recall, recollect; remind.

recorrer /rreko'rrer/ *v.* go over; read over; cover (distance).

recorte /rre'korte/ *n. m.* clipping, cutting.

recostarse /rrekos'tarse/ *v.* recline, lean back, rest.

recreación /rrekrea'θion; rrekrea'sion/ *n. f.* recreation.

recreo /rre'kreo/ *n. m.* recreation.

recriminación /rrekrimina'θion; rrekrimina'sion/ *n. f.* recrimination.

rectangular /rrektaŋgu'lar/ *a.* rectangular.

rectángulo /rrek'taŋgulo/ *n. m.* rectangle.

rectificación /rrektifika'θion; rrektifika'sion/ *n. f.* rectification.

rectificar /rrektifi'kar/ *v.* rectify.

recto /'rrekto/ *a.* straight; just, fair. **ángulo r.,** right angle.

recuento /rre'kuento/ *n. m.* recount.

recuerdo /rre'kuerðo/ *n. m.* memory; souvenir; remembrance; (*pl.*) regards.

reculada /rreku'laða/ *n. f.* recoil. **—recular,** *v.*

recuperación /rrekupera'θion; rrekupera'sion/ *n. f.* recuperation.

recuperar /rrekupe'rar/ *v.* recuperate.

recurrir /rreku'rrir/ *v.* revert; resort, have recourse.

recurso /rre'kurso/ *n. m.* resource; recourse.

red /rreð/ *n. f.* net; trap. **r. local** local area network.

redacción /rreðak'θion; rreðak'sion/ *n. f.* (editorial) staff; composition (of written material).

redactar /rreðak'tar/ *v.* draft, draw up; edit.

redactor /rreðak'tor/ **-ra** *n.* editor.

redada /rre'ðaða/ *n. f.* netful, catch, haul.

redargución /rreðargu'θion; rreðargu'sion/ *n. f.* retort. **—redargüir,** *v.*

redención /rreðen'θion; rreðen'sion/ *n. f.* redemption, salvation.

redentor /rreðen'tor/ **-ra** *n.* redeemer.

redimir /rreði'mir/ *v.* redeem.

redoblante /rreðo'βlante/ *n. m.* snare drum; snare dummer.

redonda /rre'ðonda/ *n. f.* neighborhood, vicinity.

redondo /rre'ðondo/ *a.* round, circular.

reducción /rreðuk'θion; rreðuk'sion/ *n. f.* reduction.

reducir /rreðu'θir; rreðu'sir/ *v.* reduce.

reembolso /rreem'βolso/ *n. m.* refund. **—reembolsar,** *v.*

reemplazar /rreempla'θar; rreempla'sar/ *v.* replace, supersede.

reencarnación /rreenkarna'θion; rreenkarna'sion/ *n. f.* reincarnation.

reexaminar /rreeksami'nar/ *v.* reexamine.

reexpedir /rreekspe'ðir/ *v.* forward (mail).

referencia /rrefe'renθia; rrefe'rensia/ *n. f.* reference.

referéndum /rrefe'rendum/ *n. m.* referendum.

referir /rrefe'rir/ *v.* relate, report on.

referirse /rrefe'rirse/ *v.* refer.

refinamiento /rrefina'miento/ *n. m.* refinement.

refinar /rrefi'nar/ *v.* refine.

refinería /rrefine'ria/ *n. f.* refinery.

reflejar /rrefle'har/ *v.* reflect; think, ponder.

reflejo /rre'fleho/ *n. m.* reflection; glare.

reflexión /rreflek'sion/ *n. f.* reflection, thought.

reflexionar /rrefleksio'nar/ *v.* reflect, think.

reflujo /rre'fluho/ *n. m.* ebb; ebb tide.

reforma /rre'forma/ *n. f.* reform. **—reformar,** *v.*

reformación /rreforma'θion; rreforma'sion/ *n. f.* reformation.

reformador /rreforma'ðor/ **-ra** *n.* reformer.

reforma tributaria /rre'forma triβu'taria/ tax reform.

reforzar /rrefor'θar; rrefor'sar/ *v.* reinforce, strengthen; encourage.

refractario /rrefrak'tario/ *a.* refractory.

refrán /rre'fran/ *n. m.* proverb, saying.

refrenar /rrefre'nar/ *v.* curb, rein; restrain.

refrescar /rrefres'kar/ *v.* refresh, freshen, cool.

refresco /rre'fresko/ *n. m.* refreshment; cold drink.

refrigeración /rrefrihera'θion; rrefrihera'sion/ *n. f.* refrigeration.

refrigerador /rrefrihera'ðor/ *n. m.* refrigerator.

refrigerar /rrefrihe'rar/ *v.* refrigerate.

refuerzo /rre'fuerθo; rre'fuerso/ *n. m.* reinforcement.

refugiado /rrefu'hiaðo/ **-da** refugee.

refugiarse /rrefu'hiarse/ *v.* take refuge.

refugio /rre'fuhio/ *n. m.* refuge, asylum, shelter.

refulgencia /rreful'henθia; rreful'hensia/ *n. f.* refulgence.

refulgente /rreful'hente/ *a.* refulgent.

refulgir /rreful'hir/ *v.* shine.

refunfuñar /rrefunfu'ɲar/ *v.* mutter, grumble, growl.

refutación /rrefuta'θion; rrefuta'sion/ *n. f.* refutation; rebuttal.

refutar /rrefu'tar/ *v.* refute.

regadera /rrega'ðera/ *n. f.* watering can.

regadizo /rrega'ðiθo; rrega'ðiso/ *a.* irrigable.

regadura /rrega'ðura/ *n. f.* irrigation.

regalar /rrega'lar/ *v.* give (a gift), give away.

regaliz /rrega'liθ; rrega'lis/ *n. m.* licorice.

regalo /rre'galo/ *n. m.* gift, present, **con r.,** in luxury.

regañar /rrega'ɲar/ *v.* reprove; scold.

regaño /rre'gaɲo/ *n. m.* reprimand; scolding.

regar /rre'gar/ *v.* water, irrigate.

regatear /rregate'ar/ *v.* haggle.

regateo /rrega'teo/ *n. m.* bargaining, haggling.

regazo /rre'gaθo; rre'gaso/ *n. m.* lap.

regencia /rre'henθia; rre'hensia/ *n. f.* regency.

regeneración /rrehenera'θion; rrehenera'sion/ *n. f.* regeneration.

regenerar /rrehene'rar/ *v.* regenerate.

regente /rre'hente/ **-ta** *a. & n.* regent.

régimen /'rrehimen/ *n. m.* regime; diet.

regimentar /rrehimen'tar/ *v.* regiment.

regimiento /rrehi'miento/ *n. m.* regiment.

región /rre'hion/ *n. f.* region.

regional /rrehio'nal/ *a.* regional, sectional.

regir /rre'hir/ *v.* rule; be in effect.

registrar /rrehis'trar/ *v.* register; record; search.

registro /rre'histro/ *n. m.* register; record; search.

regla /'rregla/ *n. f.* rule, regulation. **en r.,** in order.

reglamento /rregla'mento/ *n. m.* code of regulations.

regocijarse /rregoθi'harse; rregosi'harse/ *v.* rejoice, exult.

regocijo /rrego'θiho; rrego'siho/ *n. m.* rejoicing; merriment, joy.

regordete /rregor'ðete/ *a.* chubby, plump.

regresar /rregre'sar/ *v.* go back, return.

regresión /rregre'sion/ *n. f.* regression.

regresivo /rregre'siβo/ *a.* regressive.

regreso /rre'greso/ *n. m.* return.

regulación /rregula'θion; rregula'sion/ *n. f.* regulation.

regular /rregu'lar/ *a.* 1. regular; fair, middling. **—v.** 2. regulate.

regularidad /rregulari'ðað/ *n. f.* regularity.

regularmente /rregular'mente/ *adv.* regularly.

rehabilitación /rreaβilita'θion; rreaβilita'sion/ *n. f.* rehabilitation.

rehabilitar /rreaβili'tar/ *v.* rehabilitate.

rehén /rre'en/ *n. m.* hostage.

rehogar /rreo'gar/ *v.* brown.

rehusar /rreu'sar/ *v.* refuse; decline.

reina /'rreina/ *n. f.* queen.

reinado /rrei'naðo/ *n. m.* reign. **—reinar,** *v.*

reino /'rreino/ *n. m.* kingdom; realm; reign.

reír /rre'ir/ *v.* laugh.

reiteración /rreitera'θion; rreitera'sion/ *n. f.* reiteration.

reiterar /rreite'rar/ *v.* reiterate.

reja /'rreha/ *n. f.* grating, grillwork.

relación /rrela'θion; rrela'sion/ *n. f.* relation; account, report.

relacionar /rrelaθio'nar; rrelasio'nar/ *v.* relate, connect.

relajamiento /rrelaha'miento/ *n. m.* laxity, laxness.

relajar /rrela'har/ *v.* relax, slacken.

relámpago /rre'lampago/ *n. m.* lightning; flash (of lightning).

relatador /rrelata'ðor/ **-ra** *n.* teller.

relatar /rrela'tar/ *v.* relate, recount.

relativamente /rrelatiβa'mente/ *adv.* relatively.

relatividad /rrelatiβi'ðað/ *n. f.* relativity.

relativo /rrela'tiβo/ *a.* relative.

relato /rre'lato/ *n. m.* account, story.

relegación /rrelega'θion; rrelega'sion/ *n. f.* relegation.

relegar /rrele'gar/ *v.* relegate.

relevar /rrele'βar/ *v.* relieve.

relicario /rreli'kario/ *n. m.* reliquary; locket.

relieve /rre'lieβe/ *n. m.* (sculpture) relief.

religión /rreli'hion/ *n. f.* religion.

religiosidad /rrelihiosi'ðað/ *n. f.* religiosity.

religioso /rreli'hioso/ **-sa** *a.* 1. religious. **—n.** 2. *m.* member of a religious order.

reliquia /rre'likia/ *n. f.* relic.

rellenar /rreʎe'nar; rreye'nar/ *v.* refill; fill up, stuff.

relleno /rre'ʎeno; rre'yeno/ *n. m.* filling; stuffing.

reloj /rre'loh/ *n. m.* clock; watch.

reloj de pulsera /rre'loh de pul'sera/ wrist watch.

relojería /rrelohe'ria/ *n. f.* watchmaker's shop.

relojero /rrelo'hero/ **-ra** *n.* watchmaker.

relucir /rrelu'θir; rrelu'sir/ *v.* glow, shine; excel.

relumbrar /rrelum'βrar/ *v.* glitter, sparkle.

remache /rre'matʃe/ *n. m.* rivet. **—remachar,** *v.*

remar /rre'mar/ *v.* row (a boat).

rematado /rrema'taðo/ *a.* finished; sold.

remate /rre'mate/ *n. m.* end, finish; auction. **de r.,** utterly.

remedador /rremeða'ðor/ **-ra** *n.* imitator.

remedar /rreme'ðar/ *v.* imitate.

remedio /rre'meðio/ *n. m.* remedy. **—remediar,** *v.*

remendar /rremen'dar/ *v.* mend, patch.

remesa /rre'mesa/ *n. f.* shipment; remittance.

remiendo /rre'miendo/ *n. m.* patch.

remilgado /rremil'gaðo/ *a.* prudish; affected.

reminiscencia /rreminis'θenθia; rreminis'sensia/ *n. f.* reminiscence.

remitir /rremi'tir/ *v.* remit.

remo /'rremo/ *n. m.* oar.

remolacha /rremo'latʃa/ *n. f.* beet.

remolcador /rremolka'ðor/ *n. m.* tug (boat); tow truck.

remolino /rremo'lino/ *n. m.* whirl; whirlpool; whirlwind.

remolque /rre'molke/ *n. m.* tow. **—remolcar,** *v.*

remontar /rremon'tar/ *v.* ascend, go up.

remontarse /rremon'tarse/ *v.* get excited; soar. **r. a,** date from; go back to (in time).

remordimiento /rremorði'miento/ *n. m.* remorse.

remotamente /rremota'mente/ *adv.* remotely.

remoto /rre'moto/ *a.* remote.

remover /rremo'βer/ *v.* remove; stir; shake; loosen.

rempujar /rrempu'har/ *v.* jostle.

remuneración /rremunera'θion; rremunera'sion/ *n. f.* remuneration;

remunerar /rremune'rar/ v. remunerate.

renacido /rrena'θiðo; rrena'siðo/ a. reborn, born-again.

renacimiento /rrenaθi'miento; rrenasi'miento/ n. m. rebirth; renaissance.

rencor /rren'kor/ n. m. rancor, bitterness, animosity; grudge.

rencoroso /rrenko'roso/ a. rancorous, bitter.

rendición /rrendi'θion; rrendi'sion/ n. f. surrender.

rendido /rren'diðo/ a. weary, worn out.

rendir /rren'dir/ v. yield; surrender, give up; win over.

renegado /rrene'gaðo/ **-da** n. renegade.

renglón /rreŋ'glon/ n. m. line; Com. item.

reno /'rreno/ n. m. reindeer.

renombre /rre'nombre/ n. m. renown.

renovación /rrenoβa'θion; rrenoβa'sion/ n. f. renovation, renewal.

renovar /rreno'βar/ v. renew; renovate.

renta /'rrenta/ n. f. income; rent.

rentar /rren'tar/ v. yield; rent.

renuencia /rre'nuenθia; rre'nuensia/ n. f. reluctance.

renuente /rre'nuente/ a. reluctant.

renuncia /rre'nunθia; rre'nunsia/ n. f. resignation; renunciation.

renunciar /rrenun'θiar; rrenun'siar/ v. resign; renounce, give up.

reñir /rre'ɲir/ v. scold, berate; quarrel, wrangle.

reo /'rreo/ a. & n. criminal; convict.

reorganizar /rreorgani'θar; rreorgani'sar/ v. reorganize.

reparación /rrepara'θion; rrepara'sion/ n. f. reparation, atonement; repair.

reparar /rrepa'rar/ v. repair; mend; stop, stay over. **r. en,** notice; consider.

reparo /rre'paro/ n. m. repair; remark; difficulty; objection.

repartición /rreparti'θion; rreparti'sion/ n. f., **repartimiento, reparto,** m. division, distribution.

repartir /rrepar'tir/ v. divide, apportion, distribute; Theat. cast.

repaso /rre'paso/ n. m. review. —**repasar,** v.

repatriación /rrepatria'θion; rrepatria'sion/ n. f. repatriation.

repatriar /rrepa'triar/ v. repatriate.

repeler /rrepe'ler/ v. repel.

repente /rre'pente/ n. m. **de r.,** suddenly; unexpectedly.

repentinamente /rrepentina'mente/ adv. suddenly.

repentino /rrepen'tino/ a. sudden.

repercusión /rreperku'sion/ n. f. repercussion.

repertorio /rreper'torio/ n. m. repertoire.

repetición /rrepeti'θion; rrepeti'sion/ n. f. repetition; action replay.

repetidamente /rrepetiða'mente/ adv. repeatedly.

repetir /rrepe'tir/ v. repeat.

repisa /rre'pisa/ n. f. shelf.

réplica /'rreplika/ n. f. reply; objection; replica.

replicar /rrepli'kar/ v. reply; answer back.

repollo /rre'poʎo; rre'poyo/ n. m. cabbage.

reponer /rrepo'ner/ v. replace; repair.

reponerse /rrepo'nerse/ v. recover, get well.

reporte /rre'porte/ n. m. report; news.

repórter /rre'porter/ **reportero -ra** n. reporter.

reposado /rrepo'saðo/ a. tranquil, peaceful, quiet.

reposo /rre'poso/ n. m. repose, rest. —**reposar,** v.

reposte /rre'poste/ n. f. pantry.

represalia /rrepre'salia/ n. f. reprisal.

representación /rrepresenta'θion; rrepresenta'sion/ n. f. representation; Theat. performance.

representante /rrepresen'tante/ n. m. & f. representative, agent.

representar /rrepresen'tar/ v. represent; depict; Theat. perform.

representativo /rrepresenta'tiβo/ a. representative.

represión /rrepre'sion/ n. f. repression.

represivo /rrepre'siβo/ a. repressive.

reprimenda /rrepri'menda/ n. f. reprimand.

reprimir /rrepri'mir/ v. repress, quell.

reproche /rre'protʃe/ n. m. reproach. —**reprochar,** v.

reproducción /rreproðuk'θion; rreproðuk'sion/ n. f. reproduction.

reproducir /rreproðu'θir; rreproðu'sir/ v. reproduce.

reptil /rrep'til/ n. m. reptile.

república /rre'puβlika/ n. f. republic.

republicano /rrepuβli'kano/ **-na** a. & n. republican.

repudiación /rrepuðia'θion; rrepuðia'sion/ n. f. repudiation.

repudiar /rrepu'ðiar/ v. repudiate; disown.

repuesto /rre'puesto/ n. m. spare part. **de r.,** spare.

repugnancia /rrepug'nanθia; rrepug'nansia/ n. f. repugnance.

repugnante /rrepug'nante/ a. disgusting, repugnant, repulsive, revolting.

repugnar /rrepug'nar/ v. disgust.

repulsa /rre'pulsa/ n. f. refusal; repulse.

repulsivo /rrepul'siβo/ a. repulsive.

reputación /rreputa'θion; rreputa'sion/ n. f. reputation.

reputar /rrepu'tar/ v. repute; appreciate.

requerir /rreke'rir/ v. require.

requesón /rreke'son/ n. m. cottage cheese.

requisición /rrekisi'θion; rekisi'sion/ n. f. requisition.

requisito /rreki'sito/ n. m. requisite, requirement.

res /rres/ n. f. head of cattle.

resaca /rre'saka/ n. f. hangover.

resbalar /rresβa'lar/ v. slide; slip.

resbaloso /rresβa'loso/ a. slippery.

rescate /rres'kate/ n. m. rescue; ransom. —**rescatar,** v.

rescindir /rresθin'dir; rressin'dir/ v. rescind.

resentimiento /rresenti'miento/ n. m. resentment.

resentirse /rresen'tirse/ v. resent.

reserva /rre'serβa/ n. f. reserve. —**reservar,** v.

reservación /rreserβa'θion; rreserβa'sion/ n. f. reservation.

resfriado /rres'friaðo/ n. m. Med. cold.

resfriarse /rres'friarse/ v. catch cold.

resguardar /rresguar'ðar/ v. guard, protect.

residencia /rresi'ðenθia; rresi'ðensia/ n. f. residence; seat, headquarters.

residente /rresi'ðente/ a. & n. resident.

residir /rresi'ðir/ v. reside.

residuo /rre'siðuo/ n. m. remainder.

resignación /rresigna'θion; rresigna'sion/ n. f. resignation.

resignar /rresig'nar/ v. resign.

resina /rre'sina/ n. f. resin; rosin.

resistencia /rresis'tenθia; rresis'tensia/ n. f. resistance.

resistir /rresis'tir/ v. resist; endure.

resolución /rresolu'θion; rresolu'sion/ n. f. resolution.

resolutivamente /rresolutiβa'mente/ adv. resolutely.

resolver /rresol'βer/ v. resolve; solve.

resonante /rreso'nante/ a. resonant.

resonar /rreso'nar/ v. resound.

resorte /rre'sorte/ n. m. Mech. spring.

respaldar /rrespal'dar/ v. endorse; back.

respaldo /rres'paldo/ n. m. back (of a seat).

respectivo /rrespek'tiβo/ a. respective.

respecto /rres'pekto/ n. m. relation, proportion; **r. a,** concerning, regarding.

respetabilidad /rrespetaβili'ðað/ n. f. respectability.

respetable /rrespe'taβle/ a. respectable.

respeto /rres'peto/ n. m. respect. —**respetar,** v.

respetuosamente /rrespetuosa'mente/ adv. respectfully.

respetuoso /rrespe'tuoso/ a. respectful.

respiración /rrespira'θion; rrespira'sion/ n. f. respiration, breath.

respirar /rrespi'rar/ v. breathe.

resplandeciente /rresplande'θiente; rresplande'siente/ a. resplendent.

resplandor /rresplan'dor/ n. m. brightness, glitter.

responder /rrespon'der/ v. respond, answer.

responsabilidad /rresponsaβili'ðað/ n. f. responsibility.

responsable /rrespon'saβle/ a. responsible.

respuesta /rres'puesta/ n. f. answer, response, reply.

resquicio /rres'kiθio; rres'kisio/ n. m. crack, slit.

resta /'rresta/ n. f. subtraction; remainder.

restablecer /rrestaβle'θer; rrestaβle'ser/ v. restore; reestablish.

restablecerse /rrestaβle'θerse; rrestaβle'serse/ v. recover, get well.

restar /rres'tar/ v. remain; subtract.

restauración /rrestaura'θion; rrestaura'sion/ n. f. restoration.

restaurante /rrestau'rante/ n. m. restaurant.

restaurar /rrestau'rar/ v. restore.

restitución /rrestitu'θion; rrestitu'sion/ n. f. restitution.

restituir /rresti'tuir/ v. restore, give back.

resto /'rresto/ n. m. remainder, rest; (pl.) remains.

restorán /rresto'ran/ n. m. restaurant.

restregar /rrestre'gar/ v. rub hard; scrub.

restricción /rrestrik'θion; rrestrik'sion/ n. f. restriction.

restrictivo /rrestrik'tiβo/ a. restrictive.

restringir /rrestriŋ'gir/ v. restrict, curtail.

resucitar /rresuθi'tar; rresusi'tar/ v. revive, resuscitate.

resuelto /rre'suelto/ a. resolute.

resultado /rresul'taðo/ n. m. result.

resultar /rresul'tar/ v. result; turn out; ensue.

resumen /rre'sumen/ n. m. résumé, summary, **en r.,** in brief.

resumir /rresu'mir/ v. sum up.

resurgir /rresur'hir/ v. resurge, reappear.

resurrección /rresurrek'θion; rresurrek'sion/ n. f. resurrection.

retaguardia /rreta'guarðia/ n. f. rear guard.

retal /rre'tal/ n. m. remnant.

retardar /rretar'ðar/ v. retard, slow.

retardo /rre'tarðo/ n. m. delay.

retención /rreten'θion; rreten'sion/ n. f. retention.

retener /rrete'ner/ v. retain, keep; withhold.

reticencia /rreti'θenθia; rreti'sensia/ n. f. reticence.

reticente /rreti'θente; rreti'sente/ a. reticent.

retirada /rreti'raða/ n. f. retreat, retirement.

retirar /rreti'rar/ v. retire, retreat, withdraw.

retiro /rre'tiro/ n. m. retirement.

retorcer /rretor'θer; rretor'ser/ v. wring.

retórica /rre'torika/ n. f. rhetoric.

retórico /rre'toriko/ a. rhetorical.

retorno /rre'torno/ n. m. return.

retozo /rre'toθo; rre'toso/ n. m. frolic, romp. —**retozar,** v.

retozón /rreto'θon; rreto'son/ a. frisky.

retracción /rretrak'θion; rretrak'sion/ n. f. retraction.

retractar /rretrak'tar/ v. retract.

retrasar /rretra'sar/ v. delay, set back.

retrasarse /rretra'sarse/ v. be slow.

retraso /rre'traso/ n. m. delay, lag, slowness.

retratar /rretra'tar/ v. portray; photograph.

retrato /rre'trato/ n. m. portrait; picture, photograph.

retreta /rre'treta/ n. f. Mil. retreat.

retrete /rre'trete/ n. m. toilet.

retribución /rretriβu'θion; rretriβu'sion/ n. f. retribution.

retroactivo /rretroak'tiβo/ a. retroactive.

retroalimentación /rretroalimenta'θion; rretroalimenta'sion/ n. f. feedback.

retroceder /rretroθe'ðer; rretrose'ðer/ v. recede, go back, draw back, back up.

retumbar /rretum'βar/ v. resound, rumble.

reumático /rreu'matiko/ a. rheumatic.

reumatismo /rreuma'tismo/ n. m. rheumatism.

reunión /rreu'nion/ n. f. gathering, meeting, party; reunion.

reunir /rreu'nir/ v. gather, collect, bring together.

reunirse /rreu'nirse/ v. meet, assemble, get together.

reutilizar /rreutili'zar/ v. reuse.

revelación /rreβela'θion; rreβela'sion/ n. f. revelation.

revelar /rreβe'lar/ v. reveal; betray; Phot. develop.

reventa /rre'βenta/ n. f. resale.

reventar /rreβen'tar/ v. burst; split apart.

reventón /rreβen'ton/ n. m. blowout (of tire).

reverencia /rreβeren'θia; rreβeren'sia/ n. f. reverence.

reverendo /rreβe'rendo/ a. reverend.

reverente /rreβe'rente/ a. reverent.

revertir /rreβer'tir/ v. revert.

revés /rre'βes/ n. m. reverse; back, wrong side. **al r.,** just the opposite; inside out.

revisar /rreβi'sar/ v. revise; review.

revisión /rreβi'sion/ n. f. revision.

revista /rre'βista/ n. f. magazine, periodical; review.

revivir /rreβi'βir/ v. revive.

revocación /rreβoka'θion; rreβoka'sion/ n. f. revocation.

revocar /rreβo'kar/ v. revoke, reverse.

revolotear /rreβolote'ar/ v. hover.

revolución /rreβolu'θion; rreβolu'sion/ n. f. revolution.

revolucionario /rreβoluθio'nario; rreβolusio'nario/ **-ria** a. & n. revolutionary.

revolver /rreβol'βer/ v. revolve; stir, agitate.

revólver n. m. revolver, pistol.

revuelta /rre'βuelta/ n. f. revolt; turn.

rey /rrei/ n. m. king.

reyerta /rre'yerta/ n. f. quarrel, wrangle.

rezar /rre'θar; rre'sar/ v. pray.

rezongar /rreθoŋ'gar; rresoŋ'gar/ v. grumble; mutter.

ría /'rria/ n. f. estuary.

riachuelo /rria'tʃuelo/ n. m. creek.

riba /'rriβa/ n. f. embankment.

rico /'rriko/ a. rich, wealthy; delicious.

ridículamente /rriˈðikulamente/ adv. ridiculously.

ridiculizar /rriðikuliˈθar; rriðikuliˈsar/ v. ridicule.

ridículo /rriˈðikulo/ a. & m. ridiculous; ridicule.

riego /ˈrriego/ n. m. irrigation.

rienda /ˈrrienda/ n. f. rein.

riesgo /ˈrriesgo/ n. m. risk, gamble.

rifa /ˈrrifa/ n. f. raffle; lottery; scuffle.

rifle /ˈrrifle/ n. m. rifle.

rígidamente /ˈrrihiðamente/ adv. rigidly.

rigidez /rrihiˈðeθ; rrihiˈðes/ n. f. rigidity.

rígido /ˈrrihiðo/ a. rigid, stiff.

rigor /rriˈgor/ n. m. rigor.

riguroso /rriguˈroso/ a. rigorous, strict.

rima /ˈrrima/ n. f. rhyme. **—rimar,** v.

rimel /rriˈmel/ n. f. mascara.

rincón /rrinˈkon/ n. m. corner, nook.

rinoceronte /rrinoθeˈronte; rrinoseˈronte/ n. m. rhinoceros.

riña /ˈrriɲa/ n. f. quarrel, feud.

riñón /rriˈɲon/ n. m. kidney.

río /ˈrrio/ n. m. river. **r. abajo** downstream, downriver. **r. arriba,** upstream, upriver.

ripio /ˈrripio/ n. m. debris.

riqueza /rriˈkeθa; rriˈkesa/ n. f. wealth.

risa /ˈrrisa/ n. f. laugh; laughter.

risco /ˈrrisko/ n. m. cliff.

risibilidad /rrisiβiliˈðað/ n. f. risibility.

risotada /rrisoˈtaða/ n. f. peal of laughter.

risueño /rriˈsueɲo/ a. cheerful, smiling.

rítmico /ˈrritmiko/ a. rhythmical.

ritmo /ˈrritmo/ n. m. rhythm.

rito /ˈrrito/ n. m. rite.

ritual /rriˈtual/ a. & m. ritual.

rivalidad /rriβaliˈðað/ n. f. rivalry.

rivera /rriˈβera/ n. f. brook.

rizado /rriˈθaðo; rriˈsaðo/ a. curly.

rizo /ˈrriθo; ˈrriso/ n. m. curl. **—rizar,** v.

robar /rroˈβar/ v. rob, steal.

roble /ˈrroβle/ n. m. oak.

roblón /rroˈβlon/ n. m. rivet. **—roblar,** v.

robo /ˈrroβo/ n. m. robbery, theft.

robustamente /rroβustaˈmente/ adv. robustly.

robusto /rroˈβusto/ a. robust.

roca /ˈrroka/ n. f. rock; cliff.

rociada /rroˈθiaða; rroˈsiaða/ n. f. spray, sprinkle. **—rociar,** v.

rocío /rroˈθio; ˈrrosio/ n. m. dew.

rocoso /rroˈkoso/ a. rocky.

rodar /rroˈðar/ v. roll; roam.

rodear /rroðeˈar/ v. surround, encircle.

rodeo /rroˈðeo/ n. m. turn, winding; roundup.

rodilla /rroˈðiʎa; rroˈðiya/ n. f. knee.

rodillo /rroˈðiʎo; rroˈðiyo/ n. m. roller.

rodio /ˈrroðio/ n. m. rhodium.

rododendro /rroðoˈðendro/ n. m. rhododendron.

roedor /rroeˈðor/ n. m. rodent.

roer /rroˈer/ v. gnaw.

rogación /rrogaˈθion; rrogaˈsion/ n. f. request, entreaty.

rogar /rroˈgar/ v. beg, plead with, supplicate.

rojizo /rroˈhiθo; rroˈhiso/ a. reddish.

rojo /ˈrroho/ a. red.

rollizo /rroˈʎiθo; rroˈyiso/ a. chubby.

rollo /ˈrroʎo; ˈrroyo/ n. m. roll; coil.

romadizo /rromaˈðiθo; rromaˈðiso/ n. m. head cold.

romance /rroˈmanθe; rroˈmanse/ n. m. romance; ballad.

románico /rroˈmaniko/ a. Romance.

romano /rroˈmano/ **-na** a. & n. Roman.

romántico /rroˈmantiko/ a. romantic.

romería /rromeˈria/ n. f. pilgrimage; picnic.

romero /rroˈmero/ **-ra** n. pilgrim.

rompecabezas /rrompekaˈβeθas; rrompekaˈβesas/ n. m. puzzle (pastime).

romper /rromˈper/ v. break, smash, shatter; sever; tear.

rompible /rromˈpiβle/ a. breakable.

ron /rron/ n. m. rum.

roncar /rronˈkar/ v. snore.

ronco /ˈrronko/ a. hoarse.

ronda /ˈrronda/ n. f. round.

rondar /rronˈdar/ v. prowl.

ronquido /rronˈkiðo/ n. m. snore.

ronronear /rronroneˈar/ v. purr.

ronzal /rronˈθal; rronˈsal/ n. m. halter.

roña /ˈrroɲa/ n. f. scab; filth.

ropa /ˈrropa/ n. f. clothes, clothing. **r. blanca,** linen. **r. interior,** underwear.

ropa de marca /ˈrropa de ˈmarka/ designer clothing.

ropero /rroˈpero/ n. m. closet.

rosa /ˈrrosa/ n. f. rose. **r. náutica,** compass.

rosado /rroˈsaðo/ a. pink, rosy.

rosal /rroˈsal/ n. m. rose bush.

rosario /rroˈsario/ n. m. rosary.

rosbif /rrosˈβif/ n. m. roast beef.

rosca /ˈrroska/ n. f. thread (of screw).

róseo /ˈrroseo/ a. rosy.

rostro /ˈrrostro/ n. m. face, countenance.

rota /ˈrrota/ n. f. defeat; Naut. course.

rotación /rrotaˈθion; rrotaˈsion/ n. f. rotation.

rotatorio /rrotaˈtorio/ a. rotary.

rótula /ˈrrotula/ n. f. kneecap.

rotulador /rrotulaˈðor/ n. m. felt-tipped pen.

rótulo /ˈrrotulo/ n. m. label. **—rotular,** v.

rotundo /rroˈtundo/ a. round; sonorous.

rotura /rroˈtura/ n. f. break, fracture, rupture.

rozar /rroˈθar; rroˈsar/ v. rub against, chafe; graze.

rubí /rruˈβi/ n. m. ruby.

rubio /ˈrruβio/ **-bia** a. & n. blond.

rubor /rruˈβor/ n. m. blush; bashfulness.

rúbrica /ˈrruβrika/ n. f. caption; scroll.

rucho /ˈrrutʃo/ n. m. donkey.

rudeza /rruˈðeθa; rruˈðesa/ n. f. rudeness; roughness.

rudimentario /rruðimenˈtario/ a. rudimentary.

rudimento /rruðiˈmento/ n. m. rudiment.

rudo /ˈrruðo/ a. rude, rough.

rueda /ˈrrueða/ n. f. wheel.

rueda de feria /ˈrrueða de ˈferia/ Ferris wheel.

ruego /ˈrruego/ n. m. plea; entreaty.

rufián /rruˈfian/ n. m. ruffian.

rufo /ˈrrufo/ a. sandy haired.

rugir /rruˈhir/ v. bellow, roar.

rugoso /rruˈgoso/ a. wrinkled.

ruibarbo /rruiˈβarβo/ n. m. rhubarb.

ruido /ˈrruiðo/ n. m. noise.

ruidoso /rruiˈðoso/ a. noisy.

ruina /ˈrruina/ n. f. ruin, wreck.

ruinar /rruiˈnar/ v. ruin, destroy.

ruinoso /rruiˈnoso/ a. ruinous.

ruiseñor /rruiseˈɲor/ n. m. nightingale.

ruleta /rruˈleta/ n. f. roulette.

rumba /ˈrrumba/ n. f. rumba (dance or music).

rumbo /ˈrrumbo/ n. m. course, direction.

rumor /rruˈmor/ n. m. rumor; murmur.

runrún /rrunˈrun/ n. m. rumor.

ruptura /rrupˈtura/ n. f. rupture, break.

rural /rruˈral/ a. rural.

Rusia /ˈrrusia/ n. f. Russia.

ruso /ˈrruso/ **-sa** a. & n. Russian.

rústico /ˈrrustiko/ **-ca** a. & n. rustic. **en r.,** paperback f.

ruta /ˈrruta/ n. f. route.

rutina /rruˈtina/ n. f. routine.

rutinario /rrutiˈnario/ a. routine.

S

sábado /ˈsaβaðo/ n. m. Saturday.

sábalo /ˈsaβalo/ n. m. shad.

sábana /saˈβana/ n. f. sheet.

sabañon /saβaˈɲon/ n. m. chilblain.

saber /saˈβer/ n. **1.** m. knowledge. —v. **2.** know; learn, find out; know how to; taste. **a s.,** namely, to wit.

sabiduría /saβiðuˈria/ n. f. wisdom; learning.

sabio /ˈsaβio/ **-a 1.** wise; scholarly. —n. **2.** sage; scholar.

sable /ˈsaβle/ n. m. saber.

sabor /saˈβor/ n. m. flavor, taste, savor.

saborear /saβoreˈar/ v. savor, relish.

sabotaje /saβoˈtahe/ n. m. sabotage.

sabroso /saˈβroso/ a. savory, tasty.

sabueso /saˈβueso/ n. m. hound.

sacacorchos /sakaˈkortʃos/ n. m. corkscrew.

sacapuntas /sakaˈpuntas/ n. f. pencil sharpener.

sacar /saˈkar/ v. draw out; take out; take.

sacerdocio /saθerˈðoθio; saserˈðosio/ n. m. priesthood.

sacerdote /saθerˈðote; saserˈðote/ n. m. priest.

saciar /saˈθiar; saˈsiar/ v. satiate.

saco /ˈsako/ n. m. sack, bag, pouch; suit coat, jacket.

sacramento /sakraˈmento/ n. m. sacrament.

sacrificio /sakriˈfiθio; sakriˈfisio/ n. m. sacrifice. **—sacrificar,** v.

sacrilegio /sakriˈlehio/ n. m. sacrilege.

sacristán /sakrisˈtan/ n. m. sexton.

sacro /ˈsakro/ a. sacred, holy.

sacrosanto /sakroˈsanto/ a. sacrosanct.

sacudir /sakuˈðir/ v. shake, jerk, jolt.

sádico /ˈsaðiko/ a. sadistic.

sadismo /saˈðismo/ n. m. sadism.

sagacidad /sagaθiˈðað; sagasiˈðað/ n. f. sagacity.

sagaz /saˈgaθ; saˈgas/ a. sagacious, sage.

sagrado /saˈgraðo/ a. sacred, holy.

sal /sal/ n. f. salt; Colloq. wit.

sala /ˈsala/ n. f. room; living room, parlor; hall, auditorium.

salado /saˈlaðo/ a. salted, salty; Colloq. witty.

salar /saˈlar/ v. salt; steep in brine.

salario /saˈlario/ n. m. salary, wages.

salchicha /salˈtʃitʃa/ n. f. sausage.

sal de la Higuera /sal de la iˈgera/ Epsom salts.

saldo /ˈsaldo/ n. m. remainder, balance; (bargain) sale.

saldo acreedor /ˈsaldo akreeˈðor/ credit balance.

saldo deudor /ˈsaldo deuˈðor/ debit balance.

salero /saˈlero/ n. m. salt shaker.

salida /saˈliða/ n. f. exit, outlet; departure.

salida de urgencia /saˈliða de urˈhenθia; saˈliða de urˈhensia/ emergency exit, fire exit.

salir /saˈlir/ v. go out, come out; set out, leave, start; turn out, result.

salirse de /saˈlirse de/ v. get out of. **s. con la suya,** have one's own way.

salitre /saˈlitre/ n. m. saltpeter.

saliva /saˈliβa/ n. f. saliva.

salmo /ˈsalmo/ n. m. psalm.

salmón /salˈmon/ n. m. salmon.

salmonete /salmoˈnete/ n. m. red mullet.

salmuera /salˈmuera/ n. f. pickle; brine.

salobre /saˈloβre/ a. salty.

salón /saˈlon/ n. m. parlor, living room; hall. **s. de baile,** dance hall. **s. de belleza** beauty parlor.

salpicar /salpiˈkar/ v. spatter, splash.

salpullido /salpuˈʎiðo; salpuˈyiðo/ n. m. rash.

salsa /ˈsalsa/ n. f. sauce; gravy.

saltamontes /saltaˈmontes/ n. m. grasshopper.

salteador /salteaˈðor/ n. m. highwayman.

saltear /salteˈar/ v. hold up, rob; sauté.

salto /ˈsalto/ n. m. jump, leap, spring. **—saltar,** v.

saltón /salˈton/ n. m. grasshopper.

salubre /saˈluβre/ a. salubrious, healthful.

salubridad /saluβriˈðað/ n. f. health.

salud /saˈluð/ n. f. health.

saludable /saluˈðaβle/ a. healthful, wholesome.

saludar /saluˈðar/ v. greet; salute.

saludo /saˈluðo/ n. m. greeting; salutation; salute.

salutación /salutaˈθion; salutaˈsion/ n. f. salutation.

salva /ˈsalβa/ n. f. salvo.

salvación /salβaˈθion; salβaˈsion/ n. f. salvation; deliverance.

salvador /salβaˈðor/ **-ra** n. savior; rescuer.

salvaguardia /salβaˈguarðia/ n. m. safeguard.

salvaje /salˈβahe/ a. & n. savage, wild (person).

salvamento /salβaˈmento/ n. m. salvation; rescue.

salvar /salˈβar/ v. save; salvage; rescue; jump over.

salvavidas /salβaˈβiðas/ n. m. life preserver.

salvia /ˈsalβia/ n. f. sage (plant).

salvo /ˈsalβo/ a. **1.** safe. —prep. **2.** except, save (for). **s. que,** unless.

San /san/ title. Saint.

sanar /saˈnar/ v. heal, cure.

sanatorio /sanaˈtorio/ n. m. sanatorium.

sanción /sanˈθion; sanˈsion/ n. f. sanction. **—sancionar,** v.

sancochar /sankoˈtʃar/ v. parboil.

sandalia /sanˈdalia/ n. f. sandal.

sandez /sanˈdeθ; sanˈdes/ n. f. stupidity.

sandía /sanˈdia/ n. f. watermelon.

saneamiento /saneaˈmiento/ n. m. sanitation.

sangrar /saŋˈgrar/ v. bleed.

sangre /ˈsaŋgre/ n. f. blood.

sangriento /saŋˈgriento/ a. bloody.

sanguinario /saŋgiˈnario/ a. bloodthirsty.

sanidad /saniˈðað/ n. f. health.

sanitario /saniˈtario/ a. sanitary.

sano /ˈsano/ a. healthy, sound, sane; healthful, wholesome.

santidad /santiˈðað/ n. f. sanctity, holiness.

santificar /santifiˈkar/ v. sanctify.

santo /ˈsanto/ **-ta 1.** holy, saintly. —n. **2.** m. saint.

Santo -ta title. Saint.

santuario /sanˈtuario/ n. m. sanctuary, shrine.

saña /ˈsaɲa/ n. f. rage, anger.

sapiente /saˈpiente/ a. wise.

sapo /ˈsapo/ n. m. toad.

saquear /sakeˈar/ v. sack; ransack; plunder.

sarampión /saramˈpion/ n. m. measles.

sarape /saˈrape/ n. m. (Mex.) woven blanket; shawl.

sarcasmo /sarˈkasmo/ n. m. sarcasm.

sarcástico /sarˈkastiko/ a. sarcastic.

sardina /sarˈðina/ n. f. sardine.

sargento /sarˈhento/ n. m. sergeant.

sarna /ˈsarna/ n. f. itch.

sartén /sarˈten/ n. m. frying pan.

sastre /ˈsastre/ n. m. tailor.

satánico /saˈtaniko/ a. satanic.

satélite /saˈtelite/ n. m. satellite.

sátira /'satira/ *n. f.* satire.

satírico /sa'tiriko/ *a. & m.* satirical; satirist.

satirizar /satiri'θar; satiri'sar/ *v.* satirize.

sátiro /'satiro/ *n. m.* satyr.

satisfacción /satisfak'θion; satisfak'sion/ *n. f.* satisfaction.

satisfacer /satisfa'θer; satisfa'ser/ *v.* satisfy.

satisfactorio /satisfak'torio/ *a.* satisfactory.

saturación /satura'θion; satura'sion/ *n. f.* saturation.

saturar /satu'rar/ *v.* saturate.

sauce /'sauθe; 'sause/ *n. m.* willow.

sauna /'sauna/ *n. f.* sauna.

savia /'saβia/ *n. f.* sap.

saxofón /sakso'fon/ **saxófono** *n. m.* saxophone.

saya /'saya/ *n. f.* skirt.

sazón /sa'θon; sa'son/ *n. f.* season; seasoning. **a la s.,** at that time.

sazonar /saθo'nar; saso'nar/ *v.* flavor, season.

se /se/ *pron.* -self, -selves.

seca /'seka/ *n. f.* drought.

secador /seka'ðor/ **secador de pelo** *n. m.* hair dryer.

secante /se'kante/ *a.* **papel s.,** blotting paper.

secar /se'kar/ *v.* dry.

sección /sek'θion; sek'sion/ *n. f.* section.

seco /'seko/ *a.* dry; curt.

secreción /sekre'θion; sekre'sion/ *n. f.* secretion.

secretar /sekre'tar/ *v.* secrete.

secretaría /sekreta'ria/ *n. f.* secretary's office; secretariat.

secretario /sekre'tario/ **-ra** *n.* secretary.

secreto /se'kreto/ *a. & m.* secret.

secta /'sekta/ *n. f.* denomination; sect.

secuela /se'kuela/ *n. f.* result; sequel.

secuestrar /sekues'trar/ *v.* abduct, kidnap; hijack.

secuestro /se'kuestro/ *n. m.* abduction, kidnapping.

secular /seku'lar/ *a.* secular.

secundario /sekun'dario/ *a.* secondary.

sed /seð/ *n. f.* thirst. **tener s., estar con s.,** to be thirsty.

seda /'seða/ *n. f.* silk.

sedar /se'ðar/ *v.* quiet, allay.

sedativo /seða'tiβo/ *a. & m.* sedative.

sede /'seðe/ *n. f.* seat, headquarters.

sedentario /seðen'tario/ *a.* sedentary.

sedición /seði'θion; seði'sion/ *n. f.* sedition.

sedicioso /seði'θioso; seði'sioso/ *a.* seditious.

sediento /se'ðiento/ *a.* thirsty.

sedimento /seði'mento/ *n. m.* sediment.

sedoso /se'ðoso/ *a.* silky.

seducir /seðu'θir; seðu'sir/ *v.* seduce.

seductivo /seðuk'tiβo/ *a.* seductive, alluring.

segar /se'gar/ *v.* reap, harvest; mow.

seglar /seg'lar/ *n. m. & f.* layman, laywoman.

segmento /seg'mento/ *n. m.* segment.

segregar /segre'gar/ *v.* segregate.

seguida /se'giða/ *n. f.* succession. **en s.,** right away, at once.

seguido /se'giðo/ *a.* consecutive.

seguir /se'gir/ *v.* follow; continue, keep on, go on.

según /se'gun/ *prep.* **1.** according to. —*conj.* **2.** as.

segundo /se'gundo/ *a. & m.* second. —**segundar,** *v.*

seguridad /seguri'ðað/ *n. f.* safety, security; assurance.

seguro /se'guro/ *a.* **1.** safe, secure; sure, certain. —*n.* **2.** *m.* insurance.

seis /seis/ *a. & pron.* six.

seiscientos /seis'θientos; seis'sientos/ *a. & pron.* six hundred.

selección /selek'θion; selek'sion/ *n. f.* selection, choice.

seleccionar /selekθio'nar; seleksio'nar/ *v.* select, choose.

selecto /se'lekto/ *a.* select, choice, elite.

sello /'seʎo; 'seyo/ *n. m.* seal; stamp. —**sellar,** *v.*

selva /'selβa/ *n. f.* forest; jungle.

selvoso /sel'βoso/ *a.* sylvan.

semáforo /se'maforo/ *n. m.* semaphore; traffic light.

semana /se'mana/ *n. f.* week.

semana inglesa /se'mana iŋ'glesa/ five-day work week.

semanal /sema'nal/ *a.* weekly.

semana laboral /se'mana laβo'ral/ work week.

semántica /se'mantika/ *n. f.* semantics.

semblante /sem'βlante/ *n. m.* look, expression.

sembrado /sem'βraðo/ *n. m.* sown field.

sembrar /sem'βrar/ *v.* sow, seed.

semejante /seme'hante/ *a.* **1.** like, similar; such (a). —*n.* **2.** *m.* fellow man.

semejanza /seme'hanθa; seme'hansa/ *n. f.* similarity, likeness.

semejar /seme'har/ *v.* resemble.

semilla /se'miʎa; se'miya/ *n. f.* seed.

seminario /semi'nario/ *n. m.* seminary.

sémola /'semola/ *n. f.* semolina.

senado /se'naðo/ *n. m.* senate.

senador /sena'ðor/ **-ra** *n.* senator.

sencillez /senθi'ʎeθ; sensi'yes/ *n. f.* simplicity; naturalness.

sencillo /sen'θiʎo; sen'siyo/ *a.* simple, natural; single.

senda /'senda/ *n. f.* **sendero,** *m.* path, footpath.

senectud /senek'tuð/ *n. f.* old age.

senil /se'nil/ *a.* senile.

seno /'seno/ *n. m.* breast, bosom.

sensación /sensa'θion; sensa'sion/ *n. f.* sensation.

sensacional /sensaθio'nal; sensasio'nal/ *a.* sensational.

sensato /sen'sato/ *a.* sensible, wise.

sensibilidad /sensiβili'ðað/ *n. f.* sensibility; sensitiveness.

sensible /sen'siβle/ *a.* sensitive; emotional.

sensitivo /sensi'tiβo/ *a.* sensitive.

sensual /sen'sual/ *a.* sensual.

sensualidad /sensuali'ðað/ *n. f.* sensuality.

sentar /sen'tar/ *v.* seat. **s. bien,** fit well, be becoming.

sentarse /sen'tarse/ *v.* sit, sit down.

sentencia /sen'tenθia; sen'tensia/ *n. f.* (court) sentence.

sentidamente /sentiða'mente/ *adv.* feelingly.

sentido /sen'tiðo/ *n. m.* meaning, sense; consciousness.

sentido común /sen'tiðo ko'mun/ common sense.

sentimental /sentimen'tal/ *a.* sentimental.

sentimiento /senti'miento/ *n. m.* sentiment, feeling.

sentir /sen'tir/ *v.* feel, sense; hear; regret, be sorry.

seña /'seɲa/ *n. f.* sign, indication; (*pl.*) address.

señal /se'ɲal/ *n. f.* sign, signal; mark.

señalar /seɲa'lar/ *v.* designate, point out; mark.

señal de marcar /se'ɲal de mar'kar/ dial tone.

señor /se'ɲor/ *n. m.* gentleman; lord; (title) Mr., Sir.

señora /se'ɲora/ *n. f.* lady; wife; (title) Mrs., Madam.

señora de la limpieza /se'ɲora de la lim'pieθa; se'ɲora de la lim'piesa/ cleaning woman.

señorita /seɲo'rita/ *n. f.* young lady; (title) Miss.

sépalo /'sepalo/ *n. m.* sepal.

separación /separa'θion; separa'sion/ *n. f.* separation, parting.

separadamente /separaða'mente/ *adv.* separately.

separado /sepa'raðo/ *a.* separate; separated. —**separar,** *v.*

septentrional /septentrio'nal/ *a.* northern.

septiembre /sep'tiembre/ *n. m.* September.

séptimo /'septimo/ *a.* seventh.

sepulcro /se'pulkro/ *n. m.* sepulcher.

sepultar /sepul'tar/ *v.* bury, entomb.

sepultura /sepul'tura/ *n. f.* grave.

sequedad /seke'ðað/ *n. f.* dryness.

sequía /se'kia/ *n. f.* drought.

ser /ser/ *v.* be.

serenata /sere'nata/ *n. f.* serenade.

serenidad /sereni'ðað/ *n. f.* serenity.

sereno /se'reno/ *a.* **1.** serene, calm. —*n.* **2.** *m.* dew; watchman.

ser humano /ser u'mano/ *n.* human being.

serie /'serie/ *n. f.* series, sequence.

seriedad /serie'ðað/ *n. f.* seriousness.

serio /'serio/ *a.* serious. **en s.,** seriously.

sermón /ser'mon/ *n. m.* sermon.

seroso /se'roso/ *a.* watery.

serpiente /ser'piente/ *n. f.* serpent, snake.

serpiente de cascabel /ser'piente de kaska'βel/ rattlesnake.

serrano /se'rrano/ **-na** *n.* mountaineer.

serrar /se'rrar/ *v.* saw.

serrín /se'rrin/ *n. m.* sawdust.

servicial /serβi'θial; serβi'sial/ *a.* helpful, of service.

servicio /ser'βiθio; ser'βisio/ *n. m.* service; toilet.

servidor /serβi'ðor/ **-ra** *n.* servant.

servidumbre /serβi'ðumbre/ *n. f.* bondage; staff of servants.

servil /ser'βil/ *a.* servile, menial.

servilleta /serβi'ʎeta; serβi'yeta/ *n. f.* napkin.

servir /ser'βir/ *v.* serve. **s. para,** be good for.

servirse /ser'βirse/ *v.* help oneself.

sesenta /se'senta/ *a. & pron.* sixty.

sesgo /'sesgo/ *n. m.* slant. —**sesgar,** *v.*

sesión /se'sion/ *n. f.* session; sitting.

seso /'seso/ *n. m.* brain.

seta /'seta/ *n. f.* mushroom.

setecientos /sete'θientos; sete'sientos/ *a. & pron.* seven hundred.

setenta /se'tenta/ *a. & pron.* seventy.

seto /'seto/ *n. m.* hedge.

severamente /seβera'mente/ *adv.* severely.

severidad /seβeri'ðað/ *n. f.* severity.

severo /se'βero/ *a.* severe, strict, stern.

sexismo /sek'sismo/ *n. m.* sexism.

sexista /sek'sista/ *a. & n.* sexist.

sexo /'sekso/ *n. m.* sex.

sexto /'seksto/ *a.* sixth.

sexual /sek'sual/ *a.* sexual.

si /si/ *conj.* if; whether.

sí *pron.* **1.** -self, -selves. —*interj.* **2.** yes.

sico-. See **psicoanálisis, psicología,** etc.

sicómoro /siko'moro/ *n. m.* sycamore.

SIDA /'siða/ *n. m.* AIDS.

sidra /'siðra/ *n. f.* cider.

siempre /'siempre/ *adv.* always. **para s.,** forever. **s. que,** whenever; provided that.

sierra /'sierra/ *n. f.* saw; mountain range.

siervo /'sierβo/ **-va** *n.* slave; serf.

siesta /'siesta/ *n. f.* (afternoon) nap.

siete /'siete/ *a. & pron.* seven.

sifón /si'fon/ *n. m.* siphon; siphon bottle.

siglo /'siglo/ *n. m.* century.

signatura /signa'tura/ *n. f.* *Mus.* signature.

significación /signifika'θion; signifika'sion/ *n. f.* significance.

significado /signifi'kaðo/ *n. m.* meaning.

significante /signifi'kante/ *a.* significant.

significar /signifi'kar/ *v.* signify, mean.

significativo /signifika'tiβo/ *a.* significant.

signo /'signo/ *n. m.* sign, symbol; mark.

siguiente /si'giente/ *a.* following, next.

sílaba /'silaβa/ *n. f.* syllable.

silbar /sil'βar/ *v.* whistle; hiss, boo.

silbato /sil'βato/ **silbido** *n. m.* whistle.

silencio /si'lenθio; si'lensio/ *n. m.* silence, stillness.

silenciosamente /silenθiosa'mente; silensiosa'mente/ *a.* silently.

silencioso /silen'θioso; silen'sioso/ *a.* silent, still.

silicato /sili'kato/ *n. m.* silicate.

silicio /si'liθio; si'lisio/ *n. m.* silicon.

silla /'siʎa; 'siya/ *n. f.* chair; saddle.

sillón /si'ʎon; si'yon/ *n. m.* armchair.

silueta /si'lueta/ *n. f.* silhouette.

silvestre /sil'βestre/ *a.* wild, uncultivated. **fauna s.,** wildlife.

sima /'sima/ *n. f.* chasm; cavern.

simbólico /sim'boliko/ *a.* symbolic.

símbolo /'simbolo/ *n. m.* symbol.

simetría /sime'tria/ *n. f.* symmetry.

simétrico /si'metriko/ *a.* symmetrical.

símil /'simil/ **similar** *a.* similar, alike.

similitud /simili'tuð/ *n. f.* similarity.

simpatía /simpa'tia/ *n. f.* congeniality; friendly feeling.

simpático /sim'patiko/ *a.* likeable, nice, congenial.

simple /'simple/ *a.* simple.

simpleza /sim'pleθa; sim'plesa/ *n. f.* silliness; trifle.

simplicidad /simpliθi'ðað; simplisi'ðað/ *n. f.* simplicity.

simplificación /simplifika'θion; simplifika'sion/ *n. f.* simplification.

simplificar /simplifi'kar/ *v.* simplify.

simular /simu'lar/ *v.* simulate.

simultáneo /simul'taneo/ *a.* simultaneous.

sin /sin/ *prep.* without. **s. sentido,** meaningless.

sinagoga /sina'goga/ *n. f.* synagogue.

sinceridad /sinθeri'ðað; sinseri'ðað/ *n. f.* sincerity.

sincero /sin'θero; sin'sero/ *a.* sincere.

sincronizar /sinkroni'θar; sinkroni'sar/ *v.* synchronize.

sindicato /sindi'kato/ *n. m.* syndicate; labor union.

síndrome /'sindrome/ *n. m.* syndrome.

sinfonía /sinfo'nia/ *n. f.* symphony.

sinfónico /sin'foniko/ *a.* symphonic.

singular /siŋgu'lar/ *a. & m.* singular.

siniestro /si'niestro/ *a.* sinister, ominous.

sino /'sino/ *conj.* but.

sinónimo /si'nonimo/ *n. m.* synonym.

sinrazón /sinra'θon; sinra'son/ *n. f.* wrong, injustice.

sinsabor /sinsa'βor/ *n. m.* displeasure, distaste; trouble.

sintaxis /sin'taksis/ *n. f.* syntax.

síntesis /'sintesis/ *n. f.* synthesis.

sintético /sin'tetiko/ *a.* synthetic.

síntoma /'sintoma/ *n. m.* symptom.

siquiera /si'kiera/ *adv.* **ni s.,** not even.

sirena /si'rena/ *n. f.* siren.

sirviente /sir'βiente/ **-ta** *n.* servant.

sistema /sis'tema/ *n. m.* system.

sistemático /siste'matiko/ *a.* systematic.

sistematizar /sistemati'θar; sistemati'sar/ *v.* systematize.

sitiar /si'tiar/ *v.* besiege.

sitio /'sitio/ *n. m.* site, location, place, spot.

situación /situa'θion; situa'sion/ *n. f.* situation; location.
situar /si'tuar/ *v.* situate; locate.
smoking /'smokiŋg/ *n. m.* tuxedo, dinner jacket.
so /so/ *prep.* under.
soba /'soβa/ *n. f.* massage. **—sobar,** *v.*
sobaco /so'βako/ *n. m.* armpit.
sobaquero /soβa'kero/ *n. f.* armhole.
soberano /soβe'rano/ **-na** *a.* & *n.* sovereign.
soberbia /so'βerβia/ *n. f.* arrogance.
soberbio /so'βerβio/ *a.* superb; arrogant.
soborno /so'βorno/ *n. m.* bribe. **—sobornar,** *v.*
sobra /'soβra/ *n. f.* excess, surplus. **de sobra,** to spare.
sobrado /so'βraðo/ *n. m.* attic.
sobrante /so'βrante/ *a.* & *m.* surplus.
sobras /'soβras/ *n. f.pl.* leftovers.
sobre /'soβre/ *prep.* **1.** about; above, over. **—***n.* **2.** *m.* envelope.
sobrecama /soβre'kama/ *n. f.* bedspread.
sobrecargo /soβre'kargo/ *n. m.* supercargo.
sobredicho /soβre'ðitʃo/ *a.* aforesaid.
sobredosis /soβre'ðosis/ *n. f.* overdose.
sobrehumano /soβreu'mano/ *a.* superhuman.
sobrenatural /soβrenatu'ral/ *a.* supernatural, weird.
sobrepasar /soβrepa'sar/ *v.* surpass.
sobresalir /soβresa'lir/ *v.* excel.
sobretodo /soβre'toðo/ *n. m.* overcoat.
sobrevivir /soβreβi'βir/ *v.* survive, outlive.
sobriedad /soβrie'ðað/ *n. f.* sobriety; moderation.
sobrina /so'βrina/ *n. f.* niece.
sobrino /so'βrino/ *n. m.* nephew.
sobrio /'soβrio/ *a.* sober, temperate.
socarrén /soka'rren/ *n. m.* eaves.
sociable /so'θiaβle; so'siaβle/ *a.* sociable.
social /so'θial; so'sial/ *a.* social.
socialismo /soθia'lismo; sosia'lismo/ *n. m.* socialism.
socialista /soθia'lista; sosia'lista/ *a.* & *n.* socialist.
sociedad /soθie'ðað; sosie'ðað/ *n. f.* society; association.
sociedad de consumo /soθie'ðað de kon'sumo; sosie'ðað de kon'sumo/ consumer society.
socio /'soθio; 'sosio/ **-cia** *n.* associate, partner; member.
sociología /soθiolo'hia; sosiolo'hia/ *n. f.* sociology.
sociológico /soθio'lohiko; sosio'lohiko/ *a.* sociological.
sociólogo /so'θiologo; so'siologo/ **-ga** *n.* sociologist.
socorrista /soko'rrista/ *n. m.* & *f.* lifeguard.
socorro /so'korro/ *n. m.* help, aid. **—socorrer,** *v.*
soda /'soða/ *n. f.* soda.
sodio /'soðio/ *n. m.* sodium.
soez /so'eθ; so'es/ *a.* vulgar.
sofá /so'fa/ *n. m.* sofa, couch.
sofisma /so'fisma/ *n. m.* sophism.
sofista /so'fista/ *n. m.* & *f.* sophist.
sofocación /sofoka'θion; sofoka'sion/ *n. f.* suffocation.
sofocar /sofo'kar/ *v.* smother, suffocate, stifle, choke.
sofrito /so'frito/ *n. m.* sauce of sautéed tomatoes, peppers, onions, and garlic.
software /'sofθwer/ *n. m.* software.
soga /'soga/ *n. f.* rope.
soja /'soha/ *n. f.* soya.
sol /sol/ *n. m.* sun.
solada /so'laða/ *n. f.* dregs.
solanera /sola'nera/ *n. f.* sunburn.
solapa /so'lapa/ *n. f.* lapel.
solar /so'lar/ *a.* **1.** solar. **—***n.* **2.** *m.* building lot.
solaz /so'laθ; so'las/ *n. m.* solace, comfort. **—solazar,** *v.*
soldado /sol'daðo/ *n. m.* soldier.
soldar /sol'dar/ *v.* solder, weld.
soledad /sole'ðað/ *n. f.* solitude, privacy.
solemne /so'lemne/ *a.* solemn.
solemnemente /solemne'mente/ *adv.* solemnly.
solemnidad /solemni'ðað/ *n. f.* solemnity.
soler /so'ler/ *v.* be in the habit of.
solicitador /soliθita'ðor; solisita'ðor/ **-ra** *n.* applicant, petitioner.
solicitar /soliθi'tar; solisi'tar/ *v.* solicit; apply for.
solícito /so'liθito; so'lisito/ *a.* solicitous.
solicitud /soliθi'tuð; solisi'tuð/ *n. f.* solicitude; application.
sólidamente /soliða'mente/ *adv.* solidly.
solidaridad /soliðari'ðað/ *n. f.* solidarity.
solidez /soli'ðeθ; soli'ðes/ *n. f.* solidity.
solidificar /soliðifi'kar/ *v.* solidify.
sólido /'soliðo/ *a.* & *m.* solid.
soliloquio /soli'lokio/ *n. m.* soliloquy.
solitario /soli'tario/ *a.* solitary, lone.
sollozo /so'ʎoθo; so'yoso/ *n. m.* sob. **—sollozar,** *v.*
solo /'solo/ *a.* **1.** only; single; alone; lonely. **a solas,** alone. **—***n.* **2.** *m. Mus.* solo.
sólo *adv.* only, just.
solomillo /solo'miʎo; solo'miyo/ *n. m.* sirloin.
soltar /sol'tar/ *v.* release; loosen.
soltero /sol'tero/ **-ra** *a.* & *n.* single, unmarried (person).
soltura /sol'tura/ *n. f.* poise, ease, facility.
solubilidad /soluβili'ðað/ *n. f.* solubility.
solución /solu'θion; solu'sion/ *n. f.* solution.
solucionar /soluθio'nar; solusio'nar/ *v.* solve, settle.
solvente /sol'βente/ *a.* solvent.
sombra /'sombra/ *n. f.* shade; shadow. **—sombrear,** *v.*
sombra de ojos /'sombra de 'ohos/ eye shadow.
sombrerera /sombre'rera/ *n. f.* hatbox.
sombrero /som'βrero/ *n. m.* hat.
sombrilla /som'βriʎa; som'βriya/ *n. f.* parasol.
sombrío /som'βrio/ *a.* somber, bleak, gloomy.
sombroso /som'βroso/ *a.* very shady.
someter /some'ter/ *v.* subject; submit.
somnífero /som'nifero/ *n. m.* sleeping pill.
somnolencia /somno'lenθia; somno'lensia/ *n. f.* drowsiness.
son /son/ *n. m.* sound. **—sonar,** *v.*
sonata /so'nata/ *n. f.* sonata.
sondar /son'dar/ *v.* sound, fathom.
sonido /so'niðo/ *n. m.* sound.
sonoridad /sonori'ðað/ *n. f.* sonority.
sonoro /so'noro/ *a.* sonorous.
sonrisa /son'risa/ *n. f.* smile. **—sonreír,** *v.*
sonrojo /son'roho/ *n. m.* flush, blush. **—sonrojarse,** *v.*
soñador /soɲa'ðor/ **-ra** *a.* & *n.* dreamy; dreamer.
soñar /so'ɲar/ *v.* dream.
soñoliento /soɲo'liento/ *a.* sleepy.
sopa /'sopa/ *n. f.* soup.
soplar /so'plar/ *v.* blow.
soplete /so'plete/ *n. m.* blowtorch.
soplo /'soplo/ *n. m.* breath; puff, gust.
soportar /sopor'tar/ *v.* abide, bear, stand.
soprano /so'prano/ *n. m.* & *f.* soprano.
sorbete /sor'βete/ *n. m.* sherbet.
sorbo /'sorβo/ *n. m.* sip. **—sorber,** *v.*
sordera /sor'ðera/ *n. f.* deafness.
sórdidamente /sorðiða'mente/ *adv.* sordidly.
sordidez /sorði'ðeθ; sorði'ðes/ *n. f.* sordidness.
sórdido /'sorðiðo/ *a.* sordid.
sordo /'sorðo/ *a.* deaf; muffled, dull.
sordomudo /sorðo'muðo/ **-da** *a.* & *n.* deaf-mute.
sorpresa /sor'presa/ *n. f.* surprise. **—sorprender,** *v.*
sorteo /sor'teo/ *n. m.* drawing lots; raffle.
sortija /sor'tiha/ *n. f.* ring.
sosa /'sosa/ *n. f. Chem.* soda.
soso /'soso/ *a.* dull, insipid, tasteless.
sospecha /sos'petʃa/ *n. f.* suspicion.
sospechar /sospe'tʃar/ *v.* suspect.
sospechoso /sospe'tʃoso/ *a.* suspicious.
sostén /sos'ten/ *n. m.* bra, brassiere; support.
sostener /soste'ner/ *v.* hold, support; maintain.
sostenimiento /sosteni'miento/ *n. m.* sustenance.
sota /'sota/ *n. f.* jack (in cards).
sótano /'sotano/ *n. m.* basement, cellar.
soto /'soto/ *n. m.* grove.
soviet /so'βiet/ *n. m.* soviet.
soya /'soya/ *n. f.* soybean.
su /su/ *a.* his, her, its, their, your.
suave /'suaβe/ *a.* smooth; gentle, soft, mild.
suavidad /suaβi'ðað/ *n. f.* smoothness; gentleness, softness, mildness.
suavizar /suaβi'θar; suaβi'sar/ *v.* soften.
subalterno /suβal'terno/ **-na** *a.* & *n.* subordinate.
subasta /su'βasta/ *n. f.* auction.
subcampeón /suβkampe'on/ **-na** *n.* runner-up.
subconsciencia /suβkons'θienθia; suβkons'siensia/ *n. f.* subconscious.
súbdito /'suβðito/ **-ta** *n.* subject.
subestimar /suβesti'mar/ *v.* underestimate.
subida /su'βiða/ *n. f.* ascent, rise.
subilla /su'βiʎa; su'βiya/ *n. f.* awl.
subir /su'βir/ *v.* rise, climb, ascend, mount. **s. a,** amount to.
súbito /'suβito/ *a.* sudden.
subjetivo /suβhe'tiβo/ *a.* subjective.
subjuntivo /suβhun'tiβo/ *a.* & *m.* subjunctive.
sublimación /suβlima'θion; suβlima'sion/ *n. f.* sublimation.
sublimar /suβli'mar/ *v.* elevate; sublimate.
sublime /su'βlime/ *a.* sublime.
submarinismo /suβmari'nismo/ *n. m.* scuba diving.
submarino /suβma'rino/ *a.* & *m.* submarine.
subordinación /suβorðina'θion; suβorðina'sion/ *n. f.* subordination.
subordinado /suβorði'naðo/ **-da** *a.* & *n.* subordinate. **—subordinar,** *v.*
subrayar /suβra'yar/ *v.* underline.
subscri- = suscri-
subscribirse /suβskri'βirse/ *v.* subscribe; sign one's name.
subscripción /suβskrip'θion; suβskrip'sion/ *n. f.* subscription.
subsecuente /suβse'kuente/ *a.* subsequent.
subsidiario /suβsi'ðiario/ *a.* subsidiary.
subsiguiente /suβsi'giente/ *a.* subsequent.
substan- = sustan-
substi- = susti-
substraer /suβstra'er/ = subtract.
subsuelo /suβ'suelo/ *n. m.* subsoil.
subterfugio /suβter'fuhio/ *n. m.* subterfuge.
subterráneo /suβte'rraneo/ *a.* **1.** subterranean, underground. **—***n.* **2.** *m.* place underground; subway.
subtítulo /suβ'titulo/ *n. m.* subtitle.
suburbio /su'βurβio/ *n. m.* suburb.
subvención /suββen'θion; suββen'sion/ *n. f.* subsidy, grant.
subversión /suββer'sion/ *n. f.* subversion.
subversivo /suββer'siβo/ *a.* subversive.
subvertir /suββer'tir/ *v.* subvert.
subyugación /suβyuga'θion; suβyuga'sion/ *n. f.* subjugation.
subyugar /suβyu'gar/ *v.* subjugate, quell.
succión /suk'θion; suk'sion/ *n. f.* suction.
suceder /suθe'ðer; suse'ðer/ *v.* happen, occur, befall. **s. a,** succeed, follow.
sucesión /suθe'sion; suse'sion/ *n. f.* succession.
sucesivo /suθe'siβo; suse'siβo/ *a.* successive. **en lo s.,** in the future.
suceso /su'θeso; su'seso/ *n. m.* event.
sucesor /suθe'sor; suse'sor/ **-ra** *n.* successor.
suciedad /suθie'ðað; susie'ðað/ *n. f.* filth, dirt.
sucio /'suθio; 'susio/ *a.* filthy, dirty.
suculento /suku'lento/ *a.* succulent.
sucumbir /sukum'βir/ *v.* succumb.
sud /suð/ *n. m.* south.
sudadera /suða'ðera/ *n. f.* sweatshirt.
Sudáfrica /su'ðafrika/ *n. f.* South Africa.
sudafricano /suðafri'kano/ **-na** *a.* & *n.* South African.
sudamericano /suðameri'kano/ **-na** *a.* & *n.* South American.
sudar /su'ðar/ *v.* perspire, sweat.
sudeste /su'ðeste/ *n. m.* southeast.
sudoeste /suðo'este/ *n. m.* southwest.
sudor /su'ðor/ *n. m.* perspiration, sweat.
Suecia /'sueθia; 'suesia/ *n. f.* Sweden.
sueco /'sueko/ **-ca** *a.* & *n.* Swedish; Swede.
suegra /'suegra/ *n. f.* mother-in-law.
suegro /'suegro/ *n. m.* father-in-law.
suela /'suela/ *n. f.* sole.
sueldo /'sueldo/ *n. m.* salary, wages.
suelo /'suelo/ *n. m.* soil; floor; ground.
suelto /'suelto/ *a.* **1.** loose; free; odd, separate. **—***n.* **2.** loose change.
sueño /'sueɲo/ *n. m.* sleep; sleepiness; dream. **tener s.,** to be sleepy.
suero /'suero/ *n. m.* serum.
suerte /'suerte/ *n. f.* luck; chance; lot.
suéter /'sueter/ *n. m.* sweater.
suficiente /sufi'θiente; sufi'siente/ *a.* sufficient.
sufragio /su'frahio/ *n. m.* suffrage.
sufrimiento /sufri'miento/ *n. m.* suffering, agony.
sufrir /su'frir/ *v.* suffer; undergo; endure.
sugerencia /suhe'renθia; suhe'rensia/ *n. f.* suggestion.
sugerir /suhe'rir/ *v.* suggest.
sugestión /suhes'tion/ *n. f.* suggestion.
sugestionar /suhestio'nar/ *v.* influence; hypnotize.
suicida /sui'θiða; sui'siða/ *n. m.* & *f.* suicide (person).
suicidarse /suiθi'ðarse; suisi'ðarse/ *v.* commit suicide.
suicidio /sui'θiðio; sui'siðio/ *n. m.* (act of) suicide.
Suiza /'suiθa; 'suisa/ *n. f.* Switzerland.
suizo /'suiθo; 'suiso/ **-za** *a.* & *n.* Swiss.
sujeción /suhe'θion; suhe'sion/ *n. f.* subjection.
sujetador /suheta'ðor/ *n. m.* bra, brassiere.
sujetapapeles /su'hetapa'peles/ *n. m.* paper clip.
sujetar /suhe'tar/ *v.* hold, fasten, clip.
sujeto /su'heto/ *a.* **1.** subject, liable. **—***n.* **2.** *m. Gram.* subject.
sulfato /sul'fato/ *n. m.* sulfate.
sulfuro /sul'furo/ *n. m.* sulfide.
sultán /sul'tan/ *n. m.* sultan.
suma /'suma/ *n. f.* sum, amount. **en s.,** in short. **s. global,** lump sum.
sumar /su'mar/ *v.* add up.
sumaria /su'maria/ *n. f.* indictment.
sumario /su'mario/ *a.* & *m.* summary.

sumergir /sumer'hir/ v. submerge.

sumersión /sumer'sion/ n. f. submersion.

sumisión /sumi'sion/ n. f. submission.

sumiso /su'miso/ a. submissive.

sumo /'sumo/ a. great, high, utmost.

suntuoso /sun'tuoso/ a. sumptuous.

superar /supe'rar/ v. overcome, surpass.

superficial /superfi'θial; superfi'sial/ a. superficial, shallow.

superficie /super'fiθie; super'fisie/ n. f. surface.

superfluo /su'perfluo/ a. superfluous.

superhombre /super'ombre/ n. m. superman.

superintendente /superinten'dente/ n. m. & f. superintendent.

superior /supe'rior/ a. **1.** superior; upper, higher. —n. **2.** m. superior.

superioridad /superiori'ðað/ n. f. superiority.

superlativo /superla'tiβo/ n. m. & a. superlative.

superstición /supersti'θion; supersti'sion/ n. f. superstition.

supersticioso /supersti'θioso; supersti'sioso/ a. superstitious.

supervisar /superβi'sar/ v. supervise.

supervivencia /superβi'βenθia; superβi'βensia/ n. f. survival.

suplantar /suplan'tar/ v. supplant.

suplementario /suplemen'tario/ a. supplementary.

suplemento /suple'mento/ n. m. supplement. —**suplementar,** v.

suplente /su'plente/ a. & n. substitute.

súplica /'suplika/ n. f. request, entreaty, plea.

suplicación /suplika'θion; suplika'sion/ n. f. supplication; request, entreaty.

suplicar /supli'kar/ v. request, entreat; implore.

suplicio /su'pliθio; su'plisio/ n. m. torture, ordeal.

suplir /su'plir/ v. supply.

suponer /supo'ner/ v. suppose, presume, assume.

suposición /suposi'θion; suposi'sion/ n. f. supposition, assumption.

supositorio /suposi'torio/ n. m. suppository.

supremacía /suprema'θia; suprema'sia/ n. f. supremacy.

supremo /su'premo/ a. supreme.

supresión /supre'sion/ n. f. suppression.

suprimir /supri'mir/ v. suppress; abolish.

supuesto /su'puesto/ a. supposed. **por s.,** of course.

sur /sur/ n. m. south.

surco /'surko/ n. m. furrow. —**surcar,** v.

surgir /sur'hir/ v. arise; appear suddenly.

surtido /sur'tiðo/ n. m. assortment; supply, stock.

surtir /sur'tir/ v. furnish, supply.

susceptibilidad /susθeptiβili'ðað; susseptiβili'ðað/ n. f. susceptibility.

susceptible /susθep'tiβle; sussep'tiβle/ a. susceptible.

suscitar /susθi'tar; sussi'tar/ v. stir up.

suspender /suspen'der/ v. withhold; suspend; fail (in a course).

suspensión /suspen'sion/ n. f. suspension.

suspenso /sus'penso/ n. m. failing grade. **en s.,** in suspense.

suspicacia /suspi'kaθia; suspi'kasia/ n. f. suspicion, distrust.

suspicaz /suspi'kaθ; suspi'kas/ a. suspicious.

suspicazmente /suspikaθ'mente; suspikas'mente/ adv. suspiciously.

suspiro /sus'piro/ n. m. sigh. —**suspirar,** v.

sustancia /sus'tanθia; sus'tansia/ n. f. substance.

sustancial /sus'tanθial; sus'tansial/ a. substantial.

sustantivo /sustan'tiβo/ n. m. substantive, noun.

sustentar /susten'tar/ v. sustain, support.

sustento /sus'tento/ n. m. sustenance, support, living.

sustitución /sustitu'θion; sustitu'sion/ n. f. substitution.

sustituir /susti'tuir/ v. replace; substitute.

sustitutivo /sustitu'tiβo/ a. substitute.

sustituto /susti'tuto/ **-ta** n. substitute.

susto /'susto/ n. m. fright, scare.

susurro /su'surro/ n. m. rustle; whisper. —**susurrar,** v.

sutil /'sutil/ a. subtle.

sutileza /suti'leθa, suti'liðað; suti'lesa, sutili'ðað/ **sutilidad** n. f. subtlety.

sutura /su'tura/ n. f. suture.

suyo /'suyo/ a. his, hers, theirs, yours.

T

tabaco /ta'βako/ n. m. tobacco.

tábano /'taβano/ n. m. horsefly.

tabaquería /taβake'ria/ n. f. tobacco shop.

taberna /ta'βerna/ n. f. tavern, bar.

tabernáculo /taβer'nakulo/ n. m. tabernacle.

tabique /ta'βike/ n. m. dividing wall, partition.

tabla /'taβla/ n. f. board, plank; table, list. **t. de planchar,** ironing board.

tablado /ta'βlaðo/ n. m. stage, platform.

tablero /ta'βlero/ n. m. panel.

tableta /ta'βleta/ n. f. tablet.

tablilla /ta'βliʎa; ta'βliya/ n. f. bulletin board.

tabú /ta'βu/ n. m. taboo.

tabular /taβu'lar/ a. tabular.

tacaño /ta'kaɲo/ a. stingy.

tacha /'tatʃa/ n. f. fault, defect.

tachar /ta'tʃar/ v. find fault with; cross out.

tachuela /ta'tʃuela/ n. f. tack.

tácitamente /'taθitamente; 'tasitamente/ adv. tacitly.

tácito /'taθito; 'tasito/ a. tacit.

taciturno /taθi'turno; tasi'turno/ a. taciturn.

taco /'tako/ n. m. heel (of shoe); billiard cue.

tacón /ta'kon/ n. m. heel (of shoe).

táctico /'taktiko/ a. tactical.

tacto /'takto/ n. m. (sense of) touch; tact.

tafetán /tafe'tan/ n. m. taffeta.

taimado /tai'maðo/ a. sly.

tajada /ta'haða/ n. cut, slice. —**tajar,** v.

tajea /ta'hea/ n. f. channel.

tal /tal/ a. such. **con t. que.,** provided that. **t. vez,** perhaps.

taladrar /tala'ðrar/ v. drill.

taladro /ta'laðro/ n. m. Mech. drill.

talante /ta'lante/ n. m. humor, disposition.

talco /'talko/ n. m. talc.

talega /ta'lega/ n. f. bag, sack.

talento /ta'lento/ n. m. talent.

talla /'taʎa; 'taya/ n. f. engraving; stature; size (of suit).

tallador /taʎa'ðor; taya'ðor/ **-ra** n. engraver; dealer (at cards).

talle /'taʎe; 'taye/ n. m. figure; waist; fit.

taller /ta'ʎer; ta'yer/ n. m. workshop, factory.

tallo /'taʎo; 'tayo/ n. m. stem, stalk.

talón /ta'lon/ n. m. heel (of foot); (baggage) check, stub.

tamal /ta'mal/ n. m. tamale.

tamaño /ta'maɲo/ n. m. size.

tambalear /tambale'ar/ v. stagger, totter.

también /tam'bien/ adv. also, too.

tambor /tam'bor/ n. m. drum.

tamiz /ta'miθ; ta'mis/ n. m. sieve, sifter.

tampoco /tam'poko/ adv. neither, either.

tan /tan/ adv. so.

tanda /'tanda/ n. f. turn, relay.

tándem /'tandem/ n. m. tandem; pair.

tangencia /taŋ'genθia; taŋ'gensia/ n. f. tangency.

tangible /taŋ'giβle/ a. tangible.

tango /'taŋgo/ n. m. tango (dance or music).

tanque /'tanke/ n. m. tank.

tanteo /tan'teo/ n. m. estimate. —**tantear,** v.

tanto /'tanto/ a. & pron. **1.** so much, so many; as much, as many. **entre t., mientras t.,** meanwhile. **por lo t.,** therefore. **un t.,** somewhat, a bit. —n. **2.** m. point (in games) **3.** (pl.) score. **estar al t.,** to be up to date.

tañer /ta'ɲer/ v. play (an instrument); ring (bells).

tapa /'tapa/ n. f. cap, cover; snack served in a bar. —**tapar,** v.

tapadero /tapa'ðero/ n. m. stopper, lid.

tápara /'tapara/ n. f. caper.

tapete /ta'pete/ n. m. small rug, mat, cover.

tapia /'tapia/ n. f. wall.

tapicería /tapiθe'ria; tapise'ria/ n. f. tapestry.

tapioca /ta'pioka/ n. f. tapioca.

tapiz /ta'piθ; ta'pis/ n. m. tapestry; carpet.

tapizado (de pared) /tapi'θaðo de pa'reð tapi'saðo de pa'reð/ n. m. (wall) covering.

tapón /ta'pon/ n. m. plug; cork.

taquigrafía /takigra'fia/ n. f. shorthand.

taquilla /ta'kiʎa; ta'kiya/ n. f. ticket office; box office; ticket window.

tara /'tara/ n. f. hang-up.

tarántula /ta'rantula/ n. f. tarantula.

tararear /tarare'ar/ v. hum.

tardanza /tar'ðanθa; tar'ðansa/ n. f. delay; lateness.

tardar /tar'ðar/ v. delay; be late; take (of time). **a más t.,** at the latest.

tarde /'tarðe/ adv. **1.** late. —n. **2.** f. afternoon.

tardío /tar'ðio/ a. late, belated.

tarea /ta'rea/ n. f. task, assignment.

tarifa /ta'rifa/ n. f. rate; tariff; price list.

tarjeta /tar'heta/ n. f. card.

tarjeta bancaria /tar'heta ban'karia/ bank card.

tarjeta de crédito /tar'heta de 'kreðito/ credit card.

tarjeta de embarque /tar'heta de em'βarke/ boarding pass.

tarta /'tarta/ n. f. tart.

tartamudear /tartamuðe'ar/ v. stammer, falter.

tasa /'tasa/ n. f. rate.

tasación /tasa'θion; tasa'sion/ n. f. valuation.

tasar /ta'sar/ v. assess, appraise.

tasca /'taska/ n. f. bar, pub.

tasugo /ta'sugo/ n. m. badger.

tatuar /tatu'ar/ v. tattoo.

tautología /tautolo'hia/ n. f. tautology.

taxi /'taksi/ **taxímetro** n. m. taxi.

taxista /tak'sista/ n. m. & f. taxi driver.

taxonomía /taksono'mia/ n. f. taxonomy.

taza /'taθa; 'tasa/ n. f. cup.

te /te/ pron. you; yourself.

té n. m. tea.

team /tim/ n. m. team.

teátrico /te'atriko/ a. theatrical.

teatro /te'atro/ n. m. theater.

tebeo /te'βeo/ n. m. comic book.

techo /'tetʃo/ n. m. roof. —**techar,** v.

tecla /'tekla/ n. f. key (of a piano, etc.).

teclado /te'klaðo/ n. m. keyboard.

teclado numérico /te'klaðo nu'meriko/ numeric keypad.

técnica /'teknika/ n. f. technique.

técnicamente /'teknikamente/ adv. technically.

técnico /'tekniko/ a. **1.** technical; —m. **2.** repairman, technician.

tecnología /teknolo'hia/ n. f. technology.

tedio /'teðio/ n. m. tedium, boredom.

tedioso /te'ðioso/ a. tedious.

teísmo /te'ismo/ n. m. theism.

teja /'teha/ n. f. tile.

tejado /te'haðo/ n. m. roof.

tejano /te'hano/ **-na** a. & n. Texan.

tejanos /te'hanos/ n. m.pl. jeans.

tejer /te'her/ v. weave; knit.

tejido /te'hiðo/ n. m. fabric; weaving.

tejón /te'hon/ n. m. badger.

tela /'tela/ n. f. cloth, fabric, web. **t. metálica,** screen; screening. **t. vaquera,** denim.

telar /te'lar/ n. m. loom.

telaraña /tela'raɲa/ n. f. cobweb, spiderweb.

telefonista /telefo'nista/ n. m. & f. (telephone) operator.

teléfono /te'lefono/ n. m. telephone. —**telefonear,** v.

teléfono gratuito /te'lefono gra'tuito/ toll-free number.

teléfono público /te'lefono 'puβliko/ pay phone, public telephone.

teléfono rojo /te'lefono 'rroho/ hotline.

telégrafo /te'legrafo/ n. m. telegraph. —**telegrafear,** v.

telegrama /tele'grama/ n. m. telegram.

telescopio /teles'kopio/ n. m. telescope.

televisión /teleβi'sion/ n. f. television.

telón /te'lon/ n. m. Theat. curtain.

telurio /te'lurio/ n. m. tellurium.

tema /'tema/ n. m. theme, subject.

temblar /tem'blar/ v. tremble, quake; shake, shiver.

temblor /tem'blor/ n. m. tremor; shiver.

temer /te'mer/ v. fear, be afraid of, dread.

temerario /teme'rario/ a. rash.

temeridad /temeri'ðað/ n. f. temerity.

temerosamente /temerosa'mente/ adv. timorously.

temeroso /teme'roso/ a. fearful.

temor /te'mor/ n. m. fear.

témpano /'tempano/ n. m. kettledrum; iceberg.

temperamento /tempera'mento/ n. m. temperament.

temperancia /tempe'ranθia; tempe'ransia/ n. f. temperance.

temperatura /tempera'tura/ n. f. temperature.

tempestad /tempes'tað/ n. f. tempest, storm.

tempestuoso /tempes'tuoso/ a. tempestuous, stormy.

templado /tem'plaðo/ a. temperate, mild, moderate.

templanza /tem'planθa; tem'plansa/ n. f. temperance; mildness.

templar /tem'plar/ v. temper; tune (an instrument).

templo /'templo/ n. m. temple.

temporada /tempo'raða/ n. f. season, time, spell.

temporal /tempo'ral/ **temporáneo** *a.* temporary.
temprano /tem'prano/ *a.* & *adv.* early.
tenacidad /tenaθi'ðað; tenasi'ðað/ *n. f.* tenacity.
tenaz /te'naθ; te'nas/ *a.* tenacious, stubborn.
tenazmente /tenaθ'mente; tenas'mente/ *adv.* tenaciously.
tendencia /ten'denθia; tendensia/ *n. f.* tendency, trend.
tender /ten'der/ *v.* stretch, stretch out.
tendero /ten'dero/ **-ra** *n.* shopkeeper, storekeeper.
tendón /ten'don/ *n. m.* tendon, sinew.
tenebrosidad /teneβrosi'ðað/ *n. f.* gloom.
tenebroso /tene'βroso/ *a.* dark, gloomy.
tenedor /tene'ðor/ *n.* **1.** *m.* & *f.* keeper; holder. **2.** *m.* fork.
tener /te'ner/ *v.* have; own; hold. **t. que,** have to, must.
teniente /te'niente/ *n. m.* lieutenant.
tenis /'tenis/ *n. m.* tennis; (*pl.*) sneakers.
tenor /te'nor/ *n. m.* tenor.
tensión /ten'sion/ *n. f.* tension, stress, strain.
tenso /'tenso/ *a.* tense.
tentación /tenta'θion; tenta'sion/ *n. f.* temptation.
tentáculo /ten'takulo/ *n. m.* tentacle.
tentador /tenta'ðor/ *a.* alluring, tempting.
tentar /ten'tar/ *v.* tempt, lure; grope, probe.
tentativa /tenta'tiβa/ *n. f.* attempt.
tentativo /tenta'tiβo/ *a.* tentative.
teñir /te'ɲir/ *v.* tint, dye.
teología /teolo'hia/ *n. f.* theology.
teológico /teo'lohiko/ *a.* theological.
teoría /teo'ria/ *n. f.* theory.
teórico /te'oriko/ *a.* theoretical.
terapéutico /tera'peutiko/ *a.* therapeutic.
tercero /ter'θero; ter'sero/ *a.* third.
tercio /'terθio; 'tersio/ *n. m.* third.
terciopelo /terθio'pelo; tersio'pelo/ *n. m.* velvet.
terco /'terko/ *a.* obstinate, stubborn.
termal /ter'mal/ *a.* thermal.
terminación /termina'θion; termina'sion/ *n. f.* termination; completion.
terminal aérea /termi'nal 'airea/ *n. f.* air terminal.
terminar /termi'nar/ *v.* terminate, finish.
término /'termino/ *n. m.* term; end.
terminología /terminolo'hia/ *n. f.* terminology.
termómetro /ter'mometro/ *n. m.* thermometer.
termos /'termos/ *n. m.* thermos.
termostato /ter'mostato/ *n. m.* thermostat.
ternero /ter'nero/ **-ra** *n.* calf.
ternura /ter'nura/ *n. f.* tenderness.
terquedad /terke'ðað/ *n. f.* stubbornness.
terraza /te'rraθa; te'rrasa/ *n. f.* terrace.
terremoto /terre'moto/ *n. m.* earthquake.
terreno /te'rreno/ *a.* **1.** earthly, terrestrial. —*n.* **2.** *m.* ground, terrain; lot, plot.
terrible /te'rriβle/ *a.* terrible, awful.
terrífico /te'rrifiko/ *a.* terrifying.
territorio /terri'torio/ *n. m.* territory.
terrón /te'rron/ *n. m.* clod, lump; mound.
terror /te'rror/ *n. m.* terror.
terso /'terso/ *a.* smooth, glossy; terse.
tertulia /ter'tulia/ *n. f.* social gathering, party.
tesis /'tesis/ *n. f.* thesis.
tesorería /tesore'ria/ *n. f.* treasury.
tesorero /teso'rero/ **-ra** *n.* treasurer.
tesoro /te'soro/ *n. m.* treasure.
testamento /testa'mento/ *n. m.* will, testament.
testarudo /testa'ruðo/ *a.* stubborn.
testificar /testifi'kar/ *v.* testify.
testigo /tes'tigo/ *n. m.* & *f.* witness.
testimonial /testimo'nial/ *a.* testimonal.
testimonio /testi'monio/ *n. m.* testimony.
teta /'teta/ *n. f.* teat.
tetera /te'tera/ *n. f.* teapot.
tétrico /'tetriko/ *a.* sad; gloomy.
texto /'teksto/ *n. m.* text.
textura /teks'tura/ *n. f.* texture.
tez /teθ; tes/ *n. f.* complexion.
ti /ti/ *pron.* you; yourself.
tía /'tia/ *n. f.* aunt.
tibio /'tiβio/ *a.* lukewarm.
tiburón /tiβu'ron/ *n. m.* shark.
tiemblo /'tiemblo/ *n. m.* aspen.
tiempo /'tiempo/ *n. m.* time; weather; *Gram.* tense.
tienda /'tienda/ *n. f.* shop, store; tent.
tientas /'tientas/ *n. f.pl.* **andar a t.,** to grope (in the dark).
tierno /'tierno/ *a.* tender.
tierra /'tierra/ *n. f.* land; ground; earth, dirt, soil.
tieso /'tieso/ *a.* taut, stiff, hard, strong.
tiesto /'tiesto/ *n. m.* flower pot.
tiesura /tie'sura/ *n. f.* stiffness; harshness.
tifo /'tifo/ *n. m.* typhus.
tifoideo /tifoi'ðeo/ *n. m.* typhoid fever.
tigre /'tigre/ *n. m.* tiger.
tijeras /ti'heras/ *n. f.pl.* scissors.
tila /'tila/ *n. f.* linden.
timbre /'timbre/ *n. m.* seal, stamp; tone; (electric) bell.
tímidamente /'timiðamente/ *adv.* timidly.
timidez /timi'ðeθ; timi'ðes/ *n. f.* timidity.
tímido /'timiðo/ *a.* timid, shy.
timón /ti'mon/ *n. m.* rudder, helm.
tímpano /'timpano/ *n. m.* kettledrum; eardrum.
tina /'tina/ *n. f.* tub, vat.
tinaja /ti'naha/ *n. f.* jar.
tinta /'tinta/ *n. f.* ink.
tinte /'tinte/ *n. m.* tint, shade.
tintero /tin'tero/ *n. m.* inkwell.
tinto /'tinto/ *a.* wine-colored; red (of wine).
tintorería /tintore'ria/ *n. f.* dry cleaning shop.
tintorero /tinto'rero/ **-ra** *n.* dyer; dry cleaner.
tintura /tin'tura/ *n. f.* tincture; dye.
tiñoso /ti'ɲoso/ *a.* scabby; stingy.
tío /'tio/ *n. m.* uncle.
tíovivo /tio'βiβo/ *n. m.* merry-go-round.
típico /'tipiko/ *a.* typical.
tipo /'tipo/ *n. m.* type, sort; (interest) rate; *Colloq.* guy, fellow.
tipo de cambio /'tipo de 'kambio/ exchange rate.
tipo de interés /'tipo de inte'res/ interest rate.
tira /'tira/ *n. f.* strip.
tirabuzón /tiraβu'θon; tiraβu'son/ *n. m.* corkscrew.
tirada /ti'raða/ *n. f.* edition.
tirado /ti'raðo/ **-da** *a.* dirt-cheap.
tiranía /tira'nia/ *n. f.* tyranny.
tiránico /ti'raniko/ *n. m.* tyrannical.
tirano /ti'rano/ **-na** *n.* tyrant.
tirante /ti'rante/ *a.* **1.** tight, taut; tense. —*n.* **2.** *m.pl.* suspenders.
tirar /ti'rar/ *v.* throw; draw; pull; fire (a weapon).
tiritar /tiri'tar/ *v.* shiver.
tiro /'tiro/ *n. m.* throw; shot.
tirón /ti'ron/ *n. m.* pull. **de un t.,** at a stretch, at one stroke.
tísico /'tisiko/ *n.* & *a.* consumptive.
tisis /'tisis/ *n. f.* consumption, tuberculosis.
titanio /ti'tanio/ *n. m.* titanium.
títere /'titere/ *n. m.* puppet.
titilación /titila'θion; titila'sion/ *n. f.* twinkle.
titubear /tituβe'ar/ *v.* stagger; totter; waver.
titulado /titu'laðo/ *a.* entitled; so-called.
titular /titu'lar/ *a.* **1.** titular. —*v.* **2.** entitle.
título /'titulo/ *n. m.* title, headline.
tiza /'tiθa; 'tisa/ *n. f.* chalk.
tiznar /tiθ'nar; tis'nar/ *v.* smudge; stain.
toalla /to'aʎa; to'aya/ *n. f.* towel. **t. sanitaria,** sanitary napkin.
toalleta /toa'ʎeta; toa'yeta/ *n. f.* small towel.
tobillo /to'βiʎo; to'βiyo/ *n. m.* ankle.
tobogán /toβo'gan/ *n. m.* toboggan.
tocadiscos /toka'ðiskos/ *n. m.* record player.
tocadiscos compacto /toka'ðiskos kom'pakto/ **tocadiscos digital** CD player.
tocado /to'kaðo/ *n. m.* hairdo.
tocador /toka'ðor/ *n. m.* boudoir; dressing table.
tocante /to'kante/ *a.* touching. **t. a,** concerning, relative to.
tocar /to'kar/ *v.* touch; play (an instrument). **t. a uno,** be one's turn; be up to one.
tocayo /to'kayo/ **-ya** *n.* namesake.
tocino /to'θino; to'sino/ *n. m.* bacon.
tocólogo /to'kologo/ **-ga** *n.* obstetrician.
todavía /toða'βia/ *adv.* yet, still.
todo /'toðo/ *a.* **1.** all, whole. **todos los,** every. —*pron.* **2.** all, everything. **con t.,** still, however. **del t.,** wholly; at all.
todopoderoso /toðopoðe'roso/ *a.* almighty.
toldo /'toldo/ *n. m.* awning.
tolerancia /tole'ranθia; tole'ransia/ *n. f.* tolerance.
tolerante /tole'rante/ *a.* tolerant.
tolerar /tole'rar/ *v.* tolerate.
toma /'toma/ *n. f.* taking, capture, seizure.
tomaína /to'maina/ *n. f.* ptomaine.
tomar /to'mar/ *v.* take; drink. **t. el sol,** sunbathe.
tomate /to'mate/ *n. m.* tomato.
tomillo /to'miʎo; to'miyo/ *n. m.* thyme.
tomo /'tomo/ *n. m.* volume.
tonada /to'naða/ *n. f.* tune.
tonel /to'nel/ *n. m.* barrel, cask.
tonelada /tone'laða/ *n. f.* ton.
tonelaje /tone'lahe/ *n. m.* tonnage.
tónico /'toniko/ *a.* & *m.* tonic.
tono /'tono/ *n. m.* tone, pitch, shade. **darse t.,** to put on airs.
tonsila /ton'sila/ *n. f.* tonsil.
tonsilitis /tonsi'litis/ *n. f.* tonsilitis.
tontería /tonte'ria/ *n. f.* nonsense, foolishness.
tontifútbol /tonti'futβol/ *n. m.* excessively defensive strategy (in soccer).
tonto /'tonto/ **-ta** *a.* & *n.* foolish, silly; fool.
topacio /to'paθio; to'pasio/ *n. m.* topaz.
topar /to'par/ *v.* run into. **t. con,** come upon.
tópico /'topiko/ *a.* **1.** topical. —*n.* **2.** *m.* cliché.
topo /'topo/ *n. m.* mole (animal).
toque /'toke/ *n. m.* touch.
tórax /'toraks/ *n. m.* thorax.
torbellino /torβe'ʎino; torβe'yino/ *n. m.* whirlwind.
torcer /tor'θer; tor'ser/ *v.* twist; wind; distort.
toreador /torea'ðor/ **-a** *n.* toreador.
torero /to'rero/ **-ra** *n.* bullfighter.
torio /'torio/ *n. m.* thorium.
tormenta /tor'menta/ *n. f.* storm.
tormento /tor'mento/ *n. m.* torment.
tornado /tor'naðo/ *n. m.* tornado.
tornar /tor'nar/ *v.* return; turn.
tornarse en /tor'narse en/ *v.* turn into, become.
torneo /tor'neo/ *n. m.* tournament.
tornillo /tor'niʎo; tor'niyo/ *n. m.* screw.
toro /'toro/ *n. m.* bull.
toronja /to'ronha/ *n. f.* grapefruit.
torpe /'torpe/ *a.* awkward, clumsy; sluggish.
torpedero /torpe'ðero/ *n. m.* torpedo boat.
torpedo /tor'peðo/ *n. m.* torpedo.
torre /'torre/ *n. f.* tower.
torre de mando /'torre de 'mando/ control tower.
torrente /to'rrente/ *n. m.* torrent.
tórrido /'torriðo/ *a.* torrid.
torta /'torta/ *n. f.* cake; loaf.
tortilla /tor'tiʎa; tor'tiya/ *n. f.* omelet; (Mex.) tortilla, pancake.
tórtola /'tortola/ *n. f.* dove.
tortuga /tor'tuga/ *n. f.* turtle.
tortuoso /tor'tuoso/ *a.* tortuous.
tortura /tor'tura/ *n. f.* torture. —**torturar,** *v.*
tos /tos/ *n. m.* cough. —**toser,** *v.*
tosco /'tosko/ *a.* coarse, rough, uncouth.
tosquedad /toske'ðað/ *n. f.* coarseness, roughness.
tostador /tosta'ðor/ *n. m.* toaster.
tostar /'tostar/ *v.* toast; tan.
total /to'tal/ *a.* & *m.* total.
totalidad /totali'ðað/ *n. f.* totality, entirety, whole.
totalitario /totali'tario/ *a.* totalitarian.
totalmente /total'mente/ *adv.* totally; entirely.
tótem /'totem/ *n. m.* totem.
tóxico /'toksiko/ *a.* toxic.
toxicómano /toksi'komano/ **-na** *n. m.* & *f.* drug addict.
trabajador /traβaha'ðor/ **-ra** *a.* **1.** hardworking. —*n.* **2.** worker.
trabajo /tra'βaho/ *n. m.* work; labor. —**trabajar,** *v.*
trabar /tra'βar/ *v.* fasten, shackle; grasp; strike up.
tracción /trak'θion; trak'sion/ *n. f.* traction.
tracto /'trakto/ *n. m.* tract.
tractor /'trak'tor/ *n. m.* tractor.
tradición /traði'θion; traði'sion/ *n. f.* tradition.
tradicional /traðiθio'nal; traðisio'nal/ *a.* traditional.
traducción /traðuk'θion; traðuk'sion/ *n. f.* translation.
traducir /traðu'θir; traðu'sir/ *v.* translate.
traductor /traðuk'tor/ **-ra** *n.* translator.
traer /tra'er/ *v.* bring; carry; wear.
tráfico /'trafiko/ *n. m.* traffic. —**traficar,** *v.*
tragaperras /traga'perras/ *n. f.* slot machine, one-armed bandit.
tragar /tra'gar/ *v.* swallow.
tragedia /tra'heðia/ *n. f.* tragedy.
trágicamente /'trahikamente/ *adv.* tragically.
trágico /'trahiko/ **-ca** *a.* **1.** tragic. —*n.* **2.** tragedian.
trago /'trago/ *n. m.* swallow; drink.
traición /trai'θion; trai'sion/ *n. f.* treason, betrayal.
traicionar /traiθio'nar; traisio'nar/ *v.* betray.
traidor /trai'ðor/ **-ra** *a.* & *n.* traitorous; traitor.
traje /'trahe/ *n. m.* suit; dress; garb, apparel.
traje de baño /'trahe de 'baɲo/ bathing suit.
trama /'trama/ *v.* plot (of a story).
tramador /trama'ðor/ **-ra** *n.* weaver; plotter.
tramar /tra'mar/ *v.* weave; plot, scheme.
trámite /'tramite/ *n. m.* (business) deal, transaction.

tramo /'tramo/ *n. m.* span, stretch, section.

trampa /'trampa/ *n. f.* trap, snare.

trampista /tram'pista/ *n. m. & f.* cheater; swindler.

trance /'tranθe; 'transe/ *n. m.* critical moment or stage. **a todo t.,** at any cost.

tranco /'tranko/ *n. m.* stride.

tranquilidad /trankili'ðað/ *n. f.* tranquility, calm, quiet.

tranquilizante /trankili'θante; trankili'sante/ *n. m.* tranquilizer.

tranquilizar /trankili'θar; trankili'sar/ *v.* quiet, calm down.

tranquilo /tran'kilo/ *a.* tranquil, calm.

transacción /transak'θion; transak'sion/ *n. f.* transaction.

transbordador /transβorða'ðor/ *n. m.* ferry.

transbordador espacial /transβorða'ðor espa'θial; transβorða'ðor espa'sial/ space, shuttle.

transcribir /transkri'βir/ *v.* transcribe.

transcripción /transkrip'θion; transkrip'sion/ *n. f.* transcription.

transcurrir /transku'rrir/ *v.* elapse.

transeúnte /tran'seunte/ *a. & n.* transient; passerby.

transexual /transek'sual/ *a.* transsexual.

transferencia /transfe'renθia; transfe'rensia/ *n. f.* transference.

transferir /transfe'rir/ *v.* transfer.

transformación /transforma'θion; transforma'sion/ *n. f.* transformation.

transformar /transfor'mar/ *v.* transform.

transfusión /transfu'sion/ *n. f.* transfusion.

transgresión /transgre'sion/ *n. f.* transgression.

transgresor /transgre'sor/ **-ra** *n.* transgressor.

transición /transi'θion; transi'sion/ *n. f.* transition.

transigir /transi'hir/ *v.* compromise, settle; agree.

transistor /transis'tor/ *n. m.* transistor.

transitivo /transi'tiβo/ *a.* transitive.

tránsito /'transito/ *n. m.* transit, passage.

transitorio /transi'torio/ *a.* transitory.

transmisión /transmi'sion/ *n. f.* transmission; broadcast.

transmisora /transmi'sora/ *n. f.* broadcasting station.

transmitir /transmi'tir/ *v.* transmit; broadcast.

transparencia /transpa'renθia; transpa'rensia/ *n. f.* transparency.

transparente /transpa'rente/ *a.* **1.** transparent. —*n.* **2.** *m.* (window) shade.

transportación /transporta'θion; transporta'sion/ *n. f.* transportation.

transportar /transpor'tar/ *v.* transport, convey.

transporte /trans'porte/ *n. m.* transportation; transport.

tranvía /tram'bia/ *n. m.* streetcar, trolley.

trapacero /trapa'θero; trapa'sero/ **-ra** *n.* cheat; swindler.

trapo /'trapo/ *n. m.* rag.

tráquea /'trakea/ *n. f.* trachea.

tras /tras/ *prep.* after; behind.

trasegar /trase'gar/ *v.* upset, overturn.

trasero /tra'sero/ *a.* rear, back.

traslado /tras'laðo/ *n. m.* transfer. —**trasladar,** *v.*

traslapo /tras'lapo/ *n. m.* overlap. —**traslapar,** *v.*

trasnochar /trasno'tʃar/ *v.* stay up all night.

traspalar /traspa'lar/ *v.* shovel.

traspasar /traspa'sar/ *v.* go beyond; cross; violate; pierce.

trasquilar /traski'lar/ *v.* shear; clip.

trastornar /trastor'nar/ *v.* overturn, overthrow, upset.

trastorno /tras'torno/ *m.* overthrow; upheaval.

trastorno mental /tras'torno men'tal/ mental disorder.

trasvasar /trasβa'sar/ *v.* download; download.

tratado /tra'taðo/ *n. m.* treaty; treatise.

tratamiento /trata'miento/ *n. m.* treatment.

tratar /tra'tar/ *v.* treat, handle. **t. de,** deal with; try to; call (a name).

tratarse de /tra'tarse de/ *v.* be a question of.

trato /'trato/ *n. m.* treatment; manners; *Com.* deal.

través /tra'βes/ *adv.* **a t. de,** through, across. **de t.,** sideways.

travesía /traβe'sia/ *n. f.* crossing; voyage.

travestí /traβes'ti/ *n. m.* transvestite.

travestido /traβes'tiðo/ *a.* disguised.

travesura /traβe'sura/ *n. f.* prank; mischief.

travieso /tra'βieso/ *a.* naughty, mischievous.

trayectoria /trayek'toria/ *n. f.* trajectory.

trazar /tra'θar; tra'sar/ *v.* plan, devise; trace; draw.

trazo /'traθo; 'traso/ *n.* plan, outline; line, stroke.

trébol /'treβol/ *n. m.* clover.

trece /'treθe; 'trese/ *a. & pron.* thirteen.

trecho /'tretʃo/ *n. m.* space, distance, stretch.

tregua /'tregua/ *n. f.* truce; respite, lull.

treinta /'treinta/ *a. & pron.* thirty.

tremendo /tre'mendo/ *a.* tremendous.

tremer /tre'mer/ *v.* tremble.

tren /tren/ *n. m.* train.

trenza /'trenθa; 'trensa/ *n. f.* braid. —**trenzar,** *v.*

trepar /tre'par/ *v.* climb, mount.

trepidación /trepiða'θion; trepiða'sion/ *n. f.* trepidation.

tres /tres/ *a. & pron.* three.

trescientos /tres'θientos; tres'sientos/ *a. & pron.* three hundred.

triángulo /tri'angulo/ *n. m.* triangle.

triar /triar/ *v.* sort, separate.

tribu /'triβu/ *n. f.* tribe.

tribulación /triβula'θion; triβula'sion/ *n. f.* tribulation.

tribuna /tri'βuna/ *n. f.* rostrum, stand; (*pl.*) grandstand.

tribunal /triβu'nal/ *n. m.* court, tribunal.

tributario /triβu'tario/ *a. & m.* tributary.

tributo /tri'βuto/ *n. m.* tribute.

triciclo /tri'θiklo; tri'siklo/ *n. m.* tricycle.

trigo /'trigo/ *n. m.* wheat.

trigonometría /trigonome'tria/ *n. f.* trigonometry.

trigueño /tri'geɲo/ *a.* swarthy, dark.

trilogía /trilo'hia/ *n. f.* trilogy.

trimestral /trimes'tral/ *a.* quarterly.

trinchar /trin'tʃar/ *v.* carve (meat).

trinchera /trin'tʃera/ *n. f.* trench, ditch.

trineo /tri'neo/ *n. m.* sled; sleigh.

trinidad /trini'ðað/ *n. f.* trinity.

tripa /'tripa/ *n. f.* tripe, entrails.

triple /'triple/ *a.* triple. —**triplicar,** *v.*

trípode /'tripode/ *n. m.* tripod.

tripulación /tripula'θion; tripula'sion/ *n. f.* crew.

tripulante /tripu'lante/ *m & f.* crew member.

tripular /tripu'lar/ *v.* man.

triste /'triste/ *a.* sad, sorrowful; dreary.

tristemente /triste'mente/ *adv.* sadly.

tristeza /tris'teθa; tris'tesa/ *n. f.* sadness; gloom.

triunfal /triun'fal/ *a.* triumphal.

triunfante /triun'fante/ *a.* triumphant.

triunfo /'triunfo/ *n. m.* triumph; trump. —**triunfar,** *v.*

trivial /tri'βial/ *a.* trivial, commonplace.

trivialidad /triβiali'ðað/ *n. f.* triviality.

trocar /tro'kar/ *v.* exchange, switch; barter.

trofeo /tro'feo/ *n. m.* trophy.

trombón /trom'bon/ *n. m.* trombone.

trompa /'trompa/ **trompeta** *n. f.* trumpet, horn.

tronada /tro'naða/ *n. f.* thunderstorm.

tronar /tro'nar/ *v.* thunder.

tronco /'tronko/ *n. m.* trunk, stump.

trono /'trono/ *n. m.* throne.

tropa /'tropa/ *n. f.* troop.

tropel /tro'pel/ *n. m.* crowd, throng.

tropezar /trope'θar; trope'sar/ *v.* trip, stumble. **t. con,** come upon, run into.

trópico /'tropiko/ *a. & m.* tropical; tropics.

tropiezo /tro'pieθo; tro'pieso/ *n. m.* stumble; obstacle; slip, error.

trote /'trote/ *n. m.* trot. —**trotar,** *v.*

trovador /troβa'ðor/ *n. m.* troubadour.

trozo /'troθo; 'troso/ *n. m.* piece, portion, fragment; selection, passage.

trucha /'trutʃa/ *n. f.* trout.

trueco /'trueko/ **trueque** *n. m.* exchange, barter.

trueno /'trueno/ *n. m.* thunder.

trufa /'trufa/ *n. f.* truffle.

tu /tu/ *a.* **1.** your.

tú *pron.* **2.** you.

tuberculosis /tuβerku'losis/ *n. f.* tuberculosis.

tubo /'tuβo/ *n. m.* tube, pipe.

tubo de ensayo /'tuβo de en'sayo/ test tube.

tubo de escape /'tuβo de es'kape/ exhaust pipe.

tuerca /'tuerka/ *n. f. Mech.* nut.

tulipán /tuli'pan/ *n. m.* tulip.

tumba /'tumba/ *n. f.* tomb, grave.

tumbar /tum'bar/ *v.* knock down.

tumbarse /tum'βarse/ *v.* lie down.

tumbo /'tumbo/ *n. m.* tumble; somersault.

tumbona /tum'βona/ *n. f.* deck chair.

tumor /tu'mor/ *n. m.* tumor; growth.

tumulto /tu'multo/ *n. m.* tumult, commotion.

tumultuoso /tumul'tuoso/ *a.* tumultuous, boisterous.

tunante /tu'nante/ *n. m.* rascal, rogue.

tunda /'tunda/ *n. f.* spanking, whipping.

túnel /'tunel/ *n. m.* tunnel.

túnel del Canal de la Mancha /'tunel del ka'nal de la 'mantʃa/ Channel Tunnel, Chunnel.

tungsteno /tungs'teno/ *n. m.* tungsten.

túnica /'tunika/ *n. f.* tunic, robe.

tupir /tu'pir/ *v.* pack tight, stuff; stop up.

turbación /turβa'θion; turβa'sion/ *n. f.* confusion, turmoil.

turbamulta /turβa'multa/ *n. f.* mob, disorderly crowd.

turbar /tur'βar/ *v.* disturb, upset; embarrass.

turbina /tur'βina/ *n. f.* turbine.

turbio /'turβio/ *a.* turbid; muddy.

turco /'turko/ **-ca** *a. & n.* Turkish; Turk.

turismo /tu'rismo/ *n. m.* touring, (foreign) travel, tourism.

turista /tu'rista/ *n. m. & f.* tourist.

turno /'turno/ *n. m.* turn; (work) shift.

turquesa /tur'kesa/ *n. f.* turquoise.

Turquía /tur'kia/ *n. f.* Turkey.

turrón /tu'rron/ *n. m.* nougat.

tusa /'tusa/ *n. f.* corncob; corn.

tutear /tute'ar/ *v.* use the pronoun **tú,** etc., in addressing a person.

tutela /tu'tela/ *n. f.* guardianship; aegis.

tutor /tu'tor/ **-ra** *n.* tutor; guardian.

tuyo /'tuyo/ *a.* your, yours.

U

u /u/ *conj.* or.

ubre /'uβre/ *n. f.* udder.

Ucrania /u'krania/ *n. f.* Ukraine.

ucranio /u'kranio/ **-ia** *a. & n.* Ukrainian.

ufano /u'fano/ *a.* proud, haughty.

úlcera /'ulθera; 'ulsera/ *n. f.* ulcer.

ulterior /ulte'rior/ *a.* ulterior.

último /'ultimo/ *a.* last, final; ultimate; latest. **por ú.,** finally. **ú. minuto,** last minute, eleventh hour.

ultraje /ul'trahe/ *n. m.* outrage. —**ultrajar,** *v.*

ultrasónico /ultra'soniko/ *a.* ultrasonic.

umbral /um'bral/ *n. m.* threshold.

umbroso /um'broso/ *a.* shady.

un /un/ **una** *art. & a.* a, an; one; (*pl.*) some.

unánime /u'nanime/ *a.* unanimous.

unanimidad /unanimi'ðað/ *n. f.* unanimity.

unción /un'θion; un'sion/ *n. f.* unction.

ungüento /uŋ'guento/ *n. m.* ointment, salve.

único /'uniko/ *a.* only, sole; unique.

unicornio /uni'kornio/ *n. m.* unicorn.

unidad /uni'ðað/ *n. f.* unit; unity.

unidad de cuidados intensivos /uni'ðað de kui'ðaðos inten'siβos/ **unidad de vigilancia intensiva** intensive-care unit.

unidad de disco /uni'ðað de 'disko/ disk drive.

unificar /unifi'kar/ *v.* unify.

uniforme /uni'forme/ *a. & m.* uniform.

uniformidad /uniformi'ðað/ *n. f.* uniformity.

unión /u'nion/ *n. f.* union; joining.

unir /u'nir/ *v.* unite, join.

universal /uniβer'sal/ *a.* universal.

universalidad /uniβersali'ðað/ *n. f.* universality.

universidad /uniβersi'ðað/ *n. f.* university; college.

universo /uni'βerso/ *n. m.* universe.

uno /'uno/ **una** *pron.* one; (*pl.*) some.

untar /un'tar/ *v.* spread; grease; anoint.

uña /'uɲa/ *n. f.* fingernail.

urbanidad /urβani'ðað/ *n. f.* urbanity; good breeding.

urbanismo /urβa'nismo/ *n. m.* city planning.

urbano /ur'βano/ *a.* urban; urbane; well-bred.

urbe /'urβe/ *n. f.* large city.

urgencia /ur'henθia; ur'hensia/ *n. f.* urgency.

urgente /ur'hente/ *a.* urgent, pressing. **entrega u.,** special delivery.

urgir /ur'hir/ *v.* be urgent.

urna /'urna/ *n. f.* urn; ballot box; (*pl.*) polls.

urraca /u'rraka/ *n. f.* magpie.

usanza /u'sanθa; usansa/ *n. f.* usage, custom.

usar /u'sar/ *v.* use; wear.

uso /'uso/ *n. m.* use; usage; wear.

usted /us'teð/ *pron.* you.

usual /u'sual/ *a.* usual.

usualmente /usual'mente/ *adv.* usually.

usura /u'sura/ *n. f.* usury.

usurero /usu'rero/ **-ra** *n.* usurer.

usurpación /usurpa'θion; usurpa'sion/ *n. f.* usurpation.

usurpar /usur'par/ *v.* usurp.

utensilio /uten'silio/ *n. m.* utensil.

útero /'utero/ *n. m.* uterus.

útil /'util/ *a.* useful, handy.

utilidad /utili'ðað/ *n. f.* utility, usefulness.

utilizar /utili'θar; utili'sar/ *v.* use, utilize.

útilmente /util'mente/ *adv.* usefully.

utópico /u'topiko/ *a.* utopian.

uva /'uβa/ *n. f.* grape.

V

vaca /'baka/ *n. f.* cow; beef.

vacaciones /baka'θiones; baka'siones/ *n. f.pl.* vacation, holidays.

vacancia /ba'kanθia; ba'kansia/ *n. f.* vacancy.

vacante /ba'kante/ *a.* **1.** vacant. —*n.* **2.** *f.* vacancy.

vaciar /ba'θiar; ba'siar/ *v.* empty; pour out.

vacilación /baθila'θion; basila'sion/ *n. f.* vacillation, hesitation.

vacilante /baθi'lante; basi'lante/ *a.* vacillating.

vacilar /baθi'lar; basi'lar/ *v.* falter, hesitate; waver; stagger.

vacío /ba'θio; ba'sio/ *a.* **1.** empty. —*n.* **2.** *m.* void, empty space.

vacuna /ba'kuna/ *n. f.* vaccine.

vacunación /bakuna'θion; bakuna'sion/ *n. f.* vaccination.

vacunar /baku'nar/ *v.* vaccinate.

vacuo /'bakuo/ *a.* **1.** empty, vacant. —*n.* **2.** *m.* vacuum.

vadear /baðe'ar/ *v.* wade through, ford.

vado /'baðo/ *n. m.* ford.

vagabundo /baga'βundo/ **-da** *a. & n.* vagabond.

vagar /ba'gar/ *v.* wander, rove, roam; loiter.

vago /'bago/ **-ga** *a.* **1.** vague, hazy; wandering, vagrant. —*n.* **2.** vagrant, tramp.

vagón /ba'gon/ *n. m.* railroad car.

vahído /ba'iðo/ *n. m.* dizziness.

vaina /'baina/ *n. f.* sheath; pod.

vainilla /bai'niʎa; bai'niya/ *n. f.* vanilla.

vaivén /bai'βen/ *n. m.* vibration, sway.

vajilla /ba'hiʎa; ba'hiya/ *n. f.* (dinner) dishes.

valentía /balen'tia/ *n. f.* valor, courage.

valer /ba'ler/ *n.* **1.** *m.* worth. —*v.* **2.** be worth.

valerse de /ba'lerse de/ *v.* make use of, avail oneself of.

valía /ba'lia/ *n. f.* value.

validez /bali'ðeθ; bali'ðes/ *n. f.* validity.

válido /'baliðo/ *a.* valid.

valiente /ba'liente/ *a.* valiant, brave, courageous.

valija /ba'liha/ *n. f.* valise.

valioso /ba'lioso/ *a.* valuable.

valla /'baʎa; 'baya/ *n. f.* fence, barrier.

valle /'baʎe; 'baye/ *n. m.* valley.

valor /ba'lor/ *n. m.* value, worth; bravery, valor; (*pl., Com.*) securities.

valoración /balora'θion; balora'sion/ *n. f.* appraisal.

valorar /balo'rar/ *v.* value, appraise.

vals /bals/ *n. m.* waltz.

valsar /bal'sar/ *v.* waltz.

valuación /balua'θion; balua'sion/ *n. f.* valuation.

valuar /balu'ar/ *v.* value; rate.

válvula /'balβula/ *n. f.* valve.

válvula de seguridad /'balβula de seguri'ðað/ safety valve.

vandalismo /banda'lismo/ *n. m.* vandalism.

vándalo /'bandalo/ **-la** *n.* vandal.

vanidad /bani'ðað/ *n. f.* vanity.

vanidoso /bani'ðoso/ *a.* vain, conceited.

vano /'bano/ *a.* vain; inane.

vapor /ba'por/ *n. m.* vapor; steam; steamer, steamship.

vaquero /ba'kero/ **-ra** *n.* cowboy.

vara /'bara/ *n. f.* wand, stick, switch.

varadero /bara'ðero/ *n. m.* shipyard.

varar /ba'rar/ *v.* launch; be stranded; run aground.

variable /ba'riaβle/ *a.* variable.

variación /baria'θion; baria'sion/ *n. f.* variation.

variar /ba'riar/ *v.* vary.

varicela /bari'θela; bari'sela/ *n. f.* chicken pox.

variedad /barie'ðað/ *n. f.* variety.

varios /'barios/ *a. & pron. pl.* various; several.

variz /ba'riθ; ba'ris/ *n. f.* varicose vein.

varón /ba'ron/ *n. m.* man; male.

varonil /baro'nil/ *a.* manly, virile.

vasallo /ba'saʎo; ba'sayo/ *n. m.* vassal.

vasectomía /basekto'mia/ *n. f.* vasectomy.

vasija /ba'siha/ *n. f.* bowl, container (for liquids).

vaso /'baso/ *n. m.* water glass; vase. **v. de papel,** paper cup.

vástago /'bastago/ *n. m.* bud, shoot; twig; offspring.

vasto /'basto/ *a.* vast.

vecindad /beθin'dað; besin'dað/ *n. f.* **vecindario,** *m.* neighborhood, vicinity.

vecino /be'θino; be'sino/ **-na** *a. & n.* neighboring; neighbor.

vedar /be'ðar/ *v.* forbid; impede.

vega /'bega/ *n. f.* meadow.

vegetación /beheta'θion; beheta'sion/ *n. f.* vegetation.

vegetal /behe'tal/ *n. m.* vegetable.

vehemente /bee'mente/ *a.* vehement.

vehículo /be'ikulo/ *n. m.* vehicle; conveyance.

veinte /'beinte/ *a. & pron.* twenty.

vejez /be'heθ; be'hes/ *n. f.* old age.

vejiga /be'higa/ *n. f.* bladder.

vela /'bela/ *n. f.* vigil, watch; candle; sail.

velar /be'lar/ *v.* stay up, sit up; watch over.

vellón /be'ʎon; be'yon/ *n. m.* fleece.

velloso /be'ʎoso; be'yoso/ *a.* hairy; fuzzy.

velludo /be'ʎuðo; be'yuðo/ *a.* downy.

velo /'belo/ *n. m.* veil.

velocidad /beloθi'ðað; belosi'ðað/ *n. f.* velocity, speed; rate. **v. máxima,** speed limit.

velomotor /belomo'tor/ *n. m.* motorbike, moped.

veloz /be'loθ; be'los/ *a.* speedy, fast, swift.

vena /'bena/ *n. f.* vein.

venado /be'naðo/ *n. m.* deer.

vencedor /benθe'ðor; bense'ðor/ **-ra** *n.* victor.

vencer /ben'θer; ben'ser/ *v.* defeat, overcome, conquer; *Com.* become due, expire.

vencimiento /benθi'miento; bensi'miento/ *n. m.* defeat; expiration.

venda /'benda/ *n. f.* **vendaje,** *m.* bandage. —**vendar,** *v.*

vendedor /bende'ðor/ **-ra** *n.* seller, trader; sales clerk.

vender /ben'der/ *v.* sell.

vendimia /ben'dimia/ *n. f.* vintage; grape harvest.

Venecia /be'neθia; be'nesia/ *n. f.* Venice.

veneciano /bene'θiano; bene'siano/ **-na** *a. & n.* Venetian.

veneno /be'neno/ *n. m.* poison.

venenoso /bene'noso/ *a.* poisonous.

veneración /benera'θion; benera'sion/ *n. f.* veneration.

venerar /bene'rar/ *v.* venerate, revere.

venero /be'nero/ *n. m.* spring; origin.

véneto /'beneto/ *a.* Venetian.

venezolano /beneθo'lano; beneso'lano/ **-na** *a. & n.* Venezuelan.

vengador /beŋga'ðor/ **-ra** *n.* avenger.

venganza /beŋ'ganθa; beŋ'gansa/ *n. f.* vengeance, revenge.

vengar /beŋ'gar/ *v.* avenge.

venida /be'niða/ *n. f.* arrival, advent, coming.

venidero /beni'ðero/ *a.* future; coming.

venir /be'nir/ *v.* come.

venta /'benta/ *n. f.* sale; sales.

ventaja /ben'taha/ *n. f.* advantage; profit.

ventajoso /benta'hoso/ *a.* advantageous; profitable.

ventana /ben'tana/ *n. f.* window.

ventero /ben'tero/ **-ra** *n.* innkeeper.

ventilación /bentila'θion; bentila'sion/ *n. m.* ventilation.

ventilador /bentila'ðor/ *n. m.* ventilator, fan.

ventilar /benti'lar/ *v.* ventilate, air.

ventisquero /bentis'kero/ *n. m.* snowdrift; glacier.

ventoso /ben'toso/ *a.* windy.

ventura /ben'tura/ *n. f.* venture; happiness; luck.

ver /ber/ *v.* see. **tener que v. con,** have to do with.

vera /'bera/ *n. f.* edge.

veracidad /beraθi'ðað; berasi'ðað/ *n. f.* truthfulness, veracity.

verano /be'rano/ *n. m.* summer. —**veranear,** *v.*

veras /'beras/ *n. f.pl.* **de v.,** really, truly.

veraz /be'raθ; be'ras/ *a.* truthful.

verbigracia /berβi'graθia; berβi'grasia/ *adv.* for example.

verbo /'berβo/ *n. m.* verb.

verboso /ber'βoso/ *a.* verbose.

verdad /ber'ðað/ *n. f.* truth. **ser v.,** to be true.

verdadero /berða'ðero/ *a.* true, real.

verde /'berðe/ *a.* green; risqué, offcolor.

verdor /ber'ðor/ *n. m.* greenness, verdure.

verdugo /ber'ðugo/ *n. m.* hangman.

verdura /ber'ðura/ *n. f.* verdure, vegetation; (*pl.*) vegetables.

vereda /be'reða/ *n. f.* path.

veredicto /bere'ðikto/ *n. m.* verdict.

vergonzoso /bergon'θoso; bergon'soso/ *a.* shameful, embarrassing; shy, bashful.

vergüenza /ber'guenθa; ber'guensa/ *n. f.* shame; disgrace; embarrassment.

verificar /berifi'kar/ *v.* verify, check.

verja /'berha/ *n. f.* grating, railing.

verosímil /bero'simil/ *a.* likely, plausible.

verraco /be'rrako/ *n. m.* boar.

verruga /be'rruga/ *n. f.* wart.

versátil /ber'satil/ *a.* versatile.

verse /'berse/ *v.* look, appear.

versión /ber'sion/ *n. f.* version.

verso /'berso/ *n. m.* verse, stanza; line (of poetry).

verter /ber'ter/ *v.* pour, spill; shed; empty.

vertical /berti'kal/ *a.* vertical.

vertiente /ber'tiente/ *n. f.* slope; watershed.

vertiginoso /bertihi'noso/ *a.* dizzy.

vértigo /'bertigo/ *n. m.* vertigo, dizziness.

vestíbulo /bes'tiβulo/ *n. m.* vestibule, lobby.

vestido /bes'tiðo/ *n. m.* dress; clothing.

vestigio /bes'tihio/ *n. m.* vestige, trace.

vestir /bes'tir/ *v.* dress, clothe.

veterano /bete'rano/ **-na** *a. & n.* veteran.

veterinario /beteri'nario/ **-ria** *a.* **1.** veterinary. —*n.* **2.** veterinarian.

veto /'beto/ *n. m.* veto.

vetusto /be'tusto/ *a.* ancient, very old.

vez /beθ; bes/ *n. f.* time; turn. **tal v.,** perhaps. **a la v.,** at the same time. **en v. de,** instead of. **una v.,** once. **otra v.,** again.

vía /'bia/ *n. f.* track; route, way.

viaducto /bia'ðukto/ *n. m.* viaduct.

viajante /bia'hante/ *a. & n.* traveling; traveler.

viajar /bia'har/ *v.* travel; journey; tour.

viaje /'biahe/ *n. m.* trip, journey, voyage; (*pl.*) travels.

viaje de estudios /'biahe de es'tuðios/ field trip.

viajero /bia'hero/ **-ra** *n.* traveler; passenger.

viaje todo incluido /'biahe 'toðo in'kluiðo/ package tour.

viandas /'biandas/ *n. f.pl.* victuals, food.

víbora /'biβora/ *n. f.* viper.

vibración /biβra'θion; biβra'sion/ *n. f.* vibration.

vibrar /bi'βrar/ *v.* vibrate.

vicepresidente /biθepresi'ðente; bisepresi'ðente/ **-ta** *n.* vice president.

vicio /'biθio; 'bisio/ *n. m.* vice.

vicioso /bi'θioso; bi'sioso/ *a.* vicious; licentious.

víctima /'biktima/ *n. f.* victim.

victoria /bik'toria/ *n. f.* victory.

victorioso /bikto'rioso/ *a.* victorious.

vid /bið/ *n. f.* grapevine.

vida /'biða/ *n. f.* life; living.

vídeo /bi'ðeo/ *n. m.* videotape.

videocámara /biðeo'kamara/ *n. f.* video camera.

videodisco /biðeo'ðisko/ *n. m.* videodisc.

videojuego /biðeo'huego/ *n. m.* video game.

vidrio /'biðrio/ *n. m.* glass.

viejo /'bieho/ **-ja** *a. & n.* old; old person.

viento /'biento/ *n. m.* wind. **hacer v.,** to be windy.

vientre /'bientre/ *n. m.* belly.

viernes /'biernes/ *n. m.* Friday.

viga /'biga/ *n. f.* beam, rafter.

vigente /bi'hente/ *a.* in effect (prices, etc.).

vigilante /bihi'lante/ *a. & m.* vigilant, watchful; watchman.

vigilante nocturno /bihi'lante nok'turno/ night watchman.

vigilar /bihi'lar/ *v.* guard, watch over.

vigilia /bi'hilia/ *n. f.* vigil, watchfulness; *Relig.* fast.

vigor /bi'gor/ *n. m.* vigor. **en v.,** in effect, in force.

vil /bil/ *a.* vile, low, contemptible.

vileza /bi'leθa; bi'lesa/ *n. f.* baseness; vileness.

villa /'biʎa; 'biya/ *n. f.* town; country house.

villancico /biʎan'θiko; biyan'siko/ *n. m.* Christmas carol.

villanía /biʎa'nia; biya'nia/ *n. f.* villainy.

villano /bi'ʎano; bi'yano/ *n. m.* boor.

vinagre /bi'nagre/ *n. m.* vinegar.

vinagrera /bina'grera/ *n. f.* cruet.

vínculo /'binkulo/ *n. m.* link. —**vincular,** *v.*

vindicar /bindi'kar/ *v.* vindicate.

vino /'bino/ *n. m.* wine.

viña /'biɲa/ *n. f.* vineyard.

violación /biola'θion; biola'sion/ *n. f.* violation; rape.

violador /biola'ðor/ **-ra** *n. m. & f.* rapist.

violar /bio'lar/ *v.* violate; rape.

violencia /bio'lenθia; bio'lensia/ *n. f.* violence.

violento /bio'lento/ *a.* violent; impulsive.

violeta /bio'leta/ *n. f.* violet.

violín /bio'lin/ *n. m.* violin.

violón /bio'lon/ *n. m.* bass viol.

virar /bi'rar/ *v.* veer, change course.

virgen /bir'hen/ *n. f.* virgin.

viril /bi'ril/ *a.* virile, manly.

virilidad /birili'ðað/ *n. f.* virility, manhood.

virtual /bir'tual/ *a.* virtual.

virtud /bir'tuð/ *n. f.* virtue; efficacy, power.

virtuoso /bir'tuoso/ *a.* virtuous.

viruela /bi'ruela/ *n. f.* smallpox.

viruelas locas /bi'ruelas 'lokas/ *n. f.pl.* chicken pox.
virus /'birus/ *n. m.* virus.
visa /'bisa/ *n. f.* visa.
visaje /bi'sahe/ *n. m.* grimace.
visera /bi'sera/ *n. f.* visor.
visible /bi'siβle/ *a.* visible.
visión /bi'sion/ *n. f.* vision.
visionario /bisio'nario/ **-ria** *a. & n.* visionary.
visita /bi'sita/ *n. f.* visit; *m. & f.* visitor, caller. **v. con guía, v. explicada, v. programada,** guided tour.
visitación /bisita'θion; bisita'sion/ *n. f.* visitation.
visitante /bisi'tante/ *a. & n.* visiting; visitor.
visitar /bisi'tar/ *v.* visit; inspect, examine.
vislumbrar /bislum'βrar/ *v.* glimpse.
vislumbre /bis'lumbre/ *n. f.* glimpse.
viso /'biso/ *n. m.* looks; outlook.
víspera /'bispera/ *n. f.* eve, day before.
vista /'bista/ *n. f.* view; scene; sight.
vista de pájaro /'bista de 'paharo/ bird's-eye view.
vistazo /bis'taðo; bis'taso/ *n. m.* glance, glimpse.
vistoso /bis'toso/ *a.* beautiful; showy.
visual /bi'sual/ *a.* visual.
vital /bi'tal/ *a.* vital.
vitalidad /bitali'ðað/ *n. f.* vitality.
vitamina /bita'mina/ *n. f.* vitamin.
vitando /bi'tando/ *a.* hateful.
vituperar /bitupe'rar/ *v.* vituperate; revile.
viuda /'biuða/ *n. f.* widow.
viudo /'biuðo/ *n. m.* widower.
vivaz /bi'βaθ; bi'βas/ *a.* vivacious, buoyant; clever.
víveres /'biβeres/ *n. m.pl.* provisions.
viveza /bi'βeθa; bi'βesa/ *n. f.* animation, liveliness.
vívido /bi'βiðo/ *a.* vivid, bright.
vivienda /bi'βienda/ *n. f.* (living) quarters, dwelling.
vivificar /biβifi'kar/ *v.* vivify, enliven.
vivir /bi'βir/ *v.* live.

vivo /'biβo/ *a.* live, alive, living; vivid; animated, brisk.
vocablo /bo'kaβlo/ *n. m.* word.
vocabulario /bokaβu'lario/ *n. m.* vocabulary.
vocación /boka'θion; boka'sion/ *n. f.* vocation, calling.
vocal /bo'kal/ *a.* **1.** vocal. —*n.* **2.** *f.* vowel.
vocear /boθe'ar; bose'ar/ *v.* vociferate.
vodca /'boðka/ *n. m.* vodka.
vodevil /boðe'βil/ *n. m.* vaudeville.
volante /bo'lante/ *a.* **1.** flying. —*n.* **2.** *m.* memorandum; (steering) wheel.
volar /bo'lar/ *v.* fly; explode.
volcán /bol'kan/ *n. m.* volcano.
volcar /bol'kar/ *v.* upset, capsize.
voltaje /bol'tahe/ *n. m.* voltage.
voltear /bolte'ar/ *v.* turn, whirl; overturn.
voltio /'boltio/ *n. m.* volt.
volumen /bo'lumen/ *n. m.* volume.
voluminoso /bolumi'noso/ *a.* voluminous.
voluntad /bolun'tað/ *n. f.* will. **buena v.** goodwill.
voluntario /bolun'tario/ **-ria** *a. & n.* voluntary; volunteer.
voluntarioso /bolunta'rioso/ *a.* willful.
volver /bol'βer/ *v.* turn; return, go back, come back. **v. a hacer** (etc.), do (etc.) again.
volverse /bol'βerse/ *v.* turn around; turn, become.
vómito /'bomito/ *n. m.* vomit. —**vomitar,** *v.*
voracidad /boraθi'ðað; borasi'ðað/ *n. f.* voracity; greed.
voraz /bo'raθ; bo'ras/ *a.* greedy, ravenous.
vórtice /'bortiθe; 'bortise/ *n. m.* whirlpool.
vosotros /bo'sotros, bo'sotras/ **-as** *pron.pl.* you; yourselves.
votación /bota'θion; bota'sion/ *n. f.* voting; vote.
voto /'boto/ *n. m.* vote; vow. —**votar,** *v.*

voz /boθ; bos/ *n. f.* voice; word. **a voces,** by shouting. **en v. alta,** aloud.
vuelco /'buelko/ *n. m.* upset.
vuelo /'buelo/ *n. m.* flight. **v. libre,** hang gliding.
vuelo chárter /'buelo 'tʃarter/ charter flight.
vuelo regular /'buelo rregu'lar/ scheduled flight.
vuelta /'buelta/ *n. f.* turn, bend; return. **a la v. de,** around. **dar una v.,** to take a walk.
vuestro /'buestro/ *a.* your, yours.
vulgar /bul'gar/ *a.* vulgar, common.
vulgaridad /bulgari'ðað/ *n. f.* vulgarity.
vulgo /'bulgo/ *n. m.* (the) masses, (the) common people.
vulnerable /bulne'raβle/ *a.* vulnerable.

Y Z

y /i/ *conj.* and.
ya /ya/ *adv.* already; now; at once. **y. no,** no longer, any more. **y. que,** since.
yacer /ya'θer; ya'ser/ *v.* lie.
yacimiento /yaθi'miento; yasi'miento/ *n. m.* deposit.
yanqui /'yanki/ *a. & n.* North American.
yate /'yate/ *n. m.* yacht.
yegua /'yegua/ *n. f.* mare.
yelmo /'yelmo/ *n. m.* helmet.
yema /'yema/ *n. f.* yolk (of an egg).
yerba /'yerβa/ *n. f.* grass; herb.
yerno /'yerno/ *n. m.* son-in-law.
yerro /'yerro/ *n. m.* error, mistake.
yeso /'yeso/ *n. m.* plaster.
yídish /'yiðis/ *n. m.* Yiddish.
yo /yo/ *pron.* I.
yodo /'yoðo/ *n. m.* iodine.
yoduro /jo'ðuro/ *n. m.* iodide.
yonqui /'yonki/ *m. &amp. f. Colloq.* drug addict, junkie.
yugo /'yugo/ *n. m.* yoke.
yunque /'yunke/ *n. m.* anvil.

yunta /'yunta/ *n. f.* team (of animals).
zafarse /θa'farse; sa'farse/ *v.* run away, escape. **z. de,** get rid of.
zafio /'θafio; 'safio/ *a.* coarse, uncivil.
zafiro /θa'firo; sa'firo/ *n. m.* sapphire.
zaguán /θa'guan; sa'guan/ *n. m.* vestibule, hall.
zalamero /θala'mero; sala'mero/ **-ra** *n.* flatterer, wheedler.
zambullir /θambu'ʎir; sambu'yir/ *v.* plunge, dive.
zampar /θam'par; sam'par/ *v. Colloq.* gobble down, wolf down.
zanahoria /θana'oria; sana'oria/ *n. f.* carrot.
zanja /'θanha; 'sanha/ *n. f.* ditch, trench.
zapatería /θapate'ria; sapate'ria/ *n. f.* shoe store; shoemaker's shop.
zapatero /θapa'tero; sapa'tero/ *n. m.* shoemaker.
zapato /θa'pato; sa'pato/ *n. m.* shoe.
zar /θar; sar/ *n. m.* czar.
zaraza /θa'raθa; sa'rasa/ *n. f.* calico; chintz.
zarza /'θarθa; 'sarsa/ *n. f.* bramble.
zarzuela /θar'θuela; sar'suela/ *n. f.* musical comedy.
zodíaco /θo'ðiako; so'ðiako/ *n. m.* zodiac.
zona /'θona; 'sona/ *n. f.* zone.
zoología /θoolo'hia; soolo'hia/ *n. f.* zoology.
zoológico /θoo'lohiko; soo'lohiko/ *a.* zoological.
zorro /'θorro; 'sorro/ **-rra** *n.* fox.
zozobra /θo'θoβra; so'soβra/ *n. f.* worry, anxiety; capsizing.
zozobrar /θoθo'βrar; soso'βrar/ *v.* capsize; worry.
zumba /'θumba; 'sumba/ *n. f.* spanking.
zumbido /θum'βiðo; sum'βiðo/ *n. m.* buzz, hum. —**zumbar,** *v.*
zumo /'θumo; 'sumo/ *n. m.* juice. **z. de naranja,** orange juice.
zurcir /θur'θir; sur'sir/ *v.* darn, mend.
zurdo /'θurðo; 'surðo/ *a.* left-handed.
zurrar /θu'rrar; su'rrar/ *v.* flog, drub.

English–Spanish

inglés–español

A

a /ə, *when stressed* ā/ *art.* un, una.
abacus /'æbəkəs/ *n.* ábaco *m.*
abandon /ə'bændən/ *n.* **1.** desenfreno, abandono *m.* —*v.* **2.** abandonar, desamparar.
abandoned /ə'bændənd/ *a.* abandonado.
abandonment /ə'bændənmənt/ *n.* abandono, desamparo *m.*
abase /ə'beis/ *v.* degradar, humillar.
abasement /ə'beismənt/ *n.* degradación, humillación *f.*
abash /ə'bæʃ/ *v.* avergonzar.
abate /ə'beit/ *v.* menguar, moderarse.
abatement /ə'beitmənt/ *n.* disminución *f.*
abbess /'æbis/ *n.* abadesa *f.*
abbey /'æbi/ *n.* abadía *f.*
abbot /'æbət/ *n.* abad *m.*
abbreviate /ə'brivi,eit/ *v.* abreviar.
abbreviation /ə,brivi'eiʃən/ *n.* abreviatura *f.*
abdicate /'æbdı,keit/ *v.* abdicar.
abdication /,æbdı'keiʃən/ *n.* abdicación *f.*
abdomen /'æbdəmən/ *n.* abdomen *m.*
abdominal /æb'domənl/ *a.* abdominal.
abduct /æb'dʌkt/ *v.* secuestrar.
abduction /æb'dʌkʃən/ *n.* secuestración *f.*
abductor /æb'dʌktər/ *n.* secuestrador -ra.
aberrant /ə'bɛrənt, 'æbər-/ *a.* aberrante.
aberration /,æbə'reiʃən/ *n.* aberración *f.*
abet /ə'bɛt/ *v.* apoyar, favorecer.
abetment /ə'bɛtmənt/ *n.* apoyo *m.*
abettor /ə'bɛtər/ *n.* cómplice *m. & f.*
abeyance /ə'beiəns/ *n.* suspensión *f.*
abhor /æb'hɔr/ *v.* abominar, odiar.
abhorrence /æb'hɔrəns/ *n.* detestación *f.*; aborrecimiento *m.*
abhorrent /æb'hɔrənt/ *a.* detestable, aborrecible.
abide /ə'baid/ *v.* soportar. **to a. by,** cumplir con.
abiding /ə'baidiŋ/ *a.* perdurable.
ability /ə'biliti/ *n.* habilidad *f.*
abject /'æbdʒɛkt/ *a.* abyecto; desanimado.
abjuration /,æbdʒə'reiʃən/ *n.* renuncia *f.*
abjure /æb'dʒʊr/ *v.* renunciar.
ablative /'æblətiv/ *a. & n. Gram.* ablativo *m.*
ablaze /ə'bleiz/ *a.* en llamas.
able /'eibəl/ *a.* capaz; competente. **to be a.,** poder.
able-bodied /'eibəl 'bodid/ *a.* robusto.
ablution /ə'bluʃən/ *n.* ablución *f.*
ably /'eibli/ *adv.* hábilmente.
abnegate /'æbni,geit/ *v.* repudiar; negar.
abnegation /,æbni'geiʃən/ *n.* abnegación; repudiación *f.*
abnormal /æb'nɔrməl/ *a.* anormal.
abnormality /,æbnɔr'mæliti/ *n.* anormalidad, deformidad *f.*
abnormally /æb'nɔrməli/ *adv.* anormalmente.
aboard /ə'bɔrd/ *adv.* a bordo.
abode /ə'boud/ *n.* residencia *f.*
abolish /ə'boliʃ/ *v.* suprimir.
abolishment /ə'boliʃmənt/ *n.* abolición *f.*
abolition /,æbə'liʃən/ *n.* abolición *f.*
abominable /ə'bomənəbəl/ *a.* abominable.
abominate /ə'bomə,neit/ *v.* abominar, detestar.
abomination /ə,bomə'neiʃən/ *n.*
aboriginal /,æbə'ridʒənl/ *a. & n.* aborigen *f.*
abortion /ə'bɔrʃən/ *n.* aborto *m.*
abortive /ə'bɔrtiv/ *a.* abortivo.

abound /ə'baund/ *v.* abundar.
about /ə'baut/ *adv.* **1.** como. **about to,** para; a punto de. —*prep.* **2.** de, sobre, acerca de.
about-face /ə'baut,feis, ə'baut'feis/ *n. Mil.* media vuelta.
above /ə'bʌv/ *adv.* **1.** arriba. —*prep.* **2.** sobre; por encima de.
aboveboard /ə'bʌv,bɔrd/ *a. & adv.* sincero, franco.
abrasion /ə'breiʒən/ *n.* raspadura *f.; Med.* abrasión *f.*
abrasive /ə'breisiv/ *a.* raspante. *n.* abrasivo *m.*
abreast /ə'brɛst/ *adv.* de frente.
abridge /ə'bridʒ/ *v.* abreviar.
abridgment /ə'bridʒmənt/ *n.* abreviación *f.*; compendio *m.*
abroad /ə'brɔd/ *adv.* en el extranjero, al extranjero.
abrogate /'æbrə,geit/ *v.* abrogar, revocar.
abrogation /,æbrə'geiʃən/ *n.* abrogación, revocación *f.*
abrupt /ə'brʌpt/ *a.* repentino; brusco.
abruptly /ə'brʌptli/ *adv.* bruscamente, precipitadamente.
abruptness /ə'brʌptnis/ *n.* precipitación; brusquedad *f.*
abscess /'æbsɛs/ *n.* absceso *m.*
abscond /æb'skond/ *v.* fugarse.
absence /'æbsəns/ *n.* ausencia, falta *f.*
absent /'æbsənt/ *a.* ausente.
absentee /,æbsən'ti/ *a. & n.* ausente *m. & f.*
absent-minded /'æbsənt 'maindid/ *a.* distraído.
absinthe /'æbsinθ/ *n.* absenta *f.*
absolute /'æbsə,lut/ *a.* absoluto.
absolutely /,æbsə'lutli/ *adv.* absolutamente.
absoluteness /,æbsə'lutnis/ *n.* absolutismo *m.*
absolution /,æbsə'luʃən/ *n.* absolución *f.*
absolutism /'æbsəlu,tizəm/ *n.* absolutismo, despotismo *m.*
absolve /æb'zolv/ *v.* absolver.
absorb /æb'sɔrb/ *v.* absorber; preocupar.
absorbed /æb'sɔrbd/ *a.* absorbido; absorto.
absorbent /æb'sɔrbənt/ *a.* absorbente.
absorbent cotton algodón hidrófilo *m.*
absorbing /æb'sɔrbiŋ/ *a.* interesante.
absorption /æb'sɔrpʃən/ *n.* absorción; preocupación *f.*
abstain /æb'stein/ *v.* abstenerse.
abstemious /æb'stimiəs/ *a.* abstemio, sobrio.
abstinence /'æbstənəns/ *n.* abstinencia *f.*
abstract /*a, v* æb'strækt, 'æbstrækt; *n* 'æbstrækt/ *a.* **1.** abstracto. —*n.* **2.** resumen *m.* —*v.* **3.** abstraer.
abstracted /æb'stræktid/ *a.* distraído.
abstraction /æb'strækʃən/ *n.* abstracción *f.*
abstruse /æb'strus/ *a.* abstruso.
absurd /æb'sɜrd/ *a.* absurdo, ridículo.
absurdity /æb'sɜrditi/ *n.* absurdo *m.*
absurdly /æb'sɜrdli/ *adv.* absurdamente.
abundance /ə'bʌndəns/ *n.* abundancia *f.*
abundant /ə'bʌndənt/ *a.* abundante.
abundantly /ə'bʌndəntli/ *adv.* abundantemente.
abuse /*n* ə'byus; *v* ə'byuz/ *n.* **1.** abuso *m.* —*v.* **2.** abusar de; maltratar.
abusive /ə'byusiv/ *a.* abusivo.
abusively /ə'byusivli/ *adv.* abusivamente, ofensivamente.
abutment /ə'bʌtmənt/ *n.* (building) estribo, contrafuerte *m.*
abut (on) /ə'bʌt/ *v.* terminar (en); lindar (con).
abyss /ə'bis/ *n.* abismo *m.*
Abyssinian /,æbə'siniən/ *a. & n.* abisinio -nia.
acacia /ə'keiʃə/ *n.* acacia *f.*

academic /,ækə'dɛmik/ *a.* académico.
academy /ə'kædəmi/ *n.* academia *f.*
acanthus /ə'kænθəs/ *n. Bot.* acanto *m.*
accede /æk'sid/ *v.* acceder; consentir.
accelerate /æk'sɛlə,reit/ *v.* acelerar.
acceleration /æk,sɛlə'reiʃən/ *n.* aceleración *f.*
accelerator /æk'sɛlə,reitər/ *n. Auto.* acelerador *m.*
accent /'æksɛnt/ *n.* **1.** acento *m.* —*v.* **2.** acentuar.
accentuate /æk'sɛntʃu,eit/ *v.* acentuar.
accept /æk'sɛpt/ *v.* aceptar.
acceptability /æk,sɛptə'biliti/ *n.* aceptabilidad *f.*
acceptable /æk'sɛptəbəl/ *a.* aceptable.
acceptably /æk'sɛptəbli/ *adv.* aceptablemente.
acceptance /æk'sɛptəns/ *n.* aceptación *f.*
access /'æksɛs/ *n.* acceso *m.*, entrada *f.*
accessible /æk'sɛsəbəl/ *a.* accesible.
accessory /æk'sɛsəri/ *a.* **1.** accesorio. —*n.* **2.** cómplice *m. & f.*
accident /'æksidənt/ *n.* accidente *m.* **by a.,** por casualidad.
accidental /,æksi'dɛntl/ *a.* accidental.
accidentally /,æksi'dɛntli/ *adv.* accidentalmente, casualmente.
acclaim /ə'kleim/ *v.* aclamar.
acclamation /,æklə'meiʃən/ *n.* aclamación *f.*
acclimate /'æklə,meit/ *v.* aclimatar.
acclivity /ə'kliviti/ *n.* subida *f.*
accolade /'ækə,leid/ *n.* acolada *f.*
accommodate /ə'komə,deit/ *v.* acomodar.
accommodating /ə'komə,deitiŋ/ *a.* bondadoso, complaciente.
accommodation /ə,komə'deiʃən/ *n.* servicio *m.; (pl.)* alojamiento *m.*
accompaniment /ə'kʌmpənimənt/ *n.* acompañamiento *m.*
accompanist /ə'kʌmpənist/ *n.* acompañante *m. & f.*
accompany /ə'kʌmpəni/ *v.* acompañar.
accomplice /ə'komplis/ *n.* cómplice *m. & f.*
accomplish /ə'kompliʃ/ *v.* llevar a cabo; realizar.
accomplished /ə'kompliʃt/ *a.* acabado, cumplido; culto.
accomplishment /ə'kompliʃmənt/ *n.* realización *f.*; logro *m.*
accord /ə'kɔrd/ *n.* **1.** acuerdo *m.* —*v.* **2.** otorgar.
accordance /ə'kɔrdns/ *n.:* **in a. with,** de acuerdo con.
accordingly /ə'kɔrdiŋli/ *adv.* en conformidad.
according to /ə'kɔrdiŋ/ *prep.* según.
accordion /ə'kɔrdiən/ *n.* acordeón *m.*
accost /ə'kɔst/ *v.* dirigirse a.
account /ə'kaunt/ *n.* **1.** relato *m.; Com.* cuenta *f.* **on a. of,** a causa de. **on no a.,** de ninguna manera. —*v.* **2. a. for,** explicar.
accountable /ə'kauntəbəl/ *a.* responsable.
accountant /ə'kauntnt/ *n.* contador -ra.
accounting /ə'kauntiŋ/ *n.* contabilidad *f.*
accouter /ə'kutər/ *v.* equipar, ataviar.
accouterments /ə'kutərmənts/ *n.* equipo, atavío *m.*
accredit /ə'krɛdit/ *v.* acreditar.
accretion /ə'kriʃən/ *n.* aumento *m.*
accrual /ə'kruəl/ *n.* aumento, incremento *m.*
accrue /ə'kru/ *v.* provenir; acumularse.
accumulate /ə'kyumyə,leit/ *v.* acumular.
accumulation /ə,kyumyə'leiʃən/ *n.* acumulación *f.*
accumulative /ə'kyumyə,leitiv/ *a.* acumulativo.

accumulator /ə'kyumyə,leitər/ *n.* acumulador *m.*
accuracy /'ækyərəsi/ *n.* exactitud, precisión *f.*
accurate /'ækyərit/ *a.* exacto.
accursed /ə'kɜrsid, ə'kɜrst/ *a.* maldito.
accusation /,ækyu'zeiʃən/ *n.* acusación *f.*, cargo *m.*
accusative /ə'kyuzətiv/ *a. & n.* acusativo *m.*
accuse /ə'kyuz/ *v.* acusar.
accused /ə'kyuzd/ *a. & n.* acusado -da, procesado -da.
accuser /ə'kyuzər/ *n.* acusador -ra.
accustom /ə'kʌstəm/ *v.* acostumbrar.
accustomed /ə'kʌstəmd/ *a.* acostumbrado.
ace /eis/ *a.* **1.** sobresaliente. —*n.* **2.** as *m.*
acerbity /ə'sɜrbiti/ *n.* acerbidad, amargura *f.*
acetate /'æsi,teit/ *n. Chem.* acetato *m.*
acetic /ə'sitik/ *a.* acético.
acetylene /ə'sɛtl,in/ *a.* **1.** acetilénico. —*n.* **2.** *Chem.* acetileno *m.*
ache /eik/ *n.* **1.** dolor *m.* —*v.* **2.** doler.
achieve /ə'tʃiv/ *v.* lograr, llevar a cabo.
achievement /ə'tʃivmənt/ *n.* realización *f.*; hecho notable *m.*
acid /'æsid/ *a. & n.* ácido *m.*
acidify /ə'sidə,fai/ *v.* acidificar.
acidity /ə'siditi/ *n.* acidez *f.*
acidosis /,æsi'dousis/ *n. Med.* acidismo *m.*
acid rain lluvia ácida *f.*
acid test prueba decisiva.
acidulous /ə'sidʒələs/ *a.* agrio, acídulo.
acknowledge /æk'nolidʒ/ *v.* admitir; (receipt) acusar.
acme /'ækmi/ *n.* apogeo, colmo *m.*
acne /'ækni/ *n. Med.* acné *m. & f.*
acolyte /'ækə,lait/ *n.* acólito *m.*
acorn /'eikɔrn/ *n.* bellota *f.*
acoustics /ə'kustiks/ *n.* acústica *f.*
acquaint /ə'kweint/ *v.* familiarizar. **to be acquainted with,** conocer.
acquaintance /ə'kweintns/ *n.* conocimiento *m.*; (person known) conocido -da. **to make the a. of,** conocer.
acquiesce /,ækwi'ɛs/ *v.* consentir.
acquiescence /,ækwi'ɛsəns/ *n.* consentimiento *m.*
acquire /ə'kwai°r/ *v.* adquirir.
acquirement /ə'kwai°rmənt/ *n.* adquisición *f.; (pl.)* conocimientos *m.pl.*
acquisition /,ækwə'ziʃən/ *n.* adquisición *f.*
acquisitive /ə'kwizitiv/ *a.* adquisitivo.
acquit /ə'kwit/ *v.* exonerar, absolver.
acquittal /ə'kwitl/ *n.* absolución *f.*
acre /'eikər/ *n.* acre *m.*
acreage /'eikəridʒ/ número de acres.
acrid /'ækrid/ *a.* acre, punzante.
acrimonious /,ækrə'mouniəs/ *a.* acrimonioso, mordaz.
acrimony /'ækrə,mouni/ *n.* acrimonia, aspereza *f.*
acrobat /'ækrə,bæt/ *n.* acróbata *m. & f.*
acrobatic /,ækrə'bætik/ *a.* acrobático.
across /ə'krɔs/ *adv.* **1.** a través, al otro lado. —*prep.* **2.** al otro lado de, a través de.
acrostic /ə'krɔstik/ *n.* acróstico *m.*
act /ækt/ *n.* **1.** acción *f.*; acto *m.* —*v.* **2.** actuar, portarse. **act as,** hacer de. **act on,** decidir sobre.
acting /'æktiŋ/ *a.* **1.** interino. —*n.* **2.** acción *f.; Theat.* representación *f.*
actinism /'æktə,nizəm/ *n.* actinismo *m.*
actinium /æk'tiniəm/ *n. Chem.* actinio *m.*
action /'ækʃən/ *n.* acción *f.* **take a.,** tomar medidas.
action replay /'ri,plei/ repetición *f.*
activate /'æktə,veit/ *v.* activar.

activation /ˌæktəˈveiʃən/ *n.* activación *f.*

activator /ˈæktəˌveitər/ *n. Chem.* activador *m.*

active /ˈæktɪv/ *a.* activo.

activity /ækˈtɪvɪti/ *n.* actividad *f.*

actor /ˈæktər/ *n.* actor *m.*

actress /ˈæktrɪs/ *n.* actriz *f.*

actual /ˈæktʃuəl/ *a.* real, efectivo.

actuality /ˌæktʃuˈælɪti/ *n.* realidad, actualidad *f.*

actually /ˈæktʃuəli/ *adv.* en realidad.

actuary /ˈæktʃuˌɛri/ *n.* actuario *m.*

actuate /ˈæktʃuˌeit/ *v.* impulsar, mover.

acumen /əˈkyumən/ *n.* cacumen *m.*, perspicacia *f.*

acupuncture /ˈækyʊˌpʌŋktʃər/ *n.* acupuntura *f.*

acute /əˈkyut/ *a.* agudo; perspicaz.

acutely /əˈkyutli/ *adv.* agudamente.

acuteness /əˈkyutnɪs/ *n.* agudeza *f.*

adage /ˈædɪdʒ/ *n.* refrán, proverbio *m.*

adamant /ˈædəmənt/ *a.* firme.

Adam's apple /ˈædəmz/ nuez de la garganta.

adapt /əˈdæpt/ *v.* adaptar.

adaptability /əˌdæptəˈbɪlɪti/ *n.* adaptabilidad *f.*

adaptable /əˈdæptəbəl/ *a.* adaptable.

adaptation /ˌædəpˈteiʃən/ *n.* adaptación *f.*

adapter /əˈdæptər/ *n. Elec.* adaptador *m.*; *Mech.* ajustador *m.*

adaptive /əˈdæptɪv/ *a.* adaptable, acomodable.

add /æd/ *v.* agregar, añadir. **a. up,** sumar.

adder /ˈædər/ *n.* víbora; serpiente *f.*

addict /ˈædɪkt/ *n.* adicto -ta; (fan) aficionado -da.

addition /əˈdɪʃən/ *n.* adición *f.* **in a. to,** además de.

additional /əˈdɪʃənl/ *a.* adicional.

addle /ˈædl/ *v.* confundir.

address /*n* əˈdrɛs, ˈædrɛs; *v* əˈdrɛs/ *n.* **1.** dirección *f.*; señas *f.pl.*; (speech) discurso. —*v.* **2.** dirigirse a.

addressee /ˌædrɛˈsi/ *n.* destinatario -ia.

adduce /əˈdus/ *v.* aducir.

adenoid /ˈædnˌɔid/ *a.* adenoidea.

adept /əˈdɛpt/ *a.* adepto.

adeptly /əˈdɛptli/ *adv.* diestramente.

adeptness /əˈdɛptnɪs/ *n.* destreza *f.*

adequacy /ˈædɪkwəsi/ *n.* suficiencia *f.*

adequate /ˈædɪkwɪt/ *a.* adecuado.

adequately /ˈædɪkwɪtli/ *adv.* adecuadamente.

adhere /ædˈhɪər/ *v.* adherirse, pegarse.

adherence /ædˈhɪərəns/ *n.* adhesión *f.*; apego *m.*

adherent /ædˈhɪərənt/ *n.* adherente *m.*, partidario -ria.

adhesion /ædˈhiʒən/ *n.* adhesión *f.*

adhesive /ædˈhisɪv/ *a.* adhesivo. **a. tape,** esparadrapo *m.*

adhesiveness /ædˈhisɪvnɪs/ *n.* adhesividad *f.*

adieu /əˈdu/ *interj.* **1.** adiós. —*n.* **2.** despedida *f.*

adjacent /əˈdʒeisənt/ *a.* adyacente.

adjective /ˈædʒɪktɪv/ *n.* adjetivo *m.*

adjoin /əˈdʒɔin/ *v.* lindar (con).

adjoining /əˈdʒɔinɪŋ/ *a.* contiguo.

adjourn /əˈdʒɜrn/ *v.* suspender, levantar.

adjournment /əˈdʒɜrnmənt/ *n.* suspensión *f.*; *Leg.* espera *f.*

adjunct /ˈædʒʌŋkt/ *n.* adjunto *m.*; *Gram.* atributo *m.*

adjust /əˈdʒʌst/ *v.* ajustar, acomodar; arreglar.

adjuster /əˈdʒʌstər/ *n.* ajustador -ra.

adjustment /əˈdʒʌstmənt/ *n.* ajuste; arreglo *m.*

adjutant /ˈædʒətənt/ *n. Mil.* ayudante *m.*

administer /ædˈmɪnəstər/ *v.* administrar.

administration /ædˌmɪnəˈstreiʃən/ *n.* administración *f.*; gobierno *m.*

administrative /ædˈmɪnəˌstreitɪv/ *a.* administrativo.

administrator /ædˈmɪnəˌstreitər/ *n.* administrador -ra.

admirable /ˈædmərəbəl/ *a.* admirable.

admirably /ˈædmərəbli/ *adv.* admirablemente.

admiral /ˈædmərəl/ *n.* almirante *m.*

admiralty /ˈædmərəlti/ *n.* Ministerio de Marina.

admiration /ˌædməˈreiʃən/ *n.* admiración *f.*

admire /ædˈmaiᵊr/ *v.* admirar.

admirer /ædˈmaiᵊrər/ *n.* admirador -ra; enamorado -da.

admiringly /ædˈmaiᵊrɪŋli/ *adv.* admirativamente.

admissible /ædˈmɪsəbəl/ *a.* admisible, aceptable.

admission /ædˈmɪʃən/ *n.* admisión; entrada *f.*

admit /ædˈmɪt/ *v.* admitir.

admittance /ædˈmɪtn̩s/ *n.* entrada *f.*

admittedly /ædˈmɪtɪdli/ *adv.* reconocidamente.

admixture /ædˈmɪkstʃər/ *n.* mezcla *f.*

admonish /ædˈmɒnɪʃ/ *v.* amonestar.

admonition /ˌædməˈnɪʃən/ *n.* admonición *f.*

adolescence /ˌædlˈɛsəns/ *n.* adolescencia *f.*

adolescent /ˌædlˈɛsənt/ *n.* & *a.* adolescente.

adopt /əˈdɒpt/ *v.* adoptar.

adopted child /əˈdɒptɪd/ hija adoptiva *f.*, hijo adoptivo *m.*

adoption /əˈdɒpʃən/ *n.* adopción *f.*

adorable /əˈdɔrəbəl/ *a.* adorable.

adoration /ˌædəˈreiʃən/ *n.* adoración *f.*

adore /əˈdɔr/ *v.* adorar.

adorn /əˈdɔrn/ *v.* adornar.

adornment /əˈdɔrnmənt/ *n.* adorno *m.*

adrenalin /əˈdrɛnl̩ɪn/ *n.* adrenalina *f.*

adrift /əˈdrɪft/ *adv.* a la ventura.

adroit /əˈdrɔit/ *a.* diestro.

adulate /ˈædʒəˌleit/ *v.* adular.

adulation /ˌædʒəˈleiʃən/ *n.* adulación *f.*

adult /əˈdʌlt/ *a.* & *n.* adulto -a.

adulterant /əˈdʌltərənt/ *a.* & *n.* adulterante *m.*

adulterate /əˈdʌltəˌreit/ *v.* adulterar.

adulterer /əˈdʌltərər/ *n.* adúltero -ra.

adulteress /əˈdʌltərɪs/ *n.* adúltera *f.*

adultery /əˈdʌltəri/ *n.* adulterio *m.*

advance /ædˈvæns/ *n.* **1.** avance; adelanto *m.* **in a.,** de antemano, antes. —*v.* **2.** avanzar, adelantar.

advanced /ædˈvænst/ *a.* avanzado, adelantado.

advancement /ædˈvænsmənt/ *n.* adelantamiento *m.*; promoción *f.*

advantage /ædˈvæntɪdʒ/ *n.* ventaja *f.* **take a. of,** aprovecharse de.

advantageous /ˌædvənˈteidʒəs/ *a.* provechoso, ventajoso.

advantageously /ˌædvənˈteidʒəsli/ *adv.* ventajosamente.

advent /ˈædvɛnt/ *n.* venida, llegada *f.*

adventitious /ˌædvənˈtɪʃəs/ *a.* adventicio, espontáneo.

adventure /ædˈvɛntʃər/ *n.* aventura *f.*

adventurer /ædˈvɛntʃərər/ *n.* aventurero -ra.

adventurous /ædˈvɛntʃərəs/ *a.* aventurero, intrépido.

adventurously /ædˈvɛntʃərəsli/ *adv.* arriesgadamente.

adverb /ˈædvɜrb/ *n.* adverbio *m.*

adverbial /ædˈvɜrbiəl/ *a.* adverbial.

adversary /ˈædvərˌsɛri/ *n.* adversario -a.

adverse /ædˈvɜrs/ *a.* adverso.

adversely /ædˈvɜrsli/ *adv.* adversamente.

adversity /ædˈvɜrsɪti/ *n.* adversidad *f.*

advert /ædˈvɜrt/ *v.* hacer referencia a.

advertise /ˈædvərˌtaiz/ *v.* avisar, anunciar; (promote) promocionar.

advertisement /ˌædvərˈtaizmənt, ædˈvɜrtɪsmənt/ *n.* aviso, anuncio *m.*

advertiser /ˈædvərˌtaizər/ *n.* anunciante *m.* & *f.*, avisador -ra.

advertising /ˈædvərˌtaizɪŋ/ *n.* publicidad *f.*

advice /ædˈvais/ *n.* consejos *m.pl.*

advisability /ædˌvaizəˈbɪlɪti/ *n.* prudencia, propiedad *f.*

advisable /ædˈvaizəbəl/ *a.* aconsejable, prudente.

advisably /ædˈvaizəbli/ *adv.* prudentemente.

advise /ædˈvaiz/ *v.* aconsejar. **a. against,** desaconsejar.

advisedly /ædˈvaizɪdli/ *adv.* avisadamente, prudentemente.

advisement /ædˈvaizmənt/ *n.* consideración *f.*; **take under a.,** someter a estudio.

adviser /ædˈvaizər/ *n.* consejero -ra.

advocacy /ˈædvəkəsi/ *n.* abogacía; defensa *f.*

advocate /*n* ˈædvəkɪt; *v* -ˌkeit/ *n.* **1.** abogado -da. —*v.* **2.** apoyar.

aegis /ˈidʒɪs/ *n.* amparo *m.*

aerate /ˈɛəreit/ *v.* airear, ventilar.

aeration /ˌɛəˈreiʃən/ *n.* aeración, ventilación *f.*

aerial /ˈɛəriəl/ *a.* aéreo.

aerie /ˈɛəri/ *n.* nido de águila.

aeronautics /ˌɛərəˈnɔtɪks/ *n.* aeronáutica *f.*

aerosol bomb /ˈɛərəˌsɔl/ bomba insecticida.

afar /əˈfɑr/ *adv.* lejos. **from a.,** de lejos, desde lejos.

affability /ˌæfəˈbɪlɪti/ *n.* afabilidad, amabilidad *f.*

affable /ˈæfəbəl/ *a.* afable.

affably /ˈæfəbli/ *adv.* afablemente.

affair /əˈfɛər/ *n.* asunto *m.* **love a.,** aventura amorosa.

affect /əˈfɛkt/ *v.* afectar; (emotionally) conmover.

affectation /ˌæfɛkˈteiʃən/ *n.* afectación *f.*

affected /əˈfɛktɪd/ *a.* artificioso.

affecting /əˈfɛktɪŋ/ *a.* conmovedor.

affection /əˈfɛkʃən/ *n.* cariño *m.*

affectionate /əˈfɛkʃənɪt/ *a.* afectuoso, cariñoso.

affectionately /əˈfɛkʃənɪtli/ *adv.* afectuosamente, con cariño.

affiance /əˈfaiəns/ *v.* dar palabra de casamiento; **become affianced,** comprometerse.

affidavit /ˌæfɪˈdeivɪt/ *n. Leg.* declaración, deposición *f.*

affiliate /*n* əˈfɪliˌɪt; *v* əˈfɪliˌeit/ *n.* **1.** afiliado -da. —*v.* **2.** afiliar.

affiliation /əˌfɪliˈeiʃən/ *n.* afiliación *f.*

affinity /əˈfɪnɪti/ *n.* afinidad *f.*

affirm /əˈfɜrm/ *v.* afirmar.

affirmation /ˌæfərˈmeiʃən/ *n.* afirmación, aserción *f.*

affirmative /əˈfɜrmətɪv/ *n.* **1.** afirmativa *f.* —*a.* **2.** afirmativo.

affirmatively /əˈfɜrmətɪvli/ *adv.* afirmativamente, aseveradamente.

affix /*n* ˈæfɪks; *v* əˈfɪks/ *n.* **1.** *Gram.* afijo *m.* —*v.* **2.** fijar, pegar, poner.

afflict /əˈflɪkt/ *v.* afligir.

affliction /əˈflɪkʃən/ *n.* aflicción *f.*; mal *m.*

affluence /ˈæfluəns/ *n.* abundancia, opulencia *f.*

affluent /ˈæfluənt/ *a.* opulento, afluente.

afford /əˈfɔrd/ *v.* proporcionar. **be able to a.,** tener con que comprar.

affordable /əˈfɔrdəbəl/ *a.* asequible.

affront /əˈfrʌnt/ *n.* **1.** afrenta *f.* —*v.* **2.** afrentar, insultar.

afield /əˈfild/ *adv.* lejos de casa; lejos del camino; lejos del asunto.

afire /əˈfaiᵊr/ *adv.* ardiendo.

afloat /əˈflout/ *adv. Naut.* a flote.

aforementioned /əˈfɔrˌmɛnʃənd/ *a.* dicho, susodicho.

afraid /əˈfreid/ *a.* **to be a.,** tener miedo, temer.

African /ˈæfrɪkən/ *n.* & *a.* africano -na.

aft /æft/ *adv. Naut.* a popa, en popa.

after /ˈæftər/ *prep.* **1.** después de. —*conj.* **2.** después que.

aftermath /ˈæftərˌmæθ/ *n.* resultados *m.pl.*, consecuencias *f.pl.*

afternoon /ˌæftərˈnun/ *n.* tarde *f.* **good a.,** buenas tardes.

aftertaste /ˈæftərˌteist/ *n.* gustillo *m.*

afterthought /ˈæftərˌθɔt/ *n.* idea tardía.

afterward(s) /ˈæftərwərdz/ *adv.* después.

again /əˈgɛn/ *adv.* otra vez, de nuevo. **to do a.,** volver a hacer.

against /əˈgɛnst/ *prep.* contra; en contra de.

agape /əˈgeip/ *adv.* con la boca abierta.

agate /ˈægɪt/ *n.* ágata *f.*

age /eidʒ/ *n.* **1.** edad *f.* **of a.,** mayor de edad. **old a.,** vejez *f.* —*v.* **2.** envejecer.

aged /eidʒd; ˈeidʒɪd/ *a.* viejo, anciano, añejo.

ageism /ˈeidʒɪzəm/ *n.* discriminación contra las personas de edad.

ageless /ˈeidʒlɪs/ *a.* sempiterno.

agency /ˈeidʒənsi/ *n.* agencia *f.*

agenda /əˈdʒɛndə/ *n.* agenda *f.*, orden *m.*

agent /ˈeidʒənt/ *n.* agente; representante *m.* & *f.*

agglutinate /əˈglutn̩ˌeit/ *v.* aglutinar.

agglutination /əˌglutn̩ˈeiʃən/ *n.* aglutinación *f.*

aggrandize /əˈgrændaiz/ *v.* agrandar; elevar.

aggrandizement /əˈgrændɪzmənt/ *n.* engrandecimiento *m.*

aggravate /ˈægrəˌveit/ *v.* agravar; irritar.

aggravation /ˌægrəˈveiʃən/ *n.* agravamiento; empeoramiento *m.*

aggregate /ˈægrɪgɪt, -ˌgeit/ *a.* & *n.* agregado *m.*

aggregation /ˌægrɪˈgeiʃən/ *n.* agregación *f.*

aggression /əˈgrɛʃən/ *n.* agresión *f.*

aggressive /əˈgrɛsɪv/ *a.* agresivo.

aggressively /əˈgrɛsɪvli/ *adv.* agresivamente.

aggressiveness /əˈgrɛsɪvnɪs/ *n.* agresividad *f.*

aggressor /əˈgrɛsər/ *n.* agresor -ra.

aghast /əˈgæst/ *a.* horrorizado.

agile /ˈædʒəl/ *a.* ágil.

agility /əˈdʒɪlɪti/ *n.* agilidad, ligereza, prontitud *f.*

agitate /ˈædʒɪˌteit/ *v.* agitar.

agitation /ˌædʒɪˈteiʃən/ *n.* agitación *f.*

agitator /ˈædʒɪˌteitər/ *n.* agitador -ra.

agnostic /ægˈnɒstɪk/ *a.* & *n.* agnóstico -ca.

ago /əˈgou/ *adv.* hace. **two days a.,** hace dos días.

agonized /ˈægəˌnaizd/ *a.* angustioso.

agony /ˈægəni/ *n.* sufrimiento *m.*; angustia *f.*

agrarian /əˈgrɛəriən/ *a.* agrario.

agree /əˈgri/ *v.* estar de acuerdo; convenir. **a. with one,** sentar bien.

agreeable /əˈgriəbəl/ *a.* agradable.

agreeably /əˈgriəbli/ *adv.* agradablemente.

agreement /əˈgrimənt/ *n.* acuerdo *m.*

agriculture /ˈægrɪˌkʌltʃər/ *n.* agricultura *f.*

ahead /əˈhɛd/ *adv.* adelante.

aid /eid/ *n.* **1.** ayuda *f.* —*v.* **2.** ayudar.

aide /eid/ *n.* ayudante -ta.

AIDS /eidz/ *n.* SIDA *m.*

ailing /ˈeilɪŋ/ *adj.* enfermo.

ailment /ˈeilmənt/ *n.* enfermedad *f.*

aim /eim/ *n.* **1.** puntería *f.*; (purpose) propósito *m.* —*v.* **2.** apuntar.

aimless /ˈeimlɪs/ *a.* sin objeto.

air /ɛər/ *n.* **1.** aire *m.* **by a.** por avión. —*v.* **2.** ventilar, airear.

airbag /'ɛər,bæg/ n. (in automobiles) saco de aire m.
air-conditioned /'ɛər kən,dıʃənd/ a. con aire acondicionado.
air-conditioning /ɛər kən,dıʃənıŋ/ acondicionamiento del aire.
aircraft /'ɛər,kræft/ n. avión m.
aircraft carrier portaaviones m.
airfare /'ɛər,fɛər/ n. precio del billete de avión m.
airing /'ɛərıŋ/ n. ventilación f.
airline /'ɛər,lain/ n. línea aérea f.
airliner /'ɛər,lainər/ n. avión de pasajeros.
airmail /'ɛər,meil/ n. correo aéreo.
airplane /'ɛər,plein/ n. avión, aeroplano m.
air pollution contaminación atmosférica, contaminación del aire.
airport /'ɛər,port/ n. aeropuerto m.
air pressure presión atmosférica.
air raid ataque aéreo.
airsick /'ɛər,sık/ a. mareado.
air terminal terminal aérea f.
airtight /'ɛər,tait/ a. hermético.
air traffic controller controlador aéreo m.
aisle /ail/ n. pasillo m.
ajar /ə'dʒar/ a. entreabierto.
akin /ə'kın/ a. emparentado, semejante.
alacrity /ə'lækrıti/ n. alacridad, presteza f.
alarm /ə'larm/ n. 1. alarma f. —v. 2. alarmar.
alarmist /ə'larmıst/ n. alarmista m. & f.
albino /æl'bainou/ n. albino -na.
album /'ælbəm/ n. álbum m.
alcohol /'ælkə,hɔl/ n. alcohol m.
alcoholic /,ælkə'hɔlık/ a. alcohólico.
alcove /'ælkouv/ n. alcoba f.
ale /eil/ n. cerveza inglesa.
alert /ə'lɜrt/ n. 1. alarma f. **on the a.,** alerta, sobre aviso. —a. 2. listo, vivo. —v. 3. poner sobre aviso.
alfalfa /æl'fælfə/ n. alfalfa f.
algebra /'ældʒəbrə/ n. álgebra f.
alias /'eiliəs/ n. alias m.
alibi /'ælə,bai/ n. excusa f.; Leg. coartada f.
alien /'eiliən/ a. 1. ajeno, extranjero. —n. 2. extranjero -ra.
alienate /'eiliə,neit/ v. enajenar.
alight /ə'lait/ v. bajar, apearse.
align /ə'lain/ v. alinear.
alike /ə'laik/ a. 1. semejante, igual. —adv. 2. del mismo modo, igualmente.
alimentary canal /,ælə'mɛntəri/ n. tubo digestivo m.
alive /ə'laiv/ a. vivo; animado.
alkali /'ælkə,lai/ n. Chem. álcali, cali m.
alkaline /'ælkə,lain/ a. alcalino.
all /ɔl/ a. & pron. todo. **not at a.,** de ninguna manera, nada.
allay /ə'lei/ v. aquietar.
allegation /,ælı'geiʃən/ n. alegación f.
allege /ə'lɛdʒ/ v. alegar; pretender.
allegiance /ə'lidʒəns/ n. lealtad f.; (to country) homenaje m.
allegory /'ælə,gɔri/ n. alegoría f.
allergy /'ælərdʒi/ n. alergia f.
alleviate /ə'livi,eit/ v. aliviar.
alley /'æli/ n. callejón m. **bowling a.,** bolera f., boliche m.
alliance /ə'laiəns/ n. alianza f.
allied /'ælaid/ a. aliado.
alligator /'ælı,geitər/ n. caimán m.; (Mex.) lagarto m. **a. pear,** aguacate m.
allocate /'ælə,keit/ v. colocar, asignar.
allot /ə'lɒt/ v. asignar.
allotment /ə'lɒtmənt/ n. lote, porción f.
allow /ə'lau/ v. permitir, dejar.
allowance /ə'lauəns/ n. abono m.; dieta f. **make a. for,** tener en cuenta.
alloy /'ælɔi/ n. mezcla f.; (metal) aleación f.

all right está bien.
allude /ə'lud/ v. aludir.
allure /ə'lʊr/ n. 1. atracción f. —v. 2. atraer, tentar.
alluring /ə'lʊrıŋ/ a. tentador, seductivo.
allusion /ə'luʒən/ n. alusión f.
ally /n 'ælai, v ə'lai/ n. 1. aliado -da. —v. 2. aliar.
almanac /'ɔlmə,næk/ n. almanaque m.
almighty /ɔl'maiti/ a. todopoderoso.
almond /'amənd/ n. almendra f.
almost /'ɔlmoust/ adv. casi.
alms /amz/ n. limosna f.
aloft /ə'lɔft/ adv. arriba, en alto.
alone /ə'loun/ adv. solo, a solas. **to leave a.,** dejar en paz.
along /ə'lɔŋ/ prep. por; a lo largo de. **a. with,** junto con.
alongside /ə'lɔŋ'said/ adv. 1. al lado. —prep. 2. junto a.
aloof /ə'luf/ a. apartado.
aloud /ə'laud/ adv. en voz alta.
alpaca /æl'pækə/ n. alpaca f.
alphabet /'ælfə,bɛt/ n. alfabeto m.
alphabetical /,ælfə'bɛtıkəl/ a. alfabético.
alphabetize /'ælfəbı,taiz/ v. alfabetizar.
already /ɔl'rɛdi/ adv. ya.
also /'ɔlsou/ adv. también.
altar /'ɔltər/ n. altar m.
alter /'ɔltər/ v. alterar.
alteration /,ɔltə'reiʃən/ n. alteración f.
alternate /a, n 'ɔltərnıt; v -,neit/ a. 1. alterno. —n. 2. substituto -ta. —v. 3. alternar.
alternative /ɔl'tɜrnətıv/ a. 1. alternativo. —n. 2. alternativa f.
although /ɔl'ðou/ conj. aunque.
altitude /'æltı,tud/ n. altura f.
alto /'æltou/ n. contralto m.
altogether /,ɔltə'gɛðər/ adv. en junto; enteramente.
altruism /'æltru,ızəm/ n. altruismo m.
alum /'æləm/ n. alumbre m.
aluminum /ə'lumənəm/ n. aluminio m.
aluminum foil papel de aluminio m.
always /'ɔlweiz/ adv. siempre.
amalgam /ə'mælgəm/ n. amalgama f.
amalgamate /ə'mælgə,meit/ v. amalgamar.
amass /ə'mæs/ v. amontonar.
amateur /'æmə,tʃʊr/ n. aficionado -da.
amaze /ə'meiz/ v. asombrar; sorprender.
amazement /ə'meizmənt/ n. asombro m.
amazing /ə'meizıŋ/ a. asombroso, pasmoso.
ambassador /æm'bæsədər/ n. embajador -ra.
amber /'æmbər/ a. 1. ambarino. —n. 2. ámbar m.
ambidextrous /,æmbı'dɛkstrəs/ a. ambidextro.
ambiguity /,æmbı'gyuıti/ n. ambigüedad f.
ambiguous /æm'bıgyuəs/ a. ambiguo.
ambition /æm'bıʃən/ n. ambición f.
ambitious /æm'bıʃəs/ a. ambicioso.
ambulance /'æmbyələns/ n. ambulancia f.
ambush /'æmbʊʃ/ n. 1. emboscada f. —v. 2. acechar.
ameliorate /ə'milyə,reit/ v. mejorar.
amenable /ə'minəbəl/ a. tratable, dócil.
amend /ə'mɛnd/ v. enmendar.
amendment /ə'mɛndmənt/ n. enmienda f.
amenity /ə'mɛnıti/ n. amenidad f.
American /ə'mɛrıkən/ a. & n. americano -na, norteamericano -na.
amethyst /'æməθıst/ n. amatista f.
amiable /'eimiəbəl/ a. amable.
amicable /'æmıkəbəl/ a. amigable.

amid /ə'mıd/ prep. entre, en medio de.
amidships /ə'mıd,ʃıps/ adv. Naut. en medio del navío.
amiss /ə'mıs/ adv. mal. **to take a.,** llevar a mal.
amity /'æmıti/ n. amistad, armonía f.
ammonia /ə'mounyə/ n. amoníaco m.
ammunition /,æmyə'nıʃən/ n. municiones f.pl.
amnesia /æm'niʒə/ n. amnesia f.
amnesty /'æmnəsti/ n. amnistía f., indulto m.
amniocentesis /,æmniousɛn'tisıs/ n. amniocéntesis f.
amoeba /ə'mibə/ n. amiba f.
among /ə'mʌŋ/ prep. entre.
amoral /ei'mɔrəl/ a. amoral.
amorous /'æmərəs/ a. amoroso.
amorphous /ə'mɔrfəs/ a. amorfo.
amortize /'æmər,taiz/ v. Com. amortizar.
amount /ə'maunt/ n. 1. cantidad, suma f. —v. 2. **a. to,** subir a.
ampere /'æmpıər/ n. Elec. amperio m.
amphibian /æm'fıbiən/ a. & n. anfibio m.
amphitheater /'æmfə,θiətər/ n. anfiteatro, circo m.
ample /'æmpəl/ a. amplio; suficiente.
amplify /'æmplə,fai/ v. amplificar.
amputate /'æmpyu,teit/ v. amputar.
amuse /ə'myuz/ v. entretener, divertir.
amusement /ə'myuzmənt/ n. diversión f.
an /ən, when stressed an/ art. un, una.
anachronism /ə'nækrə,nızəm/ n. anacronismo, m.
analogous /ə'næləgəs/ a. análogo, parecido.
analogy /ə'nælədʒi/ n. analogía f.
analysis /ə'næləsıs/ n. análisis m.
analyst /'ænlıst/ n. analista m. & f.
analytic /,ænl'ıtık/ a. analítico.
analyze /'ænl,aiz/ v. analizar.
anarchy /'ænərki/ n. anarquía f.
anatomy /ə'nætəmi/ n. anatomía f.
ancestor /'ænsɛstər/ n. antepasado m.
ancestral /æn'sɛstrəl/ a. de los antepasados, hereditario.
ancestry /'ænsɛstri/ n. linaje, abolengo m.
anchor /'æŋkər/ n. 1. ancla f. **weigh a.,** levar el ancla. —v. 2. anclar.
anchorage /'æŋkərıdʒ/ n. Naut. ancladero, anclaje m.
anchovy /æn'tʃouvi/ n. anchoa f.
ancient /'einʃənt/ a. 1. antiguo -ua. —n. 2. antiguo -ua.
and /ænd, ənd/ conj. y, (before i-, hi-) e.
anecdote /'ænık,dout/ n. anécdota f.
anemia /ə'nimiə/ n. Med. anemia f.
anesthetic /,ænəs'θɛtık/ n. anestesia f.
anew /ə'nu/ adv. de nuevo.
angel /'eindʒəl/ n. ángel m.
anger /'æŋgər/ n. 1. ira f., enojo m. —v. 2. enfadar, enojar.
angle /'æŋgəl/ n. ángulo m.
angry /'æŋgri/ a. enojado, enfadado.
anguish /'æŋgwıʃ/ n. angustia f.
angular /'æŋgyələr/ a. angular.
aniline /'ænlın/ n. Chem. anilina f.
animal /'ænəməl/ a. & n. animal m.
animate /v 'ænə,meit; a -mıt/ v. 1. animar. —a. 2. animado.
animated /'ænə,meitıd/ a. vivo, animado.
animation /,ænə'meiʃən/ n. animación, viveza f.
animosity /,ænə'mɒsıti/ n. rencor m.
anise /'ænıs/ n. anís m.
ankle /'æŋkəl/ n. tobillo m.
annals /'ænlz/ n.pl. anales m.pl.
annex /n 'ænɛks; v ə'nɛks, 'ænɛks/ n. 1. anexo m., adición f. —v. 2. anexar.
annexation /,ænık'seiʃən/ n. anexión, adición f.
annihilate /ə'naiə,leit/ v. aniquilar, destruir.
anniversary /,ænə'vɜrsəri/ n. aniversario m.

annotate /'ænə,teit/ v. anotar.
annotation /,ænə'teiʃən/ n. anotación f., apunte m.
announce /ə'nauns/ v. anunciar.
announcement /ə'naunsmənt/ n. anuncio, aviso m.
announcer /ə'naunsər/ n. anunciador -ra; (radio) locutor -ra.
annoy /ə'nɔi/ v. molestar.
annoyance /ə'nɔiəns/ n. molestia, incomodidad f.
annual /'ænyuəl/ a. anual.
annuity /ə'nuıti/ n. anualidad, pensión f.
annul /ə'nʌl/ v. anular, invalidar.
anode /'ænoud/ n. Elec. ánodo m.
anoint /ə'nɔint/ v. untar; Relig. ungir.
anomalous /ə'nɒmələs/ a. anómalo, irregular.
anonymous /ə'nɒnəməs/ a. anónimo.
anorexia /,ænə'rɛksiə/ n. anorexia f.
another /ə'nʌðər/ a. & pron. otro.
answer /'ænsər, 'an-/ n. 1. contestación, respuesta f. —v. 2. contestar, responder. **a. for,** ser responsable de.
answerable /'ænsərəbəl/ a. discutible, refutable.
answering machine /'ænsərıŋ/ contestador automático m.
ant /ænt/ n. hormiga f.
antacid /ænt'æsıd/ a. & n. antiácido m.
antagonism /æn'tægə,nızəm/ n. antagonismo m.
antagonist /æn'tægənıst/ n. antagonista m. & f.
antagonistic /æn,tægə'nıstık/ a. antagónico, hostil.
antagonize /æn'tægə,naiz/ v. contrariar.
antarctic /ænt'arktık/ a. & n. antártico m.
antecedent /,æntə'sidnt/ a. & n. antecedente m.
antedate /'æntı,deit/ v. antedatar.
antelope /'æntl,oup/ n. antílope m., gacela f.
antenna /æn'tɛnə/ n. antena f.
antepenultimate /,æntıpı'nʌltəmıt/ a. antepenúltimo.
anterior /æn'tıəriər/ a. anterior.
anteroom /'ænti,rum/ n. antecámara f.
anthem /'ænθəm/ n. himno m.; (religious) antífona f.
anthology /æn'θɒlədʒi/ n. antología f.
anthracite /'ænθrə,sait/ n. antracita f.
anthrax /'ænθræks/ n. Med. ántrax m.
anthropology /,ænθrə'pɒlədʒi/ n. antropología f.
antiaircraft /,ænti'ɛər,kræft, ,æntai-/ a. antiaéreo.
antibody /'ænti,bɒdi/ n. anticuerpo m.
anticipate /æn'tısə,peit/ v. esperar, anticipar.
anticipation /æn,tısə'peiʃən/ n. anticipación f.
anticlerical /,ænti'klɛrıkəl, ,æntai-/ a. anticlerical.
anticlimax /,ænti'klaimæks, ,æntai-/ n. anticlímax m.
antidote /'ænti,dout/ n. antídoto m.
antifreeze /'ænti,friz/ n. anticongelante m.
antihistamine /,ænti'hıstə,min, -mın, ,æntai-/ n. antihistamínico m.
antimony /'æntə,mouni/ n. antimonio m.
antinuclear /,ænti'nukliər, æntai-/ a. antinuclear.
antipathy /æn'tıpəθi/ n. antipatía f.
antiquated /'ænti,kweitıd/ a. anticuado.
antique /æn'tik/ a. 1. antiguo. —n. 2. antigüedad f.
antiquity /æn'tıkwıti/ n. antigüedad f.
antiseptic /,æntə'sɛptık/ a. & n. antiséptico m.
antisocial /,ænti'souʃəl, æntai-/ a. antisocial.

antitoxin /ˌæntɪ'tɒksɪn/ *n. Med.* antitoxina *f.*

antler /'æntlər/ *n.* asta *f.*

anvil /'ænvɪl/ *n.* yunque *m.*

anxiety /æŋ'zaiɪti/ *n.* ansia, ansiedad *f.*

anxious /'æŋkʃəs, 'æŋʃəs/ *a.* inquieto, ansioso.

any /'ɛni/ *a.* alguno; (at all) cualquiera; (after *not*) ninguno.

anybody /'ɛniˌbɒdi/ *pron.* alguien; (at all) cualquiera; (after *not*) nadie.

anyhow /'ɛniˌhau/ *adv.* de todos modos; en todo caso.

anyone /'ɛniˌwʌn/ *pron.* = anybody.

anything /'ɛniˌθɪŋ/ *pron.* algo; (at all) cualquier cosa; (after *not*) nada.

anyway /'ɛniˌwei/ *adv.* = anyhow.

anywhere /'ɛniˌwɛər/ *adv.* en alguna parte; (at all) dondequiera; (after *not*) en ninguna parte.

apart /ə'pɑrt/ *adv.* aparte. **to take a.,** deshacer.

apartheid /ə'pɑrtheit, -hait/ *n.* apartheid *m.*

apartment /ə'pɑrtmənt/ *n.* apartamento, piso *m.*

apartment house casa de pisos *f.*

apathetic /ˌæpə'θɛtɪk/ *a.* apático.

apathy /'æpəθi/ *n.* apatía *f.*

ape /eip/ *n.* **1.** mono *-na.* **—***v.* **2.** imitar.

aperture /'æpərtʃər/ *n.* abertura *f.*

apex /'eipɛks/ *n.* ápice *m.*

aphorism /'æfəˌrɪzəm/ *n.* aforismo *m.*

apiary /'eipiˌɛri/ *n.* colmenario, abejar *m.*

apiece /ə'pis/ *adv.* por persona; cada uno.

apologetic /əˌpɒlə'dʒɛtɪk/ *a.* apologético.

apologist /ə'pɒlədʒɪst/ *n.* apologista *m.* & *f.*

apologize /ə'pɒləˌdʒaiz/ *v.* excusarse, disculparse.

apology /ə'pɒlədʒi/ *n.* excusa; apología *f.*

apoplectic /ˌæpə'plɛktɪk/ *a.* apopléctico.

apoplexy /'æpəˌplɛksi/ *n.* apoplejía *f.*

apostate /ə'pɒsteit/ *n.* apóstata *m.* & *f.*

apostle /ə'pɒsəl/ *n.* apóstol *m.*

apostolic /ˌæpə'stɒlɪk/ *a.* apostólico.

appall /ə'pɔl/ *v.* horrorizar; consternar.

apparatus /ˌæpə'rætəs/ *n.* aparato *m.*

apparel /ə'pærəl/ *n.* ropa *f.*

apparent /ə'pærənt/ *a.* aparente; claro.

apparition /ˌæpə'rɪʃən/ *n.* aparición *f.;* fantasma *m.*

appeal /ə'pil/ *n.* **1.** súplica *f.;* interés *m.; Leg.* apelación *f.* **—***v.* **2.** apelar, suplicar; interesar.

appear /ə'pɪər/ *v.* aparecer, asomar; (seem) parecer; *Leg.* comparecer.

appearance /ə'pɪərəns/ *n.* apariencia *f.,* aspecto *m.;* aparición *f.*

appease /ə'piz/ *v.* aplacar, apaciguar.

appeasement /ə'pizmənt/ *n.* apaciguamiento *m.*

appeaser /ə'pizər/ *n.* apaciguador -ra, pacificador -ra.

appellant /ə'pɛlənt/ *n.* apelante, demandante *m.* & *f.*

appellate /ə'pɛlɪt/ *a. Leg.* de apelación.

appendage /ə'pɛndɪdʒ/ *n.* añadidura *f.*

appendectomy /ˌæpən'dɛktəmi/ *n.* apendectomía *f.*

appendicitis /əˌpɛndə'saitɪs/ *n.* apendicitis *f.*

appendix /ə'pɛndɪks/ *n.* apéndice *m.*

appetite /'æpɪˌtait/ *n.* apetito *m.*

appetizer /'æpɪˌtaizər/ *n.* aperitivo *m.*

appetizing /'æpɪˌtaizɪŋ/ *a.* apetitoso.

applaud /ə'plɔd/ *v.* aplaudir.

applause /ə'plɔz/ *n.* aplauso *m.*

apple /'æpəl/ *n.* manzana *f.* **a. tree,** manzano *m.*

applesauce /'æpəlˌsɔs/ *n.* compota de manzana.

appliance /ə'plaiəns/ *n.* aparato *m.*

applicable /'æplɪkəbəl/ *a.* aplicable.

applicant /'æplɪkənt/ *n.* suplicante *m.* & *f.;* candidato -ta.

application /ˌæplɪ'keiʃən/ *n.* solicitud *f.,* (computer) programa *m.*

applied /ə'plaid/ *a.* aplicado. **a. for,** pedido.

appliqué /ˌæplɪ'kei/ *n.* (sewing) aplicación *f.*

apply /ə'plai/ *v.* aplicar. **a. for,** solicitar, pedir.

appoint /ə'pɔint/ *v.* nombrar.

appointment /ə'pɔintmənt/ *n.* nombramiento *m.;* puesto *m.*

apportion /ə'pɔrʃən/ *v.* repartir.

apposition /ˌæpə'zɪʃən/ *n. Gram.* aposición *f.*

appraisal /ə'preizəl/ *n.* valoración *f.*

appraise /ə'preiz/ *v.* evaluar; tasar; estimar.

appreciable /ə'priʃiəbəl/ *a.* apreciable; notable.

appreciate /ə'priʃiˌeit/ *v.* apreciar, estimar.

appreciation /əˌpriʃi'eiʃən/ *n.* aprecio; reconocimiento *m.*

apprehend /ˌæprɪ'hɛnd/ *v.* prender, capturar.

apprehension /ˌæprɪ'hɛnʃən/ *n.* aprensión *f.;* detención *f.*

apprehensive /ˌæprɪ'hɛnsɪv/ *a.* aprensivo.

apprentice /ə'prɛntɪs/ *n.* aprendiz -iza.

apprenticeship /ə'prɛntɪsˌʃɪp/ *n.* aprendizaje *m.*

apprise /ə'praiz/ *v.* informar.

approach /ə'proutʃ/ *n.* **1.** acceso; método *m.* **—***v.* **2.** acercarse.

approachable /ə'proutʃəbəl/ *a.* accesible.

approbation /ˌæprə'beiʃən/ *n.* aprobación *f.*

appropriate /*a* ə'prouprɪt; *v* -ˌeit/ *a.* **1.** apropiado. **—***v.* **2.** apropiar.

appropriation /əˌproupri'eiʃən/ *n.* apropiación *f.*

approval /ə'pruvəl/ *n.* aprobación *f.*

approve /ə'pruv/ *v.* aprobar.

approximate /*a* ə'prɒksəmɪt; *v* -ˌmeit/ *a.* **1.** aproximado. **—***v.* **2.** aproximar.

approximately /ə'prɒksəmɪtli/ *adv.* aproximadamente.

approximation /əˌprɒksə'meiʃən/ *n.* aproximación *f.*

appurtenance /ə'pɜrtṇəns/ *n.* dependencia *f.*

apricot /'æprɪˌkɒt/ *n.* albaricoque, damasco *m.*

April /'eiprəl/ *n.* abril *m.*

apron /'eiprən/ *n.* delantal *m.*

apropos /ˌæprə'pou/ *adv.* a propósito.

apt /æpt/ *a.* apto; capaz.

aptitude /'æptɪˌtud/ *n.* aptitud; facilidad *f.*

aquarium /ə'kwɛəriəm/ *n.* acuario *m.,* pecera *f.*

aquatic /ə'kwætɪk/ *a.* acuático.

aqueduct /'ækwɪˌdʌkt/ *n.* acueducto *m.*

aqueous /'ækwiəs/ *a.* ácueo, acuoso, aguoso.

aquiline /'ækwəˌlain/ *a.* aquilino, aguileño.

Arab /'ærəb/ *a.* & *n.* árabe *m.* & *f.*

arable /'ærəbəl/ *a.* cultivable.

arbitrary /'ɑrbɪˌtrɛri/ *a.* arbitrario.

arbitrate /'ɑrbɪˌtreit/ *v.* arbitrar.

arbitration /ˌɑrbɪ'treiʃən/ *n.* arbitraje *m.,* arbitración *f.*

arbitrator /'ɑrbɪˌtreitər/ *n.* arbitrador -ra.

arbor /'ɑrbər/ *n.* emparrado *m.*

arboreal /ɑr'bɔriəl/ *a.* arbóreo.

arc /ɑrk/ *n.* arco *m.*

arch /ɑrtʃ/ *n.* **1.** arco *m.* **—***v.* **2.** arquear, encorvar.

archaeology /ˌɑrki'ɒlədʒi/ *n.* arqueología *f.*

archaic /ɑr'keiɪk/ *a.* arcaico.

archbishop /'ɑrtʃ'bɪʃəp/ *n.* arzobispo *m.*

archdiocese /ˌɑrtʃ'daiəˌsis, -sɪs/ *n.* archidiócesis *f.*

archduke /'ɑrtʃ'duk/ *n.* archiduque *m.*

archer /'ɑrtʃər/ *n.* arquero *m.*

archery /'ɑrtʃəri/ *n.* ballestería *f.*

archipelago /ˌɑrkə'pɛləˌgou/ *n.* archipiélago *m.*

architect /'ɑrkɪˌtɛkt/ *n.* arquitecto -ta.

architectural /ˌɑrkɪ'tɛktʃərəl/ *a.* arquitectural.

architecture /'ɑrkɪˌtɛktʃər/ *n.* arquitectura *f.*

archive /'ɑrkaiv/ *n.* archivo *m.*

archway /'ɑrtʃˌwei/ *n.* arcada *f.*

arctic /'ɑrktɪk, 'ɑrtɪk/ *a.* ártico.

ardent /'ɑrdṇt/ *a.* ardiente.

ardor /'ɑrdər/ *n.* ardor *m.,* pasión *f.*

arduous /'ɑrdʒuəs/ *a.* arduo, difícil.

area /'ɛəriə/ *n.* área; extensión *f.*

area code prefijo *m.*

arena /ə'rinə/ *n.* arena *f.*

Argentine /'ɑrdʒəntɪn, -ˌtain/ *a.* & *n.* argentino -na.

argue /'ɑrgyu/ *v.* disputar; sostener.

argument /'ɑrgyəmənt/ *n.* disputa *f.;* razonamiento *m.*

argumentative /ˌɑrgyə'mɛntətɪv/ *a.* argumentoso.

aria /'ɑriə/ *n.* aria *f.*

arid /'ærɪd/ *a.* árido, seco.

arise /ə'raiz/ *v.* surgir; alzarse.

aristocracy /ˌærə'stɒkrəsi/ *n.* aristocracia *f.*

aristocrat /ə'rɪstəˌkræt/ *n.* aristócrata *m.*

aristocratic /əˌrɪstə'krætɪk/ *a.* aristocrático.

arithmetic /ə'rɪθmətɪk/ *n.* aritmética *f.*

ark /ɑrk/ *n.* arca *f.*

arm /ɑrm/ *n.* **1.** brazo *m.;* (weapon) arma *f.* **—***v.* **2.** armar.

armament /'ɑrməmənt/ *n.* armamento *m.*

armchair /'ɑrmˌtʃɛər/ *n.* sillón *m.,* butaca *f.*

armed forces /'ɑrmd 'fɔrsɪz/ fuerzas militares.

armful /'ɑrmˌfʊl/ *n.* brazada *f.*

armhole /'ɑrmˌhoul/ *n.* (sew.) sobaquera *f.*

armistice /'ɑrməstɪs/ *n.* armisticio *m.*

armor /'ɑrmər/ *n.* armadura *f.,* blindaje *m.*

armored /'ɑrmərd/ *a.* blindado.

armory /'ɑrməri/ *n.* armería *f.,* arsenal *m.*

armpit /'ɑrmˌpɪt/ *n.* axila *f.,* sobaco *m.*

army /'ɑrmi/ *n.* ejército *m.*

arnica /'ɑrnɪkə/ *n.* árnica *f.*

aroma /ə'roumə/ *n.* fragancia *f.*

aromatic /ˌærə'mætɪk/ *a.* aromático.

around /ə'raund/ *prep.* alrededor de, a la vuelta de; cerca de. **a. here,** por aquí.

arouse /ə'rauz/ *v.* despertar; excitar.

arraign /ə'rein/ *v. Leg.* procesar criminalmente.

arrange /ə'reindʒ/ *v.* arreglar; concertar; *Mus.* adaptar.

arrangement /ə'reindʒmənt/ *n.* arreglo; orden *m.*

array /ə'rei/ *n.* **1.** orden; adorno *m.* **—***v.* **2.** adornar.

arrears /ə'rɪərz/ *n.* atrasos *m.pl.*

arrest /ə'rɛst/ *n.* **1.** detención *f.* **—***v.* **2.** detener, arrestar.

arrival /ə'raivəl/ *n.* llegada *f.*

arrive /ə'raiv/ *v.* llegar.

arrogance /'ærəgəns/ *n.* arrogancia *f.*

arrogant /'ærəgənt/ *a.* arrogante.

arrogate /'ærəˌgeit/ *v.* arrogarse, usurpar.

arrow /'ærou/ *n.* flecha *f.*

arrowhead /'ærouˌhɛd/ *n.* punta de flecha *f.*

arsenal /'ɑrsənḷ/ *n.* arsenal *m.*

arsenic /'ɑrsənɪk/ *n.* arsénico *m.*

arson /'ɑrsən/ *n.* incendio premeditado.

art /ɑrt/ arte *m.* (*f.* in *pl.*); (skill) maña *f.*

arterial /ɑr'tɪəriəl/ *a.* arterial.

arteriosclerosis /ɑrˌtɪəriousklə'rousɪs/ *n.* arteriosclerosis *f.*

artery /'ɑrtəri/ *n.* arteria *f.*

artesian well /ɑr'tiʒən/ pozo artesiano.

artful /'ɑrtfəl/ *a.* astuto.

arthritis /ɑr'θraitɪs/ *n.* artritis *f.*

artichoke /'ɑrtɪˌtʃouk/ *n.* alcachofa *f.*

article /'ɑrtɪkəl/ *n.* artículo *m.*

articulate /ɑr'tɪkyəˌleit/ *v.* articular.

articulation /ɑrˌtɪkyə'leiʃən/ *n.* articulación *f.*

artifice /'ɑrtəfɪs/ *n.* artificio *m.*

artificial /ˌɑrtə'fɪʃəl/ *a.* artificial.

artificially /ˌɑrtə'fɪʃəli/ *adv.* artificialmente.

artillery /ɑr'tɪləri/ *n.* artillería *f.*

artisan /'ɑrtəzən/ *n.* artesano -na.

artist /'ɑrtɪst/ *n.* artista *m.* & *f.*

artistic /ɑr'tɪstɪk/ *a.* artístico.

artistry /'ɑrtɪstri/ *n.* arte *m.* & *f.*

artless /'ɑrtlɪs/ *a.* natural, cándido.

as /æz/ *adv.* & *conj.* como; **as... as** tan... como.

asbestos /æs'bɛstəs/ *n.* asbesto *m.*

ascend /ə'sɛnd/ *v.* ascender.

ascendancy /ə'sɛndənsi/ *n.* ascendiente *m.*

ascendant /ə'sɛndənt/ *a.* ascendente.

ascent /ə'sɛnt/ *n.* subida *f.,* ascenso *m.*

ascertain /ˌæsər'tein/ *v.* averiguar.

ascetic /ə'sɛtɪk/ *a.* **1.** ascético. **—***n.* **2.** asceta *m.* & *f.*

ascribe /ə'skraib/ *v.* atribuir.

ash /æʃ/ *n.* ceniza *f.*

ashamed /ə'ʃeimd/ *a.* avergonzado.

ashen /'æʃən/ *a.* pálido.

ashore /ə'ʃɔr/ *adv.* a tierra. **go a.,** desembarcar.

ashtray /'æʃˌtrei/ *n.* cenicero *m.*

Ash Wednesday miércoles de ceniza *m.*

Asiatic /ˌeiʒi'ætɪk/ *a.* & *n.* asiático -ca.

aside /ə'said/ *adv.* al lado. **a. from,** aparte de.

ask /æsk/ *v.* preguntar; invitar; (request) pedir. **a. for,** pedir. **a. a question,** hacer una pregunta.

askance /ə'skæns/ *adv.* de soslayo; con recelo.

asleep /ə'slip/ *a.* dormido. **to fall a.,** dormirse.

asparagus /ə'spærəgəs/ *n.* espárrago *m.*

aspect /'æspɛkt/ *n.* aspecto *m.,* apariencia *f.*

asperity /ə'spɛrɪti/ *n.* aspereza *f.*

aspersion /ə'spɜrʒən/ *n.* calumnia *f.*

asphalt /'æsfɔlt/ *n.* asfalto *m.*

asphyxia /æs'fɪksiə/ *n.* asfixia *f.*

asphyxiate /æs'fɪksiˌeit/ *v.* asfixiar, sofocar.

aspirant /'æspərənt/ *a.* & *n.* aspirante *m.* & *f.*

aspirate /'æspəˌreit/ *v.* aspirar.

aspiration /ˌæspə'reiʃən/ *n.* aspiración *f.*

aspirator /'æspəˌreitər/ *n.* aspirador *m.*

aspire /ə'spaiᵊr/ *v.* aspirar. **a. to,** ambicionar.

aspirin /'æspərɪn/ *n.* aspirina *f.*

ass /æs/ *n.* asno, burro *m.*

assail /ə'seil/ *v.* asaltar, acometer.

assailant /ə'seilənt/ *n.* asaltador -ra.

assassin /ə'sæsɪn/ *n.* asesino -na.

assassinate /ə'sæsəˌneit/ *v.* asesinar.

assassination /əˌsæsə'neiʃən/ *n.* asesinato *m.*

assault /ə'sɔlt/ *n.* **1.** asalto *m.* **—***v.* **2.** asaltar, atacar.

assay /'æsei/ *v.* examinar; ensayar.

assemblage /ə'sɛmblɪdʒ/ *n.* asamblea *f.*

assemble /ə'sɛmbəl/ *v.* juntar, convocar; (mechanism) montar.

assembly /ə'sɛmbli/ *n.* asamblea, concurrencia *f.*

assent /ə'sɛnt/ *n.* **1.** asentimiento *m.* **—***v.* **2.** asentir, convenir.

assert /ə'sɜrt/ *v.* afirmar, aseverar. **a. oneself,** hacerse sentir.

assertion /ə'sɜrʃən/ *n.* aserción, aseveración *f.*

assertive /ə'sɜrtɪv/ *a.* asertivo.

assess /ə'sɛs/ *v.* tasar, evaluar.

assessor /ə'sɛsər/ *n.* asesor -ra.

asset /'æsɛt/ *n.* ventaja *f.* **assets,** *Com.* capital *m.*

asseverate /ə'sɛvəˌreit/ *v.* aseverar, afirmar.

asseveration /əˌsɛvə'reiʃən/ *n.* aseveración *f.*

assiduous /ə'sɪdʒuəs/ *a.* asiduo.

assiduously /ə'sɪdʒuəsli/ *adv.* asiduamente.

assign /ə'sain/ *v.* asignar; destinar.

assignable /ə'sainəbəl/ *a.* asignable, transferible.

assignation /ˌæsɪg'neiʃən/ *n.* asignación *f.*

assignment /ə'sainmənt/ *n.* misión; tarea *f.*

assimilate /ə'sɪməˌleit/ *v.* asimilar.

assimilation /əˌsɪmə'leiʃən/ *n.* asimilación *f.*

assimilative /ə'sɪmələtɪv/ *a.* asimilativo.

assist /ə'sɪst/ *v.* ayudar, auxiliar.

assistance /ə'sɪstəns/ *n.* ayuda *f.*, auxilio *m.*

assistant /ə'sɪstənt/ *n.* ayudante -ta, asistente -ta.

associate /*n* ə'sousiɪt; *v* -siˌeit/ *n.* **1.** socio -cia. **—***v.* **2.** asociar.

association /əˌsousi'eiʃən/ *n.* asociación; sociedad *f.*

assonance /'æsənəns/ *n.* asonancia *f.*

assort /ə'sɔrt/ *v.* surtir con variedad.

assorted /ə'sɔrtɪd/ *a.* variado, surtido.

assortment /ə'sɔrtmənt/ *n.* surtido *m.*

assuage /ə'sweidʒ/ *v.* mitigar, aliviar.

assume /ə'sum/ *v.* suponer; asumir.

assuming /ə'sumɪŋ/ *a.* presuntuoso. **a. that,** dado que.

assumption /ə'sʌmpʃən/ *n.* suposición; *Relig.* asunción *f.*

assurance /ə'ʃʊrəns/ *n.* seguridad; confianza *f.*; garantía *f.*

assure /ə'ʃʊr/ *v.* asegurar; dar confianza.

assured /ə'ʃʊrd/ *a.* **1.** seguro. **—***a.* & *n.* **2.** *Com.* asegurado -da.

assuredly /ə'ʃʊrɪdli/ *adv.* ciertamente.

aster /'æstər/ *n.* aster *f.*

asterisk /'æstərɪsk/ *n.* asterisco *m.*

astern /ə'stɜrn/ *adv. Naut.* a popa.

asteroid /'æstəˌrɔid/ *n.* asteroide *m.*

asthma /'æzmə/ *n. Med.* asma *f.*

astigmatism /ə'stɪgməˌtɪzəm/ *n.* astigmatismo *m.*

astir /ə'stɜr/ *adv.* en movimiento.

astonish /ə'stɒnɪʃ/ *v.* asombrar, pasmar.

astonishment /ə'stɒnɪʃmənt/ *n.* asombro *m.*, sorpresa *f.*

astound /ə'staund/ *v.* pasmar, sorprender.

astral /'æstrəl/ *a.* astral, estelar.

astray /ə'strei/ *a.* desviado.

astride /ə'straid/ *adv.* a horcajadas.

astringent /ə'strɪndʒənt/ *a.* & *n.* astringente *m.*

astrology /ə'strɒlədʒi/ *n.* astrología *f.*

astronaut /'æstrəˌnɔt/ *n.* astronauta *m.* & *f.*

astronomy /ə'strɒnəmi/ *n.* astronomía *f.*

astute /ə'stut/ *a.* astuto; agudo.

asunder /ə'sʌndər/ *adv.* en dos.

asylum /ə'sailəm/ *n.* asilo, refugio *m.*

asymmetry /ei'sɪmɪtri/ *n.* asimetría *f.*

at /æt/ *prep,* a, en; cerca de.

ataxia /ə'tæksiə/ *n. Med.* ataxia *f.*

atheist /'eiθiɪst/ *n.* ateo -tea.

athlete /'æθlit/ *n.* atleta *m.* & *f.*

athletic /æθ'lɛtɪk/ *a.* atlético.

athletics /æθ'lɛtɪks/ *n.* atletismo *m.*, deportes *m.pl.*

athwart /ə'θwɔrt/ *prep.* a través de.

Atlantic /æt'læntɪk/ *a.* **1.** atlántico. **—***n.* **2.** Atlántico *m.*

Atlantic Ocean Océano Atlántico *m.*

atlas /'ætləs/ *n.* atlas *m.*

atmosphere /'ætməsˌfɪər/ *n.* atmósfera *f.*; *Fig.* ambiente *m.*

atmospheric /ˌætməs'fɛrɪk/ *a.* atmosférico.

atoll /'ætɔl/ *n.* atolón *m.*

atom /'ætəm/ *n.* átomo *m.*

atomic /ə'tɒmɪk/ *a.* atómico.

atomic bomb bomba atómica *f.*

atomic energy energía atómica, energía nuclear *f.*

atomic theory teoría atómica. *f.*

atomic weight peso atómico *m.*

atonal /ei'tounl/ *a. Mus.* atonal.

atone /ə'toun/ *v.* expiar, compensar.

atonement /ə'tounmənt/ *n.* expiación; reparación *f.*

atrocious /ə'trouʃəs/ *a.* atroz.

atrocity /ə'trɒsɪti/ *n.* atrocidad *f.*

atrophy /'ætrəfi/ *n.* **1.** *Med.* atrofia *f.* **—***v.* **2.** atrofiar.

atropine /'ætrəˌpin, -pɪn/ *n.* atropina *f.*

attach /ə'tætʃ/ *v.* juntar; prender; (hook) enganchar; *Fig.* atribuir.

attaché /ætæ'ʃei/ *n.* agregado -da.

attachment /ə'tætʃmənt/ enlace *m.*; accesorio *m.*; (emotional) afecto, cariño *m.*

attack /ə'tæk/ *n.* **1.** ataque *m.* **—***v.* **2.** atacar.

attacker /ə'tækər/ *n.* asaltador -ra.

attain /ə'tein/ *v.* lograr, alcanzar.

attainable /ə'teinəbəl/ *a.* accesible, realizable.

attainment /ə'teinmənt/ *n.* logro; *(pl.)* dotes *f.pl.*

attempt /ə'tɛmpt/ *n.* **1.** ensayo; esfuerzo *m.*; tentativa *f.* **—***v.* **2.** ensayar, intentar.

attend /ə'tɛnd/ *v.* atender; (a meeting) asistir a.

attendance /ə'tɛndəns/ *n.* asistencia; presencia *f.*

attendant /ə'tɛndənt/ *a.* **1.** concomitante. **—***n.* **2.** servidor -ra.

attention /ə'tɛnʃən/ *n.* atención *f.*; obsequio *m.* **to pay a. to,** hacer caso a.

attentive /ə'tɛntɪv/ *a.* atento.

attentively /ə'tɛntɪvli/ *adv.* atentamente.

attenuate /ə'tɛnyuˌeit/ *v.* atenuar, adelgazar.

attest /ə'tɛst/ *v.* confirmar, atestiguar.

attic /'ætɪk/ *n.* desván *m.*, guardilla *f.*

attire /ə'taiᵊr/ *n.* **1.** traje *m.* **—***v.* **2.** vestir.

attitude /'ætɪˌtud/ *n.* actitud *f.*, ademán *m.*

attorney /ə'tɜrni/ *n.* abogado -da, apoderado -da.

attract /ə'trækt/ *v.* atraer. **a. attention,** llamar la atención.

attraction /ə'trækʃən/ *n.* atracción *f.*, atractivo *m.*

attractive /ə'træktɪv/ *a.* atractivo; simpático.

attributable /ə'trɪbyʊtəbəl/ *a.* atribuible, imputable.

attribute /*n* 'ætrəˌbyut; *v* ə'trɪbyut/ *n.* **1.** atributo *m.* **—***v.* **2.** atribuir.

attrition /ə'trɪʃən/ *n.* roce, desgaste *m.*; atrición *f.*

attune /ə'tun/ *v.* armonizar.

auction /'ɔkʃən/ *n.* subasta *f.*, *S.A.* venduta *f.*

auctioneer /ˌɔkʃə'nɪər/ *n.* subastador -ra, *S.A.* martillero -ra.

audacious /ɔ'deiʃəs/ *a.* audaz.

audacity /ɔ'dæsɪti/ *n.* audacia *f.*

audible /'ɔdəbəl/ *a.* audible.

audience /'ɔdiəns/ *n.* auditorio, público *m.*; entrevista *f.*

audiovisual /ˌɔdiou'vɪʒuəl/ *a.* audiovisual.

audit /'ɔdɪt/ *n.* **1.** revisión de cuentas *f.* **—***v.* **2.** revisar cuentas.

audition /ɔ'dɪʃən/ *n.* audición *f.*

auditor /'ɔdɪtər/ *n.* interventor -ora, revisor -ora.

auditorium /ˌɔdɪ'tɔriəm/ *n.* sala *f.*; teatro *m.*

auditory /'ɔdɪˌtɔri/ *a.* & *n.* auditorio *m.*

augment /ɔg'mɛnt/ *v.* aumentar.

augur /'ɔgər/ *v.* augurar, pronosticar.

August /'ɔgəst/ *n.* agosto *m.*

aunt /ænt, ɑnt/ *n.* tía *f.*

auspice /'ɔspɪs/ *n.* auspicio *m.*

auspicious /ɔ'spɪʃəs/ *a.* favorable; propicio.

austere /ɔ'stɪər/ *a.* austero.

austerity /ɔ'stɛrɪti/ *n.* austeridad, severidad *f.*

Austrian /'ɔstriən/ *a.* & *n.* austríaco -ca.

authentic /ɔ'θɛntɪk/ *a.* auténtico.

authenticate /ɔ'θɛntɪˌkeit/ *v.* autenticar.

authenticity /ˌɔθɛn'tɪsɪti/ *n.* autenticidad *f.*

author /'ɔθər/ *n.* autor -ra, escritor -ra.

authoritarian /əˌθɔrɪ'tɛəriən/ *a.* & *n.* autoritario -ria.

authoritative /ə'θɔrɪˌteitɪv/ *a.* autoritativo; autorizado.

authoritatively /ə'θɔrɪˌteitɪvli/ *adv.* autoritativamente.

authority /ə'θɔrɪti/ *n.* autoridad *f.*

authorization /ˌɔθərə'zeiʃən/ *n.* autorización *f.*

authorize /'ɔθəˌraiz/ *v.* autorizar.

auto /'ɔtou/ *n.* auto, automóvil *m.*

autobiography /ˌɔtəbai'ɒgrəfi/ *n.* autobiografía *f.*

autocracy /ɔ'tɒkrəsi/ *n.* autocracia *f.*

autocrat /'ɔtəˌkræt/ *n.* autócrata *m.* & *f.*

autograph /'ɔtəˌgræf/ *n.* autógrafo *m.*

automatic /ˌɔtə'mætɪk/ *a.* automático.

automatically /ˌɔtə'mætɪkəli/ *adv.* automáticamente.

automobile /ˌɔtəmə'bil/ *n.* automóvil, coche *m.*

automotive /ˌɔtə'moutɪv/ *a.* automotriz.

autonomy /ɔ'tɒnəmi/ *n.* autonomía *f.*

autopsy /'ɔtɒpsi/ *n.* autopsia *f.*

autumn /'ɔtəm/ *n.* otoño *m.*

auxiliary /ɔg'zɪlyəri/ *a.* auxiliar.

avail /ə'veil/ *n.* **1. of no a.,** en vano. **—***v.* **2. a. oneself of,** aprovecharse.

available /ə'veiləbəl/ *a.* disponible.

avalanche /'ævəˌlæntʃ/ *n.* alud *m.*

avarice /'ævərɪs/ *n.* avaricia, codicia *f.*

avariciously /ˌævə'rɪʃəsli/ *adv.* avaramente.

avenge /ə'vɛndʒ/ *v.* vengar.

avenger /ə'vɛndʒər/ *n.* vengador -ra.

avenue /'ævəˌnu/ *n.* avenida *f.*

average /'ævərɪdʒ/ *a.* **1.** medio; común. **—***n.* **2.** promedio, término medio *m.* **—***v.* **3.** calcular el promedio.

averse /ə'vɜrs/ *a.* **to be a. to,** tener antipatía a, opuesto a.

aversion /ə'vɜrʒən/ *n.* aversión *f.*

avert /ə'vɜrt/ *v.* desviar; impedir.

aviary /'eiviˌɛri/ *n.* pajarera, avería *f.*

aviation /ˌeivi'eiʃən/ *n.* aviación *f.*

aviator /'eiviˌeitər/ *n.* aviador -ra.

aviatrix /ˌeivi'eitrɪks/ *n.* aviatriz *f.*

avid /'ævɪd/ *a.* ávido.

avocado /ˌævə'kɑdou, ˌɑvə-/ *n.* aguacate *m.*

avocation /ˌævə'keiʃən/ *n.* pasatiempo *f.*

avoid /ə'vɔid/ *v.* evitar.

avoidable /ə'vɔidəbəl/ *a.* evitable.

avoidance /ə'vɔidṇs/ *n.* evitación *f.*; *Leg.* anulación *f.*

avow /ə'vau/ *v.* declarar; admitir.

avowal /ə'vauəl/ *n.* admisión *f.*

avowed /ə'vaud/ *a.* reconocido; admitido.

avowedly /ə'vauɪdli/ *adv.* reconocidamente; confesadamente.

await /ə'weit/ *v.* esperar, aguardar.

awake /ə'weik/ *a.* despierto.

awaken /ə'weikən/ *v.* despertar.

award /ə'wɔrd/ *n.* **1.** premio *m.* **—***v.* **2.** otorgar.

aware /ə'wɛər/ *a.* enterado, consciente.

awash /ə'wɒʃ/ *a.* & *adv. Naut.* a flor de agua.

away /ə'wei/ *adv.* (see under verb: **go away, put away, take away,** etc.)

awe /ɔ/ *n.* pavor *m.*

awesome /'ɔsəm/ *a.* pavoroso; aterrador.

awful /'ɔfəl/ *a.* horrible, terrible, muy malo, pésimo.

awhile /ə'wail/ *adv.* por un rato.

awkward /'ɔkwərd/ *a.* torpe, desmañado; *Fig.* delicado, embarazoso.

awning /'ɔnɪŋ/ *n.* toldo *m.*

awry /ə'rai/ *a.* oblicuo, torcido.

ax /æks/ *n.* hacha *f.*

axiom /'æksiəm/ *n.* axioma *m.*

axis /'æksɪs/ *n.* eje *m.*

axle /'æksəl/ *n.* eje *m.*

ayatollah /ˌɑyə'toulə/ *n.* ayatolá *m.*

azure /'æʒər/ *a.* azul.

B

babble /'bæbəl/ *n.* **1.** balbuceo, murmullo *m.* **—***v.* **2.** balbucear.

babbler /'bæblər/ *n.* hablador -ra, charlador -ra.

baboon /bæ'bun/ *n.* mandril *m.*

baby /'beibi/ *n.* nene, bebé *m.*

baby carriage cochecito de niño *m.*

babyish /'beibiɪʃ/ *a.* infantil.

baby squid /skwɪd/ chipirón *m.*

bachelor /'bætʃələr/ *n.* soltero *m.*

bacillus /bə'sɪləs/ *n.* bacilo, microbio *m.*

back /bæk/ *adv.* **1.** atrás. **to be b.,** estar de vuelta. **b. of,** detrás de. **—***n.* **2.** espalda *f.*; (of animal) lomo *m.*

backache /'bækˌeik/ *n.* dolor de espalda *m.*

backbone /'bækˌboun/ *n.* espinazo *m.*; *Fig.* firmeza *f.*

backer /'bækər/ *n.* sostenedor -ra.

background /'bækˌgraund/ *n.* fondo *m.* antecedentes *m.pl.*

backing /'bækɪŋ/ *n.* apoyo *m.*, garantía *f.*

backlash /'bækˌlæʃ/ *n.* repercusión negativa.

backlog /'bækˌlɔg/ *n.* atrasos *m.pl.*

backpack /'bækˌpæk/ *n.* mochila *f.*

back seat asiento trasero *m.*

backstage /'bæk'steidʒ/ *n.* entre bastidores *m.*

backup /'bækˌʌp/ *n.* copia de seguridad *f.*

backward /'bækwərd/ *a.* **1.** atrasado. **—***adv.* **2.** hacia atrás.

backwardness /'bækwərdnɪs/ *n.* atraso *m.*

backwater /'bækˌwɔtər/ *n.* parte de río estancada *f.*

backwoods /'bæk'wʊdz/ *n.* región del monte apartada *f.*

bacon /'beikən/ *n.* tocino *m.*

bacteria /bæk'tɪəriə/ *n.* bacterias *f.pl.*

bacteriologist /ˌbæktɪəri'ɒlədʒɪst/ *n.* bacteriólogo -a.

bacteriology /ˌbæktɪəri'ɒlədʒi/ *n.* bacteriología *f.*

bad /bæd/ *a.* malo.

badge /bædʒ/ *n.* insignia, divisa *f.*

badger /'bædʒər/ *n.* **1.** tejón *m.* **—***v.* **2.** atormentar.

badly /'bædli/ *adv.* mal.

badness /'bædnɪs/ *n.* maldad *f.*

bad-tempered /'bæd'tɛmpərd/ *a.* de mal humor.

baffle /'bæfəl/ *v.* desconcertar.

bafflement /'bæfəlmənt/ *n.* contrariedad; confusión *f.*

bag /bæg/ n. **1.** saco m.; bolsa f. —v. **2.** ensacar, cazar.

baggage /'bægɪdʒ/ n. equipaje m. **b. check,** talón m.

baggage cart (airport) carrillo para llevar equipaje.

baggy /'bægi/ a. abotagado; bolsudo; hinchado.

bagpipe /'bæg,paip/ n. gaita f.

bail /beil/ n. **1.** fianza f. —v. **2.** desaguar.

bailiff /'beilɪf/ n. alguacil m.

bait /beit/ n. **1.** cebo m. —v. **2.** cebar.

bake /beik/ v. cocer en horno.

baked potato /beikt/ patata asada f.

baker /'beikər/ n. panadero -ra, hornero -ra.

bakery /'beikəri, 'beikri/ n. panadería f.

baking /'beikɪŋ/ n. hornada f. **b. powder,** levadura f.

balance /'bæləns/ n. balanza f.; equilibrio m.; Com. saldo m.

balcony /'bælkəni/ n. balcón m.; Theat. galería f.

bald /bɔld/ a. calvo.

baldness /'bɔldnɪs/ n. calvicie f.

bale /beil/ n. **1.** bala f. —v. **2.** embalar.

balk /bɔk/ v. frustrar; rebelarse.

Balkans /'bɔlkənz/ n. pl. Balcanes m.pl.

balky /'bɔki/ a. rebelón.

ball /bɔl/ n. bola, pelota f.; (dance) baile m.

ballad /'bæləd/ n. romance, m.; balada f.

ballast /'bæləst/ n. **1.** lastre m. —v. **2.** lastrar.

ball bearing cojinete de bolas m.

ballerina /,bælə'rinə/ n. bailarina f.

ballet /bæ'lei/ n. danza f.; ballet m.

ballistics /bə'lɪstɪks/ n. balística f.

balloon /bə'lun/ n. globo m. **b. tire,** neumático de balón.

ballot /'bælət/ n. **1.** balota f., voto m. —v. **2.** balotar, votar.

ballpoint pen /'bɔl,pɔint/ bolígrafo m.

ballroom /'bɔl,rum/ n. salón de baile m.

balm /bam/ n. bálsamo m.; ungüento m.

balmy /'bami/ a. fragante; reparador; calmante.

balsa /'bɔlsə/ n. balsa f.

balsam /'bɔlsəm/ n. bálsamo m.

balustrade /'bælə,streid/ n. barandilla f.

bamboo /bæm'bu/ n. bambú m., caña f.

ban /bæn/ n. **1.** prohibición f. —v. **2.** prohibir; proscribir.

banal /bə'næl/ a. trivial; vulgar.

banana /bə'nænə/ n. banana f., cambur m. **b. tree,** banano, plátano m.

band /bænd/ n. **1.** banda f.; (of men) banda, cuadrilla, partida f. —v. **2.** asociarse.

bandage /'bændɪdʒ/ n. **1.** vendaje m. —v. **2.** vendar.

bandanna /bæn'dænə/ n. pañuelo (grande) m.; bandana f.

bandbox /'bænd,bɒks/ n. caja de cartón.

bandit /'bændɪt/ n. bandido -da.

bandmaster /'bænd,mæstər/ n. director de una banda musical m.

bandstand /'bænd,stænd/ n. kiosco de música.

bang /bæŋ/ interj. **1.** ¡pum! —n. **2.** ruido de un golpe. —v. **3.** golpear ruidosamente.

banish /'bænɪʃ/ v. desterrar.

banishment /'bænɪʃmənt/ n. destierro m.

banister /'bænəstər/ n. pasamanos m. pl.

bank /bæŋk/ n. **1.** banco m.; (of a river) margen f. —v. **2.** depositar.

bank account cuenta bancaria f.

bankbook /'bæŋk,bʊk/ n. libreta de depósitos f.

bank card tarjeta bancaria f.

banker /'bæŋkər/ n. banquero -ra.

banking /'bæŋkɪŋ/ a. bancaria. n. banca f.

bank note billete de banco m.

bankrupt /'bæŋkrʌpt/ a. insolvente.

bankruptcy /'bæŋkrʌptsi/ n. bancarrota f.

banner /'bænər/ n. bandera f.; estandarte m.

banquet /'bæŋkwɪt/ n. banquete m.

banter /'bæntər/ n. **1.** choteo m.; zumba; burla f. —v. **2.** chotear; zumbar; burlarse.

baptism /'bæptɪzəm/ n. bautismo, bautizo m.

baptismal /bæp'tɪzməl/ a. bautismal.

Baptist /'bæptɪst/ n. bautista m. & f.

baptize /bæp'taiz, 'bæptaiz/ v. bautizar.

bar /bar/ n. **1.** barra f.; obstáculo m.; (tavern) taberna f., bar m. —v. **2.** barrear; prohibir, excluir.

barbarian /bar'bɛəriən/ a. bárbaro. n. bárbaro -ra.

barbarism /'barbə,rɪzəm/ n. barbarismo m., barbarie f.

barbarous /'barbərəs/ a. bárbaro, cruel.

barbecue /'barbɪ,kyu/ n. animal asado entero; (Mex.) barbacoa f.

barber /'barbər/ n. barbero m. **b. shop,** barbería f.

barbiturate /bar'bɪtʃərɪt/ n. barbitúrico m.

bar code código de barras m.

bare /bɛər/ a. **1.** desnudo; descubierto. —v. **2.** desnudar; descubrir.

bareback /'bɛər,bæk/ adv. sin silla.

barefoot(ed) /'bɛər,fʊtɪd/ a. descalzo.

barely /'bɛərli/ adv. escasamente, apenas.

bareness /'bɛərnɪs/ n. desnudez f.; pobreza f.

bargain /'bargən/ n. **1.** ganga f., compra ventajosa f.; contrato m. —v. **2.** regatear; negociar.

barge /bardʒ/ n. lanchón m., barcaza f.

baritone /'bærɪ,toun/ n. barítono m.

barium /'bɛəriəm/ n. bario m.

bark /bark/ n. **1.** corteza f.; (of dog) ladrido f. —v. **2.** ladrar.

barley /'barli/ n. cebada f.

barn /barn/ n. granero m.

barnacle /'barnəkəl/ n. lapa f.

barnyard /'barn,yard/ n. corral m.

barometer /bə'rɒmɪtər/ n. barómetro m.

barometric /,bærə'mɛtrɪk/ a. barométrico.

baron /'bærən/ n. barón m.

baroness /'bærənɪs/ n. baronesa f.

baronial /bə'rouniəl/ a. baronial.

baroque /bə'rouk/ a. barroco.

barracks /'bærəks/ n. cuartel m.

barrage /bə'raʒ/ n. cortina de fuego f.

barred /bard/ a. excluído; prohibido.

barrel /'bærəl/ n. barril m.; (of gun) cañón m.

barren /'bærən/ a. estéril.

barrenness /'bærən,nɪs/ n. esterilidad f.

barricade /'bærɪ,keid/ n. barricada, barrera f.

barrier /'bæriər/ n. barrera f.; obstáculo m.

barroom /'bar,rum, -,rʊm/ n. cantina f.

bartender /'bar,tɛndər/ n. tabernero; cantinero m.

barter /'bartər/ n. **1.** cambio, trueque m. —v. **2.** cambiar, trocar.

base /beis/ a. **1.** bajo, vil. —n. **2.** base f. —v. **3.** basar.

baseball /'beis,bɔl/ n. béisbol m.

baseboard /'beis,bord/ n. tabla de resguardo.

basement /'beismənt/ n. sótano m.

baseness /'beisnɪs/ n. bajeza, vileza f.

bashful /'bæʃfəl/ a. vergonzoso, tímido.

bashfully /'bæʃfəli/ adv. tímidamente; vergonzosamente.

bashfulness /'bæʃfəlnɪs/ n. vergüenza; timidez f.

basic /'beisɪk/ a. fundamental, básico.

basin /'beisən/ n. bacía f.; (of river) cuenca f.

basis /'beisɪs/ n. base f.

bask /bæsk/ v. tomar el sol.

basket /'bæskɪt/ n. cesta, canasta f.

bass /bæs/ n. (fish) lobina f.; Mus. bajo profundo m. **b. viol.** violón m.

bassinet /,bæsə'nɛt/ n. bacinete m.

bassoon /bæ'sun/ n. bajón m.

bastard /'bæstərd/ a. & n. bastardo -da; hijo -a natural.

baste /beist/ v. (sew) bastear; (cooking) pringar.

bat /bæt/ n. **1.** (animal) murciélago m.; (baseball) bate m. —v. **2.** batear.

batch /bætʃ/ n. cantidad de cosas.

bath /bæθ/ n. baño m.

bathe /beið/ v. bañar, bañarse.

bather /'beiðər/ n. bañista m. & f.

bathing resort /'beiðɪŋ/ balneario m.

bathing suit /'beiðɪŋ/ traje de baño.

bathrobe /'bæθ,roub/ n. bata de baño f.

bathroom /'bæθ,rum, -,rʊm/ n. cuarto de baño.

bathtub /'bæθ,tʌb/ n. bañera f.

baton /bə'tɒn/ n. bastón m.; Mus. batuta f.

battalion /bə'tælyən/ n. batallón m.

batter /'bætər/ n. **1.** (cooking) batido m.; (baseball) voleador m. —v. **2.** batir; derribar.

battery /'bætəri/ n. batería; Elec. pila f.

batting /'bætɪŋ/ n. agramaje, moldeaje m.

battle /'bætl/ n. **1.** batalla f.; combate m. —v. **2.** batallar.

battlefield /'bætl,fild/ n. campo de batalla.

battleship /'bætl,ʃɪp/ n. acorazado m.

bauxite /'bɒksait, 'bouzait/ n. bauxita f.

bawl /bɔl/ v. gritar; vocear.

bay /bei/ n. bahía f. v. aullar.

bayonet /'beinɛt/ n. bayoneta f.

bazaar /bə'zar/ n. bazar m., feria f.

BC abbr. (**before Christ**) a.C. (antes de Cristo).

be /bi/ v. ser; estar. (See hacer; hay; tener in Sp.-Eng. section.)

beach /bitʃ/ n. playa f.

beachcomber /'bitʃ,koumər/ n. raquero -ra m. & f.

beacon /'bikən/ n. faro m.

bead /bid/ n. cuenta f.; pl. Relig. rosario m.

beading /'bidɪŋ/ n. abalorio m.

beady /'bidi/ a. globuloso; burbujoso.

beak /bik/ n. pico m.

beaker /'bikər/ n. vaso con pico m.

beam /bim/ n. viga f.; (of wood) madero m.; (of light) rayo m.

beaming /'bimɪŋ/ a. radiante.

bean /bin/ n. haba, habichuela f., frijol m.

bear /bɛər/ n. **1.** oso -sa. —v. **2.** llevar; (endure) aguantar.

bearable /'bɛərəbəl/ a. sufrible; soportable.

beard /bɪərd/ n. barba f.

bearded /'bɪərdɪd/ a. barbado; barbudo.

beardless /'bɪərdlɪs/ a. lampiño; imberbe.

bearer /'bɛərər/ n. portador -ra.

bearing /'bɛərɪŋ/ n. porte, aguante m.

bearskin /'bɛər,skɪn/ n. piel de oso f.

beast /bist/ n. bestia f.; bruto -ta.

beat /bit/ v. golpear; batir; pulsar; (in games) ganar, vencer.

beaten /'bitn/ a. vencido; batido.

beatify /bi'ætə,fai/ v. beatificar.

beating /'bitɪŋ/ n. paliza f.

beau /bou/ n. novio m.

beautiful /'byutəfəl/ a. hermoso, bello.

beautifully /'byutəfəli/ adv. bellamente.

beautify /'byutə,fai/ v. embellecer.

beauty /'byuti/ n. hermosura, belleza f. **b. parlor,** salón de belleza.

beaver /'bivər/ n. castor m.

becalm /bi'kam/ v. calmar; sosegar; encalmarse.

because /bi'kɔz/ conj. porque. **b. of,** a causa de.

beckon /'bɛkən/ v. hacer señas.

become /bi'kʌm/ v. hacerse; ponerse.

becoming /bi'kʌmɪŋ/ a. propio, correcto; **be b.,** quedar bien, sentar bien.

bed /bɛd/ n. cama f.; lecho m.; (of river) cauce m.

bedbug /'bɛd,bʌg/ n. chinche m.

bedclothes /'bɛd,klouz, -,klouðz/ n. ropa de cama f.

bedding /'bɛdɪŋ/ n. colchones m.pl.

bedfellow /'bɛd,fɛlou/ n. compañero -ra de cama.

bedizen /bi'daizən, -'dɪzən/ v. adornar; aderezar.

bedridden /'bɛd,rɪdn/ a. postrado (en cama).

bedrock /'bɛd,rɒk/ n. (mining) lecho de roca m.; Fig. fundamento m.

bedroom /'bɛd,rum/ n. alcoba f.; (Mex.) recámara f.

bedside /'bɛd,said/ n. al lado de una cama m.

bedspread /'bɛd,sprɛd/ n. cubrecama, sobrecama f.

bedstead /'bɛd,stɛd/ n. armadura de cama f.

bedtime /'bɛd,taim/ n. hora de acostarse.

bee /bi/ n. abeja f.

beef /bif/ n. carne de vaca.

beefburger /'bif,bɜrgər/ n. hamburguesa f.

beefsteak /'bif,steik/ n. bistec, bisté m.

beehive /'bi,haiv/ n. colmena f.

beer /bɪər/ n. cerveza f.

beeswax /'biz,wæks/ n. cera de abejas.

beet /bit/ n. remolacha f.; (Mex.) betabel m.

beetle /'bitl/ n. escarabajo m.

befall /bi'fɔl/ v. suceder, sobrevenir.

befitting /bi'fɪtɪŋ/ a. conveniente; propio; digno.

before /bi'fɔr/ adv. antes. prep. de; (in front of) delante de. conj. antes que.

beforehand /bi'fɔr,hænd/ adv. de antemano.

befriend /bi'frɛnd/ v. amparar.

befuddle /bi'fʌdl/ v. confundir; aturdir.

beg /bɛg/ v. rogar, suplicar; (for alms) mendigar.

beget /bi'gɛt/ v. engendrar; producir.

beggar /'bɛgər/ n. mendigo -ga; S.A. limosnero -ra.

beggarly /'bɛgərli/ a. pobre, miserable.

begin /bi'gɪn/ v. empezar, comenzar; principiar.

beginner /bi'gɪnər/ n. principiante -ta.

beginning /bi'gɪnɪŋ/ n. principio, comienzo m.

begrudge /bi'grʌdʒ/ v. envidiar.

behalf /bi'hæf/ n.:**in, on b. of,** a favor de, en pro de.

behave /bi'heiv/ v. portarse, comportarse.

behavior /bi'heivyər/ n. conducta f.; comportamiento m.

behead /bi'hɛd/ v. decapitar.

behind /bi'haind/ adv. atrás, detrás. prep. detrás de.

behold /bi'hould/ v. contemplar.

beige /beiʒ/ a. beige.

being /'biɪŋ/ n. existencia f.; (person) ser m.

bejewel /bɪˈdʒuəl/ *v.* adornar con joyas.
belated /bɪˈleitɪd/ *a.* atrasado, tardío.
belch /bɛltʃ/ *n.* **1.** eructo *m.* —*v.* **2.** vomitar; eructar.
belfry /ˈbɛlfri/ *n.* campanario *m.*
Belgian /ˈbɛldʒən/ *a. & n.* belga *m. & f.*
Belgium /ˈbɛldʒəm/ *n.* Bélgica *f.*
belie /bɪˈlai/ *v.* desmentir.
belief /bɪˈlif/ *n.* creencia *f.*; parecer *m.*
believable /bɪˈlivəbəl/ *a.* creíble.
believe /bɪˈliv/ *v.* creer.
believer /bɪˈlivər/ *n.* creyente *m. & f.*
belittle /bɪˈlɪtl/ *v.* dar poca importancia a.
bell /bɛl/ *n.* campana *f.*; (of house) campanilla *f.*; (electric) timbre *m.*
bellboy /ˈbɛlˌbɔi/ *n.* mozo, botones *m.*
bellicose /ˈbɛlɪˌkous/ *a.* guerrero.
belligerence /bəˈlɪdʒərəns/ *n.* beligerancia *f.*
belligerent /bəˈlɪdʒərənt/ *a. & n.* beligerante *m. & f.*
belligerently /bəˈlɪdʒərəntli/ *adv.* belicosamente.
bellow /ˈbɛlou/ *v.* bramar, rugir.
bellows /ˈbɛlouz/ *n.* fuelle *m.*
belly /ˈbɛli/ *n.* vientre *m.*; panza, barriga *f.*
belong /bɪˈlɔŋ/ *v.* pertenecer.
belongings /bɪˈlɔŋɪŋz/ *n.* propiedad *f.*
beloved /bɪˈlʌvɪd/ *a.* querido, amado.
below /bɪˈlou/ *adv.* **1.** debajo, abajo. —*prep.* **2.** debajo de.
belt /bɛlt/ *n.* cinturón *m.*
bench /bɛntʃ/ *n.* banco *m.*
bend /bɛnd/ *n.* vuelta; curva *f.* *v.* encorvar, doblar.
beneath /bɪˈniθ/ *adv.* **1.** debajo, abajo. —*prep.* **2.** debajo de.
benediction /ˌbɛnɪˈdɪkʃən/ *n.* bendición *f.*
benefactor /ˈbɛnəˌfæktər/ *n.* bienhechor -ra.
benefactress /ˈbɛnəˌfæktrɪs/ *n.* bienhechora *f.*
beneficial /ˌbɛnəˈfɪʃəl/ *a.* provechoso, beneficioso.
beneficiary /ˌbɛnəˈfɪʃiˌɛri/ *n.* beneficiario -ria, beneficiado -da.
benefit /ˈbɛnəfɪt/ *n.* **1.** provecho, beneficio *m.* —*v.* **2.** beneficiar.
benevolence /bəˈnɛvələns/ *n.* benevolencia *f.*
benevolent /bəˈnɛvələnt/ *a.* benévolo.
benevolently /bəˈnɛvələntli/ *adv.* benignamente.
benign /bɪˈnain; bɪˈnɪgnənt/ *a.* benigno.
benignity /bɪˈnɪgnɪti/ *n.* benignidad; bondad *f.*
bent /bɛnt/ *a.* **1.** encorvado. **b. on,** resuelto a. —*n.* **2.** inclinación *f.*
benzene /ˈbɛnzin, bɛnˈzin/ *n.* benceno *m.*
bequeath /bɪˈkwið/ *v.* legar.
bequest /bɪˈkwɛst/ *n.* legado *m.*
berate /bɪˈreit/ *v.* reñir, regañar.
bereave /bɪˈriv/ *v.* despojar; desolar.
bereavement /bɪˈrivmənt/ *n.* privación *f.*; despojo *m.*; (mourning) luto *m.*
berry /ˈbɛri/ *n.* baya *f.*
berth /bɜrθ/ *n.* camarote *m.*; *Naut.* litera *f.*; (for vessel) amarradero *m.*
beseech /bɪˈsitʃ/ *v.* suplicar; implorar.
beseechingly /bɪˈsitʃɪŋli/ *adv.* suplicantemente.
beset /bɪˈsɛt/ *v.* acosar; rodear.
beside /bɪˈsaid/ *prep.* al lado de.
besides /bɪˈsaidz/ *adv.* además, por otra parte.
besiege /bɪˈsidʒ/ *v.* sitiar; asediar.
besieged /bɪˈsidʒd/ *a.* sitiado.
besieger /bɪˈsidʒər/ *n.* sitiador -ra.
besmirch /bɪˈsmɜrtʃ/ *v.* manchar; deshonrar.
best /bɛst/ *a. & adv.* mejor. **at b.,** a lo más.
bestial /ˈbɛstʃəl/ *a.* bestial; brutal.
bestir /bɪˈstɜr/ *v.* incitar; intrigar.
best man *n.* padrino de boda.
bestow /bɪˈstou/ *v.* conferir.
bestowal /bɪˈstouəl/ *n.* dádiva; presentación *f.*
bet /bɛt/ *n.* **1.** apuesta *f.* —*v.* **2.** -apostar.
betoken /bɪˈtoukən/ *v.* presagiar, anunciar.
betray /bɪˈtrei/ *v.* traicionar; revelar.
betrayal /bɪˈtreiəl/ *n.* traición *f.*
betroth /bɪˈtrouð/ *v.* contraer esponsales; prometerse.
betrothal /bɪˈtrouðəl/ *n.* esponsales *m.pl.*
better /ˈbɛtər/ *a. & adv.* **1.** mejor. —*v.* **2.** mejorar.
between /bɪˈtwin/ *prep.* entre, en medio de.
bevel /ˈbɛvəl/ *n.* **1.** cartabón *m.* —*v.* **2.** cortar al sesgo.
beverage /ˈbɛvərɪdʒ/ *n.* bebida *f.*; (cold) refresco *m.*
bewail /bɪˈweil/ *v.* llorar; lamentar.
beware /bɪˈwɛər/ *v.* guardarse, precaverse.
bewilder /bɪˈwɪldər/ *v.* aturdir.
bewildered /bɪˈwɪldərd/ *a.* descarriado.
bewildering /bɪˈwɪldərɪŋ/ *a.* aturdente.
bewilderment /bɪˈwɪldərmənt/ *n.* aturdimiento *m.*; perplejidad *f.*
bewitch /bɪˈwɪtʃ/ *v.* hechizar; embrujar.
beyond /biˈɒnd/ *prep.* más allá de.
biannual /baiˈænyuəl/ *a.* semianual; semestral.
bias /ˈbaiəs/ *n.* **1.** parcialidad *f.*; prejuicio *m.* **on the b.,** al sesgo. —*v.* **2.** predisponer, influir.
bib /bɪb/ *n.* babador *m.*
Bible /ˈbaibəl/ *n.* Biblia *f.*
Biblical /ˈbɪblɪkəl/ *a.* bíblico.
bibliography /ˌbɪbliˈɒgrəfi/ *n.* bibliografía *f.*
bicarbonate /baiˈkɑrbənɪt/ *n.* bicarbonato *m.*
bicentennial /ˌbaisɛnˈtɛniəl/ *a. & n.* bicentenario *m.*
biceps /ˈbaisɛps/ *n.* bíceps *m.*
bicker /ˈbɪkər/ *v.* altercar.
bicycle /ˈbaisɪkəl/ *n.* bicicleta *f.*
bicyclist /ˈbaisɪklɪst/ *n.* biciclista *m. & f.*
bid /bɪd/ *n.* **1.** proposición, oferta *f.* —*v.* **2.** mandar; ofrecer.
bidder /ˈbɪdər/ *n.* postor -ra.
bide /baid/ *v.* aguardar; esperar.
bier /bɪər/ *n.* ataúd *m.*
bifocal /baiˈfoukəl/ *a.* bifocal.
big /bɪg/ *a.* grande.
bigamist /ˈbɪgəmɪst/ *n.* bígamo -ma.
bigamy /ˈbɪgəmi/ *n.* bigamia *f.*
bigot /ˈbɪgət/ *n.* persona intolerante.
bigotry /ˈbɪgətri/ *n.* intolerancia *f.*
bikini /bɪˈkini/ *n.* bikini *m.*
bilateral /baiˈlætərəl/ *a.* bilateral.
bile /bail/ *n.* bilis *f.*
bilingual /baiˈlɪŋgwəl/ *a.* bilingüe.
bilingualism /baiˈlɪŋgwəˌlɪzəm/ *n.* bilingüismo *m.*
bilious /ˈbɪlyəs/ *a.* bilioso.
bill /bɪl/ **1.** *n.* cuenta, factura *f.*; (money) billete *m.*; (of bird) pico *m.* —*v.* **2.** facturar.
billboard /ˈbɪlˌbɔrd/ *n.* cartelera *f.*
billet /ˈbɪlɪt/ *n.* **1.** billete *m.*; *Mil.* boleta *f.* —*v.* **2.** aposentar.
billfold /ˈbɪlˌfould/ *n.* cartera *f.*
billiard balls /ˈbɪlyərd bɔlz/ bolas de billar.
billiards /ˈbɪlyərdz/ *n.* billar *m.*
billion /ˈbɪlyən/ *n.* billón *m.*
bill of health *n.* certificado de sanidad.
bill of lading /ˈleidɪŋ/ *n.* conocimiento de embarque.
bill of sale *n.* escritura de venta.
billow /ˈbɪlou/ *n.* ola; oleada *f.*
bimetallic /ˌbaiməˈtælɪk/ *a.* bimetálico.
bimonthly /baiˈmʌnθli/ *a. & adv.* bimestral.
bin /bɪn/ *n.* hucha *f.*; depósito *m.*
bind /baind/ *v.* atar; obligar; (book) encuadernar.
bindery /ˈbaindəri/ *n.* taller de encuadernación *m.*
binding /ˈbaindɪŋ/ *n.* encuadernación *f.*
bingo /ˈbɪŋgou/ *n.* bingo *m.*
binocular /bəˈnɒkyələr/ *a.* binocular. *n.pl.* gemelos *m.pl.*
biochemistry /ˌbaiouˈkɛməstri/ *n.* bioquímica *f.*
biodegradable /ˌbaioudɪˈgreidəbəl/ *a.* biodegradable.
biofeedback /ˌbaiouˈfidˌbæk/ *n.* biofeedback.
biographer /baiˈɒgrəfər/ *n.* biógrafo -fa.
biographical /ˌbaiəˈgræfɪkəl/ *a.* biográfico.
biography /baiˈɒgrəfi/ *n.* biografía *f.*
biological /ˌbaiəˈlɒdʒɪkəl/ *a.* biológico.
biologically /ˌbaiəˈlɒdʒɪkəli/ *adv.* biológicamente.
biology /baiˈɒlədʒi/ *n.* biología *f.*
bipartisan /baiˈpɑrtəzən/ *a.* bipartito.
biped /ˈbaipɛd/ *n.* bípedo *m.*
bird /bɜrd/ *n.* pájaro *m.*; ave *f.*
birdie /ˈbɜrdi/ *n.* (golf) uno bajo par *m.*
bird of prey *n.* ave de rapiña *f.*
bird's-eye view /ˈbɜrdzˌai/ *n.* vista de pájaro *f.*
birth /bɜrθ/ *n.* nacimiento *m.* **give b. to,** dar a luz.
birth certificate partida de nacimiento *f.*
birth control *n.* contracepción *f.*
birthday /ˈbɜrθˌdei/ *n.* cumpleaños *m.*
birthmark /ˈbɜrθˌmɑrk/ *n.* marca de nacimiento *f.*
birthplace /ˈbɜrθˌpleis/ *n.* natalicio *m.*
birth rate *n.* natalidad *f.*
birthright /ˈbɜrθˌrait/ *n.* primogenitura *f.*
biscuit /ˈbɪskɪt/ *n.* bizcocho *m.*
bisect /baiˈsɛkt/ *v.* bisecar.
bishop /ˈbɪʃəp/ *n.* obispo *m.*; (chess) alfil *m.*
bishopric /ˈbɪʃəprɪk/ *n.* obispado *m.*
bismuth /ˈbɪzməθ/ *n.* bismuto *m.*
bison /ˈbaisən/ *n.* bisonte *m.*
bit /bɪt/ *n.* pedacito *m.*; *Mech.* taladro *m.*; (for horse) bocado *m.*; (computer) bit *m.*
bitch /bɪtʃ/ *n.* perra *f.*
bite /bait/ *n.* **1.** bocado *m.*; picada *f.* —*v.* **2.** morder; picar.
biting /ˈbaitɪŋ/ *a.* penetrante; mordaz.
bitter /ˈbɪtər/ *a.* amargo.
bitterly /ˈbɪtərli/ *adv.* amargamente; agriamente.
bitterness /ˈbɪtərnɪs/ *n.* amargura *f.*; rencor *m.*
bivouac /ˈbɪvuˌæk/ *n.* **1.** vivaque *m.* —*v.* **2.** vivaquear.
biweekly /baiˈwikli/ *a.* quincenal.
black /blæk/ *a.* negro.
Black /blæk/ *n.* (person) negro -gra; persona de color.
blackberry /ˈblækˌbɛri/ *n.* mora *f.*
blackbird /ˈblækˌbɜrd/ *n.* mirlo *m.*
blackboard /ˈblækˌbɔrd/ *n.* pizarra *f.*
blacken /ˈblækən/ *v.* ennegrecer.
black eye *n.* ojo amoratado.
blackguard /ˈblægɑrd/ *n.* tunante; pillo *m.*
blacklist /ˈblækˌlɪst/ *n.* lista negra *f.*
blackmail /ˈblækˌmeil/ *n.* **1.** chantaje *m.* —*v.* **2.** amenazar con chantaje, chantajear.
black market mercado negro, estraperlo *m.*
black marketeer /ˌmɑrkɪˈtɪr/ estraperlista *mf.*
blackout /ˈblækˌaut/ *n.* oscurecimiento, apagamiento *m.*
blacksmith /ˈblækˌsmɪθ/ *n.* herrero -ra.
bladder /ˈblædər/ *n.* vejiga *f.*
blade /bleid/ *n.* (sword) hoja *f.*; (oar) pala *f.*; (grass) brizna *f.*
blame /bleim/ *v.* culpar, echar la culpa a.
blameless /ˈbleimlɪs/ *a.* inculpable.
blanch /blæntʃ/ *v.* blanquear; escaldar.
bland /blænd/ *a.* blando.
blank /blæŋk/ *a. & n.* en blanco.
blanket /ˈblæŋkɪt/ *n.* manta *f.*; cobertor *m.*
blare /blɛər/ *n.* sonido de trompeta. *v.* sonar como trompeta.
blaspheme /blæsˈfim/ *v.* blasfemar.
blasphemer /blæsˈfimər/ *n.* blasfemo -ma, blasfemador -ra.
blasphemous /ˈblæsfəməs/ *a.* blasfemo, impío.
blasphemy /ˈblæsfəmi/ *n.* blasfemia *f.*
blast /blæst/ *n.* **1.** barreno *m.*; (wind) ráfaga *f.* —*v.* **2.** barrenar.
blatant /ˈbleitnt/ *a.* bramante; descarado.
blaze /bleiz/ *n.* **1.** llama, hoguera *f.* —*v.* **2.** encenderse en llama.
blazing /ˈbleizɪŋ/ *a.* flameante.
bleach /blitʃ/ *n.* **1.** lejía, blanqueador. —*v.* **2.** blanquear.
bleachers /ˈblitʃərz/ *n.* asientos al aire libre.
bleak /blik/ *a.* frío y sombrío.
bleakness /ˈbliknɪs/ *n.* desolación *f.*
bleed /blid/ *v.* sangrar.
blemish /ˈblɛmɪʃ/ *n.* **1.** mancha *f.*; lunar *m.* —*v.* **2.** manchar.
blend /blɛnd/ *n.* **1.** mezcla *f.* —*v.* **2.** mezclar, combinar.
blended /ˈblɛndɪd/ *a.* mezclado.
blender /ˈblɛndər/ *n.* (for food) licuadora *f.*
bless /blɛs/ *v.* bendecir.
blessed /ˈblɛsɪd/ *a.* bendito.
blessing /ˈblɛsɪŋ/ *a.* bendición *f.*
blight /blait/ *n.* **1.** plaga *f.*; tizón *m.* —*v.* **2.** atizonar.
blind /blaind/ *a.* ciego.
blindfold /ˈblaindˌfould/ *v.* vendar los ojos.
blinding /ˈblaindɪŋ/ *a.* deslumbrante; ofuscante.
blindly /ˈblaindli/ *adv.* ciegamente.
blindness /ˈblaindnɪs/ *n.* ceguedad, ceguera *f.*
blink /blɪŋk/ *n.* **1.** guiñada *f.* —*v.* **2.** guiñar.
bliss /blɪs/ *n.* felicidad *f.*
blissful /ˈblɪsfəl/ *a.* dichoso; bienaventurado.
blissfully /ˈblɪsfəli/ *adv.* felizmente.
blister /ˈblɪstər/ *n.* ampolla *f.*
blithe /blaið/ *a.* alegre; jovial; gozoso.
blizzard /ˈblɪzərd/ *n.* nevasca *f.*
bloat /blout/ *v.* hinchar.
bloc /blɒk/ *n.* grupo (político); bloc.
block /blɒk/ *n.* **1.** bloque *m.*; (street) manzana, cuadra *f.* —*v.* **2.** bloquear.
blockade /blɒˈkeid/ *n.* **1.** bloqueo *m.* —*v.* **2.** bloquear.
blond /blɒnd/ *a. & n.* rubio -ia.
blood /blʌd/ *n.* sangre *f.*; parentesco, linaje *m.*
bloodhound /ˈblʌdˌhaund/ *n.* sabueso *m.*
bloodless /ˈblʌdlɪs/ *a.* exangüe; desangrado.
blood poisoning /ˈpɔizənɪŋ/ envenenamiento de sangre.
blood pressure presión arterial.
bloodshed /ˈblʌdˌʃɛd/ *n.* matanza *f.*
bloodthirsty /ˈblʌdˌθɜrsti/ *a.* cruel, sanguinario.
bloody /ˈblʌdi/ *a.* ensangrentado, sangriento.
bloom /blum/ *n.* **1.** flor *f.* —*v.* **2.** florecer.
blooming /ˈblumɪŋ/ *a.* lozano; fresco; floreciente.
blossom /ˈblɒsəm/ *n.* **1.** flor *f.* —*v.* **2.** florecer.

blot /blɒt/ *n.* **1.** mancha *f.* —*v.* **2.** manchar.

blotch /blɒtʃ/ *n.* **1.** mancha, roncha *f.* —*v.* **2.** manchar.

blotter /ˈblɒtər/ *n.* papel secante.

blouse /blaus/ *n.* blusa *f.*

blow /blou/ *n.* **1.** golpe *m.; Fig.* chasco *m.* —*v.* **2.** soplar.

blowout /ˈblouˌaut/ *n.* reventón de neumático *m.*

blubber /ˈblʌbər/ *n.* grasa de ballena.

bludgeon /ˈblʌdʒən/ *n.* porra *f. v.* apalear.

blue /blu/ *a.* azul; triste, melancólico.

bluebird /ˈbluˌbɜrd/ *n.* azulejo *m.*

blue jeans jeans; vaqueros *m.pl.*

blueprint /ˈbluˌprɪnt/ *n.* heliografía *f.*

bluff /blʌf/ *n.* risco *m. v.* alardear; baladronar.

bluing /ˈbluɪŋ/ *n.* añil *m.*

blunder /ˈblʌndər/ *n.* **1.** desatino *m.* —*v.* **2.** desatinar.

blunderer /ˈblʌndərər/ *n.* desatinado -da.

blunt /blʌnt/ *a.* embotado; descortés. *v.* embotar.

bluntly /ˈblʌntli/ *a.* bruscamente.

bluntness /ˈblʌntnɪs/ *n.* grosería *f.;* brusquedad.

blur /blɜr/ *n.* **1.** trazo confuso. —*v.* **2.** hacer indistinto.

blush /blʌʃ/ *n.* **1.** rubor, sonrojo *m.* —*v.* **2.** sonrojarse.

bluster /ˈblʌstər/ *n.* **1.** fanfarria *f.* —*v.* **2.** fanfarrear.

boar /bɔr/ *n.* verraco *m.* **wild b.,** jabalí.

board /bɔrd/ *n.* **1.** tabla; *Govt.* consejo *m.;* junta *f.* **b. and room,** cuarto y comida, casa y comida. —*v.* **2.** (ship) abordar.

boarder /ˈbɔrdər/ *n.* pensionista *m. & f.*

boardinghouse /ˈbɔrdɪŋ/ *n.* pensión *f.*, casa de huéspedes.

boarding pass /ˈbɔrdɪŋ/ boleto de embarque *m.*, tarjeta de embarque *f.*

boast /boust/ *n.* **1.** jactancia *f.* —*v.* **2.** jactarse.

boaster /ˈboustər/ *n.* fanfarrón -na.

boastful /ˈboustfəl/ *a.* jactancioso.

boastfulness /ˈboustfəlnɪs/ *n.* jactancia *f.*

boat /bout/ *n.* barco, buque, bote *m.*

boathouse /ˈboutˌhaus/ *n.* casilla de botes *f.*

boatswain /ˈbousən/ *n.* contramaestre *m.*

bob /bɒb/ *v.* menear.

bobbin /ˈbɒbɪn/ *n.* bobina *f.*

bobby pin /ˈbɒbi/ *n.* gancho *m.*, horquilla.

bodice /ˈbɒdɪs/ *n.* corpiño *m.*

bodily /ˈbɒdḷi/ *a.* corporal.

body /ˈbɒdi/ *n.* cuerpo *m.*

body builder culturista *mf.*

body building culturismo *m.*

bodyguard /ˈbɒdiˌgɑrd/ *n.* guardaespaldas.

bog /bɒg/ *n.* pantano *m.*

bogey /ˈbougi/ *n.* (golf) uno sobre par *m.*

Bohemian /bouˈhimiən/ *a. & n.* bohemio -mia.

boil /bɔil/ *n.* **1.** hervor *m.; Med.* divieso *m.* —*v.* **2.** hervir.

boiler /ˈbɔilər/ *n.* marmita; caldera *f.*

boiling point /ˈbɔilɪŋ/ punto de ebullición *m.*

boisterous /ˈbɔistərəs/ *a.* tumultuoso.

boisterously /ˈbɔistərəsli/ *adv.* tumultuosamente.

bold /bould/ *a.* atrevido, audaz.

boldface /ˈbouldˌfeis/ *n.* (type) letra negra.

boldly /ˈbouldli/ *adv.* audazmente; descaradamente.

boldness /ˈbouldnɪs/ *n.* atrevimiento *m.;* osadía *f.*

Bolivian /bouˈlɪviən/ *a. & n.* boliviano -na.

bologna /bəˈlouni/ *n.* salchicha *f.*, mortadela.

bolster /ˈboulstər/ *n.* **1.** travesero, cojín *m.* —*v.* **2.** apoyar, sostener.

bolt /boult/ *n.* perno *m.;* (of door) cerrojo *m.;* (lightning) rayo *m. v.* acerrojar.

bomb /bɒm/ *n.* **1.** bomba *f.* —*v.* **2.** bombardear.

bombard /bɒmˈbɑrd/ *v.* bombardear.

bombardier /ˌbɒmbərˈdɪər/ *n.* bombardero -ra.

bombardment /bɒmˈbɑrdmənt/ *n.* bombardeo *m.*

bomber /ˈbɒmər/ *n.* avión de bombardeo.

bombproof /ˈbɒmˌpruf/ *a.* a prueba de granadas.

bombshell /ˈbɒmˌʃɛl/ *n.* bomba *f.*

bonbon /ˈbɒnˌbɒn/ *n.* dulce, bombón *m.*

bond /bɒnd/ *n.* lazo *m.; Com.* bono *m.*

bondage /ˈbɒndɪdʒ/ *n.* esclavitud, servidumbre *f.*

bonded /ˈbɒndɪd/ *a.* garantizado.

bone /boun/ *n.* hueso *m.*

boneless /ˈbounlɪs/ *a.* sin huesos.

bonfire /ˈbɒnˌfaiᵊr/ *n.* hoguera, fogata *f.*

bonnet /ˈbɒnɪt/ *n.* gorra *f.*

bonus /ˈbounəs/ *n.* sobrepaga *f.*

bony /ˈbouni/ *a.* huesudo.

boo /bu/ *v.* abuchear.

book /bʊk/ *n.* libro *m.*

bookbinder /ˈbʊkˌbaindər/ *n.* encuadernador -ora.

bookcase /ˈbʊkˌkeis/ *n.* armario para libros.

bookkeeper /ˈbʊkˌkipər/ *n.* tenedor -ra de libros.

bookkeeping /ˈbʊkˌkipɪŋ/ *n.* contabilidad *f.*

booklet /ˈbʊklɪt/ *n.* folleto *m.*, libreta *f.*

bookmark /ˈbʊkˌmɑrk/ *n.* marcapáginas *m.*

bookseller /ˈbʊkˌsɛlər/ *n.* librero -ra.

bookstore /ˈbʊkˌstɔr/ *n.* librería *f.*

boom /bum/ *n. Naut.* botalón *m.;* prosperidad repentina.

boon /bun/ *n.* dádiva *f.*

boor /bʊr/ *n.* patán, rústico *m.*

boorish /ˈbʊrɪʃ/ *a.* villano.

boost /bust/ *n.* **1.** alza; ayuda *f.* —*v.* **2.** levantar, alzar; fomentar.

booster /ˈbustər/ *n.* fomentador *m.*

boot /but/ *n.* bota *f.*

bootblack /ˈbutˌblæk/ *n.* limpiabotas *m.*

booth /buθ/ *n.* cabaña; casilla *f.*

booty /ˈbuti/ *n.* botín *m.*

border /ˈbɔrdər/ *n.* **1.** borde *m.;* frontera *f.* —*v.* **2. b. on,** lindar con.

borderline /ˈbɔrdərˌlain/ *a.* marginal. *n.* margen *m.*

bore /bɔr/ *n.* lata *f.;* persona pesada. *v.* aburrir, fastidiar; *Mech.* taladrar.

boredom /ˈbɔrdəm/ *n.* aburrimiento *m.*

boric acid /ˈbɔrɪk/ *n.* ácido bórico *m.*

boring /ˈbɔrɪŋ/ *a.* aburrido, pesado.

born /bɔrn/ *a.* nacido. **be born,** nacer.

born-again /ˈbɔrn əˈgɛn/ *a.* renacido.

borrow /ˈbɒrou/ *v.* pedir prestado.

bosom /ˈbʊzəm/ *v.* seno, pecho *m.*

boss /bɒs/ *n.* jefe, patrón *m.*

botany /ˈbɒtṇi/ *n.* botánica *f.*

both /bouθ/ *pron. & a.* ambos, los dos.

bother /ˈbɒðər/ *n.* molestia *f. v.* molestar, incomodar.

bothersome /ˈbɒðərsəm/ *a.* molesto.

bottle /ˈbɒtḷ/ *n.* **1.** botella *f.* —*v.* **2.** embotellar.

bottling /ˈbɒtlɪŋ/ *n.* embotellamiento *m.*

bottom /ˈbɒtəm/ *n.* fondo *m.*

boudoir /ˈbudwɑr/ *n.* tocador *m.*

bough /bau/ *n.* rama *f.*

boulder /ˈbouldər/ *n.* canto rodado.

boulevard /ˈbʊləˌvɑrd/ *n.* bulevar *m.*

bounce /bauns/ *n.* **1.** brinco *m.* —*v.* **2.** brincar; hacer saltar.

bound /baund/ *n.* **1.** salto *m.* —*v.* **2.** limitar.

boundary /ˈbaundəri/ *n.* límite, lindero *m.*

bouquet /bouˈkei, bu-/ *n.* ramillete de flores.

bourgeois /bʊrˈʒwɑ/ *a. & n.* burgués -esa.

bout /baut/ *n.* encuentro; combate *m.*

bow /*n* bau, bou; *v* bau/ *n.* **1.** saludo *m.;* (of ship) proa *f.;* (archery) arco *m.;* (ribbon) lazo *m.* —*v.* **2.** saludar, inclinar.

bowels /ˈbauəlz/ *n.* intestinos *m.pl.;* entrañas *f.pl.*

bowl /boul/ *n.* **1.** vasija *f.;* platón *m.* —*v.* **2.** jugar a los bolos. **b. over,** derribar.

bowlegged /ˈbouˌlɛgɪd/ *a.* perniabierto.

bowling /ˈboulɪŋ/ *n.* bolos *m.pl.*

bow tie /bou/ pajarita *f.*

box /bɒks/ *n.* **1.** caja *f.; Theat.* palco *m.* —*v.* **2.** (sports) boxear.

boxcar /ˈbɒksˌkɑr/ *n.* vagón *m.*

boxer /ˈbɒksər/ *n.* boxeador -ra, pugilista *m. & f.*

boxing /ˈbɒksɪŋ/ *n.* boxeo *m.*

box office *n.* taquilla *f.*

boy /bɔi/ *n.* muchacho, chico, niño *m.*

boycott /ˈbɔikɒt/ *n.* **1.** boicoteo *m.* —*v.* **2.** boicotear.

boyhood /ˈbɔihʊd/ *n.* muchachez *f.*

boyish /ˈbɔiɪʃ/ *a.* pueril.

boyishly /ˈbɔiɪʃli/ *adv.* puerilmente.

bra /brɑ/ *n.* sujetador, sostén *m.*

brace /breis/ *n.* **1.** grapón *m.; pl.* tirantes *m.pl.* —*v.* **2.** reforzar.

bracelet /ˈbreislɪt/ *n.* brazalete *m.*, pulsera *f.*

bracket /ˈbrækɪt/ *n.* ménsula *f.*

brag /bræg/ *v.* jactarse.

braggart /ˈbrægərt/ *a.* **1.** jactancioso. —*n.* **2.** jaque *m.*

braid /breid/ *n.* **1.** trenza *f.* —*v.* **2.** trenzar.

brain /brein/ *n.* cerebro, seso *m.*

brainy /ˈbreini/ *a.* sesudo, inteligente.

brake /breik/ *n.* **1.** freno *m.* —*v.* **2.** frenar.

bran /bræn/ *n.* salvado *m.*

branch /bræntʃ, brɑntʃ/ *n.* ramo *m.;* (of tree) rama *f.*

brand /brænd/ *n.* marca *f.*

brandish /ˈbrændɪʃ/ *v.* blandir.

brand-new /ˈbrænˈnu/ *a.* enteramente nuevo.

brandy /ˈbrændi/ *n.* aguardiente, coñac *m.*

brash /bræʃ/ *a.* impetuoso.

brass /bræs/ *n.* bronce, latón *m.*

brassiere /brəˈzɪər/ *n.* corpiño, sujetador, sostén *m.*

brat /bræt/ *n.* mocoso *m.*

bravado /brəˈvɑdou/ *n.* bravata *f.*

brave /breiv/ *a.* valiente.

bravery /ˈbreivəri/ *n.* valor *m.*

brawl /brɔl/ *n.* alboroto *m. v.* alborotar.

brawn /brɔn/ *n.* músculo *m.*

bray /brei/ *v.* rebuznar.

brazen /ˈbreizən/ *a.* desvergonzado.

Brazil /brəˈzɪl/ *n.* Brasil *m.*

Brazilian /brəˈzɪlyən/ *a. & n.* brasileño -ña.

breach /britʃ/ *n.* rotura; infracción *f.*

breach of contract incumplimiento de contrato *m.*

bread /brɛd/ *n.* pan *m.*

breadth /brɛdθ/ *n.* anchura *f.*

break /breik/ *n.* **1.** rotura; pausa *f.* —*v.* **2.** quebrar, romper.

breakable /ˈbreikəbəl/ *a.* rompible, frágil.

breakage /ˈbreikɪdʒ/ *n.* rotura *f.*, destrozo *m.*

breakfast /ˈbrɛkfəst/ *n.* **1.** desayuno, almuerzo *m.* —*v.* **2.** desayunar, almorzar.

breakneck /ˈbreikˌnɛk/ *a.* rápido, precipitado, atropellado.

breast /brɛst/ *n.* (of human) pecho, seno *m.;* (of fowl) pechuga *f.*

breastbone /ˈbrɛstˌboun/ *n.* esternón *m.*

breath /brɛθ/ *n.* aliento; soplo *m.*

breathe /brið/ *v.* respirar.

breathless /ˈbrɛθlɪs/ *a.* desalentado.

breathlessly /ˈbrɛθlɪsli/ *adv.* jadeantemente, intensamente.

bred /brɛd/ *a.* criado; educado.

breeches /ˈbrɪtʃɪz/ *n.pl.* calzones; pantalones, *m.pl.*

breed /brid/ *n.* **1.** raza *f.* —*v.* **2.** engendrar; criar.

breeder /ˈbridər/ *n.* criador -ra.

breeding /ˈbridɪŋ/ *n.* cría *f.*

breeze /briz/ *n.* brisa *f.*

breezy /ˈbrizi/ *a.:* **it is b.,** hace brisa.

brevity /ˈbrɛvɪti/ *n.* brevedad *f.*

brew /bru/ *v.* fraguar; elaborar.

brewer /ˈbruər/ *n.* cervecero -ra.

brewery /ˈbruəri/ *n.* cervecería *f.*

bribe /braib/ *n.* **1.** soborno, cohecho *m.* —*v.* **2.** sobornar, cohechar.

briber /ˈbraibər/ *n.* sobornador -ra.

bribery /ˈbraibəri/ *n.* soborno, cohecho *m.*

brick /brɪk/ *n.* ladrillo *m.*

bricklayer /ˈbrɪkˌleiər/ *n.* albañil *m.*

bridal /ˈbraidl/ *a.* nupcial.

bride /braid/ *n.* novia *f.*

bridegroom /ˈbraidˌgrum/ *n.* novio *m.*

bridesmaid /ˈbraidzˌmeid/ *n.* madrina de boda.

bridge /brɪdʒ/ *n.* puente *m.*

bridged /brɪdʒd/ *a.* conectado.

bridgehead /ˈbrɪdʒˌhɛd/ *n. Mil.* cabeza de puente.

bridle /ˈbraidl/ *n.* brida *f.*

brief /brif/ *a.* breve.

briefcase /ˈbrifˌkeis/ *n.* maletín *m.*

briefly /ˈbrifli/ *adv.* brevemente.

briefness /ˈbrifnɪs/ *n.* brevedad *f.*

brier /ˈbraiər/ *n.* zarza *f.*

brig /brɪg/ *n.* bergantín *m.*

brigade /brɪˈgeid/ *n.* brigada *f.*

bright /brait/ *a.* claro, brillante.

brighten /ˈbraitṇ/ *v.* abrillantar; alegrar.

brightness /ˈbraitnɪs/ *n.* resplandor *m.*

brilliance /ˈbrɪlyəns/ *n.* brillantez *f.*

brilliant /ˈbrɪlyənt/ *a.* brillante.

brim /brɪm/ *n.* borde *m.;* (of hat) ala *f.*

brine /brain/ *n.* escabeche, *m.* salmuera *f.*

bring /brɪŋ/ *v.* traer. **b. about,** efectuar, llevar a cabo.

brink /brɪŋk/ *n.* borde *m.*

briny /ˈbraini/ *a.* salado.

brisk /brɪsk/ *a.* vivo; enérgico.

briskly /ˈbrɪskli/ *adv.* vivamente.

briskness /ˈbrɪsknɪs/ *n.* viveza *f.*

bristle /ˈbrɪsəl/ *n.* cerda *f.*

bristly /ˈbrɪsli/ *a.* hirsuto.

Britain /ˈbrɪtṇ/ *n.* **Great B.,** Gran Bretaña *f.*

British /ˈbrɪtɪʃ/ *a.* británico.

British Empire imperio británico *m.*

British Isles /ailz/ islas británicas *f.*

Briton /ˈbrɪtṇ/ *n.* inglés *m.*

brittle /ˈbrɪtl/ *a.* quebradizo, frágil.

broad /brɔd/ *a.* ancho.

broadcast /ˈbrɔdˌkæst/ *n.* **1.** radiodifusión *f.* —*v.* **2.** radiodifundir.

broadcaster /ˈbrɔdˌkæstər/ *n.* locutor -ra.

broadcloth /ˈbrɔdˌklɔθ/ *n.* paño fino.

broaden /ˈbrɔdṇ/ *v.* ensanchar.

broadly /ˈbrɔdli/ *adv.* ampliamente.

broadminded /ˈbrɔdˈmaindɪd/ *a.* tolerante, liberal.

brocade /brouˈkeid/ *n.* brocado *m.*

brocaded /brouˈkeidɪd/ *a.* espolinado.

broccoli /ˈbrɒkəli/ *n.* brécol *m.*

broil /brɔil/ *v.* asar.

broiler /ˈbrɔilər/ *n.* parrilla *f.*

broken /ˈbroukən/ *a.* roto, quebrado.

broken-hearted /ˈbroukənˈhɑrtɪd/ *a.* angustiado.

broker /'broukər/ n. corredor -ra, bolsista m. & f.

brokerage /'broukərɪdʒ/ n. corretaje m.

bronchial /'brɒŋkiəl/ a. bronquial.

bronchitis /brɒŋ'kaitis/ n. bronquitis f.

bronze /brɒnz/ n. bronce m.

brooch /broutʃ/ n. broche m.

brood /brud/ n. **1.** cría, progenie f. —v. **2.** empollar; cobijar.

brook /bruk/ n. arroyo m., quebrada f.

broom /brum/ n. escoba f.

broomstick /'brum,stɪk/ n. palo de escoba.

broth /brɔθ/ n. caldo m.

brothel /'brɒθəl/ n. burdel m.

brother /'brʌðər/ n. hermano m.

brotherhood /'brʌðər,hud/ n. fraternidad f.

brother-in-law /'brʌðər ɪn ,lɔ/ n. cuñado m.

brotherly /'brʌðərli/ a. fraternal.

brow /brau/ n. ceja; frente f.

brown /braun/ a. pardo, moreno; marrón. v. rehogar.

brown sugar azúcar moreno m.

browse /brauz/ v. curiosear; ramonear.

browser /'brauzər/ n. (Internet) nagegador m., visualizador m., visor m.

bruise /bruz/ n. **1.** contusión f. —v. **2.** magullar.

brunette /bru'nɛt/ a. & n. moreno -na, trigueño -ña.

brush /brʌʃ/ n. **1.** cepillo m.; brocha f. —v. **2.** cepillar.

brushwood /'brʌʃ,wud/ n. matorral m.

brusque /brʌsk/ a. brusco.

brusquely /'brʌskli/ adv. bruscamente.

brutal /'brutl/ a. brutal.

brutality /bru'tælɪti/ n. brutalidad f.

brutalize /'brutl,aiz/ v. embrutecer.

brute /brut/ n. bruto -ta, bestia f.

bubble /'bʌbəl/ n. ampolla f.

bucket /'bʌkɪt/ n. cubo m.

buckle /'bʌkəl/ n. hebilla f.

buckram /'bʌkrəm/ n. bucarán m.

bucksaw /'bʌk'sɔ/ n. sierra de bastidor.

buckshot /'bʌk,ʃɒt/ n. posta f.

buckwheat /'bʌk,wit/ n. trigo sarraceno.

bud /bʌd/ n. **1.** brote m. —v. **2.** brotar.

budding /'bʌdɪŋ/ a. en capullo.

budge /bʌdʒ/ v. moverse.

budget /'bʌdʒɪt/ n. presupuesto m.

buffalo /'bʌfə,lou/ n. búfalo m.

buffer /'bʌfər/ n. parachoques m.

buffet /bə'fei/ n. bufet m.; (furniture) aparador m.

buffoon /bə'fun/ n. bufón m.

bug /bʌg/ n. insecto m.; (computer) error m.

bugle /'byugəl/ n. clarín m.; corneta f.

build /bɪld/ v. construir.

builder /'bɪldər/ n. constructor -ra.

building /'bɪldɪŋ/ n. edificio m.

bulb /bʌlb/ n. bulbo m.; (of lamp) bombilla, ampolla f.

bulge /bʌldʒ/ n. abultamiento m. v. abultar.

bulging /'bʌldʒɪŋ/ a. protuberante.

bulimia /bu'limiə/ n. bulimia f.

bulk /bʌlk/ n. masa f.; grueso m.; mayoría f.

bulkhead /'bʌlk,hɛd/ n. frontón m.

bulky /'bʌlki/ a. grueso, abultado.

bull /bul/ n. toro m.

bulldog /'bul,dɔg/ n. perro de presa.

bullet /'bulɪt/ n. bala f.

bulletin /'bulɪtɪn/ n. boletín m.

bulletproof /'bulɪt,pruf/ a. a prueba de bala.

bullfight /'bul,fait/ n. corrida de toros.

bullfighter /'bul,faitər/ n. torero -ra.

bullfinch /'bul,fɪntʃ/ n. pinzón real m.

bully /'buli/ n. **1.** rufián m. —v. **2.** bravear.

bulwark /'bulwərk/ n. baluarte m.

bum /bʌm/ n. holgazán m.

bump /bʌmp/ n. **1.** golpe, choque m. —v. **2. b. into**, chocar contra.

bumper /'bʌmpər/ n. parachoques m.

bun /bʌn/ n. bollo m.

bunch /bʌntʃ/ n. racimo; montón m.

bundle /'bʌndl/ n. **1.** bulto m. —v. **2. b. up**, abrigar.

bungalow /'bʌŋgə,lou/ n. casa de un solo piso.

bungle /'bʌŋgəl/ v. estropear.

bunion /'bʌnyən/ n. juanete m.

bunk /bʌŋk/ n. litera f.

bunny /'bʌni/ n. conejito -ta.

bunting /'bʌntɪŋ/ n. lanilla; banderas f.

buoy /'bui/ n. boya f.

buoyant /'bɔiənt/ a. boyante; vivaz.

burden /'bɜrdn/ n. **1.** carga f. —v. **2.** cargar.

burdensome /'bɜrdnsəm/ a. gravoso.

bureau /'byurou/ n. (furniture) cómoda f.; departamento m.

burglar /'bɜrglər/ n. ladrón -ona.

burglarize /'bɜrglə,raiz/ v. robar.

burglary /'bɜrgləri/ n. robo m.

burial /'bɛriəl/ n. entierro m.

burlap /'bɜrlæp/ n. arpillera f.

burly /'bɜrli/ a. corpulento.

burn /bɜrn/ v. quemar; arder.

burner /'bɜrnər/ n. mechero m.

burning /'bɜrnɪŋ/ a. ardiente.

burnish /'bɜrnɪʃ/ v. pulir; acicalar.

burrow /'bɜrou/ v. minar; horadar.

burst /bɜrst/ v. reventar.

bury /'bɛri/ v. enterrar.

bus /bʌs/ n. autobús m.

bush /buʃ/ n. arbusto m.

bushy /'buʃi/ a. matoso; peludo.

business /'bɪznɪs/ n. negocios m.pl.; comercio m.

businesslike /'bɪznɪs,laik/ a. directo, práctico.

businessman /'bɪznɪs,mæn/ n. hombre de negocios, comerciante m.

businesswoman /'bɪznɪs,wumən/ n. mujer de negocios.

bust /bʌst/ n. busto; pecho m.

bustle /'bʌsəl/ n. bullicio m.; animación f.

busy /'bɪzi/ a. ocupado, atareado.

busybody /'bɪzi,bɒdi/ n. entremetido -da.

but /bʌt/ conj. pero; sino.

butcher /'butʃər/ n. carnicero -ra.

butchery /'butʃəri/ n. carnicería; matanza f.

butler /'bʌtlər/ n. mayordomo m.

butt /bʌt/ n. punta f.; cabo extremo m.

butter /'bʌtər/ n. manteca, mantequilla f.

buttercup /'bʌtər,kʌp/ n. ranúnculo m.

butterfat /'bʌtər,fæt/ n. mantequilla f.

butterfly /'bʌtər,flai/ n. mariposa f.

buttermilk /'bʌtər,mɪlk/ n. suero (de leche) m.

button /'bʌtn/ n. botón m.

buttonhole /'bʌtn,houl/ n. ojal m.

buttress /'bʌtrɪs/ n. sostén; refuerzo m.

buxom /'bʌksəm/ a. regordete.

buy /bai/ v. comprar.

buyer /'baiər/ n. comprador -ra.

buzz /bʌz/ n. **1.** zumbido m. —v. **2.** zumbar.

buzzard /'bʌzərd/ n. gallinazo m.

buzzer /'bʌzər/ n. zumbador m.; timbre m.

buzz saw n. sierra circular f.

by /bai/ prep. por; (near) cerca de, al lado de; (time) para.

by-and-by /,baiən'bai/ adv. pronto; luego.

bygone /'bai,gɔn/ a. pasado.

bylaw /'bai,lɔ/ n. estatuto, reglamento m.

bypass /'bai,pæs/ n. desvío m.

byproduct /'bai,prɒdəkt/ n. subproducto m.

bystander /'bai,stændər/ n. espectador -ra; mirón -na.

byte /bait/ n. en teoría de la información: ocho bits, byte m.

byway /'bai,wei/ n. camino desviado m.

C

cab /kæb/ n. taxi, coche de alquiler m.

cabaret /,kæbə'rei/ n. cabaret m.

cabbage /'kæbɪdʒ/ n. repollo m.

cabin /'kæbɪn/ n. cabaña f.

cabinet /'kæbənɪt/ n. gabinete; ministerio m.

cabinetmaker /'kæbənɪt,meikər/ n. ebanista m.

cable /'keibəl/ n. cable m.

cablegram /'keibəl,græm/ n. cablegrama m.

cache /kæʃ/ n. escondite m.

cackle /'kækəl/ n. charla f.; cacareo m. v. cacarear.

cacophony /kə'kɒfəni/ n. cacofonía f.

cactus /'kæktəs/ n. cacto m.

cad /kæd/ n. persona vil.

cadaver /kə'dævər/ n. cadáver m.

cadaverous /kə'dævərəs/ a. cadavérico.

caddie /'kædi/ n. (golf) ayudante m. & f.

cadence /'keidns/ n. cadencia f.

cadet /kə'dɛt/ n. cadete m.

cadmium /'kædmiəm/ n. cadmio m.

cadre /'kædri, 'kɑdrei/ n. núcleo; Mil. cuadro m.

café /kæ'fei/ n. café m., cantina f.

cafeteria /,kæfɪ'tɪəriə/ n. cafetería f.

caffeine /kæ'fin/ n. cafeína f.

cage /keidʒ/ n. jaula f. v. enjaular.

caged /keidʒd/ a. enjaulado.

caisson /'keisɒn, -sən/ n. arcón m.; Mil. furgón m.

cajole /kə'dʒoul/ v. lisonjear; adular.

cake /keik/ n. torta f.; bizcocho m.

calamitous /kə'læmɪtəs/ a. calamitoso.

calamity /kə'læmɪti/ n. calamidad f.

calcify /'kælsə,fai/ v. calcificar.

calcium /'kælsiəm/ n. calcio m.

calculable /'kælkyələbəl/ a. calculable.

calculate /'kælkyə,leit/ v. calcular.

calculating /'kælkyə,leitɪŋ/ a. interesado.

calculation /,kælkyə'leiʃən/ n. calculación f.; cálculo m.

calculus /'kælkyələs/ n. cálculo m.

caldron /'kɔldrən/ n. caldera f.

calendar /'kæləndər/ n. calendario m.

calf /kæf/ n. ternero m. (animal); pantorrilla f. (of the body).

calfskin /'kæf,skɪn/ n. piel de becerro f.

caliber /'kælɪbər/ n. calibre m.

calico /'kælɪ,kou/ n. calicó f.

caliper /'kæləpər/ n. calibrador m.

calisthenics /,kæləs'θɛnɪks/ n. calistenia, gimnasia f.

calk /kɔk/ v. calafatear; rellenar.

calker /'kɔkər/ n. calafate -ta.

call /kɔl/ n. **1.** llamada f. —v. **2.** llamar.

calligraphy /kə'lɪgrəfi/ n. caligrafía f.

calling /'kɔlɪŋ/ n. vocación f.

calling card tarjeta (de visita) f.

callously /'kæləsli/ adv. insensiblemente.

callow /'kælou/ a. sin experiencia.

callus /'kæləs/ n. callo m.

calm /kɑm/ a. **1.** tranquilo, calmado. —n. **2.** calma f. —v. **3.** calmar.

calmly /'kɑmli/ adv. serenamente.

calmness /'kɑmnɪs/ n. calma f.

caloric /kə'lɔrɪk/ a. calórico.

calorie /'kæləri/ n. caloría f.

calorimeter /,kælə'rɪmɪtər/ n. calorímetro m.

calumniate /kə'lʌmni,eit/ v. calumniar.

calumny /'kæləmni/ n. calumnia f.

Calvary /'kælvəri/ n. Calvario m.

calve /kæv/ v. parir (la vaca).

calyx /'keilɪks/ n. cáliz m.

camaraderie /,kɑmə'rɑdəri/ n. compañerismo m., compadrería f.

cambric /'keimbrɪk/ n. batista f.

camcorder /'kæm,kɔrdər/ n. videocámara f.

camel /'kæməl/ n. camello -lla.

camellia /kə'milyə/ n. camelia f.

camel's hair /'kæməlz/ pelo de camello.

cameo /'kæmi,ou/ n. camafeo m.

camera /'kæmərə/ n. cámara f.

camouflage /'kæmə,flɑʒ/ n. camuflaje m.

camouflaging /'kæmə,flɑʒɪŋ/ n. simulacro, disfraz m.

camp /kæmp/ n. **1.** campamento m. —v. **2.** acampar.

campaign /kæm'pein/ n. campaña f.

camper /'kæmpər/ n. acampado m.

campfire /'kæmp,faiər/ n. fogata de campamento.

camphor /'kæmfər/ n. alcanfor m.

camphor ball bola de alcanfor.

campus /'kæmpəs/ n. campo de colegio (o universidad), campus m.

can /kæn/ v. (be able) poder.

can /kæn/ n. **1.** lata f. —v. **2.** conservar en latas, enlatar.

Canada /'kænədə/ n. Canadá m.

Canadian /kə'neidiən/ a. & n. canadiense.

canal /kə'næl/ n. canal m.

canalize /'kænl,aiz/ v. canalizar.

canard /kə'nɑrd/ n. embuste m.

canary /kə'nɛəri/ n. canario -ria.

cancel /'kænsəl/ v. cancelar.

cancellation /,kænsə'leiʃən/ n. cancelación f.

cancer /'kænsər/ n. cáncer m.

candelabrum /,kændl'ɑbrəm/ n. candelabro m.

candid /'kændɪd/ a. cándido, sincero.

candidacy /'kændɪdəsi/ n. candidatura f.

candidate /'kændɪ,deit/ n. candidato -ta.

candidly /'kændɪdli/ adv. cándidamente.

candidness /'kændɪdnɪs/ n. candidez; sinceridad f.

candied /'kændid/ a. garapiñado.

candle /'kændl/ n. vela f.

candlestick /'kændl,stɪk/ n. candelero m.

candor /'kændər/ n. candor m.; sinceridad f.

candy /'kændi/ n. dulces m.pl.

cane /kein/ n. caña f.; (for walking) bastón m.

canine /'keinain/ a. canino.

canister /'kænəstər/ n. frasco m.; lata f.

canker /'kæŋkər/ n. llaga; úlcera f.

cankerworm /'kæŋkər,wɜrm/ n. oruga f.

canned /kænd/ a. envasado, enlatado.

canner /'kænər/ n. envasador m.

cannery /'kænəri/ n. fábrica de conservas alimenticias f.

cannibal /'kænəbəl/ n. caníbal m. & f.

cannon /'kænən/ n. cañón m.

cannonade /,kænə'neid/ n. cañoneo m.

cannoneer /,kænə'nɪər/ n. cañonero -ra.

canny /'kæni/ a. sagaz; prudente.

canoe /kə'nu/ n. canoa, piragua f.

canoeing /kə'nuɪŋ/ n. piragüismo m.

canoeist /kə'nuɪst/ n. piragüista m. & f.

canon /'kænən/ n. canon m.; Relig. canónigo m.

canonical /kə'nɒnɪkəl/ a. canónico.

canonize /'kænə,naiz/ v. canonizar.

can opener /'oupənər/ abrelatas m.

canopy /'kænəpi/ n. dosel m.

cant /kænt/ *n.* hipocresía *f.*

cantaloupe /ˈkæntlˌoup/ *n.* melón *m.*

canteen /kænˈtin/ *n.* cantina *f.*

canter /ˈkæntər/ *n.* **1.** medio galope *m.* —*v.* **2.** galopar.

cantonment /kænˈtɒnmənt/ *n. Mil.* acuartelamiento *m.*

canvas /ˈkænvəs/ *n.* lona *f.*

canyon /ˈkænyən/ *n.* cañón, desfiladero *m.*

cap /kæp/ *n.* **1.** tapa *f.*; (headwear) gorro *m.* —*v.* **2.** tapar.

capability /ˌkeipəˈbɪlɪti/ *n.* capacidad *f.*

capable /ˈkeipəbəl/ *a.* capaz.

capably /ˈkeipəbli/ *adv.* hábilmente.

capacious /kəˈpeiʃəs/ *a.* espacioso.

capacity /kəˈpæsɪti/ *n.* capacidad *f.*

cape /keip/ *n.* capa *f.*, *Geog.* cabo *m.*

caper /ˈkeipər/ *n.* zapateta *f.*; *Bot.* alcaparra *f.*

capillary /ˈkæpəˌlɛri/ *a.* capilar.

capital /ˈkæpɪtl/ *n.* capital *m.*; *Govt.* capital *f.*

capitalism /ˈkæpɪtlˌɪzəm/ *n.* capitalismo *m.*

capitalist /ˈkæpɪtlɪst/ *n.* capitalista *m.* & *f.*

capitalistic /ˌkæpɪtlˈɪstɪk/ *a.* capitalista.

capitalization /ˌkæpɪtləˈzeiʃən/ *n.* capitalización *f.*

capitalize /ˈkæpɪtlˌaiz/ *v.* capitalizar.

capital letter *n.* mayúscula *f.*

capitulate /kəˈpɪtʃəˌleit/ *v.* capitular.

capon /ˈkeipɒn/ *n.* capón *m.*

caprice /kəˈpris/ *n.* capricho *m.*

capricious /kəˈprɪʃəs/ *a.* caprichoso.

capriciously /kəˈprɪʃəsli/ *adv.* caprichosamente.

capriciousness /kəˈprɪʃəsnɪs/ *n.* capricho *m.*

capsize /ˈkæpsaiz/ *v.* zozobrar, volcar.

capsule /ˈkæpsəl/ *n.* cápsula *f.*

captain /ˈkæptən/ *n.* capitán -tana.

caption /ˈkæpʃən/ *n.* título *m.*; (motion pictures) subtítulo *m.*

captious /ˈkæpʃəs/ *a.* capcioso.

captivate /ˈkæptəˌveit/ *v.* cautivar.

captivating /ˈkæptəˌveitɪŋ/ *a.* encantador.

captive /ˈkæptɪv/ *n.* cautivo -va, prisionero -ra.

captivity /kæpˈtɪvɪti/ *n.* cautividad *f.*

captor /ˈkæptər/ *n.* apresador -ra.

capture /ˈkæptʃər/ *n.* **1.** captura *f.* —*v.* **2.** capturar.

car /kɑr/ *n.* coche, carro *m.*; (of train) vagón, coche *m.* **baggage c.,** vagón de equipajes. **parlor c.,** coche salón.

carafe /kəˈræf/ *n.* garrafa *f.*

caramel /ˈkærəməl/ *n.* caramelo *m.*

carat /ˈkærət/ *n.* quilate *m.*

caravan /ˈkærəˌvæn/ *n.* caravana *f.*

caraway /ˈkærəˌwei/ *n.* alcaravea *f.*

carbide /ˈkɑrbaid/ *n.* carburo *m.*

carbine /ˈkɑrbin/ *n.* carabina *f.*

carbohydrate /ˌkɑrbouˈhaidreit/ *n.* hidrato de carbono.

carbon /ˈkɑrbən/ *n.* carbón *m.*

carbon dioxide /daiˈɒksaid/ anhídrido carbónico.

carbon monoxide /mɒnˈɒksaid/ monóxido de carbono.

carbon paper papel carbón *m.*

carbuncle /ˈkɑrbʌŋkəl/ *n.* carbúnculo *m.*

carburetor /ˈkɑrbəˌreitər/ *n.* carburador *m.*

carcinogenic /ˌkɑrsənəˈdʒɛnɪk/ *a.* carcinogénico.

card /kɑrd/ *n.* tarjeta *f.* **playing c.,** naipe *m.*

cardboard /ˈkɑrdˌbɔrd/ *n.* cartón *m.*

cardiac /ˈkɑrdiˌæk/ *a.* cardíaco.

cardigan /ˈkɑrdɪgən/ *n.* chaqueta de punto.

cardinal /ˈkɑrdnl/ *a.* **1.** cardinal. —*n.* **2.** cardenal *m.*

cardiologist /ˌkɑrdiˈɒlədʒɪst/ *n.* cardiólogo, -ga *m.* & *f.*

care /kɛər/ *n.* **1.** cuidado. —*v.* **2. c. for,** cuidar.

careen /kəˈrin/ *v.* carenar; echarse de costado.

career /kəˈrɪər/ *n.* carrera *f.*

carefree /ˈkɛərˌfri/ *a.* descuidado.

careful /ˈkɛərfəl/ *a.* cuidadoso. **be. c.,** tener cuidado.

carefully /ˈkɛərfəli/ *adv.* cuidadosamente.

carefulness /ˈkɛərfəlnɪs/ *n.* esmero; cuidado *m.*; cautela *f.*

careless /ˈkɛərlɪs/ *a.* descuidado.

carelessly /ˈkɛərlɪsli/ *adv.* descuidadamente; negligentemente.

carelessness /ˈkɛərlɪsnɪs/ *n.* descuido *m.*

caress /kəˈrɛs/ *n.* **1.** caricia *f.* —*v.* **2.** acariciar.

caretaker /ˈkɛərˌteikər/ *n.* guardián -ana.

cargo /ˈkɑrgou/ *n.* carga *f.*

caricature /ˈkærɪkətʃər/ *n.* caricatura *f.*

caricaturist /ˈkærɪkəˌtʃʊrɪst/ *n.* caricaturista *m.* & *f.*

caries /ˈkɛəriz/ *n.* caries *f.*

carjacking /ˈkɑrˌdʒækɪŋ/ *n.* robo de coche *m.*

carload /ˈkɑrˌloud/ *a.* furgonada, vagonada.

carnal /ˈkɑrnl/ *a.* carnal.

carnation /kɑrˈneiʃən/ *n.* clavel *m.*

carnival /ˈkɑrnəvəl/ *n.* carnaval *m.*

carnivorous /kɑrˈnɪvərəs/ *a.* carnívoro.

carol /ˈkærəl/ *n.* villancico *m.*

carouse /kəˈrauz/ *v.* parrandear.

carpenter /ˈkɑrpəntər/ *n.* carpintero -ra.

carpet /ˈkɑrpɪt/ *n.* alfombra *f.*

carpeting /ˈkɑrpɪtɪŋ/ *n.* alfombrado *m.*

car pool /ˈkɑrˌpul/ uso habitual, por varias personas, de un automóvil perteneciente a una de ellas.

carriage /ˈkærɪdʒ/ *n.* carruaje; (bearing) porte *m.*

carrier /ˈkæriər/ *n.* portador -ra.

carrier pigeon paloma mensajera.

carrot /ˈkærət/ *n.* zanahoria *f.*

carrousel /ˌkærəˈsɛl/ *n.* volantín, carrusel *m.*

carry /ˈkæri/ *v.* llevar, cargar. **c. out,** cumplir, llevar a cabo.

cart /kɑrt/ *n.* carreta *f.*

cartage /ˈkɑrtɪdʒ/ *n.* acarreo, carretaje *m.*

cartel /kɑrˈtɛl/ *n.* cartel *m.*

cartilage /ˈkɑrtlɪdʒ/ *n.* cartílago *m.*

carton /ˈkɑrtn/ *n.* caja de cartón.

cartoon /kɑrˈtun/ *n.* caricatura *f.*

cartoonist /kɑrˈtunɪst/ *n.* caricaturista *m.* & *f.*

cartridge /ˈkɑrtrɪdʒ/ *n.* cartucho *m.*

carve /kɑrv/ *v.* esculpir; (meat) trinchar.

carver /ˈkɑrvər/ *n.* tallador -ra; grabador -ra.

carving /ˈkɑrvɪŋ/ *n.* entalladura *f.*; arte de trinchar. **c. knife,** trinchante *m.*

cascade /kæsˈkeid/ *n.* cascada *f.*

case /keis/ *n.* caso *m.*; (box) caja *f.* **in any c.,** sea como sea.

cash /kæʃ/ *n.* **1.** dinero contante. —*v.* **2.** efectuar, cambiar.

cashier /kæˈʃɪər/ *n.* cajero -ra.

cashmere /ˈkæʒmɪər/ *n.* casimir *m.*

casino /kəˈsinou/ *n.* casino *m.*

cask /kæsk/ *n.* barril *m.*

casket /ˈkæskɪt/ *n.* ataúd *m.*

casserole /ˈkæsəˌroul/ *n.* cacerola *f.*

cassette /kəˈsɛt/ *n.* cassette *m.*, cartucho *m.*

cast /kæst/ *n.* **1.** *Theat.* reparto de papeles. —*v.* **2.** echar; *Theat.* repartir.

castanet /ˌkæstəˈnɛt/ *n.* castañuela *f.*

castaway /ˈkæstəˌwei/ *n.* náufrago -ga.

caste /kæst/ *n.* casta *f.*

caster /ˈkæstər/ *n.* tirador *m.*

castigate /ˈkæstɪˌgeit/ *v.* castigar.

Castilian /kæˈstɪlyən/ *a.* castellano.

cast iron *n.* hierro colado *m.*

castle /ˈkæsəl/ *n.* castillo *m.*

castoff /ˈkæstˌɔf/ *a.* descartado.

casual /ˈkæʒuəl/ *a.* casual.

casually /ˈkæʒuəli/ *adv.* casualmente.

casualness /ˈkæʒuəlnɪs/ *n.* casualidad *f.*

casualty /ˈkæʒuəlti/ *n.* víctima *f.*; *Mil.* baja *f.*

cat /kæt/ *n.* gato -ta.

cataclysm /ˈkætəˌklɪzəm/ *n.* cataclismo *m.*

catacomb /ˈkætəˌkoum/ *n.* catacumba *f.*

catalogue /ˈkætlˌɔg/ *n.* catálogo *m.*

catapult /ˈkætəˌpʌlt/ *n.* catapulta *f.*

cataract /ˈkætəˌrækt/ *n.* catarata *f.*

catarrh /kəˈtɑr/ *n.* catarro *m.*

catastrophe /kəˈtæstrəfi/ *n.* catástrofe *f.*

catch /kætʃ/ *v.* alcanzar, atrapar, coger.

catchy /ˈkætʃi/ *a.* contagioso.

catechism /ˈkætɪˌkɪzəm/ *n.* catequismo *m.*

catechize /ˈkætɪˌkaiz/ *v.* catequizar.

categorical /ˌkætɪˈgɔrɪkəl/ *a.* categórico.

category /ˈkætɪˌgɔri/ *n.* categoría *f.*

cater /ˈkeitər/ *v.* abastecer; proveer. **c. to,** complacer.

caterpillar /ˈkætəˌpɪlər/ *n.* gusano *m.*

catgut /ˈkætˌgʌt/ *n.* cuerda (de tripa).

catharsis /kəˈθɑrsɪs/ *n.* catarsis, purga *f.*

cathartic /kəˈθɑrtɪk/ *a.* **1.** catártico; purgante. —*n.* **2.** purgante *m.*

cathedral /kəˈθidrəl/ *n.* catedral *f.*

cathode /ˈkæθoud/ *n.* cátodo *m.*

Catholic /ˈkæθəlɪk/ *a.* católico & *n.* católico -ca.

Catholicism /kəˈθɒləˌsɪzəm/ *n.* catolicismo *m.*

catnap /ˈkætˌnæp/ *n.* siesta corta.

catsup /ˈkætsəp, ˈkɛtʃəp/ *n.* salsa de tomate.

cattle /ˈkætl/ *n.* ganado *m.*

cattleman /ˈkætlmən, -ˌmæn/ *n.* ganadero *m.*

cauliflower /ˈkɔləˌflauər/ *n.* coliflor *m.*

causation /kɔˈzeiʃən/ *n.* causalidad *f.*

cause /kɔz/ *n.* causa *f.*

causeway /ˈkɔzˌwei/ *n.* calzada elevada *f.*; terraplén *m.*

caustic /ˈkɔstɪk/ *a.* cáustico.

cauterize /ˈkɔtəˌraiz/ *v.* cauterizar.

cautery /ˈkɔtəri/ *n.* cauterio *m.*

caution /ˈkɔʃən/ *n.* cautela *f.*

cautious /ˈkɔʃəs/ *a.* cauteloso.

cavalcade /ˌkævəlˈkeid/ *n.* cabalgata *f.*

cavalier /ˌkævəˈlɪər/ *n.* caballero *m.*

cavalry /ˈkævəlri/ *n.* caballería *f.*

cave /keiv/ **cavern** *n.* caverna, gruta *f.*

cave-in /ˈkeiv ˌɪn/ *n.* hundimiento *m.*

caviar /ˈkæviˌɑr/ *n.* caviar *m.*

cavity /ˈkævɪti/ *n.* hueco *m.*

cayman /ˈkeimən/ *n.* caimán *m.*

CD player tocadiscos compacto, tocadiscos digital *m.*

cease /sis/ *v.* cesar.

ceaseless /ˈsislɪs/ *a.* incesante.

cedar /ˈsidər/ *n.* cedro *m.*

cede /sid/ *v.* ceder.

ceiling /ˈsilɪŋ/ *n.* techo; cielo *m.*

celebrant /ˈsɛləbrənt/ *n.* celebrante -ta.

celebrate /ˈsɛləˌbreit/ *v.* celebrar.

celebration /ˌsɛləˈbreiʃən/ *n.* celebración *f.*

celebrity /səˈlɛbrɪti/ *n.* celebridad.

celerity /səˈlɛrɪti/ *n.* celeridad; prontitud *f.*

celery /ˈsɛləri/ *n.* apio *m.*

celestial /səˈlɛstʃəl/ *a.* celeste.

celibacy /ˈsɛləbəsi/ *n.* celibato -ta.

celibate /ˈsɛləbɪt/ *a.* & *n.* célibe *m.* & *f.*

cell /sɛl/ *n.* celda *f.*; *Biol.* célula *f.*

cellar /ˈsɛlər/ *n.* sótano *m.*

cellist /ˈtʃɛlɪst/ *a.* celista *m.* & *f.*

cello /ˈtʃɛlou/ *n.* violonchelo *m.*

cellophane /ˈsɛləˌfein/ *n.* celofán *m.*

cellular /ˈsɛlyələr/ *a.* celular.

cellular phone /foun/ teléfono móvil *m.*

celluloid /ˈsɛlyəˌlɔid/ *n.* celuloide *m.*

cellulose /ˈsɛlyəˌlous/ *a.* **1.** celuloso. —*n.* **2.** celulosa *f.*

Celtic /ˈkɛltɪk, ˈsɛl-/ *a.* céltico.

cement /sɪˈmɛnt/ *n.* cemento *m.*

cemetery /ˈsɛmɪˌtɛri/ *n.* cementerio *m.*; campo santo *m.*

censor /ˈsɛnsər/ *n.* censor -ra.

censorious /sɛnˈsɔriəs/ *a.* severo; crítico.

censorship /ˈsɛnsərˌʃɪp/ *n.* censura *f.*

censure /ˈsɛnʃər/ *n.* **1.** censura *f.* —*v.* **2.** censurar.

census /ˈsɛnsəs/ *n.* censo *m.*

cent /sɛnt/ *n.* centavo, céntimo *m.*

centenary /sɛnˈtɛnəri/ *a.* & *n.* centenario *m.*

centennial /sɛnˈtɛniəl/ *a.* & *n.* centenario *m.*

center /ˈsɛntər/ *n.* centro *m.*

centerfold /ˈsɛntərˌfould/ *n.* página central desplegable en una revista.

centerpiece /ˈsɛntərˌpis/ *n.* centro de mesa.

centigrade /ˈsɛntɪˌgreid/ *a.* centígrado.

centigrade thermometer termómetro centígrado.

central /ˈsɛntrəl/ *a.* central.

Central American *a.* & *n.* centroamericano -na.

centralize /ˈsɛntrəˌlaiz/ *v.* centralizar.

century /ˈsɛntʃəri/ *n.* siglo *m.*

century plant maguey *m.*

ceramic /səˈræmɪk/ *a.* cerámico.

ceramics /səˈræmɪks/ *n.* cerámica *f.*

cereal /ˈsɪəriəl/ *n.* cereal *m.*

cerebral /səˈribrəl/ *a.* cerebral.

ceremonial /ˌsɛrəˈmouniəl/ *a.* ceremonial.

ceremonious /ˌsɛrəˈmouniəs/ *a.* ceremonioso.

ceremony /ˈsɛrəˌmouni/ *n.* ceremonia *f.*

certain /ˈsɜrtn/ *a.* cierto, seguro.

certainly /ˈsɜrtnli/ *adv.* sin duda, seguramente.

certainty /ˈsɜrtnti/ *n.* certeza *f.*

certificate /sərˈtɪfɪkɪt/ *n.* certificado *m.*

certification /ˌsɜrtəfɪˈkeiʃən, sərˌtɪfə-/ *n.* certificación *f.*

certified /ˈsɜrtəˌfaid/ *a.* certificado.

certify /ˈsɜrtəˌfai/ *v.* certificar.

certitude /ˈsɜrtɪˌtyud/ *n.* certeza *f.*

cessation /sɛˈseiʃən/ *n.* cesación, descontinuación *f.*

cession /ˈsɛʃən/ *n.* cesión *f.*

chafe /tʃeif/ *v.* irritar.

chafing dish /ˈtʃeifɪŋ/ *n.* escalfador *m.*

chagrin /ʃəˈgrɪn/ *n.* disgusto *m.*

chain /tʃein/ *n.* **1.** cadena *f.* —*v.* **2.** encadenar.

chair /tʃɛər/ *n.* silla *f.*

chairman /ˈtʃɛərmən/ *n.* presidente -ta.

chairperson /ˈtʃɛərˌpɜrsən/ *n.* presidente -ta; persona que preside.

chalk /tʃɔk/ *n.* tiza *f.*

challenge /ˈtʃælɪndʒ/ *n.* **1.** desafío *m.* —*v.* **2.** desafiar.

challenger /ˈtʃælɪndʒər/ *n.* desafiador -ra.

chamber /ˈtʃeimbər/ *n.* cámara *f.*

chamberlain /ˈtʃeimbərlɪn/ *n.* camarero *m.*

chambermaid /ˈtʃeimbərˌmeid/ *n.* camarera *f.*

chameleon /kəˈmiliən/ *n.* camaleón *m.*

chamois /ˈʃæmi/ *n.* gamuza *f.*

champagne /ʃæmˈpein/ *n.* champán *m.*, champaña *f.*

champion /ˈtʃæmpiən/ *n.* **1.** campeón -na —*v.* **2.** defender.

championship /ˈtʃæmpiənˌʃɪp/ *n.* campeonato *m.*

chance /tʃæns/ n. oportunidad, ocasión f. **by c.,** por casualidad, por acaso. **take a c.,** aventurarse.

chancel /'tʃænsəl/ n. antealtar m.

chancellery /'tʃænsələri/ n. cancillería f.

chancellor /'tʃænsələr/ n. canciller m.

chandelier /ˌʃændl'ɪər/ n. araña de luces.

change /tʃeindʒ/ n. **1.** cambio; (from a bill) moneda f. —v. **2.** cambiar.

changeability /ˌtʃeindʒə'bɪliti/ n. mutabilidad f.

changeable /'tʃeindʒəbəl/ a. variable, inconstante.

changer /'tʃeindʒər/ n. cambiador -ra.

channel /'tʃænl/ n. **1.** canal m. —v. **2.** encauzar.

Channel Tunnel túnel del Canal de la Mancha m.

chant /tʃænt/ n. **1.** canto llano m. —v. **2.** cantar.

chaos /'keiɒs/ n. caos m.

chaotic /kei'ɒtɪk/ a. caótico.

chap /tʃæp/ n. **1.** Colloq. tipo m. —v. **2.** rajar.

chapel /'tʃæpəl/ n. capilla f.

chaperon /'ʃæpəˌroun/ n. acompañante -ta de señorita.

chaplain /'tʃæplɪn/ n. capellán m.

chapter /'tʃæptər/ n. capítulo m.

char /tʃɑr/ v. carbonizar.

character /'kærɪktər/ n. carácter m.

characteristic /ˌkærɪktə'rɪstɪk/ a. **1.** característico. —n. **2.** característica f.

characterization /ˌkærɪktərə'zeiʃən/ n. caracterización f.

characterize /'kærɪktəˌraiz/ v. caracterizar.

charcoal /'tʃɑrˌkoul/ n. carbón leña.

charge /tʃɑrdʒ/ n. **1.** acusación f.; ataque m. —v. **2.** cargar; acusar; atacar.

chariot /'tʃæriət/ n. carroza f.

charisma /kə'rɪzmə/ n. carisma m.

charitable /'tʃærɪtəbəl/ a. caritativo.

charitableness /'tʃærɪtəbəlnɪs/ n. caridad f.

charitably /'tʃærɪtəbli/ adv. caritativamente.

charity /'tʃærɪti/ n. caridad f.; (alms) limosna f.

charlatan /'ʃɑrlətn/ n. charlatán -na.

charlatanism /'ʃɑrlətnˌɪzəm/ n. charlatanería f.

charm /tʃɑrm/ n. **1.** encanto m.; (witchcraft) hechizo m. —v. **2.** encantar; hechizar.

charming /'tʃɑrmɪŋ/ a. encantador.

charred /tʃɑrd/ a. carbonizado.

chart /tʃɑrt/ n. tabla, esquema f.

charter /'tʃɑrtər/ n. **1.** carta f. —v. **2.** alquilar.

charter flight vuelo chárter m.

charwoman /'tʃɑrˌwumən/ n. mujer de la limpieza f.

chase /tʃeis/ n. **1.** caza f. —v. **2.** cazar; perseguir.

chaser /'tʃeisər/ n. perseguidor -ra.

chasm /'kæzəm/ n. abismo m.

chassis /'tʃæsi/ n. chasis m.

chaste /tʃeist/ a. casto.

chasten /'tʃeisən/ v. corregir, castigar.

chastise /tʃæs'taiz/ v. castigar.

chastisement /'tʃæs'taizmənt/ n. castigo m.

chastity /'tʃæstɪti/ n. castidad, pureza f.

chat /tʃæt/ n. **1.** plática, charla f. —v. **2.** platicar, charlar.

chateau /ʃæ'tou/ n. castillo m.

chattels /'tʃætlz/ n.pl. bienes m.

chatter /'tʃætər/ v. **1.** cotorrear; (teeth) rechinar. —n. **2.** cotorreo m.

chatterbox /'tʃæt,ər bɒks/ n. charlador -ra.

chauffeur /'ʃoufər/ n. chofer m.

cheap /tʃip/ a. barato.

cheapen /'tʃipən/ v. rebajar, menospreciar.

cheaply /'tʃipli/ adv. barato.

cheapness /'tʃipnɪs/ n. baratura f.

cheat /tʃit/ v. engañar.

cheater /'tʃitər/ n. engañador -ra.

check /tʃɛk/ n. **1.** verificación f.; (bank) cheque m.; (restaurant) cuenta f.; (chess) jaque m. —v. **2.** verificar.

checkers /'tʃɛkərz/ n. juego de damas.

checkmate /'tʃɛkˌmeit/ v. dar mate.

checkout counter /'tʃɛkˌaut/ caja f.

cheek /tʃik/ n. mejilla f. (of face), desfachatez f. (gall).

cheekbone /'tʃikˌboun/ n. pómulo m.

cheeky /'tʃiki/ a. fresco, descarado, chulo.

cheer /tʃɪər/ n. **1.** alegría f.; aplauso m. —v. **2.** alegrar; aplaudir.

cheerful /'tʃɪərfəl/ a. alegre.

cheerfully /'tʃɪərfəli/ adv. alegremente.

cheerfulness /'tʃɪərfəlnɪs/ n. alegría f.

cheerless /'tʃɪərlɪs/ a. triste.

cheery /'tʃɪəri/ a. alegre.

cheese /tʃiz/ n. queso m. **cottage c.,** requesón m.

chef /ʃɛf/ n. cocinero en jefe.

chemical /'kɛmɪkəl/ a. **1.** químico. —n. **2.** reactivo m.

chemically /'kɛmɪkli/ adv. químicamente.

chemist /'kɛmɪst/ n. químico -ca.

chemistry /'kɛməstri/ n. química f.

chemotherapy /ˌkimou'θɛrəpi/ n. quimioterapia f.

chenille /ʃə'nil/ n. felpilla f.

cherish /'tʃɛrɪʃ/ v. apreciar.

cherry /'tʃɛri/ n. cereza f.

cherub /'tʃɛrəb/ n. querubín m.

chess /tʃɛs/ n. ajedrez m.

chest /tʃɛst/ n. arca f.; (physiology) pecho m.

chestnut /'tʃɛs,nʌt/ n. castaña f.

chevron /'ʃɛvrən/ n. sardineta f.

chew /tʃu/ v. mascar, masticar.

chewer /'tʃuər/ n. mascador -ra.

chic /ʃik/ a. elegante, paquete.

chicanery /ʃɪ'keinəri/ n. trampería f.

chick /tʃɪk/ n. pollito -ta.

chicken /'tʃɪkən/ n. pollo m., gallina f.

chicken-hearted /'tʃɪkən 'hɑrtɪd/ a. cobarde.

chicken pox /pɒks/ viruelas locas, varicela f.

chicle /'tʃɪkəl/ n. chicle m.

chicory /'tʃɪkəri/ n. achicoria f.

chide /tʃaid/ v. regañar, reprender.

chief /tʃif/ a. **1.** principal. —n. **2.** jefe -fa.

chiefly /'tʃifli/ adv. principalmente, mayormente.

chieftain /'tʃiftən/ n. caudillo m.; (Indian c.) cacique m.

chiffon /ʃɪ'fɒn/ n. chifón m., gasa f.

chilblain /'tʃɪlblein/ n. sabañón m.

child /tʃaild/ n. niño -ña; hijo -ja.

childbirth /'tʃaild,bɜrθ/ n. parto m.

childhood /'tʃaildhud/ n. niñez f.

childish /'tʃaildɪʃ/ a. pueril.

childishness /'tʃaildɪʃnɪs/ n. puerilidad f.

childless /'tʃaildlɪs/ a. sin hijos.

childlike /'tʃaild,laik/ a. infantil.

Chilean /'tʃɪliən/ a. & n. chileno -na.

chili /'tʃɪli/ n. chile, ají m.

chill /tʃɪl/ n. **1.** frío; escalofrío m. —v. **2.** enfriar.

chilliness /'tʃɪlinɪs/ n. frialdad f.

chilly /'tʃɪli/ a. frío; friolento.

chimes /tʃaimz/ n. juego de campanas.

chimney /'tʃɪmni/ n. chimenea f.

chimpanzee /ˌtʃɪmpæn'zi, tʃɪm'pænzi/ n. chimpancé m.

chin /tʃɪn/ n. barba f.

china /'tʃainə/ n. loza f.

chinchilla /tʃɪn'tʃɪlə/ n. chinchilla f.

Chinese /tʃai'niz/ a. & n. chino -na.

chink /tʃɪŋk/ n. grieta f.

chintz /tʃɪnts/ n. zaraza f.

chip /tʃɪp/ n. **1.** astilla f. —v. **2.** astillar.

chiropodist /kɪ'rɒpədɪst/ n. pedicuro -ra.

chiropractor /'kairəˌpræktər/ n. quiropráctico -ca.

chirp /tʃɜrp/ n. **1.** chirrido m. —v. **2.** chirriar, piar.

chisel /'tʃɪzəl/ n. **1.** cincel m. —v. **2.** cincelar, talar.

chivalrous /'ʃɪvəlrəs/ a. caballeroso.

chivalry /'ʃɪvəlri/ n. caballería f.

chive /tʃaiv/ n. cebollino m.

chloride /'klɔraid/ n. cloruro m.

chlorine /'klɔrin/ n. cloro m.

chloroform /'klɔrəˌfɔrm/ n. cloroformo m.

chlorophyll /'klɔrəfɪl/ n. clorofila f.

chock-full /'tʃɒk'ful/ a. repleto, colmado.

chocolate /'tʃɒkəlɪt/ n. chocolate m.

choice /tʃɔis/ a. **1.** selecto, escogido. —n. **2.** selección f.; escogimiento m.

choir /kwaiər/ n. coro m.

choke /tʃouk/ v. sofocar, ahogar.

cholera /'kɒlərə/ n. cólera f.

choleric /'kɒlərɪk/ a. colérico, irascible.

cholesterol /kə'lɛstəˌroul/ n. colesterol m.

choose /tʃuz/ v. elegir, escoger.

chop /tʃɒp/ n. **1.** chuleta, costilla f. —v. **2.** tajar; cortar.

chopper /'tʃɒpər/ n. tajador -ra.

choppy /'tʃɒpi/ a. agitado.

choral /'kɔrəl/ a. coral.

chord /kɔrd/ n. cuerda f.; acorde m.

chore /tʃɔr/ n. tarea f., quehacer m.

choreography /ˌkɔri'ɒgrəfi, ˌkour-/ n. coreografía f.

chorister /'kɔrəstər/ n. corista m.

chorus /'kɔrəs/ n. coro m.

christen /'krɪsən/ v. bautizar.

Christendom /'krɪsəndəm/ n. cristiandad f.

Christian /'krɪsʃən/ a. & n. cristiano -na.

Christianity /ˌkrɪsʃi'ænɪti/ n. cristianismo m.

Christmas /'krɪsməs/ n. Navidad, Pascua f. **Merry C.,** felices Pascuas. **C. Eve,** Nochebuena f.

chromatic /krou'mætɪk/ a. cromático.

chromium /'kroumiəm/ n. cromo m.

chromosome /'kroumə,soum/ n. cromosoma m.

chronic /'krɒnɪk/ a. crónico.

chronicle /'krɒnɪkəl/ n. crónica f.

chronological /ˌkrɒnl'ɒdʒɪkəl/ a. cronológico.

chronology /krə'nɒlədʒi/ n. cronología f.

chrysalis /'krɪsəlɪs/ n. crisálida f.

chrysanthemum /krɪ'sænθəməm/ n. crisantemo m.

chubby /'tʃʌbi/ a. regordete, rollizo.

chuck /tʃʌk/ v. (cluck) cloquear; (throw) echar, tirar.

chuckle /'tʃʌkəl/ v. reír entre dientes.

chum /tʃʌm/ n. amigo -ga; compinche m.

chummy /'tʃʌmi/ a. íntimo.

chunk /tʃʌŋk/ n. trozo m.

chunky /'tʃʌŋki/ a. fornido, trabado.

Chunnel /'tʃʌnl/ n. túnel del Canal de la Mancha m.

church /tʃɜrtʃ/ n. iglesia f.

churchman /'tʃɜrtʃmən/ n. eclesiástico m.

churchyard /'tʃɜrtʃ,yard/ n. cementerio m.

churn /tʃɜrn/ n. **1.** mantequera f. —v. **2.** agitar, revolver.

chute /ʃut/ n. conducto; canal m.

cicada /sɪ'keidə/ n. cigarra, chicharra f.

cider /'saidər/ n. sidra f.

cigar /sɪ'gɑr/ n. cigarro, puro m.

cigarette /ˌsɪgə'rɛt/ n. cigarrillo, cigarro, pitillo m. **c. case,** cigarrillera f. **c. lighter,** encendedor m.

cinchona /sɪŋ'kounə/ n. cinchona f.

cinder /'sɪndər/ n. ceniza f.

cinema /'sɪnəmə/ n. cine m.

cinnamon /'sɪnəmən/ n. canela f.

cipher /'saifər/ n. cifra f.

circle /'sɜrkəl/ n. círculo m.

circuit /'sɜrkɪt/ n. circuito m.

circuitous /sər'kyuitəs/ a. tortuoso.

circuitously /sər'kyuitəsli/ adv. tortuosamente.

circular /'sɜrkyələr/ a. circular, redondo.

circularize /'sɜrkyələˌraiz/ v. hacer circular.

circulate /'sɜrkyəˌleit/ v. circular.

circulation /ˌsɜrkyə'leiʃən/ n. circulación f.

circulator /'sɜrkyəˌleitər/ n. diseminador -ra.

circulatory /'sɜrkyələˌtɔri/ a. circulatorio.

circumcise /'sɜrkəmˌsaiz/ v. circuncidar.

circumcision /ˌsɜrkəm'sɪʒən/ n. circuncisión f.

circumference /sər'kʌmfərəns/ n. circunferencia f.

circumlocution /ˌsɜrkəmlou'kyuʃən/ n. circunlocución f.

circumscribe /'sɜrkəmˌskraib/ v. circunscribir; limitar.

circumspect /'sɜrkəmˌspɛkt/ a. discreto.

circumstance /'sɜrkəmˌstæns/ n. circunstancia f.

circumstantial /ˌsɜrkəm'stænʃəl/ a. circunstancial, indirecto.

circumstantially /ˌsɜrkəm'stænʃəli/ adv. minuciosamente.

circumvent /ˌsɜrkəm'vɛnt/ v. evadir, evitar.

circumvention /ˌsɜrkəm'vɛnʃən/ n. trampa f.

circus /'sɜrkəs/ n. circo m.

cirrhosis /sɪ'rousɪs/ n. cirrosis f.

cistern /'sɪstərn/ n. cisterna f.

citadel /'sɪtədl/ n. ciudadela f.

citation /sai'teiʃən/ n. citación f.

cite /sait/ v. citar.

citizen /'sɪtəzən/ n. ciudadano -na.

citizenship /'sɪtəzənˌʃɪp/ n. ciudadanía f.

citric /'sɪtrɪk/ a. cítrico.

city /'sɪti/ n. ciudad f.

city hall ayuntamiento, municipio m.

city planning urbanismo m.

civic /'sɪvɪk/ a. cívico.

civics /'sɪvɪks/ n. ciencia del gobierno civil.

civil /'sɪvəl/ a. civil; cortés.

civilian /sɪ'vɪlyən/ a. & n. civil m. & f.

civility /sɪ'vɪlɪti/ n. cortesía f.

civilization /ˌsɪvələ'zeiʃən/ n. civilización f.

civilize /'sɪvəˌlaiz/ v. civilizar.

civil rights /raits/ derechos civiles m. pl.

civil service n. servicio civil oficial m.

civil war n. guerra civil f.

clabber /'klæbər/ n. **1.** cuajo m. —v. **2.** cuajarse.

clad /klæd/ a. vestido.

claim /kleim/ n. **1.** demanda; pretensión f. —v. **2.** demandar, reclamar.

claimant /'kleimənt/ n. reclamante -ta.

clairvoyance /klɛər'vɔiəns/ n. clarividencia f.

clairvoyant /klɛər'vɔiənt/ a. clarividente.

clam /klæm/ n. almeja f.

clamber /'klæmbər/ v. trepar.

clamor /'klæmər/ n. **1.** clamor m. —v. **2.** clamar.

clamorous /'klæmərəs/ a. clamoroso.

clamp /klæmp/ n. **1.** prensa de sujeción f. —v. **2.** asegurar, sujetar.

clan /klæn/ n. tribu f., clan m.

clandestine /klæn'dɛstɪn/ a. clandestino.

clandestinely /klæn'dɛstɪnli/ adv. clandestinamente.

clangor /'klæŋər, 'klæŋgər/ n. estruendo m., estrépito m.

clannish /'klænɪʃ/ a. unido; exclusivista.

clap /klæp/ v. aplaudir.

clapboard /'klæbərd, 'klæp,bɔrd/ n. chilla f.

claque /klæk/ n. claque f.

claret /'klærɪt/ n. clarete m.

clarification /ˌklærəfə'keiʃən/ n. clarificación f.

clarify /'klærə,fai/ v. clarificar.

clarinet /ˌklærə'nɛt/ n. clarinete m.

clarinetist /ˌklærə'nɛtɪst/ n. clarinetista m. & f.

clarity /'klærɪti/ n. claridad f.

clash /klæʃ/ n. **1.** choque, enfrentamiento m. —v. **2.** chocar.

clasp /klæsp/ n. **1.** broche m. —v. **2.** abrochar.

class /klæs/ n. clase f.

classic, /'klæsɪk/ **classical** a. clásico.

classicism /'klæsə,sɪzəm/ n. clasicismo m.

classifiable /'klæsə,faiəbəl/ a. clasificable, calificable.

classification /ˌklæsəfɪ'keiʃən/ n. clasificación f.

classify /'klæsə,fai/ v. clasificar.

classmate /'klæs,meit/ n. compañero -ra de clase.

classroom /'klæs,rum, -,rʊm/ n. sala de clase.

clatter /'klætər/ n. **1.** alboroto m. —v. **2.** alborotar.

clause /klɔz/ n. cláusula f.

claustrophobia /ˌklɔstrə'foubiə/ n. claustrofobia f.

claw /klɔ/ n. garra f.

clay /klei/ n. arcilla f.; barro m.

clean /klin/ a. **1.** limpio. —v. **2.** limpiar.

cleaner /'klinər/ n. limpiador -ra.

cleaning lady, cleaning woman /'klinɪŋ/ señora de la limpieza, mujer de la limpieza f.

cleanliness /'klɛnlinɪs/ n. limpieza f.

cleanse /klɛnz/ v. limpiar, purificar.

cleanser /'klɛnzər/ n. limpiador m., purificador m.

clear /klɪər/ a. claro.

clearance /'klɪərəns/ n. espacio libre. **c. sale,** venta de liquidación.

clearing /'klɪərɪŋ/ n. despejo m.; desmonte m.

clearly /'klɪərli/ adv. claramente, evidentemente.

clearness /'klɪərnɪs/ n. claridad f.

cleavage /'klividʒ/ n. resquebradura f.

cleaver /'klivər/ n. partidor m., hacha f.

clef /klɛf/ n. clave, llave f.

clemency /'klɛmənsi/ n. clemencia f.

clench /klɛntʃ/ v. agarrar.

clergy /'klɜrdʒi/ n. clero m.

clergyman /'klɜrdʒimən/ n. clérigo m.

clerical /'klɛrɪkəl/ a. clerical. **c. work,** trabajo de oficina.

clericalism /'klɛrɪkə,lɪzəm/ n. clericalismo m.

clerk /klɜrk/ n. dependiente, escribiente m.

clerkship /'klɜrkʃɪp/ n. escribanía f., secretaría f.

clever /'klɛvər/ a. diestro, hábil.

cleverly /'klɛvərli/ adv. diestramente, hábilmente.

cleverness /'klɛvərnɪs/ n. destreza f.

cliché /kli'ʃei/ n. tópico m.

client /'klaiənt/ n. cliente -ta.

clientele /ˌklaiən'tɛl/ n. clientela f.

cliff /klɪf/ n. precipicio, risco m.

climate /'klaimɪt/ n. clima m.

climatic /klai'mætɪk/ a. climático.

climax /'klaimæks/ n. colmo m., culminación f.

climb /klaim/ v. escalar; subir.

climber /'klaimər/ n. trepador -ra, escalador -ra; Bot. enredadera f.

climbing plant /'klaimɪŋ/ enredadera f.

clinch /klɪntʃ/ v. afirmar.

cling /klɪŋ/ v. pegarse.

clinic /'klɪnɪk/ n. clínica f.

clinical /'klɪnɪkəl/ a. clínico.

clinically /'klɪnɪkəli/ adv. clínicamente.

clip /klɪp/ n. **1.** grapa f. **paper c.,** gancho m. —v. **2.** prender; (shear) trasquilar.

clipper /'klɪpər/ n. recortador m.; Aero. clíper m.

clipping /'klɪpɪŋ/ n. recorte m.

clique /klik/ n. camarilla f., compadraje m.

cloak /klouk/ n. capa f., manto m.

clock /klɒk/ n. reloj m. **alarm c.,** despertador m.

clod /klɒd/ n. terrón m.; césped m.

clog /klɒg/ v. obstruir.

cloister /'klɔistər/ n. claustro m.

clone /kloun/ n. clon m. & f. v. clonar.

close /a, adv. klous; v klouz/ a. **1.** cercano. —adv. **2.** cerca. **c. to,** cerca de. —v. **3.** cerrar; tapar.

closely /'klousli/ adv. (near) de cerca; (tight) estrechamente; (care) cuidadosamente.

closeness /'klousnɪs/ n. contigüidad f., apretamiento m.; (airless) falta de ventilación f.

closet /'klɒzɪt/ n. gabinete m. **clothes c.,** ropero m.

clot /klɒt/ n. **1.** coágulo f. —v. **2.** coagularse.

cloth /klɔθ/ n. paño m.; tela f.

clothe /kloud/ v. vestir.

clothes /klouz/ n. ropa f.

clothing /'kloudɪŋ/ n. vestidos m., ropa f.

cloud /klaud/ n. nube f.

cloudburst /'klaud,bɜrst/ n. chaparrón m.

cloudiness /'klaudinɪs/ n. nebulosidad f.; obscuridad f.

cloudless /'klaudlɪs/ a. despejado, sin nubes.

cloudy /'klaudi/ a. nublado.

clove /klouv/ n. clavo m.

clover /'klouvər/ n. trébol m.

clown /klaun/ n. bufón -na, payaso -sa.

clownish /'klaunɪʃ/ a. grosero; bufonesco.

cloy /klɔi/ v. saciar, empalagar.

club /klʌb/ n. **1.** porra f.; (social) círculo, club m.; (cards) basto m. —v. **2.** golpear con una porra.

clubfoot /'klʌb,fʊt/ n. pateta m., pie zambo m.

clue /klu/ n. seña, pista f.

clump /klʌmp/ n. grupo m., masa f.

clumsiness /'klʌmzinɪs/ n. tosquedad f.; desmaña f.

clumsy /'klʌmzi/ a. torpe, desmañado.

cluster /'klʌstər/ n. **1.** grupo m.; (fruit) racimo m. —v. **2.** agrupar.

clutch /klʌtʃ/ n. **1.** Auto. embrague m. —v. **2.** agarrar.

clutter /'klʌtər/ n. **1.** confusión f. —v. **2.** poner en desorden.

coach /koutʃ/ n. **1.** coche, vagón m.; coche ordinario; (sports) entrenador m. —v. **2.** entrenar.

coachman /'koutʃmən/ n. cochero -ra.

coagulate /kou'ægyə,leit/ v. coagular.

coagulation /kou,ægyə'leiʃən/ n. coagulación f.

coal /koul/ n. carbón m.

coalesce /ˌkouə'lɛs/ v. unirse, soldarse.

coal oil n. petróleo m.

coalition /ˌkouə'lɪʃən/ n. coalición f.

coal tar n. alquitrán m.

coarse /kɔrs/ a. grosero, burdo; (material) tosco, grueso.

coarsen /'kɔrsən/ v. vulgarizar.

coarseness /'kɔrsnɪs/ n. grosería; tosquedad f.

coast /koust/ n. **1.** costa f., litoral m. —v. **2.** deslizarse.

coastal /'koustl/ a. costanero.

coast guard guardacostas m. & f.

coat /kout/ n. **1.** saco m., chaqueta f.; (paint) capa f. —v. **2.** cubrir.

coat of arms /armz/ n. escudo m.

coax /kouks/ v. instar.

cobalt /'koubɒlt/ n. cobalto m.

cobbler /'kɒblər/ n. zapatero -ra.

cobblestone /'kɒbəl,stoun/ n. guijarro m.

cobra /'koubrə/ n. cobra f.

cobweb /'kɒb,wɛb/ n. telaraña f.

cocaine /kou'kein/ n. cocaína f.

cock /kɒk/ n. (rooster) gallo m.; (water, etc.) llave f.; (gun) martillo m.

cockfight /'kɒk,fait/ n. riña de gallos f.

cockpit /'kɒk,pɪt/ n. gallera f.; reñidero de gallos m.; Aero. cabina f.

cockroach /'kɒk,routʃ/ n. cucaracha f.

cocktail /'kɒk,teil/ n. cóctel m.

cocky /'kɒki/ a. confiado, atrevido.

cocoa /'koukou/ n. cacao m.

coconut /'koukə,nʌt/ n. coco m.

cocoon /kə'kun/ n. capullo m.

cod /kɒd/ n. bacalao m.

code /koud/ n. código m.; clave f.

codeine /'koudin/ n. codeína f.

codfish /'kɒd,fɪʃ/ n. bacalao m.

codify /'kɒdə,fai/ v. compilar.

cod-liver oil /'kɒd 'lɪvər/ aceite de hígado de bacalao m.

coeducation /ˌkouɛdʒu'keiʃən/ n. coeducación f.

coequal /kou'ikwəl/ a. mutuamente igual.

coerce /kou'ɜrs/ v. forzar.

coercion /kou'ɜrʃən/ n. coerción f.

coercive /kou'ɜrsɪv/ a. coercitivo.

coexist /ˌkouɪg'zɪst/ v. coexistir.

coffee /'kɔfi/ n. café m. **c. plantation,** cafetal m. **c. shop,** café m.

coffee break pausa para el café f.

coffer /'kɔfər/ n. cofre m.

coffin /'kɔfɪn/ n. ataúd m.

cog /kɒg/ n. diente de rueda m.

cogent /'koudʒənt/ a. convincente.

cogitate /'kɒdʒɪ,teit/ v. pensar, reflexionar.

cognizance /'kɒgnəzəns/ n. conocimiento m., comprensión f.

cognizant /'kɒgnəzənt/ a. conocedor, informado.

cogwheel /'kɒg,wil/ n. rueda dentada f.

cohere /kou'hɪər/ v. pegarse.

coherent /kou'hɪərənt/ a. coherente.

cohesion /kou'hiʒən/ n. cohesión f.

cohesive /kou'hisɪv/ a. cohesivo.

cohort /'kouhɔrt/ n. cohorte f.

coiffure /kwa'fyʊr/ n. peinado, tocado m.

coil /kɔil/ n. **1.** rollo m.; Naut. adujada f. —v. **2.** enrollar.

coin /kɔin/ n. moneda f.

coinage /'kɔinidʒ/ n. sistema monetario m.

coincide /ˌkouɪn'said/ v. coincidir.

coincidence /kou'ɪnsɪdəns/ n. coincidencia; casualidad f.

coincident /kou'ɪnsɪdənt/ a. coincidente.

coincidental /kou,ɪnsɪ'dɛntl/ a. coincidental.

coincidentally /kou,ɪnsɪ'dɛntli/ adv. coincidentalmente, al mismo tiempo.

colander /'kɒləndər/ n. colador m.

cold /kould/ a. & n. frío -a; Med. resfriado m. **to be c.,** tener frío; (weather) hacer frío.

coldly /'kouldli/ adv. fríamente.

coldness /'kouldnɪs/ n. frialdad f.

collaborate /kə'læbə,reit/ v. colaborar.

collaboration /kə,læbə'reiʃən/ n. colaboración f.

collaborator /kə'læbə,reitər/ n. colaborador -ra.

collapse /kə'læps/ n. **1.** desplome m.; Med. colapso m. —v. **2.** desplomarse.

collar /'kɒlər/ n. cuello m.

collarbone /'kɒlər,boun/ n. clavícula f.

collate /kou'leit/ v. comparar.

collateral /kə'lætərəl/ a. **1.** colateral. —n. **2.** garantía f.

collation /kə'leiʃən/ n. comparación f.; (food) colación f., merienda f.

colleague /'kɒlig/ n. colega m. & f.

collect /kə'lɛkt/ v. cobrar; recoger; coleccionar.

collection /kə'lɛkʃən/ n. colección f.

collective /kə'lɛktɪv/ a. colectivo.

collectively /kə'lɛktɪvli/ adv. colectivamente, en masa.

collector /kə'lɛktər/ n. colector -ra; coleccionista m. & f.

college /'kɒlidʒ/ n. colegio m.; universidad f.

collegiate /kə'lidʒɪt/ n. colegiado m.

collide /kə'laid/ v. chocar.

collision /kə'lɪʒən/ n. choque m.

colloquial /kə'loukwiəl/ a. familiar.

colloquially /kə'loukwiəli/ adv. familiarmente.

colloquy /'kɒləkwi/ n. conversación f., coloquio m.

collusion /kə'luʒən/ n. colusión f., connivencia f.

Cologne /kə'loun/ n. Colonia f.

Colombian /kə'lʌmbiən/ a. & n. colombiano -na.

colon /'koulən/ n. colon m.; Punct. dos puntos.

colonel /'kɜrnl/ n. coronel m.

colonial /kə'louniəl/ a. colonial.

colonist /'kɒlənɪst/ n. colono -na.

colonization /ˌkɒlənə'zeiʃən/ n. colonización f.

colonize /'kɒlə,naiz/ v. colonizar.

colony /'kɒləni/ n. colonia f.

color /'kʌlər/ n. **1.** color; colorido m. —v. **2.** colorar; colorir.

coloration /ˌkʌlə'reiʃən/ n. colorido m.

colored /'kʌlərd/ a. de color.

colorful /'kʌlərfəl/ a. vívido.

colorless /'kʌlərlɪs/ a. descolorido, sin color.

colossal /kə'lɒsəl/ a. colosal.

colt /koult/ n. potro m.

column /'kɒləm/ n. columna f.

coma /'koumə/ n. coma m.

comb /koum/ n. **1.** peine m. —v. **2.** peinar.

combat /n 'kɒmbæt; v kəm'bæt/ n. **1.** combate m. —v. **2.** combatir.

combatant /kəm'bætnt/ n. combatiente -ta.

combative /kəm'bætɪv/ a. combativo.

combination /ˌkɒmbə'neiʃən/ n. combinación f.

combine /kəm'bain/ v. combinar.

combustible /kəm'bʌstəbəl/ a. & n. combustible m.

combustion /kəm'bʌstʃən/ n. combustión f.

come /kʌm/ v. venir. **c. back,** volver. **c. in,** entrar. **c. out,** salir. **c. up,** subir. **c. upon,** encontrarse con.

comedian /kə'midiən/ n. cómico -ca.

comedienne /kə,midi'ɛn/ n. cómica f., actriz f.

comedy /'kɒmidi/ n. comedia f.

comet /'kɒmɪt/ n. cometa m.

comfort /'kʌmfərt/ n. **1.** confort m.; solaz m. —v. **2.** confortar; solazar.

comfortable /'kʌmftəbəl/ a. cómodo.

comfortably /'kʌmftəbli/ adv. cómodamente.

comforter /'kʌmfərtər/ n. colcha f.

comfortingly /'kʌmfərtɪŋli/ adv. confortantemente.

comfortless /'kʌmfərtlɪs/ a. sin consuelo; sin comodidades.

comic /'kɒmɪk/ **comical** a. cómico.

comic book n. tebeo m.

coming /'kʌmɪŋ/ n. **1.** venida f., llegada f. —a. **2.** próximo, que viene, entrante.

comma /'kɒmə/ n. coma f.

command /kə'mænd/ n. **1.** mando m. —v. **2.** mandar.

commandeer /ˌkɒmən'dɪər/ v. reclutir forzosamente, expropiar.

commander /kə'mændər/ *n.* comandante -ta.

commander in chief *n.* generalísimo, jefe supremo.

commandment /kə'mændmənt/ *n.* mandato; mandamiento *m.*

commemorate /kə'memə,reit/ *v.* conmemorar.

commemoration /kə,memə'reiʃən/ *n.* conmemoración *f.*

commemorative /kə'memə,reitiv/ *a.* conmemorativo.

commence /kə'mens/ *v.* comenzar, principiar.

commencement /kə'mensmənt/ *n.* comienzo *m.*; graduación *f.*

commend /kə'mend/ *v.* encomendar; elogiar.

commendable /kə'mendəbəl/ *a.* recomendable.

commendably /kə'mendəbli/ *adv.* loablemente.

commendation /,kɒmən'deiʃən/ *n.* recomendación *f.*; elogio *m.*

commensurate /kə'mensərit/ *a.* proporcionado.

comment /'kɒment/ *n.* **1.** comentario *m.* —*v.* **2.** comentar.

commentary /'kɒmən,teri/ *n.* comentario *m.*

commentator /'kɒmən,teitər/ *n.* comentador -ra.

commerce /'kɒmərs/ *n.* comercio *m.*

commercial /kə'mɜrʃəl/ *a.* comercial.

commercialism /kə'mɜrʃə,lizəm/ *n.* comercialismo *m.*

commercialize /kə'mɜrʃə,laiz/ *v.* mercantilizar, explotar.

commercially /kə'mɜrʃəli/ *a.* & *adv.* comercialmente.

commiserate /kə'mizə,reit/ *v.* compadecerse.

commissary /'kɒmə,seri/ *n.* comisario *m.*

commission /kə'miʃən/ *n.* **1.** comisión *f.* —*v.* **2.** comisionar.

commissioner /kə'miʃənər/ *n.* comisario -ria.

commit /kə'mit/ *v.* cometer.

commitment /kə'mitmənt/ *n.* compromiso *m.*

committee /kə'miti/ *n.* comité *m.*

commodious /kə'moudiəs/ *a.* cómodo.

commodity /kə'mɒditi/ *n.* mercadería *f.*

common /'kɒmən/ *a.* común; ordinario.

commonly /'kɒmənli/ *adv.* comúnmente, vulgarmente.

Common Market Mercado Común *m.*

commonplace /'kɒmən,pleis/ *a.* trivial, banal.

common sense sentido común *m.*

commonwealth /'kɒmən,welθ/ *n.* estado *m.*; nación *f.*

commotion /kə'mouʃən/ *n.* tumulto *m.*

communal /kə'myunl/ *a.* comunal, público.

commune /'kɒmyun/ *n.* **1.** distrito municipal *m.*; comuna *f.* —*v.* **2.** conversar.

communicable /kə'myunikəbəl/ *a.* comunicable; *Med.* transmisible.

communicate /kə'myuni,keit/ *v.* comunicar.

communication /kə,myuni'keiʃən/ *n.* comunicación *f.*

communicative /kə'myuni,keitiv/ *a.* comunicativo.

communion /kə'myunyən/ *n.* comunión *f.* **take c.,** comulgar.

communiqué /kə,myuni'kei/ *n.* comunicación *f.*

communism /'kɒmyə,nizəm/ *n.* comunismo *m.*

communist /'kɒmyənist/ *n.* comunista *m.* & *f.*

communistic /,kɒmyə'nistik/ *a.* comunístico.

community /kə'myuniti/ *n.* comunidad *f.*

commutation /,kɒmyə'teiʃən/ *n.* conmutación *f.*

commuter /kə'myutər/ *n.* empleado que viaja diariamente desde su domicilio hasta la ciudad donde trabaja.

compact /*a* kəm'pækt; *n* 'kɒmpækt/ *a.* **1.** compacto. —*n.* **2.** pacto *m.*; (lady's) polvera *f.*

compact disk disco compacto *m.*

companion /kəm'pænyən/ *n.* compañero -ra.

companionable /kəm'pænyənəbəl/ *a.* sociable.

companionship /kəm'pænyən,ʃip/ *n.* compañerismo *m.*

company /'kʌmpəni/ *n.* compañía *f.*

comparable /'kɒmpərəbəl/ *a.* comparable.

comparative /kəm'pærətiv/ *a.* comparativo.

comparatively /kəm'pærətivli/ *a.* relativamente.

compare /kəm'peər/ *v.* comparar.

comparison /kəm'pærəsən/ *n.* comparación *f.*

compartment /kəm'purtmənt/ *n.* compartimiento *m.*

compass /'kʌmpəs/ *n.* compás *m.*; *Naut.* brújula *f.*

compassion /kəm'pæʃən/ *n.* compasión *f.*

compassionate /kəm'pæʃənit/ *a.* compasivo.

compassionately /kəm'pæʃənitli/ *adv.* compasivamente.

compatible /kəm'pætəbəl/ *a.* compatible.

compatriot /kəm'peitriət/ *n.* compatriota *m.* & *f.*

compel /kəm'pel/ *v.* obligar.

compensate /'kɒmpən,seit/ *v.* compensar.

compensation /,kɒmpən'seiʃən/ *n.* compensación *f.*

compensatory /kəm'pensə,tɔri/ *a.* compensatorio.

compete /kəm'pit/ *v.* competir.

competence /'kɒmpitəns/ *n.* competencia *f.*

competent /'kɒmpitənt/ *a.* competente, capaz.

competently /'kɒmpitəntli/ *adv.* competentemente.

competition /,kɒmpi'tiʃən/ *n.* concurrencia *f.*; concurso *m.*

competitive /kəm'petitiv/ *a.* competidor.

competitor /kəm'petitər/ *n.* competidor -ra.

compile /kəm'pail/ *v.* compilar.

complacency /kəm'pleisənsi/ *n.* complacencia *f.*

complacent /kəm'pleisənt/ *a.* complaciente.

complacently /kəm'pleisəntli/ *adv.* complacientemente.

complain /kəm'plein/ *v.* quejarse.

complaint /kəm'pleint/ *n.* queja *f.*

complement /'kɒmpləmənt/ *n.* complemento *m.*

complete /kəm'plit/ *a.* **1.** completo —*v.* **2.** completar.

completely /kəm'plitli/ *adv.* completamente, enteramente.

completeness /kəm'plitnis/ *n.* integridad *f.*

completion /kəm'pliʃən/ *n.* terminación *f.*

complex /kəm'pleks/ *a.* complejo.

complexion /kəm'plekʃən/ *n.* tez *f.*

complexity /kəm'pleksiti/ *n.* complejidad *f.*

compliance /kəm'plaiəns/ *n.* consentimiento *m.* **in c. with,** de acuerdo con.

compliant /kəm'plaiənt/ *a.* dócil; complaciente.

complicate /'kɒmpli,keit/ *v.* complicar.

complicated /'kɒmpli,keitid/ *a.* complicado.

complication /,kɒmpli'keiʃən/ *n.* complicación *f.*

complicity /kəm'plisiti/ *n.* complicidad *f.*

compliment /*n* 'kɒmpləmənt; *v* -,ment/ *n.* **1.** elogio *m.* *Fig.* —*v.* **2.** felicitar; echar flores.

complimentary /,kɒmplə'mentəri/ *a.* galante, obsequioso, regaloso.

comply /kəm'plai/ *v.* cumplir.

component /kəm'pounənt/ *a.* & *n.* componente *m.*

comport /kəm'pɔrt/ *v.* portarse.

compose /kəm'pouz/ *v.* componer.

composed /kəm'pouzd/ *a.* tranquilo; (made up) compuesto.

composer /kəm'pouzər/ *n.* compositor -ra.

composite /kəm'pɒzit/ *a.* compuesto.

composition /,kɒmpə'ziʃən/ *n.* composición *f.*

composure /kəm'pouʒər/ *n.* serenidad *f.*; calma *f.*

compote /'kɒmpout/ *n.* compota *f.*

compound /'kɒmpaund/ *a.* & *n.* compuesto *m.*

comprehend /,kɒmpri'hend/ *v.* comprender.

comprehensible /,kɒmpri'hensəbəl/ *a.* comprensible.

comprehension /,kɒmpri'henʃən/ *n.* comprensión *f.*

comprehensive /,kɒmpri'hensiv/ *a.* comprensivo.

compress /*n* 'kɒmpres; *v* kəm'pres/ *n.* **1.** cabezal *m.* —*v.* **2.** comprimir.

compressed /kəm'prest/ *a.* comprimido.

compression /kəm'preʃən/ *n.* presión *f.*

compressor /kəm'presər/ *n.* compresor *m.*

comprise /kəm'praiz/ *v.* comprender; abarcar.

compromise /'kɒmprə,maiz/ *n.* **1.** compromiso *m.* —*v.* **2.** comprometer.

compromiser /'kɒmprə,maizər/ *n.* compromisario *m.*

compulsion /kəm'pʌlʃən/ *n.* compulsión *f.*

compulsive /kəm'pʌlsiv/ *a.* compulsivo.

compulsory /kəm'pʌlsəri/ *a.* obligatorio.

compunction /kəm'pʌŋkʃən/ *n.* compunción *f.*; escrúpulo *m.*

computation /,kɒmpyu'teiʃən/ *n.* computación *f.*

compute /kəm'pyut/ *v.* computar, calcular.

computer /kəm'pyutər/ *n.* computadora *f.*, ordenador *m.*

computerize /kəm'pyutə,raiz/ *v.* procesar en computadora, computerizar.

computer programmer /'prougræmər/ programador -ra de ordenadores.

computer science informática *f.*

comrade /'kɒmræd/ *n.* camarada *m.* & *f.*; compañero -ra.

comradeship /'kɒmræd,ʃip/ *n.* camaradería *f.*

concave /kɒn'keiv/ *a.* cóncavo.

conceal /kən'sil/ *v.* ocultar, esconder.

concealment /kən'silmənt/ *n.* ocultación *f.*

concede /kən'sid/ *v.* conceder.

conceit /kən'sit/ *n.* amor propio; engreimiento *m.*

conceited /kən'sitid/ *a.* engreído.

conceivable /kən'sivəbəl/ *a.* concebible.

conceive /kən'siv/ *v.* concebir.

concentrate /'kɒnsən,treit/ *v.* concentrar.

concentration /,kɒnsən'treiʃən/ *n.* concentración *f.*

concentration camp campo de concentración *m.*

concept /'kɒnsept/ *n.* concepto *m.*

conception /kən'sepʃən/ *n.* concepción *f.*; concepto *m.*

concern /kən'sɜrn/ *n.* **1.** interés *m.*; inquietud *f.*; *Com.* negocio *m.* —*v.* **2.** concernir.

concerning /kən'sɜrniŋ/ *prep.* respecto a.

concert /'kɒnsərt/ *n.* concierto *m.*

concerted /kən'sɜrtid/ *a.* convenido.

concession /kən'seʃən/ *n.* concesión *f.*

conciliate /kən'sili,eit/ *v.* conciliar.

conciliation /kən,sili'eiʃən/ *n.* conciliación *f.*

conciliator /kən'sili,eitər/ *n.* conciliador -a.

conciliatory /kən'sili,ətɔri/ *a.* conciliatorio.

concise /kən'sais/ *a.* conciso.

concisely /kən'saisli/ *adv.* concisamente.

conciseness /kən'saisnis/ *n.* concisión *f.*

conclave /'kɒnkleiv/ *n.* conclave *m.*

conclude /kən'klud/ *v.* concluir.

conclusion /kən'kluʒən/ *n.* conclusión *f.*

conclusive /kən'klusiv/ *a.* conclusivo, decisivo.

conclusively /kən'klusivli/ *adv.* concluyentemente.

concoct /kɒn'kɒkt/ *v.* confeccionar.

concomitant /kɒn'kɒmitənt/ *n.* & *a.* concomitante *m.*

concord /'kɒnkɔrd/ *n.* concordia *f.*

concordat /kɒn'kɔrdæt/ *a.* concordato *m.*

concourse /'kɒnkɔrs/ *n.* concurso *m.*; confluencia *f.*

concrete /'kɒnkrit/ *a.* concreto.

concretely /kɒn'kritli/ *adv.* concretamente.

concubine /'kɒŋkyə,bain/ *n.* concubina, amiga *f.*

concur /kən'kɜr/ *v.* concurrir.

concurrence /kən'kɜrəns/ *n.* concurrencia *f.*; casualidad *f.*

concurrent /kən'kɜrənt/ *a.* concurrente.

concussion /kən'kʌʃən/ *n.* concusión *f.*; (c. of the brain) conmoción cerebral *f.*

condemn /kən'dem/ *v.* condenar.

condemnable /kən'demnəbəl/ *a.* culpable, condenable.

condemnation /,kɒndem'neiʃən/ *n.* condenación *f.*

condensation /,kɒnden'seiʃən/ *n.* condensación *f.*

condense /kən'dens/ *v.* condensar.

condenser /kən'densər/ *n.* condensador *m.*

condescend /,kɒndə'send/ *v.* condescender.

condescension /,kɒndə'senʃən/ *n.* condescendencia *f.*

condiment /'kɒndəmənt/ *n.* condimento *m.*

condition /kən'diʃən/ *n.* **1.** condición *f.*; estado *m.* —*v.* **2.** acondicionar.

conditional /kən'diʃənl/ *a.* condicional.

conditionally /kən'diʃənli/ *adv.* condicionalmente.

condole /kən'doul/ *v.* condolerse.

condolence /kən'douləns/ *n.* pésame *m.*

condom /'kɒndəm/ *n.* forro, preservativo *m.*

condominium /,kɒndə'miniəm/ *n.* condominio *m.*

condone /kən'doun/ *v.* condonar.

conducive /kən'dusiv, -'dyu-/ *a.* conducente.

conduct /*n* 'kɒndʌkt; *v* kən'dʌkt/ *n.* **1.** conducta *f.* —*v.* **2.** conducir.

conductivity /,kɒndʌk'tiviti/ *n.* conductividad *f.*

conductor /kən'dʌktər/ *n.* conductor *m.*

conduit /'kɒnduit/ *n.* caño *m.*, canal *f.*; conducto *m.*

cone /koun/ *n.* cono *m.* **ice-cream c.,** barquillo de helado.

confection /kən'fekʃən/ *n.* confitura *f.*

confectioner /kən'fekʃənər/ *n.* confitero -ra.

confectionery /kənˈfɛkʃəˌnɛri/ n. dulcería f.

confederacy /kənˈfɛdərəsi/ n. federación f.

confederate / kənˈfɛdərɪt/ a. & n. confederado m.

confederation /kənˌfɛdəˈreiʃən/ n. confederación f.

confer /kənˈfɜr/ v. conferenciar; conferir.

conference /ˈkɒnfərəns/ n. conferencia f.; congreso m.

confess /kənˈfɛs/ v. confesar.

confession /kənˈfɛʃən/ n. confesión f.

confessional /kənˈfɛʃənḷ/ n. **1.** confesionario m. —a. **2.** confesional.

confessor /kənˈfɛsər/ n. confesor m.

confetti /kənˈfɛti/ n. confetti m.

confidant /ˈkɒnfɪˌdænt/ **confidante** n. confidente m. & f.

confide /kənˈfaid/ v. confiar.

confidence /ˈkɒnfɪdəns/ n. confianza f.

confident /ˈkɒnfɪdənt/ a. confiado; cierto.

confidential /ˌkɒnfɪˈdɛnʃəl/ a. confidencial.

confidentially /ˌkɒnfɪˈdɛnʃəli/ adv. confidencialmente, en secreto.

confidently /ˈkɒnfɪdəntli/ adv. confiadamente.

confine /kənˈfain/ n. **1.** confín m. —v. **2.** confinar; encerrar.

confirm /kənˈfɜrm/ v. confirmar.

confirmation /ˌkɒnfərˈmeiʃən/ n. confirmación f.

confiscate /ˈkɒnfəˌskeit/ v. confiscar.

confiscation /ˌkɒnfəˈskeiʃən/ n. confiscación f.

conflagration /ˌkɒnfləˈgreiʃən/ n. incendio m.

conflict /n ˈkɒnflɪkt; v kənˈflɪkt/ n. **1.** conflicto m. —v. **2.** oponerse; estar en conflicto.

conform /kənˈfɔrm/ v. conformar.

conformation /ˌkɒnfərˈmeiʃən/ n. conformación f.

conformer /kənˈfɔrmər/ n. conformista m. & f.

conformist /kənˈfɔrmɪst/ n. conformista m. & f.

conformity /kənˈfɔrmɪti/ n. conformidad f.

confound /kɒnˈfaund/ v. confundir.

confront /kənˈfrʌnt/ v. confrontar.

confrontation /ˌkɒnfrənˈteiʃən/ n. enfrentamiento m.

confuse /kənˈfyuz/ v. confundir.

confusion /kənˈfyuʒən/ n. confusión f.

congeal /kənˈdʒil/ v. congelar, helar.

congealment /kənˈdʒilmənt/ n. congelación f.

congenial /kənˈdʒinyəl/ a. congenial.

congenital /kənˈdʒɛnɪtḷ/ a. congénito.

congenitally /kənˈdʒɛnɪtḷi/ adv. congenitalmente.

congestion /kənˈdʒɛstʃən/ n. congestión f.

conglomerate /v kənˈglɒməˌreit; a, n kənˈglɒmərɪt/ v. **1.** conglomerar. —a. & n. **2.** conglomerado.

conglomeration /kənˌglɒməˈreiʃən/ n. conglomeración f.

congratulate /kənˈgrætʃəˌleit/ v. felicitar.

congratulation /kənˌgrætʃəˈleiʃən/ n. felicitación f.

congratulatory /kənˈgrætʃələˌtɔri/ a. congratulatorio.

congregate /ˈkɒŋgrɪˌgeit/ v. congregar.

congregation /ˌkɒŋgrɪˈgeiʃən/ n. congregación f.

congress /ˈkɒŋgrɪs/ n. congreso m.

conic /ˈkɒnɪk/ n. **1.** cónica f. —a. **2.** cónico.

conjecture /kənˈdʒɛktʃər/ n. **1.** conjetura f. —v. **2.** conjeturar.

conjugal /ˈkɒndʒəgəl/ a. conyugal, matrimonial.

conjugate /ˈkɒndʒəˌgeit/ v. conjugar.

conjugation /ˌkɒndʒəˈgeiʃən/ n. conjugación f.

conjunction /kənˈdʒʌŋkʃən/ n. conjunción f.

conjunctive /kənˈdʒʌŋktɪv/ n. **1.** Gram. conjunción f. —a. **2.** conjuntivo.

conjunctivitis /kənˌdʒʌŋktəˈvaitɪs/ n. conjuntivitis f.

conjure /ˈkɒndʒər/ v. conjurar.

connect /kəˈnɛkt/ v. juntar; relacionar.

connection /kəˈnɛkʃən/ n. conexión f.

connivance /kəˈnaivəns/ n. consentimiento m.

connive /kəˈnaiv/ v. disimular.

connoisseur /ˌkɒnəˈsɜr/ n. perito -ta.

connotation /ˌkɒnəˈteiʃən/ n. connotación f.

connote /kəˈnout/ v. connotar.

connubial /kəˈnubiəl/ a. conyugal.

conquer /ˈkɒŋkər/ v. conquistar.

conquerable /ˈkɒŋkərəbəl/ a. conquistable, vencible.

conqueror /ˈkɒŋkərər/ n. conquistador -ra.

conquest /ˈkɒŋkwɛst/ n. conquista f.

conscience /ˈkɒnʃəns/ n. conciencia f.

conscientious /ˌkɒnʃiˈɛnʃəs/ a. concienzudo.

conscientiously /ˌkɒnʃiˈɛnʃəsli/ adv. escrupulosamente.

conscientious objector /ɒbˈdʒɛktər/ objetor de conciencia m.

conscious /ˈkɒnʃəs/ a. consciente.

consciously /ˈkɒnʃəsli/ adv. con conocimiento.

consciousness /ˈkɒnʃəsnɪs/ n. conciencia f.

conscript /n ˈkɒnskrɪpt; v kənˈskrɪpt/ n. **1.** conscripto m., recluta m. —v. **2.** reclutar, alistar.

conscription /kənˈskrɪpʃən/ n. conscripción f., alistamiento m.

consecrate /ˈkɒnsɪˌkreit/ v. consagrar.

consecration /ˌkɒnsɪˈkreiʃən/ n. consagración f.

consecutive /kənˈsɛkyətɪv/ a. consecutivo, seguido.

consecutively /kənˈsɛkyətɪvli/ adv. consecutivamente, de seguida.

consensus /kənˈsɛnsəs/ n. consenso m., acuerdo general m.

consent /kənˈsɛnt/ n. **1.** consentimiento m. —v. **2.** consentir.

consequence /ˈkɒnsɪˌkwɛns/ n. consecuencia f.

consequent /ˈkɒnsɪˌkwɛnt/ a. consiguiente.

consequential /ˌkɒnsɪˈkwɛnʃəl/ a. importante.

consequently /ˈkɒnsɪˌkwɛntli/ adv. por lo tanto, por consiguiente.

conservation /ˌkɒnsərˈveiʃən/ n. conservación f.

conservatism /kənˈsɜrvəˌtɪzəm/ n. conservatismo m.

conservative /kənˈsɜrvətɪv/ a. conservador, conservativo.

conservatory /kənˈsɜrvəˌtɔri/ n. (plants) invernáculo m.; (school) conservatorio m.

conserve /kənˈsɜrv/ v. conservar.

consider /kənˈsɪdər/ v. considerar. **C. it done!** ¡Dalo por hecho!

considerable /kənˈsɪdərəbəl/ a. considerable.

considerably /kənˈsɪdərəbli/ adv. considerablemente.

considerate /kənˈsɪdərɪt/ a. considerado.

considerately /kənˈsɪdərɪtli/ adv. consideradamente.

consideration /kənˌsɪdəˈreiʃən/ n. consideración f.

considering /kənˈsɪdərɪŋ/ prep. visto que, en vista de.

consign /kənˈsain/ v. consignar.

consignment /kənˈsainmənt/ n. consignación f., envío m.

consist /kənˈsɪst/ v. consistir.

consistency /kənˈsɪstənsi/ n. consistencia f.

consistent /kənˈsɪstənt/ a. consistente.

consolation /ˌkɒnsəˈleiʃən/ n. consolación f.

consolation prize premio de consuelo m.

console /ˈkɒnsoul/ v. consolar.

consolidate /kənˈsɒlɪˌdeit/ v. consolidar.

consommé /ˌkɒnsəˈmei/ n. caldo m.

consonant /ˈkɒnsənənt/ n. consonante f.

consort /n ˈkɒnsɔrt; v kənˈsɔrt/ n. **1.** cónyuge m. & f.; socio. —v. **2.** asociarse.

conspicuous /kənˈspɪkyuəs/ a. conspicuo.

conspicuously /kənˈspɪkyuəsli/ adv. visiblemente, llamativamente.

conspicuousness /kənˈspɪkyuəsnɪs/ n. visibilidad f.; evidencia f.; fama f.

conspiracy /kənˈspɪrəsi/ n. conspiración f.; complot m.

conspirator /kənˈspɪrətər/ n. conspirador -ra.

conspire /kənˈspaiʳr/ v. conspirar.

conspirer /kənˈspaiʳrər/ n. conspirante m. & f.

constancy /ˈkɒnstənsi/ n. constancia f., lealtad f.

constant /ˈkɒnstənt/ a. constante.

constantly /ˈkɒnstəntli/ adv. constantemente, de continuo.

constellation /ˌkɒnstəˈleiʃən/ n. constelación f.

consternation /ˌkɒnstərˈneiʃən/ n. consternación f.

constipate /ˈkɒnstəˌpeit/ v. estreñir.

constipated /ˈkɒnstəˌpeitɪd/ a. estreñido, m.

constipation /ˌkɒnstəˈpeiʃən/ n. estreñimiento, m.

constituency /kənˈstɪtʃuənsi/ n. distrito electoral m.

constituent /kənˈstɪtʃuənt/ a. **1.** constituyente. —n. **2.** elector m.

constitute /ˈkɒnstɪˌtut/ v. constituir.

constitution /ˌkɒnstɪˈtuʃən/ n. constitución f.

constitutional /ˌkɒnstɪˈtuʃənḷ/ a. constitucional.

constrain /kənˈstrein/ v. constreñir.

constraint /kənˈstreint/ n. constreñimiento m., compulsión f.

constrict /kənˈstrɪkt/ v. apretar, estrechar.

construct /kənˈstrʌkt/ v. construir.

construction /kənˈstrʌkʃən/ n. construcción f.

constructive /kənˈstrʌktɪv/ a. constructivo.

constructively /kənˈstrʌktɪvli/ adv. constructivamente; por deducción.

constructor /kənˈstrʌktər/ n. constructor m.

construe /kənˈstru/ v. interpretar.

consul /ˈkɒnsəl/ n. cónsul m.

consular /ˈkɒnsələr/ a. consular.

consulate /ˈkɒnsəlɪt/ n. consulado m.

consult /kənˈsʌlt/ v. consultar.

consultant /kənˈsʌltənt/ n. consultor -ora.

consultation /ˌkɒnsəlˈteiʃən/ n. consulta f.

consume /kənˈsum/ v. consumir.

consumer /kənˈsumər/ n. consumidor -ra.

consumer society sociedad de consumo f.

consummation /ˌkɒnsəˈmeiʃən/ n. consumación f.

consumption /kənˈsʌmpʃən/ n. consumo m.; Med. tisis.

consumptive /kənˈsʌmptɪv/ n. **1.** tísico m. —a. **2.** consuntivo.

contact /ˈkɒntækt/ n. **1.** contacto m. —v. **2.** ponerse en contacto con.

contact lens lentilla f.

contagion /kənˈteidʒən/ n. contagio m.

contagious /kənˈteidʒəs/ a. contagioso.

contain /kənˈtein/ v. contener.

container /kənˈteinər/ n. envase m.

contaminate /kənˈtæməˌneit/ v. contaminar.

contemplate /ˈkɒntəmˌpleit/ v. contemplar.

contemplation /ˌkɒntəmˈpleiʃən/ n. contemplación f.

contemplative /kənˈtɛmplətɪv/ a. contemplativo.

contemporary /kənˈtɛmpəˌrɛri/ n. & a. contemporáneo -nea.

contempt /kənˈtɛmpt/ n. desprecio m.

contemptible /kənˈtɛmptəbəl/ a. vil, despreciable.

contemptuous /kənˈtɛmptʃuəs/ a. desdeñoso.

contemptuously /kənˈtɛmptʃuəsli/ adv. desdeñosamente.

contend /kənˈtɛnd/ v. contender; competir.

contender /kənˈtɛndər/ n. competidor -ra.

content /a, v kənˈtɛnt; n ˈkɒntɛnt/ a. **1.** contento. —n. **2.** contenido m. —v. **3.** contentar.

contented /kənˈtɛntɪd/ a. contento.

contention /kənˈtɛnʃən/ n. contención f.

contentment /kənˈtɛntmənt/ n. contentamiento m.

contest /n ˈkɒntɛst; v kənˈtɛst/ n. **1.** concurso m. —v. **2.** disputar.

contestable /kənˈtɛstəbəl/ a. contestable.

context /ˈkɒntɛkst/ n. contexto m.

contiguous /kənˈtɪgyuəs/ a. contiguo.

continence /ˈkɒntṇəns/ n. continencia f., castidad f.

continent /ˈkɒntṇənt/ n. continente m.

continental /ˌkɒntṇˈɛntḷ/ a. continental.

contingency /kənˈtɪndʒənsi/ n. eventualidad f., casualidad f.

contingent /kənˈtɪndʒənt/ a. contingente.

continual /kənˈtɪnyuəl/ a. continuo.

continuation /kənˌtɪnyuˈeiʃən/ n. continuación f.

continue /kənˈtɪnyu/ v. continuar.

continuity /ˌkɒntṇˈuɪti/ n. continuidad f.

continuous /kənˈtɪnyuəs/ a. continuo.

continuously /kənˈtɪnyuəsli/ adv. continuamente.

contour /ˈkɒntʊr/ n. contorno m.

contraband /ˈkɒntrəˌbænd/ n. contrabando m.

contraception /ˌkɒntrəˈsɛpʃən/ n. contracepción f.

contraceptive /ˌkɒntrəˈsɛptɪv/ n. & a. anticeptivo m.

contract /n ˈkɒntrækt; v kənˈtrækt/ n. **1.** contrato m. —v. **2.** contraer.

contraction /kənˈtrækʃən/ n. contracción f.

contractor /ˈkɒntræktər/ n. contratista m. & f.

contradict /ˌkɒntrəˈdɪkt/ v. contradecir.

contradiction /ˌkɒntrəˈdɪkʃən/ n. contradicción f.

contradictory /ˌkɒntrəˈdɪktəri/ a. contradictorio.

contralto /kənˈtræltou/ n. contralto m.

contrary /ˈkɒntrɛri/ a. & n. contrario -ria.

contrast /n ˈkɒntræst; v kənˈtræst/ n. **1.** contraste m. —v. **2.** contrastar.

contribute /kənˈtrɪbyut/ v. contribuir.

contribution /ˌkɒntrəˈbyuʃən/ n. contribución f.

contributor /kənˈtrɪbyətər/ n. contribuidor -ra.

contributory /kənˈtrɪbyəˌtɔri/ a. contribuyente.

contrite /kən'trait/ a. contrito.

contrition /kən'trıʃən/ n. contrición f.

contrivance /kən'traivəns/ n. aparato m.; estratagema f.

contrive /kən'traiv/ v. inventar, tramar; darse maña.

control /kən'troul/ n. 1. control m. —v. 2. controlar.

controllable /kən'trouləbəl/ a. controlable, dominable.

controller /kən'troulər/ n. interventor -ra; contralor -ra.

control tower torre de mando f.

controversial /ˌkɒntrə'vɜrʃəl/ a. contencioso.

controversy /'kɒntrəˌvɜrsi/ n. controversia f.

contusion /kən'tuʒən/ n. contusión f.

convalesce /ˌkɒnvə'lɛs/ v. convalecer.

convalescence /ˌkɒnvə'lɛsəns/ n. convalecencia f.

convalescent /ˌkɒnvə'lɛsənt/ n. convaleciente m. & f.

convalescent home clínica de reposo f.

convene /kən'vin/ v. juntarse; convocar.

convenience /kən'vinyəns/ n. comodidad f.

convenient /kən'vinyənt/ a. cómodo; oportuno.

conveniently /kən'vinyəntli/ adv. cómodamente.

convent /'kɒnvɛnt/ n. convento m.

convention /kən'vɛnʃən/ n. convención f.

conventional /kən'vɛnʃənl/ a. convencional.

conventionally /kən'vɛnʃənli/ adv. convencionalmente.

converge /kən'vɜrdʒ/ v. convergir.

convergence /kən'vɜrdʒəns/ n. convergencia f.

convergent /kən'vɜrdʒənt/ a. convergente.

conversant /kən'vɜrsənt/ a. versado; entendido (de).

conversation /ˌkɒnvər'seiʃən/ n. conversación, plática f.

conversational /ˌkɒnvər'seiʃənl/ a. de conversación.

conversationalist /ˌkɒnvər'seiʃənlıst/ n. conversador -ra.

converse /kən'vɜrs/ v. conversar.

conversely /kən'vɜrsli/ adv. a la inversa.

convert /n 'kɒnvɜrt; v kən'vɜrt/ n. 1. convertido da-. —v. 2. convertir.

converter /kən'vɜrtər/ n. convertidor m.

convertible /kən'vɜrtəbəl/ a. convertible.

convex /kɒn'vɛks/ a. convexo.

convey /kən'vei/ v. transportar; comunicar.

conveyance /kən'veiəns/ n. transporte; vehículo m.

conveyor /kən'veiər/ n. conductor m.; Mech. transportador m.

conveyor belt correa transportadora f.

convict /n 'kɒnvıkt; v kən'vıkt/ n. 1. reo m. —v. 2. declarar culpable.

conviction /kən'vıkʃən/ n. convicción f.

convince /kən'vıns/ v. convencer.

convincing /kən'vınsıŋ/ a. convincente.

convivial /kən'vıviəl/ a. convival.

convocation /ˌkɒnvə'keiʃən/ n. convocación; asamblea f.

convoke /kən'vouk/ v. convocar, citar.

convoy /'kɒnvɔi/ n. convoy m.; escolta f.

convulse /kən'vʌls/ v. convulsionar; agitar violentamente.

convulsion /kən'vʌlʃən/ n. convulsión f.

convulsive /kən'vʌlsıv/ a. convulsivo.

cook /kʊk/ n. 1. cocinero -ra. —v. 2. cocinar, cocer.

cookbook /'kʊkˌbʊk/ n. libro de cocina m.

cookie /'kʊki/ n. galleta dulce f.

cool /kul/ a. 1. fresco. —v. 2. refrescar.

cooler /'kulər/ n. enfriadera f.

coolness /'kulnıs/ n. frescura f.

coop /kup/ n. 1. jaula f. chicken c., gallinero m. —v. 2. enjaular.

cooperate /kou'ɒpəˌreit/ v. cooperar.

cooperation /kouˌɒpə'reiʃən/ n. cooperación f.

cooperative /kou'ɒpərətıv/ a. cooperativo.

cooperatively /kou'ɒpərətıvli/ adv. cooperativamente.

coordinate /kou'ɔrdnˌeit/ v. coordinar.

coordination /kouˌɔrdn'eiʃən/ n. coordinación f.

coordinator /kou'ɔrdnˌeitər/ n. coordinador -ra.

cope /koup/ v. contender. c. with, superar, hacer frente a.

copier /'kɒpiər/ n. copiadora f.

copious /'koupiəs/ a. copioso, abundante.

copiously /'koupiəsli/ adv. copiosamente.

copiousness /'koupiəsnıs/ n. abundancia f.

copper /'kɒpər/ n. cobre m.

copy /'kɒpi/ n. 1. copia f.; ejemplar m. —v. 2. copiar.

copyist /'kɒpiıst/ n. copista m. & f.

copyright /'kɒpiˌrait/ n. derechos de propiedad literaria m.pl.

coquetry /'koukıtri/ n. coquetería f.

coquette /kou'kɛt/ n. coqueta f.

coral /'kɔrəl/ n. coral m.

cord /kɔrd/ n. cuerda f.

cordial /'kɔrdʒəl/ a. cordial.

cordiality /kɔr'dʒælıti/ n. cordialidad f.

cordially /'kɔrdʒəli/ adv. cordialmente.

cordon off /'kɔrdn/ v. acordonar.

cordovan /'kɔrdəvən/ n. cordobán m.

corduroy /'kɔrdəˌrɔi/ n. pana f.

core /kɔr/ n. corazón m.; centro m.

cork /kɔrk/ n. corcho m.

corkscrew /'kɔrkˌskru/ n. tirabuzón m.

corn /kɔrn/ n. maíz m.

cornea /'kɔrniə/ n. córnea f.

corned beef /kɔrnd/ carne acecinada f.

corner /'kɔrnər/ n. rincón m.; (of street) esquina f.

cornet /kɔr'nɛt/ n. corneta f.

cornetist /kɔr'nɛtıst/ n. cornetín m.

cornice /'kɔrnıs/ n. cornisa f.

cornstarch /'kɔrnˌstɑrtʃ/ n. maicena f.

corollary /'kɔrəˌlɛri/ n. corolario m.

coronary /'kɔrəˌnɛri/ a. coronario.

coronation /ˌkɔrə'neiʃən/ n. coronación f.

corporal /'kɔrpərəl/ a. 1. corpóreo. —n. 2. cabo m.

corporate /'kɔrpərıt/ a. corporativo.

corporation /ˌkɔrpə'reiʃən/ n. corporación f.

corps /kɔr/ n. cuerpo m.

corpse /kɔrps/ n. cadáver m.

corpulent /'kɔrpyələnt/ a. corpulento.

corpuscle /'kɔrpəsəl/ n. corpúsculo m.

corral /kə'ræl/ n. 1. corral m. —v. 2. acorralar.

correct /kə'rɛkt/ a. 1. correcto. —v. 2. corregir.

correction /kə'rɛkʃən/ n. corrección; enmienda f.

corrective /kə'rɛktıv/ n. & a. correctivo.

correctly /kə'rɛktli/ adv. correctamente.

correctness /kə'rɛktnıs/ n. exactitud f.

correlate /'kɔrəˌleit/ v. correlacionar.

correlation /ˌkɔrə'leiʃən/ n. correlación f.

correspond /ˌkɔrə'spɒnd/ v. corresponder.

correspondence /ˌkɔrə'spɒndəns/ n. correspondencia f.

correspondence course curso por correspondencia m.

correspondence school escuela por correspondencia f.

correspondent /ˌkɔrə'spɒndənt/ a. & n. correspondiente m. & f.

corresponding /ˌkɔrə'spɒndıŋ/ a. correspondiente.

corridor /'kɔrıdər/ n. corredor, pasillo m.

corroborate /kə'rɒbəˌreit/ v. corroborar.

corroboration /kəˌrɒbə'reiʃən/ n. corroboración f.

corroborative /kə'rɒbəˌreitıv/ a. corroborante.

corrode /kə'roud/ v. corroer.

corrosion /kə'rouʒən/ n. corrosión f.

corrugate /'kɔrəˌgeit/ v. arrugar; ondular.

corrupt /kə'rʌpt/ a. 1. corrompido. —v. 2. corromper.

corruptible /kə'rʌptəbəl/ a. corruptible.

corruption /kə'rʌpʃən/ n. corrupción f.

corruptive /kə'rʌptıv/ a. corruptivo.

corset /'kɔrsıt/ n. corsé m., (girdle) faja f.

cortege /kɔr'tɛʒ/ n. comitiva f., séquito m.

corvette /kɔr'vɛt/ n. corbeta f.

cosmetic /kɒz'mɛtık/ a. & n. cosmético m.

cosmic /'kɒzmık/ a. cósmico.

cosmonaut /'kɒzməˌnɒt/ n. cosmonauta m. & f.

cosmopolitan /ˌkɒzmə'pɒlıtn/ a. & n. cosmopolita m. & f.

cosmos /'kɒzməs/ n. cosmos m.

cost /kɒst/ n. 1. coste m.; costa f. —v. 2. costar.

Costa Rican /'kɒstə'rikən/ a. & n. costarricense m. & f.

costly /'kɒstli/ a. costoso, caro.

costume /'kɒstum/ n. traje; disfraz m.

costume jewelry bisutería f., joyas de fantasía f.pl.

cot /kɒt/ n. catre m.

coterie /'koutəri/ n. camarilla f.

cotillion /kə'tılyən/ n. cotillón m.

cottage /'kɒtıdʒ/ n. casita f.

cottage cheese requesón m.

cotton /'kɒtn/ n. algodón m.

cottonseed /'kɒtnˌsid/ n. semilla del algodón f.

couch /kautʃ/ n. sofá m.

cougar /'kugər/ n. puma f.

cough /kɒf/ n. 1. tos f. —v. 2. toser.

council /'kaunsəl/ n. consejo, concilio m.

counsel /'kaunsəl/ n. 1. consejo; (law) abogado -da. —v. 2. aconsejar. to keep one's c., no decir nada.

counselor /'kaunsələr/ n. consejero -ra; (law) abogado -da.

count /kaunt/ n. 1. cuenta f.; (title) conde m. —v. 2. contar.

countenance /'kauntnəns/ n. 1. aspecto m.; cara f. —v. 2. aprobar.

counter /'kauntər/ adv. 1. c. to, contra, en contra de. —n. 2. mostrador m.

counteract /ˌkauntər'ækt/ v. contrarrestar.

counteraction /ˌkauntər'ækʃən/ n. neutralización f.

counterbalance /'kauntərˌbæləns/ n. 1. contrapeso m. —v. 2. contrapesar.

counterfeit /'kauntərˌfıt/ a. 1. falsificado. —v. 2. falsear.

countermand /ˌkauntər'mænd/ v. contramandar.

counteroffensive /ˌkauntərə'fɛnsıv/ n. contraofensiva f.

counterpart /'kauntərˌpɑrt/ n. contraparte f.

counterproductive /ˌkauntərprə'dʌktıv/ a. contraproducente.

countess /'kauntıs/ n. condesa f.

countless /'kauntlıs/ a. innumerable.

country /'kʌntri/ n. campo m.; Pol. país m.; (homeland) patria f.

country code distintivo del país m.

countryman /'kʌntrimən/ n. paisano m. fellow c., compatriota m.

countryside /'kʌntriˌsaid/ n. campo, paisaje m.

county /'kaunti/ n. condado m.

coupé /kup/ n. cupé m.

couple /'kʌpəl/ n. 1. par m. —v. 2. unir.

coupon /'kupɒn/ n. cupón, talón m.

courage /'kɜrıdʒ/ n. valor m.

courageous /kə'reidʒəs/ a. valiente.

course /kɔrs/ n. curso m. of c., por supuesto, desde luego.

court /kɔrt/ n. 1. corte f.; cortejo m.; (of law) tribunal m. —v. 2. cortejar.

courteous /'kɜrtiəs/ a. cortés.

courtesy /'kɜrtəsi/ n. cortesía f.

courthouse /'kɔrtˌhaus/ n. palacio de justicia m., tribunal m.

courtier /'kɔrtiər/ n. cortesano m.

courtly /'kɔrtli/ a. cortés, galante.

courtroom /'kɔrtˌrum, -ˌrʊm/ n. sala de justicia f.

courtship /'kɔrtʃıp/ n. cortejo m.

courtyard /'kɔrtˌyɑrd/ n. patio m.

cousin /'kʌzən/ n. primo -ma.

covenant /'kʌvənənt/ n. contrato, convenio m.

cover /'kʌvər/ n. 1. cubierta, tapa f. —v. 2. cubrir, tapar.

cover charge precio del cubierto m.

covet /'kʌvıt/ v. ambicionar, suspirar por.

covetous /'kʌvıtəs/ a. codicioso.

cow /kau/ n. vaca f.

coward /'kauərd/ n. cobarde m. & f.

cowardice /'kauərdıs/ n. cobardía f.

cowardly /'kauərdli/ a. cobarde.

cowboy /'kauˌbɔi/ n. vaquero, gaucho m.

cower /'kauər/ v. agacharse (de miedo).

cowhide /'kauˌhaid/ n. cuero m.

coy /kɔi/ a. recatado, modesto.

coyote /kai'outi/ n. coyote m.

cozy /'kouzi/ a. cómodo y agradable.

crab /kræb/ n. cangrejo m.

crab apple n. manzana silvestre f.

crack /kræk/ n. 1. hendedura f.; (noise) crujido m. —v. 2. hender; crujir.

cracker /'krækər/ n. galleta f.

cradle /'kreidl/ n. cuna f.

craft /kræft/ n. arte m.

craftsman /'kræftsmən/ n. artesano -na.

craftsmanship /'kræftsmənˌʃıp/ n. artesanía f.

crafty /'kræfti/ a. ladino.

crag /kræg/ n. despeñadero m.; peña f.

cram /kræm/ v. rellenar, hartar.

cramp /kræmp/ n. calambre m.

cranberry /'krænˌbɛri/ n. arándano m.

crane /krein/ n. (bird) grulla f.; Mech. grúa f.

cranium /'kreiniəm/ n. cráneo m.

crank /kræŋk/ n. Mech. manivela f.

cranky /'kræŋki/ a. chiflado, caprichoso.

crash /kræʃ/ n. 1. choque; estallido m. —v. 2. estallar.

crate /kreit/ n. canasto m.

crater /'kreitər/ n. cráter m.

crave /kreiv/ v. desear; anhelar.

craven /'kreivən/ a. cobarde.

craving /'kreivıŋ/ n. sed m., anhelo m.

crawl /krɔl/ v. andar a gatas, arrastrarse.

crayon /'kreiən/ n. creyón; lápiz m.

crazy /'kreizi/ a. loco.

creak /krik/ v. crujir.
creaky /'kriki/ a. crujiente.
cream /krim/ n. crema f.
cream cheese queso crema m.
creamery /'krimɔri/ n. lechería f.
creamy /'krimi/ a. cremoso.
crease /kris/ n. **1.** pliegue m. —v. **2.** plegar.
create /kri'eit/ v. crear.
creation /kri'eiʃɔn/ n. creación f.
creative /kri'eitiv/ a. creativo, creador.
creator /kri'eitɔr/ n. creador -ra.
creature /'kritʃɔr/ n. criatura f.
credence /'kridns/ n. creencia f.
credentials /krɪ'dɛnʃɔlz/ n. credenciales f.pl.
credibility /ˌkredɔ'bɪlɪti/ n. credibilidad f.
credible /'kredɔbɔl/ a. creíble.
credit /'kredɪt/ n. **1.** crédito m. **on c.,** al fiado. —v. **2.** Com. abonar.
creditable /'kredɪtɔbɔl/ a. fidedigno.
credit balance saldo acreedor.
credit card n. tarjeta de crédito f.
creditor /'kredɪtɔr/ n. acreedor -ra.
credit union banco cooperativo m.
credo /'kridou/ n. credo m.
credulity /krɔ'dulɪti/ n. credulidad f.
credulous /'kredʒɔlɔs/ a. crédulo.
creed /krid/ n. credo m.
creek /krik/ n. riachuelo m.
creep /krip/ v. gatear.
cremate /'krimeit/ v. incinerar.
crematory /'krimɔˌtɔri/ n. crematorio m.
creosote /'kriɔˌsout/ n. creosota f.
crepe /kreip/ n. crespón m.
crepe paper papel crespón m.
crescent /'kresɔnt/ a. n. creciente f.
crest /krest/ n. cresta; cima f.; (heraldry) timbre m.
cretonne /krɪ'tɒn/ n. cretona f.
crevice /'krevɪs/ n. grieta f.
crew /kru/ n. tripulación f.
crew member tripulante m. & f.
crib /krɪb/ n. pesebre m.; cuna.
cricket /'krɪkɪt/ n. grillo m.
crime /kraim/ n. crimen m.
criminal /'krɪmɔnl/ a. & n. criminal m. & f.
criminologist /ˌkrɪmɔ'nɒlɔdʒɪst/ n. criminólogo -ga, criminalista m. & f.
criminology /ˌkrɪmɔ'nɒlɔdʒi/ n. criminología f.
crimson /'krɪmzɔn, -sɔn/ a. & n. carmesí m.
cringe /krɪndʒ/ v. encogerse, temblar.
cripple /'krɪpɔl/ n. **1.** lisiado -da. —v. **2.** estropear, lisiar.
crisis /'kraisɪs/ n. crisis f.
crisp /krɪsp/ a. crespo, fresco.
crispness /'krɪspnɪs/ n. encrespadura f.
crisscross /'krɪs,krɒs/ a. entrelazado.
criterion /krai'tɪriɔn/ n. criterio m.
critic /'krɪtɪk/ n. crítico -ca.
critical /'krɪtɪkɔl/ a. crítico.
criticism /'krɪtɔ,sɪzɔm/ n. crítica; censura f.
criticize /'krɪtɔ,saiz/ v. criticar; censurar.
critique /krɪ'tik/ n. crítica f.
croak /krouk/ n. **1.** graznido m. —v. **2.** graznar.
crochet /krou'ʃei/ n. **1.** crochet m. —v. **2.** hacer crochet.
crochet work ganchillo m.
crock /krɒk/ n. cazuela f.; olla de barro.
crockery /'krɒkɔri/ n. loza f.
crocodile /'krɒkɔ,dail/ n. cocodrilo m.
crony /'krouni/ n. compinche m.
crooked /'krukɪd/ a. encorvado; deshonesto.
croon /krun/ v. canturrear.
crop /krɒp/ n. cosecha f.
croquet /krou'kei/ n. juego de croquet m.
croquette /krou'ket/ n. croqueta f.
cross /krɒs/ a. **1.** enojado, mal hu-

morado. —n. **2.** cruz f. —v. **3.** cruzar, atravesar.
crossbreed /'krɒs,brid/ n. **1.** mestizo m. —v. **2.** cruzar (animales o plantas).
cross-examine /'krɒs ɪg,zæmɪn/ v. interrogar.
cross-eyed /'krɒs ,aid/ a. bizco.
cross-fertilization /'krɒs ,fɜrtlɔ'zeiʃɔn/ n. alogamia f.
crossing /'krɒsɪŋ/ **crossroads** n. cruce m.
cross section corte transversal m.
crosswalk /'krɒs,wɔk/ n. paso cebra m.
crossword puzzle /'krɒs ,wɜrd/ crucigrama m.
crotch /krɒtʃ/ n. bifurcación f.; Anat. bragadura f.
crouch /krautʃ/ v. agacharse.
croup /krup/ n. Med. crup m.
croupier /'krupiɔr/ n. crupié m. & f.
crow /krou/ n. cuervo m.
crowd /kraud/ n. **1.** muchedumbre f.; tropel m. —v. **2.** apretar.
crowded /'kraudɪd/ a. lleno de gente.
crown /kraun/ n. **1.** corona f. —v. **2.** coronar.
crown prince príncipe heredero m.
crucial /'kruʃɔl/ a. crucial.
crucible /'krusɔbɔl/ n. crisol m.
crucifix /'krusɔfɪks/ n. crucifijo m.
crucifixion /ˌkrusɔ'fɪkʃɔn/ n. crucifixión f.
crucify /'krusɔ,fai/ v. crucificar.
crude /krud/ a. crudo; (oil) bruto.
crudeness /'krudnɪs/ a. crudeza.
cruel /'kruɔl/ a. cruel.
cruelty /'kruɔlti/ n. crueldad f.
cruet /'kruɪt/ n. vinagrera f.
cruise /kruz/ n. **1.** viaje por mar. —v. **2.** navegar.
cruiser /'kruzɔr/ n. crucero m.
crumb /krʌm/ n. miga; migaja f.
crumble /'krʌmbɔl/ v. desmigajar; desmoronar.
crumple /'krʌmpɔl/ v. arrugar; encogerse.
crusade /kru'seid/ n. cruzada f.
crusader /kru'seidɔr/ n. cruzado m.
crush /krʌʃ/ v. aplastar.
crust /krʌst/ n. costra; corteza f.
crustacean /krʌ'steiʃɔn/ n. crustáceo m.
crutch /krʌtʃ/ n. muleta f.
cry /krai/ n. **1.** grito m. —v. **2.** gritar; (weep) llorar.
cryosurgery /ˌkraiou'sɜrdʒɔri/ n. criocirugía f.
crypt /krɪpt/ n. gruta f., cripta f.
cryptic /'krɪptɪk/ a. secreto.
cryptography /krɪp'tɒgrɔfi/ n. criptografía f.
crystal /'krɪstl/ n. cristal m.
crystalline /'krɪstlɪn/ a. cristalino, transparente.
crystallize /'krɪstl,aiz/ v. cristalizar.
cub /kʌb/ n. cachorro m.
Cuban /'kyubɔn/ n. & a. cubano -na.
cube /kyub/ n. cubo m.
cubic /'kyubɪk/ a. cúbico.
cubicle /'kyubɪkɔl/ n. cubículo m.
cubic measure medida de capacidad f.
cubism /'kyubɪzɔm/ n. cubismo m.
cuckoo /'kuku/ n. cuco m.
cucumber /'kyukʌmbɔr/ n. pepino m.
cuddle /'kʌdl/ v. abrazar.
cudgel /'kʌdʒɔl/ n. palo m.
cue /kyu/ n. apunte m.; (billiards) taco m.
cuff /kʌf/ n. puño de camisa. **c. links,** gemelos.
cuisine /kwɪ'zin/ n. arte culinario m.
culinary /'kyulɔ,neri/ a. culinario.
culminate /'kʌlmɔ,neit/ v. culminar.
culmination /ˌkʌlmɔ'neiʃɔn/ n. culminación f.
culpable /'kʌlpɔbɔl/ a. culpable.
culprit /'kʌlprɪt/ n. criminal; delincuente m. & f.
cult /kʌlt/ n. culto m.

cultivate /'kʌltɔ,veit/ v. cultivar.
cultivated /'kʌltɔ,veitɪd/ a. cultivado.
cultivation /ˌkʌltɔ'veiʃɔn/ n. cultivo m.; cultivación f.
cultivator /'kʌltɔ,veitɔr/ n. cultivador -ra.
cultural /'kʌltʃɔrɔl/ a. cultural.
culture /'kʌltʃɔr/ n. cultura f.
cultured /'kʌltʃɔrd/ a. culto.
cumbersome /'kʌmbɔrsɔm/ a. pesado, incómodo.
cumulative /'kyumyɔlɔtɪv/ a. acumulativo.
cunning /'kʌnɪŋ/ a. **1.** astuto. —n. **2.** astucia f.
cup /kʌp/ n. taza, jícara f.
cupboard /'kʌbɔrd/ n. armario, aparador m.
cupidity /kyu'pɪdɪti/ n. avaricia f.
curable /'kyurɔbɔl/ a. curable.
curator /kyu'reitɔr/ n. guardián -ana.
curb /kɜrb/ n. **1.** freno m. —v. **2.** refrenar.
curd /kɜrd/ n. cuajada f.
curdle /'kɜrdl/ v. cuajarse, coagularse.
cure /kyur/ n. **1.** remedio m. —v. **2.** curar, sanar.
curfew /'kɜrfyu/ n. toque de queda m.
curio /'kyuri,ou/ n. objeto curioso.
curiosity /ˌkyuri'ɒsɪti/ n. curiosidad f.
curious /'kyuriɔs/ a. curioso.
curl /kɜrl/ n. **1.** rizo m. —v. **2.** rizar.
curly /'kɜrli/ a. rizado.
currant /'kɜrɔnt/ n. grosella f.
currency /'kɜrɔnsi/ n. circulación f.; dinero m.
current /'kɜrɔnt/ a. & n. corriente f.
current events /ɪ'vɛnts/ actualidades f.pl.
currently /'kɜrɔntli/ adv. corrientemente.
curriculum /kɔ'rɪkyɔlɔm/ n. plan de estudio m.
curse /kɜrs/ n. **1.** maldición f. —v. **2.** maldecir.
cursor /'kɜrsɔr/ n. cursor m.
cursory /'kɜrsɔri/ a. sumario.
curt /kɜrt/ a. brusco.
curtail /kɔr'teil/ v. reducir; restringir.
curtain /'kɜrtn/ n. cortina f.; Theat. telón m.
curtsy /'kɜrtsi/ n. **1.** reverencia f. —v. **2.** hacer una reverencia.
curvature /'kɜrvɔtʃɔr/ n. curvatura f.
curve /kɜrv/ n. **1.** curva f. —v. **2.** encorvar.
cushion /'kuʃɔn/ n. cojín m.; almohada f.
cuspidor /'kʌspɪ,dɔr/ n. escupidera f.
custard /'kʌstɔrd/ n. flan m.; natillas f.pl.
custodian /kʌ'stoudiɔn/ n. custodio m.
custody /'kʌstɔdi/ n. custodia f.
custom /'kʌstɔm/ n. costumbre f.
customary /'kʌstɔ,meri/ a. acostumbrado, usual.
customer /'kʌstɔmɔr/ n. cliente m. & f.
customhouse /'kʌstɔm,haus/ **customs** n. aduana f.
customs duty /'kʌstɔmz/ derechos de aduana m.pl.
customs officer /'kʌstɔmz/ agente de aduana m. & f.
cut /kʌt/ n. **1.** corte m.; cortada f.; tajada f.; (printing) grabado m. —v. **2.** cortar; tajar.
cute /kyut/ a. mono, lindo.
cut glass cristal tallado m.
cuticle /'kyutɪkɔl/ n. cutícula f.
cutlery /'kʌtlɔri/ n. cuchillería f.
cutlet /'kʌtlɪt/ n. chuleta f.
cutter /'kʌtɔr/ n. cortador -ra; Naut. cúter m.
cutthroat /'kʌt,θrout/ n. asesino -na.
cyberpunk /'saibɔr,pʌŋk/ n. ciberpunk m. & f.
cyberspace /'saibɔr,speis/ n. ciberespacio m.
cyclamate /'saiklɔ,meit, 'sɪklɔ-/ n. ciclamato m.

cycle /'saikɔl/ n. ciclo m.
cyclist /'saiklɪst/ n. ciclista m. & f.
cyclone /'saikloun/ n. ciclón, huracán m.
cyclotron /'saiklɔ,trɒn, 'sɪklɔ-/ n. ciclotrón m.
cylinder /'sɪlɪndɔr/ n. cilindro m.
cylindrical /sɪ'lɪndrɪkɔl/ a. cilíndrico.
cymbal /'sɪmbɔl/ n. címbalo m.
cynic /'sɪnɪk/ n. cínico -ca.
cynical /'sɪnɪkɔl/ a. cínico.
cynicism /'sɪnɔ,sɪzɔm/ n. cinismo m.
cypress /'saiprɔs/ n. ciprés m. **c. nut,** piñuela f.
cyst /sɪst/ n. quiste m.

D

dad /dæd/ n. papá m., papito m.
daffodil /'dæfɔdɪl/ n. narciso m.
dagger /'dægɔr/ n. puñal m.
dahlia /'dælyɔ/ n. dalia f.
daily /'deili/ a. diario, cotidiano.
daintiness /'deintɪnɪs/ n. delicadeza f.
dainty /'deinti/ a. delicado.
dairy /'dɛɔri/ n. lechería, quesería f.
dais /'deiɪs/ n. tablado m.
daisy /'deizi/ n. margarita f.
dale /deil/ n. valle m.
dally /'dæli/ v. holgar; perder el tiempo.
dam /dæm/ n. presa f.; dique m.
damage /'dæmɪdʒ/ n. **1.** daño m. —v. **2.** dañar.
damask /'dæmɔsk/ n. damasco m.
damn /dæm/ v. condenar.
damnation /dæm'neiʃɔn/ n. condenación f.
damp /dæmp/ a. húmedo.
dampen /'dæmpɔn/ v. humedecer.
dampness /'dæmpnɪs/ n. humedad f.
damsel /'dæmzɔl/ n. doncella f.
dance /dæns/ n. **1.** baile m.; danza f. —v. **2.** bailar.
dance hall salón de baile m.
dancer /'dænsɔr/ n. bailador -ra; (professional) bailarín -na.
dancing /'dænsɪŋ/ n. baile m.
dandelion /'dændl,aiɔn/ n. amargón m.
dandruff /'dændrɔf/ n. caspa f.
dandy /'dændi/ n. petimetre m.
danger /'deindʒɔr/ n. peligro m.
dangerous /'deindʒɔrɔs/ a. peligroso.
dangle /'dæŋgɔl/ v. colgar.
Danish /'deinɪʃ/ a. & n. danés -sa; dinamarqués -sa.
dapper /'dæpɔr/ a. gallardo.
dare /dɛɔr/ v. atreverse, osar.
daredevil /'dɛɔr,devɔl/ n. atrevido m., -da f.
daring /'dɛɔrɪŋ/ a. **1.** atrevido. —n. **2.** osadía f.
dark /dɑrk/ a. **1.** obscuro; moreno. —n. **2.** obscuridad f.
darken /'dɑrkɔn/ v. obscurecer.
darkness /'dɑrknɪs/ n. obscuridad f.
darkroom /'dɑrk,rum, -,rʊm/ n. cámara obscura f.
darling /'dɑrlɪŋ/ a. & n. querido -da, amado -da.
darn /dɑrn/ v. zurcir.
darning needle /'dɑrnɪŋ/ aguja de zurcir m.
dart /dɑrt/ n. dardo m.
dartboard /'dɑrt,bɔrd/ n. diana f.
dash /dæʃ/ n. arranque m.; Punct. guión m.
data /'deitɔ/ n. datos m.
database /'deitɔbeis/ n. base de datos m.
data processing /'prɒsesɪŋ/ proceso de datos m.
date /deit/ n. fecha f.; (engagement) cita f.; (fruit) dátil m.
daughter /'dɔtɔr/ n. hija f.
daughter-in-law /'dɔ,tɔr ɪn lɔ/ n. nuera f.
daunt /dɔnt, dɑnt/ v. intimidar.
dauntless /'dɔntlɪs/ a. intrépido.

davenport /'dævən,pɔrt/ n. sofá m.

dawn /dɔn/ n. **1.** alba, madrugada f. —v. **2.** amanecer.

day /dei/ n. día m. **good d.,** buenos días.

daybreak /'dei,breik/ n. alba, madrugada f.

daydream /'dei,drim/ n. fantasía f.

daylight /'dei,lait/ n. luz del día.

daze /deiz/ v. aturdir.

dazzle /'dæzəl/ v. deslumbrar.

deacon /'dikən/ n. diácono m.

dead /dɛd/ a. muerto.

deaden /'dɛdn/ v. amortecer.

dead end atolladero m. (impasse); callejón sin salida m. (street).

deadline /'dɛd,lain/ n. fecha límite f.

deadlock /'dɛd,lɒk/ n. paro m.

deadly /'dɛdli/ a. mortal.

deaf /dɛf/ a. sordo.

deafen /'dɛfən/ v. ensordecer.

deafening /'dɛfənɪŋ/ a. ensordecedor.

deaf-mute /'dɛf 'myut/ n. sordomudo -da.

deafness /'dɛfnɪs/ n. sordera f.

deal /dil/ n. **1.** trato m.; negociación f. **a great d., a good d.,** mucho. —v. **2.** tratar; negociar.

dealer /'dilər/ n. comerciante m., (at cards) tallador -ra.

dean /din/ n. decano -na.

dear /dɪər/ a. querido; caro.

dearth /dɜrθ/ n. escasez f.

death /dɛθ/ n. muerte f.

death certificate partida de defunción f.

deathless /'dɛθlɪs/ a. inmortal.

debacle /də'bakəl/ n. desastre m.

debase /dɪ'beis/ v. degradar.

debatable /dɪ'beitəbəl/ a. discutible.

debate /dɪ'beit/ n. **1.** debate m. —v. **2.** disputar, deliberar.

debauch /dɪ'bɔtʃ/ v. corromper.

debilitate /dɪ'bɪlɪ,teit/ v. debilitar.

debit /'dɛbɪt/ n. débito m.

debit balance saldo deudor m.

debonair /,dɛbə'nɛər/ a. cortés; alegre, vivo.

debris /dei'bri/ n. escombros m.pl.

debt /dɛt/ n. deuda f. **get into d.** endeudarse.

debtor /'dɛtər/ n. deudor -ra.

debug /di'bʌg/ v. depurar, limpiar.

debunk /dɪ'bʌŋk/ v. desacreditar; desenmascarar.

debut /dei'byu/ n. debut, estreno m.

debutante /'dɛbyu,tɑnt/ n. debutante f.

decade /'dɛkeid/ n. década f.

decadence /'dɛkədəns/ n. decadencia f.

decadent /'dɛkədənt/ a. decadente.

decaffeinated /di'kæfɪ,neitɪd/ a. descafeinado.

decalcomania /dɪ,kælkə'meiniə/ n. calcomanía f.

decanter /dɪ'kæntər/ n. garrafa f.

decapitate /dɪ'kæpɪ,teit/ v. descabezar.

decay /dɪ'kei/ n. **1.** descaecimiento m.; (dental) caries f. —v. **2.** decaer; (dental) cariarse.

deceased /dɪ'sist/ a. muerto, difunto.

deceit /dɪ'sit/ n. engaño m.

deceitful /dɪ'sitfəl/ a. engañoso.

deceive /dɪ'siv/ v. engañar.

December /dɪ'sɛmbər/ n. diciembre m.

decency /'disənsi/ n. decencia f.; decoro m.

decent /'disənt/ a. decente.

decentralize /di'sɛntrə,laiz/ v. descentralizar.

deception /dɪ'sɛpʃən/ n. decepción f.

deceptive /dɪ'sɛptɪv/ a. decepcionante.

decibel /'dɛsə,bɛl/ n. decibelio m.

decide /dɪ'said/ v. decidir.

decimal /'dɛsəməl/ a. decimal.

decipher /dɪ'saifər/ v. descifrar.

decision /dɪ'sɪʒən/ n. decisión f.

decisive /dɪ'saisɪv/ a. decisivo.

deck /dɛk/ n. cubierta f.

deck chair tumbona f.

declamation /,dɛklə'meiʃən/ n. declamación f.

declaration /,dɛklə'reiʃən/ n. declaración f.

declarative /dɪ'klærətɪv/ a. declarativo.

declare /dɪ'klɛər/ v. declarar.

declension /dɪ'klɛnʃən/ n. declinación f.

decline /dɪ'klain/ n. **1.** decadencia f. —v. **2.** decaer; negarse; *Gram.* declinar.

decompose /,dikəm'pouz/ v. descomponer.

decongestant /,dikən'dʒɛstənt/ n. descongestionante m.

decorate /'dɛkə,reit/ v. decorar, adornar.

decoration /,dɛkə'reiʃən/ n. decoración f.

decorative /'dɛkərətɪv/ a. decorativo.

decorator /'dɛkə,reitər/ n. decorador -ra.

decorous /'dɛkərəs/ a. correcto.

decorum /dɪ'kɔrəm/ n. decoro m.

decrease /dɪ'kris/ v. disminuir.

decree /dɪ'kri/ n. decreto m.

decrepit /dɪ'krɛpɪt/ a. decrépito.

decry /dɪ'krai/ v. desacreditar.

dedicate /'dɛdɪ,keit/ v. dedicar; consagrar.

dedication /,dɛdɪ'keiʃən/ n. dedicación; dedicatoria f.

deduce /dɪ'dus/ v. deducir.

deduction /dɪ'dʌkʃən/ n. rebaja; deducción f.

deductive /dɪ'dʌktɪv/ a. deductivo.

deed /did/ n. acción; hazaña f.

deem /dim/ v. estimar.

deep /dip/ a. hondo, profundo.

deepen /'dipən/ v. profundizar, ahondar.

deep freeze congelación f.

deeply /'dipli/ adv. profundamente.

deer /dɪər/ n. venado, ciervo m.

deface /dɪ'feis/ v. mutilar.

defamation /,dɛfə'meiʃən/ n. calumnia f.

defame /dɪ'feim/ v. difamar.

default /dɪ'fɔlt/ n. **1.** defecto m. —v. **2.** faltar.

defeat /dɪ'fit/ n. **1.** derrota f. —v. **2.** derrotar.

defeatism /dɪ'fitɪzəm/ n. derrotismo m.

defect /'difɛkt, dɪ'fɛkt/ n. defecto m.

defective /dɪ'fɛktɪv/ a. defectivo.

defend /dɪ'fɛnd/ v. defender.

defendant /dɪ'fɛndənt/ n. acusado -da.

defender /dɪ'fɛndər/ n. defensor -ra.

defense /dɪ'fɛns/ n. defensa f.

defensive /dɪ'fɛnsɪv/ a. defensivo.

defer /dɪ'fɜr/ v. aplazar; deferir.

deference /'dɛfərəns/ n. deferencia f.

defiance /dɪ'faiəns/ n. desafío m.

defiant /dɪ'faiənt/ a. desafiador.

deficiency /dɪ'fɪʃənsi/ n. defecto m.

deficient /dɪ'fɪʃənt/ a. deficiente.

deficit /'dɛfəsɪt/ n. déficit, descubierto m.

defile /dɪ'fail/ n. **1.** desfiladero m. —v. **2.** profanar.

define /dɪ'fain/ v. definir.

definite /'dɛfənɪt/ a. exacto; definitivo.

definitely /'dɛfənɪtli/ adv. definitivamente.

definition /,dɛfə'nɪʃən/ n. definición f.

definitive /dɪ'fɪnɪtɪv/ a. definitivo.

deflate /dɪ'fleiʃən/ n. desinflación f.

deflect /dɪ'flɛkt/ v. desviar.

deform /dɪ'fɔrm/ v. deformar.

deformity /dɪ'fɔrmiti/ n. deformidad f.

defraud /dɪ'frɔd/ v. defraudar.

defray /dɪ'frei/ v. costear.

defrost /dɪ'frɔst/ v. descongelar.

deft /dɛft/ a. diestro.

defy /dɪ'fai/ v. desafiar.

degenerate /a dɪ'dʒɛnərɪt; v -,reit/ a. **1.** degenerado. —v. **2.** degenerar.

degeneration /dɪ,dʒɛnə'reiʃən/ n. degeneración f.

degradation /,dɛgrɪ'deiʃən/ n. degradación f.

degrade /dɪ'greid/ v. degradar.

degree /dɪ'gri/ n. grado m.

deign /dein/ v. condescender.

deity /'diɪti/ n. deidad f.

dejected /dɪ'dʒɛktɪd/ a. abatido.

dejection /dɪ'dʒɛkʃən/ n. tristeza f.

delay /dɪ'lei/ n. **1.** retardo m., demora f. —v. **2.** tardar, demorar.

delegate /n 'dɛlɪgɪt; v -,geit/ n. **1.** delegado -da. —v. **2.** delegar.

delegation /,dɛlɪ'geiʃən/ n. delegación f.

delete /dɪ'lit/ v. suprimir, tachar.

deliberate /a dɪ'lɪbərɪt; v -ə,reit/ a. **1.** premeditado. —v. **2.** deliberar.

deliberately /dɪ'lɪbərɪtli/ adv. deliberadamente.

deliberation /dɪ,lɪbə'reiʃən/ n. deliberación f.

deliberative /dɪ'lɪbərətɪv/ a. deliberativo.

delicacy /'dɛlɪkəsi/ n. delicadeza f.

delicate /'dɛlɪkɪt/ a. delicado.

delicious /dɪ'lɪʃəs/ a. delicioso.

delight /dɪ'lait/ n. deleite m.

delightful /dɪ'laitfəl/ a. deleitoso.

delinquency /dɪ'lɪŋkwənsi/ n. delincuencia f.

delinquent /dɪ'lɪŋkwənt/ a. & n. delincuente. m. & f.

delirious /dɪ'lɪəriəs/ a. delirante.

deliver /dɪ'lɪvər/ v. entregar.

deliverance /dɪ'lɪvərəns/ n. liberación; salvación f.

delivery /dɪ'lɪvəri/ n. entrega f.; *Med.* parto m.

delude /dɪ'lud/ v. engañar.

deluge /'dɛlyudʒ/ n. inundación f.

delusion /dɪ'luʒən/ n. decepción f.; engaño m.

delve /dɛlv/ v. cavar, sondear.

demagogue /'dɛmə,gɒg/ n. demagogo -ga.

demand /dɪ'mænd/ n. **1.** demanda f. —v. **2.** demandar; exigir.

demarcation /,dimɑr'keiʃən/ n. demarcación f.

demeanor /dɪ'minər/ n. conducta f.

demented /dɪ'mɛntɪd/ a. demente, loco.

demilitarize /di'mɪlɪtə,raiz/ v. desmilitarizar.

demobilize /di'moubə,laiz/ v. desmovilizar.

democracy /dɪ'mɒkrəsi/ n. democracia f.

democrat /'dɛmə,kræt/ n. demócrata m. & f.

democratic /,dɛmə'krætɪk/ a. democrático.

demolish /dɪ'mɒlɪʃ/ v. demoler.

demon /'dimən/ n. demonio m.

demonstrate /'dɛmən,streit/ v. demostrar.

demonstration /,dɛmən'streiʃən/ n. demostración f.

demonstrative /də'mɒnstrətɪv/ a. demostrativo.

demoralize /dɪ'mɔrə,laiz, -'mɒr-/ v. desmoralizar.

demure /dɪ'myor/ a. modesto, serio.

den /dɛn/ n. madriguera, caverna f.

denature /di'neitʃər/ v. alterar.

denial /dɪ'naiəl/ n. negación f.

denim /'dɛnəm/ n. dril, tela vaquera.

Denmark /'dɛnmɑrk/ n. Dinamarca f.

denomination /dɪ,nɒmə'neiʃən/ n. denominación; secta f.

denote /dɪ'nout/ v. denotar.

denounce /dɪ'nauns/ v. denunciar.

dense /dɛns/ a. denso, espeso; estúpido.

density /'dɛnsiti/ n. densidad f.

dent /dɛnt/ n. **1.** abolladura f. —v. **2.** abollar.

dental /'dɛntl/ a. dental.

dentist /'dɛntɪst/ n. dentista m. & f.

dentistry /'dɛntəstri/ n. odontología f.

denture /'dɛntʃər/ n. dentadura f.

denunciation /dɪ,nʌnsi'eiʃən/ n. denunciación f.

deny /dɪ'nai/ v. negar, rehusar.

deodorant /di'oudərənt/ n. desodorante m.

depart /dɪ'pɑrt/ v. partir; irse, marcharse.

department /dɪ'pɑrtmənt/ n. departamento m.

departmental /dɪ,pɑrt'mɛntl/ a. departamental.

department store grandes almacenes m.pl.

departure /dɪ'pɑrtʃər/ n. salida; desviación f.

depend /dɪ'pɛnd/ v. depender.

dependability /dɪ,pɛndə'bɪliti/ n. confiabilidad f.

dependable /dɪ'pɛndəbəl/ a. confiable.

dependence /dɪ'pɛndəns/ n. dependencia f.

dependent /dɪ'pɛndənt/ a. & n. dependiente m. & f.

depict /dɪ'pɪkt/ v. pintar; representar.

deplete /dɪ'plit/ v. agotar.

deplorable /dɪ'plɔrəbəl/ a. deplorable.

deplore /dɪ'plɔr/ v. deplorar.

deport /dɪ'pɔrt/ v. deportar.

deportation /,dipɔr'teiʃən/ n. deportación f.

deportment /dɪ'pɔrtmənt/ n. conducta f.

depose /dɪ'pouz/ v. deponer.

deposit /dɪ'pɒzɪt/ n. **1.** depósito m. (of money); yacimiento (of ore, etc.) m. —v. **2.** depositar.

depositor /dɪ'pɒzɪtər/ n. depositante m. & f.

depot /'dipou/ n. depósito m.; (railway) estación f.

depravity /dɪ'prævɪti/ n. depravación f.

deprecate /'dɛprɪ,keit/ v. deprecar.

depreciate /dɪ'priʃi,eit/ v. depreciar.

depreciation /dɪ,priʃi'eiʃən/ n. depreciación f.

depredation /,dɛprə'deiʃən/ n. depredación f.

depress /dɪ'prɛs/ v. deprimir; desanimar.

depression /dɪ'prɛʃən/ n. depresión f.

deprive /dɪ'praiv/ v. privar.

depth /dɛpθ/ n. profundidad, hondura f.

depth charge carga de profundidad f.

deputy /'dɛpyəti/ n. diputado -da.

deride /dɪ'raid/ v. burlar.

derision /dɪ'rɪʒən/ n. burla f.

derivation /,dɛrə'veiʃən/ n. derivación f.

derivative /dɪ'rɪvətɪv/ a. derivativo.

derive /dɪ'raiv/ v. derivar.

dermatologist /,dɜrmə'tɒlədʒɪst/ n. dermatólogo -ga.

derogatory /dɪ'rɒgə,tɔri/ a. derogatorio.

derrick /'dɛrɪk/ n. grúa f.

descend /dɪ'sɛnd/ v. descender, bajar.

descendant /dɪ'sɛndənt/ n. descendiente m. & f.

descent /dɪ'sɛnt/ n. descenso m.; origen m.

describe /dɪ'skraib/ v. describir.

description /dɪ'skrɪpʃən/ n. descripción f.

descriptive /dɪ'skrɪptɪv/ a. descriptivo.

desecrate /'dɛsɪ,kreit/ v. profanar.

desert /n 'dɛzərt; v dɪ'zɜrt/ n. **1.** desierto m. —v. **2.** abandonar.

deserter /dɪ'zɜrtər/ n. desertor -ra.

desertion /dɪ'zɜrʃən/ n. deserción f.

deserve /dɪ'zɜrv/ v. merecer.

design /dɪ'zain/ *n.* **1.** diseño *m.* —*v.* **2.** diseñar.
designate /'dɛzɪg,neit/ *v.* señalar, apuntar; designar.
designation /,dɛzɪg'neiʃən/ *n.* designación *f.*
designer /dɪ'zainər/ *n.* diseñador -ra; (technical) proyectista *m.* & *f.*
designer clothes, designer clothing ropa de marca *f.*
desirability /dɪ,zaiᵊrə'bɪlɪti/ *n.* conveniencia *f.*
desirable /dɪ'zaiᵊrəbəl/ *a.* deseable.
desire /dɪ'zaiᵊr/ *n.* **1.** deseo *m.* —*v.* **2.** desear.
desirous /dɪ'zaiᵊrəs/ *a.* deseoso.
desist /dɪ'sɪst/ *v.* desistir.
desk /dɛsk/ *n.* escritorio *m.*
desk clerk recepcionista *m.* & *f.*
desktop computer /'dɛsk,tɒp/ computadora de sobremesa *f.*, ordenador de sobremesa *f.*
desolate /*a* 'dɛsəlɪt; *v* -,leit/ *a.* **1.** desolado. —*v.* **2.** desolar.
desolation /,dɛsə'leiʃən/ *n.* desolación, ruina *f.*
despair /dɪ'spɛər/ *n.* **1.** desesperación *f.* —*v.* **2.** desesperar.
despatch /dɪ'spætʃ/ **dispatch** *n.* **1.** despacho *m.*; prontitud *f.* —*v.* **2.** despachar.
desperado /,dɛspə'rɑdou/ *n.* bandido *m.*
desperate /'dɛspərɪt/ *a.* desesperado.
desperation /,dɛspə'reiʃən/ *n.* desesperación *f.*
despicable /'dɛspɪkəbəl/ *a.* vil.
despise /dɪ'spaiz/ *v.* despreciar.
despite /dɪ'spait/ *prep.* a pesar de.
despondent /dɪ'spɒndənt/ *a.* abatido; desanimado.
despot /'dɛspət/ *n.* déspota *m.* & *f.*
despotic /dɛs'pɒtɪk/ *a.* despótico.
dessert /dɪ'zɜrt/ *n.* postre *m.*
destination /,dɛstə'neiʃən/ *n.* destinación *f.*
destine /'dɛstɪn/ *v.* destinar.
destiny /'dɛstəni/ *n.* destino *m.*
destitute /'dɛstɪ,tut/ *a.* destituído, indigente.
destitution /,dɛstɪ'tuʃən/ *n.* destitución *f.*
destroy /dɪ'strɔi/ *v.* destrozar, destruir.
destroyer /dɪ'strɔiər/ *n.* destruidor -ra; (naval) destructor *m.*
destruction /dɪ'strʌkʃən/ *n.* destrucción *f.*
destructive /dɪ'strʌktɪv/ *a.* destructivo.
desultory /'dɛsəl,tɔri/ *a.* inconexo; casual.
detach /dɪ'tætʃ/ *v.* separar, desprender.
detachment /dɪ'tætʃmənt/ *n.* *Mil.* destacamento; desprendimiento *m.*
detail /dɪ'teil/ *n.* **1.** detalle *m.* —*v.* **2.** detallar.
detain /dɪ'tein/ *v.* detener.
detect /dɪ'tɛkt/ *v.* descubrir.
detection /dɪ'tɛkʃən/ *n.* detección *f.*
detective /dɪ'tɛktɪv/ *n.* detective *m.* & *f.*
deténte /dei'tɑnt/ *n.* distensión *f.*; *Pol.* deténte.
detention /dɪ'tɛnʃən/ *n.* detención; cautividad *f.*
deter /dɪ'tɜr/ *v.* disuadir.
detergent /dɪ'tɜrdʒənt/ *n.* & *a.* detergente *m.*
deteriorate /dɪ'tɪəriə,reit/ *v.* deteriorar.
deterioration /dɪ,tɪəriə'reiʃən/ *n.* deterioración *f.*
determination /dɪ,tɜrmə'neiʃən/ *n.* determinación *f.*
determine /dɪ'tɜrmɪn/ *v.* determinar.
deterrence /dɪ'tɜrəns/ *n.* disuasión *f.*
detest /dɪ'tɛst/ *v.* detestar.
detonate /'dɛtn̩,eit/ *v.* detonar.
detour /'ditʊr/ *n.* desvío *m.* *v.* desviar.
detract /dɪ'trækt/ *v.* disminuir.
detriment /'dɛtrəmənt/ *n.* detrimento *m.*, daño *m.*
detrimental /,dɛtrə'mɛntl̩/ *a.* dañoso.
devaluate /di'vælyu,eit/ *v.* depreciar.
devastate /'dɛvə,steit/ *v.* devastar.
develop /dɪ'vɛləp/ *v.* desarrollar; *Phot.* revelar.
developing nation /dɪ'vɛləpɪŋ/ nación en desarrollo.
development /dɪ'vɛləpmənt/ *n.* desarrollo *m.*
deviate /'divi,eit/ *v.* desviar.
deviation /,divi'eiʃən/ *n.* desviación *f.*
device /dɪ'vais/ *n.* aparato; artificio *m.*
devil /'dɛvəl/ *n.* diablo, demonio *m.*
devious /'diviəs/ *a.* desviado.
devise /dɪ'vaiz/ *v.* inventar.
devoid /dɪ'vɔid/ *a.* desprovisto.
devote /dɪ'vout/ *v.* dedicar, consagrar.
devoted /dɪ'voutɪd/ *a.* devoto.
devotee /,dɛvə'ti/ *n.* aficionado -da.
devotion /dɪ'vouʃən/ *n.* devoción *f.*
devour /dɪ'vaur/ *v.* devorar.
devout /dɪ'vaut/ *a.* devoto.
dew /du/ *n.* rocío, sereno *m.*
dexterity /dɛk'stɛrɪti/ *n.* destreza *f.*
dexterous /'dɛkstrəs/ *a.* diestro.
diabetes /,daiə'bitɪs/ *n.* diabetes *f.*
diabolic /,daiə'bɒlɪk/ *a.* diabólico.
diadem /'daiə,dɛm/ *n.* diadema *f.*
diagnose /'daiəg,nous/ *v.* diagnosticar.
diagnosis /,daiəg'nousɪs/ *n.* diagnóstico *m.*
diagonal /dai'ægənl̩/ *n.* diagonal *f.*
diagram /'daiə,græm/ *n.* diagrama *m.*
dial /'daiəl/ *n.* **1.** cuadrante *m.*, carátula *f.* —*v.* **2. dial up** marcar.
dialect /'daiə,lɛkt/ *n.* dialecto *m.*
dialing code /'daiəlɪŋ/ prefijo *m.*
dialogue /'daiə,lɔg/ *n.* diálogo *m.*
dial tone señal de marcar *f.*
diameter /dai'æmɪtər/ *n.* diámetro *m.*
diamond /'daimənd/ *n.* diamante, brillante *m.*
diaper /'daipər/ *n.* pañal *m.*
diarrhea /,daiə'riə/ *n.* diarrea *f.*
diary /'daiəri/ *n.* diario *m.*
diathermy /'daiə,θɜrmi/ *n.* diatermia *f.*
dice /dais/ *n.* dados *m.pl.*
dictate /'dɪkteit/ *n.* **1.** mandato *m.* —*v.* **2.** dictar.
dictation /dɪk'teiʃən/ *n.* dictado *m.*
dictator /'dɪkteitər/ *n.* dictador -ra.
dictatorship /dɪk'teitər,ʃɪp/ *n.* dictadura *f.*
diction /'dɪkʃən/ *n.* dicción *f.*
dictionary /'dɪkʃə,nɛri/ *n.* diccionario *m.*
die /dai/ *n.* **1.** matriz *f.*; (game) dado *m.* —*v.* **2.** morir.
diet /'daiɪt/ *n.* dieta *f.*
dietary /'daiɪ,tɛri/ *a.* dietético.
dietitian /,daiɪ'tɪʃən/ *n.* & *a.* dietético -ca.
differ /'dɪfər/ *v.* diferir.
difference /'dɪfərəns/ *n.* diferencia *f.* **to make no d.,** no importar.
different /'dɪfərənt/ *a.* diferente, distinto.
differential /,dɪfə'rɛnʃəl/ *n.* diferencial *f.*
differentiate /,dɪfə'rɛnʃi,eit/ *v.* diferenciar.
difficult /'dɪfɪ,kʌlt/ *a.* difícil.
difficulty /'dɪfɪ,kʌlti/ *n.* dificultad *f.*
diffident /'dɪfɪdənt/ *a.* tímido.
diffuse /dɪ'fyuz/ *v.* difundir.
diffusion /dɪ'fyuʒən/ *n.* difusión *f.*
dig /dɪg/ *v.* cavar.
digest /*n* 'daidʒɛst; *v* dɪ'dʒɛst, dai-/ *n.* **1.** extracto *m.* —*v.* **2.** digerir.
digestible /dɪ'dʒɛstəbəl, dai-/ *a.* digerible.
digestion /dɪ'dʒɛstʃən, dai-/ *n.* digestión *f.*
digestive /dɪ'dʒɛstɪv, dai-/ *a.* digestivo.
digital /'dɪdʒɪtl̩/ *a.* digital.
digitalis /,dɪdʒɪ'tælɪs/ *n.* digital *f.*
dignified /'dɪgnə,f aid/ *a.* digno.
dignify /'dɪgnə,fai/ *v.* dignificar.
dignitary /'dɪgnɪ,tɛri/ *n.* dignatario -ria.
dignity /'dɪgnɪti/ *n.* dignidad *f.*
digress /dɪ'grɛs, dai-/ *v.* divagar.
digression /dɪ'grɛʃən, dai-/ *n.* digresión *f.*
dike /daik/ *n.* dique *m.*
dilapidated /dɪ'læpɪ,deitɪd/ *a.* dilapidado.
dilapidation /dɪ,læpə'deiʃən/ *n.* dilapidación *f.*
dilate /dai'leit/ *v.* dilatar.
dilatory /'dɪlə,tɔri/ *a.* dilatorio.
dilemma /dɪ'lɛmə/ *n.* dilema *m.*
dilettante /'dɪlɪ,tɑnt/ *n.* diletante *m.* & *f.*
diligence /'dɪlɪdʒəns/ *n.* diligencia *f.*
diligent /'dɪlɪdʒənt/ *a.* diligente, aplicado.
dilute /dɪ'lut, dai-/ *v.* diluir.
dim /dɪm/ *a.* **1.** oscuro. —*v.* **2.** oscurecer.
dimension /dɪ'mɛnʃən/ *n.* dimensión *f.*
diminish /dɪ'mɪnɪʃ/ *v.* disminuir.
diminution /,dɪmə'nuʃən/ *n.* disminución *f.*
diminutive /dɪ'mɪnyətɪv/ *a.* diminutivo.
dimness /'dɪmnɪs/ *n.* oscuridad *f.*
dimple /'dɪmpəl/ *n.* hoyuelo *m.*
din /dɪn/ *n.* alboroto, estrépito *m.*
dine /dain/ *v.* comer, cenar.
diner /'dainər/ *n.* coche comedor *m.*
dingy /'dɪndʒi/ *a.* deslucido, deslustrado.
dining room /'dainɪŋ/ comedor *m.*
dinner /'dɪnər/ *n.* comida, cena *f.*
dinosaur /'dainə,sɔr/ *n.* dinosauro *m.*
diocese /'daiəsɪs/ *n.* diócesis *f.*
dip /dɪp/ *v.* sumergir, hundir.
diphtheria /dɪf'θɪəriə/ *n.* difteria *f.*
diploma /dɪ'ploumə/ *n.* diploma *m.*
diplomacy /dɪ'plouməsi/ *n.* diplomacia *f.*
diplomat /'dɪplə,mæt/ *n.* diplomático -ca.
diplomatic /,dɪplə'mætɪk/ *a.* diplomático.
dipper /'dɪpər/ *n.* cucharón *m.*
dire /daiᵊr/ *a.* horrendo.
direct /dɪ'rɛkt, dai-/ *a.* **1.** directo. —*v.* **2.** dirigir.
direction /dɪ'rɛkʃən, 'dai-/ *n.* dirección *f.*
directive /dɪ'rɛktɪv, dai-/ *n.* directiva *f.*
directly /dɪ'rɛktli, dai-/ *adv.* directamente.
director /dɪ'rɛktər, dai-/ *n.* director -ra.
directory /dɪ'rɛktəri, dai-/ *n.* directorio *m.*, guía *f.*
dirigible /'dɪrɪdʒəbəl/ *n.* dirigible *m.*
dirt /dɜrt/ *n.* basura *f.*; (earth) tierra *f.*
dirt-cheap /'dɜrt 'tʃip/ *a.* tirado.
dirty /'dɜrti/ *a.* sucio.
dis /dɪs/ *v.* *Colloq.* ofender, faltar al respeto.
disability /,dɪsə'bɪlɪti/ *n.* inhabilidad *f.*
disable /dɪs'eibəl/ *v.* incapacitar.
disabuse /,dɪsə'byuz/ *v.* desengañar.
disadvantage /,dɪsəd'væntɪdʒ/ *n.* desventaja *f.*
disagree /,dɪsə'gri/ *v.* desconvenir; disentir.
disagreeable /,dɪsə'griəbəl/ *a.* desagradable.
disagreement /,dɪsə'grimənt/ *n.* desacuerdo *m.*
disappear /,dɪsə'pɪər/ *v.* desaparecer.
disappearance /,dɪsə'pɪərəns/ *n.* desaparición *f.*
disappoint /,dɪsə'pɔint/ *v.* disgustar, desilusionar.
disappointment /,dɪsə'pɔintmənt/ *n.* disgusto *m.*, desilusión *f.*
disapproval /,dɪsə'pruvəl/ *n.* desaprobación *f.*
disapprove /,dɪsə'pruv/ *v.* desaprobar.
disarm /dɪs'ɑrm/ *v.* desarmar.
disarmament /dɪs'ɑrməmənt/ *n.* desarme *m.*
disarrange /,dɪsə'reindʒ/ *v.* desordenar; desarreglar.
disaster /dɪ'zæstər/ *n.* desastre *m.*
disastrous /dɪ'zæstrəs/ *a.* desastroso.
disavow /,dɪsə'vau/ *v.* repudiar.
disavowal /,dɪsə'vauəl/ *n.* repudiación *f.*
disband /dɪs'bænd/ *v.* dispersarse.
disbelieve /,dɪsbɪ'liv/ *v.* descreer.
disburse /dɪs'bɜrs/ *v.* desembolsar, pagar.
discard /dɪ'skɑrd/ *v.* descartar.
discern /dɪ'sɜrn/ *v.* discernir.
discerning /dɪ'sɜrnɪŋ/ *a.* discernidor, perspicaz.
discernment /dɪ'sɜrnmənt/ *n.* discernimiento *m.*
discharge /dɪs'tʃɑrdʒ/ *v.* descargar; despedir.
disciple /dɪ'saipəl/ *n.* discípulo -la.
disciplinary /'dɪsəplə,nɛri/ *a.* disciplinario.
discipline /'dɪsəplɪn/ *n.* disciplina *f.*
disclaim /dɪs'kleim/ *v.* repudiar.
disclaimer /dɪs'kleimər/ *n.* negación *f.*
disclose /dɪ'sklouz/ *v.* revelar.
disclosure /dɪ'sklouʒər/ *n.* revelación *f.*
disco /'dɪskou/ *n.* discoteca *f.*
discolor /dɪs'kʌlər/ *v.* descolorar.
discomfort /dɪs'kʌmfərt/ *n.* incomodidad *f.*
disconcert /,dɪskən'sɜrt/ *v.* desconcertar.
disconnect /,dɪskə'nɛkt/ *v.* desunir; desconectar.
disconnected /,dɪskə'nɛktɪd/ *a.* desunido.
disconsolate /dɪs'kɒnsəlɪt/ *a.* desconsolado.
discontent /,dɪskən'tɛnt/ *n.* descontento *m.*
discontented /,dɪskən'tɛntɪd/ *a.* descontento.
discontinue /,dɪskən'tɪnyu/ *v.* descontinuar.
discord /'dɪskɔrd/ *n.* discordia *f.*
discordant /dɪs'kɔrdənt/ *a.* disonante.
discotheque /'dɪskə,tɛk/ *n.* discoteca *f.*
discount /'dɪskaunt/ *n.* descuento *m.*
discourage /dɪ'skɜrɪdʒ/ *v.* desalentar, desanimar.
discouragement /dɪ'skɜrɪdʒmənt/ *n.* desaliento, desánimo *m.*
discourse /'dɪskɔrs/ *n.* discurso *m.*
discourteous /dɪs'kɜrtiəs/ *a.* descortés.
discourtesy /dɪs'kɜrtəsi/ *n.* descortesía *f.*
discover /dɪ'skʌvər/ *v.* descubrir.
discoverer /dɪ'skʌvərər/ *n.* descubridor -ra.
discovery /dɪ'skʌvəri/ *n.* descubrimiento *m.*
discreet /dɪ'skrit/ *a.* discreto.
discrepancy /dɪ'skrɛpənsi/ *n.* discrepancia *f.*
discretion /dɪ'skrɛʃən/ *n.* discreción *f.*
discriminate /dɪ'skrɪm,əneit/ *v.* distinguir. **d. against** discriminar contra.
discrimination /dɪ,skrɪmə'neiʃən/ *n.* discernimiento *m.*; discriminación *f.*
discuss /dɪ'skʌs/ *v.* discutir.
discussion /dɪ'skʌʃən/ *n.* discusión *f.*
disdain /dɪs'dein/ *n.* **1.** desdén *m.* —*v.* **2.** desdeñar.
disdainful /dɪs'deinfəl/ *a.* desdeñoso.
disease /dɪ'ziz/ *n.* enfermedad *f.*, mal *m.*
disembark /,dɪsɛm'bɑrk/ *v.* desembarcar.

disentangle /ˌdɪsɛn'tæŋgəl/ v. desenredar.

disfigure /dɪs'fɪgyər/ v. desfigurar.

disgrace /dɪs'greis/ n. **1.** vergüenza; deshonra f. —v. **2.** deshonrar.

disgraceful /dɪs'greisfəl/ a. vergonzoso.

disguise /dɪs'gaiz/ n. **1.** disfraz m. —v. **2.** disfrazar.

disgust /dɪs'gʌst/ n. **1.** repugnancia —v. **2.** fastidiar; repugnar.

dish /dɪʃ/ n. plato m.

dishearten /dɪs'hɑrtn/ v. desanimar; descorazonar.

dishonest /dɪs'ɒnɪst/ a. deshonesto.

dishonesty /dɪs'ɒnəsti/ n. deshonestidad f.

dishonor /dɪs'ɒnər/ n. **1.** deshonra f. —v. **2.** deshonrar.

dishonorable /dɪs'ɒnərəbəl/ a. deshonroso.

dishwasher /'dɪʃ,wɒʃər/ n. lavaplatos m.

disillusion /ˌdɪsɪ'luʒən/ n. **1.** desengaño m. —v. **2.** desengañar.

disinfect /ˌdɪsɪn'fɛkt/ v. desinfectar.

disinfectant /ˌdɪsɪn'fɛktənt/ n. desinfectante m.

disinherit /ˌdɪsɪn'hɛrɪt/ v. desheredar.

disintegrate /dɪs'ɪntə,greit/ v. desintegrar.

disinterested /dɪs'ɪntə,rɛstɪd, -trɪstɪd/ a. desinteresado.

disk /dɪsk/ n. disco m.

disk drive disquetera f.

diskette /dɪ'skɛt/ n. disquete m.

disk jockey pinchadiscos m. & f.

dislike /dɪs'laik/ n. **1.** antipatía f. —v. **2.** no gustar de.

dislocate /'dɪslou,keit/ v. dislocar.

dislodge /dɪs'lɒdʒ/ v. desalojar; desprender.

disloyal /dɪs'lɔiəl/ a. desleal; infiel.

disloyalty /dɪs'lɔiəlti/ n. deslealtad f.

dismal /'dɪzməl/ a. lúgubre.

dismantle /dɪs'mæntl/ v. desmantelar, desmontar.

dismay /dɪs'mei/ n. **1.** consternación f. —v. **2.** consternar.

dismiss /dɪs'mɪs/ v. despedir.

dismissal /dɪs'mɪsəl/ n. despedida f.

dismount /dɪs'maunt/ v. apearse, desmontarse.

disobedience /ˌdɪsə'bidiəns/ n. desobediencia f.

disobedient /ˌdɪsə'bidiənt/ a. desobediente.

disobey /ˌdɪsə'bei/ v. desobedecer.

disorder /dɪs'ɔrdər/ n. desorden m.

disorderly /dɪs'ɔrdərli/ a. desarreglado, desordenado.

disown /dɪs'oun/ v. repudiar.

dispassionate /dɪs'pæʃənɪt/ a. desapasionado; templado.

dispatch /dɪ'spætʃ/ n. **1.** despacho m. —v. **2.** despachar.

dispel /dɪ'spɛl/ v. dispersar.

dispensary /dɪ'spɛnsəri/ n. dispensario m.

dispensation /ˌdɪspən'seiʃən/ n. dispensación f.

dispense /dɪ'spɛns/ v. dispensar.

dispersal /dɪ'spɜrsəl/ n. dispersión f.

disperse /dɪ'spɜrs/ v. dispersar.

displace /dɪs'pleis/ v. dislocar.

display /dɪ'splei/ n. **1.** despliegue m., exhibición f. —v. **2.** desplegar, exhibir.

displease /dɪs'pliz/ v. disgustar; ofender.

displeasure /dɪs'plɛʒər/ n. disgusto, sinsabor m.

disposable /dɪs'pouzəbəl/ a. disponible; desechable.

disposal /dɪs'pouzəl/ n. disposición f.

dispose /dɪ'spouz/ v. disponer.

disposition /ˌdɪspə'zɪʃən/ n. disposición f.; índole f., genio m.

dispossess /ˌdɪspə'zɛs/ v. desposeer.

disproportionate /ˌdɪsprə'pɔrʃənɪt/ a. desproporcionado.

disprove /dɪs'pruv/ v. confutar.

dispute /dɪ'spyut/ n. **1.** disputa f. —v. **2.** disputar.

disqualify /dɪs'kwɒlə,fai/ v. inhabilitar.

disregard /ˌdɪsrɪ'gɑrd/ n. **1.** desatención f. —v. **2.** desatender.

disrepair /ˌdɪsrɪ'pɛər/ n. descompostura f.

disreputable /dɪs'rɛpyətəbəl/ a. desacreditado.

disrespect /ˌdɪsrɪ'spɛkt/ n. falta de respeto, f., desacato m.

disrespectful /ˌdɪsrɪ'spɛktfəl/ a. irrespetuoso.

disrobe /dɪs'roub/ v. desvestir.

disrupt /dɪs'rʌpt/ v. romper; desbaratar.

dissatisfaction /ˌdɪssætɪs'fækʃən/ n. descontento m.

dissatisfy /dɪs'sætɪs,fai/ v. descontentar.

dissect /dɪ'sɛkt/ v. disecar.

dissemble /dɪ'sɛmbəl/ v. disimular.

disseminate /dɪ'sɛmə,neit/ v. diseminar.

dissension /dɪ'sɛnʃən/ n. disensión f.

dissent /dɪ'sɛnt/ n. **1.** disensión f. —v. **2.** disentir.

dissertation /ˌdɪsər'teiʃən/ n. disertación f.

dissimilar /dɪ'sɪmələr/ a. desemejante.

dissipate /'dɪsə,peit/ v. disipar.

dissipation /ˌdɪsə'peiʃən/ n. disipación f.; libertinaje m.

dissolute /'dɪsə,lut/ a. disoluto.

dissolution /ˌdɪsə'luʃən/ n. disolución f.

dissolve /dɪ'zɒlv/ v. disolver; derretirse.

dissonant /'dɪsənənt/ a. disonante.

dissuade /dɪ'sweid/ v. disuadir.

distance /'dɪstəns/ n. distancia f. **at a d., in the d.,** a lo lejos.

distant /'dɪstənt/ a. distante, lejano.

distaste /dɪs'teist/ n. disgusto, sinsabor m.

distasteful /dɪs'teistfəl/ a. desagradable.

distill /dɪ'stɪl/ v. destilar.

distillation /ˌdɪstl'eiʃən/ n. destilación f.

distillery /dɪ'stɪləri/ n. destilería f.

distinct /dɪ'stɪŋkt/ a. distinto.

distinction /dɪ'stɪŋkʃən/ n. distinción f.

distinctive /dɪ'stɪŋktɪv/ a. distintivo; característico.

distinctly /dɪ'stɪŋktli/ adv. distintamente.

distinguish /dɪ'stɪŋgwɪʃ/ v. distinguir.

distinguished /dɪ'stɪŋgwɪʃt/ a. distinguido.

distort /dɪ'stɔrt/ v. falsear; torcer.

distract /dɪ'strækt/ v. distraer.

distraction /dɪ'strækʃən/ n. distracción f.

distraught /dɪ'strɔt/ a. aturrullado; demente.

distress /dɪ'strɛs/ n. **1.** dolor m. —v. **2.** afligir.

distressing /dɪ'strɛsɪŋ/ a. penoso.

distribute /dɪ'strɪbyut/ v. distribuir.

distribution /ˌdɪstrə'byuʃən/ n. distribución f.; reparto m.

distributor /dɪ'strɪbyətər/ n. distribuidor -ra.

district /'dɪstrɪkt/ n. distrito m.

distrust /dɪs'trʌst/ n. **1.** desconfianza f. —v. **2.** desconfiar.

distrustful /dɪs'trʌstfəl/ a. desconfiado; sospechoso.

disturb /dɪ'stɜrb/ v. incomodar; inquietar.

disturbance /dɪ'stɜrbəns/ n. disturbio m.

disturbing /dɪ'stɜrbɪŋ/ a. inquietante.

ditch /dɪtʃ/ n. zanja f.; foso m.

divan /dɪ'væn/ n. diván m.

dive /daiv/ n. **1.** clavado m.; Colloq. leonera f. —v. **2.** echar un clavado; bucear.

diver /'daivər/ n. buzo m.

diverge /dɪ'vɜrdʒ/ v. divergir.

divergence /dɪ'vɜrdʒəns/ n. divergencia f.

divergent /dɪ'vɜrdʒənt/ a. divergente.

diverse /dɪ'vɜrs/ a. diverso.

diversion /dɪ'vɜrʒən/ n. diversión f.; pasatiempo m.

diversity /dɪ'vɜrsɪti/ n. diversidad f.

divert /dɪ'vɜrt/ v. desviar; divertir.

divest /dɪ'vɛst/ v. desnudar, despojar.

divide /dɪ'vaid/ v. dividir.

dividend /'dɪvɪ,dɛnd/ n. dividendo m.

divine /dɪ'vain/ a. divino.

divinity /dɪ'vɪnɪti/ n. divinidad f.

division /dɪ'vɪʒən/ n. división f.

divorce /dɪ'vɔrs/ n. **1.** divorcio m. —v. **2.** divorciar.

divorcee /dɪvɔr'sei/ n. divorciado -da.

divulge /dɪ'vʌldʒ/ v. divulgar, revelar.

dizziness /'dɪzinɪs/ n. vértigo, mareo m.

dizzy /'dɪzi/ a. mareado.

DNA abbr. (deoxyribonucleic acid) ADN (ácido deoxirríbonucleico) m.

do /du/ v. hacer.

docile /'dɒsəl/ a. dócil.

dock /dɒk/ n. **1.** muelle m. **dry d.,** astillero m. —v. **2.** entrar en muelle.

doctor /'dɒktər/ n. médico m.; doctor -ra.

doctorate /'dɒktərɪt/ n. doctorado m.

doctrine /'dɒktrɪn/ n. doctrina f.

document /'dɒkyəmənt/ n. documento m.

documentary /ˌdɒkyə'mɛntəri/ a. documental.

documentation /ˌdɒkyəmən'teiʃən/ n. documentación f.

dodge /dɒdʒ/ n. **1.** evasión f. —v. **2.** evadir.

dodgem /'dɒdʒɪm/ n. coche de choque m.

doe /dou/ n. gama f.

dog /dɔg/ n. perro -a.

dogma /'dɔgmə/ n. dogma m.

dogmatic /dɔg'mætɪk/ a. dogmático.

dogmatism /'dɔgmə,tɪzəm/ n. dogmatismo m.

doily /'dɔili/ n. servilletita f.

doleful /'doulfəl/ a. triste.

doll /dɒl/ n. muñeca -co.

dollar /'dɒlər/ n. dólar m.

dolorous /'doulərəs/ a. lastimoso.

dolphin /'dɒlfɪn/ n. delfín m.

domain /dou'mein/ n. dominio m.

dome /doum/ n. domo m.

domestic /də'mɛstɪk/ a. doméstico.

domesticate /də'mɛstɪ,keit/ v. domesticar.

domicile /'dɒmə,sail/ n. domicilio m.

dominance /'dɒmənəns/ n. dominación f.

dominant /'dɒmənənt/ a. dominante.

dominate /'dɒmə,neit/ v. dominar.

domination /ˌdɒmə'neiʃən/ n. dominación f.

domineer /ˌdɒmə'nɪər/ v. dominar.

domineering /ˌdɒmə'nɪərɪŋ/ a. tiránico, mandón.

dominion /də'mɪnyən/ n. dominio; territorio m.

domino /'dɒmə,nou/ n. dominó m.

donate /'douneit/ v. donar; contribuir.

donation /dou'neiʃən/ n. donación f.

donkey /'dɒŋki/ n. asno, burro m.

doom /dum/ n. **1.** perdición, ruina f. —v. **2.** perder, ruinar.

door /dɔr/ n. puerta f.

doorman /'dɔr,mæn, -mən/ n. portero m.

doormat /'dɔr,mæt/ n. felpudo m.

doorway /'dɔr,wei/ n. entrada f.

dope /doup/ n. Colloq. narcótico m.; idiota m.

dormant /'dɔrmənt/ a. durmiente; inactivo.

dormitory /'dɔrmɪ,tɔri/ n. dormitorio m.

dosage /'dousɪdʒ/ n. dosificación f.

dose /dous/ n. dosis f.

dot /dɒt/ n. punto m.

dotted line /'dɒtɪd/ línea de puntos f.

double /'dʌbəl/ a. **1.** doble. —v. **2.** duplicar.

double bass /beis/ contrabajo m.

double-breasted /'dʌbəl 'brɛstɪd/ a. cruzado.

double-cross /'dʌbəl 'krɔs/ v. traicionar.

doubly /'dʌbli/ adv. doblemente.

doubt /daut/ n. **1.** duda f. —v. **2.** dudar.

doubtful /'dautfəl/ a. dudoso, incierto.

doubtless /'dautlɪs/ a. **1.** indudable. —adv. **2.** sin duda.

dough /dou/ n. pasta, masa f.

doughnut /'dounət, -,nʌt/ n. buñuelo m.

dove /dʌv/ n. paloma f.

dowager /'dauədʒər/ n. viuda (con título) f.

down /daun/ adv. **1.** abajo. —prep. **2.** **d. the street,** etc. calle abajo, etc.

downcast /'daun,kæst/ a. cabizbajo.

downfall /'daun,fɔl/ n. ruina, perdición f.

downhearted /'daun'hɑrtɪd/ a. descorazonado.

download /'daun,loud/ v. bajar, descargar.

downpour /'daun,pɔr/ n. chaparrón m.

downright /'daun,rait/ a. absoluto, completo.

downriver /'daun'rɪvər/ adv. aguas abajo, río abajo.

downstairs /'daun'stɛərz/ adv. **1.** abajo. —n. **2.** primer piso.

downstream /'daun'strim/ adv. aguas abajo, río abajo.

downtown /'daun'taun/ adv. al centro, en el centro.

downward /'daunwərd/ a. **1.** descendente. —adv. **2.** hacia abajo.

dowry /'dauri/ n. dote f.

doze /douz/ v. dormitar.

dozen /'dʌzən/ n. docena f.

draft /dræft/ n. **1.** dibujo m.; Com. giro m.; Mil. conscripción f. —v. **2.** dibujar; Mil. reclutar.

draftee /dræf'ti/ n. conscripto m.

draft notice notificación de reclutamiento f.

drag /dræg/ v. arrastrar.

dragon /'drægən/ n. dragón m.

drain /drein/ n. **1.** desaguadero m. —v. **2.** desaguar.

drainage /'dreinɪdʒ/ n. drenaje m.

drain board escurridero m.

drama /'drɑmə, 'dræmə/ n. drama m.

dramatic /drə'mætɪk/ a. dramático.

dramatics /drə'mætɪks/ n. dramática f.

dramatist /'dræmətɪst, 'drɑmə-/ n. dramaturgo -ga.

dramatize /'dræmə,taiz, 'drɑmə-/ v. dramatizar.

drape /dreip/ n. cortinas f.pl. v. vestir; adornar.

drapery /'dreipəri/ n. colgaduras f.pl.; ropaje m.

drastic /'dræstɪk/ a. drástico.

draw /drɔ/ v. dibujar; atraer. **d. up,** formular.

drawback /'drɔ,bæk/ n. desventaja f.

drawer /drɔr/ n. cajón m.

drawing /'drɔɪŋ/ n. dibujo m.; rifa f.

dread /drɛd/ n. **1.** terror m. —v. **2.** temer.

dreadful /'drɛdfəl/ a. terrible.

dreadfully /'drɛdfəli/ adv. horrendamente.

dream /drim/ n. **1.** sueño, ensueño m. —v. **2.** soñar.

dreamer /'drimər/ n. soñador -ra; visionario -ia.

dreamy /'drimi/ a. soñador, contemplativo.

dreary /'drɪəri/ a. monótono y pesado.

dredge /drɛdʒ/ n. **1.** rastra f. —v. **2.** rastrear.
dregs /drɛgz/ n. sedimento m.
drench /drɛntʃ/ v. mojar.
dress /drɛs/ n. **1.** vestido; traje m. —v. **2.** vestir.
dresser /'drɛsər/ n. (furniture) tocador.
dressing /'drɛsɪŋ/ n. Med. curación f.; (cookery) relleno m., salsa f.
dressing gown bata f.
dressing table tocador m.
dressmaker /'drɛs,meikər/ n. modista m. & f.
drift /drɪft/ n. **1.** tendencia f.; Naut. deriva f. —v. **2.** Naut. derivar; (snow) amontonarse.
drill /drɪl/ n. **1.** ejercicio m.; Mech. taladro m. —v. **2.** Mech. taladrar.
drink /drɪŋk/ n. **1.** bebida f. —v. **2.** beber, tomar.
drinkable /'drɪŋkəbəl/ a. potable, bebible.
drip /drɪp/ v. gotear.
drive /draiv/ n. **1.** paseo m. —v. **2.** impeler; Auto. guiar, conducir.
drive-in (movie theater) /'draiv,ɪn/ n. autocine, autocinema m.
driver /'draivər/ n. conductor -ra; chofer m. **d.'s license,** permiso de conducir.
driveway /'draiv,wei/ n. entrada para coches.
drizzle /'drɪzəl/ n. **1.** llovizna f. —v. **2.** lloviznar.
dromedary /'drɒmɪ,dɛri/ n. dromedario m.
droop /drup/ v. inclinarse.
drop /drɒp/ n. **1.** gota f. —v. **2.** soltar; dejar caer.
dropout /'drɒp,aut/ n. joven que abandona sus estudios.
dropper /'drɒpər/ n. cuentagotas f.
dropsy /'drɒpsi/ n. hidropesía f.
drought /draut/ n. sequía f.
drove /drouv/ n. manada f.
drown /draun/ v. ahogar.
drowse /drauz/ v. adormecer.
drowsiness /'drauzinɪs/ n. somnolencia f.
drowsy /'drauzi/ a. soñoliento.
drudge /drʌdʒ/ n. ganapán m.
drudgery /'drʌdʒəri/ n. trabajo penoso.
drug /drʌg/ n. **1.** droga f. —v. **2.** narcotizar.
drug addict drogadicto -ta, toxicómano -na m. & f.
druggist /'drʌgɪst/ n. farmacéutico -ca, boticario -ria.
drugstore /'drʌg,stɔr/ n. farmacia, botica, droguería f.
drum /drʌm/ n. tambor m.
drummer /'drʌmər/ n. tambor m.
drumstick /'drʌm,stɪk/ n. palillo m.; Leg. pierna f.
drunk /drʌŋk/ a. & n. borracho, -a.
drunkard /'drʌŋkərd/ n. borrachón m.
drunken /'drʌŋkən/ a. borracho; ebrio.
drunkenness /'drʌŋkənnɪs/ n. embriaguez f.
dry /drai/ a. **1.** seco, árido. —v. **2.** secar.
dry cell n. pila seca f.
dry cleaner tintorero -ra.
dryness /'drainɪs/ n. sequedad f.
dual /'duəl/ a. doble.
dubious /'dubiəs/ a. dudoso.
duchess /'dʌtʃɪs/ n. duquesa f.
duck /dʌk/ n. **1.** pato m. —v. **2.** zambullir; (avoid) esquivar.
duct /dʌkt/ n. canal m.
due /du/ a. **1.** debido; Com. vencido. —n. **2. dues** cuota f.
duel /'duəl/ n. duelo m.
duelist /'duəlɪst/ n. duelista f.
duet /du'ɛt/ n. dúo m.
duke /duk/ n. duque m.
dull /dʌl/ a. apagado, desteñido; sin punta; Fig. pesado, soso.

dullness /'dʌlnɪs/ n. estupidez; pesadez f.; deslustre m.
duly /'duli/ adv. debidamente.
dumb /dʌm/ a. mudo; Colloq. estúpido.
dumbwaiter /'dʌm,weitər/ n. montaplatos m.
dumfound /dʌm'faund/ v. confundir.
dummy /'dʌmi/ n. maniquí m.
dump /dʌmp/ n. **1.** depósito m. —v. **2.** descargar.
dune /dun/ n. duna f.
dungeon /'dʌndʒən/ n. calabozo m.
dunk /dʌŋk/ v. mojar.
dupe /dup/ v. engañar.
duplicate /a, n 'duplɪkɪt; v -,keit/ a. & n. **1.** duplicado m. —v. **2.** duplicar.
duplication /,duplɪ'keiʃən/ n. duplicación f.
duplicity /du'plɪsɪti/ n. duplicidad f.
durability /,durə'bɪlɪti/ n. durabilidad f.
durable /'durəbəl/ a. durable, duradero.
duration /du'reiʃən/ n. duración f.
duress /du'rɛs/ n. compulsión f.; encierro m.
during /'durɪŋ/ prep. durante.
dusk /dʌsk/ n. crepúsculo m.
dusky /'dʌski/ a. oscuro; moreno.
dust /dʌst/ n. **1.** polvo m. —v. **2.** polvorear; despolvorear.
dusty /'dʌsti/ a. empolvado.
Dutch /dʌtʃ/ a. holandés -sa.
dutiful /'dutəfəl/ a. respetuoso.
dutifully /'dutəfəli/ adv. respetuosamente, obedientemente.
duty /'duti/ n. deber m.; Com. derechos m.pl.
duty-free /'duti 'fri/ a. libre de derechos.
dwarf /dwɔrf/ n. **1.** enano -na. —v. **2.** achicar.
dwell /dwɛl/ v. habitar, residir. **d. on,** espaciarse en.
dwelling /'dwɛlɪŋ/ n. morada, casa f.
dwindle /'dwɪndl/ v. disminuirse.
dye /dai/ n. **1.** tintura f. —v. **2.** teñir.
dyer /'daiər/ n. tintorero -ra.
dynamic /dai'næmɪk/ a. dinámico.
dynamite /'dainə,mait/ n. dinamita f.
dynamo /'dainə,mou/ n. dínamo m.
dynasty /'dainəsti/ n. dinastía f.
dysentery /'dɪsən,tɛri/ n. disentería f.
dyslexia /dɪs'lɛksiə/ n. dislexia f.
dyslexic /dɪs'lɛksɪk/ a. disléxico.
dyspepsia /dɪs'pɛpʃə/ n. dispepsia f.

E

each /itʃ/ a. **1.** cada. —pron. **2.** cada uno -na. **e. other,** el uno al otro.
eager /'igər/ a. ansioso.
eagerly /'igərli/ adv. ansiosamente.
eagerness /'igərnɪs/ n. ansia f.
eagle /'igəl/ n. águila f.
ear /ɪər/ n. oído m.; (outer) oreja f.; (of corn) mazorca f.
earache /'ɪər,eik/ n. dolor de oído m.
earl /ɜrl/ n. conde m.
early /'ɜrli/ a. & adv. temprano.
earn /ɜrn/ v. ganar.
earnest /'ɜrnɪst/ a. serio.
earnestly /'ɜrnɪstli/ adv. seriamente.
earnings /'ɜrnɪŋz/ n. ganancias f.pl.; Com. ingresos m.pl.
earphone /'ɪər,foun/ n. auricular m.
earring /'ɪər,rɪŋ/ n. pendiente, arete m.
earth /ɜrθ/ n. tierra f.
earthquake /'ɜrθ,kweik/ n. terremoto m.
ease /iz/ n. **1.** reposo m.; facilidad f. —v. **2.** aliviar.
easel /'izəl/ n. caballete m.
easily /'izəli/ adv. fácilmente.
east /ist/ n. oriente, este m.
Easter /'istər/ n. Pascua Florida.
eastern /'istərn/ a. oriental.
eastward /'istwərd/ adv. hacia el este.

easy /'izi/ a. fácil.
eat /it/ v. comer.
eau de Cologne /'ou də kə'loun/ colonia f.
eaves /ivz/ n. socarrén m.
ebb /ɛb/ n. **1.** menguante f. —v. **2.** menguar.
ebony /'ɛbəni/ n. ébano m.
eccentric /ɪk'sɛntrɪk/ a. excéntrico.
eccentricity /,ɛksən'trɪsɪti/ n. excentricidad f.
ecclesiastic /ɪ,klizi'æstɪk/ a. & n. eclesiástico m.
echelon /'ɛʃə,lɒn/ n. escalón m.
echo /'ɛkou/ n. eco m.
eclipse /ɪ'klɪps/ n. **1.** eclipse m. —v. **2.** eclipsar.
ecological /,ɛkə'lɒdʒɪkəl/ a. ecológico.
ecology /ɪ'kɒlədʒi/ n. ecología f.
economic /,ɛkə'nɒmɪk, ,ikə-/ a. económico.
economical /,ɛkə'nɒmɪkəl, ,ikə-/ a. económico.
economics /,ɛkə'nɒmɪks, ,ikə-/ n. economía política.
economist /ɪ'kɒnəmɪst/ n. economista m. & f.
economize /ɪ'kɒnə,maiz/ v. economizar.
economy /ɪ'kɒnəmi/ n. economía f.
ecstasy /'ɛkstəsi/ n. éxtasis m.
Ecuadorian /,ɛkwə'dɔriən/ a. & n. ecuatoriano -na.
ecumenical /,ɛkyu'mɛnɪkəl/ a. ecuménico.
eczema /'ɛksəmə/ n. eczema f.
eddy /'ɛdi/ n. **1.** remolino m. —v. **2.** remolinar.
edge /ɛdʒ/ n. **1.** filo; borde m. **e. one's way,** abrirse paso.
edible /'ɛdəbəl/ a. comestible.
edict /'idɪkt/ n. edicto m.
edifice /'ɛdəfɪs/ n. edificio m.
edify /'ɛdə,fai/ v. edificar.
edition /ɪ'dɪʃən/ n. edición f.
editor /'ɛdɪtər/ n. redactor -ra.
editorial /,ɛdɪ'tɔriəl/ n. editorial m. **e. board,** consejo de redacción m. **e. staff,** redacción f.
educate /'ɛdʒu,keit/ v. educar.
education /,ɛdʒu'keiʃən/ n. instrucción; enseñanza f.
educational /,ɛdʒu'keiʃənl/ a. educativo.
educator /'ɛdʒu,keitər/ n. educador -ra, pedagogo -ga.
eel /il/ n. anguila f.
efface /ɪ'feis/ v. tachar.
effect /ɪ'fɛkt/ n. **1.** efecto m. **in e.,** en vigor. —v. **2.** efectuar, realizar.
effective /ɪ'fɛktɪv/ a. eficaz; efectivo; en vigor.
effectively /ɪ'fɛktɪvli/ adv. eficazmente.
effectiveness /ɪ'fɛktɪvnɪs/ n. efectividad f.
effectual /ɪ'fɛktʃuəl/ a. eficaz.
effeminate /ɪ'fɛmənɪt/ a. afeminado.
efficacy /'ɛfɪkəsi/ n. eficacia f.
efficiency /ɪ'fɪʃənsi/ n. eficiencia f.
efficient /ɪ'fɪʃənt/ a. eficaz.
efficiently /ɪ'fɪʃəntli/ adv. eficazmente.
effigy /'ɛfɪdʒi/ n. efigie f.
effort /'ɛfərt/ n. esfuerzo m.
effrontery /ɪ'frʌntəri/ n. impudencia f.
effusive /ɪ'fyusɪv/ a. efusivo.
egg /ɛg/ n. huevo m. **fried e.,** huevo frito. **soft-boiled e.,** h. pasado por agua. **scrambled eggs,** huevos revueltos.
eggplant /'ɛg,plænt/ n. berenjena f.
egg white clara de huevo f.
egoism /'igou,ɪzəm/ **egotism** n. egoísmo m.
egoist /'igouɪst/ **egotist** n. egoísta m. & f.
egotism /'igə,tɪzəm/ n. egotismo m.
egotist /'igətɪst/ n. egotista m. & f.
Egypt /'idʒɪpt/ n. Egipto m.

Egyptian /ɪ'dʒɪpʃən/ a. & n. egipcio -ia.
eight /eit/ a. & pron. ocho.
eighteen /'ei'tin/ a. & pron. dieciocho.
eighth /eitθ, eiθ/ a. octavo.
eightieth /'eitiiθ/ n. octogésimo m.
eighty /'eiti/ a. & pron. ochenta.
either /'iðər/ a. & pron. **1.** cualquiera de los dos. —adv. **2.** tampoco. —conj. **3. either... or,** o... o.
ejaculate /ɪ'dʒækyə,leit/ v. exclamar; eyacular.
ejaculation /ɪ,dʒækyə'leiʃən/ n. eyaculación f.
eject /ɪ'dʒɛkt/ v. expeler; eyectar.
ejection /ɪ'dʒɛkʃən/ n. expulsión f.; eyección f.
elaborate /a ɪ'læbərɪt; v -ə,reit/ a. **1.** elaborado. —v. **2.** elaborar; ampliar.
elapse /ɪ'læps/ v. transcurrir; pasar.
elastic /ɪ'læstɪk/ a. & n. elástico m.
elasticity /ɪlæ'stɪsɪti/ n. elasticidad f.
elate /ɪ'leit/ v. exaltar.
elation /ɪ'leiʃən/ n. exaltación f.
elbow /'ɛlbou/ n. codo m.
elder /'ɛldər/ a. **1.** mayor. —n. **2.** anciano -na.
elderly /'ɛldərli/ a. de edad.
eldest /'ɛldɪst/ a. mayor.
elect /ɪ'lɛkt/ v. elegir.
election /ɪ'lɛkʃən/ n. elección f.
elective /ɪ'lɛktɪv/ a. electivo.
electorate /ɪ'lɛktərɪt/ n. electorado m.
electric /ɪ'lɛktrɪk/ **electrical** a. eléctrico.
electrician /ɪlɛk'trɪʃən/ n. electricista m. & f.
electricity /ɪlɛk'trɪsɪti/ n. electricidad f.
electrocardiogram /ɪ,lɛktrou'kɑrdiə,græm/ n. electrocardiograma m.
electrocute /ɪ'lɛktrə,kyut/ v. electrocutar.
electrode /ɪ'lɛktroud/ n. electrodo m.
electrolysis /ɪlɛk'trɒləsɪs/ n. electrólisis f.
electron /ɪ'lɛktrɒn/ n. electrón m.
electronic /ɪlɛk'trɒnɪk/ a. electrónico.
electronics /ɪlɪk'trɒnɪks/ n. electrónica f.
elegance /'ɛlɪgəns/ n. elegancia f.
elegant /'ɛlɪgənt/ a. elegante.
elegy /'ɛlɪdʒi/ n. elegía f.
element /'ɛləmənt/ n. elemento m.
elemental /,ɛlə'mɛntl/ a. elemental.
elementary /,ɛlə'mɛntəri/ a. elemental.
elephant /'ɛləfənt/ n. elefante -ta.
elevate /'ɛlə,veit/ v. elevar.
elevation /,ɛlə'veiʃən/ n. elevación f.
elevator /'ɛlə,veitər/ n. ascensor m.
eleven /ɪ'lɛvən/ a. & pron. once.
eleventh /ɪ'lɛvənθ/ a. undécimo.
eleventh hour último minuto m.
elf /ɛlf/ n. duende m.
elicit /ɪ'lɪsɪt/ v. sacar; despertar.
eligibility /,ɛlɪdʒə'bɪlɪti/ n. elegibilidad f
eligible /'ɛlɪdʒəbəl/ a. elegible.
eliminate /ɪ'lɪmə,neit/ v. eliminar.
elimination /ɪ,lɪmə'neiʃən/ n. eliminación f.
elixir /ɪ'lɪksər/ n. elixir m.
elk /ɛlk/ n. alce m., anta m.
elm /ɛlm/ n. olmo m.
elocution /,ɛlə'kyuʃən/ n. elocución f.
elongate /ɪ'lɔŋgeit/ v. alargar.
elope /ɪ'loup/ v. fugarse.
eloquence /'ɛləkwəns/ n. elocuencia f.
eloquent /'ɛləkwənt/ a. elocuente.
eloquently /'ɛləkwəntli/ adv. elocuentemente.
else /ɛls/ adv. más. **someone e.,** otra persona. **something e.,** otra cosa. **or e.,** de otro modo.
elsewhere /'ɛls,wɛər/ adv. en otra parte.

elucidate /ɪ'lusɪ,deit/ v. elucidar.
elude /ɪ'lud/ v. eludir.
elusive /ɪ'lusɪv/ a. evasivo.
emaciated /ɪ'meiʃi,eitɪd/ a. demacrado, enflaquecido.
e-mail /'i,meil/ n. correo electrónico m.
emanate /'ɛmə,neit/ v. emanar.
emancipate /ɪ'mænsə,peit/ v. emancipar.
emancipation /ɪ,mænsə'peiʃən/ n. emancipación f.
emancipator /ɪ'mænsə,peitər/ n. libertador -ra.
embalm /ɛm'bɑm/ v. embalsamar.
embankment /ɛm'bæŋkmənt/ n. malecón, dique m.
embargo /ɛm'bɑrgou/ n. embargo m.
embark /ɛm'bɑrk/ v. embarcar.
embarrass /ɛm'bærəs/ v. avergonzar; turbar.
embarrassing /ɛm'bærəsɪŋ/ a. penoso, vergonzoso.
embarrassment /ɛm'bærəsmənt/ n. turbación f.; vergüenza f.
embassy /'ɛmbəsi/ n. embajada f.
embellish /ɛm'bɛlɪʃ/ v. hermosear, embellecer.
embellishment /ɛm'bɛlɪʃmənt/ n. embellecimiento m.
embezzle /ɛm'bɛzəl/ v. desfalcar, malversar.
emblem /'ɛmbləm/ n. emblema m.
embody /ɛm'bɒdi/ v. incorporar; personificar.
embrace /ɛm'breis/ n. **1.** abrazo m. —v. **2.** abrazar.
embroider /ɛm'brɔidər/ v. bordar.
embroidery /ɛm'brɔidəri, -dri/ n. bordado m.
embryo /'ɛmbri,ou/ n. embrión m.
embryonic /,ɛmbri'ɒnɪk/ a. embrionario.
emerald /'ɛmərəld/ n. esmeralda f.
emerge /ɪ'mɜrdʒ/ v. salir.
emergency /ɪ'mɜrdʒənsi/ n. emergencia f.
emergency brake freno de auxilio m.
emergency exit salida de urgencia f.
emergency landing aterrizaje forzoso m.
emergent /ɪ'mɜrdʒənt/ a. emergente.
emery /'ɛməri/ n. esmeril m.
emetic /ɪ'mɛtɪk/ n. emético m.
emigrant /'ɛmɪgrənt/ a. & n. emigrante m. & f.
emigrate /'ɛmɪ,greit/ v. emigrar.
emigration /,ɛmə'greiʃən/ n. emigración f.
eminence /'ɛmənəns/ n. altura; eminencia f.
eminent /'ɛmənənt/ a. eminente.
emissary /'ɛmə,sɛri/ n. emisario m.
emission /ɪ'mɪʃən/ n. emisión f.
emit /ɪ'mɪt/ v. emitir.
emolument /ɪ'mɒlyəmənt/ n. emolumento m.
emotion /ɪ'mouʃən/ n. emoción f.
emotional /ɪ'mouʃənl/ a. emocional; sentimental.
emperor /'ɛmpərər/ n. emperador m.
emphasis /'ɛmfəsɪs/ n. énfasis m. or f.
emphasize /'ɛmfə,saiz/ v. acentuar, recalcar.
emphatic /ɛm'fætɪk/ a. enfático.
empire /'ɛmpaiər/ n. imperio m.
empirical /ɛm'pɪrɪkəl/ a. empírico.
employ /ɛm'plɔi/ v. emplear.
employee /ɛm'plɔii/ n. empleado -da.
employer /ɛm'plɔiər/ n. patrón -ona.
employment /ɛm'plɔimənt/ n. empleo m.
employment agency agencia de colocaciones f.
empower /ɛm'pauər/ v. autorizar.
emptiness /'ɛmptinɪs/ n. vaciedad; futilidad f.
empty /'ɛmpti/ a. **1.** vacío. —v. **2.** vaciar.
emulate /'ɛmyə,leit/ v. emular.
emulsion /ɪ'mʌlʃən/ n. emulsión f.

enable /ɛn'eibəl/ v. capacitar; permitir.
enact /ɛn'ækt/ v. promulgar, decretar.
enactment /ɛn'æktmənt/ n. ley f., estatuto m.
enamel /ɪ'næməl/ n. **1.** esmalte m. —v. **2.** esmaltar.
enamored /ɪ'næmərd/ a. enamorado.
enchant /ɛn'tʃænt/ v. encantar.
enchantment /ɛn'tʃæntmənt/ n. encanto m.
encircle /ɛn'sɜrkəl/ v. circundar.
enclose /ɛn'klouz/ v. encerrar. **enclosed,** (in letter) adjunto.
enclosure /ɛn'klouʒər/ n. recinto m.; (in letter) incluso m.
encompass /ɛn'kʌmpəs/ v. circundar.
encounter /ɛn'kauntər/ n. **1.** encuentro m. —v. **2.** encontrar.
encourage /ɛn'kɜridʒ/ v. animar.
encouragement /ɛn'kɜridʒmənt/ n. estímulo m.
encroach /ɛn'kroutʃ/ v. usurpar; meterse.
encryption /ɛn'krɪpʃən/ n. encriptación f., cifrado m.
encyclical /ɛn'sɪklɪkəl/ n. encíclica f.
encyclopedia /ɛn,saiklə'pidiə/ n. enciclopedia f.
end /ɛnd/ n. **1.** fin, término, cabo; extremo; (aim) propósito m. —v. **2.** acabar; terminar.
endanger /ɛn'deindʒər/ v. poner en peligro.
endear /ɛn'diər/ v. hacer querer.
endeavor /ɛn'dɛvər/ n. **1.** esfuerzo m. —v. **2.** esforzarse.
ending /'ɛndɪŋ/ n. conclusión f.
endless /'ɛndlɪs/ a. sin fin.
endocrine gland /'ɛndəkrɪn/ glándula endocrina f.
endorse /ɛn'dɔrs/ v. endosar; apoyar.
endorsement /ɛn'dɔrsmənt/ n. endoso m.
endow /ɛn'dau/ v. dotar, fundar.
endowment /ɛn'daumənt/ n. dotación f., fundación f.
endurance /ɛn'durəns/ n. resistencia f.
endure /ɛn'dur/ v. soportar, resistir, aguantar.
enema /'ɛnəmə/ n. enema; lavativa f.
enemy /'ɛnəmi/ n. enemigo -ga.
energetic /,ɛnər'dʒɛtɪk/ a. enérgico.
energy /'ɛnərdʒi/ n. energía f.
enervate /'ɛnər,veit/ v. enervar.
enervation /,ɛnər'veiʃən/ n. enervación f.
enfold /ɛn'fould/ v. envolver.
enforce /ɛn'fɔrs/ v. ejecutar.
enforcement /ɛn'fɔrsmənt/ n. ejecución f.
engage /ɛn'geidʒ/ v. emplear; ocupar.
engaged /ɛn'geidʒd/ a. (to marry) prometido.
engagement /ɛn'geidʒmənt/ n. combate; compromiso; contrato m.; cita f.
engine /'ɛndʒən/ n. máquina f. (railroad) locomotora f.
engineer /,ɛndʒə'nɪər/ n. ingeniero -ra; maquinista m.
engineering /,ɛndʒə'nɪərɪŋ/ n. ingeniería f.
England /'ɪŋglənd/ n. Inglaterra f.
English /'ɪŋglɪʃ/ a. & n. inglés -esa.
English Channel Canal de la Mancha m.
Englishman /'ɪŋglɪʃmən/ n. inglés m.
Englishwoman /'ɪŋglɪʃ,wumən/ n. inglesa f.
engrave /ɛn'greiv/ v. grabar.
engraver /ɛn'greivər/ n. grabador m.
engraving /ɛn'greivɪŋ/ n. grabado m.
engross /ɛn'grous/ v. absorber.
enhance /ɛn'hæns/ v. aumentar en valor; realzar.
enigma /ə'nɪgmə/ n. enigma m.
enigmatic /,ɛnɪg'mætɪk/ a. enigmático.
enjoy /ɛn'dʒɔi/ v. gozar de; disfrutar de. **e. oneself,** divertirse.
enjoyable /ɛn'dʒɔiəbəl/ a. agradable.
enjoyment /ɛn'dʒɔimənt/ n. goce m.

enlarge /ɛn'lɑrdʒ/ v. agrandar; ampliar.
enlargement /ɛn'lɑrdʒmənt/ n. ensanchamiento m., ampliación f.
enlarger /ɛn'lɑrdʒər/ n. amplificador m.
enlighten /ɛn'laitn/ v. informar.
enlightenment /ɛn'laitnmənt/ n. esclarecimiento m.; cultura f.
enlist /ɛn'lɪst/ v. reclutar; alistarse.
enlistment /ɛn'lɪstmənt/ n. alistamiento m.
enliven /ɛn'laivən/ v. avivar.
enmesh /ɛn'mɛʃ/ v. entrampar.
enmity /'ɛnmɪti/ n. enemistad f.
enormity /ɪ'nɔrmɪti/ v. enormidad f.
enormous /ɪ'nɔrməs/ a. enorme.
enough /ɪ'nʌf/ a. & adv. bastante. **to be e.,** bastar.
enrage /ɛn'reidʒ/ v. enfurecer.
enrich /ɛn'rɪtʃ/ v. enriquecer.
enroll /ɛn'roul/ v. registrar; matricularse.
enrollment /ɛn'roulmənt/ n. matriculación f.
ensign /'ɛnsən/ n. bandera f.; (naval) subteniente m.
enslave /ɛn'sleiv/ v. esclavizar.
ensue /ɛn'su/ v. seguir, resultar.
entail /ɛn'teil/ v. acarrear, ocasionar.
entangle /ɛn'tæŋgəl/ v. enredar.
enter /'ɛntər/ v. entrar.
enterprise /'ɛntər,praiz/ n. empresa f.
enterprising /'ɛntər,praizɪŋ/ a. emprendedor.
entertain /,ɛntər'tein/ v. entretener; divertir.
entertainment /,ɛntər'teinmənt/ n. entretenimiento m.; diversión f.
enthrall /ɛn'θrɔl/ v. esclavizar; cautivar.
enthusiasm /ɛn'θuzi,æzəm/ n. entusiasmo m.
enthusiast /ɛn'θuzi,æst, -ɪst/ n. entusiasta m. & f.
enthusiastic /ɛn,θuzi'æstɪk/ a. entusiasmado.
entice /ɛn'tais/ v. inducir.
entire /ɛn'taiər/ a. entero.
entirely /ɛn'taiərli/ adv. enteramente.
entirety /ɛn'taiərti/ n. totalidad f.
entitle /ɛn'taitl/ v. autorizar; (book) titular.
entity /'ɛntɪti/ n. entidad f.
entrails /'ɛntreilz/ n. entrañas f.pl.
entrance /ɛn'træns/ n. entrada f.
entrance examination examen de ingreso m.
entrant /'ɛntrənt/ n. competidor -ra.
entreat /ɛn'trit/ v. rogar, suplicar.
entreaty /ɛn'triti/ n. ruego m., súplica f.
entrench /ɛn'trɛntʃ/ v. atrincherar.
entrust /ɛn'trʌst/ v. confiar.
entry /'ɛntri/ n. entrada f.; Com. partida f.
entry blank hoja de inscripción f.
enumerate /ɪ'numə,reit/ v. enumerar.
enumeration /ɪ,numə'reiʃən/ n. enumeración f.
enunciate /ɪ'nʌnsi,eit/ v. enunciar.
enunciation /ɪ,nʌnsi'eiʃən/ n. enunciación f.
envelop /ɛn'vɛləp/ v. envolver.
envelope /'ɛnvə,loup/ n. sobre m.; cubierta f.
enviable /'ɛnviəbəl/ a. envidiable.
envious /'ɛnviəs/ a. envidioso.
environment /ɛn'vairənmənt/ n. ambiente m.
environmentalist /ɛn,vairən'mɛntlɪst/ n. ambientalista, ecologista m. & f.
environmental protection /ɛn,vairən'mɛntəl/ protección del ambiente.
environs /ɛn'vairənz/ n. alrededores m.
envoy /'ɛnvɔi/ n. enviado m.
envy /'ɛnvi/ n. **1.** envidia f. —v. **2.** envidiar.
eon /'iən/ n. eón m.

ephemeral /ɪ'fɛmərəl/ a. efímero.
epic /'ɛpɪk/ a. **1.** épico. —n. **2.** epopeya f.
epicure /'ɛpɪ,kyur/ n. epicúreo m.
epidemic /,ɛpɪ'dɛmɪk/ a. **1.** epidémico. —n. **2.** epidemia f.
epidermis /,ɛpɪ'dɜrmɪs/ n. epidermis f.
epigram /'ɛpɪ,græm/ n. epigrama f.
epilepsy /'ɛpə,lɛpsi/ n. epilepsia f.
epilogue /'ɛpə,lɔg/ n. epílogo m.
episode /'ɛpə,soud/ n. episodio m.
epistle /ɪ'pɪsəl/ n. epístola f.
epitaph /'ɛpɪ,tæf/ n. epitafio m.
epithet /'ɛpə,θɛt/ n. epíteto m.
epitome /ɪ'pɪtəmi/ n. epítome m.
epoch /'ɛpək/ n. época, era f.
Epsom salts /'ɛpsəm/ n.pl. sal de la Higuera f.
equal /'ikwəl/ a. & n. **1.** igual m. —v. **2.** igualar; equivaler.
equality /ɪ'kwɒlɪti/ n. igualdad f.
equalize /'ikwə,laiz/ v. igualar.
equanimity /,ikwə'nɪmɪti/ n. ecuanimidad f.
equate /ɪ'kweit/ v. igualar.
equation /ɪ'kweiʒən/ n. ecuación f.
equator /ɪ'kweitər/ n. ecuador m.
equatorial /,ikwə'tɔriəl/ a. ecuatorial.
equestrian /ɪ'kwɛstriən/ n. **1.** jinete m. —a. **2.** ecuestre.
equilibrium /,ikwə'lɪbriəm/ n. equilibrio m.
equinox /'ikwə,nɒks/ n. equinoccio m.
equip /ɪ'kwɪp/ v. equipar.
equipment /ɪ'kwɪpmənt/ n. equipo m.
equitable /'ɛkwɪtəbəl/ a. equitativo.
equity /'ɛkwɪti/ n. equidad, justicia f.
equivalent /ɪ'kwɪvələnt/ a. & n. equivalente m.
equivocal /ɪ'kwɪvəkəl/ a. equívoco, ambiguo.
era /'ɪərə, 'ɛrə/ n. era, época, edad f.
eradicate /ɪ'rædɪ,keit/ v. extirpar.
erase /ɪ'reis/ v. borrar.
eraser /ɪ'reisər/ n. borrador m.
erasure /ɪ'reiʃər/ n. borradura f.
erect /ɪ'rɛkt/ a. **1.** derecho, erguido. —v. **2.** erigir.
erection /ɪ'rɛkʃən/ **erectness** n. erección f.
ermine /'ɜrmɪn/ n. armiño m.
erode /ɪ'roud/ v. corroer.
erosion /ɪ'rouʒən/ n. erosión f.
erotic /ɪ'rɒtɪk/ a. erótico.
err /ɜr, ɛr/ v. equivocarse.
errand /'ɛrənd/ n. encargo, recado m.
errant /'ɛrənt/ a. errante.
erratic /ɪ'rætɪk/ a. errático.
erroneous /ə'rouniəs/ a. erróneo.
error /'ɛrər/ n. error m.
erudite /'ɛryu,dait/ a. erudito.
erudition /,ɛryu'dɪʃən/ n. erudición f.
eruption /ɪ'rʌpʃən/ n. erupción, irrupción f.
erysipelas /,ɛrə'sɪpələs/ n. erisipela f.
escalate /'ɛskə,leit/ v. escalar; intensificarse.
escalator /'ɛskə,leitər/ n. escalera mecánica f.
escapade /'ɛskə,peid/ n. escapada; correría f.
escape /ɪ'skeip/ n. **1.** fuga, huída f. **fire e.,** escalera de salvamento. —v. **2.** escapar; fugarse.
eschew /ɛs'tʃu/ v. evadir.
escort /n 'ɛskɔrt; v ɪ'skɔrt/ n. **1.** escolta f. —v. **2.** escoltar.
escrow /'ɛskrou/ n. plica f.
escutcheon /ɪ'skʌtʃən/ n. escudo de armas m.
esophagus /ɪ'sɒfəgəs/ n. esófago m.
esoteric /,ɛsə'tɛrɪk/ a. esotérico.
especially /ɪ'spɛʃəli/ adv. especialmente.
espionage /'ɛspiə,nɑʒ/ n. espionaje m.
espresso /ɛ'sprɛsou/ n. café exprés, m.
essay /'ɛsei/ n. ensayo m.

essayist /'ɛseiɪst/ n. ensayista m. & f.

essence /'ɛsəns/ n. esencia f.; perfume m.

essential /ə'sɛntʃəl/ a. esencial.

essentially /ə'sɛntʃəli/ adv. esencialmente.

establish /ɪ'stæblɪʃ/ v. establecer.

establishment /ɪ'stæblɪʃmənt/ n. establecimiento m.

estate /ɪ'steit/ n. estado m.; hacienda f.; bienes m.pl.

esteem /ɪ'stim/ n. 1. estima f. —v. 2. estimar.

estimable /'ɛstəməbəl/ a. estimable.

estimate /n 'ɛstə,mit/ v -,meit/ n. 1. cálculo; presupuesto m. —v. 2. estimar.

estimation /,ɛstə'meiʃən/ n. estimación f.; cálculo m.

estrange /ɪ'streindʒ/ v. extrañar; enajenar.

estuary /'ɛstʃu,ɛri/ n. estuario m.

etch /ɛtʃ/ v. grabar al agua fuerte.

etching /'ɛtʃɪŋ/ n. aguafuerte.

eternal /ɪ'tɜrnl/ a. eterno.

eternity /ɪ'tɜrnɪti/ n. eternidad f.

ether /'iθər/ n. éter m.

ethereal /ɪ'θɪriəl/ a. etéreo.

ethical /'ɛθɪkəl/ a. ético.

ethics /'ɛθɪks/ n. ética f.

ethnic /'ɛθnɪk/ a. étnico.

etiquette /'ɛtɪkɪt/ n. etiqueta f.

etymology /,ɛtə'mɒlədʒi/ n. etimología f.

eucalyptus /,yukə'lɪptəs/ n. eucalipto m.

eugenic /yu'dʒɛnɪk/ a. eugenésico.

eugenics /yu'dʒɛnɪks/ n. eugenesia f.

eulogize /'yulə,dʒaiz/ v. elogiar.

eulogy /'yulədʒi/ n. elogio m.

eunuch /'yunək/ n. eunuco m.

euphonious /yu'founiəs/ a. eufónico.

Europe /'yurəp/ n. Europa f.

European /,yurə'piən/ a. & n. europeo -pea.

euthanasia /,yuθə'neiʒə, -ʒiə, -ziə/ n. eutanasia f.

evacuate /ɪ'vækyu,eit/ v. evacuar.

evade /ɪ'veid/ v. evadir.

evaluate /ɪ'vælyu,eit/ v. evaluar.

evaluation /ɪ,vælyu'eiʃən/ n. valoración f.

evangelist /ɪ'vændʒəlɪst/ n. evangelista m. & f.

evaporate /ɪ'væpə,reit/ v. evaporarse.

evaporation /ɪ,væpə'reiʃən/ n. evaporación f.

evasion /ɪ'veiʒən/ n. evasión f.

evasive /ɪ'veisɪv/ a. evasivo.

eve /iv/ n. víspera f.

even /'ivən/ a. 1. llano; igual. —adv. 2. aun; hasta. **not e.**, ni siquiera.

evening /'ivnɪŋ/ n. noche, tarde f. **good e.!** ¡buenas tardes! ¡buenas noches!

evening class clase nocturna f.

evenness /'ivənnɪs/ n. uniformidad f.

even number número par m.

event /ɪ'vɛnt/ n. acontecimiento, suceso m.

eventful /ɪ'vɛntfəl/ a. memorable.

eventual /ɪ'vɛntʃuəl/ a. eventual.

ever /'ɛvər/ adv. alguna vez; (after not) nunca. **e. since**, desde que.

everlasting /,ɛvər'læstɪŋ/ a. eterno.

every /'ɛvri/ a. cada, todos los.

everybody /'ɛvri,bɒdi, -,bʌdi/ pron. todo el mundo; cada uno.

everyday /'ɛvri,dei/ a. ordinario, de cada día.

everyone /'ɛvri,wʌn/ pron. todo el mundo; cada uno; cada cual.

everything /'ɛvri,θɪŋ/ pron. todo m.

everywhere /'ɛvri,wɛər/ adv. por todas partes, en todas partes.

evict /ɪ'vɪkt/ v. expulsar.

eviction /ɪ'vɪkʃən/ n. evicción f.

evidence /'ɛvɪdəns/ n. evidencia f.

evident /'ɛvɪdənt/ a. evidente.

evidently /'ɛvɪdəntli/ adv. evidentemente.

evil /'ivəl/ a. 1. malo; maligno. —n. 2. mal m.

evince /ɪ'vɪns/ v. revelar.

evoke /ɪ'vouk/ v. evocar.

evolution /,ɛvə'luʃən/ n. evolución f.

evolve /ɪ'vɒlv/ v. desenvolver; desarrollar.

ewe /yu/ n. oveja f.

exact /ɪg'zækt/ a. 1. exacto. —v. 2. exigir.

exacting /ɪg'zæktɪŋ/ a. exigente.

exactly /ɪg'zæktli/ adv. exactamente.

exaggerate /ɪg'zædʒə,reit/ v. exagerar.

exaggeration /ɪg,zædʒə'reiʃən/ n. exageración f.

exalt /ɪg'zɔlt/ v. exaltar.

exaltation /,ɛgzɔl'teiʃən/ n. exaltación f.

examination /ɪg,zæmə'neiʃən/ n. examen m.; (legal) interrogatorio m.

examine /ɪg'zæmɪn/ v. examinar.

example /ɪg'zæmpəl/ n. ejemplo m.

exasperate /ɪg'zæspə,reit/ v. exasperar.

exasperation /ɪg,zæspə'reiʃən/ n. exasperación f.

excavate /'ɛkskə,veit/ v. excavar, cavar.

exceed /ɪk'sid/ v. exceder.

exceedingly /ɪk'sidɪŋli/ adv. sumamente, extremadamente.

excel /ɪk'sɛl/ v. sobresalir.

excellence /'ɛksələns/ n. excelencia f.

Excellency /'ɛksələnsi/ n. (title) Excelencia f.

excellent /'ɛksələnt/ a. excelente.

except /ɪk'sɛpt/ prep. 1. salvo, excepto. —v. 2. exceptuar.

exception /ɪk'sɛpʃən/ n. excepción f.

exceptional /ɪk'sɛpʃənl/ a. excepcional.

excerpt /'ɛksɜrpt/ n. extracto m.

excess /ɪk'sɛs, 'ɛksɛs/ n. exceso m.

excessive /ɪk'sɛsɪv/ a. excesivo.

exchange /ɪks'tʃeindʒ/ n. 1. cambio; canje m. **stock e.**, bolsa f. **telephone e.**, central telefónica. —v. 2. cambiar, canjear, intercambiar.

exchangeable /ɪks'tʃeindʒəbəl/ a. cambiable.

exchange rate tipo de cambio m.

excise /n 'ɛksaiz; v ɪk'saiz/ n. 1. sisa f. —v. 2. extirpar.

excite /ɪk'sait/ v. agitar; provocar; emocionar.

excitement /ɪk'saitmənt/ n. agitación, conmoción f.

exciting /ɪk'saitɪŋ/ a. emocionante.

exclaim /ɪk'skleim/ v. exclamar.

exclamation /,ɛksklə'meiʃən/ n. exclamación f.

exclamation mark punto de admiración m.

exclude /ɪk'sklud/ v. excluir.

exclusion /ɪk'skluʒən/ n. exclusión f.

exclusive /ɪk'sklusɪv/ a. exclusivo.

excommunicate /,ɛkskə'myunɪ,keit/ v. excomulgar, descomulgar.

excommunication /,ɛkskə,myunɪ'keiʃən/ n. excomunión f.

excrement /'ɛkskrəmənt/ n. excremento m.

excruciating /ɪk'skruʃi,eitɪŋ/ a. penosísimo.

exculpate /'ɛkskʌl,peit/ v. exculpar.

excursion /ɪk'skɜrʒən/ n. excursión, jira f.

excuse /n ɪk'skyus; v ɪk'skyuz/ n. 1. excusa f. —v. 2. excusar, perdonar, disculpar; dispensar.

execrable /'ɛksɪkrəbəl/ a. execrable.

execute /'ɛksɪ,kyut/ v. ejecutar.

execution /,ɛksɪ'kyuʃən/ n. ejecución f.

executioner /,ɛksɪ'kyuʃənər/ n. verdugo m.

executive /ɪg'zɛkyətɪv/ a. & n. ejecutivo -va.

executor /ɪg'zɛkyətər/ n. testamentario m.

exemplary /ɪg'zɛmpləri/ a. ejemplar.

exemplify /ɪg'zɛmplə,fai/ v. ejemplificar.

exempt /ɪg'zɛmpt/ a. 1. exento. —v. 2. exentar.

exercise /'ɛksər,saiz/ n. 1. ejercicio m. —v. 2. ejercitar.

exert /ɪg'zɜrt/ v. esforzar.

exertion /ɪg'zɜrʃən/ n. esfuerzo m.

exhale /ɛks'heil/ v. exhalar.

exhaust /ɪg'zɔst/ n. 1. Auto. escape m. —v. 2. agotar.

exhaustion /ɪg'zɔstʃən/ n. agotamiento m.

exhaustive /ɪg'zɔstɪv/ a. exhaustivo.

exhaust pipe tubo de escape m.

exhibit /ɪg'zɪbɪt/ n. 1. exhibición, exposición f. —v. 2. exhibir.

exhibition /,ɛksə'bɪʃən/ n. exhibición f.

exhilarate /ɪg'zɪlə,reit/ v. alegrar; estimular.

exhort /ɪg'zɔrt/ v. exhortar.

exhortation /,ɛgzɔr'teiʃən/ n. exhortación f.

exhume /ɪg'zum/ v. exhumar.

exigency /'ɛksɪdʒənsi/ n. exigencia f., urgencia f.

exile /n 'ɛgzail/ n. 1. destierro m., (person) desterrado m. —v. 2. desterrar.

exist /ɪg'zɪst/ v. existir.

existence /ɪg'zɪstəns/ n. existencia f.

existent /ɪg'zɪstənt/ a. existente.

exit /'ɛgzɪt, 'ɛksɪt/ n. salida f.

exodus /'ɛksədəs/ n. éxodo m.

exonerate /ɪg'zɒnə,reit/ v. exonerar.

exorbitant /ɪg'zɔrbɪtənt/ a. exorbitante.

exorcise /'ɛksɔr,saiz/ v. exorcizar.

exotic /ɪg'zɒtɪk/ a. exótico.

expand /ɪk'spænd/ v. dilatar; ensanchar.

expanse /ɪk'spæns/ n. espacio m.; extensión f.

expansion /ɪk'spænʃən/ n. expansión f.

expansion slot ranura de expansión f.

expansive /ɪk'spænsɪv/ a. expansivo.

expatiate /ɪk'speiʃi,eit/ v. espaciar.

expatriate /n, a ɛks'peitriɪt; v ɛks'peitri,eit/ n. & a. 1. expatriado m. —v. 2. expatriar.

expect /ɪk'spɛkt/ v. esperar; contar con.

expectancy /ɪk'spɛktənsi/ n. esperanza f.

expectation /,ɛkspɛk'teiʃən/ n. esperanza f.

expectorate /ɪk'spɛktə,reit/ v. expectorar.

expediency /ɪk'spidiənsi/ n. conveniencia f.

expedient /ɪk'spidiənt/ a. 1. oportuno. —n. 2. expediente m.

expedite /'ɛkspɪ,dait/ v. acelerar, despachar.

expedition /,ɛkspɪ'dɪʃən/ n. expedición f.

expel /ɪk'spɛl/ v. expeler; expulsar.

expend /ɪk'spɛnd/ v. desembolsar, expender.

expenditure /ɪk'spɛndɪtʃər/ n. desembolso; gasto m.

expense /ɪk'spɛns/ n. gasto m.; costa f.

expensive /ɪk'spɛnsɪv/ a. caro, costoso.

expensively /ɪk'spɛnsɪvli/ adv. costosamente.

experience /ɪk'spɪriəns/ n. 1. experiencia f. —v. 2. experimentar.

experienced /ɪk'spɪriənst/ a. experimentado, perito.

experiment /n ɪk'spɛrəmənt; v -,mɛnt/ n. 1. experimento m. —v. 2. experimentar.

experimental /ɪk,spɛrə'mɛntl/ a. experimental.

expert /'ɛkspɜrt/ a. & n. experto -ta.

expertise /,ɛkspər'tiz/ n. pericia f.

expiate /'ɛkspi,eit/ v. expiar.

expiration /,ɛkspə'reiʃən/ n. expiración f.

expiration date fecha de caducidad f.

expire /ɪk'spaiər/ v. expirar; Com. vencerse.

explain /ɪk'splein/ v. explicar.

explanation /,ɛksplə'neiʃən/ n. explicación f.

explanatory /ɪk'splænə,tɔri/ a. explicativo.

expletive /'ɛksplɪtɪv/ n. 1. interjección f. —a. 2. expletivo.

explicit /ɪk'splɪsɪt/ a. explícito, claro.

explode /ɪk'sploud/ v. estallar, volar; refutar.

exploit /ɪk'splɔit/ n. 1. hazaña f. —v. 2. explotar.

exploitation /,ɛksplɔi'teiʃən/ n. explotación f.

exploration /,ɛksplə'reiʃən/ n. exploración f.

exploratory /ɪk'splɔrə,tɔri/ a. exploratorio.

explore /ɪk'splɔr/ v. explorar.

explorer /ɪk'splɔrər/ n. explorador -ra.

explosion /ɪk'splouʒən/ n. explosión f.

explosive /ɪk'splousɪv/ a. explosivo.

export /n 'ɛkspɔrt; v ɪk'spɔrt/ n. 1. exportación f. —v. 2. exportar.

exportation /,ɛkspɔr'teiʃən/ n. exportación f.

expose /ɪk'spouz/ v. exponer; descubrir.

exposition /,ɛkspə'zɪʃən/ n. exposición f.

expository /ɪk'spɒzɪ,tɔri/ a. expositivo.

expostulate /ɪk'spɒstʃə,leit/ v. altercar.

exposure /ɪk'spouʒər/ n. exposición f.

expound /ɪk'spaund/ v. exponer, explicar.

express /ɪk'sprɛs/ a. & n. 1. expreso m. **e. company,** compañía de porteo. —v. 2. expresar.

expression /ɪk'sprɛʃən/ n. expresión f.

expressive /ɪk'sprɛsɪv/ a. expresivo.

expressly /ɪk'sprɛsli/ adv. expresamente.

expressman /ɪk'sprɛsmən, -,mæn/ n. empresario de expresos m.

expressway /ɪk'sprɛs,wei/ n. autopista f.

expropriate /ɛks'proupri,eit/ v. expropriar.

expulsion /ɪk'spʌlʃən/ n. expulsión f.

expunge /ɪk'spʌndʒ/ v. borrar, expurgar.

expurgate /'ɛkspər,geit/ v. expurgar.

exquisite /ɪk'skwɪzɪt/ a. exquisito.

extant /'ɛkstənt/ a. existente.

extemporaneous /ɪk,stɛmpə'reiniəs/ a. improvisado.

extend /ɪk'stɛnd/ v. extender.

extension /ɪk'stɛnʃən/ n. extensión f.

extensive /ɪk'stɛnsɪv/ a. extenso.

extensively /ɪk'stɛnsɪvli/ adv. extensamente.

extent /ɪk'stɛnt/ n. extensión f.; grado m. **to a certain e.,** hasta cierto punto.

extenuate /ɪk'stɛnyu,eit/ v. extenuar.

exterior /ɪk'stɪriər/ a. & n. exterior m.

exterminate /ɪk'stɜrmə,neit/ v. exterminar.

extermination /ɪk,stɜrmə'neiʃən/ n. exterminio m.

external /ɪk'stɜrnl/ a. externo, exterior.

extinct /ɪk'stɪŋkt/ a. extinto.

extinction /ɪk'stɪŋkʃən/ n. extinción f.

extinguish /ɪk'stɪŋgwɪʃ/ v. extinguir, apagar.

extol /ɪk'stoul/ v. alabar.

extort /ɪk'stɔrt/ v. exigir dinero sin derecho.

extortion /ɪk'stɔrʃən/ n. extorsión f.

extra /'ɛkstrə/ a. 1. extraordinario;

adicional. —*n.* **2.** (newspaper) extra *m.*
extract /*n* 'ɛkstrækt; *v* ɪk'strækt/ *n.* **1.** extracto *m.* —*v.* **2.** extraer.
extraction /ɪk'strækʃən/ *n.* extracción *f.*
extraneous /ɪk'streiniəs/ *a.* extraño; ajeno.
extraordinary /ɪk'strɔrdn̩ˌɛri/ *a.* extraordinario.
extravagance /ɪk'strævəgəns/ *n.* extravagancia *f.*
extravagant /ɪk'strævəgənt/ *a.* extravagante.
extreme /ɪk'strim/ *a.* & *n.* extremo *m.*
extremity /ɪk'strɛmɪti/ *n.* extremidad *f.*
extricate /'ɛkstrɪˌkeit/ *v.* desenredar.
exuberant /ɪg'zubərənt/ *a.* exuberante.
exude /ɪg'zud/ *v.* exudar.
exult /ɪg'zʌlt/ *v.* regocijarse.
exultant /ɪg'zʌltn̩t/ *a.* triunfante.
eye /ai/ *n.* **1.** ojo *m.* —*v.* **2.** ojear.
eyeball /'aiˌbɔl/ *n.* globo del ojo.
eyebrow /'aiˌbrau/ *n.* ceja *f.*
eyeglasses /'aiˌglæsɪz/ *n.* lentes *m.pl.*
eyelash /'aiˌlæʃ/ *n.* pestaña *f.*
eyelid /'aiˌlɪd/ *n.* párpado *m.*
eyeliner /'aiˌlainər/ *n.* lápiz de ojos *m.*
eye shadow *n.* sombra de ojos *f.*
eyesight /'aiˌsait/ *n.* vista *f.*

F

fable /'feibəl/ *n.* fábula; ficción *f.*
fabric /'fæbrɪk/ *n.* tejido *m.*, tela *f.*
fabricate /'fæbrɪˌkeit/ *v.* fabricar.
fabulous /'fæbyələs/ *a.* fabuloso.
façade /fə'sɑd/ *n.* fachada *f.*
face /feis/ *n.* **1.** cara *f.* **make faces,** hacer muecas. —*v.* **2.** encararse con. **f. the street,** dar a la calle.
facet /'fæsɪt/ *n.* faceta *f.*
facetious /fə'siʃəs/ *a.* chistoso.
facial /'feiʃəl/ *n.* **1.** masaje facial *m.* —*a.* **2.** facial.
facile /'fæsɪl/ *a.* fácil.
facilitate /fə'sɪlɪˌteit/ *v.* facilitar.
facility /fə'sɪlɪti/ *n.* facilidad *f.*
facsimile /fæk'sɪməli/ *n.* facsímile *m.*
fact /fækt/ *n.* hecho *m.* **in f.,** en realidad.
faction /'fækʃən/ *n.* facción *f.*
factor /'fæktər/ *n.* factor *m.*
factory /'fæktəri/ *n.* fábrica *f.*
factual /'fæktʃuəl/ *a.* verdadero.
faculty /'fækəlti/ *n.* facultad *f.*
fad /fæd/ *n.* boga; novedad *f.*
fade /feid/ *v.* desteñirse; (flowers) marchitarse.
fail /feil/ *n.* **1. without f.,** sin falla. —*v.* **2.** fallar; fracasar. **not to f. to,** no dejar de.
failure /'feilyər/ *n.* fracaso *m.*
faint /feint/ *a.* **1.** débil; vago; pálido. —*n.* **2.** desmayo *m.* —*v.* **3.** desmayarse.
faintly /'feintli/ *adv.* débilmente; indistintamente.
fair /fɛər/ *a.* **1.** razonable, justo; (hair) rubio; (weather) bueno. —*n.* **2.** feria *f.*
fairly /'fɛərli/ *adv.* imparcialmente; regularmente; claramente; bellamente.
fairness /'fɛərnɪs/ *n.* justicia *f.*
fair play juego limpio *m.*
fairway /'fɛərˌwei/ *n.* (golf) calle *f.*
fairy /'fɛəri/ *n.* hada *f.*, duende *m.*
faith /feiθ/ *n.* fe; confianza *f.*
faithful /'feiθfəl/ *a.* fiel.
fake /feik/ *a.* **1.** falso; postizo. —*n.* **2.** imitación; estafa *f.* —*v.* **3.** imitar; fingir.
faker /'feikœr/ *n.* imitador *m.*; farsante *m.*
falcon /'fɔlkən/ *n.* halcón *m.*
fall /fɔl/ *n.* **1.** caída; catarata *f.*; (season) otoño *m.*; (in price) baja *f.* —*v.* **2.** caer; bajar. **f. asleep,** dormirse; **f. in love,** enamorarse.
fallacious /fə'leiʃəs/ *a.* falaz.
fallacy /'fæləsi/ *n.* falacia *f.*
fallible /'fæləbəl/ *a.* falible.
fallout /'fɔlˌaut/ *n.* lluvia radiactiva, polvillo radiactivo.
fallow /'fælou/ *a.* sin cultivar; barbecho.
false /fɔls/ *a.* falso; postizo.
falsehood /'fɔlshʊd/ *n.* falsedad; mentira *f.*
falseness /'fɔlsnɪs/ *n.* falsedad, perfidia *f.*
false teeth /tiθ/ dentadura postiza *f.*
falsetto /fɔl'sɛtou/ *n.* falsete *m.*
falsification /ˌfɔlsəfɪ'keiʃən/ *n.* falsificación *f.*
falsify /'fɔlsəfai/ *v.* falsificar.
falter /'fɔltər/ *v.* vacilar; (in speech) tartamudear.
fame /feim/ *n.* fama *f.*
familiar /fə'mɪlyər/ *a.* familiar; conocido. **be f. with,** estar familiarizado con.
familiarity /fəˌmɪli'ærɪti/ *n.* familiaridad *f.*
familiarize /fə'mɪlyəˌraiz/ *v.* familiarizar.
family /'fæməli/ *n.* familia; especie *f.*
family name apellido *m.*
family tree árbol genealógico *m.*
famine /'fæmɪn/ *n.* hambre; carestía *f.*
famished /'fæmɪʃt/ *a.* hambriento.
famous /'feiməs/ *a.* famoso, célebre.
fan /fæn/ *n.* abanico; ventilador *m.* (sports) aficionado -da.
fanatic /fə'nætɪk/ *a.* & *n.* fanático -ca.
fanatical /fə'nætɪkəl/ *a.* fanático.
fanaticism /fə'nætəˌsɪzəm/ *n.* fanatismo *m.*
fanciful /'fænsɪfəl/ *a.* caprichoso; fantástico.
fancy /'fænsi/ *a.* **1.** fino, elegante. **f. foods,** novedades *f.pl.* —*n.* **2.** fantasía *f.*; capricho *m.* —*v.* **3.** imaginar.
fanfare /'fænfɛər/ *n.* fanfarria *f.*
fang /fæŋ/ *n.* colmillo *m.*
fan heater estufa de aire *f.*
fantastic /fæn'tæstɪk/ *a.* fantástico.
fantasy /'fæntəsi/ *n.* fantasía *f.*
FAQ /fæk/ *n.* (Frequently Asked Questions) preguntas más frecuentes *f. pl.*
far /fɑr/ *a.* **1.** lejano, distante. —*adv.* **2.** lejos. **how f.,** a qué distancia. **as f. as,** hasta. **so f., thus f.,** hasta aquí.
farce /fɑrs/ *n.* farsa *f.*
fare /fɛər/ *n.* pasaje *m.*
farewell /ˌfɛər'wɛl/ *n.* **1.** despedida *f.* **to say f.** despedirse. —*interj.* **2.** ¡adiós!
farfetched /'fɑr'fɛtʃt/ *a.* forzado, inverosímil.
farm /fɑrm/ *n.* **1.** granja; hacienda *f.* —*v.* **2.** cultivar, labrar la tierra.
farmer /'fɑrmər/ *n.* labrador, agricultor *m.*
farmhouse /'fɑrmˌhaus/ *n.* hacienda, alquería *f.*
farming /'fɑrmɪŋ/ *n.* agricultura *f.*; cultivo *m.*
fart /fɑrt/ *n.* *Colloq.* pedo *m.*
fascinate /'fæsəˌneit/ *v.* fascinar, embelesar.
fascination /ˌfæsə'neiʃən/ *n.* fascinación *f.*
fascism /'fæʃˌɪzəm/ *n.* fascismo *m.*
fashion /'fæʃən/ *n.* **1.** moda; costumbre; guisa *f.* **be in f.,** estilarse. —*v.* **2.** formar.
fashionable /'fæʃənəbəl/ *a.* de moda, en boga.
fashion show desfile de modas, pase de modelos *m.*
fast /fæst/ *a.* **1.** rápido, veloz; (watch) adelantado; (color) firme. —*adv.* **2.** ligero, de prisa. —*n.* **3.** ayuno *m.* —*v.* **4.** ayunar.
fasten /'fæsən/ *v.* afirmar; atar; fijar.
fastener /'fæsənər/ *n.* asegurador *m.*
fastidious /fæ'stɪdiəs/ *a.* melindroso.
fat /fæt/ *a.* **1.** gordo. —*n.* **2.** grasa, manteca *f.*
fatal /'feitl/ *a.* fatal.
fatality /fei'tælɪti/ *n.* fatalidad *f.*
fatally /'feitl̩i/ *adv.* fatalmente.
fate /feit/ *n.* destino *m.*; suerte *f.*
fateful /'feitfəl/ *a.* fatal; ominoso.
father /'fɑðər/ *n.* padre *m.*
fatherhood /'fɑðərˌhʊd/ *n.* paternidad *f.*
father-in-law /'fɑˌðər ɪn lɔ/ *n.* suegro *m.*
fatherland /'fɑðərˌlænd/ *n.* patria *f.*
fatherly /'fɑðərli/ *a.* **1.** paternal. —*adv.* **2.** paternalmente.
fathom /'fæðəm/ *n.* **1.** braza *f.* —*v.* **2.** sondar; *Fig.* penetrar en.
fatigue /fə'tig/ *n.* **1.** fatiga *f.*, cansancio *m.* —*v.* **2.** fatigar, cansar.
fatten /'fætn̩/ *v.* engordar, cebar.
faucet /'fɔsɪt/ *n.* grifo *m.*, llave *f.*
fault /fɔlt/ *n.* culpa *f.*; defecto *m.* **at f.,** culpable.
faultless /'fɔltlɪs/ *a.* sin tacha, perfecto.
faultlessly /'fɔltlɪsli/ *adv.* perfectamente.
faulty /'fɔlti/ *a.* defectuoso, imperfecto.
fauna /'fɔnə/ *n.* fauna *f.*
favor /'feivər/ *n.* **1.** favor *m.* —*v.* **2.** favorecer.
favorable /'feivərəbəl/ *a.* favorable.
favorite /'feivərɪt/ *a.* & *n.* favorito -ta.
favoritism /'feivərɪˌtɪzəm/ *n.* favoritismo *m.*
fawn /fɔn/ *n.* **1.** cervato *m.* —*v.* **2.** halagar, adular.
fax /fæks/ *n.* **1.** fax *m.* —*v.* **2.** mandar un fax.
faze /feiz/ *v.* desconcertar.
fear /fɪər/ *n.* **1.** miedo, temor *m.* —*v.* **2.** temer.
fearful /'fɪərfəl/ *a.* temeroso, medroso.
fearless /'fɪərlɪs/ *a.* intrépido; sin temor.
fearlessness /'fɪərlɪsnɪs/ *n.* intrepidez *f.*
feasible /'fizəbəl/ *a.* factible.
feast /fist/ *n.* banquete *m.*; fiesta *f.*
feat /fit/ *n.* hazaña *f.*; hecho *m.*
feather /'fɛðər/ *n.* pluma *f.*
feature /'fitʃər/ *n.* **1.** facción *f.*; rasgo *m.*; (movies) película principal *f.*, largometraje *m.* —*v.* **2.** presentar como atracción especial.
February /'fɛbruˌɛri, 'fɛbyu-/ *n.* febrero *m.*
federal /'fɛdərəl/ *a.* federal.
federation /ˌfɛdə'reiʃən/ *n.* confederación, federación *f.*
fee /fi/ *n.* honorarios *m.pl.*
feeble /'fibəl/ *a.* débil.
feeble-minded /'fibəl 'maindɪd/ *a.* imbécil.
feebleness /'fibəlnɪs/ *a.* debilidad *f.*
feed /fid/ *n.* **1.** pasto *m.* —*v.* **2.** alimentar; dar de comer. **fed up with,** harto de.
feedback /'fidˌbæk/ *n.* feedback *m.*, retroalimentación *f.*
feel /fil/ *n.* **1.** sensación *f.* —*v.* **2.** sentir; palpar. **f. like,** tener ganas de.
feeling /'filɪŋ/ *n.* sensación; sentimiento.
feign /fein/ *v.* fingir.
felicitate /fɪ'lɪsɪˌteit/ *v.* felicitar.
felicitous /fɪ'lɪsɪtəs/ *a.* feliz.
felicity /fɪ'lɪsɪti/ *n.* felicidad *f.*, dicha *f.*
feline /'filain/ *a.* felino.
fellow /'fɛlou/ *n.* compañero; socio *m.*; *Colloq.* tipo *m.*
fellowship /'fɛlouˌʃɪp/ *n.* compañerismo; (for study) beca *f.*
felon /'fɛlən/ *n.* reo *m.* & *f.*, felón -ona.
felony /'fɛləni/ *n.* felonía *f.*
felt /fɛlt/ *n.* fieltro *m.*
felt-tipped pen /'fɛlt ˌtɪpt/ rotulador *m.*
female /'fimeil/ *a.* & *n.* hembra *f.*
feminine /'fɛmənɪn/ *a.* femenino.
feminist /'fɛmənɪst/ *a.* & *n.* feminista *m.* & *f.*
fence /fɛns/ *n.* **1.** cerca *f.* —*v.* **2.** cercar.
fender /'fɛndər/ *n.* guardabarros *m.pl.*
ferment /*n* 'fɜrmɛnt; *v* fər'mɛnt/ *n.* **1.** fermento *m.*; *Fig.* agitación *f.* —*v.* **2.** fermentar.
fermentation /ˌfɜrmɛn'teiʃən/ *n.* fermentación *f.*
fern /fɜrn/ *n.* helecho *m.*
ferocious /fə'rouʃəs/ *a.* feroz, fiero.
ferociously /fə'rouʃəsli/ *adv.* ferozmente.
ferocity /fə'rɒsɪti/ *n.* ferocidad, fiereza *f.*
Ferris wheel /'fɛrɪs/ rueda de feria *f.*
ferry /'fɛri/ *n.* transbordador *m.*, barca de transporte.
fertile /'fɜrtl/ *a.* fecundo; (land) fértil.
fertility /fər'tɪlɪti/ *n.* fertilidad *f.*
fertilization /ˌfɜrtl̩ə'zeiʃən/ *n.* fertilización *f.*
fertilize /'fɜrtl̩ˌaiz/ *v.* fertilizar, abonar.
fertilizer /'fɜrtl̩ˌaizər/ *n.* abono *m.*
fervency /'fɜrvənsi/ *n.* ardor *m.*
fervent /'fɜrvənt/ *a.* fervoroso.
fervently /'fɜrvəntli/ *adv.* fervorosamente.
fervid /'fɜrvɪd/ *a.* férvido.
fervor /'fɜrvər/ *n.* fervor *m.*
fester /'fɛstər/ *v.* ulcerarse.
festival /'fɛstəvəl/ *n.* fiesta *f.*
festive /'fɛstɪv/ *a.* festivo.
festivity /fɛ'stɪvɪti/ *n.* festividad *f.*
festoon /fɛ'stun/ *n.* **1.** festón *m.* —*v.* **2.** festonear.
fetch /fɛtʃ/ *v.* ir por; traer.
fete /feit/ *n.* **1.** fiesta *f.* —*v.* **2.** festejar.
fetid /'fɛtɪd/ *a.* fétido.
fetish /'fɛtɪʃ/ *n.* fetiche *m.*
fetter /'fɛtər/ *n.* **1.** grillete *m.* —*v.* **2.** engrillar.
fetus /'fitəs/ *n.* feto *m.*
feud /fyud/ *n.* riña *f.*
feudal /'fyudl/ *a.* feudal.
feudalism /'fyudl̩ˌɪzəm/ *n.* feudalismo *m.*
fever /'fivər/ *n.* fiebre *f.*
feverish /'fivərɪʃ/ *a.* febril.
feverishly /'fivərɪʃli/ *adv.* febrilmente.
few /fyu/ *a.* pocos. **a. f.,** algunos, unos cuantos.
fiancé, fiancée /ˌfiɑn'sei/ *n.* novio -via.
fiasco /fi'æskou/ *n.* fiasco *m.*
fiat /'fiɑt/ *n.* fiat *m.*, orden *f.*
fib /fɪb/ *n.* **1.** mentira *f.* —*v.* **2.** mentir.
fiber /'faibər/ *n.* fibra *f.*
fibrous /'faibrəs/ *a.* fibroso.
fickle /'fɪkəl/ *a.* caprichoso.
fickleness /'fɪkəlnɪs/ *n.* inconstancia *f.*
fiction /'fɪkʃən/ *n.* ficción *f.*; (literature) novelas *f.pl.*
fictitious /fɪk'tɪʃəs/ *a.* ficticio.
fidelity /fɪ'dɛlɪti/ *n.* fidelidad *f.*
fidget /'fɪdʒɪt/ *v.* inquietar.
field /fild/ *n.* campo *m.*
field trip viaje de estudios *m.*
fiend /find/ *n.* demonio *m.*
fiendish /'findɪʃ/ *a.* diabólico, malvado.
fierce /fɪərs/ *a.* fiero, feroz.
fiery /'faiəri/ *a.* ardiente.
fiesta /fi'ɛstə/ *n.* fiesta *f.*
fife /faif/ *n.* pífano *m.*
fifteen /'fɪf'tin/ *a.* & *pron.* quince.
fifteenth /'fɪf'tinθ/ *n.* & *a.* décimoquinto.
fifth /fɪfθ/ *a.* quinto.
fifty /'fɪfti/ *a.* & *pron.* cincuenta.
fig /fɪg/ *n.* higo *m.* **f. tree,** higuera *f.*
fight /fait/ *n.* **1.** lucha, pelea *f.* —*v.* **2.** luchar, pelear.
fighter /'faitər/ *n.* peleador -ra, luchador -ra.

figment /'fɪgmənt/ n. invención f.
figurative /'fɪgyərətɪv/ a. metafórico.
figuratively /'fɪgyərətɪvli/ adv. figuradamente.
figure /'fɪgyər/ n. **1.** figura; cifra f. —v. **2.** figurar; calcular.
filament /'fɪləmənt/ n. filamento m.
file /faɪl/ n. **1.** archivo m.; (instrument) lima f.; (row) fila f. —v. **2.** archivar; limar.
file cabinet archivador m.
filial /'fɪlɪəl/ a. filial.
filigree /'fɪlə,gri/ n. filigrana f.
fill /fɪl/ v. llenar.
fillet /'fɪlɪt/ n. filete m.
filling /'fɪlɪŋ/ n. relleno m.; (dental) empastadura f. **f. station,** gasolinera f.
film /fɪlm/ n. **1.** película f., film m. —v. **2.** filmar.
filter /'fɪltər/ n. **1.** filtro m. —v. **2.** filtrar.
filth /fɪlθ/ n. suciedad, mugre f.
filthy /'fɪlθi/ a. sucio.
fin /fɪn/ n. aleta f.
final /'faɪnl/ a. **1.** final, último. —n. **2.** examen final. **finals** (sports) final f.
finalist /'faɪnlɪst/ n. finalista m. & f.
finally /'faɪnli/ adv. finalmente.
finances /'faɪnænsəz/ n. recursos, fondos m.pl.
financial /fɪ'nænʃəl/ a. financiero.
financier /,fɪnən'sɪər, ,faɪnən-/ n. financiero -ra.
find /faɪnd/ n. **1.** hallazgo m. —v. **2.** hallar; encontrar. **f. out,** averiguar, enterarse, saber.
fine /faɪn/ a. **1.** fino; bueno. —adv. **2.** muy bien. —n. **3.** multa f. —v. **4.** multar.
fine arts /ɑrts/ bellas artes f.pl.
finery /'faɪnəri/ n. gala f., adorno m.
finesse /fɪ'nɛs/ n. **1.** artificio m. —v. **2.** valerse de artificio.
finger /'fɪŋgər/ n. dedo m.
finger bowl n. enjuagatorio m.
fingernail /'fɪŋgər,neɪl/ n. uña f.
fingerprint /'fɪŋgər,prɪnt/ n. **1.** impresión digital f. —v. **2.** tomar las impresiones digitales.
finicky /'fɪnɪki/ a. melindroso.
finish /'fɪnɪʃ/ n. **1.** conclusión f. —v. **2.** acabar, terminar.
finished /'fɪnɪʃt/ a. acabado.
finite /'faɪnaɪt/ a. finito.
fir /fɜr/ n. abeto m.
fire /faɪər/ n. **1.** fuego; incendio m. —v. **2.** disparar, tirar; Colloq. despedir.
fire alarm n. alarma de incendio f.
firearm /'faɪər,ɑrm/ n. arma de fuego.
firecracker /'faɪər,krækər/ n. triquitraque m., buscapiés m., petardo m.
fire engine bomba de incendios f.
fire escape escalera de incendios f.
fire exit salida de urgencia f.
fire extinguisher /ɪk'stɪŋgwɪʃər/ matafuego m.
firefly /'faɪər,flaɪ/ n. luciérnaga f.
fireman /'faɪərmən/ n. bombero m.; (railway) fogonero m.
fireplace /'faɪər,pleɪs/ n. hogar, fogón m.
fireproof /'faɪər,pruf/ a. incombustible.
fireside /'faɪər,saɪd/ n. hogar, fogón m.
fireworks /'faɪər,wɜrks/ n. fuegos artificiales.
firm /fɜrm/ a. **1.** firme. —n. **2.** firma, empresa f.
firmness /'fɜrmnɪs/ n. firmeza f.
first /fɜrst/ a. & adv. primero. **at f.,** al principio.
first aid primeros auxilios.
first-class /'fɜrst 'klæs/ a. de primera clase.
fiscal /'fɪskəl/ a. fiscal.
fish /fɪʃ/ n. **1.** (food) pescado m.; (alive) pez m. —v. **2.** pescar.
fisherman /'fɪʃərmən/ n. pescador m.
fishhook /'fɪʃ,hʊk/ n. anzuelo m.

fishing /'fɪʃɪŋ/ n. pesca f. **go f.,** ir de pesca.
fishmonger /'fɪʃ,mʌŋgər/ n. pescadero m.
fish store pescadería f.
fission /'fɪʃən/ n. fisión f.
fissure /'fɪʃər/ n. grieta f., quebradura f.; fisura.
fist /fɪst/ n. puño m.
fit /fɪt/ a. **1.** capaz; justo. —n. **2.** corte, talle m.; Med. convulsión f. —v. **3.** caber; quedar bien, sentar bien.
fitful /'fɪtfəl/ a. espasmódico; caprichoso.
fitness /'fɪtnɪs/ n. aptitud; conveniencia f.
fitting /'fɪtɪŋ/ a. **1.** conveniente. **be f.,** convenir. —n. **2.** ajuste m.
fitting room probador m.
five /faɪv/ a. & pron. cinco.
five-day work week /faɪv 'deɪ/ semana inglesa f.
fix /fɪks/ n. **1.** apuro m. —v. **2.** fijar; arreglar; componer, reparar.
fixation /fɪk'seɪʃən/ n. fijación f.; fijeza f.
fixed /fɪkst/ a. fijo.
fixture /'fɪkstʃər/ n. instalación; guarnición f.
flabby /'flæbi/ a. flojo.
flaccid /'flæksɪd, 'flæsɪd/ a. flojo; flácido.
flag /flæg/ n. bandera f.
flagellant /'flædʒələnt/ n. & a. flagelante m.
flagon /'flægən/ n. frasco m.
flagrant /'fleɪgrənt/ a. flagrante.
flagrantly /'fleɪgrəntli/ adv. notoriamente.
flair /flɛər/ n. aptitud especial f.
flake /fleɪk/ n. **1.** escama f.; copo de nieve. —v. **2.** romperse en láminas.
flamboyant /flæm'bɔɪənt/ a. flamante, llamativo.
flame /fleɪm/ n. **1.** llama f. —v. **2.** llamear.
flaming /'fleɪmɪŋ/ a. llameante, flamante.
flamingo /flə'mɪŋgoʊ/ n. flamenco m.
flammable /'flæməbəl/ a. inflamable.
flank /flæŋk/ n. **1.** ijada f.; Mil. flanco m. —v. **2.** flanquear.
flannel /'flænl/ n. franela f.
flap /flæp/ n. **1.** cartera f. —v. **2.** aletear; sacudirse.
flare /flɛər/ n. **1.** llamarada f. —v. **2.** brillar; Fig. enojarse.
flash /flæʃ/ n. **1.** resplandor m.; (lightning) rayo, relámpago m.; Fig. instante m. —v. **2.** brillar.
flashcube /'flæʃ,kyub/ n. cubo de flash m.
flashlight /'flæʃ,laɪt/ n. linterna (eléctrica).
flashy /'flæʃi/ a. ostentoso.
flask /flæsk/ n. frasco m.
flat /flæt/ a. **1.** llano; (tire) desinflado. —n. **2.** llanura f.; apartamento m.
flatness /'flætnɪs/ n. llanura f.
flatten /'flætn/ v. aplastar, allanar; abatir.
flatter /'flætər/ v. adular, lisonjear.
flatterer /'flætərər/ n. lisonjero -ra; zalamero -ra.
flattery /'flætəri/ n. adulación, lisonja f.
flaunt /flɔnt/ v. ostentar.
flavor /'fleɪvər/ n. **1.** sabor m. —v. **2.** sazonar.
flavoring /'fleɪvərɪŋ/ n. condimento m.
flaw /flɔ/ n. defecto m.
flax /flæks/ n. lino m.
flay /fleɪ/ v. despellejar; excoriar.
flea /fli/ n. pulga f.
flea market rastro m.
fleck /flɛk/ n. **1.** mancha f. —v. **2.** varetear.
flee /fli/ v. huir.
fleece /flis/ n. **1.** vellón m. —v. **2.** esquilar.

fleet /flit/ a. **1.** veloz. —n. **2.** flota f.
fleeting /'flitɪŋ/ a. fugaz, pasajero.
flesh /flɛʃ/ n. carne f.
fleshy /'flɛʃi/ a. gordo; carnoso.
flex /flɛks/ n. **1.** doblez m. —v. **2.** doblar.
flexibility /,flɛksə'bɪlɪti/ n. flexibilidad f.
flexible /'flɛksəbəl/ a. flexible.
flier /'flaɪər/ n. aviador -ra.
flight /flaɪt/ n. vuelo m.; fuga f.
flight attendant n. azafata f.; ayudante de vuelo m.
flimsy /'flɪmzi/ a. débil.
flinch /flɪntʃ/ v. acobardarse.
fling /flɪŋ/ v. lanzar.
flint /flɪnt/ n. pedernal m.
flip /flɪp/ v. lanzar.
flippant /'flɪpənt/ a. impertinente.
flippantly /'flɪpəntli/ adv. impertinentemente.
flirt /flɜrt/ n. **1.** coqueta f. —v. **2.** coquetear, flirtear.
flirtation /flɜr'teɪʃən/ n. coqueteo m.
float /floʊt/ v. flotar.
flock /flɒk/ n. **1.** rebaño m. —v. **2.** congregarse.
flog /flɒg/ v. azotar.
flood /flʌd/ n. **1.** inundación f. —v. **2.** inundar.
floor /flɔr/ n. **1.** suelo, piso m. —v. **2.** derribar.
floppy disk /'flɒpi/ floppy, m., disquete, m.
floral /'flɔrəl/ a. floral.
florid /'flɔrɪd/ a. florido.
florist /'flɔrɪst/ n. florista m. & f.
flounce /flaʊns/ n. **1.** (sewing) volante m. —v. **2.** pernear.
flounder /'flaʊndər/ n. rodaballo m.
flour /flaʊər/ n. harina f.
flourish /'flɜrɪʃ/ n. **1.** Mus. floreo m. —v. **2.** florecer; prosperar; blandir.
flow /floʊ/ n. **1.** flujo m. —v. **2.** fluir.
flow chart organigrama m.
flower /'flaʊər/ n. **1.** flor f. —v. **2.** florecer.
flowerpot /'flaʊər,pɒt/ n. maceta f.
flowery /'flaʊəri/ a. florido.
fluctuate /'flʌktʃu,eɪt/ v. fluctuar.
fluctuation /,flʌktʃu'eɪʃən/ n. fluctuación f.
flue /flu/ n. humero m.
fluency /'fluənsi/ n. fluidez f.
fluent /'fluənt/ a. fluido; competente.
fluffy /'flʌfi/ a. velloso.
fluid /'fluɪd/ a. & n. fluido m.
fluidity /flu'ɪdɪti/ n. fluidez f.
fluoroscope /'flʊrə,skoup/ n. fluoroscopio m.
flurry /'flɜri/ n. agitación f.
flush /flʌʃ/ a. **1.** bien provisto. —n. **2.** sonrojo m. —v. **3.** limpiar con un chorro de agua; sonrojarse.
flute /flut/ n. flauta f.
flutter /'flʌtər/ n. **1.** agitación f. —v. **2.** agitarse.
flux /flʌks/ n. flujo m.
fly /flaɪ/ n. **1.** mosca f. —v. **2.** volar.
flying saucer /'flaɪɪŋ/ platillo volante m.
foam /foʊm/ n. **1.** espuma f. —v. **2.** espumar.
focal /'foʊkəl/ a. focal.
focus /'foʊkəs/ n. **1.** enfoque m. —v. **2.** enfocar.
fodder /'fɒdər/ n. forraje m., pienso m.
foe /foʊ/ n. adversario -ria, enemigo -ga.
fog /fɒg/ n. niebla f.
foggy /'fɒgi/ a. brumoso.
foil /fɔɪl/ v. frustrar.
foist /fɔɪst/ v. imponer.
fold /foʊld/ n. **1.** pliegue m. —v. **2.** doblar, plegar.
foldable /'foʊldəbəl/ a. plegable.
folder /'foʊldər/ n. circular m.; (for filing) carpeta f.
folding /'foʊldɪŋ/ a. plegable.
foliage /'foʊliɪdʒ/ n. follaje m.
folio /'foʊli,oʊ/ n. infolio; folio m.

folklore /'foʊk,lɔr/ n. folklore m.
folks /foʊks/ n. gente; familia f.
follicle /'fɒlɪkəl/ n. folículo m.
follow /'fɒloʊ/ v. seguir.
follower /'fɒloʊər/ n. partidario -ria.
folly /'fɒli/ n. locura f.
foment /foʊ'mɛnt/ v. fomentar.
fond /fɒnd/ a. cariñoso, tierno. **be f. of,** ser aficionado a.
fondle /'fɒndl/ v. acariciar.
fondly /'fɒndli/ adv. tiernamente.
fondness /'fɒndnɪs/ n. afición f.; cariño m.
food /fud/ n. alimento m.; comida f.
foodie /'fudi/ n. Colloq. gastrónomo -ma, gourmet m. & f.
food poisoning /'pɔɪzənɪŋ/ intoxicación alimenticia f.
foodstuffs /'fud,stʌfs/ n.pl. comestibles, víveres m.pl.
fool /ful/ **1.** tonto -ta; bobo -ba; bufón -ona. —v. **2.** engañar.
foolhardy /'ful,hɑrdi/ a. temerario.
foolish /'fulɪʃ/ a. bobo, tonto, majadero.
foolproof /'ful,pruf/ a. seguro.
foot /fʊt/ n. pie m.
footage /'fʊtɪdʒ/ n. longitud en pies.
football /'fʊt,bɔl/ n. fútbol, balompié m.
footbridge /'fʊt,brɪdʒ/ n. puente para peatones m.
foothold /'fʊt,hoʊld/ n. posición establecida.
footing /'fʊtɪŋ/ n. base f., fundamento m.
footlights /'fʊt,laɪts/ n.pl. luces del proscenio.
footnote /'fʊt,noʊt/ n. nota al pie de una página.
footpath /'fʊt,pæθ/ n. sendero m.
footprint /'fʊt,prɪnt/ n. huella f.
footstep /'fʊt,stɛp/ n. paso m.
footstool /'fʊt,stul/ n. escañuelo m., banqueta f.
fop /fɒp/ n. petimetre m.
for /fɔr; unstressed fər/ prep. **1.** para; por. **as f.,** en cuanto a. **what f.,** ¿para qué? —conj. **2.** porque, pues.
forage /'fɔrɪdʒ/ n. **1.** forraje m. —v. **2.** forrajear.
foray /'fɔreɪ/ n. correría f.
forbear /fɔr,bɛər/ v. cesar; abstenerse.
forbearance /fɔr'bɛərəns/ n. paciencia f.
forbid /fər'bɪd/ v. prohibir.
forbidding /fər'bɪdɪŋ/ a. repugnante.
force /fɔrs/ n. **1.** fuerza f. —v. **2.** forzar.
forced landing /fɔrst/ aterrizaje forzoso m.
forceful /'fɔrsfəl/ a. fuerte; enérgico.
forcible /'fɔrsəbəl/ a. a la fuerza; enérgico.
ford /fɔrd/ n. **1.** vado m. —v. **2.** vadear.
fore /fɔr/ a. **1.** delantero. —n. **2.** delantera f.
fore and aft de popa a proa.
forearm /fɔr'ɑrm/ n. antebrazo m.
forebears /'fɔr,bɛərz/ n.pl. antepasados m.pl.
forebode /fɔr'boʊd/ v. presagiar.
foreboding /fɔr'boʊdɪŋ/ n. presentimiento m.
forecast /'fɔr,kæst/ n. **1.** pronóstico m.; profecía f. —v. **2.** pronosticar.
forecastle /'foʊksəl/ n. Naut. castillo de proa.
forefathers /'fɔr,fɑðərz/ n. antepasados m.pl.
forefinger /'fɔr,fɪŋgər/ n. índice m.
forego /fɔr'goʊ/ v. renunciar.
foregone /fɔr'gɒn/ a. predeterminado.
foreground /'fɔr,graʊnd/ n. primer plano.
forehead /'fɔrɪd/ n. frente f.
foreign /'fɔrɪn/ a. extranjero.
foreign aid n. ayuda exterior f.
foreigner /'fɔrənər/ n. extranjero -ra; forastero -ra.

foreleg /'fɔrˌlɛg/ *n.* pierna delantera.
foreman /'fɔrmən/ *n.* capataz, jefe de taller *m.*
foremost /'fɔrˌmoust/ *a.* **1.** primero. —*adv.* **2.** en primer lugar.
forenoon /'fɔrˌnun/ *n.* mañana *f.*
forensic /fə'rɛnsɪk/ *a.* forense.
forerunner /'fɔrˌrʌnər/ *n.* precursor -ra.
foresee /fɔr'si/ *v.* prever.
foreshadow /fɔr'ʃædou/ *v.* prefigurar, anunciar.
foresight /'fɔrˌsait/ *n.* previsión *f.*
forest /'fɔrɪst/ *n.* bosque *m.*; selva *f.*
forestall /fɔr'stɔl/ *v.* anticipar; prevenir.
forester /'fɔrəstər/ *n.* silvicultor -ra; guardamontes *m.pl.* & *f.pl.*
forestry /'fɔrəstri/ *n.* silvicultura *f.*
foretell /fɔr'tɛl/ *v.* predecir.
forever /fɔr'ɛvər/ *adv.* por siempre, para siempre.
forevermore /fɔrˌɛvər'mɔr/ *adv.* siempre.
forewarn /fɔr'wɔrn/ *v.* advertir, avisar.
foreword /'fɔrˌwɜrd/ *n.* prefacio *m.*
forfeit /'fɔrfɪt/ *n.* **1.** prenda; multa *f.* —*v.* **2.** perder.
forfeiture /'fɔrfɪtʃər/ *n.* decomiso *m.*, multa *f.*; pérdida.
forgather /fɔr'gæðər/ *v.* reunirse.
forge /fɔrdʒ/ *n.* **1.** fragua *f.* —*v.* **2.** forjar; falsear.
forger /'fɔrdʒər/ *n.* forjador -ra; falsificador -ra.
forgery /'fɔrdʒəri/ *n.* falsificación *f.*
forget /fər'gɛt/ *v.* olvidar.
forgetful /fər'gɛtfəl/ *a.* olvidadizo.
forgive /fər'gɪv/ *v.* perdonar.
forgiveness /fər'gɪvnɪs/ *n.* perdón *m.*
fork /fɔrk/ *n.* **1.** tenedor *m.*; bifurcación *f.* —*v.* **2.** bifurcarse.
forlorn /fɔr'lɔrn/ *a.* triste.
form /fɔrm/ *n.* **1.** forma *f.*; (document) formulario *m.* —*v.* **2.** formar.
formal /'fɔrməl/ *a.* formal; ceremonioso. **f. dance,** baile de etiqueta. **f. dress,** traje de etiqueta.
formality /fɔr'mælɪti/ *n.* formalidad *f.*
formally /'fɔrməli/ *adv.* formalmente.
format /'fɔrmæt/ *n.* formato *m.*
formation /fɔr'meiʃən/ *n.* formación *f.*
formative /'fɔrmətɪv/ *a.* formativo.
formatting /'fɔrmætɪŋ/ *n.* formateo *m.*
former /'fɔrmər/ *a.* anterior; antiguo. **the f.,** aquél.
formerly /'fɔrmərli/ *adv.* antiguamente.
formidable /'fɔrmɪdəbəl/ *a.* formidable.
formless /'fɔrmlɪs/ *a.* sin forma.
formula /'fɔrmyələ/ *n.* fórmula *f.*
formulate /'fɔrmyəˌleit/ *v.* formular.
formulation /ˌfɔrmy'leiʃən/ *n.* formulación *f.*; expresión *f.*
forsake /fɔr'seik/ *v.* abandonar.
fort /fɔrt/ *n.* fortaleza *f.*; fuerte *m.*
forte /'fɔrtei/ *a.* & *adv. Mus.* forte; fuerte.
forth /fɔrθ/ *adv.* adelante. **back and f.,** de aquí allá. **and so f.,** etcétera.
forthcoming /'fɔrθ'kʌmɪŋ/ *a.* futuro, próximo.
forthright /'fɔrθˌrait/ *a.* franco.
forthwith /ˌfɔrθ'wɪθ/ *adv.* inmediatamente.
fortification /ˌfɔrtəfɪ'keiʃən/ *n.* fortificación *f.*
fortify /'fɔrtəˌfai/ *v.* fortificar.
fortissimo /fɔr'tɪsəˌmou/ *a.* & *adv. Mus.* fortísimo.
fortitude /'fɔrtɪˌtud/ *n.* fortaleza; fortitud *f.*
fortnight /'fɔrtˌnait/ *n.* quincena *f.*
fortress /'fɔrtrɪs/ *n.* fuerte *m.*, fortaleza *f.*
fortuitous /fɔr'tuɪtəs/ *a.* fortuito.
fortunate /'fɔrtʃənɪt/ *a.* afortunado.
fortune /'fɔrtʃən/ *n.* fortuna; suerte *f.*
fortune-teller /'fɔrtʃən ˌtɛlər/ *n.* sortílego -ga, adivino -na.
forty /'fɔrti/ *a.* & *pron.* cuarenta.
forum /'fɔrəm/ *n.* foro *m.*
forward /'fɔrwərd/ *a.* **1.** delantero; atrevido. —*adv.* **2.** adelante. —*v.* **3.** trasmitir, reexpedir.
foster /'fɔstər/ *n.* **1. f. child,** hijo adoptivo. —*v.* **2.** fomentar; criar.
foul /faul/ *a.* sucio; impuro.
found /faund/ *v.* fundar.
foundation /faun'deiʃən/ *n.* fundación *f.*; (of building) cimientos *m.pl.*
founder /'faundər/ *n.* **1.** fundador -ra. —*v.* **2.** irse a pique.
foundry /'faundri/ *n.* fundición *f.*
fountain /'fauntn̩/ *n.* fuente *f.*
fountain pen pluma estilográfica, plumafuente *f.*
four /fɔr/ *a.* & *pron.* cuatro.
fourteen /'fɔr'tin/ *a.* & *pron.* catorce.
fourth /fɔrθ/ *a.* & *n.* cuarto *m.*
fowl /faul/ *n.* ave *f.*
fox /fɒks/ *n.* zorro -rra.
fox-trot /'fɒksˌtrɒt/ *n.* foxtrot *m.*
foxy /'fɒksi/ *a.* astuto.
foyer /'fɔiər/ *n.* salón de entrada.
fracas /'freikəs, 'frækəs/ *n.* riña *f.*
fraction /'frækʃən/ *n.* fracción *f.*
fracture /'fræktʃər/ *n.* **1.** fractura, rotura *f.* —*v.* **2.** fracturar, romper.
fragile /'frædʒəl/ *a.* frágil.
fragment /'frægmənt/ *n.* fragmento, trozo *m.*
fragmentary /'frægmənˌtɛri/ *a.* fragmentario.
fragrance /'freigrəns/ *n.* fragancia *f.*
fragrant /'freigrənt/ *a.* fragante.
frail /freil/ *a.* débil, frágil.
frailty /'freilti/ *n.* debilidad, fragilidad *f.*
frame /freim/ *n.* **1.** marco; armazón; cuadro; cuerpo *m.* —*v.* **2.** fabricar; formar; encuadrar.
frame-up /'freim ˌʌp/ *n. Colloq.* conspiración *f.*
framework /'freimˌwɜrk/ *n.* armazón *m.*
France /fræns/ *n.* Francia *f.*
franchise /'fræntʃaiz/ *n.* franquicia *f.*
frank /fræŋk/ *a.* **1.** franco. —*n.* **2.** carta franca. —*v.* **3.** franquear.
frankfurter /'fræŋkfərtər/ *n.* salchicha *f.*
frankly /'fræŋkli/ *adv.* francamente.
frankness /'fræŋknɪs/ *n.* franqueza *f.*
frantic /'fræntɪk/ *a.* frenético.
fraternal /frə'tɜrnl̩/ *a.* fraternal.
fraternity /frə'tɜrnɪti/ *n.* fraternidad *f.*
fraternization /ˌfrætərnə'zeiʃən/ *n.* fraternización *f.*
fraternize /'frætərˌnaiz/ *v.* confraternizar.
fratricide /'frætrɪˌsaid/ *n.* fratricida *m.* & *f.*; fratricidio *m.*
fraud /frɔd/ *n.* fraude *m.*
fraudulent /'frɔdʒələnt/ *a.* fraudulento.
fraudulently /'frɔdʒələntli/ *adv.* fraudulentamente.
fraught /frɔt/ *a.* cargado.
freak /frik/ *n.* rareza *f.*; monstruosidad.
freckle /'frɛkəl/ *n.* peca *f.*
freckled /'frɛkəld/ *a.* pecoso.
free /fri/ *a.* **1.** libre; gratis. —*v.* **2.** libertar, librar.
freedom /'fridəm/ *n.* libertad *f.*
freeze /friz/ *v.* helar, congelar.
freezer /'frizər/ *n.* heladora *f.*
freezing point /'frizɪŋ/ punto de congelación *m.*
freight /freit/ *n.* **1.** carga *f.*; flete *m.* —*v.* **2.** cargar; fletar.
freighter /'freitər/ *n. Naut.* fletador *m.*
French /frɛntʃ/ *a.* & *n.* francés -esa.
Frenchman /'frɛntʃmən/ *n.* francés *m.*
Frenchwoman /'frɛntʃˌwʊmən/ *n.* francesa *f.*
frenzied /'frɛnzid/ *a.* frenético.
frenzy /'frɛnzi/ *n.* frenesí *m.*
frequency /'frikwənsi/ *n.* frecuencia *f.*
frequency modulation /ˌmɒdʒə'leiʃən/ modulación de frequencia.
frequent /'frikwənt/ *a.* frecuente.
frequently /'frikwəntli/ *adv.* frecuentemente.
fresco /'frɛskou/ *n.* fresco.
fresh /frɛʃ/ *a.* fresco. **f. water,** agua dulce.
freshen /'frɛʃən/ *v.* refrescar.
freshness /'frɛʃnɪs/ *n.* frescura *f.*
fret /frɛt/ *v.* quejarse, irritarse; *Mus.* traste *m.*
fretful /'frɛtfəl/ *a.* irritable.
fretfully /'frɛtfəli/ *adv.* de mala gana.
fretfulness /'frɛtfəlnɪs/ *n.* mal humor.
friar /'fraiər/ *n.* fraile *m.*
fricassee /ˌfrɪkə'si/ *n.* fricasé *m.*
friction /'frɪkʃən/ *n.* fricción *f.*
Friday /'fraidei/ *n.* viernes *m.* **Good F.,** Viernes Santo *m.*
fried /fraid/ *a.* frito.
friend /frɛnd/ *n.* amigo -ga.
friendless /'frɛndlɪs/ *a.* sin amigos.
friendliness /'frɛndlinɪs/ *n.* amistad *f.*
friendly /'frɛndli/ *a.* amistoso.
friendship /'frɛndʃɪp/ *n.* amistad *f.*
fright /frait/ *n.* susto *m.*
frighten /'fraitn̩/ *v.* asustar, espantar.
frightful /'fraitfəl/ *a.* espantoso.
frigid /'frɪdʒɪd/ *a.* frígido; frío.
frill /frɪl/ *n.* (sewing) lechuga *f.*
fringe /frɪndʒ/ *n.* fleco; borde *m.*
frisky /'frɪski/ *a.* retozón.
fritter /'frɪtər/ *n.* fritura *f.*
frivolity /frɪ'vɒlɪti/ *n.* frivolidad *f.*
frivolous /'frɪvələs/ *a.* frívolo.
frivolousness /'frɪvələsnɪs/ *n.* frivolidad *f.*
frock /frɒk/ *n.* vestido de mujer. **f. coat,** levita *f.*
frog /frɒg/ *n.* rana *f.*
frolic /'frɒlɪk/ *n.* **1.** retozo *m.* —*v.* **2.** retozar.
from /frʌm, *unstressed* frəm/ *prep.* de; desde.
front /frʌnt/ *n.* frente; (of building) fachada *f.* **in f. of,** delante de.
frontal /'frʌntl̩/ *a.* frontal.
front door puerta principal *f.*
frontier /frʌn'tɪər/ *n.* frontera *f.*
front seat asiento delantero *m.*
frost /frɔst/ *n.* helada, escarcha *f.*
frosty /'frɔsti/ *a.* helado.
froth /frɔθ/ *n.* espuma *f.*
frown /fraun/ *n.* **1.** ceño *m.* —*v.* **2.** fruncir el entrecejo.
frowzy /'frauzi/ *a.* desaliñado.
frozen /'frouzən/ *a.* helado; congelado.
fructify /'frʌktəˌfai/ *v.* fructificar.
frugal /'frugəl/ *a.* frugal.
frugality /fru'gælɪti/ *n.* frugalidad *f.*
fruit /frut/ *n.* fruta *f.*; (benefits) frutos *m.pl.* **f. tree,** árbol frutal.
fruitful /'frutfəl/ *a.* productivo.
fruition /fru'ɪʃən/ *n.* fruición *f.*
fruitless /'frutlɪs/ *a.* inútil, en vano.
fruit salad macedonia de frutas *f.*
fruit store frutería *f.*
frustrate /'frʌstreit/ *v.* frustrar.
frustration /frʌ'streiʃən/ *n.* frustración *f.*
fry /frai/ *v.* freír.
fuel /'fyuəl/ *n.* combustible *m.*
fugitive /'fyudʒɪtɪv/ *a.* & *n.* fugitivo -va.
fugue /fyug/ *n.* fuga *f.*
fulcrum /'fʊlkrəm/ *n.* fulcro *m.*
fulfill /fʊl'fɪl/ *v.* cumplir.
fulfillment /fʊl'fɪlmənt/ *n.* cumplimiento *m.*; realización *f.*
full /fʊl/ *a.* lleno; completo; pleno.
full name nombre y apellidos.
fullness /'fʊlnɪs/ *n.* plenitud *f.*
fulminate /'fʌlməˌneit/ *v.* volar; fulminar.
fulmination /ˌfʌlmə'neiʃən/ *n.* fulminación *f.*; detonación *f.*
fumble /'fʌmbəl/ *v.* chapucear.
fume /fyum/ *n.* **1.** humo *m.* —*v.* **2.** humear.
fumigate /'fyumɪˌgeit/ *v.* fumigar.
fumigator /'fyumɪˌgeitər/ *n.* fumigador *m.*
fun /fʌn/ *n.* diversión *f.* **to make f. of,** burlarse de. **to have f.,** divertirse.
function /'fʌŋkʃən/ *n.* **1.** función *f.* —*v.* **2.** funcionar.
functional /'fʌŋkʃənl̩/ *a.* funcional.
fund /fʌnd/ *n.* fondo *m.*
fundamental /ˌfʌndə'mɛntl̩/ *a.* fundamental.
funeral /'fyunərəl/ *n.* funeral *m.*
funeral home, funeral parlor funeraria *f.*
fungus /'fʌŋgəs/ *n.* hongo *m.*
funnel /'fʌnl̩/ *n.* embudo *m.*; (of ship) chimenea *f.*
funny /'fʌni/ *a.* divertido, gracioso. **to be f.,** tener gracia.
fur /fɜr/ *n.* piel *f.*
furious /'fyʊriəs/ *a.* furioso.
furlough /'fɜrlou/ *n.* permiso *m.*
furnace /'fɜrnɪs/ *n.* horno *m.*
furnish /'fɜrnɪʃ/ *v.* surtir, proveer; (a house) amueblar.
furniture /'fɜrnɪtʃər/ *n.* muebles *m.pl.*
furrow /'fɜrou/ *n.* **1.** surco *m.* —*v.* **2.** surcar.
further /'fɜrðər/ *a.* & *adv.* **1.** más. —*v.* **2.** adelantar, fomentar.
furthermore /'fɜrðərˌmɔr/ *adv.* además.
fury /'fyʊri/ *n.* furor *m.*; furia *f.*
fuse /fyuz/ *n.* **1.** fusible *m.* —*v.* **2.** fundir.
fuss /fʌs/ *n.* **1.** alboroto *m.* —*v.* **2.** preocuparse por pequeñeces.
fussy /'fʌsi/ *a.* melindroso.
futile /'fyutl̩/ *a.* fútil.
future /'fyutʃər/ *a.* **1.** futuro. —*n.* **2.** porvenir *m.*
futurology /ˌfyutʃə'rɒlədʒi/ *n.* futurología *f.*
fuzzy logic /'fʌzi/ lógica matizada *f.*
FYI *abbr.* (For Your Information) para su información.

G

gag /gæg/ *n.* chiste *m.*; mordaza *f.*
gaiety /'geiɪti/ *n.* alegría *f.*
gain /gein/ *n.* **1.** ganancia *f.* —*v.* **2.** ganar.
gait /geit/ *n.* paso *m.*
gale /geil/ *n.* ventarrón *m.*
gall /gɔl/ *n.* hiel *f.*; *Fig.* amargura *f.*; descaro *m.*
gallant /'gælənt, gə'lænt, -'lɑnt/ *a.* **1.** galante. —*n.* **2.** galán *m.*
gallery /'gæləri/ *n.* galería *f.*; *Theat.* paraíso *m.*
gallon /'gælən/ *n.* galón *m.*
gallop /'gæləp/ *n.* **1.** galope *m.* —*v.* **2.** galopar.
gallows /'gælouz/ *n.* horca *f.*
gamble /'gæmbəl/ *n.* **1.** riesgo *m.* —*v.* **2.** jugar, aventurar.
game /geim/ *n.* juego *m.*; (match) partida *f.*; (hunting) caza *f.*
gang /gæŋ/ *n.* cuadrilla; pandilla *f.*
gangster /'gæŋstər/ *n.* rufián *m.*
gap /gæp/ *n.* raja *f.*
gape /geip/ *v.* boquear.
garage /gə'rɑʒ/ *n.* garaje *m.*
garbage /'gɑrbɪdʒ/ *n.* basura *f.*
garden /'gɑrdn̩/ *n.* jardín *m.*; (vegetable) huerta *f.*
gardener /'gɑrdnər/ *n.* jardinero -ra.
gargle /'gɑrgəl/ *n.* **1.** gárgara *f.* —*v.* **2.** gargarizar.
garland /'gɑrlənd/ *n.* guirnalda *f.*
garlic /'gɑrlɪk/ *n.* ajo *m.*
garment /'gɑrmənt/ *n.* prenda de vestir.
garrison /'gærəsən/ *n.* guarnición *f.*

garter /'gɑrtər/ n. liga f.; ataderas f. pl.

gas /gæs/ n. gas m.

gasohol /'gæsə,hɔl, -,hɒl/ n. gasohol m.

gasoline /,gæsə'lin/ n. gasolina f.

gasp /gæsp/ n. **1.** boqueada f. —v. **2.** boquear.

gas station gasolinera f.

gate /geit/ n. puerta; entrada; verja f.

gather /'gæðər/ v. recoger; inferir; reunir.

gaudy /'gɔdi/ a. brillante; llamativo.

gauge /geidʒ/ n. **1.** manómetro, indicador m. —v. **2.** medir; estimar.

gaunt /gɔnt/ a. flaco.

gauze /gɔz/ n. gasa f.

gay /gei/ a. **1.** alegre; homosexual. —n. **2.** homosexual.

gaze /geiz/ n. **1.** mirada f. —v. **2.** mirar con fijeza.

gear /giər/ n. engranaje m. **in g.,** en juego.

gearshift /'giər,ʃift/ n. palanca de cambio f.

gem /dʒɛm/ n. joya f.

gender /'dʒɛndər/ n. género m.

general /'dʒɛnərəl/ a. & n. general m.

generality /,dʒɛnə'ræliti/ n. generalidad f.

generalize /'dʒɛnərə,laiz/ v. generalizar.

generation /,dʒɛnə'reiʃən/ n. generación f.

generator /'dʒɛnə,reitər/ n. generador m.

generosity /,dʒɛnə'rɒsiti/ n. generosidad f.

generous /'dʒɛnərəs/ a. generoso.

genetic /dʒə'nɛtik/ a. genético.

genial /'dʒinyəl/ a. genial.

genius /'dʒinyəs/ n. genio m.

genocide /'dʒɛnə,said/ n. genocidio m.

gentle /'dʒɛntl/ a. suave; manso; benigno.

gentleman /'dʒɛntlmən/ n. señor; caballero m.

gentleness /'dʒɛntlnis/ n. suavidad f.

genuine /'dʒɛnyuin/ a. genuino.

genuineness /'dʒɛnyuinnis/ n. pureza f.

geographical /,dʒiə'græfikəl/ a. geográfico.

geography /dʒi'ɒgrəfi/ n. geografía f.

geometric /,dʒiə'mɛtrik/ a. geométrico.

geranium /dʒə'reiniəm/ n. geranio m.

germ /dʒɜrm/ n. germen; microbio m.

German /'dʒɜrmən/ a. & n. alemán -mana.

Germany /'dʒɜrməni/ n. Alemania f.

gesticulate /dʒɛ'stikyə,leit/ v. gesticular.

gesture /'dʒɛstʃər/ n. **1.** gesto m. —v. **2.** gesticular, hacer gestos.

get /gɛt/ v. obtener; conseguir; (become) ponerse. **go and g.,** ir a buscar; **g. away,** irse; descargar. **g. together,** reunirse. **g. on,** subirse; **g. off,** bajarse; **g. up,** levantarse; **g. there,** llegar.

ghastly /'gæstli/ a. pálido; espantoso.

ghost /goust/ n. espectro, fantasma m.

giant /'dʒaiənt/ n. gigante m.

gibberish /'dʒibəriʃ/ n. galimatías, m.

gift /gift/ n. regalo, don; talento m.

gigabyte /'gigə,bait, 'dʒig-/ n. giga m.

gild /gild/ v. dorar.

gin /dʒin/ n. ginebra f.

ginger /'dʒindʒər/ n. jengibre m.

gingerbread /'dʒindʒər,brɛd/ n. pan de jengibre.

gingham /'giŋəm/ n. guinga f.

gird /gɜrd/ v. ceñir.

girdle /'gɜrdl/ n. faja f.

girl /gɜrl/ n. muchacha, niña, chica f.

give /giv/ v. dar; regalar. **g. back,** devolver. **g. up,** rendirse; renunciar.

giver /'givər/ n. dador -ra; donador -ra.

glacier /'gleiʃər/ n. glaciar; ventisquero m.

glad /glæd/ a. alegre, contento. **be g.,** alegrarse.

gladly /'glædli/ adj. con mucho gusto.

gladness /'glædnis/ n. alegría f.; placer m.

glamor /'glæmər/ n. encanto m.; elegancia f.

glamorous /'glæmərəs/ a. encantador; elegante.

glamour /'glæmər/ n. encanto m.; elegancia f.

glance /glæns/ n. **1.** vistazo m., ojeada f. —v. **2.** ojear.

gland /glænd/ n. glándula f.

glare /glɛər/ n. **1.** reflejo; brillo m. —v. **2.** deslumbrar; echar miradas indignadas.

glass /glæs/ n. vidrio; vaso m.; (eyeglasses), lentes, anteojos m.pl.

gleam /glim/ n. **1.** fulgor m. —v. **2.** fulgurar.

glee /gli/ n. alegría f.; júbilo m.

glide /glaid/ v. deslizarse.

glimpse /glimps/ n. **1.** vislumbre, vistazo m. —v. **2.** vislumbrar, ojear.

glisten /'glisən/ n. **1.** brillo m. —v. **2.** brillar.

glitter /'glitər/ n. **1.** resplandor m. —v. **2.** brillar.

globe /gloub/ n. globo; orbe m.

gloom /glum/ n. oscuridad; tristeza f.

gloomy /'glumi/ a. oscuro; sombrío, triste.

glorify /'glɔrə,fai/ v. glorificar.

glorious /'glɔriəs/ a. glorioso.

glory /'glɔri/ n. gloria, fama f.

glossary /'glɒsəri/ n. glosario m.

glove /glʌv/ n. guante m.

glove compartment guantera f.

glow /glou/ n. **1.** fulgor m. —v. **2.** relucir; arder.

glucose /'glukous/ f. glucosa.

glue /glu/ n. **1.** cola f., pegamento m. —v. **2.** encolar, pegar.

glum /glʌm/ a. de mal humor.

glutton /'glʌtn/ n. glotón -ona.

gnaw /nɔ/ v. roer.

GNP (abbr. **gross national product**), **PNB** (producto nacional bruto).

go /gou/ v. ir, irse. **g. away,** irse, marcharse. **g. back,** volver, regresar. **g. down,** bajar. **g. in,** entrar. **g. on,** seguir. **g. out,** salir. **g. up,** subir.

goal /goul/ n. meta f.; objeto m.

goalkeeper /'goul,kipər/ n. guardameta mf.

goat /gout/ n. cabra f.

goblet /'gɒblit/ n. copa f.

God /gɒd/ n. Dios m.

gold /gould/ n. oro m.

golden /'gouldən/ a. áureo.

gold-plated /'gould ,pleitid/ a. chapado en oro.

golf /gɒlf/ n. golf m.

golf course campo de golf m.

golfer /'gɒlfər/ n. golfista m. & f.

good /gud/ a. **1.** bueno. —n. **2.** bienes m.pl.; Com. géneros m.pl.

good-bye /,gud'bai/ n. **1.** adiós m. —interj. **2.** ¡adiós!, ¡hasta la vista!, ¡hasta luego! **say g. to,** despedirse de.

goodness /'gudnis/ n. bondad f.

goodwill /'gud'wil/ n. buena voluntad. f.

goose /gus/ n. ganso m.

gooseberry /'gus,bɛri/ n. uva crespa f.

gooseneck /'gus,nɛk/ n. **1.** cuello de cisne m. —a. **2.** curvo.

goose step /'gus,stɛp/ paso de ganso m.

gore /gɔr/ n. **1.** sangre f. —v. **2.** acornear.

gorge /gɔrdʒ/ n. **1.** gorja f. —v. **2.** engullir.

gorgeous /'gɔrdʒəs/ a. magnífico; precioso.

gorilla /gə'rilə/ n. gorila m.

gory /'gɔri/ a. sangriento.

gosling /'gɒzliŋ/ n. gansarón m.

gospel /'gɒspəl/ n. evangelio m.

gossamer /'gɒsəmər/ n. **1.** telaraña f. —a. **2.** delgado.

gossip /'gɒsəp/ n. **1.** chisme m. —v. **2.** chismear.

Gothic /'gɒθik/ a. gótico.

gouge /gaudʒ/ n. **1.** gubia f. —v. **2.** escoplear.

gourd /gɔrd/ n. calabaza f.

gourmand /gur'mɑnd/ n. glotón m.

gourmet /gur'mei/ a. gastrónomo -ma.

govern /'gʌvərn/ v. gobernar.

governess /'gʌvərnis/ n. aya, institutriz f.

government /'gʌvərnmənt, -ərmənt/ n. gobierno m.

governmental /,gʌvərn'mɛntl, ,gʌvər-/ a. gubernamental.

governor /'gʌvərnər/ n. gobernador -ra.

governorship /'gʌvərnər,ʃip/ n. gobernatura f.

gown /gaun/ n. vestido m. **dressing g.,** bata f.

grab /græb/ v. agarrar, arrebatar.

grace /greis/ n. gracia; gentileza; merced f.

graceful /'greisfəl/ a. agraciado.

graceless /'greislis/ a. réprobo; torpe.

gracious /'greiʃəs/ a. gentil, cortés.

grackle /'grækəl/ n. grajo m.

grade /greid/ n. **1.** grado; nivel m.; pendiente; nota; calidad f. —v. **2.** graduar.

grade crossing n. paso a nivel m.

gradual /'grædʒuəl/ a. gradual, paulatino.

gradually /'grædʒuəli/ adv. gradualmente.

graduate /n 'grædʒuit; v -,eit/ n. **1.** graduado -da, diplomado -da. —v. **2.** graduar; diplomarse.

graft /græft/ n. **1.** injerto m.; soborno público. —v. **2.** injertar.

graham /'greiəm/ a. centeno; acemita.

grail /greil/ n. grial m.

grain /grein/ n. grano; cereal m.

grain alcohol n. alcohol de madera m.

gram /græm/ n. gramo m.

grammar /'græmər/ n. gramática f.

grammarian /grə'mɛəriən/ n. gramático -ca.

grammar school n. escuela elemental f.

grammatical /grə'mætikəl/ a. gramatical.

gramophone /'græmə,foun/ n. gramófono m.

granary /'greinəri/ n. granero m.

grand /grænd/ a. grande, ilustre; estupendo.

grandchild /'græn,tʃaild/ n. nieto -ta.

granddaughter /'græn,dɔtər/ n. nieta f.

grandee /græn'di/ n. noble m.

grandeur /'grændʒər/ n. grandeza f.

grandfather /'græn,fɑðər/ n. abuelo m.

grandiloquent /græn'diləkwənt/ a. grandílocuo.

grandiose /'grændi,ous/ a. grandioso.

grand jury jurado de acusación, jurado de juicio m.

grandly /'grændli/ adv. grandiosamente.

grandmother /'græn,mʌðər/ n. abuela f.

grand opera ópera grande f.

grandparents /'grænd,pɛərənts/ n. abuelos m.pl.

grandson /'græn,sʌn/ n. nieto m.

grandstand /'græn,stænd/ n. andanada f., tribuna f.

grange /greindʒ/ n. granja f.

granger /'greindʒər/ n. labriego m.

granite /'grænit/ n. granito m.

granny /'græni/ n. abuelita f.

grant /grænt/ n. **1.** concesión; subvención f. —v. **2.** otorgar; conceder; conferir. **take for granted,** tomar por cierto.

granular /'grænyələr/ a. granular.

granulate /'grænyə,leit/ v. granular.

granulation /,grænyə'leiʃən/ n. granulación f.

granule /'grænyul/ n. gránulo m.

grape /greip/ n. uva f.

grapefruit /'greip,frut/ n. toronja f.

grape harvest vendimia f.

grapeshot /'greip,ʃɒt/ n. metralla f.

grapevine /'greip,vain/ n. vid; parra f.

graph /græf/ n. gráfica f.

graphic /'græfik/ a. gráfico.

graphite /'græfait/ n. grafito m.

graphology /græ'fɒlədʒi/ n. grafología f.

grapple /'græpəl/ v. agarrar.

grasp /græsp/ n. **1.** puño; poder; conocimiento m. —v. **2.** empuñar, agarrar; comprender.

grasping /'græspiŋ/ a. codicioso.

grass /græs/ n. hierba f.; (marijuana) marijuana f.

grasshopper /'græs,hɒpər/ n. saltamontes m.

grassy /'græsi/ a. herboso.

grate /greit/ n. reja f.

grateful /'greitfəl/ a. agradecido.

gratify /'grætə,fai/ v. satisfacer.

grating /'greitiŋ/ n. **1.** enrejado m. —a. **2.** discordante.

gratis /'grætis/ adv. & a. gratis.

gratitude /'græti,tud/ n. agradecimiento m.

gratuitous /grə'tuitəs/ adj. gratuito.

gratuity /grə'tuiti/ n. propina f.

grave /greiv/ a. **1.** grave. —n. **2.** sepultura; tumba f.

gravel /'grævəl/ n. cascajo m.

gravely /'greivli/ adv. gravemente.

gravestone /'greiv,stoun/ n. lápida sepulcral f.

graveyard /'greiv,yɑrd/ n. cementerio m.

gravitate /'grævi,teit/ v. gravitar.

gravitation /,grævi'teiʃən/ n. gravitación f.

gravity /'græviti/ n. gravedad; seriedad f.

gravure /grə'vyur/ n. fotograbado m.

gravy /'greivi/ n. salsa f.

gray /grei/ a. gris; (hair) cano.

grayish /'greiiʃ/ a. pardusco.

gray matter substancia gris f.

graze /greiz/ v. rozar; (cattle) pastar.

grazing /'greiziŋ/ a. pastando.

grease /gris/ n. **1.** grasa f. —v. **2.** engrasar.

greasy /'grisi/ a. grasiento.

great /greit/ a. grande, ilustre; estupendo.

Great Dane /dein/ mastín danés m.

great-grandfather /,greit 'græn,fɑðər/ n. bisabuelo.

great-grandmother /,greit 'græn,mʌðər/ f. bisabuela.

greatness /'greitnis/ n. grandeza f.

Greece /gris/ n. Grecia f.

greed /grid/ **greediness** n. codicia, voracidad f.

greedy /'gridi/ a. voraz.

Greek /grik/ a. & n. griego -ga.

green /grin/ a. & n. verde m. **greens,** n. verduras f.pl.

greenery /'grinəri/ n. verdor m.

greenhouse /'grin,haus/ n. invernáculo m.

greenhouse effect n. efecto invernáculo m.

greet /grit/ v. saludar.

greeting /'gritiŋ/ n. saludo m.

gregarious /gri'gɛəriəs/ a. gregario; sociable.

grenade /gri'neid/ n. granada; bomba f.

greyhound /'grei,haund/ n. galgo m.

grid /grid/ n. parrilla f.

griddle /'gridl/ n. tortera f.

griddlecake /'gridl,keik/ n. tortita de harina f.

gridiron /'grɪd,aiərn/ *n.* parrilla *f.*; campo de fútbol *m.*

grief /grif/ *n.* dolor *m.*; pena *f.*

grievance /'grivəns/ *n.* pesar; agravio *m.*

grieve /griv/ *v.* afligir.

grievous /'grivəs/ *a.* penoso.

grill /grɪl/ *n.* **1.** parrilla *f.* —*v.* **2.** asar a la parrilla.

grillroom /'grɪl,rum, -,rʊm/ *n.* parrilla *f.*

grim /grɪm/ *a.* ceñudo.

grimace /'grɪməs/ *n.* **1.** mueca *f.* —*v.* **2.** hacer muecas.

grime /graim/ *n.* mugre *f.*

grimy /'graimi/ *a.* sucio; mugroso.

grin /grɪn/ *n.* **1.** sonrisa *f.* —*v.* **2.** sonreír.

grind /graind/ *v.* moler; afilar.

grindstone /'graind,stoun/ *n.* amoladera *f.*

gringo /'grɪŋgou/ *n.* gringo; yanqui *m.*

grip /grɪp/ *n.* **1.** maleta *f.* —*v.* **2.** agarrar.

gripe /graip/ *v.* **1.** agarrar. —*n.* **2.** asimiento *m.*, opresión *f.*

grippe /grɪp/ *n.* gripe *f.*

grisly /'grɪzli/ *a.* espantoso.

grist /grɪst/ *n.* molienda *f.*

gristle /'grɪsəl/ *n.* cartílago *m.*

grit /grɪt/ *n.* arena *f.*; entereza *f.*

grizzled /'grɪzəld/ *a.* tordillo.

groan /groun/ *n.* **1.** gemido *m.* —*v.* **2.** gemir.

grocer /'grousər/ *n.* abacero *m.*

grocery /'grousəri/ *n.* tienda de comestibles, abacería; (Carib.) bodega *f.*

grog /grɒg/ *n.* brebaje *m.*

groggy /'grɒgi/ *a.* medio borracho; vacilante.

groin /groin/ *n.* ingle *f.*

groom /grum/ *n.* (of horses) establero; (at wedding) novio *m.*

groove /gruv/ *n.* **1.** estría *f.* —*v.* **2.** acanalar.

grope /group/ *v.* tentar; andar a tientas.

gross /grous/ *a.* **1.** grueso; grosero. —*n.* **2.** gruesa *f.*

grossly /'grousli/ *adv.* groseramente.

gross national product producto nacional bruto *m.*

grossness /'grousnɪs/ *n.* grosería *f.*

grotesque /grou'tɛsk/ *a.* grotesco.

grotto /'grɒtou/ *n.* gruta *f.*

grouch /grautʃ/ *n.* gruñón; descontento *m.*

ground /graund/ *n.* tierra *f.*; terreno; suelo; campo; fundamento *m.*

ground floor planta baja *f.*

groundhog /'graund,hɒg/ *n.* marmota *f.*

groundless /'graundlɪs/ *a.* infundado.

groundwork /'graund,wɜrk/ *n.* base *f.*, fundamento *m.*

group /grup/ *n.* **1.** grupo *m.* —*v.* **2.** agrupar.

groupie /'grupi/ *n.* persona aficionada que acompaña a un grupo de música moderna.

grouse /graus/ *v.* quejarse

grove /grouv/ *n.* arboleda *f.*

grovel /'grɒvəl/ *v.* rebajarse; envilecerse.

grow /grou/ *v.* crecer; cultivar.

growl /graul/ *n.* **1.** gruñido *m.* —*v.* **2.** gruñir.

grown /groun/ *a.* crecido; desarrollado.

grownup /'groun,ʌp/ *n.* adulto -ta.

growth /grouθ/ *n.* crecimiento *m.*; vegetación *f.*; *Med.* tumor *m.*

grub /grʌb/ *n.* gorgojo *m.*, larva *f.*

grubby /'grʌbi/ *a.* gorgojoso, mugriento.

grudge /grʌdʒ/ *n.* rencor *m.* **bear a g.**, guardar rencor.

gruel /'gruəl/ *n.* **1.** atole *m.* —*v.* **2.** agotar.

gruesome /'grusəm/ *a.* horripilante.

gruff /grʌf/ *a.* ceñudo.

grumble /'grʌmbəl/ *v.* quejarse.

grumpy /'grʌmpi/ *a.* gruñón; quejoso.

grunt /grʌnt/ *v.* gruñir.

guarantee /,gærən'ti/ *n.* **1.** garantía *f.* —*v.* **2.** garantizar.

guarantor /'gærən,tɔr/ *n.* fiador -ra.

guaranty /'gærən,ti/ *n.* garantía *f.*

guard /gard/ *n.* **1.** guardia *m.* & *f.* —*v.* **2.** vigilar.

guarded /'gardɪd/ *a.* cauteloso.

guardhouse /'gard,haus/ *n.* prisión militar *f.*

guardian /'gardiən/ *n.* guardián -ana.

guardianship /'gardiən,ʃɪp/ *n.* tutela *f.*

guardsman /'gardzmən/ *n.* centinela *m.*

guava /'gwavə/ *n.* guayaba *f.*

gubernatorial /,gubərnə'tɔriəl/ *a.* gubernativo.

guerrilla /gə'rɪlə/ *n.* guerrilla *f.*; guerrillero, -ra.

guess /gɛs/ *n.* **1.** conjetura *f.* —*v.* **2.** adivinar; *Colloq.* creer.

guesswork /'gɛs,wɜrk/ *n.* conjetura *f.*

guest /gɛst/ *n.* huésped *m.* & *f.*

guest room alcoba de huéspedes *f.*, alcoba de respeto *f.*, cuarto para invitados *m.*

guffaw /gʌ'fɔ/ *n.* risotada *f.*

guidance /'gaidns/ *n.* dirección *f.*

guide /gaid/ *n.* **1.** guía *m.* & *f.* —*v.* **2.** guiar.

guidebook /'gaid,bʊk/ *n.* guía *f.*

guided tour /'gaidɪd/ visita explicada, visita programada, visita con guía *f.*

guideline /'gaid,lain/ *n.* pauta *f.*

guidepost /'gaid,poust/ *n.* poste indicador *m.*

guild /gɪld/ *n.* gremio *m.*

guile /gail/ *n.* engaño *m.*

guillotine /'gɪlə,tin/ *n.* **1.** guillotina *f.* —*v.* **2.** guillotinar.

guilt /gɪlt/ *n.* culpa *f.*

guiltily /'gɪltəli/ *adv.* culpablemente.

guiltless /'gɪltlɪs/ *a.* inocente.

guilty /'gɪlti/ *a.* culpable.

guinea fowl /'gɪni/ gallina de Guinea *f.*

guinea pig /'gɪni/ cobayo *m.*, conejillo de Indias *m.*

guise /gaiz/ *n.* modo *m.*

guitar /gɪ'tar/ *n.* guitarra *f.*

guitarist /gɪ'tarɪst/ *n.* guitarrista *m.* & *f.*

gulch /gʌltʃ/ *n.* quebrada *f.*

gulf /gʌlf/ *n.* golfo *m.*

gull /gʌl/ *n.* gaviota *f.*

gullet /'gʌlɪt/ *n.* esófago *m.*; zanja *f.*

gullible /'gʌləbəl/ *a.* crédulo.

gully /'gʌli/ *n.* barranca *f.*

gulp /gʌlp/ *n.* **1.** trago *m.* —*v.* **2.** tragar.

gum /gʌm/ *n.* **1.** goma *f.*; *Anat.* encía *f.* **chewing g.**, chicle *m.* —*v.* **2.** engomar.

gumbo /'gʌmbou/ *n.* quimbombó *m.*

gummy /'gʌmi/ *a.* gomoso.

gun /gʌn/ *n.* fusil, revólver *m.*

gunboat /'gʌn,bout/ *n.* cañonero *m.*

gunman /'gʌnmən/ *n.* bandido *m.*

gunner /'gʌnər/ *n.* artillero *m.*

gun permit licencia de armas *f.*

gunpowder /'gʌn,paudər/ *n.* pólvora *f.*

gunshot /'gʌn,ʃɒt/ *n.* escopetazo *m.*

gunwale /'gʌnḷ/ *n.* borda *f.*

gurgle /'gɜrgəl/ *n.* **1.** gorgoteo *m.* —*v.* **2.** gorgotear.

guru /'guru, gʊ'ru/ *n.* gurú *m.*

gush /gʌʃ/ *n.* **1.** chorro *m.* —*v.* **2.** brotar, chorrear.

gusher /'gʌʃər/ *n.* pozo de petróleo *m.*

gust /gʌst/ *n.* soplo *m.*; ráfaga *f.*

gustatory /'gʌstə,tɔri/ *a.* gustativo.

gusto /'gʌstou/ *n.* gusto; placer *m.*

gusty /'gʌsti/ *a.* borrascoso.

gut /gʌt/ *n.* intestino *m.*, tripa *f.*

gutter /'gʌtər/ *n.* canal; zanja *f.*

guttural /'gʌtərəl/ *a.* gutural.

guy /gai/ *n.* tipo *m.*

guzzle /'gʌzəl/ *v.* engullir; tragar.

gym /dʒɪm/ *n.* gimnasio *m.*

gymnasium /gɪm'naziəm/ *n.* gimnasio *m.*

gymnast /'dʒɪmnæst/ *n.* gimnasta *m.* & *f.*

gymnastic /dʒɪm'næstɪk/ *a.* gimnástico.

gymnastics /dʒɪm'næstɪks/ *n.* gimnasia *f.*

gynecologist /,gainɪ'kɒlədʒɪst/ *n.* ginecólogo, -ga *m.* & *f.*

gynecology /,gainɪ'kɒlədʒi/ *n.* ginecología *f.*

gypsum /'dʒɪpsəm/ *n.* yeso *m.*

Gypsy /'dʒɪpsi/ *a.* & *n.* gitano -na.

gyrate /'dʒaireit/ *v.* girar.

gyroscope /'dʒairə,skoup/ *n.* giroscopio *m.*

H

habeas corpus /'heibiəs 'kɔrpəs/ habeas corpus *m.*

haberdasher /'hæbər,dæʃər/ *n.* camisero *m.*

haberdashery /'hæbər,dæʃəri/ *n.* camisería *f.*

habiliment /hə'bɪləmənt/ *n.* vestuario *m.*

habit /'hæbɪt/ *n.* costumbre *f.*, hábito *m.* **be in the h. of,** estar acostumbrado a; soler.

habitable /'hæbɪtəbəl/ *a.* habitable.

habitat /'hæbɪ,tæt/ *n.* habitación *f.*, ambiente *m.*

habitation /,hæbɪ'teiʃən/ *n.* habitación *f.*

habitual /hə'bɪtʃuəl/ *a.* habitual.

habituate /hə'bɪtʃu,eit/ *v.* habituar.

habitué /hə'bɪtʃu,ei/ *n.* parroquiano *m.*

hack /hæk/ *n.* **1.** coche de alquiler. —*v.* **2.** tajar.

hacker /'hækər/ *n.* pirata *m.* & *f.*

hackneyed /'hæknid/ *a.* trillado.

hacksaw /'hæk,sɔ/ *n.* sierra para cortar metal *f.*

haddock /'hædək/ *n.* merluza *f.*

haft /hæft/ *n.* mango *m.*

hag /hæg, hɑg/ *n.* bruja *f.*

haggard /'hægərd/ *a.* trasnochado.

haggle /'hægəl/ *v.* regatear.

hail /heil/ *n.* **1.** granizo; (greeting) saludo *m.* —*v.* **2.** granizar; saludar.

Hail Mary /'mɛəri/ Ave María *f.*

hailstone /'heil,stoun/ *n.* piedra de granizo *f.*

hailstorm /'heil,stɔrm/ *n.* granizada *f.*

hair /hɛər/ *n.* pelo; cabello *m.*

haircut /'hɛər,kʌt/ *n.* corte de pelo.

hairdo /'hɛər,du/ *n.* peinado *m.*

hairdresser /'hɛər,drɛsər/ *n.* peluquero *m.*

hair dryer /'draiər/ secador de pelo, secador *m.*

hairpin /'hɛər,pɪn/ *n.* horquilla *f.*; gancho *m.*

hair's-breadth /'hɛərz,brɛdθ/ *n.* ancho de un pelo *m.*

hairspray /'hɛərsprei/ *n.* aerosol para cabello.

hairy /'hɛəri/ *a.* peludo.

halcyon /'hælsiən/ *n.* **1.** alcedón *m.* —*a.* **2.** tranquilo.

hale /heil/ *a.* sano.

half /hæf/ *a.* **1.** medio. —*n.* **2.** mitad *f.*

half-and-half /'hæf ən 'hæf/ *a.* mitad y mitad.

half-baked /'hæf 'beikt/ *a.* medio crudo.

half-breed /'hæf ,brid/ *n.* mestizo *m.*

half brother *n.* medio hermano *m.*

half-hearted /'hæf'hartɪd/ *a.* sin entusiasmo.

half-mast /'hæf 'mæst/ *a.* & *n.* media asta *m.*

halfpenny /'heipəni/ *n.* medio penique *m.*

halfway /'hæf'wei/ *adv.* a medio camino.

half-wit /'hæf ,wɪt/ *n.* bobo *m.*

halibut /'hæləbət/ *n.* hipogloso *m.*

hall /hɔl/ *n.* corredor *m.*; (for assembling) sala *f.* **city h.,** ayuntamiento *m.*

hallmark /'hɔl,mark/ *n.* marca del contraste *f.*

hallow /'hælou/ *v.* consagrar.

Halloween /,hælə'win/ *n.* víspera de Todos los Santos *f.*

hallucination /hə,lusə'neiʃən/ *n.* alucinación *f.*

hallway /'hɔl,wei/ *n.* pasadizo *m.*

halo /'heilou/ *n.* halo *m.*; corona *f.*

halt /hɔlt/ *a.* **1.** cojo. —*n.* **2.** parada *f.* —*v.* **3.** parar. —*interj.* **4.** ¡alto!

halter /'hɔltər/ *n.* cabestro *m.*

halve /hæv/ *v.* dividir en dos partes.

halyard /'hælyərd/ *n.* driza *f.*

ham /hæm/ *n.* jamón *m.*

hamburger /'hæm,bɜrgər/ *n.* albóndiga *f.*

hamlet /'hæmlɪt/ *n.* aldea *f.*

hammer /'hæmər/ *n.* **1.** martillo *m.* —*v.* **2.** martillar.

hammock /'hæmək/ *n.* hamaca *f.*

hamper /'hæmpər/ *n.* canasta *f.*, cesto *m.*

hamstring /'hæm,strɪŋ/ *n.* **1.** tendón de la corva *m.* —*v.* **2.** desjarretar.

hand /hænd/ *n.* **1.** mano *f.* **on the other h.,** en cambio. —*v.* **2.** pasar. **h. over,** entregar.

handbag /'hænd,bæg/ *n.* cartera *f.*

handball /'hænd,bɔl/ *n.* pelota *f.*

handbook /'hænd,bʊk/ *n.* manual *m.*

handbrake /'hændbreik/ *n.* freno de mano *m.*

handcuff /'hænd,kʌf/ *n.* esposa *v.* esposar.

handful /'hændfʊl/ *n.* puñado *m.*

handicap /'hændi,kæp/ *n.* desventaja *f.*

handicraft /'hændi,kræft/ *n.* artífice *m.*; destreza manual.

handiwork /'hændi,wɜrk/ *n.* artefacto *m.*

handkerchief /'hæŋkərtʃɪf/ *n.* pañuelo *m.*

handle /'hændḷ/ *n.* **1.** mango *m.* —*v.* **2.** manejar.

hand luggage equipaje de mano *m.*

handmade /'hænd'meid/ *a.* hecho a mano.

handmaid /'hænd,meid/ *n.* criada de mano, sirvienta *f.*

hand organ organillo *m.*

handsome /'hænsəm/ *a.* guapo; hermoso.

hand-to-hand /'hænd tə 'hænd/ *adv.* de mano a mano.

handwriting /'hænd,raitɪŋ/ *n.* escritura *f.*

handy /'hændi/ *a.* diestro; útil; a la mano.

hang /hæŋ/ *v.* colgar; ahorcar.

hangar /'hæŋər/ *n.* hangar *m.*

hangdog /'hæŋ,dɒg/ *a.* & *n.* camastrón *m.*

hanger /'hæŋər/ *n.* colgador, gancho *m.*

hanger-on /'hæŋər 'ɒn/ *n.* dependiente; mogollón *m.*

hang glider /'glaidər/ aparato para vuelo libre, delta, ala delta.

hanging /'hæŋɪŋ/ *n.* **1.** ahorcadura *f.* —*a.* **2.** colgante.

hangman /'hæŋmən/ *n.* verdugo *m.*

hangnail /'hæŋ,neil/ *n.* padrastro *m.*

hang out *v.* enarbolar.

hangover /'hæŋ,ouvər/ *n.* resaca *f.*

hangup /'hæŋʌp/ *n.* tara (psicológica) *f.*

hank /hæŋk/ *n.* madeja *f.*

hanker /'hæŋkər/ *v.* ansiar; apetecer.

haphazard /,hæp'hæzərd/ *a.* casual.

happen /'hæpən/ *v.* acontecer, suceder, pasar.

happening /'hæpənɪŋ/ *n.* acontecimiento *m.*

happiness /'hæpinɪs/ *n.* felicidad; dicha *f.*

happy /'hæpi/ *a.* feliz; contento; dichoso.

happy-go-lucky /'hæpi gou 'lʌki/ a. & n. descuidado m.

harakiri /'hɑrə'kɪəri/ n. harakiri (suicidio japonés) m.

harangue /hə'ræŋ/ n. **1.** arenga f. —v. **2.** arengar.

harass /hə'ræs/ v. acosar; atormentar.

harbinger /'hɑrbɪndʒər/ n. presagio m.

harbor /'hɑrbər/ n. **1.** puerto; albergue m. —v. **2.** abrigar.

hard /hɑrd/ a. **1.** duro; difícil. —adv. **2.** mucho.

hard coal antracita m.

hard disk disco duro m.

harden /'hɑrdn̩/ v. endurecer.

hard-headed /'hɑrd 'hɛdɪd/ a. terco.

hard-hearted /'hɑrd'hɑrtɪd/ a. empedernido.

hardiness /'hɑrdinɪs/ n. vigor m.

hardly /'hɑrdli/ adv. apenas.

hardness /'hɑrdnɪs/ n. dureza; dificultad f.

hardship /'hɑrdʃɪp/ n. penalidad f.; trabajo m.

hardware /'hɑrd,wɛər/ n. hardware m.; (computer) quincalla f.

hardwood /'hɑrd,wʊd/ n. madera dura f.

hardy /'hɑrdi/ a. fuerte, robusto.

hare /hɛər/ n. liebre f.

harebrained /'hɛər,breind/ a. tolondro.

harelip /'hɛər,lɪp/ n. **1.** labio leporino m. —a. **2.** labihendido.

harem /'hɛərəm/ n. harén m.

hark /hɑrk/ v. escuchar; atender.

Harlequin /'hɑrləkwɪn/ n. arlequín m.

harlot /'hɑrlət/ n. ramera f.

harm /hɑrm/ n. **1.** mal, daño; perjuicio m. —v. **2.** dañar.

harmful /'hɑrmfəl/ a. dañoso.

harmless /'hɑrmlɪs/ a. inocente.

harmonic /hɑr'mɒnɪk/ a. armónico m.

harmonica /hɑr'mɒnɪkə/ n. armónica f.

harmonious /hɑr'mouniəs/ a. armonioso.

harmonize /'hɑrmə,naiz/ v. armonizar.

harmony /'hɑrməni/ n. armonía f.

harness /'hɑrnɪs/ n. arnés m.

harp /hɑrp/ n. arpa f.

harpoon /hɑr'pun/ n. arpón m.

harridan /'hɑridn̩/ n. vieja regañona f.

harrow /'hærou/ n. **1.** rastro m.; grada f. —v. **2.** gradar.

harry /'hæri/ v. acosar.

harsh /hɑrʃ/ a. áspero.

harshness /'hɑrʃnɪs/ n. aspereza f.

harvest /'hɑrvɪst/ n. **1.** cosecha f. —v. **2.** cosechar.

hash /hæʃ/ n. picadillo m.

hashish /'hæʃiʃ/ n. haxis m.

hasn't /'hæzənt/ v. no tiene (neg. + tener).

hassle /'hæsəl/ n. lío m., molestia f.; controversia f.

hassock /'hæsək/ n. cojín m.

haste /heist/ n. prisa f.

hasten /'heisən/ v. apresurarse, darse prisa.

hasty /'heisti/ a. apresurado.

hat /hæt/ n. sombrero m.

hat box /hæt,bɒks/ sombrerera f.

hatch /hætʃ/ n. **1.** Naut. cuartel m. —v. **2.** incubar; Fig. tramar.

hatchery /'hætʃəri/ n. criadero m.

hatchet /'hætʃɪt/ n. hacha pequeña.

hate /heit/ n. **1.** odio m. —v. **2.** odiar, detestar.

hateful /'heitfəl/ a. detestable.

hatred /'heitrɪd/ n. odio m.

haughtiness /'hɔtinɪs/ n. arrogancia f.

haughty /'hɔti/ a. altivo.

haul /hɔl/ n. **1.** (fishery) redada f. —v. **2.** tirar, halar.

haunch /hɔntʃ/ n. anca f.

haunt /hɔnt/ n. **1.** lugar frecuentado. —v. **2.** frecuentar, andar por.

have /hæv; unstressed həv, əv/ v. tener; haber.

haven /'heivən/ n. puerto; asilo m.

haven't /'hævənt/ v. no tiene (neg. + tener).

havoc /'hævək/ n. ruina f.

hawk /hɔk/ n. halcón m.

hawker /'hɔkər/ n. buhonero m.

hawser /'hɔzər/ n. cable m.

hawthorn /'hɔ,θɔrn/ n. espino m.

hay /hei/ n. heno m.

hay fever n. fiebre del heno f.

hayfield /'heifild/ n. henar m.

hayloft /'hei,lɔft/ n. henil m.

haystack /'hei,stæk/ n. hacina de heno f.

hazard /'hæzərd/ n. **1.** azar m. —v. **2.** aventurar.

hazardous /'hæzərdəs/ a. peligroso.

haze /heiz/ n. niebla f.

hazel /'heizəl/ n. avellano m.

hazelnut /'heizəl,nʌt/ avellana f.

hazy /'heizi/ a. brumoso.

he /hei/ pron. él m.

head /hɛd/ n. **1.** cabeza f.; jefe m. —v. **2.** dirigir; encabezar.

headache /'hɛd,eik/ n. dolor de cabeza m.

headband /'hɛd,bænd/ n. venda para cabeza f.

headfirst /'hɛd'fɜrst/ adv. de cabeza.

headgear /'hɛd,gɪər/ n. tocado m.

headlight /'hɛd,lait/ n. linterna delantera f., farol de tope m.

headline /'hɛd,lain/ n. encabezado m.

headlong /'hɛd,lɔŋ/ a. precipitoso.

head-on /'hɛd 'ɒn/ adv. de frente.

headphones /'hɛd,founz/ n.pl. auriculares m.pl.

headquarters /'hɛd,kwɔrtərz/ n. jefatura f.; Mil. cuartel general.

headstone /'hɛd,stoun/ n. lápida mortuoria f.

headstrong /'hɛd,strɔŋ/ a. terco.

headwaiter /'hɛd'weitər/ jefe de comedor m. & f.

headwaters /'hɛd,wɔtərz/ n. cabeceras f.pl.

headway /'hɛd,wei/ n. avance m., progreso m.

headwork /'hɛd,wɜrk/ n. trabajo mental m.

heady /'hɛdi/ a. impetuoso.

heal /hil/ v. curar, sanar.

health /hɛlθ/ n. salud f.

healthful /'hɛlθfəl/ a. saludable.

healthy /'hɛlθi/ a. sano; salubre.

heap /hip/ n. montón m.

hear /hɪr/ v. oír. **h. from,** tener noticias de. **h. about, h. of,** oír hablar de.

hearing /'hɪərɪŋ/ n. oído m.

hearing aid n. audífono m.

hearsay /'hɪər,sei/ n. rumor m.

hearse /hɜrs/ n. ataúd m.

heart /hɑrt/ n. corazón; ánimo m. **by h.,** de memoria. **have h. trouble** padecer del corazón.

heartache /'hɑrt,eik/ n. angustia f.

heart attack ataque cardíaco, infarto, infarto de miocardio m.

heartbreak /'hɑrt,breik/ n. angustia f.; pesar m.

heartbroken /'hɑrt,broukən/ a. acongojado.

heartburn /'hɑrt,bɜrn/ n. acedía f., ardor de estómago m.

heartfelt /'hɑrt,fɛlt/ a. sentido.

hearth /hɑrθ/ n. hogar m., chimenea f.

heartless /'hɑrtlɪs/ a. empedernido.

heartsick /'hɑrt,sɪk/ a. desconsolado.

heart-stricken /'hɑrt 'strɪkən/ a. afligido.

heart-to-heart /'hɑrt tə 'hɑrt/ adv. franco; sincero.

hearty /'hɑrti/ a. cordial; vigoroso.

heat /hit/ n. **1.** calor; ardor m.; calefacción f. —v. **2.** calentar.

heated /'hitɪd/ a. acalorado.

heater /'hitər/ n. calentador m.

heath /hiθ/ n. matorral m.

heathen /'hiðən/ a. & n. pagano -na.

heather /'hɛðər/ n. brezo m.

heating /'hitɪŋ/ n. calefacción f.

heatstroke /'hit,strouk/ n. insolación f.

heat wave onda de calor f.

heave /hiv/ v. tirar.

heaven /'hɛvən/ n. cielo m.

heavenly /'hɛvənli/ a. divino.

heavy /'hɛvi/ a. pesado; oneroso.

Hebrew /'hibru/ a. & n. hebreo -ea.

hectic /'hɛktɪk/ a. turbulento.

hedge /hɛdʒ/ n. seto m.

hedgehog /'hɛdʒ,hɒg/ n. erizo m.

hedonism /'hidn̩,izəm/ n. hedonismo m.

heed /hid/ n. **1.** cuidado m. —v. **2.** atender.

heedless /'hidlɪs/ a. desatento; incauto.

heel /hil/ n. talón m.; (of shoe) tacón m.

heifer /'hɛfər/ n. novilla f.

height /hait/ n. altura f.

heighten /'haitn̩/ v. elevar; exaltar.

heinous /'heinəs/ a. nefando.

heir /ɛər/ **heiress** n. heredero -ra.

helicopter /'hɛli,kɒptər/ n. helicóptero m.

heliotrope /'hiliə,troup/ n. heliotropo m.

helium /'hiliəm/ n. helio m.

hell /hɛl/ n. infierno m.

Hellenism /'hɛlə,nizəm/ n. helenismo m.

hellish /'hɛlɪʃ/ a. infernal.

hello /hɛ'lou/ interj. ¡hola!; (on telephone) aló; bueno.

helm /hɛlm/ n. timón m.

helmet /'hɛlmɪt/ n. yelmo, casco m.

helmsman /'hɛlmzmən/ n. limonero m.

help /hɛlp/ n. **1.** ayuda f. **help!** ¡socorro! —v. **2.** ayudar. **h. oneself,** servirse. **can't help (but),** no poder menos de.

helper /'hɛlpər/ n. ayudante m.

helpful /'hɛlpfəl/ a. útil; servicial.

helpfulness /'hɛlpfəlnɪs/ n. utilidad f.

helpless /'hɛlplɪs/ a. imposibilitado.

hem /hɛm/ n. **1.** ribete m. —v. **2.** ribetear.

hemisphere /'hɛmɪ,sfɪər/ n. hemisferio m.

hemlock /'hɛm,lɒk/ n. abeto m.

hemoglobin /'himə,gloubɪn/ n. hemoglobina f.

hemophilia /,himə'fɪliə/ n. hemofilia f.

hemorrhage /'hɛmərɪdʒ/ n. hemorragia f.

hemorrhoids /'hɛmə,rɔidz/ n. hemorroides f.pl.

hemp /hɛmp/ n. cáñamo m.

hemstitch /'hɛm,stɪtʃ/ n. **1.** vainica f. —v. **2.** hacer una vainica.

hen /hɛn/ n. gallina f.

hence /hɛns/ adv. por lo tanto.

henceforth /,hɛns'fɔrθ/ adv. de aquí en adelante.

henchman /'hɛntʃmən/ n. paniaguado m.

henna /'hɛnə/ n. alheña f.

hepatitis /,hɛpə'taitɪs/ n. hepatitis f.

her /hɜr; unstressed hər, ər/ a. **1.** su. —pron. **2.** ella; la; le.

herald /'hɛrəld/ n. heraldo m.

heraldic /hɛ'rældɪk/ a. heráldico.

heraldry /'hɛrəldri/ n. heráldica f.

herb /ɜrb; esp. Brit. hɜrb/ n. yerba, hierba f.

herbaceous /hɜr'beiʃəs, ɜr-/ a. herbáceo.

herbarium /hɜr'bɛəriəm, ɜr-/ n. herbario m.

herd /hɜrd/ n. **1.** hato, rebaño m. —v. **2.** reunir en hatos.

here /hɪr/ adv. aquí; acá.

hereafter /hɪər'æftər/ adv. en lo futuro.

hereby /hɪər'bai/ adv. por éstas, por la presente.

hereditary /hə'rɛdi,tɛri/ a. hereditario.

heredity /hə'rɛditi/ n. herencia f.

herein /hɪər'ɪn/ adv. aquí dentro; incluso.

heresy /'hɛrəsi/ n. herejía f.

heretic /'hɛritɪk/ a. **1.** herético. —n. **2.** hereje m. & f.

heretical /hə'rɛtɪkəl/ a. herético.

heretofore /,hɪərtə'fɔr/ adv. hasta ahora.

herewith /hɪər'wɪθ/ adv. con esto, adjunto.

heritage /'hɛritɪdʒ/ n. herencia f.

hermetic /hɜr'mɛtɪk/ a. hermético.

hermit /'hɜrmɪt/ n. ermitaño m.

hernia /'hɜrniə/ n. hernia f.

hero /'hɪərou/ n. héroe m.

heroic /hɪ'rouɪk/ a. heroico.

heroically /hɪ'rouɪkəli/ adv. heroicamente.

heroin /'hɛrouɪn/ n. heroína f.

heroine /'hɛrouɪn/ n. heroína f.

heroism /'hɛrou,ɪzəm/ n. heroísmo m.

heron /'hɛrən/ n. garza f.

herring /'hɛrɪŋ/ n. arenque m.

hers /hɜrz/ pron. suyo, de ella.

herself /hər'sɛlf/ pron. sí, sí misma, se. **she h.,** ella misma. **with h.,** consigo.

hertz /hɜrts/ n. hertzio m.

hesitancy /'hɛzɪtənsi/ n. hesitación f.

hesitant /'hɛzɪtənt/ a. indeciso.

hesitate /'hɛzi,teit/ v. vacilar.

hesitation /,hɛzi'teiʃən/ n. duda; vacilación f.

heterogeneous /,hɛtərə'dʒiniəs/ a. heterogéneo.

heterosexual /,hɛtərə'sɛkʃuəl/ a. heterosexual.

hexagon /'hɛksə,gɒn/ n. hexágono m.

hibernate /'haibər,neit/ v. invernar.

hibernation /,haibər'neiʃən/ n. invernada f.

hibiscus /hai'bɪskəs/ n. hibisco m.

hiccup /'hɪkʌp/ n. **1.** hipo m. —v. **2.** tener hipo.

hickory /'hɪkəri/ n. nogal americano m.

hidden /'hɪdn̩/ a. oculto; escondido.

hide /haid/ n. **1.** cuero m.; piel f. —v. **2.** esconder; ocultar.

hideous /'hɪdiəs/ a. horrible.

hide-out /'haid ,aut/ n. escondite m.

hiding place /'haidɪŋ/ escondrijo m.

hierarchy /'haiə,rɑrki/ n. jerarquía f.

high /hai/ a. alto, elevado; (in price) caro.

highbrow /'hai,brau/ n. erudito m.

highfalutin /,haifə'lutn̩/ a. pomposo, presumido.

high fidelity de alta fidelidad.

highlighter /'hai,laitər/ n. marcador m.

highly /'haili/ adv. altamente; sumamente.

high school escuela secundaria f.

highway /'hai,wei/ n. carretera f.; camino real m.

hijacker /'hai,dʒækər/ n. secuestrador, pirata de aviones m.

hike /haik/ n. caminata f.

hilarious /hɪ'lɛəriəs/ a. alegre, bullicioso.

hilarity /hɪ'læriti/ n. hilaridad f.

hill /hɪl/ n. colina f.; cerro m.; **down h.,** cuesta abajo. **up h.,** cuesta arriba.

hilly /'hɪli/ a. accidentado.

hilt /hɪlt/ n. puño m. **up to the h.,** a fondo.

him /hɪm/ pron. él; lo; le.

himself /hɪm'sɛlf/ pron. sí, sí mismo; se. **he h.,** él mismo. **with h.,** consigo.

hinder /'hɪndər/ v. impedir.

hindmost /'haind,moust/ a. último.

hindquarter /'haind,kwɔrtər/ n. cuarto trasero m.

hindrance /'hɪndrəns/ n. obstáculo m.

hinge /hɪndʒ/ n. **1.** gozne m. —v. **2.** engoznar. **h. on,** depender de.

hint /hɪnt/ n. **1.** insinuación f.; indicio m. —v. **2.** insinuar.

hip /hɪp/ *n.* cadera *f.*
hippopotamus /ˌhɪpəˈpɒtəməs/ *n.* hipopótamo *m.*
hire /haiᵊr/ *v.* alquilar.
his /hɪz; *unstressed* ɪz/ *a.* **1.** su. —*pron.* **2.** suyo, de él.
Hispanic /hɪˈspænɪk/ *a.* hispano.
hiss /hɪs/ *v.* silbar, sisear.
historian /hɪˈstɔriən/ *n.* historiador *m.*
historic /hɪˈstɔrɪk/ **historical** *a.* histórico.
history /ˈhɪstəri/ *n.* historia *f.*
histrionic /ˌhɪstriˈɒnɪk/ *a.* histriónico.
hit /hɪt/ *n.* **1.** golpe *m.; Colloq.* éxito *m.*; (Internet) hit *m.* —*v.* **2.** golpear.
hitch /hɪtʃ/ *v.* amarrar; enganchar.
hitchhike /ˈhɪtʃˌhaik/ *v.* hacer autostop.
hitchhiker /ˈhɪtʃˌhaikər/ *n.* autostopista *f.*
hitchhiking /ˈhɪtʃˌhaikɪŋ/ *n.* autostop *m.*
hither /ˈhɪðər/ *adv.* acá, hacia acá.
hitherto /ˈhɪðərˌtu/ *adv.* hasta ahora.
hive /haiv/ *n.* colmena *f.*
hives /haivz/ *n.* urticaria *f.*
hoard /hɔrd/ *n.* **1.** acumulación *f.* —*v.* **2.** acaparar; atesorar.
hoarse /hɔrs/ *a.* ronco.
hoax /houks/ *n.* **1.** engaño *m.* —*v.* **2.** engañar.
hobby /ˈhɒbi/ *n.* afición *f.*, pasatiempo *m.*
hobgoblin /ˈhɒbˌgɒblɪn/ *n.* trasgo *m.*
hobnob /ˈhɒbˌnɒb/ *v.* tener intimidad.
hobo /ˈhoubou/ *n.* vagabundo *m.*
hockey /ˈhɒki/ *n.* hockey *m.* **ice-h.,** hockey sobre hielo.
hod /hɒd/ *n.* esparavel *m.*
hodgepodge /ˈhɒdʒˌpɒdʒ/ *n.* baturrillo *m.;* mezcolanza *f.*
hoe /hou/ *n.* **1.** azada *f.* —*v.* **2.** cultivar con azada.
hog /hɔg/ *n.* cerdo, puerco *m.*
hoist /hɔist/ *n.* **1.** grúa *f.*, elevador *m.* —*v.* **2.** elevar, enarbolar.
hold /hould/ *n.* **1.** presa *f.;* agarro *m.; Naut.* bodega *f.* **to get h. of,** conseguir, apoderarse de. —*v.* **2.** tener; detener; sujetar; celebrar.
holder /ˈhouldər/ *n.* tenedor *m.* **cigarette h.,** boquilla *f.*
holdup /ˈhouldˌʌp/ *n.* salteamiento *m.*
hole /houl/ *n.* agujero; hoyo; hueco *m.*
holiday /ˈhɒlɪˌdei/ *n.* día de fiesta.
holiness /ˈhoulinɪs/ *n.* santidad *f.*
Holland /ˈhɒlənd/ *n.* Holanda *f.*
hollow /ˈhɒlou/ *a.* **1.** hueco. —*n.* **2.** cavidad *f.* —*v.* **3.** ahuecar; excavar.
holly /ˈhɒli/ *n.* acebo *m.*
hollyhock /ˈhɒliˌhɒk/ *n.* malva real *f.*
holocaust /ˈhɒləˌkɔst/ *n.* holocausto *m.*
hologram /ˈhɒləˌgræm/ *n.* holograma *m.*
holography /həˈlɒgrəfi/ *n.* holografía *f.*
holster /ˈhoulstər/ *n.* pistolera *f.*
holy /ˈhouli/ *a.* santo.
holy day disanto *m.*
Holy See Santa Sede *f.*
Holy Spirit Espíritu Santo *m.*
Holy Week Semana Santa *f.*
homage /ˈhɒmɪdʒ/ *n.* homenaje *m.*
home /houm/ *n.* casa, morada *f;* hogar *m.* **at h.,** en casa. **to go h.,** ir a casa.
home appliance electrodoméstica *m.*
home computer ordenador doméstico *m.*, computadora doméstica *f.*
homeland /ˈhoumˌlænd/ *n.* patria *f.*
homely /ˈhoumli/ *a.* feo; casero.
home rule *n.* autonomía *f.*
homesick /ˈhoumˌsɪk/ *a.* nostálgico.
homespun /ˈhoumˌspʌn/ *a.* casero; tocho.
homeward /ˈhoumwərd/ *adv.* hacia casa.
homework /ˈhoumˌwɜrk/ *n.* deberes *m.pl.*
homicide /ˈhɒməˌsaid/ *n.* homicida *m. & f.*
homily /ˈhɒməli/ *n.* homilía *f.*
homogeneous /ˌhouməˈdʒiniəs/ *a.* homogéneo.
homogenize /həˈmɒdʒəˌnaiz/ *v.* homogenezar.
homosexual /ˌhouməˈsɛkʃuəl/ *n. & a.* homosexual *m.*
Honduras /hɒnˈdʊrəs/ *n.* Honduras *f.*
hone /houn/ *n.* **1.** piedra de afilar *f.* —*v.* **2.** afilar.
honest /ˈɒnɪst/ *a.* honrado, honesto; sincero.
honestly /ˈɒnɪstli/ *adv.* honradamente; de veras.
honesty /ˈɒnəsti/ *n.* honradez, honestidad *f.*
honey /ˈhʌni/ *n.* miel *f.*
honeybee /ˈhʌniˌbi/ *n.* abeja obrera *f.*
honeymoon /ˈhʌniˌmun/ *n.* luna de miel.
honeysuckle /ˈhʌniˌsʌkəl/ *n.* madreselva *f.*
honor /ˈɒnər/ *n.* **1.** honra *f.;* honor *m.* —*v.* **2.** honrar.
honorable /ˈɒnərəbəl/ *a.* honorable; ilustre.
honorary /ˈɒnəˌrɛri/ *a.* honorario.
hood /hʊd/ *n.* capota; capucha *f.; Auto.* cubierta del motor.
hoodlum /ˈhudləm/ *n.* pillo *m.*, rufián *m.*
hoodwink /ˈhʊdˌwɪŋk/ *v.* engañar.
hoof /hʊf/ *n.* pezuña *f.*
hook /hʊk/ *n.* **1.** gancho *m.* —*v.* **2.** enganchar.
hooligan /ˈhulɪgən/ *n.* gamberro -rra.
hoop /hup/ *n.* cerco *m.*
hop /hɒp/ *n.* **1.** salto *m.* —*v.* **2.** saltar.
hope /houp/ *n.* **1.** esperanza *f.* —*v.* **2.** esperar.
hopeful /ˈhoupfəl/ *a.* lleno de esperanzas.
hopeless /ˈhouplɪs/ *a.* desesperado; sin remedio.
horde /hɔrd/ *n.* horda *f.*
horehound /ˈhɔrˌhaund/ *n.* marrubio *m.*
horizon /həˈraizən/ *n.* horizonte *m.*
horizontal /ˌhɔrəˈzɒntl̩/ *a.* horizontal.
hormone /ˈhɔrmoun/ *n.* hormona *f.*
horn /hɔrn/ *n.* cuerno *m.;* (music) trompa *f.; Auto.* bocina *f.*
hornet /ˈhɔrnɪt/ *n.* avispón *m.*
horny /ˈhɔrni/ *a.* córneo; calloso.
horoscope /ˈhɔrəˌskoup/ *n.* horóscopo *m.*
horrendous /həˈrɛndəs/ *a.* horrendo.
horrible /ˈhɔrəbəl/ *a.* horrible.
horrid /ˈhɔrɪd/ *a.* horrible.
horrify /ˈhɔrəˌfai/ *v.* horrorizar.
horror /ˈhɔrər/ *n.* horror *m.*
horror film película de terror *f.*
hors d'oeuvre /ɔr ˈdɜrv/ *n.* entremés *m.*
horse /hɔrs/ *n.* caballo *m.* **to ride a h.,** cabalgar.
horseback /ˈhɔrsˌbæk/ *n.* **on h.,** a caballo. **to ride h.,** montar a caballo.
horseback riding equitación *f.*
horsefly /ˈhɔrsˌflai/ *n.* tábano *m.*
horsehair /ˈhɔrsˌhɛər/ *n.* pelo de caballo *m.;* tela de crin *f.*
horseman /ˈhɔrsmən/ *n.* jinete *m.*
horsemanship /ˈhɔrsmənˌʃɪp/ *n.* manejo *m.*, equitación *f.*
horsepower /ˈhɔrsˌpauər/ *n.* caballo de fuerza *m.*
horse race carrera de caballos *f.*
horseradish /ˈhɔrsˌrædɪʃ/ *n.* rábano picante *m.*
horseshoe /ˈhɔrsˌʃu/ *n.* herradura *f.*
hortatory /ˈhɔrtəˌtɔri/ *a.* exhortatorio.
horticulture /ˈhɔrtɪˌkʌltʃər/ *n.* horticultura *f.*
hose /houz/ *n.* medias *f.pl.;* (garden) manguera *f.*
hosiery /ˈhouʒəri/ *n.* calcetería *f.*
hospitable /ˈhɒspɪtəbəl/ *a.* hospitalario.
hospital /ˈhɒspɪtl̩/ *n.* hospital *m.*
hospitality /ˌhɒspɪˈtælɪti/ *n.* hospitalidad *f.*
hospitalization /ˌhɒspɪtl̩ɪˈzeiʃən/ *n.* hospitalización *f.*
hospitalize /ˈhɒspɪtl̩ˌaiz/ *v.* hospitalizar.
host /houst/ *n.* anfitrión *m.*, dueño de la casa; *Relig.* hostia *f.*
hostage /ˈhɒstɪdʒ/ *n.* rehén *m.*
hostel /ˈhɒstl̩/ *n.* hostería *f.*
hostelry /ˈhɒstl̩ri/ *n.* fonda *f.*, parador *m.*
hostess /ˈhoustɪs/ *n.* anfitriona *f.*, dueña de la casa.
hostile /ˈhɒstl̩/ *a.* hostil.
hostility /hɒˈstɪlɪti/ *n.* hostilidad *f.*
hot /hɒt/ *a.* caliente; (sauce) picante. **to be h.,** tener calor; (weather) hacer calor.
hotbed /ˈhɒtˌbɛd/ *n.* estercolero *m.* *Fig.* foco *m.*
hot dog perrito caliente *m.*
hotel /houˈtɛl/ *n.* hotel *m.*
hotelier /ˌoutəlˈyei, ˌhoutl̩ˈɪər/ *n.* hotelero -ra.
hot-headed /ˈhɒt ˈhɛdɪd/ *a.* turbulento, alborotadizo.
hothouse /ˈhɒtˌhaus/ *n.* invernáculo *m.*
hot-water bottle /ˈhɒt ˈwɔtər/ bolsa de agua caliente *f.*
hound /haund/ *n.* **1.** sabueso *m.* —*v.* **2.** perseguir; seguir la pista.
hour /auᵊr/ *n.* hora *f.*
hourglass /ˈauᵊrˌglæs/ *n.* reloj de arena *m.*
hourly /ˈauᵊrli/ *a.* **1.** por horas. —*adv.* **2.** a cada hora.
house /*n* haus; *v* hauz/ *n.* **1.** casa *f.; Theat.* público *m.* —*v.* **2.** alojar, albergar.
housefly /ˈhausˌflai/ *n.* mosca ordinaria *f.*
household /ˈhausˌhould/ *n.* familia; casa *f.*
housekeeper /ˈhausˌkipər/ *n.* ama de llaves.
housemaid /ˈhausˌmeid/ *n.* criada *f.*, sirvienta *f.*
housewife /ˈhausˌwaif/ *n.* ama de casa.
housework /ˈhausˌwɜrk/ *n.* tareas domésticas.
hovel /ˈhʌvəl/ *n.* choza *f.*
hover /ˈhʌvər/ *v.* revolotear.
hovercraft /ˈhʌvərˌkræft/ *n.* aerodeslizador *m.*
how /hau/ *adv.* cómo. **h. much,** cuánto. **h. many,** cuántos. **h. far,** a qué distancia.
however /hauˈɛvər/ *adv.* como quiera; sin embargo.
howl /haul/ *n.* **1.** aullido *m.* —*v.* **2.** aullar.
HTML *abbr.* (HyperText Markup Language) Lenguaje de Marcado de Hipertexto *m.*
hub /hʌb/ *n.* centro *m.;* eje *m.* **h. of a wheel,** cubo de la rueda *m.*
hubbub /ˈhʌbʌb/ *n.* alboroto *m.*, bulla *f.*
hue /hyu/ *n.* matiz; color *m.*
hug /hʌg/ *n.* **1.** abrazo *m.* —*v.* **2.** abrazar.
huge /hyudʒ/ *a.* enorme.
hulk /hʌlk/ *n.* casco de buque *m.*
hull /hʌl/ *n.* **1.** cáscara *f.;* (naval) casco *m.* —*v.* **2.** decascarar.
hum /hʌm/ *n.* **1.** zumbido *m.* —*v.* **2.** tararear; zumbar.
human /ˈhyumən/ *a. & n.* humano -na.
human being ser humano *m.*
humane /hyuˈmein/ *a.* humano, humanitario.
humanism /ˈhyuməˌnɪzəm/ *n.* humanidad *f.;* benevolencia *f.*
humanitarian /hyuˌmænɪˈtɛəriən/ *a.* humanitario.
humanity /hyuˈmænɪti/ *n.* humanidad *f.*
humanly /ˈhyumənli/ *a.* humanamente.
humble /ˈhʌmbəl/ *a.* humilde.
humbug /ˈhʌmˌbʌg/ *n.* farsa *f.*, embaucador *m.*
humdrum /ˈhʌmˌdrʌm/ *a.* monótono.
humid /ˈhyumɪd/ *a.* húmedo.
humidity /hyuˈmɪdɪti/ *n.* humedad *f.*
humiliate /hyuˈmɪliˌeit/ *v.* humillar.
humiliation /hyuˌmɪliˈeiʃən/ *n.* mortificación *f.;* bochorno *m.*
humility /hyuˈmɪlɪti/ *n.* humildad *f.*
humor /ˈhyumər/ *n.* **1.** humor; capricho *m.* —*v.* **2.** complacer.
humorist /ˈhyumərɪst/ *n.* humorista *m.*
humorous /ˈhyumərəs/ *a.* divertido.
hump /hʌmp/ *n.* joroba *f.*
humpback /ˈhʌmpˌbæk/ *n.* jorobado *m.*
humus /ˈhyuməs/ *n.* humus *m.*
hunch /hʌntʃ/ *n.* giba *f.;* (idea) corazonada *f.*
hunchback /ˈhʌntʃˌbæk/ *n.* jorobado *m.*
hundred /ˈhʌndrɪd/ *a. & pron.* **1.** cien, ciento. **200,** doscientos. **300,** trescientos. **400,** cuatrocientos. **500,** quinientos. **600,** seiscientos. **700,** setecientos. **800,** ochocientos. **900,** novecientos. —*n.* **2.** centenar *m.*
hundredth /ˈhʌndrɪdθ/ *n. & a.* centésimo *m.*
Hungarian /hʌŋˈgɛəriən/ *a. & n.* húngaro -ra.
Hungary /ˈhʌŋgəri/ Hungría *f.*
hunger /ˈhʌŋgər/ *n.* hambre *f.*
hunger strike huelga de hambre *f.*
hungry /ˈhʌŋgri/ *a.* hambriento. **to be h.,** tener hambre.
hunt /hʌnt/ *n.* **1.** caza *f.* —*v.* **2.** cazar. **h. up,** buscar.
hunter /ˈhʌntər/ *n.* cazador *m.*
hunting /ˈhʌntɪŋ/ *n.* caza *f.* **to go h.,** ir de caza.
hurdle /ˈhɜrdl̩/ *n.* zarzo *m.*, valla *f.;* dificultad *f.*
hurl /hɜrl/ *v.* arrojar.
hurricane /ˈhɜrɪˌkein/ *n.* huracán *m.*
hurry /ˈhɜri/ *n.* **1.** prisa *f.* **to be in a h.,** tener prisa. —*v.* **2.** apresurar; darse prisa.
hurt /hɜrt/ *n.* **1.** daño, perjuicio *m.* —*v.* **2.** dañar; lastimar; doler; ofender.
hurtful /ˈhɜrtfəl/ *a.* perjudicial, dañino.
hurtle /ˈhɜrtl̩/ *v.* lanzar.
husband /ˈhʌzbənd/ *n.* marido, esposo *m.*
husk /hʌsk/ *n.* **1.** cáscara *f.* —*v.* **2.** descascarar.
husky /ˈhʌski/ *a.* fornido.
hustle /ˈhʌsəl/ *v.* empujar.
hustle and bustle ajetreo *m.*
hut /hʌt/ *n.* choza *f.*
hyacinth /ˈhaiəsɪnθ/ *n.* jacinto *m.*
hybrid /ˈhaibrɪd/ *a.* híbrido.
hydrangea /haiˈdreindʒə/ *n.* hortensia *f.*
hydraulic /haiˈdrɔlɪk/ *a.* hidráulico.
hydroelectric /ˌhaidrouɪˈlɛktrɪk/ *a.* hidroeléctrico.
hydrogen /ˈhaidrədʒən/ *n.* hidrógeno *m.*
hydrophobia /ˌhaidrəˈfoubiə/ *n.* hidrofobia. *f.*
hydroplane /ˈhaidrəˌplein/ *n.* hidroavión *m.*
hydrotherapy /ˌhaidrəˈθɛrəpi/ *n.* hidroterapia *f.*
hyena /haiˈinə/ *n.* hiena *f.*
hygiene /ˈhaidʒin/ *n.* higiene *f.*
hygienic /ˌhaidʒiˈɛnɪk/ *a.* higiénico.
hymn /hɪm/ *n.* himno *m.*
hymnal /ˈhɪmnl̩/ *n.* himnario *m.*
hype /haip/ *n.* *Colloq.* **1.** bomba publicitario *f.* —*v.* **2.** promocionar a bombo y platillo.
hypercritical /ˌhaipərˈkrɪtɪkəl/ *a.* hipercrítico.
hyperlink /ˈhaipərˌlɪŋk/ *n.* (Internet) hiperenlace *m.*
hypermarket /ˈhaipərˌmɑrkɪt/ *n.* hipermercado *m.*
hypertension /ˌhaipərˈtɛnʃən/ *n.* hipertensión *f.*

hypertext /'haɪpər,tɛkst/ *n.* (Internet) hipertexto *m.*
hyphen /'haɪfən/ *n.* guión *m.*
hyphenate /'haɪfə,neɪt/ *v.* separar con guión.
hypnosis /hɪp'noʊsɪs/ *n.* hipnosis *f.*
hypnotic /hɪp'nɒtɪk/ *a.* hipnótico.
hypnotism /'hɪpnə,tɪzəm/ *n.* hipnotismo *m.*
hypnotize /'hɪpnə,taɪz/ *v.* hipnotizar.
hypochondria /,haɪpə'kɒndriə/ *n.* hipocondría *f.*
hypochondriac /,haɪpə'kɒndri,æk/ *n. & a.* hipocondríaco *m.*
hypocrisy /hɪ'pɒkrəsi/ *n.* hipocresía *f.*
hypocrite /'hɪpəkrɪt/ *n.* hipócrita *m. & f.*
hypocritical /,hɪpə'krɪtɪkəl/ *a.* hipócrita.
hypodermic /,haɪpə'dɜrmɪk/ *a.* hipodérmico.
hypotenuse /haɪ'pɒtṇ,us/ *n.* hipotenusa *f.*
hypothesis /haɪ'pɒθəsɪs/ *n.* hipótesis *f.*
hypothetical /,haɪpə'θɛtɪkəl/ *a.* hipotético.
hysterectomy /,hɪstə'rɛktəmi/ *n.* histerectomía *f.*
hysteria /hɪ'stɛriə/ **hysterics** *n.* histeria *f.*
hysterical /hɪ'stɛrɪkəl/ *a.* histérico.

I

I /aɪ/ *pron.* yo.
iambic /aɪ'æmbɪk/ *a.* yámbico.
ice /aɪs/ *n.* hielo *m.*
iceberg /'aɪsbɜrg/ *n.* iceberg *m.*
icebox /'aɪs,bɒks/ *n.* refrigerador *m.*
ice cream helado, mantecado *m.;* **i.-c. cone,** barquillo de helado; **i.-c. parlor** heladería *f.*
ice cube cubito de hielo *m.*
ice skate patín de cuchilla *m.*
icon /'aɪkɒn/ *n.* icón *m.*
icy /'aɪsi/ *a.* helado; indiferente.
idea /aɪ'diə/ *n.* idea *f.*
ideal /aɪ'diəl/ *a.* ideal.
idealism /aɪ'diə,lɪzəm/ *n.* idealismo *m.*
idealist /aɪ'diəlɪst/ *n.* idealista *m. & f.*
idealistic /aɪ,diə'lɪstɪk/ *a.* idealista.
idealize /aɪ'diə,laɪz/ *v.* idealizar.
ideally /aɪ'diəli/ *adv.* idealmente.
identical /aɪ'dɛntɪkəl/ *a.* idéntico.
identifiable /aɪ,dɛntɪ'faɪəbəl/ *a.* identificable.
identification /aɪ,dɛntəfɪ'keɪʃən/ *n.* identificación *f.* **i. papers,** cédula de identidad *f.*
identify /aɪ'dɛntə,faɪ/ *v.* identificar.
identity /aɪ'dɛntɪti/ *n.* identidad *f.*
ideology /,aɪdi'ɒlədʒi/ *n.* ideología *f.*
idiocy /'ɪdiəsi/ *n.* idiotez *f.*
idiom /'ɪdiəm/ *n.* modismo *m.;* idioma *m.*
idiot /'ɪdiət/ *n.* idiota *m. & f.*
idiotic /,ɪdi'ɒtɪk/ *a.* idiota, tonto.
idle /'aɪdl/ *a.* desocupado; perezoso.
idleness /'aɪdḷnɪs/ *n.* ociosidad, pereza *f.*
idol /'aɪdl/ *n.* ídolo *m.*
idolatry /aɪ'dɒlətri/ *n.* idolatría *f.*
idolize /'aɪdḷ,aɪz/ *v.* idolatrar.
idyl /'aɪdl/ *n.* idilio *m.*
idyllic /aɪ'dɪlɪk/ *a.* idílico.
if /ɪf/ *conj.* si. **even if,** aunque.
ignite /ɪg'naɪt/ *v.* encender.
ignition /ɪg'nɪʃən/ *n.* ignición *f.*
ignoble /ɪg'noʊbəl/ *a.* innoble, indigno.
ignominious /,ɪgnə'mɪniəs/ *a.* ignominioso.
ignoramus /,ɪgnə'reɪməs/ *n.* ignorante *m.*
ignorance /'ɪgnərəns/ *n.* ignorancia *f.*
ignorant /'ɪgnərənt/ *a.* ignorante. **to be i. of,** ignorar.

ignore /ɪg'nɔr/ *v.* desconocer, pasar por alto.
ill /ɪl/ *a.* enfermo, malo.
illegal /ɪ'ligəl/ *a.* ilegal.
illegible /ɪ'lɛdʒəbəl/ *a.* ilegible.
illegibly /ɪ'lɛdʒəbli/ *a.* ilegiblemente.
illegitimacy /,ɪlɪ'dʒɪtəməsi/ *n.* ilegitimidad *f.*
illegitimate /,ɪlɪ'dʒɪtəmɪt/ *a.* ilegítimo; desautorizado.
illicit /ɪ'lɪsɪt/ *a.* ilícito.
illiteracy /ɪ'lɪtərəsi/ *n.* analfabetismo *m.*
illiterate /ɪ'lɪtərɪt/ *a. & n.* analfabeto -ta.
illness /'ɪlnɪs/ *n.* enfermedad, maldad *f.*
illogical /ɪ'lɒdʒɪkəl/ *a.* ilógico.
illuminate /ɪ'lumə,neɪt/ *v.* iluminar.
illumination /ɪ,lumə'neɪʃən/ *n.* iluminación *f.*
illusion /ɪ'luʒən/ *n.* ilusión *f.;* ensueño *m.*
illusive /ɪ'lusɪv/ *a.* ilusivo.
illustrate /'ɪlə,streɪt/ *v.* ilustrar; ejemplificar.
illustration /,ɪlə'streɪʃən/ *n.* ilustración *f.;* ejemplo; grabado *m.*
illustrative /ɪ'lʌstrətɪv/ *a.* ilustrativo.
illustrious /ɪ'lʌstriəs/ *a.* ilustre.
image /'ɪmɪdʒ/ *n.* imagen, estatua *f.*
imagery /'ɪmɪdʒri/ *n.* imaginación *f.*
imaginable /ɪ'mædʒənəbəl/ *a.* imaginable.
imaginary /ɪ'mædʒə,nɛri/ *a.* imaginario.
imagination /ɪ,mædʒə'neɪʃən/ *n.* imaginación *f.*
imaginative /ɪ'mædʒənətɪv/ *a.* imaginativo.
imagine /ɪ'mædʒɪn/ *v.* imaginarse, figurarse.
imam /ɪ'mɑm/ *n.* imán *m.*
imbecile /'ɪmbəsɪl/ *n. & a.* imbécil *m.*
imitate /'ɪmɪ,teɪt/ *v.* imitar.
imitation /,ɪmɪ'teɪʃən/ *n.* imitación *f.*
imitative /'ɪmɪ,teɪtɪv/ *a.* imitativo.
immaculate /ɪ'mækyəlɪt/ *a.* inmaculado.
immanent /'ɪmənənt/ *a.* inmanente.
immaterial /,ɪmə'tɪəriəl/ *a.* inmaterial; sin importancia.
immature /'ɪmə'tʃʊr/ *a.* inmaduro.
immediate /ɪ'midɪt/ *a.* inmediato.
immediately /ɪ'midɪtli/ *adv.* inmediatamente.
immense /ɪ'mɛns/ *a.* inmenso.
immerse /ɪ'mɜrs/ *v.* sumergir.
immigrant /'ɪmɪgrənt/ *n.* inmigrante *m. & f.*
immigrate /'ɪmɪ,greɪt/ *v.* inmigrar.
imminent /'ɪmənənt/ *a.* inminente.
immobile /ɪ'moʊbəl/ *a.* inmóvil.
immoderate /ɪ'mɒdərɪt/ *a.* inmoderado.
immodest /ɪ'mɒdɪst/ *a.* inmodesto; atrevido.
immoral /ɪ'mɔrəl/ *a.* inmoral.
immorality /,ɪmə'rælɪti/ *n.* inmoralidad *f.*
immorally /ɪ'mɔrəli/ *adv.* licenciosamente.
immortal /ɪ'mɔrtḷ/ *a.* inmortal.
immortality /,ɪmɔr'tælɪti/ *n.* inmortalidad *f.*
immortalize /ɪ'mɔrtḷ,aɪz/ *v.* inmortalizar.
immune /ɪ'myun/ *a.* inmune.
immunity /ɪ'myunɪti/ *n.* inmunidad *f.*
immunize /'ɪmyə,naɪz/ *v.* inmunizar.
impact /'ɪmpækt/ *n.* impacto *m.*
impair /ɪm'pɛər/ *v.* empeorar, perjudicar.
impale /ɪm'peɪl/ *v.* empalar.
impart /ɪm'pɑrt/ *v.* impartir, comunicar.
impartial /ɪm'pɑrʃəl/ *a.* imparcial.
impatience /ɪm'peɪʃəns/ *n.* impaciencia *f.*
impatient /ɪm'peɪʃənt/ *a.* impaciente.
impede /ɪm'pid/ *v.* impedir, estorbar.

impediment /ɪm'pɛdəmənt/ *n.* impedimento *m.*
impel /ɪm'pɛl/ *v.* impeler.
impenetrable /ɪm'pɛnɪtrəbəl/ *a.* impenetrable.
impenitent /ɪm'pɛnɪtənt/ *n. & a.* impenitente *m.*
imperative /ɪm'pɛrətɪv/ *a.* imperativo.
imperceptible /,ɪmpər'sɛptəbəl/ *a.* imperceptible.
imperfect /ɪm'pɜrfɪkt/ *a.* imperfecto.
imperfection /,ɪmpər'fɛkʃən/ *n.* imperfección *f.*
imperial /ɪm'pɪəriəl/ *a.* imperial.
imperialism /ɪm'pɪəriə,lɪzəm/ *n.* imperialismo *m.*
imperious /ɪm'pɪəriəs/ *a.* imperioso.
impersonal /ɪm'pɜrsənḷ/ *a.* impersonal.
impersonate /ɪm'pɜrsə,neɪt/ *v.* personificar; imitar.
impersonation /ɪm,pɜrsə'neɪʃən/ *n.* personificación *f.;* imitación *f.*
impertinence /ɪm'pɜrtṇəns/ *n.* impertinencia *f.*
impervious /ɪm'pɜrviəs/ *a.* impermeable.
impetuous /ɪm'pɛtʃuəs/ *a.* impetuoso.
impetus /'ɪmpɪtəs/ *n.* ímpetu *m.,* impulso *m.*
impinge /ɪm'pɪndʒ/ *v.* tropezar; infringir.
implacable /ɪm'plækəbəl/ *a.* implacable.
implant /ɪm'plænt/ *v.* implantar; inculcar.
implement /'ɪmpləmənt/ *n.* herramienta *f.*
implicate /'ɪmplɪ,keɪt/ *v.* implicar; embrollar.
implication /,ɪmplɪ'keɪʃən/ *n.* inferencia *f.;* complicidad *f.*
implicit /ɪm'plɪsɪt/ *a.* implícito.
implied /ɪm'plaɪd/ *a.* implícito.
implore /ɪm'plɔr/ *v.* implorar.
imply /ɪm'plaɪ/ *v.* significar; dar a entender.
impolite /,ɪmpə'laɪt/ *a.* descortés.
import /n 'ɪmpɔrt; v ɪm'pɔrt/ *n.* **1.** importación *f.* —*v.* **2.** importar.
importance /ɪm'pɔrtns/ *n.* importancia *f.*
important /ɪm'pɔrtṇt/ *a.* importante.
importation /,ɪmpɔr'teɪʃən/ *n.* importación *f.*
importune /,ɪmpɔr'tun/ *v.* importunar.
impose /ɪm'poʊz/ *v.* imponer.
imposition /,ɪmpə'zɪʃən/ *n.* imposición *f.*
impossibility /ɪm,pɒsə'bɪlɪti/ *n.* imposibilidad *f.*
impossible /ɪm'pɒsəbəl/ *a.* imposible.
impotence /'ɪmpətəns/ *n.* impotencia *f.*
impotent /'ɪmpətənt/ *a.* impotente.
impregnable /ɪm'prɛgnəbəl/ *a.* impregnable.
impregnate /ɪm'prɛgneɪt/ *v.* impregnar; fecundizar.
impresario /,ɪmprə'sɑri,oʊ/ *n.* empresario *m.*
impress /ɪm'prɛs/ *v.* impresionar.
impression /ɪm'prɛʃən/ *n.* impresión *f.*
impressive /ɪm'prɛsɪv/ *a.* imponente.
imprison /ɪm'prɪzən/ *v.* encarcelar.
imprisonment /ɪm'prɪzənmənt/ *n.* prisión, encarcelación *f.*
improbable /ɪm'prɒbəbəl/ *a.* improbable.
impromptu /ɪm'prɒmptu/ *a.* extemporáneo.
improper /ɪm'prɒpər/ *a.* impropio.
improve /ɪm'pruv/ *v.* mejorar; progresar.
improvement /ɪm'pruvmənt/ *n.* mejoramiento; progreso *m.*
improvise /'ɪmprə,vaɪz/ *v.* improvisar.
impudent /'ɪmpyədənt/ *a.* descarado.
impugn /ɪm'pyun/ *v.* impugnar.

impulse /'ɪmpʌls/ *n.* impulso *m.*
impulsive /ɪm'pʌlsɪv/ *a.* impulsivo.
impunity /ɪm'pyunɪti/ *n.* impunidad *f.*
impure /ɪm'pyʊr/ *a.* impuro.
impurity /ɪm'pyʊrɪti/ *n.* impureza *f.;* deshonestidad *f.*
impute /ɪm'pyut/ *v.* imputar.
in /ɪn/ *prep.* **1.** en; dentro de. —*adv.* **2.** adentro.
inadvertent /,ɪnəd'vɜrtṇt/ *a.* inadvertido.
inalienable /ɪn'eilyənəbəl/ *a.* inalienable.
inane /ɪ'neɪn/ *a.* mentecato.
inaugural /ɪn'ɔgyərəl/ *a.* inaugural.
inaugurate /ɪn'ɔgyə,reɪt/ *v.* inaugurar.
inauguration /ɪn,ɔgyə'reɪʃən/ *n.* inauguración *f.*
Inca /'ɪŋkə/ *n.* inca *m.*
incandescent /,ɪnkən'dɛsənt/ *a.* incandescente.
incantation /,ɪnkæn'teɪʃən/ *n.* encantación *f.,* conjuro *m.*
incapacitate /,ɪnkə'pæsɪ,teɪt/ *v.* incapacitar.
incarcerate /ɪn'kɑrsə,reɪt/ *v.* encarcelar.
incarnate /ɪn'kɑrnɪt/ *a.* encarnado; personificado.
incarnation /,ɪnkɑr'neɪʃən/ *n.* encarnación *f.*
incendiary /ɪn'sɛndi,ɛri/ *a.* incendario.
incense /ɪn'sɛns/ *n.* **1.** incienso *m.* —*v.* **2.** indignar.
incentive /ɪn'sɛntɪv/ *n.* incentivo *m.*
inception /ɪn'sɛpʃən/ *n.* comienzo *m.*
incessant /ɪn'sɛsənt/ *a.* incesante.
incest /'ɪnsɛst/ *n.* incesto *m.*
inch /ɪntʃ/ *n.* pulgada *f.*
incidence /'ɪnsɪdəns/ *n.* incidencia *f.*
incident /'ɪnsɪdənt/ *n.* incidente *m.*
incidental /,ɪnsɪ'dɛntḷ/ *a.* incidental.
incidentally /,ɪnsɪ'dɛntḷi/ *adv.* incidentalmente; entre paréntesis.
incinerate /ɪn'sɪnə,reɪt/ *v.* incinerar.
incinerator /ɪn'sɪnə,reɪtər/ *n.* incinerador *m.*
incipient /ɪn'sɪpiənt/ *a.* incipiente.
incision /ɪn'sɪʒən/ *n.* incisión *f.;* cortadura *f.*
incisive /ɪn'saɪsɪv/ *a.* incisivo; mordaz.
incisor /ɪn'saɪzər/ *n.* incisivo *m.*
incite /ɪn'saɪt/ *v.* incitar, instigar.
inclination /,ɪnklə'neɪʃən/ *n.* inclinación *f.;* declive *m.*
incline /n 'ɪnklaɪn; v ɪn'klaɪn/ *n.* **1.** pendiente *m.* —*v.* **2.** inclinar.
inclose /ɪn'kloʊz/ *v.* incluir.
include /ɪn'klud/ *v.* incluir, englobar.
including /ɪn'kludɪŋ/ *prep.* incluso.
inclusive /ɪn'klusɪv/ *a.* inclusivo.
incognito /,ɪnkɒg'nitoʊ/ *n. & adv.* incógnito *m.*
income /'ɪnkʌm/ *n.* renta *f.;* ingresos *m.pl.*
income tax impuesto sobre la renta *m.*
incomparable /ɪn'kɒmpərəbəl/ *a.* incomparable.
inconvenience /,ɪnkən'vinyəns/ *n.* **1.** incomodidad *f.* —*v.* **2.** incomodar.
inconvenient /,ɪnkən'vinyənt/ *a.* incómodo.
incorporate /ɪn'kɔrpə,reɪt/ *v.* incorporar; dar cuerpo.
incorrigible /ɪn'kɔrɪdʒəbəl/ *a.* incorregible.
increase /ɪn'kris/ *v.* crecer; aumentar.
incredible /ɪn'krɛdəbəl/ *a.* increíble.
incredulity /,ɪnkrɪ'dulɪti/ *n.* incredulidad *f.*
incredulous /ɪn'krɛdʒələs/ *a.* incrédulo.
increment /'ɪnkrəmənt/ *n.* incremento *m.,* aumento *m.*
incriminate /ɪn'krɪmə,neɪt/ *v.* incriminar.
incrimination /ɪn,krɪmə'neɪʃən/ *n.* incriminación *f.*
incrust /ɪn'krʌst/ *v.* incrustar.

incubator /ˈɪnkyəˌbeitər/ *n.* incubadora *f.*
inculcate /ɪnˈkʌlkeit/ *v.* inculcar.
incumbency /ɪnˈkʌmbənsi/ *n.* incumbencia *f.*
incumbent /ɪnˈkʌmbənt/ *a.* obligatorio; colocado sobre.
incur /ɪnˈkɜr/ *v.* incurrir.
incurable /ɪnˈkyʊrəbəl/ *a.* incurable.
indebted /ɪnˈdɛtɪd/ *a.* obligado; adeudado.
indeed /ɪnˈdid/ *adv.* verdaderamente, de veras. **no i.,** de ninguna manera.
indefatigable /ˌɪndɪˈfætɪgəbəl/ *a.* incansable.
indefinite /ɪnˈdɛfənɪt/ *a.* indefinido.
indefinitely /ɪnˈdɛfənɪtli/ *adv.* indefinidamente.
indelible /ɪnˈdɛləbəl/ *a.* indeleble.
indemnify /ɪnˈdɛmnəˌfai/ *v.* indemnizar.
indemnity /ɪnˈdɛmnɪti/ *n.* indemnificación *f.*
indent /ɪnˈdɛnt/ *n.* **1.** diente *f.*, mella *f.* **—***v.* **2.** indentar, mellar.
indentation /ˌɪndɛnˈteiʃən/ *n.* indentación *f.*
independence /ˌɪndɪˈpɛndəns/ *n.* independencia *f.*
independent /ˌɪndɪˈpɛndənt/ *a.* independiente.
in-depth /ˈɪn ˈdɛpθ/ *adj.* en profundidad.
index /ˈɪndɛks/ *n.* índice *m.;* (of book) tabla *f.*
index card ficha *f.*
index finger dedo índice *m.*
India /ˈɪndiə/ *n.* India *f.*
Indian /ˈɪndiən/ *a.* & *n.* indio -dia.
indicate /ˈɪndɪˌkeit/ *v.* indicar.
indication /ˌɪndɪˈkeiʃən/ *n.* indicación *f.*
indicative /ɪnˈdɪkətɪv/ *a.* & *n.* indicativo *m.*
indict /ɪnˈdait/ *v.* encausar.
indictment /ɪnˈdaitmənt/ *n.* (law) sumaria; denuncia *f.*
indifference /ɪnˈdɪfərəns/ *n.* indiferencia *f.*
indifferent /ɪnˈdɪfərənt/ *a.* indiferente.
indigenous /ɪnˈdɪdʒənəs/ *a.* indígena.
indigent /ˈɪndɪdʒənt/ *a.* indigente, pobre.
indigestion /ˌɪndɪˈdʒɛstʃən/ *n.* indigestión *f.*
indignant /ɪnˈdɪgnənt/ *a.* indignado.
indignation /ˌɪndɪgˈneiʃən/ *n.* indignación *f.*
indignity /ɪnˈdɪgnɪti/ *n.* indignidad *f.*
indirect /ˌɪndəˈrɛkt/ *a.* indirecto.
indiscreet /ˌɪndɪˈskrit/ *a.* indiscreto.
indiscretion /ˌɪndɪˈskrɛʃən/ *n.* indiscreción *f.*
indiscriminate /ˌɪndɪˈskrɪmənɪt/ *a.* promiscuo.
indispensable /ˌɪndɪˈspɛnsəbəl/ *a.* indispensable.
indisposed /ˌɪndɪˈspouzd/ *a.* indispuesto.
individual /ˌɪndəˈvɪdʒuəl/ *a.* & *n.* individuo *m.*
individuality /ˌɪndəˌvɪdʒuˈælɪti/ *n.* individualidad *f.*
individually /ˌɪndəˈvɪdʒuəli/ *adv.* individualmente.
indivisible /ˌɪndəˈvɪzəbəl/ *a.* indivisible.
indoctrinate /ɪnˈdɒktrəˌneit/ *v.* doctrinar, enseñar.
indolent /ˈɪndl̩ənt/ *a.* indolente.
indoor /ˈɪnˌdɔr/ *a.* **1.** interior. **indoors** **—***adv.* **2.** en casa; bajo techo.
indorse /ɪnˈdɔrs/ *v.* endosar.
induce /ɪnˈdus/ *v.* inducir, persuadir.
induct /ɪnˈdʌkt/ *v.* instalar, iniciar.
induction /ɪnˈdʌkʃən/ *n.* introducción *f.;* instalación *f.*
inductive /ɪnˈdʌktɪv/ *a.* inductivo; introductor.
indulge /ɪnˈdʌldʒ/ *v.* favorecer. **i. in,** entregarse a.
indulgence /ɪnˈdʌldʒəns/ *n.* indulgencia *f.*
indulgent /ɪnˈdʌldʒənt/ *a.* indulgente.
industrial /ɪnˈdʌstriəl/ *a.* industrial.
industrialist /ɪnˈdʌstriəlɪst/ *n.* industrial *m.*
industrial park polígono industrial *m.*
industrious /ɪnˈdʌstriəs/ *a.* industrioso, trabajador.
industry /ˈɪndəstri/ *n.* industria *f.*
inedible /ɪnˈɛdəbəl/ *a.* incomible.
ineligible /ɪnˈɛlɪdʒəbəl/ *a.* inelegible.
inept /ɪnˈɛpt/ *a.* inepto.
inert /ɪnˈɜrt/ *a.* inerte.
inertia /ɪnˈɜrʃə/ *n.* inercia *f.*
inevitable /ɪnˈɛvɪtəbəl/ *a.* inevitable.
inexpensive /ˌɪnɪkˈspɛnsɪv/ *a.* económico.
inexplicable /ɪnˈɛksplɪkəbəl/ *a.* inexplicable.
infallible /ɪnˈfæləbəl/ *a.* infalible.
infamous /ˈɪnfəməs/ *a.* infame.
infamy /ˈɪnfəmi/ *n.* infamia *f.*
infancy /ˈɪnfənsi/ *n.* infancia *f.*
infant /ˈɪnfənt/ *n.* nene *m.;* criatura *f.*
infantile /ˈɪnfənˌtail/ *a.* infantil.
infantry /ˈɪnfəntri/ *n.* infantería *f.*
infatuated /ɪnˈfætʃuˌeitɪd/ *a.* infatuado.
infatuation /ɪnˌfætʃuˈeiʃən/ *a.* encaprichamiento *m.*
infect /ɪnˈfɛkt/ *v.* infectar.
infection /ɪnˈfɛkʃən/ *n.* infección *f.*
infectious /ɪnˈfɛkʃəs/ *a.* infeccioso.
infer /ɪnˈfɜr/ *v.* inferir.
inference /ˈɪnfərəns/ *n.* inferencia *f.*
inferior /ɪnˈfɪəriər/ *a.* inferior.
infernal /ɪnˈfɜrnl̩/ *a.* infernal.
inferno /ɪnˈfɜrnou/ *n.* infierno *m.*
infest /ɪnˈfɛst/ *v.* infestar.
infidel /ˈɪnfɪdl̩/ *n.* **1.** infiel *m.* & *f.;* pagano -na. **—***a.* **2.** infiel.
infidelity /ˌɪnfɪˈdɛlɪti/ *n.* infidelidad *f.*
infiltrate /ɪnˈfɪltreit/ *v.* infiltrar.
infinite /ˈɪnfənɪt/ *a.* infinito.
infinitesimal /ˌɪnfɪnɪˈtɛsəməl/ *a.* infinitesimal.
infinitive /ɪnˈfɪnɪtɪv/ *n.* & *a.* infinitivo *m.*
infinity /ɪnˈfɪnɪti/ *n.* infinidad *f.*
infirm /ɪnˈfɜrm/ *a.* enfermizo.
infirmary /ɪnˈfɜrməri/ *n.* hospital *m.*, enfermería *f.*
infirmity /ɪnˈfɜrmɪti/ *n.* enfermedad *f.*
inflame /ɪnˈfleim/ *v.* inflamar.
inflammable /ɪnˈflæməbəl/ *a.* inflamable.
inflammation /ˌɪnfləˈmeiʃən/ *n.* inflamación *f.*
inflammatory /ɪnˈflæməˌtɔri/ *a.* inflamante; *Med.* inflamatorio.
inflate /ɪnˈfleit/ *v.* inflar.
inflation /ɪnˈfleiʃən/ *n.* inflación *f.*
inflection /ɪnˈflɛkʃən/ *n.* inflexión *f.;* (of the voice) modulación de la voz *f.*
inflict /ɪnˈflɪkt/ *v.* infligir.
infliction /ɪnˈflɪkʃən/ *n.* imposición *f.*
influence /ˈɪnfluəns/ *n.* **1.** influencia *f.* **—***v.* **2.** influir en.
influential /ˌɪnfluˈɛnʃəl/ *a.* influyente.
influenza /ˌɪnfluˈɛnzə/ *n.* gripe *f.*
influx /ˈɪnˌflʌks/ *n.* afluencia *f.*
inform /ɪnˈfɔrm/ *v.* informar. **i. oneself,** enterarse.
informal /ɪnˈfɔrməl/ *a.* informal.
information /ˌɪnfərˈmeiʃən/ *n.* informaciones *f.pl.*
information technology *n.* informática *f.*
infrastructure /ˈɪnfrəˌstrʌktʃər/ *n.* infraestructura *f.*
infringe /ɪnˈfrɪndʒ/ *v.* infringir.
infuriate /ɪnˈfyʊriˌeit/ *v.* enfurecer.
ingenious /ɪnˈdʒinyəs/ *a.* ingenioso.
ingenuity /ˌɪndʒəˈnuɪti/ *n.* ingeniosidad; destreza *f.*
ingredient /ɪnˈgridiənt/ *n.* ingrediente *m.*
inhabit /ɪnˈhæbɪt/ *v.* habitar.
inhabitant /ɪnˈhæbɪtənt/ *n.* habitante *m.* & *f.*
inhale /ɪnˈheil/ *v.* inhalar.
inherent /ɪnˈhɪərənt/ *a.* inherente.
inherit /ɪnˈhɛrɪt/ *v.* heredar.
inheritance /ɪnˈhɛrɪtəns/ *n.* herencia *f.*
inhibit /ɪnˈhɪbɪt/ *v.* inhibir.
inhibition /ˌɪnɪˈbɪʃən/ *n.* inhibición *f.*
inhuman /ɪnˈhyumən/ *a.* inhumano.
inimical /ɪˈnɪmɪkəl/ *a.* hostil.
inimitable /ɪˈnɪmɪtəbəl/ *a.* inimitable.
iniquity /ɪˈnɪkwɪti/ *n.* iniquidad *f.*
initial /ɪˈnɪʃəl/ *a.* & *n.* inicial *f.*
initiate /ɪˈnɪʃiˌeit/ *v.* iniciar.
initiation /ɪˌnɪʃiˈeiʃən/ *n.* iniciación *f.*
initiative /ɪˈnɪʃiətɪv/ *n.* iniciativa *f.*
inject /ɪnˈdʒɛkt/ *v.* inyectar.
injection /ɪnˈdʒɛkʃən/ *n.* inyección *f.*
injunction /ɪnˈdʒʌŋkʃən/ *n.* mandato *m.;* (law) embargo *m.*
injure /ˈɪndʒər/ *v.* herir; lastimar; ofender.
injurious /ɪnˈdʒʊriəs/ *a.* perjudicial.
injury /ˈɪndʒəri/ *n.* herida; afrenta *f.;* perjuicio *m.*
injustice /ɪnˈdʒʌstɪs/ *n.* injusticia *f.*
ink /ɪŋk/ *n.* tinta *f.*
inland /ˈɪnlænd/ *a.* **1.** interior. **—***adv.* **2.** tierra adentro.
inlet /ˈɪnlɛt/ *n.* entrada *f.;* ensenada *f.;* estuario *m.*
inmate /ˈɪnˌmeit/ *n.* residente *m.* & *f.;* (of a prison) preso -sa.
inn /ɪn/ *n.* posada *f.;* mesón *m.*
inner /ˈɪnər/ *a.* interior. **i. tube,** cámara de aire.
innocence /ˈɪnəsəns/ *n.* inocencia *f.*
innocent /ˈɪnəsənt/ *a.* inocente.
innocuous /ɪˈnɒkyuəs/ *a.* innocuo.
innovation /ˌɪnəˈveiʃən/ *n.* innovación *f.*
innuendo /ˌɪnyuˈɛndou/ *n.* insinuación *f.*
innumerable /ɪˈnumərəbəl/ *a.* innumerable.
inoculate /ɪˈnɒkyəˌleit/ *v.* inocular.
inoculation /ɪˌnɒkyəˈleiʃən/ *n.* inoculación *f.*
input /ˈɪnˌpʊt/ *n.* aducto *m.*, ingreso *m.*, entrada *f.*
inquest /ˈɪnkwɛst/ *n.* indagación *f.*
inquire /ɪnˈkwaiᵊr/ *v.* preguntar; inquirir.
inquiry /ɪnˈkwaiᵊri/ *n.* pregunta; investigación *f.*
inquisition /ˌɪnkwəˈzɪʃən/ *n.* escudriñamiento *m.;* (church) Inquisición *f.*
insane /ɪnˈsein/ *a.* loco. **to go i.,** perder la razón; volverse loco.
insanity /ɪnˈsænɪti/ *n.* locura *f.*, demencia *f.*
inscribe /ɪnˈskraib/ *v.* inscribir.
inscription /ɪnˈskrɪpʃən/ *n.* inscripción; dedicatoria *f.*
insect /ˈɪnsɛkt/ *n.* insecto *m.*
insecticide /ɪnˈsɛktəˌsaid/ *n.* & *a.* insecticida *m.*
inseparable /ɪnˈsɛpərəbəl/ *a.* inseparable.
insert /ɪnˈsɜrt/ *v.* insertar, meter.
insertion /ɪnˈsɜrʃən/ *n.* inserción *f.*
inside /ˌɪnˈsaid/ *a.* & *n.* **1.** interior *m.* **—***adv.* **2.** adentro, por dentro. **i. out,** al revés. **—***prep.* **3.** dentro de.
insidious /ɪnˈsɪdiəs/ *a.* insidioso.
insight /ˈɪnˌsait/ *n.* perspicacia *f.;* comprensión *f.*
insignia /ɪnˈsɪgniə/ *n.* insignias *f.pl.*
insignificance /ˌɪnsɪgˈnɪfɪkəns/ *n.* insignificancia *f.*
insignificant /ˌɪnsɪgˈnɪfɪkənt/ *a.* insignificante.
insinuate /ɪnˈsɪnyuˌeit/ *v.* insinuar.
insinuation /ɪnˌsɪnyuˈeiʃən/ *n.* insinuación *f.*
insipid /ɪnˈsɪpɪd/ *a.* insípido.
insist /ɪnˈsɪst/ *v.* insistir.
insistence /ɪnˈsɪstəns/ *n.* insistencia *f.*
insistent /ɪnˈsɪstənt/ *a.* insistente.
insolence /ˈɪnsələns/ *n.* insolencia *f.*
insolent /ˈɪnsələnt/ *a.* insolente.
insomnia /ɪnˈsɒmniə/ *n.* insomnio *m.*
inspect /ɪnˈspɛkt/ *v.* inspeccionar, examinar.
inspection /ɪnˈspɛkʃən/ *n.* inspección *f.*
inspector /ɪnˈspɛktər/ *n.* inspector -ora.
inspiration /ˌɪnspəˈreiʃən/ *n.* inspiración *f.*
inspire /ɪnˈspaiᵊr/ *v.* inspirar.
install /ɪnˈstɔl/ *v.* instalar.
installation /ˌɪnstəˈleiʃən/ *n.* instalación *f.*
installment /ɪnˈstɔlmənt/ *n.* plazo *m.*
instance /ˈɪnstəns/ *n.* ocasión *f.* **for i.,** por ejemplo.
instant /ˈɪnstənt/ *a.* & *n.* instante *m.*
instantaneous /ˌɪnstənˈteiniəs/ *a.* instantáneo.
instant coffee café soluble *m.*
instantly /ˈɪnstəntli/ *adv.* al instante.
instead /ɪnˈstɛd/ *adv.* en lugar de eso. **i. of,** en vez de, en lugar de.
instigate /ˈɪnstɪˌgeit/ *v.* instigar.
instill /ɪnˈstɪl/ *v.* instilar.
instinct /ɪnˈstɪŋkt/ *n.* instinto *m.* **by i.** por instinto.
instinctive /ɪnˈstɪŋktɪv/ *a.* instintivo.
instinctively /ɪnˈstɪŋktɪvli/ *adv.* por instinto.
institute /ˈɪnstɪˌtut/ *n.* **1.** instituto *m.* **—***v.* **2.** instituir.
institution /ˌɪnstɪˈtuʃən/ *n.* institución *f.*
instruct /ɪnˈstrʌkt/ *v.* instruir.
instruction /ɪnˈstrʌkʃən/ *n.* instrucción *f.*
instructive /ɪnˈstrʌktɪv/ *a.* instructivo.
instructor /ɪnˈstrʌktər/ *n.* instructor -ora.
instrument /ˈɪnstrəmənt/ *n.* instrumento *m.*
instrumental /ˌɪnstrəˈmɛntl̩/ *a.* instrumental.
insufficient /ˌɪnsəˈfɪʃənt/ *a.* insuficiente.
insular /ˈɪnsələr/ *a.* insular; estrecho de miras.
insulate /ˈɪnsəˌleit/ *v.* aislar.
insulation /ˌɪnsəˈleiʃən/ *n.* aislamiento *m.*
insulator /ˈɪnsəˌleitər/ *n.* aislador *m.*
insulin /ˈɪnsəlɪn/ *n.* insulina *f.*
insult /*n.* ˈɪnsʌlt; *v.* ɪnˈsʌlt/ *n.* **1.** insulto *m.* **—***v.* **2.** insultar.
insuperable /ɪnˈsupərəbəl/ *a.* insuperable.
insurance /ɪnˈʃʊrəns/ *n.* seguro *m.*
insure /ɪnˈʃʊr, -ˈʃɜr/ *v.* asegurar.
insurgent /ɪnˈsɜrdʒənt/ *a.* & *n.* insurgente *m.* & *f.*
insurrection /ˌɪnsəˈrɛkʃən/ *n.* insurrección *f.*
intact /ɪnˈtækt/ *a.* intacto.
intangible /ɪnˈtændʒəbəl/ *a.* intangible, impalpable.
integral /ˈɪntɪgrəl/ *a.* íntegro.
integrate /ˈɪntɪˌgreit/ *v.* integrar.
integrity /ɪnˈtɛgrɪti/ *n.* integridad *f.*
intellect /ˈɪntl̩ˌɛkt/ *n.* intelecto *m.*
intellectual /ˌɪntl̩ˈɛktʃuəl/ *a.* & *n.* intelectual *m.* & *f.*
intelligence /ɪnˈtɛlɪdʒəns/ *n.* inteligencia *f.*
intelligence quotient /ˈkwouʃənt/ coeficiente intelectual *m.*
intelligent /ɪnˈtɛlɪdʒənt/ *a.* inteligente.
intelligible /ɪnˈtɛlɪdʒəbəl/ *a.* inteligible.
intend /ɪnˈtɛnd/ *v.* pensar; intentar; destinar.
intense /ɪnˈtɛns/ *a.* intenso.
intensify /ɪnˈtɛnsəˌfai/ *v.* intensificar.
intensity /ɪnˈtɛnsɪti/ *n.* intensidad *f.*
intensive /ɪnˈtɛnsɪv/ *a.* intensivo.
intensive-care unit /ɪnˈtɛnsɪvˈkɛər/ unidad de cuidados intensivos, unidad de vigilancia intensiva *f.*
intent /ɪnˈtɛnt/ *n.* intento *m.*

intention /ɪn'tɛnʃən/ *n.* intención *f.*

intentional /ɪn'tɛnʃənl̩/ *a.* intencional.

intercede /ˌɪntər'sid/ *v.* interceder.

intercept /ˌɪntər'sɛpt/ *v.* interceptar; detener.

interchange /ˌɪntər'tʃendʒ/ *v.* intercambiar.

interchangeable /ˌɪntər'tʃeindʒəbəl/ *a.* intercambiable.

intercourse /'ɪntərˌkɔrs/ *n.* tráfico *m.*; comunicación *f.*; coito *m.*

interest /'ɪntərɪst/ *n.* **1.** interés *m.* —*v.* **2.** interesar.

interesting /'ɪntərəstɪŋ/ *a.* interesante.

interest rate *n.* tipo de interés *m.*

interface /'ɪntərˌfeis/ *n.* interfaz.

interfere /ˌɪntər'fɪər/ *v.* entremeterse, intervenir. **i. with,** estorbar.

interference /ˌɪntər'fɪərəns/ *n.* intervención *f.*; obstáculo *m.*

interior /ɪn'tɪəriər/ *a.* interior.

interject /ˌɪntər'dʒɛkt/ *v.* interponer; intervenir.

interjection /ˌɪntər'dʒɛkʃən/ *n.* interjección *f.*; interposición *f.*

interlude /'ɪntərˌlud/ *n.* intervalo *m.*; *Theat.* intermedio *m.*; (music) interludio *m.*

intermediary /ˌɪntər'midiˌɛri/ *n.* intermediario -ria.

intermediate /ˌɪntər'midiˌeit/ *a.* intermedio.

interment /ɪn'tɜrmənt/ *n.* entierro.

intermission /ˌɪntər'mɪʃən/ *n.* intermisión *f.*; *Theat.* entreacto *m.*

intermittent /ˌɪntər'mɪtn̩t/ *a.* intermitente.

intern /ɪn'tɜrn/ *n.* **1.** interno -na, internado -da. —*v.* **2.** internar.

internal /ɪn'tɜrnl̩/ *a.* interno.

international /ˌɪntər'næʃənl̩/ *a.* internacional.

internationalism /ˌɪntər'næʃənl̩ˌɪzəm/ *n.* internacionalismo *m.*

Internet, the /'ɪntərˌnɛt/ *n.* el Internet *m.*

interpose /ˌɪntər'pouz/ *v.* interponer.

interpret /ɪn'tɜrprɪt/ *v.* interpretar.

interpretation /ɪnˌtɜrprɪ'teiʃən/ *n.* interpretación *f.*

interpreter /ɪn'tɜrprɪtər/ *n.* intérprete *m.* & *f.*

interrogate /ɪn'tɛrəˌgeit/ *v.* interrogar.

interrogation /ɪnˌtɛrə'geiʃən/ *n.* interrogación; pregunta *f.*

interrogative /ˌɪntə'rɒgətɪv/ *a.* interrogativo.

interrupt /ˌɪntə'rʌpt/ *v.* interrumpir.

interruption /ˌɪntə'rʌpʃən/ *n.* interrupción *f.*

intersect /ˌɪntər'sɛkt/ *v.* cortar.

intersection /ˌɪntər'sɛkʃən/ *n.* intersección *f.*; (street) bocacalle *f.*

intersperse /ˌɪntər'spɜrs/ *v.* entremezclar.

interval /'ɪntərvəl/ *n.* intervalo *m.*

intervene /ˌɪntər'vin/ *v.* intervenir.

intervention /ˌɪntər'venʃən/ *n.* intervención *f.*

interview /'ɪntərˌvyu/ *n.* **1.** entrevista *f.* —*v.* **2.** entrevistar.

interviewer /'ɪntərˌvyuər/ *n.* entrevistador -ora *m.* & *f.*

intestine /ɪn'tɛstɪn/ *n.* intestino *m.*

intimacy /'ɪntəməsi/ *n.* intimidad; familiaridad *f.*

intimate /'ɪntəmɪt/ *a.* **1.** íntimo, familiar. —*n.* **2.** amigo -ga íntimo -ma. —*v.* **3.** insinuar.

intimidate /ɪn'tɪmɪˌdeit/ *v.* intimidar.

intimidation /ɪnˌtɪmɪ'deiʃən/ *n.* intimidación *f.*

into /'ɪntu; *unstressed* -tʊ, -tə/ *prep.* en, dentro de.

intonation /ˌɪntou'neiʃən/ *n.* entonación *f.*

intone /ɪn'toun/ *v.* entonar.

intoxicate /ɪn'tɒksɪˌkeit/ *v.* embriagar.

intoxication /ɪnˌtɒksɪ'keiʃən/ *n.* embriaguez *f.*

intravenous /ˌɪntrə'vinəs/ *a.* intravenoso.

intrepid /ɪn'trɛpɪd/ *a.* intrépido.

intricacy /'ɪntrɪkəsi/ *n.* complejidad *f.*; enredo *m.*

intricate /'ɪntrɪkɪt/ *a.* intrincado; complejo.

intrigue /ɪn'trig; *n. also* 'ɪntrig/ *n.* **1.** intriga *f.* —*v.* **2.** intrigar.

intrinsic /ɪn'trɪnsɪk/ *a.* intrínseco.

introduce /ˌɪntrə'dus/ *v.* introducir; (a person) presentar.

introduction /ˌɪntrə'dʌkʃən/ *n.* presentación; introducción *f.*

introductory /ˌɪntrə'dʌktəri/ *a.* introductor; preliminar. **i. offer,** ofrecimiento de presentación *m.*

introvert /'ɪntrəˌvɜrt/ *n.* & *a.* introvertido -da.

intrude /ɪn'trud/ *v.* entremeterse.

intruder /ɪn'trudər/ *n.* intruso -sa.

intuition /ˌɪntu'ɪʃən/ *n.* intuición *f.*

intuitive /ɪn'tuɪtɪv/ *a.* intuitivo.

inundate /'ɪnənˌdeit/ *v.* inundar.

invade /ɪn'veid/ *v.* invadir.

invader /ɪn'veidər/ *n.* invasor -ra.

invalid /ɪn'vælɪd/ *a.* & *n.* inválido -da.

invariable /ɪn'vɛəriəbəl/ *a.* invariable.

invasion /ɪn'veiʒən/ *n.* invasión *f.*

invective /ɪn'vɛktɪv/ *n.* **1.** invectiva *f.* —*a.* **2.** ultrajante.

inveigle /ɪn'veigəl/ *v.* seducir.

invent /ɪn'vɛnt/ *v.* inventar.

invention /ɪn'vɛnʃən/ *n.* invención *f.*

inventive /ɪn'vɛntɪv/ *a.* inventivo.

inventor /ɪn'vɛntər/ *n.* inventor -ra.

inventory /'ɪnvənˌtɔri/ *n.* inventario *m.*

invertebrate /ɪn'vɜrtəbrɪt/ *n.* & *a.* invertebrado *m.*

invest /ɪn'vɛst/ *v.* investir; *Com.* invertir.

investigate /ɪn'vɛstɪˌgeit/ *v.* investigar.

investigation /ɪnˌvɛstɪ'geiʃən/ *n.* investigación *f.*

investment /ɪn'vɛstmənt/ *n.* inversión *f.*

investor /ɪn'vɛstər/ *n.* inversor, -ra.

inveterate /ɪn'vɛtərɪt/ *a.* inveterado.

invidious /ɪn'vɪdiəs/ *a.* abominable, odioso, injusto.

invigorate /ɪn'vɪgəˌreit/ *v.* vigorizar, fortificar.

invincible /ɪn'vɪnsəbəl/ *a.* invencible.

invisible /ɪn'vɪzəbəl/ *a.* invisible.

invitation /ˌɪnvɪ'teiʃən/ *n.* invitación *f.*

invite /ɪn'vait/ *v.* invitar, convidar.

invocation /ˌɪnvə'keiʃən/ *n.* invocación *f.*

invoice /'ɪnvɔis/ *n.* factura *f.*

invoke /ɪn'vouk/ *v.* invocar.

involuntary /ɪn'vɒlənˌtɛri/ *a.* involuntario.

involve /ɪn'vɒlv/ *v.* envolver; implicar.

involved /ɪn'vɒlvd/ *a.* complicado.

invulnerable /ɪn'vʌlnərəbəl/ *a.* invulnerable.

inward /'ɪnwərd/ *adv.* hacia adentro.

inwardly /'ɪnwərdli/ *adv.* interiormente.

iodine /'aiəˌdain/ *n.* iodo *m.*

IQ *abbr.* CI (coeficiente intelectual) *m.*

irate /ai'reit/ *a.* encolerizado.

Ireland /'aiᵊrlənd/ *n.* Irlanda *f.*

iris /'airɪs/ *n.* *Anat.* iris *m.*; (botany) flor de lis *f.*

Irish /'airɪʃ/ *a.* irlandés.

irk /ɜrk/ *v.* fastidiar.

iron /'aiərn/ *n.* **1.** hierro *m.*; (appliance) plancha *f.* —*v.* **2.** planchar.

ironical /ai'rɒnɪkəl/ *a.* irónico.

ironing board /'aiərnɪŋ/ tabla de planchar *f.*

irony /'airəni/ *n.* ironía *f.*

irrational /ɪ'ræʃənl̩/ *a.* irracional; ilógico.

irregular /ɪ'rɛgyələr/ *a.* irregular.

irregularity /ɪˌrɛgyə'lærɪti/ *n.* irregularidad *f.*

irrelevant /ɪ'rɛləvənt/ *a.* ajeno.

irresistible /ˌɪrɪ'zɪstəbəl/ *a.* irresistible.

irresponsible /ˌɪrɪ'spɒnsəbəl/ *a.* irresponsable.

irreverent /ɪ'rɛvərənt/ *a.* irreverente.

irrevocable /ɪ'rɛvəkəbəl/ *a.* irrevocable.

irrigate /'ɪrɪˌgeit/ *v.* regar; *Med.* irrigar.

irrigation /ˌɪrɪ'geiʃən/ *n.* riego *m.*

irritability /ˌɪrɪtə'bɪlɪti/ *n.* irritabilidad *f.*

irritable /'ɪrɪtəbəl/ *a.* irritable.

irritant /'ɪrɪtn̩t/ *n.* & *a.* irritante *m.*

irritate /'ɪrɪˌteit/ *v.* irritar.

irritation /ˌɪrɪ'teiʃən/ *n.* irritación *f.*

island /'ailənd/ *n.* isla *f.*

isolate /'aisəˌleit/ *v.* aislar.

isolation /ˌaisə'leiʃən/ *n.* aislamiento *m.*

isosceles /ai'sɒsəˌliz/ *a.* isósceles.

issuance /'ɪʃuəns/ *n.* emisión *f.*; publicación *f.*

issue /'ɪʃu/ *n.* **1.** emisión; edición; progenie *f.*; número *m.*; punto en disputa. —*v.* **2.** emitir; publicar.

isthmus /'ɪsməs/ *n.* istmo *m.*

it /ɪt/ *pron.* ello; él, ella; lo, la.

Italian /ɪ'tælyən/ *a.* & *n.* italiano -na.

Italy /'ɪtl̩i/ *n.* Italia *f.*

itch /ɪtʃ/ *n.* **1.** picazón *f.* —*v.* **2.** picar.

item /'aitəm/ *n.* artículo; detalle *m.*; inserción *f.*; *Com.* renglón *m.*

itemize /'aitəˌmaiz/ *v.* detallar.

itinerant /ai'tɪnərənt/ *n.* **1.** viandante *m.* —*a.* **2.** ambulante.

itinerary /ai'tɪnəˌrɛri/ *n.* itinerario *m.*

its /ɪts/ *a.* su.

itself /ɪt'sɛlf/ *pron.* sí; se.

ivory /'aivəri/ *n.* marfil *m.*

ivy /'aivi/ *n.* hiedra *f.*

J

jab /dʒæb/ *n.* **1.** pinchazo *m.* —*v.* **2.** pinchar.

jack /dʒæk/ *n.* (for lifting) gato *m.*; (cards) sota *f.*

jackal /'dʒækəl/ *n.* chacal *m.*

jackass /'dʒækˌæs/ *n.* asno *m.*

jacket /'dʒækɪt/ *n.* chaqueta *f.*; saco *m.*

jack-of-all-trades /'dʒæk əv 'ɔl 'treidz/ *n.* estuche *m.*

jade /dʒeid/ *n.* (horse) rocín *m.*; (woman) picarona *f.*; (mineral) jade *m.*

jaded /'dʒeidɪd/ *a.* rendido.

jagged /'dʒægɪd/ *a.* mellado.

jaguar /'dʒægwɑr/ *n.* jaguar *m.*

jail /dʒeil/ *n.* cárcel *f.*

jailer /'dʒeilər/ *n.* carcelero *m.*

jam /dʒæm/ *n.* **1.** conserva *f.*; aprieto, apretón *m.* —*v.* **2.** apiñar, apretar; trabar.

janitor /'dʒænɪtər/ *n.* portero *m.*

January /'dʒænyuˌɛri/ *n.* enero *m.*

Japan /dʒə'pæn/ *n.* Japón *m.*

Japanese /ˌdʒæpə'niz/ *a.* & *n.* japonés -esa.

jar /dʒɑr/ *n.* **1.** jarro *m.* —*v.* **2.** chocar; agitar.

jargon /'dʒɑrgən/ *n.* jerga *f.*

jasmine /'dʒæzmɪn/ *n.* jazmín *m.*

jaundice /'dʒɔndɪs/ *n.* ictericia *f.*

jaunt /dʒɔnt/ *n.* paseo *m.*

javelin /'dʒævlɪn/ *n.* jabalina *f.*

jaw /dʒɔ/ *n.* quijada *f.*

jay /dʒei/ *n.* grajo *m.*

jazz /dʒæz/ *n.* jazz *m.*

jealous /'dʒɛləs/ *a.* celoso. **to be j.,** tener celos.

jealousy /'dʒɛləsi/ *n.* celos *m.pl.*

jeans /dʒinz/ *n.* vaqueros, tejanos *m.pl.*

jeer /dʒɪər/ *n.* **1.** burla *f.*, mofa *f.* —*v.* **2.** burlar, mofar.

jelly /'dʒɛli/ *n.* jalea *f.*

jellyfish /'dʒɛliˌfɪʃ/ *n.* aguamar *m.*

jeopardize /'dʒɛpərˌdaiz/ *v.* arriesgar.

jeopardy /'dʒɛpərdi/ *n.* riesgo *m.*

jerk /dʒɜrk/ *n.* **1.** sacudida *f.* —*v.* **2.** sacudir.

jerky /'dʒɜrki/ *a.* espasmódico.

Jerusalem /dʒɪ'rusələm/ *n.* Jerusalén *m.*

jest /dʒɛst/ *n.* **1.** broma *f.* —*v.* **2.** bromear.

jester /'dʒɛstər/ *n.* bufón -ona; burlón -ona.

Jesuit /'dʒɛʒuɪt/ *a.* & *n.* jesuita *m.*

Jesus Christ /'dʒizəs 'kraist/ *n.* Jesucristo *m.*

jet /dʒɛt/ *n.* chorro *m.*; (gas) mechero *m.*

jet lag *n.* defase horario *m.*, inadaptación horaria *f.*

jetsam /'dʒɛtsəm/ *n.* echazón *f.*

jettison /'dʒɛtəsən/ *v.* echar al mar.

jetty /'dʒɛti/ *n.* muelle *m.*

Jew /dʒu/ *n.* judío -día.

jewel /'dʒuəl/ *n.* joya *f.*

jeweler /'dʒuələr/ *n.* joyero -ra.

jewelry /'dʒuəlri/ *n.* joyas *f.pl.* **j. store,** joyería *f.*

Jewish /'dʒuɪʃ/ *a.* judío.

jib /dʒɪb/ *n.* *Naut.* foque *m.*

jiffy /'dʒɪfi/ *n.* instante *m.*

jig /dʒɪg/ *n.* jiga *f.* **j-saw,** sierra de vaivén *f.*

jilt /dʒɪlt/ *v.* dar calabazas.

jingle /'dʒɪŋgəl/ *n.* **1.** retintín *m.*; rima pueril *f.* —*v.* **2.** retiñir.

jinx /dʒɪŋks/ *n.* **1.** aojo *m.* —*v.* **2.** aojar.

jittery /'dʒɪtəri/ *a.* nervioso.

job /dʒɒb/ *n.* empleo *m.*

jobber /'dʒɒbər/ *n.* destajista *m.* & *f.*, corredor *m.*

jockey /'dʒɒki/ *n.* jockey *m.*

jocular /'dʒɒkyələr/ *a.* jocoso.

jog /dʒɒg/ *n.* empujoncito *m.* *v.* empujar; estimular. **j. along,** ir a un trote corto.

join /dʒɔin/ *v.* juntar; unir.

joiner /'dʒɔinər/ *n.* ebanista *m.*

joint /dʒɔint/ *n.* juntura *f.*

jointly /'dʒɔintli/ *adv.* conjuntamente.

joke /dʒouk/ *n.* **1.** broma, chanza *f.*; chiste *m.* —*v.* **2.** bromear.

joker /'dʒoukər/ *n.* bromista *m.* & *f.*; comodín *m.*

jolly /'dʒɒli/ *a.* alegre, jovial.

jolt /dʒoult/ *n.* **1.** sacudido *m.* —*v.* **2.** sacudir.

jonquil /'dʒɒŋkwɪl/ *n.* junquillo *m.*

jostle /'dʒɒsəl/ *v.* empujar.

journal /'dʒɜrnl̩/ *n.* diario *m.*; revista *f.*

journalism /'dʒɜrnl̩ˌɪzəm/ *n.* periodismo *m.*

journalist /'dʒɜrnl̩ɪst/ *n.* periodista *m.* & *f.*

journey /'dʒɜrni/ *n.* **1.** viaje *m.*; jornada *f.* —*v.* **2.** viajar.

journeyman /'dʒɜrnimən/ *n.* jornalero *m.*, oficial *m.*

jovial /'dʒouviəl/ *a.* jovial.

jowl /dʒaul/ *n.* carrillo *m.*

joy /dʒɔi/ *n.* alegría *f.*

joyful /'dʒɔifəl/ **joyous** *a.* alegre, gozoso.

jubilant /'dʒubələnt/ *a.* jubiloso.

jubilee /'dʒubəˌli/ *n.* jubileo *m.*

Judaism /'dʒudiˌɪzəm/ *n.* judaísmo *m.*

judge /dʒʌdʒ/ *n.* **1.** juez *m.* & *f.* —*v.* **2.** juzgar.

judgment /'dʒʌddʒmənt/ *n.* juicio *m.*

judicial /dʒu'dɪʃəl/ *a.* judicial.

judiciary /dʒu'dɪʃiˌɛri/ *a.* judiciario.

judicious /dʒu'dɪʃəs/ *a.* juicioso.

jug /dʒʌg/ *n.* jarro *m.*

juggle /'dʒʌgəl/ *v.* escamotear.

juice /dʒus/ *n.* jugo, zumo *m.*

juicy /'dʒusi/ *a.* jugoso.

July /dʒu'lai/ *n.* julio *m.*

jumble /'dʒʌmbəl/ *n.* **1.** revoltillo *m.* —*v.* **2.** arrebujar, revolver.

jump /dʒʌmp/ *n.* **1.** salto *m.* —*v.* **2.** saltar, brincar.

junction /'dʒʌŋkʃən/ *n.* confluencia *f.*; (railway) empalme *m.*
juncture /'dʒʌŋktʃər/ *n.* juntura *f.*; coyuntura *f.*
June /dʒun/ *n.* junio *m.*
jungle /'dʒʌŋgəl/ *n.* jungla, selva *f.*
junior /'dʒunyər/ *a.* menor; más joven. **Jr.,** hijo.
juniper /'dʒunəpər/ *n.* enebro *m.*
junk /dʒʌŋk/ *n.* basura *f.*
junket /'dʒʌŋkɪt/ *n.* **1.** leche cuajada *f.* —*v.* **2.** festejar.
junkie /'dʒʌŋki/ *n. Colloq.* yonqui *m. & f.*, toxicómano -na.
junk mail *n.* porpaganda indeseada *f.*, correo basura *m.*
jurisdiction /ˌdʒʊrɪs'dɪkʃən/ *n.* jurisdicción *f.*
jurisprudence /ˌdʒʊrɪs'prudns/ *n.* jurisprudencia *f.*
jurist /'dʒʊrɪst/ *n.* jurista *m. & f.*
juror /'dʒʊrər/ *n.* jurado -da.
jury /'dʒʊri/ *n.* jurado *m.*
just /dʒʌst/ *a.* **1.** justo; exacto. —*adv.* **2.** exactamente; (only) sólo. **j. now,** ahora mismo. **to have j.,** acabar de.
justice /'dʒʌstɪs/ *n.* justicia *f.*; (person) juez *m. & f.*
justifiable /'dʒʌstəˌfaiəbəl/ *a.* justificable.
justification /ˌdʒʌstəfɪ'keiʃən/ *n.* justificación *f.*
justify /'dʒʌstəˌfai/ *v.* justificar.
jut /dʒʌt/ *v.* sobresalir.
jute /dʒut/ *n.* yute *m.*
juvenile /'dʒuvənl/ *a.* juvenil.
juvenile delinquency delincuencia de menores, delincuencia juvenil *f.*

K

kaleidoscope /kə'laidəˌskoup/ *n.* calidoscopio *m.*
kangaroo /ˌkæŋgə'ru/ *n.* canguro *m.*
karakul /'kærəkəl/ *n.* caracul *m.*
karat /'kærət/ *n.* quilate *m.*
karate /kə'rɑti/ *n.* karate *m.*
keel /kil/ *n.* **1.** quilla *f.* —*v.* **2. to k. over,** volcarse.
keen /kin/ *a.* agudo; penetrante.
keep /kip/ *v.* mantener, retener; guardar; preservar. **k. on,** seguir, continuar.
keeper /'kipər/ *n.* guardián *m.*
keepsake /'kipˌseik/ *n.* recuerdo *m.*
keg /kɛg/ *n.* barrilito *m.*
kennel /'kɛnl/ *n.* perrera *f.*
kerchief /'kɜrtʃɪf/ *n.* pañuelo *m.*
kernel /'kɜrnl/ *n.* pepita *f.*; grano *m.*
kerosene /'kɛrəˌsin/ *n.* kerosén *m.*
ketchup /'kɛtʃəp/ *n.* salsa de tomate *f.*
kettle /'kɛtl/ *n.* caldera, olla *f.*
kettledrum /'kɛtlˌdrʌm/ *n.* tímpano *m.*
key /ki/ *n.* llave *f.*; (music) clave *f.*; (piano) tecla *f.*
keyboard /'kiˌbɔrd/ *n.* teclado *m.*
keyhole /'kiˌhoul/ *n.* bocallave *f.*
keypad /'kiˌpæd/ *n.* teclado *m.*
khaki /'kæki/ *a.* caqui.
kick /kɪk/ *n.* **1.** patada *f.* —*v.* **2.** patear; *Colloq.* quejarse.
kid /kɪd/ *n.* **1.** cabrito *m.*; *Colloq.* niño -ña, chico -ca. —*v.* **2.** *Colloq.* bromear.
kidnap /'kɪdnæp/ *v.* secuestrar.
kidnaper /'kɪdnæpər/ *n.* secuestrador -ora.
kidnaping /'kɪdnæpɪŋ/ *n.* rapto, secuestro *m.*
kidney /'kɪdni/ *n.* riñón *m.*
kidney bean *n.* frijol *m.*
kill /kɪl/ *v.* matar.
killer /'kɪlər/ *n.* matador -ora.
killjoy /'kɪldʒɔi/ *n.* aguafiestas *m. & f.*
kiln /kɪl/ *n.* horno *m.*
kilogram /'kɪləˌgræm/ *n.* kilogramo *m.*
kilohertz /'kɪləˌhɜrts/ *n.* kilohercio *m.*
kilometer /kɪ'lɒmɪtər/ *n.* kilómetro *m.*
kilowatt /'kɪləˌwɒt/ *n.* kilovatio *m.*
kin /kɪn/ *n.* parentesco *m.*; parientes *m.pl.*
kind /kaind/ *a.* **1.** bondadoso, amable. —*n.* **2.** género *m.*; clase *f.* **k. of,** algo, un poco.
kindergarten /'kɪndərˌgɑrtn/ *n.* kindergarten *m.*
kindle /'kɪndl/ *v.* encender.
kindling /'kɪndlɪŋ/ *n.* encendimiento *m.* **k.-wood,** leña menuda *f.*
kindly /'kaindli/ *a.* bondadoso.
kindness /'kaindnɪs/ *n.* bondad *f.*
kindred /'kɪndrɪd/ *n.* parentesco *m.*
kinetic /kɪ'nɛtɪk/ *a.* cinético.
king /kɪŋ/ *n.* rey *m.*
kingdom /'kɪŋdəm/ *n.* reino *m.*
king prawn langostino *m.*
kink /kɪŋk/ *n.* retorcimiento *m.*
kinky /'kɪŋki/ *a. Colloq.* pervertidillo; (hair) rizado.
kiosk /'kiɒsk/ *n.* kiosco *m.*
kiss /kɪs/ *n.* **1.** beso *m.* —*v.* **2.** besar.
kitchen /'kɪtʃən/ *n.* cocina *f.*
kite /kait/ *n.* cometa *f.*
kitten /'kɪtn/ *n.* gatito -ta.
kleptomania /ˌklɛptə'meiniə/ *n.* cleptomanía *f.*
kleptomaniac /ˌklɛptə'meiniæk/ *n.* cleptómano -na.
klutz /klʌts/ *n. Colloq.* torpe, patoso -sa.
knack /næk/ *n.* don *m.*, destreza *f.*
knapsack /'næpˌsæk/ *n.* alforja *f.*
knead /nid/ *v.* amasar.
knee /ni/ *n.* rodilla *f.*
kneecap /'niˌkæp/ *n.* rodillera, rótula *f.*
kneel /nil/ *v.* arrodillarse.
knickers /'nɪkərz/ *n.* calzón corto *m.*, pantalones *m.pl.*
knife /naif/ *n.* cuchillo *m.*
knight /nait/ *n.* caballero *m.*; (chess) caballo *m.*
knit /nɪt/ *v.* tejer.
knob /nɒb/ *n.* tirador *m.*
knock /nɒk/ *n.* **1.** golpe *m.*; llamada *f.* —*v.* **2.** golpear; tocar, llamar.
knot /nɒt/ *n.* **1.** nudo; lazo *m.* —*v.* **2.** anudar.
knotty /'nɒti/ *a.* nudoso.
know /nou/ *v.* saber; (a person) conocer.
knowledge /'nɒlɪdʒ/ *n.* conocimiento, saber *m.*
knuckle /'nʌkəl/ *n.* nudillo *m.* **k. bone,** jarrete *m.* **to k. under,** ceder a.
Koran /kə'rɑn/ *n.* Corán *m.*
Korea /kə'riə/ *n.* Corea *f.*
Korean /kə'riən/ *a. & n.* coreano.

L

label /'leibəl/ *n.* **1.** rótulo *m.* —*v.* **2.** rotular; designar.
labor /'leibər/ *n.* **1.** trabajo *m.*; la clase obrera. —*v.* **2.** trabajar.
laboratory /'læbrəˌtɔri/ *n.* laboratorio *m.*
laborer /'leibərər/ *n.* trabajador, obrero *m.*
laborious /lə'bɔriəs/ *a.* laborioso, difícil.
labor union gremio obrero, sindicato *m.*
labyrinth /'læbərɪnθ/ *n.* laberinto *m.*
lace /leis/ *n.* **1.** encaje *m.*; (of shoe) lazo *m.* —*v.* **2.** amarrar.
lacerate /'læsəˌreit/ *v.* lacerar, lastimar.
laceration /ˌlæsə'reiʃən/ *n.* laceración *f.*, desgarro *m.*
lack /læk/ *n.* **1.** falta *f.* **l. of respect,** desacato *m.* —*v.* **2.** faltar, carecer.
lackadaisical /ˌlækə'deizɪkəl/ *a.* indiferente; soñador.
laconic /lə'kɒnɪk/ *a.* lacónico.
lacquer /'lækər/ *n.* **1.** laca *f.*, barniz *m.* —*v.* **2.** laquear, barnizar.
lactic /'læktɪk/ *a.* láctico.
lactose /'læktous/ *n.* lactosa *f.*
ladder /'lædər/ *n.* escalera *f.*
ladle /'leidl/ *n.* **1.** cucharón *m.* —*v.* **2.** servir con cucharón.
lady /'leidi/ *n.* señora, dama *f.*
ladybug /'leidiˌbʌg/ *n.* mariquita *f.*
lag /læg/ *n.* **1.** retraso *m.* —*v.* **2.** quedarse atrás.
lagoon /lə'gun/ *n.* laguna *f.*
laid-back /'leid 'bæk/ *a.* de buen talante, ecuánime, pacífico.
laity /'leiɪti/ *n.* laicado *m.*
lake /leik/ *n.* lago *m.*
lamb /læm/ *n.* cordero *m.*
lame /leim/ *a.* **1.** cojo; estropeado. —*v.* **2.** estropear, lisiar; incapacitar.
lament /lə'mɛnt/ *n.* **1.** lamento *m.* —*v.* **2.** lamentar.
lamentable /lə'mɛntəbəl/ *a.* lamentable.
lamentation /ˌlæmən'teiʃən/ *n.* lamento *m.*; lamentación *f.*
laminate /'læməˌneit/ *a.* laminado. *v.* laminar.
lamp /læmp/ *n.* lámpara *f.*
lampoon /læm'pun/ *n.* **1.** pasquín *m.* —*v.* **2.** pasquinar.
lance /læns/ *n.* **1.** lanza *f.* —*v.* **2.** *Med.* abrir.
land /lænd/ *n.* **1.** país *m.*; tierra *f.* **native l.,** patria *f.* —*v.* **2.** desembarcar; (plane) aterrizar.
landholder /'lændˌhouldər/ *n.* hacendado -da.
landing /'lændɪŋ/ *n.* (of stairs) descanso, descansillo *m.*; (ship) desembarcadero *m.*; (airplane) aterrizaje *m.*
landlady /'lændˌleidi/ **landlord** *n.* propietario -ria.
landmark /'lændˌmɑrk/ *n.* mojón *m.*, señal *f.*; rasgo sobresaliente *m.*
landscape /'lændˌskeip/ *n.* paisaje *m.*
landslide /'lændˌslaid/ *n.* derrumbe *m.*
lane /lein/ *n.* senda *f.*
language /'læŋgwɪdʒ/ *n.* lengua *f.*, idioma; lenguaje *m.*
languid /'læŋgwɪd/ *a.* lánguido.
languish /'læŋgwɪʃ/ *v.* languidecer.
languor /'læŋgər/ *n.* languidez *f.*
lanky /'læŋki/ *a.* larguirucho; desgarbado.
lanolin /'lænlɪn/ *n.* lanolina *f.*
lantern /'læntərn/ *n.* linterna *f.*; farol *m.*
lap /læp/ *n.* **1.** regazo *m.*; falda *f.* —*v.* **2.** lamer.
lapel /lə'pɛl/ *n.* solapa *f.*
lapse /læps/ *n.* **1.** lapso *m.* —*v.* **2.** pasar; decaer; caer en error.
laptop computer /'læpˌtɒp/ ordenador portátil *m.*
larceny /'lɑrsəni/ *n.* ratería *f.*
lard /lɑrd/ *n.* manteca de cerdo *f.*
large /lɑrdʒ/ *a.* grande.
largely /'lɑrdʒli/ *adv.* ampliamente; mayormente; muy.
largo /'lɑrgou/ *n. & a. Mus.* largo *m.*
lariat /'læriət/ *n.* lazo *m.*
lark /lɑrk/ *n.* (bird) alondra *f.*
larva /'lɑrvə/ *n.* larva *f.*
laryngitis /ˌlærən'dʒaitɪs/ *n.* laringitis *f.*
larynx /'lærɪŋks/ *n.* laringe *f.*
lascivious /lə'sɪviəs/ *a.* lascivo.
laser /'leizər/ *n.* láser *m.*
lash /læʃ/ *n.* **1.** azote, latigazo *m.* —*v.* **2.** azotar.
lass /læs/ *n.* doncella *f.*
lassitude /'læsɪˌtud/ *n.* lasitud *f.*
lasso /'læsou/ *n.* **1.** lazo *m.* —*v.* **2.** enlazar.
last /læst/ *a.* **1.** pasado; (final) último. **at l.,** por fin. **l. but one,** penúltimo. **l. but two,** antepenúltimo. —*v.* **2.** durar.
lasting /'læstɪŋ/ *a.* duradero.
latch /lætʃ/ *n.* aldaba *f.*
late /leit/ *a.* **1.** tardío; (deceased) difunto. **to be l.,** llegar tarde. —*adv.* **2.** tarde.
lately /'leitli/ *adv.* recientemente.
latent /'leitnt/ *a.* latente.
lateral /'lætərəl/ *a.* lateral.
lather /'læðər/ *n.* **1.** espuma de jabón. —*v.* **2.** enjabonar.
Latin /'lætn/ *n.* latín *m.*
Latin America /ə'mɛrɪkə/ Hispanoamérica, América Latina *f.*
Latin American hispanoamericano -na.
latitude /'lætɪˌtud/ *n.* latitud *f.*
latrine /lə'trin/ *n.* letrina *f.*
latter /'lætər/ *a.* posterior. **the l.,** éste.
lattice /'lætɪs/ *n.* celosía *f.*
laud /lɔd/ *v.* loar.
laudable /'lɔdəbəl/ *a.* laudable.
laudanum /'lɔdnəm/ *n.* láudano *m.*
laudatory /'lɔdəˌtɔri/ *a.* laudatorio.
laugh /læf/ *n.* **1.** risa, risotada *f.* —*v.* **2.** reír. **l. at,** reírse de.
laughable /'læfəbəl/ *a.* risible.
laughter /'læftər/ *n.* risa *f.*
launch /lɔntʃ/ *n.* **1.** *Naut.* lancha *f.* —*v.* **2.** lanzar.
launder /'lɔndər/ *v.* lavar y planchar la ropa.
laundry /'lɔndri/ *n.* lavandería *f.*
laundryman /'lɔndriˌmæn/ *n.* lavandero -ra.
laureate /'lɔriɪt/ *n. & a.* laureado -da.
laurel /'lɔrəl/ *n.* laurel *m.*
lava /'lɑvə/ *n.* lava *f.*
lavatory /'lævəˌtɔri/ *n.* lavatorio *m.*
lavender /'lævəndər/ *n.* lavándula *f.*
lavish /'lævɪʃ/ *a.* **1.** pródigo. —*v.* **2.** prodigar.
law /lɔ/ *n.* ley *f.*; derecho *m.*
lawful /'lɔfəl/ *a.* legal.
lawless /'lɔlɪs/ *a.* sin ley.
lawn /lɔn/ *n.* césped; prado *m.*
lawn mower /'mouər/ *n.* cortacésped *m. & f.*
lawsuit /'lɔˌsut/ *n.* pleito *m.*
lawyer /'lɔyər/ *n.* abogado *m. & f.*
lax /læks/ *a.* flojo, laxo.
laxative /'læksətɪv/ *n.* purgante *m.*
laxity /'læksɪti/ *n.* laxidad *f.*; flojedad *f.*
lay /lei/ *a.* **1.** secular. —*v.* **2.** poner.
layer /'leiər/ *n.* capa *f.*
layman /'leimən/ *n.* lego, seglar *m.*
lazy /'leizi/ *a.* perezoso.
lead /lɛd , lid/ *n.* **1.** plomo *m.*; *Theat.* papel principal. **to take the l.,** tomar la delantera. —*v.* **2.** conducir; dirigir.
leaden /'lɛdn/ *a.* plomizo; pesado; abatido.
leader /'lidər/ *n.* líder *m. & f.*; jefe *m. & f.*; director -ora.
leadership /'lidərˌʃɪp/ *n.* dirección *f.*
leaf /lif/ *n.* hoja *f.*
leaflet /'liflɪt/ *n. Bot.* hojilla *f.*; folleto *m.*
league /lig/ *n.* liga; (measure) legua *f.*
leak /lik/ *n.* **1.** escape; goteo *m.* —*v.* **2.** gotear; *Naut.* hacer agua.
leakage /'likɪdʒ/ *n.* goteo *m.*, escape *m.*, pérdida *f.*
leaky /'liki/ *a.* llovedizo, resquebrajado.
lean /lin/ *a.* **1.** flaco, magro. —*v.* **2.** apoyarse, arrimarse.
leap /lip/ *n.* **1.** salto *m.* —*v.* **2.** saltar.
leap year *n.* año bisiesto *m.*
learn /lɜrn/ *v.* aprender; saber.
learned /'lɜrnɪd/ *a.* erudito.
learning /'lɜrnɪŋ/ *n.* erudición *f.*, instrucción *f.*
lease /lis/ *n.* **1.** arriendo *m.* —*v.* **2.** arrendar.
leash /liʃ/ *n.* **1.** correa *f.* —*v.* **2.** atraillar.
least /list/ *a.* menor; mínimo. **the l.,** lo menos. **at l.,** por lo menos.
leather /'lɛðər/ *n.* cuero *m.*
leathery /'lɛðəri/ *a.* coriáceo.
leave /liv/ *n.* **1.** licencia *f.* **to take l.,** despedirse. —*v.* **2.** dejar; (depart) salir, irse. **l. out,** omitir.
leaven /'lɛvən/ *n.* **1.** levadura *f.* —*v.* **2.** fermentar, imbuir.
lecherous /'lɛtʃərəs/ *a.* lujurioso.
lecture /'lɛktʃər/ *n.* conferencia *f.*
lecturer /'lɛktʃərər/ *n.* conferencista *m. & f.*; catedrático -ca.
ledge /lɛdʒ/ *n.* borde *m.*; capa *f.*
ledger /'lɛdʒər/ *n.* libro mayor *m.*

lee /li/ n. sotavento m.

leech /litʃ/ n. sanguijuela f.

leek /lik/ n. puerro m.

leer /lɪər/ v. mirar de soslayo.

leeward /'liwərd/ a. sotavento.

left /lɛft/ a. izquierdo. **the l.,** la izquierda. **to be left,** quedarse.

left-handed /'lɛft 'hændɪd/ a. zurdo.

leftist /'lɛftɪst/ n. izquierdista m. & f.

leftovers /'lɛft,ouvərz/ n. sobras f.pl.

leg /lɛg/ n. pierna f.

legacy /'lɛgəsi/ n. legado m., herencia f.

legal /'ligəl/ a. legal.

legalize /'ligə,laiz/ v. legalizar.

legation /lɪ'geiʃən/ n. legación, embajada f.

legend /'lɛdʒənd/ n. leyenda f.

legendary /'lɛdʒən,dɛri/ a. legendario.

legible /'lɛdʒəbəl/ a. legible.

legion /'lidʒən/ n. legión f.

legislate /'lɛdʒɪs,leit/ v. legislar.

legislation /,lɛdʒɪs'leiʃən/ n. legislación f.

legislator /'lɛdʒɪs,leitər/ n. legislador -ra.

legislature /'lɛdʒɪs,leitʃər/ n. legislatura f.

legitimate /lɪ'dʒɪtəmɪt/ a. legítimo.

legume /'lɛgyum/ n. legumbre f.

leisure /'liʒər/ n. desocupación f.; horas libres.

leisurely /'liʒərli/ a. **1.** deliberado. —adv. **2.** despacio.

lemon /'lɛmən/ n. limón m.

lemonade /,lɛmə'neid/ n. limonada f.

lend /lɛnd/ v. prestar.

length /lɛŋkθ/ n. largo m.; duración f.

lengthen /'lɛŋkθən/ v. alargar.

lengthwise /'lɛŋkθ,waiz/ adv. a lo largo.

lengthy /'lɛŋkθi/ a. largo.

lenient /'liniənt/ a. indulgente.

lens /lɛnz/ n. lente m. or f.

Lent /lɛnt/ n. cuaresma f.

Lenten /'lɛntn/ a. cuaresmal.

lentil /'lɛntɪl/ n. lenteja f.

leopard /'lɛpərd/ n. leopardo m.

leotard /'liə,tɑrd/ n. mallas f.pl.

leper /'lɛpər/ n. leproso -sa.

leprosy /'lɛprəsi/ n. lepra f.

lesbian /'lɛzbiən/ n. lesbiana f.

lesion /'liʒən/ n. lesión f.

less /lɛs/ a. & adv. menos.

lessen /'lɛsən/ v. disminuir.

lesser /'lɛsər/ a. menor; más pequeño.

lesson /'lɛsən/ n. lección f.

lest /lɛst/ conj. para que no.

let /lɛt/ v. dejar; permitir; arrendar.

letdown /'lɛt,daun/ n. decepción f.

lethal /'liθəl/ a. letal.

lethargic /lə'θɑrdʒɪk/ a. letárgico.

lethargy /'lɛθərdʒi/ n. letargo m.

letter /'lɛtər/ n. carta; (of alphabet) letra f.

letterhead /'lɛtər,hɛd/ n. membrete m.

lettuce /'lɛtɪs/ n. lechuga f.

leukemia /lu'kimiə/ n. leucemia f.

levee /'lɛvi, lɛ'vi/ n. recepción f.

level /'lɛvəl/ a. **1.** llano, nivelado. —n. **2.** nivel m.; llanura f. —v. **3.** allanar; nivelar.

lever /'lɛvər/ n. palanca f.

levity /'lɛvɪti/ n. levedad f.

levy /'lɛvi/ n. **1.** leva f. —v. **2.** imponer.

lewd /lud/ a. lascivo.

lexicon /'lɛksɪ,kɒn/ n. léxico m.

liability /,laiə'bɪlɪti/ n. riesgo m.; obligación f.

liable /'laiəbəl/ a. sujeto; responsable.

liaison /li'eizən/ n. vinculación f., enlace m.; concubinaje m.

liar /'laiər/ n. embustero -ra.

libel /'laibəl/ n. **1.** libelo m. —v. **2.** difamar.

libelous /'laibələs/ a. difamatorio.

liberal /'lɪbərəl/ a. liberal; generoso.

liberalism /'lɪbərə,lɪzəm/ n. liberalismo m.

liberality /,lɪbə'rælɪti/ n. liberalidad f.

liberate /'lɪbə,reit/ v. libertar.

liberty /'lɪbərti/ n. libertad f.

libidinous /lɪ'bɪdnəs/ a. libidinoso.

librarian /lai'brɛəriən/ n. bibliotecario -ria.

library /'lai,brɛri/ n. biblioteca f.

libretto /lɪ'brɛtou/ n. libreto m.

license /'laisəns/ n. licencia f.; permiso m.

licentious /lai'sɛnʃəs/ a. licencioso.

lick /lɪk/ v. lamer.

licorice /'lɪkərɪʃ, 'lɪkrɪʃ, 'lɪkərɪs/ n. regaliz m.

lid /lɪd/ n. tapa f.

lie /lai/ n. **1.** mentira f. —v. **2.** mentir. **l. down,** acostarse, echarse.

lieutenant /lu'tɛnənt/ n. teniente m.

life /laif/ n. vida f.

lifeboat /'laif,bout/ n. bote salvavidas m.

life buoy boya f.

lifeguard /'laif,gɑrd/ socorrista m. & f.

life insurance seguro de vida m.

life jacket chaleco salvavidas m.

lifeless /'laiflɪs/ a. sin vida.

life preserver /prɪ'zɜrvər/ salvavidas m.

lifestyle /'laifstail/ n. modo de vida m.

lift /lɪft/ v. levantar, alzar, elevar.

ligament /'lɪgəmənt/ n. ligamento m.

ligature /'lɪgətʃər/ n. ligadura f.

light /lait/ a. **1.** ligero; liviano; (in color) claro. —n. **2.** luz; candela f. —v. **3.** encender; iluminar.

light bulb bombilla f.

lighten /'laitn/ v. aligerar; aclarar; iluminar.

lighter /'laitər/ n. encendedor m.

lighthouse /'lait,haus/ n. faro m.

lightness /'laitnɪs/ n. ligereza; agilidad f.

lightning /'laitnɪŋ/ n. relámpago m.

like /laik/ a. **1.** semejante. —prep. **2.** como. —v. **3. I like...** me gusta, me gustan... **I should like,** quisiera.

likeable /'laikəbəl/ a. simpático, agradable.

likelihood /'laikli,hʊd/ n. probabilidad f.

likely /'laikli/ a. probable; verosímil.

liken /'laikən/ v. comparar; asemejar.

likeness /'laiknɪs/ n. semejanza f.

likewise /'laik,waiz/ adv. igualmente.

lilac /'lailək/ n. lila f.

lilt /lɪlt/ n. **1.** cadencia alegre f. —v. **2.** cantar alegremente.

lily /'lɪli/ n. lirio m.

lily of the valley muguete m.

limb /lɪm/ n. rama f.

limber /'lɪmbər/ a. flexible. **to l. up,** ponerse flexible.

limbo /'lɪmbou/ n. limbo m.

lime /laim/ n. cal f.; (fruit) limoncito m., lima f.

limestone /'laim,stoun/ n. piedra caliza f.

limewater /'laim,wɔtər/ n. agua de cal f.

limit /'lɪmɪt/ n. **1.** límite m. —v. **2.** limitar.

limitation /,lɪmɪ'teiʃən/ n. limitación f.

limitless /'lɪmɪtlɪs/ a. ilimitado.

limousine /'lɪmə,zin/ n. limusina f.

limp /lɪmp/ n. **1.** cojera f. —a. **2.** flojo. —v. **3.** cojear.

limpid /'lɪmpɪd/ a. límpido.

line /lain/ n. **1.** línea; fila; raya f.; (of print) renglón m. —v. **2.** forrar; rayar.

lineage /'lɪnɪdʒ/ n. linaje m.

lineal /'lɪniəl/ a. lineal.

linear /'lɪniər/ a. linear, longitudinal.

linen /'lɪnən/ n. lienzo, lino m.; ropa blanca.

liner /'lainər/ n. vapor m.

linger /'lɪŋgər/ v. demorarse.

lingerie /,lɑnʒə'rei/ n. ropa blanca f.

linguist /'lɪŋgwɪst/ n. lingüista m. & f.

linguistic /lɪŋ'gwɪstɪk/ a. lingüístico.

liniment /'lɪnəmənt/ n. linimento m.

lining /'lainɪŋ/ n. forro m.

link /lɪŋk/ n. **1.** eslabón; vínculo m. —v. **2.** vincular.

linoleum /lɪ'nouliəm/ n. linóleo m.

linseed /'lɪn,sid/ n. linaza f.; simiente de lino f.

lint /lɪnt/ n. hilacha f.

lion /'laiən/ n. león m.

lip /lɪp/ n. labio m.

liposuction /'lɪpə,sʌkʃən, 'laipə-/ n. liposucción f.

lipstick /'lɪp,stɪk/ n. lápiz de labios.

liqueur /lɪ'kɜr/ n. licor m.

liquid /'lɪkwɪd/ a. & n. líquido m.

liquidate /'lɪkwɪ,deit/ v. liquidar.

liquidation /,lɪkwɪ'deiʃən/ n. liquidación f.

liquor /'lɪkər/ n. licor m.

lisp /lɪsp/ n. **1.** ceceo m. —v. **2.** cecear.

list /lɪst/ n. **1.** lista f. —v. **2.** registrar.

listen (to) /'lɪsən/ v. escuchar.

listless /'lɪstlɪs/ a. indiferente.

litany /'lɪtni/ n. letanía f.

liter /'litər/ n. litro m.

literal /'lɪtərəl/ a. literal.

literary /'lɪtə,rɛri/ a. literario.

literate /'lɪtərɪt/ a. alfabetizado.

literature /'lɪtərətʃər/ n. literatura f.

litigant /'lɪtɪgənt/ n. & a. litigante m. & f.

litigation /,lɪtɪ'geiʃən/ n. litigio, pleito m.

litter /'lɪtər/ n. **1.** litera f.; cama de paja. —v. **2.** poner en desorden.

little /'lɪtl/ a. pequeño; (quantity) poco.

little finger meñique m.

liturgical /lɪ'tɜrdʒɪkəl/ a. litúrgico.

liturgy /'lɪtərdʒi/ n. liturgia f.

live /a laiv; v lɪv/ a. **1.** vivo. —v. **2.** vivir.

livelihood /'laivli,hʊd/ n. subsistencia f.

lively /'laivli/ a. vivo; rápido; animado.

liver /'lɪvər/ n. hígado m.

livery /'lɪvəri/ n. librea f.

livestock /'laiv,stɒk/ n. ganadería f.

livid /'lɪvɪd/ a. lívido.

living /'lɪvɪŋ/ a. **1.** vivo. —n. **2.** sustento m. **to earn (make) a living,** ganarse la vida.

living room salón m.

lizard /'lɪzərd/ n. lagarto m., lagartija f.

llama /'lɑmə/ n. llama f.

load /loud/ n. **1.** carga f. —v. **2.** cargar.

loaf /louf/ n. **1.** pan m. —v. **2.** holgazanear.

loam /loum/ n. marga f.

loan /loun/ n. **1.** préstamo m. —v. **2.** prestar.

loathe /louð/ v. aborrecer, detestar.

loathsome /'louðsəm/ a. repugnante.

lobby /'lɒbi/ n. vestíbulo m.

lobe /loub/ n. lóbulo m.

lobster /'lɒbstər/ n. langosta f.

local /'loukəl/ a. local.

local area network red local f.

locale /lou'kæl/ n. localidad f.

locality /lou'kælɪti/ n. localidad f., lugar m.

localize /'loukə,laiz/ v. localizar.

locate /'loukeit/ v. situar; hallar.

location /lou'keiʃən/ n. sitio m.; posición f.

lock /lɒk/ n. **1.** cerradura f.; (pl.) cabellos m.pl. —v. **2.** cerrar con llave.

locker /'lɒkər/ n. cajón m.; ropero m.

locket /'lɒkɪt/ n. guardapelo m.; medallón m.

lockjaw /'lɒk,dʒɔ/ n. trismo m.

locksmith /'lɒk,smɪθ/ n. cerrajero -ra.

locomotive /,loukə'moutɪv/ n. locomotora f.

locust /'loukəst/ n. cigarra f., saltamontes m.

locution /lou'kyuʃən/ n. locución f.

lode /loud/ n. filón m., veta f.

lodge /lɒdʒ/ n. **1.** logia; (inn) posada f. —v. **2.** fijar; alojar, morar.

lodger /'lɒdʒər/ n. inquilino m.

lodging /'lɒdʒɪŋ/ n. alojamiento m.

loft /lɔft/ n. desván, sobrado m.

lofty /'lɔfti/ a. alto; altivo.

log /lɔg/ n. tronco de árbol; Naut. barquilla f.

loge /louʒ/ n. palco m.

logic /'lɒdʒɪk/ n. lógica f.

logical /'lɒdʒɪkəl/ a. lógico.

loin /lɔin/ n. lomo m.

loincloth /'lɔin,klɔθ/ n. taparrabos m.

loiter /'lɔitər/ v. haraganear.

lone /loun/ a. solitario.

loneliness /'lounlinɪs/ n. soledad f.

lonely, /'lounli/ **lonesome** a. solo y triste.

lonesome /'lounsəm/ a. solitario, aislado.

long /lɔŋ/ a. **1.** largo. **a l. time,** mucho tiempo. —adv. **2.** mucho tiempo. **how l.,** cuánto tiempo. **no longer,** ya no. —v. **3. l. for,** anhelar.

long-distance call /'lɔŋ 'dɪstəns/ conferencia interurbana f.

longevity /lɒn'dʒɛvɪti/ n. longevidad f.

long-haired /'lɔŋ 'hɛərd/ a. melenudo.

longing /'lɔŋɪŋ/ n. anhelo m.

longitude /'lɒndʒɪ,tud/ n. longitud m.

look /lʊk/ n. **1.** mirada f.; aspecto m. —v. **2.** parecer; mirar. **l. at,** mirar. **l. for,** buscar. **l. like,** parecerse a. **l. out!,** ¡cuidado! **l. up,** buscar; ir a ver, venir a ver.

looking glass /'lʊkɪŋ/ espejo m.

loom /lum/ n. **1.** telar m. —v. **2.** asomar.

loop /lup/ n. vuelta f.

loophole /'lup,houl/ n. aspillera f.; Fig. callejuela, evasiva f., efugio m.

loose /lus/ a. suelto; flojo.

loose change suelto m.

loosen /'lusən/ v. soltar; aflojar.

loot /lut/ n. **1.** botín m., saqueo m. —v. **2.** saquear.

lopsided /'lɒp'saidɪd/ a. desequilibrado.

loquacious /lou'kweiʃəs/ a. locuaz.

lord /lɔrd/ n. señor m.; (Brit. title) lord m.

lordship /'lɔrdʃɪp/ n. señorío m.

lose /luz/ v. perder. **l. consciousness,** perder el concimiento.

loss /lɔs/ n. pérdida f.

lost /lɔst/ a. perdido.

lot /lɒt/ n. suerte f. **building l.,** solar m. **a lot (of), lots of,** mucho.

lotion /'louʃən/ n. loción f.

lottery /'lɒtəri/ n. lotería f.

loud /laud/ a. **1.** fuerte; ruidoso. —adv. **2.** alto.

loudspeaker /'laud,spikər/ n. altavoz m.

lounge /laundʒ/ n. sofá m.; salón de fumar m.

louse /laus/ n. piojo m.

love /lʌv/ n. **1.** amor m. **in l.,** enamorado. **to fall in l.,** enamorarse. **l. at first sight,** flechazo m. —v. **2.** querer; amar; adorar.

lovely /'lʌvli/ a. hermoso.

lover /'lʌvər/ n. amante m. & f.

low /lou/ a. bajo; vil.

low-cut /'lou 'kʌt/ a. escotado.

lower /'louər/ v. bajar; (in price) rebajar.

lower-case letter /'louər 'keis/ minúscula f.

lowly /'louli/ a. humilde.

low neckline /'nɛk,lain/ escote m.

loyal /'lɔiəl/ a. leal, fiel.

loyalist /'lɔiəlɪst/ n. lealista m. & f.

loyalty /'lɔiəlti/ n. lealtad f.

lozenge /'lɒzɪndʒ/ n. pastilla f.

lubricant /'lubrɪkənt/ n. lubricante m.

lubricate /'lubrɪ,keit/ v. engrasar, lubricar.

lucid /'lusɪd/ a. claro, lúcido.

luck /lʌk/ *n.* suerte; fortuna *f.*
lucky /ˈlʌki/ *a.* afortunado. **to be l.,** tener suerte.
lucrative /ˈlukrətɪv/ *a.* lucrativo.
ludicrous /ˈludɪkrəs/ *a.* rídiculo.
luggage /ˈlʌgɪdʒ/ *n.* equipaje *m.*
lukewarm /ˈlukˈwɔrm/ *a.* tibio.
lull /lʌl/ *n.* **1.** momento de calma. —*v.* **2.** calmar.
lullaby /ˈlʌləˌbai/ *n.* arrullo *m.*
lumbago /lʌmˈbeigou/ *n.* lumbago *m.*
lumber /ˈlʌmbər/ *n.* madera *f.*
luminous /ˈlumənəs/ *a.* luminoso.
lump /lʌmp/ *n.* protuberancia *f.;* (of sugar) terrón *m.*
lump sum suma global *f.*
lunacy /ˈlunəsi/ *n.* locura *f.*
lunar /ˈlunər/ *a.* lunar.
lunatic /ˈlunətɪk/ *a.* & *n.* loco -ca.
lunch, luncheon /lʌntʃ; ˈlʌntshən;/ *n.* **1.** merienda *f.*, almuerzo *m.* —*v.* **2.** merendar, almorzar.
lunch box /ˈlʌntʃˌbɒks/ fiambrera *f.*
lung /lʌŋ/ *n.* pulmón *m.*
lunge /lʌndʒ/ *n.* **1.** estocada, arremetida *f.* —*v.* **2.** dar un estocada, arremeter.
lure /lʊr/ *v.* atraer.
lurid /ˈlʊrɪd/ *a.* sensacional; espeluznante.
lurk /lɜrk/ *v.* esconderse; espiar.
luscious /ˈlʌʃəs/ *a.* sabroso, delicioso.
lust /lʌst/ *n.* sensualidad; codicia *f.*
luster /ˈlʌstər/ *n.* lustre *m.*
lustful /ˈlʌstfəl/ *a.* sensual, lascivo.
lusty /ˈlʌsti/ *a.* vigoroso.
lute /lut/ *n.* laúd *m.*
Lutheran /ˈluθərən/ *n.* & *a.* luterano -na.
luxuriant /lʌgˈʒʊriənt/ *a.* exuberante, frondoso.
luxurious /lʌgˈʒʊriəs/ *a.* lujoso.
luxury /ˈlʌkʃəri/ *n.* lujo *m.*
lying /ˈlaiɪŋ/ *a.* mentiroso.
lymph /lɪmf/ *n.* linfa *f.*
lynch /lɪntʃ/ *v.* linchar.
lyre /laiᵊr/ *n.* lira *f.*
lyric /ˈlɪrɪk/ *a.* lírico.
lyricism /ˈlɪrəˌsɪzəm/ *n.* lirismo *m.*

M

macabre /məˈkɑbrə/ *a.* macabro.
macaroni /ˌmækəˈrouni/ *n.* macarrones *m.*
machine /məˈʃin/ *n.* máquina *f.*
machine gun ametralladora *f.*
machinery /məˈʃinəri/ *n.* maquinaria *f.*
machinist /məˈʃinɪst/ *n.* maquinista *m.* & *f.*, mecánico *m.*
macho /ˈmɑtʃou/ *a.* machista.
mackerel /ˈmækərəl/ *n.* escombro *m.*
macro /ˈmækrou/ *n.* (computer) macro *m.*
mad /mæd/ *a.* loco; furioso.
madam /ˈmædəm/ *n.* señora *f.*
mafia /ˈmɑfiə/ *n.* mafia *f.*
magazine /ˌmægəˈzin/ *n.* revista *f.*
magic /ˈmædʒɪk/ *a.* **1.** mágico. —*n.* **2.** magia *f.*
magician /məˈdʒɪʃən/ *n.* mágico *m.*
magistrate /ˈmædʒəˌstreit/ *n.* magistrado, -da.
magnanimous /mægˈnænəməs/ *a.* magnánimo.
magnate /ˈmægneit/ *n.* magnate *m.*
magnesium /mægˈniziəm/ *n.* magnesio *m.*
magnet /ˈmægnɪt/ *n.* imán *m.*
magnetic /mægˈnɛtɪk/ *a.* magnético.
magnificence /mægˈnɪfəsəns/ *n.* magnificencia *f.*
magnificent /mægˈnɪfəsənt/ *a.* magnífico.
magnify /ˈmægnəˌfai/ *v.* magnificar.
magnifying glass /ˈmægnəˌfaiɪŋ/ lupa *f.*
magnitude /ˈmægnɪˌtud/ *n.* magnitud *f.*
magpie /ˈmægˌpai/ *n.* hurraca *f.*
mahogany /məˈhɒgəni/ *n.* caoba *f.*
maid /meid/ *n.* criada *f.* **old m.,** solterona *f.*
maiden /ˈmeidn̩/ *a.* soltera.
mail /meil/ *n.* **1.** correo *m.* **air m.,** correo aéreo. **by return m.,** a vuelta de correo. —*v.* **2.** echar al correo.
mailbox /ˈmeilˌbɒks/ *n.* buzón *m.*
mailman /ˈmeilˌmæn/ *n.* cartero *m.*
maim /meim/ *v.* mutilar.
main /mein/ *a.* principal.
mainframe /ˈmeinˌfreim/ *n.* componente central de una computadora.
mainland /ˈmeinˌlænd/ *n.* continente *m.*
maintain /meinˈtein/ *v.* mantener; sostener.
maintenance /ˈmeintənəns/ *n.* mantenimiento; sustento *m.;* conservación *f.*
maître d' /ˌmeiˈtər di, ˌmeitrə, ˌmɛtrə/ *n.* jefe de sala *m.* & *f.*
maize /meiz/ *n.* maíz *m.*
majestic /məˈdʒɛstɪk/ *a.* majestuoso.
majesty /ˈmædʒəsti/ *n.* majestad *f.*
major /ˈmeidʒər/ *a.* **1.** mayor. —*n.* **2.** *Mil.* comandante *m.;* (study) especialidad *f.*
majority /məˈdʒɔrɪti/ *n.* mayoría *f.*
make /meik/ *n.* **1.** marca *f.* —*v.* **2.** hacer; fabricar; (earn) ganar.
maker /ˈmeikər/ *n.* fabricante *m.*
makeshift /ˈmeikˌʃɪft/ *a.* provisional.
make-up /ˈmeikˌʌp/ *n.* cosméticos *m. pl.*
malady /ˈmælədi/ *n.* mal *m.*, enfermedad *f.*
malaria /məˈlɛəriə/ *n.* paludismo *m.*
male /meil/ *a.* & *n.* macho *m.*
malevolent /məˈlɛvələnt/ *a.* malévolo.
malice /mælɪs/ *n.* malicia *f.*
malicious /məˈlɪʃəs/ *a.* malicioso.
malign /məˈlain/ *v.* **1.** difamar. —*a.* **2.** maligno.
malignant /məˈlɪgnənt/ *a.* maligno.
malnutrition /ˌmælnuˈtrɪʃən/ *n.* desnutrición *f.*
malt /mɔlt/ *n.* malta *f.*
mammal /ˈmæməl/ *n.* mamífero *m.*
man /mæn/ *n.* hombre; varón *m.* *v.* tripular.
manage /ˈmænɪdʒ/ *v.* manejar; dirigir; administrar; arreglárselas. **m. to,** lograr.
management /ˈmænɪdʒmənt/ *n.* dirección, administración *f.*
manager /ˈmænɪdʒər/ *n.* director -ora.
mandate /ˈmændeit/ *n.* mandato *m.*
mandatory /ˈmændəˌtɔri/ *a.* obligatorio.
mandolin /ˈmændlɪn/ *n.* mandolina *f.*
mane /mein/ *n.* crines *f. pl.*
maneuver /məˈnuvər/ *n.* **1.** maniobra *f.* —*v.* **2.** maniobrar.
manganese /ˈmæŋgəˌnis, -ˌniz/ *n.* manganeso *m.*
manger /ˈmeindʒər/ *n.* pesebre *m.*
mangle /ˈmæŋgəl/ *n.* **1.** rodillo, exprimidor *m.* —*v.* **2.** mutilar.
manhood /ˈmænhʊd/ *n.* virilidad *f.*
mania /ˈmeiniə/ *n.* manía *f.*
maniac /ˈmeiniˌæk/ *a.* & *n.* maniático -ca; maníaco -ca.
manicure /ˈmænɪˌkyʊr/ *n.* manicura *f.*
manifest /ˈmænəˌfɛst/ *a.* & *n.* **1.** manifiesto *m.* —*v.* **2.** manifestar.
manifesto /ˌmænəˈfɛstou/ *n.* manifiesto *m.*
manifold /ˈmænəˌfould/ *a.* **1.** muchos. —*n.* **2.** *Auto.* tubo múltiple.
manipulate /məˈnɪpyəˌleit/ *v.* manipular.
mankind /ˈmænˈkaind/ *n.* humanidad *f.*
manly /ˈmænli/ *a.* varonil.
manner /ˈmænər/ *n.* manera *f.*, modo *m.* **manners,** modales *m. pl.*
mannerism /ˈmænəˌrɪzəm/ *n.* manerismo *m.*
mansion /ˈmænʃən/ *n.* mansión *f.*
mantel /ˈmæntl̩/ *n.* manto de chimenea.
mantle /ˈmæntl̩/ *n.* manto *m.*
manual /ˈmænyuəl/ *a.* & *n.* manual *m.*
manufacture /ˌmænyəˈfæktʃər/ *v.* fabricar.
manufacturer /ˌmænyəˈfæktʃərər/ *n.* fabricante *m.*
manufacturing /ˌmænyəˈfæktʃərɪŋ/ *n.* fabricación *f.*
manure /məˈnʊr/ *n.* abono, estiércol *m.*
manuscript /ˈmænyəˌskrɪpt/ *n.* manuscrito *m.*
many /ˈmɛni/ *a.* muchos. **how m.,** cuántos. **so m.,** tantos. **too m.,** demasiados. **as m. as,** tantos como.
map /mæp/ *n.* mapa *m.*
maple /ˈmeipəl/ *n.* arce *m.*
mar /mɑr/ *v.* estropear; desfigurar.
marble /ˈmɑrbəl/ *n.* mármol *m.*
march /mɑrtʃ/ *n.* **1.** marcha *f.* —*v.* **2.** marchar.
March /mɑrtʃ/ *n.* marzo *m.*
mare /mɛər/ *n.* yegua *f.*
margarine /ˈmɑrdʒərɪn/ *n.* margarina *f.*
margin /ˈmɑrdʒɪn/ *n.* margen *m.* or *f.*
marijuana /ˌmærəˈwɑnə/ *n.* marijuana *f.*
marine /məˈrin/ *a.* **1.** marino. —*n.* **2.** soldado de marina.
mariner /ˈmærənər/ *n.* marinero *m.*
marionette /ˌmæriəˈnɛt/ *n.* marioneta *f.*
marital /ˈmærɪtl̩/ *a.* marital.
maritime /ˈmærɪˌtaim/ *a.* marítimo.
mark /mɑrk/ *n.* **1.** marca *f.* —*v.* **2.** marcar.
market /ˈmɑrkɪt/ *n.* mercado *m.* **meat m.,** carnicería *f.* **stock m.,** bolsa *f.*, *v.* comercializar.
marmalade /ˈmɑrməˌleid/ *n.* mermelada *f.*
maroon /məˈrun/ *a.* & *n.* color rojo oscuro. *v.* dejar abandonado.
marquis /ˈmɑrkwɪs/ *n.* marqués *m.*
marriage /ˈmærɪdʒ/ *n.* matrimonio *m.*
marriage certificate partida de matrimonio *f.*
married /ˈmærid/ *a.* casado. **to get m.,** casarse.
marrow /ˈmærou/ *n.* médula *f.;* substancia *f.*
marry /ˈmæri/ *v.* casarse con; casar.
marsh /mɑrʃ/ *n.* pantano *m.*
marshal /ˈmɑrʃəl/ *n.* mariscal *m.*
marshmallow /ˈmɑrʃˌmɛlou/ *n.* malvarisco *m.;* bombón de altea *m.*
martial /ˈmɑrʃəl/ *a.* marcial. **m. law,** gobierno militar.
martyr /ˈmɑrtər/ *n.* mártir *m.* & *f.*
martyrdom /ˈmɑrtərdəm/ *n.* martirio *m.*
marvel /ˈmɑrvəl/ *n.* **1.** maravilla *f.* —*v.* **2.** maravillarse.
marvelous /ˈmɑrvələs/ *a.* maravilloso.
mascara /mæˈskærə/ *n.* rímel *m.*
mascot /ˈmæskɒt/ *n.* mascota *f.*
masculine /ˈmæskyəlɪn/ *a.* masculino.
mash /mæʃ/ *v.* majar. **mashed potatoes,** puré de papas *m.*
mask /mæsk/ *n.* máscara *f.*
mason /ˈmeisən/ *n.* albañil *m.*
masquerade /ˌmæskəˈreid/ *n.* mascarada *f.*
mass /mæs/ *n.* masa *f.; Relig.* misa *f.* **to say m.,** cantar misa. **m. production,** producción en serie.
massacre /ˈmæsəkər/ *n.* **1.** carnicería, matanza *f.* —*v.* **2.** matar atrozmente, destrozar.
massage /məˈsɑʒ/ *n.* **1.** masaje *m.;* soba *f.* —*v.* **2.** sobar.
masseur /məˈsɜr/ *n.* masajista *m.* & *f.*
massive /ˈmæsɪv/ *a.* macizo, sólido.
mast /mæst/ *n.* palo, árbol *m.*
master /ˈmæstər/ *n.* **1.** amo; maestro *m.* —*v.* **2.** domar, dominar.
masterpiece /ˈmæstərˌpis/ *n.* obra maestra *f.*
master's degree /ˈmæstərz/ maestría *f.*
mastery /ˈmæstəri/ *n.* maestría *f.*
mat /mæt/ *n.* **1.** estera; palleta *f.* —*v.* **2.** enredar.
match /mætʃ/ *n.* **1.** igual *m;* fósforo *m.;* (sport) partida, contienda *f.;* (marriage) noviazgo; casamiento. —*v.* **2.** ser igual a; igualar.
matchbox /ˈmætʃˌbɒks/ caja de cerillas, caja de fósforos *f.*
mate /meit/ *n.* **1.** consorte *m.* & *f.;* compañero -ra. —*v.* **2.** igualar; casar.
material /məˈtɪəriəl/ *a.* & *n.* material *m.* **raw materials,** materias primas.
materialism /məˈtɪəriəˌlɪzəm/ *n.* materialismo *m.*
materialize /məˈtɪəriəˌlaiz/ *v.* materializar.
maternal /məˈtɜrnl̩/ *a.* materno.
maternity /məˈtɜrnɪti/ *n.* maternidad *f.*
maternity hospital maternidad *f.*
mathematical /ˌmæθəˈmætɪkəl/ *a.* matemático.
mathematics /ˌmæθəˈmætɪks/ *n.* matemáticas *f.pl.*
matinee /ˌmætn̩ˈei/ *n.* matiné *f.*
matrimony /ˈmætrəˌmouni/ *n.* matrimonio *m.*
matron /ˈmeitrən/ *n.* matrona; directora *f.*
matter /ˈmætər/ *n.* **1.** materia *f.;* asunto *m.* **what's the m.?,** ¿qué pasa? —*v.* **2.** importar.
mattress /ˈmætrɪs/ *n.* colchón *m.*
mature /məˈtʃʊr/ *a.* **1.** maduro. —*v.* **2.** madurar.
maturity /məˈtʃʊrɪti/ *n.* madurez *f.*
maudlin /ˈmɔdlɪn/ *a.* sentimental en exceso; sensiblero.
maul /mɔl/ *v.* aporrear.
maxim /ˈmæksɪm/ *n.* máxima *f.*
maximum /ˈmæksəməm/ *a.* & *n.* máximo.
may /mei/ *v.* poder.
May /mei/ *n.* mayo *m.*
maybe /ˈmeibi/ *adv.* quizá, quizás, tal vez.
mayonnaise /ˌmeiəˈneiz/ *n.* mayonesa *f.*
mayor /ˈmeiər/ *n.* alcalde *m.* alcaldesa *f.*
maze /meiz/ *n.* laberinto *m.*
me /mi/ *pron.* mí; me. **with me,** conmigo.
meadow /ˈmɛdou/ *n.* prado *m.;* vega *f.*
meager /ˈmigər/ *a.* magro; pobre.
meal /mil/ *n.* comida; (flour) harina *f.*
mean /min/ *a.* **1.** bajo; malo. —*n.* **2.** medio (see also **means**). —*v.* **3.** significar; querer decir.
meander /miˈændər/ *v.* (river) serpentear; (person) deambular.
meaning /ˈminɪŋ/ *n.* sentido, significado *m.*
meaningless /ˈminɪŋlɪs/ *a.* sin sentido.
means /minz/ *n.pl.* medios, recursos *m.* **by all m.,** sin falta. **by no m.,** de ningún modo. **by m. of,** por medio de.
meanwhile /ˈminˌwail/ *adv.* mientras tanto.
measles /ˈmizəlz/ *n.* sarampión *m.*
measure /ˈmɛʒər/ *n.* **1.** medida *f.;* (music) compás *m.* —*v.* **2.** medir.
measurement /ˈmɛʒərmənt/ *n.* medida, dimensión *f.*
meat /mit/ *n.* carne *f.*
mechanic /məˈkænɪk/ *n.* mecánico *m.* & *f.*
mechanical /məˈkænɪkəl/ *a.* mecánico.
mechanism /ˈmɛkəˌnɪzəm/ *n.* mecanismo *m.*
mechanize /ˈmɛkəˌnaiz/ *v.* mecanizar.
medal /ˈmɛdl̩/ *n.* medalla *f.*

meddle /'mɛdl/ v. meterse, entremeterse.

mediate /'midɪˌeit/ v. mediar.

medical /'mɛdɪkəl/ a. médico.

medicine /'mɛdəsɪn/ n. medicina f.

medicine chest botiquín m.

medieval /ˌmidi'ivəl/ a. medieval.

mediocre /ˌmidi'oukər/ a. mediocre.

mediocrity /ˌmidi'ɒkrɪti/ n. mediocridad f.

meditate /'mɛdɪˌteit/ v. meditar.

meditation /ˌmɛdɪ'teiʃən/ n. meditación f.

Mediterranean /ˌmɛdɪtə'reiniən/ n. Mediterráneo m.

medium /'midiəm/ a. **1.** mediano, medio. —n. **2.** medio m.

medley /'mɛdli/ n. mezcla f., ensalada f.

meek /mik/ a. manso; humilde.

meekness /'miknɪs/ n. modestia; humildad f.

meet /mit/ a. **1.** apropiado. —n. **2.** concurso m. —v. **3.** encontrar; reunirse; conocer.

meeting /'mitɪŋ/ n. reunión f.; mitin m.

megahertz /'mɛgəˌhɜrts/ n. megahercio m.

megaphone /'mɛgəˌfoun/ n. megáfono m.

melancholy /'mɛlənˌkɒli/ a. **1.** melancólico. —n. **2.** melancolía f.

mellow /'mɛlou/ a. suave; blando; maduro.

melodious /mə'loudiəs/ a. melodioso.

melodrama /'mɛləˌdrɑmə/ n. melodrama m.

melody /'mɛlədi/ n. melodía f.

melon /'mɛlən/ n. melón m.

melt /mɛlt/ v. derretir.

meltdown /'mɛltˌdaun/ n. fundición resultante de un accidente en un reactor nuclear.

member /'mɛmbər/ n. socio -ia; miembro m. **m. of the crew,** tripulante m. & f.

membership /'mɛmbərˌʃɪp/ n. número de miembros.

membrane /'mɛmbrein/ n. membrana f.

memento /mə'mɛntou/ n. recuerdo m.

memoir /'mɛmwɑr/ n. memoria f.

memorable /'mɛmərəbəl/ a. memorable.

memorandum /ˌmɛmə'rændəm/ n. memorándum, volante m.

memorial /mə'mɔriəl/ a. **1.** conmemorativo. —n. **2.** memorial m.

memorize /'mɛməˌraiz/ v. aprender de memoria.

memory /'mɛməri/ n. memoria f.; recuerdo m.

menace /'mɛnɪs/ n. **1.** amenaza f. —v. **2.** amenazar.

mend /mɛnd/ v. reparar, remendar.

menial /'miniəl/ a. **1.** servil. —n. **2.** sirviente -ta.

meningitis /ˌmɛnɪn'dʒaitɪs/ n. meningitis f.

menopause /'mɛnəˌpɔz/ n. menopausia f.

menstruation /ˌmɛnstru'eiʃən/ n. menstruación f.

menswear /'mɛnzˌwɛər/ n. ropa de caballeros f.

mental /'mɛntl/ a. mental.

mental disorder trastorno mental m.

mentality /mɛn'tæliti/ n. mentalidad f.

menthol /'mɛnθɔl/ n. mentol m.

mention /'mɛnʃən/ n. **1.** mención f. —v. **2.** mencionar.

menu /'mɛnyu/ n. menú m., lista f.

mercantile /'mɜrkənˌtil/ a. mercantil.

mercenary /'mɜrsəˌnɛri/ a. & n. mercenario -ria.

merchandise /'mɜrtʃənˌdaiz/ n. mercancía f.

merchant /'mɜrtʃənt/ a. **1.** mercante. —n. **2.** comerciante m.

merciful /'mɜrsɪfəl/ a. misericordioso, compasivo.

merciless /'mɜrsɪlɪs/ a. cruel, inhumano.

mercury /'mɜrkyəri/ n. mercurio m.

mercy /'mɜrsi/ n. misericordia; merced f.

mere /mɪər/ a. mero, puro.

merely /'mɪərli/ adv. solamente; simplemente.

merge /mɜrdʒ/ v. unir, combinar.

merger /'mɜrdʒər/ n. consolidación, fusión f.

meringue /mə'ræŋ/ n. merengue m.

merit /'mɛrɪt/ n. **1.** mérito m. —v. **2.** merecer.

meritorious /ˌmɛrɪ'tɔriəs/ a. meritorio.

mermaid /'mɜrˌmeid/ n. sirena f.

merriment /'mɛrɪmənt/ n. regocijo m.

merry /'mɛri/ a. alegre, festivo.

merry-go-round /'mɛri gou ˌraund/ n. caballitos m. pl.; tíovivo m.

mesh /mɛʃ/ n. malla f.

mess /mɛs/ n. **1.** lío m.; confusión f.; Mil. salón comedor; rancho m. —v. **2. m. up,** ensuciar; enredar.

message /'mɛsɪdʒ/ n. mensaje, recado m.

messenger /'mɛsəndʒər/ n. mensajero -ra.

messy /'mɛsi/ a. confuso; desarreglado.

metabolism /mə'tæbəˌlɪzəm/ n. metabolismo m.

metal /'mɛtl/ n. metal m.

metallic /mə'tælɪk/ a. metálico.

metaphysics /ˌmɛtə'fɪzɪks/ n. metafísica f.

meteor /'mitiər/ n. meteoro m.

meteorology /ˌmitiə'rɒlədʒi/ n. meteorología f.

meter /'mitər/ n. contador, medidor; (measure) metro m.

method /'mɛθəd/ n. método m.

meticulous /mə'tɪkyələs/ a. meticuloso.

metric /'mɛtrɪk/ a. métrico.

metropolis /mɪ'trɒpəlɪs/ n. metrópoli f.

metropolitan /ˌmɛtrə'pɒlɪtn̩/ a. metropolitano.

Mexican /'mɛksɪkən/ a. & n. mexicano -na.

Mexico /'mɛksɪˌkou/ n. México m.

mezzanine /'mɛzəˌnin/ n. entresuelo m.

microbe /'maikroub/ n. microbio m.

microchip /'maikrouˌtʃɪp/ n. microchip m.

microfiche /'maikrəˌfiʃ/ n. microficha f.

microfilm /'maikrəˌfɪlm/ n. microfilm m.

microform /'maikrəˌfɔrm/ n. microforma f.

microphone /'maikrəˌfoun/ n. micrófono m.

microscope /'maikrəˌskoup/ n. microscopio m.

microscopic /ˌmaikrə'skɒpɪk/ a. microscópico.

mid /mɪd/ a. medio.

middle /'mɪdl/ a. & n. medio m. **in the m. of,** en medio de, a mediados de.

middle-aged /eidʒd/ a. de edad madura.

Middle East Medio Oriente m.

middle finger dedo corazón m.

midget /'mɪdʒɪt/ n. enano -na.

midnight /'mɪdˌnait/ n. medianoche f.

midwife /'mɪdˌwaif/ n. comadrona, partera f.

might /mait/ n. poder m., fuerza f.

mighty /'maiti/ a. poderoso.

migraine /'maigrein/ n. migraña f.; jaqueca f.

migrate /'maigreit/ v. emigrar.

migration /mai'greiʃən/ n. emigración f.

migratory /'maigrəˌtɔri/ a. migratorio.

mild /maild/ a. moderado, suave; templado.

mildew /'mɪlˌdu/ n. añublo m., moho m.

mile /mail/ n. milla f.

mileage /'maildʒ/ n. kilometraje m.

militant /'mɪlɪtənt/ a. militante.

militarism /'mɪlɪtəˌrɪzəm/ n. militarismo m.

military /'mɪlɪˌtɛri/ a. militar.

militia /mɪ'lɪʃə/ n. milicia f.

milk /mɪlk/ n. **1.** leche f. —v. **2.** ordeñar.

milk chocolate chocolate con leche m.

milkman /'mɪlkˌmæn/ n. lechero m.

milk shake batido m.

milky /'mɪlki/ a. lácteo; lechoso.

mill /mɪl/ n. **1.** molino m.; fábrica f. —v. **2.** moler.

miller /'mɪlər/ n. molinero -ra.

millimeter /'mɪləˌmitər/ n. milímetro m.

milliner /'mɪlənər/ n. sombrerero -ra.

millinery /'mɪləˌnɛri/ n. sombrerería f.

million /'mɪlyən/ n. millón m.

millionaire /ˌmɪlyə'nɛər/ n. millonario -ria.

mimic /'mɪmɪk/ n. **1.** mimo -ma. —v. **2.** imitar.

mind /maind/ n. **1.** mente; opinión f. —v. **2.** obedecer. **never m.,** no se ocupe.

mindful /'maindfəl/ a. atento.

mine /main/ pron. **1.** mío. —n. **2.** mina f. —v. **3.** minar.

miner /'mainər/ n. minero -ra.

mineral /'mɪnərəl/ a. & n. mineral m.

mineral water agua mineral f.

mine sweeper /'main ˌswipər/ dragaminas f.

mingle /'mɪŋgəl/ v. mezclar.

miniature /'mɪniətʃər/ n. miniatura f.

miniaturize /'mɪniətʃəˌraiz/ v. miniaturizar.

minibus /'mɪniˌbʌs/ n. microbús m.

minicab /'mɪniˌkæb/ n. microtaxi m.

minimize /'mɪnəˌmaiz/ v. menospreciar.

minimum /'mɪnəməm/ a. & n. mínimo m.

mining /'mainɪŋ/ n. minería f.

minister /'mɪnəstər/ n. **1.** ministro -tra; Relig. pastor m. —v. **2.** ministrar.

ministry /'mɪnəstri/ n. ministerio m.

mink /mɪŋk/ n. visón m.; (fur) piel de visón m.

minor /'mainər/ a. **1.** menor. —n. **2.** menor de edad.

minority /mɪ'nɔrɪti/ n. minoría f.

minstrel /'mɪnstrəl/ n. juglar m.

mint /mɪnt/ n. **1.** menta f.; casa de moneda. —v. **2.** acuñar.

minus /'mainəs/ prep. menos.

minute /mai'nut/ a. **1.** minucioso. —n. **2.** minuto, momento m.

miracle /'mɪrəkəl/ n. milagro m.

miraculous /mɪ'rækyələs/ a. milagroso.

mirage /mɪ'rɑʒ/ n. espejismo m.

mire /maiər/ n. lodo m.

mirror /'mɪrər/ n. espejo m.

mirth /mɜrθ/ n. alegría; risa f.

misbehave /ˌmɪsbɪ'heiv/ v. portarse mal.

miscellaneous /ˌmɪsə'leiniəs/ a. misceláneo.

mischief /'mɪstʃɪf/ n. travesura, diablura f.

mischievous /'mɪstʃəvəs/ a. travieso, dañino.

miser /'maizər/ n. avaro -ra.

miserable /'mɪzərəbəl/ a. miserable; infeliz.

miserly /'maizərli/ a. avariento, tacaño.

misfortune /mɪs'fɔrtʃən/ n. desgracia f., infortunio, revés m.

misgiving /mɪs'gɪvɪŋ/ n. recelo m., desconfianza f.

mishap /'mɪsˌhæp/ n. desgracia f., contratiempo m.

mislay /mɪs'lei/ v. perder.

mislead /mɪs'lid/ v. extraviar, despistar; pervertir.

misplaced /mɪs'pleist/ a. extraviado.

mispronounce /ˌmɪsprə'nouns/ v. pronunciar mal.

miss /mɪs/ n. **1.** señorita f. —v. **2.** perder; echar de menos, extrañar. **be missing,** faltar.

missile /'mɪsəl/ n. proyectil m.

mission /'mɪʃən/ n. misión f.

missionary /'mɪʃəˌnɛri/ n. misionero -ra.

mist /mɪst/ n. niebla, bruma f.

mistake /mɪ'steik/ n. equivocación f.; error m. **to make a m.,** equivocarse.

mistaken /mɪ'steikən/ a. equivocado.

mister /'mɪstər/ n. señor m.

mistletoe /'mɪsəlˌtou/ n. muérdago m.

mistreat /mɪs'trit/ v. maltratar.

mistress /'mɪstrɪs/ n. ama; señora; concubina f.

mistrust /mɪs'trʌst/ v. desconfiar; sospechar.

misty /'mɪsti/ a. nebuloso, brumoso.

misunderstand /ˌmɪsʌndər'stænd/ v. entender mal.

misuse /mɪs'yuz/ v. maltratar; abusar.

mite /mait/ n. pizca f., blanca f.

mitten /'mɪtn̩/ n. mitón, confortante m.

mix /mɪks/ v. mezclar. **m. up,** confundir.

mixer /'mɪksər/ (for food), n. batidora f.

mixture /'mɪkstʃər/ n. mezcla, mixtura f.

mix-up /'mɪksˌʌp/ n. confusión f.

moan /moun/ n. **1.** quejido, gemido m. —v. **2.** gemir.

mob /mɒb/ n. muchedumbre f.; gentío m.

mobilization /ˌmoubələ'zeiʃən/ n. movilización f.

mobilize /'moubəˌlaiz/ v. movilizar.

mock /mɒk/ v. burlar.

mockery /'mɒkəri/ n. burla f.

mod /mɒd/ a. a la última; en boga.

mode /moud/ n. modo m.

model /'mɒdl/ n. **1.** modelo m. —v. **2.** modelar.

modem /'moudəm/ n. módem m.

moderate /a 'mɒdərɪt; v -əˌreit/ a. **1.** moderado. —v. **2.** moderar.

moderation /ˌmɒdə'reiʃən/ n. moderación; sobriedad f.

modern /'mɒdərn/ a. moderno.

modernize /'mɒdərˌnaiz/ v. modernizar.

modest /'mɒdɪst/ a. modesto.

modesty /'mɒdəsti/ n. modestia f.

modify /'mɒdəˌfai/ v. modificar.

modulate /'mɒdʒəˌleit/ v. modular.

moist /mɔist/ a. húmedo.

moisten /'mɔisən/ v. humedecer.

moisture /'mɔistʃər/ n. humedad f.

moisturize /'mɔistʃəˌraiz/ v. hidratar.

molar /'moulər/ n. molar m.

molasses /mə'læsɪz/ n. melaza f.

mold /mould/ n. **1.** molde; moho m. —v. **2.** moldar, formar; enmohecerse.

moldy /'mouldi/ a. mohoso.

mole /'moulei/ n. lunar m.; (animal) topo m.

molecule /'mɒlɪˌkyul/ n. molécula f.

molest /mə'lɛst/ v. molestar.

mollify /'mɒləˌfai/ v. molificar.

moment /'moumənt/ n. momento m.

momentary /'moumənˌtɛri/ a. momentáneo.

momentous /mou'mɛntəs/ a. importante.

monarch /'mɒnərk/ n. monarca m. & f.

monarchy /'mɒnərki/ n. monarquía f.

monastery /'mɒnəˌstɛri/ n. monasterio m.

Monday /'mʌndei/ n. lunes m.

monetary /'mɒnɪˌtɛri/ a. monetario.

money /ˈmʌni/ *n.* dinero *m.* **m. order,** giro postal.

mongrel /ˈmʌŋgrəl/ *n.* **1.** mestizo *m.* —*a.* **2.** mestizo, cruzado.

monitor /ˈmɒnɪtər/ *n.* amonestador *m.*; (computer) consola *f.*, pantalla *f.*

monk /mʌŋk/ *n.* monje *m.*

monkey /ˈmʌŋki/ *n.* mono -na.

monocle /ˈmɒnəkəl/ *n.* monóculo *m.*

monologue /ˈmɒnəˌlɔg/ *n.* monólogo *m.*

monopolize /məˈnɒpəˌlaiz/ *v.* monopolizar.

monopoly /məˈnɒpəli/ *n.* monopolio *m.*

monosyllable /ˈmɒnəˌsɪləbəl/ *n.* monosílabo *m.*

monotone /ˈmɒnəˌtoun/ *n.* monotonía *f.*

monotonous /məˈnɒtn̩əs/ *a.* monótono.

monotony /məˈnɒtn̩i/ *n.* monotonía *f.*

monsoon /mɒnˈsun/ *n.* monzón *m.*

monster /ˈmɒnstər/ *n.* monstruo *m.*

monstrosity /mɒnˈstrɒsɪti/ *n.* monstruosidad *f.*

monstrous /ˈmɒnstrəs/ *a.* monstruoso.

month /mʌnθ/ *n.* mes *m.*

monthly /ˈmʌnθli/ *a.* mensual.

monument /ˈmɒnyəmənt/ *n.* monumento *m.*

monumental /ˌmɒnyəˈmɛntl̩/ *a.* monumental.

mood /mud/ *n.* humor *m.*; *Gram.* modo *m.*

moody /ˈmudi/ *a.* caprichoso, taciturno.

moon /mun/ *n.* luna *f.*

moonlight /ˈmunˌlait/ *n.* luz de la luna.

moonlighting /ˈmunˌlaitɪŋ/ *n.* pluriempleo *m.*

moor /mʊr/ *n.* **1.** párano *m.* —*v.* **2.** anclar.

Moor /mʊr/ *n.* moro -ra.

mop /mɒp/ *n.* **1.** fregasuelos *m.*, fregona *f.*, (*S.A.*) trapeador *m.* —*v.* **2.** fregar, (*S.A.*) trapear.

moped /ˈmouˌpɛd/ *n.* (vehicle) velomotor *m.*

moral /ˈmɔrəl/ *a.* **1.** moral. —*n.* **2.** moraleja *f.* **morals,** moralidad *f.*

morale /məˈræl/ *n.* espíritu *m.*

moralist /ˈmɔrəlɪst/ *n.* moralista *m.* & *f.*

morality /məˈrælɪti/ *n.* moralidad, ética *f.*

morbid /ˈmɔrbɪd/ *a.* mórbido.

more /mɔr/ *a.* & *adv.* más. **m. and m.,** cada vez más.

moreover /mɔrˈouvər/ *adv.* además.

morgue /mɔrg/ *n.* necrocomio *m.*

morning /ˈmɔrnɪŋ/ *n.* mañana *f.* **good m.,** buenos días.

Morocco /məˈrɒkou/ *n.* Marruecos *m.*

morose /məˈrous/ *a.* malhumorado.

morphine /ˈmɔrfin/ *n.* morfina *f.*

morsel /ˈmɔrsəl/ *n.* bocado *m.*

mortal /ˈmɔrtl̩/ *a.* & *n.* mortal *m.* & *f.*

mortality /mɔrˈtælɪti/ *n.* mortalidad *f.*

mortar /ˈmɔrtər/ *n.* mortero *m.*

mortgage /ˈmɔrgɪdʒ/ *n.* **1.** hipoteca *f.* —*v.* **2.** hipotecar.

mortify /ˈmɔrtəˌfai/ *v.* mortificar.

mosaic /mouˈzeiɪk/ *n.* & *a.* mosaico *m.*

mosque /mɒsk/ *n.* mezquita *f.*

mosquito /məˈskitou/ *n.* mosquito *m.*

moss /mɔs/ *n.* musgo *m.*

most /moust/ *a.* **1.** más. —*adv.* **2.** más; sumamente. —*pron.* **3. m. of,** la mayor parte de.

mostly /ˈmoustli/ *adv.* principalmente; en su mayor parte.

motel /mouˈtɛl/ *n.* motel *m.*

moth /mɔθ/ *n.* polilla *f.*

mother /ˈmʌðər/ *n.* madre *f.*

mother-in-law /ˈmʌðər ɪn ˌlɔ/ *n.* suegra *f.*

motif /mouˈtif/ *n.* tema *m.*

motion /ˈmouʃən/ *n.* **1.** moción *f.*; movimiento *m.* —*v.* **2.** hacer señas.

motionless /ˈmouʃənlɪs/ *a.* inmóvil.

motion picture película *f.*

motivate /ˈmoutəˌveit/ *v.* motivar.

motive /ˈmoutɪv/ *n.* motivo *m.*

motor /ˈmoutər/ *n.* motor *m.*

motorboat /ˈmoutərˌbout/ *n.* lancha motora *f.*, autobote, motorbote *m.*, gasolinera *f.*

motorcycle /ˈmoutərˌsaikəl/ *n.* motocicleta *f.*

motorcyclist /ˈmoutərˌsaiklɪst/ *n.* motociclista *m.* & *f.*

motorist /ˈmoutərɪst/ *n.* motorista *m.* & *f.*

motto /ˈmɒtou/ *n.* lema *m.*

mound /maund/ *n.* terrón; montón *m.*

mount /maunt/ *n.* **1.** monte *m.*; (horse) montura *f.* —*v.* **2.** montar; subir.

mountain /ˈmauntn̩/ *n.* montaña *f.*

mountaineer /ˌmauntn̩ˈɪər/ *n.* montañés *m.*

mountainous /ˈmauntn̩əs/ *a.* montañoso.

mourn /mɔrn/ *v.* lamentar, llorar; llevar luto.

mournful /ˈmɔrnfəl/ *a.* triste.

mourning /ˈmɔrnɪŋ/ *n.* luto; lamento *m.*

mouse /maus/ *n.* ratón, ratoncito *m.*

mouth /mauθ/ *n.* boca *f.*; (of river) desembocadura *f.*

mouthwash /ˈmauθˌwɔʃ/ *n.* enjuague bucal *m.*

movable /ˈmuvəbəl/ *a.* movible, movedizo.

move /muv/ *n.* **1.** movimiento *m.*; mudanza *f.* —*v.* **2.** mover; mudarse; emocionar, conmover. **m. away,** quitar; alejarse; mudarse.

movement /ˈmuvmənt/ *n.* movimiento *m.*

movie /ˈmuvi/ *n.* película *f.* **m. theater, movies,** cine *m.*

moving /ˈmuvɪŋ/ *a.* conmovedor; persuasivo.

mow /mou/ *v.* guadañar, segar.

Mr. /ˈmɪstər/ *title.* Señor (Sr.).

Mrs. /ˈmɪsəz/ *title.* Señora (Sra.).

much /mʌtʃ/ *a.* & *adv.* mucho. **how m.,** cuánto. **so m.,** tanto. **too m.,** demasiado. **as m. as,** tanto como.

mucilage /ˈmyusəlɪdʒ/ *n.* mucílago *m.*

mucous /ˈmyukəs/ *a.* mucoso.

mucous membrane *n.* membrana mucosa *f.*

mud /mʌd/ *n.* fango, lodo *m.*

muddy /ˈmʌdi/ *a.* **1.** lodoso; turbio. —*v.* **2.** ensuciar; enturbiar.

muff /mʌf/ *n.* manguito *m.*

muffin /ˈmʌfɪn/ *n.* panecillo *m.*

mug /mʌg/ *n.* cubilete *m.*

mugger /ˈmʌgər/ *n.* asaltante *m.* & *f.*

mulatto /məˈlætou/ *n.* mulato *m.*

mule /myul/ *n.* mula *f.*

mullah /ˈmʌlə/ *n.* mullah *m.*

multicultural /ˌmʌltiˈkʌltʃərəl, ˌmʌltai-/ *a.* multicultural.

multinational /ˌmʌltiˈnæʃənl̩, ˌmʌltai-/ *a.* multinacional.

multiple /ˈmʌltəpəl/ *a.* múltiple.

multiplication /ˌmʌltəplɪˈkeiʃən/ *n.* multiplicación *f.*

multiplicity /ˌmʌltəˈplɪsɪti/ *n.* multiplicidad *f.*

multiply /ˈmʌltəpli/ *v.* multiplicar.

multitasking /ˌmʌltiˈtæskɪŋ, ˌmʌltai-/ *n.* multitarea *f.*

multitude /ˈmʌltɪˌtud/ *n.* multitud *f.*

mummy /ˈmʌmi/ *n.* momia *f.*

mumps /mʌmps/ *n.* paperas *f.pl.*

municipal /myuˈnɪsəpəl/ *a.* municipal.

munificent /myuˈnɪfəsənt/ *a.* munífico.

munitions /myuˈnɪʃənz/ *n.* municiones *m.pl.*

mural /ˈmyʊrəl/ *a.* & *n.* mural *m.*

murder /ˈmɜrdər/ *n.* **1.** asesinato; homicidio *m.* —*v.* **2.** asesinar.

murderer /ˈmɜrdərər/ *n.* asesino -na.

murmur /ˈmɜrmər/ *n.* **1.** murmullo *m.* —*v.* **2.** murmurar.

muscle /ˈmʌsəl/ *n.* músculo *m.*

muscular /ˈmʌskyələr/ *a.* muscular.

muse /myuz/ *n.* **1.** musa *f.* —*v.* **2.** meditar.

museum /myuˈziəm/ *n.* museo *m.*

mushroom /ˈmʌʃrum/ *n.* seta *f.*, hongo *m.*

music /ˈmyuzɪk/ *n.* música *f.*

musical /ˈmyuzɪkəl/ *a.* musical; melodioso.

musician /myuˈzɪʃən/ *n.* músico -ca.

Muslim /ˈmʌzlɪm/ *a.* & *n.* musulmano.

muslin /ˈmʌzlɪn/ *n.* muselina *f.*; percal *m.*

mussel /ˈmʌsəl/ *n.* mejillón *m.*

must /mʌst/ *v.* deber; tener que.

mustache /ˈmʌstæʃ/ *n.* bigotes *m.pl.*

mustard /ˈmʌstərd/ *n.* mostaza *f.*

muster /ˈmʌstər/ *n.* **1.** *Mil.* revista *f.* —*v.* **2.** reunir, juntar.

mute /myut/ *a.* & *n.* mudo -da.

mutilate /ˈmyutl̩ˌeit/ *v.* mutilar.

mutiny /ˈmyutn̩i/ *n.* **1.** motín *m.* —*v.* **2.** amotinarse.

mutt /mʌt/ *n.* *Colloq.* chucho *m.*

mutter /ˈmʌtər/ *v.* refunfuñar, gruñir.

mutton /ˈmʌtn̩/ *n.* carnero *m.*

mutual /ˈmyutʃuəl/ *a.* mutuo.

muzzle /ˈmʌzəl/ *n.* **1.** hocico *m.*; bozal *m.* —*v.* **2.** embozar.

my /mai/ *a.* mi.

myriad /ˈmɪriəd/ *n.* miríada *f.*

myrtle /ˈmɜrtl̩/ *n.* mirto *m.*

myself /maiˈsɛlf/ *pron.* mí, mí mismo; me. **I m.,** yo mismo.

mysterious /mɪˈstɪəriəs/ *a.* misterioso.

mystery /ˈmɪstəri/ *n.* misterio *m.*

mystic /ˈmɪstɪk/ *a.* místico.

mystify /ˈmɪstəˌfai/ *v.* confundir.

myth /mɪθ/ *n.* mito *m.*

mythical /ˈmɪθɪkəl/ *a.* mítico.

mythology /mɪˈθɒlədʒi/ *n.* mitología *f.*

N

nag /næg/ *n.* **1.** jaca *f.* —*v.* **2.** regañar; sermonear.

nail /neil/ *n.* **1.** clavo *m.*; (finger) uña *f.* **n. polish,** esmalte para las uñas. —*v.* **2.** clavar.

naïve /nɑˈiv/ *a.* ingenuo.

naked /ˈneikɪd/ *a.* desnudo.

name /neim/ *n.* **1.** nombre *m.*; reputación *f.* —*v.* **2.** nombrar, mencionar.

namely /ˈneimli/ *adv.* a saber; es decir.

namesake /ˈneimˌseik/ *n.* tocayo *m.*

nanny /ˈnæni/ *n.* niñera *f.*

nap /næp/ *n.* siesta *f.* **to take a n.,** echar una siesta.

naphtha /ˈnæfθə, ˈnæp-/ *n.* nafta *f.*

napkin /ˈnæpkɪn/ *n.* servilleta *f.*

narcissus /nɑrˈsɪsəs/ *n.* narciso *m.*

narcotic /nɑrˈkɒtɪk/ *a.* & *n.* narcótico *m.*

narrate /ˈnæreit/ *v.* narrar.

narrative /ˈnærətɪv/ *a.* **1.** narrativo. —*n.* **2.** cuento, relato *m.*

narrow /ˈnærou/ *a.* estrecho, angosto. **n.-minded,** intolerante.

nasal /ˈneizəl/ *a.* nasal.

nasty /ˈnæsti/ *a.* desagradable.

nation /ˈneiʃən/ *n.* nación *f.*

national /ˈnæʃənl̩/ *a.* nacional.

nationalism /ˈnæʃənl̩ˌɪzəm/ *n.* nacionalismo *m.*

nationality /ˌnæʃəˈnælɪti/ *n.* nacionalidad *f.*

nationalization /ˌnæʃənləˈzeiʃən/ *n.* nacionalización *f.*

nationalize /ˈnæʃənl̩ˌaiz, ˈnæʃnəˌlaiz/ *v.* nacionalizar.

native /ˈneitɪv/ *a.* **1.** nativo. —*n.* **2.** natural; indígena *m.* & *f.*

nativity /nəˈtɪvɪti/ *n.* natividad *f.*

natural /ˈnætʃərəl/ *a.* natural.

naturalist /ˈnætʃərəlɪst/ *n.* naturalista *m.* & *f.*

naturalize /ˈnætʃərəˌlaiz/ *v.* naturalizar.

naturalness /ˌnætʃərəlnɪs/ *n.* naturalidad *f.*

nature /ˈneitʃər/ *n.* naturaleza *f.*; índole *f.*; humor *m.*

naughty /ˈnɔti/ *a.* travieso, desobediente.

nausea /ˈnɔziə, -ʒə/ *n.* náusea *f.*

nauseous /ˈnɔʃəs/ *a.* nauseoso.

nautical /ˈnɔtɪkəl/ *a.* náutico.

naval /ˈneivəl/ *a.* naval.

nave /neiv/ *n.* nave *f.*

navel /ˈneivəl/ *n.* ombligo *m.*

navigable /ˈnævɪgəbəl/ *a.* navegable.

navigate /ˈnævɪˌgeit/ *v.* navegar.

navigation /ˌnævɪˈgeiʃən/ *n.* navegación *f.*

navigator /ˈnævɪˌgeitər/ *n.* navegante *m.* & *f.*

navy /ˈneivi/ *n.* marina *f.*

navy blue azul marino *m.*

near /nɪər/ *a.* **1.** cercano, próximo. —*adv.* **2.** cerca. —*prep.* **3.** cerca de.

nearby /ˈnɪərˈbai/ *a.* **1.** cercano. —*adv.* **2.** cerca.

nearly /ˈnɪərli/ *adv.* casi.

nearsighted /ˈnɪərˌsaitɪd/ *a.* corto de vista.

neat /nit/ *a.* aseado; ordenado.

neatness /ˈnitnɪs/ *n.* aseo *m.*

nebulous /ˈnɛbyələs/ *a.* nebuloso.

necessary /ˈnɛsəˌsɛri/ *a.* necesario.

necessity /nəˈsɛsɪti/ *n.* necesidad *f.*

neck /nɛk/ *n.* cuello *m.*

necklace /ˈnɛklɪs/ *n.* collar *m.*

necktie /ˈnɛkˌtai/ *n.* corbata *f.*

nectar /ˈnɛktər/ *n.* néctar *m.*

nectarine /ˌnɛktəˈrin/ *n.* nectarina *f.*

need /nid/ *n.* **1.** necesidad; (poverty) pobreza *f.* —*v.* **2.** necesitar.

needle /ˈnidl̩/ *n.* aguja *f.*

needless /ˈnidlɪs/ *a.* innecesario, inútil.

needy /ˈnidi/ *a.* indigente, necesitado, pobre.

nefarious /nɪˈfɛəriəs/ *a.* nefario.

negative /ˈnɛgətɪv/ *a.* negativo. *n.* negativa *f.*

neglect /nɪˈglɛkt/ *n.* **1.** negligencia *f.*; descuido *m.* —*v.* **2.** descuidar.

negligee /ˌnɛglɪˈʒei/ *n.* negligé *m.*, bata de casa *f.*

negligent /ˈnɛglɪdʒənt/ *a.* negligente, descuidado.

negligible /ˈnɛglɪdʒəbəl/ *a.* insignificante.

negotiate /nɪˈgouʃiˌeit/ *v.* negociar.

negotiation /nɪˌgouʃiˈeiʃən/ *n.* negociación *f.*

Negro /ˈnigrou/ *n.* negro -ra.

neighbor /ˈneibər/ *n.* vecino -na.

neighborhood /ˈneibərˌhʊd/ *n.* vecindad *f.*

neither /ˈniðər, ˈnai-/ *a.* & *pron.* **1.** ninguno de los dos. —*adv.* **2.** tampoco. —*conj.* **3. neither... nor,** ni... ni.

neon /ˈniɒn/ *n.* neón *m.* **n. light,** tubo neón *m.*

nephew /ˈnɛfyu/ *n.* sobrino *m.*

nerve /nɜrv/ *n.* nervio *m.*; *Colloq.* audacia *f.*

nervous /ˈnɜrvəs/ *a.* nervioso.

nervous breakdown /ˈbreikˌdaun/ crisis nerviosa *f.*

nest /nɛst/ *n.* nido *m.*

net /nɛt/ *a.* **1.** neto. —*n.* **2.** red *f.* **hair n.,** albanega, redecilla *f.* *v.* redar; *Com.* ganar.

netiquette /ˈnɛtɪkɪt/ *n.* etiqueta de la red *f.*

netting /ˈnɛtɪŋ/ *n.* red *m.*; obra de malla *f.*

network /ˈnɛtˌwɜrk/ *n.* (radio) red radiodifusora.

neuralgia /nʊˈrældʒə/ *n.* neuralgia *f.*

neurology /nʊˈrɒlədʒi/ *n.* neurología *f.*

neurotic /nʊˈrɒtɪk/ *a.* neurótico.

neutral /ˈnutrəl/ *a.* neutral.
neutrality /nuˈtrælɪti/ *n.* neutralidad *f.*
neutron /ˈnutrɒn/ *n.* neutrón *m.*
neutron bomb bomba de neutrones *f.*
never /ˈnɛvər/ *adv.* nunca, jamás; **n. mind,** no importa.
nevertheless /ˌnɛvərðəˈlɛs/ *adv.* no obstante, sin embargo.
new /nu/ *a.* nuevo.
newbie /ˈnubi/ *n. Colloq.* novato -ta, inexperto -ta.
news /nuz/ *n.* noticias *f.pl.*
newsboy /ˈnuzˌbɔi/ *n.* vendedor -ra de periódicos.
news bulletin boletín informativo *m.*
news flash *n.* noticia de última hora *f.*
newsgroup /ˈnuzˌgrup/ *n.* grupo de discusion *m.*
newsletter /ˈnuzˌlɛtər/ *n.* hoja informativa *f.*
newspaper /ˈnuzˌpeipər/ *n.* periódico *m.*
New Testament Nuevo Testamento *m.*
new year *n.* año nuevo *m.*
next /nɛkst/ *a.* **1.** próximo; siguiente; contiguo. —*adv.* **2.** luego, después. **n. door,** al lado. **n. to,** al lado de.
next-to-the-last /ˈnɛkst tə ðə ˈlæst/ *a.* penúltimo.
nibble /ˈnɪbəl/ *v.* picar.
nice /nis/ *a.* simpático, agradable; amable; hermoso; exacto.
nick /nɪk/ *n.* muesca *f.*, picadura *f.* **in the n. of time,** a punto.
nickel /ˈnɪkəl/ *n.* níquel *m.*
nickname /ˈnɪkˌneim/ *n.* **1.** apodo, mote *m.* —*v.* **2.** apodar.
nicotine /ˈnɪkəˌtin/ *n.* nicotina *f.*
niece /nis/ *n.* sobrina *f.*
niggardly /ˈnɪgərdli/ *a.* mezquino.
night /nait/ *n.* noche *f.* **good n.,** buenas noches. **last n.,** anoche. **n. club,** cabaret *m.*
nightclub /ˈnaitˌklʌb/ *n.* cabaret *m.*
nightclub owner cabaretero -ra *m. & f.*
nightgown /ˈnaitˌgaun/ *n.* camisa de dormir.
nightingale /ˈnaitṇˌgeil, ˈnaitɪŋ-/ *n.* ruiseñor *m.*
nightly /ˈnaitli/ *adv.* todas las noches.
nightmare /ˈnaitˌmɛər/ *n.* pesadilla *f.*
night school escuela nocturna *f.*
night watchman vigilante nocturno *m.*
nimble /ˈnɪmbəl/ *a.* ágil.
nine /nain/ *a. & pron.* nueve.
nineteen /ˈnainˈtin/ *a. & pron.* diecinueve.
ninety /ˈnainti/ *a. & pron.* noventa.
ninth /nainθ/ *a.* noveno.
nipple /ˈnɪpəl/ *n.* teta *f.*; pezón *m.*
nitrogen /ˈnaitrədʒən/ *n.* nitrógeno *m.*
no /nou/ *a.* **1.** ninguno. **no one,** nadie. —*adv.* **2.** no.
nobility /nouˈbɪlɪti/ *n.* nobleza *f.*
noble /ˈnoubəl/ *a. & n.* noble *m.*
nobleman /ˈnoubəlmən/ *n.* noble *m.*
nobody /ˈnouˌbɒdi/ *pron.* nadie.
nocturnal /nɒkˈtɜrnḷ/ *a.* nocturno.
nocturne /ˈnɒktɜrn/ *n.* nocturno *m.*
nod /nɒd/ *n.* **1.** seña con la cabeza. —*v.* **2.** inclinar la cabeza; (doze) dormitar.
no-frills /ˈnou ˈfrɪlz/ *a.* sin extras.
noise /nɔiz/ *n.* ruido *m.*
noiseless /ˈnɔizlɪs/ *a.* silencioso.
noisy /ˈnɔizi/ *a.* ruidoso.
nominal /ˈnɒmənḷ/ *a.* nominal.
nominate /ˈnɒməˌneit/ *v.* nombrar.
nomination /ˌnɒməˈneiʃən/ *n.* nombramiento *m.*, nominación *f.*
nominee /ˌnɒməˈni/ *n.* candidato -ta.
nonaligned /ˌnɒnəˈlaind/ (in political sense), *a.* no alineado.
nonchalant /ˌnɒnʃəˈlɑnt/ *a.* indiferente.
noncombatant /ˌnɒnkəmˈbætnt/ *n.* no combatiente *m.*
noncommittal /ˌnɒnkəˈmɪtḷ/ *a.* evasivo; reservado.
nondescript /ˌnɒndɪˈskrɪpt/ *a.* difícil de describir.
none /nʌn/ *pron.* ninguno.
nonentity /nɒnˈɛntɪti/ *n.* nulidad *f.*
nonpartisan /nɒnˈpɑrtəzən/ *a.* sin afiliación.
non-proliferation /ˌnɒnprəˌlɪfəˈreiʃən/ *n.* no proliferación *m.*
nonsense /ˈnɒnsɛns/ *n.* tontería *f.*
nonsmoker /nɒnˈsmoukər/ *n.* no fumador -dora.
noodle /ˈnudl/ *n.* fideo *m.*
noon /nun/ *n.* mediodía *m.*
noose /nus/ *n.* lazo corredizo *m.*; dogal *m.*
nor /nɔr; *unstressed* nər/ *conj.* ni.
normal /ˈnɔrməl/ *a.* normal.
north /nɔrθ/ *n.* norte *m.*
North America /əˈmɛrɪkə/ Norte América *f.*
North American *a. & n.* norteamericano -na.
northeast /ˌnɔrθˈist; *Naut.* ˌnɔr-/ *n.* nordeste *m.*
northern /ˈnɔrðərn/ *a.* septentrional.
North Pole *n.* Polo Norte *m.*
northwest /ˌnɔrθˈwɛst; *Naut.* ˌnɔr-/ *n.* noroeste *m.*
Norway /ˈnɔrwei/ *n.* Noruega *f.*
Norwegian /nɔrˈwidʒən/ *a. & n.* noruego -ga.
nose /nouz/ *n.* nariz *f.*
nosebleed /ˈnouzˌblid/ *n.* hemorragia nasal *f.*
nostalgia /nɒˈstældʒə/ *n.* nostalgia *f.*
nostril /ˈnɒstrəl/ *n.* ventana de la nariz; (pl.) narices *f.pl.*
not /nɒt/ *adv.* no. **n. at all,** de ninguna manera. **n. even,** ni siquiera.
notable /ˈnoutəbəl/ *a.* notable.
notary /ˈnoutəri/ *n.* notario *m.*
notation /nouˈteiʃən/ *n.* notación *f.*
notch /nɒtʃ/ *n.* muesca *f.*; corte *m.*
note /nout/ *n.* **1.** nota *f.*; apunte *m.* —*v.* **2.** notar.
notebook /ˈnoutˌbʊk/ *n.* libreta *f.*, cuaderno *m.*
noted /ˈnoutɪd/ *a.* célebre.
notepaper /ˈnoutˌpeipər/ *n.* papel de notas *m.*
noteworthy /ˈnoutˌwɜrði/ *a.* notable.
nothing /ˈnʌθɪŋ/ *pron.* nada.
notice /ˈnoutɪs/ *n.* **1.** aviso *m.*; noticia *f.* —*v.* **2.** observar, fijarse en.
noticeable /ˈnoutɪsəbəl/ *a.* notable.
notification /ˌnoutəfɪˈkeiʃən/ *n.* notificación *f.*
notify /ˈnoutəˌfai/ *v.* notificar.
notion /ˈnouʃən/ *n.* noción; idea *f.*; (pl.) novedades *f.pl.*
notoriety /ˌnoutəˈraiɪti/ *n.* notoriedad *f.*
notorious /nouˈtɔriəs/ *a.* notorio.
noun /naun/ *n.* nombre, sustantivo *m.*
nourish /ˈnɜrɪʃ/ *v.* nutrir, alimentar.
nourishment /ˈnɜrɪʃmənt/ *n.* nutrimento; alimento *m.*
novel /ˈnɒvəl/ *a.* **1.** nuevo, original. —*n.* **2.** novela *f.*
novelist /ˈnɒvəlɪst/ *n.* novelista *m. & f.*
novelty /ˈnɒvəlti/ *n.* novedad *f.*
November /nouˈvɛmbər/ *n.* noviembre *m.*
novena /nouˈvinə/ *n.* novena *f.*
novice /ˈnɒvɪs/ *n.* novicio -cia, novato -ta.
novocaine /ˈnouvəˌkein/ *n.* novocaína *f.*
now /nau/ *adv.* ahora. **n. and then,** de vez en cuando. **by n.,** ya. **from n. on,** de ahora en adelante. **just n.,** ahorita. **right n.,** ahora mismo.
nowadays /ˈnauəˌdeiz/ *adv.* hoy día, hoy en día, actualmente.
nowhere /ˈnouˌwɛər/ *adv.* en ninguna parte.
nozzle /ˈnɒzəl/ *n.* boquilla *f.*
nuance /ˈnuɑns/ *n.* matiz *m.*
nuclear /ˈnukliər/ *a.* nuclear.
nuclear energy energía nuclear *f.*
nuclear warhead /ˈwɔrˌhɛd/ cabeza nuclear *f.*
nuclear waste desechos nucleares *m.pl.*
nucleus /ˈnukliəs/ *n.* núcleo *m.*
nude /nud/ *a.* desnudo.
nuisance /ˈnusəns/ *n.* molestia *f.*
nuke /nuk/ *n.* bomba atómica *f.*
nullify /ˈnʌləˌfai/ *v.* anular.
number /ˈnʌmbər/ *n.* **1.** número *m.*; cifra *f.* **license n.,** matrícula *f.* —*v.* **2.** numerar, contar.
numeric /nuˈmɛrɪk/ **numerical** *a.* numérico.
numeric keypad /nuˈmɛrɪk/ teclado numérico *m.*
numerous /ˈnumərəs/ *a.* numeroso.
nun /nʌn/ *n.* monja *f.*
nuptial /ˈnʌpʃəl/ *a.* nupcial.
nurse /nɜrs/ *n.* **1.** enfermera *f.*; (child's) ama, niñera *f.* —*v.* **2.** criar, alimentar, amamantar; cuidar.
nursery /ˈnɜrsəri/ *n.* cuarto destinado a los niños; *Agr.* plantel, criadero *m.*
nursery school jardín de infancia *m.*
nurture /ˈnɜrtʃər/ *v.* nutrir.
nut /nʌt/ *n.* nuez *f.*; *Mech.* tuerca *f.*
nutcracker /ˈnʌtˌkrækər/ *n.* cascanueces *m.*
nutrition /nuˈtrɪʃən/ *n.* nutrición *f.*
nutritious /nuˈtrɪʃəs/ *a.* nutritivo.
nylon /ˈnailɒn/ *n.* nilón *m.*
nymph /nɪmf/ *n.* ninfa *f.*

O

oak /ouk/ *n.* roble *m.*
oar /ɔr/ *n.* remo *m.*
OAS *abbr.* (Organization of American States) OEA (Organización de los Estados Americanos) *f.*
oasis /ouˈeisɪs/ *n.* oasis *m.*
oat /out/ *n.* avena *f.*
oath /ouθ/ *n.* juramento *m.*
oatmeal /ˈoutˌmil/ *n.* harina de avena *f.*
obedience /ouˈbidiəns/ *n.* obediencia *f.*
obedient /ouˈbidiənt/ *a.* obediente.
obese /ouˈbis/ *a.* obeso, gordo.
obey /ouˈbei/ *v.* obedecer.
obituary /ouˈbɪtʃuˌɛri/ *n.* obituario *m.*
object /*n* ˈɒbdʒɪkt; *v* əbˈdʒɛkt/ *n.* **1.** objeto *m.*; *Gram.* complemento *m.* —*v.* **2.** oponerse; objetar.
objection /əbˈdʒɛkʃən/ *n.* objeción *f.*
objectionable /əbˈdʒɛkʃənəbəl/ *a.* censurable.
objective /əbˈdʒɛktɪv/ *a. & n.* objetivo *m.*
obligation /ˌɒblɪˈgeiʃən/ *n.* obligación *f.*
obligatory /əˈblɪgəˌtɔri/ *a.* obligatorio.
oblige /əˈblaidʒ/ *v.* obligar; complacer.
oblique /əˈblik/ *a.* oblicuo.
obliterate /əˈblɪtəˌreit/ *v.* borrar; destruir.
oblivion /əˈblɪviən/ *n.* olvido *m.*
oblong /ˈɒbˌlɔŋ/ *a.* oblongo.
obnoxious /əbˈnɒkʃəs/ *a.* ofensivo, odioso.
obscene /əbˈsin/ *a.* obsceno, indecente.
obscure /əbˈskyʊr/ *a.* **1.** obscuro. —*v.* **2.** obscurecer.
observance /əbˈzɜrvəns/ *n.* observancia; ceremonia *f.*
observation /ˌɒbzɜrˈveiʃən/ *n.* observación *f.*
observatory /əbˈzɜrvəˌtɔri/ *n.* observatorio *m.*
observe /əbˈzɜrv/ *v.* observar; celebrar.
observer /əbˈzɜrvər/ *n.* observador -ra.
obsession /əbˈsɛʃən/ *n.* obsesión *f.*
obsolete /ˌɒbsəˈlit/ *a.* anticuado.
obstacle /ˈɒbstəkəl/ *n.* obstáculo *m.*
obstetrician /ˌɒbstɪˈtrɪʃən/ *n.* obstétrico -ca, tocólogo -ga *m. & f.*
obstinate /ˈɒbstənɪt/ *a.* obstinado, terco.
obstruct /əbˈstrʌkt/ *v.* obstruir, impedir.
obstruction /əbˈstrʌkʃən/ *n.* obstrucción *f.*
obtain /əbˈtein/ *v.* obtener, conseguir.
obtuse /əbˈtus/ *a.* obtuso.
obviate /ˈɒbviˌeit/ *v.* obviar.
obvious /ˈɒbviəs/ *a.* evidente, obvio.
occasion /əˈkeiʒən/ *n.* **1.** ocasión *f.* —*v.* **2.** ocasionar.
occasional /əˈkeiʒənḷ/ *a.* ocasional.
occult /əˈkʌlt/ *a.* oculto.
occupant /ˈɒkyəpənt/ *n.* ocupante *m. & f.*; inquilino -na.
occupation /ˌɒkyəˈpeiʃən/ *n.* ocupación *f.*; empleo *m.*
occupy /ˈɒkyəˌpai/ *v.* ocupar; emplear.
occur /əˈkɜr/ *v.* ocurrir.
occurrence /əˈkɜrəns/ *n.* ocurrencia *f.*
ocean /ˈouʃən/ *n.* océano *m.*
o'clock /əˈklɒk/ **it's one o.,** es la una. **it's two o.,** son las dos, etc. **at... o.,** a las...
octagon /ˈɒktəˌgɒn/ *n.* octágono *m.*
octave /ˈɒktɪv/ *n.* octava *f.*
October /ɒkˈtoubər/ *n.* octubre *m.*
octopus /ˈɒktəpəs/ *n.* pulpo *m.*
oculist /ˈɒkyəlɪst/ *n.* oculista *m. & f.*
odd /ɒd/ *a.* impar; suelto; raro.
odd number número impar *m.*
odious /ˈoudiəs/ *a.* odioso.
odor /ˈoudər/ *n.* olor *m.*; fragancia *f.*
of /əv/ *prep.* de.
off /ɔf/ *adv.* (see under verb: **stop off, take off,** etc.)
offend /əˈfɛnd/ *v.* ofender.
offender /əˈfɛndər/ *n.* ofensor -ra; delincuente *m. & f.*
offense /əˈfɛns/ *n.* ofensa *f.*; crimen *m.*
offensive /əˈfɛnsɪv/ *a.* **1.** ofensivo. —*n.* **2.** ofensiva *f.*
offer /ˈɔfər/ *n.* **1.** oferta *f.* —*v.* **2.** ofrecer.
offering /ˈɔfərɪŋ/ *n.* oferta *f.*
office /ˈɔfɪs/ *n.* oficina *f.*; despacho *m.*; oficio, cargo *m.*
officer /ˈɔfəsər/ *n.* oficial *m. & f.* **police o.,** agente de policía *m. & f.*
official /əˈfɪʃəl/ *a.* **1.** oficial. —*n.* **2.** oficial *m. & f.*, funcionario -ria.
officiate /əˈfɪʃiˌeit/ *v.* oficiar.
officious /əˈfɪʃəs/ *a.* oficioso.
offspring /ˈɔfˌsprɪŋ/ *n.* hijos *m.pl.*; progenie *f.*
often /ˈɔfən/ *adv.* muchas veces, a menudo. **how o.,** con qué frecuencia.
oil /ɔil/ *n.* **1.** aceite; óleo; petróleo *m.* —*v.* **2.** aceitar; engrasar.
oil refinery /rɪˈfainəri/ destilería de petróleo *f.*
oil tanker /ˈtæŋkər/ petrolero *m.*
oily /ˈɔili/ *a.* aceitoso.
ointment /ˈɔintmənt/ *n.* ungüento *m.*
okay /ˈouˈkei, ˌouˈkei/ *adv.* bien; de acuerdo.
old /ould/ *a.* viejo; antiguo. **o. man, o. woman,** viejo -ja.
old-fashioned /ˈould ˈfæʃənd/ *a.* fuera de moda, anticuado.
Old Testament Antiguo Testamento *m.*
olive /ˈɒlɪv/ *n.* aceituna, oliva *f.*
ombudsman /ˈɒmbədzmən/ *n.* ombudsman *m.*
omelet /ˈɒmlɪt/ *n.* tortilla de huevos.
omen /ˈoumən/ *n.* agüero *m.*
ominous /ˈɒmənəs/ *a.* ominoso, siniestro.
omission /ouˈmɪʃən/ *n.* omisión *f.*; olvido *m.*
omit /ouˈmɪt/ *v.* omitir.
omnibus /ˈɒmnəˌbʌs/ *n.* ómnibus *m.*
omnipotent /ɒmˈnɪpətənt/ *a.* omnipotente.
on /ɒn/ *prep.* **1.** en, sobre, encima de. —*adv.* **2.** adelante.

once /wʌns/ *adv.* una vez. **at o.,** en seguida. **o. in a while,** de vez en cuando.
one /wʌn/ *a. & pron.* uno -na.
one-armed bandit /ˈwʌn ˌɑrmd/ tragaperras *f.*
oneself /wʌnˈsɛlf/ *pron.* sí mismo -ma; se. **with o.,** consigo.
onion /ˈʌnyən/ *n.* cebolla *f.*
on-line /ˈɒn ˈlain/ *a.* conectado.
only /ˈounli/ *a.* **1.** único, solo. *—adv.* **2.** sólo, solamente.
onward /ˈɒnwərd/ *adv.* adelante.
opal /ˈoupəl/ *n.* ópalo *m.*
opaque /ouˈpeik/ *a.* opaco.
open /ˈoupən/ *a.* **1.** abierto; franco. **o. air,** aire libre. *—v.* **2.** abrir.
opening /ˈoupənɪŋ/ *n.* abertura *f.*
opera /ˈɒpərə/ *n.* ópera *f.* **o. glasses,** anteojos de ópera; gemelos *m.pl.*
operate /ˈɒpəˌreit/ *v.* operar.
operation /ˌɒpəˈreiʃən/ *n.* operación *f.* **to have an o.,** operarse, ser operado.
operative /ˈɒpərətɪv/ *a.* eficaz, operativo.
operator /ˈɒpəˌreitər/ *n.* operario -ria. **elevator o.,** ascensorista *m. & f.* **telephone o.,** telefonista *m. & f.*
operetta /ˌɒpəˈrɛtə/ *n.* opereta *f.*
ophthalmic /ɒfˈθælmɪk, ɒp-/ *a.* oftálmico.
opinion /əˈpɪnyən/ *n.* opinión *f.*
opponent /əˈpounənt/ *n.* antagonista *m. & f.*
opportunism /ˌɒpərˈtunɪzəm/ *n.* oportunismo *m.*
opportunity /ˌɒpərˈtunɪti/ *n.* ocasión, oportunidad *f.*
oppose /əˈpouz/ *v.* oponer.
opposite /ˈɒpəzɪt/ *a.* **1.** opuesto, contrario. *—prep.* **2.** al frente de. *—n.* **3.** contrario *m.*
opposition /ˌɒpəˈzɪʃən/ *n.* oposición *f.*
oppress /əˈprɛs/ *v.* oprimir.
oppression /əˈprɛʃən/ *n.* opresión *f.*
oppressive /əˈprɛsɪv/ *a.* opresivo.
optic /ˈɒptɪk/ *a.* óptico.
optical disc /ˈɒptɪkəl ˈdɪsk/ disco óptico *m.*
optical illusion /ˈɒptɪkəl/ ilusión de óptica *f.*
optician /ɒpˈtɪʃən/ *n.* óptico -ca.
optics /ˈɒptɪks/ *n.* óptica *f.*
optimism /ˈɒptəˌmɪzəm/ *n.* optimismo.
optimistic /ˌɒptəˈmɪstɪk/ *a.* optimista.
option /ˈɒpʃən/ *n.* opción, elección *f.*
optional /ˈɒpʃənl̩/ *a.* discrecional, facultativo.
optometry /ɒpˈtɒmɪtri/ *n.* optometría *f.*
opulent /ˈɒpyələnt/ *a.* opulento.
or /ɔr/ *conj.* o, (before *o-, ho-*) u.
oracle /ˈɔrəkəl/ *n.* oráculo *m.*
oral /ˈɔrəl/ *a.* oral, vocal.
orange /ˈɔrɪndʒ/ *n.* naranja *f.*
orange juice jugo de naranja, zumo de naranja *m.*
orange squeezer /ˈskwizər/ *n.* exprimidora de naranjas *f.*
oration /ɔˈreiʃən/ *n.* discurso *m.;* oración *f.*
orator /ˈɔrətər/ *n.* orador -ra.
oratory /ˈɔrəˌtɔri/ *n.* oratoria *f.;* (church) oratorio *m.*
orbit /ˈɔrbɪt/ *n.* órbita *f.*
orchard /ˈɔrtʃərd/ *n.* huerto *m.*
orchestra /ˈɔrkəstrə/ *n.* orquesta *f.* **o. seat,** butaca *f.*
orchid /ˈɔrkɪd/ *n.* orquídea *f.*
ordain /ɔrˈdein/ *v.* ordenar.
ordeal /ɔrˈdil/ *n.* prueba *f.*
order /ˈɔrdər/ *n.* orden, *m. or f.;* clase *f.; Com.* pedido *m.* **in o. that,** para que. *v.* ordenar; mandar; pedir.
order blank hoja de pedidos *f.*
orderly /ˈɔrdərli/ *a.* ordenado.
ordinance /ˈɔrdn̩əns/ *n.* ordenanza *f.*
ordinary /ˈɔrdn̩ˌɛri/ *a.* ordinario.
ordination /ˌɔrdn̩ˈeiʃən/ *n.* ordenación *f.*
ore /ɔr/ *n.* mineral *m.*
organ /ˈɔrgən/ *n.* órgano *m.*
organdy /ˈɔrgəndi/ *n.* organdí *m.*
organic /ɔrˈgænɪk/ *a.* orgánico.
organism /ˈɔrgəˌnɪzəm/ *n.* organismo *m.*
organist /ˈɔrgənɪst/ *n.* organista *m. & f.*
organization /ˌɔrgənəˈzeiʃən/ *n.* organización *f.*
organize /ˈɔrgəˌnaiz/ *v.* organizar.
orgy /ˈɔrdʒi/ *n.* orgía *f.*
orient /ˈɔriənt/ *n.* **1.** oriente *m.* *—v.* **2.** orientar.
Orient /ˈɔriənt/ *n.* Oriente *m.*
Oriental /ˌɔriˈɛntl̩/ *a.* oriental.
orientation /ˌɔriənˈteiʃən/ *n.* orientación *f.*
origin /ˈɔrɪdʒɪn/ *n.* origen *m.*
original /əˈrɪdʒənl̩/ *a. & n.* original *m.*
originality /əˌrɪdʒəˈnælɪti/ *n.* originalidad *f.*
ornament /*n* ˈɔrnəmənt; *v* -ˌmɛnt/ *n.* **1.** ornamento *m.* *—v.* **2.** ornamentar.
ornamental /ˌɔrnəˈmɛntl̩/ *a.* ornamental, decorativo.
ornate /ɔrˈneit/ *a.* ornado.
ornithology /ˌɔrnəˈθɒlədʒi/ *n.* ornitología *f.*
orphan /ˈɔrfən/ *a. & n.* huérfano -na.
orphanage /ˈɔrfənɪdʒ/ *n.* orfanato *m.*
orthodox /ˈɔrθəˌdɒks/ *a.* ortodoxo.
ostentation /ˌɒstɛnˈteiʃən/ *n.* ostentación *f.*
ostentatious /ˌɒstɛnˈteiʃəs/ *a.* ostentoso.
ostrich /ˈɔstrɪtʃ/ *n.* avestruz *f.*
other /ˈʌðər/ *a. & pron.* otro. **every o. day,** un día sí otro no.
otherwise /ˈʌðərˌwaiz/ *adv.* de otra manera.
ought /ɔt/ *v.* deber.
ounce /auns/ *n.* onza *f.*
our /auᵊr; *unstressed* ɑr/ **ours** *a. & pron.* nuestro.
ourselves /ɑrˈsɛlvz/ *pron.* nosotros -as; mismos -as; nos.
oust /aust/ *v.* desalojar.
ouster /ˈaustər/ *n.* desahucio *m.*
out /aut/ *adv.* **1.** fuera, afuera. **out of,** fuera de. *—prep.* **2.** por.
outbreak /ˈautˌbreik/ *n.* erupción *f.*
outcast /ˈautˌkæst/ *n.* paria *m. & f.*
outcome /ˈautˌkʌm/ *n.* resultado *m.*
outdoors /ˌautˈdɔrz/ *adv.* fuera de casa; al aire libre.
outer /ˈautər/ *a.* exterior, externo.
outfit /ˈautˌfɪt/ *n.* **1.** equipo; traje *m.* *—v.* **2.** equipar.
outgrowth /ˈautˌgrouθ/ *n.* resultado *m.*
outing /ˈautɪŋ/ *n.* paseo *m.*
outlaw /ˈautˌlɔ/ *n.* **1.** bandido *m.* *—v.* **2.** proscribir.
outlet /ˈautlɛt/ *n.* salida *f.*
outline /ˈautˌlain/ *n.* **1.** contorno; esbozo *m.;* silueta *f.* *—v.* **2.** esbozar.
outlive /ˌautˈlɪv/ *v.* sobrevivir.
out-of-court settlement /ˈautəvˌkɔrt/ arreglo pacífico *m.*
out-of-date /ˈaut əv ˈdeit/ *a.* anticuado.
out of focus *a.* desenfocado.
outpost /ˈautˌpoust/ *n.* puesto avanzado.
output /ˈautˌput/ *n.* capacidad *f.;* producción *f.*
outrage /ˈautreidʒ/ *n.* **1.** ultraje *m.;* atrocidad *f.* *—v.* **2.** ultrajar.
outrageous /autˈreidʒəs/ *a.* atroz.
outrun /ˌautˈrʌn/ *v.* exceder.
outside /*a, prep, adv* ˌautˈsaid; *n* ˈautˈsaid/ *a. & n.* **1.** exterior *m.* *—adv.* **2.** afuera, por fuera. *—prep.* **3.** fuera de.
outskirt /ˈautˌskɜrt/ *n.* borde *m.*
outward /ˈautwərd/ *adv.* hacia afuera.
outwardly /ˈautwərdli/ *adv.* exteriormente.
oval /ˈouvəl/ *a.* **1.** oval, ovalado. *—n.* **2.** óvalo *m.*
ovary /ˈouvəri/ *n.* ovario *m.*
ovation /ouˈveiʃən/ *n.* ovación *f.*
oven /ˈʌvən/ *n.* horno *m.*
over /ˈouvər/ *prep.* **1.** sobre, encima de; por. *—adv.* **2. o. here,** aquí. **o. there,** allí, por allí. **to be o.,** estar terminado.
overcoat /ˈouvərˌkout/ *n.* abrigo, sobretodo *m.*
overcome /ˌouvərˈkʌm/ *v.* superar, vencer.
overdose /ˈouvərˌdous/ *n.* sobredosis *f.*
overdue /ˌouvərˈdu/ *a.* retrasado.
overflow /*n* ˈouvərˌflou; *v* ˌouvərˈflou/ *n.* **1.** inundación *f.* *—v.* **2.** inundar.
overhaul /ˌouvərˈhɔl/ *v.* repasar.
overhead /ˈouvərˈhɛd/ *adv.* arriba, en lo alto.
overkill /ˈouvərˌkɪl/ *n.* efecto mayor que el pretendido.
overlook /ˌouvərˈlʊk/ *v.* pasar por alto.
overnight /ˈouvərˈnait/ *adv.* **to stay or stop o.,** pasar la noche.
overpower /ˌouvərˈpauər/ *v.* vencer.
overrule /ˌouvərˈrul/ *v.* predominar.
overrun /ˌouvərˈrʌn/ *v.* invadir.
oversee /ˌouvərˈsi/ *v.* superentender.
oversight /ˈouvərˌsait/ *n.* descuido *m.*
overt /ouˈvɜrt/ *a.* abierto.
overtake /ˌouvərˈteik/ *v.* alcanzar.
overthrow /*n* ˈouvərˌθrou; *v* ˌouvərˈθrou/ *n.* **1.** trastorno *m.* *—v.* **2.** trastornar.
overture /ˈouvərtʃər/ *n. Mus.* obertura *f.*
overturn /ˌouvərˈtɜrn/ *v.* trastornar.
overview /ˈouvərˌvyu/ *n.* visión de conjunto *f.*
overweight /ˈouvərˌweit/ *a.* demasiado pesado.
overwhelm /ˌouvərˈwɛlm/ *v.* abrumar.
overwork /ˌouvərˈwɜrk/ *v.* trabajar demasiado.
owe /ou/ *v.* deber. **owing to,** debido a.
owl /aul/ *n.* búho *m.,* lechuza *f.*
own /oun/ *a.* **1.** propio. *—v.* **2.** poseer.
owner /ˈounər/ *n.* dueño -ña.
ox /ɒks/ *n.* buey *m.*
oxygen /ˈɒksɪdʒən/ *n.* oxígeno *m.*
oxygen tent tienda de oxígeno *f.*
oyster /ˈɔistər/ *n.* ostra *f.*

P

pace /peis/ *n.* **1.** paso *m.* *—v.* **2.** pasearse. **p. off,** medir a pasos.
pacific /pəˈsɪfɪk/ *a.* pacífico.
Pacific Ocean Océano Pacífico *m.*
pacifier /ˈpæsəˌfaiər/ *n.* pacificador *m.;* (baby p.) chupete *m.*
pacifism /ˈpæsəˌfɪzəm/ *n.* pacifismo *m.*
pacifist /ˈpæsəfɪst/ *n.* pacifista *m. & f.*
pacify /ˈpæsəˌfai/ *v.* pacificar.
pack /pæk/ *n.* **1.** fardo; paquete *m.;* (animals) muta *f.* **p. of cards,** baraja *f.* *—v.* **2.** empaquetar; (baggage) empacar.
package /ˈpækɪdʒ/ *n.* paquete, bulto *m.*
package tour viaje todo incluido *m.*
pact /pækt/ *n.* pacto *m.*
pad /pæd/ *n.* **1.** colchoncillo *m.* **p. of paper,** bloc de papel. *—v.* **2.** rellenar.
paddle /ˈpædl̩/ *n.* **1.** canalete *m.* *—v.* **2.** remar.
padlock /ˈpædˌlɒk/ *n.* candado *m.*
pagan /ˈpeigən/ *a. & n.* pagano -na.
page /peidʒ/ *n.* página *f.;* (boy) paje *m.*
pageant /ˈpædʒənt/ *n.* espectáculo *m.;* procesión *f.*
pail /peil/ *n.* cubo *m.*
pain /pein/ *n.* dolor *m.* **to take pains,** esmerarse.
painful /ˈpeinfəl/ *a.* doloroso; penoso.
pain killer /ˈpeinˌkɪlər/ analgésico *m.*
paint /peint/ *n.* **1.** pintura *f.* *—v.* **2.** pintar.
painter /ˈpeintər/ *n.* pintor -ra.
painting /ˈpeintɪŋ/ *n.* pintura *f.;* cuadro *m.*
pair /pɛər/ *n.* **1.** par *m.;* pareja *f.* *—v.* **2.** parear. **p. off,** emparejarse.
pajamas /pəˈdʒɑməz, -ˈdʒæməz/ *n.* pijama *m.*
palace /ˈpælɪs/ *n.* palacio *m.*
palatable /ˈpælətəbəl/ *a.* sabroso, agradable.
palate /ˈpælɪt/ *n.* paladar *m.*
palatial /pəˈleiʃəl/ *a.* palaciego, suntuoso.
pale /peil/ *a.* pálido. **to turn pale,** palidecer.
paleness /ˈpeilnɪs/ *n.* palidez *f.*
palette /ˈpælɪt/ *n.* paleta *f.*
pallbearer /ˈpɔlˌbɛərər/ *n.* portador del féretro, portaféretro *m.*
pallid /ˈpælɪd/ *a.* pálido.
palm /pɑm/ *n.* palma *f.* **p. tree,** palmera *f.*
palpitate /ˈpælpɪˌteit/ *v.* palpitar.
paltry /ˈpɔltri/ *a.* miserable.
pamper /ˈpæmpər/ *v.* mimar.
pamphlet /ˈpæmflɪt/ *n.* folleto *m.*
pan /pæn/ *n.* cacerola *f.*
panacea /ˌpænəˈsiə/ *n.* panacea *f.*
Pan-American /ˌpænəˈmɛrɪkən/ *a.* panamericano.
pane /pein/ *n.* hoja de vidrio *f.,* cuadro *m.*
panel /ˈpænl̩/ *n.* tablero *m.*
pang /pæŋ/ *n.* dolor; remordimiento *m.*
panic /ˈpænɪk/ *n.* pánico *m.*
panorama /ˌpænəˈræmə, -ˈrɑmə/ *n.* panorama *m.*
pant /pænt/ *v.* jadear.
panther /ˈpænθər/ *n.* pantera *f.*
pantomime /ˈpæntəˌmaim/ *n.* pantomima *f.;* mímica *f.*
pantry /ˈpæntri/ *n.* despensa *f.*
pants /pænts/ *n.* pantalones, *m.pl.*
panty hose /ˈpæntiˌhouz/ *n.* pantys, pantimedias *f. pl.* (medias hasta la cintura).
papal /ˈpeipəl/ *a.* papal.
paper /ˈpeipər/ *n.* papel; periódico; artículo *m.*
paperback /ˈpeipərˌbæk/ *n.* libro en rústica *m.*
paper clip sujetapapeles *m.*
paper cup vaso de papel *m.*
paper hanger /ˈpeipərˌhæŋər/ empapelador -ra.
paper money papel moneda *m.*
paperweight /ˈpeipərˌweit/ pisapapeles *m.*
papier-mâché /ˌpeipərməˈʃei, pɑˌpyei-/ *n.* cartón piedra *m.*
paprika /pæˈprikə, pə-, pɑ-, ˈpæprɪkə/ *n.* pimentón *m.*
par /pɑr/ *n.* paridad *f.; Com.* par *f.*
parable /ˈpærəbəl/ *n.* parábola *f.*
parachute /ˈpærəˌʃut/ *n.* paracaídas *m.*
parade /pəˈreid/ *n.* **1.** desfile *m.,* procesión *f.* *—v.* **2.** desfilar.
paradise /ˈpærəˌdais/ *n.* paraíso *m.*
paradox /ˈpærəˌdɒks/ *n.* paradoja *f.*
paraffin /ˈpærəfɪn/ *n.* parafina *f.*
paragraph /ˈpærəˌgræf/ *n.* párrafo *m.*
parakeet /ˈpærəˌkit/ *n.* perico *m.*
parallel /ˈpærəˌlɛl/ *a.* **1.** paralelo. *—v.* **2.** correr parejas con.
paralysis /pəˈrælәsɪs/ *n.* parálisis *f.*
paralyze /ˈpærəˌlaiz/ *v.* paralizar.
paramedic /ˌpærəˈmɛdɪk/ *n.* paramédico -ca.
parameter /pəˈræmɪtər/ *n.* parámetro *m.*
paramount /ˈpærəˌmaunt/ *a.* supremo.
paraphrase /ˈpærəˌfreiz/ *n.* **1.** paráfrasis *f.* *—v.* **2.** parafrasear.
paraplegic /ˌpærəˈplidʒɪk/ *n.* parapléjico -ca.
parasite /ˈpærəˌsait/ *n.* parásito *m.*

parboil /'par,bɔil/ v. sancochar.
parcel /'parsəl/ n. paquete m. **p. of land,** lote de terreno.
parchment /'partʃmənt/ n. pergamino m.
pardon /'pardṇ/ n. **1.** perdón m. —v. **2.** perdonar.
pare /peər/ v. pelar.
parentage /'peərəntɪdʒ, 'pær-/ n. origen m.; extracción f.
parenthesis /pə'rɛnθəsɪs/ n. paréntesis m.
parents /'peərənts/ n. padres m.pl.
parish /'pærɪʃ/ n. parroquia f.
Parisian /pə'rɪʒən, -'riʒən, -'rɪziən/ a. & n. parisiense m. & f.
parity /'pærɪti/ n. igualdad, paridad f.
park /park/ n. **1.** parque m. —v. **2.** estacionar.
parking lot /'parkɪŋ/ n. estacionamiento, aparcamiento m.
parking meter /'parkɪŋ/ parquímetro m.
parking space /'parkɪŋ/ estacionamiento, aparcamiento m.
parkway /'park,wei/ n. bulevar m.; autopista f.
parley /'parli/ n. conferencia f.; Mil. parlamento m.
parliament /'parləmənt/ n. parlamento m.
parliamentary /,parlə'mɛntəri, -tri; sometimes ,parlyə-/ a. parlamentario.
parlor /'parlər/ n. sala f., salón m.
parochial /pə'roukiəl/ a. parroquial.
parody /'pærədi/ n. **1.** parodia f. —v. **2.** parodiar.
parole /pə'roul/ n. **1.** palabra de honor f.; Mil. santo y seña. —v. **2.** poner en libertad bajo palabra.
paroxysm /'pærək,sɪzəm/ n. paroxismo m.
parrot /'pærət/ n. loro, papagayo m.
parsimony /'parsə,mouni/ n. parsimonia f.
parsley /'parsli/ n. perejil m.
parson /'parsən/ n. párroco m.
part /part/ n. **1.** parte f.; Theat. papel m. —v. **2.** separarse, partirse. **p. with,** desprenderse de.
partake /par'teik/ v. tomar parte.
partial /'parʃəl/ a. parcial.
participant /par'tɪsəpənt/ n. participante m. & f.
participate /par'tɪsə,peit/ v. participar.
participation /par,tɪsə'peiʃən/ n. participación f.
participle /'partə,sɪpəl, -səpəl/ n. participio m.
particle /'partɪkəl/ n. partícula f.
particular /pər'tɪkyələr/ a. & n. particular m.
parting /'partɪŋ/ n. despedida f.
partisan /'partəzən, -sən/ a. & n. partidario -ria.
partition /par'tɪʃən, pər-/ n. tabique m. v. dividir, partir.
partly /'partli/ adv. en parte.
partner /'partnər/ n. socio -cia; compañero -ra.
partridge /'partrɪdʒ/ n. perdiz f.
party /'parti/ n. tertulia, fiesta f.; grupo m.; (political) partido m.
pass /pæs/ n. **1.** pase; (mountain) paso m. —v. **2.** pasar. **p. away,** fallecer.
passable /'pæsəbəl/ a. transitable; regular.
passage /'pæsɪdʒ/ n. pasaje; (corridor) pasillo m.
passé /pæ'sei/ a. anticuado.
passenger /'pæsəndʒər/ n. pasajero -ra.
passenger ship buque de pasajeros m.
passerby /'pæsər'bai/ n. transeúnte m. & f.
passion /'pæʃən/ n. pasión f.
passionate /'pæʃənɪt/ a. apasionado.
passive /'pæsɪv/ a. pasivo.
passport /'pæsport/ n. pasaporte m.

password /'pæs,wɜrd/ n. código m., clave m., contraseña f.
past /pæst/ a. & n. **1.** pasado m. —prep. **2.** más allá de; después de.
paste /peist/ n. **1.** pasta f. —v. **2.** empastar; pegar.
pasteurize /'pæstʃə,raiz/ v. pasteurizar.
pastime /'pæs,taim/ n. pasatiempo m.; diversión f.
pastor /'pæstər/ n. pastor m.
pastrami /pə'strami/ n. pastrón m.
pastry /'peistri/ n. pastelería f.
pasture /'pæstʃər/ n. **1.** pasto m.; pradera f. —v. **2.** pastar.
pat /pæt/ n. **1.** golpecillo m. **to stand p.,** mantenerse firme. —v. **2.** dar golpecillos.
patch /pætʃ/ n. **1.** remiendo m. —v. **2.** remendar.
patent /'pætṇt/ a. & n. **1.** patente m. —v. **2.** patentar.
patent leather /'pætnt, 'pætṇ/ charol m.
paternal /pə'tɜrnḷ/ a. paterno, paternal.
paternity /pə'tɜrniti/ n. paternidad f.
path /pæθ/ n. senda f.
pathetic /pə'θɛtɪk/ a. patético.
pathology /pə'θɒlədʒi/ n. patología f.
pathos /'peiθɒs/ n. rasgo conmovedor m.
patience /'peiʃəns/ n. paciencia f.
patient /'peiʃənt/ a. **1.** paciente. —n. **2.** enfermo -ma, paciente m. & f.
patio /'pæti,ou/ n. patio m.
patriarch /'peitri,ark/ n. patriarca m.
patriot /'peitriət/ n. patriota m. & f.
patriotic /,peitri'ɒtɪk/ a. patriótico.
patriotism /'peitriə,tɪzəm/ n. patriotismo m.
patrol /pə'troul/ n. **1.** patrulla f. —v. **2.** patrullar.
patrolman /pə'troulmən/ n. vigilante m.; patrullador m.
patron /'peitrən/ n. patrón m.
patronize /'peitrə,naiz/ v. condescender; patrocinar; ser cliente de.
pattern /'pætərn/ n. modelo m.
pauper /'pɔpər/ n. indigente m. & f.
pause /pɔz/ n. **1.** pausa f. —v. **2.** pausar.
pave /peiv/ v. pavimentar. **p. the way,** preparar el camino.
pavement /'peivmənt/ n. pavimento m.
pavilion /pə'vɪlyən/ n. pabellón m.
paw /pɔ/ n. **1.** pata f. —v. **2.** patear.
pawn /pɔn/ n. **1.** prenda f.; (chess) peón de ajedrez m. —v. **2.** empeñar.
pay /pei/ v. **1.** pago; sueldo, salario m.; —v. **2.** pagar. **p. back,** pagar; vengarse de. **p. cash,** pagar en metálico.
payee /pei'i/ n. destinatario -ria m. & f.
payment /'peimənt/ n. pago m.; recompensa f.
pay phone teléfono público m.
pea /pi/ n. guisante m.
peace /pis/ n. paz f.
peaceable /'pisəbəl/ a. pacífico.
peaceful /'pisfəl/ a. tranquilo.
peach /pitʃ/ n. durazno, melocotón m.
peacock /'pi,kɒk/ n. pavo real m.
peak /pik/ n. pico, cumbre; máximo m.
peal /pil/ n. repique; estruendo m. **p. of laughter,** risotada f.
peanut /'pi,nʌt/ n. maní, cacahuete m.
pear /peər/ n. pera f.
pearl /pɜrl/ n. perla f.
peasant /'pɛzənt/ n. campesino -na.
pebble /'pɛbəl/ n. guija f.
peck /pɛk/ n. **1.** picotazo m. —v. **2.** picotear.
peckish /'pɛkɪʃ/ a. tener un poco de hambre.
peculiar /pɪ'kyulyər/ a. peculiar.
pecuniary /pɪ'kyuni,ɛri/ a. pecuniario.
pedagogue /'pɛdə,gɒg/ n. pedagogo -ga.

pedagogy /'pɛdə,goudʒi, -,gɒdʒi/ n. pedagogía f.
pedal /'pɛdl/ n. pedal m.
pedant /'pɛdṇt/ n. pedante m. & f.
peddler /'pɛdlər/ n. buhonero m.
pedestal /'pɛdəstḷ/ n. pedestal m.
pedestrian /pə'dɛstriən/ n. peatón -na.
pedestrian crossing paso de peatones m.
pediatrician /,pidiə'trɪʃən/ n. pediatra m. & f.
pediatrics /,pidi'ætrɪks/ n. puericultura f.
pedigree /'pɛdɪ,gri/ n. genealogía f.
peek /pik/ n. **1.** atisbo m. —v. **2.** atisbar.
peel /pil/ n. **1.** corteza f.; (fruit) pellejo m. —v. **2.** descortezar; pelar.
peep /pip/ n. **1.** ojeada f. —v. **2.** mirar, atisbar.
peer /pɪər/ n. **1.** par m. —v. **2.** mirar fijamente.
peg /pɛg/ n. clavija; estaquilla f.; gancho m.
pelt /pɛlt/ n. **1.** pellejo m. —v. **2.** apedrear; (rain) caer con fuerza.
pelvis /'pɛlvɪs/ n. pelvis f.
pen /pɛn/ n. pluma f.; corral m. **fountain p.,** pluma fuente.
penalty /'pɛnlti/ n. pena; multa f.; castigo m.
penance /'pɛnəns/ n. penitencia f. **to do p.,** penar.
penchant /'pɛntʃənt;/ n. propensión f.
pencil /'pɛnsəl/ n. lápiz m.
pencil sharpener /'ʃarpənər/ sacapuntas m.
pending /'pɛndɪŋ/ a. pendiente. **to be p.,** pender.
penetrate /'pɛni,treit/ v. penetrar.
penetration /,pɛni'treiʃən/ n. penetración f.
penicillin /,pɛnə'sɪlɪn/ n. penicilina f.
peninsula /pə'nɪnsələ, -'nɪnsyələ/ n. península f.
penitent /'pɛnɪtənt/ n. & a. penitente m. & f.
penknife /'pɛn,naif/ n. cortaplumas f.
penniless /'pɛnɪlɪs/ a. indigente.
penny /'pɛni/ n. penique m.
pension /'pɛnʃən/ n. pensión f.
pensive /'pɛnsɪv/ a. pensativo.
penultimate /pɪ'nʌltəmɪt/ a. penúltimo.
penury /'pɛnyəri/ n. penuria f.
people /'pipəl/ n. **1.** gente f.; (of a nation) pueblo m. —v. **2.** poblar.
pepper /'pɛpər/ n. pimienta f.; (plant) pimiento m.
per /pɜr; unstressed pər/ prep. por.
perambulator /pər'æmbyə,leitər/ n. cochecillo de niño m.
perceive /pər'siv/ v. percibir.
percent /pər'sɛnt/ adv. por ciento.
percentage /pər'sɛntɪdʒ/ n. porcentaje m.
perceptible /pər'sɛptəbəl/ a. perceptible.
perception /pər'sɛpʃən/ n. percepción f.
perch /pɜrtʃ/ n. percha f.; (fish) perca f.
perdition /pər'dɪʃən/ n. perdición f.
peremptory /pə'rɛmptəri/ a. perentorio, terminante.
perennial /pə'rɛniəl/ a. perenne.
perfect /a. 'pɜrfɪkt; v. pər'fɛkt/ a. **1.** perfecto. —v. **2.** perfeccionar.
perfection /pər'fɛkʃən/ n. perfección f.
perfectionist /pər'fɛkʃənɪst/ a. & n. perfeccionista m. & f.
perforation /,pɜrfə'reiʃən/ n. perforación f.
perform /pər'fɔrm/ v. hacer; ejecutar; Theat. representar.
performance /pər'fɔrməns/ n. ejecución f.; Theat. representación f.
perfume /n. 'pɜrfyum; v. pər'fyum/ n. **1.** perfume m.; fragancia f. —v. **2.** perfumar.

perfunctory /pər'fʌŋktəri/ a. perfunctorio, superficial.
perhaps /pər'hæps/ adv. quizá, quizás, tal vez.
peril /'pɛrəl/ n. peligro m.
perilous /'pɛrələs/ a. peligroso.
perimeter /pə'rɪmɪtər/ n. perímetro m.
period /'pɪəriəd/ n. período m.; Punct. punto m.
periodic /,pɪəri'ɒdɪk/ a. periódico.
periodical /,pɪəri'ɒdɪkəl/ n. revista f.
periphery /pə'rɪfəri/ n. periferia f.
perish /'pɛrɪʃ/ v. perecer.
perishable /'pɛrɪʃəbəl/ a. perecedero.
perjury /'pɜrdʒəri/ n. perjurio m.
permanent /'pɜrmənənt/ a. permanente. **p. wave,** ondulado permanente.
permeate /'pɜrmi,eit/ v. penetrar.
permissible /pər'mɪsəbəl/ a. permisible.
permission /pər'mɪʃən/ n. permiso m.
permit /n. 'pɜrmɪt; v. pər'mɪt/ n. **1.** permiso m. —v. **2.** permitir.
pernicious /pər'nɪʃəs/ a. pernicioso.
perpendicular /,pɜrpən'dɪkyələr/ n. & a. perpendicular f.
perpetrate /'pɜrpɪ,treit/ v. perpetrar.
perpetual /pər'pɛtʃuəl/ a. perpetuo.
perplex /pər'plɛks/ v. confundir.
perplexity /pər'plɛksɪti/ n. perplejidad f.
persecute /'pɜrsɪ,kyut/ v. perseguir.
persecution /,pɜrsɪ'kyuʃən/ n. persecución f.
perseverance /,pɜrsə'vɪərəns/ n. perseverancia f.
persevere /,pɜrsə'vɪər/ v. perseverar.
persist /pər'sɪst/ v. persistir.
persistent /pər'sɪstənt/ a. persistente.
person /'pɜrsən/ n. persona f.
personage /'pɜrsənɪdʒ/ n. personaje m.
personal /'pɜrsənḷ/ a. personal.
personality /,pɜrsə'nælɪti/ n. personalidad f.
personnel /,pɜrsə'nɛl/ n. personal m.
perspective /pər'spɛktɪv/ n. perspectiva f.
perspiration /'pɜrspə'reiʃən/ n. sudor m.
perspire /pər'spaiᵊr/ v. sudar.
persuade /pər'sweid/ v. persuadir.
persuasive /pər'sweisɪv/ a. persuasivo.
pertain /pər'tein/ v. pertenecer.
pertinent /'pɜrtnənt/ a. pertinente.
perturb /pər'tɜrb/ v. perturbar.
peruse /pə'ruz/ v. leer con cuidado.
pervade /pər'veid/ v. penetrar; llenar.
perverse /pər'vɜrs/ a. perverso.
perversion /pər'vɜrʒən/ n. perversión f.
pessimism /'pɛsə,mɪzəm/ n. pesimismo m.
pester /'pɛstər/ v. molestar; fastidiar.
pesticide /'pɛstə,said/ n. pesticida m.
pestilence /'pɛstḷəns/ n. pestilencia f.
pet /pɛt/ n. **1.** favorito -ta.; animal doméstico m. —v. **2.** mimar.
petal /'pɛtḷ/ n. pétalo m.
petition /pə'tɪʃən/ n. **1.** petición, súplica f. —v. **2.** pedir, suplicar.
petrify /'pɛtrə,fai/ v. petrificar.
petroleum /pə'trouliəm/ n. petróleo m.
petticoat /'pɛti,kout/ n. enagua f.
petty /'pɛti/ a. mezquino, insignificante.
petulant /'pɛtʃələnt/ a. quisquilloso.
pew /pyu/ n. banco de iglesia m.
pewter /'pyutər/ n. peltre m.
phantom /'fæntəm/ n. espectro, fantasma m.
pharmacist /'farməsɪst/ n. farmacéutico -ca, boticario -ria.
pharmacy /'farməsi/ n. farmacia, botica f.
phase /feiz/ n. fase f.
pheasant /'fɛzənt/ n. faisán m.

phenomenal /fɪˈnɒmənl/ *a.* fenomenal.
phenomenon /fɪˈnɒməˌnɒn/ *n.* fenómeno *f.*
philanthropy /fɪˈlænθrəpi/ *n.* filantropía *f.*
philately /fɪˈlætl̩i/ *n.* filatelia *f.*
philosopher /fɪˈlɒsəfər/ *n.* filósofo -fa.
philosophical /ˌfɪləˈsɒfɪkəl/ *a.* filosófico.
philosophy /fɪˈlɒsəfi/ *n.* filosofía *f.*
phlegm /flɛm/ *n.* flema *f.*
phlegmatic /flɛgˈmætɪk/ *a.* flemático.
phobia /ˈfoubiə/ *n.* fobia *f.*
phone /foun/ *n.* teléfono *m.*
phonetic /fəˈnɛtɪk/ *a.* fonético.
phonograph /ˈfounəˌgræf/ *n.* fonógrafo *m.*
phosphorus /ˈfɒsfərəs/ *n.* fósforo *m.*
photocopier /ˈfoutəˌkɒpiər/ *n.* fotocopiadora *f.*
photocopy /ˈfoutəˌkɒpi/ *n.* **1.** fotocopia *f.* —*v.* **2.** fotocopiar.
photoelectric /ˌfoutouɪˈlɛktrɪk/ *a.* fotoeléctrico.
photogenic /ˌfoutəˈdʒɛnɪk/ *a.* fotogénico.
photograph /ˈfoutəˌgræf/ *n.* **1.** fotografía *f.* —*v.* **2.** fotografiar; retratar.
photography /fəˈtɒgrəfi/ *n.* fotografía *f.*
phrase /freiz/ *n.* **1.** frase *f.* —*v.* **2.** expresar.
physical /ˈfɪzɪkəl/ *a.* físico.
physician /fɪˈzɪʃən/ *n.* médico *m.* & *f.*
physics /ˈfɪzɪks/ *n.* física *f.*
physiology /ˌfɪziˈɒlədʒi/ *n.* fisiología *f.*
physiotherapy /ˌfɪziouˈθɛrəpi/ *n.* fisioterapia *f.*
physique /fɪˈzik/ *n.* físico *m.*
pianist /piˈænɪst, ˈpiənɪst/ *n.* pianista *m.* & *f.*
piano /piˈænou/ *n.* piano *m.*
picayune /ˌpɪkəˈyun/ *a.* insignificante.
piccolo /ˈpɪkəˌlou/ *n.* flautín *m.*
pick /pɪk/ *n.* **1.** pico *m.* —*v.* **2.** escoger. **p. up,** recoger.
picket /ˈpɪkɪt/ *n.* piquete *m.*
pickle /ˈpɪkəl/ *n.* **1.** salmuera *f.;* encurtido *m.* —*v.* **2.** escabechar.
pickpocket /ˈpɪkˌpɒkɪt/ *n.* cortabolsas *m.* & *f.*
picnic /ˈpɪknɪk/ *n.* picnic *m.*
picture /ˈpɪktʃər/ *n.* **1.** cuadro; retrato *m.;* fotografía *f.;* (movie) película *f.* —*v.* **2.** imaginarse.
picturesque /ˌpɪktʃəˈrɛsk/ *a.* pintoresco.
pie /pai/ *n.* pastel *m.*
piece /pis/ *n.* pedazo *m.;* pieza *f.*
pieceworker /ˈpisˌwɜrkər/ *n.* destajero -ra, destajista *m.* & *f.*
pier /pɪər/ *n.* muelle *m.*
pierce /pɪərs/ *v.* perforar; pinchar; traspasar.
piety /ˈpaiɪti/ *n.* piedad *f.*
pig /pɪg/ *n.* puerco, cerdo, lechón *m.*
pigeon /ˈpɪdʒən/ *n.* paloma *f.*
pigeonhole /ˈpɪdʒənˌhoul/ *n.* casilla *f.*
pigment /ˈpɪgmənt/ *n.* pigmento *m.*
pile /pail/ *n.* **1.** pila *f.;* montón *m.;* *Med.* hemorroides *f.pl.* —*v.* **2.** amontonar.
pilfer /ˈpɪlfər/ *v.* ratear.
pilgrim /ˈpɪlgrɪm/ *n.* peregrino -na, romero -ra.
pilgrimage /ˈpɪlgrəmɪdʒ/ *n.* romería *f.*
pill /pɪl/ *n.* píldora *f.*
pillage /ˈpɪlɪdʒ/ *n.* **1.** pillaje *m.* —*v.* **2.** pillar.
pillar /ˈpɪlər/ *n.* columna *f.*
pillow /ˈpɪlou/ *n.* almohada *f.*
pillowcase /ˈpɪlouˌkeis/ *n.* funda de almohada *f.*
pilot /ˈpailət/ *n.* **1.** piloto *m.* & *f.* —*v.* **2.** pilotar.
pimple /ˈpɪmpəl/ *n.* grano *m.*
pin /pɪn/ *n.* **1.** alfiler; broche *m.;* *Mech.* clavija *f.* —*v.* **2.** prender. **p. up,** fijar.
pinafore /ˈpɪnəˌfɔr/ *n.* delantal (de niña) *m.*
pinch /pɪntʃ/ *n.* **1.** pellizco *m.* —*v.* **2.** pellizcar.
pine /pain/ *n.* **1.** pino *m.* —*v.* **2. p. away,** languidecer. **p. for,** anhelar.
pineapple /ˈpaiˌnæpəl/ *n.* piña *f.,* ananás *m.pl.*
pink /pɪŋk/ *a.* rosado.
pinky /ˈpɪŋki/ *n.* meñique *m.*
pinnacle /ˈpɪnəkəl/ *n.* pináculo *m.;* cumbre *f.*
pint /paint/ *n.* pinta *f.*
pioneer /ˌpaiəˈnɪər/ *n.* pionero -ra.
pious /ˈpaiəs/ *a.* piadoso.
pipe /paip/ *n.* pipa *f.;* tubo; (of organ) cañón *m.*
pipeline /ˈpaipˌlain/ *n.* oleoducto *m.*
piper /ˈpaipər/ *n.* flautista *m.* & *f.*
piquant /ˈpikənt/ *a.* picante.
pirate /ˈpairət/ *n.* pirata *m.*
pistol /ˈpɪstl̩/ *n.* pistola *f.*
piston /ˈpɪstən/ *n.* émbolo, pistón *m.*
pit /pɪt/ *n.* hoyo *m.;* (fruit) hueso *m.*
pitch /pɪtʃ/ *n.* **1.** brea *f.;* grado de inclinación; (music) tono *m.;* —*v.* **2.** lanzar; (ship) cabecear.
pitchblende /ˈpɪtʃˌblɛnd/ *n.* pechblenda *f.*
pitcher /ˈpɪtʃər/ *n.* cántaro *m.;* (baseball) lanzador -ra.
pitchfork /ˈpɪtʃˌfɔrk/ *n.* horca *f.;* tridente *m.*
pitfall /ˈpɪtˌfɔl/ *n.* trampa *f.,* hoya cubierta *f.*
pitiful /ˈpɪtɪfəl/ *a.* lastimoso.
pitiless /ˈpɪtɪlɪs/ *a.* cruel.
pituitary gland /pɪˈtuɪˌtɛri/ glándula pituitaria *f.*
pity /ˈpɪti/ *n.* **1.** compasión, piedad *f.* **to be a p.,** ser lástima. —*v.* **2.** compadecer.
pivot /ˈpɪvət/ *n.* **1.** espiga *f.,* pivote *m.;* punto de partida *m.* —*v.* **2.** girar sobre un pivote.
pizza /ˈpitsə/ *n.* pizza *f.*
placard /ˈplækɑrd/ *n.* **1.** cartel *m.* —*v.* **2.** fijar carteles.
placate /ˈpleikeit/ *v.* aplacar.
place /pleis/ *n.* **1.** lugar, sitio, puesto *m.* —*v.* **2.** colocar, poner.
placid /ˈplæsɪd/ *a.* plácido.
plagiarism /ˈpleidʒəˌrɪzəm/ *n.* plagio *m.*
plague /pleig/ *n.* **1.** plaga, peste *f.* —*v.* **2.** atormentar.
plain /plein/ *a.* **1.** sencillo; puro; evidente. —*n.* **2.** llano *m.*
plaintiff /ˈpleintɪf/ *n.* demandante *m.* & *f.*
plan /plæn/ *n.* **1.** plan, propósito *m.* —*v.* **2.** planear; pensar; planificar. **p. on,** contar con.
plane /plein/ *n.* **1.** plano; (tool) cepillo *m.* —*v.* **2.** allanar; acepillar.
planet /ˈplænɪt/ *n.* planeta *m.*
planetarium /ˌplænɪˈtɛəriəm/ *n.* planetario *m.*
plank /plæŋk/ *n.* tablón *m.*
planning /ˈplænɪŋ/ *n.* planificación *f.*
plant /plænt/ *n.* **1.** mata, planta *f.* —*v.* **2.** sembrar, plantar.
plantation /plænˈteiʃən/ *n.* plantación *f.* **coffee p.,** cafetal *m.*
planter /ˈplæntər/ *n.* plantador; hacendado *m.*
plasma /ˈplæzmə/ *n.* plasma *m.*
plaster /ˈplæstər/ *n.* **1.** yeso; emplasto *m.* —*v.* **2.** enyesar; emplastar.
plastic /ˈplæstɪk/ *a.* plástico.
plate /pleit/ *n.* **1.** plato *m.;* plancha de metal. —*v.* **2.** planchear.
plateau /plæˈtou/ *n.* meseta *f.*
platform /ˈplætfɔrm/ *n.* plataforma *f.*
platinum /ˈplætn̩əm/ *n.* platino *m.*
platitude /ˈplætɪˌtud/ *n.* perogrullada *f.*
platter /ˈplætər/ *n.* fuente *f.,* platel *m.*
plaudit /ˈplɔdɪt/ *n.* aplauso *m.*
plausible /ˈplɔzəbəl/ *a.* plausible.
play /plei/ *n.* **1.** juego *m.;* *Theat.* pieza *f.* —*v.* **2.** jugar; (music) tocar; *Theat.* representar. **p. a part,** hacer un papel.
player /ˈpleiər/ *n.* jugador -ra; (music) músico -ca.; *Theat.* actor *m.,* actriz *f.*
playful /ˈpleifəl/ *a.* juguetón.
playground /ˈpleiˌgraund/ *n.* campo de deportes; patio de recreo.
playmate /ˈpleiˌmeit/. *n.* compañero -ra de juego.
playwright /ˈpleiˌrait/ *n.* dramaturgo -ga.
plea /pli/ *n.* ruego *m.;* súplica *f.;* (legal) declaración *f.*
plead /plid/ *v.* suplicar; declararse. **p. a case,** defender un pleito.
pleasant /ˈplɛzənt/ *a.* agradable.
please /pliz/ *v.* **1.** gustar, agradar. **Pleased to meet you,** Mucho gusto en conocer a Vd. —*adv.* **2.** por favor. **Please...** Haga el favor de..., Tenga la bondad de..., Sírvase...
pleasure /ˈplɛʒər/ *n.* gusto, placer *m.*
pleat /plit/ *n.* **1.** pliegue *m.* —*v.* **2.** plegar.
plebiscite /ˈplɛbəˌsait/ *n.* plebiscito *m.*
pledge /plɛdʒ/ *n.* **1.** empeño *m.* —*v.* **2.** empeñar.
plentiful /ˈplɛntɪfəl/ *a.* abundante.
plenty /ˈplɛnti/ *n.* abundancia *f.* **p. of,** bastante. **p. more,** mucho más.
pleurisy /ˈplʊrəsi/ *n.* pleuritis *f.*
pliable, pliant /ˈplaiəbəl; ˈplaiənt/ *a.* flexible.
pliers /ˈplaiərz/ *n.pl.* alicates *m.pl.*
plight /plait/ *n.* apuro, aprieto *m.*
plot /plɒt/ *n.* **1.** conspiración; (of a story) trama; (of land) parcela *f.* —*v.* **2.** conspirar; tramar.
plow /plau/ *n.* **1.** arado *m.* —*v.* **2.** arar.
pluck /plʌk/ *n.* **1.** valor *m.* —*v.* **2.** arrancar; desplumar.
plug /plʌg/ *n.* **1.** tapón; *Elec.* enchufe *m.* **spark p.,** bujía *f.* —*v.* **2.** tapar.
plum /plʌm/ *n.* ciruela *f.*
plumage /ˈplumɪdʒ/ *n.* plumaje *m.*
plumber /ˈplʌmər/ *n.* fontanero -era, plomero -era.
plume /plum/ *n.* pluma *f.*
plump /plʌmp/ *a.* regordete.
plunder /ˈplʌndər/ *n.* **1.** botín *m.;* despojos *m.pl.* —*v.* **2.** saquear.
plunge /plʌndʒ/ *v.* zambullir; precipitar.
plural /ˈplʊrəl/ *a.* & *n.* plural *m.*
plus /plʌs/ *prep.* más.
plutocrat /ˈplutəˌkræt/ *n.* plutócrata *m.* & *f.*
pneumatic /nʊˈmætɪk/ *a.* neumático.
pneumonia /nʊˈmounyə/ *n.* pulmonía *f.*
poach /poutʃ/ *v.* (eggs) escalfar; invadir; cazar en vedado.
pocket /ˈpɒkɪt/ *n.* **1.** bolsillo *m.* —*v.* **2.** embolsar.
pocketbook /ˈpɒkɪtˌbʊk/ *n.* cartera *f.*
podiatry /pəˈdaiətri/ *n.* podiatría *f.*
poem /ˈpouəm/ *n.* poema *m.*
poet /ˈpouɪt/ *n.* poeta *m.* & *f.*
poetic /pouˈɛtɪk/ *a.* poético.
poetry /ˈpouɪtri/ *n.* poesía *f.*
poignant /ˈpɔinyənt/ *a.* conmovedor.
point /pɔint/ *n.* **1.** punta *f.;* punto *m.* —*v.* **2.** apuntar. **p. out,** señalar.
pointed /ˈpɔintɪd/ *a.* puntiagudo; directo.
pointless /ˈpɔintlɪs/ *a.* inútil.
poise /pɔiz/ *n.* **1.** equilibrio *m.;* serenidad *f.* —*v.* **2.** equilibrar; estar suspendido.
poison /ˈpɔizən/ *n.* **1.** veneno *m.* —*v.* **2.** envenenar.
poisonous /ˈpɔizənəs/ *a.* venenoso.
poke /pouk/ *n.* **1.** empuje *m.,* hurgonada *f.* —*v.* **2.** picar; haronear.
Poland /ˈpoulənd/ *n.* Polonia *f.*
polar /ˈpoulər/ *a.* polar.
pole /poul/ *n.* palo; *Geog.* polo *m.*
polemical /pəˈlɛmɪkəl/ *a.* polémico.
police /pəˈlis/ *n.* policía *f.*
policeman /pəˈlismən/ *n.* policía *m.*
policy /ˈpɒləsi/ *n.* política *f.* **insurance p.,** póliza de seguro.
Polish /ˈpɒlɪʃ/ *a.* & *n.* polaco -ca.
polish /ˈpɒlɪʃ/ *n.* **1.** lustre *m.* —*v.* **2.** pulir, lustrar.
polite /pəˈlait/ *a.* cortés.
politic /ˈpɒlɪtɪk/ **political** *a.* político.
politician /ˌpɒlɪˈtɪʃən/ *n.* político -ca.
politics /ˈpɒlɪtɪks/ *n.* política *f.*
poll /poul/ *n.* encuesta *f.;* (pl.) urnas *f.pl.*
pollen /ˈpɒlən/ *n.* polen *m.*
pollute /pəˈlut/ *v.* contaminar.
pollution /pəˈluʃən/ *n.* contaminación *f.*
polo /ˈpoulou/ *n.* polo *m.*
polyester /ˌpɒliˈɛstər/ *n.* poliéster *m.*
polygamy /pəˈlɪgəmi/ *n.* poligamia *f.*
polygon /ˈpɒliˌgɒn/ *n.* polígono *m.*
pomp /pɒmp/ *n.* pompa *f.*
pompous /ˈpɒmpəs/ *a.* pomposo.
poncho /ˈpɒntʃou/ *n.* poncho *m.*
pond /pɒnd/ *n.* charca *f.*
ponder /ˈpɒndər/ *v.* ponderar, meditar.
ponderous /ˈpɒndərəs/ *a.* ponderoso, pesado.
pontiff /ˈpɒntɪf/ *n.* pontífice *m.*
pontoon /pɒnˈtun/ *n.* pontón *m.*
pony /ˈpouni/ *n.* caballito *m.*
ponytail /ˈpouniˌteil/ *n.* cola de caballo *f.*
poodle /ˈpudl̩/ *n.* caniche *m.*
pool /pul/ *n.* charco *m.* **swimming p.,** piscina *f.*
poor /pʊr/ *a.* pobre; (not good) malo.
pop /pɒp/ *n.* chasquido *m.*
popcorn /ˈpɒpˌkɔrn/ *n.* rosetas de maíz, palomitas de maíz *f.pl.*
pope /poup/ *n.* papa *m.*
poppy /ˈpɒpi/ *n.* amapola *f.*
popsicle /ˈpɒpsɪkəl/ *n.* polo *m.*
popular /ˈpɒpyələr/ *a.* popular.
popularity /ˌpɒpyəˈlærɪti/ *n.* popularidad *f.*
population /ˌpɒpyəˈleiʃən/ *n.* población *f.*
porcelain /ˈpɔrsəlɪn/ *n.* porcelana *f.*
porch /pɔrtʃ/ *n.* pórtico *m.;* galería *f.*
pore /pɔr/ *n.* poro *m.*
pork /pɔrk/ *n.* carne de puerco.
pornography /pɔrˈnɒgrəfi/ *n.* pornografía *f.*
porous /ˈpɔrəs/ *a.* poroso, esponjoso.
port /pɔrt/ *n.* puerto; *Naut.* babor *m.* **p. wine,** oporto *m.*
portable /ˈpɔrtəbəl/ *a.* portátil.
portal /ˈpɔrtl̩/ *n.* portal *m.*
portend /pɔrˈtɛnd/ *v.* pronosticar.
portent /ˈpɔrtɛnt/ *n.* presagio *m.,* portento *m.*
porter /ˈpɔrtər/ *n.* portero *m.*
portfolio /pɔrtˈfouliˌou/ *n.* cartera *f.*
porthole /ˈpɔrtˌhoul/ *n.* porta *f.*
portion /ˈpɔrʃən/ *n.* porción *f.*
portly /ˈpɔrtli/ *a.* corpulento.
portrait /ˈpɔrtrɪt/ *n.* retrato *m.*
portray /pɔrˈtrei/ *v.* pintar.
Portugal /ˈpɔrtʃəgəl/ *n.* Portugal *m.*
Portuguese /ˌpɔrtʃəˈgiz/ *a.* & *n.* portugués -esa.
pose /pouz/ *n.* **1.** postura; actitud *f.* —*v.* **2.** posar. **p. as,** pretender ser.
position /pəˈzɪʃən/ *n.* posición *f.*
positive /ˈpɒzɪtɪv/ *a.* positivo.
possess /pəˈzɛs/ *v.* poseer.
possession /pəˈzɛʃən/ *n.* posesión *f.*
possessive /pəˈzɛsɪv/ *a.* posesivo.
possibility /ˌpɒsəˈbɪlɪti/ *n.* posibilidad *f.*
possible /ˈpɒsəbəl/ *a.* posible.
post /poust/ *n.* **1.** poste; puesto *m.* —*v.* **2.** fijar; situar; echar al correo.
postage /ˈpoustɪdʒ/ *n.* porte de correo. **p. stamp,** sello *m.*
postal /ˈpoustl̩/ *a.* postal.
post card tarjeta postal.
poster /ˈpoustər/ *n.* cartel, letrero *m.*
posterior /pɒˈstɪəriər/ *a.* posterior.
posterity /pɒˈstɛrɪti/ *n.* posteridad *f.*
postgraduate /poustˈgrædʒuɪt/ *a.* & *n.* postgraduado -da.

postmark /'poust,mɑrk/ n. matasellos m.

post office correos m.pl.

postpone /poust'poun/ v. posponer, aplazar.

postscript /'poust,skrɪpt/ n. posdata f.

posture /'pɒstʃər/ n. postura f.

pot /pɒt/ n. olla, marmita; (marijuana) marijuana, hierba f. **flower p.,** tiesto m.

potassium /pə'tæsiəm/ n. potasio m.

potato /pə'teitou/ n. patata, papa f. **sweet p.,** batata f.

potent /'poutn̩t/ a. potente, poderoso.

potential /pə'tɛnʃəl/ a. & n. potencial f.

potion /'pouʃən/ n. poción, pócima f.

pottery /'pɒtəri/ n. alfarería f.

pouch /pautʃ/ n. saco m.; bolsa f.

poultry /'poultri/ n. aves de corral.

pound /paund/ n. **1.** libra f. —v. **2.** golpear.

pour /pɔr/ v. echar; verter; llover a cántaros.

poverty /'pɒvərti/ n. pobreza f.

powder /'paudər/ n. **1.** polvo m.; (gun) pólvora f. —v. **2.** empolvar; pulverizar.

power /'pauər/ n. poder m.; potencia f.

powerful /'pauərfəl/ a. poderoso, fuerte.

powerless /'pauərlɪs/ a. impotente.

practical /'præktɪkəl/ a. práctico.

practical joke inocentada f.

practically /'præktɪkli/ adv. casi; prácticamente.

practice /'præktɪs/ n. **1.** práctica; costumbre; clientela f. —v. **2.** practicar; ejercer.

practiced /'præktɪst/ a. experto.

practitioner /præk'tɪʃənər/ n. practicante m. & f.

pragmatic /præg'mætɪk/ a. pragmático.

prairie /'prɛəri/ n. llanura; S.A. pampa f.

praise /preiz/ n. **1.** alabanza f. —v. **2.** alabar.

prank /præŋk/ n. travesura f.

prawn /prɔn/ n. gamba f.

pray /prei/ v. rezar; (beg) rogar.

prayer /'preiər/ n. oración; súplica f., ruego m.

preach /pritʃ/ v. predicar; sermonear.

preacher /'pritʃər/ n. predicador m.

preamble /'pri,æmbəl/ n. preámbulo m.

precarious /prɪ'kɛəriəs/ a. precario.

precaution /prɪ'kɔʃən/ n. precaución f.

precede /prɪ'sid/ v. preceder, anteceder.

precedent /n. 'prɛsɪdənt; a. prɪ'sidn̩t/ n. & a. precedente m.

precept /'prisɛpt/ n. precepto m.

precinct /'prisɪŋkt/ n. recinto m.

precious /'prɛʃəs/ a. precioso.

precipice /'prɛsəpɪs/ n. precipicio m.

precipitate /prɪ'sɪpɪ,teit/ v. precipitar.

precise /prɪ'sais/ a. preciso, exacto.

precision /prɪ'sɪʒən/ n. precisión f.

preclude /prɪ'klud/ v. evitar.

precocious /prɪ'kouʃəs/ a. precoz.

precooked /prɪ'kʊkt/ a. precocinado.

predatory /'prɛdə,tɔri/ a. de rapiña, rapaz.

predecessor /'prɛdə,sɛsər/ n. predecesor -ra, antecesor -ra.

predicament /prɪ'dɪkəmənt/ n. dificultad f.; apuro m.

predict /prɪ'dɪkt/ v. pronosticar, predecir.

predictable /prɪ'dɪktəbəl/ a. previsible.

predilection /,prɛdl̩'ɛkʃən/ n. predilección f.

predispose /,pridɪ'spouz/ v. predisponer.

predominant /prɪ'dɒmənənt/ a. predominante.

prefabricate /pri'fæbrɪ,keit/ v. fabricar de antemano.

preface /'prɛfɪs/ n. prefacio m.

prefer /prɪ'fɜr/ v. preferir.

preferable /'prɛfərəbəl/ a. preferible.

preference /'prɛfərəns/ n. preferencia f.

prefix /'prifɪks/ n. **1.** prefijo m. —v. **2.** prefijar.

pregnant /'prɛgnənt/ a. preñada.

prehistoric /,prihɪ'stɔrɪk/ a. prehistórico.

prejudice /'prɛdʒədɪs/ n. prejuicio m.

prejudiced /'prɛdʒədɪst/ a. (S.A.) prejuiciado.

preliminary /prɪ'lɪmə,nɛri/ a. preliminar.

prelude /'prɛlyud/ n. preludio m.

premature /,primə'tʃʊr/ a. prematuro.

premeditate /prɪ'mɛdɪ,teit/ v. premeditar.

premier /prɪ'mɪər/ n. primer ministro.

première /prɪ'mɪər/ n. estreno m.

premise /'prɛmɪs/ n. premisa f.

premium /'primiəm/ n. premio m.

premonition /,primə'nɪʃən/ n. presentimiento m.

prenatal /pri'neitl̩/ a. prenatal.

preparation /,prɛpə'reiʃən/ n. preparativo m.; preparación f.

preparatory /prɪ'pærə,tɔri/ a. preparatorio. **p. to,** antes de.

prepare /prɪ'pɛər/ v. preparar.

preponderant /prɪ'pɒndərənt/ a. preponderante.

preposition /,prɛpə'zɪʃən/ n. preposición f.

preposterous /prɪ'pɒstərəs/ a. prepóstero, absurdo.

prerequisite /prɪ'rɛkwəzɪt/ n. requisito previo.

prerogative /prɪ'rɒgətɪv/ n. prerrogativa f.

prescribe /prɪ'skraib/ v. prescribir; Med. recetar.

prescription /prɪ'skrɪpʃən/ n. prescripción; Med. receta f.

presence /'prɛzəns/ n. presencia f.; porte m.

present /a, n 'prɛzənt; v prɪ'zɛnt/ a. **1.** presente. **to be present at,** asistir a. —a. **2.** presente; (gift) regalo m. **at p.,** ahora, actualmente. **for the p.,** por ahora. —v. **3.** presentar.

presentable /prɪ'zɛntəbəl/ a. presentable.

presentation /,prɛzən'teiʃən/ n. presentación; introducción f.; Theat. representación f.

presently /'prɛzəntli/ adv. luego; dentro de poco.

preservative /prɪ'zɜrvətɪv/ a. & n. preservativo m.

preserve /prɪ'zɜrv/ n. **1.** conserva f.; (hunting) vedado m. —v. **2.** preservar.

preside /prɪ'zaid/ v. presidir.

presidency /'prɛzɪdənsi/ n. presidencia f.

president /'prɛzɪdənt/ n. presidente -ta.

press /prɛs/ n. **1.** prensa f. —v. **2.** apretar; urgir; (clothes) planchar.

pressing /'prɛsɪŋ/ a. urgente.

pressure /'prɛʃər/ n. presión f.

pressure cooker /'kʊkər/ cocina de presión f.

prestige /prɛ'stiʒ/ n. prestigio m.

presume /prɪ'zum/ v. presumir, suponer.

presumptuous /prɪ'zʌmptʃuəs/ a. presuntuoso.

presuppose /,prisə'pouz/ v. presuponer.

pretend /prɪ'tɛnd/ v. fingir. **p. to the throne,** aspirar al trono.

pretense /prɪ'tɛns, 'pritɛns/ n. pretensión f.; fingimiento m.

pretension /prɪ'tɛnʃən/ n. pretensión f.

pretentious /prɪ'tɛnʃəs/ a. presumido.

pretext /'pritɛkst/ n. pretexto m.

pretty /'prɪti/ a. **1.** bonito, lindo. —adv. **2.** bastante.

prevail /prɪ'veil/ v. prevalecer.

prevailing /prɪ'veilɪŋ/ **prevalent** a. predominante.

prevent /prɪ'vɛnt/ v. impedir; evitar.

prevention /prɪ'vɛnʃən/ n. prevención f.

preventive /prɪ'vɛntɪv/ a. preventivo.

preview /'pri,vyu/ n. vista anticipada f.

previous /'priviəs/ a. anterior, previo.

prey /prei/ n. presa f.

price /prais/ n. precio m.

priceless /'praislɪs/ a. sin precio.

prick /prɪk/ n. **1.** punzada f. —v. **2.** punzar.

pride /praid/ n. orgullo m.

priest /prist/ n. sacerdote, cura m.

prim /prɪm/ a. estirado, remilgado.

primary /'praimɛri/ a. primario, principal.

prime /praim/ a. **1.** primero. —n. **2.** flor f. —v. **3.** alistar.

prime minister primer ministro m. & f.

primitive /'prɪmɪtɪv/ a. primitivo.

prince /prɪns/ n. príncipe m.

Prince Charming Príncipe Azul m.

princess /'prɪnsɪs/ n. princesa f.

principal /'prɪnsəpəl/ a. **1.** principal. —n. **2.** principal m. & f.; director -ra.

principle /'prɪnsəpəl/ n. principio m.

print /prɪnt/ n. **1.** letra de molde f.; (art) grabado m. —v. **2.** imprimir, estampar.

printer /'prɪntər/ n. impresora f.

printing /'prɪntɪŋ/ n. impresión; **p. office,** imprenta f.

printing press prensa f.

printout /'prɪnt,aut/ n. impreso producido por una computadora, impresión f.

priority /prai'ɔrɪti/ n. prioridad, precedencia f.

prism /'prɪzəm/ n. prisma m.

prison /'prɪzən/ n. prisión, cárcel f.

prisoner /'prɪzənər/ n. presidiario -ria, prisionero -ra, preso -sa.

pristine /'prɪstin/ a. inmaculado.

privacy /'praivəsi/ n. soledad f.

private /'praivɪt/ a. **1.** particular. —n. **2.** soldado raso. **in p.,** en particular.

privation /prai'veiʃən/ n. privación f.

privet /'prɪvɪt/ n. ligustro m.

privilege /'prɪvəlɪdʒ/ n. privilegio m.

privy /'prɪvi/ n. letrina f.

prize /praiz/ n. **1.** premio m. —v. **2.** apreciar, estimar.

probability /,prɒbə'bɪliti/ n. probabilidad f.

probable /'prɒbəbəl/ a. probable.

probate /'proubeit/ a. testamentario.

probation /prou'beiʃən/ n. prueba f.; probación f.; libertad condicional f.

probe /proub/ n. **1.** indagación f. —v. **2.** indagar; tentar.

probity /'proubɪti/ n. probidad f.

problem /'prɒbləm/ n. problema m.

procedure /prə'sidʒər/ n. procedimiento m.

proceed /prə'sid/ v. proceder; proseguir.

process /'prɒsɛs/ n. proceso m.

procession /prə'sɛʃən/ n. procesión f.

proclaim /prou'kleim/ v. proclamar, anunciar.

proclamation /,prɒklə'meiʃən/ n. proclamación f.; decreto m.

procrastinate /prou'kræstə,neit/ v. dilatar.

procure /prou'kyur/ v. obtener, procurar.

prodigal /'prɒdɪgəl/ n. & a. pródigo -ga.

prodigy /'prɒdɪdʒi/ n. prodigio m.

produce /prə'dus/ v. producir.

product /'prɒdəkt/ n. producto m.

production /prə'dʌkʃən/ n. producción f.

productive /prə'dʌktɪv/ a. productivo.

profane /prə'fein/ a. **1.** profano. —v. **2.** profanar.

profanity /prə'fænɪti/ n. profanidad f.

profess /prə'fɛs/ v. profesar; declarar.

profession /prə'fɛʃən/ n. profesión f.

professional /prə'fɛʃən̩l/ a. & n. profesional m. & f.

professor /prə'fɛsər/ n. profesor -ra; catedrático -ca.

proficient /prə'fɪʃənt/ a. experto, proficiente.

profile /'proufail/ n. perfil m.

profit /'prɒfɪt/ n. **1.** provecho m.; ventaja f.; Com. ganancia f. —v. **2.** aprovechar; beneficiar.

profitable /'prɒfɪtəbəl/ a. provechoso, ventajoso, lucrativo.

profiteer /,prɒfɪ'tɪər/ n. **1.** explotador -ra. —v. **2.** explotar.

profound /prə'faund/ a. profundo, hondo.

profuse /prə'fyus/ a. pródigo; profuso.

prognosis /prɒg'nousɪs/ n. pronóstico m.

program /'prougræm/ n. programa m.

progress /n. 'prɒgrɛs; v. prə'grɛs/ n. **1.** progresos m.pl. **in p.,** en marcha. —v. **2.** progresar; marchar.

progressive /prə'grɛsɪv/ a. progresivo; progresista.

prohibit /prou'hɪbɪt/ v. prohibir.

prohibition /,prouə'bɪʃən/ n. prohibición f.

prohibitive /prou'hɪbɪtɪv/ a. prohibitivo.

project /n. 'prɒdʒɛkt; v. prə'dʒɛkt/ n. **1.** proyecto m. —v. **2.** proyectar.

projectile /prə'dʒɛktɪl/ n. proyectil m.

projection /prə'dʒɛkʃən/ n. proyección f.

projector /prə'dʒɛktər/ n. proyector m.

proliferation /prə,lɪfə'reiʃən/ n. proliferación f.

prolific /prə'lɪfɪk/ a. prolífico.

prologue /'proulɒg/ n. prólogo m.

prolong /prə'lɒŋ/ v. prolongar.

prominent /'prɒmənənt/ a. prominente; eminente.

promiscuous /prə'mɪskyuəs/ a. promiscuo.

promise /'prɒmɪs/ n. **1.** promesa f. —v. **2.** prometer.

promote /prə'mout/ v. fomentar; estimular; adelantar; promocionar.

promotion /prə'mouʃən/ n. promoción f.; adelanto m.

prompt /prɒmpt/ a. **1.** puntual. —v. **2.** impulsar; Theat. apuntar. —adv. **3.** pronto.

promulgate /'prɒməl,geit/ v. promulgar.

pronoun /'prou,naun/ n. pronombre m.

pronounce /prə'nauns/ v. pronunciar.

pronunciation /prə,nʌnsi'eiʃən/ n. pronunciación f.

proof /pruf/ n. prueba f.

proof of purchase certificado de compra m.

proofread /'pruf,rid/ v. corregir pruebas.

prop /prɒp/ n. **1.** apoyo, m. —v. **2.** sostener.

propaganda /,prɒpə'gændə/ n. propaganda f.

propagate /'prɒpə,geit/ v. propagar.

propel /prə'pɛl/ v. propulsar.

propeller /prə'pɛlər/ n. hélice f.

propensity /prə'pɛnsɪti/ n. tendencia f.

proper /'prɒpər/ a. propio; correcto.

property /'prɒpərti/ n. propiedad f.

prophecy /'prɒfəsi/ n. profecía f.

prophesy /'prɒfə,sai/ v. predecir, profetizar.

prophet /'prɒfɪt/ n. profeta m.

prophetic /prə'fɛtɪk/ a. profético.

propitious /prə'pɪʃəs/ a. propicio.

proponent /prə'pounənt/ n. & a. proponente m.

proportion /prə'pɔrʃən/ n. proporción f.

proportionate /prə'pɔrʃənit/ a. proporcionado.

proposal /prə'pouzəl/ n. propuesta; oferta f.; (marriage) declaración f.

propose /prə'pouz/ v. proponer; pensar; declararse.

proposition /ˌprɒpə'zɪʃən/ n. proposición f.

proprietor /prə'praiitər/ n. propietario -ria, dueño -ña.

propriety /prə'praiiti/ n. corrección f., decoro m.

prosaic /prou'zeiik/ a. prosaico.

proscribe /prou'skraib/ v. proscribir.

prose /prouz/ n. prosa f.

prosecute /'prɒsɪˌkyut/ v. acusar, procesar.

prospect /'prɒspɛkt/ n. perspectiva; esperanza f.

prospective /prə'spɛktɪv/ a. anticipado, presunto.

prosper /'prɒspər/ v. prosperar.

prosperity /prɒ'spɛriti/ n. prosperidad f.

prosperous /'prɒspərəs/ a. próspero.

prostate gland /'prɒsteit/ glándula prostática f.

prostitute /'prɒstɪˌtut/ n. 1. prostituta f. —v. 2. prostituir.

prostrate /'prɒstreit/ a. 1. postrado. —v. 2. postrar.

protect /prə'tɛkt/ v. proteger; amparar.

protection /prə'tɛkʃən/ n. protección f.; amparo m.

protective /prə'tɛktɪv/ a. protector.

protector /prə'tɛktər/ n. protector -ora.

protégé /'prouteˌʒei/ n. protegido -da.

protein /'proutin, -tiin/ n. proteína f.

protest /n. 'proutɛst; v. prə'tɛst, 'proutɛst/ n. 1. protesta f. —v. 2. protestar.

Protestant /'prɒtəstənt/ a. & n. protestante m. & f.

protocol /'proutəˌkɔl/ n. protocolo m.

proton /'proutɒn/ n. protón m.

protract /prou'trækt/ v. alargar, demorar.

protrude /prou'trud/ v. salir fuera.

protuberance /prou'tubərəns/ n. protuberancia f.

proud /praud/ a. orgulloso.

prove /pruv/ v. comprobar.

proverb /'prɒvərb/ n. proverbio, refrán m.

provide /prə'vaid/ v. proporcionar; proveer.

provided /prə'vaidid/ conj. con tal que.

providence /'prɒvɪdəns/ n. providencia f.

province /'prɒvɪns/ n. provincia f.

provincial /prə'vɪnʃəl/ a. 1. provincial. —n. 2. provinciano -na.

provision /prə'vɪʒən/ n. 1. provisión f.; (pl.) comestibles m.pl. —v. 2. abastecer.

provocation /ˌprɒvə'keiʃən/ n. provocación f.

provoke /prə'vouk/ v. provocar.

prowess /'prauis/ n. proeza f.

prowl /praul/ v. rondar.

prowler /'praulər/ n. merodeador -dora m. & f.

proximity /prɒk'sɪmiti/ n. proximidad f.

proxy /'prɒksi/ n. delegado -da. **by p.,** mediante apoderado.

prudence /'prudns/ n. prudencia f.

prudent /'prudnt/ a. prudente, cauteloso.

prune /prun/ n. ciruela pasa f.

pry /prai/ v. atisbar; curiosear; Mech. alzaprimar.

psalm /sɑm/ n. salmo m.

pseudonym /'sudnɪm/ n. seudónimo m.

psychedelic /ˌsaiki'dɛlɪk/ a. psiquedélico.

psychiatrist /sɪ'kaiətrɪst, sai-/ n. psiquiatra m. & f.

psychiatry /sɪ'kaiətri, sai-/ n. psiquiatría f.

psychoanalysis /ˌsaikouə'næləsɪs/ n. psicoanálisis m.

psychoanalyst /ˌsaikou'ænlɪst/ n. psicoanalista m. & f.

psychological /ˌsaikə'lɒdʒɪkəl/ a. psicológico.

psychology /sai'kɒlədʒi/ n. psicología f.

psychosis /sai'kousɪs/ n. psicosis f.

ptomaine /'toumein/ n. tomaína f.

pub /pʌb/ n. bar m.

public /'pʌblɪk/ a. & n. público m.

publication /ˌpʌblɪ'keiʃən/ n. publicación; revista f.

publicity /pʌ'blisiti/ n. publicidad f.

publicity agent publicista m. & f.

publish /'pʌblɪʃ/ v. publicar.

publisher /'pʌblɪʃər/ n. editor -ora.

pudding /'pudɪŋ/ n. pudín m.

puddle /'pʌdl/ n. charco, lodazal m.

Puerto Rican /'pwɛrtə 'rikən, 'pɔr-/ a. & n. puertorriqueño -ña.

Puerto Rico /'pwɛrtə rikou, 'pɔrtə/ Puerto Rico m.

puff /pʌf/ n. 1. soplo m.; (of smoke) bocanada f. **powder p.,** polvera f. —v. 2. jadear; echar bocanadas. **p. up,** hinchar; Fig. engreír.

pugnacious /pʌg'neiʃəs/ a. pugnaz.

puh-lease! /pʌ 'liz/ ¡Favor!

pull /pul/ n. 1. tirón m.; Colloq. influencia f. —v. 2. tirar; halar.

pulley /'puli/ n. polea f., motón m.

pulmonary /'pʌlmə,nɛri/ a. pulmonar.

pulp /pʌlp/ n. pulpa; (of fruit) carne f.

pulpit /'pulpɪt, 'pʌl-/ n. púlpito m.

pulsar /'pʌlsɑr/ n. pulsar m.

pulsate /'pʌlseit/ v. pulsar.

pulse /pʌls/ n. pulso m.

pump /pʌmp/ n. 1. bomba f. —v. 2. bombear. **p. up,** inflar.

pumpkin /'pʌmpkɪn/ n. calabaza f.

pun /pʌn/ n. juego de palabras.

punch /pʌntʃ/ n. 1. puñetazo; Mech. punzón; (beverage) ponche m. —v. 2. dar puñetazos; punzar.

punch bowl ponchera f.

punctual /'pʌŋktʃuəl/ a. puntual.

punctuate /'pʌŋktʃu,eit/ v. puntuar.

puncture /'pʌŋktʃər/ n. 1. pinchazo m., perforación f. —v. 2. pinchar, perforar.

pungent /'pʌndʒənt/ a. picante, pungente.

punish /'pʌnɪʃ/ v. castigar.

punishment /'pʌnɪʃmənt/ n. castigo m.

punitive /'pyunɪtɪv/ a. punitivo.

puny /'pyuni/ a. encanijado.

pupil /'pyupəl/ n. alumno -na; Anat. pupila f.

puppet /'pʌpɪt/ n. muñeco m.

puppy /'pʌpi/ n. perrito -ta.

purchase /'pʌrtʃəs/ n. 1. compra f. —v. 2. comprar.

purchasing power /'pʌrtʃəsɪŋ/ poder adquisitivo m.

pure /pyur/ a. puro.

purée /pyu'rei/ n. puré m.

purge /pʌrdʒ/ v. purgar.

purify /'pyurə,fai/ v. purificar.

puritanical /ˌpyurɪ'tænɪkəl/ a. puritano.

purity /'pyuriti/ n. pureza f.

purple /'pʌrpəl/ a. 1. purpúreo. —n. 2. púrpura f.

purport /n. 'pʌrpɔrt; v. pər'pɔrt/ n. 1. significación f. —v. 2. significar.

purpose /'pʌrpəs/ n. propósito m. **on p.,** de propósito.

purr /pʌr/ v. ronronear.

purse /pʌrs/ n. bolsa f.

pursue /pər'su/ v. perseguir.

pursuit /pər'sut/ n. caza; busca; ocupación f. **p. plane,** avión de caza m.

push /puʃ/ n. 1. empuje; impulso m. —v. 2. empujar.

put /put/ v. poner, colocar. **p. away,** guardar. **p. in,** meter. **p. off,** dejar. **p. on,** ponerse. **p. out,** apagar. **p. up with,** aguantar.

putrid /'pyutrɪd/ a. podrido.

putt /pʌt/ n. (golf) golpe corto m.

puzzle /'pʌzəl/ n. 1. enigma; rompecabezas m. —v. 2. dejar perplejo. **p. out,** descifrar.

pyramid /'pɪrəmɪd/ n. pirámide f.

pyromania /ˌpairə'meiniə/ n. piromanía f.

Q

quack /kwæk/ n. 1. (doctor) curandero -ra; (duck) graznido m. —v. 2. graznar.

quadrangle /'kwɒd,ræŋgəl/ n. cuadrángulo m.

quadraphonic /ˌkwɒdrə'fɒnɪk/ a. cuatrifónico.

quadruped /'kwɒdru,pɛd/ a. & n. cuadrúpedo m.

quail /kweil/ n. 1. codorniz f. —v. 2. descorazonarse.

quaint /kweint/ a. curioso.

quake /kweik/ n. 1. temblor m. —v. 2. temblar.

qualification /ˌkwɒləfɪ'keiʃən/ n. requisito m.; (pl.) preparaciones f.pl.

qualified /'kwɒlə,faid/ a. calificado, competente; preparado.

qualify /'kwɒlə,fai/ v. calificar, modificar; llenar los requisitos.

quality /'kwɒliti/ n. calidad f.

quandary /'kwɒndəri, -dri/ n. incertidumbre f.

quantity /'kwɒntiti/ n. cantidad f.

quarantine /'kwɒrən,tin, 'kwɔr-, ,kwɒrən'tin, ,kwɔr-/ n. cuarentena f.

quarrel /'kwɔrəl, 'kwɒr-/ n. 1. riña, disputa f. —v. 2. reñir, disputar.

quarry /'kwɔri, 'kwɒri/ n. cantera; (hunting) presa f.

quarter /'kwɔrtər/ n. cuarto m.; (pl.) vivienda f.

quarterly /'kwɔrtərli/ a. 1. trimestral. —adv. 2. por cuartos.

quartet /kwɔr'tɛt/ n. cuarteto m.

quartz /kwɔrts/ n. cuarzo m.

quasar /'kweizɑr/ n. cuasar m.

quaver /'kweivər/ v. temblar.

queen /kwin/ n. reina f.; (chess) dama f.

queer /kwɪər/ a. extraño, raro.

quell /kwɛl/ v. reprimir.

quench /kwɛntʃ/ v. apagar.

query /'kwɪəri/ n. 1. pregunta f. —v. 2. preguntar.

quest /kwɛst/ n. busca f.

question /'kwɛstʃən/ n. 1. pregunta; cuestión f. **q. mark,** signo de interrogación. —v. 2. preguntar; interrogar; dudar.

questionable /'kwɛstʃənəbəl/ a. dudoso.

questionnaire /ˌkwɛstʃə'nɛər/ n. cuestionario m.

quiche /kiʃ/ n. quiche f.

quick /kwɪk/ a. rápido.

quicken /'kwɪkən/ v. acelerar.

quicksand /'kwɪk,sænd/ n. arena movediza.

quiet /'kwaiit/ a. 1. quieto, tranquilo; callado. **be q., keep q.,** callarse. —n. 2. calma; quietud f. —v. 3. tranquilizar. **q. down,** callarse; calmarse.

quilt /kwɪlt/ n. colcha f.

quinine /'kwainain/ n. quinina f.

quintet /kwɪn'tɛt/ n. Mus. quinteto m.

quip /kwɪp/ n. 1. pulla f. —v. 2. echar pullas.

quit /kwɪt/ v. dejar; renunciar a. **q. doing** (etc.) dejar de hacer (etc.).

quite /kwait/ adv. bastante; completamente. **not q.,** no precisamente; no completamente.

quiver /'kwɪvər/ n. 1. aljaba f.; temblor m. —v. 2. temblar.

quixotic /kwɪk'sɒtɪk/ a. quijotesco.

quorum /'kwɔrəm/ n. quórum m.

quota /'kwoutə/ n. cuota f.

quotation /kwou'teiʃən/ n. citación; Com. cotización f. **q. marks,** comillas f.pl.

quote /kwout/ v. citar; Com. cotizar.

R

rabbi /'ræbai/ n. rabí, rabino m.

rabbit /'ræbɪt/ n. conejo m.

rabble /'ræbəl/ n. canalla f.

rabid /'ræbɪd/ a. rabioso.

rabies /'reibiz/ n. hidrofobia f.

race /reis/ n. 1. raza; carrera f. —v. 2. echar una carrera; correr de prisa.

race track /'reis,træk/ hipódromo m.

rack /ræk/ n. 1. (cooking) pesebre m.; (clothing) colgador m. —v. 2. atormentar.

racket /'rækɪt/ n. (noise) ruido m.; (tennis) raqueta f.; (graft) fraude organizado.

radar /'reidɑr/ n. radar m.

radiance /'reidiəns/ n. brillo m.

radiant /'reidiənt/ a. radiante.

radiate /'reidi,eit/ v. irradiar.

radiation /ˌreidi'eiʃən/ n. irradiación f.

radiator /'reidi,eitər/ n. calorífero m.; Auto. radiador m.

radical /'rædɪkəl/ a. & n. radical m.

radio /'reidi,ou/ n. radio m. or f. **r. station,** estación radiodifusora f.

radioactive /ˌreidiou'æktɪv/ a. radioactivo.

radio cassette radiocasete m.

radish /'rædɪʃ/ n. rábano m.

radium /'reidiəm/ n. radio m.

radius /'reidiəs/ n. radio m.

raffle /'ræfəl/ n. 1. rifa, lotería f. —v. 2. rifar.

raft /ræft/ n. balsa f.

rafter /'ræftər/ n. viga f.

rag /ræg/ n. trapo m.

ragamuffin /'rægə,mʌfɪn/ n. galopín m.

rage /reidʒ/ n. 1. rabia f. —v. 2. rabiar.

ragged /'rægɪd/ a. andrajoso; desigual.

raid /reid/ n. Mil. correría f.

rail /reil/ n. baranda f.; carril m. **by r.,** por ferrocarril.

railroad /'reil,roud/ n. ferrocarril m.

rain /rein/ n. 1. lluvia f. —v. 2. llover.

rainbow /'rein,bou/ n. arco iris m.

raincoat /'rein,kout/ n. impermeable m.; gabardina f.

rainfall /'rein,fɔl/ n. precipitación f.

rainy /'reini/ a. lluvioso.

raise /reiz/ n. 1. aumento m. —v. 2. levantar, alzar; criar.

raisin /'reizɪn/ n. pasa f.

rake /reik/ n. 1. rastro m. —v. 2. rastrillar.

rally /'ræli/ n. 1. reunión f. —v. 2. reunirse.

ram /ræm/ n. carnero m.

ramble /'ræmbəl/ v. vagar.

ramp /ræmp/ n. rampa f.

rampart /'ræmpart/ n. terraplén m.

ranch /ræntʃ/ n. rancho m.

rancid /'rænsɪd/ a. rancio.

rancor /'ræŋkər/ n. rencor m.

random /'rændəm/ a. fortuito. **at r.,** a la ventura.

range /reindʒ/ n. 1. extensión f.; alcance m.; estufa; sierra f.; terreno de pasto. —v. 2. recorrer; extenderse.

rank /ræŋk/ n. 1. espeso; rancio. —n. 2. fila f.; grado m. —v. 3. clasificar.

ransack /'rænsæk/ v. saquear.

ransom /'rænsəm/ n. 1. rescate m. —v. 2. rescatar.

rap /ræp/ n. 1. golpecito m. —v. 2. golpear.

rapid /'ræpɪd/ a. rápido.

rapist /ˈreipɪst/ *n.* violador -dora *m. & f.*

rapport /ræˈpɔr/ *n.* armonía *f.*

rapture /ˈræptʃər/ *n.* éxtasis *m.*

rare /rɛər/ *a.* raro; (of food) a medio cocer.

rascal /ˈræskəl/ *n.* pícaro, bribón *m.*

rash /ræʃ/ *a.* **1.** temerario. —*n.* **2.** erupción *f.*

raspberry /ˈræzˌbɛri/ *n.* frambuesa *f.*

rat /ræt/ *n.* rata *f.*

rate /reit/ *n.* **1.** velocidad; tasa *f.*; precio *m.*; (of exchange; of interest) tipo *m.* **at any r.,** de todos modos. —*v.* **2.** valuar.

rather /ˈræðər/ *adv.* bastante; más bien, mejor dicho.

ratify /ˈrætəˌfai/ *v.* ratificar.

ratio /ˈreiʃou/ *n.* razón; proporción *f.*

ration /ˈræʃən, ˈreiʃən/ *n.* **1.** ración *f.* —*v.* **2.** racionar.

rational /ˈræʃənl/ *a.* racional.

rattle /ˈrætl/ *n.* **1.** ruido *m.*; matraca *f.* **r. snake,** culebra de cascabel, serpiente de cascabel *f.* —*v.* **2.** matraquear; rechinar.

raucous /ˈrɔkəs/ *a.* ronco.

ravage /ˈrævɪdʒ/ *v.* pillar; destruir; asolar.

rave /reiv/ *v.* delirar; entusiasmarse.

ravel /ˈrævəl/ *v.* deshilar.

raven /ˈreivən/ *n.* cuervo *m.*

ravenous /ˈrævənəs/ *a.* voraz.

raw /rɔ/ *a.* crudo; verde.

ray /rei/ *n.* rayo *m.*

rayon /ˈreiɒn/ *n.* rayón *m.*

razor /ˈreizər/ *n.* navaja de afeitar. **r. blade,** hoja de afeitar.

reach /ritʃ/ *n.* **1.** alcance *m.* —*v.* **2.** alcanzar.

react /riˈækt/ *v.* reaccionar.

reaction /riˈækʃən/ *n.* reacción *f.*

reactionary /riˈækʃəˌnɛri/ *a.* **1.** reaccionario. —*n.* **2.** *Pol.* retrógrado *m.*

read /rid/ *v.* leer.

reader /ˈridər/ *n.* lector -ra; libro de lectura *m.*

readily /ˈrɛdli/ *adv.* fácilmente.

reading /ˈridɪŋ/ *n.* lectura *f.*

ready /ˈrɛdi/ *a.* listo, preparado; dispuesto.

ready-cooked /ˈrɛdi ˌkʊkt/ *a.* precocinado.

real /reiˈɑl/ *a.* verdadero; real.

real estate bienes inmuebles, *m.pl.*

real-estate agent /ˈriəl ɪˈsteit/ agente inmobiliario *m.*, agente inmobiliaria *f.*

realist /ˈriəlɪst/ *n.* realista *m. & f.*

realistic /ˌriəˈlɪstɪk/ *a.* realista.

reality /riˈælɪti/ *n.* realidad *f.*

realization /ˌriələˈzeiʃən/ *n.* comprensión; realización *f.*

realize /ˈriəˌlaiz/ *v.* darse cuenta de; realizar.

really /ˈriəli/ *adv.* de veras; en realidad.

realm /rɛlm/ *n.* reino; dominio *m.*

reap /rip/ *v.* segar, cosechar.

rear /rɪər/ *a.* **1.** posterior. —*n.* **2.** parte posterior. —*v.* **3.** criar; levantar.

reason /ˈrizən/ *n.* **1.** razón; causa *f.*; motivo *m.* —*v.* **2.** razonar.

reasonable /ˈrizənəbəl/ *a.* razonable.

reassure /ˌriəˈʃʊr/ *v.* calmar, tranquilizar.

rebate /ˈribeit/ *n.* rebaja *f.*

rebel /*n.* ˈrɛbəl; *v.* rɪˈbɛl/ *n.* **1.** rebelde *m. & f.* —*v.* **2.** rebelarse.

rebellion /rɪˈbɛlyən/ *n.* rebelión *f.*

rebellious /rɪˈbɛlyəs/ *a.* rebelde.

rebirth /riˈbɜrθ/ *n.* renacimiento *m.*

rebound /rɪˈbaund/ *v.* repercutir; resaltar.

rebuff /rɪˈbʌf/ *n.* **1.** repulsa *f.* —*v.* **2.** rechazar.

rebuke /rɪˈbyuk/ *n.* **1.** reprensión *f.* —*v.* **2.** reprender.

rebuttal /rɪˈbʌtl/ *n.* refutación *f.*

recalcitrant /rɪˈkælsɪtrənt/ *a.* recalcitrante.

recall /rɪˈkɔl/ *v.* recordar; acordarse de; hacer volver.

recapitulate /ˌrikəˈpɪtʃəˌleit/ *v.* recapitular.

recede /rɪˈsid/ *v.* retroceder.

receipt /rɪˈsit/ *n.* recibo *m.*; (com., pl.) ingresos *m.pl.*

receive /rɪˈsiv/ *v.* recibir.

receiver /rɪˈsivər/ *n.* receptor *m.*

recent /ˈrisənt/ *a.* reciente.

recently /ˈrisəntli/ *adv.* recién.

receptacle /rɪˈsɛptəkəl/ *n.* receptáculo *m.*

reception /rɪˈsɛpʃən/ *n.* acogida; recepción *f.*

receptionist /rɪˈsɛpʃənɪst/ *n.* recepcionista *m. & f.*

receptive /rɪˈsɛptɪv/ *a.* receptivo.

recess /rɪˈsɛs, ˈrisɛs/ *n.* nicho; retiro; recreo *m.*

recipe /ˈrɛsəpi/ *n.* receta *f.*

recipient /rɪˈsɪpiənt/ *n.* recibidor -ra, recipiente *m. & f.*

reciprocate /rɪˈsɪprəˌkeit/ *v.* corresponder; reciprocar.

recite /rɪˈsait/ *v.* recitar.

reckless /ˈrɛklɪs/ *a.* descuidado; imprudente.

reckon /ˈrɛkən/ *v.* contar; calcular.

reclaim /rɪˈkleim/ *v.* reformar; *Leg.* reclamar.

recline /rɪˈklain/ *v.* reclinar; recostar.

recognition /ˌrɛkəgˈnɪʃən/ *n.* reconocimiento *m.*

recognize /ˈrɛkəgˌnaiz/ *v.* reconocer.

recoil /*n.* ˈriˌkɔil; *v.* rɪˈkɔil/ *n.* **1.** culatada *f.* —*v.* **2.** recular.

recollect /ˌrɛkəˈlɛkt/ *v.* recordar, acordarse de.

recommend /ˌrɛkəˈmɛnd/ *v.* recomendar.

recommendation /ˌrɛkəmɛnˈdeiʃən/ *n.* recomendación *f.*

recompense /ˈrɛkəmˌpɛns/ *n.* **1.** recompensa *f.* —*v.* **2.** recompensar.

reconcile /ˈrɛkənˌsail/ *v.* reconciliar.

recondition /ˌrikənˈdɪʃən/ *v.* reacondicionar.

reconsider /ˌrikənˈsɪdər/ *v.* considerar de nuevo.

reconstruct /ˌrikənˈstrʌkt/ *v.* reconstruir.

record /*n.* ˈrɛkərd, *v.* rɪˈkɔrd/ *n.* **1.** registro; (sports) record *m.* **phonograph r.,** disco *m.* —*v.* **2.** registrar.

record player tocadiscos *m.*

recount /rɪˈkaunt/ *v.* relatar; contar.

recover /rɪˈkʌvər/ *v.* recobrar; restablecerse.

recovery /rɪˈkʌvəri/ *n.* recobro *m.*; recuperación *f.*

recruit /rɪˈkrut/ *n.* **1.** recluta *m.* —*v.* **2.** reclutar.

rectangle /ˈrɛkˌtæŋgəl/ *n.* rectángulo *m.*

rectify /ˈrɛktəˌfai/ *v.* rectificar.

recuperate /rɪˈkupəˌreit/ *v.* recuperar.

recur /rɪˈkɜr/ *v.* recurrir.

recycle /riˈsaikəl/ *v.* reciclar.

red /rɛd/ *a.* rojo, colorado.

redeem /rɪˈdim/ *v.* redimir, rescatar.

redemption /rɪˈdɛmpʃən/ *n.* redención *f.*

redhead /ˈrɛdˌhɛd/ *n.* pelirrojo -ja.

red mullet /ˈmʌlɪt/ salmonete *m.*

reduce /rɪˈdus/ *v.* reducir.

reduction /rɪˈdʌkʃən/ *n.* reducción *f.*

reed /rid/ *n.* caña *f.*, *S.A.* bejuco *m.*

reef /rif/ *n.* arrecife, escollo *m.*

reel /ril/ *n.* **1.** aspa *f.*, carrete *m.* —*v.* **2.** aspar.

refer /rɪˈfɜr/ *v.* referir.

referee /ˌrɛfəˈri/ *n.* árbitro *m. & f.*

reference /ˈrɛfərəns/ *n.* referencia *f.*

refill /*n.* ˈriˌfɪl; *v.* riˈfɪl/ *n.* **1.** relleno *m.* —*v.* **2.** rellenar.

refine /rɪˈfain/ *v.* refinar.

refinement /rɪˈfainmənt/ *n.* refinamiento *m.*; cultura *f.*

reflect /rɪˈflɛkt/ *v.* reflejar; reflexionar.

reflection /rɪˈflɛkʃən/ *n.* reflejo *m.*; reflexión *f.*

reflex /ˈriflɛks/ *a.* reflejo.

reform /rɪˈfɔrm/ *n.* **1.** reforma *f.* —*v.* **2.** reformar.

reformation /ˌrɛfərˈmeiʃən/ *n.* reformación *f.*

refractory /rɪˈfræktəri/ *a.* refractario.

refrain /rɪˈfrein/ *n.* **1.** estribillo *m.* —*v.* **2.** abstenerse.

refresh /rɪˈfrɛʃ/ *v.* refrescar.

refreshment /rɪˈfrɛʃmənt/ *n.* refresco *m.*

refrigerator /rɪˈfrɪdʒəˌreitər/ *n.* refrigerador *m.*

refuge /ˈrɛfyudʒ/ *n.* refugio *m.*

refugee /ˌrɛfyʊˈdʒi/ *n.* refugiado -da.

refund /*n* ˈrifʌnd; *v* riˈfʌnd/ *n.* **1.** reembolso *m.* —*v.* **2.** reembolsar.

refusal /rɪˈfyuzəl/ *n.* negativa *f.*

refuse /*n* ˈrɛfyus; *v* rɪˈfyuz/ *n.* **1.** basura *f.* —*v.* **2.** negarse, rehusar.

refute /rɪˈfyut/ *v.* refutar.

regain /riˈgein/ *v.* recobrar. **r. consciousness,** recobrar el conocimiento.

regal /ˈrigəl/ *a.* real.

regard /rɪˈgɑrd/ *n.* **1.** aprecio; respeto *m.* **with r. to,** con respecto a. —*v.* **2.** considerar; estimar.

regarding /rɪˈgɑrdɪŋ/ *prep.* en cuanto a, acerca de.

regardless (of) /rɪˈgɑrdlɪs/ a pesar de.

regent /ˈridʒənt/ *n.* regente *m. & f.*

regime /rəˈʒim, rei-/ *n.* régimen *m.*

regiment /*n.* ˈrɛdʒəmənt; *v.* -ˌmɛnt/ *n.* **1.** regimiento *m.* —*v.* **2.** regimentar.

region /ˈridʒən/ *n.* región *f.*

register /ˈrɛdʒəstər/ *n.* **1.** registro *m.* **cash r.,** caja registradora *f.* —*v.* **2.** registrar; matricularse; (a letter) certificar.

registration /ˌrɛdʒəˈstreiʃən/ *n.* registro *m.*; matrícula *f.*

regret /rɪˈgrɛt/ *n.* **1.** pena *f.* —*v.* **2.** sentir, lamentar.

regular /ˈrɛgyələr/ *a.* regular; ordinario.

regularity /ˌrɛgyəˈlærɪti/ *n.* regularidad *f.*

regulate /ˈrɛgyəˌleit/ *v.* regular.

regulation /ˌrɛgyəˈleiʃən/ *n.* regulación *f.*

regulator /ˈrɛgyəˌleitər/ *n.* regulador *m.*

rehabilitate /ˌrihəˈbɪlɪˌteit, ˌriə-/ *v.* rehabilitar.

rehearse /rɪˈhɜrs/ *v.* repasar; *Theat.* ensayar.

reheat /riˈhit/ *v.* recalentar.

reign /rein/ *n.* **1.** reino, reinado *m.* —*v.* **2.** reinar.

reimburse /ˌriɪmˈbɜrs/ *v.* reembolsar.

rein /rein/ *n.* **1.** rienda *f.* —*v.* **2.** refrenar.

reincarnation /ˌriɪnkɑrˈneiʃən/ *n.* reencarnación *f.*

reindeer /ˈreinˌdɪər/ *n.* reno *m.*

reinforce /ˌriɪnˈfɔrs, -ˈfours/ *v.* reforzar.

reinforcement /ˌriɪnˈfɔrsmənt, -ˈfours-/ *n.* refuerzo *m.*; armadura *f.*

reiterate /riˈɪtəˌreit/ *v.* reiterar.

reject /rɪˈdʒɛkt/ *v.* rechazar.

rejoice /rɪˈdʒɔis/ *v.* regocijarse.

rejoin /rɪˈdʒɔin/ *v.* reunirse con; replicar.

rejuvenate /rɪˈdʒuvəˌneit/ *v.* rejuvenecer.

relapse /*v.* rɪˈlæps; *n. also* ˈrilæps/ *v.* **1.** recaer. —*n.* **2.** recaída *f.*

relate /rɪˈleit/ *v.* relatar, contar; relacionar. **r. to,** llevarse bien con.

relation /rɪˈleiʃən/ *n.* relación *f.*; pariente *m. & f.*

relative /ˈrɛlətɪv/ *a.* **1.** relativo. —*n.* **2.** pariente *m. & f.*

relativity /ˌrɛləˈtɪvɪti/ *n.* relatividad *f.*

relax /rɪˈlæks/ *v.* descansar; relajar.

relay /ˈrilei; *v. also* rɪˈlei/ *n.* **1.** relevo *m.* —*v.* **2.** retransmitir.

release /rɪˈlis/ *n.* **1.** liberación *f.* —*v.* **2.** soltar.

relent /rɪˈlɛnt/ *v.* ceder.

relevant /ˈrɛləvənt/ *a.* pertinente.

reliability /rɪˌlaiəˈbɪlɪti/ *n.* veracidad *f.*

reliable /rɪˈlaiəbəl/ *a.* responsable; digno de confianza.

relic /ˈrɛlɪk/ *n.* reliquia *f.*

relief /rɪˈlif/ *n.* alivio; (sculpture) relieve *m.*

relieve /rɪˈliv/ *v.* aliviar.

religion /rɪˈlɪdʒən/ *n.* religión *f.*

religious /rɪˈlɪdʒəs/ *a.* religioso.

relinquish /rɪˈlɪŋkwɪʃ/ *v.* abandonar.

relish /ˈrɛlɪʃ/ *n.* **1.** sabor; condimento *m.* —*v.* **2.** saborear.

reluctant /rɪˈlʌktənt/ *a.* renuente.

rely /rɪˈlai/ *v.* **r. on,** confiar en; contar con; depender de.

remain /rɪˈmein/ *n.* **1.** (pl.) restos *m.pl.* —*v.* **2.** quedar, permanecer.

remainder /rɪˈmeindər/ *n.* resto *m.*

remark /rɪˈmɑrk/ *n.* **1.** observación *f.* —*v.* **2.** observar.

remarkable /rɪˈmɑrkəbəl/ *a.* notable.

remedial /rɪˈmidiəl/ *a.* reparador.

remedy /ˈrɛmɪdi/ *n.* **1.** remedio *m.* —*v.* **2.** remediar.

remember /rɪˈmɛmbər/ *v.* acordarse de, recordar.

remembrance /rɪˈmɛmbrəns/ *n.* recuerdo *m.*

remind /rɪˈmaind/ *v.* **r. of,** recordar.

reminisce /ˌrɛməˈnɪs/ *v.* pensar en o hablar de cosas pasadas.

remiss /rɪˈmɪs/ *a.* remiso; flojo.

remit /rɪˈmɪt/ *v.* remitir.

remorse /rɪˈmɔrs/ *n.* remordimiento *m.*

remote /rɪˈmout/ *a.* remoto.

remote control mando a distancia *m.*

removal /rɪˈmuvəl/ *n.* alejamiento *m.*; eliminación *f.*

remove /rɪˈmuv/ *v.* quitar; remover.

renaissance /ˌrɛnəˈsɑns/ *n.* renacimiento *m.*

rend /rɛnd/ *v.* hacer pedazos; separar.

render /ˈrɛndər/ *v.* dar; rendir; *Theat.* interpretar.

rendezvous /ˈrɑndəˌvu, -dei-/ *n.* cita *f.*

rendition /rɛnˈdɪʃən/ *n.* interpretación, rendición *f.*

renege /rɪˈnɪg, -ˈnɛg/ *v.* renunciar; faltar a su palabra, no cumplir una promesa.

renew /rɪˈnu, -ˈnyu/ *v.* renovar.

renewal /rɪˈnuəl, -ˈnyu-/ *n.* renovación; *Com.* prórroga *f.*

renounce /rɪˈnauns/ *v.* renunciar a.

renovate /ˈrɛnəˌveit/ *v.* renovar.

renown /rɪˈnaun/ *n.* renombre *m.*, fama *f.*

rent /rɛnt/ *n.* **1.** alquiler *m.* —*v.* **2.** arrendar, alquilar.

repair /rɪˈpɛər/ *n.* **1.** reparo *m.* —*v.* **2.** reparar.

repairman /rɪˈpɛərˌmæn/ *n.* técnico *m.*

repatriate /riˈpeitriˌeit/ *v.* repatriar.

repay /rɪˈpei/ *v.* pagar; devolver.

repeat /rɪˈpit/ *v.* repetir.

repel /rɪˈpɛl/ *v.* repeler, repulsar.

repent /ˈripənt, rɪˈpɛnt/ *v.* arrepentirse.

repentance /rɪˈpɛntns, -ˈpɛntəns/ *n.* arrepentimiento *m.*

repercussion /ˌripərˈkʌʃən, ˌrɛpər-/ *n.* repercusión *f.*

repertoire /ˈrɛpərˌtwɑr/ *n.* repertorio *m.*

repetition /ˌrɛpɪˈtɪʃən/ *n.* repetición *f.*

replace /rɪˈpleis/ *v.* reemplazar.

replenish /rɪˈplɛnɪʃ/ *v.* rellenar; surtir de nuevo.

reply /rɪˈplai/ *n.* **1.** respuesta *f.* —*v.* **2.** replicar; contestar.

report /rɪˈpɔrt, -ˈpourt/ *n.* **1.** informe *m.* —*v.* **2.** informar, contar; denunciar; presentarse.

reporter /rɪˈpɔrtər, -ˈpour-/ *n.* repórter *m. & f.*, reportero -ra.

repose /rɪˈpouz/ *n.* **1.** reposo *m.* —*v.* **2.** reposar; reclinar.

reprehensible /ˌrɛprɪˈhɛnsəbəl/ *a.* reprensible.
represent /ˌrɛprɪˈzɛnt/ *v.* representar.
representation /ˌrɛprɪzɛnˈteiʃən, -zən-/ *n.* representación *f.*
representative /ˌrɛprɪˈzɛntətɪv/ *a.* **1.** representativo. —*n.* **2.** representante *m.* & *f.*
repress /rɪˈprɛs/ *v.* reprimir.
reprimand /ˈrɛprəˌmænd, -ˌmɑnd/ *n.* **1.** regaño *m.* —*v.* **2.** regañar.
reprisal /rɪˈpraizəl/ *n.* represalia *f.*
reproach /rɪˈproutʃ/ *n.* **1.** reproche *m.* —*v.* **2.** reprochar.
reproduce /ˌriprəˈdus, -ˈdyus/ *v.* reproducir.
reproduction /ˌriprəˈdʌkʃən/ *n.* reproducción *f.*
reproof /rɪˈpruf/ *n.* censura *f.*
reprove /rɪˈpruv/ *v.* censurar, regañar.
reptile /ˈrɛptɪl, -tail/ *n.* reptil *m.*
republic /rɪˈpʌblɪk/ *n.* república *f.*
republican /rɪˈpʌblɪkən/ *a.* & *n.* republicano -na.
repudiate /rɪˈpyudiˌeit/ *v.* repudiar.
repulsive /rɪˈpʌlsɪv/ *a.* repulsivo, repugnante.
reputation /ˌrɛpyəˈteiʃən/ *n.* reputación; fama *f.*
repute /rɪˈpyut/ *n.* **1.** reputación *f.* —*v.* **2.** reputar.
request /rɪˈkwɛst/ *n.* **1.** súplica *f.*, ruego *m.* —*v.* **2.** pedir; rogar, suplicar.
require /rɪˈkwaiᵊr/ *v.* requerir; exigir.
requirement /rɪˈkwaiᵊrmənt/ *n.* requisito *m.*
requisite /ˈrɛkwəzɪt/ *a.* **1.** necesario. —*n.* **2.** requisito *m.*
requisition /ˌrɛkwəˈzɪʃən/ *n.* requisición *f.*
rescind /rɪˈsɪnd/ *v.* rescindir, anular.
rescue /ˈrɛskyu/ *n.* **1.** rescate *m.* —*v.* **2.** rescatar.
research /rɪˈsɜrtʃ, ˈrisɜrtʃ/ *n.* investigación *f.*
researcher /rɪˈsɜrtʃər/ *n.* investigador -dora.
resemble /rɪˈzɛmbəl/ *v.* parecerse a, asemejarse a.
resent /rɪˈzɛnt/ *v.* resentirse de.
reservation /ˌrɛzərˈveiʃən/ *n.* reservación *f.*
reserve /rɪˈzɜrv/ *n.* **1.** reserva *f.* —*v.* **2.** reservar.
reservoir /ˈrɛzərˌvwɑr, -ˌvwɔr, -ˌvɔr, ˈrɛzə-/ *n* depósito; tanque *m.*
reside /rɪˈzaid/ *v.* residir, morar.
residence /ˈrɛzɪdəns/ *n.* residencia, morada *f.*
resident /ˈrɛzɪdənt/ *n.* residente *m.* & *f.*
residue /ˈrɛzɪˌdu/ *n.* residuo *m.*
resign /rɪˈzain/ *v.* dimitir; resignar.
resignation /ˌrɛzɪgˈneiʃən/ *n.* dimisión; resignación *f.*
resist /rɪˈzɪst/ *v.* resistir.
resistance /rɪˈzɪstəns/ *n.* resistencia *f.*
resolute /ˈrɛzəˌlut/ *a.* resuelto.
resolution /ˌrɛzəˈluʃən/ *n.* resolución *f.*
resolve /rɪˈzɒlv/ *v.* resolver.
resonant /ˈrɛzənənt/ *a.* resonante.
resort /rɪˈzɔrt/ *n.* **1.** recurso; expediente *m.* **summer r.,** lugar de veraneo. —*v.* **2.** acudir, recurrir.
resound /rɪˈzaund/ *v.* resonar.
resource /ˈrisɔrs/ *n.* recurso *m.*
respect /rɪˈspɛkt/ *n.* **1.** respeto *m.* **with r. to,** con respecto a. —*v.* **2.** respetar.
respectable /rɪˈspɛktəbəl/ *a.* respetable.
respectful /rɪˈspɛktfəl/ *a.* respetuoso.
respective /rɪˈspɛktɪv/ *a.* respectivo.
respiration /ˌrɛspəˈreiʃən/ *n.* respiración *f.*
respite /ˈrɛspɪt/ *n.* pausa, tregua *f.*
respond /rɪˈspɒnd/ *v.* responder.
response /rɪˈspɒns/ *n.* respuesta *f.*
responsibility /rɪˌspɒnsəˈbɪlɪti/ *n.* responsabilidad *f.*
responsible /rɪˈspɒnsəbəl/ *a.* responsable.
responsive /rɪˈspɒnsɪv/ *a.* sensible a.
rest /rɛst/ *n.* **1.** descanso; reposo *m.*; (music) pausa *f.* **the r.,** el resto, lo demás; los demás. —*v.* **2.** descansar; recostar.
restaurant /ˈrɛstərənt, -təˌrɑnt, -trɑnt/ *n.* restaurante *m.*
restful /ˈrɛstfəl/ *a.* tranquilo.
restitution /ˌrɛstɪˈtuʃən, -ˈtyu-/ *n.* -restitución *f.*
restless /ˈrɛstlɪs/ *a.* inquieto.
restoration /ˌrɛstəˈreiʃən/ *n.* restauración *f.*
restore /rɪˈstɔr, -ˈstour/ *v.* restaurar.
restrain /rɪˈstrein/ *v.* refrenar.
restraint. /rɪˈstreint/ *n.* limitación, restricción *f.*
restrict /rɪˈstrɪkt/ *v.* restringir, limitar.
rest room aseos *m.pl.*
result /rɪˈzʌlt/ *n.* **1.** resultado *m.* —*v.* **2.** resultar.
resume /rɪˈzum/ *v.* reasumir; empezar de nuevo.
résumé /ˈrɛzʊˌmei/ *n.* resumen *m.*
resurgent /rɪˈsɜrdʒənt/ *a.* resurgente.
resurrect /ˌrɛzəˈrɛkt/ *v.* resucitar.
resuscitate /rɪˈsʌsɪˌteit/ *v.* resucitar.
retail /ˈriteil/ *n.* **at r.,** al por menor.
retain /rɪˈtein/ *v.* retener.
retaliate /rɪˈtæliˌeit/ *v.* vengarse.
retard /rɪˈtɑrd/ *v.* retardar.
retention /rɪˈtɛnʃən/ *n.* retención *f.*
reticent /ˈrɛtəsənt/ *a.* reticente.
retire /rɪˈtaiᵊr/ *v.* retirar.
retirement /rɪˈtaiᵊrmənt/ *n.* jubilación *f.*
retort /rɪˈtɔrt/ *n.* **1.** réplica; *Chem.* retorta *f.* —*v.* **2.** replicar.
retreat /rɪˈtrit/ *n.* **1.** retiro *m.*; *Mil.* retirada, retreta *f.* —*v.* **2.** retirarse.
retribution /ˌrɛtrəˈbyuʃən/ *n.* retribución *f.*
retrieve /rɪˈtriv/ *v.* recobrar.
return /rɪˈtɜrn/ *n.* **1.** vuelta *f.*, regreso; retorno *m.* **by r. mail,** a vuelta de correo. —*v.* **2.** volver, regresar; devolver.
reunion /riˈyunyən/ *n.* reunión *f.*
rev /rɛv/ *n.* **1.** revolución *f.* —*v.* **2.** (motor) acelerar.
reveal /rɪˈvil/ *v.* revelar.
revelation /ˌrɛvəˈleiʃən/ *n.* revelación *f.*
revenge /rɪˈvɛndʒ/ *n.* venganza *f.* **to get r.,** vengarse.
revenue /ˈrɛvənˌyu, -əˌnu/ *n.* renta *f.*
revere /rɪˈvɪər/ *v.* reverenciar, venerar.
reverence /ˈrɛvərəns, ˈrɛvrəns/ *n.* **1.** reverencia *f.* —*v.* **2.** reverenciar.
reverend /ˈrɛvərənd, ˈrɛvrənd/ *a.* **1.** reverendo. —*n.* **2.** pastor *m.*
reverent /ˈrɛvərənt, ˈrɛvrənt/ *a.* reverente.
reverse /rɪˈvɜrs/ *a.* **1.** inverso. —*n.* **2.** revés, inverso *m.* —*v.* **3.** invertir; revocar.
revert /rɪˈvɜrt/ *v.* revertir.
review /rɪˈvyu/ *n.* **1.** repaso *m.*; revista *f.* —*v.* **2.** repasar; *Mil.* revistar.
revise /rɪˈvaiz/ *v.* revisar.
revision /rɪˈvɪʒən/ *n.* revisión *f.*
revival /rɪˈvaivəl/ *n.* reavivamiento *m.*
revive /rɪˈvaiv/ *v.* avivar; revivir, resucitar.
revoke /rɪˈvouk/ *v.* revocar.
revolt /rɪˈvoult/ *n.* **1.** rebelión *f.* —*v.* **2.** rebelarse.
revolting /rɪˈvoultɪŋ/ *a.* repugnante.
revolution /ˌrɛvəˈluʃən/ *n.* revolución *f.*
revolutionary /ˌrɛvəˈluʃəˌnɛri/ *a.* & *n.* revolucionario -ria.
revolve /rɪˈvɒlv/ *v.* girar; dar vueltas.
revolver /rɪˈvɒlvər/ *n.* revólver *m.*
revolving door /rɪˈvɒlvɪŋ/ puerta giratoria *f.*
reward /rɪˈwɔrd/ *n.* **1.** pago *m.*; recompensa *f.* —*v.* **2.** recompensar.
rhetoric /ˈrɛtərɪk/ *n.* retórica *f.*
rheumatism /ˈruməˌtɪzəm/ *n.* reumatismo *m.*
rhinoceros /raiˈnɒsərəs/ *n.* rinoceronte *m.*
rhubarb /ˈrubɑrb/ *n.* ruibarbo *m.*
rhyme /raim/ *n.* **1.** rima *f.* —*v.* **2.** rimar.
rhythm /ˈrɪðəm/ *n.* ritmo *m.*
rhythmical /ˈrɪðmɪkəl/ *a.* rítmico.
rib /rɪb/ *n.* costilla *f.*
ribbon /ˈrɪbən/ *n.* cinta *f.*
rib cage caja torácica *f.*
rice /rais/ *n.* arroz *m.*
rich /rɪtʃ/ *a.* rico.
rid /rɪd/ *v.* librar. **get r. of,** deshacerse de, quitarse.
riddle /ˈrɪdl/ *n.* enigma; rompecabezas *m.*
ride /raid/ *n.* **1.** paseo (a caballo, en coche, etc.) *m.* —*v.* **2.** cabalgar; ir en coche.
ridge /rɪdʒ/ *n.* cerro *m.*; arruga *f.*; (of a roof) caballete *m.*
ridicule /ˈrɪdɪˌkyul/ *n.* **1.** ridículo *m.* —*v.* **2.** ridiculizar.
ridiculous /rɪˈdɪkyələs/ *a.* ridículo.
riding /ˈraidɪŋ/ *n.* equitación *f.*
riding school picadero *m.*
rifle /ˈraifəl/ *n.* **1.** fusil *m.* —*v.* **2.** robar.
rig /rɪg/ *n.* **1.** aparejo *m.* —*v.* **2.** aparejar.
right /rait/ *a.* **1.** derecho; correcto. **to be r.,** tener razón. —*adv.* **2.** bien, correctamente. **r. here,** etc., aquí mismo, etc. **all r.,** está bien, muy bien. —*n.* **3.** derecho *m.*; justicia *f.* **to the r.,** a la derecha. —*v.* **4.** corregir; enderezar.
righteous /ˈraitʃəs/ *a.* justo.
rigid /ˈrɪdʒɪd/ *a.* rígido.
rigor /ˈrɪgər/ *n.* rigor *m.*
rigorous /ˈrɪgərəs/ *a.* riguroso.
rim /rɪm/ *n.* margen *m. or f.*; borde *m.*
ring /rɪŋ/ *n.* **1.** anillo *m.*; sortija *f.*; círculo; campaneo *m.* —*v.* **2.** cercar; sonar; tocar.
ring finger dedo anular *m.*
rinse /rɪns/ *v.* enjuagar, lavar.
riot /ˈraiət/ *n.* motín; alboroto *m.*
rip /rɪp/ *n.* **1.** rasgadura *f.* —*v.* **2.** rasgar; desgarrar.
ripe /raip/ *a.* maduro.
ripen /ˈraipən/ *v.* madurar.
ripoff /ˈrɪpˌɔf/ *n.* robo, atraco *m.*
ripple /ˈrɪpəl/ *n.* **1.** onda *f.* —*v.* **2.** ondear.
rise /raiz/ *n.* **1.** subida *f.* —*v.* **2.** ascender; levantarse; (moon) salir.
risk /rɪsk/ *n.* **1.** riesgo *m.* —*v.* **2.** arriesgar.
rite /rait/ *n.* rito *m.*
ritual /ˈrɪtʃuəl/ *a.* & *n.* ritual *m.*
rival /ˈraivəl/ *n.* rival *m.* & *f.*
rivalry /ˈraivəlri/ *n.* rivalidad *f.*
river /ˈrɪvər/ *n.* río *m.*
rivet /ˈrɪvɪt/ *n.* **1.** remache, roblón *m.* —*v.* **2.** remachar, roblar.
road /roud/ *n.* camino *m.*; carretera *f.*
roadside /ˈroudˌsaid/ *n.* borde de la carretera *m.*
roam /roum/ *v.* vagar.
roar /rɔr, rour/ *n.* **1.** rugido, bramido *m.* —*v.* **2.** rugir, bramar.
roast /roust/ *n.* **1.** asado *m.* —*v.* **2.** asar.
rob /rɒb/ *v.* robar.
robber /ˈrɒbər/ *n.* ladrón -na.
robbery /ˈrɒbəri/ *n.* robo *m.*
robe /roub/ *n.* manto *m.*
robin /ˈrɒbɪn/ *n.* petirrojo *m.*
robust /rouˈbʌst, ˈroubʌst/ *a.* robusto.
rock /rɒk/ *n.* **1.** roca, peña *f.*; (music) rock *m.*, música (de) rock *f.* —*v.* **2.** mecer; oscilar.
rocker /ˈrɒkər/ *n.* mecedora *f.*
rocket /ˈrɒkɪt/ *n.* cohete *m.*
rocking chair /ˈrɒkɪŋ/ mecedora *f.*
Rock of Gibraltar /dʒɪˈbrɔltər/ Peñón de Gibraltar *m.*
rocky /ˈrɒki/ *a.* pedregoso.
rod /rɒd/ *n.* varilla *f.*
rodent /ˈroudnt/ *n.* roedor *m.*
rogue /roug/ *n.* bribón, pícaro *m.*
roguish /ˈrougɪʃ/ *a.* pícaro.
role /roul/ *n.* papel *m.*
roll /roul/ **1.** rollo *m.*; lista *f.*; panecillo *m.* **to call the r.,** pasar lista. —*v.* **2.** rodar. **r. up,** enrollar. **r. up one's sleeves,** arremangarse.
roller /ˈroulər/ *n.* rodillo, cilindro *m.*
roller skate patín de ruedas *m.*
Roman /ˈroumən/ *a.* & *n.* romano -na.
romance /rouˈmæns, ˈroumæns/ *a.* **1.** románico. —*n.* **2.** romance *m.*; amorío *m.*
romantic /rouˈmæntɪk/ *a.* romántico.
romp /rɒmp/ *v.* retozar; jugar.
roof /ruf, rʊf/ *n.* **1.** techo *m.*; —*v.* **2.** techar.
room /rum, rʊm/ *n.* **1.** cuarto *m.*, habitación *f.*; lugar *m.* —*v.* **2.** alojarse.
roommate /ˈrumˌmeit, ˈrʊm-/ *n.* compañero -ra de cuarto.
rooster /ˈrustər/ *n.* gallo *m.*
root /rut/ *n.* raíz *f.* **to take r.,** arraigar.
rootless /ˈrutlɪs/ *a.* desarraigado.
rope /roup/ *n.* cuerda, soga *f.*
rose /rouz/ *n.* rosa *f.*
rosy /ˈrouzi/ *a.* róseo, rosado.
rot /rɒt/ *n.* **1.** putrefacción *f.* —*v.* **2.** pudrirse.
rotary /ˈroutəri/ *a.* giratorio; rotativo.
rotate /ˈrouteit/ *v.* girar; alternar.
rotation /rouˈteiʃən/ *n.* rotación *f.*
rotten /ˈrɒtn/ *a.* podrido.
rouge /ruʒ/ *n.* colorete *m.*
rough /rʌf/ *a.* áspero; rudo; grosero; aproximado.
round /raund/ *a.* **1.** redondo. **r. trip,** viaje de ida y vuelta. —*n.* **2.** ronda *f.*; (boxing) asalto *m.*
rouse /rauz/ *v.* despertar.
rout /raut, rut/ *n.* **1.** derrota *f.* —*v.* **2.** derrotar.
route /rut, raut/ *n.* ruta, vía *f.*
routine /ruˈtin/ *a.* **1.** rutinario. —*n.* **2.** rutina *f.*
rove /rouv/ *v.* vagar.
rover /ˈrouvər/ *n.* vagabundo -da.
row /rou/ *n.* **1.** fila *f.* —*v.* **2.** *Naut.* remar.
rowboat /ˈrouˌbout/ *n.* bote de remos.
rowdy /ˈraudi/ *a.* alborotado.
royal /ˈrɔiəl/ *a.* real.
royalty /ˈrɔiəlti/ *n.* realeza *f.*; (pl.) regalías *f.pl.*
rub /rʌb/ *v.* frotar. **r. against,** rozar. **r. out,** borrar.
rubber /ˈrʌbər/ *n.* goma *f.*; caucho *m.*; (pl.) chanclos *m.pl.*, zapatos de goma.
rubbish /ˈrʌbɪʃ/ *n.* basura *f.*; (nonsense) tonterías *f.pl.*
ruby /ˈrubi/ *n.* rubí *m.*
rudder /ˈrʌdər/ *n.* timón *m.*
ruddy /ˈrʌdi/ *a.* colorado.
rude /rud/ *a.* rudo; grosero; descortés.
rudiment /ˈrudəmənt/ *n.* rudimento *m.*
rudimentary /ˌrudəˈmɛntəri, -tri/ *a.* rudimentario.
rue /ru/ *v.* deplorar; lamentar.
ruffian /ˈrʌfiən, ˈrʌfyən/ *n.* rufián, bandolero *m.*
ruffle /ˈrʌfəl/ *n.* **1.** volante fruncido. —*v.* **2.** fruncir; irritar.
rug /rʌg/ *n.* alfombra *f.*
rugged /ˈrʌgɪd/ *a.* áspero; robusto.
ruin /ˈruɪn/ *n.* **1.** ruina *f.* —*v.* **2.** arruinar.
ruinous /ˈruənəs/ *a.* ruinoso.
rule /rul/ *n.* **1.** regla *f.* **as a r.,** por regla general. —*v.* **2.** gobernar; mandar; rayar.
ruler /ˈrulər/ *n.* gobernante *m.* & *f.*; soberano -na; regla *f.*
rum /rʌm/ *n.* ron *m.*
rumble /ˈrʌmbəl/ *v.* retumbar.
rumor /ˈrumər/ *n.* rumor *m.*
rumpus /ˈrʌmpəs/ *n.* lío, jaleo, escándalo *m.*
run /rʌn/ *v.* correr; hacer correr. **r. away,** escaparse. **r. into,** chocar con.

runner /'rʌnər/ n. corredor -ra; mensajero -ra.

runner-up /'rʌnər 'ʌp/ n. subcampeón -ona.

runproof /'rʌnpruf/ a. indesmallable.

rupture /'rʌptʃər/ n. 1. rotura; hernia f. —v. 2. reventar.

rural /'rʊrəl/ a. rural, campestre.

rush /rʌʃ/ n. 1. prisa f.; Bot. junco m. —v. 2. ir de prisa.

rush hour hora punta f.

Russia /'rʌʃə/ n. Rusia f.

Russian /'rʌʃən/ a. & n. ruso -sa.

rust /rʌst/ n. 1. herrumbre f. —v. 2. aherrumbrarse.

rustic /'rʌstɪk/ a. rústico.

rustle /'rʌsəl/ n. 1. susurro m. —v. 2. susurrar.

rusty /'rʌsti/ a. mohoso.

rut /rʌt/ n. surco m.

ruthless /'ruθlɪs/ a. cruel, inhumano.

rye /rai/ n. centeno m.

rye bread pan de centeno m.

S

saber /'seibər/ n. sable m.

sable /'seibəl/ n. cebellina f.

sabotage /'sæbə,taʒ/ n. sabotaje m.

sachet /sæ'ʃei/ n. perfumador m.

sack /sæk/ n. 1. saco m. —v. 2. Mil. saquear.

sacred /'seikrɪd/ a. sagrado, santo.

sacrifice /'sækrə,fais/ n. 1. sacrificio m. —v. 2. sacrificar.

sacrilege /'sækrəlɪdʒ/ n. sacrilegio m.

sad /sæd/ a. triste.

saddle /'sædl/ n. 1. silla de montar. —v. 2. ensillar.

sadness /'sædnɪs/ n. tristeza f.

safe /seif/ a. 1. seguro; salvo. —n. 2. caja de caudales.

safeguard /'seif,gard/ n. 1. salvaguardia m. —v. 2. proteger, poner a salvo.

safety /'seifti/ n. seguridad, protección f.

safety belt cinturón de seguridad m.

safety pin imperdible m.

safety valve /vælv/ válvula de seguridad f.

sage /seidʒ/ a. 1. sabio, sagaz. —n. 2. sabio m.; Bot. salvia f.

sail /seil/ n. 1. vela f.; paseo por mar. —v. 2. navegar; embarcarse.

sailboat /'seil,bout/ n. barco de vela.

sailor /'seilər/ n. marinero m.

saint /seint/ n. santo -ta.

sake /seik/ n. **for the s. of,** por; por el bien de.

salad /'sæləd/ n. ensalada f. **s. bowl,** ensaladera f.

salad dressing aliño m.

salary /'sæləri/ n. sueldo, salario m.

sale /seil/ n. venta f.

salesman /'seilzmən/ n. vendedor m.; viajante de comercio.

sales tax /seilz/ impuesto sobre la venta.

saliva /sə'laivə/ n. saliva f.

salmon /'sæmən/ n. salmón m.

salt /sɔlt/ n. 1. salado. —n. 2. sal f. —v. 3. salar.

salute /sə'lut/ n. 1. saludo m. —v. 2. saludar.

salvage /'sælvɪdʒ/ v. salvar, recobrar.

salvation /sæl'veiʃən/ n. salvación f.

salve /sæv/ n. emplasto, ungüento m.

same /seim/ a. & pron. mismo. **it's all the s.,** lo mismo da.

sample /'sæmpəl/ n. 1. muestra f. —v. 2. probar.

sanatorium /,sænə'tɔriəm/ n. sanatorio m.

sanctify /'sæŋktə,fai/ v. santificar.

sanction /'sæŋkʃən/ n. 1. sanción f. —v. 2. sancionar.

sanctity /'sæŋktɪti/ n. santidad f.

sanctuary /'sæŋktʃu,eri/ n. santuario, asilo m.

sand /sænd/ n. arena f.

sandal /'sændl/ n. sandalia f.

sandpaper /'sænd,peipər/ n. papel de lija m.

sandwich /'sændwɪtʃ, 'sæn-/ n. emparedado, sándwich m.

sandy /'sændi/ a. arenoso; (color) rufo.

sane /sein/ a. cuerdo; sano.

sanitary /'sæni,teri/ a. higiénico, sanitario. **s. napkin,** toalla sanitaria.

sanitation /,sæni'teiʃən/ n. saneamiento m.

sanity /'sæniti/ n. cordura f.

Santa Claus /'sæntə klɔz/ Papá Noel m.

sap /sæp/ n. 1. savia f.; Colloq. estúpido, bobo m. —v. 2. agotar.

sapphire /'sæfaiər/ n. zafiro m.

sarcasm /'sarkæzəm/ n. sarcasmo m.

sardine /sar'din/ n. sardina f.

sash /sæʃ/ n. cinta f.

satellite /'sætl,ait/ n. satélite m.

satellite dish antena parabólica f.

satin /'sætn/ n. raso m.

satire /'sætaiər/ n. sátira f.

satisfaction /,sætis'fækʃən/ n. satisfacción; recompensa f.

satisfactory /,sætis'fæktəri/ a. satisfactorio.

satisfy /'sætis,fai/ v. satisfacer. **be satisfied that...,** estar convencido de que.

saturate /'sætʃə,reit/ v. saturar.

Saturday /'sætər,dei/ n. sábado m.

sauce /sɔs/ n. salsa; compota f.

saucer /'sɔsər/ n. platillo m.

saucy /'sɔsi/ a. descarado, insolente.

sauna /'sɔnə/ n. sauna f.

sausage /'sɔsidʒ/ n. salchicha f.

savage /'sævidʒ/ a. & n. salvaje m. & f.

save /seiv/ v. 1. salvar; guardar; ahorrar, economizar. —prep. 2. salvo, excepto.

savings /'seivɪŋz/ n. ahorros m.pl.

savings account cuenta de ahorros m.

savings bank caja de ahorros f.

savior /'seivyər/ n. salvador -ora.

savor /'seivər/ n. 1. sabor m. —v. 2. saborear.

savory /'seivəri/ a. sabroso.

saw /sɔ/ n. 1. sierra f. —v. 2. aserrar.

saxophone /'sæksə,foun/ n. saxofón, saxófono, m.

say /sei/ v. decir; recitar.

saying /'seiɪŋ/ n. dicho, refrán m.

scaffold /'skæfəld/ n. andamio; (gallows) patíbulo m.

scald /skɔld/ v. escaldar.

scale /skeil/ n. 1. escala; (of fish) escama f.; (pl.) balanza f. —v. 2. escalar; escamar.

scalp /skælp/ n. pericráneo m. v. escalpar.

scan /skæn/ v. hojear, repasar; (poetry) escandir; (computer) escanear, digitalizar.

scandal /'skændl/ n. escándalo m.

scanner /'skænər/ n. escáner m.

scant /skænt/ a. escaso.

scar /skar/ n. cicatriz f.

scarce /skɛərs/ a. escaso; raro.

scarcely /'skɛərsli/ adv. & conj. apenas.

scare /skɛər/ n. 1. susto m. —v. 2. asustar. **s. away,** espantar.

scarf /skarf/ n. pañueleta, bufanda f.

scarlet /'skarlɪt/ n. escarlata f.

scarlet fever escarlatina f.

scatter /'skætər/ v. esparcir; dispersar.

scavenger /'skævɪndʒər/ n. basurero m.

scenario /sɪ'nɛəri,ou, -'nar-/ n. escenario m.

scene /sin/ n. vista f., paisaje m.; Theat. escena f. **behind the scenes,** entre bastidores.

scenery /'sinəri/ n. paisaje m.; Theat. decorado m.

scent /sɛnt/ n. 1. olor, perfume; (sense) olfato m. —v. 2. perfumar; Fig. sospechar.

schedule /'skɛdʒul, -ʊl, -uəl/ n. 1. programa, horario m. —v. 2. fijar la hora para.

scheme /skim/ n. 1. proyecto; esquema m. —v. 2. intrigar.

scholar /'skɒlər/ n. erudito -ta; becado -da.

scholarship /'skɒlər,ʃɪp/ n. beca; erudición f.

school /skul/ n. 1. escuela f.; colegio m.; (of fish) banco m. —v. 2. enseñar.

sciatica /sai'ætɪkə/ n. ciática f.

science /'saiəns/ n. ciencia f.

science fiction ciencia ficción.

scientific /,saiən'tɪfɪk/ a. científico.

scientist /'saiəntɪst/ n. científico -ca.

scissors /'sɪzərz/ n. tijeras f. pl.

scoff /skɔf, skɒf/ v. mofarse, burlarse.

scold /skould/ v. regañar.

scoop /skup/ n. 1. cucharón m.; cucharada f. —v. 2. **s. out,** recoger, sacar.

scope /skoup/ n. alcance; campo m.

score /skɔr/ n. 1. tantos m. pl.; (music) partitura f. —v. 2. marcar, hacer tantos.

scorn /skɔrn/ n. 1. desprecio m. —v. 2. despreciar.

scornful /'skɔrnfəl/ a. desdeñoso.

Scotland /'skɒtlənd/ n. Escocia f.

Scottish /'skɒtɪʃ/ a. escocés.

scour /skauər/ v. fregar, estregar.

scourge /skɜrdʒ/ n. azote m.; plaga f.

scout /skaut/ n. 1. explorador -ra. —v. 2. explorar, reconocer.

scramble /'skræmbəl/ n. 1. rebatiña f. —v. 2. bregar. **scrambled eggs,** huevos revueltos.

scrap /skræp/ n. 1. migaja f.; pedacito m.; Colloq. riña f. **s. metal,** hierro viejo m. **s. paper,** papel borrador. —v. 2. desechar; Colloq. reñir.

scrapbook /'skræp,bʊk/ n. álbum de recortes m.

scrape /skreip/ n. 1. lío, apuro m. —v. 2. raspar; (feet) restregar.

scratch /skrætʃ/ n. 1. rasguño m. —v. 2. rasguñar; rayar.

scream /skrim/ n. 1. grito, chillido m. —v. 2. gritar, chillar.

screen /skrin/ n. biombo m.; (for window) tela metálica; (movie) pantalla f.

screw /skru/ n. 1. tornillo m. —v. 2. atornillar.

screwdriver /'skru,draivər/ n. destornillador m.

scribble /'skrɪbəl/ v. hacer garabatos.

scroll /skroul/ n. rúbrica f.; rollo de papel.

scroll bar n. barra de enrollar f.

scrub /skrʌb/ v. fregar, estregar.

scruple /'skrupəl/ n. escrúpulo m.

scrupulous /'skrupyələs/ a. escrupuloso.

scuba diving /'skubə 'daivɪŋ/ submarinismo m.

sculptor /'skʌlptər/ n. escultor -ra.

sculpture /'skʌlptʃər/ n. 1. escultura f. —v. 2. esculpir.

scythe /saið/ n. guadaña f.

sea /si/ n. mar m. or f.

seabed /'si,bɛd/ n. lecho marino m.

sea breeze brisa marina f.

seafood /'si,fud/ n. mariscos m.pl.

seal /sil/ n. 1. sello m.; (animal) foca f. —v. 2. sellar.

seam /sim/ n. costura f.

seamy /'simi/ a. sórdido.

seaplane /'si,plein/ n. hidroavión m.

seaport /'si,pɔrt/ n. puerto de mar.

search /sɜrtʃ/ n. 1. registro m. **in s. of,** en busca de. —v. 2. registrar. **s. for,** buscar.

search engine motor de búsqueda m., buscador m., indexador de información m.

seasick /'si,sɪk/ a. mareado. **to get s.,** marearse.

season /'sizən/ n. 1. estación; sazón; temporada f. —v. 2. sazonar.

seasoning /'sizənɪŋ/ n. condimento m.

season ticket abono m.

seat /sit/ n. 1. asiento m.; residencia, sede f.; Theat. localidad f. **s. belt,** cinturón de seguridad. —v. 2. sentar. **be seated,** sentarse.

seaweed /'si,wid/ n. alga, alga marina f.

second /'sɛkənd/ a. & n. 1. segundo m. —v. 2. apoyar, segundar.

secondary /'sɛkən,dɛri/ a. secundario.

secret /'sikrɪt/ a. & n. secreto m.

secretary /'sɛkrɪ,tɛri/ n. secretario -ria; Govt. ministro -tra; (furniture) papelera f.

sect /sɛkt/ n. secta f.; partido m.

section /'sɛkʃən/ n. sección, parte f.

sectional /'sɛkʃənl/ a. regional, local.

secular /'sɛkyələr/ a. secular.

secure /sɪ'kyʊr/ a. 1. seguro. —v. 2. asegurar; obtener; Fin. garantizar.

security /sɪ'kyʊriti/ n. seguridad; garantía f.

sedative /'sɛdətɪv/ a. & n. sedativo m.

seduce /sɪ'dus/ v. seducir.

see /si/ v. ver; comprender. **s. off,** despedirse de. **s. to,** encargarse de.

seed /sid/ n. 1. semilla f. —v. 2. sembrar.

seek /sik/ v. buscar. **s. to,** tratar de.

seem /sim/ v. parecer.

seep /sip/ v. colarse.

segment /'sɛgmənt/ n. segmento m.

segregate /'sɛgrɪ,geit/ v. segregar.

seize /siz/ v. agarrar; apoderarse de.

seldom /'sɛldəm/ adv. rara vez.

select /sɪ'lɛkt/ a. 1. escogido, selecto. —v. 2. elegir, seleccionar.

selection /sɪ'lɛkʃən/ n. selección f.

selective /sɪ'lɛktɪv/ a. selectivo.

selfish /'sɛlfɪʃ/ a. egoísta.

selfishness /'sɛlfɪʃnɪs/ n. egoísmo m.

sell /sɛl/ v. vender.

semester /sɪ'mɛstər/ n. semestre m.

semicircle /'sɛmi,sɜrkəl/ n. semicírculo m.

semolina /,sɛmə'linə/ n. sémola f.

senate /'sɛnɪt/ n. senado m.

senator /'sɛnətər/ n. senador -ra.

send /sɛnd/ v. mandar, enviar; (a wire) poner. **s. away,** despedir. **s. back,** devolver. **s. for,** mandar buscar. **s. off,** expedir. **s. word,** mandar recado.

senile /'sinail/ a. senil.

senior /'sinyər/ a. mayor; más viejo. **Sr.,** padre.

senior citizen persona de edad avanzada.

sensation /sɛn'seiʃən/ n. sensación f.

sensational /sɛn'seiʃənl/ a. sensacional.

sense /sɛns/ n. 1. sentido; juicio m. —v. 2. percibir; sospechar.

sensible /'sɛnsəbəl/ a. sensato, razonable.

sensitive /'sɛnsɪtɪv/ a. sensible; sensitivo.

sensual /'sɛnʃuəl/ a. sensual.

sentence /'sɛntns/ n. 1. frase; Gram. oración; Leg. sentencia f. —v. 2. condenar.

sentiment /'sɛntəmənt/ n. sentimiento m.

sentimental /,sɛntə'mɛntl/ a. sentimental.

separate /a. 'sɛpərɪt; v. -,reit/ a. 1. separado; suelto. —v. 2. separar, dividir.

separation /,sɛpə'reiʃən/ n. separación f.

September /sɛp'tɛmbər/ n. septiembre m.

sequence /'sikwəns/ n. serie f. **in s.,** seguidos.

serenade /,sɛrə'neid/ n. 1. serenata f. —v. 2. dar serenata a.

serene /sə'rin/ a. sereno; tranquilo.

sergeant /'sardʒənt/ n. sargento m.

serial /ˈsɪəriəl/ *a.* en serie, de serie.

series /ˈsɪəriz/ *n.* serie *f.*

serious /ˈsɪəriəs/ *a.* serio; grave.

sermon /ˈsɜrmən/ *n.* sermón *m.*

serpent /ˈsɜrpənt/ *n.* serpiente *f.*

servant /ˈsɜrvənt/ *n.* criado -da; servidor -ra.

serve /sɜrv/ *v.* servir.

server /ˈsɜrvər/ *n.* servidor *m.*

service /ˈsɜrvɪs/ *n.* **1.** servicio *m.* **at the s. of,** a las órdenes de. **be of s.,** servir; ser útil. —*v.* **2.** *Auto.* reparar.

service station estación de servicio *f.*

session /ˈsɛʃən/ *n.* sesión *f.*

set /sɛt/ *a.* **1.** fijo. —*n.* **2.** colección *f.;* (of a game) juego; *Mech.* aparato; *Theat.* decorado *m.* —*v.* **3.** poner, colocar; fijar; (sun) ponerse. **s. forth,** exponer. **s. off, s. out,** salir. **s. up,** instalar; establecer.

settle /ˈsɛtl̩/ *v.* solucionar; arreglar; establecerse.

settlement /ˈsɛtl̩mənt/ *n.* caserío; arreglo; acuerdo *m.*

settler /ˈsɛtlər/ *n.* poblador -ra.

seven /ˈsɛvən/ *a.* & *pron.* siete.

seventeen /ˈsɛvənˈtin/ *a.* & *pron.* diecisiete.

seventh /ˈsɛvənθ/ *a.* séptimo.

seventy /ˈsɛvənti/ *a.* & *pron.* setenta.

sever /ˈsɛvər/ *v.* desunir; romper.

several /ˈsɛvərəl/ *a.* & *pron.* varios.

severance pay /ˈsɛvərəns/ indemnización de despido.

severe /səˈvɪər/ *a.* severo; grave.

severity /səˈvɛrɪti/ *n.* severidad *f.*

sew /sou/ *v.* coser.

sewer /ˈsuər/ *n.* cloaca *f.*

sewing /ˈsouɪŋ/ *n.* costura *f.*

sewing basket costurero *m.*

sewing machine máquina de coser *f.*

sex /sɛks/ *n.* sexo *m.*

sexism /ˈsɛksɪzəm/ *n.* sexismo *m.*

sexist /ˈsɛksɪst/ *a.* & *n.* sexista *m.* & *f.*

sexton /ˈsɛkstən/ *n.* sacristán *m.*

sexual /ˈsɛkʃuəl/ *a.* sexual.

shabby /ˈʃæbi/ *a.* haraposo, desaliñado.

shade /ʃeid/ *n.* **1.** sombra *f.;* tinte *m.;* (window) transparente *m.* —*v.* **2.** sombrear.

shadow /ˈʃædou/ *n.* sombra *f.*

shady /ˈʃeidi/ *a.* sombroso; sospechoso.

shaft /ʃæft/ *n.* (columna) fuste; *Mech.* asta *f.*

shake /ʃeik/ *v.* sacudir; agitar; temblar. **s. hands with,** dar la mano a.

shallow /ˈʃælou/ *a.* poco hondo; superficial.

shame /ʃeim/ *n.* **1.** vergüenza *f.* **be a s.,** ser una lástima. —*v.* **2.** avergonzar.

shameful /ˈʃeimfəl/ *a.* vergonzoso.

shampoo /ʃæmˈpu/ *n.* champú *m.*

shape /ʃeip/ *n.* **1.** forma *f.;* estado *m.* —*v.* **2.** formar.

share /ʃɛər/ *n.* **1.** parte; (stock) acción *f.* **2** —*v.* **2.** compartir.

shareholder /ˈʃɛərˌhouldər/ *n.* accionista *m.* & *f.*

shareware /ˈʃɛərˌwɛər/ *n.* programas compartidos *m.pl.*

shark /ʃɑrk/ *n.* tiburón *m.*

sharp /ʃɑrp/ *a.* agudo; (blade) afilado.

sharpen /ˈʃɑrpən/ *v.* aguzar; afilar.

shatter /ˈʃætər/ *v.* estrellar; hacer pedazos.

shave /ʃeiv/ *n.* **1.** afeitada *f.* —*v.* **2.** afeitarse.

shawl /ʃɔl/ *n.* rebozo, chal *m.*

she /ʃi/ *pron.* ella *f.*

sheaf /ʃif/ *n.* gavilla *f.*

shear /ʃɪər/ *v.* cizallar.

shears /ʃɪərz/ *n.* cizallas *f.pl.*

sheath /ʃiθ/ *n.* vaina *f.*

shed /ʃɛd/ *n.* **1.** cobertizo *m.* —*v.* **2.** arrojar, quitarse.

sheep /ʃip/ *n.* oveja *f.*

sheet /ʃit/ *n.* sábana; (of paper) hoja *f.*

shelf /ʃɛlf/ *n.* estante, *m.,* repisa *f.*

shell /ʃɛl/ *n.* **1.** cáscara; (sea) concha *f.;* *Mil.* proyectil *m.* —*v.* **2.** desgranar; bombardear.

shellac /ʃəˈlæk/ *n.* laca *f.*

shelter /ˈʃɛltər/ *n.* **1.** albergue; refugio *m.* —*v.* **2.** albergar; amparar.

shepherd /ˈʃɛpərd/ *n.* pastor *m.*

sherry /ˈʃɛri/ *n.* jerez *m.*

shield /ʃild/ *n.* **1.** escudo *m.* —*v.* **2.** amparar.

shift /ʃɪft/ *n.* **1.** cambio; (work) turno *m.* —*v.* **2.** cambiar, mudar. **s. for oneself,** arreglárselas.

shine /ʃain/ *n.* **1.** brillo, lustre *m.* —*v.* **2.** brillar; (shoes) lustrar.

shiny /ˈʃaini/ *a.* brillante, lustroso.

ship /ʃɪp/ *n.* **1.** barco *m.,* nave *f.* —*v.* **2.** embarcar; *Com.* enviar.

shipment /ˈʃɪpmənt/ *n.* envío; embarque *m.*

shirk /ʃɜrk/ *v.* faltar al deber.

shirt /ʃɜrt/ *n.* camisa *f.*

shiver /ˈʃɪvər/ *n.* **1.** temblor *m.* —*v.* **2.** temblar.

shock /ʃɒk/ *n.* **1.** choque *m.* —*v.* **2.** chocar.

shoe /ʃu/ *n.* zapato *m.*

shoelace /ˈʃuˌleis/ *n.* lazo *m.;* cordón de zapato.

shoemaker /ˈʃuˌmeikər/ *n.* zapatero *m.*

shoot /ʃut/ *v.* tirar; (gun) disparar. **s. away, s. off,** salir disparado.

shop /ʃɒp/ *n.* tienda *f.*

shopping /ˈʃɒpɪŋ/ *n.* **to go s.,** hacer compras, ir de compras.

shop window escaparate *m.*

shore /ʃɔr/ *n.* orilla; playa *f.*

short /ʃɔrt/ *a.* corto; breve; (in stature) pequeño, bajo. **a s. time,** poco tiempo. **in s.,** en suma.

shortage /ˈʃɔrtɪdʒ/ *n.* escasez; falta *f.*

shorten /ˈʃɔrtn̩/ *v.* acortar, abreviar.

shortly /ˈʃɔrtli/ *adv.* en breve, dentro de poco.

shorts /ʃɔrts/ *n.* calzoncillos *m. pl.*

shot /ʃɒt/ *n.* tiro, disparo *m.*

shoulder /ˈʃouldər/ *n.* **1.** hombro *m.* —*v.* **2.** asumir; cargar con.

shoulder blade *n.* omóplato *m.,* paletilla *f.*

shout /ʃaut/ *n.* **1.** grito *m.* —*v.* **2.** gritar.

shove /ʃʌv/ *n.* **1.** empujón *m.* —*v.* **2.** empujar.

shovel /ˈʃʌvəl/ *n.* **1.** pala *f.* —*v.* **2.** traspalar.

show /ʃou/ *n.* **1.** ostentación *f.;* *Theat.* función *f.;* espectáculo *m.* —*v.* **2.** enseñar, mostrar; verse. **s. up,** destacarse; *Colloq.* asomar.

shower /ˈʃauər/ *n.* chubasco *m.;* (bath) ducha *f.* *v.* ducharse.

shrapnel /ˈʃræpnl̩/ *n.* metralla *f.*

shrewd /ʃrud/ *a.* astuto.

shriek /ʃrik/ *n.* **1.** chillido *m.* —*v.* **2.** chillar.

shrill /ʃrɪl/ *a.* chillón, agudo.

shrimp /ʃrɪmp/ *n.* camarón *m.*

shrine /ʃrain/ *n.* santuario *m.*

shrink /ʃrɪŋk/ *v.* encogerse, contraerse. **s. from,** huir de.

shroud /ʃraud/ *n.* **1.** mortaja *f.* —*v.* **2.** *Fig.* ocultar.

shrub /ʃrʌb/ *n.* arbusto *m.*

shudder /ˈʃʌdər/ *n.* **1.** estremecimiento *m.* —*v.* **2.** estremecerse.

shun /ʃʌn/ *v.* evitar, huir de.

shut /ʃʌt/ *v.* cerrar. **s. in,** encerrar. **s. up,** *Colloq.* callarse.

shutter /ˈʃʌtər/ *n.* persiana *f.*

shy /ʃai/ *a.* tímido, vergonzoso.

sick /sɪk/ *a.* enfermo. **s. of,** aburrido de, cansado de.

sickness /ˈsɪknɪs/ *n.* enfermedad *f.*

side /said/ *n.* **1.** lado; partido *m.;* parte *f.;* *Anat.* costado *m.* —*v.* **2. s. with,** ponerse del lado de.

sidewalk /ˈsaidˌwɔk/ *n.* acera, vereda *f.*

siege /sidʒ/ *n.* asedio *m.*

sieve /sɪv/ *n.* cedazo *m.*

sift /sɪft/ *v.* cerner.

sigh /sai/ *n.* **1.** suspiro *m.* —*v.* **2.** suspirar.

sight /sait/ *n.* **1.** vista *f.;* punto de interés *m.* **lose s. of,** perder de vista. —*v.* **2.** divisar.

sign /sain/ *n.* **1.** letrero; señal, seña *f.* —*v.* **2.** firmar. **s. up,** inscribirse.

signal /ˈsɪgnl̩/ *n.* **1.** señal *f.* —*v.* **2.** hacer señales.

signature /ˈsɪgnətʃər/ *n.* firma *f.*

significance /sɪgˈnɪfɪkəns/ *n.* significación *f.*

significant /sɪgˈnɪfɪkənt/ *a.* significativo.

significant other pareja *m.* & *f.*

signify /ˈsɪgnəˌfai/ *v.* significar.

silence /ˈsailəns/ *n.* **1.** silencio *m.* —*v.* **2.** hacer callar.

silent /ˈsailənt/ *a.* silencioso; callado.

silk /sɪlk/ *n.* seda *f.*

silken /ˈsɪlkən/ **silky** *a.* sedoso.

sill /sɪl/ *n.* umbral de puerta *m.,* solera *f.*

silly /ˈsɪli/ *a.* necio, tonto.

silo /ˈsailou/ *n.* silo *m.*

silver /ˈsɪlvər/ *n.* plata *f.*

silver-plated /ˈsɪlvər ˈpleitɪd/ *a.* chapado en plata.

silverware /ˈsɪlvərˌwɛər/ *n.* vajilla de plata *f.*

similar /ˈsɪmələr/ *a.* semejante, parecido.

similarity /ˌsɪməˈlærɪti/ *n.* semejanza *f.*

simple /ˈsɪmpəl/ *a.* sencillo, simple.

simplicity /sɪmˈplɪsɪti/ *n.* sencillez *f.*

simplify /ˈsɪmpləˌfai/ *v.* simplificar.

simulate /ˈsɪmyəˌleit/ *v.* simular.

simultaneous /ˌsaiməlˈteiniəs/ *a.* simultáneo.

sin /sɪn/ *n.* **1.** pecado *m.* —*v.* **2.** pecar.

since /sɪns/ *adv.* **1.** desde entonces. —*prep.* **2.** desde. —*conj.* **3.** desde que; puesto que.

sincere /sɪnˈsɪər/ *a.* sincero.

sincerely /sɪnˈsɪərli/ *adv.* sinceramente.

sincerity /sɪnˈsɛrɪti/ *n.* sinceridad *f.*

sinew /ˈsɪnyu/ *n.* tendón *m.*

sinful /ˈsɪnfəl/ *a.* pecador.

sing /sɪŋ/ *v.* cantar.

singe /sɪndʒ/ *v.* chamuscar.

singer /ˈsɪŋər/ *n.* cantante *m.* & *f.*

single /ˈsɪŋgəl/ *a.* solo; (room) sencillo; (unmarried) soltero. **s. room,** habitación individual.

singular /ˈsɪŋgyələr/ *a.* & *n.* singular *m.*

sinister /ˈsɪnəstər/ *a.* siniestro.

sink /sɪŋk/ *n.* **1.** fregadero *m.* —*v.* **2.** hundir; *Fig.* abatir.

sinner /ˈsɪnər/ *n.* pecador -ra.

sinuous /ˈsɪnyuəs/ *a.* sinuoso.

sinus /ˈsainəs/ *n.* seno *m.*

sip /sɪp/ *n.* **1.** sorbo *m.* —*v.* **2.** sorber.

siphon /ˈsaifən/ *n.* sifón *m.*

sir /sɜr/ *title.* señor.

siren /ˈsairən/ *n.* sirena *f.*

sirloin /ˈsɜrlɔin/ *n.* solomillo *m.*

sisal /ˈsaisəl, ˈsɪsəl/ *n.* henequén *m.*

sister /ˈsɪstər/ *n.* hermana *f.*

sister-in-law /ˈsɪstərɪnˌlɔ/ *n.* cuñada *f.*

sit /sɪt/ *v.* sentarse; posar. **be sitting,** estar sentado. **s. down,** sentarse. **s. up,** incorporarse; quedar levantado.

site /sait/ *n.* sitio, local *m.*

sitting /ˈsɪtɪŋ/ *n.* sesión *f.* *a.* sentado.

situate /ˈsɪtʃuˌeit/ *v.* situar.

situation /ˌsɪtʃuˈeiʃən/ *n.* situación *f.*

sit-up /ˈsɪt ˌʌp/ *n.* abdominal *m.*

six /sɪks/ *a.* & *pron.* seis.

sixteen /ˈsɪksˈtin/ *a.* & *pron.* dieciséis.

sixth /sɪksθ/ *a.* sexto.

sixty /ˈsɪksti/ *a.* & *pron.* sesenta.

size /saiz/ *n.* tamaño; (of shoe, etc.) número *m.;* talla *f.*

sizing /ˈsaizɪŋ/ *n.* upreso *m.;* sisa, cola de retazo *f.*

skate /skeit/ *n.* **1.** patín *m.* —*v.* **2.** patinar.

skateboard /ˈskeitˌbɔrd/ *n.* monopatín *m.*

skein /skein/ *n.* madeja *f.*

skeleton /ˈskɛlɪtn̩/ *n.* esqueleto *m.*

skeptic /ˈskɛptɪk/ *n.* escéptico -ca.

skeptical /ˈskɛptɪkəl/ *a.* escéptico.

sketch /skɛtʃ/ *n.* **1.** esbozo *m.* —*v.* **2.** esbozar.

ski /ski/ *n.* **1.** esquí *m.* —*v.* **2.** esquiar.

skid /skɪd/ *v.* **1.** resbalar. —*n.* **2.** varadera *f.*

skill /skɪl/ *n.* destreza, habilidad *f.*

skillful /ˈskɪlfəl/ *a.* diestro, hábil.

skim /skɪm/ *v.* rasar; (milk) desnatar. **s. over, s. through,** hojear.

skin /skɪn/ *n.* **1.** piel; (of fruit) corteza *f.* —*v.* **2.** desollar.

skin doctor dermatólogo -ga *m.* & *f.*

skip /skɪp/ *n.* **1.** brinco *m.* —*v.* **2.** brincar. **s. over,** pasar por alto.

skirmish /ˈskɜrmɪʃ/ *n.* escaramuza *f.*

skirt /skɜrt/ *n.* falda *f.*

skull /skʌl/ *n.* cráneo *m.*

skunk /skʌŋk/ *n.* zorrillo *m.*

sky /skai/ *n.* cielo *m.*

skylight /ˈskaiˌlait/ *n.* tragaluz *m.*

skyscraper /ˈskaiˌskreipər/ *n.* rascacielos *m.*

slab /slæb/ *n.* tabla *f.*

slack /slæk/ *a.* flojo; descuidado.

slacken /ˈslækən/ *v.* relajar.

slacks /slæks/ *n.* pantalones flojos.

slam /slæm/ *n.* **1.** portazo *m.* —*v.* **2.** cerrar de golpe. **slamming on the brakes,** frenazo *m.*

slander /ˈslændər/ *n.* **1.** calumnia *f.* —*v.* **2.** calumniar.

slang /slæŋ/ *n.* jerga *f.*

slant /slænt/ *n.* **1.** sesgo *m.* —*v.* **2.** sesgar.

slap /slæp/ *n.* **1.** bofetada, palmada *f.* —*v.* **2.** dar una bofetada.

slash /slæʃ/ *n.* **1.** cuchillada *f.* —*v.* **2.** acuchillar.

slat /slæt/ *n.* **1.** tablilla *f.* —*v.* **2.** lanzar.

slate /sleit/ *n.* **1.** pizarra *f.;* lista de candidatos. —*n.* **2.** destinar.

slaughter /ˈslɔtər/ *n.* **1.** matanza *f.* —*v.* **2.** matar.

slave /sleiv/ *n.* esclavo -va.

slavery /ˈsleivəri/ *n.* esclavitud *f.*

Slavic /ˈslɑvɪk/ *a.* eslavo.

slay /slei/ *v.* matar, asesinar.

sled /slɛd/ *n.* trineo *m.*

sleek /slik/ *a.* liso y brillante.

sleep /slip/ *n.* **1.** sueño *m.* **to get much s.,** dormir mucho. —*v.* **2.** dormir.

sleeping car /ˈslipɪŋ/ coche cama.

sleeping pill /ˈslipɪŋ/ pastilla para dormir, somnífero *m.*

sleepy /ˈslipi/ *a.* soñoliento. **to be s.,** tener sueño.

sleet /slit/ *n.* **1.** cellisca *f.* —*v.* **2.** cellisquear.

sleeve /sliv/ *n.* manga *f.*

slender /ˈslɛndər/ *a.* delgado.

slice /slais/ *n.* **1.** rebanada; (of meat) tajada *f.* —*v.* **2.** rebanar; tajar.

slide /slaid/ *v.* resbalar, deslizarse.

slide rule regla de cálculo *f.*

slight /slait/ *n.* **1.** desaire *m.* —*a.* **2.** pequeño; leve. —*v.* **3.** desairar.

slim /slɪm/ *a.* delgado.

slime /slaim/ *n.* lama *f.*

sling /slɪŋ/ *n.* **1.** honda *f.;* *Med.* cabestrillo *m.* —*v.* **2.** tirar.

slink /slɪŋk/ *v.* escabullirse.

slip /slɪp/ *n.* **1.** imprudencia; (garment) combinación *f.;* (of paper) trozo *m.;* ficha *f.* —*v.* **2.** resbalar; deslizar. **s. up,** equivocarse.

slipper /ˈslɪpər/ *n.* chinela *f.*

slippery /ˈslɪpəri/ *a.* resbaloso.

slit /slɪt/ *n.* **1.** abertura *f.* —*v.* **2.** cortar.

slogan /ˈslougən/ *n.* lema *m.*

slope /sloup/ *n.* **1.** declive *m.* —*v.* **2.** inclinarse.

sloppy /ˈslɒpi/ *a.* desaliñado, chapucero.

slot /slɒt/ *n.* ranura *f.*

slot machine tragaperras *f.*
slouch /slautʃ/ *n.* **1.** patán *m.* —*v.* **2.** estar gacho.
slovenly /'slʌvənli/ *a.* desaliñado.
slow /slou/ *a.* **1.** lento; (watch) atrasado. —*v.* **2. s. down, s. up,** retardar; ir más despacio.
slowly /'slouli/ *adv.* despacio.
slowness /'slounɪs/ *n.* lentitud *f.*
sluggish /'slʌgɪʃ/ *a.* perezoso, inactivo.
slum /slʌm/ *n.* barrio bajo *m.*
slumber /'slʌmbər/ *v.* dormitar.
slur /slɜr/ *n.* **1.** estigma *m.* —*v.* **2.** menospreciar.
slush /slʌʃ/ *n.* fango *m.*
sly /slai/ *a.* taimado. **on the s.** a hurtadillas.
smack /smæk/ *n.* **1.** manotada *f.* —*v.* **2.** manotear.
small /smɔl/ *a.* pequeño.
small letter minúscula *f.*
smallpox /'smɔl,pɒks/ *n.* viruela *f.*
smart /smɑrt/ *a.* **1.** listo; elegante. —*v.* **2.** escocer.
smash /smæʃ/ *v.* aplastar; hacer pedazos.
smear /smɪər/ *n.* **1.** mancha; difamación *f.* —*v.* **2.** manchar; difamar.
smell /smɛl/ *n.* **1.** olor; (sense) olfato *m.* —*v.* **2.** oler.
smelt /smɛlt/ *n.* **1.** eperlano *m.* —*v.* **2.** fundir.
smile /smail/ *n.* **1.** sonrisa *f.* —*v.* **2.** sonreír.
smite /smait/ *v.* afligir; apenar.
smock /smɒk/ *n.* camisa de mujer *f.*
smoke /smouk/ *n.* **1.** humo *m.* —*v.* **2.** fumar; (food) ahumar.
smokestack /'smouk,stæk/ *n.* chimenea *f.*
smolder /'smouldər/ *v.* arder sin llama.
smooth /smuð/ *a.* **1.** liso; suave; tranquilo. —*v.* **2.** alisar.
smother /'smʌðər/ *v.* sofocar.
smug /smʌg/ *a.* presumido.
smuggle /'smʌgəl/ *v.* pasar de contrabando.
snack /snæk/ *n.* bocadillo *m.*
snag /snæg/ *n.* nudo; obstáculo *m.*
snail /sneil/ *n.* caracol *m.*
snake /sneik/ *n.* culebra, serpiente *f.*
snap /snæp/ *n.* **1.** trueno *m.* —*v.* **2.** tronar; romper.
snapshot /'snæp,ʃɒt/ *n.* instantánea *f.*
snare /snɛər/ *n.* trampa *f.*
snarl /snɑrl/ *n.* **1.** gruñido *m.* —*v.* **2.** gruñir; (hair) enredar.
snatch /snætʃ/ *v.* arrebatar.
sneak /snik/ *v.* ir, entrar, salir (etc.) a hurtadillas.
sneaker /'snikər/ *n.* sujeto ruín *m.* zapatilla de tenis.
sneer /snɪər/ *n.* **1.** mofa *f.* —*v.* **2.** mofarse.
sneeze /sniz/ *n.* **1.** estornudo *m.* —*v.* **2.** estornudar.
snicker /'snɪkər/ *n.* risita *f.*
snob /snɒb/ *n.* esnob *m.*
snore /snɔr/ *n.* **1.** ronquido *m.* —*v.* **2.** roncar.
snow /snou/ *n.* **1.** nieve *f.* —*v.* **2.** nevar.
snowball /'snou,bɔl/ *n.* bola de nieve *f.*
snowdrift /'snou,drift/ *n.* ventisquero *m.*
snowplow /'snou,plau/ *n.* quitanieves *m.*
snowstorm /'snou,stɔrm/ *n.* nevasca *f.*
snub /snʌb/ *v.* desairar.
snug /snʌg/ *a.* abrigado y cómodo.
so /sou/ *adv.* **1.** así; (also) también. **so as to,** para. **so that,** para que. **so... as,** tan... como. **so... that,** tan... que. —*conj.* **2.** así es que.
soak /souk/ *v.* empapar.
soap /soup/ *n.* **1.** jabón *m.* —*v.* **2.** enjabonar.
soap powder jabón en polvo *m.*
soar /sɔr/ *v.* remontarse.

sob /sɒb/ *n.* **1.** sollozo *m.* —*v.* **2.** sollozar.
sober /'soubər/ *a.* sobrio; pensativo.
sociable /'souʃəbəl/ *a.* sociable.
social /'souʃəl/ *a.* **1.** social. —*n.* **2.** tertulia *f.*
socialism /'souʃə,lɪzəm/ *n.* socialismo *m.*
socialist /'souʃəlɪst/ *a. & n.* socialista *m. & f.*
society /sə'saiɪti/ *n.* sociedad; compañía *f.*
sociological /,sousiə'lɒdʒɪkəl/ *a.* sociológico.
sociologist /,sousi,ɒlədʒɪst/ *n.* sociólogo -ga *m. & f.*
sociology /,sousi'ɒlədʒi/ *n.* sociología *f.*
sock /sɒk/ *n.* **1.** calcetín; puñetazo *m.* —*v.* **2.** dar un puñetazo a.
socket /'sɒkɪt/ *n.* cuenca *f.; Elec.* enchufe *m.*
sod /sɒd/ *n.* césped *m.*
soda /'soudə/ *n.* soda; *Chem.* sosa *f.*
sodium /'soudiəm/ *n.* sodio *m.*
sofa /'soufə/ *n.* sofá *m.*
soft /sɔft/ *a.* blando; fino; suave.
soft drink bebida no alcohólica.
soften /'sɔfən/ *v.* ablandar; suavizar.
software /'sɔft,wɛər/ *n.* software *m.;* programa *m.*
soil /sɔil/ *n.* **1.** suelo *m.* —*v.* **2.** ensuciar.
sojourn /'soudʒɜrn/ *n.* morada *f.,* estancia *f.*
solace /'sɒlɪs/ *n.* **1.** solaz *m.* —*v.* **2.** solazar.
solar /'soulər/ *a.* solar.
solar system sistema solar *m.*
solder /'sɒdər/ *v.* **1.** soldar. —*n.* **2.** soldadura *f.*
soldier /'souldʒər/ *n.* soldado *m. & f.*
sole /soul/ *n.* **1.** suela; (of foot) planta *f.;* (fish) lenguado *m.* —*a.* **2.** único.
solemn /'sɒləm/ *a.* solemne.
solemnity /sə'lɛmnɪti/ *n.* solemnidad *f.*
solicit /sə'lɪsɪt/ *v.* solicitar.
solicitous /sə'lɪsɪtəs/ *a.* solícito.
solid /'sɒlɪd/ *a. & n.* sólido *m.*
solidify /sə'lɪdə,fai/ *v.* solidificar.
solidity /sə'lɪdɪti/ *n.* solidez *f.*
solitary /'sɒlɪ,tɛri/ *a.* solitario.
solitude /'sɒlɪ,tud/ *n.* soledad *f.*
solo /'soulou/ *n.* solo *m.*
soloist /'soulouɪst/ *n.* solista *m. & f.*
soluble /'sɒlyəbəl/ *a.* soluble.
solution /sə'luʃən/ *n.* solución *f.*
solve /sɒlv/ *v.* solucionar; resolver.
solvent /'sɒlvənt/ *a.* solvente.
somber /'sɒmbər/ *a.* sombrío.
some /sʌm; *unstressed* səm/ *a. & pron.* algo (de), un poco (de); alguno; (pl.) algunos, unos.
somebody, someone /'sʌmbɒdi, 'sʌm,wʌn/ *pron.* alguien.
somehow /'sʌm,hau/ *adv.* de algún modo.
someone /'sʌm,wʌn/ *n.* alguien o alguno.
somersault /'sʌmər,sɔlt/ *n.* salto mortal *m.*
something /'sʌm,θɪŋ/ *pron.* algo, alguna cosa.
sometime /'sʌm,taim/ *adv.* alguna vez.
sometimes /'sʌm,taimz/ *adv.* a veces, algunas veces.
somewhat /'sʌm,wʌt/ *adv.* algo, un poco.
somewhere /'sʌm,wɛər/ *adv.* en (*or* a) alguna parte.
son /sʌn/ *n.* hijo *m.*
song /sɔŋ/ *n.* canción *f.*
son-in-law /'sʌn ɪn ,lɔ/ *n.* yerno *m.*
soon /sun/ *adv.* pronto. **as s. as possible,** cuanto antes. **sooner or later,** tarde o temprano. **no sooner... than,** apenas... cuando.
soot /sʊt/ *n.* hollín *m.*
soothe /suð/ *v.* calmar.
soothingly /'suðɪŋli/ *adv.* tiernamente.

sophisticated /sə'fɪstɪ,keitɪd/ *a.* sofisticado.
sophomore /'sɒfə,mɔr/ *n.* estudiante de segundo año *m.*
soprano /sə'prænou/ *n.* soprano *m. & f.*
sorcery /'sɔrsəri/ *n.* encantamiento *m.*
sordid /'sɔrdɪd/ *a.* sórdido.
sore /sɔr/ *n.* **1.** llaga *f.* —*a.* **2.** lastimado; *Colloq.* enojado. **to be s.,** doler.
sorority /sə'rɔrɪti, -'rɒr-/ *n.* hermandad de mujeres *f.*
sorrow /'sɒrou/ *n.* pesar, dolor *m.,* aflicción *f.*
sorrowful /'sɒrəfəl/ *a.* doloroso; afligido.
sorry /'sɒri/ *a.* **to be s.,** sentir, lamentar. **to be s. for,** compadecer.
sort /sɔrt/ *n.* **1.** tipo *m.;* clase, especie *f.* **s. of,** algo, un poco. —*v.* **2.** clasificar.
soul /soul/ *n.* alma *f.*
sound /saund/ *a.* **1.** sano; razonable; firme. —*n.* **2.** sonido *m.* —*v.* **3.** sonar; parecer.
soundproof /'saund,pruf/ *a.* insonorizado. *v.* insonorizar.
soundtrack /'saund,træk/ *n.* banda sonora *f.*
soup /sup/ *n.* sopa *f.*
sour /sauᵊr/ *a.* agrio; ácido; rancio.
source /sɔrs/ *n.* fuente; causa *f.*
south /sauθ/ *n.* sur *m.*
South Africa /'æfrɪkə/ Sudáfrica *f.*
South African *a. & n.* sudafricano.
South America /ə'mɛrɪkə/ Sudamérica, América del Sur.
South American *a. & n.* sudamericano -na.
southeast /,sauθ'ist; *Naut.* ,sau-/ *n.* sudeste *m.*
southern /'sʌðərn/ *a.* meridional.
South Pole *n.* polo sur *m.*
southwest /,sauθ'wɛst; *Naut.* ,sau-/ *n.* sudoeste *m.*
souvenir /,suvə'nɪər/ *n.* recuerdo *m.*
sovereign /'sɒvrɪn/ *n.* soberano -na.
sovereignty /'sɒvrɪnti/ *n.* soberanía *f.*
Soviet Russia Rusia soviética *f.*
sow /sau/ *n.* **1.** puerca *f.* —*v.* **2.** sembrar.
space /speis/ *n.* **1.** espacio *m.* —*v.* **2.** espaciar.
space out *v.* escalonar.
spaceship /'speis,ʃɪp/ *n.* nave espacial, astronave *f.*
space shuttle /'ʃʌtl/ transbordador espacial *m.*
spacious /'speiʃəs/ *a.* espacioso.
spade /speid/ *n.* **1.** laya; (cards) espada *f.* —*v.* **2.** layar.
spaghetti /spə'gɛti/ *n.* espaguetis *m. pl.*
Spain /spein/ *n.* España *f.*
span /spæn/ *n.* **1.** tramo *m.* —*v.* **2.** extenderse sobre.
Spaniard /'spænyərd/ *n.* español -ola.
Spanish /'spænɪʃ/ *a. & n.* español -ola.
spank /spæŋk/ *v.* pegar.
spanking /'spæŋkɪŋ/ *n.* tunda, zumba *f.*
spar /spɑr/ *v.* altercar.
spare /spɛər/ *a.* **1.** de repuesto. —*v.* **2.** perdonar; ahorrar; prestar. **have... to s.,** tener... de sobra.
spare tire neumático de recambio *m.*
spark /spɑrk/ *n.* chispa *f.*
sparkle /'spɑrkəl/ *n.* **1.** destello *m.* —*v.* **2.** chispear. **sparkling wine,** vino espumoso.
spark plug /'spɑrk,plʌg/ *n.* bujía *f.*
sparrow /'spærou/ *n.* gorrión *m.*
sparse /spɑrs/ *a.* esparcido.
spasm /'spæzəm/ *n.* espasmo *m.*
spasmodic /spæz'mɒdɪk/ *a.* espasmódico.
spatter /'spætər/ *v.* salpicar; manchar.
speak /spik/ *v.* hablar.
speaker /'spikər/ *n.* conferenciante *m. & f.*

spear /spɪər/ *n.* lanza *f.*
spearmint /'spɪər,mɪnt/ *n.* menta romana *f.*
special /'spɛʃəl/ *a.* especial. **s. delivery,** entrega inmediata, entrega urgente.
specialist /'spɛʃəlɪst/ *n.* especialista *m. & f.*
specialty /'spɛʃəlti/ *n.* especialidad *f.*
species /'spiʃiz, -siz/ *n.* especie *f.*
specific /spɪ'sɪfɪk/ *a.* específico.
specify /'spɛsə,fai/ *v.* especificar.
specimen /'spɛsəmən/ *n.* espécimen *m.;* muestra *f.*
spectacle /'spɛktəkəl/ *n.* espectáculo *m.;* (pl.) lentes, anteojos *m. pl.*
spectacular /spɛk'tækyələr/ *a.* espectacular, aparatoso.
spectator /'spɛkteitər/ *n.* espectador -ra.
spectrum /'spɛktrəm/ *n.* espectro *m.*
speculate /'spɛkyə,leit/ *v.* especular.
speculation /,spɛkyə'leiʃən/ *n.* especulación *f.*
speech /spitʃ/ *n.* habla *f.;* lenguaje; discurso *m.* **part of s.,** parte de la oración.
speechless /'spitʃlɪs/ *a.* mudo.
speed /spid/ *n.* **1.** velocidad; rapidez *f.* —*v.* **2. s. up,** acelerar, apresurar.
speed limit velocidad máxima *f.*
speedometer /spi'dɒmɪtər/ *n.* velocímetro *m.*
speedy /'spidi/ *a.* veloz, rápido.
spell /spɛl/ *n.* **1.** hechizo; rato; *Med.* ataque *m.* —*v.* **2.** escribir; relevar.
spelling /'spɛlɪŋ/ *n.* ortografía *f.*
spend /spɛnd/ *v.* gastar; (time) pasar.
spendthrift /'spɛnd,θrɪft/ *a. & n.* pródigo; manirroto *m.*
sphere /sfɪər/ *n.* esfera *f.*
spice /spais/ *n.* **1.** especia *f.* —*v.* **2.** especiar.
spider /'spaidər/ *n.* araña *f.*
spider web telaraña *f.*
spike /spaik/ *n.* alcayata *f.;* punta *f.,* clavo *m.*
spill /spɪl/ *v.* derramar. *n.* caída *f.,* vuelco *m.*
spillway /'spɪl,wei/ *n.* vertedero *m.*
spin /spɪn/ *v.* hilar; girar.
spinach /'spɪnɪtʃ/ *n.* espinaca *f.*
spine /spain/ *n.* espina dorsal *f.*
spinet /'spɪnɪt/ *n.* espineta *f.*
spinster /'spɪnstər/ *n.* solterona *f.*
spiral /'spairəl/ *a. & n.* espiral *f.*
spire /spaiᵊr/ *n.* caracol *m.,* espiral *f.*
spirit /'spɪrɪt/ *n.* espíritu; ánimo *m.*
spiritual /'spɪrɪtʃuəl/ *a.* espiritual.
spiritualism /'spɪrɪtʃuə,lɪzəm/ *n.* espiritismo *m.*
spirituality /,spɪrɪtʃu'ælɪti/ *n.* espiritualidad *f.*
spit /spɪt/ *v.* escupir.
spite /spait/ *n.* despecho *m.* **in s. of,** a pesar de.
splash /splæʃ/ *n.* **1.** salpicadura *f.* —*v.* **2.** salpicar.
splendid /'splɛndɪd/ *a.* espléndido.
splendor /'splɛndər/ *n.* esplendor *m.*
splice /splais/ *v.* **1.** empalmar. —*n.* **2.** empalme *m.*
splint /splɪnt/ *n.* tablilla *f.*
splinter /'splɪntər/ *n.* **1.** astilla *f.* —*v.* **2.** astillar.
split /splɪt/ *n.* **1.** división *f.* —*v.* **2.** dividir, romper en dos.
splurge /splɜrdʒ/ *v.* **1.** fachendear. —*n.* **2.** fachenda *f.*
spoil /spɔil/ *n.* **1.** (pl.) botín *m.* —*v.* **2.** echar a perder; (a child) mimar.
spoke /spouk/ *n.* rayo (de rueda) *m.*
spokesman /'spouksmən/ *n.* portavoz *m. & f.*
spokesperson /'spouks,pɜrsən/ *n.* portavoz *m. & f.*
sponge /spʌndʒ/ *n.* esponja *f.*
sponsor /'spɒnsər/ *n.* **1.** patrocinador *m.* —*v.* **2.** patrocinar; costear.
spontaneity /,spɒntə'niiti, -'nei-/ *n.* espontaneidad *f.*

spontaneous /spɒn'teiniəs/ a. espontáneo.
spool /spul/ n. carrete m.
spoon /spun/ n. cuchara f.
spoonful /'spunfʊl/ n. cucharada f.
sporadic /spə'rædɪk/ a. esporádico.
sport /spɔrt/ n. deporte m.
sport jacket chaqueta deportiva f.
sports center /spɔrts/ pabellón de deportes, polideportivo m.
sportsman /'spɔrtsmən/ a. 1. deportivo. —n. 2. deportista m. & f.
spot /spɒt/ n. 1. mancha f.; lugar, punto m. —v. 2. distinguir.
spouse /spaus/ n. esposo -sa.
spout /spaut/ n. 1. chorro; (of teapot) pico m. —v. 2. correr a chorro.
sprain /sprein/ n. 1. torcedura f., esguince m. —v. 2. torcerse.
sprawl /sprɔl/ v. tenderse.
spray /sprei/ n. 1. rociada f. —v. 2. rociar.
spread /sprɛd/ n. 1. propagación; extensión; (for bed) colcha f. —v. 2. propagar; extender.
spreadsheet /'sprɛd,ʃit/ n. hoja de cálculo f.
spree /spri/ n. parranda f.
sprig /sprɪg/ n. ramita f.
sprightly /'spraitli/ a. garboso.
spring /sprɪŋ/ n. resorte, muelle m.; (season) primavera f.; (of water) manantial m.
springboard /'sprɪŋ,bɔrd/ n. trampolín m.
spring onion cebolleta f.
sprinkle /'sprɪŋkəl/ v. rociar; (rain) lloviznar.
sprint /sprɪnt/ n. carrera f.
sprout /spraut/ n. retoño m.
spry /sprai/ a. ágil.
spun /spʌn/ a. hilado.
spur /spɜr/ n. 1. espuela f. **on the s. of the moment,** sin pensarlo. —v. 2. espolear.
spurious /'spyʊriəs/ a. espurio.
spurn /spɜrn/ v. rechazar, despreciar.
spurt /spɜrt/ n. 1. chorro m.; esfuerzo supremo. —v. 2. salir en chorro.
spy /spai/ 1. espía m. & f. —v. 2. espiar.
squabble /'skwɒblɪŋ/ n. 1. riña f. —v. 2. reñir.
squad /skwɒd/ n. escuadra f.
squadron /'skwɒdrən/ n. escuadrón m.
squalid /'skwɒlɪd/ a. escuálido.
squall /skwɔl/ n. borrasca f.
squalor /'skwɒlər/ n. escualidez f.
squander /'skwɒndər/ v. malgastar.
square /skwɛər/ a. 1. cuadrado. —n. 2. cuadrado m.; plaza f.
square dance n. contradanza f.
squat /skwɒt/ v. agacharse.
squeak /skwik/ n. 1. chirrido m. —v. 2. chirriar.
squeamish /'skwimɪʃ/ a. escrupuloso.
squeeze /skwiz/ n. 1. apretón m. —v. 2. apretar; (fruit) exprimir.
squirrel /'skwɜrəl// n. ardilla f.
squirt /skwɜrt/ n. 1. chisguete m. —v. 2. jeringar.
stab /stæb/ n. 1. puñalada f. —v. 2. apuñalar.
stability /stə'bɪlɪti/ n. estabilidad f.
stabilize /'steibə,laiz/ v. estabilizar.
stable /'steibəl/ a. 1. estable, equilibrado. —n. 2. caballeriza f.
stack /stæk/ n. 1. pila f. —v. 2. apilar.
stadium /'steidiəm/ n. estadio m.
staff /stæf/ n. personal m. **editorial s.,** cuerpo de redacción. **general s.,** estado mayor.
stag /stæg/ n. ciervo m.
stage /steidʒ/ n. 1. etapa; Theat. escena f. —v. 2. representar.
stagflation /stæg'fleiʃən/ n. estagflación.
stagger /'stægər/ v. (teeter) tambalear; (space out) escalonar.
stagnant /'stægnənt/ a. estancado.
stagnate /'stægneit/ v. estancarse.
stain /stein/ n. 1. mancha f. —v. 2. manchar.
stainless steel /'steinlɪs/ acero inoxidable m.
staircase /'stɛər,keis/ **stairs** n. escalera f.
stake /steik/ n. estaca; (bet) apuesta f. **at s.,** en juego; en peligro.
stale /steil/ a. rancio.
stalemate /'steil,meit/ n. estancación f.; tablas f.pl.
stalk /stɔk/ n. caña f.; (of flower) tallo m. v. acechar.
stall /stɔl/ n. 1. tenderete; (for horse) pesebre m. —v. 2. demorar; (motor) atascar.
stallion /'stælyən/ n. S.A. garañón m.
stalwart /'stɔlwərt/ a. fornido.
stamina /'stæmənə/ n. vigor m.
stammer /'stæmər/ v. tartamudear.
stamp /stæmp/ n. 1. sello m., estampilla f. —v. 2. sellar.
stamp collecting /kə'lɛktɪŋ/ filatelia f.
stampede /stæm'pid/ n. estampida f.
stand /stænd/ n. 1. puesto m.; posición; (speaker's) tribuna; (furniture) mesita f. —v. 2. estar; estar de pie; aguantar. **s. up,** pararse, levantarse.
standard /'stændərd/ a. 1. normal, corriente. —n. 2. norma f. **s. of living,** nivel de vida.
standardize /'stændər,daiz/ v. uniformar.
standing /'stændɪŋ/ a. fijo; establecido.
standpoint /'stænd,pɔint/ n. punto de vista m.
staple /'steipəl/ n. materia prima f.; grapa f.
stapler /'steiplər/ n. grapadora f.
star /stɑr/ n. estrella f.
starboard /'stɑrbərd/ n. estribor m.
starch /stɑrtʃ/ n. 1. almidón m.; (in diet) fécula f. —v. 2. almidonar.
stare /stɛər/ v. mirar fijamente.
stark /stɑrk/ a. 1. severo. —adv. 2. completamente.
start /stɑrt/ n. 1. susto; principio m. —v. 2. comenzar, empezar; salir; poner en marcha; causar.
startle /'stɑrtl̩/ v. asustar.
starvation /stɑr'veiʃən/ n. hambre f.
starve /stɑrv/ v. morir de hambre.
state /steit/ n. 1. estado m. —v. 2. declarar, decir.
statement /'steitmənt/ n. declaración f.
stateroom /'steit,rum/ n. camarote m.
statesman /'steitsmən/ n. estadista m.
static /'stætɪk/ a. 1. estático. —n. 2. estática f.
station /'steiʃən/ n. estación f.
stationary /'steiʃə,nɛri/ a. estacionario, fijo.
stationery /'steiʃə,nɛri/ n. papel de escribir.
statistics /stə'tɪstɪks/ n. estadística f.
statue /'stætʃu/ n. estatua f.
stature /'stætʃər/ n. estatura f.
status /'steitəs, 'stætəs/ n. condición, estado m.
statute /'stætʃut/ n. ley f.
staunch /stɔntʃ/ a. fiel; constante.
stay /stei/ n. 1. estancia; visita f. —v. 2. quedar, permanecer; parar, alojarse. **s. away,** ausentarse. **s. up,** velar.
steadfast /'stɛd,fæst/ a. inmutable.
steady /'stɛdi/ a. 1. firme; permanente; regular. —v. 2. sostener.
steak /steik/ n. biftec, bistec m.
steal /stil/ v. robar. **s. away,** escabullirse.
stealth /stɛlθ/ n. cautela f.
steam /stim/ n. vapor m.
steamboat /'stim,bout/ **steamer, steamship** n. vapor m.
steel /stil/ n. 1. acero m. —v. 2. **s. oneself,** fortalecerse.
steep /stip/ a. escarpado, empinado.
steeple /'stipəl/ n. campanario m.
steer /stɪər/ n. 1. buey m. —v. 2. guiar, manejar.
stellar /'stɛlər/ a. astral.
stem /stɛm/ n. 1. tallo m. —v. 2. parar. **s. from,** emanar de.
stencil /'stɛnsəl/ n. 1. estarcido. —v. 2. estarcir.
stenographer /stə'nɒgrəfər/ n. estenógrafo -fa.
stenography /stə'nɒgrəfi/ n. taquigrafía f.
step /stɛp/ n. 1. paso m.; medida f.; (stairs) escalón m. —v. 2. pisar. **s. back,** retirarse.
stepladder /'stɛp,lædər/ n. escalera de mano f.
stereophonic /,stɛriə'fɒnɪk/ a. estereofónico.
stereotype /'stɛriə,taip/ n. 1. estereotipo m. —v. 2. estereotipar.
sterile /'stɛrɪl/ a. estéril.
sterilize /'stɛrə,laiz/ v. esterilizar.
sterling /'stɜrlɪŋ/ a. esterlina, genuino.
stern /stɜrn/ n. 1. popa f. —a. 2. duro, severo.
stethoscope /'stɛθə,skoup/ n. estetoscopio m.
stevedore /'stivɪ,dɔr/ n. estibador m.
stew /stu/ n. 1. guisado m. —v. 2. estofar.
steward /'stuərd/ n. camarero.
stewardess /'stuərdɪs/ n. azafata f., aeromoza f.
stick /stɪk/ n. 1. palo, bastón m. —v. 2. pegar; (put) poner, meter.
sticky /'stɪki/ a. pegajoso.
stiff /stɪf/ a. tieso; duro.
stiffness /'stɪfnɪs/ n. tiesura f.
stifle /'staifəl/ v. sofocar; Fig. suprimir.
stigma /'stɪgmə/ n. estigma m.
still /stɪl/ a. 1. quieto; silencioso. **to keep s.,** quedarse quieto. —adv. 2. todavía, aún; no obstante. —n. 3. alambique m.
stillborn /'stɪl,bɔrn/ n. & a. nacido -da muerto -ta.
still life n. naturaleza muerta f.
stillness /'stɪlnɪs/ n. silencio m.
stilted /'stɪltɪd/ a. afectado, artificial.
stimulant /'stɪmyələnt/ a. & n. estimulante m.
stimulate /'stɪmyə,leit/ v. estimular.
stimulus /'stɪmyələs/ n. estímulo m.
sting /stɪŋ/ n. 1. picadura f. —v. 2. picar.
stingy /'stɪndʒi/ a. tacaño.
stipulate /'stɪpyə,leit/ v. estipular.
stir /stɜr/ n. 1. conmoción f. —v. 2. mover. **s. up,** conmover; suscitar.
stitch /stɪtʃ/ n. 1. puntada f. —v. 2. coser.
stock /stɒk/ n. surtido f.; raza f.; (finance) acciones. f.pl. **in s.,** en existencia. **to take s. in,** tener fe en.
stock exchange bolsa f.
stockholder /'stɒk,houldər/ n. accionista m. & f.
stocking /'stɒkɪŋ/ n. media f.
stockyard /'stɒk,yɑrd/ n. corral de ganado m.
stodgy /'stɒdʒi/ a. pesado.
stoical /'stouɪkəl/ a. estoico.
stole /stoul/ n. estola f.
stolid /'stɒlɪd/ a. impasible.
stomach /'stʌmək/ n. estómago m.
stomachache /'stʌmək,eik/ n. dolor de estómago m.
stone /stoun/ n. piedra f.
stool /stul/ n. banquillo m.
stoop /stup/ v. encorvarse; Fig. rebajarse. espaldas encorvadas f.pl.
stop /stɒp/ n. 1. parada f. **to put a s. to,** poner fin a. —v. 2. parar; suspender; detener; impedir. **s. doing** (etc.), dejar de hacer (etc.).
stopgap /'stɒp,gæp/ n. recurso provisional m.
stopover /'stɒp,ouvər/ n. parada f.
stopwatch /'stɒp,wɒtʃ/ n. cronómetro m.
storage /'stɔrɪdʒ/ n. almacenaje m.
store /stɔr/ n. 1. tienda; provisión f. **department s.,** almacén m. —v. 2. guardar; almacenar.
store window escaparate m.
stork /stɔrk/ n. cigüeña f.
storm /stɔrm/ n. tempestad, tormenta f.
stormy /'stɔrmi/ a. tempestuoso.
story /'stɔri/ n. cuento; relato m.; historia f. **short s.,** cuento.
stout /staut/ a. corpulento.
stove /stouv/ n. hornilla; estufa f.
straight /streit/ a. 1. recto; derecho. —adv. 2. directamente.
straighten /'streitn̩/ v. enderezar. **s. out,** poner en orden.
straightforward /,streit'fɔrwərd/ a. recto, sincero.
strain /strein/ n. 1. tensión f. —v. 2. colar.
strainer /'streinər/ n. colador m.
strait /streit/ n. estrecho m.
strand /strænd/ n. 1. hilo m. —v. 2. **be stranded,** encallarse.
strange /streindʒ/ a. extraño; raro.
stranger /'streindʒər/ n. extranjero -ra; forastero -ra; desconocido -da.
strangle /'stræŋgəl/ v. estrangular.
strap /stræp/ n. correa f.
stratagem /'strætədʒəm/ n. estratagema f.
strategic /strə'tidʒɪk/ a. estratégico.
strategy /'strætɪdʒi/ n. estrategia f.
stratosphere /'strætə,sfɪər/ n. estratosfera f.
straw /strɔ/ n. paja f.
strawberry /'strɔ,bɛri/ n. fresa f.
stray /strei/ a. 1. vagabundo. —v. 2. extraviarse.
streak /strik/ n. 1. racha; raya f.; lado m. —v. 2. rayar.
stream /strim/ n. corriente f.; arroyo m.
street /strit/ n. calle f.
streetcar /'strit,kɑr/ n. tranvía m.
street lamp /'strit,læmp/ n. farol m.
strength /strɛŋkθ, strɛnθ/ n. fuerza m.
strengthen /'strɛŋkθən, 'strɛn-/ v. reforzar.
strenuous /'strɛnyuəs/ a. estrenuo.
streptococcus /,strɛptə'kɒkəs/ n. estreptococo m.
stress /strɛs/ n. 1. tensión f.; énfasis m. —v. 2. recalcar; acentuar.
stretch /strɛtʃ/ n. 1. trecho m. **at one s.,** de un tirón. —v. 2. tender; extender; estirarse.
stretcher /'strɛtʃər/ n. camilla f.
strew /stru/ v. esparcir.
stricken /'strɪkən/ a. agobiado.
strict /strɪkt/ a. estricto; severo.
stride /straid/ n. 1. tranco m.; (fig., pl.) progresos. —v. 2. andar a trancos.
strife /straif/ n. contienda f.
strike /straik/ n. 1. huelga f. —v. 2. pegar; chocar con; (clock) dar.
striker /'straikər/ n. huelguista m. & f.
string /strɪŋ/ n. cuerda f.; cordel m.
string bean n. habichuela f.
stringent /'strɪndʒənt/ a. estricto.
strip /strɪp/ n. 1. tira f. —v. 2. despojar; desnudarse.
stripe /straip/ n. raya f.; Mil. galón m.
strive /straiv/ v. esforzarse.
stroke /strouk/ n. golpe m.; (swimming) brazada f.; Med. ataque m. **s. of luck,** suerte f.
stroll /stroul/ n. 1. paseo m. —v. 2. pasearse.
stroller /'stroulər/ n. vagabundo m.; cochecito (de niño).
strong /strɔŋ/ a. fuerte.
stronghold /'strɔŋ,hould/ n. fortificación f.
structure /'strʌktʃər/ n. estructura f.
struggle /'strʌgəl/ n. 1. lucha f. —v. 2. luchar.
strut /strʌt/ n. 1. pavonada f. —v. 2. pavonear.
stub /stʌb/ n. 1. cabo; (ticket) talón

m. —*v.* **2. s. on one's toes,** tropezar con.
stubborn /'stʌbərn/ *a.* testarudo.
stucco /'stʌkou/ *n.* **1.** estuco *m.* —*v.* **2.** estucar.
student /'studnt/ *n.* alumno -na, estudiante -ta.
studio /'studi,ou/ *n.* estudio *m.*
studious /'studiəs/ *a.* aplicado; estudioso.
study /'stʌdi/ *n.* **1.** estudio *m.* —*v.* **2.** estudiar.
stuff /stʌf/ *n.* **1.** cosas *f.pl.* —*v.* **2.** llenar; rellenar.
stuffing /'stʌfɪŋ/ *n.* relleno *m.*
stumble /'stʌmbəl/ *v.* tropezar.
stump /stʌmp/ *n.* cabo; tocón; muñón *m.*
stun /stʌn/ *v.* aturdir.
stunt /stʌnt/ *n.* **1.** maniobra sensacional *f.* —*v.* **2.** impedir crecimiento.
stupendous /stu'pɛndəs/ *a.* estupendo.
stupid /'stupɪd/ *a.* estúpido.
stupidity /stu'pɪdɪti/ *n.* estupidez *f.*
stupor /'stupər/ *n.* estupor *m.*
sturdy /'stɜrdi/ *a.* robusto.
stutter /'stʌtər/ *v.* **1.** tartamudear. —*n.* **2.** tartamudeo *m.*
sty /stai/ *n.* pocilga *f.*; *Med.* orzuelo.
style /stail/ *n.* estilo *m.*; moda *f.*
stylish /'stailɪʃ/ *a.* elegante; a la moda.
suave /swɑv/ *a.* afable, suave.
subconscious /sʌb'kɒnʃəs/ *a.* subconsciente.
subdue /səb'du/ *v.* dominar.
subject /*n.* 'sʌbdʒɪkt; *v.* səb'dʒɛkt/ *n.* **1.** tema *m.*; (of study) materia *f.*; *Pol.* súbdito -ta; *Gram.* sujeto *m.* —*v.* **2.** someter.
subjugate /'sʌbdʒə,geit/ *v.* sojuzgar, subyugar.
subjunctive /səb'dʒʌŋktɪv/ *a.* & *n.* subjuntivo *m.*
sublimate /'sʌblə,meit/ *v.* sublimar.
sublime /sə'blaim/ *a.* sublime.
submarine /,sʌbmə'rin/ *a.* & *n.* submarino *m.*
submerge /səb'mɜrdʒ/ *v.* sumergir.
submission /səb'mɪʃən/ *n.* sumisión *f.*
submit /səb'mɪt/ *v.* someter.
subnormal /sʌb'nɔrməl/ *a.* subnormal.
subordinate /*a, n* sə'bɔrdnɪt; *v* -dn,eit/ *a.* & *n.* **1.** subordinado -da. —*v.* **2.** subordinar.
subscribe /səb'skraib/ *v.* aprobar; abonarse.
subscriber /səb'skraibər/ *n.* abonado -da *m.* & *f.*
subscription /səb'skrɪpʃən/ *n.* abono *m.*
subsequent /'sʌbsɪkwənt/ *a.* subsiguiente.
subservient /səb'sɜrviənt/ *a.* servicial.
subside /səb'said/ *v.* apaciguarse, menguar.
subsidy /'sʌbsɪdi/ *n.* subvención *f.*
subsoil /'sʌb,sɔil/ *n.* subsuelo *m.*
substance /'sʌbstəns/ *n.* sustancia *f.*
substantial /səb'stænʃəl/ *a.* sustancial; considerable.
substitute /'sʌbstɪ,tut/ *a.* **1.** sustitutivo. —*n.* **2.** sustituto -ta. —*v.* **3.** sustituir.
substitution /,sʌbstɪ'tuʃən/ *n.* sustitución *f.*
subterfuge /'sʌbtər,fyudʒ/ *n.* subterfugio *m.*
subtitle /'sʌb,taitḷ/ *n.* subtítulo *m.*
subtle /'sʌtḷ/ *a.* sutil.
subtract /səb'trækt/ *v.* sustraer.
suburb /'sʌbɜrb/ *n.* suburbio *m.*; (pl.) afueras *f.pl.*
subversive /səb'vɜrsɪv/ *a.* subversivo.
subway /'sʌb,wei/ *n.* metro *m.*
succeed /sək'sid/ *v.* lograr, tener éxito; (in office) suceder a.
success /sək'sɛs/ *n.* éxito *m.*
successful /sək'sɛsfəl/ *a.* próspero; afortunado.
succession /sək'sɛʃən/ *n.* sucesión *f.*
successive /sək'sɛsɪv/ *a.* sucesivo.
successor /sək'sɛsər/ *n.* sucesor -ra; heredero -ra.
succor /'sʌkər/ *n.* **1.** socorro *m.* —*v.* **2.** socorrer.
succumb /sə'kʌm/ *v.* sucumbir.
such /sʌtʃ/ *a.* tal.
suck /sʌk/ *v.* chupar.
suction /'sʌkʃən/ *n.* succión *f.*
sudden /'sʌdṇ/ *a.* repentino, súbito. **all of a s.,** de repente.
suds /sʌdz/ *n.* jabonaduras *f. pl.*
sue /su/ *v.* demandar.
suffer /'sʌfər/ *v.* sufrir; padecer.
suffice /sə'fais/ *v.* bastar.
sufficient /sə'fɪʃənt/ *a.* suficiente.
suffocate /'sʌfə,keit/ *v.* sofocar.
sugar /'ʃʊgər/ *n.* azúcar *m.*
sugar bowl azucarero *m.*
suggest /səg'dʒɛst/ *v.* sugerir.
suggestion /səg'dʒɛstʃən/ *n.* sugerencia *f.*
suicide /'suə,said/ *n.* suicidio *m.*; (person) suicida *m.* & *f.* **to commit s.,** suicidarse.
suit /sut/ *n.* **1.** traje; (cards) palo; (law) pleito *m.* —*v.* **2.** convenir a.
suitable /'sutəbəl/ *a.* apropiado; que conviene.
suitcase /'sut,keis/ *n.* maleta *f.*
suite /swit/ *n.* serie *f.*, séquito *m.*
suitor /'sutər/ *n.* pretendiente *m.*
sullen /'sʌlən/ *a.* hosco.
sum /sʌm/ *n.* **1.** suma *f.* —*v.* **2. s. up,** resumir.
summarize /'sʌmə,raiz/ *v.* resumir.
summary /'sʌməri/ *n.* resumen *m.*
summer /'sʌmər/ *n.* verano *m.*
summon /'sʌmən/ *v.* llamar; (law) citar.
summons /'sʌmənz/ *n.* citación *f.*
sumptuous /'sʌmptʃuəs/ *a.* suntuoso.
sun /sʌn/ *n.* **1.** sol *m.* —*v.* **2.** tomar el sol.
sunbathe /'sʌn,beið/ *v.* tomar el sol.
sunburn /'sʌn,bɜrn/ *n.* quemadura de sol.
sunburned /'sʌn,bɜrnd/ *a.* quemado por el sol.
Sunday /'sʌndei/ *n.* domingo *m.*
sunken /'sʌŋkən/ *a.* hundido.
sunny /'sʌni/ *a.* asoleado. **s. day,** día de sol. **to be s.,** (weather) hacer sol.
sunshine /'sʌn,ʃain/ *n.* luz del sol.
suntan /'sʌn,tæn/ *n.* bronceado *m.* **s. lotion,** loción bronceadora *f.*, bronceador *m.*
superb /sʊ'pɜrb/ *a.* soberbio.
superficial /,supər'fɪʃəl/ *a.* superficial.
superfluous /sʊ'pɜrfluəs/ *a.* superfluo.
superhuman /,supər'hyumən/ *a.* sobrehumano.
superintendent /,supərɪn'tɛndənt/ *n.* superintendente *m.* & *f.*; (of building) conserje *m.*; (of school) director -ra general.
superior /sə'pɪəriər/ *a.* & *n.* superior *m.*
superiority /sə,pɪəri'ɔrɪti/ *n.* superioridad *f.*
superlative /sə'pɜrlətɪv/ *a.* superlativo.
supernatural /,supər'nætʃərəl/ *a.* sobrenatural.
supersede /,supər'sid/ *v.* reemplazar.
superstar /'supər,stɑr/ *n.* superestrella *m.* & *f.*
superstition /,supər'stɪʃən/ *n.* superstición *f.*
superstitious /,supər'stɪʃəs/ *a.* supersticioso.
supervise /'supər,vaiz/ *v.* supervisar.
supper /'sʌpər/ *n.* cena *f.*
supplement /'sʌpləmənt/ *n.* **1.** suplemento *m.* —*v.* **2.** suplementar.
supply /sə'plai/ *n.* **1.** provisión *f.*; *Com.* surtido *m.*; *Econ.* existencia *f.* —*v.* **2.** suplir; proporcionar.
support /sə'pɔrt/ *n.* **1.** sustento; apoyo *m.* —*v.* **2.** mantener; apoyar.
suppose /sə'pouz/ *v.* suponer. **be supposed to,** deber.
suppository /sə'pɒzɪ,tɔri/ *n.* supositorio *m.*
suppress /sə'pres/ *v.* suprimir.
suppression /sə'prɛʃən/ *n.* supresión *f.*
supreme /sə'prim/ *a.* supremo.
sure /ʃʊr, ʃɜr/ *a.* seguro, cierto. **for s.,** con seguridad. **to make s.,** asegurarse.
surety /'ʃʊrɪti, 'ʃɜr-/ *n.* garantía *f.*
surf /sɜrf/ *n.* **1.** oleaje *m.* —*v.* **2.** (Internet) navegar; (sport) surfear.
surface /'sɜrfɪs/ *n.* superficie *f.*
surfboard /'sɜrf,bɔrd/ *n.* tabla de surf *f.*
surfer /'sɜrfər/ *n.* (Internet) usuario -ria, navegante *m.* & *f.*; (sport) surfero -ra.
surge /sɜrdʒ/ *v.* surgir.
surgeon /'sɜrdʒən/ *n.* cirujano -na.
surgery /'sɜrdʒəri/ *n.* cirugía *f.*
surmise /sər'maiz/ *v.* suponer.
surmount /sər'maunt/ *v.* vencer.
surname /'sɜr,neim/ *n.* apellido *m.*
surpass /sər'pæs/ *v.* superar.
surplus /'sɜrplʌs/ *a.* & *n.* sobrante *m.*
surprise /sər'praiz, sə-/ *n.* **1.** sorpresa —*v.* **2.** sorprender. **I am surprised...,** me extraña...
surrender /sə'rɛndər/ *n.* **1.** rendición *f.* —*v.* **2.** rendir.
surround /sə'raund/ *v.* rodear, circundar.
surveillance /sər'veiləns/ *n.* vigilancia *f.*
survey /*n.* 'sɜrvei; *v.* sər'vei/ *n.* **1.** examen; estudio *m.* —*v.* **2.** examinar; (land) medir.
survival /sər'vaivəl/ *n.* supervivencia *f.*
survive /sər'vaiv/ *v.* sobrevivir.
susceptible /sə'sɛptəbəl/ *a.* susceptible.
suspect /*v.* sə'spɛkt; *n.* 'sʌspɛkt/ *v.* **1.** sospechar. —*n.* **2.** sospechoso -sa.
suspend /sə'spɛnd/ *v.* suspender.
suspense /sə'spɛns/ *n.* incertidumbre *f.* **in s.,** en suspenso.
suspension /sə'spɛnʃən/ *n.* suspensión *f.*
suspension bridge *n.* puente colgante *m.*
suspicion /sə'spɪʃən/ *n.* sospecha *f.*
suspicious /sə'spɪʃəs/ *a.* sospechoso.
sustain /sə'stein/ *v.* sustentar; mantener.
swallow /'swɒlou/ *n.* **1.** trago *m.*; (bird) golondrina *f.* —*v.* **2.** tragar.
swamp /swɒmp/ *n.* **1.** pantano *m.* —*v.* **2.** *Fig.* abrumar.
swan /swɒn/ *n.* cisne *m.*
swap /swɒp/ *n.* **1.** trueque *m.* —*v.* **2.** cambalachear.
swarm /swɔrm/ *n.* enjambre *m.*
swarthy /'swɔrði/ *a.* moreno.
sway /swei/ *n.* **1.** predominio *m.* —*v.* **2.** bambolearse; *Fig.* influir en.
swear /swɛər/ *v.* jurar. **s. off,** renunciar a.
sweat /swɛt/ *n.* **1.** sudor *m.* —*v.* **2.** sudar.
sweater /'swɛtər/ *n.* suéter *m.*
sweatshirt /'swɛt,ʃɜrt/ *n.* sudadera *f.*
Swede /swid/ *n.* sueco -ca.
Sweden /'swidṇ/ *n.* Suecia *f.*
Swedish /'swidɪʃ/ *a.* sueco.
sweep /swip/ *v.* barrer.
sweet /swit/ *a.* **1.** dulce; amable, simpático. —*n.* **2.** (pl.) dulces *m. pl.*
sweetheart /'swit,hɑrt/ *n.* novio -via.
sweetness /'switnɪs/ *n.* dulzura *f.*
sweet-toothed /'swit ,tuθt/ *a.* goloso.
swell /swɛl/ *a.* **1.** *Colloq.* estupendo, excelente. —*n.* **2.** (of the sea) oleada *f.* —*v.* **3.** hincharse; aumentar.
swelter /'swɛltər/ *v.* sofocarse de calor.
swift /swɪft/ *a.* rápido, veloz.
swim /swɪm/ *n.* **1.** nadada *f.* —*v.* **2.** nadar.
swimming /'swɪmɪŋ/ *n.* natación *f.*
swimming pool alberca, piscina *f.*
swindle /'swɪndḷ/ *n.* **1.** estafa *f.* —*v.* **2.** estafar.
swine /swain/ *n.* puercos *m.pl.*
swing /swɪŋ/ *n.* **1.** columpio *m.* **in full s.,** en plena actividad. —*v.* **2.** mecer; balancear.
swirl /swɜrl/ *n.* **1.** remolino *m.* —*v.* **2.** arremolinar.
Swiss /swɪs/ *a.* & *n.* suizo -za.
switch /swɪtʃ/ *n.* **1.** varilla *f.*; *Elec.* llave *f.*, conmutador *m.*; (railway) cambiavía *m.* —*v.* **2.** cambiar; trocar.
switchboard /'swɪtʃ,bɔrd/ *n.* cuadro conmutador *m.*, centralita *f.*
Switzerland /'swɪtsərlənd/ *n.* Suiza *f.*
sword /sɔrd/ *n.* espada *f.*
syllable /'sɪləbəl/ *n.* sílaba *f.*
symbol /'sɪmbəl/ *n.* símbolo *m.*
sympathetic /,sɪmpə'θɛtɪk/ *a.* compasivo. **to be s.,** tener simpatía.
sympathy /'sɪmpəθi/ *n.* lástima; condolencia *f.*
symphony /'sɪmfəni/ *n.* sinfonía *f.*
symptom /'sɪmptəm/ *n.* síntoma *m.*
synagogue /'sɪnə,gɒg/ *n.* sinagoga *f.*
synchronize /'sɪŋkrə,naiz/ *v.* sincronizar.
syndicate / 'sɪndɪkɪt/ *n.* sindicato *m.*
syndrome /'sɪndroum, -drəm/ *n.* síndrome *m.*
synonym /'sɪnənɪm/ *n.* sinónimo *m.*
synthetic /sɪn'θɛtɪk/ *a.* sintético.
syringe /sə'rɪndʒ/ *n.* jeringa *f.*
syrup /'sɪrəp, 'sɜr-/ *n.* almíbar; *Med.* jarabe *m.*
system /'sɪstəm/ *n.* sistema *m.*
systematic /,sɪstə'mætɪk/ *a.* sistemático.

T

tabernacle /'tæbər,nækəl/ *n.* tabernáculo *m.*
table /'teibəl/ *n.* mesa; (list) tabla *f.*
tablecloth /'teibəl,klɔθ/ *n.* mantel *m.*
table of contents /'kɒntɛnts/ índice de materias *m.*
tablespoon /'teibəl,spun/ *n.* cuchara *f.*
tablespoonful /'teibəlspun,fʊl/ *n.* cucharada *f.*
tablet /'tæblɪt/ *n.* tableta; *Med.* pastilla *f.*
tack /tæk/ *n.* tachuela *f.*
tact /tækt/ *n.* tacto *m.*
tag /tæg/ *n.* etiqueta *f.*, rótulo *m.*
tail /teil/ *n.* cola *f.*, rabo *m.*
tailor /'teilər/ *n.* sastre *m.*
take /teik/ *v.* tomar; llevar. **t. a bath,** bañarse. **t. a shower,** ducharse. **t. away,** quitar. **t. off,** quitarse. **t. out,** sacar. **t. long,** tardar mucho.
tale /teil/ *n.* cuento *m.*
talent /'tælənt/ *n.* talento *m.*
talk /tɔk/ *n.* **1.** plática, habla *f.*; discurso *m.* —*v.* **2.** hablar.
talkative /'tɔkətɪv/ *a.* locuaz.
tall /tɔl/ *a.* alto.
tame /teim/ *a.* **1.** manso, domesticado. —*v.* **2.** domesticar.
tamper /'tæmpər/ *v.* **t. with,** entremeterse en.
tampon /'tæmpɒn/ *n.* tampón *m.*
tan /tæn/ *a.* **1.** color de arena. —*v.* **2.** curtir; tostar. *n.* bronceado.
tangerine /,tændʒə'rin/ *n.* clementina *f.*
tangible /'tændʒəbəl/ *a.* tangible.
tangle /'tæŋgəl/ *n.* **1.** enredo *m.* —*v.* **2.** enredar.
tank /tæŋk/ *n.* tanque *m.*
tap /tæp/ *n.* **1.** golpe ligero. —*v.* **2.** golpear ligeramente; decentar.
tape /teip/ *n.* cinta *f.*

tape recorder /rɪ'kɔrdər/ magnetófono *m.*, grabadora *f.*
tapestry /'tæpəstri/ *n.* tapiz *m.*; tapicería *f.*
tar /tɑr/ *n.* **1.** brea *f.* —*v.* **2.** embrear.
target /'tɑrgɪt/ *n.* blanco *m.*
tarnish /'tɑrnɪʃ/ *n.* **1.** deslustre *m.* —*v.* **2.** deslustrar.
tarpaulin /tɑr'pɔlɪn, 'tɑrpəlɪn/ *n.* lona *f.*
task /tæsk/ *n.* tarea *f.*
taste /teist/ *n.* **1.** gusto; sabor *m.* —*v.* **2.** gustar; probar. **t. of,** saber a.
tasty /'teisti/ *a.* sabroso.
tattoo /tæ'tu/ *v.* tatuar.
taut /tɔt/ *a.* tieso.
tavern /'tævərn/ *n.* taberna *f.*
tax /tæks/ *n.* **1.** impuesto *m.* —*v.* **2.** imponer impuestos.
tax collector *n.* recaudador -ra *m.* & *f.*
taxi /'tæksi/ *n.* taxi, taxímetro *m.* **t. driver,** taxista *m.* & *f.*
taxpayer /'tæks,peiər/ *n.* contribuyente *m.* & *f.*
tax reform reforma tributaria *f.*
tax return declaración de la renta *f.*
tea /ti/ *n.* té *m.*
teach /titʃ/ *v.* enseñar.
teacher /'titʃər/ *n.* maestro -tra, profesor -ra.
team /tim/ *n.* equipo *m.*; pareja *f.*
tear /tɪər/ *n.* **1.** rasgón *m.*; lágrima *f.* —*v.* **2.** rasgar, lacerar. **t. apart,** separar.
tease /tiz/ *v.* atormentar; embromar.
teaspoon /'ti,spun/ *n.* cucharita *f.*
technical /'tɛknɪkəl/ *a.* técnico.
technician /tɛk'nɪʃən/ *n.* técnico -ca *m.* & *f.*
technique /tɛk'nik/ *n.* técnica *f.*
technology /tɛk'nɒlədʒi/ *n.* tecnología *f.*
teddy bear /'tɛdi/ oso de felpa *m.*
tedious /'tidiəs/ *a.* tedioso.
telegram /'tɛlɪ,græm/ *n.* telegrama *m.*
telegraph /'tɛlɪ,græf/ *n.* **1.** telégrafo *m.* —*v.* **2.** telegrafiar.
telephone /'tɛlə,foun/ *n.* **1.** teléfono *m.* **t. book,** directorio telefónico. —*v.* **2.** telefonear; llamar por teléfono.
telescope /'tɛlə,skoup/ *n.* **1.** telescopio *m.* —*v.* **2.** enchufar.
television /'tɛlə,vɪʒən/ *n.* televisión *f.*
tell /tɛl/ *v.* decir; contar; distinguir.
temper /'tɛmpər/ *n.* **1.** temperamento, genio *m.* —*v.* **2.** templar.
temperament /'tɛmpərəmənt, -prəmənt/ *n.* temperamento.
temperamental /,tɛmpərə'mɛntl̩, -prə'mɛn-/ *a.* sensitivo, emocional.
temperance /'tɛmpərəns/ *n.* moderación; sobriedad *f.*
temperate /'tɛmpərɪt/ *a.* templado.
temperature /'tɛmpərətʃər/ *n.* temperatura *f.*
tempest /'tɛmpɪst/ *n.* tempestad *f.*
tempestuous /tɛm'pɛstʃuəs/ *a.* tempestuoso.
temple /'tɛmpəl/ *n.* templo *m.*
temporary /'tɛmpə,rɛri/ *a.* temporal, temporario.
tempt /tɛmpt/ *v.* tentar.
temptation /tɛmp'teiʃən/ *n.* tentación *f.*
ten /tɛn/ *a.* & *pron.* diez.
tenant /'tɛnənt/ *n.* inquilino -na.
tend /tɛnd/ *v.* tender. **t. to,** atender.
tendency /'tɛndənsi/ *n.* tendencia *f.*
tender /'tɛndər/ *a.* **1.** tierno. —*v.* **2.** ofrecer.
tenderness /'tɛndərnɪs/ *n.* ternura *f.*
tennis /'tɛnɪs/ *n.* tenis *m.*
tennis court cancha de tenis, pista de tenis *f.*
tenor /'tɛnər/ *n.* tenor *m.*
tense /tɛns/ *a.* **1.** tenso. —*n.* **2.** *Gram.* tiempo *m.*
tent /tɛnt/ *n.* tienda, carpa *f.*
tenth /tɛnθ/ *a.* décimo.
term /tɜrm/ *n.* **1.** término; plazo *m.* —*v.* **2.** llamar.
terminal /'tɜrmənl̩/ *n.* terminal *f.*
terrace /'tɛrəs/ *n.* terraza *f.*
terrible /'tɛrəbəl/ *a.* terrible, espantoso; pésimo.
territory /'tɛrɪ,tɔri/ *n.* territorio *m.*
terror /'tɛrər/ *n.* terror, espanto, pavor *m.*
test /tɛst/ *n.* **1.** prueba *f.*; examen *m.* —*v.* **2.** probar; examinar.
testament /'tɛstəmənt/ *n.* testamento *m.*
testify /'tɛstə,fai/ *v.* atestiguar, testificar.
testimony /'tɛstə,mouni/ *n.* testimonio *m.*
test tube tubo de ensayo *m.*
text /tɛkst/ *n.* texto; tema *m.*
textbook /'tɛkst,bʊk/ *n.* libro de texto.
textile /'tɛkstail/ *a.* **1.** textil. —*n.* **2.** tejido *m.*
texture /'tɛkstʃər/ *n.* textura *f.*; tejido *m.*
than /ðæn, ðɛn; *unstressed* ðən, ən/ *conj.* que; de.
thank /θæŋk/ *v.* agradecer, dar gracias; **thanks, th. you,** gracias.
thankful /'θæŋkfəl/ *a.* agradecido; grato.
that /ðæt; *unstressed* ðət/ *a.* **1.** ese, aquel. —*dem. pron.* **2.** ése, aquél; eso, aquello. —*rel. pron.* & *conj.* **3.** que.
the /*stressed* ði; *unstressed before a consonant* ðə, *unstressed before a vowel* ði/ *art.* el, la, los, las; lo.
theater /'θiətər/ *n.* teatro *m.*
theft /θɛft/ *n.* robo *m.*
their /ðɛər; *unstressed* ðər/ *a.* su.
theirs /ðɛərz/ *pron.* suyo, de ellos.
them /ðɛm; *unstressed* ðəm, əm/ *pron.* ellos, ellas; los, las; les.
theme /θim/ *n.* tema; *Mus.* motivo *m.*
themselves /ðəm'sɛlvz, ,ðɛm-/ *pron.* sí, sí mismos -as. **they th.,** ellos mismos, ellas mismas. **with th.,** consigo.
then /ðɛn/ *adv.* entonces, después; pues.
thence /ðɛns/ *adv.* de allí.
theology /θi'ɒlədʒi/ *n.* teología *f.*
theory /'θiəri/ *n.* teoría *f.*
there /ðɛər; *unstressed* ðər/ *adv.* allí, allá, ahí. **there is, there are,** hay.
therefore /'ðɛər,fɔr/ *adv.* por lo tanto, por consiguiente.
thermometer /θər'mɒmɪtər/ *n.* termómetro *m.*
thermostat /'θɜrmə,stæt/ *n.* termostato *m.*
they /ðei/ *pron.* ellos, ellas.
thick /θɪk/ *a.* espeso, grueso, denso; torpe.
thicken /'θɪkən/ *v.* espesar, condensar.
thief /θif/ *n.* ladrón -na.
thigh /θai/ *n.* muslo *m.*
thimble /'θɪmbəl/ *n.* dedal *m.*
thin /θɪn/ *a.* **1.** delgado; raro; claro; escaso. —*v.* **2.** enrarecer; adelgazar.
thing /θɪŋ/ *n.* cosa *f.*
thingamabob /'θɪŋəmə,bɒb/ *n.* *Colloq.* chisme *m.*
think /θɪŋk/ *v.* pensar; creer.
thinker /'θɪŋkər/ *n.* pensador -ra.
third /θɜrd/ *a.* tercero.
Third World Tercer Mundo *m.*
thirst /θɜrst/ *n.* sed *f.*
thirsty /'θɜrsti/ *a.* sediento. **to be th.,** tener sed.
thirteen /'θɜr'tin/ *a.* & *pron.* trece.
thirty /'θɜrti/ *a.* & *pron.* treinta.
this /ðɪs/ *a.* **1.** este. —*pron.* **2.** éste; esto.
thoracic cage /θɔ'ræsɪk/ *n.* caja torácica *f.*
thorn /θɔrn/ *n.* espina *f.*
thorough /'θɜrou/ *a.* completo; cuidadoso.
though /ðou/ *adv.* **1.** sin embargo. —*conj.* **2.** aunque. **as th.,** como si.
thought /θɔt/ *n.* pensamiento *m.*
thoughtful /'θɔtfəl/ *a.* pensativo; considerado.
thousand /'θauzənd/ *a.* & *pron.* mil.
thread /θrɛd/ *n.* hilo *m.*; (of screw) rosca *f.*
threat /θrɛt/ *n.* amenaza *f.*
threaten /'θrɛtn̩/ *v.* amenazar.
three /θri/ *a.* & *pron.* tres.
thrift /θrɪft/ *n.* economía, frugalidad *f.*
thrill /θrɪl/ *n.* **1.** emoción *f.* —*v.* **2.** emocionar.
thrive /θraiv/ *v.* prosperar.
throat /θrout/ *n.* garganta *f.*
throne /θroun/ *n.* trono *m.*
through /θru/ *prep.* **1.** por; a través de; por medio de. —*a.* **2.** continuo. **th. train,** tren directo. **to be th.,** haber terminado.
throughout /θru'aut/ *prep.* **1.** por todo, durante todo. —*adv.* **2.** en todas partes; completamente.
throw /θrou/ *n.* **1.** tiro *m.* —*v.* **2.** tirar, lanzar. **th. away,** arrojar. **th. out,** echar.
thrust /θrʌst/ *n.* **1.** lanzada *f.* —*v.* **2.** empujar.
thumb /θʌm/ *n.* dedo pulgar, pulgar *m.*
thumbtack /'θʌm,tæk/ *n.* chincheta *f.*
thunder /'θʌndər/ *n.* **1.** trueno *m.* —*v.* **2.** tronar.
Thursday /'θɜrzdei/ *n.* jueves *m.*
thus /ðʌs/ *adv.* así, de este modo.
thwart /θwɔrt/ *v.* frustrar.
ticket /'tɪkɪt/ *n.* billete, boleto *m.* **t. window,** taquilla *f.* **round trip t.,** billete de ida y vuelta.
tickle /'tɪkəl/ *n.* **1.** cosquilla *f.* —*v.* **2.** hacer cosquillas a.
ticklish /'tɪklɪʃ/ *a.* cosquilloso.
tide /taid/ *n.* marea *f.*
tidy /'taidi/ *a.* **1.** limpio, ordenado. —*v.* **2.** poner en orden.
tie /tai/ *n.* **1.** corbata *f.*; lazo; (game) empate *m.* —*v.* **2.** atar; anudar.
tier /tɪər/ *n.* hilera *f.*
tiger /'taigər/ *n.* tigre *m.*
tight /tait/ *a.* apretado; tacaño.
tighten /'taitn̩/ *v.* estrechar, apretar.
tile /tail/ *n.* teja *f.*; azulejo *m.*
till /tɪl/ *prep.* **1.** hasta. —*conj.* **2.** hasta que. —*n.* **3.** cajón *m.* —*v.* **4.** cultivar, labrar.
tilt /tɪlt/ *n.* **1.** inclinación; justa *f.* —*v.* **2.** inclinar; justar.
timber /'tɪmbər/ *n.* madera *f.*; (beam) madero *m.*
time /taim/ *n.* tiempo *m.*; vez *f.*; (of day) hora *f,*; *v.* *cronometrar.*
timetable /'taim,teibəl/ *n.* horario, itinerario *m.*
time zone huso horario *m.*
timid /'tɪmɪd/ *a.* tímido.
timidity /tɪ'mɪdɪti/ *n.* timidez *f.*
tin /tɪn/ *n.* estaño *m.*; hojalata *f.* **t. can,** lata *f.*
tin foil papel de estaño *m.*
tint /tɪnt/ *n.* **1.** tinte *m.* —*v.* **2.** teñir.
tiny /'taini/ *a.* chiquito, pequeñito.
tip /tɪp/ *n.* **1.** punta; propina *f.* —*v.* **2.** inclinar; dar propina a.
tire /taiᵊr/ *n.* **1.** llanta, goma *f.*, neumático *m.* —*v.* **2.** cansar.
tired /taiᵊrd/ *a.* cansado.
tissue /'tɪʃu/ *n.* tejido *m.* **t. paper,** papel de seda.
title /'taitl̩/ *n.* **1.** título *m.* —*v.* **2.** titular.
to /tu; *unstressed* tʊ, tə/ *prep.* a; para.
toast /toust/ *n.* **1.** tostada *f.*; (drink) brindis *m.* —*v.* **2.** tostar; brindar.
toaster /'toustər/ *n.* tostador *m.*
tobacco /tə'bækou/ *n.* tabaco *m.* **t. shop,** tabaquería *f.*
toboggan /tə'bɒgən/ *n.* tobogán *m.*
today /tə'dei/ *adv.* hoy.
toe /tou/ *n.* dedo del pie.
together /tə'gɛðər/ *a.* **1.** juntos. —*adv.* **2.** juntamente.
toil /tɔil/ *n.* **1.** trabajo *m.* —*v.* **2.** afanarse.
toilet /'tɔilɪt/ *n.* tocado; excusado, retrete *m.* **t. paper,** papel higiénico.
token /'toukən/ *n.* señal *f.*
tolerance /'tɒlərəns/ *n.* tolerancia *f.*
tolerate /'tɒlə,reit/ *v.* tolerar.
toll-free number /'toul 'fri/ teléfono gratuito *m.*
tomato /tə'meitou/ *n.* tomate *m.*
tomb /tum/ *n.* tumba *f.*
tomorrow /tə'mɔrou/ *adv.* mañana. **day after t.,** pasado mañana.
ton /tʌn/ *n.* tonelada *f.*
tone /toun/ *n.* tono *m.*
tongue /tʌŋ/ *n.* lengua *f.*
tonic /'tɒnɪk/ *n.* tónico *m.*
tonight /tə'nait/ *adv.* esta noche.
tonsil /'tɒnsəl/ *n.* amígdala *f.*
too /tu/ *adv.* también. **t. much,** demasiado. **t. many,** demasiados.
tool /tul/ *n.* herramienta *f.*
tooth /tuθ/ *n.* diente *m.*; (back) muela *f.*
toothache /'tuθ,eik/ *n.* dolor de muela.
toothbrush /'tuθ,brʌʃ/ *n.* cepillo de dientes.
toothpaste /'tuθ,peist/ *n.* crema dentífrica, pasta dentífrica.
top /tɒp/ *n.* **1.** parte de arriba. —*v.* **2.** cubrir; sobrepasar.
topic /'tɒpɪk/ *n.* *S.A.* tópico *m.*
topical /'tɒpɪkəl/ *a.* tópico.
torch /tɔrtʃ/ *n.* antorcha *f.*
torment /*n.* 'tɔrmɛnt; *v.* tɔr'mɛnt/ *n.* **1.** tormento *m.* —*v.* **2.** atormentar.
torrent /'tɔrənt/ *n.* torrente *m.*
torture /'tɔrtʃər/ *n.* **1.** tortura *f.* —*v.* **2.** torturar.
toss /tɔs/ *v.* tirar; agitar.
total /'toutl̩/ *a.* **1.** total, entero. —*n.* **2.** total *m.*
touch /tʌtʃ/ *n.* **1.** tacto *m.* **in t.,** en comunicación. —*v.* **2.** tocar; conmover.
tough /tʌf/ *a.* tosco; tieso; fuerte.
tour /tʊr/ *n.* **1.** viaje *m.* —*v.* **2.** viajar.
tourist /'tʊrɪst/ *n.* turista *m.* & *f.* *a.* turístico.
tournament /'tʊrnəmənt/ *n.* torneo *m.*
tow /tou/ *n.* **1.** remolque *m.* —*v.* **2.** remolcar.
toward /tɔrd, tə'wɔrd/ *prep.* hacia.
towel /'tauəl/ *n.* toalla *f.*
tower /'tauər/ *n.* torre *f.*
town /taun/ *n.* pueblo *m.*
town meeting cabildo abierto *m.*
tow truck grúa *f.*
toy /tɔi/ *n.* **1.** juguete *m.* —*v.* **2.** jugar.
trace /treis/ *n.* **1.** vestigio; rastro *m.* —*v.* **2.** trazar; rastrear; investigar.
track /træk/ *n.* **1.** huella, pista *f.* **race t.,** hipódromo *m.* —*v.* **2.** rastrear.
tract /trækt/ *n.* trecho; tracto *m.*
tractor /'træktər/ *n.* tractor *m.*
trade /treid/ *n.* **1.** comercio, negocio; oficio; canje *m.* —*v.* **2.** comerciar, negociar; cambiar.
trader /'treidər/ *n.* comerciante *m.*
tradition /trə'dɪʃən/ *n.* tradición *f.*
traditional /trə'dɪʃənl̩/ *a.* tradicional.
traffic /'træfɪk/ *n.* **1.** tráfico *m.* —*v.* **2.** traficar.
traffic jam atasco, embotellamiento *m.*
traffic light semáforo *m.*
tragedy /'trædʒɪdi/ *n.* tragedia *f.*
tragic /'trædʒɪk/ *a.* trágico.
trail /treil/ *n.* **1.** sendero; rastro *m.* —*v.* **2.** rastrear; arrastrar.
train /trein/ *n.* **1.** tren *m.* —*v.* **2.** enseñar; disciplinar; (sport) entrenarse.
traitor /'treitər/ *n.* traidor -ora.
tramp /træmp/ *n.* **1.** caminata *f.*; vagabundo *m.* —*v.* **2.** patear.
tranquil /'træŋkwɪl/ *a.* tranquilo.
tranquilizer /'træŋkwə,laizər/ *n.* tranquilizante *m.*
tranquillity /træŋ'kwɪlɪti/ *n.* tranquilidad *f.*
transaction /træn'sækʃən/ *n.* transacción *f.*
transfer /*n.* 'trænsfər, *v.* træns'fɜr/ *n.* **1.** traslado *m.*; boleto de transbordo. —*v.* **2.** trasladar, transferir.
transform /træns'fɔrm/ *v.* transformar.

transfusion /træns'fyuʒən/ n. transfusión f.

transistor /træn'zɪstər/ n. transistor m.

transition /træn'zɪʃən/ n. transición f.

translate /træns'leit/ v. traducir.

translation /træns'leiʃən/ n. traducción f.

transmit /træns'mɪt/ v. transmitir.

transparent /træns'pɛərənt/ a. transparente.

transport /n. 'trænspɔrt, v. træns'pɔrt/ n. **1.** transporte m. —v. **2.** transportar.

transportation /ˌtrænspər'teiʃən/ n. transporte m.

transsexual /træns'sɛkʃuəl/ a. & n. transexual m. & f.

transvestite /træns'vɛstait/ n. travestí m. & f.

trap /træp/ n. **1.** trampa f. —v. **2.** atrapar.

trash /træʃ/ n. desecho m.; basura f.

trash can cubo de la basura m.

travel /'trævəl/ n. **1.** tráfico m.; (pl.) viajes m. pl. —v. **2.** viajar.

travel agency agencia de viajes f.

traveler /'trævələr/ n. viajero -ra.

traveler's check /'trævələrz/ cheque de viaje m.

tray /trei/ n. bandeja f.

tread /trɛd/ n. **1.** pisada f.; (of a tire) cubierta f. —v. **2.** pisar.

treason /'trizən/ n. traición f.

treasure /'trɛʒər/ n. tesoro m.

treasurer /'trɛʒərər/ n. tesorero -ra.

treasury /'trɛʒəri/ n. tesorería f.

treat /trit/ v. tratar; convidar.

treatment /'tritmənt/ n. trato, tratamiento m.

treaty /'triti/ n. tratado, pacto m.

tree /tri/ n. árbol m.

tremble /'trɛmbəl/ v. temblar.

tremendous /trɪ'mɛndəs/ a. tremendo.

trench /trɛntʃ/ n. foso m.; Mil. trinchera f.

trend /trɛnd/ n. **1.** tendencia f. —v. **2.** tender.

trespass /'trɛspəs, -pæs/ v. traspasar; violar.

triage /tri'aʒ/ n. clasificación de los heridos después del combate.

trial /'traiəl/ n. prueba f.; Leg. proceso, juicio m.

triangle /'trai,æŋgəl/ n. triángulo m.

tribulation /ˌtrɪbyə'leiʃən/ n. tribulación f.

tributary /'trɪbyə,tɛri/ a. n. tributario m.

tribute /'trɪbyut/ n. tributo m.

trick /trɪk/ n. **1.** engaño m.; maña f.; (cards) baza f. —v. **2.** engañar.

trifle /'traifəl/ n. **1.** pequeñez f. —v. **2.** juguetear.

trigger /'trɪgər/ n. gatillo m.

trim /trɪm/ a. **1.** ajustado; acicalado. —n. **2.** adorno m. —v. **3.** adornar; ajustar; cortar un poco.

trinket /'trɪŋkɪt/ n. bagatela, chuchería f.

trip /trɪp/ n. **1.** viaje m. —v. **2.** tropezar.

triple /'trɪpəl/ a. **1.** triple —v. **2.** triplicar.

tripod /'traipɒd/ n. trípode m.

trite /trait/ a. banal.

triumph /'traiəmf/ n. **1.** triunfo m. —v. **2.** triunfar.

triumphant /trai'ʌmfənt/ a. triunfante.

trivial /'trɪviəl/ a. trivial.

trolley /'troli/ n. tranvía m.

trombone /trɒm'boun/ n. trombón m.

troop /trup/ n. tropa f.

trophy /'troufi/ n. trofeo m.

tropical /'trɒpɪkəl/ a. tropical.

tropics /'trɒpɪks/ n. trópico m.

trot /trɒt/ n. **1.** trote m. —v. **2.** trotar.

trouble /'trʌbəl/ n. **1.** apuro m.; congoja; aflicción f. —v. **2.** molestar; afligir.

troublesome /'trʌbəlsəm/ a. penoso, molesto.

trough /trɒf/ n. artesa f.

trousers /'trauzərz/ n. pantalones, calzones m.pl.

trout /traut/ n. trucha f.

truce /trus/ n. tregua f.

truck /trʌk/ n. camión m.

true /tru/ a. verdadero, cierto, verdad.

truffle /'trʌfəl/ n. trufa f.

trumpet /'trʌmpɪt/ n. trompeta, trompa f.

trunk /trʌŋk/ n. baúl m.; (of a tree) tronco m.

trust /trʌst/ n. **1.** confianza f. —v. **2.** confiar.

trustworthy /'trʌst,wɜrði/ a. digno de confianza.

truth /truθ/ n. verdad f.

truthful /'truθfəl/ a. veraz.

try /trai/ n. **1.** prueba f.; ensayo m. —v. **2.** tratar; probar; ensayar; Leg. juzgar. **t. on,** probarse.

T-shirt /'ti,ʃɜrt/ n. camiseta f.

tub /tʌb/ n. tina f.

tube /tub/ n. tubo m.

tuberculosis /tu,bɜrkyə'lousɪs/ n. tuberculosis f.

tuck /tʌk/ n. **1.** recogido m. —v. **2.** recoger.

Tuesday /'tuzdei/ n. martes m.

tug /tʌg/ n. **1.** tirada f.; (boat) remolcador m. —v. **2.** tirar de.

tuition /tu'ɪʃən/ n. matrícula, colegiatura f.

tumble /'tʌmbəl/ n. **1.** caída f. —v. **2.** caer, tumbar; voltear.

tumult /'tumʌlt/ n. tumulto, alboroto m.

tuna /'tʌni/ n. atún m.

tune /tun/ n. **1.** tono m.; melodía, canción f. —v. **2.** templar.

tunnel /'tʌnl/ n. túnel m.

turf /tɜrf/ n. césped m.

Turkey /'tɜrki/ n. Turquía f.

Turkish /'tɜrkɪʃ/ a. turco.

turmoil /'tɜrmɔil/ n. disturbio m.

turn /tɜrn/ n. **1.** vuelta f.; giro; turno m. —v. **2.** volver, tornear, girar; **t. into,** transformar. **t. around,** volverse. **t. on,** encender; abrir. **t. off, t. out,** apagar.

turnip /'tɜrnɪp/ n. nabo m.

turret /'tɜrɪt/ n. torrecilla f.

turtle /'tɜrtl/ n. tortuga f.

turtleneck sweater /'tɜrtl,nɛk/ jersey de cuello alto m.

tutor /'tutər/ n. **1.** tutor -ra. —v. **2.** enseñar.

tweezers /'twizərz/ n. pl. pinzas f. pl.

twelve /twɛlv/ a. & pron. doce.

twenty /'twɛnti/ a. & pron. veinte.

twice /twais/ adv. dos veces.

twig /twɪg/ n. varita; ramita f.; vástago m.

twilight /'twai,lait/ n. crepúsculo m.

twin /twɪn/ n. gemelo -la.

twine /twain/ n. **1.** guita f. —v. **2.** torcer.

twinkle /'twɪŋkəl/ v. centellear.

twist /twɪst/ v. torcer.

two /tu/ a. & pron. dos.

type /taip/ n. **1.** tipo m. —v. **2.** escribir a máquina.

typewriter /'taip,raitər/ n. máquina de escribir.

typhoid fever /'taifɔid/ fiebre tifoidea.

typical /'tɪpɪkəl/ a. típico.

typist /'taipɪst/ n. mecanógrafo -fa.

tyranny /'tɪrəni/ n. tiranía f.

tyrant /'tairənt/ n. tirano -na.

U

udder /'ʌdər/ n. ubre f.

UFO abbr. (unidentified flying object) OVNI m. (objeto volador no identificado).

ugly /'ʌgli/ a. feo.

Ukraine /yu'krein/ n. Ucrania f.

Ukrainian /yu'kreiniən/ a. & n. ucranio.

ulcer /'ʌlsər/ n. úlcera f.

ulterior /ʌl'tɪəriər/ a. ulterior.

ultimate /'ʌltəmɪt/ a. último.

ultrasonic /ˌʌltrə'sɒnɪk/ a. ultrasónico.

umbrella /ʌm'brɛlə/ n. paraguas m. **sun u.,** quitasol m.

umpire /'ʌmpaiər/ n. árbitro m.

unable /ʌn'eibəl/ a. incapaz. **to be u.,** no poder.

unanimous /yu'nænəməs/ a. unánime.

uncertain /ʌn'sɜrtn/ a. incierto, inseguro.

uncle /'ʌŋkəl/ n. tío m.

unconscious /ʌn'kɒnʃəs/ a. inconsciente; desmayado.

uncover /ʌn'kʌvər/ v. descubrir.

undeniable /ˌʌndɪ'naiəbəl/ a. innegable.

under /'ʌndər/ adv. **1.** debajo, abajo. —prep. **2.** bajo, debajo de.

underestimate /ˌʌndər'ɛstə,meit/ v. menospreciar; subestimar.

undergo /ˌʌndər'gou/ v. sufrir.

underground /'ʌndər,graund,/ a. subterráneo; clandestino.

underline /'ʌndər,lain/ v. subrayar.

underneath /ˌʌndər'niθ/ adv. **1.** por debajo. —prep. **2.** debajo de.

undershirt /'ʌndər,ʃɜrt/ n. camiseta f.

understand /ˌʌndər'stænd/ v. entender, comprender.

undertake /ˌʌndər'teik/ v. emprender.

underwear /'ʌndər,wɛər/ n. ropa interior.

undo /ʌn'du/ v. deshacer; desatar.

undress /ʌn'drɛs/ v. desnudar, desvestir.

uneasy /ʌn'izi/ a. inquieto.

uneven /ʌn'ivən/ a. desigual.

unexpected /ˌʌnɪk'spɛktɪd/ a. inesperado.

unfair /ʌn'fɛər/ a. injusto.

unfit /ʌn'fɪt/ a. incapaz; inadecuado.

unfold /ʌn'fould/ v. desplegar; revelar.

unforgettable /ˌʌnfər'gɛtəbəl/ a. inolvidable.

unfortunate /ʌn'fɔrtʃənɪt/ a. desafortunado, desgraciado.

unfurnished /ʌn'fɜrnɪʃt/ a. desamueblado.

unhappy /ʌn'hæpi/ a. infeliz.

uniform /'yunə,fɔrm/ a. & n. uniforme m.

unify /'yunə,fai/ v. unificar.

union /'yunyən/ n. unión f. **labor u.,** sindicato de obreros.

unique /yu'nik/ a. único.

unisex /'yunə,sɛks/ a. unisex.

unit /'yunɪt/ n. unidad f.

unite /yu'nait/ v. unir.

United Nations /yu'naitɪd 'neiʃənz/ Naciones Unidas f. pl.

United States /yu'naitɪd 'steits/ Estados Unidos m. pl.

unity /'yunɪti/ n. unidad f.

universal /ˌyunə'vɜrsəl/ a. universal.

universe /'yunə,vɜrs/ n. universo m.

university /ˌyunə'vɜrsɪti/ n. universidad f.

unleaded /ʌn'lɛdɪd/ a. sin plomo.

unless /ʌn'lɛs/ conj. a menos que, si no es que.

unlike /ʌn'laik/ a. disímil.

unload /ʌn'loud/ v. descargar.

unlock /ʌn'lɒk/ v. abrir.

unplug /ʌn'plʌg/ v. desenchufar.

unpopular /ʌn'pɒpyələr/ a. impopular.

unreasonable /ʌn'rizənəbəl/ a. desrazonable.

unscrew /ʌn'skru/ v. desatornillar.

untie /ʌn'tai/ v. desatar; soltar.

until /ʌn'tɪl/ prep. **1.** hasta. —conj. **2.** hasta que.

unusual /ʌn'yuʒuəl/ a. raro, inusitado.

up /ʌp/ adv. **1.** arriba. —prep. **2.** **u. the street,** etc. calle arriba, etc.

uphold /ʌp'hould/ v. apoyar; defender.

upholster /ʌp'houlstər, ə'poul-/ v. entapizar.

upload /'ʌp,loud/ n. **1.** ascenso de archivos m. —v. **2.** subir, cargar.

upon /ə'pɒn/ prep. sobre, encima de.

upper /'ʌpər/ a. superior.

upper-case letter /'ʌpər 'keis/ mayúscula f.

upright /'ʌp,rait/ a. derecho, recto.

upriver /'ʌp'rɪvər/ adv. río arriba.

uproar /'ʌp,rɔr/ n. alboroto, tumulto m.

upset /n. 'ʌp,sɛt; v. ʌp'sɛt/ n. **1.** trastorno m. —v. **2.** trastornar.

upsetting /ʌp'sɛtɪŋ/ a. inquietante.

upstream /'ʌp'strim/ adv. aguas arriba, contra la corriente, río arriba.

uptight /'ʌp'tait/ a. (psicológicamente) tenso, tieso.

upward /'ʌpwərd/ adv. hacia arriba.

urge /ɜrdʒ/ n. **1.** deseo m. —v. **2.** instar.

urgency /'ɜrdʒənsi/ n. urgencia f.

urgent /'ɜrdʒənt/ a. urgente. **to be u.,** urgir.

us /ʌs/ pron. nosotros -as; nos.

use /n. yus; v. yuz/ n. **1.** uso m. —v. **2.** usar, emplear. **u. up,** gastar, agotar. **be used to,** estar acostumbrado a.

useful /'yusfəl/ a. útil.

useless /'yuslɪs/ a. inútil, inservible.

user-friendly /'yuzər 'frɛndli/ a. amigable.

username /'yuzər'neim/ n. nombre de usuario m.

usher /'ʌʃər/ n. **1.** acomodador -ora. —v. **2.** introducir.

usual /'yuʒuəl/ a. usual.

utensil /yu'tɛnsəl/ n. utensilio m.

utmost /'ʌt,moust/ a. sumo, extremo.

utter /'ʌtər/ a. **1.** completo. —v. **2.** proferir; dar.

utterance /'ʌtərəns/ n. expresión f.

V

vacancy /'veikənsi/ n. vacante f.

vacant /'veikənt/ a. desocupado, libre.

vacation /vei'keiʃən/ n. vacaciones f. pl.

vaccinate /'væksə,neit/ v. vacunar.

vacuum /'vækyum/ n. vacuo, vacío m. **v. cleaner,** aspiradora f.

vagrant /'veigrənt/ a. & n. vagabundo- a.

vague /veig/ a. vago.

vain /vein/ a. vano; vanidoso. **in v.,** en vano.

valiant /'vælyənt/ a. valiente.

valid /'vælɪd/ a. válido.

valley /'væli/ n. valle m.

valor /'vælər/ n. valor m.; valentía f.

valuable /'vælyuəbəl/ a. valioso. **to be v.,** valer mucho.

value /'vælyu/ n. **1.** valor, importe m. —v. **2.** valorar; estimar.

van /væn/ n. furgoneta f.

vandal /'vændl/ n. vándalo m.

vandalism /'vændl,ɪzəm/ n. vandalismo m.

vanish /'vænɪʃ/ v. desaparecer.

vanity /'vænɪti/ n. vanidad f. **v. case,** polvera f.

vanquish /'væŋkwɪʃ/ v. vencer.

vapor /'veipər/ n. vapor m.

variation /ˌvɛəri'eiʃən/ n. variación f.

varicose vein /'vɛri,kous/ variz f.

variety /və'raiɪti/ n. variedad f.

various /'vɛəriəs/ a. varios; diversos.

varnish /'vɑrnɪʃ/ n. **1.** barniz m. —v. **2.** barnizar.

vary /'vɛəri/ v. variar; cambiar.

vase /veis, veiz, vɑz/ n. florero; jarrón m.

vasectomy /væ'sɛktəmi/ *n.* vasectomía *f.*

vassal /'væsəl/ *n.* vasallo *m.*

vast /væst/ *a.* vasto.

vat /væt/ *n.* tina *f.*, tanque *m.*

VAT /væt/ *n.* IVA (impuesto sobre el valor añadido).

vault /vɔlt/ *n.* bóveda *f.*

vegetable /'vɛdʒtəbəl/ *a. & n.* vegetal *m.*; (pl.) legumbres, verduras *f. pl.*

vehement /'viəmənt/ *a.* vehemente.

vehicle /'viɪkəl or, sometimes,* 'vihɪ-/ *n.* vehículo *m.*

veil /veil/ *n.* **1.** velo *m.* —*v.* **2.** velar.

vein /vein/ *n.* vena *f.*

velocity /və'lɒsiti/ *n.* velocidad *f.*

velvet /'vɛlvɪt/ *n.* terciopelo *m.*

Venetian /və'niʃən/ *a. & n.* veneciano.

vengeance /'vɛndʒəns/ *n.* venganza *f.*

Venice /'vɛnɪs/ *n.* Venecia *f.*

vent /vɛnt/ *n.* apertura *f.*

ventilate /'vɛntl̩,eit/ *v.* ventilar.

venture /'vɛntʃər/ *n.* ventura *f.*

verb /vɜrb/ *n.* verbo *m.*

verbose /vər'bous/ *a.* verboso.

verdict /'vɜrdɪkt/ *n.* veredicto, fallo *m.*

verge /vɜrdʒ/ *n.* borde *m.*

verify /'vɛrə,fai/ *v.* verificar.

versatile /'vɜrsətl̩/ *a.* versátil.

verse /vɜrs/ *n.* verso *m.*

version /'vɜrʒən/ *n.* versión *f.*

vertical /'vɜrtɪkəl/ *a.* vertical.

very /'vɛri/ *a.* **1.** mismo. —*adv.* **2.** muy.

vessel /'vɛsəl/ *n.* vasija *f.*; barco *m.*

vest /vɛst/ *n.* chaleco *m.*

veteran /'vɛtərən/ *a. & n.* veterano -na.

veto /'vitou/ *n.* veto *m.*

vex /vɛks/ *v.* molestar.

via /'vaiə, 'viə/ *prep.* por la vía de; por.

viaduct /'vaiə,dʌkt/ *n.* viaducto *m.*

vibrate /'vaibreit/ *v.* vibrar.

vibration /vai'breiʃən/ *n.* vibración *f.*

vice /vais/ *n.* vicio *m.*

vicinity /vɪ'sɪnɪti/ *n.* vecindad *f.*

vicious /'vɪʃəs/ *a.* vicioso.

victim /'vɪktəm/ *n.* víctima *f.*

victor /'vɪktər/ *n.* vencedor -ora.

victorious /vɪk'tɔriəs/ *a.* victorioso.

victory /'vɪktəri/ *n.* victoria *f.*

video camera /'vɪdi,ou/ videocámara *f.*

videoconference /'vɪdiou,kɒnfərəns/ videoconferencia *f.*

videodisc /'vɪdiou,dɪsk/ *n.* videodisco *m.*

video game /'vɪdi,ou/ videojuego *m.*

videotape /'vɪdiou,teip/ *n.* vídeo *m.*, magnetoscopio *m.*

view /vyu/ *n.* **1.** vista *f.* —*v.* **2.** ver.

viewpoint /'vyu,pɔint/ *n.* punto de vista *m.*

vigil /'vɪdʒəl/ *n.* vigilia, vela *f.*

vigilant /'vɪdʒələnt/ *a.* vigilante.

vigor /'vɪgər/ *n.* vigor *m.*

vile /vail/ *a.* vil, bajo.

village /'vɪlɪdʒ/ *n.* aldea *f.*

villain /'vɪlən/ *n.* malvado -da.

vindicate /'vɪndɪ,keit/ *v.* vindicar.

vine /vain/ *n.* parra, vid *f.*

vinegar /'vɪnɪgər/ *n.* vinagre *m.*

vintage /'vɪntɪdʒ/ *n.* vendimia *f.*

violate /'vaiə,leit/ *v.* violar.

violation /,vaiə'leiʃən/ *n.* violación *f.*

violence /'vaiələns/ *n.* violencia *f.*

violent /'vaiələnt/ *a.* violento.

violin /,vaiə'lɪn/ *n.* violín *m.*

virgin /'vɜrdʒɪn/ *n.* virgen *f.*

virile /'vɪrəl/ *a.* viril.

virtual /'vɜrtʃuəl/ *a.* virtual.

virtual memory memoria virtual *f.*

virtual reality realidad virtual *f.*

virtue /'vɜrtʃu/ *n.* virtud *f.*

virtuous /'vɜrtʃuəs/ *a.* virtuoso.

virus /'vairəs/ *n.* virus *m.*

visa /'vizə/ *n.* visa *f.*

visible /'vɪzəbəl/ *a.* visible.

vision /'vɪʒən/ *n.* visión *f.*

visit /'vɪzɪt/ *n.* **1.** visita *f.* —*v.* **2.** visitar.

visitor /'vɪzɪtər/ *n.* visitante *m. & f.*

visual /'vɪʒuəl/ *a.* visual.

vital /'vaitl̩/ *a.* vital.

vitality /vai'tælɪti/ *n.* vitalidad, energía vital *f.*

vitamin /'vaitəmɪn/ *n.* vitamina *f.*

vivacious /vɪ'veiʃəs, vai-/ *a.* vivaz.

vivid /'vɪvɪd/ *a.* vivo; gráfico.

vocabulary /vou'kæbyə,lɛri/ *n.* vocabulario *m.*

vocal /'voukəl/ *a.* vocal.

vodka /'vɒdkə/ *n.* vodca *m.*

vogue /voug/ *n.* boga; moda *f.* **be in vogue** estilarse.

voice /vɔis/ *n.* **1.** voz *f.* —*v.* **2.** expresar.

voice mail correo de voz *m.*

voice recognition reconocimiento de voz *m.*

void /vɔid/ *a.* **1.** vacío. —*n.* **2.** vacío *m.* —*v.* **3.** invalidar.

voltage /'voultidʒ/ *n.* voltaje *m.*

volume /'vɒlyum/ *n.* volumen; tomo *m.*

voluntary /'vɒlən,tɛri/ *a.* voluntario.

volunteer /,vɒlən'tɪər/ *n.* **1.** voluntario -ria. —*v.* **2.** ofrecerse.

vomit /'vɒmɪt/ *v.* vomitar.

vote /vout/ *n.* **1.** voto *m.* —*v.* **2.** votar.

voter /'voutər/ *n.* votante *m. & f.*

vouch /vautʃ/ *v.* **v. for,** garantizar.

vow /vau/ *n.* **1.** voto *m.* —*v.* **2.** jurar.

vowel /'vauəl/ *n.* vocal *f.*

voyage /'vɔiɪdʒ/ *n.* viaje *m.*

vulgar /'vʌlgər/ *a.* vulgar; común; soez.

vulnerable /'vʌlnərəbəl/ *a.* vulnerable.

W

wade /weid/ *v.* vadear.

wag /wæg/ *v.* menear.

wage /weidʒ/ *n.* **1.** (pl.) sueldo, salario *m.* —*v.* **2. w. war,** hacer guerra.

wagon /'wægən/ *n.* carreta *f.*

wail /weil/ *n.* **1.** lamento, gemido *m.* —*v.* **2.** lamentar, gemir.

waist /weist/ *n.* cintura *f.*

wait /weit/ *n.* **1.** espera *f.* —*v.* **2.** esperar. **w. for,** esperar. **w. on,** atender.

waiter /'weitər/ *n.* **waitress** *n.* camarero -ra.

waiting room /'weitɪŋ/ sala de espera.

wake /weik/ *v.* **w. up,** despertar.

walk /wɔk/ *n.* **1.** paseo *m.*; vuelta; caminata *f.*; modo de andar. —*v.* **2.** andar; caminar; ir a pie.

wall /wɔl/ *n.* pared; muralla *f.*

wallcovering /'wɔl,kʌvəriŋ/ *n.* tapizado de pared *m.*

wallet /'wɒlɪt/ *n.* cartera *f.*

wallpaper /'wɔl,peipər/ *n.* **1.** empapelado *m.* —*v.* **2.** empapelar.

walnut /'wɔl,nʌt/ *n.* nuez *f.*

waltz /wɔlts/ *n.* vals *m.*

wander /'wɒndər/ *v.* vagar.

want /wɒnt/ *n.* **1.** necesidad *f.* —*v.* **2.** querer.

war /wɔr/ *n.* guerra *f.*

ward /wɔrd/ *n.* **1.** *Pol.* barrio *m.*; (hospital) cuadra *f.* —*v.* **2. w. off,** parar.

warehouse /'wɛər,haus/ *n.* almacén *m.*

wares /wɛərz/ *n.* mercancías *f.pl.*

warlike /'wɔr,laik/ *a.* belicoso.

warm /wɔrm/ *a.* **1.** caliente; *Fig.* caluroso. **to be w.,** tener calor; (weather) hacer calor. —*v.* **2.** calentar.

warmth /wɔrmθ/ *n.* calor *m.*

warn /wɔrn/ *v.* advertir.

warning /'wɔrnɪŋ/ *n.* aviso *m.*

warp /wɔrp/ *v.* alabear.

warrant /'wɔrənt, 'wɒr-/ *v.* justificar.

warrior /'wɔriər/ *n.* guerrero -ra.

warship /'wɔr,ʃɪp/ *n.* navío de guerra, buque de guerra *m.*

wash /wɒʃ/ *v.* lavar.

washing machine /'wɒʃɪŋ/ máquina de lavar, lavadora *f.*

wasp /wɒsp/ *n.* avispa *f.*

waste /weist/ *n.* **1.** gasto *m.*; desechos *m.pl.* —*v.* **2.** gastar; perder.

watch /wɒtʃ/ *n.* **1.** reloj *m.*; *Mil.* guardia *f.* —*v.* **2.** observar, mirar. **w. for,** esperar. **w. out for,** tener cuidado con. **w. over,** guardar; velar por.

watchful /'wɒtʃfəl/ *a.* desvelado.

watchmaker /'wɒtʃ,meikər/ *n.* relojero -ra.

watchman /'wɒtʃmən/ *n.* sereno *m.*

water /'wɔtər/ *n.* **1.** agua *f.* **w. color,** acuarela *f.* —*v.* **2.** aguar.

waterbed /'wɔtər,bɛd/ *n.* cama de agua *f.*

waterfall /'wɔtər,fɔl/ *n.* catarata *f.*

watering can /'wɔtəriŋ/ regadera *f.*

waterproof /'wɔtər,pruf/ *a.* impermeable.

wave /weiv/ *n.* **1.** onda; ola *f.* —*v.* **2.** ondear; agitar; hacer señas.

waver /'weivər/ *v.* vacilar.

wax /wæks/ *n.* **1.** cera *f.* —*v.* **2.** encerar.

way /wei/ *n.* camino; modo *m.*, manera *f.* **in a w.,** hasta cierto punto. **a long w.,** muy lejos. **by the w.,** a propósito. **this w.,** por aquí. **that w.,** por allí. **which w.,** por dónde.

we /wi/ *pron.* nosotros -as.

weak /wik/ *a.* débil.

weaken /'wikən/ *v.* debilitar.

weakness /'wiknɪs/ *n.* debilidad *f.*

wealth /wɛlθ/ *n.* riqueza *f.*

wealthy /'wɛlθi/ *a.* adinerado.

wean /win/ *v.* destetar.

weapon /'wɛpən/ *n.* arma *f.*

wear /wɛər/ *n.* **1.** uso; desgaste *m.*; (clothes) ropa *f.* —*v.* **2.** usar, llevar. **w. out,** gastar; cansar.

weary /'wɪəri/ *a.* cansado, rendido.

weather /'wɛðər/ *n.* tiempo *m.*

weave /wiv/ *v.* tejer.

weaver /'wivər/ *n.* tejedor -ra.

web /wɛb/ *n.* **1.** tela *f.*

Web /wɛb/ *n.* **2.** (Internet) malla *f.*; telaraña *f.*, web *m.*

wedding /'wɛdɪŋ/ *n.* boda *f.*

wedge /wɛdʒ/ *n.* cuña *f.*

Wednesday /'wɛnzdei/ *n.* miércoles *m.*

weed /wid/ *n.* maleza *f.*

week /wik/ *n.* semana *f.*

weekday /'wik,dei/ *n.* día de trabajo.

weekend /'wik,ɛnd/ *n.* fin de semana.

weekly /'wikli/ *a.* semanal.

weep /wip/ *v.* llorar.

weigh /wei/ *v.* pesar.

weight /weit/ *n.* peso *m.*

weightless /'weitlɪs/ *v.* ingrávido.

weightlessness /'weitlɪsnɪs/ *n.* ingravidez *f.*

weird /wɪərd/ *a.* misterioso, extraño.

welcome /'wɛlkəm/ *a.* **1.** bienvenido. **you're w.,** de nada, no hay de qué. —*n.* **2.** acogida, bienvenida *f.* —*v.* **3.** acoger, recibir bien.

welfare /'wɛl,fɛər/ *n.* bienestar *m.*

well /wɛl/ *a.* **1.** sano, bueno. —*adv.* **2.** bien; pues. —*n.* **3.** pozo *m.*

well-done /'wɛl 'dʌn/ *a.* (food) bien cocido.

well-known /'wɛl 'noun/ *a.* bien conocido.

well-mannered /'wɛl 'mænərd/ *a.* educado.

west /wɛst/ *n.* oeste, occidente *m.*

western /'wɛstərn/ *a.* occidental.

westward /'wɛstwərd/ *adv.* hacia el oeste.

wet /wɛt/ *a.* **1.** mojado. **to get w.,** mojarse. —*v.* **2.** mojar.

whale /weil/ *n.* ballena *f.*

what /wʌt; unstressed wət/ *a.* **1.** qué; cuál. —*interrog. pron.* **2.** qué. —*rel. pron.* **3.** lo que.

whatever /wʌt'ɛvər/ *a.* **1.** cualquier. —*pron.* **2.** lo que; todo lo que.

wheat /wit/ *n.* trigo *m.*

wheel /wil/ *n.* rueda *f.* **steering w.,** volante *m.*

when /wɛn; unstressed wən/ *adv.* **1.** cuándo. —*conj.* **2.** cuando.

whenever /wɛn'ɛvər/ *conj.* siempre que, cuando quiera que.

where /wɛər/ *adv.* **1.** dónde, adónde. —*conj.* **2.** donde.

wherever /wɛər'ɛvər/ *conj.* dondequiera que, adondequiera que.

whether /'wɛðər/ *conj.* si.

which /wɪtʃ/ *a.* **1.** qué. —*interrog. pron.* **2.** cuál. —*rel. pron.* **3.** que; el cual; lo cual.

whichever /wɪtʃ'ɛvər/ *a. & pron.* cualquiera que.

while /wail/ *conj.* **1.** mientras; mientras que. —*n.* **2.** rato *m.*

whip /wɪp/ *n.* **1.** látigo *m.* —*v.* **2.** azotar.

whipped cream /wɪpt/ nata batida *f.*

whirl /wɜrl/ *v.* girar.

whirlpool /'wɜrl,pul/ *n.* vórtice *m.*

whirlwind /'wɜrl,wɪnd/ *n.* torbellino *m.*

whisk broom /wɪsk/ escobilla *f.*

whisker /'wɪskər/ *n.* bigote *m.*

whiskey /'wɪski/ *n.* whisky *m.*

whisper /'wɪspər/ *n.* **1.** cuchicheo *m.* —*v.* **2.** cuchichear.

whistle /'wɪsəl/ *n.* **1.** pito; silbido *m.* —*v.* **2.** silbar.

white /wait/ *a.* **1.** blanco. —*n.* **2.** (of egg) clara *f.*

who /hu/ **whom** *interrog. pron.* **1.** quién. —*rel. pron.* **2.** que; quien.

whoever /hu'ɛvər/ **whomever** *pron.* quienquiera que.

whole /houl/ *a.* **1.** entero. **the wh.,** todo el. —*n.* **2.** totalidad *f.* **on the wh.,** por lo general.

wholesale /'houl,seil/ *n.* **at wh.,** al por mayor.

wholesaler /'houl,seilər/ *n.* mayorista *m. & f.*

wholesome /'houlsəm/ *a.* sano, saludable.

wholly /'houli/ *adv.* enteramente.

whose /huz/ *interrog. adj.* **1.** de quién. —*rel. adj.* **2.** cuyo.

why /wai/ *adv.* por qué; para qué.

wicked /'wɪkɪd/ *a.* malo, malvado.

wickedness /'wɪkɪdnɪs/ *n.* maldad *f.*

wide /waid/ *a.* **1.** ancho; extenso. —*adv.* **2. w. open,** abierto de par en par.

widen /'waidn̩/ *v.* ensanchar; extender.

widespread /'waid'sprɛd/ *a.* extenso.

widow /'wɪdou/ *n.* viuda *f.*

widower /'wɪdouər/ *n.* viudo *m.*

width /wɪdθ/ *n.* anchura *f.*

wield /wild/ *v.* manejar, empuñar.

wife /waif/ *n.* esposa, señora, mujer *f.*

wig /wɪg/ *n.* peluca *f.*

wild /waild/ *a.* salvaje; bárbaro.

wilderness /'wɪldərnɪs/ *n.* desierto *m.*

wildlife /'waild,laif/ *n.* fauna silvestre *f.*

will /wɪl/ *n.* **1.** voluntad *f.*; testamento *m.* —*v.* **2.** querer; determinar; *Leg.* legar.

willful /'wɪlfəl/ *a.* voluntarioso; premeditado.

willing /'wɪlɪŋ/ *a.* **to be w.,** estar dispuesto.

willingly /'wɪlɪŋli/ *adv.* de buena gana.

wilt /wɪlt/ *v.* marchitar.

win /wɪn/ *v.* ganar.

wind /wɪnd/ *n.* **1.** viento *m.* —*v.* **2.** torcer; dar cuerda a.

windmill /'wɪnd,mɪl/ *n.* molino de viento *m.*

window /'wɪndou/ *n.* ventana; (of car) ventanilla *f.*; (of shop or store) escaparate *m.*

windshield /'wɪnd,ʃild/ *n.* parabrisas *m.*

windy /'wɪndi/ *a.* ventoso. **to be w.,** (weather) hacer viento.

wine /wain/ *n.* vino *m.*

wing /wɪŋ/ *n.* ala *f.; Theat.* bastidor *m.*

wink /wɪŋk/ *n.* **1.** guiño *m.* —*v.* **2.** guiñar.

winner /'wɪnər/ *n.* ganador -ra.

winter /'wɪntər/ *n.* invierno *m.*

wipe /waip/ *v.* limpiar; (dry) secar. **w. out,** destruir.

wire /waiˀr/ *n.* **1.** alambre; hilo; telegrama *m.* —*v.* **2.** telegrafiar.

wireless /'waiˀrlɪs/ *n.* telégrafo sin hilos.

wisdom /'wɪzdəm/ *n.* juicio *m.;* sabiduría *f.*

wise /waiz/ *a.* sensato, juicioso; sabio.

wish /wɪʃ/ *n.* **1.** deseo; voto *m.* —*v.* **2.** desear; querer.

wit /wɪt/ *n.* ingenio *m.,* sal *f.*

witch /wɪtʃ/ *n.* bruja *f.*

with /wɪθ, wɪð/ *prep.* con.

withdraw /wɪð'drɔ, wɪθ-/ *v.* retirar.

wither /'wɪðər/ *v.* marchitar.

withhold /wɪθ'hould, wɪð-/ *v.* retener, suspender.

within /wɪð'ɪn, wɪθ-/ *adv.* **1.** dentro, por dentro. —*prep.* **2.** dentro de; en.

without /wɪð'aut, wɪθ-/ *adv.* **1.** fuera, por fuera. —*prep.* **2.** sin.

witness /'wɪtnɪs/ *n.* **1.** testigo; testimonio *m.* & *f.* —*v.* **2.** presenciar; atestar.

witty /'wɪti/ *a.* ingenioso, gracioso, ocurrente.

wizard /'wɪzərd/ *n.* hechicero *m.*

woe /wou/ *n.* dolor *m.;* pena *f.*

wolf /wʊlf/ *n.* lobo -ba.

woman /'wʊmən/ *n.* mujer *f.*

womb /wum/ *n.* entrañas *f.pl.,* matriz *f.*

wonder /'wʌndər/ *n.* **1.** maravilla; admiración *f.* **for a w.,** por milagro. **no w.,** no es extraño. —*v.* **2.** preguntarse; maravillarse.

wonderful /'wʌndərfəl/ *a.* maravilloso; estupendo.

woo /wu/ *v.* cortejar.

wood /wʊd/ *n.* madera; (for fire) leña *f.*

wooden /'wʊdn/ *a.* de madera.

wool /wʊl/ *n.* lana *f.*

word /wɜrd/ *n.* **1.** palabra *f.* **the words** (of a song), la letra. —*v.* **2.** expresar.

word processing /'prɒsɛsɪŋ/ procesamiento de textos *m.*

word processor /'prɒsɛsər/ procesador de textos *m.*

work /wɜrk/ *n.* **1.** trabajo *m.;* (of art) obra *f.* —*v.* **2.** trabajar; obrar; funcionar.

worker /'wɜrkər/ *n.* trabajador -ra; obrero -ra.

workman /'wɜrkmən/ *n.* obrero *m.*

work station estación de trabajo *f.*

work week /'wɜrk,wik/ semana laboral *f.*

world /wɜrld/ *n.* mundo *m.* **w. war,** guerra mundial.

worldly /'wɜrldli/ *a.* mundano.

worldwide /'wɜrld'waid/ *a.* mundial.

worm /wɜrm/ *n.* gusano *m.*

worn /wɔrn/ *a.* usado. **w. out,** gastado; cansado, rendido.

worrisome /'wɜrisəm/ *a.* inquietante.

worry /'wɜri/ *n.* **1.** preocupación *f.* —*v.* **2.** preocupar.

worrying /'wɜriɪŋ/ *a.* inquietante.

worse /wɜrs/ *a.* peor. **to get w.,** empeorar.

worship /'wɜrʃɪp/ *n.* **1.** adoración *f.* —*v.* **2.** adorar.

worst /wɜrst/ *a.* peor.

worth /wɜrθ/ *a.* **1. to be w.,** valer. —*n.* **2.** valor *m.*

worthless /'wɜrθlɪs/ *a.* sin valor.

worthy /'wɜrði/ *a.* digno.

wound /wund/ *n.* **1.** herida *f.* —*v.* **2.** herir.

wrap /ræp/ *n.* **1.** (pl.) abrigos *m. pl.* —*n.* **2.** envolver.

wrapping /'ræpɪŋ/ *n.* cubierta *f.*

wrath /ræθ/ *n.* ira, cólera *f.*

wreath /riθ/ *n.* guirnalda; corona *f.*

wreck /rɛk/ *n.* **1.** ruina *f.;* accidente *m.* —*v.* **2.** destrozar, arruinar.

wrench /rɛntʃ/ *n.* llave *f.* **monkey w.,** llave inglesa.

wrestle /'rɛsəl/ *v.* luchar.

wretched /'rɛtʃɪd/ *a.* miserable.

wring /rɪŋ/ *v.* retorcer.

wrinkle /'rɪŋkəl/ *n.* **1.** arruga *f.* —*v.* **2.** arrugar.

wrist /rɪst/ *n.* muñeca *f.* **w. watch,** reloj de pulsera.

write /rait/ *v.* escribir. **w. down,** apuntar.

writer /'raitər/ *n.* escritor -ra.

writhe /raið/ *v.* contorcerse.

writing paper /'raitɪŋ/ papel de escribir *m.*

wrong /rɒŋ/ *a.* **1.** equivocado; incorrecto. **to be w.,** equivocarse; no tener razón. —*adv.* **2.** mal, incorrectamente. —*n.* **3.** agravio *m.* **right and w.,** el bien y el mal. —*v.* **4.** agraviar, ofender.

WWW *abbr.* (World Wide Web) malla mundial *f.*

X Y Z

x-ray /'ɛks,rei/ *n.* **1.** rayo X *m.,* radiografía, *f.* —*v.* **2.** radiografiar.

xylophone /'zailə,foun/ *n.* xilófono *m.*

yacht /yɒt/ *n.* yate *m.*

yard /yɑrd/ *n.* patio, corral *m.;* (measure) yarda *f.*

yarn /yɑrn/ *n.* hilo.

yawn /yɔn/ *n.* **1.** bostezo *m.* —*v.* **2.** bostezar.

year /yiər/ *n.* año *m.*

yearly /'yiərli/ *a.* anual.

yearn /yɜrn/ *v.* anhelar.

yell /yɛl/ *n.* **1.** grito *m.* —*v.* **2.** gritar.

yellow /'yɛlou/ *a.* amarillo.

yes /yɛs/ *adv.* sí.

yesterday /'yɛstər,dei/ *adv.* ayer.

yet /yɛt/ *adv.* todavía, aún.

Yiddish /'yɪdɪʃ/ *n.* yídish *m.*

yield /yild/ *v.* producir; ceder.

yogurt /'yougərt/ *n.* yogur *m.*

yoke /youk/ *n.* yugo *m.*

yolk /youk/ *n.* yema *f.*

you /yu; *unstressed* yʊ, yə/ *pron.* usted, (pl.) ustedes; lo, la, los, las; les; (familiar) tú, (pl.) vosotros -as; ti; te, (pl.) os. **with y.,** contigo, con usted.

young /yʌŋ/ *a.* joven.

youngster /'yʌŋstər/ *n.* muchacho -cha *m.* & *f.*

your /yʊr, yɔr; *unstressed* yər/ *a.* su; (familiar) tu; (pl.) vuestro.

yours /yʊrz, yɔrz/ *pron.* suyo; (familiar) tuyo; (pl.) vuestro.

yourself -selves /yʊr'sɛlf, yɔr- yər-/ *pron.* sí; se; (familiar) ti; te. **with y.,** consigo; contigo. **you y.,** usted mismo, ustedes mismos; tú mismo, vosotros mismos.

youth /yuθ/ *n.* juventud *f.;* (person) joven *m.* & *f.*

youth club club juvenil *m.*

youthful /'yuθfəl/ *a.* juvenil.

yuppie /'yʌpi/ *n.* yuppie *m.* & *f.*

zap /zæp/ *v.* desintegrar, aniquilar.

zeal /zil/ *n.* celo, fervor *m.*

zealous /'zɛləs/ *a.* celoso, fervoroso.

zero /'zɪərou/ *n.* cero *m.*

zest /zɛst/ *n.* gusto *m.*

zip code /zɪp/ número de distrito postal.

zipper /'zɪpər/ *m.* cremallera *f.*

zone /zoun/ *n.* zona *f.*

zoo /zu/ *n.* jardín zoológico.

SPANISH IRREGULAR VERBS

Infinitive	Present	Future	Preterit	Past Part.
andar	ando	andaré	anduve	andado
caber	quepo	cabré	cupe	cabido
caer	caigo	caeré	caí	caído
conducir	conduzco	conduciré	conduje	conducido
dar	doy	daré	di	dado
decir	digo	diré	dije	dicho
estar	estoy	estaré	estuve	estado
haber	he	habré	hube	habido
hacer	hago	haré	hice	hecho
ir	voy	iré	fui	ido
jugar	juego	jugaré	jugué	jugado
morir	muero	moriré	morí	muerto
oir	oigo	oiré	oí	oído
poder	puedo	podré	pude	podido
poner	pongo	pondré	puse	puesto
querer	quiero	querré	quise	querido
saber	sé	sabré	supe	sabido
salir	salgo	saldré	salí	salido
ser	soy	seré	fui	sido
tener	tengo	tendré	tuve	tenido
traer	traigo	traeré	traje	traído
valer	valgo	valdré	valí	valido
venir	vengo	vendré	vine	venido
ver	veo	veré	vi	visto

LAS FORMAS DEL VERBO INGLÉS

1. Se forma la 3ª persona singular del tiempo presente exactamente al igual que el plural de los sustantivos, añadiendo **-es** o **-s** a la forma sencilla según las mismas reglas, así:

(1)	teach	pass	wish	fix	buzz		
	teaches	passes	wishes	fixes	buzzes		
(2)	place	change	judge	please	freeze		
	places	changes	judges	pleases	freezes		
(3a)	find	sell	clean	hear	love	buy	know
	finds	sells	cleans	hears	loves	buys	knows
(3b)	think	like	laugh	stop	hope	meet	want
	thinks	likes	laughs	stops	hopes	meets	wants
(4)	cry	try	dry	carry	deny		
	cries	tries	dries	carries	denies		

Cinco verbos muy comunes tienen 3ª persona singular irregular:

| (5) | go | do | say | have | be |
| | goes | does | says | has | is |

2. Se forman el tiempo pasado y el participio de modo igual, añadiendo a la forma sencilla la terminación **-ed** o **-d** según las reglas que siguen:

(1) Si la forma sencilla termina en **-d** o **-t**, se le pone **-ed** como sílaba aparte:

| end | fold | need | load | want | feast | wait | light |
| ended | folded | needed | loaded | wanted | feasted | waited | lighted |

(2) Si la forma sencilla termina en cualquier otra consonante, se añade también **-ed** pero sin hacer sílaba aparte:

LAS FORMAS DEL VERBO INGLÉS

(2a)
bang	sail	seem	harm	earn	weigh
banged	sailed	seemed	harmed	earned	weighed

(2b)
lunch	work	look	laugh	help	pass
lunched	worked	looked	laughed	helped	passed

(3) Si la forma sencilla termina en **-e**, se le pone sólo **-d**:

(3a)
hate	taste	waste	guide	fade	trade
hated	tasted	wasted	guided	faded	traded

(3b)
free	judge	rule	name	dine	scare
freed	judged	ruled	named	dined	scared

(3c)
place	force	knife	like	hope	base
placed	forced	knifed	liked	hoped	based

(4) Una **-y** final que sigue a cualquier consonante se cambia en **-ie** al añadir la **-d** del pasado/participio:

cry	try	dry	carry	deny
cried	tried	dried	carried	denied

3. Varios verbos muy comunes forman el tiempo pasado y el participio de manera irregular. Pertenecen a tres grupos.

(1) Los que tienen una sola forma irregular para el tiempo pasado y el participio, como los siguientes:

bend	bleed	bring	build	buy	catch	creep	deal
bent	bled	brought	built	bought	caught	crept	dealt

dig	feed	feel	fight	find	flee	get	hang
dug	fed	felt	fought	found	fled	got	hung

have	hear	hold	keep	lead	leave	lend	lose
had	heard	held	kept	led	left	lent	lost

make	mean	meet	say	seek	sell	send	shine
made	meant	met	said	sought	sold	sent	shone

shoot	sit	sleep	spend	stand	strike	sweep	teach
shot	sat	slept	spent	stood	struck	swept	taught

(2) Los que tienen una forma irregular para el tiempo pasado y otra forma irregular para el participio, como los siguientes:

be	beat	become	begin	bite
was	beat	became	began	bit
been	beaten	become	begun	bitten

blow	break	choose	come	do
blew	broke	chose	came	did
blown	broken	chosen	come	done

draw	drink	drive	eat	fall
drew	drank	drove	ate	fell
drawn	drunk	driven	eaten	fallen

fly	forget	freeze	give	go
flew	forgot	froze	gave	went
flown	forgotten	frozen	given	gone

grow	hide	know	ride	ring
grew	hid	knew	rode	rang
grown	hidden	known	ridden	rung

rise	run	see	shake	shrink
rose	ran	saw	shook	shrank
risen	run	seen	shaken	shrunk

sing	sink	speak	steal	swear
sang	sank	spoke	stole	swore
sung	sunk	spoken	stolen	sworn

LAS FORMAS DEL VERBO INGLÉS

swim	tear	throw	wear	write
swam	tore	threw	wore	wrote
swum	torn	thrown	worn	written

(3) Los que no varían del todo, con la forma sencilla que funciona también como pasado/participio; entre éstos son de mayor frecuencia:

bet	burst	cast	cost	cut
hit	hurt	let	put	quit
read	set	shed	shut	slit
spit	split	spread	thrust	wet

EL PLURAL DEL SUSTANTIVO INGLÉS

A la forma singular se añade la terminición -**es** o -**s** de acuerdo con las reglas siguientes.

(1) Si el singular termina en -**ch, -s, -sh, -x** o -**z,** se le pone -**es** como sílaba aparte:

match	glass	dish	box	buzz
matches	glasses	dishes	boxes	buzzes

(2) Si el singular termina en -**ce, -ge, -se,** or -**ze,** se le pone una -**s** que con la vocal precedente forma sílaba aparte:

face	page	house	size
faces	pages	houses	sizes

(3) Una -**y** final que sigue a cualquier consonante se cambia en -**ie** a ponérsele la -**s** del plural:

sky	city	lady	ferry	penny
skies	cities	ladies	ferries	pennies

(4) Los siguientes sustantivos comunes tienen plural irregular:

man	woman	child	foot	mouse	goose
men	women	children	feet	mice	geese
wife	knife	life	half	leaf	deer
wives	knives	lives	halves	leaves	deer

WEIGHTS AND MEASURES/PESOS Y MEDIDAS

1 centímetro	=	.3937 inches	1 kilolitro	=	264,18 gallons
1 metro	=	39.37 inches	1 inch	=	2,54 centímetros
1 kilómetro	=	.621 mile	1 foot	=	,305 metros
1 centigramo	=	.1543 grain	1 mile	=	1,61 kilómetros
1 gramo	=	15.432 grains	1 grain	=	,065 gramos
1 kilogramo	=	2.2046 pounds	1 pound	=	,455 kilogramos
1 tonelada	=	2.204 pounds	1 ton	=	,907 toneladas
1 centilitro	=	.338 ounces	1 ounce	=	2,96 centilitros
1 litro	=	1.0567 quart (liquid); .908 quart (dry)	1 quart	=	1,13 litros
			1 gallon	=	4,52 litros

NUMBERS/NÚMEROS

Cardinal/Cardinales

one	1	uno, una		thirty-one	31	treinta y uno
two	2	dos		thirty-two	32	treinta y dos
three	3	tres		forty	40	cuarenta
four	4	cuatro		fifty	50	cincuenta
five	5	cinco		sixty	60	sesenta
six	6	seis		seventy	70	setenta
seven	7	siete		eighty	80	ochenta
eight	8	ocho		ninety	90	noventa
nine	9	nueve		one hundred	100	cien
ten	10	diez		one hundred one	101	ciento uno
eleven	11	once		one hundred two	102	ciento dos
twelve	12	doce		two hundred	200	doscientos, -as
thirteen	13	trece		three hundred	300	trescientos, -as
fourteen	14	catorce		four hundred	400	cuatrocientos, -as
fifteen	15	quince		five hundred	500	quinientos, -as
sixteen	16	dieciséis		six hundred	600	seiscientos, -as
seventeen	17	diecisiete		seven hundred	700	setecientos, -as
eighteen	18	dieciocho		eight hundred	800	ochocientos, -as
nineteen	19	diecinueve		nine hundred	900	novecientos, -as
twenty	20	veinte		one thousand	1,000	mil
twenty-one	21	veinte y uno (or veintiuno)		two thousand	2,000	dos mil
				one hundred thousand	100,000	cien mil
twenty-two	22	veinte y dos (or veintidós)		one million	1,000,000	un millón
thirty	30	treinta		two million	2,000,000	dos millones

Ordinal/Ordinales

first	1st / 1°	primero
second	2nd / 2°	segundo
third	3rd / 3°	tercero
fourth	4th / 4°	cuarto
fifth	5th / 5°	quinto
sixth	6th / 6°	sexto
seventh	7th / 7°	séptimo
eighth	8th / 8°	octavo
ninth	9th / 9°	noveno
tenth	10th / 10°	décimo

Days of the Week/Días de la Semana

Sunday	domingo
Monday	lunes
Tuesday	martes
Wednesday	miércoles
Thursday	jueves
Friday	viernes
Saturday	sábado

Signs/Señales

By appointment	Cita previa	**No admittance**	Entrada prohibida
Caution	Precaución	**No entry**	Dirección prohibida
Closed	Cerrado	**No thoroughfare**	Prohibido el paso/ Calle cerrada
Closed for repairs	Cerrado por refaccíon	**No parking**	Se prohíbe estacionar
Danger	Peligro	**No smoking**	Prohibido fumar
Do not disturb	No molesten	**No tipping**	No se admiten propinas
Down (on elevator)	Para bajar	**Not working**	No funciona
Driveway	Vado permante/Paso de carruajes	**One way**	Dirección única
Dumping prohibited	Se prohíbe arrojar la basura	**Open**	Abierto
		People working	Trabajadores
Entrance	Entrada	**Post no bills**	Se prohíbe fijar carteles
Exit	Salida	**Road closed**	Paso cerrado
For immediate occupancy	De ocupación inmediata	**Road repairs**	Camino en reparación
For sale	Se vende	**Same-day service**	En el día
Go (traffic)	Siga	**Slow**	Despacio
Inquire within	Se dan informaciones	**Slow down**	Moderar su velocidad
Keep to the left	Tome su izquierda	**Stop**	Alto
Keep to the right	Tome su derecha	**This way to...**	Dirección a...
Ladies'/Women's room	El cuarto de damas	**Town ahead**	Poblado próximo
Men	Señores, Hombres, Caballeros	**Up (on elevator)**	Para subir
		Wet paint	Recién pintado
Men's room	El servicio	**Women**	Señoras, Mujeres, Damas
Narrow road	Camino estrecho		

FOOD TERMS/ALIMENTOS

apple	manzana	lemonade	limonada
artichoke	alcachofa	lettuce	lechuga
asparagus	espárrago	liver	hígado
bacon	tocino	lobster	langosta
baked	al horno	meat	carne
banana	banana	melon	melón
bean	habichuela	milk	leche
beer	cerveza	mushroom	seta
beet	remolacha	noodle	fideo
biscuit	bizcocho	nut	nuez
boiled	hervido	omelet	tortilla de huevos
bread	pan	onion	cebolla
broccoli	bróculi	orange	naranja
broiled	a la parrilla	peach	melocotón
butter	mantequilla	pear	pera
cake	torta	pepper	pimienta
carrot	zanahoria	pie	pastel
cauliflower	coliflor	pork	carne de puerco
celery	apio	potato	patata
cheese	queso	rice	arroz
chicken	pollo	roast beef	rosbif
chocolate	chocolate	roasted	asado
coffee	café	salad	ensalada
cognac	coñac	salmon	salmón
cookie	galleta dulce	salt	sal
crab	cangrejo	sandwich	sándwich
cream	crema	sauce	salsa
cucumber	pepino	scrambled eggs	huevos revueltos
dessert	postre	shrimp	camarón
drink	bebida	soda	soda
duck	pato	sole	lenguado
egg	huevo	soup	sopa
fillet	filete	spinach	espinaca
fish	pescado	steak	biftec
fowl	ave	strawberry	fresa
fried	frito	stuffed	relleno
fruit	fruta	sugar	azúcar
goose	ganso	tea	té
grape	uva	tomato	tomate
grapefruit	toronja	trout	trucha
ham	jamón	tuna	atún
hamburger	hamburguesa	turkey	pavo
ice cream	helado	veal	ternera
jelly	jalea	vegetable	legumbre
juice	jugo	water	agua
lamb	cordero	wine	vino

Colors/Colores

Black	Negro		**Pink**	Rosa
Blue	Azul		**Purple**	Morado
Brown	Marron		**Red**	Rojo
Gold	Dorado		**Silver**	Plateado
Gray	Gris		**White**	Blanco
Green	Verde		**Yellow**	Amarillo
Orange	Anarajado			

Animals/Animales

Bear	El Oso		**Kangaroo**	El Canguro
Bird	El Pajaro		**Lion**	El Leon
Camel	El Camello		**Lizard**	La Lagartija
Cat	El Gato		**Monkey**	El Mono
Cow	La Vaca		**Owl**	El Buho
Deer	El Venado		**Peacock**	El Pavoreal
Dog	El Perro		**Pig**	El Cerdo
Donkey	El Burro		**Rabbit**	El Conejo
Duck	El Pato		**Raccoon**	El Mapache
Elephant	El Elefante		**Rhinoceros**	El Rinoceronte
Fox	El Zorro		**Rooster**	La Gallo
Giraffe	La Jirafa		**Sheep**	La Oveja
Goat	La Cabra		**Snake**	La Serpiente
Goose	El Ganso		**Tiger**	El Tigre
Gorilla	El Gorila		**Turkey**	El Pavo
Hippo	El Hipopotamo		**Wolf**	El Lobo
Horse	El Caballo		**Zebra**	La Cebra

Clothing/Vestidos

Dress	El Vestido		**Scarf**	La Bufanda
Gloves	Los Guantes		**Shirt**	La Camisa
Hat	El Sombrero		**Shoes**	Los Zapatos
Jacket	La Chaqueta		**Socks**	Los Calcetines
Jeans	Los Jeans		**Tie**	La Corbata
Pants	Los Pantalones			

WORD FIND: BODY PARTS

Instructions: The Spanish words for various body parts are listed below with their English translations. Can you find and circle all the Spanish body parts in the Word Find below?

B	C	D	O	M	E	E	H	Ñ	J	K	A	N	F	Q	G	I	A	F	I
K	B	B	A	N	G	L	M	E	J	I	L	L	A	S	Y	L	Y	J	C
A	N	R	E	I	P	N	C	I	B	C	Q	A	T	Y	L	E	E	L	G
L	O	H	A	K	M	E	F	R	O	E	S	V	D	I	H	Ñ	Q	L	H
G	E	I	K	Z	J	K	G	L	C	Ñ	I	F	B	K	P	G	O	T	Ñ
F	L	G	A	Ñ	O	E	I	M	A	V	G	R	O	D	I	L	L	A	Ñ
I	B	I	N	O	L	J	Q	T	T	D	A	Y	G	J	E	Y	P	R	A
Q	T	D	P	D	L	N	X	Ñ	A	B	D	V	A	H	T	W	D	C	D
R	B	V	I	I	E	L	Z	K	J	B	C	J	M	A	I	F	Q	S	C
J	O	S	H	S	U	Ñ	I	P	D	Q	C	G	O	V	J	I	H	K	Q
D	R	J	Y	D	C	U	R	B	W	K	I	Q	T	Q	D	U	O	M	Y
L	X	B	O	F	B	C	A	D	O	V	Ñ	V	S	Ñ	G	S	M	D	I
Z	A	E	U	S	F	A	N	V	R	T	O	Ñ	E	H	C	I	B	Y	X
X	C	Q	L	C	B	J	M	H	E	F	B	N	O	T	I	G	R	F	Q
O	T	H	I	V	L	J	K	C	J	S	E	P	F	A	E	F	O	Ñ	Ñ
O	P	E	C	H	O	F	Ñ	X	A	Q	J	E	R	X	Z	O	Z	A	H
P	K	F	S	D	A	T	B	G	S	F	R	U	E	B	U	A	N	P	E
B	Q	Q	O	A	I	U	N	B	Ñ	D	I	E	N	T	E	S	J	A	H
Ñ	A	C	E	Ñ	U	M	K	V	J	T	Q	P	T	S	T	C	L	L	M
Z	J	E	L	C	H	I	Ñ	D	G	C	A	B	E	Z	A	N	F	O	D

BODY PARTS/LAS PARTES DEL CUERPO

Barbilla	Chin	**Mejillas**	Cheeks
Boca	Mouth	**Muñeca**	Wrist
Brazo	Arm	**Nariz**	Nose
Codo	Elbow	**Ojos**	Eyes
Cuello	Neck	**Orejas**	Ears
Cabeza	Head	**Pecho**	Chest
Dientes	Teeth	**Pie**	Foot
Estomago	Stomach	**Pierna**	Leg
Frente	Forehead	**Rodilla**	Knee
Hombro	Shoulder	**Tobillo**	Ankle
Mano	Hand		

WORD FIND: MONTHS OF THE YEAR

Instructions: The Spanish words for the months of the year are listed below with their English translations. Can you find and circle all the Spanish months in the Word Find below?

```
A C K I N D J H M B L H C M I O D E I B
F I L F A M O K P N E Q D T F L S Q A K
C K E P A G O S T O S S I J V Z O H R M
N J Ñ H M O R N O F J D C R X R L T T E
O M J F T D H B S C I I I W E Ñ U O T L
V P U R L E R S A Y T C L R Y H G Z S J
I A L V A F H U J H R I B G Ñ D U R G H
E K I O W S R E M T D E B A T Z X A W Q
M S O Z J X B H J X F M K H Ñ K Ñ M Z K
B Q B U C G R E R G L B J E I Y O E A P
R O W P D D K N E M W R Ñ B D X Ñ J Y G
E V Y H T J F E I V I E P G L A W M V R
M A X B A X J R L F O L Ñ Z L L I R B A
E E R B U T C O A L C H T A Y Z P O X Q
G Q C E N Z R K Y S M G L Ñ H Ñ I Z L S
B J Q H R J M M N A Y A K T Ñ G B J J C
F A O S V E H Y V N M R C Ñ K M U F K N
D L T F L T U H L B Ñ I Ñ D Y A V H T I
H O I N U J I R Q X W Z G S Q L E S T A
C K H A L P I O A K S E P T I E M B R E
```

MONTHS OF THE YEAR/MESES DEL AÑO

Enero	January		**Julio**	July
Febrero	February		**Agosto**	August
Marzo	March		**Septiembre**	September
Abril	April		**Octubre**	October
Mayo	May		**Noviembre**	November
Junio	June		**Diciembre**	December

Body Parts/Las Partes del Cuerpo Answer Key

Months of the Year/Meses del Año Answer Key

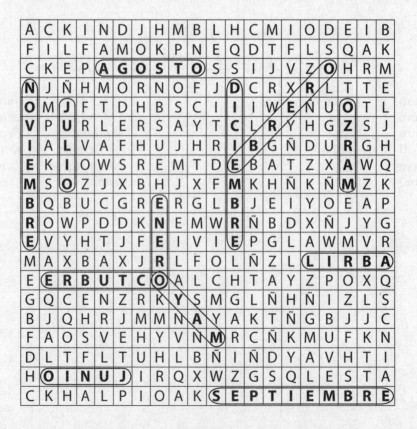

USEFUL PHRASES/LOCUCIONES ÚTILES

Good day, Good morning.   Buenos días.
Good afternoon.   Buenas tardes.
Good night, Good evening.   Buenas noches.
Hello.   ¡Hola!
Welcome!   ¡Bienvenido!
See you later.   Hasta luego.
Goodbye.   ¡Adiós!
How are you?   ¿Cómo está usted?
I'm fine, thank you.   Estoy bien, gracias.
I'm pleased to meet you.   Mucho gusto en conocerle.
May I introduce...   Quisiera presentar...
Thank you very much.   Muchas gracias.
You're welcome.   De nada *or* No hay de qué.
Please.   Por favor.
Excuse me.   Con permiso.
Good luck.   ¡Buena suerte!
To your health.   ¡Salud!

Please help me.   Ayúdeme, por favor.
I don't know.   No sé.
I don't understand.   No entiendo.
Do you understand?   ¿Entiende usted?
I don't speak Spanish.   No hablo español.
Do you speak English?   ¿Habla usted inglés?
How do you say... in Spanish?   ¿Cómo se dice... en español?
What do you call this?   ¿Cómo se llama esto?
Speak slowly, please.   Hable despacio, por favor.
Please repeat.   Repita, por favor.
I don't like it.   No me gusta.
I am lost.   Ando perdido; Me he extraviado.

What is your name?   ¿Cómo se llama usted?
My name is...   Me llamo...
I am an American.   Soy americano; Soy estadounidense.
Where are you from?   ¿De dónde es usted?
I'm from...   Soy de...

How is the weather?   ¿Qué tiempo hace?
It's cold (hot) today.   Hace frío (calor) hoy.
What time is it?   ¿Qué hora es?

How much is it?   ¿Cuánto es?
It is too much.   Es demasiado.
What do you wish?   ¿Qué desea usted?
I want to buy...   Quiero comprar...
May I see something better?   ¿Puedo ver algo mejor?
May I see something cheaper?   ¿Puedo ver algo menos caro?
It is not exactly what I want.   No es exactamente lo que quiero.

I'm hungry.   Tengo hambre.
I'm thirsty.   Tengo sed.
Where is there a restaurant?   ¿Dónde hay un restaurante?

I have a reservation.   Tengo una reservación.
I would like...   Quisiera...; Me gustaría...
Please give me...   Por favor, déme usted...
Please bring me...   Por favor, tráigame usted...
May I see the menu?   ¿Puedo ver el menú?
The bill, please.   La cuenta, por favor.
Is service included in the bill?   ¿El servicio está incluido en la cuenta?
Where is there a hotel?   ¿Dónde hay un hotel?
Where is the post office?   ¿Dónde está el correo?
Is there any mail for me?   ¿Hay correo para mí?
Where can I mail this letter?   ¿Dónde puedo echar esta carta al correo?

Take me to...   Lléveme a...
I believe I am ill.   Creo que estoy enfermo.
Please call a doctor.   Por favor, llame al médico.
Please call the police.   Por favor, llame a la policía.
I want to send a telegram.   Quiero poner un telegrama.
As soon as possible.   Cuanto antes.

Round trip.   Ida y vuelta.
Please help me with my luggage.   Por favor, ayúdeme con mi equipaje.
Where can I get a taxi?   ¿Dónde hay taxi?
What is the fare to...   ¿Cuánto es el pasaje hasta...?
Please take me to this address.   Por favor, lléveme a esta dirección.
Where can I change my money?   ¿Dónde puedo cambiar mi dinero?
Where is the nearest bank?   ¿Dónde está el banco más cercano?
Can you accept my check?   ¿Puede aceptar usted mi cheque?
Do you accept traveler's checks?   ¿Aceptan cheques de viaje?
What is the postage?   ¿Cuánto es el franqueo?
Where is the nearest drugstore?   ¿Dónde está la farmacia más cercana?
Where is the men's (women's) room?   ¿Dónde está el servicio de caballeros (de señoras)?
Please let me off at...   Por favor, déjeme bajar en...

Right away.   ¡Pronto!
Help.   ¡Socorro!
Who is it?   ¿Quién es?
Just a minute!   ¡Un momento no más!
Come in.   ¡Pase usted!
Pardon me.   Dispense usted.
Stop.   ¡Pare!
Look out.   ¡Cuidado!
Hurry.   ¡De prisa! *or* ¡Dése prisa!
Go on.   ¡Siga!
To (on, at) the right.   A la derecha.
To (on, at) the left.   A la izquierda.
Straight ahead.   Adelante.

INTRODUCTION TO THE SAT SPANISH SUBJECT TESTS

What Are The Spanish Subject Tests?

There are two different Spanish Subject Tests, the traditional Spanish Subject Test and a newer test called Spanish with Listening Subject Test. Both SAT Spanish Subject Tests are hour-long, multiple-choice exams that are supposed to measure your knowledge of Spanish. In fact, the College Board claims that the subject tests "...provide a reliable measure of your academic achievement" and "can help in assessing how well prepared you are for different programs of college study." Do the SAT Spanish Subject Tests really accomplish this? Absolutely not. If you want to know how well you speak Spanish, you should try reading a Spanish newspaper, watching a Spanish television show, or speaking Spanish with a native speaker. Each of these activities will give you a better idea of how well you speak the language than will the results of the SAT Spanish Subject Tests.

Why Should You Take a Spanish Subject Test?

Other than wanting to get a higher score than one of your friends, there are only two good reasons to take an SAT Spanish Subject Test. The first of these reasons is that one of the colleges to which you are applying either requires or strongly recommends that you take several different SAT Subject Tests. If this is the case, you will want to make sure that you pick the three subjects that will best demonstrate your academic achievement. Evaluate your own strengths and weaknesses, and contact colleges to see which tests they suggest or require. The second reason you might take the SAT Spanish Subject Test is that one of the colleges to which you're applying plans to use the Spanish Subject Test as a placement exam.

When Should You Take It?

The first thing you need to decide is whether to take one of the Spanish Subject Tests. These tests are appropriate for students who have completed a minimum of two years of high school Spanish or the equivalent.

The second thing you need to decide is whether to take the Spanish Subject Test or the Spanish with Listening Subject Test. If you have a lot of experience speaking Spanish, you might want to take the Spanish with Listening Subject Test. If you learned most of your Spanish from reading a book, you should probably take the Spanish Test that does not contain a listening section.

The Spanish Subject Test is given five times each year: October, December, January, May, and June. The Spanish with Listening Subject Test is given only once each year, in November.

Structure of the Test

Both the Spanish and the Spanish with Listening Subject Tests contain 85 multiple-choice questions. You'll have one hour to complete each of the tests, but you do not necessarily need to finish either test to get a good score. The structure of each test is as follows:

Spanish Subject Test: Spanish

The Spanish Subject Test contains three sections that measure different skills. Each section is weighted equally and contains approximately the same number of questions (between 27 and 29). The three sections are:

- Part A: Vocabulary and Structure
- Part B: Paragraph Completion
- Part C: Reading Comprehension

Spanish Subject Test: Spanish with Listening

The Spanish with Listening Subject Test consists of two sections: the Listening section and the Reading section. The Listening section contains about 35 questions and must be completed in about 20 minutes. The Reading section contains about 50 questions and must be completed in 40 minutes. Each of these two sections contains questions that measure different skills. The specific format is as follows:

Listening Section

- Part A: Pictures—You will be presented with a picture and asked to select the sentence that best reflects what someone in the picture might say or what is portrayed in the picture.

- Part B: Rejoinders—You will listen to a short conversation and then select the answer choice that represents the most likely continuation of the conversation.
- Part C: Selections—You will be asked to listen to extensive selections and then choose the best possible answer.

Reading Section
- Part A: Vocabulary and Structure
- Part B: Paragraph Completion
- Part C: Reading Comprehension

Scoring

Your overall score on either the Spanish Subject Test or the Spanish with Listening Subject Test is based on the number of questions you answer correctly minus the number of questions you answer incorrectly. You get no credit and lose no points for questions you leave blank. On the Spanish Subject Test, the result of this simple calculation (# correct – of number incorrect) represents your raw score. Raw scores can range from –28 to 85. On the Spanish with Listening Subject Test, you receive several different scores: a raw score for each section, a scaled score for each section (20–80), and an overall scaled score (200–800).

Both Spanish Subject Tests are scored on a 200–800 scale. Just like with the SAT, the lowest possible score is a 200 (even if you answer every question incorrectly) and the highest possible score is an 800 (which you can get even if you miss a question or two).

Final Thoughts

Preparation is the key to success—not just on this test, but in everything you do. If you want to succeed on the Spanish Subject Test or any other test, make sure you understand the content, practice the strategies, and develop an overall plan to attain your target score. You may want to read a Spanish newspaper (looking up the words you don't know in a dictionary), listen to Spanish-language radio stations or television programs, or engage in conversations in Spanish with your classmates, friends, or family members.

Finally, RELAX. Once you've finished preparing, there's no need to stress about the tests. Just make sure you get plenty of sleep the night before the test, eat a balanced breakfast, walk into the test center with a feeling of confidence, and do your best. In the end, your score is just a number. These tests will never be able to measure the most important aspect of your academic potential: your determination.

Strategies for Cracking the Exam

Pacing

Since your earliest days in school, you were probably taught that when you take a test, finishing is important. Standardized tests, however, are a completely different ball game. The folks who write these tests are interested in how fast you can work, and they design the tests so that it's nearly impossible to finish on time. Because you're so accustomed to the idea that finishing is crucial, you may pressure yourself to answer every question. Have you ever stopped to consider how much sense this makes? It's not as if you get a special prize for finishing! In fact, in order to finish, you usually have to rush through questions, and as a result you make careless errors that could be avoided. Doesn't it make more sense to slow down a bit, answer the questions you're sure of, and leave a few blanks? Well, let's see how pacing yourself on the Spanish Subject Tests relates to actual scores:

Pacing Chart

To Get a Score of	Answer About	Leave This Many Blank
400	13	72
450	26	59
500	38	47
550	48	37
600	58	27
650	68	17
700	78	7
750 & up	85	0

Understand that the pacing chart assumes that you'll make fewer than six mistakes, and it doesn't take guesses into account. If you take your time, pick your questions carefully, and learn to guess effectively, making fewer than six errors really isn't as tough as it might sound.

You should walk into your test with a target score in mind and a pacing strategy that reflects the score you're shooting for. Remember, this is your test, and that means you can answer the questions you want, when you want, how you want, and still get an excellent score. If you want to leave most (or all) of the reading comprehension blank and concentrate on the other questions, go ahead. If you're good at the reading comprehension, but not so good on the grammar, then do more of the reading comprehension and less of the grammar sentence completions. If all the other students at your test site want to race frantically to the end of the test and make careless mistakes along the way, that's their problem. You're going to be sitting there, cool and relaxed, just taking your time, and getting a great score.

When Should You Guess?

A lot of people talk about the "guessing penalty" on the SAT and the SAT Subject Tests. What they really mean is that there's no advantage to random guessing. The truth is, there really isn't a penalty either.

Each question on the Spanish Subject Test and the Spanish with Listening Subject Test has four answer choices. If you answer a question correctly, you will receive 1 raw-score point. If you get a question wrong, you will lose 1/3 of a raw-score point. If you were to randomly guess on four questions with four answer choices each, odds are you would get one question right and three questions wrong. How would this affect your raw score?

1 question correct = +1 point

3 questions incorrect = –1/3 × 3 = –1 point

Total impact on overall score = 0

So should you guess? Sometimes. If you can eliminate one or more incorrect answer choices, the odds become more favorable. Imagine if you were able to eliminate two answer choices and then randomly guess on the remaining two answer choices for four different problems. In this case, you would likely get two questions right and two questions wrong. How would this affect your raw score?

2 questions correct = +2 points

2 questions incorrect = –1/3 × 2 = –2/3 points

Total impact on overall score = +1 1/3 points

The moral of this story is this: If you can eliminate even one answer choice, you should guess. If you can't eliminate any answer choices, there's no reason to guess. You'll just be wasting valuable time.

Three-Pass System

Because the test is written for students with varying levels of expertise in Spanish, the questions vary in difficulty. Unfortunately, they aren't arranged in any particular order of difficulty. There are questions that are much easier than others, but it's up to you to find them if you want to take advantage of them.

The Three-Pass System Says the Following:

- 1st Pass—Go through an entire section of the test from beginning to end, but only answer the easiest questions, that is, those on which you thoroughly understand all the vocabulary, etc. Skip anything that looks as if it's going to give you grief.
- 2nd Pass—Go back to the beginning of the same section and take a shot at those questions where you knew some, but not all, of the vocabulary.
- 3rd Pass—Use the Process of Elimination (which you'll learn about in a moment) on the remaining questions in that section to eliminate some answers. Then take a guess. If you can't eliminate anything, leave the question blank.

Taking a section of the test this way will keep you from getting stuck on a tough question early in the section and spending too much time on it. Your time should be spent both answering questions you're sure of and guessing intelligently, not banging your head against the wall in an attempt to crack a tough question.

Note: The Three-Pass System will not work on the Listening section of the Spanish with Listening Subject Test. During that section, you will be listening to an audiocassette and you must answer the questions in the order in which they appear (or leave them blank).

POE—Process of Elimination

The usefulness of the Process of Elimination is one of the gifts of a multiple-choice exam. The idea is simple: There are three wrong answers and only one right one; so it is easier to find answers to eliminate. If you can eliminate answers that you know are wrong, you will eventually stumble upon the right answer because it'll be the only one left. POE is going to vary a bit for the different question types, but the general idea is always the same.

Excerpted from *Cracking the SAT Subject Test Spanish, 2007–2008 Edition,* ISBN 978-0-375-76595-7, Random House, March 2007

NOTES/NOTAS

NOTES/NOTAS

NOTES/NOTAS

NOTES/NOTAS

NOTES/NOTAS

NOTES/NOTAS